b164236892

The Routledge Handbook of Irish Criminology

The Routledge Handbook of Irish Criminology is the first edited collection of its kind to bring together the work of leading Irish criminologists in a single volume. While Irish criminology can be characterised as a nascent but dynamic discipline, it has much to offer the Irish and international reader due to the unique historical, cultural, political, social and economic arrangements that exist on the island of Ireland.

The Handbook consists of 30 chapters, which offer original, comprehensive and critical reviews of theory, research, policy and practice in a wide range of subject areas. The chapters are divided into four thematic sections:

1. *Understanding crime* examines specific offence types, including homicide, gangland crime and white-collar crime, and the theoretical perspectives used to explain them.
2. *Responding to crime* explores criminal justice responses to crime, including crime prevention, restorative justice, approaches to policing and trial as well as post-conviction issues such as imprisonment, community sanctions and rehabilitation.
3. *Contexts of crime* investigates the social, political and cultural contexts of the policymaking process, including media representations, politics, the role of the victim and the impact of gender.
4. *Emerging ideas* focuses on innovative ideas that prompt a reconsideration of received wisdom on particular topics, including sexual violence and ethnicity.

Charting the key contours of the criminological enterprise on the island of Ireland and placing the Irish material in the context of the wider European and international literature, this book is essential reading for those involved in the study of Irish criminology and international and comparative criminal justice.

Deirdre Healy is a Lecturer in Criminology at the UCD Sutherland School of Law, University College Dublin.

Claire Hamilton is a Senior Lecturer in Law at Maynooth University.

Yvonne Daly is a Senior Lecturer in Criminal Law and the Law of Evidence in the School of Law and Government at Dublin City University.

Michelle Butler is a Lecturer in Criminology in the School of Sociology, Social Policy and Social Work, Queen's University Belfast.

The Routledge Handbook of Irish Criminology

Edited by Deirdre Healy, Claire Hamilton,
Yvonne Daly and Michelle Butler

Routledge
Taylor & Francis Group

LONDON AND NEW YORK

First published 2016
by Routledge
2 Park Square, Milton Park, Abingdon, Oxon, OX14 4RN

and by Routledge
711 Third Avenue, New York, NY 10017

Routledge is an imprint of the Taylor & Francis Group, an informa business

British Library Cataloguing in Publication Data
A catalogue record for this book is available from the British Library

Library of Congress Cataloging in Publication Data
 The Routledge handbook of Irish criminology / edited by Deirdre Healy, Claire Hamilton, Yvonne Daly and Michelle Butler.
  pages cm
Includes bibliographical references.
 1. Criminology--Ireland. 2. Criminal justice, Administration of--Ireland. I. Healy, Deirdre.
 HV9960.I73R68 2016
 364.9417--dc23

                                                2015020245

ISBN: 978-1-138-01943-0 (hbk)
ISBN: 978-1-315-77900-3 (ebk)

Typeset in Bembo Std by
Servis Filmsetting Ltd, Stockport, Cheshire

MIX
Paper from
responsible sources
FSC   FSC® C013056
www.fsc.org

Printed and bound in Great Britain by
TJ International Ltd, Padstow, Cornwall

Contents

Contents

List of figures

List of tables

Contributors

Editors

Michelle Butler is a Lecturer in Criminology in the School of Sociology, Social Policy and Social Work, Queen's University Belfast. She is a former graduate of University College Dublin and the University of Kent at Canterbury and holds a Doctorate in Criminology from the University of Cambridge. Her research interests include imprisonment, criminological psychology, identity, shame, masculinity and violence. To date she has been involved in a number of research projects in England, the Republic of Ireland and Northern Ireland, exploring issues such as imprisonment, identity, violence, young people on remand, fear of crime and vulnerable people in the criminal justice system.

Yvonne Daly is a Senior Lecturer in Criminal Law and the Law of Evidence in the School of Law and Government at Dublin City University and a member of DCU's Socio-Legal Research Centre. Her research focuses on the pre-trial investigative process, with particular regard to the rights to silence and legal advice, and to the rules on improperly obtained evidence. She has published widely and is co-author of *Irish Criminal Justice: Theory, process and procedure* (Clarus Press, 2010). She is a Board Member of the Association for Criminal Justice Research and Development (ACJRD) and Vice-Chair of the Royal Irish Academy's Ethical, Political, Legal and Philosophical Studies Committee.

Claire Hamilton practised as a barrister in criminal law until 2004, when she became a full-time academic. She is currently a Senior Lecturer in Law at Maynooth University, having previously worked as a lecturer in criminology in Dublin Institute of Technology and Queen's University Belfast. Her research interests lie in the area of penology, particularly comparative penology. She has published three books, the most recent being *Reconceptualising Penality: A comparative perspective on punitiveness in Ireland, Scotland and New Zealand* (Ashgate, 2014). She has written widely on various criminological topics in national and international journals.

Deirdre Healy is a Lecturer in Criminology at the UCD Sutherland School of Law, University College Dublin. Her teaching and research interests include desistance, reintegration, community sanctions, criminological theory and victimisation. She has a track record of high-quality publications in peer-reviewed international and Irish journals, and her work has attracted interest from policymakers and practitioners as well as academics. She has published two books: *The Dynamics of Desistance: Charting pathways through change* (Routledge, 2012) and *Rape and Justice in Ireland* (with Conor Hanly and Stacey Scriver; Liffey Press, 2009).

Chapter Authors

Jackie Bates-Gaston is a Chartered and Registered forensic psychologist. She was a Senior Lecturer in Psychology at the University of Ulster and an Honorary Professor at Heriot-Watt University for over ten years. In 1991 she became the first psychologist in the Northern Ireland Prison Service, where she developed and implemented interventions and services for both staff and offenders. In 2014 she was awarded Senior Practitioner in Forensic Psychology by the British Psychological Society. Her proudest achievement is being mother of her three children, whose generosity of spirit she constantly admires.

Cormac Behan teaches criminology at the Centre for Criminological Research, University of Sheffield. His research interests include penal history, prisoners' rights, comparative penology and prison education. Before taking up this position, he taught politics and history in Irish prisons for fourteen years. He has served on the executive boards of the Correctional Education Association and the European Prison Education Association.

Lynsey Black is a PhD student at Trinity College Dublin researching women sentenced to death in post-Independence Ireland. The study seeks to understand how these death-sentenced women were discursively produced and how this production influenced juridical disposal. The research also explores wider themes of sexuality, institutional confinement and paternalism in Ireland. She has also carried out research on the representation of crime in the media, and the media use and construction of issues of gender and crime particularly. She has previously worked as a part-time assistant lecturer at Dublin Institute of Technology and at the Irish Penal Reform Trust.

Matt Bowden is an urban sociologist and a Lecturer in Sociology at Dublin Institute of Technology. He is course co-ordinator of the MA in Criminology, specialising in criminological theory, policing, crime prevention and urban security governance. His current research interests are in the areas of security fields and security capital as the stratifying dynamics of inclusion and exclusion. His book *Crime, Disorder and Symbolic Violence: Governing the urban periphery* was published in 2014 by Palgrave Macmillan.

Denis Bracken is Professor of Social Work at the University of Manitoba. He has held visiting posts at DeMontfort University, the Glasgow School of Social Work, Trinity College Dublin and University College Dublin. His research interests include criminal justice social work, desistance, and probation practice with Indigenous peoples and ethnic minorities in criminal justice. Currently he is Associate Dean of the Faculty of Social Work responsible for undergraduate and distance education. He has been the Director of the University's Inner City Social Work program, and more recently was the Rector of St. Paul's College at the University of Manitoba.

Damien Brennan trained and worked as a Psychiatric Nurse and Nurse Tutor in mental hospitals in Dublin. He undertook his PhD at the Department of Sociology, Trinity College Dublin, which detailed and critiqued mental hospital use in Ireland. As Assistant Professor at the School of Nursing and Midwifery, Trinity College, his teaching and research focus on the Sociology of Health and Illness, particularly mental health. He is the author of *Irish Insanity 1800–2000* (Routledge, 2014) which asserts that there was no epidemic of mental illness in Ireland; rather extensive Irish asylum/mental hospital institutional confinement occurred in response to social forces.

Elaine A. Byrne is based at the Global Irish Studies Centre, University of New South Wales. She is the author of *Political Corruption in Ireland 1922–2010: A crooked harp?* (Manchester University Press, 2012). Dr Byrne is a specialist on governance for the European Commission and a journalist with *The Sunday Business Post*. She has published on deliberative democracy, Irish political parties and twentieth-century Irish history.

Liz Campbell is Senior Lecturer in Criminal Law and Evidence at the University of Edinburgh. Her principal areas of research are criminal law and justice, with a particular interest in the legal responses to organised crime, DNA databases and the presumption of innocence. Dr Campbell's current research projects focus on the definitions of organised crime, and on organised crime and corruption. She is the author of *Organised Crime and the Law* (Hart, 2013) and has published widely in domestic and international journals like the *Modern Law Review*, *New Criminal Law Review* and *Criminal Law Review*. She frequently provides expert commentary for local and national media on her areas of study. She contributes to the blog www.humanrights.ie and tweets at @lizjcampbell.

Nicola Carr is a Lecturer in Criminology in the School of Sociology, Social Policy and Social Work, Queen's University Belfast. Her main research areas are probation and community sanctions and youth justice. Along with colleagues she is currently working on a number of research projects including a study funded by the British Academy on young people's experiences of paramilitary violence in Northern Ireland. She is co-author of the book *Understanding Criminal Justice: A critical introduction* (Routledge, 2012).

Johnny Connolly is a criminologist in the Alcohol and Drugs Research Unit of the Health Research Board. He has researched and written on community policing, drugs and crime and alternatives to imprisonment.

Una Convery is a Lecturer in the School of Criminology, Politics and Social Policy at Ulster University. Her teaching and research interests include victims of crime, prisoners' families, youth justice and women in the criminal justice system. She has published on the rights of children in custody and the history of the Irish youth justice systems.

John Devaney, PhD, is a Senior Lecturer in social work within the School of Sociology, Social Policy and Social Work at Queen's University Belfast. He joined the university in 2006 after a twenty-year career as a social worker and senior manager in social care in Northern Ireland. His research interests lie in the areas of the safeguarding of children from abuse and neglect, familial violence, the development of child welfare policy and the impact of childhood adversity across the lifecourse. He has published widely on issues related to child abuse and neglect, and domestic violence. He is a member of the Safeguarding Board for Northern Ireland. He is also national chair of the British Association for the Study and Prevention of Child Abuse and Neglect.

Stephanie Holt is a Lecturer in Social Work in the School of Social Work and Social Policy, Trinity College Dublin. Before moving to Trinity, she was a child and family social worker in West Dublin. She has held the post of Director of Postgraduate Teaching and Learning in the School since 2011 and has had lead responsibility for the development of Trinity's first fully online postgraduate programme – the Postgraduate Diploma in Applied Social Studies. Her primary research interests include domestic violence, intimate partner homicide and family support.

Niamh Hourigan is Senior Lecturer at the School of Sociology and Philosophy, University College Cork. She is the author of *Rule-breakers: Why 'being there' trumps 'being fair' in Ireland* (Gill and Macmillan, 2015) and a number of journal articles, expert reports and co-edited books. Her 2011 edited collection *Understanding Limerick: Social exclusion and change* presented the findings of her three-year research project on fear, feuding and intimidation by gangs in Limerick city. She is a former editor of the *Irish Journal of Sociology* and a frequent contributor to the Irish print and broadcast media on the themes of crime and deviance.

John Jackson is Professor of Comparative Criminal Law and Procedure at the University of Nottingham. He was previously Dean of UCD School of Law and Professor of Public Law at Queen's University Belfast. From 1998 to 2000 he was an Independent Assessor on the Criminal Justice Review Group established under the Good Friday/Belfast Agreement, and he is presently a Parole Commissioner for Northern Ireland. He is the author of a number books, articles and research reports on criminal justice and criminal evidence. His latest book (with Sarah Summers) is *The Internationalisation of Criminal Evidence* (Cambridge University Press, 2012).

Marie Keenan is a systemic psychotherapist, restorative justice practitioner, researcher and Lecturer at the School of Applied Social Science, University College Dublin, and a member of the Advisory Board of UCD's Criminology Institute. She is joint principal investigator with KU Leuven on a European Commission-funded Daphne III project on 'Developing Integrated Responses to Sexual Violence: An interdisciplinary research project on the potential of restorative justice'. Her recent publications include *Child Sexual Abuse in the Catholic Church: Gender, power and organizational culture* (Oxford University Press, 2012), *Broken Faith: Why hope matters* (Bern: Peter Lang, 2013; co-edited with Pat Claffey and Joe Egan) and *Sexual Trauma and Abuse: Restorative and transformative possibilities?* (University College Dublin, 2014).

Shane Kilcommins is a Professor of Law at the University of Limerick. His most recent book publications include: *Crime, Punishment and the Search for Order in Ireland* (2004, co-author), *Terrorism, Rights and the Rule of Law* (2008), *Criminal Law in Ireland* (2010, co-author), *Regulatory Crime in Ireland* (2010, co-editor) and *Integrative Learning: International research and practice* (Routledge, 2015, co-editor). He has written various articles on penology and criminal justice in journals such as: *Criminology and Criminal Justice*, the *European Journal of Criminology*, the *International Review of Victimology* and the *Howard Journal of Criminal Justice*.

Kristian Lasslett is Lecturer in Criminology at the University of Ulster and sits on the Executive Board of the International State Crime Initiative (www.statecrime.org). His research has featured in a range of international journals including the *British Journal of Criminology*, *State Crime* and *Theoretical Criminology*. His first monograph, *State Crime on the Margins of Empire*, was published by Pluto Press in 2014. His current research focuses on land confiscation, forced eviction and corruption, in addition to war, memory and post-conflict reconstruction. He is editor of The State Crime Testimony Project, and is shortly launching the Land Confiscation and Forced Eviction Research Lab.

Niamh Maguire is a Lecturer in Criminology at Waterford Institute of Technology. She completed her undergraduate studies in law at Trinity College Dublin and later completed her PhD there in 2008. She is professionally qualified as a barrister and also holds an MSc in Criminology and Criminal Justice from Edinburgh University. Her PhD thesis explored the practice and philosophy of punishment in Ireland, focusing on the sentencing practices of Irish judges. She continues to research and publish on this and on other topics including penal decision-making, probation and community sanctions, and offender supervision in comparative contexts.

Siobhán McAlister is a Lecturer in Criminology in the School of Sociology, Social Policy and Social Work at Queen's University Belfast. She is a Programme Director for the MSc Youth Justice and convenes a range of postgraduate and undergraduate modules including: Youth and Social Justice; Qualitative Research with Children and Young People; Childhood and Youth Research in Practice. Prior to this, she worked as a researcher in academia and the voluntary sector for over ten years. Her research interests are in the broad fields of marginalisation, criminalisation and social justice, with a particular focus on children, young people and communities.

Ciaran McCullagh was formerly a Senior Lecturer in Sociology in University College Cork. He is a graduate of the LSE and holds a Doctorate from the National University of Ireland. He has published widely in the field of criminology and wrote one of the first texts on crime in Ireland (*Crime in Ireland*, Cork University Press, 1996), and has also published work on the media (*Media Power*, Palgrave, 2002). His most recent publications are on cultural understandings of crime and criminals and on the 'wired' family.

T.J. McIntyre is a Lecturer in the UCD Sutherland School of Law where his research focuses on the intersection of information technology, crime and civil liberties. He is also the chair of civil liberties group Digital Rights Ireland. He is co-author of *Criminal Law* (Dublin: Round Hall, 2012). He holds a BCL from University College Dublin, an LLM from University College London and a PhD from the University of Edinburgh. He qualified as a barrister in the Honorable Society of King's Inns and was later admitted as a solicitor. He is a member of the New York Bar.

Luke Moffett, LLB, LLM, PhD, is a Lecturer at Queen's University Belfast School of Law. His research focuses on the rights of victims of criminal and political violence in Northern Ireland, Uganda and the International Criminal Court. His book *Justice for Victims before the International Criminal Court* is published by Routledge (2014). He has kindly received funding from the Socio-Legal Studies Association to examine the reform of victim impact statements in Northern Ireland.

Aogán Mulcahy teaches in the School of Sociology at University College Dublin. His research interests include policing and legitimacy; culture and social control; and crime, community and marginalisation. He has conducted research on policing in a number of different countries and contexts, and his publications include *Policing Northern Ireland* (2006) and *Policing and the Condition of England* (with Ian Loader, 2003).

Kieran O'Dwyer is a practising consultant and researcher and has been active in the field of restorative justice for over fifteen years. He completed a PhD degree in University College Dublin in 2008 which researched the Garda programme of restorative justice for young offenders. He is a Board member of Restorative Justice Services and a chair of its offender reparation panels. He is also a member of the Restorative Practices Strategic Forum. He was formerly Head of Research in the Garda Síochána and Director of Regimes in the Irish Prison Service.

Sara Parsons has been Deputy Head of the Garda Síochána Analysis Service (GSAS) since 2007. The GSAS, which is based at Garda Headquarters, Phoenix Park, Dublin 8, provides a range of supports to operational policing, including monitoring crime trends. Previously, she spent four years with the National Crime Council, an advisory group to the Minister for Justice. Her research there covered topics such as the time taken to investigate and prosecute murder and rape cases, community courts and domestic abuse.

Brian Payne is a Senior Lecturer in Criminology at the University of Gloucestershire. His primary research interests lie in the areas of transnational organised crime, community policing and restorative justice. Prior to taking up this post, he was a Research Fellow at Keele University and worked on a major research council project entitled 'North–South Irish Responses to Transnational Organised Crime'. His doctoral research was undertaken at Queen's University Belfast and explored the construction of partnerships between a community-based restorative justice project and the police in Nationalist/Republican communities of West Belfast.

Andrew Percy is a Senior Lecturer in Criminology and Director of the Centre for Research on Transitions, Identity and Wellbeing at Queen's University Belfast. His main research interests include adolescent alcohol, drug use and crime. His work has been published in leading journals including: *Addiction, Drug & Alcohol Dependence* and the *International Journal of Drug Policy*. He is currently Associate Editor of *Journal of Adolescence*.

Christina Quinlan is a Lecturer in Research Methods, Criminology and Sociology. She has taught Research Methods at Dublin City University for a number of years. Her areas of interest include social research methods, gender, and crime and punishment. She has written extensively on women and criminal justice, research methodologies, feminist methodologies, visual methods, action research and ethnography. She has long been an activist in penal reform. She has published *Inside: Ireland's women's prisons, past and present* (2011), and in 2015 she co-authored her second major textbook on business research methods.

Mary Rogan is the Head of Law at Dublin Institute of Technology. She writes on the politics of punishment, penal policymaking, prison law and prisoners' rights. She is the author of *Prison Policy in Ireland: Politics, penal-welfarism and political imprisonment* (Routledge, 2011) and *Prison Law* (Bloomsbury, 2014). She is a representative of Ireland on the International Penal and Penitentiary Foundation and is a barrister.

Bill Rolston is an Emeritus Professor with the Transitional Justice Institute at Ulster University. He was previously Director of the Institute. He has researched and written widely on Northern Ireland society and politics over many years, with his focus most recently being on legacy issues arising out of the conflict. Published books and articles have covered such issues as state killings, victims and memory, the right to truth, politically motivated ex-prisoners and the experiences of sons and daughters of political activists.

Andrea Ryan is Director of the Centre for Criminal Justice and a lecturer at the School of Law, University of Limerick. Her research expertise lies in the areas of the European Convention on Human Rights, EU criminal justice, criminal evidence, comparative criminal procedure, criminal law and sentencing. She has published widely in these areas, most recently *Towards a System of European Criminal Justice: The problem of admissibility of evidence* (Routledge, 2014).

Mairéad Seymour is a Senior Lecturer in the School of Languages, Law and Social Sciences at the Dublin Institute of Technology. Her teaching and research interests include youth crime and justice, community disposals, offender compliance, reintegration, restorative justice and comparative criminal justice. Her book *Youth Justice in Context: Community, compliance and young people* (Routledge, 2013) explores the notion of compliance in relation to offender supervision in comparative jurisdictions and from the perspectives of young people and the youth justice professionals who supervise them.

Sarah Skedd has an MA in Criminology from Dublin Institute of Technology. She is a Crime and Policing Analyst with An Garda Síochána. Her areas of work include national homicide statistics for the Republic of Ireland, as well as providing detailed analytical support to individual homicide, and other serious crime, investigations.

John Topping is a Lecturer in Criminology at Ulster University where he also acts as Criminology Subject Director within the School of Criminology, Politics and Social Policy and is a member of the Institute for Research in Social Sciences (IRiSS). He specialises in police research with a particular focus upon community policing, security governance, police training and public order policing. He has acted as consultant for the Police Service of Northern Ireland on community policing training and acted as an adviser to the Office of the Police Ombudsman for Northern Ireland (OPONI) in regard to informal police complaints resolution. He also sits on the Board of Directors for Community Restorative Justice Ireland (CRJI), the leading community-based restorative justice organisation in the jurisdiction.

Barry Vaughan has worked as a lecturer on criminal justice issues in various colleges in Ireland and England. He has co-authored two books on criminal justice matters in Ireland: *Crime, Punishment and the Search for Order in Ireland* (Institute of Public Administration, 2004) and *Terrorism, Rights and the Rule of Law: Negotiating justice in Ireland* (Willan, 2008). He has also written numerous articles on various criminological topics in international journals as well as a number of reports for public bodies.

Foreword

For many years to come, *The Routledge Handbook of Irish Criminology* will be the authoritative source of knowledge about Irish criminology and criminal justice systems. The singular and plural are intentional.

In an international context, there appears to be something that reasonably can be described as Irish criminology, an offshoot of Britain's. The affinity is not surprising given that Northern Ireland remains part of the United Kingdom, criminology is a relatively new academic specialty, the fledgling departments are located in law schools and many criminologists received their graduate educations in Britain.

Interests of individuals are inevitably idiosyncratic but, as a whole, Irish criminology has proclivities for qualitative methods, critical mindsets and social theory and accords lesser emphasis to quantitative data, statistical modeling and etiological explanation. These tendencies can be seen by comparing references to works of David Garland, Loic Wacquant and Ian Loader with those for David P. Farrington, Robert J. Sampson and Lawrence Sherman. In these respects Irish criminology shares central tendencies with British and Commonwealth criminology and differs from American criminology. Much of continental Europe falls in between, but most countries have a richer blend than in Ireland or Britain of quantitative and qualitative methods, critical and operational mindsets, and social and etiological theories.

Criminology, but criminal justice systems. Although British influences can be seen in laws and institutional practices, overall the Irish Republic is its own place. The imprisonment rate, despite modest recent rises, is much lower than those in England or Scotland, and crime has not in recent decades been a continuing field for ideological and political conflict. Northern Ireland by contrast, like Scotland, suffered from the politicization and centralization of criminal justice policy under Britain's recent Labour government. Despite lower-than-English imprisonment rates, and gentler-and-kinder juvenile justice policies, Northern Ireland's institutions more conspicuously bear the stigmata of British rule and mentalities than do the Republic's.

The Handbook, like a fly in amber, provides opportunity to examine a facet of the island's history at a particular time. In coming years it will provide a baseline for measuring the evolution of Irish criminology and criminal justice systems. Both will develop, of course, but whether they converge in ways that are distinctive to Ireland, or that more strongly reveal common British influence, or whether they do not converge at all remains to be seen. My money is on the first, distinctly Irish, future. The Handbook's summaries will some day make the answer clearer than would otherwise have been possible.

Even imagining a handbook of Irish criminology demonstrates an ambition to achieve a common Irishness. I can think of no comparable effort elsewhere for so small a place. The *Oxford Handbook of Criminology* has always had England, Wales and Scotland (60 million people) as its frame of reference. There are European and American criminology handbooks, but those are continents. *Crime and Justice* volumes explore Dutch (16 million) and Scandinavian (25 million) criminologies. The closest small-country (11 million) volume I've found is *Crime and Punishment in Contemporary Greece* (2011), edited by Leonidas K. Cheliotis and Sappho Xenakis. It covers many fewer subjects.

May Irish criminology thrive and Irish criminology emerge. Let the rumble begin.

Michael Tonry
McKnight Presidential Professor in Criminal Law
and Policy, University of Minnesota, USA

Acknowledgements

We would like to acknowledge the support of various people and institutions that assisted us with the preparation of the Handbook: Dublin City University, Maynooth University, Queen's University Belfast and University College Dublin, which provided administrative and financial assistance for various aspects of the project. In particular, this book received financial support from the Faculty of Humanities and Social Sciences Book Publication Scheme at Dublin City University, from the Maynooth University Publications Fund and from the UCD Sutherland School of Law. In addition, we would like to thank Liz Campbell, Tim Hope, Mick Ryan and Michael Tonry who provided invaluable insights, guidance and feedback on our work; and Clare Cresswell, Joe Garrihy, Donna McNamara, Morgane Nerrou and Louise Rooney for acting as rapporteurs at *The Routledge Handbook of Irish Criminology* conference and/or assisting with copy-editing tasks. We are grateful to Eric Boylan and Hideta Nagai for giving us permission to use their work as our cover image and to the following publishers who granted us permission to reproduce extracts from their publications, namely Ashgate, the Irish Probation Service, the Irish Province of the Society of Jesus and Sage. We would also like to thank Routledge for their faith in us and this project. Most of all, we are deeply indebted to the contributors whose enthusiasm and commitment made our work as editors easy and whose expertise enabled us to produce a comprehensive and high-quality edited collection.

Introduction

Claire Hamilton and Deirdre Healy

With criminology 'booming' around the world (Bosworth and Hoyle, 2011), the position of Irish criminology may appear somewhat anomalous. Long dubbed an 'absentee discipline' (O'Donnell, 2005: 99), accounts of the development of criminology, at least in the Republic, have frequently sought to emphasise its embryonic nature, the lack of a proper infrastructure and the limited number of academic positions in the specialism (e.g. Rolston and Tomlinson, 1982; O'Donnell, 2005; Kilcommins *et al.*, 2004). With a slow but steady increase in the number of programmes offering criminology and criminal justice, however, and a growing number of academics and postgraduate students working in the area, it may well be time to revisit the Cinderella status of Irish criminology. Indeed, the impetus to write this book derived substantially from a desire to collate and showcase that burgeoning knowledge, particularly those accounts which go beyond purely local imperatives to engage issues of general interest in criminology. We hope in this introductory chapter to provide a brief history of ideas of the discipline as well as a critical perspective on the position of Irish criminology today. Before we undertake a fuller discussion of Irish criminology, it is necessary to provide a brief overview of the origins and development of the criminal justice systems in the two jurisdictions for those readers less familiar with its history. Having cleared the ground thus, the potential contribution of Irish criminology to broader theory and comparative criminology is discussed, highlighting in particular the unique features which may contradict received wisdom.

Criminal justice since 1922

The history of criminal justice in pre-partition Ireland, like its political history more generally, is intimately linked with that of its former colonial master. Indeed, in many ways the nation's distinctive law and order problems (deriving from the quasi-political nature of much of the crime) may have forced its early development, resulting in the establishment of a professional police force and centralised system of prosecution well in advance of England and Wales (McEldowney, 1990). While certain distinctive structures have emerged, to this day the criminal justice system bears strong similarities to the British system, including significant areas of criminal law which remain governed by common law and older British legislation. Indeed, the same may also be said of more recent legislation with one important legacy of the past being 'an ingrained tendency to look to London for political inspiration' (O'Donnell, 2005: 103).

For those readers unfamiliar, the greater part of the island of Ireland is occupied by the Republic of Ireland (population 4.6 million approximately), with the north-eastern part of the island remaining part of the United Kingdom (Northern Ireland's population is now 1.8 million approximately). Ireland's nearest neighbour, Britain, occupied the island for nearly 800 years, with independence being achieved only with the end of the war of independence in 1922. The period following this conflict affirmed legal arrangements for the partition of the island into Northern Ireland (six counties) and what was then called the Irish Free State (26 counties). Each part of the island retained its own Parliament as well as its own system of courts. While both legal systems have their roots in the British common law tradition, the Republic adopted a written constitution in 1937. It is with respect to *Bunreacht na Eireann* (lit: the basic law of the state) that the latter's legal system most closely approximates the American model, providing as it does for supremacy over both common law and legislation. The Northern Irish legal system continues to resemble strongly the British system, with Dickson (2005) observing that the process of assimilation between the content of the law in Northern Ireland and England and Wales has, if anything, been fortified in the last number of decades.

Following partition, the troubled relationship with Britain continued to cast a dark shadow over life on the island, with political violence breaking out in Northern Ireland in 1968 after clashes over the civil rights campaign.[1] The campaign, which took the form of protests and marches calling for a fair voting system, an end to religious discrimination and general equality for all the people of Northern Ireland, met with a violent response from loyalists and the police, attracting condemnation from around the world. The thirty-year period of political and civil unrest which followed, colloquially known as 'the Troubles/Conflict', saw the deaths of over 3,500 people, with many thousands more injured. The cessation of violence in 1994 and the signing of the Good Friday Agreement in 1998 cleared the way for a new Northern Ireland Assembly, the first Assembly to sit there since the suspension of the Stormont Parliament by Westminster in 1972. While the Assembly was suspended between 2002 and 2007 (pending cross-party agreement on policing and decommissioning of weapons), all the major political parties are currently in their second consecutive term of sharing executive power.[2] Indeed, of particular note from a criminological perspective, the devolution of justice and policing to the Northern Ireland executive occurred in April 2010, together with the appointment of the first Justice Minister.

Despite the violent history of the island, 'ordinary' crime rates in both jurisdictions are low by international standards (although we note the findings of studies suggesting high rates of self-reported delinquency and victimisation (see e.g. Enzmann *et al.*, 2010)). This apparent paradox has been the subject of some criminological interest, with Brewer *et al.* (1997: 5) observing 'the seemingly absurd contrasts: the most picturesque of English market towns ... have levels of ordinary crime which exceed strife-torn Belfast'. Most famously, Rutgers University academic Freda Adler described the Republic of Ireland as one of her 'nations not obsessed with crime' in a book which appeared in 1983. Perhaps it was a form of complacency borne from this 'policeman's paradise' (Brady, 1974: 240) which caused such a lag in public reactions when crime rates did begin their inevitable rise. Crime levels in both jurisdictions started to increase in the 1960s and accelerated with the drugs epidemic which exploded in the 1980s in the Republic and a decade later in Northern Ireland (see Skedd, *infra*). Yet, as Kilcommins *et al.* (2004) observe, such increases were not reflected in public opinion polls in the Republic, which continued to rank crime far below issues such as unemployment, emigration and the political situation in Northern Ireland. This state of affairs was also mirrored north of the border, where the all-consuming nature of the political situation meant that little attention was devoted to 'ordinary' crime (Greer, 2003).

The picture surrounding both states in the early years of their existence is thus one of relative inertia surrounding criminal justice policy. Writing of the forty-year period after partition, Rogan (2011, *infra*) notes the almost total lack of interest in penal affairs in both jurisdictions, variously described (with regard to the Republic) as 'calcification' (Kilcommins *et al.*, 2004: 41) or 'stagnation' (O'Donnell, 2008). While in the Republic pioneering Minster for Justice Charles Haughey set in train a number of important changes to the penal system in the 1960s – *viz.*, improvements in youth diversion, probation and rehabilitation in prisons – this momentum was not sustained. That said, it would be misleading to characterise these decades as a time of unbroken complacency about criminal matters. The overspill in paramilitary violence relating to Northern Ireland contributed to a rise in the number of more serious crimes such as armed robberies and the increased use of firearms (armed robberies in the Republic increased from 12 at the start of 'the Conflict' in 1969 to 228 in 1979: see Mulcahy, 2002). Moreover, every now and then, the general inertia in this area was shattered by a 'crime crisis', such as those relating to joyriding in the 1980s or the raft of reforms to sexual offences legislation which followed the Lavinia Kerwick rape case in 1992 (see O'Mahony, 1996, 1998; O'Connell, 1998). The sound and fury attending these events usually dissipated fairly quickly, however, and, with the brief exception of the 1997 general election (discussed below), no sustained effort has been made to fashion a more resolutely critical law and order stance in the manner observed in England and Wales since 1979 (Downes and Morgan, 1994; Kilcommins *et al.*, 2004).

The situation in Northern Ireland differed insofar as the turbulent decades of the 1970s and 1980s saw the introduction of controversial measures such as non-jury (Diplock) courts and the significant extension of police powers under special powers legislation. These innovations, among others, gave rise to the argument that the jurisdiction provided a 'testing ground' for the extension of authoritarian powers through the use of repressive technologies and policies soon to be transplanted elsewhere (Hillyard, 1985). Hillyard's 'contagion thesis' has generally been well received in criminological circles (see Daly and Jackson, *infra*; for criticisms, see also Mulcahy, 2005) and indeed revived in a contemporary context (see, for example, Pantazis and Pemberton, 2009, on the Muslim 'suspect community' in Britain). A hindsight view of the evolution of the criminal justice systems on the island of Ireland and Britain also vindicates Hillyard's concerns to quite a significant degree. In the Republic, the current incarnation of the juryless Special Criminal Court was established to hear cases of a paramilitary nature in 1972 and was subsequently extended to defendants suspected of involvement in organised criminal activity. Legislation providing for extended periods of detention and incursions on the right to silence for ordinary criminal offences has also been enacted, drawing on an important symbolic fusion between subversive crime and 'narco-terrorism' (Hamilton, 2011). Similarly, in Britain, 'temporary' emergency legislation enacted to deal with Irish terrorism in 1974 was constantly renewed and extended before eventually being made permanent in the Anti Terrorism, Crime and Security Act 2001.

The apathy of the earlier decades with regard to 'ordinary' crime was rapidly shed in the mid-1990s which marked a watershed in both jurisdictions. In the Republic, the murder of investigative journalist Veronica Guerin, allegedly by a group of major drug-dealing Dublin criminals, was the catalyst for a crime package which included an innovative new civil forfeiture procedure as well as significant increases in police numbers and prison places (O'Donnell and O'Sullivan, 2003; Hamilton, 2007). In sharp contrast to the low priority accorded to crime in previous soundings, opinion polls now showed crime to be a key issue for the public (Kilcommins *et al.*, 2004). With an election looming in 1997, the evident public concern that a journalist could be the target of a contract killing in broad daylight on a public highway was doggedly exploited by

Fianna Fáil in opposition. The shadow minister promised to 'wage war on crime' and 'to give the streets of the country back to the Irish people' (Hamilton, 2007: 102). His chosen strategy for doing so was the rather elastic concept of 'zero tolerance' policing, an approach which it was claimed had achieved impressive results in New York City (O'Donnell and O'Sullivan, 2003). This period of intensified concern did not last, however, and the trend towards *ad hoc* policy-making in criminal justice has continued in the ensuing decades, most recurrently in relation to violence perpetrated by organised criminal gangs (see further Campbell, 2010, *infra*).

North of the border, the period following the 1994 ceasefires also allowed space for social problems artificially suppressed by the political conflict to emerge (Hollywood, 1997; Greer, 2003). Changes in patterns of drug use, and particularly an expansion in the heroin market, led to significant media attention around the problem of drug consumption (McElrath, 2004; see Connolly and Percy, *infra*). To a considerable degree, this focus on 'ordinary' crime has continued in tandem with the normalisation of the political situation, with Tomlinson (2012: 442) noting that the 'ideologies and practices of counter terrorism no longer dominate the business of criminal justice'. Radical reforms of the police service following the report of the Patten Commission (1999) have resulted in a focus on 'policing with the community' as a form of normalised policing. While the expectations of the community have often exceeded what can realistically be achieved (or the available resources), progress has been such that the Police Service of Northern Ireland (PSNI) is now recognised as a model for police reform generally (Mulcahy, 2013, *infra*). The Criminal Justice Review, which reported to the government in 2000, undertook a similar process of 'normalisation' across a wide range of criminal justice institutions and procedures, including the prosecution system, methods of adjudication, restorative justice, juvenile justice and sentencing. It produced 294 recommendations, the most significant of which concerned juvenile justice, judicial appointments and the establishment of a new prosecution service (on youth justice more generally, see Convery and Seymour, *infra*).

Despite the distorting effect of the Conflict on the conduct of 'ordinary' criminal business, it may be said that, on balance, more significant points of convergence than divergence emerge from an assessment of criminal justice in the two jurisdictions. In a very real sense, the influence of the Conflict extended beyond the Northern Irish criminal justice system and into crime control in the Republic. Chapters within this Handbook talk about the 'chilling effect' of political violence on media reporting (Black, *infra*); a closed and secretive civil service culture, driven in part by fear (Rogan, *infra*); and a preference for 'front-end' crime control measures as administered by the police (Hamilton, *infra*). Both jurisdictions have also benefitted from improved policing accountability mechanisms since the conclusion of the Good Friday Agreement and concomitant human rights acts, with developments in Northern Ireland exerting what has been described as a 'magnetic pull' on developments south of the border (Vaughan and Kilcommins, 2008: 17). Another point of convergence can be located in the field of youth justice. While England has pursued policies which have sought to 'responsibilise' young offenders (and their parents) and have resulted in higher custody rates and greater coercion in the community, Northern Ireland and the Republic of Ireland may be said to have pursued a very different path through their continued commitment to rehabilitative policies and restorative justice (Hamilton *et al.*, 2014; Convery and Seymour, *infra*; O'Dwyer and Payne, *infra*).

The challenge of Irish criminology to criminological research

Writing recently in *Theoretical Criminology*, Katja Aas (2012) urges criminology to embrace the 'view from the periphery'. For her, and others critical of North Atlantic domination in the analogous field of sociology (Connell, 2006), the orientation of much criminological theorising is skewed towards the 'metropole', while the range of potentially productive insights afforded by other, less influential, jurisdictions remains un- or under-explored. Set in small post-colonial societies on the fringes of Western Europe, the Irish and Northern Irish cases provide a good demonstration of the perils of extrapolating from the US or even English example. Particularly over the past decade or so, there has emerged a significant body of work on 'Hibernian exception-alism' to broader punitive trends, ranging in focus from the continued emphasis on rehabilitation (Healy and O'Donnell, 2005) and the individuated justice system (Vaughan and Kilcommins, 2008; Hamilton, 2014a) to the more 'diluted and distinct' culture of control evident in contem-porary policy and practice (Kilcommins et al., 2004: 292; see also Griffin and O'Donnell, 2012; O'Donnell and Jewkes, 2011). These studies are important in the challenge that they present to universalistic claims of punitiveness, not simply because they advance arguments of the 'it hasn't happened here' variety (Hallsworth and Lea, 2008), but also because they illustrate the complex-ities which inhere in the penal field. Griffin and O'Donnell's (2012: 625) account of parole in the Republic of Ireland, for example, does well to remind us that flexibility and informality in the Irish criminal justice system cut both ways:

> [A]ccru[ing] to the advantage of the prisoner as they did in the 1970s and 1980s, when the average life sentence equated to 7.5 years in custody … [or operating] in the opposite direction, as the lifers now serving an additional decade behind bars might attest.

The account thus problematises traditional critiques equating actuarialism with a more punitive approach, as well as highlighting the complex relationship between policy intentions and effects (Daems, 2007; see further Hamilton, infra).

The unique social, political and cultural arrangements that exist within Northern Ireland and the Republic of Ireland have also created novel challenges for theory and practice. For example, Hourigan (2011, infra) identifies two distinctive features of criminal gang structures in the Republic of Ireland, namely, the close family relationships that underpin gang membership and the complex relationships that exist between gangs, dissident groups and the state. The widespread use of social control mechanisms in the Republic of Ireland, especially in the historical context, also warrants particular attention. For example Keenan's (2012, infra) seminal study illustrates the ways in which the institutional culture of the Catholic Church contributed to the emergence and concealment of child sexual abuse, Brennan (infra) sheds light on the historical processes that underpinned the unusually high committal rates to psychiatric institutions before the 1960s, while Quinlan (infra) reflects on the role of patriarchal social structures in the control of women. Likewise, the history and impact of the Conflict in Northern Ireland necessitates the inclusion of additional layers of analysis even in studies of relatively mainstream criminological topics, such as the poverty-crime nexus (see McAlister and Healy, infra) and state crime (see Byrne et al., infra). On the other hand, some criminological topics that are extremely popular elsewhere have attracted little attention here. Writing about white-collar crime in Northern Ireland, McCullagh (infra) notes 'the apparent absence of such crime in the jurisdiction' due to its under-developed corporate sector. Similarly, Bracken (infra) observes that the need to respond to ethnic diversity within the criminal justice system in the Republic of Ireland is only beginning to be recognised.

Certain criminological studies drawing on the Irish and Northern Irish cases also offer the-oretical insights into the conceptualisation and operationalisation of core criminological con-cepts such as punishment, particularly for comparative and transnational researchers. Hamilton's (2014a, 2014b) research on the multidimensional measurement of punishment, for example, illustrates that countries which appear very punitive when viewed through the traditional lens of imprisonment rates may take on quite a different complexion when assessed on a much broader range of criteria and vice versa. The importance of including what she terms 'front-end' variables concerning the nature and intensity of street-level law enforcement is particularly critical in understanding 'punishment' in jurisdictions which may not have the resources to put into prison building (Neapolitan, 2001). O'Sullivan and O'Donnell's (2007, 2012) work on historical levels of 'coercive confinement' in the Republic of Ireland also holds much contemporary relevance for theoretical work around new forms of confinement such as detention and deportation centres (Aas and Bosworth, 2013). Both of these accounts raise issues about forms of punishment which may not qualify as 'punishment' as seen through the prism of current western theory, yet which are intended as punishments or have distinct punitive elements (Aas, 2012). Similar challenges around conceptual boundaries are thrown up by the Northern Irish research on 'policing' (broadly conceived) and 'crime prevention'. Topping and Byrne's (2014) research on community-based policing, for example, suggests that for those involved it may be more appropriately understood as 'community development', 'good relations' or 'social justice' (see further Bowden and Topping, *infra*).

The case of Northern Ireland also raises the broader question of its theoretical value as a 'society in transition'. Aas's (2012: 9) critique of the transitional label – 'that they can be seen as a metropolitan translation for "not yet like us" and thus not yet of interest' – finds an application in criticisms of the neglect of Northern Ireland in broader criminological discussions (Brewer *et al.*, 1997). Yet the singular and (out of necessity) often innovative paths in penal policy taken in post-conflict societies such as Northern Ireland present valuable opportunities to test the validity of western criminological assumptions. Those interested in desistance, for example, will no doubt find much to interest them in the strikingly low reconviction rate associated with those political prisoners released on licence after the Good Friday Agreement (see further Behan and Bates-Gaston, *infra*; Healy, *infra*). The role played by restorative justice in both reducing levels of violence in the community in the period following the ceasefires and in reducing the youth detention rate in Northern Ireland is also a topic which holds much criminological interest (see further McEvoy and Mika, 2002; Jacobson and Gibbs, 2009; O'Dwyer and Payne, *infra*). It may be that, rather than transitional societies being sidelined as exceptional societies or societies 'in waiting', they offer insights as 'harbingers of a global future' (Comaroff and Comaroff, 2006: 42). Indeed, as already noted, the idea of transitional societies or societies experiencing conflict as *sui generis* or irrelevant to mainstream criminology is turned on its head by work such as Hillyard's on the 'contagion' effect of government policies in Northern Ireland. Plentiful material for theoretical reflection may also be found in research detailing the implicit challenges to state sovereignty presented by the involvement of the community sector in policing Northern Ireland (see further Bowden and Topping, *infra*). The plurality of actors involved in policing 'from below' as well as 'from above' and the manner in which they are accommodated by the state may well provide valuable lessons for theory construction more broadly, particularly in light of the increasingly 'negotiated' nature of contemporary criminal justice (Vaughan and Kilcommins, 2010).

The state of Irish criminology

The above discussion is strongly suggestive of a body of Irish criminological scholarship which not only draws significant inspiration from external research, but also makes original and important contributions to knowledge. In light of this, and as previously noted, the aim of the *Routledge Handbook of Irish Criminology* is to showcase and critically review this emerging corpus of research. The title immediately posits the assumption that there is a single or unified 'Irish criminology', something which is contestable, particularly since the Handbook covers two separate jurisdictions. Undeniably, there is a sense in which the preoccupations of criminologists north and south of the border diverge, with Northern Irish researchers tending to focus predominantly on the Conflict, often analysing traditional criminological topics through this lens. In contrast, researchers in the Republic of Ireland are more concerned with topics related to criminal justice policy development and historical issues. This has been very helpfully described by Professor Mick Ryan, one of our advisers in this project, as a bifurcation between what he sees as a 'transitional' criminology in Northern Ireland and a more 'modernising' approach south of the border. Yet, as he goes on to point out, there is nothing wrong with discussing Irish 'criminologies' rather than a single criminology if that reflects what is actually happening on the ground. Moreover, although the aim of the Handbook is not to impose a false unity, a welcome outcome is to recognise the synergies that exist between criminological research and crime control policy in the two jurisdictions. As noted above, in a very real sense the Conflict strongly influenced the way in which criminal justice was and is done in the Republic as well as in Northern Ireland.

A further consideration is the heterogeneity of the field. As will become apparent to readers of the Handbook, contributors employed multiple theoretical perspectives and a variety of methods in the preparation of the chapters. This diversity is unsurprising given their range of disciplinary backgrounds, which include sociology, psychology, law, political science, history and medicine. This issue clearly mirrors wider debates on the extent to which it is meaningful to talk about a unified criminology, with existential dilemmas regarding the status of criminology now well-rehearsed internationally. Whereas some scholars believe that criminology constitutes a self-contained disciplinary field, many regard it as a substratum of other, more established, disciplines. Indeed, it has become a truism to refer to criminology as a hybrid, cross-disciplinary or rendezvous subject. For example, Loader and Sparks (2012: 10) describe criminology as being 'organised around a social problem which serves as a crossroads for exchange between researchers trained in more basic disciplines (sociology, psychology, law, philosophy, history, economics, political science) and is repeatedly animated and rejuvenated by ideas and concepts imported from outside'. Similarly, Bosworth and Hoyle (2011: 6) portray criminology as a transgressive field because it 'pilfers knowledge and methodologies from the key disciplines that originally produced criminologists: namely sociology, psychology and law'. They urge criminological scholars to adopt a more reflexive approach in their work and to critically reflect on the aims, methodologies, consequences (intended and unintended) and key debates in the field. The potential impact of the wider institutional context on knowledge production and consumption should also be considered, including the role of institutions that fund research, control access to data, employ criminologists and decide to use or ignore criminological findings (Loader and Sparks, 2012). Nevertheless, it is widely agreed that criminology is enlivened by its manifold origins which open up rich, diverse seams of knowledge to scholars in the field (Loader and Sparks, 2012; Bosworth and Hoyle, 2011).

From the 1990s onwards, the criminological enterprise expanded rapidly in Europe and the US, primarily due to rising public and political concern about crime and criminal justice issues (Loader and Sparks, 2012). In contrast, criminology in Northern Ireland and the Republic of Ireland remains underdeveloped. In fact, O'Donnell (2005: 99) described criminology in the Republic of Ireland as an 'absentee discipline' on the basis that: there was only one dedicated academic post in the field; the quality of criminal justice data was poor; state support for criminological research was scarce; there were no specialist journals or societies; and indigenous scholarship barely made ripples in national or international debates. Lockhart (2014) made similar observations in relation to Northern Ireland. Applying O'Donnell's (2005) indicators today, it would appear that criminology on the island of Ireland has experienced substantial growth in the past decade. First, there are now approximately 80 academics (along with a handful of international scholars) actively engaged in criminological research. In addition, many academic institutions now offer undergraduate, postgraduate or doctoral courses in criminology, criminal justice and other related disciplines (we counted over 30 programmes with criminological components). That all of the major academic institutions on the island of Ireland are represented in criminological pedagogy and research highlights the influence and dynamism of the discipline in 2015.

Second, criminal justice data are more readily available and of better quality than a decade ago. Although criminal justice agencies in the Republic of Ireland began to computerise their records at the turn of the century, the involvement of the Central Statistics Office in the compilation of recorded crime and recidivism statistics from 2003 onwards further improved data quality and analysis, albeit from a very low base.[3] In addition, a number of important innovations enhanced access to research resources, including NUI Maynooth's All-Island Research Observatory (AIRO), which creates spatial maps of key socio-economic factors such as crime, and the UCD Irish Social Science Data Archive (ISSDA), which stores and disseminates quantitative data sets in the social sciences. Despite these positive developments, there is still significant scope for improvement. Although criminal justice agencies now publish statistics in a timely fashion, these data only include basic information such as counts and demographic profiles. While useful, such information cannot provide insights into the lives and experiences of people in contact with the criminal justice system. In addition, there is no dedicated government research agency, although some criminal justice agencies, including the Probation Service and An Garda Síochána, have established research, statistical or information units. Indeed, the fact that the National Crime Council (1999–2008) was one of the few 'quangos' to be culled under the austerity programme (which was introduced in an effort to reduce government spending in the aftermath of the 2008 recession) illustrates political lack of interest in criminological research. Moreover, and as is the case in many jurisdictions, researchers often encounter resistance from gatekeepers when attempting to access research sites; a response which may be due to a limited understanding of the utility of empirical research among policymakers and practitioners, at least within some state agencies. Finally, aside from the Irish Research Council and European funding bodies, funding streams for criminological research remain limited, with little or no funding currently available from the Department of Justice and Equality.

The statistical and research infrastructure in Northern Ireland is somewhat better developed, perhaps due to influence of the managerialist philosophy which became a central feature of criminal justice policymaking in the United Kingdom during the late 1990s. For instance, the Department of Justice Northern Ireland (DOJNI), in conjunction with the Northern Ireland Statistics and Research Agency (NISRA), publishes regular surveys on topics such as victimisation and witness satisfaction and also produces occasional research reports. In addition, these organisations act as clearing houses for the statistics produced by individual criminal justice agencies, compiling and disseminating statistics on a wide range of topics, including police-recorded crime, prison populations, the operation of the criminal courts and re-offending (an important drawback being that some of these statistics relate only to the last ten years). Another key data source is the Northern Ireland Neighbourhood Information Service (NINIS), which provides micro-level statistics and maps for a range of social indicators including crime. Furthermore, a number of research repositories have recently been set up, including the Northern Ireland Qualitative Archive (NIQA) and the Online Research Bank (ORB). There are also more opportunities for research funding available to Northern Irish scholars, who can apply to funding bodies in the United Kingdom such as the British Academy and the Economic and Social Research Council (ESRC), and also to locally based sources such as the Office of the First Minister and Deputy First Minister (OFMDFM).

Third, it is still the case that there are no specialist criminology journals or societies, which means that Irish and Northern Irish scholars must publish their work in related disciplines.

Consequently, the field is quite fragmented and, to a certain extent, exists in disciplinary silos. Key publication outlets include the *Irish Jurist*, *Irish Criminal Law Journal*, *Probation Journal* (jointly published by the Irish Probation Service and the Northern Ireland Probation Service), the *Northern Ireland Legal Quarterly*, the *Irish Journal of Psychological Medicine* and the *Irish Journal of Sociology*. Nevertheless, a north-south criminology conference, which has been in existence for about a decade, provides an important annual forum for research dissemination and networking.

Fourth, the visibility and impact of Irish criminological research has grown slowly but steadily over the last ten years, although its influence on national policy development remains very limited. This problem is of course not unique to this island, and the growing gap between policymakers and criminological researchers is well-documented elsewhere (see e.g. Garland, 2001). On a more positive note, Irish and Northern Irish scholars regularly make significant contributions to international theoretical and research debates. Reflecting this, contemporary international texts now frequently contain chapters on the Republic of Ireland and/or Northern Ireland (e.g. Robinson and McNeill, 2015; Tonry, 2014; Gelsthorpe and Morgan, 2013).

The Handbook

Irish criminology is therefore best characterised as a nascent but dynamic discipline, no longer in its infancy but in its adolescence. Yet, despite various advances in the field, there has been no text of sufficient quality, depth and scope to meet the needs of professionals working in the field. We aimed to address this deficit by producing a comprehensive and authoritative guide to Irish criminology.

Our first task was to decide which scholars would be invited to contribute to the Handbook, and we opted to approach scholars from a variety of disciplinary backgrounds to reflect the multi-disciplinary nature of the field. This created challenges for contributors who not only had to marry the research literatures of two very different jurisdictions but also their own theoretical and methodological preferences. Nevertheless, the approach encouraged them to engage in comparative and cross-disciplinary analysis, and we feel that the chapters are stronger as a result. In addition, efforts were made to be as inclusive as possible by recruiting a cross-section of both early-stage and established scholars. Finally, we endeavoured to achieve a good jurisdictional balance but, despite our best efforts, a small number of chapters focus on one jurisdiction more than the other. This imbalance is primarily explained by a dearth of research on some topics in one of the jurisdictions.

Our invitations to prospective contributors received an overwhelmingly positive response, perhaps reflecting widespread recognition of the need for this book, as well as the close and supportive culture that exists among criminologists on this island. Although we did not attempt to directly incorporate the perspectives of people who commit crime, their voices are represented by the evocative cover image that was designed by artist and former prisoner Eric Boylan, who based the image on a photograph taken by Hideta Nagai.

Another key issue concerned the terminology that would be used to describe the two jurisdictions. This poses particular problems when dealing with societies in transition, where sovereignty may be contested. Ultimately, we opted for the legal names of the jurisdictions; that is, 'Northern Ireland' and the 'Republic of Ireland.' We felt that 'Northern Ireland' constituted the least politically loaded term but recognise that some scholars may take issue with this designation. Also, references to the 'Republic of Ireland' may sound strange to Irish ears since most people refer to the country as simply 'Ireland' (its constitutional name). Nevertheless, the designation is used to draw a clear distinction between the two jurisdictions for the benefit of international readers.

Overview

The Handbook, which is the first of its kind to amalgamate, analyse and compare Irish and Northern Irish literatures, contains a collection of 30 high-quality chapters authored by leading experts who were carefully selected on the basis of their expertise and standing in the field. The Handbook is divided into four thematic sections:

I. **Understanding crime:** This section explores the extent to which general crime trends in Northern Ireland and the Republic of Ireland mirror those observed elsewhere. It also analyses patterns of specific criminal behaviours such as homicide, cybercrime and gangland crime. The theoretical explanations used to understand these behaviours are critically reviewed to investigate whether international perspectives are applicable in a different setting.

II. **Responding to crime:** This section examines criminal justice responses to crime, beginning with efforts to prevent crime, through policing and criminal trial, and on to post-conviction issues such as imprisonment and community sanctions. Modern themes such as the emerging focus on restorative justice and innovations in youth justice policy and practice are examined and situated in the context of European and international literature.

III. **Contexts of crime:** The topics in this section investigate the mediating factors that influence the criminal justice policymaking process, including the quality of media representation, the role of the victim and the views of individual ministers. International influences are also examined, such as the influence of membership of the European Union and the impact of the now-dominant neoliberal economic model.

IV. **Emerging ideas:** This section focuses on innovative ideas and practices that originated in Northern Ireland and the Republic of Ireland but impacted significantly on international debates; in some cases, even prompting a reconsideration of received wisdom on particular topics. It considers subjects such as child sexual abuse in the Catholic Church, the use of psychiatric institutions as sites of social control and ethnic diversity.

References

Aas, K. (2012) 'The Earth Is One but the World Is Not: Criminological theory and its geopolitical divisions', *Theoretical Criminology*, 16(1): 5–20.

Aas, K. and Bosworth, M. (2013) *The Borders of Punishment: Migration, citizenship and social exclusion*. Oxford: Oxford University Press.

Adler, F. (1983) *Nations Not Obsessed with Crime*. Littleton, CO: Rothman.

Bosworth, M. and Hoyle, C. (2011) *What Is Criminology?* Oxford: Oxford University Press.

Brady, C. (1974) *Guardians of the Peace*. Dublin: Prendeville Publishing.

Brewer, J. D., Lockhart, B. and Rodgers, P. (1997) *Crime in Ireland 1945–95: Here be dragons*. Oxford: Oxford University Press.

Campbell, L. (2010) 'Responding to Gun Crime in Ireland', *British Journal of Criminology*, 50(3): 414–434.

Comaroff, J. L. and Comaroff, J. (2006) 'Law and Disorder in the Postcolony: An introduction' in J. L. Comaroff and J. Comaroff, (eds) *Law and Disorder in the Postcolony*. Chicago: University of Chicago Press.

Connell, R. (2006) 'Northern Theory: The political geography of general social theory', *Theory and Society*, 35(2): 237–264.

Daems, T. (2007) 'Deconstructing Punitiveness: Review: Natasha A. Frost (2006): The Punitive State: Crime, Punishment and Imprisonment across the United States. New York, LFB Scholarly Publishing', *Crime, Law and Social Change*, 47(2): 129–133.

Dickson, B. (2005) *The Legal System of Northern Ireland*. Belfast: SLS Legal Publications.

Downes, D. and Morgan, R. (1994) 'Hostages to Fortune: The politics of law and order in post-war Britain' in M. Maguire *et al.* (eds), *Oxford Handbook of Criminology*. Oxford: Oxford University Press.

Enzmann, D., Marshall, I-H., Killias, M., Junger-Tas, J. and Steketee, M. (2010) 'Self Reported Youth Delinquency in Europe and Beyond: First results of the Second International Self-Report Delinquency Study in the context of police and vicitmisation data', *European Journal of Criminology*, 7(2): 159–183.

Ferriter, D. (2004) *The Transformation of Ireland*. London: Profile Books.

Garland, D. (2001) *The Culture of Control: Crime and social order in contemporary society*. Oxford: Oxford University Press.

Gelsthorpe, L. and Morgan, R. (eds) (2013) *Handbook of Probation*. Abingdon: Routledge.

Greer, C. (2003) *Sex Crime in the Media: Sex offending and the press in a divided society*. Cullompton: Willan.

Griffin, D. and O'Donnell, I. (2012) 'The Life Sentence and Parole', *British Journal of Criminology*, 52(3): 611–629.

Hallsworth, S. and Lea, J. (2008) 'Confronting the Criminology of Complacency: A rejoinder to some recent critiques of the "punitive turn"'. [Online] Available at: www.bunker8.pwp.blueyonder.co.uk/misc/complacency.html [accessed 13 April 2014].

Hamilton, C. (2007) *The Presumption of Innocence and Irish Criminal Law: Whittling the golden thread*. Dublin: Irish Academic Press.

—— (2011) 'Organised Criminals as "Agents of Obligation": The case of Ireland', *European Journal on Criminal Policy and Research*, 17(4): 253–266.

—— (2014a) *Reconceptualising Penality: A comparative perspective on punitiveness in Ireland, Scotland and New Zealand*. Farnham: Ashgate.

—— (2014b) 'Reconceptualising Penality: Towards a multidimensional test for punitiveness', *British Journal of Criminology*, 52(4): 321–343.

Hamilton, C., Carr, N. and Fitzgibbon, W. (2014) 'Practice Cultures in Youth Justice: A comparative perspective', Practitioners' Forum: Youth Justice. London Metropolitan University. 4 June.

Healy, D. and O'Donnell, I. (2005) 'Probation in the Republic of Ireland: Context and challenges', *Probation Journal*, 52(1): 56–68.

Hillyard, P. (1985) 'Lessons from Ireland' in B. Fine and R. Millar (eds) *Policing the Miners' Strike*. London: Lawrence and Wishart.

—— (1987) 'The Normalization of Special Powers: From Northern Ireland to Britain', in P. Scraton (ed) *Law, Order and the Authoritarian State*. Milton Keynes: Open University Press.

Hollywood, B. (1997) 'Dancing in the Dark: Ecstasy, the dance culture, and moral panic in post ceasefire Northern Ireland', *Critical Criminology*, 8(1): 62–77.

Hourigan, N. (2011) *Understanding Limerick: Social Exclusion and Change*. Cork: Cork University Press.

Jacobson, J. and Gibbs, P. (2009) *Making Amends: Restorative justice in Northern Ireland*. London: Prison Reform Trust.

Keenan, M. (2012) *Child Sexual Abuse and the Catholic Church: Gender, power, organizational culture*. New York: Oxford University Press.

Kilcommins, S., O'Donnell, I., O'Sullivan, E. and Vaughan, B. (2004) *Crime, Punishment and the Search for Order in Ireland*. Dublin: Institute of Public Administration.

Loader, I. and Sparks, R. (2012) 'Situating Criminology: On the production and consumption of knowledge about crime and justice.' in M. Maguire, R. Morgan and R. Reiner (eds) *The Oxford Handbook of Criminology*. 5th ed. Oxford: Oxford University Press.

Lockhart, B. (2014) 'Crime Statistics and Survey in Northern Ireland'. Available at: http://www.cain.ulst.ac.uk/othelem/research/esrc7.htm [accessed 24 March 2015].

McEldowney, J. F. (1990) 'Some Aspects of Law and Police in the Administration of Criminal Justice in Nineteenth-Century Ireland' in J.F. McEldowney and P. O'Higgins (eds) *The Common Law Tradition: Essays in Irish legal history*. Dublin: Irish Academic Press.

McElrath, K. (2004) 'Drug Use and Drug Markets in the Context of Political Conflict: The case of Northern Ireland', *Addiction, Research and Theory*, 12(4): 577–590.

McEvoy, K. and Mika, H. (2002) 'Restorative Justice and the Critique of Informalism in Northern Ireland', *British Journal of Criminology*, 42(3): 534–562.

Mulcahy, A. (2002) 'The Impact of the Northern Troubles on Criminal Justice in the Irish Republic' in P. O'Mahony (ed) *Criminal Justice in Ireland*. Dublin: Institute of Public Administration.

—— (2005) 'The "Other" Lessons from Ireland? Policing, political violence and policy transfer', *European Journal of Criminology*, 2(2): 185–209.

—— (2013) 'Great Expectations and Complex Realities: Assessing the impact and implications of the police reform process in Northern Ireland' in J. Brown (ed.) *The Future of Policing*. London: Routledge.

Neapolitan, J. (2001) 'An Examination of Cross-national Variation in Punitiveness', *International Journal of Offender Therapy and Comparative Criminology*, 45(6): 691–710.

O'Connell, M. (1998) 'Stop This Madness: And tone down the headlines too'. *Magill*, 1 January.

O'Donnell, I. (2005) 'Crime and Justice in the Republic of Ireland', *European Journal of Criminology*, 2(1): 99–131.

—— (2008) 'Stagnation and Change in Irish Penal Policy', *Howard Journal of Criminal Justice*, 47(2): 121–133.

O'Donnell, I. and Jewkes, Y. (2011) 'Going Home for Christmas: Prisoners, a taste of freedom and the press', *The Howard Journal of Criminal Justice*, 50(1): 75–91.

O'Donnell, I. and O'Sullivan, E. (2003) 'The Politics of Intolerance – Irish Style', *British Journal of Criminology*, 43(1): 41–62.

O'Mahony, P. (1996) *Criminal Chaos: Seven crises in Irish criminal justice*. Dublin: Round Hall Sweet and Maxwell.

—— (1998) 'Losing the Plot'. *Magill*, 1 January.

O'Sullivan, E. and O'Donnell, I. (2007) 'Coercive Confinement in the Republic of Ireland: The waning of a culture of control', *Punishment & Society*, 9(1): 27–48.

—— (2012) *Coercive Confinement in Ireland: Patients, prisoners and penitents*. Manchester: Manchester University Press.

Pantazis, C. and Pemberton, S. (2009) 'From the Old to the New "Suspect Community": Examining the impact of recent UK counter terrorism legislation', *British Journal of Criminology*, 49(5): 464–666.

Robinson, G. and McNeill, F. (eds) (2015) *Community Punishment: European perspectives*. Abingdon: Routledge.

Rogan, M. (2011) *Prison Policy in Ireland: Politics, penal-welfarism and political imprisonment*. Abingdon: Routledge.

Rolston, B. and Tomlinson, M. (1982) 'Spectators at the "Carnival of Reaction"'? in M. Kelly, L. O'Dowd and J. Wickham (eds) *Power, Conflict and Inequality*. Dublin: Turoe Press.

Tomlinson, M. (2012) 'From Counter-terrorism to Criminal Justice: Transformation or business as usual?', *Howard Journal of Criminal Justice*, 51(5): 442–457.

Tonry, M. (2014) *Oxford Handbooks Online in Criminology and Criminal Justice*. New York: Oxford.

Topping, J. R. and Byrne, J. (2014) '"Shadow Policing": The boundaries of community-based "policing" in Northern Ireland', *Policing and Society*. DOI:10.1080/10439463.2014.989152.

Vaughan, B. and Kilcommins, S. (2008) *Terrorism, Rights and the Rule of Law: Negotiating justice in Ireland*. Cullompton: Willan.

—— (2010) 'The Governance of Crime and the Negotiation of Justice', *Criminology and Criminal Justice*, 10(1): 59–75.

Notes

1 For a detailed history, see D. Ferriter (2004) *The Transformation of Ireland*. London: Profile Books.

2 At the time of writing, however, Northern Ireland's power-sharing executive is close to collapse following suggestions that members of the Irish Republican Army (IRA) may have been involved in a recent murder.

3 PRIS (Prisoner Records Information System) was introduced in 2001 (IPS, 2002) and PULSE (Police Using Leading Systems Effectively) in 1999 (CSO, 2008).

Part I
Understanding crime

1

Crime trends

Sara Parsons[1]

Introduction

The *Oxford English Dictionary* defines crime as 'an action or omission which constitutes an offence and is punishable by law'. However, whilst a contravention of legislation might sound simple to define and record, it is far from so in reality. What constitutes a crime will vary from country to country and over time. What was once defined as criminal is repealed or decriminalised due to social and cultural developments. For example, suicide was decriminalised in Northern Ireland in 1966[2] and in the Republic of Ireland in 1993.[3] Similarly, new criminal offences are enacted. These may stem from new technologies, which facilitate new methods of offending, or from general trends and behaviours in society which the legislature seeks to reduce or curtail. Additionally, a crime only becomes a crime 'when influential human beings have decided what meaning to attribute to it' (Box, 1981: 162).

This chapter considers police-recorded crime statistics between 1963 and 2013 in the Republic of Ireland and Northern Ireland, both independently and in an international context. It considers briefly the impact of reporting rates and attitudes towards the police on the recorded crime figures over recent years. Following this, the results from domestic and international crime victimisation surveys in both jurisdictions are examined. A number of factors which may contribute to increases or decreases in crime, such as the proportion of young males in each jurisdiction, are discussed. The contrasts and similarities between police-recorded and victim-reported crime are outlined, and some possible explanations are offered for the divergent trends evident. Finally, areas in need of additional research are proposed.

Examining trends in crime – data sources and limitations

A myriad of issues must be considered when seeking to analyse crime statistics both within and across different jurisdictions. The most basic of these relates to the fact that there is no way to measure with complete accuracy the number of crimes which are committed in any country. Hypothetically, there is a true crime rate, which consists of all acts that contravene legislation and hence are legally defined as criminal. To be 'counted' however, a criminal act must not only constitute a contravention of law but must also be reported and recorded as such.

The decision to report a crime

A person or entity who has been the victim of a crime may not necessarily report their victimisation to the police for a variety of reasons. In terms of crimes against property, a victim may choose not to report because they believe the crime is too minor, or there has been no/limited financial loss. Typically, such crimes include vandalism/criminal damage and attempted burglaries (van Dijk *et al.*, 2007a; CSO, 2010; PSNI, 2014). In terms of crimes against the person, a victim may choose not to report because they do not wish to subject themselves to the intrusion of a criminal investigation, feel ashamed, believe the crime was too trivial or because it happened a substantial period of time ago. Typically, such crimes include victims of sexual, domestic or child abuse (McGee *et al.*, 2002; Watson and Parsons, 2005).

Unreported crime

Nevertheless, certain unreported crimes may come to the attention of the police during the course of their day-to-day duties or as a result of specific enforcement initiatives. Such enforcement initiatives can lead to substantial, if short-term, increases in recorded crimes. There is a correlation therefore between reporting rates, policing priorities and activity and the amount of crime recorded.

There will also be a number of crimes which have occurred that are not reported or disclosed at all, for example, crimes that do not have a direct victim or that have an offender who is already in conflict with the law. However, even if a crime is reported to the police, it must be recorded as such before it will appear in a jurisdiction's crime statistics.

The decision to record a crime

Just because a crime has been reported or the police are aware a crime has taken place, it does not necessarily mean that the crime will be recorded. Two factors impact at this stage. The first is police discretion and the second relates to the nuances of police recording systems and procedures.

Discretion is a legitimate police power which is used to decide which course of action to take in a given situation. That decision may be to take no action. This may be motivated by a number of factors, including a desire to avoid criminalising people for offences which have come to police attention. Whilst the law can guide many police actions, it cannot provide absolute clarity for every situation a police officer will encounter; police must also use their own judgement. A police officer:

> [C]annot decide to arrest, warn, caution … a suspect simply by taking into account the legal facts of the case. Consequently, he has to introduce other criteria: these usually reflect his personal values, beliefs and prejudices, and those of the social group with whom he identifies.
>
> *(Box, 1981: 171)*

Police officer training, instructions from supervisors and policies of the police service will also influence the level of discretion employed. Whilst discretion is essential to enable the police to function efficiently, it is also a contentious issue. It can be difficult to ensure that discretion is employed in a fair and consistent manner and that the police are accountable for the discretionary decisions they make. Academic authors have noted that police attention and interaction, both with suspects and victims, can be disproportionately focused and '[T]ypically comprises individuals and groups who are marginalised in some way (people who are on low incomes, young in age, and of ethnic minority background are typically over-represented)' (Healy *et al.*, 2013: 16). This is often because these groups spend more time in public places and hence are more likely to come to police attention.

The second issue is that the total amount of crime reported to the police is not the same as the total amount of crime recorded (or counted) by the police. Many jurisdictions have formal recording procedures and crime counting rules. In the Republic of Ireland and Northern Ireland, a crime must be recorded if, on the balance of probability, the police believe a crime occurred and there is no credible evidence to the contrary.[4] Crime counting rules also apply in both jurisdictions; a significant example of this is the primary/principal offence rule. This dictates that when multiple criminal acts are committed within one episode, only the most serious offence[5] is counted. Both jurisdictions give primacy to offences against the person over offences against property. So, for example, if a home is entered, the householder is raped and their car stolen, the rape will be counted. It is important to note that the police record reported crimes for operational use. Hence, whilst they provide some representation of police workload, they do not, nor are they intended to, represent the total level of crime which actually occurs. During periods where there are no substantial changes in crime counting and recording rules or in victim reporting rates, police crime statistics can also be useful to ascertain general trends in crime.

The police are not the only agencies responsible for law enforcement however; others include Revenue – Irish Tax and Customs, Her Majesty's Revenue and Customs, as well as An Post/ BBC/TV Licensing. Offences reported to/recorded by other law enforcement agencies may be published, for example, in lists of tax defaulters published by the respective revenue services. Where settlements are reached these acts may not be officially labelled as 'criminal'.

Measuring crimes not reported to the police

Crime victimisation surveys are used to elicit details of crimes not reported to the police. They do not, however, include the full range of the criminal law, as some offences are deemed too sensitive for inclusion, such as sexual offences or offences against children. There are also surveys conducted by the private and/or commercial sector which attempt to measure crimes against businesses,[6] as there may be some reluctance to report such crimes due to commercial sensitivities. Other crimes may be disclosed to certain other agencies or services but not to the police or crime victims' surveys. An example of such disclosure would be experience of rape if victims attended for medical treatment or to make use of other support services. Some such agencies publish details of the use of their services which may be useful when considering victimisation trends.[7]

The configuration of crime statistics

The outer circle in Figure 1.1 represents the absolute total amount of crime in any jurisdiction. The various internal shapes show the configuration from different sources of reported and recorded crime. The area of the circle not covered by any internal shape represents all crime which is unrecorded via any source.

The first source of data considered when examining crime trends in the Republic of Ireland and Northern Ireland are police-recorded crime statistics. As outlined, these must be considered in the context of the rules pertaining to recording; the most significant issues are outlined briefly below and sources of additional information are provided.

17

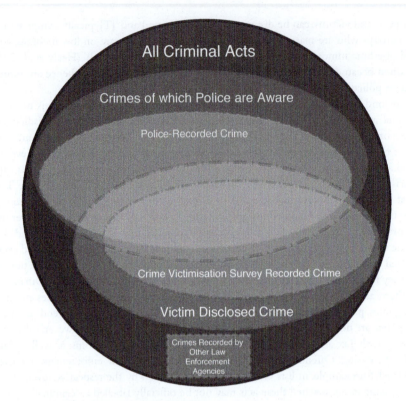

Figure 1.1 The configuration of crime statistics

Police-recorded crime statistics

The Police Service of Northern Ireland (PSNI),[8] in common with all constabularies in England and Wales, adheres to the Home Office crime recording standards.[9] These state that all notifiable offences (previously, indictable offences) are recorded and published in crime statistics.[10] Notifiable offences are all those which could possibly be tried by a jury (i.e. in a Crown Court or higher) and also includes some less serious offences, such as minor thefts. The crime statistics do not include details of non-notifiable offences.[11] Figures are published by the PSNI in annual reports and figures dating back to 1968 and are available online.[12]

The Garda Annual Reports from 1922 to 2005 include full details of the number of recorded indictable offences[13] in the Republic of Ireland. Indictable offences have a similar meaning to Northern Ireland, in that they could be tried by a jury (i.e. in the Circuit Court or higher). Whilst not publishing figures on the total number of non-indictable offences recorded, the Garda Síochána did publish figures on the numbers of persons proceeded against for non-indictable offences. The Central Statistics Office (CSO) took responsibility for the publication of crime statistics in 2006 and introduced a new Irish Crime Classification System (ICCS). Under the ICCS, statistics on all crime recorded by the Garda Síochána (both what was previously indictable and non-indictable) were published for the first time. This led to a substantial increase in the overall total crime figures. The CSO has since published crime statistics according to the ICCS dating back to 2003. This chapter uses CSO-supplied indictable recorded crime figures for 2003 to 2013.

In both jurisdictions, over the time period examined, there have been changes to the crime counting rules used by the respective police services.[14] Additionally, new computerised crime recording systems have been introduced (ICIS[15] and NICHE in Northern Ireland, PULSE[16] in the Republic of Ireland). Both of these factors create breaks in the data series. It would be expected also that the improvements in recording brought about by the new systems would lead to increases in recorded crime figures.

Trends in police-recorded crime statistics

Trends between 1963 and 2013

Crime trends over a fifty-year span (from 1963 to 2013, the most recent available) were examined to provide a long-term view within each jurisdiction. This time period also encompasses significant social and cultural changes. At the macro level, there have been differing trends in the population of the Republic of Ireland and Northern Ireland. With the exception of some dips in the late eighties and early nineties, the population of the Republic of Ireland has grown incrementally from under 3,000,000 to over 4,500,000. In Northern Ireland, the population remained around 1,500,000 until the early eighties (with some reductions in the seventies) and has since grown slowly to over 1,800,000. There has been significant political and civil conflict in Northern Ireland[17] from the late sixties until the late nineties, which also impacted the Republic of Ireland.

Both jurisdictions have become more densely populated and urbanised. Household sizes have reduced dramatically, but the number of rooms per household has increased. From a time when most homes did not have a television, washing machine or landline telephone, there has been a substantial increase in the number of electronic appliances invented and present in the majority of homes – from video cassette recorders to DVD players; games consoles to music players and mobile phones. Car ownership has also greatly increased. In the Republic of Ireland particularly, the 'Celtic Tiger' roared, and then the economy fell into a deep and prolonged recession. There have been peaks in unemployment, in both jurisdictions during the eighties and again since 2009, which are now beginning to decline again.[18] All of these changes in society and the increased availability of tempting targets have influenced crime trends to some extent.

In 1963 the Gardaí recorded 16,203 crimes in the Republic of Ireland, and the Royal Ulster Constabulary (RUC) recorded 10,859 crimes in Northern Ireland. By 2013, there were 113,019 crimes[19], officially recorded in the Republic of Ireland and 102,746 in Northern Ireland. Crudely considering the total time period, recorded crime increased by almost seven times in the Republic of Ireland (698 per cent) and over nine times in Northern Ireland (946 per cent). Figures 1.2 and 1.3 present the annual figures for both jurisdictions. What is striking is the remarkably similar trends evident in both jurisdictions from 1963 until the end of the century and the divergent trends since the start of the twenty-first century.

In both jurisdictions, recorded crime rose in the late sixties and into the early seventies with 1973 showing a decrease. There is a further sustained period of upward trends during the mid-seventies before a slight plateau is reached in the late seventies. The early eighties in the Republic of Ireland saw the upward trends continue until a peak in 1983; by this time 102,387 crimes were recorded. During the course of these twenty years (1963–83), recorded crime increased more than six times (632 per cent). In Northern Ireland, whilst there are also increases in the early to mid-eighties, the peak does not occur until three years later in 1986, when 68,255 crimes were recorded. Similarly to the Republic, recorded crime in Northern Ireland increased more than sixfold (629 per cent) over the course of these twenty-three years

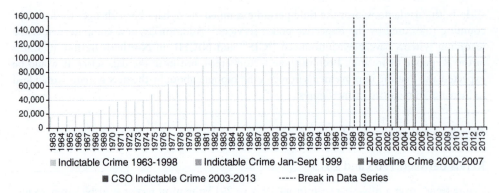

Figure 1.2 Total recorded indictable crime in the Republic of Ireland (Garda Síochána and CSO) 1963–2013

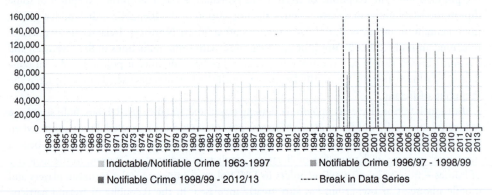

Figure 1.3 Total recorded indictable/notifiable crime in Northern Ireland (RUC and PSNI) 1963–2013[20]

(1963–86). Into the late eighties and the early nineties, trends in both jurisdictions continue to display similarities; there are decreases for a number of years, followed by increases into the new decade. Both jurisdictions record new highs in 1995, although for both all that has happened in reality is the reductions seen in the mid/late eighties have been eroded, and crime figures have returned to slightly above their levels at the last peak in the eighties. In 1995 there were 102,484 crimes in the Republic of Ireland and 68,808 in Northern Ireland.

Much of the increase in the Republic of Ireland in the early eighties is attributed to the emergence of the use of illegal drugs, including heroin, as 'addicts frequently involved themselves in all sorts of theft and property crime to acquire money to feed the habit' (Brewer *et al.*, 1997: 47). Indeed, there were peaks in the numbers of people charged with non-indictable drug offences in 1983 and 1995 – both years when recorded indictable crime also spiked. In Northern Ireland, drug use had less of an impact on the overall crime trends. This has been linked to the fact that there was greater use of recreational drugs, such as cannabis and ecstasy, rather than those which were more expensive and addictive, such as heroin and cocaine (Brewer *et al.*, 1997). Instead, the political and civil conflict played a part in the increases in crime; it had 'a knock-on effect on other crimes in the North. Property crime, rape and other sex crimes, and burglary, for example, all rose but not exponentially so during the worst years of "the troubles"' (Brewer *et al.*, 1997: 214).

In the late nineties and the early part of the new millennium there were significant changes in crime recording systems and practices (as well as in counting rules in Northern Ireland); these generated substantially higher numbers of crimes recorded in both jurisdictions, which should not be compared directly with the preceding years. What is apparent, considering the period after the changes, is the divergent trends emerging in each jurisdiction. In the Republic of Ireland, Garda-recorded indictable crime has increased since the turn of the century, with a possible levelling off or plateau emerging since 2011. As shall be seen later in the chapter, this is purely a by-product of the definition of indictable crime – when ICCS-recorded crime is examined, trends have decreased since 2008. In Northern Ireland, recorded crime has decreased since 2002 and also demonstrates a possible plateau emerging since 2011.

Figures 1.4 and 1.5 chart the recorded crime statistics on the basis of year-on-year percentage change. Both jurisdictions are more prone to annual increases in crime than decreases, and the increases tend to be of a larger magnitude than the decreases.

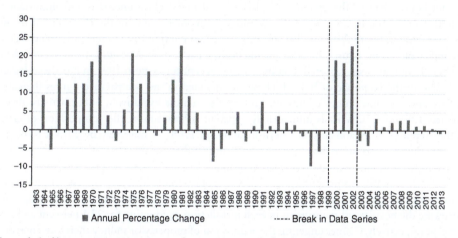

Figure 1.4 Year-on-year percentage change in recorded indictable crime in the Republic of Ireland 1963–2013 (exc. 1999)[21]

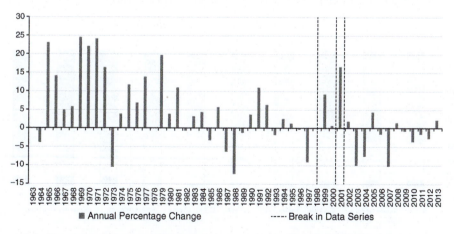

Figure 1.5 Year-on-year percentage change in recorded indictable/notifiable crime in Northern Ireland 1963–2013 (exc. 1998)[22]

The overall similarities between the two jurisdictions, highlighted in the earlier discussion, are also emphasised here, with 1973, 1985/88 and 1997 displaying pronounced decreases. Likewise, the contrasting trends of the two jurisdictions over the last ten years are evident. The Republic of Ireland records mainly increases but of a far lower magnitude year-on-year than in previous periods of rises in crime. Northern Ireland records mainly decreases which far outweigh any increases in crime.

The composition of police/Gardaí-recorded crime

In order to gain a more detailed understanding of patterns in crime, it is useful to consider the composition in terms of broad offence groups. The total police-recorded crime figures for Northern Ireland and the Republic of Ireland were examined by considering trends within the most comparable groups possible.[23] In this section therefore, the figures for the Republic of Ireland 2003–2013 are as published by the CSO according to the ICCS.[24] These ICCS figures are not comparable to the previous Garda-recorded indictable crime. It is also important to note that under the ICCS crime types considered, recorded crime in the Republic of Ireland increased from 2003 to 2008 and has since decreased, in contrast to the increasing trend seen in the indictable crime figures. In both jurisdictions, separate figures relating to indictable drugs offences have only been reported in comparatively recent times: from 1991 in Northern Ireland and 1994 in the Republic of Ireland. These are included in the comparative figures thereafter, as they are not only crimes of interest but are also, almost exclusively, police-activity-driven (Figures 1.6 and 1.7). What is immediately apparent is how similar the composition of crime in the Republic of Ireland and Northern Ireland is in 1968.[25] Conversely, by 2013 it is striking how much the composition has changed – in both jurisdictions this change coincides with, and is driven partly by, the revisions to crime recording.

In 1968, in both jurisdictions, the majority of police-recorded crime consists of thefts: 61.5 per cent in the Republic of Ireland and 53.4 per cent in Northern Ireland. Robberies and burglaries are the next largest constituent in each jurisdiction, accounting for 27.1 per cent and 33.8 per cent respectively. Crimes targeting the acquisition of property or money therefore constitute almost nine out of every ten recorded crimes in both jurisdictions. Offences against the person represent 5 per cent of crime in the Republic of Ireland and 4.2 per cent in Northern Ireland, with the remainder consisting of miscellaneous other indictable offences.[26]

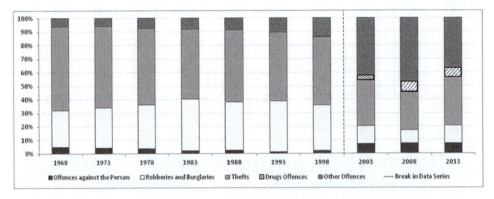

Figure 1.6 The composition of total Garda- and ICCS-recorded crime in the Republic of Ireland 1968–2013

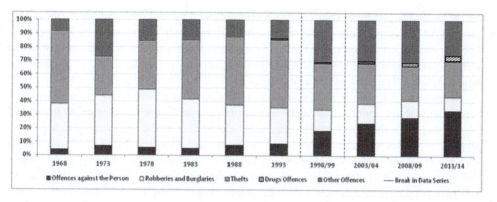

Figure 1.7 The composition of total police-recorded crime in Northern Ireland 1968–2013

Some key trends in acquisitive crime

It is beyond the scope of this chapter to examine multiple crime types in detail; instead some key trends in acquisitive crimes are noted. Arguably, the most serious of these are robberies. Trends in robbery were influenced and increased due, at least in part, to the political and civil conflict in Northern Ireland,[27] stemming from the need to finance actions related to the Conflict. In Northern Ireland, 50 robberies were recorded in 1968, and the figure escalated to 109 in 1970, 640 in 1971 and 2,310 in 1972 (a forty-sixfold increase on 1968). There were some reductions in the mid to late seventies, but robberies remained above 1,200 per year until another spike in 1981, when 2,731 robberies were recorded, and higher levels (over 1,800) were sustained until the late eighties. Similar trends were evident in the Republic of Ireland. In 1968 there were 101 robberies recorded, they then almost trebled between 1970 and 1972 to 618 (a sixfold increase on 1968). These higher levels of robberies were sustained in the early seventies and increased further throughout the seventies. Increases of similar scale were also seen in the early to mid-eighties.[28] These periods of increases in both jurisdictions coincide with heightened activity and increases in the number of people killed and injured in the Conflict.[29] The need to fund actions related to the Conflict has been highlighted by commentators as reflecting 'the impact of the "Troubles" in Northern Ireland that resulted in the increased organised criminal activity in the Republic of Ireland to finance terrorism' (Young, 2005: 62).

Historically in both jurisdictions, breaking-and-entering/burglaries from warehouses/shops/ non-domestic buildings were more prevalent than those targeting residential dwellings. Burglaries of private/residential dwellings outnumber those from non-residential buildings for the first time in 1976 in the Republic of Ireland and in 1988 in Northern Ireland.[30] The majority of thefts in both jurisdictions throughout the time period were from and of vehicles, from shops and other miscellaneous/low-value thefts. Thefts from the person have become much more prevalent in the recorded crime statistics, particularly in the Republic of Ireland, in recent years.

The impact of changes in police recording practices

A marked change occurs in the Republic of Ireland in 2003, when proportions are considered according to the ICCS, which includes a range of less serious offences. This is reflected by the largest proportionate group in 2013 being 'other offences' at 37 per cent (this group consists mainly of public-disorder-related offences, such as drunkenness and criminal damage). Thefts are the second largest proportion, 35.5 per cent, followed by robberies and burglaries at 13.1 per cent. All acquisitive crime has therefore reduced dramatically in proportion to 48.6 per cent. This is a result of the change to the ICCS only; the number of recorded robberies, burglaries and thefts increased between 1998 and 2003. Offences against the person represent 7.5 per cent and drugs offences 6.9 per cent of the total.

The most notable change in the composition of crime in Northern Ireland occurred in 1998 coinciding with the introduction of the new counting rules. Given the changes which moved towards recording the number of victims rather than offences, the substantial increase in the proportion of offences against the person is to be expected. The period after this also coincides with the ceasefires in the Northern Ireland Conflict, the Good Friday Agreement of 1998 as well as the disbanding of the RUC and the establishment of the PSNI in 2001. These factors may have led to some fundamental shifts in relations between the police and the public at this time. Reporting rates and attitudes towards the police are examined in greater detail in the next section.

Even so, further increases in the proportion of crimes against the person in Northern Ireland are apparent; between 2003 and 2013 these increased from 24 per cent to 33.7 per cent. By 2013 crimes targeting the acquisition of property or money constituted 36.3 per cent of all notifiable crime (actual figures also reduced over this time period). Drugs offences account for 4.6 per cent, and other offences have decreased proportionally since the introduction of the new counting rules from 29.8 percent in 2003 to 25.4 per cent in 2013.

Reporting rates and reasons for not reporting crime to the police/Gardaí

Crime victimisation surveys from the Republic of Ireland and Northern Ireland asked respondents whether they reported victimisation to the Gardaí/police and reasons for not reporting. Aggregate reporting rates were higher in the Republic of Ireland than Northern Ireland. In the Garda Research Unit's Public Attitudes Surveys (PAS) (2002) reporting rates for the most recent crime experienced ranged between 79 per cent (in 2003) and 88 per cent (in 1998). Considering the longest possible time period after the crime recording changes, reporting rates increased by 5 per cent[31] whilst ICCS recorded crime increased by 20 per cent. This suggests that increases in crime during this time were not only due to more crimes being reported. In the Northern Ireland Crime Survey (NICS), reporting rates have ranged between 37 per cent (in 2005/06) and 48 per cent (in 2001/02). Considering the longest possible time period after the crime recording changes (between 2003/04 and 2012/13), reporting rates increased by 6 per cent[32] whilst police-recorded crime decreased by 22 per cent. Hence reductions in recorded crime were not due to fewer crimes being reported.

The aggregate reporting rates found in the PAS were consistently higher than those found by the CSO in their Crime and Victimisation Surveys for individual crime types. Some of this difference may be attributable to the fact that respondents were aware the PAS was being conducted on behalf of the Gardai. At the incident level, the CSO found reporting rates in the Republic of Ireland generally increased between 2003 and 2010[33] (CSO, 2010). In Northern Ireland reporting rates between 2003/04 and 2012/13 have varied, reporting rates for household crimes have reduced[34] but for personal crimes have increased[35] (PSNI, 2013). Changes in the rates at which crimes are reported to the police may be indicative of improved confidence in the police or increasing seriousness of offences. Equally, they could be due to changes in levels of tolerance for certain types of crime generally. In both jurisdictions, the majority of respondents indicated that they did not report victimisation because they believed it was not serious enough, or there was no loss, or they believed the Police/Gardaí would/could do nothing. In Northern

Ireland, the proportion stating that they did not report through fear of reprisal declined between 2006 and 2010 and may be revealing of both the changing nature of society and the relationship between the public and the police. A small proportion of respondents in Northern Ireland did not report due to a dislike or fear of police or a previous bad experience of the police or courts (PSNI, 2013).[36]

Attitudes towards the police/Gardaí

Differing reporting rates can reflect differing relationships between the police and the populace. In the Republic of Ireland, the Garda PAS reported high but decreasing levels of satisfaction with the Garda Síochána[37] from 2002 to the most recent survey in 2008. The absence of a neutral response to this question may have served to boost the positive ratings. The CSO Crime and Victimisation Surveys asked respondents how they would rate the Gardaí in their local area. As with reporting rates generally, positive ratings are lower than those in the PAS. A similar trend is evident, however, with ratings of good and very good declining.[38] Throughout all years, Irish nationals have been more likely to give positive ratings than non-Irish nationals.

In Northern Ireland, attitudes towards the police were measured by the Northern Ireland Statistics and Research Agency (2000–2003) and subsequently the Northern Ireland Policing Board as part of the Omnibus Survey (2003–2013). Between 2000 and 2003 positive ratings declined.[39] The more recent Omnibus Survey provided respondents with a range of rating options[40] and the proportions of respondents stating that the police did a very or fairly good job have increased.[41] Positive ratings increased amongst both Protestant and Catholic respondents.

A somewhat paradoxical relationship between attitudes towards the policing services and reporting rates is therefore evident in both jurisdictions. In Northern Ireland, whilst positive attitudes towards the police have increased, reporting rates have decreased for certain household-related crimes but have increased for personal crimes. In the Republic of Ireland, there have been reductions in positive ratings and increases in reporting rates.

Recent trends in police/Gardaí-recorded crime (2003–2013)

Trends over the last ten years merit more detailed examination and allow for comparison with victimisation survey trends. Northern Ireland has recorded a general downward trend and the Republic of Ireland[42] a general upward trend until 2008, followed by a downward trend (Figures 1.8 and 1.9).

Populations in both jurisdictions have increased over the ten years between 2003 and 2013. In the Republic of Ireland, the population increased by 15 per cent, and recorded crime increased by 27 per cent to the peak in 2008. But overall recorded crime in 2013 and 2003 are broadly the same (increased by 1 per cent) (Figure 1.10). In Northern Ireland, the population has also increased but to a lesser extent, by 7 per cent, and recorded crime decreased by 20 per cent (Figure 1.11).

Figure 1.12 shows the total number of crimes per 100,000 population for both jurisdictions. In the Republic of Ireland, rates increased from 5,506 crimes per 100,000 population in 2003 to 6,179 per 100,000 in 2008, before falling to 4,832 per 100,000 population in 2013. In other words, recorded crime in the Republic of Ireland increased up until 2008, since when it has decreased in real terms. The year 2008 also coincides with the start of the economic recession in the Republic of Ireland (and elsewhere) and will be examined further later in the chapter.

In Northern Ireland, rates steadily declined over ten years, from 7,505 crimes per 100,000 population in 2003 to 5,615 per 100,000 in 2013. This trend shows that recorded crime in

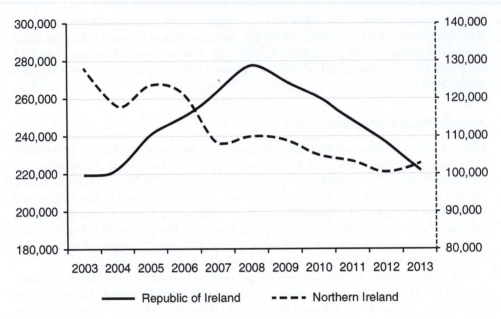

Figure 1.8   Total recorded ICCS/notifiable crime 2003–2013

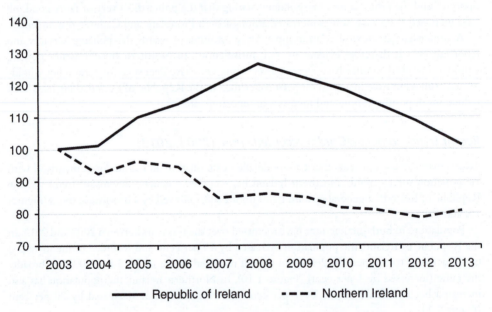

Figure 1.9   Indexed trends in recorded ICCS/notifiable crime (2003 = 100)

Northern Ireland has decreased in real terms. Due to all the issues created by differing legal systems and recording practices it is very difficult to compare crime rates across jurisdictions accurately. Suffice it to say, it is likely that the slightly higher rates in Northern Ireland are driven to some extent by the victim-focused recording. Rates in both jurisdictions are closer in 2013 than 2003 and were almost identical in 2008, but there have been no substantive changes to recording practices or counting rules during this timeframe.

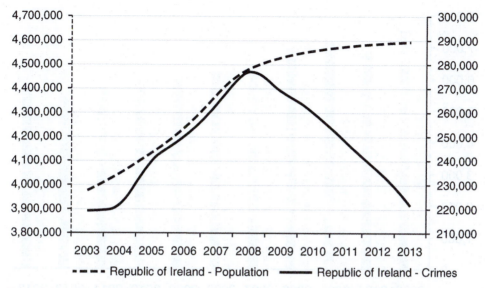

Figure 1.10 Total population and ICCS crimes in the Republic of Ireland 2003–2013

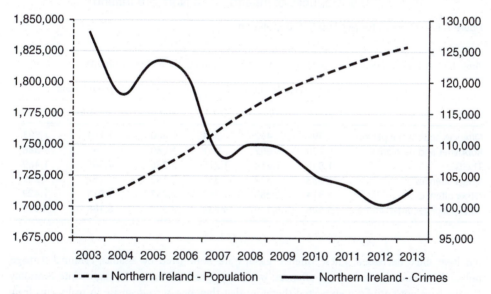

Figure 1.11 Total population and notifiable crime in Northern Ireland 2003–2013

These rates are based upon the total number of police-recorded crimes and may mask very different trends in particular crime types. Whilst it is not feasible to report on every type of crime, broad incident groupings allow a closer examination of changes in crime rates (Table 1.1).

The crime rates show that in both jurisdictions there were reductions in the majority of groupings in real terms in 2013 compared to 2003. Drugs offences, which are enforcement-driven, are the exception and increased overall in both jurisdictions. In Northern Ireland, there were consistent decreases for robberies and burglaries, thefts and other offences. In the Republic of Ireland rates for offences against the person, other offences and the overall rate peaked in 2008

27

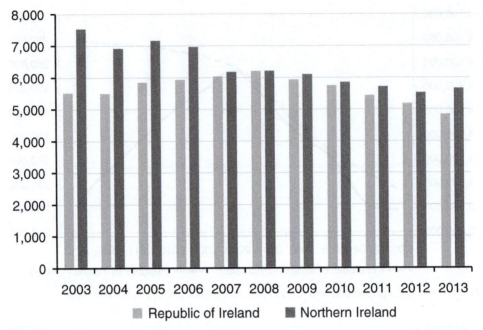

Figure 1.12   Crime rates per 100,000 population

Table 1.1   Police-recorded crime rates per 100,000 population between 2003 and 2013

Offence group	Republic of Ireland			Northern Ireland		
	2003	*2008*	*2013*	*2003/04*	*2008/09*	*2013/14*
Offences against the person	394	462	364	1,800	1,754	1,893
Robberies and burglaries	720	602	631	1,080	786	566
Thefts	1,845	1,714	1,715	2,236	1,565	1,469
Drugs offences	233	522	335	152	167	259
Other offences	2,314	2,880	1,787	2,237	1,915	1,429
Total police-recorded crime	5,506	6,179	4,832	7,505	6,188	5,615

but have since decreased. These offence groups are dominated by assaults, criminal damage, public disorder and drunkenness offences, which are often related to the night-time economy. It is perhaps not entirely unexpected therefore that they began to decrease in real terms from 2008, when one considers that disposable incomes have also fallen as a result of the economic recession, which was particularly pronounced in the Republic of Ireland.[43]

International research has previously indicated that the proportion of young males in a society can have a direct correlation with crime rates, as they typically form a key offending cohort (e.g. Tomlinson *et al.*, 1988; Watson, 2000; Ulmer and Steffensmeier, 2014). The relationship between age and offending varies depending upon the type of crime being considered (Laub and Sampson, 2003). Population estimates for males aged between 15 and 24 years (as well as between 15 and 29 years) from 2003 to 2013 were also examined (Figures 1.13 and 1.14). Whilst the population of the Republic of Ireland overall increased during this time (by 15 per cent), the proportion of young males (15–24 years) actually decreased by 15 per cent, largely driven by emigration following the recession and associated growth in unemployment. There were 67,868 crimes per 100,000 males aged 15–24 in 2003, but, given the reduction in the number of young males and similar total recorded crime figure, this had increased (by 20 per cent) to 81,230 by 2013. All other factors being equal, this increase reveals that on average there was a higher rate of offending amongst young males in the Republic of Ireland in 2013 than was the case in 2003.

Whilst the population in Northern Ireland overall increased (by 7 per cent), the population of young males has remained broadly stable, decreasing by 0.6 per cent between 2003 and 2013. Crime rates amongst young males during this time fell substantially, from 101,691 crimes per 100,000 males aged 15–24 in 2003 to 82,173 in 2013 (down 19 per cent). Hence, the converse to the Republic of Ireland is true, and, all other factors being equal, on average there was a lower rate of offending among young males in Northern Ireland in 2013 than 2003.

There may also be some limited indications to support international findings in respect of peak offending ages for different types of crime. Along with the sizeable reductions in rates amongst 15- to 24-year-olds, the most notable reductions in crime rates in Northern Ireland were amongst property crimes, which tend to have younger peak ages. Similarly, rates amongst those aged 25 to 29 years (the difference between the two age groupings shown) were higher in

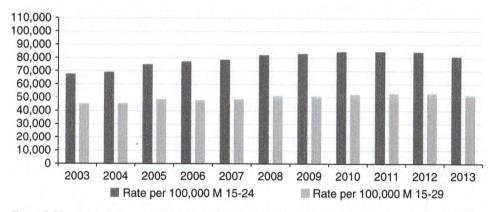

Figure 1.13   Crime rates per 100,000 males aged 15–24 years and 15–29 years in the Republic of Ireland

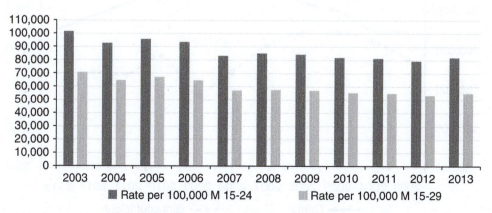

Figure 1.14   Crime rates per 100,000 males aged 15–24 years and 15–29 years in Northern Ireland

the Republic of Ireland in 2013 compared to 2003. As seen earlier, the overall rates within drugs and other offences (which include public order and criminal damage) were also higher in the Republic of Ireland. This is consistent with Laub and Sampson's (2003) findings of an older peak offending age for drug and alcohol related offences.

Some argue that the unequal distribution of wealth can give rise to higher levels of crime. Essentially, the larger the gap between the richest and the poorest people in a country, the greater the propensity for crime. The Gini coefficient is used to measure inequality of income distribution; values range between 0 and 100 per cent, the higher the number the greater the inequality.[44] Figures for Northern Ireland are not available separately, so figures for the whole of the United Kingdom[45] were used as a proxy measure (Figures 1.15 and 1.16).

The findings for Northern Ireland are more apparent and more aligned to that which might be expected – that is, as inequality decreases, so too does crime. This also makes sense in the context of the significant reductions in acquisitive crime seen in Northern Ireland. In the Republic of Ireland, there is a weaker but negative correlation between the two measures – as inequality decreases, crime rises and vice versa. This apparent contradiction (lower crime associated with higher inequality) has been noted by Healy *et al.*, who suggest, 'it may be that the total crime figure conceals different patterns for different offences' (Healy *et al.*, 2013: 2). The correlations between the Gini coefficients and the various crime group-ings for the Republic of Ireland were also examined, but all demonstrate the same negative correlation. Indeed there is a stronger negative correlation for both thefts and robberies and burglaries.

The Republic of Ireland is not unique in this somewhat unexpected outcome; the International Crime Victimisation Survey has also found such differences (van Dijk *et al.*, 2007b). As this finding is based on all victim-reported (as opposed to police-recorded) crime, it suggests that there is something inherently different about the interplay between crime trends and eco-nomic inequality in different countries.

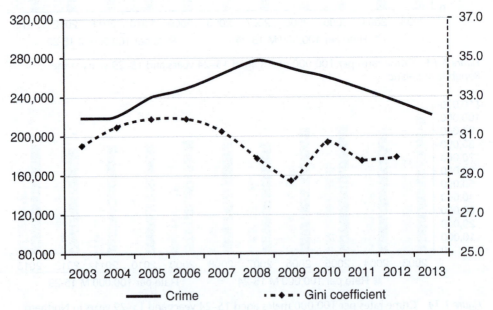

Figure 1.15 Total ICCS crime and Gini coefficient scores – Republic of Ireland

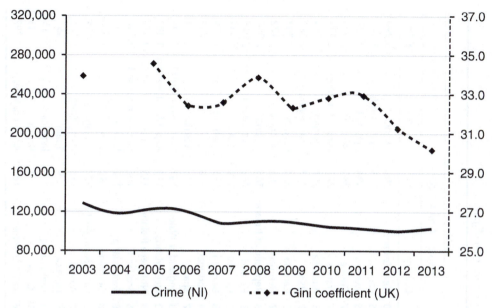

Figure 1.16 Total notifiable crime and Gini coefficient scores – Northern Ireland

International and European comparisons of police-recorded crime

The United Nations Office on Drugs and Crime (UNODC) administers regular Surveys on Crime Trends and the Operation of Criminal Justice Systems (CTS) internationally. Specific definitions for individual crime types are provided by the UNODC to try to ensure consistency in the police-recorded crime figures returned.

The latest CTS was conducted in 2013 and was used to compare the rankings of a number of countries in terms of rates of particular crimes per 100,000 population[46] which were reported to police and occurred in 2012.[47] Twenty-six countries were selected for examination here, including a range of international common law countries such as the United States of America, Canada, Australia and New Zealand. Where data were available, efforts were made to include at least one country from each continent; hence, Kenya, Jamaica and Hong Kong are also included, but it is acknowledged that countries from Eastern Europe and the former Soviet bloc are not represented (UNODC, 2014). Table 1.2 shows the full results with countries sorted by descending rank for each crime type.

The Republic of Ireland features higher in the rankings than Northern Ireland in each crime type and is generally mid-ranking out of the 26 countries. Both jurisdictions are below the average of all 26 countries considered for all crime types with the exception of thefts of motor vehicles in the Republic of Ireland. Interestingly, particularly given the dominance of property crime in recorded crime in the Republic of Ireland, both jurisdictions appear towards the bottom half of the rankings for all other thefts (excluding thefts of motor vehicles). The most substantial difference between the Republic of Ireland and Northern Ireland is evident in assaults. The major reason for this difference though would seem to be linked to differences in interpretation as to the figures which should be supplied. The UNODC (2014) states that assaults should include 'physical attack against the body of another person resulting in serious bodily injury'. From the raw figures provided, it appears that in Northern Ireland assaults resulting in more

Table 1.2 Rankings of 26 selected countries by highest rates per 100,000 population from police-recorded crime figures

Crimes in 2012 (UNODC CTS)

	Assaults		Robbery		Burglary		Thefts of Motor Vehicles		All Other Thefts	
	Country	Rate	Country	Rate	Country	Rate	Country	Rate	Country	Rate
1	Scotland	1,208	Belgium	1,728	Netherlands	1,780	New Zealand	399	Sweden	3,990
2	Sweden	915	Spain	1,075	Greece	1,505	Italy	323	Netherlands	3,877
3	Finland	707	France	194	Denmark	1,445	Sweden	304	Denmark	3,429
4	Belgium	646	Portugal	175	New Zealand	1,187	Greece	280	Norway	2,673
5	Germany	628	England & Wales	115	Austria	1,007	France	279	England & Wales	2,331
6	England & Wales	549	USA	112	Belgium	973	Australia	254	Germany	2,289
7	Luxembourg (2011)	531	Italy	103	Australia	929	USA	227	New Zealand	2,280
8	Netherlands	339	Jamaica	100	Sweden	926	Canada	224	Belgium	2,207
9	Australia (2011)	306	Sweden	97	Switzerland	922	Denmark	185	Australia	2,172
10	France	302	Netherlands	88	England & Wales	813	**Republic of Ireland**	**183**	Finland	2,095
11	**Republic of Ireland**	**294**	Canada	79	Luxembourg (2011)	693	Finland	163	Switzerland	2,016
12	Portugal	256	Luxembourg (2011)	77	USA	663	Norway	159	USA	1,937
13	USA	240	Switzerland	76	**Republic of Ireland**	**608**	Belgium	155	Scotland	1,779
14	New Zealand	228	**Republic of Ireland**	**62**	France	564	Portugal	150	Italy	1,752
15	Jamaica	205	Germany	59	**Northern Ireland**	**522**	Spain	145	Austria	1,731
16	Denmark	171	**Northern Ireland**	**57**	Canada	503	England & Wales	141	Luxembourg (2011)	1,649
17	Canada	152	Greece	54	Germany	500	Netherlands	119	**Republic of Ireland**	**1,487**
18	Italy	114	Denmark	53	Portugal	413	**Northern Ireland**	**115**	Canada	1,470
19	Hong Kong	103	Austria	48	Scotland	405	Scotland	108	**Northern Ireland**	**1,306**
20	**Northern Ireland**	**70**	New Zealand	47	Norway	348	Switzerland	102	France	1,247
21	Norway	56	Scotland	34	Spain	348	Germany	85	Greece	1,070
22	Austria	48	Finland	30	Finland	333	Luxembourg (2011)	77	Portugal	964
23	Greece	41	Norway	30	Jamaica	122	Austria	53	Hong Kong	471
24	Spain	37	Australia (2011)	17	Hong Kong	59	Jamaica	9	Spain	354
25	Kenya	34	Hong Kong	9	Kenya	4	Hong Kong	8	Jamaica	115
26	Switzerland	7	Kenya	8	Italy	N/A	Kenya	3	Kenya	33
Average	All 26 Countries	315	All 26 Countries	174	All 26 Countries	676	All 26 Countries	163	All 26 Countries	1,797

minor injuries (occasioning actual bodily harm) were excluded. For the Republic of Ireland, figures for assaults causing harm as well as minor assaults appear to have been included. This highlights the vagaries of comparing crime statistics across jurisdictions and the discrepancies which can arise even when steps are taken to limit same. The final crime type examined was robbery (from a person) which includes force or the threat of force; the Republic of Ireland and Northern Ireland are both mid-ranking.

The *European Sourcebook of Crime and Criminal Justice Statistics* (Aebi *et al.*, 2010, 2014) is compiled by a group of experts and devotes extra effort to trying to overcome recording and definition differences. As an additional verification of rankings for police-recorded crime statistics, the two most recent Sourcebooks were used to look at trends in the same five offence types between 2003 and 2007 as well as between 2007 and 2011.[48] The mean rates per 100,000 population for all countries were also considered (Table 1.3).

The trends found broadly confirm the earlier findings. Northern Ireland has seen consistent decreases across a number of crime types since 2003 and tends to have rates above the mean for all Sourcebook countries for burglary, thefts of motor vehicles and total thefts. Assault rates in Northern Ireland increased in both time periods, and, despite the engagement of national experts, the impact of differing definitions used by both jurisdictions is also apparent here. The Republic of Ireland is higher than the mean of all countries for all crime types except robbery. As outlined, police-recorded crime can only give us an indication of trends in crimes which have been reported. In order to consider both reported and unreported crime, it is necessary to consider trends evident in the findings of crime victimisation surveys.

Crime victimisation surveys

In the Republic of Ireland, the Central Statistics Office conducted nationally representative crime victimisation surveys on an ad hoc basis in 1998, 2003, 2006 and 2010. All included adults aged 18 and over and asked about experiences of certain types of crime.[49] The Garda Research Unit also commissioned independent research companies to conduct Public Attitudes Surveys, completed using a variety of methodologies (telephone and face-to-face interviews) with nationally representative samples of adults aged 18 years and over. Public Attitudes Surveys were completed in 1999, 2000, 2002 and each year from 2005 to 2008.[50] The primary focus of these surveys has been on attitudes towards crime and policing as well as experiences of reporting crime to the Gardaí; they also asked about crime victimisation.

In Northern Ireland, the Department of Justice has run a crime victimisation survey (Northern Ireland Crime Survey) since 1994/5, initially on an ad hoc basis (also conducted in 1998, 2001 and 2003/04) and annually since 2005. As with the CSO, it uses continuous data collection and asks adults aged 16 years and over about their experiences of crime.[51] A greater range of crime types are included in the Northern Ireland Crime Survey, which mirrors the Crime Survey of England and Wales.

Recent crime victimisation trends (1998–2012)

The respective surveys allow for comparisons of victimisation rates of overall experiences of crime at the household level up to 2010. The proportion of households stating that they had been victims (of crimes covered in the respective surveys) in the twelve months prior to interview decreased in both jurisdictions. Decreases were more pronounced in Northern Ireland; declining from 16 per cent of households in 2003 to 10 per cent of households in 2010. This is consistent with the decreases in police-recorded crime. In the Republic of Ireland, the proportion of

Table 1.3 European Sourcebook changes in police/Garda-recorded crime and rates per 100,000 population

| | European Sourcebook of Crime and Criminal Justice Statistics 2010 and 2014 | | | | | | | | | | | | | | |
| | Assault (bodily injury) | | | Robbery | | | Burglary | | | Theft of motor vehicle | | | Total thefts | | |
	% 03–07	% 07–11	Rate 2011	% 03–07	% 07–11	Rate 2011	% 03–07	% 07–11	Rate 2011	% 03–07	% 07–11	Rate 2011	% 03–07	% 07–11	Rate 2011
Republic of Ireland	13	-10	317	-28	26	61	-12	10	604	-8	-28	227	-2	0	2,288
Northern Ireland	31	78	55	-44	4	68	-31	-11	586	-40	-33	127	-32	-2	1,992
Mean			260			73			541			106			1,890
Minimum			2 (Georgia)			2 (Albania)			9 (Serbia)			2 (Armenia/Georgia/Serbia)			102 (Turkey)
Maximum			1,396 (Scotland)			411 (Serbia)			1,650 (Denmark)			366 (Sweden)			5,701 (Sweden)

households decreased consistently from 12 per cent in 2003 to 9 per cent in 2010.[52] As shown earlier, according to the recorded crime statistics for the Republic of Ireland, overall crime peaked in 2008 and then declined. This could suggest that crimes against the person peaked later than crimes against households in the Republic of Ireland.

Figures 1.17 and 1.18 show the percentages reporting victimisation of any crime as well as household and personal victimisation for certain types of crime.[53] In the Republic of Ireland, the CSO recorded reductions in victimisation for households experiencing thefts from vehicles (3.5 per cent to 2 per cent) and for persons experiencing thefts and/or assaults (5.2 per cent to 4 per cent) in each survey from 2003 to 2010.[54] There was a sharp rise in levels of personal crime (assaults and/or thefts) between 1998, when it was 2.4 per cent, and 2003, when it was 5.2 per cent.[55] In Northern Ireland general reductions in victimisation were recorded in most crime types year-on-year since the peaks in 2003. The percentage of households experiencing thefts from cars reduced from 2.6 per cent to 0.8 per cent and thefts of cars fell from 1.4 per cent (in 2001) to 0.2 per cent. Thefts and/or assaults were experienced by 6.3 per cent in 2003 and have since decreased to 3.2 per cent.

The surveys also show that the proportions of people stating they had been the victim of any crime are higher in Northern Ireland than the Republic of Ireland, particularly in the earlier years examined. Victimisation rates in both jurisdictions have converged in more recent years. In 2008 the victimisation rate in Northern Ireland was 13.4 per cent; in the Republic of Ireland it was 9.2 per cent. The fact that adults aged 16 and over are included in the NICS will account for some of the higher victimisation rate found in Northern Ireland.

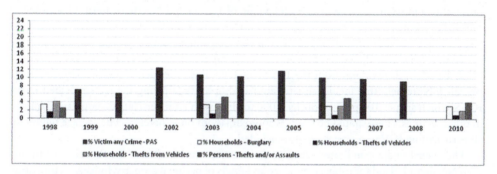

Figure 1.17 Household and personal victimisation rates in the Republic of Ireland 1982/83 and 1998–2010

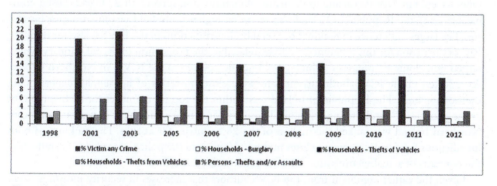

Figure 1.18 Household and personal victimisation rates in Northern Ireland 1998–2012

International and European comparisons of crime victimisation

The International Crime Victims Survey (ICVS) was initiated in 1987 by a number of European criminologists to produce victimisation estimates to facilitate research and international comparisons. There have been five sweeps of the survey to date co-ordinated by the United Nations. Northern Ireland participated in four of the five sweeps whilst the Republic of Ireland only participated in the 2004/05 sweep. This allows for comparison between both jurisdictions in a European and international context for this one fixed point in time.[56]

The overriding finding from the ICVS over the years has been that 'most of the countries about which trend data are available [participation in multiple sweeps] show a distinct downward trend in the level of victimisation since 1995 or 2000' (van Dijk et al., 2007a: 12). Whilst only figures for one sweep are available, the Republic of Ireland is flagged as the exception to this trend, at least in respect of theft of personal property, as noted earlier, 'high rates in Ireland are in line with the steep upward trend in this type of crime observed in national victimisation surveys conducted in Ireland' (van Dijk et al., 2007b: 41). As was also seen in the more recent CSO surveys, victimisation rates have subsequently decreased, though they are still not as low as those recorded in 1998. It could be, therefore, that the Republic of Ireland has simply not seen the decrease in victimisation until some years later than the majority of other countries, at least in respect of thefts from the person.

Whilst the universal drop in victimisation rates across the Western world is often quoted by commentators, there has been debate as to what factors are driving these reductions. The authors of the ICVS report note that one key factor appears to have been the increase in crime prevention and security measures. The Republic of Ireland and Northern Ireland had some of the highest proportions of households with burglar alarms fitted, 49 per cent and 38 per cent respectively, compared to an average across all ICVS countries of 16 per cent.

Table 1.4 includes the same 26 countries as included in the comparison of police-recorded crime based on the findings from the ICVS 2004/05. Both prevalence and incidence rates are provided. Note here that incidence rates are based upon multiplying the rates provided in the ICVS, which are per 100 population, by 1,000 to align with rates per 100,000 population quoted in other sections. These should be taken as approximations only therefore. The average figures for all participating ICVS countries are also included.

The overall findings indicate that victimisation rates were higher in the Republic of Ireland than Northern Ireland for robbery, burglary and thefts of personal property. Indeed, victimisation in the Republic of Ireland was considerably above the average of all ICVS countries for all crime types considered. Northern Ireland was above the average of all ICVS countries for all crime types except burglary. Reverting to the national victimisation surveys for 2003 (the closest comparable year), the Republic of Ireland also recorded higher household victimisation for burglaries. The largest difference in rankings between both jurisdictions in the ICVS is also for burglary. Part of the reason for this difference could be related to the proportion of overall burglary which targets non-domestic premises (which would not be covered in the ICVS) in Northern Ireland. As reflected in the ICVS, both jurisdictions were closer in terms of households experiencing theft of a vehicle. The Republic of Ireland was within the top six countries for all five types of crime considered[57] and the highest ranked country for robbery and thefts of personal property. Northern Ireland was ranked the highest of the 26 countries for assaults. The rankings of both jurisdictions for assaults are much closer in the ICVS than in the police-recorded CTS, reflecting the contrasts of actual victimisation vis-à-vis police-recorded crime.

Given the earlier argument from the ICVS authors that increases in security measures could be driving reductions in some crime types, it is striking to note the comparatively high rankings

Table 1.4 Rankings of 26 selected countries by highest prevalence – ICVS and EU ICS

Crimes in 2004/'05 (ICVS & EU ICS)

	Assaults			Robbery			Burglary			Theft of a car			Thefts of personal property		
	Country	Prev.	Rate	Country	Prev.	Rate	Country	Prev.	Rate	Country	Prev.	Rate	Country	Prev.	Rate
1	Northern Ireland	6.8	9,800	Republic of Ireland	2.2	3,000	England & Wales	3.5	4,600	England & Wales	1.8	2,300	Republic of Ireland	7.2	7,700
2	England & Wales	5.8	8,100	England & Wales	1.4	2,600	New Zealand	3.2	3,900	New Zealand	1.8	1,900	England & Wales	6.3	7,500
3	Republic of Ireland	4.9	8,000	Greece	1.4	1,900	Denmark	2.7	3,500	Portugal	1.5	1,600	Switzerland	5.9	N/A
4	New Zealand	4.9	7,100	Spain	1.3	1,700	USA	2.5	4,100	Northern Ireland	1.4	1,300	Greece	5.3	6,100
5	USA	4.3	8,300	Belgium	1.2	1,400	Australia	2.5	3,100	Denmark	1.3	1,300	Northern Ireland	5.1	6,400
6	Netherlands	4.3	8,000	New Zealand	1.1	1,500	Republic of Ireland	2.3	2,400	Republic of Ireland	1.2	1,200	Norway	4.8	5,900
7	Australia	3.8	5,900	Sweden	1.1	1,200	Italy	2.1	2,800	Australia	1.1	1,200	USA	4.8	5,800
8	Scotland	3.8	5,700	Northern Ireland	1.1	1,100	Canada	2.0	2,600	USA	1.1	1,200	New Zealand	4.1	4,800
9	Belgium	3.6	7,100	Portugal	1.0	1,100	Belgium	1.8	2,100	Spain	1.0	1,500	Canada	4.0	5,300
10	Sweden	3.5	5,200	Australia	0.9	1,300	Greece	1.8	2,000	Italy	1.0	1,100	Netherlands	3.7	4,200
11	Denmark	3.3	5,500	Denmark	0.9	1,200	Luxembourg	1.7	2,200	Netherlands	1.0	1,000	Australia	3.6	4,300
12	Canada	3.0	4,800	Scotland	0.9	1,000	Switzerland	1.6	2,100	Canada	0.8	800	Hong Kong	3.6	4,100
13	Norway	2.9	5,000	Switzerland	0.8	1,300	France	1.6	1,800	Norway	0.7	900	Belgium	3.4	4,100
14	Germany	2.7	4,200	France	0.8	900	Scotland	1.5	2,200	France	0.6	700	Austria	3.4	3,700
15	Switzerland	2.5	4,300	Canada	0.8	800	Portugal	1.4	1,900	Luxembourg	0.6	600	France	3.3	3,900
16	Greece	2.4	5,200	Norway	0.8	800	Northern Ireland	1.4	1,600	Belgium	0.5	600	Denmark	3.3	3,800
17	Luxembourg	2.3	3,700	Luxembourg	0.7	800	Netherlands	1.3	1,400	Sweden	0.5	500	Germany	3.0	3,900
18	Finland	2.2	4,000	USA	0.6	1,100	Norway	1.2	1,400	Finland	0.4	500	Luxembourg	2.9	5,000
19	France	2.1	3,400	Netherlands	0.5	800	Austria	0.9	1,200	Scotland	0.3	400	Scotland	2.9	3,200
20	Austria	1.8	2,900	Austria	0.4	500	Germany	0.9	1,100	Greece	0.3	300	Sweden	2.4	3,100
21	Spain	1.6	2,800	Germany	0.4	500	Finland	0.8	1,200	Germany	0.2	200	Italy	2.4	2,500
22	Hong Kong	1.2	2,000	Hong Kong	0.4	400	Spain	0.8	1,100	Switzerland	0.2	200	Finland	2.3	2,600
23	Portugal	0.9	1,100	Finland	0.3	400	Sweden	0.7	800	Austria	0.1	100	Spain	2.1	2,200
24	Italy	0.8	1,100	Italy	0.3	300	Hong Kong	0.6	600	Hong Kong	0.0	N/A	Portugal	1.6	1,700
25	Jamaica	N/A	N/A	Jamaica	N/A	N/A	Jamaica	N/A	N/A	Jamaica	N/A	N/A	Jamaica	N/A	N/A
26	Kenya	N/A	N/A	Kenya	N/A	N/A	Kenya	N/A	N/A	Kenya	N/A	N/A	Kenya	N/A	N/A
Average	All ICVS Countries	3.0	5,100	All ICVS Countries	1.0	1,300	All ICVS Countries	1.8	2,300	All ICVS Countries	0.8	900	All ICVS Countries	3.8	4,400

of the Republic of Ireland and Northern Ireland for burglary. As noted, the proportions of households in these jurisdictions stating that they had burglar alarms installed were amongst the highest recorded and considerably above average rates (and use had increased in Northern Ireland over different sweeps).

When considering just countries amongst the 18 member states of the European Union at that time, both the Republic of Ireland and Northern Ireland had statistically significantly higher rates of victimisation than average. The authors note the following factors:

- Levels of crime were most elevated in the Republic of Ireland, the United Kingdom, Estonia, The Netherlands and Denmark;
- Urbanisation is associated with high levels of crime, but not in the Republic of Ireland, which has a relatively low level of urbanisation;
- The proportion of young people in the population is associated with high levels of crime; however, whilst the correlation is positive it is statistically insignificant;
- There is a moderately strong correlation between levels of assaults/threats and beer consumption per 100,000 population (van Dijk et al., 2007b).

There are also some interesting variations in the proportions of people who indicated that they reported their experience of these crimes to the police in the Republic of Ireland and Northern Ireland (Table 1.5).

Similarly to the domestic crime victimisation surveys, reporting rates are higher for those crimes which are likely to have incurred significant financial loss and/or will result in an insurance claim (that is, burglary and theft of a car). Reporting rates are notably lower – and, in the case of the Republic of Ireland, below the average of all ICVS participating countries – for assaults, robberies and other thefts of personal property. The relatively high proportions of respondents reporting experience of assaults and robbery to the police in Northern Ireland is striking both in comparison to the Republic of Ireland and also to the ICVS average.

The ICVS victimisation findings were also compared to the CTS (police-recorded crime) for 2004. The rates per population and the rankings of both jurisdictions were much lower in the CTS (similarly to the 2012 CTS, both jurisdictions were mid to lower ranking). The only exception to this was for burglaries in Northern Ireland, which was ranked sixteenth in the ICVS but moved up to ninth in the CTS. This is due in part to the fact that the CTS includes burglaries of all types of premises, not just residential. Even when allowing for under-reporting, the police-recorded rates for personal crimes are substantially lower than those found in the ICVS. The respective positions of the Republic of Ireland and Northern Ireland were also reversed in each crime type; for crimes in which the Republic of Ireland had higher levels of victimisation in the ICVS, Northern Ireland records higher levels in the CTS and vice versa. This is partly due to the higher reporting rates found in Northern Ireland and also to the different crime recording rules applied by the police.

Table 1.5 Percentage of respondents who reported experience of crime to the police/Gardaí

	Assaults	Robbery	Burglary	Theft of a car	Thefts of personal property
Republic of Ireland	31%	38%	85%	86%	40%
Northern Ireland	51%	67%	88%	95%	43%
Average (all ICVS countries)	33%	46%	74%	83%	46%

Source: ICVS and van Dijk et al., 2007a.

Conclusions

Examining trends in crime – data preferences and possibilities

Different data sources can provide seemingly conflicting information in respect of crime trends. It is often possible to explain some of these differences with closer scrutiny of definitions and parameters within the data. Different sources will be more (or less) useful depending upon research aims. The most reliable measure of actual experience of crime is to be found in crime victimisation surveys. Police-recorded crime tells us very little about actual crime victimisation but has more benefit when it comes to considering trends and enforcement-driven incidents, particularly over longer periods of time. Cross-national comparisons, however, are fraught with discrepancies in definitions, counting rules and recording practices (see Aebi, 2008; O'Connell, 2007; Patrick, 2011). For all sources, it is preferable to be able to consider data from a number of years rather than just one fixed point in time.

Possible explanations of crime trends and areas for further research

Routine activities

Cohen and Felson's (1979) routine activities theory can contribute to our understanding of changes in the crime trends seen in the Republic of Ireland and Northern Ireland, particularly in the last century. Suitable victims or targets were present in increasing numbers at the same time as capable guardians were being dispersed (for example, as more women took up paid employment outside the home). Just as the proliferation of electronic appliances in our homes in the eighties and nineties contributed to a rise in residential burglaries, undoubtedly the fact that we now carry many devices around with us has contributed to the increases in thefts and robberies from the person, noted in the Republic of Ireland in particular, more recently. Newly emerging technologies also present new opportunities for crime; for example, contact-less payment cards are growing in prevalence and have led to the emerging phenomenon of 'digital pick-pocketing'.

In the same way, just as the introduction and usage of target-hardening measures for vehicles (such as immobilisers) contributed to reductions in their theft, so 'kill switches' and clone-proof wallets/clothing will lead to reductions in the theft of mobile phones/devices as well as financial account details.[58] Similarly, the fact that young people are spending increasing amounts of time at home online has been mooted as a possible explanation for the declining crime rates seen in many countries in recent years. In due course, though, this very behaviour could lead to increases in different types of crime committed by young people as they have 'more opportunities to engage in computer related offences ... such as illegal downloading, ... hacking, ... credit card or computer fraud' (Aebi and Linde, 2010: 269).

Alcohol consumption

The ICVS found a correlation between violent crime and beer consumption. According to the World Health Organisation's Global Health Observatory Data Repository, alcohol consumption in both Northern Ireland and the Republic of Ireland peaked in 2004 since which time it has decreased in both jurisdictions. The same source also records high but declining consumption rates amongst other high-crime countries (as per the ICVS).[59] O'Donnell (2005) has highlighted that drinking patterns are important: in particular binge drinking and the potential effects on violent crime. The relationship between alcohol consumption and crime victimisation merits further research.

Attitudes towards the law and law enforcement

Whilst post-colonial societies have generally been described as having an ambiguous relationship with authority, there does seem to be a somewhat liberal perspective towards lower-end rules and regulations in the Republic of Ireland. There are degrees of wrongness rather than a clear-cut, black-and-white moral code; something of an expectation that the letter of the law will not and should not always be followed or applied. It is perhaps best summed up in the words of an author who is primarily focusing on family law, but whose more general comments seem applicable here: 'the lofty aspirations of the formal law are mitigated by a certain lack of rigour in their application' (Duncan, 1994: 449). Duncan (1994: 452) goes on to note, 'there is still in this country [Ireland] a certain pride attached to the exercise of personal discretion in the face of strict rules'. Could it be that the offending populations within higher-crime countries are more inclined to believe 'some rules are meant to be broken'? It was beyond the confines of this chapter to consider the use of police discretion, but the ICVS has noted that 'countries with the lowest numbers of police-recorded crimes include Estonia and Ireland, both countries with levels of crime significantly above the European mean, according to the EU ICS' [60] (van Dijk et al., 2007b: 24). Research could usefully examine if the lower victimisation in police-recorded crime in these countries is in part attributable not only to lower reporting and recording rates but also to a greater use of discretion amongst the police to avoid criminalising people.

Social cohesion

Increased social cohesion and self-control or personal responsibility may contribute to reductions in victimisation. Tonry (2005) has highlighted the work of Elias and Eisner regarding a declining tolerance of violence over the long term. So, whereas once assaults were seen in the context of actual physical violence only, in more recent times it is commonly regarded that any form of threatening or abusive behaviour constitutes an assault. At the same time as this decline in tolerance, there has been an increase in self-discipline which has extended from improved personal health to improved behaviour towards others (Tonry, 2005). In the Republic of Ireland and Northern Ireland, the fact that reporting of crimes against the person to the police has increased may point to lower tolerance of violent or threatening crime. In this context, whether the higher assault victimisation rates in both jurisdictions are driven predominantly by alcohol consumption therefore also merits further exploration.

In Northern Ireland, there is some sign of increasing social cohesion from the small reduction in the proportions of people stating 'fear of reprisal' as a reason not to report crime. Likewise, in the increasing proportions, amongst both Catholics and Protestants expressing positive attitudes towards the police, there are tentative signs that the conflicts of the past are being left behind. In the same vein, could more positive attitudes towards the police lead to greater compliance with the law generally? If so, and if such trends were to continue, we might expect to see further reductions in crime.

In the Republic of Ireland, evidence is limited by the infrequency of crime victimisation surveys. It is possible that the recession has served to increase camaraderie amongst certain groups of the population. Through a shared sense of 'tough times', perhaps too there is less propensity to commit crime? Equally, rather than stay and experience unemployment, many young people (males in particular) have emigrated, and this has happened to a far greater extent than amongst their predecessors in the last recession of the eighties. Also absent more recently has been any very substantial escalation in the use of addictive illegal drugs,[61] such as heroin, which combined with unemployment to drive increases in the eighties. For some of those young males who have remained, however, there is perhaps less social cohesion and growing discontent, as reflected in the increase in the crime rates amongst those aged 15 to 24 years.

Future victimisation surveys

The absence of a victimisation survey for five years in the Republic of Ireland and of the ICVS in all jurisdictions for over a decade has left a gap in our knowledge. The participation of the Republic of Ireland in only one sweep to date also restricts the ability to consider victimisation trends over time in an international context. It would be useful to examine if decreases in crime are being driven by greater reductions in repeat victimisation in either or both jurisdictions. It is to be hoped that future victimisation surveys in the Republic of Ireland, as well as further rounds of the ICVS in both jurisdictions, will be undertaken. It will then be possible to examine what trends emerge and to explore some of the possible explanations proffered here in greater detail.

Bibliography

Aebi, M. F. (2008) 'Measuring the Influence of Statistical Counting Rules on Cross National Differences in Recorded Crime' in K. Aromaa and M. Heiskanen (eds) *Crime and Criminal Justice Systems in Europe and North America*. Helsinki: HEUNI.

Aebi, M. F., Akdeniz, G., Barclay, G., Campistol, C., Caneppele, S., Gruszczyńska, B., Harrendorf, S., Heiskanen, M., Hysi, V., Jehle, J. M., Jokinen, A., Kensey, A., Killias, M., Lewis, C. G., Savona, E., Smit, P. and Þórisdóttir, R. (2014) *European Sourcebook of Crime and Criminal Justice Statistics 2014*. 5th ed. Helsinki: HEUNI.

Aebi, M. F., Aubusson de Cavarlay, B., Barclay, G., Gruszczyńska, B., Harrendorf, S., Heiskanen, M., Hysi, V., Jaquier, V., Jehle, J. M., Killias, M., Shostko, O., Smit, P. and Þórisdóttir, R. (2010) *European Sourcebook of Crime and Criminal Justice Statistics 2010*. 4th ed. The Hague: Boom Legal Publishers.

Aebi, M. F. and Linde, A. (2010) 'Is There a Crime Drop in Western Europe?', *European Journal of Criminal Policy Research*, 16: 251–277.

Aromaa, K. and Heiskanen, M. (2008) *Crime and Criminal Justice Systems in Europe and North America 1995–2004*. Helsinki: HEUNI.

Bacik, I. and O'Connell, M. (1998) *Crime and Poverty in Ireland*. Dublin: Round Hall Sweet and Maxwell.

Bottoms, A. E. (1994) 'Environmental Criminology' in M. Maguire, R. Morgan and R. Reiner (1994) *The Oxford Handbook of Criminology*. Oxford: Clarendon Press.

Box, S. (1981) *Deviance, Reality and Society*. 2nd ed. London: Holt, Rinehart and Winston.

Brady, C. (2014) *The Guarding of Ireland: The Garda Síochána and the Irish State 1960–2014*. Dublin: Gill and Macmillan.

Breen, R. and Rothman, D. B. (1985) *Crime Victimisation in the Republic of Ireland*. Dublin: ESRI.

Brewer, J., Lockhart, B. and Rodgers, P. (1996) 'Crime in Ireland Since the Second World War', *Journal of the Statistical and Social Inquiry Society of Ireland*, XXVII(III): 135–175.

—— (1997) *Crime in Ireland 1945–95: Here Be Dragons*. Oxford: Clarendon Press.

Browne, C. (2008) *Garda Public Attitudes Survey 2008*. Templemore: Garda Síochána.

Campbell, P. and Cadogan, G. (2013) *Experience of Crime: Findings from the 2012/13 Northern Ireland Crime Survey*. Belfast: Department of Justice.

Central Statistics Office (CSO) (1999) *Quarterly National Household Survey, Crime and Victimisation September–November 1998*. Dublin: Central Statistics Office.

—— (2004) *Quarterly National Household Survey, Crime and Victimisation Quarter 4 1998 and 2003*. Dublin: Central Statistics Office.

—— (2006) *Crime and Victimisation Quarterly, National Household Survey 2006 (including results for 1998 and 2003)*. Dublin: Central Statistics Office.

—— (2010) *Crime and Victimisation Quarterly, National Household Survey 2010.* Dublin: Central Statistics Office.

—— (2011) *Recorded Crime Quarter 4 2010.* Dublin: Central Statistics Office.

—— 'Population Estimates for Ireland'. Available from: http://www.cso.ie/px/pxeirestat/Database/eirestat/Annual%20Population%20Estimates/Annual%20Population%20Estimates_statbank.asp?SP=Annual%20Population%20Estimates&Planguage=0.

Central Statistics Office and Northern Ireland Statistics and Research Agency (2014) *Census 2011 Ireland and Northern Ireland.* Available from: http://www.cso.ie/en/media/csoie/releasespublications/documents/population/2011/Cen2011IrelandNorthernIreland.pdf.

Clarke, R.V. (1999) *Hot Products: Understanding, Anticipating and Reducing Demand for Stolen Goods.* London: Home Office.

Clarke, S. (2013) *Trends in Crime and Criminal Justice, 2010.* Eurostat Statistics in Focus 18/2013: European Commission.

Clutterbuck, R. (1997) *Public Safety and Civil Liberties.* Basingstoke: Macmillan.

Cohen, L. E. and Felson, M. (1979) 'Social Change and Crime Rate Trends: A Routine Activity Approach', *American Sociological Review*, 44: 588–608.

Coogan, T. P. (2003) *Ireland in the Twentieth Century.* London: Arrow Books.

Cowen, N. (2010) *Comparisons of Crime in OECD Countries.* Available at: www.civitas.org.uk (accessed 17 June 2014).

Crime Reduction Unit, School of Forensic and Investigative Sciences, University of Central Lancashire (2013) *Crime against Small Businesses in Northern Ireland.* Belfast: Skills for Justice.

Duncan, W. (1994) 'Law and the Irish Psyche: The Conflict between Aspiration and Experience', *The Irish Journal of Psychology*, 15(2 & 3): 448–455.

Ellison, G., Pino, N. W. and Shirlow, P. (2012) 'Assessing the Determinants of Public Confidence in the Police: A Case Study of a Post-Conflict Community in Northern Ireland' *Criminology and Criminal Justice*, 13(5): 552–576.

Enzmann, D., Haen Marshall, I., Killias, M., Junger-tas, J., Steketee, M. and Gruszczynska, B. (2010) 'Self-Reported Youth Delinquency in Europe and Beyond: First Results of the Second International Self-Report Delinquency Study in the Context of Police and Victimisation Data', *European Journal of Criminology*, 7(2): 159–183.

Eurostat – Statistical Office for the European Union, 'Gini Coefficient Statistics'. Available at: http://ec.europa.eu/eurostat/tgm/table.do?tab=table&init=1&plugin=1&pcode=tessi190&language=en.

Farrell, G., Tilley, N., Tseloni, A. and Mailley, J. (2010) 'Explaining and Sustaining the Crime Drop: Clarifying the Role of Opportunity-Related Theories' *Crime Prevention and Community Safety*, 12(1): 24–41.

Garda Inspectorate (2014) *Crime Investigation.* Dublin: Garda Inspectorate.

Garda Research Unit (2002) *Garda Public Attitudes Survey 2002 Results.* Templemore: Garda Síochána.

Garda Síochána (2001) *Annual Report of An Garda Síochána 2000.* Dublin: Garda Síochána.

—— (2002) *Annual Report of An Garda Síochána 2001.* Dublin: Garda Síochána.

—— (2003) *Annual Report of An Garda Síochána 2002.* Dublin: Garda Síochána.

—— (2004) *Annual Report of An Garda Síochána 2003.* Dublin: Garda Síochána.

—— (2005) *Annual Report of An Garda Síochána 2004.* Dublin: Garda Síochána.

—— (2006) *Annual Report of An Garda Síochána 2005.* Dublin: Garda Síochána.

—— (2007) *Annual Report of An Garda Síochána 2006.* Dublin: Garda Síochána.

—— (2008) *Annual Report of An Garda Síochána 2007.* Dublin: Garda Síochána.

Garland, D. (1996) 'The Limits of the Sovereign State: Strategies of Crime Control in Contemporary Society' *The British Journal of Criminology*, 36(4): 445–471.

Goldstein, H. (1990) *Problem-Oriented Policing.* Philadelphia: Temple University Press.

Harie-Bick, J., Sheptycki, J. and Wardak, A. (2005) 'Introduction: Transnational and Comparative Criminology in a Global Perspective', J. Sheptycki and A. Wardak (eds) *Transnational and Comparative Criminology.* London: Glasshouse Press.

Healy, D., Mulcahy, A. and O'Donnell, D. (2013) *Crime, Punishment and Inequality in Ireland.* AIAS, GINI Discussion Paper 93. Available at: www.gini-research.org.

HMIC (2014) *Crime-Recording: Making the Victim Count. The Final Report of an Inspection of Crime Data Integrity in Police Forces in England and Wales.* Available at: http://www.justiceinspectorates.gov.uk/hmic.

Hughes, G. (1998) *Understanding Crime Prevention: Social Control, Risk and Late Modernity.* Buckinghamshire: Open University Press.

Irish Small and Medium Enterprises Association (2014) *ISME National Crime Survey 2014.* Dublin: ISME.

Kennedy, P. and Browne, C. (2006) *Garda Public Attitudes Survey 2006*. Templemore: Garda Síochána.

—— (2007) *Garda Public Attitudes Survey 2007*. Templemore: Garda Síochána.

Kilcommins, S., O'Donnell, I., O'Sullivan, E. and Vaughan, B. (2004) *Crime, Punishment and the Search for Order in Ireland*. Dublin: Institute of Public Administration.

Knepper, P. (2014) 'Falling Crime Rates: What Happened Last Time', *Theoretical Criminology*, doi: 10.1177/1362480614541290 (accessed 7 July 2014).

Knox, C. (2002) '"See No Evil, Hear No Evil" Insidious Paramilitary Violence in Northern Ireland' *British Journal of Criminology*, 42:164–185.

Laub, J. H. and Sampson, R. (2003) *Shared Beginnings, Divergent Lives: Delinquent Boys Aged 70*. Cambridge: Harvard University Press.

Lee, S. (2010) 'Trends in Admission to Hospital for Assault in Northern Ireland, 1996/97–2008/09' *Journal of Public Health*, 33(3): 439–444.

MacDonald, L. (1976) *The Sociology of Law and Order*. London: Faber and Faber.

Maguire, M. (2007) 'Crime Data and Statistics', in M. Maguire, R. Morgan and R. Reiner. 4th ed. *The Oxford Handbook of Criminology*. New York: Oxford University Press Inc.

Mayhew, P. (2014) *Crime Data Integrity: Literature Review of Crime Recording*. Available at: http://www.justiceinspectorates.gov.uk/hmic.

McGee, H., Garavan, R., de Barra, M., Byrne, J. and Conroy, R. (2002) *The SAVI Report: Sexual Abuse and Violence in Ireland*. Dublin: Liffey Press.

Morris, D. (1994) *The Human Zoo*. London: Vintage.

Mosher, C. J., Miethe, T. D. and Hart, T. C. (2011) 2nd ed. *The Mismeasure of Crime*. Thousand Oaks, CA: Sage.

Mulcahy, A. (2007) 'The Impact of the Northern "Troubles" on Criminal Justice in the Irish Republic' in P. O'Mahony (ed.) *Criminal Justice in Ireland*. Dublin: Institute of Public Administration.

National Audit Office (2012) *Comparing International Criminal Justice Systems: Briefing for the House of Commons Justice Committee*. London: National Audit Office.

Newman, S. and Lonsdale, S. (1996) *Human Jungle*. London: Ebury Press.

Northern Ireland Policing Board (2005) *Public Perceptions of the Police, DPPs and the Northern Ireland Policing Board: Report based on the Northern Ireland Policing Board Module of the April 2005 Omnibus Survey*. Belfast: Northern Ireland Policing Board.

—— (2007) *Public Perceptions of the Police, DPPs and the Northern Ireland Policing Board: Report based on the Northern Ireland Policing Board Module of the April 2007 Omnibus Survey*. Belfast: Northern Ireland Policing Board.

—— (2009) *Public Perceptions of the Police, DPPs and the Northern Ireland Policing Board: Report based on the Northern Ireland Policing Board Module of the April 2009 Omnibus Survey*. Belfast: Northern Ireland Policing Board.

—— (2013) *Public Perceptions of the Police, DPPs and the Northern Ireland Policing Board: Report based on the Northern Ireland Policing Board Module of the January 2013 Omnibus Survey*. Belfast: Northern Ireland Policing Board.

Northern Ireland Statistics and Research Agency, 'Population Estimates for Northern Ireland'. Available at: http://www.nisra.gov.uk/demography/default.asp17.htm.

—— (2001) *Community Attitudes Survey Bulletin January – December 2000*. Belfast: Northern Ireland Statistics and Research Agency.

—— (2002) *Community Attitudes Survey Bulletin January – December 2001*. Belfast: Northern Ireland Statistics and Research Agency.

—— (2003) *Community Attitudes Survey Bulletin January – December 2002*. Belfast: Northern Ireland Statistics and Research Agency.

—— (2004) *Community Attitudes Survey Bulletin January – December 2003*. Belfast: Northern Ireland Statistics and Research Agency.

O'Connell, M. (2007) 'Assessment of the Crime Rate in Ireland – Issues and Considerations' in P. O'Mahony (ed.) *Criminal Justice in Ireland*. Dublin: Institute of Public Administration.

O'Donnell, I. (2005) 'Violence and Social Change in the Republic of Ireland' *International Journal of the Sociology of Law*, 33: 101–117.

O'Donnell, I. and O'Sullivan, E. (2001) *Crime Control in Ireland: The Politics of Intolerance*. Cork: Cork University Press.

O'Donnell, I., O'Sullivan, E. and Healy, D. (eds) (2005) *Crime and Punishment in Ireland 1922–2003: A Statistical Sourcebook*. Dublin: Institute of Public Administration.

Office of the New York State Attorney General (2014) *Secure Our Smartphones Initiative: One Year Later*. New York: New York Office of the Attorney General.

Office for National Statistics, 'Population Estimates for England and Wales and Scotland'. Available at: http://www.ons.gov.uk/ons/publications/re-reference-tables.html?edition=tcm%3A77-319259.

Organisation for Economic Co-operation and Development (2014) *Society at a Glance: OECD Social Indicators 2014*. OECD Publishing.

Patrick, R. (2011) '"Reading Tea Leaves": An Assessment of the Reliability of Police Recorded Crime Statistics' *The Police Journal*, 84(1): 47–67.

Pease, K. (1994) 'Crime Prevention' in M. Maguire, R. Morgan and R. Reiner. 1st ed. *The Oxford Handbook of Criminology*. Oxford: Clarendon Press.

Police Service of Northern Ireland (PSNI) (2013) *Trends in Police Recorded Crime in Northern Ireland 1998/99 to 2012/13*. Belfast: Police Service of Northern Ireland.

—— (2014) *User Guide to Police Recorded Crime Statistics in Northern Ireland (last updated May 2014)* Belfast: Police Service of Northern Ireland.

Ratcliffe, J. H. (2008) *Intelligence-Led Policing*. Cullompton: Willan Publishing.

Reiner, R. (2000) *The Politics of the Police*. 3rd ed. Oxford: Oxford University Press.

Shaw, M., van Dijk, J. and Rhomberg, W. (2003) 'Determining Trends in Global Crime and Justice: An Overview of Results from the United Nations Surveys of Crime Trends and Operations of Criminal Justice Systems' *Forum on Crime and Society*, 3(1): 35–63.

Simmel, G. (1950) 'The Metropolis and Mental Life' in K. H. Wolff (ed.) *The Sociology of Georg Simmel*. Harmondsworth: Penguin.

Skolnick, J. H. and Woodworth, J. R. (1967) 'Bureaucracy, Information and Social Control' in D. J. Boruda (ed.) *The Police: Six Sociological Essays*. London: John Wiley.

Sullivan, S. (1998) 'From Theory to Practice: The Patterns of Violence in Northern Ireland 1969–1994' *Irish Political Studies*, 13(1): 76–99.

Tomlinson, M. Varley, T. and McCullagh, C. (eds) (1988) *Whose Law and Order? Aspects of Crime and Social Control in Irish Society*. Belfast: Sociological Association of Ireland.

Tonry, M. (2005) 'Why Are Europe's Crime Rates Falling?' *Criminology in Europe*, 4(2): 1 and 8–11.

Tseloni, A., Mailley, J., Farrell, G. and Tilley, N. (2010) 'Exploring the International Decline in Crime Rates' *European Journal of Criminology*, 7(5): 375–394.

UCD Institute of Criminology (2001) *Crime in Ireland*. Dublin: The Stationery Office.

Ulmer, J. T. and Steffensmeier, D. (2014) 'The Age and Crime Relationship: Social Variation, Social Explanations' in K. M. Beaver, J. C. Barnes and B. B. Boutwell (eds) *The Nurture Versus Biosocial Debate in Criminology: On the Origins of Criminal Behaviour and Criminality*. Thousand Oaks, CA: Sage.

UNODC (2014) *Criminal Justice Statistics*. Available at: http://www.unodc.org/unodc/en/data-and-analysis/statistics/crime.html (accessed 15 May 2014).

van Dijk, J., van Kesteren, J. and Smit, P. (2007a) *Crime Victimisation in International Perspective: Key Findings from the 2004–05 ICVS and EU ICS*. The Hague: Boom Legal Publishers.

van Dijk, J.J.M., Manchin, R., van Kesteren, J., Nevala, S., Hideg, G. (2007b) *The Burden of Crime in the EU. Research Report: A Comparative Analysis of the European Crime and Safety Survey (EU ICS) 2005*. Brussels: Gallop Europe.

Watson, D. (2000) *Victims of Recorded Crime in Ireland: Results of the 1996 Survey*. Dublin: Oak Tree Press.

Watson, D. and Parsons, S. (2005) *Domestic Abuse of Women and Men in Ireland: Report on the National Study of Domestic Abuse*. Dublin: Stationery Office.

Welsh Enterprise Unit (2008) *Putting the Economy Back on Track: Crimes against Business*. London: Federation of Small Businesses.

Wesfelt, L. and Estrada, F. (2005) 'International Crime Trends: Sources of Comparative Crime Data and Post-War Trends in Europe' in J. Sheptycki and A. Wardak (eds) *Transnational and Comparative Criminology*. London: Glasshouse Press.

Wood, J. and Kempa, M. (2005) 'Understanding Global Trends in Policing: Explanatory and Normative Dimensions' in J. Sheptycki and A. Wardak (eds) *Transnational and Comparative Criminology*. London: Glasshouse Press.

World Health Organisation, Global Health Observatory Data Repository. Available at: http://apps.who.int/gho/data/node.main.A1026?lang=en.

Young, P. (2005) 'The Use of National Crime Statistics in Comparative Research: Ireland and Scotland Compared' in J. Sheptycki and A. Wardak (eds) *Transnational and Comparative Criminology*. London: Glasshouse Press.

Appendix – key data sources

Information	Source
Crime statistics – Republic of Ireland	Garda Síochána *Annual Reports* (1922–2005). Most recent available from: http://www.garda.ie/Controller.aspx?Page=90&Lang=1
	O'Donnell, I., O'Sullivan, E. and Healy, D. (2005) *Crime and Punishment in Ireland 1922–2003: A Statistical Sourcebook*. Dublin: Institute of Public Administration.
	Central Statistics Office (2003–2013): http://www.cso.ie/px/pxeirestat/ DATABASE/Eirestat/Recorded%20Crime/Recorded%20Crime_statbank. asp?sp=Recorded%20Crime&Planguage=0
Crime statistics – Northern Ireland	Annual Reports of the Chief Constable, Royal Ulster Constabulary (1968– 2001/02): http://www.psni.police.uk/index/updates/updates_statistics/ updates_crime_statistics/updates_crime_statistics_archive.htm
	Police Service of Northern Ireland – Trends in Police Recorded Crime in Northern Ireland (1998/99–2013/14): http://www.psni.police.uk/index/ updates/updates_statistics/updates_crime_statistics.htm
	Brewer, J.D., Lockhart, B. and Rodgers, P. (1997) *Crime in Ireland 1945– 95: Here Be Dragons*. Oxford: Clarendon Press.
Crime statistics – international	United Nations Office on Drugs and Crime: http://www.unodc.org/ unodc/en/data-and-analysis/statistics/crime.html
	Eurostat: http://ec.europa.eu/eurostat/web/crime/database
	European Sourcebook of Crime and Criminal Justice Statistics: http://www.heuni.fi/en/index/tiedotteet/2014/09/ europeansourcebookofcrimeandcriminaljusticestatistics2014published.html
Crime victimisation and attitudes towards Gardaí surveys – Republic of Ireland	Central Statistics Office – Crime and Victimisation: Quarterly National Household Surveys (1998, 2003, 2006 and 2010): http://www.cso.ie/en/ releasesandpublications/crimeandjustice/
	Garda Public Attitudes Surveys (2002, 2006, 2007 and 2008): http:// www.garda.ie/Controller.aspx?Page=93&Lang=1
Crime victimisation and attitudes towards police surveys – Northern Ireland	Department of Justice, Northern Ireland: http://www.dojni.gov.uk/ northern-ireland-crime-survey-s-r
	Central Survey Unit, Northern Ireland Statistics and Research Agency (2000–2003): http://www.csu.nisra.gov.uk/survey.asp114.htm
	Northern Ireland Policing Board Modules of the Omnibus Surveys (2003–2013): http://www.csu.nisra.gov.uk/survey.asp79.htm
Crime victimisation surveys – international	United Nations Integrated Crime and Justice Research Institute for links to data: http://www.unicri.it/services/library_documentation/publications/ icvs/data/
	van Dijk, J., van Kesteren, J. and Smit, P. (2007a) *Crime Victimisation in International Perspective: Key Findings from the 2004–05 ICVS and EU ICS*. The Hague: Boom Legal Publishers. Available at: http://unicri. it/services/library_documentation/publications/icvs/publications/ ICVS2004_05report.pdf
	van Dijk, J.J.M., Manchin, R., van Kesteren, J., Nevala, S., Hideg, G. (2007b) *The Burden of Crime in the EU. Research Report: A Comparative Analysis of the European Crime and Safety Survey (EU ICS) 2005*. Brussels: Gallop Europe. Available at: http://vorige.nrc.nl/redactie/binnenland/ Misdaad.pdf

Notes

1 The views expressed in this chapter are those of the author alone based on publicly available data.
2 Criminal Justice (Northern Ireland) Act, 1966 (following the Suicide Act, 1961 in England and Wales).
3 Criminal Law (Suicide) Act, 1993.
4 A recent report published by Her Majesty's Inspectorate of Constabularies in England and Wales estimated that 19 per cent of crimes reported to the police went unrecorded (HMIC, 2014: 49). Under-recording rates were found to be higher for victims of violence against the person (33 per cent) and sexual offences (26 per cent). Whilst based on a small sample, it is important to note that in the ROI the Garda Síochána Inspectorate has recently stated it believes '*there are systemic failures in Garda Síochána recording practices and non-compliance with the Crime Counting Rules*' (Garda Inspectorate, 2014, part 4: 30). Subsequently to the completion of this chapter and following from the Garda Inspectorate Report, the CSO completed a review of Garda crime statistics. This found that 20 per cent of crimes reported via computer aided dispatch Garda areas and 16 per cent of crimes reported to the remaining paper record based Garda areas were not recorded on PULSE. See CSO, 2015, 'Review of the Quality of Crime Statistics' for further details.
5 The most serious being that to which the greatest penalty applies.
6 For example, the Irish Small and Medium Enterprises Association's 'Annual Business Crime Reports', the Federation of Small Businesses 'Crimes against Business' and the 'Crime against Small Businesses in NI' reports.
7 See for example, National Rape Crisis Statistics reports produced by the Rape Crisis Network Ireland.
8 The Royal Ulster Constabulary until 2001.
9 Whilst the PSNI does not fall within the jurisdiction of the Home Office, the same recording practices are followed, and the same counting rules are applied. See PSNI 2014 for full details.
10 For ease of reference, throughout this chapter the term 'indictable offences' will be used to cover all police-recorded indictable/notifiable crimes in the ROI and/or Northern Ireland (NI).
11 Non-notifiable (previously summary) offences are described as those of less severity, such as disorderly conduct and road traffic offences.
12 See appendix table for details of all key data sources used in this chapter.
13 Following the introduction of PULSE (see note 17), the categories of indictable and non-indictable crimes were replaced by headline and non-headline crime groupings. Figures on headline offences were published in the Garda Annual Reports from 2000 to 2005.
14 There have been two substantial changes in NI which are of most relevance. The first occurred in 1998, when the Home Office Counting Rules for Recorded Crime were expanded to include additional less serious offences and to move to victim-based counts (as opposed to offence-based). The second was in 2002, when a new National Crime Recording Standard (NCRS) was introduced which also incorporated more low-level crime into the recorded statistics. In 2001 the PSNI had introduced the new ICIS (see note 15) recording system, which improved data collection and coverage; as a result the impact of the introduction of the NCRS was lessened.
15 Integrated Crime Information System.
16 Police Using Leading Systems Effectively.
17 Commonly referred to as 'The Conflict'. There is little agreement as to the exact start date of the Conflict, but most note it as beginning in 1968 or 1969.
18 Figures from Eurostat show substantial rises in unemployment in the ROI and the UK between 2008 and 2009. Rates peaked in 2011 and 2012 and showed decreases in 2013 (the most recent figures available). Unemployment in the ROI peaked at almost 15 per cent in 2011 and 2012 and at 8 per cent in the UK in 2011. It was around 5 per cent in both jurisdictions in 2005–07.
19 Figure based on indictable crime figures provided by the CSO.
20 PSNI figures are based on financial years; figures are aligned to the preceding calendar year: that is, figures for April 2012 to March 2013 are presented for 2012.
21 Crime statistics for 1999 are only available for January to September; hence there is a substantial difference recorded which artificially skews the percentage change and is excluded from the chart. (Compared to 1998, the nine months of 1999 recorded a 28 per cent reduction.)
22 Crime statistics for 1998 are under the new Home Office Crime Counting Rules, which increased the number of offences reported and artificially skews the percentage change, so are excluded from the chart. (Compared to 1997, 1998/99 recorded crime figures increased by 75 per cent.)

23 Individual crime types were examined and amalgamated to create these crime groups. For example, in NI kidnapping and false imprisonment was recorded under 'other indictable offences', but was amalgamated into the 'crimes against the person' group for this analysis.

24 For comparability with NI this excludes Groups four and fourteen. Group sixteen, which covers offences not elsewhere classified, which are generally less serious offences, is also excluded.

25 Only aggregate crime figures were available for NI between 1963 and 1967, hence this section focuses on 1968–2013.

26 Lesser volume should not be taken to infer lesser significance. Offences against the person clearly have the potential to have a greater impact upon and cause more harm to the injured party.

27 Other crime types, such as homicides, weapons and explosives offences, crimes linked to organised crime generally (for example, involvement in the illegal drugs trade) and even vandalism of homes left vacant were also increased due to the Conflict. Homicide is considered in another chapter of this book (see Skedd, *infra*).

28 It is also important to note that the definition of robbery in the ROI was amended by The Criminal Law (Jurisdiction) Act, 1976, to include the notion that the injured party was in fear of violence (i.e. actual, physical violence did not have to occur, it just had to be threatened), which would have led to some increase in these figures also.

29 The Conflict Archive on the Internet (CAIN) website contains information and source material on the Northern Ireland Conflict from 1968 to the present. See http://cain.ulster.ac.uk.

30 Excludes attempted burglaries in NI, which were reported separately, and it cannot be determined whether these were against residential dwellings or other properties.

31 From 79 per cent in 2003 to 84 per cent in 2007 as recorded in the PAS published the following years.

32 From 41 per cent in 2003/04 to 47 per cent in 2012/13.

33 For thefts from vehicles reporting rates increased from 60 per cent to 67 per cent; for thefts without violence they increased from 54 per cent to 63 per cent; for thefts with violence they increased from 59 per cent to 64 per cent; for assaults they increased from 51 per cent to 55 per cent. In the case of burglary, specific reporting rates are included only for burglaries occurring whilst someone was at home. However, the report does note the proportion of all households not reporting burglary decreased from 30 per cent in 2006 to 25 per cent in 2010; this implies an increase in the rates of households reporting burglaries (from 70 to 75 per cent).

34 Reporting rates for vandalism in NI are an exception, and have increased from 37 per cent in 2003 to 57 per cent in 2012. Reporting rates for burglary were 75 per cent in 2003/04 and 68 per cent 2012/13; for vehicle related thefts they were 57 per cent in 2003/04 and 48 per cent in 2012/13 (increases and decreases were recorded in the interim in both).

35 In terms of all personal crime, reporting rates have increased from 37 per cent in 2003/04 to 46 per cent in 2012/13.

36 Three per cent in each year.

37 Satisfaction levels ranged between 80 and 86 per cent, based on a four-point Likert scale with no neutral option: Very satisfied; Satisfied; Dissatisfied; Very dissatisfied.

38 Positive ratings were 63 per cent in 1998 and 51 per cent in 2006, based on a five-point Likert scale: Very good; Good; Average; Poor; Very Poor. The answer options were changed in the 2010 survey and the rating of average removed; this has likely increased the proportion of respondents giving a good rating – 67 per cent of respondents. The EU Crime and Safety Survey, discussed further later in this chapter, has also found respondents in the ROI to be amongst the most favourable in 18 European countries when rating the performance of local police in controlling crime (78 per cent of respondents in the ROI were satisfied, the fourth-highest following Finland: 90 per cent, Denmark: 82 per cent, and Austria: 81 per cent, and an EU average of 67 per cent).

39 Respondents were simply asked if they agreed or disagreed that the police in their area did a good job. Overall proportions agreeing declined from 72 per cent in 2000 to 65 per cent in 2003.

40 Based on a three-point Likert scale: Very/fairly good; Neither good nor poor; Very/fairly poor.

41 From 62 per cent to 70 per cent.

42 ICCS recorded crime figures are used in this section. As previously, for comparability with NI this excludes Groups four and fourteen. Group sixteen, covering offences not elsewhere classified, which are generally less serious offences, is also excluded.

43 For CSO estimates of household disposable income per person see: http://www.cso.ie/px/pxeirestat/ Statire/SelectVarVal/Define.asp?Maintable=CIA01&Planguage=0.

44 Gini coefficients taken from Eurostat and updated to those most recently available (released 15 January 2015). No figure available for the UK for 2004. Breaks in the time series for the UK in 2005 and 2012. No figure available for Ireland for 2013.

45 The Institute for Fiscal Studies and other commentators in the UK state that income patterns in NI are similar to those in Great Britain.

46 Rates per 100,000 population as provided in the CTS data, except for England & Wales, Scotland and Northern Ireland. For these countries the Office for National Statistics mid-year population estimates were used to calculate rates per 100,000 population according to total crime figures reported in the CTS.

47 There were a small number of exceptions to this where data was only available for 2011. When this is the case it is highlighted in the table.

48 In the 2014 Sourcebook a total of 46 countries were included in the project; they include countries in Europe, Russia and many ex-Soviet countries.

49 Findings relate to the twelve months preceding the survey.

50 Findings relate to the calendar year preceding the survey.

51 Findings relate to the twelve months preceding the survey.

52 These victimisation rates are from the CSO Survey. The PAS showed similar trends; victimisation decreased from 12.5 per cent in 2002 to 9.2 per cent in 2008.

53 Note that data are not available for all years, and for ease of presentation these years are excluded in each chart.

54 There were also possible reductions in households experiencing thefts of vehicles from 1.2 per cent to 1 per cent; due to rounding of figures to the nearest whole number in 2006 and 2010, it is not possible to determine the exact change in proportions.

55 Personal crime victimisation declined to 4 per cent in 2010.

56 Response rates to the survey were low, particularly where random digit dialling (RDD) was used, which includes the ROI and NI, and were comparable in both jurisdictions. The average response rate for the entire ICVS was 51 per cent; this dropped to 46.3 per cent in the RDD EU countries. The response rate was 42 per cent for the ROI and 41 per cent in NI.

57 The second International Self-Report Delinquency (ISRD-2) Study also ranks the ROI highest of all participating countries in terms of the last year prevalence of total self-reported delinquency amongst 12- to 15-year-olds at 40.1 per cent (see Enzmann et al., 2010). Data collection for ISRD-2 was between November, 2005 and February, 2007. NI did not participate in the second study but there was a city sample of Belfast included in the first ISRD in 1992. This found self-report, last year prevalence rates of offending to be 47.3 per cent in Belfast, the lowest of the seven city samples (the highest being Athens at 85.1 per cent).

58 See, for example, Office of the New York State Attorney General (2014).

59 These are the ROI, the UK, Estonia, The Netherlands and Denmark.

60 Reporting rates for the ROI have been quoted earlier. Reporting rates for Estonia: assaults, 26 per cent; robbery, 39 per cent; burglary, 52 per cent; theft of a car, 58 per cent; thefts of personal property, 29 per cent.

61 There is nonetheless still a very significant drug problem in the ROI.

2

Homicide

Sarah Skedd[1]

Introduction

While considerable attention has been devoted to homicide (and violent crime in general) by various sectors of the media, the subject has been relatively understudied within the realm of criminology (Levi, Maguire and Brookman, 2007). Research in the field has been dominated by US-focused studies, though there is a growing body of European scholarship (Kivivuori, Suonpää and Lehti, 2014). Existing Irish research on homicide is limited and somewhat outdated. The studies of homicide case files in the Republic of Ireland carried out by Dooley (1995, 2001), though detailed, are limited to the period from 1972 to 1996. Given that political unrest has historically been a motivating factor behind many homicides, the bulk of research in Northern Ireland has been focused on what is commonly referred to as 'the Conflict' or the 'security situation', with less analysis dedicated to non-political homicides. While international research is useful in developing an understanding of Irish homicide, any interpretation of such must take into account the social and political circumstances that are unique to the island of Ireland.

This chapter begins by briefly outlining the legal construct of homicide in both Northern Ireland and the Republic of Ireland before moving on to discuss relevant theories on homicide. Next, the broad trends in the recorded homicide figures of both jurisdictions are examined and contrasted with international patterns. The concentration of homicide in certain areas and its distribution across particular sections of the population is then considered. Finally, the impact of organised crime is discussed, and it is argued that some of the differences observed between the island of Ireland and other European countries are due to this phenomenon.

What is homicide?

While the term 'homicide' is most commonly associated with, or used as a synonym for, murder, it is in fact a broader term that comprises a range of offences related to unlawful death. Homicide in both the Republic of Ireland and Northern Ireland consists of the offences of Murder, Manslaughter and Infanticide (Central Statistics Office [CSO], 2014a; Police Service of Northern Ireland [PSNI], 2013). In Northern Ireland, there is a further offence of Corporate

49

Manslaughter. Homicide in the Republic of Ireland also includes offences linked to dangerous driving causing death, while equivalent offences in Northern Ireland are classed under Other Violence with Injury. Internationally, definitions of homicide vary less than for other crime groups (Clarke, 2013). The United Nations Office on Drugs and Crime (UNODC) (2014) subdivides intentional homicide into three further categories, namely, Socio-political (such as terrorism), Inter-personal (including domestic incidents and male-on-male confrontational violence), and that which is related to other types of criminal activity (for example, homicides which occur during a robbery, or in the course of an organised crime group conducting its business). While these subheadings may not be part of the legal terminology of homicide, they are useful for understanding the differing motivations for such incidents.

Unlike many other crime types, the recorded figures for homicide are generally considered to be reasonably accurate reflections of what has occurred (PSNI, 2013; Office of National Statistics [ONS], 2014). Homicide is regarded as an ideal offence category for making global comparisons; incidents are typically reported to and recorded by the police, making it likely that changes in the rate over time are a reflection of actual change (Kilcommins *et al.*, 2004; Schwartz, 2010; Clarke, 2013; UNODC, 2014). However, the category is not entirely without its 'dark figure'; there are various scenarios in which an unlawful death may occur but may not be recorded. Brookman (2005) outlines a number of these, referring, *inter alia*, to missing persons and errors in identifying the cause of death. A notable UK example of the latter is that of the English doctor Harold Shipman, who killed 172 patients over a number of years, with the incidents eventually recorded as homicides in the 2002/03 figures (ONS, 2014). Missing person cases are unlikely to be recorded as homicides, given that other explanations could account for their disappearance, including intentional disappearance, suicide and accidental death or misadventure.

In some cases where the cause of death is known, the incident is not classed as a homicide because it is not widely recognised as such within a particular society. Brookman (2005: 3) argues that homicide is essentially a 'socially constructed concept' and is heavily mediated by perceptions of victimisation and culpability. Corporate killings, which include workplace deaths caused by negligence, are often not seen as 'real crime' (Brookman, 2005). In addition, deaths of civilians resulting from contact with the police are rarely recorded as homicides. A total of 1,487 deaths resulting from police contact have been identified in England and Wales, with just 13 resulting in a verdict of unlawful killing between 1990 and 2011 (Inquest, 2014a, 2014b). On the other hand, violent acts that would normally be considered abhorrent can, in certain circumstances, be legitimised; for example, terrorism may be rationalised as being a necessary tool in overthrowing oppression (Levi *et al.*, 2007).

Homicide and criminological theory

As with crime more generally, there is no single criminological theory that satisfactorily or comprehensively explains the phenomena of homicide and violence. An analysis of recent European publications on homicide demonstrates that virtually all major criminological theories have been used to explain homicide patterns, though some have proven more popular than others (Kivivuori *et al.*, 2014). Theoretical approaches have come from a variety of perspectives, including those focusing on the attributes of individuals and those considering the effects of wider forces external to the person.

Wolfgang's (1958) study of homicide in the American city of Philadelphia made a number of observations about the distribution and characteristics of homicide. In particular, certain sections of the population – African Americans and males – were disproportionately affected both as victims and offenders, though the gender balance evened out when only intimate partner homicides were considered. Gender also had an effect on where homicides took place, with females most commonly killing or killed at home, while men killed other men in public areas, such as streets. Wolfgang's (1958) study further demonstrated that victims and offenders were not necessarily mutually exclusive groups, since over a quarter of homicides were victim-precipitated, in that the eventual victim made the first violent move. The study, however, was limited by the availability of data, so it was not possible to examine issues such as the role of socio-economic class, ethnicity or the influence of alcohol (Collings, 1958). Luckenbill's (1977) research examined the circumstances surrounding homicide, described as the 'social occasion' and the 'dynamic interchange'. The 'social occasion' in which homicide occurred was invariably leisure-related and unconstrained by external limitations, as would be the case in work or at structured gatherings. Homicide occurred primarily in the home, at or near bars, or at other unsupervised public spaces, predominantly in the evenings and at weekends. These circumstances bear some similarity to the spatio-temporal convergence of offenders and targets described by Cohen and Felson's (1979) routine activities theory. While routine activities theory is content with assuming the presence of a motivated offender, Luckenbill (1977) identified various stages of a 'dynamic interchange' common to homicide incidents. The interchange begins with the eventual victim doing or saying something that the offender takes offence to, followed by a failure by either participant to back down or apologise, resulting in a commitment to fight that ends with death. The two-sided, spontaneous and leisure-based scenario has been particularly homed in on in studies of confrontational male-on-male homicide (Polk, 1994; Brookman, 2005). While the applicability of 'dynamic interchange' theory to incidents involving young children or innocent injured parties (who did not seek to cause offence or contribute to starting a fight) may seem tenuous, Luckenbill (1977) surmounts this by positing that it is the offender's interpretation of the victim's behaviour, regardless of how accurate this is, that is relevant.

A key aspect of Luckenbill's (1977) findings is the conceptualisation of victims as not necessarily passive or, in some cases, inadvertent participants in their own demise. Wolfgang (1967) carried out further work on the subject of victim precipitation, which revealed a number of differences between such incidents and the general pool of homicides studied. In particular, these cases featured a greater proportion of male victims of female offenders than in the overall study, that victims were more likely to have consumed alcohol and to have previous police or arrest records than other victims. Wolfgang's (1967) observations have been reaffirmed by additional US research, which found that victims who had previous criminal histories were more likely than those without to have died in victim-precipitated homicides and, furthermore, to be demographically more similar to offenders than to other victims in terms of age, gender and race (Muftic and Hunt, 2013). A Dutch study examining the influence of event characteristics and victim behaviour found that certain factors, including victim precipitation, alcohol use by victims and the absence of moderating third parties was predictive of lethal incidents (Ganpat, van der Leun and Nieuwbeerta, 2013).

Despite the valuable contribution of Luckenbill's (1977) work in understanding the build-up to homicide events, it does not go far enough in explaining why offenders (and victims, to a somewhat lesser extent) are more likely to be male. Polk (1994) suggested that confrontational violence between males is largely the result of the willingness of males to both challenge the honour of other men and to defend their own. Gilligan (2001: 67) contends that this willingness to pursue violence is motivated by shame – 'overwhelming, and otherwise inescapable and ineradicable shame'. Violence is intrinsically linked to notions of masculinity; a man is afforded honour for his ability to use violence when challenged and experiences shame if perceived as passive or weak. As female honour is traditionally associated with passivity and chastity rather than violence, women are not as driven to mitigate their experiences of shame through acts of violence (Gilligan, 2001). Jones (2008) also considered the influence of shame, arguing that males are less likely than women to have a secure sense of self and thus feel an imperative to prove their masculinity. He also suggested that there is an evolutionary connection between masculinity and violence, the legacy of an age when a man's toughness determined his social position and access to resources and mates. The themes of shame and evolution were apparent in rationalisations for violence made by bar fighters seeking to normalise their activities (Copes, Hochstetler and Forsyth, 2013).

In accounting for why the majority of people do not resort to violence, Gilligan (2001) proposes that violence is only used to allay feelings of shame where internal feelings of self-esteem are insufficient to do so. Factors such as gender, poverty and discrimination due to race and age can increase the likelihood of being exposed to levels of disrespect that could over-power a person's sense of self-worth. For example, having sufficient access to economic resources can provide a male with a stable basis on which to assert his masculinity, with violence being the resort of males whose masculinity is problematised by their lack of economic resources (Polk, 1994). Various studies have outlined the ways in which socio-economic marginalisation or upheaval can contribute to the development of subcultures based around the violent expression of masculinity (see Bourgois, 1996; Mears et al., 2013). While Gilligan's theory of shame as the primary motivator for violence is informative, it does not adequately explain violence associated with filicide, which may be better understood as resulting from severe strain caused by social and economic isolation and depression, rather than from shame (Wilczynski, 1995; Alt and Wells, 2010). At the other end of the spectrum, shame would also appear to be an inappropriate explanation for some of the purposive, systemic violence associated with organised crime, which is focused on control and financial gain.

The concepts of anomie and strain have also proved influential in studies of homicide. Merton (1938) theorised that a cultural emphasis on the achievement of particular goals, combined with a failure to provide some people with the means or motivation to legitimately achieve these goals, creates a form of strain that can result in resorting to alternative, possibly illegitimate, methods of goal attainment. More recently, institutional anomie theory (Messner and Rosenfeld, 1997) asserts that the dominance of economic priorities at the bureaucratic level of a society facilitates higher crime rates by diminishing the relevance of non-economic bodies, such as the family or schools, which foster social control and attachments. Messner and Rosenfeld (1997) found that countries with lower homicide rates tended to have higher levels of social welfare supports. A longitudinal comparison of European nations over a period spanning the region's phase of economic prosperity and subsequent decline found that welfare spending was linked to homicide rates (McCall and Brauer, 2014). Gilligan (2001) also identified high economic inequity and the stigmatisation of welfare services as triggers of shame which in turn led to the US experiencing higher homicide rates compared to other developed countries with lower inequality rates.

Moreover, levels of social capital, trust and political legitimacy can influence homicide rates independently of socio-economic measures such as deprivation and inequality. Rosenfeld, Messner and Baumer (2001) found that levels of social capital (measured through civic engagement and social trust) had a significant effect on homicide rates, even when taking into account other influential variables such as deprivation and population structure. Low levels of social cohesion and higher levels of socio-economic disadvantage were also found to be associated with a higher likelihood of homicide victimisation when tested at a neighbourhood level in the Netherlands (Nieuwbeerta et al., 2008). In a cross-national study, Nivette and Eisner (2013) found that the effects of political legitimacy on homicide were approximately as strong as the effects of factors such as economic inequality, and they concluded that levels of legitimacy could impact upon social control mechanisms, the distribution of social resources and the ability or willingness of people to trust in the police to resolve conflict. Looking specifically at organised crime, van Dijk (2007) argues that the quality of rule of law, particularly the police and courts system, plays a significant role in determining the prevalence of organised crime in that state.

There is a further body of theoretical work that moves away from the theoretical explanations of homicide described so far, arguing that they are insufficient for explaining the observed trends. A comparison of European homicide rates from 1960 to 2010 against commonly used predictors of homicide, such as unemployment, GDP and population age structure, did not reveal any match in trends (Aebi and Linde, 2014). Eisner (2008) argues that the various theories and perspectives outlined earlier in this chapter fail to adequately account for upward trends in homicide in the latter half of the twentieth century, as they do not take into account the longer-term historical trends or the broad similarities across Western countries for various categories of violence. Eisner (2003, 2008) attributed the significant decline in homicide observed across Europe from the fifteenth century to the mid-twentieth century to the reduction in homicides committed by elite males and in male-on-male homicide which occurred in public spaces. He emphasised the increased centralisation of power to the State as increasing levels of self-control and social control by providing an alternate method of conflict resolution. The continued decline in homicide which occurred alongside rapid developments in technology, industrialisation and urbanisation that accompanied the shift into modernity casts doubt on theories which identify these factors as causes of violence (Eisner, 2008). Instead, Eisner (2008) proposes that culturally established expectations for acceptable conduct of life are more influential, with self-control, domesticity and respectability becoming increasingly important between 1850 and 1950. While Eisner (2003, 2008) argued that homicide rates have largely been governed by changing patterns of violence involving young males, Aebi and Linde (2014) found that changing homicide patterns tended to affect both genders and various age groups proportionately. Aebi and Linde (2014) identify the 1960s as heralding a massive shift in lifestyles and attitudes, one product of which was both males and females spending more time in public spaces and thus increasing their risk of victimisation.

Irish homicide trends

The rate of homicide in the Republic of Ireland and Northern Ireland has been calculated by Eurostat at 1.3 and 1.42 per 100,000 respectively for the three-year period from 2008 to 2010 (Clarke, 2013). At first glance, these rates appear low when compared against the global homicide rate of 6.2 per 100,000, though it must be borne in mind that this figure includes nations experiencing high levels of political and social instability (UNODC, 2014). Homicide rates across Europe average at 3.0 per 100,000 (UNODC, 2014) but vary considerably, from as low as 0.31 per 100,000 in Iceland to as high as 7.7 per 100,000 in Lithuania (Clarke, 2013). The rates recorded in both the Republic of Ireland and Northern Ireland are somewhat higher than many of our nearest geographic neighbours, with the exception of Belgium and Scotland, where homicide rates exceeded 1.7 per 100,000 (Clarke, 2013).

Republic of Ireland[2]

What is immediately striking about recorded homicide figures in the Republic of Ireland is the relatively high rate between 1927 and 1937 compared with the subsequent three decades (see Figure 2.1). This was in part driven by high recordings of manslaughter, reflecting the fact that, prior to the introduction of a specific offence of dangerous driving causing death in 1962, such incidents were recorded as manslaughter (Brewer, Lockhart and Rodgers, 1997). From 1947 onwards, it is possible to distinguish the manslaughters recorded as a result of traffic fatalities from

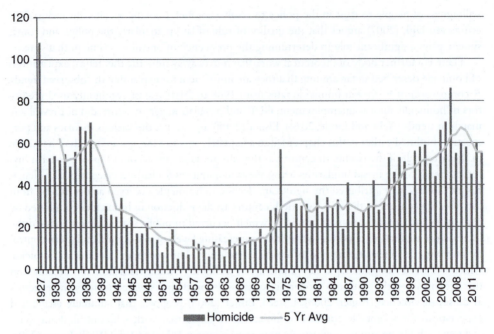

Figure 2.1   Homicide: Republic of Ireland 1927–2013

others, the effect of which is visible on the chart. However, a sharp and sustained reduction in recorded homicide occurred in 1938, almost a decade earlier. O'Donnell (2005) suggested that the War of Independence and Civil War may have contributed to higher numbers of homicides in the years immediately afterwards, followed by a drop in homicide which coincided with the commencement of the Second World War.

The decline in homicide rates observed until the mid-twentieth century and subsequent rise is broadly consistent with the wider European trend described by Eisner (2003, 2008). O'Donnell (2005) adds to Eisner's (2008) thesis by suggesting that there were circumstances specific to the Republic of Ireland which influenced the development of a particular code of life that was unique to this country. In particular, he identifies the effect of the famine on demographics, the increase in social control exerted by the Roman Catholic Church, the respect afforded to celibacy and late marriage and, separately, a growing respect for infant life which accompanied industrialisation and increased prosperity. While Eisner (2003, 2008) argues that European homicide trends declined as a result of a reduction in violent behaviour by elite males, O'Donnell (2005) suggests that the decrease in the Republic of Ireland was driven by a reduction in infanticides perpetrated by poor women. Infanticide was a considerable problem in the nineteenth century, but has declined significantly (Kilcommins *et al.*, 2004). In the ten years between 1927 and 1936, 92 murders were recorded where the victims were under one year old, reducing to 93 in the subsequent 30 years. There were further rapid drops in the following decades, with 28 cases recorded between 1967 and 1996, and just one case between 1997 and 2014. Unlike the broader homicide trend, 90 per cent of offenders in such incidents between 1927 and 1946 were female (O'Donnell, Sullivan and Healy, 2005). O'Donnell (2005) notes that the decline of infanticide began prior to the decline in the stigma against unmarried mothers and also preceded legislative changes such as the Adoption Act 1953 and the Social Welfare Act 1973, which introduced social welfare payments for unmarried mothers. While the numbers of homicides recorded each year in the Republic of Ireland are too low to show the trend, infanticide and neonaticide remain internationally the most common forms of child killing: largely attributable to post-natal mental health disorders in the west, and a preference for male children in some cultures (O'Hagan, 2014).

While other jurisdictions experienced steady increases from the mid-sixties to early nineties, the trend in the Republic of Ireland was more staggered, with the early seventies and early nineties identified as key watersheds (O'Donnell, 2002; Kilcommins et al., 2004). According to Young, O'Donnell and Clare (2001), even excluding the deaths from the Dublin and Monaghan bombings in 1974, the early 1970s heralded an increase in the yearly number of homicides that never returned to previous levels. The average rate of homicide was low compared to other European countries, yet between 1950 and 1998 the rate of homicide per 100,000 of population increased by approximately 600 per cent, from slightly over 0.2 to just under 1.4 (Dooley, 1995; Young et al., 2001). Eisner (2008) attributed the Europe-wide upswing in homicide rates to changes in modes of living, which included increased alcohol consumption and leisure time, and decreased social control mechanisms in social locations. Indeed, the Republic of Ireland recorded the highest per capita rise in alcohol consumption in Europe between 1989 and 1999 (O'Donnell, 2002). O'Donnell (2002) also proposed that the rise in homicide in the Republic of Ireland corresponded to the increase in marginalisation and anomie that accompanied unequally distributed economic prosperity of the Celtic Tiger. Homicide rates in the Republic of Ireland peaked between 2005 and 2007 and have since declined, though there are substantial year-on-year variations. The downturn in homicide rates appears to have commenced somewhat later than in other European countries, with England and Wales, France, Germany, the Netherlands, Hungary and Finland all recording declining rates shortly after the beginning of the millennium (UNODC, 2014; ONS, 2014). The relationship between the recent economic decline and homicide rates in Ireland has not yet been fully explored.

Northern Ireland[3]

Overall homicide trends in Northern Ireland (see Figure 2.2), available from 1968 onwards, are considerably different to those of the Republic of Ireland and indeed the rest of Europe, with peak rates being experienced in the 1970s. Recorded incidents of homicide declined in the late seventies and early 1980s before increasing slightly into the mid 1990s. Since then, the average rate has continued to gradually decline.

It is impossible to discuss homicide in Northern Ireland without considering the impact of socio-political violence during the Conflict. In excess of 3,000 people[4] have been killed in Northern Ireland since 1969 as a result of political violence (Brewer et al., 1997; Brookman, 2005; PSNI, 2013; Fay, Morrissey and Smyth, 1999), which led Belfast to have the highest homicide rate in the EU (Kilcommins et al., 2004). The peaks and troughs in homicide rates in Northern Ireland are closely linked to the political and social dynamics of the jurisdiction. Fay et al. (1999) explain that the introduction of internment in August 1971 was a significant trigger, with a sudden increase in homicides from this time, which continued into 1972 with a peak of 376 incidents recorded, many of which were multiple deaths resulting from bombings (Brewer et al., 1997). The ceasefires announced by Republican and Loyalist groups in 1994 led to a significant reduction in homicides in the following year, with deaths linked to the security situation dropping from 54 in 1994/95 to 12 in the following year (PSNI, 2014a). It has been estimated that 357 people, 194 of whom were not paramilitaries, were killed by members of the security forces (police and army) between 1969 and 1993 (Mulcahy, 2006). Deaths resulting from the activities of members of the security forces were not typically considered to be homicides,

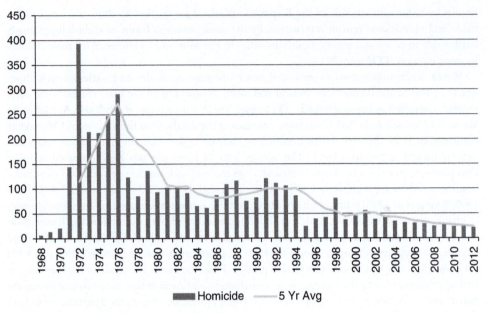

Figure 2.2 Homicide: Northern Ireland 1968–2012

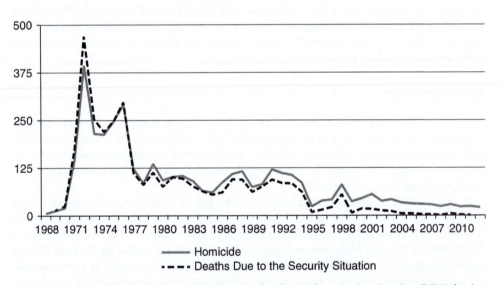

Figure 2.3 Recorded homicide compared to deaths due to the security situation (PSNI data)

a reminder of Brookman's (2005) assertion that homicide is a socially constructed concept. The number of deaths in Northern Ireland due to political unrest exceeded the number of recorded homicides between 1972 and 1976 (see Figure 2.3).[5] The two lines follow remarkably similar trends throughout the 1980s and 1990s, with the number of security situation deaths recorded each year in the single figures since 2004.

With homicides related to political violence dominating both statistics and discussion, it can be difficult to extract an image of non-political homicide trends in Northern Ireland. Brewer *et al.*

(1997) state that there was an average of 13 murders per year since 1969 which were not related to the Conflict, though this can be difficult to state definitely, as sectarian murders are not differentiated from others in official figures. Comparison of PSNI (2014a) figures from 2004/05 to 2012/13 for deaths related to the security situation to the list of deaths compiled by CAIN (Melaugh, 2015) indicates that such incidents are likely to be recorded as homicides (for example, none of the deaths appear to be perpetrated by members of the security services). On this basis, it is possible to estimate that there was an average of 24 homicides per year in Northern Ireland between 2004/05 and 2012/13 which were not related to the security situation, with a high of 37 in 2004/05, a low of 18 in 2012/13 and substantial variation in between. However, there is also the possibility that the prevalence of political violence had a knock-on effect on levels of general violence.

Noting an increase in domestic as well as political homicides since the commencement of civil unrest, Lyons and Harbinson (1986: 196) speculate that this was influenced by 'the availability of weapons and the general atmosphere of violence'. The proliferation of weapons, particularly firearms, appears to have a significant effect on the rate of domestic homicide during the Conflict, with McWilliams (1997) noting that many victims of firearm-related domestic homicides were the wives of members of the security services. The chronicle of deaths maintained by CAIN includes a number of further incidents which may, peripherally or otherwise, be linked to paramilitary groups or their members (Melaugh, 2015). Nivette and Eisner (2013) have proposed that countries with low levels of political legitimacy, leading to, *inter alia*, reduced trust in the police and inequitable allocation of resources, experience higher homicide rates. The effect of disputed political legitimacy on non-political violence, such as domestic incidents, is exemplified in Northern Ireland. McWilliams (1997) explains that it could be difficult for victims who were married to members of the security forces to get an adequate response from their husbands' colleagues, while women in Republican areas could face the additional problem of being dubbed an informer by their own community. Alternate law enforcement services provided by paramilitaries do not appear to have been any more effective than the legitimate system, with McWilliams (1997: 87) explaining that 'women felt that the various police forces, both official and unofficial, would only condemn or punish the offender for his violent behaviour in the home if he was well known to them for his anti-social or offensive behaviour outside the home'.

Distribution of homicide

While the various studies of homicide discussed above may not have agreed on the causes or explanations of violence, there appears to be a general consensus that homicide is not evenly distributed. Certain subsections of the population tend to feature more prominently than others: in particular, young people, males and those who live in socio-economically deprived urban areas (World Health Organisation, 2010). While a lack of detailed and consistent information in relation to both the Republic of Ireland and Northern Ireland has hampered analysis and interpretation of trends, it is possible to begin to develop a picture of Irish homicide and compare it to international trends and research.[6]

Geographic distribution

A breakdown of homicide figures by police administrative areas indicates that certain areas experience higher levels than others. In Northern Ireland (see Table 2.1), the PSNI districts covering Belfast city recorded almost a quarter of all homicides in the 11 years between 2003/04 and 2013/14, though the low number of homicides recorded each year means there can be substantial year-on-year percentage variations (PSNI, 2014b). As the PSNI data did not drill down to

Table 2.1 Homicides by police administrative areas – Northern Ireland 2003/04–2013/14 (PSNI, 2014b)

District	Areas	%
A District	North Belfast, West Belfast	12.1
B District	South Belfast, East Belfast	12.4
C District	Ards, Castlereagh, North Down and Down	11.1
D District	Carrickfergus, Antrim, Lisburn, Newtownabbey	11.4
E District	Armagh, Banbridge, Craigavon, Newry and Mourne	14.1
F District	Cookstown, Omagh, Fermanagh, Dungannon and South Tyrone	14.8
G District	Foyle, Limavady, Magherafelt and Strabane	12.8
H District	Larne, Ballymena, Ballymoney, Coleraine and Moyle	11.4

Table 2.2 Homicides by Garda regions – Republic of Ireland 2003–2013 (CSO, 2014d)

Region	Divisions	%
Dublin Metropolitan Region	DMR Northern, Western, Southern, Eastern, North Central, South Central	44.3
Eastern Region	Meath, Westmeath, Kildare, Wicklow, Laois/Offaly	9.4
Northern Region	Louth, Cavan/Monaghan, Sligo/Leitrim, Donegal	9.1
South Eastern Region	Tipperary, Waterford, Kilkenny/Carlow, Wexford	10.6
Southern Region	Cork City, Cork North, Cork West, Kerry, Limerick	19.4
Western Region	Clare, Galway, Mayo, Roscommon/Longford	7.2

the area level, it has not been possible to establish whether or not homicide is clustered primarily in urban or rural areas outside of Belfast. There appears to have been a shift in the distribution of homicide from Belfast to other districts; previous research has indicated that Belfast, particularly the North and West of the city, typically experienced about 50 per cent of murders in Northern Ireland between 1945 and 1995, though this could reduce if rural paramilitaries were particularly active (Brewer *et al.*, 1997; Fay *et al.*, 1999).

In the Republic of Ireland (see Table 2.2), homicide primarily affects Garda divisions which include large urban areas or commuter belts, such as Dublin, Limerick, Cork and Louth (CSO, 2014b; Kilcommins *et al.*, 2004; Dooley, 1995, 2001). Dublin is disproportionately affected by homicide; 44 per cent of homicides between 2003 and 2013 were recorded in this region, whereas the 2011 Census indicated that 28 per cent of the population lives in the Dublin city and county (CSO, 2012). The imbalance is continued within the confines of the Dublin region, with the DMR Eastern division recording just 10 incidents out of 285 in the 11-year period, compared with 89 in the DMR Western division, 60 in the DMR Northern, and 49, 42 and 35 in the South Central, North Central and Southern divisions respectively (CSO, 2014b).

The Pobal HP Deprivation Index, which was constructed using data relating to demographic profiles, social class composition and labour market situation from the 2011 Census, indicates that the electoral districts contained within the boundaries of the DMR Eastern division are predominantly classed as affluent (Haase and Pratschke, 2012). In contrast, large pockets of the Northern, Western and Southern divisions are considered to be either disadvantaged or very disadvantaged. While many of the electoral wards of the North Central and South Central divisions are not classed as disadvantaged, these areas constitute the social and leisure hubs of the city centre. However, the Pobal HP Deprivation Index also identified pockets of disadvantage in rural areas, particularly in the north-west of the country, where there is not a high rate of homicide.

There are also inconsistencies in the relationship between homicide rates and deprivation in Northern Ireland. While both Belfast police districts have recorded similar proportions of homicides, the A district, covering the North and West of the city, has considerably higher levels of deprivation (Northern Ireland Statistics and Research Agency, 2010). Research examining the links between violence and deprivation in Northern Ireland during the Conflict (Fay *et al.*, 1999) reached the conclusion that the relationship was by no means simple. While there appears to be some relationship between the rate of homicide in an area and levels of deprivation and disadvantage, the lack of consistency would suggest that there are other contributing factors. For example, lower levels of social cohesion, along with disadvantage, have been associated with higher homicide rates (Nieuwbeerta *et al.*, 2008). Similarly, levels of social capital can influence homicide rates, even when controlling for factors such as deprivation (Rosenfeld *et al.*, 2001). Considering the link between urban areas and homicide, the UNODC (2014) suggests that some of the risk factors associated with cities, such as greater economic inequality and the presence of gangs or organised crime groups, may be partially counteracted by protective factors, such as a greater policing presence, wider educational opportunities and closer medical facilities.

Gender distribution

Homicide in the island of Ireland is primarily a male-perpetrated offence. For incidents in the Republic of Ireland recorded between 2003 and 2013 (see Figure 2.4), 91.8 per cent of offenders (where known) were male, a ratio which is broadly consistent with earlier data (O'Donnell, 2005; Dooley, 1995, 2001). Over a nine-year period in Northern Ireland, 94 per cent of those convicted of homicide were male (Appleby *et al.*, 2011), though it must be borne in mind that women may be less likely than men to be convicted (Dooley, 1995). In addition, many homicide offenders are young: the median age of those convicted in Northern Ireland between 2000 and 2008 was 27 (Appleby *et al.*, 2011), while in the Republic of Ireland 54.4 per cent of homicide offenders were aged under 30. Males are also more likely to be the victims of homicide, with the Republic of Ireland and Northern Ireland recording similar proportions, at 79.6 per cent

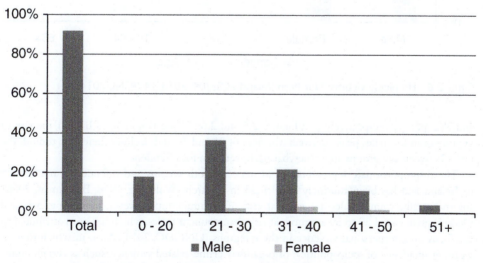

Figure 2.4 Homicide offenders: Republic of Ireland 2003–2013 (CSO, 2014c)

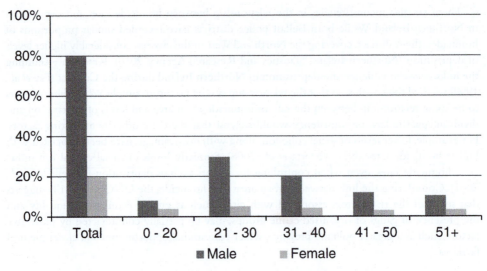

Figure 2.5 Homicide victims: Republic of Ireland 2003–2013 (CSO, 2014d)

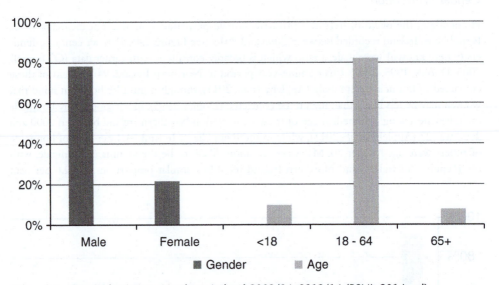

Figure 2.6 Homicide victims: Northern Ireland 2003/04–2013/14 (PSNI, 2014c, d)

and 78.2 per cent respectively (see Figures 2.5 and 2.6). In the Republic of Ireland, the risk of victimisation for males peaks between the ages of 21 and 30 and declines thereafter, though the ratios between age groups are somewhat narrower than for offenders.

The disproportionate representation of males as both victims and offenders is not unique to Ireland and has been routinely confirmed in research (Wolfgang, 1958; Brookman, 2005). Internationally, young males are most at risk of victimisation; however, in Europe, Asia and Oceania, males aged 30 to 59 are more at risk than younger males, which has been attributed to the focus on interpersonal violence in these regions (UNODC, 2014). Areas in which there is a greater incidence of socio-political or organised-crime-related violence, such as certain countries in the Americas, tend to have more male victims aged 15 to 29; this bears some similarity to the experience in Northern Ireland, in which 91.8 per cent of victims were male, half of which were aged in their twenties or thirties (UNODC, 2014; Fay *et al.*, 1999).

While Luckenbill's (1977) conceptualisation of homicide is as a situated transaction aimed to describe all non-felony-related homicides, the focus on leisure-based social occasions and the preservation of honour provide a useful springboard for a specific discussion on male-on-male homicide. To a certain degree, the focus on leisure highlights the role of alcohol consumption. The frequent association of alcohol with homicide is well chronicled internationally, with various studies noting its prevalence in approximately 50 per cent of cases (Wolfgang, 1958; O'Donnell, 2002; Brookman, 2005; Miles, 2012; UNODC, 2014). While alcohol consumption is by no means solely the preserve of male-on-male confrontational homicide, Dooley (1995, 2001) noted that a significant proportion of male-on-male homicides in the Republic of Ireland between 1972 and 1996 took place at night and involved the intoxication of at least one participant, and in 32.3 per cent of all homicides both the victim and offender were intoxicated. Research in Northern Ireland has found that 49 per cent of those convicted for homicide offences had a history of alcohol misuse, a higher percentage than was recorded in either Scotland or England and Wales (Appleby *et al.*, 2011). An all-Ireland Drug Prevalence Survey has found that half of the surveyed population could be classed as engaging in harmful drinking practices, with greater proportions of males and those aged between 18 and 24 affected (National Advisory Committee on Drugs [NACD], 2012). More specifically, 57 per cent of males and a third of females were found to engage in risky single occasion drinking – better known as binge-drinking – at least once per month, as did 45 per cent of those aged 18 to 24 (NACD, 2012). Research has found evidence of a history of binge-drinking in convicted male homicide offenders (Miles, 2012), while, at a macro-level, national cultures of risky drinking practices have been associated with higher homicide rates (Bye, 2008).

Though the Drug Prevalence Survey cited above indicates that approximately a third of females participate in risky drinking behaviours, they comprise a much smaller proportion of homicide offenders and victims. This would indicate that alcohol is not the only factor driving Irish homicide rates. Research on convicted homicide offenders in England and Wales has suggested that intoxication interacts with other factors, such as immediate situational factors and longer-term experiences of deprivation and violence (Miles, 2012). This brings us to the 'honour' component of Luckenbill's theory, the preservation of which Gilligan (2001) contends is driven by the effects of shame on masculinity. Hourigan's (2011) exploration of community violence in disadvantaged social housing estates in Limerick explains how young men who were alienated from mainstream sources of status, such as employment, sought to affirm their masculinity by being associated with the much-feared local criminal groups (see Chapter 7). McWilliams (1997) highlights the significance of masculine pride, in explaining that some young males subjected to paramilitary punishments in Northern Ireland would have preferred to receive a physical punishment, such as knee-capping, rather than be humiliated in front of the community. Physical injury and a war wound, it seems, are preferable to a dent in one's mental construction of masculinity.

As is the case internationally, females feature in Irish homicide statistics as victims more than as offenders. Females comprise slightly over 8 per cent of homicide offenders in the Republic of Ireland, and were victims in 19.8 and 21.5 per cent of cases in the Republic of Ireland and Northern Ireland respectively (see Figures 2.4–2.6). The proportion of female victims in the Republic of Ireland has decreased; between 1972 and 1996, approximately 28 per cent of victims were female (Dooley, 1995, 2001). The Republic of Ireland and Northern Ireland differ from European averages regarding the percentage of female victims, with the UNODC (2014) reporting that 28 per cent of homicide victims in the region were female. Countries with low homicide rates (below 1.0 per 100,000) have still greater proportions of female victims, including New Zealand (40 per cent) and Japan, where female victims outnumber males (UNODC, 2014). In contrast, the percentage of female victims is lower in the Americas (12 per cent); this is not to say that intimate partner or domestic homicide is any less prevalent in the Americas, but rather that other categories of homicide, such as organised crime, drives the male victimisation rate upwards (UNODC, 2014). It is possible that the higher rates of organised crime and political violence in the Republic of Ireland and Northern Ireland contribute to a lower percentage of female victims.

Female offenders in the Republic of Ireland have tended to be older than their male counterparts, with numbers peaking in the 31–40 age range. The ages of female victims are more evenly distributed across the various age ranges than any other group. The age profile of female victims in the Republic of Ireland appears broadly similar to that of other jurisdictions (UNODC, 2014). The differing age profiles of males and females may be explained by reference to the types of homicides that women tend to be involved in. Homicides involving women, either as a perpetrator or a victim, are more likely to be domestically situated and involve intimate partners (Brookman, 2005; Schwartz, 2010; UNODC, 2014). While the CSO and PSNI data do not provide motives for homicides, advocacy groups claim that 62 per cent of women killed in the Republic of Ireland between 1996 and 2013 died in their homes, with over half killed by a current or former partner, while approximately a third of homicides recorded in Northern Ireland in 2011/12 had a domestic motivation (Women's Aid, 2014; Women's Aid NI, 2014). An earlier Northern Ireland study suggested that men and women had an almost equal risk of experiencing non-political homicide, though it should be borne in mind that the study was confined to cases where the offender had been referred for psychiatric assessment (Lyons and Harbinson, 1986). Previous research on homicide in the Republic of Ireland between 1972 and 1996 found that when women did kill they were significantly more likely to kill an intimate partner than males were (Dooley, 1995, 2001). A study of middle- to high-income nations has conservatively estimated intimate partner homicides to account for one in seven incidents: 6.3 per cent of male homicides, rising to 38.6 per cent of female homicides – a pronounced difference between genders (Stockl et al., 2013). Canadian research has found that intimate partner homicide is significantly different to other types of homicide, with an increased likelihood of female victims, older offenders and evidence of planning or revenge (Juodis et al., 2014). Stamatel (2014) also noted that both victims and offenders in intimate partner homicide tended to be older. Domestic violence experienced by the female is a common precursor to intimate partner homicides, regardless of whether the offender in the homicide is male or female (Wykes, 1995; Walklate, 1995; Juodis et al., 2014).

Female perpetrators are known to feature as offenders in incidents of filicide more so than in other cases, though males are more likely to be the perpetrators in familicide cases, where the entire family is killed (Brookman, 2005; Alt and Wells, 2010; Schwartz, 2010; O'Hagan, 2014). Tallant (2011) outlines a number of Irish cases of filicide and familicide which have occurred in recent years; as in other jurisdictions, there have been incidents where children have been killed by their mothers as well as by male parents. Internationally, the killing of children by strangers is considered to be a rare event; the perpetrators of such crimes are usually close relatives, such as parents or step-parents (Brookman, 2005; Alt and Wells, 2010; ONS, 2014).

Various motivations have been proposed to explain why or how a parent could resort to killing their child, many of which can be linked to mental or emotional difficulties, or socio-economic strain. In the cases described by Tallant (2011) there are several incidents in which young single mothers who were dependent on social welfare and experiencing some level of social isolation took their own lives and that of their child. In further cases, perpetrated by both genders, it is believed that the motivation was a perceived fear of not being able to protect or support their families into the future. Wilczynski (1995:172–3) outlines circumstances common in filicide cases:

> [P]ut simply, misery, isolation and instability are strongly correlated with filicide. Numerous social stresses are a very prominent feature of filicidal parents' histories, such as financial or housing problems, youthful parenthood, marital conflict, lack of preparation for parenthood and children who are difficult to care for.

Alt and Wells (2010) describe offenders as frequently being young adults experiencing stresses related to finances and a lack of work, alcohol or drugs.

Filicide that occurs in the context of parental separation tends to be different to those driven by socio-economic strain (Tallant, 2011; O'Hagan, 2014). There are also some notable overlaps with trends in intimate partner homicide, with offenders in both scenarios tending to be older than the 'typical' homicide offender (O'Hagan, 2014; Juodis et al., 2014; Stamatel, 2014). Despite the incidents seeming to occur suddenly, O'Hagan (2014) suggests that such incidents are in fact premeditated and well planned around custodial arrangements, and often motivated by a desire to exact revenge upon the former partner (see also Juodis et al. [2014] on intimate partner homicides).

Organised crime

It has been suggested that the arrival of the drugs trade (particularly heroin) in the Republic of Ireland has had a greater impact than terrorism on the type of serious crime experienced in the country, with professional homicides (excluding paramilitary violence) and the use of firearms in revenge attacks or minor disputes rare phenomena before the late 1970s (Brewer et al., 1997; O'Mahony, 2008). Referring to Goldstein et al.'s (1992) study of homicide in New York, O'Mahony (2008) notes that a greater proportion of homicides are the result of systemic violence employed by organised crime groups to further their business objectives, rather than violence triggered by the psychosomatic effects of drug-taking or economic compulsion to support a habit. Organised crime homicides differ from other male-on-male homicides in that they are more likely to be planned, purposive events, with common motivations centring on the control of both people and illegal markets and the need to uphold respect for group leaders (Hopkins, Tilley and Gibson, 2013; UNODC, 2014; see also Hourigan, infra).

While neither the CSO nor PSNI label incidents as being linked to organised crime or otherwise, various books and newspaper articles have made reference to the numbers of homicides linked to organised crime or dissident activity in the Republic of Ireland in recent years. O'Mahony (2008) estimated that over 100 homicides were linked to gangland activity in the preceding decade. More recently, six murders were linked to organised crime or dissident activity in 2011, increasing to 16 in 2012, and reducing to nine the following year (Brady, 2012, 2013, 2014). These figures indicate that organised crime groups have been linked to approximately 19 per cent of homicides in the three-year period. In contrast, 1 per cent of homicides in Europe as a whole and 30 per cent in the Americas are linked to organised crime (UNODC, 2014). Brookman (2005) estimated that gang-related homicides involving firearms and relating to the drugs trade have accounted for approximately 1 percent of murders in England and Wales, while just 2.4 per cent of homicides recorded in 2005/06 were linked to organised crime (Hopkins et al., 2013). The rates observed in the Republic of Ireland are more similar to those of Italy, where between 10 and 15 per cent of homicides have been linked to Mafia activity (UNODC, 2014).

Organised crime appears to be linked to the development of a 'gun culture' in the Republic of Ireland that exceeds the direct activities of organised crime groups, through the importation of firearms alongside drug consignments and in providing access to firearms to group members and associates (O'Mahony, 2008). In 2006, for example, there were at least three homicides committed with firearms which, while not directly linked to organised crime, could be traced back to people connected with such groups (O'Mahony, 2008). A similar situation was observed in Northern Ireland during the Conflict; while firearms were predominantly used in homicides related to the security situation, the increased availability of such weapons led to them also being used in incidents that were not politically motivated (McWilliams, 1997; Lyons and Harbinson, 1986).

The recent fluctuations in organised-crime-related homicides bear similarities to variations in the number of homicides involving firearms. The significant increase in organised-crime-related homicides in 2012 was accompanied by the number of homicides committed using firearms increasing from 14 in 2011 to 21 in 2012 (CSO, 2014e). The decrease in firearm-perpetrated homicides in 2013 was similar to the decrease in the number of organised-crime-linked murders. Firearms are a relatively common feature of homicides in the Republic of Ireland, despite a restrictive gun ownership policy. A steady increase has been recorded in the percentage of homicides involving firearms since the 1970s, rising from 18.9 per cent between 1972 and 1991 to 27.2 per cent between 1992 and 1996, and further increasing to 33.4 per cent between 2003 and 2013 (Dooley, 1995, 2001; CSO, 2014e). An increase in injuries relating to handgun shootings has also been reported in Dublin hospitals (Murphy et al., 2014). While the PSNI data did not provide information on the use of firearms, the prevalence of firearms in homicides related to conflict since 2002 is evident (Melaugh, 2015). The pervasiveness of such weapons is much lower in England and Wales, featuring in approximately 6 per cent of homicides per year (Brookman, 2005; ONS, 2014). Across Europe, firearms are used in 13 per cent of homicides (UNODC, 2014). O'Mahony (2008: 62) notes that it is an 'unwelcome distinction' that the Republic of Ireland is more akin to the US than the UK in terms of firearm-related homicides. Approximately 69 per cent of murders recorded in 2012 in the US involved firearms (Federal Bureau of Investigation, 2012), perhaps unsurprising given that firearms are widely legal to own. Krug, Powell and Dahlberg's (1998) study found that the US recorded significantly higher rates of firearm homicides than economically similar countries in Europe, Asia and Oceania. Within the US, research has found higher levels of firearm ownership to be correlated with higher levels of firearm homicide in particular areas (Blumstein and Rosenfeld, 2008).

In discussing the place of violence within organised crime groups, Dorn, Levi and King (2005) describe it as both necessary and dangerous. The preservation of masculinity and honour is as important to the group as it is to the individual; a successful organised crime group must be able to maintain its reputation and command respect in the face of competition from other groups. While a capacity for violence is important, actually resorting to violence can be regarded as problematic for group leaders, in that it attracts unwanted attention from the police and could deter potential business partners and customers (Dorn et al., 2005). Organised crime groups in the Republic of Ireland are not afraid of resorting to violence and intimidation, which has at times escalated into series of tit-for-tat killings between rival groups (O'Mahony, 2008: 61). Among the more infamous feuds are the Crumlin/Drimnagh feud, linked to up to 24 deaths, most of which occurred between 2001 and 2009 (Sunday Independent, 2013), and the Limerick feuds (McCullagh, 2011). O'Mahony suggests that members of organised groups may enjoy the notoriety garnered from the media attention associated with their crimes and feel a need to live up to their reputations. This appears inconsistent with research in the UK, in which external attention is regarded as being bad for business (Dorn, Oette and White, 1998; Hopkins et al., 2013).

A perhaps unique aspect to the landscape of organised crime in both Northern Ireland and the Republic is the friction between criminal groups and paramilitary organisations. The role of paramilitary groups in providing an alternate system of criminal justice in Northern Ireland was established during the Conflict, with such groups targeting perpetrators of a range of crimes, from petty to more serious offences, with punishments ranging from warnings to beatings and death (Knox, 2000; Conway, 1997). Both Republican and Loyalist paramilitary groups have been linked to the murders – often involving firearms – of drug dealers in Belfast since 1994 (Brewer et al., 1997; Melaugh, 2015). Informal criminal justice systems flourished for several reasons, relating to the lack of legitimacy of and distrust towards the RUC in Republican areas; fears concerning rising levels of minor crime; and the perception that the formal justice system was too slow and too soft on crime (Knox, 2000). The relationship between paramilitary and organised crime groups also exists in the Republic of Ireland, though it is somewhat convoluted. Paramilitary groups have been linked to campaigns targeting local drug dealers, but there have also been allegations made that such groups are participating in organised criminality by taxing dealers or by arranging safe passage for products (Brewer et al., 1997). There have been several alleged revenge homicides both within paramilitary groups and involving organised crime groups based in the Republic of Ireland since 2012 (Williams, 2012; O'Keeffe, 2012; Melaugh, 2015).

While there is a lack of detailed research, it is possible that the comparatively high level of organised crime homicide in the Republic of Ireland results from a combination of factors, including a relatively small and thus highly competitive potential market, the cycle of revenge attacks in various feuds and an apparently ready supply of firearms coupled perhaps with an increasingly pervasive gun culture in some sections of the population. While paramilitary and organised crime groups have been shown to clash, there is the possibility that the legacy of socio-political violence has contributed to an environment in which organised crime can flourish.

Conclusion

In many regards the Republic of Ireland and Northern Ireland reflect the trends and characteristics that define homicide in other Western or developed countries, particularly in relation to interpersonal violence. Despite the data limitations there are indications of similar experiences of intimate partner or family homicide, and male-on-male confrontational violence. The over-representation of males, particularly those who are young, is as much a feature of Irish homicide as it is globally. However, as O'Donnell (2005) noted, there are events and circumstances specific to each country which have the potential to uniquely shape that nation's trends in violent crime. While theories relating to both the situational factors and the effects of social inequality appear to be beneficial in developing our understanding of Irish homicide, further research is required to explore the extent to which local factors – such as the economic boom and bust associated with the Celtic Tiger, the history of political violence and the rise of organised crime – are contributing to a specifically Irish picture of homicide.

References

Aebi, M. F. and Linde, A. (2014) 'The persistence of lifestyles: Rates and correlates of homicide in Western Europe from 1960 to 2010', European Journal of Criminology, 552–577.

Alt, B. L. and Wells, S. K. (2010) When Caregivers Kill: Understanding Child Murder by Parents and Other Guardians. Plymouth: Rowman & Littlefield Publishers.

Appleby, L., Kapur, N., Shaw, J., et al. (2011) The National Confidential Inquiry into Suicide and Homicide by People with Mental Illness: Suicide and Homicide in Northern Ireland. Manchester: The University of Manchester.

Blumstein, A. and Rosenfeld, R. (2008) 'Factors contributing to US crime trends', *Understanding Crime Trends: Workshop Report* (pp. 13–43). Washington, DC: National Academies Press.

Bourgois, P. (1996) 'In search of masculinity: Violence, respect and sexuality among Puerto Rican crack dealers in East Harlem', *British Journal of Criminology*, 36(3): 412–427.

Brady, T. (2012) 'Firearm killings soar as gangland murders treble in just 12 months'. *Irish Independent*, 28 December. Available from: http://www.independent.ie/irish-news/firearm-killings-soar-as-gang-land-murders-treble-in-just-12-months-28951917.html (accessed 29 June 2014).

—— (2013) 'Gangland killings down but murder toll still high at 51'. *Irish Independent*, 30 December. Available from: http://www.independent.ie/irish-news/gangland-killings-down-but-murder-toll-still-high-at-51-29874083.html (accessed 29 June 2014).

—— (2014) 'Murder rate rises 66pc in 2014 as 20 killed'. *Irish Independent*, 5 May. Available from: http://www.independent.ie/irish-news/murder-rate-rises-66pc-in-2014-as-20-killed-30244139.html (accessed 29 June 2014).

Brewer, J. D., Lockhart, B. and Rodgers, P. (1997) *Crime in Ireland 1945–95: Here Be Dragons*. Oxford: Oxford University Press.

Brookman, F. (2005) *Understanding Homicide*. London: Sage Publications.

Bye, E. K. (2008) 'Alcohol and homicide in Eastern Europe: A time analysis of six countries', *Homicide Studies*, 7–27.

Central Statistics Office (CSO) (2006) *Standard Report on Methods and Quality (v1) for Garda Recorded Crime Statistics*. Cork: Central Statistics Office.

—— (2012) *Population Classified by Area*. Dublin: Stationery Office.

—— (2014a) *CJA01: Recorded Crime Offences by Type of Offence and Year*. Available at: http://www.cso.ie/px/pxeirestat/Statire/SelectVarVal/Define.asp?maintable=CJA01&PLanguage=0 (accessed 29 June 2014).

—— (2014b) *CJQ03: Recorded Crime Offences by Garda Division, Type of Offence and Quarter*. Available at: http://www.cso.ie/px/pxeirestat/Statire/SelectVarVal/Define.asp?maintable=CJQ03&PLanguage=0 (accessed 29 June 2014).

—— (2014c) *Group 011 Offences by Gender of Offender, 2003–2013*. Personal Communication, 26 June 2014.

—— (2014d) *Group 011 Offences by Gender of Victim, 2003–2013*. Personal Communication, 26 June 2014.

—— (2014e) *Firearm Involved Group 01 and 03 2003–2013*. Personal Communication, 22 May 2014.

Clarke, S. (2013) *Trends in Crime and Criminal Justice, 2010*. Luxembourg: Eurostat.

Cohen, L. E. and Felson, M. (1979) 'Social change and crime rate trends: A routine activity approach', *American Sociological Review*, 44(4): 558–608.

Collings, J. R. (1958) 'Book review: Patterns in criminal homicide by Marvin E. Wolfgang', *California Law Review*: 862–865.

Conway, P. (1997) 'A response to paramilitary policing in Northern Ireland', *Critical Criminology*, 8(1): 109–121.

Copes, H., Hochstetler, A. and Forsyth, C. J. (2013) 'Peaceful warriors: Codes for violence among adult male bar fighters', *Criminology*: 761–794.

Dooley, E. (1995) *Homicide in Ireland 1972–1991*. Dublin: Stationery Office.

—— (2001) *Homicide in Ireland 1992–1996*. Dublin: Stationery Office.

Dorn, N., Levi, M. and King, L. (2005) *Literature Review of Upper Level Drug Trafficking*. UK: Home Office.

Dorn, N., Oette, L. and White, S. (1998) 'Drug importation and the bifurcation of risk', *British Journal of Criminology*, 38: 537–560.

Eisner, M. (2003) 'Long-term historical trends in violent crime', *Crime and Justice*: 83–142.

—— (2008) 'Modernity strikes back? A historical perspective on the latest increase in interpersonal violence', *International Journal of Conflict and Violence*: 289–316.

Fay, M. T., Morrissey, M. and Smyth, M. (1999) *Northern Ireland's Troubles: The Human Costs*. London: Pluto Press.

Federal Bureau of Investigation (2012) *Crime in the United States 2012*. Available at: http://www.fbi.gov/about-us/cjis/ucr/crime-in-the-u.s/2012/crime-in-the-u.s.-2012 (accessed 28 June 2014).

Ganpat, S. M., van der Leun, J. and Nieuwbeerta, P. (2013) 'The influence of event characteristics and actors' behaviour on the outcome of violent events: Comparing lethal with non-lethal events', *British Journal of Criminology*: 685–704.

Gilligan, J. (2001) *Preventing Violence*. London: Thames and Hudson.

Goldstein, P.J., Brownstein, H.H. and Ryan, P.J. (1992) 'Drug related homicide in New York: 1984 and 1988', *Crime and Delinquency*, 38(4): 459–476.

Haase, T. and Pratschke, J. (2012) *The Pobal HP Deprivation Index*. Retrieved from Pobal: https://www.pobal.ie/Pages/New-Measures.aspx (accessed 29 June 2014).

Hopkins, M., Tilley, N. and Gibson, K. (2013) 'Homicide and organized crime in England', *Homicide Studies*: 291–313.

Hourigan, N. (2011) 'Organised crime and community violence: Understanding Limerick's "regime of fear"' in N. Hourigan, *Understanding Limerick: Social Exclusion and Change* (pp. 74–102). Cork: Cork University Press.

Inquest (2014a) 'Deaths in police custody'. Available at: http://www.inquest.org.uk/statistics/deaths-in-police-custody (accessed 28 June 2014).

—— (2014b) 'Unlawful killing verdicts and prosecutions'. Available at: http://www.inquest.org.uk/statistics/unlawful-killing-verdicts-and-prosecutions (accessed 28 June 2014).

Jones, D. W. (2008) *Understanding Criminal Behaviour: Psychosocial Approaches to Criminology*. Cullompton, Devon: Willan Publishing.

Juodis, M., Starzomski, A., Porter, S. and Woodworth, M. (2014) 'A comparison of domestic and non-domestic homicides: Further evidence for distinct dynamics and heterogeneity of domestic homicide perpetrators', *Journal of Family Violence*: 299–313.

Kilcommins, S., O'Donnell, I., O'Sullivan, E. and Vaughan, B. (2004) *Crime, Punishment and the Search for Order in Ireland*. Dublin: Institute of Public Administration.

Kivivuori, J., Suonpää, K. and Lehti, M. (2014) 'Patterns and theories of European homicide research', *European Journal of Criminology*: 530–551.

Knox, C. (2000) 'The "deserving" victims of political violence: "Punishment" attacks in Northern Ireland', *Criminology and Criminal Justice*, 1(2): 181–199.

Krug, E., Powell, K. and Dahlberg, L. (1998) 'Firearm-related death in the United States and 35 other high- and upper-middle-income countries', *International Journal of Epidemiology*, 27: 214–221.

Levi, M., Maguire, F. and Brookman, F. (2007) 'Violent crime' in M. Maguire, R. Morgan and R. Reiner, *The Oxford Handbook of Criminology*, 4th ed. (pp. 687–732). Oxford: Oxford University Press.

Luckenbill, D. F. (1977) 'Criminal homicide as a situated transaction', *Society for the Study of Social Problems*, 25(2): 176–186.

Lyons, H. and Harbinson, H. (1986) 'A comparison of political and non-political murderers in Northern Ireland, 1974–1984', *Medicine, Science and the Law*, 26(3): 193–198.

McCall, P. L. and Brauer, J. R. (2014) 'Social welfare support and homicide: Longitudinal analyses of European countries from 1994 to 2010', *Social Science Research*: 90–107.

McCullagh, C. (2011) 'Getting a fix on crime in Limerick' in N. Hourigan, *Understanding Limerick: Social Exclusion and Change* (pp. 23–37). Cork: Cork University Press.

McWilliams, M. (1997) 'Violence against women and political conflict: The Northern Ireland experience', *Critical Criminology*, 8(1): 78–92.

Mears, D. P., Stewart, E. A., Siennick, S. E. and Simons, R. L. (2013) 'The code of the street and inmate violence: Investigating the salience of imported belief systems', *Criminology*: 695–728.

Melaugh, M. (2015, 7 January) 'Violence – Draft list of deaths related to the Conflict from 2002'. Available at: http://cain.ulst.ac.uk/issues/violence/deathsfrom2002draft.htm (accessed 26 January 2015).

Merton, R. K. (1938) 'Social structure and anomie', *American Sociological Review*, 3(5): 672–682.

Messner, S. F. and Rosenfeld, R. (1997) 'Political restraint of the market and levels of criminal homicide: A cross-national application of institutional anomie theory', *Social Forces*: 1393–1416.

Miles, C. (2012) 'Intoxication and homicide: A context-specific approach', *British Journal of Criminology*: 870–888.

Muftic, L. R. and Hunt, D. E. (2013) 'Victim precipitation: Further understanding the linkage between victimization and offending in homicide', *Homicide Studies*: 239–254.

Mulcahy, A. (2006) *Policing Northern Ireland: Conflict, Legitimacy and Reform*. Cullompton: Willan Publishing.

Murphy, I., Lavelle, L., Ní Mhurchú, E., McCarthy, R. and Heffernan, E. (2014) 'Imaging of gunshot injuries in a west Dublin teaching hospital: A ten year review', *Irish Medical Journal*: 244–245.

National Advisory Committee on Drugs (NACD) (2012) *Drug Use in Ireland and Northern Ireland: Alcohol Consumption and Alcohol-Related Harm in Ireland 2010/2011 Drug Prevalence Survey*. National Advisory Committee on Drugs.

Nieuwbeerta, P., McCall, P. L., Elffers, H. and Wittebrood, K. (2008) 'Neighborhood characteristics and individual homicide risks: Effects of social cohesion, confidence in the police, and socioeconomic disadvantage', *Homicide Studies*: 90–116.

Nivette, A. E. and Eisner, M. (2013) 'Do legitimate polities have fewer homicides? A cross-national analysis', *Homicide Studies*: 3–26.

Northern Ireland Statistics and Research Agency (NISRA) (2010) 'Northern Ireland multiple deprivation measure 2010'. Available at: http://www.nisra.gov.uk/deprivation/archive/Updateof2005Measures/NIMDM_2010_Report.pdf (accessed 25 January 2015).

O'Donnell, I. (2002) 'Unlawful killing past and present', *Irish Jurist*: 56–90.

—— (2005) 'Lethal violence in Ireland, 1841 to 2003: Famine, celibacy and parental pacification', *British Journal of Criminology*: 671–695.

O'Donnell, I., O'Sullivan, E. and Healy, D. (2005) *Crime and Punishment in Ireland 1922 to 2003: A Statistical Sourcebook*. Dublin: Institute of Public Administration.

Office of National Statistics (ONS) (2014) *Focus on Violent Crime and Sexual Offences 2012/13*. London: Office of National Statistics.

O'Hagan, K. (2014) *Filicide-Suicide: The Killing of Children in the Context of Separation, Divorce and Custody Disputes*. Basingstoke: Palgrave Macmillan.

O'Keeffe, C. (2012) 'Dublin's gangland in state of violent flux'. *Irish Examiner*, 6 December: http://www.irishexaminer.com/ireland/dublins-gangland-in-state-of-violent-flux-216056.html (accessed 29 June 2014).

O'Mahony, P. (2008) *The Irish War on Drugs: The Seductive Folly of Prohibition*. Manchester: Manchester University Press.

Police Service of Northern Ireland (PSNI) (2012) 'Deaths due to the security situation in Northern Ireland 1969–29 February 2012'. Available at: http://www.psni.police.uk/deaths_cy.pdf (accessed 26 June 2014).

—— (2013) 'Trends in police recorded crime in Northern Ireland 1998/99 to 2011/12'. Available at: http://www.psni.police.uk/police_recorded_crime_in_northern_ireland_1998-99_to_2012-13.xls (accessed 14 June 2014).

—— (2014a) *Police Recorded Security Situation Statistics Annual Report Covering the Period 1st April 2013–31st March 2014*. Belfast: Police Service of Northern Ireland.

—— (2014b) 'Number of crimes recorded in Northern Ireland for financial years 2003–04 to 2013–14 for the offences of homicide, attempted murder and threats to kill/conspiracy to murder by policing district'. Personal Communication, 8 July 2014.

—— (2014c) 'Number of crimes recorded in Northern Ireland for financial years 2003–04 to 2013–14 for the offences of homicide, attempted murder and threats to kill/conspiracy to murder by victim's gender'. Personal Communication, 8 July 2014.

—— (2014d) 'Number of crimes recorded in Northern Ireland for financial years 2003–04 to 2013–14 for the offences of homicide, attempted murder and threats to kill/conspiracy to murder by victim's age'. Personal Communication, 8 July 2014.

Polk, K. (1994) 'Masculinity, honour and confrontational homicide' in T. Newburn and E. A. Stanko, *Just Boys Doing Business? Men, Masculinities and Crime* (pp. 166–188). London: Routledge.

Rosenfeld, R., Messner, S. F. and Baumer, E. P. (2001) 'Social capital and homicide', *Social Forces*: 283–309.

Schwartz, J. (2010) 'Murder in a comparative context' in C. Ferguson, *Violent Crime: Clinical and Social Implications* (pp. 276–297). London: Sage Publications.

Stamatel, J. P. (2014) 'Explaining variations in female homicide victimization rates across Europe', *European Journal of Criminology*: 578–598.

Stockl, H., Devries, K., Rotstein, N., Campbell, J., Watts, C. and Garcia Moreno, C. (2013) 'The global prevalence of intimate partner homicide: A systematic review', *The Lancet*, 382: 859–865.

Sunday Independent (2013) 'Gangland executioners continue to escape justice', *Irish Independent*, 11 August. Available from: http://www.independent.ie/irish-news/gangland-executioners-continue-to-escape-justice-29489375.html (accessed 29 June 2014).

Tallant, N. (2011) *Flesh and Blood: Familicides and Murder Suicides That Haunt Ireland*. Dublin: Hachette Books Ireland.

United Nations Office on Drugs and Crime (UNODC) (2014) *Global Study on Homicide 2013*. Vienna: United Nations.

van Dijk, J. (2007) 'Mafia markers: Assessing organised crime and its impact upon societies', *Trends in Organized Crime*, (10): 39–56.

Walklate, S. (1995) *Gender and Crime: An Introduction*. Hemel Hempstead: Prentice Hall/Harvester Wheatsheaf.

Wilczynski, A. (1995) 'Child killing by parents: Social, legal and gender issues' in R. E. Dobash, R. P. Dobash and L. Noaks, *Gender and Crime* (pp. 167–180). Cardiff: University of Wales Press.

Williams, P. (2012) 'Paul Williams on the life and crimes of Godfather Eamon Kelly', *Irish Independent*, 5 December. Available from: http://www.independent.ie/irish-news/paul-williams-on-the-life-and-crimes-of-godfather-eamon-kelly-28943522.html (accessed 29 June 2014).

Wolfgang, M. E. (1958) *Patterns in Criminal Homicide*. Philadelphia: University of Pennsylvania Press.

—— (1967) 'Victim-precipitated criminal homicide' in M. E. Wolfgang, *Studies in Homicide* (pp. 72–87). New York: Harper and Row.

Women's Aid. (2014) 'National and international statistics'. Available at: http://www.womensaid.ie/policy/natintstats.html#X-201209171232213 (accessed 27 June 2014).

Women's Aid Northern Ireland (2014) 'Domestic violence statistics'. Available at: http://www.womensaidni.org/domestic-violence/domestic-violence-statistics/ (accessed 27 June 2014).

World Health Organisation (2010) *European Report on Preventing Violence and Knife Crime Among Young People*. Copenhagen: World Health Organisation.

Wykes, M. (1995) 'Passion, marriage and murder: Analysing the press discourse' in R. E. Dobash, R. P. Dobash and L. Noaks, *Gender and Crime* (pp. 49–76). Cardiff: University of Wales Press.

Young, P., O'Donnell, I. and Clare, E. (2001) *Crime in Ireland*. Dublin: Stationery Office.

Notes

1 The views expressed in this chapter are those of the author alone, based on publicly available data.

2 Data regarding homicide and related offences in the Republic of Ireland comes from a variety of sources. Since 2006 the Central Statistics Office has been responsible for the publication of official Garda crime statistics, on a quarterly and annual basis (CSO 2006). Before 2006 crime statistics were reported in the Annual Reports of An Garda Síochána. To smooth out some of the annual fluctuations in homicide figures and thus reveal a more general trend, a five-year rolling average line has been added to Figure 2.1. Figure 2.1 was compiled using data from the CSO (2014a) and O'Donnell, O'Sullivan and Healy (2005).

3 Data regarding homicide and related offences in Northern Ireland comes from a variety of sources. Recent data for Northern Ireland is reported by the Statistics Branch of the PSNI, with earlier data dating from 1968 onwards collected from the Chief Constable's Annual Reports (PSNI 2013). To smooth out some of the annual fluctuations in homicide figures and thus reveal a more general trend, a five-year rolling average line has been added to Figure 2.2.

4 There are differing reports as to the number of victims of the Conflict, depending on the criteria applied for inclusion. The official figures (those currently reported by the PSNI) are quite narrowly defined and are limited to deaths occurring in Northern Ireland only. Other reports (such as Fay *et al.*, 1999) adopted wider criteria, including not only deaths outside Northern Ireland but also deaths resulting from road traffic and other accidents connected to the security forces.

5 Figure 2.3 has been generated from PSNI (2012, 2013) figures. PSNI figures are limited to those which occurred in Northern Ireland and which are directly related to the Conflict.

6 There was differing information available from the CSO and PSNI regarding the breakdown of homicide figures into various demographic subsections. While the CSO provides combined figures regarding gender and age, the PSNI data deals with these attributes separately for victims and does not provide information relating to offenders at all. The CSO data is also somewhat more detailed than the PSNI data in terms of the age ranges elaborated upon and on the geographic levels for which figures are available. Analysis is constrained by the limitations of both data sets, but more so for Northern Ireland.

3

Understanding domestic abuse and sexual violence

Prevalence, policy and practice

Stephanie Holt and John Devaney

Introduction

Whilst domestic abuse and sexual violence are not new phenomena, the past thirty years have seen increasing public awareness and a growing political consensus that something needs to be done, even if what should be done is less clear. Until relatively recently across the European Union, domestic violence was viewed as a private matter demanding minimal state intervention (European Union Agency for Fundamental Rights, 2014). It is only since the 1990s that domestic abuse and sexual violence have been understood as fundamental human rights concerns warranting legal and political responses. At both national and international levels, governments in most industrialised nations have developed and ratified a range of policy initiatives and strategies designed to reduce the incidence and prevalence of both domestic abuse and sexual violence (Council of Europe, 2011). This has also been the case in both jurisdictions on the island of Ireland.

It is now widely acknowledged that domestic abuse and sexual violence are common (European Union Agency for Fundamental Rights, 2014) and that they present significant social, health and legal issues to society as a whole (World Health Organisation, 2000; 2013). At a transnational level, the Europe Commission and the Council of Europe have devoted considerable time and money to discussing the issue of violence of a sexual nature and violence and abuse within intimate relationships and agreeing how these should be tackled. This has filtered down to national governments, with many countries having strategies designed to tackle domestic abuse and sexual violence at both a societal and individual level. These strategies typically consist of three complementary strands. Firstly, to introduce measures to prevent violence and abuse from occurring in the first instance or to limit its recurrence. Next, where domestic abuse or sexual violence does occur, to ensure that victims receive prompt and comprehensive support; and, finally, to ensure that those who perpetrate such violence and abuse are held to account for their behaviour.

It is now acknowledged that domestic and sexual violence cover abuse across genders, regardless of age, ethnicity or sexuality. It is also broadly accepted that men are more likely to be perpetrators of such abuse and violence and that women tend to suffer more severe abuse over a longer period of time (European Union Agency for Fundamental Rights, 2014).

In this chapter we set out the policy landscape regarding domestic abuse and sexual violence in both jurisdictions of the island of Ireland. We then discuss the competing theoretical paradigms that inform understandings of why such abuse and violence occur, before moving on to highlight some of the approaches to dealing with these issues. In doing so, we recognise that there is a balance to be sought between understanding the impact of such abuse and violence at an individual level and responding at both an individual and societal level to these issues.

Defining domestic abuse and sexual violence

Over time our understanding about the presentation, dynamics and impact of domestic abuse and sexual violence has developed, resulting in the need to define what is it that society needs to tackle. This however has not been a trouble-free endeavour, with definitions and understanding of both forms of violence varying across studies, regions and cultural settings (European Union Agency for Fundamental Rights, 2014). With regard to domestic abuse, terms such as 'inter-parental conflict', 'common couple violence', 'patriarchal terrorism' and 'intimate partner abuse' can be employed interchangeably across studies and regions, a risky endeavour which can result in assumptions being made that all terms mean the same thing. This requires some further discussion.

Accepting that 'inter-parental conflict' is normal and unavoidable in intimate relationships, Cummings and Davies (2002: 34) describe it as encompassing any 'disputes, disagreements or expressions of untoward emotions over everyday matters between parents'. They qualify this statement by observing that this normal, everyday acceptable behaviour does not involve any form of violence and that the process of observing constructive inter-parental conflict resolution may be of benefit to children (Cummings and Davies, 2002; Grych and Fincham, 2001). Broadening out this definition, Grych and Fincham (2001: 18) define inter-parental conflict as 'an enormously wide ranging construct encompassing events viewed as common everyday stressors to events viewed as significant life traumas', which can be understood as either an integral part of the couple's behaviour or alternatively as a high or low conflict state that can negatively affect children.

Feminist theories consider the issue of gender as critical to an understanding of domestic abuse, asserting that the intimate abuse of women arises in the context of their partners' need to control women as opposed necessarily to conflict or disagreement (Yllo, 1993). Both international conventions and domestic research and policy documents also consider the issue of gender worthy of significant attention and discussion. The United Nations Declaration on the Elimination of all forms of Violence against Women 1993 (CEDAW) (Article 1 of the Convention) considers 'gender-based violence, that is, violence that is directed against a woman because she is a woman or that affects women disproportionately. It includes acts that inflict physical, mental, or sexual harm or suffering, threats of such acts, coercion and other deprivations of liberty'.

This gendered perspective of domestic abuse which reflects an understanding of this phenomenon as the intimate context within which *women* are abused by *men*, underpins this chapter and may be legitimised based on empirical data concerning the nature and impact of this behaviour. Firstly, the numeric extent of women abuse exceeds that of the intimate abuse of men (Walby and Allen, 2004; Watson and Parsons, 2005; WHO 2013). Secondly, the impact of the abuse is likely to be greater for women than men, both emotionally and injuriously (European Union Agency for Fundamental Rights, 2014). Thirdly, women are at far greater risk of serious and lethal abuse at the hands of their male partner than men are at risk from their female partner (Watson and Parsons, 2005; WHO, 2013).

The National Office for the Prevention of Domestic, Sexual and Gender Based Violence in the Republic of Ireland (COSC) recognises that there are three different dimensions of abuse which characterise domestic abuse: physical, sexual and emotional abuse. The National Strategy on Domestic, Sexual and Gender Based Violence (Department of Justice, Equality and Law Reform, 2010: 2) further states that:

> Behaviours that commonly occur in situations of domestic violence include various forms of physical violence such as kicking, punching, slapping, smothering or choking, biting, throwing, and threatening with an object. The use of isolation can be a key device, for example where the abuser restricts communication between the victim-survivor and those who are close to the person. Domestic violence often includes the use and abuse of children, as well as economic abuse. Controlling and intimidating behaviour, including threats and blaming the victim, are common forms of emotional abuse. Older people can experience abuse by carers and those in a position of trust.

For the purpose of this chapter, the term 'domestic abuse' is employed and refers to the intimate context within which one partner is abused by another. A continuum of domestic abuse may be considered as a framework to support our understanding of the shifting sands of this complex and dynamic phenomenon. However, there is little agreement within the literature on the nature and form this continuum should take. For example, Jouriles et al. (2002) suggest that the continuum could reflect the increase in severity of abuse from calm rational disagreement at one end and frequent, heated and poorly resolved disputes at the more destructive end. Other authors are critical when the focus on severity highlights the physical aspect of violence as more harmful relative to non-violent abuse (Kelly, 1987). In the context of this chapter, a continuum of domestic abuse may be usefully employed to examine how violence and abuse are defined and conceptualised and explore how those definitions and understandings change over time and over place (Kelly, 1987).

Although, as outlined above, domestic abuse can include sexual violence, it is important to highlight that domestic and sexual violence, whilst sharing similarities, are not one and the same thing. Sexual violence refers to:

> Assaults that have an explicit sexual content and includes a variety of forms including rape, sexual assault and sexual harassment. These forms of sexual violence can be perpetrated by family members, current and former sexual partners, other relatives and friends, acquaintances (including colleagues and clients), those in a variety of authority positions, and strangers. The many possible combinations of location and relationships mean that sexual violence can be in private or public locations, and in terms of rape, for example, can include many forms – marital rape, familial/incestuous rape, acquaintance/date rape, stranger rape, gang rape, custodial rape, and rape as a war crime.
>
> *(Department of Justice, Equality and Law Reform, 2010: 2)*

Sexual violence in Northern Ireland has been defined as 'any behaviour perceived to be of a sexual nature which is unwanted or takes place without consent or understanding' (Department of Health, Social Services and Public Safety, 2008: 17). Drawing upon findings from the 2008/09 Northern Ireland Crime Survey (French and Freel, 2009), sexual violence has been conceptualised as stalking or sexual harassment (obscene or threatening messages; obscene, threatening, nuisance or silent phone calls; someone loitering outside home or workplace; or being followed around and watched); sexual victimisation (indecent exposure; sexual threats; being forced by someone to watch pornography; or unwanted sexual touching or groping); and serious sexual assault (forced or attempted sexual intercourse or other sexual activity).

Therefore, a critical distinction is that some forms of sexual violence may occur between strangers, or those sharing accommodation but not in a relationship with one another. It can also be perpetrated by an adult against a child, and frequently is.

The extent of domestic abuse and sexual violence

In recent years successive governments have sought to gather data on the prevalence and incidence of domestic abuse and sexual violence and the presentation of these phenomena – who is affected, in what ways and by whom. Without such information it is difficult for policy-makers to develop strategies to tackle such issues and to prioritise a budget to fund their plans.

Prevalence of domestic abuse

Reflecting the European Union and indeed international experience (European Union Agency for Fundamental Rights, 2014; WHO, 2013), the existence and extent of domestic abuse has been largely hidden within society, compounded by a dearth of systematic and nationally representative information on the prevalence and impact of domestic abuse amongst both men and women. Indeed, while much of the earlier research in the Republic of Ireland focused primarily on the experience of women (McWilliams and McKiernan, 1993; Kelleher and O'Connor, 1995), it is only in recent years that the voice and experience of men has been sought and represented (McKeown and Kidd, 2002; Paul, Smith and Long, 2006; Sweet, 2010).

While there is growing consensus on how to measure the extent of domestic and sexual violence, methodological issues have been shown to influence the depth and breadth of data forthcoming (WHO, 2013; Hussain *et al.*, 2015). In Northern Ireland the most comprehensive statistics on domestic abuse were published in the Northern Ireland Crime Survey (a continuous, representative personal interview survey of the experiences and perceptions of crime of 3,856 adults living in private households throughout Northern Ireland). In this survey females reported a higher victimisation rate than males (18 per cent compared with 10 per cent) (Carmichael, 2008). In Northern Ireland, three in ten victims believed that their worst incident had been seen and/or heard by their children. This survey also reported that 21 per cent of female victims had suffered threats and/or force from a partner while they were pregnant. Victims claimed that half (50 per cent) of the perpetrators were under the influence of alcohol and 9 per cent were under the influence of drugs at the time of their worst incident. Analysis of repeat victimisation in Northern Ireland revealed that 59 per cent of all victims experienced domestic abuse from the same perpetrator on more than one occasion, with 35 per cent victimised four times or more. Over three-fifths (64 per cent) of victims sustained injuries as a result of their 'worst' incident. The most frequently reported type of injury was 'mental or emotional problems' – reported by a third (34 per cent) of the victims recalling their worst incident (Carmichael, 2008). A comparable study involving 3,077 adults in the Republic of Ireland was conducted in 2003 and established that 15 per cent of female respondents and 6 per cent of male respondents experienced severe abusive behaviour of a physical, sexual or emotional nature from a partner at some point in their lives (Watson and Parsons, 2005). Eleven per cent of the Irish population had experienced a pattern of abusive behaviour with actual or potential severe impact (Watson and Parsons, 2005).

The evidence from international surveys suggests that only between 10 per cent and 15 per cent of women experiencing domestic abuse actually report it to the police, therefore recorded crime statistics represent the tip of the iceberg, and the scale of the problem is likely to be far greater (Watson and Parsons, 2005). The Northern Ireland survey reinforces this point, with victims reporting that the police only knew about 20 per cent of the worst incidents of domestic abuse, and in the Republic of Ireland survey only 29 per cent of women and 5 per cent of men reported incidents of domestic abuse to An Garda Síochána. In fact, fewer than 25 per cent of those severely abused reported to An Garda Síochána, and 33 per cent of those who had been severely abused have never told anybody. For those who did not report the abuse to the police, the most common reasons given (based on data gathered in England, as comparable data does not exist in either jurisdiction in the island of Ireland) are that the abuse was too trivial or not worth reporting (42 per cent), it was a private, family matter and not the business of the police (34 per cent) or the victim did not think the police could help (15 per cent) (Smith *et al.*, 2012). While these findings mirror those of the CSO Quarterly National Household Survey regarding the reasons given by victims of what we might call 'ordinary' crime, there have, however, also been criticisms of the way that the police have responded to the issue of domestic abuse, although it is recognised that significant improvements have been made over time (e.g. Criminal Justice Inspection Northern Ireland, 2013a).

A major limitation of the crime surveys that have been undertaken in Northern Ireland is the lack of information on children's victimisation. One useful additional source of information has been the prevalence survey of child maltreatment undertaken by the NSPCC across the United Kingdom in 2009 (Radford *et al.*, 2011). Respondents reported that 12 per cent of children under age 11, 18 per cent of 11–17-year-olds and 24 per cent of 18–24-year-olds had been exposed to domestic violence between adults in their homes during childhood. Three per cent of children under the age of 11 and 3 per cent of the 11–17-year-olds reported exposure to domestic violence in the year prior to the survey. Overall, 24 per cent of young adults reported witnessing at least one episode of violence between their parents, with 5 per cent of the children reporting that the violence was frequent and ongoing (Radford *et al.*, 2011). This equates to 19,000 children in Northern Ireland being exposed to frequent and ongoing domestic violence.

Risk of severe abuse for both men and women in the Republic of Ireland was found by Watson and Parson's (2005) crime survey to increase with the presence of children, with this enhanced threat significantly higher for women when compared with men. This, the authors suggest, may arise from the increased stress of parenthood, greater difficulty leaving a relationship or restricted options for moving on when children are involved. This report also notes that nearly three-quarters of women seeking refuge from domestic abuse are accompanied by children, and that the risk of severe abuse for women who have children increases by more than 50 per cent at the point of separation.

While it is not known exactly how many children in the Republic of Ireland live with domestic abuse, research conducted by Kelleher and O'Connor in 1999 on the enforcement of domestic violence legislation in the Republic of Ireland found that in 52.3 per cent of cases where An Garda Síochána were called out to domestic abuse situations, children had either directly witnessed the abusive incident or had been in the house at the time of the incident. The available international research evidence suggests that many abusive households contain children (Mullender *et al.*, 2002; Weinehall, 2005), with US research estimating that almost four-fifths (78 per cent) of abusive households include children (Buckner, Bearslee and Bassuk, 2004).

Two Irish studies have, to date, explored the impact of exposure to domestic abuse on children (Buckley, Whelan and Holt, 2006; Hogan and O'Reilly, 2007). These studies suggest that children who live in households where their mothers are abused by partners or ex-partners are significantly affected and experience 'considerable distress' (Mullender *et al.*, 2002). There is also clear empirical evidence that children are at risk of physical and sexual abuse by their mother's abuser (Weinehall, 2005). Growing up in an abusive home environment can critically jeopardise the developmental progress and personal ability of children (Holt, Buckley and Whelan, 2008), the cumulative effect of which may be carried into adulthood and can contribute significantly to the cycle of adversity and violence (Cunningham and Baker, 2004).

Prevalence of sexual violence

The findings in Northern Ireland are that a fifth (19.4 per cent) of people currently aged 16–64 years have experienced at least one type of sexual violence or abuse in their lifetimes. Women (25.6 per cent) are twice as likely as men (12.3 per cent) to have had such an experience. Of the three sexual violence and abuse offence groups, sexual victimisation (12.9 per cent) has the highest lifetime prevalence rate, ahead of stalking or sexual harassment (9.7 per cent) and serious sexual assault (3.9 per cent). Within these groups, the most prevalent offence types are: indecent exposure (7 per cent); obscene, threatening, nuisance or silent phone calls (5.9 per cent); and obscene or threatening messages (3.9 per cent). Serious sexual assault is more likely than sexual victimisation to be a repeat offence and to involve the same perpetrators. Two-fifths (40 per cent) of serious sexual assault victims have experienced this four or more times, compared with 24 per cent of those affected by sexual victimisation. For nine-tenths of victims of sexual victimisation (91 per cent) or serious sexual assault (90 per cent), the perpetrators were exclusively male. The survey found that three-fifths of sexual victimisation (63 per cent) or serious sexual assault (58 per cent) victims have told someone about the incidents. Victims of sexual victimisation are most likely to have told a family member other than their husband, wife or partner (48 per cent), a friend or neighbour (43 per cent) or the police (27 per cent). Four-fifths (80 per cent) of victims of serious sexual assault sustained physical injuries, emotional problems or other conditions, compared with 37 per cent of victims of sexual victimisation. Most victims of sexual victimisation or serious sexual assault had not knowingly been under the influence of alcohol or drugs. For both offence groups, four-fifths (81 per cent) of victims had not been drinking, and 95 per cent or more had not taken drugs. Almost half the victims of serious sexual assault (47 per cent) believed the perpetrators had taken alcohol, compared with 31 per cent of those sexually victimised. They were much less likely to believe the perpetrators had taken drugs (11 per cent and 8 per cent respectively) (French and Freel, 2009).

Prevalence data on sexual violence in the Republic of Ireland can be drawn primarily from three sources. The Sexual Abuse and Violence in Ireland (SAVI) report produced by McGee et al. (2002) is based on a population survey of 3,000 adults, providing information on the prevalence of sexual violence for men and women in the Republic of Ireland. It specifically highlighted that 42 per cent of women and 28 per cent of men reported some form of sexual abuse or assault in their lifetime, with nearly 30 per cent of women and 25 per cent of men reporting varying levels of sexual abuse in childhood. Furthermore, while 24 per cent of women reported sexual abuse by their partner or ex-partner, the comparable finding for men was just over 1 per cent. It specifically highlighted that 42 per cent of women and 28 per cent of men reported some form of sexual abuse or assault in their lifetime, with nearly 30 per cent of women and 25 per cent of men reporting varying levels of sexual abuse in childhood. Further data is available from the CSO on recorded crime statistics and data gathered within the Irish Courts System (Court Services Annual Report, 2013). In addition to the findings of the SAVI report as outlined earlier, 20 per cent of girls and 16 per cent of boys in the Republic experience contact sexual abuse in childhood, with 24 per cent of perpetrators of sexual violence against adult women partners or former partners. However, only 1 per cent of men and 8 per cent of women reported their experience of sexual violence to An Garda Síochána, and 47 per cent of those reporting sexual abuse in the SAVI report had never told anybody.

In a study by the NSPCC (Radford *et al.*, 2011) contact and non-contact sexual abuse by a parent or guardian towards a child or young person was relatively rarely reported; 1.5 per cent of females aged 18 to 24 years reported sexual abuse had happened during childhood. The relatively higher rate of reporting for the young adults (compared to the younger children) may reflect a greater ability to position and to disclose their childhood experiences as being 'sexual abuse'. It is also likely that more sexual abuse is experienced in the later teenage years (Radford *et al.*, 2011). During the financial year 2011/12, the Police Service of Northern Ireland recorded 22 assaults of a sexual nature on boys aged 13 to 15 years and 82 assaults on girls of a similar age. There were 152 rapes of girls under 16 years and 34 rapes of boys recorded during this same time period (Police Service of Northern Ireland, 2012).

In summary, both domestic abuse and sexual violence are common and affect both adults and children. The main difference is that some sexual offences are committed by individuals who are strangers to the victim, but overall this is a small proportion of the incidents that occur. The majority of both domestic abuse and sexual violence is perpetrated by individuals known to the victim and often by people with whom the victim has had a close family relationship.

Theoretical perspectives on domestic and sexual violence

Over recent decades there have been a range of theories advanced to help explain domestic abuse and sexual violence, with some of them having greater or lesser support and sometimes, but not always, sustained by empirical evidence. When violence between intimate partners emerged as a recognisable issue in the mid-1970s empirical knowledge was very limited. But over the past thirty years a growing body of research has demonstrated the existence of different types or patterns of domestic abuse and sexual violence, and we therefore need to develop our understanding of what causes and sustains these abusive behaviours in order to develop effective interventions (Emery, 2011). To date, research in the area of domestic abuse and sexual violence has focused on a number of explanations.

Sociological and political explanations of violence in general and domestic abuse and sexual violence in particular tend to focus largely on structural and cultural factors that affect the behaviours of groups and individuals (Alvarez and Bachman, 2014). It is argued that domestic abuse and sexual violence is common, that it is based in gender inequality and the oppression of women within society and that it affects women of all social standings, effectively cutting across stratifications of ethnicity and socioeconomic status (Laing, Humphreys and Kavanagh, 2013). From this perspective domestic abuse and sexual violence arises and is sustained by broader societal systems of male dominance, power and privilege rooted in a need, alongside societal endorsement, for men to control and dominate their families, their female partners and women at large. Behind the abusive acts lie men's need for power and control in their intimate relationships, that is, being in charge and getting their own way. These behaviours and beliefs are underpinned by a set of ideas about how the world should operate, creating high expectations for the behaviour of one's partner or even former partner (Laing *et al.*, 2013). There are, though, several criticisms of the feminist theorising linking patriarchy and violence against women (Hunnicutt, 2009). It is argued that it implies a 'false universalism' and that it simplifies power relations. Men are portrayed as a singular group, which does not help to explain why only a minority of men use violence against women in societies characterised as patriarchal. However, Hunnicutt (2009) goes on to argue that the concept of patriarchy is useful in keeping the gaze directed toward social contexts rather than towards individual men who are motivated to dominate.

Psychopathological explanations suggest that individuals who are aggressive have some sort of personality disorder or mental illness that might get in the way of normal self-consciousness about using violence (Dutton, 1999; Jasinski, 2000). Psychological theories usually focus on childhood adversity and/or other traumatic or experiential events that can shape individuals to become abusive in their close relationships. While context is important, it is factors at the level of the individual which are the most salient in explaining why some people behave in ways which are outside societal norms. For example, some good evidence suggests that violent behaviour in intimate relationships can be linked to a variety of mental health conditions, such as post-traumatic stress disorder (PTSD), personality disorders, alcohol problems, anxiety and depressive disorders and schizophrenia and other psychoses (Taft *et al.*, 2007; Bell and Orcutt, 2009; Fazel *et al.*, 2009). However, not all male perpetrators of domestic abuse or sexual violence will evidence personality psychopathology, and the majority of individuals with these psychological traits will not perpetrate abuse or violence towards others.

Other theorists believe that sexual offending behaviours develop in part because of conditioning or learning. In other words, just as it is believed that individuals 'learn' appropriate or socially acceptable means of sexual behaviour or sexual expression, behavioural theorists indicate that deviant sexual interests or behaviours can also be learned (Alvarez and Bachman, 2014). For example, a father who commits domestic violence in the home is modelling hostile and aggressive attitudes and behaviours toward women, and consequently children who are exposed to that kind of environment may learn to act in similar ways as part of their developmental experiences (Burton, Miller and Shill, 2002). A different type of behavioural theory involves conditioning, whereby over time an individual's sexual interests or arousal patterns become strengthened through certain types of experiences (such as being sexually abused as a child) or reinforcers (Alvarez and Bachman, 2014). When someone masturbates to fantasies that are deviant, for example, it tends to strengthen their interest or arousal to those unhealthy or inappropriate fantasies, which ultimately may lead to offending (Akins, 2004). Alternatively, others have put forward notions based on psychological theories of cognition premised on the concept of faulty thinking. Whilst there are a number of competing theorisations of cognitive distortions in relation to sexual offending, in essence they present a framework for an understanding of how those who perpetrate sexual offences are able to rationalise their behaviour in ways that overcome societies' norms. For example, Ó Ciardha and Ward (2013) in their summary and critique of research on cognitive distortions highlight five key schema that sexual abusers of children use: children are seen as sexual objects (children are capable of desiring and enjoying sex and have adult sexual motivations), the nature of harm (sexual molesting is not harmful or is beneficial), uncontrollability (offending behaviour is outside the offender's control), entitlement (the offender's needs or wants supersede those of others) and dangerous world (the world is a hostile and dangerous place where no one or only children can be trusted). In relation to rapists the schema centre on women as being unknowable (women are inherently different to men and should be treated with suspicion, or women are dangerous), women are sex objects (created to service the sexual needs of men), along with schema related to the male sex drive as uncontrollable, the entitlement of men and a dangerous world.

An extensive literature documents biological correlates of general aggression and violence (Alvarez and Bachman, 2014), but there has been less focus on biological correlates of domestic abuse or sexual violence. Pinto *et al.* (2010) have identified literature which looks at the underlying biological mechanisms that aid our understanding of the perpetration of domestic violence. Firstly, there is some evidence to indicate that traumatic head injury results in an increase in violence within intimate relationships. Secondly, research has sought to explore the role of neurochemicals, metabolic characteristics and endocrine factors in domestic abuse and sexual violence. There is substantial evidence that high testosterone levels are associated with a high probability of aggression, including domestic abuse and sexual violence. However, the association is complicated by the influence of a range of moderating and mediating variables, including substance use and sensation-seeking (Alvarez and Bachman, 2014).

Many of these theories are appealing in helping professionals to understand why some individuals act in abusive or violent ways towards others. However, each theory has its limitations, and it is believed that a number of factors interact in a manner that leads to offending. Researchers have proposed more comprehensive and integrated theories about what leads to the initiation and, in some cases, the continuation of abusive behaviour. For example, it is argued that sexual offending behaviours are the result of a combination of biological, developmental, cognitive, environmental and cultural influences, individual vulnerabilities and situational factors. It is suggested that negative developmental influences occurring early in life, such as maltreatment or exposure to violence in the home, have a significant impact on one's ability to form close, meaningful relationships. This has a further negative impact on problem-solving, emotional management, self-esteem, self-control and other important coping skills and qualities (Smallbone and McKillop, 2014).

Space does not allow a fuller discussion of the many theories informing our understanding of what causes and sustains domestic abuse and sexual violence. However, it is important to engage with these theoretical perspectives as they shape how we believe that we should respond in dealing with these complex issues.

Responding to domestic and sexual violence

The present policy response to domestic abuse and sexual violence in Northern Ireland can be traced back to 1975 to the United Kingdom Parliamentary Select Committee on Violence in Marriage (McWilliams and McKiernan, 1993). The Committee emerged in the wake of the very public lobbying by women's groups, and in particular Women's Aid, around the rights of women to be safe and to be protected by the state. In Northern Ireland, this resulted in the passing of the Domestic Proceedings (Northern Ireland) Order 1980 that provided the legal right for women to occupy the matrimonial home and provided wives with protection and exclusion orders against their husbands (and in 1984 the legislation was extended to cover co-habitees). These civil orders gave the police a clearly defined role in intervening and protecting individuals at risk of abuse and violence from their partners. The role of police officers was further enhanced by the power of arrest attached to all relevant orders made in the Magistrates Court, although the Family Law (Northern Ireland) Order 1992 was required to be passed to make the breach of protection or exclusion orders a criminal offence. The Select Committee on Violence in Marriage also highlighted that some women might not be able to stay in the family home, and that local authorities should provide accommodation as a temporary measure and afford victims of domestic abuse priority status for rehousing.

In 1992 a further Select Committee on Domestic Violence was established to explore what more should be done by public bodies in meeting the needs of victims of domestic abuse. In Northern Ireland, the Department of Health and Social Services commissioned a study to assess the help-seeking behaviours of women who had experienced domestic abuse and to appraise the responses of various agencies with whom they came into contact. Whilst the resulting report highlighted examples of good practice, it also highlighted a patchwork of services, operating independently and without due regard to the need for, or operation of, other services. This led to many women and children not having their need for safety or services adequately identified and met. As McWilliams and McKiernan (1993: vii) note, 'domestic violence is often minimised or missed altogether, or viewed with embarrassment as an invasion of privacy, or with alarm as an extension to an already heavy workload'. The report went on to highlight that help-seeking and help-giving were often shaped by traditional beliefs that valued the maintenance of the family and the subordination of women. The authors also recognised that 'The Troubles' were likely to overshadow domestic violence and the response to this serious issue.

The signing of the Good Friday Agreement in 1998 began the process of returning policy-making to the Northern Ireland Assembly. The newly formed political party, The Women's Coalition, along with activists in the voluntary and community sector, lobbied for the development of strategies to tackle both domestic abuse and sexual violence. In 2005 the first Northern Ireland strategy to specifically address domestic violence was published (Department of Health, Social Services and Public Safety, 2005) followed by the first strategy to address sexual violence (Department of Health, Social Services and Public Safety, 2008). Both strategies sought to achieve similar outcomes, namely a reduction in the prevalence and incidence of domestic abuse and sexual violence; better access to and availability of support for victims; and swifter and more comprehensive responses to those who perpetrate abuse or violence.

The delivery of both strategies was overseen by high-level committees comprising senior civil servants, senior managers from public agencies, such as the police, education and social services, and representatives from the voluntary and community sector involved in supporting victims. The two committees were accountable to an inter-Ministerial group of the lead Government Departments. However, in reality, the inter-Ministerial group has rarely met (The Detail, 2013).

Within a couple of years of the publication of the sexual violence strategy it was recognised that many of the issues facing victims of either domestic abuse or sexual violence were similar, that many victims of domestic abuse also experienced sexual violence, and that many of the services working with both victims and perpetrators were the same. Therefore, from 2012 the Action Plans for both strategies were merged and a single high-level committee was established to oversee the delivery of the objectives in the combined Action Plan. In 2014, the Department of Health, Social Services and Public Safety and the Department of Justice consulted on a new domestic abuse and sexual violence strategy for Northern Ireland (Department of Health, Social Services and Public Safety, 2013).

It is only in the past four decades that the enormity of the impact and consequences of domestic abuse has begun to be realised and translated into policy, law reform and service provision in the Republic of Ireland. This development and metamorphosis was initiated and remains firmly rooted in the Irish Women's Liberation Movement which started in the 1970s. It was against this backdrop of fervent activity, ideology and consciousness-raising that an awareness of the existence of violence against women emerged.

A number of studies published in the eighties and nineties were instrumental in influencing the development of domestic abuse services and raising awareness of the complexities of dealing with this problem. Kelleher and O'Connor's seminal research in 1999 highlighted for the first time the widespread incidence of violence against women and its prevalence in all social classes and regions. Following on from this, violence against women, in particular domestic abuse, emerged as a major issue in the consultation process on the Department of Health's Policy Document on Women's Health. The Government set up the Task Force on Violence Against Women in 1996 whose aim was to develop a co-ordinated response to violence against women, with a particular focus on domestic abuse. The report of the Task Force was published in 1997. Then regional committees were established in 1998 in order to monitor practices and policies relating to domestic abuse, and the National Helpline operated by Women's Aid was extended to 24 hours, seven days a week, providing a comprehensive service. Both the Report of the Kilkenny Incest Investigation 1993 and the West of Ireland Farmer case 1998 highlighted the problem of domestic abuse and the inter-relationship between it and child protection concerns. The Kilkenny Incest Investigation was the first major child abuse inquiry in the state and was the biggest catalyst for legal reform and policy development the state had ever seen (expanded on in the 'Key turning points' section). The West of Ireland Farmer case 1998 involved the conviction in 1996 of a father of six children on charges of physical and sexual assaults of his children. Four of the six children in this family were subjected to horrific abuse. The abuse began in 1976, when the three oldest children were aged seven, six and four, and continued until 1993. From 1979 social workers, the family GP and the Gardaí were aware of the physical abuse of children in this family, but there was no engagement between the family and social services between 1984 and 1993, when the full extent of the physical abuse was revealed by the children, three of whom were then adults.

In 1993 the Second Commission on the Status of Women highlighted the concern that women's health needs were not always met by the health services. In response, the Department of Health published a policy document on women's health arising from extensive consultation with women, leading to violence against women being raised as a serious health problem. Furthermore, the published strategy 'A Plan for Women's Health' 1997–1999 contains an action plan for the board in line with recommendations from the Task Force on Violence Against Women 1997. The increasing recognition of domestic abuse as a problem is reflected in the continuing development by the Eastern Health Board of policies, procedures and services in the field of women's health and domestic abuse.

The 1970s saw the opening of the first refuges and the enactment of the first piece of legislation to help abused women (Family Law (Maintenance of Spouses and Children) Act, 1976), with significant changes to the legislative remedies available emerging in the 1990s. The Domestic Violence Sexual Assault Investigation Unit (DVSAIU) was established in March 1993 for the Dublin Metropolitan Area, and in 1997 it was placed under the National Bureau of Criminal Investigation and given a countrywide brief. In 1994 the Garda Síochána introduced their Policy document on Domestic Violence Intervention. This was amended in 1997 and stipulates that the Gardaí shall arrest without warrant in cases of breach of a domestic violence order. In 1996 the Working Party on the Legal and Judicial Process for Victims of Sexual and Other Crimes of Violence Against Women and Children produced its report, recommending the training of Gardaí, the introduction of a Code of Behaviour and the establishment of special Sexual Assault Units, amongst others.

Despite these developments in the 1970s, 1980s and 1990s, responsibility for services in relation to violence against women was divided between a number of different Government Departments, with successive studies and reports referred to in this section underlining the importance of welding the separate response of the different public agencies into a coherent national strategy. In response to this identified need, Cosc, the National Office for the Prevention of Domestic, Sexual and Gender-based Violence, was established in June 2007 with the key responsibility to ensure the delivery of a well-co-ordinated 'whole of Government' response to domestic, sexual and gender-based violence. The office is situated within the Department of Justice and Equality but has been given a remit to address domestic, sexual and gender-based violence from a cross-government perspective, rather than solely from that of the justice sector. Cosc's role covers co-ordination across the justice, health, housing, education, family support and community sectors. This work includes close interaction with non-governmental organisations (NGOs) and the development of the first National Strategy on Domestic, Sexual and Gender-based Violence 2010–2014.

In the Republic of Ireland the last four decades have witnessed the emergence of child welfare as a key issue in Irish social policy, with significant developments in child protection procedures and guidelines reflecting a growing awareness of the problem of child abuse and the evolving construction of the child at risk (Buckley and O'Nolan, 2013). This has reflected an emerging social construction of child abuse as a significant social issue, with the definition of child abuse evolving from the narrow focus on physical abuse in the 1970s, to a recognition of the incidence and problem of sexual abuse of children in the 1980s. While 'interference with children' had been a topic of discussion as far back as the 1930s, when it was seen as an unpleasant example of depravity in the country, it was not until the 1980s that the Department of Health began to seriously address the issue of child sexual abuse (O'Sullivan, 2009).

In both jurisdictions, the overriding paradigm is that domestic abuse and sexual violence should be seem as criminal acts, and the primary response to perpetrators of these acts by the state should be criminal sanctions (McAlinden, 2012; Devaney, 2014). Whilst both domestic abuse and sexual violence can cause significant harm, there are problems with responding within a primarily criminal justice paradigm. Firstly, some victims state that they do not want the person who has victimised them to be prosecuted, for a variety of reasons, sometimes linked to the nature of the relationship between the victim and their abuser and sometimes linked to the operation of the criminal justice itself (Smith *et al.*, 2012). Secondly, some of the behaviours that are abusive, such as coercive control or grooming, are not easy to prosecute, due to the nature of evidence that can be presented and tested in court (McAlinden, 2012). Therefore there has been much debate about how criminal justice agencies can better collect and present evidence in court and the operation of the legal processes in court to ensure that victims are provided with the opportunity to meaningfully present their evidence and to be protected from overzealous cross examination (Rape Crisis Network Ireland, 2010). As noted by McAlinden (2012) the underpinning ideology is predicated on the risk, both past and future, that individuals who are abusive present. Whilst the risk that individuals present is an important consideration, the demonisation of individuals can have the unintended consequence of increasing risk, as those who present with abusive behaviour may be less likely to seek help.

Key turning points

Throughout the last thirty years public concern and political action have been driven by a number of high-profile events that have required policy-makers and politicians to take action, both within each jurisdiction and between the two jurisdictions.

For example, in the early 1980s allegations surfaced that a number of adolescent boys had been subjected to sexual abuse while residing in a state-run residential care home in Northern Ireland. The resultant inquiries led to a number of positive and very far-reaching recommendations about the running and oversight of children's homes, although to this day concerns still exist about the involvement of high-profile public figures and the collusion of government agencies in the abuse and subsequent cover up (Moore, 1996).

It is worth reminding ourselves why the example of sexual offending is emblematic of the need for political as well as professional action in respect of cross-border co-operation over issues of sexual offenders and child protection on the island of Ireland (Devaney and Reid, 2012). In 1994 the conviction of Brendan Smyth, a Catholic Priest who had ministered on both sides of the border, resulted in the fall of the Irish government and a crisis in the Catholic Church over the mishandling of complaints about Smyth stretching back over four decades. It later became apparent that the totally inappropriate and irresponsible response by the Church authorities to allegations and disclosures of child abuse manifest in the Smyth case was widespread, with the Catholic Church seeking to avoid bad publicity at all costs by dealing with these matters internally, rather than involving the police and social services (Ryan, 2009). The National Board for Safeguarding Children in the Catholic Church was established in 2006 by the Irish Bishops to provide advice on best practice in safeguarding children and to monitor the implementation of safeguarding policy in the Church across both jurisdictions on the island of Ireland. The National Board has set out the Church's clear expectations about the minimum standards to be applied in all the work of the Church (National Board for Safeguarding Children in the Catholic Church in Ireland, 2008) and has undertaken audits of safeguarding within each diocese in the Republic of Ireland.

A number of high-profile events south of the border raised public awareness of the issue of child sexual abuse and need for policies and procedures to respond to the issue. The Kilkenny Incest Investigation was the first major child abuse inquiry in the state and was the biggest catalyst for legal reform and policy development the state had ever seen. The event that brought the Kilkenny case into the public domain in 1993 was the trial and subsequent conviction of a father for incest against his daughter. The trial and subsequent inquiry highlighted a number of concerns regarding both policy development and legislative issues concerning the protection and welfare of children. More than 100 contacts had occurred between the family and Health and Social Services before the abuse ended – in fact in late 1982/early 1983, the victim had disclosed to a social worker her physical and sexual abuse at the hands of her father. Because she was over 16 at that time, and no longer a child in the eyes of the law, no legal action could be taken to remove her from her parents' care. (Incidentally, her mother was also the victim of domestic abuse.)

The biggest development arising from the Kilkenny case was the full implementation of the Child Care Act 1991 which raised the age of a child from 16 to 18 years of age, with 32 million euros pledged to resource services sufficiently in order to operate it.

Interventions

The development of strategies to tackle domestic abuse and sexual violence in both jurisdictions on the island of Ireland has led to improvements in the provision of services and interventions for both victims and perpetrators. Of interest to this chapter is the difference in the drivers of support services in the two jurisdictions, where victim support services in the Republic of Ireland tend to be delivered by NGOs, rather than state agencies (although they are usually at least partially state-funded (see http://www.csvc.ie/)), which contrasts with Northern Ireland.

Key initiatives in Northern Ireland on domestic abuse and sexual violence have been the introduction of Multi-Agency Risk Assessment Conferences (MARAC) from 2009 and the opening of the Rowan regional Sexual Assault Referral Centre (SARC) in 2013. The main aim of the MARAC is to reduce the risk of serious harm or homicide for victims assessed as being at high risk of domestic abuse through professionals sharing information and agreeing a safety plan for a victim (Robbins *et al.*, 2014). Since 2010 over 7,000 victims of domestic abuse have been considered at MARACs in Northern Ireland. The Rowan SARC provides support for those who have suffered sexual violence through the provision of a range of support and services 24 hours a day, 365 days a year to children, young people, women and men who have been sexually abused, assaulted or raped, whether this has happened in the past or more recently. Services include forensic medical examination, screening for sexually transmitted infections, support in making a report to the police and onward referral to specialist counselling and support services. Central to the success of these services are the Independent Advisory and Support Services for the victim, generally known as and referred to as an Independent Domestic Violence Advisor (IDVA) and Independent Sexual Violence Advisor (ISVA). These specialist roles are designed to ensure that victims have a primary point of contact in relation to the range of services with which they may be in contact. They typically work with individuals at greatest risk as part of the multidisciplinary network of agencies involved with victims.

Complementing the work undertaken with victims, the strategies in relation to domestic and sexual violence in Northern Ireland have also sought to provide a more comprehensive response to those who perpetrate abuse. The Criminal Justice Inspection Northern Ireland (CJINI), an independent statutory inspectorate with responsibility for inspecting all aspects of the criminal justice system in Northern Ireland apart from the judiciary, completed inspections in 2010 relating to domestic abuse (CJINI, 2010a) and sexual violence (CJINI, 2010b). Both reports highlighted various examples of good practice within and between criminal justice agencies and their partners in health, social services and the voluntary sector. However, both inspection reports also highlighted the need for improvements in the detection and prosecution of instances of violence and abuse and the ways in which victims are supported by criminal justice organisations. In 2013, the CJINI published follow-up reviews of their inspection recommendations in relation to domestic abuse (CJINI, 2013a) and sexual violence (CJINI, 2013b). The reports were quite critical, highlighting that progress against a number of the recommendations in the earlier reports was slow. The current retrenchment of publicly funded services will undoubtedly undermine the progress made in recent years.

The main agencies working with perpetrators of domestic abuse or sexual violence are the Irish Probation Service and the Probation Board for Northern Ireland (PBNI). The PBNI offers a range of programmes for adults and young people aimed at challenging and changing offender behaviour required to reduce the likelihood of re-offending. Participation in specific programmes can be voluntary or can be an additional requirement of a Court disposal such as a Probation Order, Community Service Order or Custody Probation Order. In relation to domestic abuse and sexual violence, the PBNI works in partnership with a number of statutory and voluntary organisations, such as the police, social services and Women's Aid in the delivery of some of its offending behaviour programmes. Specific programmes include the Building Better Relationships Programme, a 28-week-based group work programme for men mandated by court to attend.

The Irish Government currently spends approximately €650,000 per annum funding a number of organisations to provide domestic violence perpetrator programmes across the Republic of Ireland. A variety of mandated and non-mandated programmes are in existence, with the mandate for attendance coming from the courts, partners or spouses or social services. A total of 12 programmes delivered by three different bodies are currently operating in conjunction with linked contact services for the partners of the men. The main objectives of such programmes are to increase the participant's understanding of his offending behaviour by examining his attitudes and belief system, the effect his behaviour has on others and to provide the participant with information on how to change abusive behaviour by exploration of non-controlling and non-violent ways of relating to women. An important and core aspect of the programmes is a dedicated partner contact element. Dedicated partner contact workers are contracted by the programme management to work with any partner or ex-partner of the men who wish to be involved. This work informs the programme facilitators of the safety of partners of the men on the programmes and allows them to challenge any man whose behaviour outside the programme is not matching his statements in the programme. The partner contact worker also provides practical support and advice to women in violent/controlling relationships, such as support services that she may wish to access.

With regard to the development of interventions concerning sex offending, Wilson, McCann and Templeton (2013) chart the development of the multi-agency model for Sex Offender Risk Assessment and Management (SORAM) in the Republic of Ireland from its origins in co-working a small number of very high-risk cases in 2007/8 to the national roll-out of the programme in May 2013. Specifically highlighted by the authors and of interest to this chapter is the corresponding introduction of an all-island system of risk assessment, in addition to the establishment of a cross-jurisdictional 'All-Island and UK committee', considered to support best practice, training and research.

Internationally, such group-based programmes are the main form of intervention with perpetrators of domestic abuse, though the evidence base of effectiveness is rather limited. A recent survey of 54 programmes for working with perpetrators of domestic abuse in 19 countries across Europe has highlighted that there is a wide disparity in both the approaches to this work and the robustness of the evidence informing the programme design due to the poor quality of many studies (Hamilton, Koehler and Lösel 2012). A systematic review by Smedslund and colleagues (2011) found that, at best, group-based programmes work for some male perpetrators in some circumstances some of the time, but for whom, how and when was still very unclear. Gondolf (2012), a proponent of group-based programmes, has argued that programmes do work but that we need to better understand what components are likely to work for particular individuals and for certain groups of offenders. He subscribes to the view that perpetrators of domestic abuse are a heterogeneous group and, as such, individuals are likely to be differentially responsive to treatment as they have both differing patterns of behaviour and motivations for their behaviour (Emery, 2011).

One of the weaknesses of group-based programmes is that they were originally developed by and have evolved through an ideological perspective on the root causes of domestic abuse rather than an empirical model of intervention development. Unlike other approaches to behavioural change involving, for example, the cessation of smoking or substance use, interventions have been derived primarily from the accounts of those who are the victims of the behaviour, rather than those who engage in the problematic behaviour. Whilst victims have a role in informing our understanding of the manifestation of domestic abuse, to best understand the factors causing and sustaining abusive behaviour requires more detailed investigation with the perpetrators of these behaviours.

Secondly, Westmarland and Kelly (2013) convincingly argue that current measures of whether programmes have been successful (such as no subsequent police callouts or self-reported incidents of physical violence by either perpetrators or their current or former partners) are limited. Based on interviews with men on programmes, their partners/ex-partners, programme staff and funders and commissioners, they argue that a broader range of outcome measures could be considered. This includes changes in the nature of abusive and controlling behaviour (not just incidents of physical violence), improvements in communication between couples, improvements in parenting and reductions in harmful behaviours such as substance use.

Conclusion

Significant progress has been made over the last thirty years in raising awareness and understanding of domestic abuse and sexual violence in both jurisdictions on the island of Ireland. In more recent years both Governments have taken responsibility for developing cross-government multi-sector strategies designed to provide effective responses to these issues in the immediate and longer term. Whilst much has been achieved, the ongoing very high rates of victimisation highlight the importance for both Governments of keeping these issues at the forefront of their social responsibilities. Scholars and activists in both parts of the island have made a significant contribution to our understanding of these issues by illuminating the abuse and violence that takes place regularly within our communities and in simultaneously making these social issues political – that is, holding politicians and policy-makers to account for how these issues are public rather than private affairs that deserve public policy responses. While the volume of research on these issues has been relatively small there is no doubting the influence that much of this work has had, primarily because it has been conducted by researchers in collaboration with activists. At a time when the question is being asked of the relevance and impact of research, it is encouraging to see how studies have sought to address our need to know about and understand the complex phenomena of sexual violence and domestic abuse, and for this knowledge to inform the response of service providers and policy-makers.

Given the current period of financial austerity and the rolling back of public services it is very possible that the situation may deteriorate rather than improve over the next decade. The financial retrenchment has affected services provided by the voluntary and community sector hardest, but there is also plenty of evidence of statutory services struggling to cope with the volume and complexity of work related to both domestic abuse and sexual violence. However, in spite of this difficult context, many victims of abuse and violence continue to be supported, and initiatives developed and implemented over the last decade continue to be available. The history of domestic abuse and sexual violence has been one characterised by a struggle at an individual and societal level, and this struggle, which has resulted in so much progress, will not abate.

References

Akins, C.K. (2004) 'The Role of Pavlovian Conditioning in Sexual Behavior: A Comparative Analysis of Human and Nonhuman Animals', *International Journal of Comparative Psychology*, 17: 241–262.

Alvarez, A. and Bachman, R. (2014) *Violence: The enduring problem*, (Second edition). London: Sage Publications.

Bell, K.M. and Orcutt, H.K. (2009) 'Posttraumatic stress disorder and male-perpetrated intimate partner violence', *Journal of the American Medical Association*, 302: 562–564.

Buckley, H. and O'Nolan, C. (2013) *An examination of recommendations from inquiries into events in families and their interactions with state services and their impact on policy and practice*. Dublin: Department of Child & Youth Affairs and Irish Research Council.

Buckley, H., Whelan, S. and Holt, S. (2006) *Listen to Me! Children's Experiences of Domestic Violence*. Trinity College Dublin: Children's Research Centre.

Buckner, J.C., Bearslee, W.R. and Bassuk, E.L. (2004) 'Exposure to violence and low-income children's mental health: Direct, moderated, and mediated relations', *American Journal of Orthopsychiatry*, 74(4): 413–423.

Burton, D.L., Miller, D.L. and Shill, C.T. (2002) 'A social learning theory comparison of the sexual victimization of adolescent sexual offenders and nonsexual offending male delinquents', *Child Abuse and Neglect*, 26(9): 893–907.

Campbell, J.C. (2002) Health consequences of intimate partner violence, *The Lancet*, 359(9314):1331–1336.

Carmichael, M. (2008) *Experiences of domestic violence: Findings from the 2006/07 Northern Ireland crime survey*. Belfast: NISRA.

Council of Europe (2011) *Convention on preventing and combatting violence against women and domestic violence*. Strasbourg: Council of Europe.

Court Services Annual Report (2013) Dublin: Court Services.

Criminal Justice Inspection Northern Ireland (2010a) *Domestic violence and abuse – a thematic inspection of the handling of domestic violence and abuse by the criminal justice system in Northern Ireland*. Belfast: CJINI.

—— (2010b) *Sexual violence and abuse – a thematic inspection of the handling of domestic violence and abuse by the criminal justice system in Northern Ireland*. Belfast: CJINI.

—— (2013a) *Domestic violence and abuse – a follow up review*. Belfast: CJINI.

—— (2013b) *Domestic violence and abuse – a follow up review*. Belfast: CJINI.

Cummings, E. M. and Davies, P. T. (2002) 'Effects of Marital Conflict on Children: Recent Advances and Emerging Themes in Process-orientated Research', *Journal of Child Psychology and Psychiatry*, 43(1): 31–63.

Cunningham, A. and Baker, L. (2004) *What About Me! Seeking to Understand a Child's View of Violence in the Family*. London, Ontario: Centre for Children & Families in the Justice System.

Department of Health, Social Services and Public Safety (2005) *Tackling violence at home – A strategy for addressing domestic violence and abuse in Northern Ireland*. Belfast: DHSSPS.

—— (2008) *Tackling sexual violence and abuse – A strategy for addressing domestic violence and abuse in Northern Ireland*. Belfast: DHSSPS.

—— (2013) *Stopping domestic and sexual violence and abuse in Northern Ireland 2013–2020*. Belfast: DHSSPS.

Department of Justice, Equality and Law Reform (2010) *National Strategy on Domestic, Sexual and Gender-based Violence 2010–2014*. Dublin: Stationery Office.

Devaney, J. (2014) 'Male perpetrators of domestic violence: How should we hold them to account?', *The Political Quarterly*, 85(4): 480–486.

Devaney, J. and Reid, C. (2012) 'Two countries, one border: The challenges and opportunities for protecting children on an all-island basis – a critical turning point', in K. Burns and D. Lynch (eds) *Children's Rights and Child Protection: Critical Times, Critical Issues in Ireland*. Manchester: Manchester University Press.

Dutton, D. G. (1999) 'Traumatic origins of intimate rage', *Aggression & Violent Behaviour*, 4(4): 431–447.

Emery, C. (2011) 'Disorder or deviant order? Re-theorizing domestic violence in terms of order, power and legitimacy: A typology', *Aggression and Violent Behaviour*, 16: 525–540.

European Union Agency for Fundamental Rights (2014) *Violence Against Women: An EU-wide Survey*. Luxembourg: FRA.

Fazel, S., Gulati, G., Linsell, L., Geddes, J.R. and Grann, M. (2009) 'Schizophrenia and Violence: Systematic Review and Meta-Analysis', *PLOS Medicine* 6(8): e1000120.

French, B. and Freel, R. (2009) *Experience of Sexual Violence and Abuse: Findings from the 2008/09 Northern Ireland Crime Survey*. Belfast: NISRA.

Gondolf, E.W. (2012) *The Future of Batterer Programs: Reassessing Evidence Based Practice*. Boston: Northeastern University Press.

Grych, J. H. and Fincham, F. D. (eds) (2001) *Interparental Conflict and Child Development: Theory Research and Application*. Cambridge: Cambridge University Press.

Hamilton, L., Koehler, J.A. and Lösel, F.A. (2012) 'Domestic Violence Perpetrator Programs in Europe, Part I: A Survey of Current Practice', *International Journal of Offender Therapy and Comparative Criminology*, XX(X): 1–17.

Hogan, F. and O'Reilly, M. (2007) *Listening to Children: Children's Stories of Domestic Violence*. Dublin: Office of the Minister for Children.

Holt, S., Buckley, H. and Whelan, S. (2008) 'The impact of exposure to domestic violence on children and young people: A review of the literature', *Child Abuse & Neglect*: 32(8): 797–810.

Hunnicutt, G. (2009) 'Varieties of patriarchy and violence against women: Resurrecting "patriarchy" as a theoretical tool', *Violence Against Women*, 15(5): 553–573.

Hussain, N., Sprague, S., Madden, K., Hussain, F.N., Pindiprolu, B. and Bhandari, M. (2015) 'A comparison of the types of screening tool administration methods used for the detection of intimate partner violence: A systematic review and meta-analysis', *Trauma, Violence and Abuse*, 16(1): 60–69.

Jasinski, J. L. (2000) 'Theoretical explanations for violence against women', in C.M. Renzetti, J.L. Edleson and R. K. Bergen (eds) *Sourcebook on violence against women*. Thousand Oaks, CA: Sage Publications.

Johnson, M. (2000) 'Conflict and control: Gender symmetry and asymmetry in domestic violence'. Paper presented at the National Institute of Justice Gender Symmetry Workshop, Arlington, VA.

Jouriles, E.N., McDonald, R., Swank, P.R., Norwood, W.D. and Buzy, W.M. (2002) *Men's Domestic Violence and Other Forms of Deviant Behavior, Final Report*. Texas: University of Houston.

Kelleher, P. and O'Connor, M. (1995) *Making the Links: Towards an Integrated Strategy for the Elimination of Violence Against Women in Intimate Relationships with Men*. Dublin: Women's Aid.

—— (1999) *Safety & Sanctions: Domestic Violence and the Enforcement of Law in Ireland*. Dublin: Attic Press.

Kelly, L. (1987) 'The Continuum of Sexual Violence'. in J. Hanmer and M. Maynard *Women, Violence and Social Control*. London: MacMillan Press.

Laing, L., Humphreys, C. and Kavanagh, K. (2013) *Social Work and Domestic Violence: Developing Critical and Reflective Practice*. London: Sage Publications.

McAlinden, A.M. (2012) *'Grooming' and the Sexual Abuse of Children*, Oxford: OUP.

McGee, H.R., Garavan, R., de Barra, G.M., Byrne, J. and Conroy, R. (2002) *The SAVI Report: A National Study of Irish Experiences. Beliefs and Attitudes Concerning Sexual Violence*. Dublin: Liffey Press.

McGuinness, C. (1993) *Report of the Kilkenny Incest Investigation*. Dublin: Stationery Office.

McKeown, K. and Kidd, P. (2002) *Men and Domestic Violence: What Research Tells Us*. Dublin: Department of Health & Children.

McWilliams, M. and McKiernan, J. (1993) *Bringing it out in the open: Domestic violence in Northern Ireland.* Belfast: HMSO.

Moore, C. (1996) *The Kincora scandal: Political cover-up and intrigue in Northern Ireland.* Dublin: Marino Books.

Mullender, A., Hague, G., Iman, U., Kelly, L., Malos, E. and Regan, L. (2002) *Children's Perspectives on Domestic Violence.* London: Sage.

National Board for Safeguarding Children in the Catholic Church in Ireland (2008) *Standards and Guidance.* Dublin: NBSCCCI.

Ó Ciardha, C. and Ward, T. (2013) 'Theories of cognitive distortions in sexual offending: What the current research tells us', *Trauma, Violence and Abuse,* 14(1): 5–21.

O'Sullivan, E. (2009) 'Residential child welfare in Ireland, 1965–2008: An outline of policy, legislation and practice', in: *Commission to Inquire into Child Abuse, Report of the Commission to Inquire into Child Abuse (Volumes I–V).* Dublin: Government Publications.

Paul, G., Smith, S.M. and Long, J. (2006) 'Experience of intimate partner violence among women and men attending general practices in Dublin, Ireland: A cross-sectional survey', *European Journal of General Practice,* 12(2): 66–69.

Pinto, L.A., Sullivan, E.L., Rosenbaum, A., Wyngarden, N., Umhau, J.C., Miller, M.W. and Taft, C.T. (2010) 'Biological correlates of intimate partner violence perpetration', *Aggression and Violent Behaviour,* 15: 387–398.

Police Service of Northern Ireland (2012) *Domestic and Sexual Offences – Response to a Freedom of Information Request.* Belfast: PSNI. Available at: http://www.psni.police.uk/domestic_sexual_offences.pdf (accessed 28 October 2014).

Radford, L., Corral, S., Bradley, C., Fisher, H., Collishaw, S., Bassett, C. and Howat, N. (2011) *Child Abuse and Neglect in the UK Today.* London: NSPCC.

Rape Crisis Network Ireland (2010) 'Rape and Justice in Ireland Handbook'. Available at: http://www.rcni.ie/wp-content/uploads/RAJIHandbook.pdf (accessed 22 March 2015).

Robbins, R., McLaughlin, H., Banks, C., Bellamy, C. and Thackray, D. (2014) 'Domestic violence and multi-agency risk assessment conferences (MARACs): A scoping review', *The Journal of Adult Protection,* 16(6).

Ryan, S. (2009) *Commission to Inquire into Child Abuse Report (Volumes I–V).* Dublin: The Stationery Office.

Smallbone, S. and McKillop, N. (2014) 'Evidence informed approaches to preventing sexual violence', in P.D. Donnelly and C.L. Ward (eds) *Oxford Textbook of Violence Prevention: Epidemiology, Evidence and Policy.* Oxford: Oxford University Press.

Smedslund, G., Dalsbø, T., Steiro, A., Winsvold, A. and Clench-Aas, J. (2011) 'Cognitive behavioural therapy for men who physically abuse their female partner', *Cochrane Database of Systematic Reviews Issue 2.* Art. No.: CD006048.pub2.

Smith, K., Osborne, S., Lau, I. and Britton, A. (2012) *Homicides, Firearm Offences and Intimate Violence 2010/11: Supplementary Volume 2 to Crime in England and Wales 2010/11.* London: Home Office.

Sweet, D. (2010) 'Towards Gender Equality: Men's Advisory Project, Belfast.' Available at: http://www.mapni.co.uk/research/ (accessed 10 November 2014).

Taft, C.T., Kaloupek, D.G., Schumm, J.A., Marshall, A.D., Panuzio, J. and Keane, T.M. (2007) 'Posttraumatic stress disorder symptoms, physiological reactivity, alcohol problems, and aggression among military veterans', *Journal of Abnormal Psychology,* 116: 498–507.

The Detail (2013) 'Murder, rape, kidnap and assault: A year of domestic abuse in Northern Ireland'. Available at: http://www.thedetail.tv/issues/293/domestic-abuse-data/murder-rape-kidnap-and-assault-a-year-of-domestic-abuse-in-northern-ireland (accessed 29 October 2014).

Walby, S. and Allen, J. (2004) 'Domestic Violence, Sexual Assault & Stalking: Findings from the British Crime Survey', *Home Office Research Study 276.* London: Home Office

Watson, D. and Parsons, S. (2005) *Domestic Abuse of Women and Men in Ireland: Report on the National Study of Domestic Abuse.* Dublin: National Crime Council.

Weinehall, K. (2005) '"Take my father away from home": Children growing up in the proximity of violence', in M. Eriksson, M. Hester, S. Keskinen and K. Pringle *Tackling Men's Violence in Families: Nordic Issues and Dilemmas.* Bristol: Policy Press.

Westmarland, N. and Kelly, L. (2013) 'Why Extending Measurements of "Success" in Domestic Violence Perpetrator Programmes Matters for Social Work', *British Journal of Social Work,* 43(6): 1092–1110.

Wilson, M., McCann, J. and Templeton, R. (2013) 'SORAM: Towards a Multi-agency Model of Sex Offender Risk Assessment and Management', *Irish Probation Journal,* 10: 177–192.

World Health Organisation (WHO) (2000) *World Report on Violence and Health*. Geneva: WHO.
—— (2013) *Global and regional estimates of violence against women: Prevalence and health effects of intimate partner violence and non-partner sexual violence*. Geneva: WHO.
Yllo, K.A. (1993) 'Through a feminist lens: Gender, power and violence', in R.J. Gelles and D.R. Loseke (eds) *Current Controversies on Family Violence*. Newbury Park, CA: Sage Publications.

4

Plus ça change

White-collar and corporate crime in and after the crisis

Ciaran McCullagh

Introduction

The recent crisis of international and national capitalisms has reinvigorated the political and social debate around white-collar and corporate crime. But it has done little to resolve the issues that beset the study of such behaviour. These include the conceptual problems that surround the definition of corporate crime, the uneven nature of the translation of the notion of corporate social harm into legal frameworks and prohibitions and the apparent absence of systematic and effective responses to such crimes. The intention of this article is to examine these issues in the context of the Republic of Ireland and Northern Ireland.

However this process is surrounded by an overarching problem. Corporate crime is a topic that has produced more heat than light. There have been spirited, if irregular, public and media debates with repeated expressions of outrage at the behaviour of bankers (particularly in the Republic of Ireland in the wake of the collapse of its banking system) and at the failure to imprison anyone responsible. But this has had little impact on the production of criminological research that would illuminate the issues surrounding such crime. Research on crime, by its nature, is sporadic and unsystematic, and that on white-collar crime even more so. Hence this chapter will raise more questions than the existing research allows us to answer.

We begin with the question of what kinds of behaviour the terms white-collar and corporate crime embrace and what attempts to give these terms coherence imply for the study of such crime. First however we need to address an issue that will be recurrent in this chapter, that is, the question of white-collar and corporate crime in one of the jurisdictions under consideration here: Northern Ireland.

Corporate crime – Northern Ireland, an exceptional state – once again?

Northern Ireland presents a number of problems for students of white-collar and corporate crime. The main one is the apparent absence of such crime in the jurisdiction. As Graham Ellison (private communication) puts it, 'to have corporate crime you have to have a corporate sector' and the Northern Ireland economy simply does not have one. Though structural changes are underway, the economy still remains dependent on the lifeblood of a subsidy from the government of the United Kingdom, and so is heavily dependent on state services for its sustenance. The UK and international banks that were implicated in the recent crises of reckless lending and interest rate manipulation had branches in Northern Ireland. But they are being investigated in London, and this is where they may face prosecution. There is some evidence, though, of a new activism with the first successful prosecution for corporate manslaughter in Northern Ireland secured in May 2012 (McKeown, 2012: 10). It is probably the case that future editions of this book will have more material to deal with from this jurisdiction. However what is perhaps the most significant issue here is the national focus of the discussion. It is one that, given the nature of the crimes under consideration, is of increasingly limited utility. These crimes tend to be increasingly global in nature and will require an appropriate global framework of study. The problem is that the crimes are global but at the moment systems of regulation tend to be largely national (see Nelken, 2012).

Issues of definition

The term white-collar crime has its origins in the writings of Edwin Sutherland (1939), who used it to refer to a crime 'committed by a person of respectability in the course of his occupation' (Sutherland, 1939: 9). Sutherland intended the concept to embrace a diverse range of activities such as tax evasion, stock exchange manipulation, breaches of anti-trust legislation, false advertising and price-fixing between companies. What these actions had in common, he contended, was that they were against the law and their purpose was profit for the employer. Such crimes, he concluded, were frequent, widespread and routine in the world of business in the United States.

His formulation has been criticised on a number of grounds. A particularly pertinent set of criticisms has focused on the standard that is used to define a white-collar crime. Tappan (1947), for example, was unhappy that the label of 'crime' should be extended to cover behaviours that did not fall under the terms of the criminal law. Violations of civil and administrative law were cases in point. He was also unhappy that Sutherland (1939) defined people as criminals whose criminality had not been established in the criminal courts and argued for a more rigorous benchmark. For behaviour to be considered white-collar crime, it had to have been successfully adjudicated on by the courts and to have been the subject of a criminal conviction.

The difficulty in Tappan's (1947) position is that it overlooks the fact that the criminal law is a social product, and as such open to shaping by a range of influences, but disproportionately so by those of powerful social forces and social actors. As Yeager (1995: 250) puts it, 'potential white-collar or business defendants are commonly involved in the active shaping of the very legal definitions being applied to their behaviour by enforcement officials'. Working with a strict legal definition of crime ignores this and with it the role that these powerful social elites play in shaping the nature of the law and in shaping where the distinction is drawn between criminal and corporate offences and between legal corporate behaviour and illegal corporate behaviour.

This leads to a further issue. Many analysts wish the term to include the behaviours of corporations and powerful individuals and groups, which have demonstrably negative social consequences, but which are not illegal in the strict sense of being against the criminal law. Many of the activities that analysts would like to embrace under the term 'crimes of the powerful' (Pearce, 1976) are not unequivocally criminal, as they are not violations of the existing criminal law. If the injuriousness of certain behaviours is independent of whether they are prohibited by the law or not, by what standards can they be judged to be crimes, and how defensible are these standards?

A number of attempts have been made to identify appropriate standards. One of these is by Hermann and Julia Schwendinger (1970) who mobilise the concept of 'human rights'. They argue that there are certain basic immutable human rights, and any behaviour that violates them is a crime, irrespective of how this behaviour is regarded by the legal system. The most fundamental one, they suggest, is 'the right to security of one's person' and anything that interferes with this should be defined as criminal. Thus, they would regard as crime actions such as murder and conventional crimes of violence but also war, genocide, poverty, hunger, economic exploitation and inequality as well as inadequate social and educational facilities, all of which can in different ways result in early, needless and avoidable death.

A second and somewhat more contemporary attempt uses the notion of 'social harm'. Thus Dorling and his colleagues (2008: 11) argue that the concept of crime should include the physical, financial, economic, emotional, psychological, sexual and cultural harms that particular behaviours cause irrespective of how the law regards them. This would help 'to focus upon harms caused by chronic conditions or states of affairs, such as exposure to airborne pollutants, poor diet, institutionalised racism and homophobia' (Dorling *et al.*, 2008: 17). They arrive in the same place as the Schwendingers but by a different route.

These solutions are attractive in that they bring behaviours that are harmful but not illegal into the remit of criminology, but they are not entirely unproblematic. They both work from views of human rights and social harms which may depend as much on political commitment as on analytical introspection. Cohen (2003) argues that the attempt to use a concept of human rights puts together behaviours that are not moral equivalents, for example, genocide and economic exploitation. Genocide he contends (2003: 543), 'is more self-evidently criminal than economic exploitation'. Using a concept of human rights in this way can lead to a situation where a category like state crime is 'simply anything we might not like at the time' (Cohen, 2003: 543). The same problem arises with the use of social harms. For some critics the harms identified as part of the criminogenic nature of capitalism may simply be aspects of the costs of modern life (see Reiman, 2006). In designating such harms as criminal we run the risk of preaching to the converted. As Robert Meier (1986: 415) puts it, 'while expressions of moral outrage are perhaps good politics, they are unsatisfactory science'.

So we return full circle to the arguments of Paul Tappan (1947). If we extend the term 'crime' beyond actions that are labelled by the law as crimes and beyond individuals judged by the courts to be criminal, then, as Slapper and Tombs (1999: 6–7) put it, 'one enters the sphere of normative reasoning or moralizing [...] [O]nce one vacates the terrain of ... the criminal law, strictly defined, who then is to make judgments about what constitutes crime-as-social harm, not least in morally pluralistic societies'.

A working definition?

Given these difficulties is it possible to arrive at a working definition of the phenomenon? To do this we need to respect two factors. The first is the need to recognise that what is included under the rubric of white-collar crime confuses two distinct and different kinds of crime (DeKeseredy, 2011). One is 'occupational crime', where organisational resources and occupational position are used to commit crime. Here the gain is personal and accrues to the individual employee or occupation-holder. Thus it includes embezzlement, defrauding of customers and clients and robbing expenses, inventory or time from employers. The victim can be the corporation itself or the public that does business with it, and the offender is not necessarily a powerful individual, simply someone at a level in the organisation where criminal opportunities are available to them.

By contrast, 'corporate crime' is where owners, employers and employees use the resources of the organisation and of their occupational position to commit crime where the benefit is to the corporation: for example, to further organisational goals such as profit maximisation. If the object of occupational crime is personal gain, the object of corporate crime is primarily corporate or organisational gain. This includes corporate negligence or forms of violence – as, for example, where workers are knowingly exposed to dangerous working conditions, or where the public is put at risk through the sale of dangerous products or by the flouting of pollution laws. It also covers corporate theft, where the public is robbed through over-pricing of goods, deceptive advertising, the kinds of collusion between corporations that results in price-fixing, or through more conventionally recognised forms of fraud.

The second factor is introduced by Slapper and Tombs (1999). For them, the behaviour involved must be punishable 'by the state, regardless of whether it is punished under administrative, civil or criminal law' (Slapper and Tombs, 1999: 19). This element is essential to circumvent the distinction between the different kinds of law applied to corporate behaviour and protects against the importation of political commitments in the guise of sociological truisms. Thus, for the purposes of this chapter, white-collar crime is any offence that breaks the law when it uses organisational resources for personal benefit. Corporate crime by contrast is any offence that breaks the law and which involves the use of organisational resources for the benefit of the organisation. In the first kind of crime, the beneficiary is the individual and in the second, the organisation.

Operationalising the terms

If we define crime in this fairly legalistic way, it may resolve some conceptual issues but it creates in turn a range of problems for empirical work. We encounter two major ones. The first is that of counting the amount of such crime that goes on, and the second is the question of the kind of law that covers white-collar and corporate criminality. The discussion will begin with the issue of counting.

Questions of data: the amount of white-collar and corporate crime

David Nelken (2012: 623–624) points out that it is relatively easy to find examples of white-collar and corporate crimes. But we have no means of knowing how representative these examples are of the overall volume of white-collar and corporate crime, as we simply do not know the precise level of such offences. For the most part, such crimes are not included in official crime statistics, largely because of the range of institutions that deal with them, ranging from health and safety officials, through medical and legal disciplinary tribunals to the police force. This leads to serious and largely irresolvable problems in amalgamating and interpreting the figures from the respective agencies.

In both jurisdictions, for example, the police record data on frauds, but there is no way of telling if these are social welfare frauds, individual business frauds or frauds committed by corporations. The data recorded by enforcement agencies can also be an indication of their own level of activity and their own level of proactive investigation of criminal behaviour, rather than a measure of the actual amount of criminal behaviour that occurs. Typically, there are many reasons why those who are victims of business crimes may not report them to enforcement agencies. The damage that it would do to their businesses is an active disincentive. Equally, some enforcement organisations may not see theirs as a law-enforcement role, but as more of an educational role. For them, criminal investigation and prosecution is a last resort; hence, the number of prosecutions they take to the courts or other sanctioning bodies may not be an indication of the level of offences that come to their notice.

There is also a danger of double counting, as reports are passed between different agencies and in the process become incidents for some and crimes for others. An example is the case of 'rogue' solicitors Michael Lynn and Thomas Byrne, who had systematically robbed their clients, most notably through taking multiple loans on the same properties, using their clients' money to fund their own property dealings and engaging in massive tax fraud (see McDonald, 2010). Byrne's debts totalled €57 million and those of Lynn were in the region of €80 million. This eventually came to the attention of the Commercial Court in Dublin when the banks, realising that they were in difficulty, tried to recoup their loans. When the cases came before Judge Kelly, he immediately referred them to the Garda Fraud Squad. It is impossible to ascertain how these were counted by the various agencies through which they proceeded before their arrival at the Fraud Squad, but, as McDonald (2010: 36) says, 'the banks had been defrauded on a massive scale, but none of them had made a complaint to the Gardaí'.

Finally, the size, expertise and motivation of enforcers are important elements in the production of figures on offences and on offending across jurisdictions. As McDonald (2010) has pointed out, serious failures in the regulation of the banks allowed the collapse that signalled the end of the Celtic Tiger. Indeed, the behaviour of the regulator became a reason for a non-custodial sentence in the only case so far against the banks. The trial of Anglo Irish executives in 2014 found that they had committed offences under section 60 of the Companies Act. This prohibits banks (or indeed any company) from lending money to people to buy its own shares. Though both men were found guilty by a jury, the judge, Martin Nolan, said that '[I]t would be most unjust to jail these two men when I feel that a State agency had led the two men into error and illegality' (McDonald, 2014: 12). The State agency was the Financial Regulator (McDonald, 2014).

How corporate and white-collar crime comes to the attention of the authorities

The problem of counting these kinds of crime also arises from the manner in which they come to the attention of the relevant authorities, a problem that is universal in all jurisdictions. The conventional wisdom in criminology is that most crime comes to police attention through the reporting of victims. This is captured by the terminology used by the Gardaí in the Republic of Ireland where official crime statistics are headed 'crimes that became known to the Gardaí'. That used by the PSNI refers to 'police recorded crime'. Both categories allow for the possibility that more crime occurs than is 'made known' to or recorded by the police. With corporate crime, the situation is different, largely because, while citizens are its victims, they may be unaware of this unwanted form of status, and so be unable to report the offence.

For what they are worth, there are only two categories in crime statistics in Northern Ireland that come close to white-collar and corporate offences. The first is Other Frauds. This covers fraud by company directors, false accounting and failing to disclose information. The recorded number of such offences rose by just over 8 per cent between 2013 and 2014. But, the absolute number of such offences remains small, 2,612 in 2014, when compared to, for example, 35,469 theft offences. The second is Corporate Manslaughter. The Corporate Manslaughter and Corporate Homicide Act became law in Northern Ireland in 2007. This refers to a situation where 'an organisation is deemed responsible for a person's death'. There has only been one conviction under this Act; it occurred in 2010. There were no recorded offences in this category in either 2013 or 2014 (see www.psni.police.uk).

There is currently no equivalent legislation on corporate manslaughter in the Republic of Ireland. Here, the closest category in crime statistics to white-collar or corporate crime is 'fraud, deception and related offences'. However, as this also includes welfare fraud, its representativeness for the crimes under consideration here is somewhat undependable. The number of such recorded offences fell from 5,791 in 2012 to 4,827 in 2013. This compares with the rise in theft from 76,402 in 2012 to 78,763 in 2013 (CSO, 2014).

Due to the absence of research on corporate and white-collar crime in Northern Ireland, this analysis focuses primarily on the Republic of Ireland. Here corporate or white-collar crime comes to the attention of the police and of regulatory bodies in a number of ways. One is by accident. The extra-curricular activities of supermarket owner Ben Dunne, in Florida in July 1992, involved the use of a prostitute and an alleged attempt to commit suicide by jumping from the 17th floor of a hotel while under the influence of cocaine. This resulted in his arrest by the police and precipitated a series of events back in Ireland that culminated in the establishment of the Moriarty Tribunal to investigate payments to politicians (Cullen, 2002).

It also comes to police and public attention through the activities of whistle-blowers. In the Republic of Ireland the encouragement and protection of whistle-blowers – that is, people who report suspicious and criminal behaviour in the organisations they work in – is poorly developed, though there have been important examples of such behaviour. It was a solicitor who worked with Michael Lynn who drew the attention of the authorities to his behaviour (McDonald, 2010). There may also be what Fleming (2010: 36) has called 'a cultural and historical aversion to whistle blowing given the dubious status and often short lives of those who were perceived as informers to the occupying British powers in the nineteenth and early twentieth century'. In Northern Ireland, the problem of short lives persists in relation to informing on political offenders, but there does not appear to be a tradition of corporate whistle-blowing. Legislative defects are currently being addressed in the Republic of Ireland through the Protected Disclosures Act 2014, but legislative solutions may not fully resolve this issue. Even in jurisdictions where whistleblowers are legally protected they are not necessarily, or indeed generally, treated as heroes (see Wax, 2013).

The third way in which such crimes come to public attention is when people within organisations report their concerns to the relevant regulatory authorities, which then investigate them. The instigation of investigations into suspicious companies is part of the remit of the Office of the Director of Corporate Enforcement (ODCE) in the Republic of Ireland. In addition to an informational and educational role, it has a duty to investigate 'unlawful and irresponsible behaviour insofar as it relates to company law' (ODCE, 2013). The bulk of these reports come from bodies with statutory reporting obligations, such as auditors and liquidators, who are obliged to report suspected criminality. As we shall see below, they may not be very good at it. But the office also receives complaints from the public about indictable crimes. In 2012 they received 252 such complaints, amounting to 11 per cent of what they define as 'external inputs'. However, this does not mean that there were 252 crimes, as many reports were about the same alleged offence (ODCE, 2013). Section 19 of the Criminal Justice Act 2011 widened the obligation on people to report about offences like fraudulent trading, insider dealing and the withholding of information or property from liquidators to An Garda Síochána. Nobody reported anything to them under these headings in 2012, and since 2005 the number of offences here never reached more than low single digits.

A key form of 'external input' is public, or what one might term victim, complaints. These have varied from 284 in 2005 to 252 in 2013, with highs of 422 in 2011 and 344 in 2006. However, the majority of these were dismissed because of insufficient evidence. Indeed, most charges or reports made to the office were dealt with by civil procedures, and only small numbers were the subject of criminal proceedings. Though the use of criminal proceedings has increased in recent years, the numbers involved are still small.

Finally, there are those crimes reported to the police. These tend to be small in number, and it is not possible to tell from the relevant statistics whether these are crimes for individual or organisational benefit, or how they have come to the attention of the police. It is not possible to discover if they have been reported directly by victims or referred to the police by other agencies, such as the ODCE. However, a senior counsel involved with such offences in the Republic of Ireland said that many of the files sent to the Garda Fraud Squad are never read and so unlikely to become the object of a police investigation (O'Toole, 2014b).

What is clear from this is that the modes of discovering and reporting on white-collar and corporate crime ensure that they are dealt with through processes that do not dramatise their possible criminality and so ensure that they generally escape the attention of the police and, most notably, of the criminal courts. There is also a lack of consistency in their reporting that makes comparative analysis impossible.

The case of the auditors who did not bark

We have discussed above the role of 'external inputs' in bringing illegal business behaviour to the attention of the authorities. It is worth pursuing in more detail the role of one important external input, that of auditors. As Larsson (2005) points out, it is the task of auditors to patrol the corporation. Their job is to see that published accounts represent the real state of the company and that the company has complied with the relevant laws under which it operates. This means their relationship with their employers is potentially an adversarial one. They work for the companies that they audit, but their real employer is the public good. The idea is that the public does not need to be concerned about corporate fraud because the auditors are on the case.

In his analysis of the banking collapse in the Republic of Ireland, the Governor of the Central Bank noted that the problems in the banks had been building up over a period of time, so accountants and auditors 'should have been more alert to weaknesses in the banks' lending and financial position' (Holohan, 2010: vi). Kinsella (2013) has shown how in 2006 and 2007 all of the major banks in the Republic of Ireland were judged by their auditors to be in good health. One year later they were all in receipt of transfusions from the state. 'You would imagine,' he says, 'that an auditor doing his or her job in 2006 might have sounded warnings that something was wrong' (Kinsella, 2013: 27).

He draws attention in particular to the role of KPMG, one of the big four global auditors (Kinsella, 2013). They were the auditors of AIB over the period from 2006 to 2011, 'not exactly', as Kinsella (2013: 27) remarks, 'the bank's golden years'. They also were auditors to the Irish Nationwide Building Society from 2006 to 2009. These were profitable contracts, and, despite what later emerged about banking practices at Irish Nationwide in particular, they never raised issues publicly about them. In 2009 Irish Nationwide was nationalised and integrated into the Irish Bank Resolution Corporation, the rebranded name for Anglo-Irish Bank. Now Kinsella adds, KPMG is overseeing the liquidation of IBRC bank. 'Quite a turnaround, wouldn't you say?' (Kinsella, 2013: 27).

The Commission of Investigation into the Banking Sector (2011: vi) says that '[T]he problem of clean audits followed by a threat of closure a short time later is not new nor is it limited to Ireland'. What is different, however, about other jurisdictions is the willingness to talk about the behaviour of accountants and auditors in the language of criminality. Fooks (2003: 17) shows how the collapse of Enron and other large corporations 'uncovered a corporate America beset by deception, false accounting and bankruptcy'. Accountants and auditors were shown to have signed off on accounts that they knew were false, to have colluded in the creation of false accounts and failed to report such frauds to the relevant authorities. They were also subject to criminal prosecutions. There is little evidence in the Republic of Ireland of a willingness to discuss the behaviour of auditors in these terms.

The problem of the law

The behaviour of auditors was by no means unique to the Republic of Ireland, but it is here that the second problem arises: that of the law covering corporate misbehaviour. Many kinds of such misbehaviour are simply not dealt with in the law in the Republic of Ireland, whether it is of a criminal, civil or administrative nature. Key aspects of banking behaviour, for example, are not covered by the law in any form. There is considerable evidence that across all of the banks there were inadequate checks on lending, symbolised most strikingly by the absence of key documentation and securities against the loans that were given. It is also clear that many banks lent money, not on the basis of stringent credit-checking, but on the grounds that others were doing it, and so they had to in order to maintain market share. But the courts have ruled that the tort of reckless lending does not exist in Irish law (Cox, 2014). The crime of recklessness in general does not exist in law either. There is a concept of reckless trading in Irish law, and arguably a case could be made against bankers for that. But it can only be used where the company involved is a failed one: that is, in receivership or liquidation. However, the way in which the authorities dealt with the failure of Irish banks – through a bank guarantee – meant that, technically, in law they were not failed companies.

Steps are being taken in England, and through that in Northern Ireland, to remedy this defect. There are plans to introduce a charge of reckless banking – that is, 'reckless misconduct in the management of a bank, an offence that will carry a maximum sentence of seven years in prison' (see James and Scuffham, 2013). The authorities are also planning a back-up power to ensure that banks play by the new rules. If they do not, the legal capacity will exist to separate their retail side from riskier activities such as investment management (James and Scuffham, 2013). There does not as yet appear to be the appetite in the Republic of Ireland for such legal reforms. Those that have been introduced are in the area of competition law. The provisions of the Competition Amendment Act (2012) include the setting up of a single body for consumer protection and increased maximum prison sentences and increased fines for anti-competitive offences. But, as prison sentences for such offences are rare, it is not clear where the deterrent is here.

The Criminal Justice Bill introduced in May 2014 was highlighted as a series of measures to combat white-collar crime. However, it dealt mainly with procedural matters to reduce delays in the investigation of white-collar crime, and some of its provisions are of a contestable nature. For example, it gives the Gardaí the right to suspend the detention periods that are permitted under other criminal laws so that a 72-hour detention period can be broken into shorter periods, presumably to allow the authorities to check details that might have emerged in questioning: essentially a trial within a trial. It says a lot for the level of deterioration in discussions of civil liberties in the Republic of Ireland that such a power can be passed into law, largely without any significant protest.

What remains to be seen here is whether the regulatory cycle mentioned by Croall (2009) will come into play here. She has noted that when regulatory change is introduced in response to an apparent crisis, it is followed by pressures to dilute, modify or reverse new regulations and laws. There is some evidence that this may be on the way in the Republic of Ireland. Alan McCarthy, a lawyer with an expertise in competition, procurement and EU law, has questioned whether we need more regulation. Writing about the Competition and Consumer Protection Bill 2014, he argues:

> [i]t is hard not to draw the conclusion that the Bill will graft another layer of extensive regulation on business in Ireland where effective powers and mechanisms for enforcing and applying competition law, consumer protection and merger control already largely exist.
>
> *(McCarthy, 2014: 7)*

Conclusions on quantities

The implications of these considerations are that we cannot say definitively how much illegal white-collar and corporate criminality goes on, whether it has increased or not, or whether the increased concern about it comes from the fact that it has become more newsworthy. Changes in relevant figures may occur for numerous reasons, not least the recent tendency to deal with such behaviour in a formal and legal manner, rather than in an informal and private manner between corporations and regulators, as may have been the practice in the past. Either way, as Nelken (2012: 625) states, it illustrates the 'artificiality of all definitions of crime' – something which, of course, is also true of all crime statistics.

Investigating and prosecuting white-collar and corporate crime

When white-collar and corporate crime surmounts the range of obstacles to becoming public, how is it investigated? The most distinctive mode of investigation in the Republic of Ireland is the Tribunal of Inquiry. There have been a significant number in the recent past (see Murphy, 2005). These are dealt with in Chapter 8, but it is relevant here to mention the McCracken Tribunal, which uncovered what became known as the Ansbacher accounts. These were secret bank accounts set up in the Cayman Islands by wealthy Irish politicians, businessmen and other public figures as a means of tax evasion. The names of those involved included former directors of semi-state bodies such as Aer Lingus, the national airline, and of Bord Fáilte, a government agency established to promote tourism, as well as a former director of the Central Bank and a managing director and chairman of one of the Republic's biggest companies, Cement Roadstone Holding. Organised tax evasion reached, it seems, into the heart of the Irish state.

The Tribunal of Inquiry method of investigation has been criticised on a number of grounds, most colourfully by developer and whistle-blower Tom Gilmartin – who said that tribunals were 'about as useful as tits on a bull' (Connolly, 2013: 12) – but also by others on the grounds of cost, time and effectiveness. What is most relevant in the current context is the inability to use the information collected by tribunals as the basis for a criminal prosecution. The reports of the various tribunals have been sent to the Gardaí and the Office of the Director of Public Prosecutions (DPP), but to what purpose is unclear. Transparency International (2009: paragraph 16) have stated that '[t]he Gardaí will have to uncover evidence of wrongdoing again with a fresh investigation into the circumstances surrounding the case. This is because evidence and testimony presented at a Tribunal of Inquiry cannot be used to secure a criminal conviction against a witness in the tribunal'. Essentially, the crime has to be reinvestigated and, as this is a huge undertaking, it is unlikely to result in criminal prosecutions.

It is instructive in this regard to note that nobody was prosecuted over the Ansbacher accounts. It is also instructive that the decision in the High Court action, where a ruling of corruption against a planner by the Flood Tribunal was overturned, now potentially opens up the space for all of those accused of offences by the tribunal to challenge its findings, effectively undermining the conclusions that the tribunal arrived at (Cullen, 2014).

A second mode of investigation is through the use of court-appointed inspectors, but one of the most striking recent examples of this continues to be controversial. Insider dealing or trading is a serious offence under the law in the Republic of Ireland and Northern Ireland. In the Republic the sentence for a conviction on indictment is fines of up to €10,000 and/or ten years in prison (Shipsey, 2010). In July 2007 the Supreme Court made a finding of insider dealing against Jim Flavin, the Executive Chairman of DCC, an industrial holding company. It held that he had access to price-sensitive information, and hence his trading in the shares of Fyffes was unlawful (Shipsey, 2010). The Director of Corporate Enforcement applied to the High Court to appoint an inspector to investigate a number of transactions in the company. The person chosen was Bill Shipsey, a senior counsel (Shipsey, 2010).

Shipsey concluded that, although the Director of Corporate Enforcement believed that what was going on was insider dealing, the Director was wrong. 'The suggestion by the Director that the 1995 transactions could have amounted to a breach of Section 108 of the Companies Act, 1990', he said, 'did not withstand scrutiny' (Shipsey, 2010: 896). He concluded that, 'on the basis of all the evidence which I have heard from all of the witnesses and from Mr Flavin himself, that there was no deliberate wrongdoing or dishonesty on his part' (Shipsey, 2010: 911). Although the Supreme Court held that Flavin had engaged in insider dealing, the court-appointed inspector said that his behaviour was 'an error of appreciation and judgment' (Shipsey, 2010: 957).

Whatever the report contains about the nature of the interpretations of the law and related matters, what is unique here is the mode through which the offences were dismissed. It was based on the interpretation by the inspector of the motives of those involved. These motives were established at a series of interviews which, given the mode of investigation, were not conducted under caution. By contrast, in conventional criminal proceedings, interviews with suspects are, theoretically at least, conducted under caution, and matters of guilt or innocence are (again, theoretically at least) a matter for juries, as are interpretations of the intentions of those involved. Many conventional criminals would consider getting caught as an 'error of appreciation and judgment', but criminal courts have been less understanding. The overarching reality behind all of this is that, as of 2010, and despite ten years of existence, the Office of the Director of Corporate Enforcement (ODCE) has 'never secured a single successful prosecution for insider dealing or market abuse' (McDonald, 2010: 232).

The third mode of investigation is through the many specialised agencies such as the Health and Safety Authority and the Garda Bureau of Fraud Investigation, but, for the most part, their investigations do not lead to criminal prosecutions or criminal adjudications. The Health and Safety Authority's function would appear to be largely educational and advisory in nature, while we have seen that questions arise about the ability of the Garda Bureau of Fraud Investigation to investigate and prosecute white-collar crime. Also, the Central Bank reported 689 cases where it suspected that criminal offences had been committed in the financial services and banks under its supervision between 2009 and 2013. So far, this has led to just two prosecutions and one conviction (Creighton, 2014).

Moreover, many of these organisations have suffered serious budget cuts in the last few years. The budget of the Garda Bureau of Fraud Investigation was cut by over 20 per cent in the period from 2008 to 2011, while that of the Office of the Director of Corporate Enforcement (ODCE) was cut by 11.6 per cent from 2010 to 2013 (Byrne, 2013). In its 2012 Annual Report, the ODCE said that it was limited by resources in its capacity to engage in 'the examination of complaints received from members of the public, auditors' and professional bodies' statutory reports and to proactively seek to address other areas of potential risk' (see Byrne, 2013: 10). Arguably this is a good illustration of the contrast made by Kilcommins between the underfunded treatment of white-collar crime and the elaborate legal and policing apparatus constructed to tackle so-called 'organised crime' (McDonald, 2010: 232), such as seven-day detention for questioning and, particularly, the use of the Special Criminal Court, set up to deal with terrorist offences, to try offenders accused of organised crime.

But even here we need to be careful. It is the case that budget cuts have affected the ability to pursue the kinds of crime discussed here. But the spectre of social class continues to be important. It is relevant to point out that 'approximately 620 staff' in the Department of Social Protection 'are directly assigned to control activities', i.e. the detection of social welfare fraud (Department of Social Protection, 2011: 69). By contrast the 'approved staff complement' in the Office of the Director of Corporate Enforcement in 2014 was 44.4 (see http://www.odce.ie).

The final mode of investigation and prosecution is the show trial. Michael Levi (2009) has detailed how, despite the fact that white-collar and corporate crime and their perpetrators might seem like prime candidates for moral panics, they have remained largely untouched by them or by the cultures of control that such panics inspire. A key element here is the manner in which the 'monstering' that is central to the construction of a moral panic works with this kind of crime. Moral panics involving these crimes pick on an atypical, limited and easily isolated range of individuals and diffuse responsibility for the crisis on to them. The kind of media coverage of people like Michael Lynn, the criminal solicitor, embodies elements of this. He had engaged in mortgage fraud of around €80 million, got money from almost all the banks that operated in the Republic of Ireland and had absconded to a range of foreign countries, largely in an attempt to avoid being returned to face charges. McDonald (2010) describes going to meet him to Portugal. He appears behind her in the airport 'wearing an orange T-shirt, shorts and a mile-wide *sneer*' and 'he reappeared, *sauntering* back to the jeep. He paused and eyeballed Seamus and me before *swaggering* away' (McDonald, 2010: 2–5, emphasis added).

Similarly Michael Fingleton, the former chief executive of Irish Nationwide Building Society, known in tabloid land as 'Fingers', is an ideal candidate for a folk devil. He had run the building society in a high-handed fashion, giving loans that appeared to be insufficiently backed up by the relevant protections to journalists, politicians and public figures. When the bank was nationalised to prevent its collapse in 2009 he retired with a pension, believed to be in the region of €27 million and a bonus of €1 million. The cost to the Exchequer of the collapse of Irish Nationwide is said to be in the region of €5.4 billion (the full account is in Lyons and Curran, 2013). According to Fingleton himself, he has become a social pariah. In a recent newspaper interview, he described his difficulty in getting high-quality legal representation (Molloy, 2014). 'If he had murdered someone', we are told, 'it would have been easier to get a barrister to take the case' (Molloy, 2014: 15). He is also being shunned by many of the business people whom he helped out. The 'friend' who gave the *Irish Independent* (Irish newspaper) this information said, '[T]here are three developers that I know of who would still call him to ask how he's getting on. The rest of them don't want to know' (Molloy, 2014: 15).

What is interesting about these two 'ideal' folk devils and what make them so suitable for that role, is that they are very much outsiders in the financial world with social backgrounds that are by no means typical of the Irish elite. So they do not need to be presented as 'typical' bankers or solicitors, and it is open to the media and others to describe them as 'rogue' elements and as aberrations in their respective professions. Despite McDonald's (2010) claim that the kind of behaviour that Lynn was involved in differed from that of other solicitors only in its scope rather than its kind, it is Lynn that was 'outed'. Similarly, Michael Fingleton was described in a Seanad debate in 2010 as 'representing the unacceptable face of capitalism' (Government of Ireland, Seanad

Eireann, 2010: paragraph 3).Yet again it is by no means clear that Fingleton's behaviour differed radically from that of other banks and other bankers. The cost of bailing out the mainstream and respectable Allied Irish Bank was almost as much as that for Anglo and considerably more than that for Irish Nationwide. Like most of the other banks, AIB was also guilty of reckless lending (O'Toole, 2014a). But those connected with it have successfully avoided the stigma that is being attached to Fingleton. This may not be unconnected to the fact that, as O'Toole has argued about AIB, 'Fine Gael blue bloods like Peter Sutherland and Dermot Gleeson did much to shape its culture' (O'Toole, 2014b: 12). So, despite behaving in ways that are uncomfortably close to those of the other major bankers, it is Fingleton who became one of the leading villains of the crisis.

Hence the nature of the moral panic around these people is such as to diffuse the responsibility onto a limited number of individuals, and these tend by background, education and career to be outsiders in those sections of the financial world that considered itself more respectable. They became in effect 'signal offenders', embodying in their persona and behaviour all of the qualities that were supposed to have led to the crisis. The effect is, as Levi (2009: 65) remarks, 'to enable elites to feel comfortable when they (the others that is) are depicted as "criminals"'. The other effect is to localise the problem and sanitise the legal and banking sectors. Get rid of the bad guys, and then it can go back to business as usual.

An essential element in this is the show trial, the limited prosecutions of people involved in the creation of the crisis: in effect an opportunity to exorcise the nouveau bankers and lawyers and give the business back to the respectable ones. The problem of reckless behaviour among bankers is neutralised by a series of symbolic degradation ceremonies that successfully isolate the problem by displacing it onto social outsiders and insulate the normal business and banking classes. It is undoubtedly the case that the limited resources of many enforcement agencies restricts the numbers of prosecutions that they can bring to court, but to limit the scope of the analysis to resources alone would seriously restrict our understanding of the degree to which the pursuit of white-collar crime may also have a function of protecting long-standing elites.

Punishing white-collar criminals

Generally speaking, white-collar or corporate criminals in the Republic of Ireland have been successful in evading prosecution, and, in the limited number of cases prosecuted, they have been successful in avoiding a prison sentence. The Competition Authority imposed €600,000 in fines over a 15-year period but nobody has gone to prison for competition offences. Similarly, although the chairperson of the Revenue Commissioners said that 289 cases of illegality had been identified in the biggest example of tax evasion identified in the Republic of Ireland, the Ansbacher affair, nobody has been prosecuted for it, and so nobody served prison time (Byrne, 2013). As we have seen, the judge in the trial of the two directors of Anglo Irish Bank found guilty of giving illegal loans to property developers said that it would be unjust to imprison them. This is despite rulings from the courts that prison sentences might be appropriate for such crimes (McDonald, 2010).

The issue of price-fixing is instructive. There is a public perception that this practice is wide-spread in certain industries, and particularly among professional groups or in what is termed the non-trading sector. It first became a criminal offence in 1996. The relevant law was amended in 2002 to give it more strength, with the provisions for increased fines and longer prison sentences. However, one of the few industries in which it has been successfully legally established that such cartels operate is in the motor industry.

The Irish Ford Dealers Association in Munster (Southwest of the Republic of Ireland) had a price-fixing arrangement that was described by the trial judge as of 'shocking sophistication' (for the details see Curtis and McNally, 2007). The dealers set agreed limits on the discounting they would offer potential purchasers by issuing garages with price guides and then policing the system to ensure compliance. They used fake customers to test it out by getting them to make price queries in garages that were part of the scheme. Oddly enough, only one person was prosecuted here. The other members of the cartel were not. That one person, Denis Manning, was the secretary to the Dealers Association, and he was found guilty in February 2007, fined €30,000 and given a suspended 12-month prison sentence. Writing about the Manning judgement, Curtis and McNally (2007: 41) concluded that it:

> [A]ppears just proportionately marginally more punitive than the *Connaught Oil* threshold and yet could be considered more lenient, in light of the legislative guidelines of the 2002 Act which allows for 'fines up to €4 million and up to 5 years imprisonment' for breaches of its provisions.

The problem would seem to lie somewhere in the gap between enforcement intentions and sentencing outcomes. The reality is that the favoured enforcement strategy is one based on compliance rather than on sanctioning (Curtis and McNally, 2007:41). It is a strategy that also finds favour with the legal profession. First Law in the Republic of Ireland organised a debate on the motion 'Is jail the way to go' after *DPP v Duffy*. The Duffy case was held to be groundbreaking in the Republic of Ireland, as it showed that prison may be an appropriate sanction for white-collar crime, rather than the system of fines that previously had been in place. The motion was defeated. There was substantial agreement as, in the words of McDonald (2011: 33), '[y]ou won't do time for "white-collar" crime', and for the most part, members of the legal profession are in agreement with this.

The failure to impose prison sentences for these kinds of crime is at least highly questionable. It contributes to the perception that there is a law for the rich and a law for the poor. To borrow a phrase from Reiman (1995) the feeling is that 'the rich get rich, and the poor get prison'.

But there is an argument that fines are actually the more appropriate way to deal with corporate crime. If these are sufficiently large, then they will lead to desistance among corporate offenders. Hence their regular use in the cases that we have looked at here. They are also widely used in conventional crime, but here they are accompanied by a significant use of prison sentences. This, however, is not the case with corporate crime. Arguably, there are hidden assumptions about social class involved here. People without economic resources can only be successfully punished by the forfeit of what they may have a lot of, namely time. Better-off people have financial resources, and so it is punishment enough to deprive them of some of these resources.

But it is not that simple. It is not clear how effective fines are in dealing with financial institutions like banks. As we have seen, the major banks in the Republic of Ireland could be classified as serial offenders, so fines have not proved a deterrent. That may well be because the fines do not dent bank profits, but are recouped from customers through higher interest rates and increased bank charges. The victim ends up paying for the crime. Or else the fines may be too small. Allied Irish Bank made a settlement of IRL£90 million following its encouragement of tax evasion through the abuse of DIRT tax.[1] According to Creaton (2000), this amounted to five weeks of bank profits.

It is undoubtedly necessary to change the ways in which we respond to the deviance of the powerful. It is also important to recognise, as Sutherland (1939) did in the United States, that many Irish white-collar and corporate offenders are both recidivist and serial. 'Just two years after avoiding prosecution for a variety of crimes', Protess (2014: 1) tells us, 'some of the world's biggest banks are suspected of having broken their promises to behave'. The same names and the same institutions come up repeatedly in any long-term analysis of the problem. Hence the argument that a taste of prison may be appropriate with such hardened and repeat offenders. The notion of a taste of prison for rich and powerful offenders has pleasing and populist overtones. But if prison does not represent a solution for ordinary offenders, it is not a solution for corporate and other white-collar offenders either.

Irene Lynch Fannon (2010) has argued that we need to be more creative in looking for appropriate sanctions for corporate offenders. This may be true, but the same level of creativity needs also to be applied to ordinary offenders as well. Perhaps, as Nelken (1994: 383–384) has suggested, the solution is to approach the problem from the other end of the penal equation. Rather than extending the methods used to deal with ordinary criminals to business and corporate ones, maybe we could apply the methods by which we deal with business and corporate crime to our dealings with conventional crime. 'It is usually necessary', Nelken (1994: 383) says, 'for an offender accused of ordinary crime to suffer the stigma of a conviction before consideration is given to compliance, whereas the opposite is true for business offenders'. With them the process is one in which a 'series of attempts at compliance [act] as a prelude to prosecution' (Nelken, 1994: 384), a process he describes as regulation without stigmatisation. This is not entirely absent from our treatment of ordinary crime. But its further extension into the response to ordinary crime would bring about more equality in our treatment of offenders from different backgrounds without at the same time surrendering to visceral demands for punitive prison sentences.

Conclusion

This article has illustrated how white-collar and corporate crime is dealt with on the island of Ireland. The way in which we respond to such crime, especially in the Republic of Ireland, is designed to understate the level of such offences, understate their criminality and, with one of two notable exceptions, shy away from the use of imprisonment for such offences and for such offenders. The literature on corporate crime would suggest that this way of dealing with such crimes differs in degree rather than kind from those operating in other countries like the United Kingdom and the United States. But there may be a bit more to it than that.

One of the most striking insights about white-collar and corporate crime and about the inability to use criminal law against them, is the problem of pursuing twentieth-century criminality in twenty-first century organisations with nineteenth-century law. This kind of law, with its individualised concept of *mens rea*, makes it difficult to pursue large organisations, in particular, as it requires the establishment of the existence of an 'organising mind' behind corporate crimes. This may be difficult to do with large scale and complex organisations, though, as John Braithwaite (1984) has pointed out, establishing lines of responsibility has not proved quite so difficult for pay and remuneration purposes.

But it does mean that smaller firms and commercial entitles are more open to having the law used against them. Take the offence of corporate manslaughter. It proved impossible to establish a case against Townsend Thoresen, the owners of the *Herald of Free Enterprise*, which capsized on 6 March 1987, killing 193 passengers and crew. The directors were charged with corporate manslaughter but the case collapsed (Chan, 2011). The judge ruled that the negligence involved could not be attributed to a controlling mind (Chan, 2011: 5). Indeed, the only successful prosecution of a corporation for manslaughter in England was of an outdoor adventure centre in Lyme Regis where four teenagers died in a drowning accident. The owner was successfully prosecuted because he was in direct control of the centre (Chan, 2011).

So, intentionally or not, the laws on corporate manslaughter, and possibly on other forms of white-collar and corporate crime, favour large corporations. Rather than acting as an inhibitor of their behaviour, it would appear that the law is an ally of corporate power. This interpretation is not new. Gabriel Kolko (1963) pointed this out when he showed how large corporations were involved in the campaign for federal regulation of the meat and railroad industries, because of the potential that such regulations had to restore and maintain confidence in meat products among the public and also to drive small competitors out of business. The reforms of the so-called progressive period in American politics were 'usually initiated by the needs of interested business, and political intervention into the economy was frequently merely a response to the demands of particular businessmen ... the regulatory movements were usually initiated by the dominant industries to be regulated' (Kolko, 1963: 2–3). The law, here as elsewhere, is for the small people.

References

Braithwaite, J. (1984) *Corporate Crime in the Pharmaceutical Industry*, London: Routledge and Kegan Paul.

Byrne, E. (2013) 'Ireland's White-Collar Crime Oversight Agencies: Fit for Purpose?' Available at www.elaine.ie. (accessed 4 August 2014).

Chan, S. P. (2011) 'History of Corporate Manslaughter: Five Key Cases'. *Daily Telegraph*, 18 February, p. 5.

Cohen, S. (2003) 'Human Rights and Crimes of the State', pp. 543–560, in E. McLoughlin, J. Muncie and J. Pratt (eds), *Criminological Perspectives: Essential Readings*. London: Sage.

Commission of Investigation into the Banking Sector (2011) *Misjudging Risk: Causes of the Systemic Banking Crisis in Ireland*. Dublin: Central Bank.

Connolly, F. (2013) *Tom Gilmartin*. Dublin: Gill and Macmillan.

Cox, A. (2014) 'High Court Confirms No Tort of "Reckless Lending"'. *Group Briefing*, June, p. 1.

Creaton, S. (2000) 'AIB settlement on DIRT largest in history of State'. *Irish Times*, 4 October, p. 1.

Creighton, L. (2014) 'Enforcement of White Collar Crime Needs to Change'. Available at www.lucindacreighton.ie (accessed 26 October 2014).

Croall, H. (2009) *Understanding White Collar Crime*. London: Open University Press.

CSO (2014) 'Recorded Crime Offences'. Available at www.cso.ie/crime statistics (accessed 25 March 2015).

Cullen, P. (2002) *With a Little Help from My Friends*. Dublin: Gill and Macmillan.

—— (2014) 'Redmond Ruling Opens Up Challenges to Tribunal Findings'. *Irish Times*, 20 December, p. 1.

Curtis, M. E. and McNally, J. (2007) 'The Classic Cartel – Hatchback Sentence'. *The Competition Law Review*, 4(1): 41–50.

DeKeseredy, W. (2011) *Contemporary Critical Criminology*. New York: Routledge.

Department of Social Protection (2011) *Comprehensive Review of Expenditure*. Dublin: Dept. of Social Protection.

Dorling, D., Gordon, D., Hillyard, P., Pantazis, C., Pemberton, S. and Tombs, S. (2008) *Criminal obsessions: Why harm matters more than crime*, 2nd ed. London: Centre for Crime and Justice Studies.

Fleming, L. (2010) 'Whistleblowing and White Collar Crime', *Accountancy Ireland*, 42(6): 36–37.

Fooks, G. (2003) 'Auditors and the Permissive Society: Market Failure, Globalisation and Financial Regulation in the US', *Risk Management*, 5(2): 17–26.

Government of Ireland. Seanad Eireann (2010) *Parliamentary Debates*, Vol. 202, No. 4, 27 April.

Holohan, P. (2010) *The Irish Banking Crisis*. Dublin: Central Bank.

Ireland, High Court (2002) *Report of the Inspectors Appointed to Enquire into the Affairs of Ansbacher (Cayman) Limited* (Also known as the McCracken Tribunal). Dublin: The Stationery Office.

James, W. and Scuffham, M. (2013) 'UK "reckless banking" charge to carry seven-year jail term', *Reuters*, 1 October.

Kinsella, S. (2013) 'Behaviour of our auditors during crash can't be ignored any longer'. *Irish Independent*, 19 February, p. 27.

Kolko, G. (1963) *The Triumph of Conservatism*. New York: Free Press.

Larsson, B. (2005) 'Patrolling the Corporation – The Auditors' Duty to Report Crime in Sweden', *International Journal of the Sociology of Law*, 33(1): 53–70.

Levi, M. (2009) 'Suite revenge? The shaping of folk devils and moral panics about white-collar crimes', *British Journal of Criminology*, 49(1): 48–67.

Lynch Fannon, I. (2010) 'Controlling Risk Taking – Whose Job Is It Anyway?', in S. Kilcommins and U. Kilkelly (eds) *Regulatory Crime in Ireland*. Dublin: Lonsdale Law Publishing.

Lyons, T. and Curran, R. (2013) *Fingers: The Man Who Brought Down Irish Nationwide and Cost Us €5.4 bn*. Dublin: Gill and Macmillan.

McCarthy, A. (2014) 'Do we need more layers of competition regulation'. *Irish Times*, 23 June, p.7.

McDonald, D. (2010) *Bust: How the Courts Have Exposed the Rotten Heart of the Irish Economy*. Dublin: Penguin Ireland.

—— (2011) 'You won't do time for "white-collar" crime – No laws seem to cover it'. *Irish Independent*, 9 June, p. 33.

—— (2014) 'Verdict in Anglo Trial'. *Irish Independent*, 31 July.

McKeown, L. (2012) 'Huge fine for first Ulster company guilty in corporate manslaughter case'. *Belfast Telegraph*, 9 May, p. 10.

Meier, R. (1986) 'Review Essay', *Criminology*, 24(2): 415–420.

Molloy, T. (2014) 'Whatever became of Michael Fingleton', *Sunday Independent*, 16 February, p. 15.

Murphy, G. (2005) 'Payments for No Political Response? Political Corruption and Tribunals of Inquiry in Ireland, 1991–2003' in J. Garrard and J. Newell (eds), *Scandals in Past and Contemporary Politics*. Manchester University Press, pp.91–105.

Nelken, D. (1994) 'White Collar Crime' in M. Maguire, R. Morgan and R. Reiner (eds), *Oxford Handbook of Criminology*, 1st ed. Oxford: Clarendon Press.

—— (2012) 'White Collar and Corporate Crime', pp. 623–659, in M. Maguire, R. Morgan and R. Reiner (eds), *Oxford Handbook of Criminology*: Oxford University Press.

ODCE (2013) *Annual Report the Office of the Director of Corporate Enforcement*. Dublin: Office of the Director of Corporate Enforcement.

O'Toole, F. (2014a) 'John Bruton represents Fine Gael values – and those values are in deep trouble', *Irish Times*, 12 August, p. 12.

—— (2014b) 'Four things that haven't changed since the crash', *Irish Times*, 23 September, p. 12.

Pearce, F. (1976) *Crimes of the Powerful*. London: Pluto Press.

Protess, B. (2014) 'Prosecutors Suspect Repeat Offenses on Wall Street', *New York Times*, 29 October, p. 1.

PSNI (Police Service of Northern Ireland) (2015) 'Police Recorded Crime'. Available at www.psni.police. uk. (Accessed 25 March 2015).

Reiman, J. H. (1995) *The rich get richer and the poor get prison: Ideology, class, and criminal justice*. Boston: Allyn & Bacon.

—— (2006) 'Beyond Criminology', *British Journal of Criminology*, 46(2): 362–36.

Schwendinger, H. and Schwendinger, J. (1970) 'Defenders of Order or Guardians of Human Rights?', *Issues in Criminology*, 5(2): 123–157.

Shipsey, W. (2010) *Inspectors Report into the Affairs of DCC*. Dublin: Office of Corporate Enforcement.

Slapper, G. and Tombs, S. (1999) *Corporate Crime*. Harlow: Longman.

Sutherland, E. (1939) *White Collar Crime*. New York: Holt Rinehart and Winston.

Tappan, P. (1947) 'Who Is the Criminal', *American Sociological Review*, 12: 96–102.

Transparency International (2009) *National Integrity Systems: Country Study: Ireland*. Berlin: Transparency Secretariat. Available at http://www.transparency.ie/sites/default/files/NIS_Full_Report_Ireland_2009. pdf (accessed 10 July 2014).

Wax, E. (2013) 'After the Whistle: Revealers of Government Secrets Share How Their Lives Have Changed', *Washington Post*, 28 July. Available at http://www.washingtonpost.com/lifestyle/style/after-the-whistle-revealers-of-government-secrets-share-how-their-lives-have-changed/2013/07/28/23d82596-f613-11e2-9434-60440856fadf_story.html (accessed: 6 July 2015).

Yeager, P. (1995) 'Law, Crime, and Inequality: The Regulatory State', in J. Hagan and R. D. Peterson (eds), *Crime and Inequality*. Stanford, CA: Stanford University Press.

Note

1 DIRT tax, properly called Deposit Interest Retention Tax, is a tax on interest earned on bank deposits in the Republic of Ireland.

5

Cybercrime
Towards a research agenda

T.J. McIntyre

Introduction

The study of cybercrime in the Republic of Ireland has generally been outward rather than inward looking. There is a growing literature *from* the Republic of Ireland, yet there has been relatively little written on cybercrime *in* the Republic. Research such as that of Kirwan and Power (2011, 2013), Conway (2006) and Taylor and Quayle (2008) has for the most part taken a broad international perspective, and there has been less attention to topics such as the ways in which Irish law addresses cybercrime, its prevalence or the manner in which the criminal justice system has responded – though with some exceptions, such as the work of Clark and Hyland (2007), O'Donnell and Milner (2007) and Kelleher and Murray (2007).

There are several reasons for this. In some cases it reflects the technical orientation of the research, as in the University College Dublin (UCD) Centre for Cybersecurity & Cybercrime Investigation, which focuses on areas such as forensic analysis. In other cases the authors explicitly or implicitly treat the issues presented by particular aspects of cybercrime – such as child abuse images – as largely homogenous across different countries (see e.g. Taylor and Quayle, 2003). Throughout the literature, there has been an influential view that cybercrime is an inherently international phenomenon, so that equally its regulation and study should presumptively take an international approach (Prins, 2006).

In light of these factors one might ask: why take a specifically Irish perspective? The answer – as with other aspects of Internet governance – is that there are important features at the domestic level which otherwise risk being overlooked. A business-friendly (and low-tax) environment has led to a cluster of Internet giants such as Google, Facebook, Microsoft and Twitter setting up regional headquarters in Dublin. Irish law and practice is particularly significant for the way in which it might regulate those firms and their users. Despite this, the Republic of Ireland is an outlier in having failed to update its cybercrime laws – the most important law in this area dates back to 1991 and is in urgent need of reform (McIntyre, 2005). Similarly, the Garda response to cybercrime has gone largely unexamined, despite significant resource and management problems which have resulted in delays of several years in examining seized computers (Garda Síochána Inspectorate, 2014).

This chapter addresses this gap in the literature by discussing current issues which are specific to the Republic of Ireland against a wider international context. The aim is to provide an introduction to the legal and regulatory framework around cybercrime, highlighting the work which has already been done as well as identifying topics which merit further research. The focus is on the substantive law and the manner in which it has been enforced – procedural issues (such as Garda powers to compel decryption of encrypted files[1]) are not considered.

The geographic scope of the chapter might call for a few words. Why focus on the Republic of Ireland when this Handbook generally takes an all-island perspective? While the constraints imposed by the word limit are a factor, the main consideration is that the substantive law in Northern Ireland largely reflects that of England and Wales and the wider United Kingdom.[2] Because of this, Northern Ireland is already well served by an extensive literature on cybercrime in the United Kingdom generally (see e.g. Edwards *et al.,* 2010). That said, there are issues relating to the policing of cybercrime in Northern Ireland which call for more examination, and the Policing Board has recently commissioned research on the prevalence of cybercrime which may provide the starting point for further work (Northern Ireland Policing Board, 2014).

Defining 'cybercrime'

What do we mean by 'cybercrime'? Is it a new type of crime which requires us to develop new concepts for understanding it or new laws to control it? There is a well-known and ongoing debate between those such as Grabosky (2001) who see computer crimes as largely a case of 'old wine in new bottles' and those who with Yar (2005) see the unique features of the online environment as giving rise to 'a new and distinctive form of criminal activity'. In some ways, however, the difference between the two sides may be more apparent than real – even those who argue against cybercrime as a new form of crime generally accept a pragmatic need for new legislation to address the particular challenges of scale, jurisdiction and evidence which it presents (Brenner, 2001).

This debate as to whether cybercrime is a distinct type of crime is in part an issue of terminology, as the term tends to be applied indiscriminately to any crime involving the use of computers. In response, Wall has developed an influential classification which identifies three generations of cybercrime (2007a, 2007b). The first generation is made up of 'traditional' or 'ordinary crimes' committed using computers – for example, where email is used to co-ordinate a kidnapping. The second generation consists of 'hybrid crimes' – traditional crimes which are given new reach, scope or impact due to the Internet. Child abuse images exemplify these crimes – while they predated the Internet, their dissemination has increased exponentially online. The third generation he terms 'true cybercrimes' – those which could not exist without the Internet. Examples include denial of service attacks and the distribution of malware. A common feature of most true cybercrimes is that they feature technology as a *target* of crime and not merely an *instrument* of crime (Casey, 2011). Applying this classification, this chapter will consider those issues presented by Wall's second and third generations of cybercrime.

Extent of cybercrime

It is exceptionally difficult to put a figure on the prevalence or cost of cybercrime. The international experience has been that the available statistics are generally fragmentary and inconsistent in the methodologies used and the Republic of Ireland is no exception (Galetsas, 2007; Anderson *et al.,* 2012; McGuire and Dowling, 2013).

At the level of the individual user, the best available sources are the Eurobarometer series of cyber security reports. These are based on surveys of the general population throughout Europe and ask to what extent the respondents have been the victims of various types of cybercrimes. The most recent, carried out in 2014, places the Republic of Ireland overall somewhat above the EU average for the extent of cybercrime (TNS Opinion & Social, 2015). For example: 40 per cent of those surveyed reported receiving phishing attacks ('emails or phone calls fraudulently asking for access to your computer, logins, etc.') compared to an EU average of 31 per cent, while 16 per cent reported their social media or email account being hacked (EU average 12 per cent); 9 per cent reported being the victim of identity theft online (EU average 7 per cent); and 7 per cent reported being the victim of ransomware ('being asked for a payment in return for getting back control of your device') against an EU average of 8 per cent.

As regards businesses, the most up-to-date sources of information are surveys carried out by security vendors who have an interest in talking up the scale of the threat (Deloitte, 2013; PwC, 2014). Consequently, while the surveys contain useful impressionistic information it is difficult to place much reliance on their wider findings. For example, one PwC survey which identified cybercrime in the Republic of Ireland as doubling between 2011 and 2014 was based on a definition which equated infection by a virus and illegal downloading of music with much more serious offences (PwC, 2014). Unfortunately, a more sophisticated survey by UCD and the Information Systems Security Association (ISSA) ran only twice – in 2006 and 2008 – before it was discontinued (O. O'Connor and Gladyshev, 2006; O. O'Connor, 2008). Nevertheless, that survey is still valuable for establishing a baseline indicating a high level of threat for Irish organisations – in the 2008 survey 25 per cent of respondents reported suffering at least one external intrusion in 2007, while 32 per cent experienced external intrusions within the previous five years.

The official sources do not take us much further. Because Irish law generally conceptualises cybercrimes as mere variants of more traditional crimes, the Irish Crime Classification System (ICCS) recognises only one distinct cybercrime – the offence of unauthorised access to data (Central Statistics Office, 2008). The most recent Garda recorded crime statistics show this as increasing from seven recorded offences in 2008 to 35 in 2012 (Central Statistics Office, 2014, p. 85). Other cybercrimes are subsumed into the more general criminal damage or dishonesty offences. For example, a prosecution of two students for defacing a political party's website shortly before the 2011 general election was charged as criminal damage and therefore would not be apparent from the statistics (Stack, 2013). A further complication is that the recorded crime statistics do not reflect reports made to other state bodies with investigation and prosecution functions – particularly the Data Protection Commissioner – and there is no statistical data available in relation to these.

There is slightly more clarity in the case of child abuse image offences. Although these statistics are not divided between online and offline crimes, in practice almost all such offences involve the Internet, and we can identify a growth in recorded offences from 46 in 2008 to 313 in 2012 (Central Statistics Office, 2014). In addition, this area was the subject of extensive empirical work by O'Donnell and Milner (2007), who have provided detailed figures for investigations and prosecutions over the period from 2000 to 2004 inclusive, including the number and nature of the images involved, profiles of the offenders and analysis of sentencing (O'Donnell and Milner, 2007). They found, for example, that the number of suspects over that period spiked from six in 2000 to 104 in 2002 following information received from a United States investigation into those purchasing access to child abuse images. Of the cases examined by O'Donnell and Milner (2007), the large majority (79 per cent) related to simple possession; 8 per cent involved distribution or production; 4 per cent involved child trafficking for sexual exploitation; and 2 per cent involved allowing a child to be used for pornography.[3]

Cybercrime figures are generally skewed by under-reporting, whether to avoid publicity, because incidents are perceived as too trivial to report, or for other reasons. Gardaí recognise that businesses prefer to avoid reporting cybercrime and have encouraged informal meetings with victims for intelligence-gathering rather than prosecution purposes (Smith, 2005). The 2006 and 2008 ISSA/UCD surveys confirmed that Irish organisations generally do not involve law enforcement – for example, where internal personnel were involved, just 18 per cent of organisations reported the matter to police, with the majority letting the matter rest following the dismissal or resignation of the employee (O. O'Connor and Gladyshev, 2006). It is therefore probable that the recorded crime statistics significantly understate the extent of offences.

There are, however, recent developments which may lead to greater reporting of cybercrime and indirectly to more reliable statistics. As we shall see later in this chapter, legislation in 2011 introduced mandatory reporting of certain types of cybercrime (broadly speaking, data breaches in the telecommunications sector, criminal damage to data and crimes of dishonesty). Failure to report is itself a crime. As organisations become more aware of this responsibility it is likely that the number of crimes recorded will increase significantly.

Policing of cybercrime

Garda Síochána

The primary responsibility for investigating cybercrime in the Republic of Ireland lies with the Computer Crimes Investigation Unit (CCIU) in the Garda Bureau of Fraud Investigation (GBFI). Cases involving child abuse images are the responsibility of the Paedophile Investigation Unit (PIU) in the National Bureau of Criminal Investigation (Garda Síochána Inspectorate, 2014). Both units have a mixed role, carrying out some complex investigations themselves and also providing support to other investigations carried out in local districts.

This split structure has been criticised, and in 2005 Eugene Gallagher, then deputy director of the GBFI, described it as leading to investigations which were 'reactive and fragmented'. Instead, Gallagher recommended that the Garda Síochána should proceed with internal proposals for a dedicated National Cyber-Crime Unit, following the UK model (Gallagher, 2005). To date, however, there has been no structural reform.

These units have had significant resource problems. Jewkes and Andrews (2005) have highlighted the demands presented by investigation of child abuse images, and in an Irish context these have been further exacerbated by limited funding. In 2014 the Garda Inspectorate reported that the PIU had only one computer set up to receive and download evidence, which could be tied up for days at a time dealing with a single case (Garda Síochána Inspectorate, 2014). That report also noted that the PIU used a paper system for managing investigations, raising the possibility that two investigators could be looking at the same suspect unbeknown to each other.

The position in the CCIU has been equally problematic. One of the main tasks of the CCIU is the forensic analysis of seized computers and mobile phones. This work has, however, grown exponentially, as the investigation of almost all serious crimes now involves the seizure and analysis of multiple computing devices (PCs, laptops and a range of smartphones and tablets). The result has been a two- to four-year delay in analysing these devices, jeopardising a number of prosecutions (Garda Síochána Inspectorate, 2014; Mooney, 2014). As of 2013, there were 25 Gardaí allocated to the CCIU and – following media attention – a further eight were promised in 2014 (Rogers, 2014). It remains to be seen whether this increase will be sufficient to eliminate the backlog.

Apart from resource problems the Garda Inspectorate has also highlighted difficulties in the way in which the CCIU and PIU interact with local investigators (Garda Síochána Inspectorate, 2014). For example, the CCIU has reported that it is struggling with unnecessary examinations of devices and would prefer that investigating Gardaí carry out preliminary checks at the point of search or seizure to assess whether a device is likely to contain any evidence. The Inspectorate has suggested that this approach should be developed by following the practice in some other jurisdictions of including computer analysts on searches or providing Gardaí with triage tools which would automate the process of carrying out initial inspections.

This suggestion is, however, somewhat unrealistic so long as local policing itself also suffers from limited access to technology and training. In 2012 it emerged that two in every five Garda stations were not networked and did not have access to the PULSE database or internal email, while the 2014 Garda Inspectorate report found that even in networked stations not all Gardaí had access to external email (Garda Síochána Inspectorate, 2014; Reilly, 2012). It is not surprising, therefore, that there has been a practice among Gardaí of using personal devices to get work done – which, quite apart from the security concerns it presents, suggests that in many cases local stations are not adequately equipped to respond to even basic types of cybercrime (Stack and Carty, 2013).

Data Protection Commissioner

The Data Protection Commissioner (DPC) is adopting an increasingly important role in policing cybercrime. While the DPC has always had a prosecution function for certain data protection breaches, until recently the DPC – in common with most Irish regulators – showed a strong preference for soft enforcement measures and the use of civil rather than criminal procedures. This began to change from 2007 onwards, when there was a policy change to move towards prosecutions for spam – unsolicited marketing text messages, telephone calls and emails (Data Protection Commissioner, 2008). More recently, the DPC has brought prosecutions in a number of serious cases involving private investigators selling on personal information wrongfully obtained from Department of Social Protection, Garda and Health Service Executive databases (McGuire, 2014; E. Edwards, 2014; Tuite and Kennedy, 2012). Although resource-intensive, the trend towards more prosecutions seems set to continue, following a government decision in 2014 to prioritise data protection by doubling funding for the DPC (McMahon, 2014).

Private policing

The focus in this chapter is on the role of the state in regulating the Internet through the use of the criminal law. But this must be seen against a context of Internet governance, where the state plays only a limited part (Riley, 2013). Wall, for example, has highlighted the range of policing functions carried out by Internet service providers, social networking sites, online marketplaces, payment providers and users themselves and has argued that the public police must develop a new understanding of their role as one node in the wider network of Internet security (Wall, 2007b). Looking at the same phenomenon, Yar (2010) has identified private policing online as posing particular threats to accountability (as private actors take on law enforcement roles without being answerable to democratic institutions) and equity (as Internet security may become a commodity to be purchased, rather than a public good). Consequently, any analysis of Internet policing would not be complete without some mention of the ways in which law-enforcement functions have been taken on by private entities.

Hotline.ie

The best known Irish instance of private policing is the system operated by the Internet Service Providers' Association of Ireland (ISPAI) which establishes a code of practice for Internet service providers (ISPs), a public website for reporting illegal content (Hotline.ie) and general public awareness programmes around staying safe online (Internet Service Providers' Association of Ireland, 2014). This was established following the 1998 Department of Justice *Report on Illegal and Harmful Use of the Internet* which recommended the establishment of a self-regulatory system and has remained essentially unchanged since (Working Group on the Illegal and Harmful Use of the Internet, 1998). The system is funded in part by industry and in part by European Union Safer Internet programmes. It works closely with Gardaí and the Department of Justice and Equality, though it has no legislative basis (Clark and Hyland, 2007). It requires Irish ISPs to remove content hosted by them which the Hotline service deems to be 'probably illegal' – that is, in violation of the criminal law – but in practice focuses on child abuse images and incitement to hatred.

Similar systems in other jurisdictions have been criticised for the way in which they involve private bodies making assessments of legality (Laidlaw, 2012). However the Hotline.ie system has mostly escaped such criticism, due largely to the pragmatic way in which the ISPAI has resisted any expansion of its remit: because it is limited to material hosted by ISPAI members and does not deal with site blocking, it does not attempt to take on a wider censorship role for Irish Internet users. Indeed, it has been argued that self-regulatory systems of this sort can promote freedom of expression by establishing consistent decision-making and enabling ISPs to resist arbitrary demands for censorship (L. Edwards, 2009).

Internet blocking

Internet blocking is one of the most controversial examples of private policing internationally, and the Irish experience is set to follow suit (Demeyer *et al.*, 2012). From 2008 onwards, Irish mobile operators have deployed blocking systems preventing access to websites alleged to host child abuse images (GSMA, 2008; GSMA Mobile Alliance Against Child Sexual Abuse Content, 2008; van Turnhout, 2013). In 2014, following pressure from the Garda Síochána and the Department of Justice, UPC became the first fixed line broadband provider to do likewise (Duncan, 2014; UPC, 2014). These blocking systems are, however, of questionable legality (Akdeniz, 2011; McIntyre, 2013). Unlike the better known case of file-sharing websites, where ISPs block access on foot of court orders, this type of blocking takes place without any prior notice, judicial involvement or legislative basis.[4]

The Garda/UPC blocking system is particularly problematic. In that system UPC have agreed to block sites designated by the Garda Síochána as containing child abuse images. The blocking appears to take place at the domain level, rather than the page or image level (e.g. blocking *all* access to example.com, not merely the particular images on example.com/users/johndoe/illegalmaterial.html), making it likely that there will be over-blocking of innocent content. The system is essentially the same as a previous Dutch model – which was abandoned in 2008 following a government study finding that it was ineffective and also contrary to the European Convention on Human Rights in lacking a statutory basis (Stol *et al.*, 2009).

For the same reason, this system would not seem to meet the requirements of Directive 2011/93/EU on combating the sexual abuse and sexual exploitation of children and child pornography. Article 25 of that Directive permits the use of blocking by member states, but subject to the requirement that any blocking measures:

[M]ust be set by transparent procedures and provide adequate safeguards, in particular to ensure that the restriction is limited to what is necessary and proportionate, and that users are informed of the reason for the restriction. Those safeguards shall also include the possibility of judicial redress.

The structural over-blocking in the Garda/UPC system and lack of any legal basis or judicial redress make it likely that it would fail this requirement unless it can be classed as merely a 'voluntary industry action', so as to fall outside the scope of the Directive.[5] In a 2013 report Senator Jillian van Turnhout – an advocate of blocking – noted these issues and recommended that a specific legal basis should be put in place for any Irish blocking system (van Turnhout, 2013). It is unfortunate that her points and the wider international experience appear to have been ignored.

Legislative framework

Irish law does not recognise a distinct concept of cybercrime and does not have any statute dedicated to computer or Internet crime. Although specific legislation has been promised many times since the Republic of Ireland signed the Council of Europe Convention on Cybercrime in 2002,[6] successive Ministers for Justice have failed to deliver. As a result, the Republic is an outlier internationally – all other EU member states bar Greece, Poland and Sweden have ratified the Convention, while in the wider common-law world both Australia and the United States have ratified the Convention, and Canada is set to do so shortly (Grigsby, 2014).

This failure to legislate is surprising given the central role of information technology in the Irish economy and is doubly so given that it has also put the Republic of Ireland in breach of its EU obligations. While the Cybercrime Convention is not binding on the Republic until it is ratified, key parts of the Convention are reflected in two European instruments – the 2005 Framework Decision on attacks against information systems[7] (which should have been transposed by March 2007) and the 2013 Directive on attacks against information systems (which should be transposed by September 2015).[8] At the time of writing, a bill to transpose the 2013 Directive and enable ratification of the Convention is expected in late 2015 – making it almost certain the state will fail to meet the September 2015 deadline also (Kehoe, 2015).

The lack of standalone legislation means that cybercrimes are for the most part conceptualised as variants of more traditional offences, with varying degrees of success. A full account of these crimes is beyond the scope of this chapter, and in any event is unnecessary given that there have been a number of pieces written on the individual offences (Clark, 1994; Clark and Hyland, 2007; Kelleher and Murray, 2007, pt. 7–8; Koops and Robinson, 2011; McIntyre, 2008, 2005; Murray, 2001; Ryan et al., 2013; Ryan and Harbison, 2010). However, it will be useful to survey the main offences to highlight the most important issues which they present. We will do so using the four-part classification of the Cybercrime Convention before going on to consider other cybercrimes falling outside the scope of the Convention (the following sections are based in part on McIntyre, 2008).

Offences against the confidentiality, integrity and availability of computer data and systems

The first category of offences required by the Cybercrime Convention are 'the core of computer-related offences … representing the basic threats … to which electronic data processing and communicating systems are exposed' (Council of Europe, 2001, para. 35). There are five types of offence under this heading: illegal access to a computer system, illegal interception of data, interference with data, system interference and misuse of devices.

In this category the Republic of Ireland has few matching offences. Most are contained in the Criminal Damage Act 1991, which, despite predating the modern Internet, is still the most important law in this area. That act was not drafted with computers in mind but was initially intended to address damage to tangible, physical property. The provisions regarding cybercrime were shoehorned in at a late stage in the drafting in a way which has caused difficulties since (McIntyre, 2005). For example, the terms 'operate' and 'computer' are not defined in the 1991 Act – leading Murray to argue that it may be unconstitutionally vague (Murray, 1995). Similarly, offences under the 1991 Act are not defined in terms of whether an individual is authorised or permitted to do something, but rather depend on whether the individual acts 'without lawful excuse', a term which is only partially defined in Section 6. This leaves it unclear whether an offence is committed if, for example, a website user does not abide by the site terms of use (Licken, 1998).

Illegal access to a computer system

Illegal access under Article 2 of the Convention is closely matched by the offence of unauthorised access under Section 5 of the Criminal Damage Act 1991 which provides:

> A person who without lawful excuse operates a computer (a) within the State with intent to access any data kept either within or outside the State, or (b) outside the State with intent to access any data kept within the State, shall, whether or not he accesses any data, be guilty of an offence.

This Section has extraterritorial effect and covers those based abroad who target Irish computers as well as purely domestic attackers. It is an attempt offence in that it criminalises those who operate a computer with intent to access any data, whether or not they succeed in doing so. It is, however, problematic.

We have already seen that the terms 'operate' and 'computer' are not defined in the Act. Similarly, it is unclear what is meant by 'lawful excuse' in this context. Does it refer to entitlement to operate the computer, to access the data, or to both? The partial definition of 'lawful excuse' in Section 6 asks whether there is consent to 'accessing of the data concerned' – not merely whether *operation of the computer* is with consent. This appears to say that a person is guilty of an offence if they use their own computer to view a file which, as a matter of civil law, they are not entitled to view. If so, this might mean that a journalist would be guilty of unauthorised access by opening a file emailed to them by a whistle-blower (Kelleher and Murray, 2007).

A practical issue is that the offence is summary only and carries a maximum term of imprisonment of three months. As a result, many investigative powers (which generally apply only to serious offences) will not be available and any proceedings must be commenced within six months from the date of the offence (Kelleher and Murray, 2007). It will be difficult for prosecutors to finalise charges in this complex area in that time, particularly given the resource constraints outlined in this chapter.

Illegal interception of data

Irish law does not have a direct counterpart to the offence of illegal interception of data under Article 3 of the Convention. The closest offence is interception of telecommunications contrary to Section 98 of the Postal Telecommunications Services Act 1983 (Hall, 1993). This prohibits interception or disclosure of telecommunications messages being transmitted by 'authorised undertakings', meaning those public telecoms operators who are required to be authorised by ComReg (including, for example, all landline and mobile operators).

This is much narrower than the Convention offence and will not apply to communications being transmitted by an entity which is not an 'authorised undertaking'. For example, a webmail provider such as Gmail would not be covered, nor a university in providing Internet access to staff and students, nor a social networking site in respect of private messages between its members. In those situations, if a person were to read users' messages no offence would be committed under Section 98 – leaving many communications unprotected by the law (Kelleher, 2006, p. 454).

The reference in Section 98 to messages 'being transmitted' also presents problems. This appears to suggest that only messages in transit are covered: stored messages, such as voicemail messages which have been listened to but left on the server, may not be protected by the Section.[9] If so, this presents some difficult questions of interpretation. For example, is an email 'being transmitted' until such time as it is read by the recipient (Kelleher, 2006)? To date there appears to have been only one prosecution under Section 98 – a District Court case involving a civil servant who was found guilty of listening to voicemails left on the mobile phone of her former supervisor (Tuite, 2013). That case did not, however, address the 'being transmitted' issue, leaving us without any guidance on this point.

Data interference

The Article 4 Convention offence of interference with data is roughly matched by criminal damage to data under Section 2 of the 1991 Act. Section 2 is not specific to computers but is a general offence committed by a person who without lawful excuse damages 'any property' either intentionally or recklessly. It is extended to computers by the very wide definition of 'property' in Section 1 to include data[10] as well as tangible property. 'Damage' to data is then defined to include any 'addition, alteration, corruption, erasure or movement' of that data.

This is an expansive offence: unlike criminal damage to tangible property (which requires some adverse effect) criminal damage to data will include any modification of any information stored on a computer whether or not it causes any interference with the system. Because of this it can potentially be used against a wide range of conduct. In one of the very few cases on this issue a man was convicted of criminal damage to his ex-girlfriend's Facebook page and fined €2,000 after he used her phone to log into her account and post a status update in her name saying that she was a 'whore' – the fine reflecting the reputational harm rather than any monetary or proprietary damage (Barrett and Mishkin, 2014).

System interference

Article 5 of the Convention requires states to establish offences relating to the 'serious hindering without right of the functioning of a computer system'. This addresses denial of service attacks, which aim to prevent users from accessing a particular website or service, usually by flooding servers with traffic in a way which prevents them from functioning by using up bandwidth, processing power or storage capacity. The most common variant is the distributed denial of service attack, which uses a large number of compromised computers as the springboard for the attack (Burden and Palmer, 2003; Houle and Weaver, 2001).

There is no direct counterpart to Article 5 in Irish law, meaning that any denial of service attack could only be prosecuted indirectly. For example, suppose that A sets out to hinder communications with B by sending several million emails to B. The effect is not only to use up B's bandwidth but also to use up his storage capacity. In this case, it might be possible to charge A with criminal damage under Section 2 of the Criminal Damage Act 1991, on the basis that A has damaged B's data within the meaning of Section 1 by adding to it without lawful excuse.[11] It is, however, undesirable to rely on this roundabout way of prosecuting, as slight variations in the structure of attacks may mean that there is no appropriate offence to charge.

Misuse of devices

Article 6 of the Cybercrime Convention requires states to establish secondary offences relating to the production, sale, possession, distribution, etc. of 'hacking tools' and passwords or access codes. This aims to reduce cybercrime by limiting the availability of these tools on the 'black market', supposedly making it more difficult for attacks to be carried out (Council of Europe, 2001).

This is an extremely controversial provision, often criticised as based on a simplistic belief that it is possible to categorise software as inherently good or evil. Instead, as Sommer notes, 'the difficulty is that many hacking tools are indistinguishable from utilities that are essential for the maintenance and security of computers and networks' (Sommer, 2006, p. 68). Consequently, there is concern that poorly drafted 'hacking tool' laws may criminalise the work of researchers and other professionals in information security (McEwan, 2008).

While Irish law does not specifically deal with 'hacking tools' and passwords, it may be possible to prosecute in individual cases using Section 4 of the Criminal Damage Act 1991. That Section provides:

> A person (in this Section referred to as the possessor) who has any thing in his custody or under his control intending without lawful excuse to use it or cause or permit another to use it ... to damage any property belonging to some other person ... shall be guilty of an offence.

Bearing in mind that the definition of property under the 1991 Act includes data, this Section may be wide enough to criminalise possession of software which is intended to damage data.[12] But note that this Section does not criminalise creation, possession, sale or distribution *per se* – in every case it must be shown that the defendant had an intention to use the item to damage data (or to allow another person to do so). This creates two related problems for prosecutors. From an evidential point of view, they will face a difficulty in demonstrating that an accused person had the necessary intention. Moreover, the intention which must be shown is an intention to damage property – a mere intention to carry out an unauthorised access would not suffice. If, for example, A were found to be in possession of a username and password belonging to B, this would not be an offence under Section 4 if A's intention was merely to view B's data.

Computer-related offences

Computer-related forgery

The first 'computer-related' offence provided for by the Convention is computer-related forgery.[13] The Explanatory Report to the Cybercrime Convention summarises this as 'creating a parallel offence to the forgery of tangible documents' to fill 'gaps in criminal law related to traditional forgery, which requires visual readability of statements, or declarations embodied in a document and which does not apply to electronically stored data' (Council of Europe, 2001, para. 81). It is largely addressed in Irish law by forgery under Section 25 of the Criminal Justice (Theft and Fraud Offences) Act 2001, which provides:

> A person is guilty of forgery if he or she makes a false instrument with the intention that it shall be used to induce another person to accept it as genuine and, by reason of so accepting it, to do some act, or to make some omission, to the prejudice of that person or any other person.

The 2001 Act was drafted with computer crime in mind, and consequently Section 24 defines 'instrument' in a way which is intended to be technology-neutral as including any 'disk, tape, sound track or other device on or in which information is recorded or stored by mechanical, electronic or other means'. Similarly, Section 31(3) deals with the requirement that a person be deceived by providing that inducing a person to accept an item as genuine will include 'inducing a machine to respond to the instrument ... as if it were a genuine instrument'.

Computer-related fraud

The offence of computer-related fraud under Article 8 of the Convention roughly corresponds to the offence of dishonest use of a computer under Section 9 of the Criminal Justice (Theft and Fraud Offences) Act 2001, which provides:

> A person who dishonestly, whether within or outside the State, operates or causes to be operated a computer within the State with the intention of making a gain for himself or herself or another, or of causing loss to another, is guilty of an offence.

On the face of it, this appears to be a very far-reaching provision which would cover most situations where 'a person lawfully has a computer but uses it for a dishonest purpose'.[14] However, ambiguous drafting means that, when examined more closely, the offence may be narrower. The offence is committed only where a person dishonestly operates a computer. Dishonesty is defined in Section 2 to mean 'without a claim of right made in good faith'. Consequently (while the Section is not entirely clear) it appears to apply only where a person operates a computer without a claim of right made in good faith – that is, without authorisation. If, for example, A uses his own computer to print a forged cheque, this would be a 'dishonest use of a computer' in a colloquial sense but would not be operation of a computer without a claim of right as required by this offence.

Content-related offences

Article 9 of the Cybercrime Convention requires states to establish offences relating to the producing, making available, distributing, procuring and possession of child pornography through computer systems. These are largely already covered by the Child Trafficking and Pornography Act 1998. That act was generally viewed as forward looking for its time – for example, in providing technology-neutral definitions of offences and avoiding subjective terms such as 'obscene', 'indecent' and 'offensive' – and has largely been unproblematic in practice (Clark and Hyland, 2007; O'Donnell and Milner, 2007).

That said, a number of changes are needed to take account of new trends in offending – for example, a shift away from downloading and possession of images and towards streaming video and even live footage of children being abused. These changes have been addressed at international level by the Council of Europe Convention on Protection of Children against Sexual Exploitation and Sexual Abuse[15] and by Directive 2011/93/EU on combating the sexual abuse and sexual exploitation of children and child pornography. In 2014 the Department of Justice published a general scheme of a Sexual Offences Bill which will implement the Directive and enable the Convention to be ratified. This will, for example, extend the 1998 Act to criminalise 'obtaining access to child pornography', making it an offence to watch a streaming video as well as to possess such a video (Department of Justice and Equality, 2014).

Offences related to infringements of copyright and related rights

Article 10 of the Cybercrime Convention requires states to criminalise certain infringements of copyright and related rights where these are committed 'wilfully, on a commercial scale and by means of a computer system'. This is done in the Republic of Ireland by Section 140 of the Copyright and Related Rights Act 2000, which predates the Convention and criminalises the making for sale, selling, making available in the course of a business, etc., of infringing copies of works (Clark *et al.*, 2010: 417–421). This Section has most commonly been used to prosecute tangible infringements – pirated copies of DVDs and CDs for example – and there does not appear to be any reported case of it being used in the Republic of Ireland to prosecute copyright infringement online.

Other offences

One limitation of the Cybercrime Convention is that it is primarily focused on crimes against property and crimes of dishonesty. Apart from child abuse images it does not specifically address crimes against the individual. However, two such cybercrimes are particularly topical and should be mentioned also – disclosure of personal data and online harassment.

Disclosure of personal data

There is a widespread problem in the Republic of Ireland, where individuals in large organisations – including state bodies such as Revenue, the Garda Síochána and the Department of Social Protection – abuse their access to databases of sensitive personal information (Kennedy, 2011, 2012; Tighe, 2011; Brady, 2014; N. O'Connor, 2014). In addition to simple snooping, this has included passing on information to private investigators and others. Historically, these cases have not generally been dealt with using the criminal law, but, as we have already seen, the DPC has begun to prosecute a number of cases involving private investigators.

The most important offence in these cases is Section 22 of the Data Protection Acts 1988 and 2003, which provides that a person is guilty of an offence if they (a) obtain access to personal data without the authority of the data controller or data processor by whom it is kept, and (b) disclose that data to another person. This will include obtaining data by 'blagging' or 'pretexting' – that is, extracting information by pretending to be a person with a legitimate need for the information.

However the limitations of that offence must be noted. First, it applies to outsiders only – subsection (2) excludes 'a person who is an employee or agent of the data controller or data processor concerned'. It does not address insiders who snoop, though it is possible that they might be guilty of unauthorised access by doing so. Second, it requires onward disclosure of the information. It is not an offence under Section 22 to obtain personal data if it is not then passed on to a third party.[16] Finally, and perhaps most importantly, the sanctions may not be adequate to deter what has become a very lucrative business. Section 22 does not carry a custodial sentence and as a practical matter will almost always be prosecuted in the District Court where fines will be relatively low – indeed, in a number of cases the Probation Act has been applied (Brennan, 2011; E. Edwards, 2014; McGuire, 2014; Tuite and Kennedy, 2012). The introduction of custodial sentences for the equivalent offence has been recommended in the United Kingdom and could be considered here also, even if only at the summary level (Society for Computers and Law, 2012).

Harassment and cyberbullying

Online harassment or 'cyberbullying' has become more common in recent years with the growth in social media, and there has been particular concern about its prevalence amongst children (O'Neill *et al.*, 2011; O'Neill and Dinh, 2013). It has been an emotive and high-profile issue in the Republic of Ireland since late 2012, when the suicides of two teenage girls were linked to comments made about them on social media. Since then we have seen the issue considered by the Oireachtas Joint Committee on Transport and Communications (2013), the Special Rapporteur on Child Protection (2013), the Internet Content Governance Advisory Group (2014) and most recently the Law Reform Commission (2014).

In each of these contexts largely the same questions are being asked. To what extent should the law criminalise crude or offensive speech online? Should the law differentiate between messages directed *to* a person and messages *about* a person? Is the criminal law an appropriate response to misbehaviour by children themselves? Are civil law remedies adequate to protect against harassment and to respond to invasions of privacy? How should the law deal with so-called 'revenge pornography', or as it is more accurately termed 'non-consensual distribution of private sexual images' (McGlynn and Rackley, 2014)? What procedures should be in place to identify individuals who post messages anonymously or pseudonymously? Is this an area best addressed by legal controls, technological measures such as user blocking and/or private policing by social media firms?

Without entering into the current debate in detail, we should note that the criminal offence currently most often used to prosecute cyberbullying is Section 10 of the Non-Fatal Offences Against the Person Act 1997. This creates an offence of harassment and prohibits the harassment of a person 'by any means' by 'persistently following, watching, pestering, besetting or communicating with him or her'. The reference to communication 'by any means' is technology-neutral and permits prosecutions to be brought where the harassment takes place electronically. While the crime statistics do not break out cases of online harassment, a search of newspaper archives reveals many cases where defendants have been convicted of harassment by email, text messages, tweets and even indirectly by posting fake posts in the name of the victim (Cunningham, 2010; Fallon, 2014; Magee and Ferguson, 2014). While there have been some claims that the substantive law is inadequate to address online harassment, these are belied by the number of successful prosecutions which have been brought. Instead, it seems more likely that the main obstacle may be a lack of resources to pursue these cases.

That said, there is nevertheless a possible issue with this offence in the requirement that the harassment be 'persistent'. While this is important in setting a threshold of seriousness, it may mean that some grave harms escape its scope. Consider, for example, a once-off public posting of private sexual images. This would not meet the persistence requirement, notwithstanding that it would be experienced as extremely humiliating and demeaning. There is a good case for a separate crime to deal with this type of exposure of private material, as in the new English offence of disclosing private sexual photographs and films with intent to cause distress.[17]

Mandatory reporting of cybercrime

A significant and distinctive aspect of Irish law is the way in which it increasingly provides for mandatory reporting of crimes. Although the common law offence of misprision of felony (failing to report a felony) was repealed in 1997,[18] it has since been largely replaced with specific statutory duties to report serious offences against the person or property,[19] offences against children and other vulnerable persons[20] and, most importantly for our purposes, the majority of crimes of dishonesty and cybercrimes.[21]

The duty to report cybercrimes is contained in Section 19 of the Criminal Justice Act 2011, which was adopted following the Irish banking crisis. It creates a criminal offence where a person fails to volunteer information to police, as follows:

> A person shall be guilty of an offence if he or she has information which he or she knows or believes might be of material assistance in—
> (a) preventing the commission by any other person of a relevant offence, or
> (b) securing the apprehension, prosecution or conviction of any other person for a relevant offence,
> and fails without reasonable excuse to disclose that information as soon as it is practicable to do so to a member of the Garda Síochána.

What crimes must be reported? The duty relates to 'relevant offences', a term defined exceptionally widely to include approximately 130 crimes.[22] These range from insider dealing and market manipulation offences to simple theft. Although the expressed aim of the 2011 Act was to deal with complex white-collar crime, this provision goes significantly further and includes essentially all crimes of dishonesty. Crucially, Schedule 2 specifically includes dishonest use of a computer[23] and criminal damage to data[24] in its scope.

The effect of the 2011 Act is that mandatory reporting will now apply to almost all cybercrimes involving dishonesty or cybercrimes where the computer is a target (apart from simple unauthorised access or disclosure of data). For example, fraud by an employee using a computer system, 419 fraud emails, phishing emails and the use of trojans, ransomware or other malware will all constitute one or other relevant offences.

This creates a remarkably invasive though often underappreciated duty. It applies to 'all persons' – unlike other reporting obligations, which may be limited to certain professions or positions – and applies to the victims of cybercrime themselves. It is prospective as well as retrospective – it applies to information which might prevent the commission of future offences as well as information which might assist in prosecuting past offences. It applies to information which 'might' be of material assistance, not merely information of clear importance. It is not limited to responding to questioning but creates an affirmative obligation to volunteer information to a Garda 'as soon as is practicable'. It also leaves undefined what might constitute a 'reasonable excuse' for failure to provide information.

The constitutionality of this provision has been questioned by McDowell (2011), but so long as it remains in force it will have a significant effect in the area of cybercrime. At a practical level it has led to a large number of reports being made to Gardaí on a precautionary basis, leading to complaints that the Garda Bureau of Fraud Investigation has been 'swamped' with information which it cannot use (McDonald, 2014).

It also has significant implications for criminological and information security research in this area, where it is now unclear when researchers must volunteer information to Gardaí and to what extent assurances of confidentiality might be given to subjects. In light of the 2011 Act, it is questionable whether, for example, researchers based in this jurisdiction could replicate the ethnographic work carried out by Coleman (2014), who studied the Anonymous movement through close and frequent contact with its members. By talking to those who have committed or might commit cybercrimes, researchers in many cases will place themselves in a position of having information which 'might be of material assistance' to Gardaí with no certainty as to whether they have a 'reasonable excuse' for failing to report that information. There is every possibility that this provision will make the Irish Internet less rather than more secure, by acting as a deterrent to research into cybercrime.

Duty to report data breaches

A separate duty to report should also be mentioned. There is an international trend in the area of data protection law to require that individuals and regulators should be notified of security breaches affecting personal data. In the European Union this is now mandatory in the case of breaches in the telecommunications sector, and if the current proposed Data Protection Regulation is adopted it will be extended to data breaches in other industries also (Burdon *et al.*, 2012; Wong, 2013, chap. 6). This is not a duty to report crime *per se* – it applies equally to simple carelessness resulting in the loss of personal data – but it will nevertheless apply to many types of cybercrime where user information is put at risk.

Conclusion

The aim of this chapter has been to provide a brief survey of the key aspects of cybercrime in the Republic of Ireland. At the level of the substantive law, the overall picture is one of a confused statutory landscape, in which many of the substantive offences are essentially *ad hoc*, tacked on to unrelated legislation and lacking consistency with each other. This is exacerbated by the small number of prosecutions brought and an almost complete lack of reported judgments. In many cases newspaper reports of cases are the only materials available to assess how the offences have been interpreted in practice, and there is still a level of ambiguity as to basic elements of the offences. The forthcoming legislation to implement the Directive on attacks against Information Systems and to enable ratification of the Cybercrime Convention represents a rare opportunity to bring coherence to this area, and it is disappointing that it has not been the subject of any public consultation.

Looking at the wider context, there is a clear need for more research into the prevalence of cybercrime in the Republic of Ireland. The Police Service of Northern Ireland now provides separate statistics for crimes which were committed in whole or in part through a computer or computer network, and it would be desirable for the Garda Síochána to follow this lead (Young, 2014). As regards the policing of cybercrime, more work needs to be done on the way in which the Garda investigates cybercrime and the division of responsibilities between the CCIU/PIU and local investigations. While some reform of the law is undoubtedly necessary, the 2014 Garda Inspectorate report suggests that the most pressing need is for more resources rather than more laws.

References

Akdeniz, Y. (2011) *Freedom of Expression on the Internet: Study of legal provisions and practices related to freedom of expression, the free flow of information and media pluralism on the Internet in OSCE participating States.* Organisation for Security and Cooperation in Europe.

Anderson, R., Barton, C., Bohme, R., Clayton, R., van Eeten, M.J., Levi, M., Moore, T. and Savage, S. (2012) 'Measuring the Cost of Cybercrime'. Presented at the Workshop on the Economics of Information Security, Berlin.

Barrett, C., Mishkin, S. (2014) 'Ex-boyfriend fined €2,000 for Facebook "frape"'. *Financial Times.*

Brady, T. (2014) 'Gardai checked private files on model more than 80 times'. *Irish Independent.*

Brennan, D. (2011) 'Insurer's private eye admits tax data breach'. *Irish Independent.*

Brenner, S.W. (2001) 'Is There Such a Thing as "Virtual Crime"?', *Berkeley Journal of Criminal Law*, 4: 3.

Burden, K., Palmer, C. (2003) 'Internet crime: Cyber crime – A new breed of criminal?' *Computer Law and Security Report*, 19: 222.

Burdon, M., Lane, B. and von Nessen, P. (2012) 'Data breach notification law in the EU and Australia – Where to now?', *Computer Law & Security Review*, 28: 296–307.

Casey, E. (2011) *Digital Evidence and Computer Crime: Forensic Science, Computers, and the Internet*, 3rd ed. Waltham, MA: Academic Press.

Central Statistics Office (2008) *Irish Crime Classification System.* Dublin.

—— (2014) *Garda Recorded Crime Statistics.* Dublin.

Clark, R. (1994) 'Computer Related Crime in Ireland', *Eur. J. Crime Crim. L. & Crim Just.*, 2: 252.

Clark, R. and Hyland, M. (2007) *The Criminalisation of Child Pornography in Irish Law: A report to the department of justice, equality and law reform.* Dublin: School of Law, University College Dublin.

Clark, R., Smyth, S. and Hall, N. (2010) *Intellectual Property Law in Ireland*, 3rd ed. Dublin: Bloomsbury Professional.

Coleman, G. (2014) *Hacker, Hoaxer, Whistleblower, Spy: The Many Faces of Anonymous.* London: Verso Books.

Conway, M. (2006) 'Terrorism and the Internet: New Media – New Threat?' *Parliamentary Affairs*, 59: 283–298.

Council of Europe (2001) 'Explanatory Report to the Convention on Cybercrime' (*ETS No. 185*) Available at: http://conventions.coe.int/Treaty/EN/Reports/Html/185.htm (accessed 27 January 2015).

Cunningham, G. (2010) 'Dad is guilty of hounding professor in emails blitz'. *Evening Herald.*

Data Protection Commissioner (2008) *Annual Report 2007.* Dublin.

Deloitte (2013) *Irish Information Security and Cybercrime Survey 2013.* Dublin: Deloitte.

Demeyer, K., Lievens, E. and Dumortier, J. (2012) 'Blocking and Removing Illegal Child Sexual Content: Analysis from a Technical and Legal Perspective'. *Policy & Internet*, 4:1.

Department of Justice and Equality (2014) *Heads of Criminal Law (Sexual Offences) Bill 2014.* Available at: URL http://www.justice.ie/en/JELR/Pages/PR14000349 (accessed 28 January 2015).

Duncan, P. (2014) 'Garda and UPC agreement will restrict access to sites with child porn images'. *Irish Times.*

Edwards, E. (2014) 'Private investigator fined €5,000 for accessing Garda data'. *Irish Times.* Available at: URL http://www.irishtimes.com/news/crime-and-law/private-investigator-fined-5-000-for-accessing-garda-data-1.2012999 (Accessed 24 November 2014).

Edwards, L. (2009) 'Pornography, Censorship and the Internet', in L. Edwards and C. Waelde (eds) *Law and the Internet.* Oxford: Hart Publishing.

Edwards, L., Rauhofer, J. and Yar, M. (2010) 'Recent developments in UK cybercrime law', in Y. Jewkes and M. Yar (eds) *Handbook of Internet Crime.* Cullompton: Willan: 413–436.

Fallon, J. (2014) 'Man who posted "vile messages" to ex-girlfriend avoids jail'. *Irish Examiner.*

Galetsas, A. (2007) *Statistical data on network security.* Brussels: European Commission.

Gallagher, E. (2005) 'The State's response to the threats posed by cyber-crime – is it adequate or ineffectual?' *Communique: Management Journal of an Garda Síochána, 20.*

Garda Síochána Inspectorate (2014) *Crime Investigation.* Dublin.

Grabosky, P N (2001) 'Virtual Criminality: Old Wine in New Bottles?' *Social & Legal Studies* 10: 243–249.

Grigsby, A. (2014) 'Coming Soon: Another Country to Ratify the Budapest Convention'. *Council on Foreign Relations – Net Politics.*

GSMA (2008) 'GSMA Launches Mobile Alliance Against Child Sexual Abuse'. *GSM World.* Available at: URL http://www.gsmworld.com/newsroom/press-releases/2008/775.htm (accessed 18 March 2010).

GSMA Mobile Alliance Against Child Sexual Abuse Content (2008) 'Implementation of Filtering of Child Sexual Abuse Images in Operator Networks', November 2008. Available at: www.gsmworld.com/documents/GSMA_Child_Tech_Doc.pdf.

Hall, E. (1993) *The Electronic Age: Telecommunications in Ireland.* Dublin: Oak Tree Press.

Houle, K. and Weaver, G. (2001) *Trends in Denial of Service Attack Technology.* Pittsburgh: CERT Coordination Center.

Internet Content Governance Advisory Group (2014) *Report of the Internet Content Governance Advisory Group*. Dublin: Department of Communications, Energy and Natural Resources.

Internet Service Providers' Association of Ireland (2014) *Hotline.ie Annual Report 2013*. Dublin.

Jewkes, Y. and Andrews, C. (2005) 'Policing the filth: The problems of investigating online child pornography in England and Wales', *Policing & Society*, 15: 42.

Joint Committee on Transport and Communications (2013) *Addressing the Growth of Social Media and Tackling Cyberbullying*. Dublin: Houses of the Oireachtas.

Kehoe, P. (2015) 'Government Legislation Programme Spring/Summer 2015'. *Department of the Taoiseach*. Available at: URL http://www.taoiseach.gov.ie/eng/Taoiseach_and_Government/Government_Legislation_Programme/Government_Legislative_Programme_Spring_Summer_2015.pdf (accessed 25 January 2015).

Kelleher, D. (2006) *Privacy and Data Protection Law in Ireland*. Dublin: Tottel.

Kelleher, D. and Murray, K. (2007) *Information Technology Law in Ireland*, 2nd ed. Dublin: Tottel.

Kennedy, E. (2011) 'Gardai probe Revenue officials over tax scam'. *Irish Independent*.

——— (2012) 'Snooping civil servants who gave out personal data keep their jobs'. *Irish Independent*.

Kirwan, G. and Power, A. (2011) 'Hacking: Legal and Ethical Aspects of an Ambiguous Activity', in A. Dudley, J. Braman and G. Vincenti (eds) *Investigating Cyber Law and Cyber Ethics: Issues, Impacts and Practices*. Hershey, PA : Information Science Reference.

——— (2013) *Cybercrime: The Psychology of Online Offenders*. Cambridge: Cambridge University Press.

Koops, B. J. and Robinson, T. (2011) 'Cybercrime law', in E. Casey (ed), *Digital Evidence and Computer Crime*. Waltham, MA: Academic Press.

Laidlaw, E. (2012) 'The responsibilities of free speech regulators: an analysis of the Internet Watch Foundation', *International Journal of Law and Information Technology*, 20(4): 312.

Law Reform Commission (2014) *Issues paper on 'Cyber-crime affecting personal safety, privacy and reputation including cyber-bullying'*. Dublin: Law Reform Commission.

Licken, E. (1998) 'Case prompts fears over Web use'. *Irish Times*.

Magee, J. and Ferguson, F. (2014) 'Woman in custody after harassing wife of former colleague'. *Independent.ie*. Available at: URL http://www.independent.ie/irish-news/courts/woman-in-custody-after-harrassing-wife-of-former-colleague-30422355.html (accessed 15 July 2014).

McDonald, D. (2014) 'There's never been a better time for white-collar crime, warns lawyer'. *Irish Independent*.

McDowell, M. (2011) 'Law means we are all informers'. *Irish Independent*.

McEwan, N. (2008) 'The Computer Misuse Act 1990: lessons from its past and predictions for its future'. *Criminal Law Review*, 955.

McGlynn, C. and Rackley, E. (2014) *Revenge Pornography Briefing*. Durham: Durham University Law School.

McGuire, E. (2014) 'Private investigators admit "blagging" credit union data'. *The Irish Times*.

McGuire, M. and Dowling, S. (2013) *Cyber crime: a review of the evidence (No. 75)*. London: Home Office.

McIntyre, T.J. (2005) 'Computer Crime in Ireland: A critical assessment of the substantive law' *Irish Criminal Law Journal*, 15(1).

——— (2008) 'Cybercrime in Ireland', in P.C. Reich (ed), *Cybercrime and Security*. Oxford: Oxford University Press.

——— (2013) 'Child Abuse Images and Cleanfeeds: Assessing Internet Blocking Systems', in I. Brown (ed), *Research Handbook on Governance of the Internet*. Cheltenham: Edward Elgar.

McMahon, A. (2014) 'Data protection gets funding doubled'. *Irish Times*.

Mooney, J. (2014) 'Garda computer backlog leads to three-year delay in child porn cases'. *The Sunday Times*.

Murray, K. (1995) 'Computer Misuse Law in Ireland'. *Irish Law Times*, 13: 114.

——— (2001) 'The Criminal Justice (Theft and Fraud Offences) Bill 2000 and the Internet'. *Irish Law Times*, 19: 143.

Northern Ireland Policing Board (2014) *Public Confidence in the Policing of Cybercrime*. Belfast: Millward Brown Ulster.

O'Connor, N. (2014) 'Probe into civil servant who snooped on dozens of women for "curiosity"'. *Irish Independent*.

O'Connor, O. (2008) *2nd ISSA / UCD Irish Cybercrime Survey*. Dublin: University College Dublin.

O'Connor, O. and Gladyshev, P. (2006) *ISSA / UCD Irish Cybercrime Survey*. Dublin: University College Dublin.

O'Donnell, I. and Milner, C. (2007) *Child Pornography: Crime, Computers and Society*. Cullompton: Willan.

O'Neill, B. and Dinh, T. (2013) 'Cyberbullying among 9–16 year olds in Ireland (No. 5)', *Digital Childhoods Working Paper Series*. Dublin: Dublin Institute of Technology.

O'Neill, B., Grehan, S. and Ólafsson, K. (2011) *Risks and Safety for Children on the Internet: the Ireland Report.* London: LSE.

Prins, C. (2006) 'Should ICT Regulation Be Undertaken at an International Level?', in B. J. Koops, M. Lips, C. Prins and M. Schellekens (eds) *Starting Points for ICT Regulation: Deconstructing Prevalent Policy One-Liners, Information Technology and Law.* The Hague: T.M.C. Asser Press.

PwC (2014) *Economic Crime: A Persisting Threat in Ireland.* Dublin: PricewaterhouseCoopers.

Reilly, G. (2012) 'Two out of five Garda stations don't have email access'. *TheJournal.ie.* Available at: URL http://www.thejournal.ie/two-out-of-five-garda-stations-dont-have-email-access-353291-Feb2012/ (accessed 25 January 2015).

Riley, M.C. (2013) 'Anarchy, State, or Utopia?: Checks and Balances in Internet Governance', *IEEE Internet Computing,* 17: 10–17. doi:10.1109/MIC.2013.24

Rogers, S. (2014) 'Garda child porn forensics unit to get extra staff'. *Irish Examiner.*

Ryan, P. and Harbison, A. (2010) 'The law on computer fraud in Ireland – development of the law and dishonesty'. *Computers and Law.*

Ryan, P., O'Brien, C. and Harbison, A. (2013) 'Cybercrime in Ireland – Recent Legislative Developments'. *Computers and Law.*

Smith, G. (2005) 'Cybercrime victims urged to enlist police help'. *SiliconRepublic.com. Available at:* http://www.siliconrepublic.com/enterprise/item/4333-cybercrime-victims-urged-to (accessed 17 January 2015).

Society for Computers and Law (2012) 'Blagging Convictions: Comments from the ICO'. *Computers and Law.* Available at: http://www.scl.org/site.aspx?i=ne25223 (accessed 29 January 2015).

Sommer, P. (2006) 'Criminalising hacking tools'. *Digital Investigation,* 3: 68–72.

Special Rapporteur on Child Protection (2013) *Sixth Report.* Dublin: Department of Children and Youth Affairs.

Stack, S. (2013) 'Students who hacked the Fine Gael website hand over €5,000 each'. *Irish Independent.*

Stack, S. and Carty, E. (2013) 'Gardaí picket closed-door talks over public-sector pay'. *Irish Independent.*

Stol, W., Kaspersen, R., Kerstens, J., Leukfeldt, R. and Lodder, A. (2009) 'Governmental filtering of websites: The Dutch case'. *Computer Law & Security Review,* 25: 251.

Taylor, M. and Quayle, E. (2003) *Child Pornography: An Internet Crime.* Hove: Brunner-Routledge.

—— (2008) 'Criminogenic qualities of the Internet in the collection and distribution of abuse images of children', *Irish Journal of Psychology,* 29: 119.

Tighe, M. (2011) 'Garda accused of bugging her ex-boyfriend'. *The Sunday Times.*

TNS Opinion & Social (2015) *Eurobarometer 423: Cyber Security.* Brussels: European Commission.

Tuite, T. (2013) 'Civil servant who hacked boss's phone walks free'. *Irish Independent.* Available at: http://www.independent.ie/irish-news/courts/civil-servant-who-hacked-bosss-phone-walks-free-29294982.html (accessed 17 July 2014).

Tuite, T. and Kennedy, E. (2012) 'Data leak insurers escape criminal conviction'. *Irish Independent.*

UPC (2014) *Press Release: UPC first major ISP to introduce safeguard measures for child sexual abuse material.* Available at: http://www.upc.ie/pdf/pressrelease/safeguard-measures.pdf (accessed 24 January 2015).

van Turnhout, J. (2013) Online Child Abuse Material: Effective Strategies to Tackle Online Child Abuse Material. Available at: http://www.jillianvanturnhout.ie/online-cam/

Wall, D. (2007a) *Cybercrime: The Transformation of Crime in the Information Age.* Cambridge: Polity Press.

—— (2007b) 'Policing Cybercrimes: Situating the Public Police in Networks of Security within Cyberspace', *Police Practice and Research,* 8(2): 183–205.

Wong, R. (2013) *Data Security Breaches and Privacy in Europe.* London: Springer.

Working Group on the Illegal and Harmful Use of the Internet (1998) *Illegal and Harmful Use of the Internet: First Report of the Working Group.* Dublin: The Stationery Office.

Yar, M. (2005) 'The Novelty of "Cybercrime": An Assessment in Light of Routine Activity Theory'. *European Journal of Criminology,* 2: 407–427.

—— (2010) 'The private policing of Internet crime', in Y. Jewkes and M. Yar (eds) *Handbook of Internet Crime.* Cullompton: Willan.

Young, D. (2014) 'Police's "pop-up shop" to advise public over online crime threat'. *Belfast Telegraph.*

Notes

1 See, e.g., Sections 48 and 52 of the Criminal Justice (Theft and Fraud Offences) Act 2001.
2 Although Northern Ireland is a separate jurisdiction with devolved powers in relation to policing and

criminal justice, those powers only came into effect in April 2010 with the adoption of the Northern Ireland Act 1998 (Devolution of Policing and Justice Functions) Order 2010. Most laws relating to cybercrime were adopted in Westminster before that date, and the law in Northern Ireland has yet to diverge significantly.

3 Numbers do not sum to 100 per cent, as some respondents did not specify the offence involved.

4 Compare *EMI v UPC* [2013] IEHC 274, in which the High Court ordered a number of ISPs to block access to The Pirate Bay – but only on the basis of a statutory provision allowing this to be done.

5 Recital 47 provides an ambiguous carve-out from Article 25: 'The measures undertaken by Member States in accordance with this Directive in order to remove or, where appropriate, block websites containing child pornography could be based on various types of public action, such as legislative, non-legislative, judicial or other. In that context, this Directive is without prejudice to voluntary action taken by the Internet industry to prevent the misuse of its services or to any support for such action by Member States'.

6 CETS No. 185.

7 Council Framework Decision 2005/222/JHA of 24 February 2005 on attacks against information systems.

8 Directive 2013/40/EU of the European Parliament and of the Council of 12 August 2013 on attacks against information systems and replacing Council Framework Decision 2005/222/JHA.

9 Compare *Edmonson, Weatherup, Brooks, Coulson & Kuttner v R* [2013] EWCA Crim 1026, holding that 'phone hacking' of stored voicemails was within the scope of the (differently worded) UK Regulation of Investigatory Powers Act 2000.

10 Defined as 'information in a form in which it can be accessed by means of a computer'.

11 Compare the English decision in *DPP v Lennon* [2006] EWHC 1201, holding that, while a public email address carries an implied consent to receive emails, this does not extend to emails which are deliberately sent to disrupt a system.

12 Assuming that 'thing' is wide enough to cover software as well as tangible items.

13 Article 7.

14 See the comments of the Minister for Justice at 168 *Seanad Debates* Col. 1130.

15 CETS no. 201.

16 Compare Section 55(1) of the UK Data Protection Act 1998 which criminalises simple obtaining of personal data, subject to some exceptions.

17 Section 33, Criminal Justice and Courts Act 2015. There is, as yet, no equivalent offence in Northern Ireland.

18 Section 3, Criminal Law Act 1997.

19 Section 9, Offences Against the State (Amendment) Act 1998.

20 Section 2, Criminal Justice (Withholding of Information on Offences Against Children and Vulnerable Persons) Act 2012.

21 Section 19, Criminal Justice Act 2011.

22 Schedule 2.

23 Section 9, Criminal Justice (Theft and Fraud Offences) Act, 2001.

24 Criminal Damage Act 1991.

6

Crime, conflict and poverty

Siobhán McAlister and Deirdre Healy

Introduction

The typical prisoner in Northern Ireland and the Republic of Ireland is a young single male with few formal educational qualifications, limited employment experience, poor mental and physical health and a heightened risk of poverty and welfare dependency (PRT, 2014; IPRT, 2012). The concentration of social problems within the prison population raises important questions about the relationship between poverty, social exclusion and crime, a topic that has preoccupied criminological scholars for almost a century. As will be shown in this chapter, some posit an association between crime rates and economic conditions or economic deprivation, whereas others consider how processes of law, order and punishment selectively and disproportionately impact the most materially disadvantaged. These studies show that, while economic deprivation is *statistically* related to crime, the relationship between poverty, social exclusion, crime and conflict is complex.

In the 1930s the Chicago School posited a causal connection between crime and poverty. Shaw and McKay (1942) studied the ecology of Chicago city and discovered that delinquency and poverty were concentrated in particular areas, namely the zone of transition that encircled the central business district. They concluded that social problems, including poverty, generated criminality by fracturing the informal social controls that normally regulate behaviour and by allowing *criminal traditions*, or subcultures, to flourish. Two key mechanisms appear to explain the relationship between community disorganisation and crime, namely limited social capital and low collective efficacy, which increase crime by reducing the availability of conventional social opportunities and allowing delinquent opportunity structures and subcultures to flourish (Kingston, Huizinga and Elliot, 2009). Subcultures can be defined as the 'knowledge, beliefs, values, codes, tastes and prejudices' that are unique to a particular social group (Cohen (1955) cited in Downes, 2013: 1). According to Thornton (1997: 2), members of subcultures are often portrayed in the literature as 'disenfranchised, disaffected' youths, whose 'shadowy, subterranean activities contrast dramatically with the "enlightened" civil decencies of the "public"'. In other words, their status as 'outsiders' is treated as their defining characteristic. Subcultural groups may experience spatial as well as normative segregation; for example when members colonise parts of neighbourhoods, creating 'no-go' areas for other residents. Furthermore, the prefix 'sub' implies that subcultures are inferior to mainstream culture, perhaps as a result of social class, ethnicity or age.

Other theorists locate the causes of crime not in the ecology of disadvantaged communities but in the wider socio-cultural arrangements of society. Merton (1938) argued that a state of anomie, or normlessness, occurs when cultural aspirations become divorced from the institutional norms that regulate the means for attaining these goals. Specifically, he observed that economic wealth is promoted as the ultimate symbol of success within American culture, but that social structures create barriers to its achievement, at least among the lower social classes. Under anomic conditions, people are more likely to employ illicit but effective means to achieve culturally prescribed goals. In this way, 'a cardinal American virtue, "ambition", promotes a cardinal American vice, "deviant behaviour"' (Merton, 1968: 200). More recently, Messner and Rosenfeld (1997: 86) extended Merton's analysis, proposing that crime rates increase when 'the competitive, individualistic and materialistic message of the American Dream' tilts the institutional balance of power towards the economy. This weakens the ability of other social institutions, such as the family or education system, to exert social control over people's behaviour. However, empirical tests suggest that this process may be culturally specific and may apply primarily to advanced Western countries (see e.g. Chamlin and Cochran, 2007).

Relative deprivation theories extend this perspective by explaining crime as a consequence of some social groups feeling relatively deprived in comparison to others. Relative deprivation is most strongly felt when inequalities are wide (Young, 1999) and when comparisons can be easily made (Lea and Young, 1993). Feelings of unfairness, resentment or frustration occur when there is a gap between goals and means, or when there is a perceived lack of power in the face of injustice (see Webber, 2007). It is the *subjective* nature of relative deprivation (rather than 'objectively' defined inequality) and *collective* perceptions and responses to injustices, that differentiate it from 'anomie' which tends to focus on *individual* adaptations and responses. Political as well as economic marginalisation is also key to this theory as those experiencing relative deprivation lack 'voice' or political representation.

Young (1999, 2003) argues that the greater ontological insecurity and market individualism of late modern life has exacerbated relative deprivation and broadened its impact. Relative deprivation is no longer limited to 'gazing upwards' at the 'included' and feeling injustice; it is also about 'gazing downwards' at 'the excluded' and feeling resentment. Because of increased insecurity for all, 'gazing downwards' creates a sense of vindictiveness whereby it is perceived that 'those below one on the social hierarchy' have an easy time of it (e.g. they receive benefits without hard work) (Young, 1999: 9).

While recognising structural factors to varying degrees, some believe that the structural analyses of the aforementioned theories did not go far enough. Taylor, Walton and Young (1973) argued that a comprehensive theory must also consider the political, social and economic conditions that elicit criminality and shape the social reaction to it. They were interested in understanding the role of power structures, inequality and social exclusion in crime causation as well as the 'political initiatives that give rise to (or abolish) legislation [and] ensure the enforcement of that legislation' (Taylor et al., 1973: 273). Recent empirical studies support Taylor et al.'s (1973) contention that structural factors impact on legislative and sentencing decisions. For example, Barak, Leighton and Cotton (2014) demonstrated that class, ethnicity and gender influence both the definition of crime and the operation of the criminal justice system.

There is also evidence that structural factors shape the lives and experiences of residents in deprived areas in ways that may encourage criminality. Wacquant (2007) examined the origins of the hyper-ghetto, a novel site of social exclusion that emerged in the working-class banlieues of Paris and the ghettos of Chicago from the 1970s onwards. The hyper-ghetto is:

[A] bounded, ethnically uniform socio-spatial formation born of the forcible relegation of a negatively typed population to a reserved territory within which this population develops an array of specific institutions operating both as a functional substitute for, and as a protective buffer against, the dominant institutions of the encompassing society.

(Wacquant, 2007: 49)

Its physical environment consists of dilapidated, burnt-out and abandoned buildings, rubbish-strewn streets and a pervasive atmosphere of lawlessness and danger. 'Territorial stigmatisation' ensures that the names of hyper-ghettoes come to symbolise social failure in the public imagination (Wacquant, Slater and Pereira, 2014: 1272). Furthermore, residents of these 'sociomoral purgatories' are portrayed by politicians and the media as inherently deviant and irredeemably damaged, which legitimises their criminalisation, control and punishment (Wacquant et al., 2014: 1271).

Wacquant (2007) rejected the notion that the origins of the hyper-ghetto lay in the individual pathology of its residents or in its socio-spatial arrangements. Instead, his theory implicated the structural changes associated with the transition to late modernity. In the case of the American hyper-ghetto, for example, employment opportunities for residents were decimated when manufacturing industries relocated from urban centres to suburban or international sites, while the state-sponsored flight of 'white' residents to the suburbs enabled upwardly mobile African American families to migrate to better neighbourhoods, leaving the unemployed and welfare-dependent behind. This analysis suggests that the relationship between poverty and crime may be more tenuous than previously thought and could at least partly reflect the structural biases of the social and criminal justice spheres.

Related work in the UK has focused on the criminalisation of social policy. This notes a move away from concern with problematic social and economic conditions (Rodger, 2008) to a focus on the alleged moral and behavioural deficits of structurally disadvantaged groups (Young, 1999). Thus, social problems become individualised and problematised, and marginalised groups recast as 'burdensome', 'unworthy' and 'threats to law and order' (Grover, 2011). Stigmatisation, othering and resentment, alongside increased perceptions of insecurity and 'politically derived anxieties' (Goldson and Muncie, 2006: x) about crime and disorder, have justified the extension of regulatory mechanisms in social and criminal justice policy including: greater welfare conditionality; increased surveillance, regulation; and more punitive punishments. Extended powers of governance targeting 'problem' or 'risky' groups and intervening early and pre-emptively to manage risk, have brought 'new categories of people and behaviour into the control system' (Brown 2004: 208), and redefined social justice issues as criminal justice problems. For example, Haydon (2014) reports that most of the children referred to Early Intervention for the Prevention of Offending Programmes in Northern Ireland were not previously known to the police, but instead had a range of family, school and community issues. She concluded that redefining welfare needs as 'criminogenic risk factors ... potentially label children at a young age and net-widen: bringing to the attention of state agencies, including the police, those experiencing difficulties at home, in school and in their communities' (Haydon and McAlister, 2015: 315).

Regulatory tools are not implemented equally, and the process of 'imposed social exclusion, and criminalisation, is not class neutral' (White and Cunneen, 2006: 24). Antisocial behaviour 'is "found" in largely social housing areas' not because of individual or neighbourhood pathology, but 'because the physical presence of "investigatory" people and technology ensures that it will be' (Brown, 2004: 210). More generally, the unemployed, working-class young people, the homeless and 'troubled families' have been the focus of much policy intervention (Rodger, 2008).

Stigmatising social policies and popular discourses reinforce social exclusion and social injustice (Squires and Stephen, 2005) and feed back into 'marginalisation and unemployment which lie at the heart of much ... criminality' (White and Cunneen, 2006: 19). Furthermore, criminalisation processes 'serve to entrench further the unemployability, alienation and social outsider status of members of these communities' (White and Cunneen, 2006: 19). This societal, as well as economic marginalisation may lead to frustration and resentment and to criminal responses (Young, 1999). However, these reactions to social exclusion may be culturally specific. For example Pfundmair *et al.* (2015) found that people living in societies with individualistic cultures tended to use what the authors defined as 'antisocial' strategies to cope with social exclusion, whereas those from societies with collectivist cultures were largely unaffected by the experience of social exclusion.

The international literature reveals the complex relationship between crime, conflict and poverty. Rather than a causal relationship, it appears that raised expectations, inequalities or a sense of injustice, alongside an understanding of the role of social and cultural factors, may provide a better understanding of crime and disorder. Further, that criminal justice policies, processes and practices (by design or consequence) impact disproportionately on the poorest sections of the population is evident. Finally, that system contact can further exacerbate social exclusion, potentially leading to more crime, is one of the ironies of contemporary responses to crime (McAra and McVie, 2007).

The next sections explore the relationship between poverty, inequality, crime and conflict in Northern Ireland and the Republic of Ireland. The discussion begins with an examination of trends in poverty and inequality. Next, the relationship between poverty, inequality and conflict in Northern Ireland is explored with a particular emphasis on the relationship between inequality, protest and political violence. This is followed by a review of research in the Republic of Ireland which critically reflects on the association between socio-economic factors and crime rates at the structural and community level.

A word on definitions

The terms 'poverty', 'social exclusion' and 'inequality' are often used interchangeably, even though they describe different phenomena. On its website the Office for Social Inclusion (undated) in the Republic of Ireland differentiates between poverty, defined as 'deprivation due to a lack of resources, both material and non-material', social exclusion defined as 'being unable to participate in society because of a lack of resources that are normally available to the general population' and inequality, a relative concept that is left undefined (but which usually refers to income inequality). There are some similarities in definitions in Northern Ireland, particularly evidenced in OFMDFM's (2006: 14) definition of social exclusion as:

> [W]hat can happen to people who are subject to the most severe problems. Social exclusion has to do with poverty and joblessness – but it is more than that. It is about being cut off from the social and economic life of our community.

For the sake of comparison, Table 6.1 illustrates recent trends in poverty based on household income in the Republic and Northern Ireland.[1] As is the case with comparative research more generally, these trends must be interpreted with caution, since the experience of poverty may vary between jurisdictions as a result of social, cultural and historical differences. In addition, population-level poverty rates may conceal variation across gender, religion, disability and age. Nevertheless, some general trends can be discerned. Unsurprisingly, poverty trends in the

Table 6.1 Trends in poverty (%)

Republic of Ireland

2004	2005	2006	2007	2008	2009	2010	2011	2012	2013
19.4	18.3	17.0	16.5	14.4	14.1	14.7	16.0	16.5	15.2

Northern Ireland

2003/4	2004/5	2005/6	2006/7	2007/8	2008/9	2009/10	2010/11	2011/12	2012/13
20	20	20	19	20	20	22	20	21	19

Note: Republic of Ireland figures are compiled from the Central Statistics Office Statbank, available at www.cso.ie; Northern Ireland figures are taken from the Northern Ireland Poverty Bulletin 2012/13 (NISRA, 2014).

Table 6.2 Trends in inequality

	2004	*2005*	*2006*	*2007*	*2008*	*2009*	*2010*	*2011*	*2012*	*2013*
Ireland	31.5	31.9	31.9	31.3	29.9	28.8	30.7	29.8	29.9	30.0
UK	n/a	34.6	32.5	32.6	33.9	32.4	32.9	33.0	31.3	30.2
EU (27 countries)	n/a	30.6	30.3	30.6	30.9	30.5	30.4	30.7	30.4	30.5

Note: Taken from Eurostat http://appsso.eurostat.ec.europa.eu/nui/setupDownloads.do

Republic of Ireland closely mirror the pattern of economic boom and bust, with the rate falling steadily between 2004 and 2009 but increasing slightly in subsequent years. Conversely, the poverty rate in Northern Ireland remained relatively stable throughout this period. Overall, poverty in Northern Ireland is significantly higher than in the Republic.

The explanation for these differences is not clear but may be related to the fact that the poverty threshold is calculated relative to median income, a method that may conceal changes in real income levels. Indeed, recent analyses show that households in Northern Ireland experienced a 10 per cent decline in incomes since the recession, partly because of a shift towards part-time employment opportunities within the labour market, greater disability levels among the populace, higher long-term unemployment rates and public expenditure cuts (JRF, 2014). Conversely, political commitment to welfare provision in the Republic of Ireland has weathered current economic trends. Although real incomes also declined, Watson and Maître (2014) estimated that social transfers reduced the (pre-transfer) poverty rate by 71 per cent in 2011 compared to 53 per cent in 2004.[2]

Table 6.2 charts inequality trends in both jurisdictions between 2004 and 2013. The relatively stable rates in the Republic of Ireland can probably be explained by the protective effects of social transfers. Although separate figures are not published for Northern Ireland, inequality rates for the United Kingdom as a whole declined during this period as a result of reduced real earnings and changes in tax and welfare regimes (ONS, 2013). Overall, rates of inequality in both jurisdictions are in line with EU averages.

While the Gini Coefficient is one of the most consistent measures of income and wealth inequality, it can also be used to measure 'disparities [in] ... other social phenomena such as inequality in education' (Hillyard et al., 2003: 42). There is some debate as to which measure constitutes the most useful proxy for economic disadvantage. Some prefer 'poverty' because the extent of inequality becomes irrelevant when all incomes are increasing, whereas others highlight the need to study inequality because of its relationship with a range of social problems, including crime (see Hillyard, Rolston and Tomlinson (2005) for a comprehensive review of this debate). Quantitative measures of poverty and inequality have also been criticised for providing an over-simplistic picture. Martin (2010) argues that qualitative studies may be better equipped to capture the underlying causal relationships between poverty, inequality and crime, their multi-dimensional characteristics and interactions with other social processes.

In light of these considerations, Hillyard *et al.* (2003: 13) developed a 'consensual poverty approach' based on 'items and activities people in Northern Ireland think everyone should be able to afford and should not have to do without'. In some respects, this merges measures of poverty, deprivation and social exclusion. Social exclusion is particularly important, as it recognises a range of social factors beyond material deprivation, including social, political, spatial and cultural disenfranchisement (Young, 2003). Similarly, O'Connor and Staunton (2015) advocate a holistic measure of inequality that captures income and wealth distribution, the impact of welfare and taxation policies, labour market accessibility and cost of living. The World Bank (2014/2015) has also devised a multi-dimensional poverty index comprising measures of the prevalence and intensity of poverty, 'at risk of poverty' and income inequality (although neither Northern Ireland nor the Republic of Ireland have been analysed using this index). Some analysts favour definitions that focus on the *presence* of social wellbeing rather than the *absence* of poverty (see e.g. World Bank, 2013).

With these caveats in mind, the next section explores the relationship between poverty, inequality and crime in Northern Ireland and the Republic of Ireland from a critical, empirical and qualitative perspective.

Poverty, conflict and relative deprivation in Northern Ireland

Research on the links between poverty, inequality and crime is lacking in Northern Ireland. Likewise, the burgeoning literature on poverty largely ignores issues of crime or criminalisation. Reflecting these preoccupations, this section focuses on the relationship between 'crime', conflict and poverty. Such analysis is relevant to contemporary criminology because definitions of 'crime' and mechanisms of control are redefined during periods of conflict and experienced unevenly. The old adage that crime is a social and cultural construct has particular resonance. Behaviours that might otherwise be defined as 'crime' in the context of political conflict might instead be defined as matters of safety (Mulvenna, 2012). Added to this, that inequalities (real or perceived) feature historically and contemporaneously make Northern Ireland a useful case study for the analysis of crime, disorder and violence in the context of relative deprivation and marginalisation.

That there is a relationship between poverty, inequality and conflict is well established (Goodhand, 2003) but there is less agreement on the direction of this relationship. Demonstrating this, Collier *et al.* (2003) detail how low-income countries are more prone to civil war, and also that the experience of civil war has adverse consequences for a country's development. Demonstrating a focus on relative deprivation, Goodhand (2003) outlines how inequality and unfair treatment generate grievances which may lead to violent conflict. Among the factors contributing to 'grievance formation' are historical inequalities and discrimination often founded in colonialism and state bias towards particular groups (Goodhand, 2003: 642). Violence may be a response to social, political and economic grievance, but also provide a sense of purpose and status (Goodhand, 2003), which could explain the continuation of violence among some working-class young men in 'post-conflict' Northern Ireland.

Poverty and political violence

Despite its history of violent conflict, there is a dearth of research and policy focus on the relationship between poverty and conflict in Northern Ireland (Hillyard *et al.*, 2005; Horgan, 2005). That said, the onset and impacts of the Conflict have been linked to economic, political and social marginalisation. Hancock (1998: paragraph 7) notes that, despite the long-standing minority position of the Catholic/Nationalist population dating back to partition, the level of ethnic violence tended to 'coincide with downturns in the local economy'. Connecting with relative deprivation theory and radical criminology, it is when perceptions of inequality and injustice are high that social protest and violence are most likely to erupt. While areas of discrimination were identified, the sense of relative deprivation was most intensely felt when, through the civil rights movement, the Catholic/Nationalist community became aware of their unequal position and the resistance from the Protestant/Unionist majority to efforts to redress this (Fitzduff and O'Hagan, 2000; Hancock, 1998).

Historical and 'horizontal inequalities' and feelings of discrimination have, therefore, been regularly cited as a cause of the Conflict (Ferguson and Michaelsen, 2013). Taking this analysis a step further, Honaker (2008: 18) argues that 'the sectarian differences in unemployment rates was [sic] a leading predictor of violence in Northern Ireland'. In particular, he notes that disparities in unemployment were a regularly invoked grievance of Republican paramilitaries. Others suggest that violent responses to civil rights demonstrations and the introduction of internment in 1971 crystallised feelings of inequality and unfairness and sparked the most recent period of violent conflict (Hancock, 1998).

While there is less evidence that material poverty caused the Conflict, there is considerable evidence to suggest the overlaying of conflict with poverty. Running concurrently with the Conflict was a process of deindustrialisation which significantly affected the economy and employment opportunities. It also had significant impacts at a local level, particularly in working-class inner-city Protestant/Unionist areas (Mulvenna, 2012). The combined impacts of the Conflict and poverty are, however, evident in communities across the ethno-national divide. A recent mapping of Conflict-related deaths with area-based multiple deprivation measures found that areas that had the greatest incidence of violence currently experience deprivation rates 25 per cent higher than those where there was little or no violence (Ferguson and Michaelsen, 2013).

Hillyard *et al.*'s (2003, 2005) public survey of poverty and social exclusion provides the most comprehensive picture of the impacts of the Conflict. This revealed that almost one half of respondents knew someone who had been killed. Further:

> [A]n estimated 80,000 households are affected by the loss of a close relative and 50,000 households contain someone injured in the conflict. Around 28,000 people have been forced to leave work because of intimidation, threats or harassment, and 54,000 households have been forced to move house for similar reasons.
>
> *(Hillyard et al., 2005: 6)*

They also found a relationship between poverty and various experiences of the Conflict. In particular their measure of 'extreme violence' – which 'combined the most serious types of violence: killings (relative), injuries (self and relative), and witnessing an incident (murder)' – was significantly related to poverty (Hillyard *et al.*, 2005: 144). Further studies support the view that political violence and its consequences were experienced most intensely in materially deprived areas. Interface communities, which experience high levels of violence, are traditionally located in working-class Catholic/Nationalist and Protestant/Unionist communities. Given the persistent low-level inter-community violence in these areas, which occasionally flares into serious violence, some 'have become deprived and ghettoized, with low rates of employment and high levels of poverty' (Hargie, O'Donnell and McMullan, 2011: 880).

Added to the violence were high levels of paramilitary regulation and control in working-class communities. Due to a legitimacy deficit and absence of formal policing in some areas, Loyalist and Republican paramilitaries engaged in processes of 'local crime management' (Brewer, Lockhart and Rodgers, 1997). Brewer et al. (1997: 7) explain that: '[c]ivil unrest can produce high levels of in-group solidarity, ghettoization in housing and more socially homogeneous districts, which significantly affects the levels of reporting of ordinary crime and facilitates management of crime locally by the community itself'. Such 'management' typically involved threatening or punishing 'anti-community', 'anti-social' or 'criminal' behaviour. Research demonstrates that young people were among the main victims of such attacks (Smyth et al., 2004). While official records are incomplete, these show that between 1991 and 1997 alone, 120 young people were shot and 234 were physically assaulted by paramilitary groups (Horgan and Rodgers, 2000). All lived in areas of high deprivation.

The paramilitary regulation and control that may have kept non-conflict-related crime at bay, or at least led to under-reporting, may have amounted to 'criminal activity' but was rarely defined as such. Interestingly, Brewer et al. (1997) suggest that the Conflict and the 'ghettoization' of ethno-national groups into single-identity areas mitigated some of the worst effects of social disadvantage and poverty. In some areas, strong community structures, extended family networks, shared local and cultural in-group identities and a sense of solidarity in the face of adversity led to tight-knit communities which, in addition to paramilitary regulation and control, acted as methods of social control (Brewer et al., 1997). This impression of community life in working-class conflict-affected areas is, however, less evident in Protestant/Unionist communities (Brewer et al., 1997; Leonard, 2004; Mulvenna, 2012) and may also provide an over-positive image of Catholic/Nationalist communities. This will be returned to shortly.

Legacies of the Conflict

While the long-term impacts of the Conflict are not yet fully known, there is evidence of a range of legacies to date. Violence and disruption undermined economic growth leading to a lack of inward investment and the withdrawal of existing industries (Hillyard et al., 2005). This negatively impacted the job market and contributed to a low-wage economy (Horgan and Monteith, 2009). Yet, poverty, industrial decline and the economic impacts of the Conflict were not on the policy agenda at the height of violence and civil unrest (Hillyard et al., 2005). The narrow policy focus and proportion of public spending dedicated to counter-terrorism also impacted on public service investment (Tomlinson, 2012). Furthermore, high levels of mental ill-health are attributed to poverty and the Conflict (Horgan, 2005; Horgan and Monteith, 2009). How this impacts on the ability of people to undertake paid employment (Horgan, 2005) is evidence of the ways in which violent conflict reproduces poverty and inequality. It is little surprise, then, that those communities most affected by the Conflict remain among the most impoverished (Ferguson and Michaelsen, 2013).

Contrary to the image of some conflict-affected areas as strong, cohesive communities, Mulvenna (2012) illustrates how the impacts of deindustrialisation, violence, population mobility (due to housing redevelopment and population movement) and the controlling influence of paramilitaries embedded poverty and marginalisation in working-class Protestant/Unionist communities. These destabilised what was once a firm working-class Protestant identity and led to 'an absence of strong, benign and effective local leadership' (Mulvenna, 2012: 428). Paramilitaries, in particular, contributed to 'Protestant working-class areas becoming "sink estates" ... characterised by unemployment, lack of aspiration, poverty and the breakdown of the family as a unit' (Mulvenna, 2012: 428). The legacies are evident today in high unemployment rates and low educational attainment. The fragmentation of some Protestant communities alongside greater discontent with the Good Friday Belfast Agreement may therefore have eroded the traditional community networks which help sustain neighbourhoods in times of change (Leonard, 2004). That said, while there is some suggestion that Catholic/Nationalist communities are more collectivist than Protestant/Unionist communities, Cairns, Van Tal and Williamson (2004) found few significant differences in levels of social capital.

Reflecting the exclusion of communities in what has been defined as a top-down settlement negotiated by those with political power, the transitional process has been divorced from 'the social needs and interests of those communities most affected by violent conflict' (Tomlinson, 2012: 443). McAlister, Scraton and Haydon (2009) found that communities felt excluded from the transition, and forgotten about during the process. There was resentment towards the rhetoric of peace as they made efforts, with limited resources, support or recognition, to deal with the economic, social and emotional legacies of the Conflict. Such disillusionment is problematic as 'the disappointment of raised expectation of improvement in quality of life in communities worst affected by conflict can compromise support for the settlement' (Smyth, 2004: 558–559). Societies that have experienced conflict 'are more vulnerable to future violence' (Goodhand, 2003: 630), which makes the level of disappointment, discontent and frustration particularly worrying.

Within the communities in McAlister et al.'s (2009) research there were underlying tensions and unresolved hurt related to the past, along with fears and uncertainties about the future. Despite a decline in political violence and paramilitary presence, residents felt less safe than they had in the past and believed that crime and antisocial behaviour were increasing. While frustrations and to some extent resentments (with political leaders and the political settlement) were evident across the ethno-national divide, perceptions of relative deprivation, injustice and unfairness were particularly pronounced in Protestant/Unionist communities. The belief was regularly expressed that the Protestant/Unionist population 'lost out' in the transition from conflict (see also Nolan et al., 2015). Moves towards equality and transparency – such as the devolution of policing and justice; equal representation; investment in communities most affected by the Conflict (many of which were Catholic/Nationalist); the establishment of a parades commission; restrictions on expressions of cultural tradition – were viewed as unfair, discriminatory and/or punishing. The perception that the cultural identity of one ethno-national group (Irish) is being increasingly recognised and preserved, while that of the other (British) is being eroded, has at times culminated in acts of collective violence directed towards the police and Nationalist/Republican communities. Perceptions of relative deprivation and collective grievances manifested most recently in protests against the decision in December 2012 to remove the union flag from Belfast City Hall except on designated days.[3] The street protests, some resulting in violence, persisted for four months (Nolan et al., 2015).

That young people have been prominent in protests and street disturbances is instructive (Ferguson and Michaelsen, 2013; Smyth et al., 2004). The sense of being marginalised within the peace process may be particularly strong among young people, as they are formally 'excluded from meaningful participation in political structures' (Hargie et al., 2011: 881). Furthermore, fears and uncertainties in communities have consolidated around young people who often feel 'alienated, marginalised and stigmatised by their own communities' (Smyth et al., 2004: 59-60). Thus, the exclusion some feel *within* their communities adds to their sense of political, economic and social exclusion. While often defined as 'recreational', research with children and young people demonstrates that their involvement in sectarian violence and collective protest is grounded in and reflective of the cultural and historical context within which they live. Violence as a means of defending territory and expressing resistance has a long tradition in Northern Ireland (Leonard, 2010; McAlister *et al.*, 2009). Among working-class young men, violence directed towards the police or 'the other community' is often an expression of discontent and grievance with past or current treatment, a means of asserting cultural (and masculine) identity and resistance to perceived inequalities (Haydon, McAlister and Scraton, 2012). The focal points of protests and violence also evidence their political basis. The police, the 'other community', churches and Orange Halls, council buildings and offices are a symbolic embodiment of the group's discontent (see Grover, 2011).

During the Conflict, masculinity became closely connected to place, culture and violence (Mulvenna, 2012; Reilly, 2004). Consequently, young men who were excluded from the transitional process and unprepared for change are experiencing a collective sense of loss (McAlister *et al.*, 2009). The further erosion of employment opportunities and a strong sense of relative deprivation, coupled with perceived threats to their cultural identity, particularly in Protestant/Unionist communities, have brought some violent responses. These are reflective of traditional, working-class male responses in a divided society – violence and sectarianism to defend and assert cultural and masculine identity. That young people talk of the excitement or 'buzz' of rioting (Leonard, 2010; Lloyd, 2009) should not overshadow the other emotions that drive it – hurt, anger, fear, injustice (Grover, 2011). Marginalising and stigmatising discourses of 'recreational rioting' decontextualise and depoliticise this behaviour. Those involved are pathologised and 'othered' as 'bigots', 'criminal gangs', those wanting to drag us back to 'the dark days'.

Negatively labelled and 'excluded from citizenship' (Young (2002) cited in Grover, 2010), the behaviour of the minority has led to the demonisation of a social group. At a time when peace is unstable and fear of crime high, denying the significance of structural and material circumstances leads to calls for authoritarian responses (Haydon *et al.*, 2012). Thus, contrary to adults' perceptions of a 'policing vacuum', working-class young people regularly report extensive contact with the police (Byrne, Conway and Ostermeyer, 2005; McAlister *et al.*, 2009; Smyth *et al.*, 2004). Added to this is the informal regulation and punishment that 'anti-social' behaviour still brings. Indeed some young people experience extreme levels of surveillance, and at times double punishment by a twin system of 'justice' – formal criminal justice *and* informal paramilitary justice (McAlister and Carr, 2014). Although publically defined as 'criminals', young people are disproportionly the victims of crime. Demonisation can increase victimisation by bringing young people to the attention of paramilitaries. Punitive sanctions of any kind 'increase the criminalisation of children and young people while failing to address social injustice' (Haydon *et al.*, 2012: 516).

Crime, poverty and inequality in the Republic of Ireland

Criminological analysis of the relationship between crime and poverty in the Republic of Ireland tends to mirror international research and theoretical development. The first wave of criminological research explored the impact of socio-economic changes on crime and was conceptually linked with structural theories, such as anomie. McCullagh (1996) proposed that economic growth between the 1960s and 1990s increased the rates of property and white-collar crime. He suggested that greater household wealth, coupled with increased consumerism, created new incentives and opportunities for young working-class males to engage in property crime. Furthermore, because traditional sources of employment for unskilled urban dwellers were in decline, crime offered an alternative means to achieve economic success. At the same time, increased business activity enhanced criminal opportunities for corporations and their employees, while weak corporate regulation meant that white-collar crimes could be committed with impunity. McCullagh's (1996) theory is innovative because it attempts to explain both 'ordinary' and white-collar crime through a single theoretical lens. It was not, however, empirically tested and its tenets have been questioned by others.

O'Donnell and O'Sullivan (2001) believed that McCullagh's (1996) theory had merit but could not explain the crime drop that occurred during the 1990s – also a period of rapid socio-economic change. They observed that economic prosperity tends to reduce property crime in the short term, because people have greater access to legitimate economic opportunities. However, they agreed with McCullagh (1996) that property crime could rise in the long term because higher consumer spending enhances the attractiveness of criminal opportunities. Drawing on Field's (1990) analysis of crime in England and Wales, O'Donnell and O'Sullivan (2001) theorised that violent victimisation would increase during periods of prosperity because people are more likely to socialise outside the home. More recently, Campbell (2010) attributed the increase in gun crime during the Celtic Tiger years to relative deprivation. She proposed that the cultural preoccupation with wealth (the Irish Dream), coupled with a nascent neoliberal ideology, alienated residents in disadvantaged communities because they were structurally excluded from economic achievement. Consistent with the tenets of relative deprivation theory, she argues that the neoliberal ethos entails a materialistic and individualistic culture and limits state intervention in economic and social life, which in turn weakens social capital, heightens inequality and reduces legitimate opportunities for success.

Others argue that protective as well as risk factors should be considered. Adler (1983) studied ten 'nations not obsessed with crime', including the Republic of Ireland, in order to uncover the socio-economic factors that protect against high crime rates. Although she found no statistical relationship between crime and standard socio-economic indicators, her qualitative analysis showed that low-crime nations had strong informal social control mechanisms that acted as a buffer against criminality. Adler (2000: 272) claimed that these social conditions elicited *synnomie*, or 'norm conformity, cohesion, intact social controls and norm integration'. However, O'Donnell and O'Sullivan (2001) rejected her thesis on the basis that crime rates did not increase during the 1990s despite a weakening of informal social controls. Recently, Stamatel (2014) revisited the ten nations originally studied by Adler (1983) and discovered that crime rates remained low and relatively stable despite the dramatic social transformations that had occurred in the intervening years. She concluded that low crime rates are produced, not by socio-economic factors, but by strong and stable political systems that promote shared values and strengthen social institutions.

These macro-level perspectives are consistent with the tenets of strain theory, because they posit a causal link between crime, culture, structural factors and the institutional balance of power. As discussed earlier, the relationship between crime and poverty is complex and not fully understood. Recent ethnographic studies have provided new and more nuanced insights into the lived experience of poverty, social exclusion and crime.

Community, crime and social exclusion

Hourigan (2011) conducted an insightful ethnographic study of several social housing estates in Limerick city, which is situated in the mid-west region of the country. Residents in these communities are affected by a range of problems, including crime and antisocial behaviour, limited public transport links, a dilapidated urban environment, educational and vocational disadvantage, stigmatisation and poor service coordination (Fitzgerald, 2007). Like Wacquant (2007), Hourigan

(2011) discovered that external factors – rather than individual or spatial pathology – influenced the evolution of disadvantaged communities. Although the estates were initially built to house former tenement dwellers and working-class families, the government offered financial incentives to encourage working-class families to leave the estates during the 1980s in an effort to free up social housing stock. In addition, a series of local factory closures reduced the number of employment opportunities available to residents. These events simultaneously deepened disadvantage and resulted in an exodus of social capital from the area. The departure of working-class families also created a power vacuum that was subsequently filled by 'local crime families' who exercised control through violence and intimidation. Residents felt helpless to challenge their dominance and encouraged children to adopt a 'hard man' identity in an effort to protect them from harm. The 'hard man' identity combined 'physical toughness with quick thinking, a capacity for "slagging" and/or verbal abuse, and a highly attuned awareness of danger' (Hourigan, 2011: 63). Ironically, residents' adoption of this identity ultimately perpetuated the cycle of fear, crime and violence (see also Hourigan, *infra*, and Campbell, *infra*).

Hourigan's (2011) analysis also highlighted the double exclusion experienced by disadvantaged families within these communities. Advantaged families constituted about two-thirds of the population and were described as stable, non-criminal and upwardly mobile. On the other hand, disadvantaged families were 'dysfunctional', 'criminal' and highly stigmatised. This is consistent with Wacquant *et al.*'s (2014) finding that residents in disadvantaged communities may exaggerate small differences between themselves and 'problem residents' as a means of coping with territorial stigmatisation. Hourigan's (2011) study reveals that the relationship between poverty and criminality is not straightforward. Although poverty contributed to criminality in these communities, it only affected a small proportion of the population. It may be that others cope with poverty using alternative, non-criminal strategies or, alternatively, possess protective factors that promote resilience and act as a buffer against feelings of exclusion. Indeed, Merton (1968) suggests that conformity is the most common response to anomic conditions. Nevertheless, a 'blemish of place' may exacerbate poverty and social exclusion within already disadvantaged communities (Wacquant, 2007). Indeed, Griffin and Kelleher (2010: 30) found that chronic unemployment limited access to conventional adult masculine identities, as highlighted in the quote from the following participant: '[i]t emotionally affects a man that he cannot support a family'. Although the men wanted to work, they experienced difficulties finding employment because of their lack of education and the stigma attached to their address.

Norris's (2014) ten-year prospective study of seven social housing communities highlighted a more positive dimension of social life in disadvantaged communities. They introduced the concept of *liveability* to describe 'the extent to which neighbourhoods succeed in attracting and retaining residents and giving them environments they like to live in, as opposed to becoming so rundown and unpopular that they undermine residents' quality of life' (Norris and Fahey, 2014: 220). Despite a history of entrenched deprivation, the majority developed into liveable communities characterised by social cohesion, community engagement, a sense of collective efficacy and an upwardly mobile population (Fahey, Norris and Field, 2014; Corcoran, 2014). Nevertheless, the residents distinguished between respectable and unsafe areas, again highlighting the double exclusion experienced by certain families. A small number of communities were classed as 'troubled' because they were home to 'problem families' who experienced mental health problems, engaged in criminality and substance misuse, avoided structured leisure activities, lived in transient accommodation and possessed weak social bonds (Corcoran, 2014). Residents in these communities noted how their quality of life was undermined by criminal and antisocial behaviour, noisy parties and neglect of properties (O'Gorman, 2014).

135

Most of the research considered so far has focused on the lives of 'the respectable majority' in disadvantaged communities. In contrast, Ilan's (2013) ethnographic study explored the experiences of marginalised young people living in a disadvantaged community in Dublin's north-inner city. He discovered that so-called 'problem' youths and their families experienced a range of difficulties, including death, addiction, criminality, evictions, mental health issues, exclusion and stigmatisation. To counteract the effects of social exclusion, the youths formed a loose and porous friendship group, the Crew, whose membership conferred a range of benefits, including a sense of belonging, respect, status and insulation from social condemnation. However, membership also generated mutual obligations: for example, failure to show group loyalty was punished with insults or a refusal to share criminal proceeds. The Crew espoused the subcultural values typically found in street culture, including opposition to authority, rejection of mainstream norms and hyper-masculinity. They embraced 'the transgressive thrill of delinquent acts' to escape at least temporarily from the tedium of a life with limited prospects (Ilan, 2007: 30). Unlike the subcultures studied by the Chicago School, the Crew's activities were not confined to specific geographical locations but traversed a vast swathe of territory that encompassed their local community, the city centre and the suburbs. The Crew often travelled to affluent suburbs to commit crime and to suburban social housing estates to engage in joyriding. During these trips, they deployed their subcultural identity to access *street social capital*; that is, to gain entry into markets in illicit trade, defuse potentially violent situations and form friendships within other offending networks. Despite the variety of rewards it offered, the subculture ultimately exacerbated social exclusion among its members. The Crew were loath to rescind their subcultural outlook because it represented 'a creative and viscerally satisfying response to the marginality generated by the confluence of their biographies, class, gender and youth' (Ilan, 2007: 37). Consequently, they resisted rehabilitation workers' efforts to change their attitudes, values and behaviours and thereby risked further criminalisation and punishment.

Ilan (2011) also examined the politics of urban governance, arguing that community leaders and state agents were primarily concerned with protecting the reputation of the community rather than addressing more important issues such as social exclusion and serious criminality. In order to knife off their troubled past, residents and community leaders stressed the difference between *rough* and *respectable* micro-communities within the area. 'Rough' residents, including the Crew, were seen to threaten the community's progress towards prosperity and respectability whereas 'respectable' residents embraced conventional middle-class values, including individualism, upward mobility and consumerism. In particular, community leaders lionised a small number of young adult residents as exemplars of respectability within the community, but the reality was less clear-cut. Other less influential residents regarded their prosperity as evidence of serious criminality and complained about constant police raids and all-night parties at their houses. Furthermore, even 'respectable' community members engaged in welfare fraud, participated in the informal economy and endorsed violent conflict resolution. Consequently, Ilan (2011) characterised their drive for respectability as an 'aspirational' rather than an actual identity.

These studies provide important insights into the possible inter-relationships between poverty, social exclusion and criminality as well as the lived experience of residents in disadvantaged communities. That people living within 'geographies of despair' experience a range of adverse consequences, including victimisation, illness (mental and physical) and unemployment, has led some to argue that poverty constitutes a human-rights issue (Cook, 2006: 9). These studies also demonstrate how stigmatising discourses of poverty that focus on the alleged moral and behavioural deficits of 'the poor' are repeated within working-class communities, evidenced by the defining of troubled families as 'troublesome' and disadvantage as 'dysfunction'. The distinction between 'them' and 'us' was apparent in all of these studies through the adoption of the

'rough'/'respectable' binary. This internal class divide may be necessitated by historical constructions of 'the poor' because: 'Respectability … would not be of concern if the working classes
(black or white) had not been consistently classified as dangerous, polluting, threatening, revolu-
tionary, pathological and without respect' (Skeggs, 1997: 1).

A desire to distance oneself from such negative and pervasive images is, therefore, neither
new nor surprising. At a time of austerity, however, this can 'harden attitudes to social welfare
in general and to people in poverty specifically' (Mooney, 2011: 4). One might also suggest that
divisiveness serves to limit the possibility of collective action, resistance and revolt by diverting attention from challenging structural issues to the values and behaviours of 'dangerous
classes'/'troubled families'/'problem youth'.

Discussion and conclusion

The profile of the prison population and the location of 'high-crime areas' suggests that the
relationships between non-conflict-related crime and poverty in Northern Ireland and the
Republic of Ireland are in line with international trends. However, the Conflict and its legacy
overlays poverty and disadvantage, and thereby brings an additional dimension to the analysis.
While the outbreak of the most recent period of conflict (from 1969 to 1994) might be easily
traced to the social, political and economic disadvantage of the Catholic/Nationalist population,
relative deprivation and radical criminology may also prove useful in the analysis of violence
since the ceasefires. Not only was there a gap between expectations and experiences within
affected communities, but the perception of loss within the Protestant/Unionist community
legitimated continued protest and violence. In addition, civil unrest and armed conflict may also
symbolise resistance to inequalities and grievances, while the state response in Northern Ireland
could be described as 'criminalising resistance'.

Despite these differences, some broad cross-cutting themes can be identified. That the
Conflict impacted the poorest communities is not entirely different to the impacts of 'crime' on
multiply deprived communities in the Republic of Ireland and elsewhere. That young men with
limited opportunities, voice, sense of identity and belonging might be 'easily drawn in' to quasi-
paramilitary/dissident groups, or low-level violence and protest, may also have some similarities
to the involvement of working-class young men elsewhere becoming involved in militant groups
or subcultures. Indeed similar methods of survival or resistance were employed by residents in
Hourigan's (2011) social housing estates and McAlister *et al.*'s (2009) conflict-affected areas and,
in both cases, perpetuated their exclusion. While it might be tempting to also draw comparisons
between the actions of 'gangs' in communities in the Republic of Ireland and those of paramilitaries in Northern Ireland, exporting and applying US and other locally specific concepts must
be cautioned against. It risks oversimplification and decontextualisation and the comparison of
social and political motivations which are inherently different and diverse, particularly when
groupings have specific political ideologies and goals. While there are clear cultural variations in
these processes, some further broad themes of commonality include the following:

(1) 'crime' (of whatever nature) in multiply deprived communities exacerbates poverty and
    social exclusion;
(2) political and policy responses tend to problematise 'youth', rather than address deeper struc-
    tural causes of crime and disadvantage;
(3) some within disadvantaged communities experience double exclusion and punishment;
(4) masculinity is implicated in crime;
(5) crime and disorder are often responses to inequalities; and

(6) structural factors shape community life, particularly their internal and external identities and reputations.

Although indigenous research largely supports international findings on poverty, conflict and crime, the literature adds to knowledge in several ways. Firstly, several of the studies reviewed show that high crime is not an inevitable by-product of socio-economic processes. In fact, social cohesion, political stability and a communitarian societal structure can dampen criminal potential in society (e.g. Stamatel, 2014; Norris and Fahey, 2014; Adler, 2000), although some suggest that these characteristics may not reduce re-offending rates (O'Donnell, Baumer and Hughes, 2008). However, strong and cohesive communities of this kind can be limiting, reproducing exclusive identities (see McAlister *et al.*, 2014), while informal methods of 'crime management' can be arbitrary and violent. Multiply deprived communities also continue to experience 'territorial stigmatisation' (Wacquant *et al.*, 2014) despite socially inclusive policy language and regeneration schemes which focused mainly on improving the urban environment rather than addressing governance issues and the socio-economic causes of community deterioration (see Hourigan, 2011; Treadwell-Shine and Norris, 2006).

Secondly, the discourses of poverty in both the Republic of Ireland and Northern Ireland differ from the narratives of their Anglophone counterparts which tend to emphasise risk and individual responsibility rather than welfarism (see Introduction). That both the Republic of Ireland and Northern Ireland largely avoided this ideological shift suggests that alternative narratives can exist within a late modern society. A devolved administration, the 'post-conflict' discourse of rights and a strong voluntary sector and lobbying culture in Northern Ireland may have aided in resisting the proliferation of risk (Dwyer and McAlister, 2013). Nevertheless, the demonisation, and in some cases criminalisation, of those seen to threaten the peace process in Northern Ireland or the veneer of respectability in disadvantaged communities in the Republic of Ireland reflects trends in individualising behaviour. That some people have been left behind and feel like 'outsiders', creating a sense of relative deprivation that may manifest in responses which resemble historical forms of resistance, is not therefore overly surprising. Demonisation is a useful tool in the process of denial, as it diverts attention from social, economic and political exclusion, from the legacies of the Conflict and the failures of government to address these effectively.

Some scholars have argued that the culture of the Republic of Ireland militates against welfare provision in other ways. Martin (2010) suggested that Catholic, liberal and conservative values construct poverty as a moral failure that should be resolved through individual and community responsibilisation rather than state intervention. In recent times, the austerity narrative that emerged in the wake of the recession has focused attention on the cost of welfare provision and downplayed its role in social protection (Healy, 2015; see also Considine and Dukelow, 2010). Moreover, a series of austerity budgets reduced public expenditure by €18 billion since 2008 (O'Sullivan, 2014). Nevertheless, social welfare rates have been protected and, as O'Sullivan (2014) notes, the reductions in public expenditure primarily affected capital expenditure rather than front-line services. In addition, welfarist principles and practices survive in the policies and practices of many state agencies, including the Probation Service (Healy, 2015), and public support for welfarism remains high (ESS, 2012). In fact, the recession has generated greater public awareness of issues related to social justice, poverty and inequality (Healy, 2012). On the basis of this evidence, it is likely that the welfare narrative will endure for the foreseeable future.

At the same time, it must be acknowledged that recent socio-economic developments increased the vulnerability of marginalised social groups. Harford (2010) discovered that the recession impacted deeply on disadvantaged communities, as the meagre benefits gained during the Celtic Tiger years were reversed, and unskilled work opportunities, including those in the informal economy, were decimated. In Northern Ireland an analysis of how tax and benefit reforms will impact income groups reveals that those in lower income quartiles will lose more as a proportion of their income than the same income groups in the UK, mainly due to a higher proportion of low-income households receiving Disability Living Allowance and a higher proportion of households with children (Browne, Hood and Joyce, 2013: 13). At the time of writing, political disagreement has placed the reform programme in jeopardy.

In both jurisdictions young people and men have been profoundly affected by the recession (McGinnity *et al.*, 2014; McQuaid, Hollywood and Canduela, 2010). This is worrying because it suggests that offenders, most of whom are young, male and from disadvantaged communities, may find it especially difficult to achieve social inclusion in the current economic climate. There is widespread agreement among criminologists that a lack of stable, high-quality employment opportunities can increase re-offending by fracturing ties to conventional institutions (Farrall, Bottoms and Shapland, 2010). However, this argument must be considered in the context of the crime drop that occurred across the Anglophone world, including the Republic of Ireland and Northern Ireland, from the 1990s onwards, despite dramatic social upheavals (van Dijk, Tseloni and Farrell, 2012; see also Skedd, *infra*). This suggests that traditional socio-economic indicators, such as inequality, may have less explanatory value in the contemporary context (e.g. Healy, Mulcahy and O'Donnell, 2013; van Dijk *et al.*, 2012). This chapter has shown that there are links between poverty, conflict and crime, but that these are more complex, nuanced and tenuous than initially thought. It is hoped that this review will inspire further work on this topic in both jurisdictions.

References

Adler, F. (1983) *Nations Not Obsessed with Crime*. Littleton CO: Fred B. Rothman.
—— (2000) 'Synnomie to anomie: A macro-sociological formulation', in F. Adler and W. Laufer (eds) *The Legacy of Anomie Theory*. Piscataway NJ: Transaction Publishers.
Barak, G., Leighton, P. and Cotton, A. (2014) *Class, Race, Gender and Crime: The Social Realities of Justice in America*. Lanham MD: Rowman & Littlefield.
Brewer, J., Lockhart, B. and Rodgers, P. (1997) *Crime in Ireland 1945–1995: Here Be Dragons*. Oxford: Clarendon Press.
Brown, A. (2004) 'Anti-social behaviour, crime control and social control', *The Howard Journal of Criminal Justice*, 43(2): 203–211.
Browne, J., Hood, A. and Joyce, R. (2013) *Child and Working-Age Poverty in Northern Ireland from 2010 to 2020. IFS Report R78*. London: Institute for Fiscal Studies. Available at http://www.ifs.org.uk/comms/r78.pdf
Byrne, J., Conway, M. and Ostermeyer, M. (2005) *Young People's Attitudes and Experiences of Policing, Violence and Community Safety in North Belfast*. Belfast: Northern Ireland Policing Board.
Cairns, E., Van Tal, J. and Williamson, A. (2004) *Social Capital, Collectivism-Individualism and Community Background in Northern Ireland*. Coleraine: Centre for Voluntary Action, University of Ulster. Available at: http://www.ofmdfmni.gov.uk/socialcapital.pdf (accessed 24 March 2015).
Campbell, L. (2010) 'Responding to gun crime in Ireland', *British Journal of Criminology*, 50(3): 414–434.
Chamlin, M. and Cochran, J. (2007) 'An evaluation of the assumptions that underlie institutional anomie theory', *Theoretical Criminology*, 11(1): 39–61.
Collier, P., Elliott, V., Hegre, H., Hoeffler, A., Reynal-Querol, M. and Sambanis, N. (2003) *Breaking the Conflict Trap: Civil War and Development Policy*. Washington: World Bank.
Considine, M. and Dukelow, F. (2010) 'Introduction: Boom to bust, Irish social policy in challenging times', *Irish Journal of Public Policy*, 2(1). Available at http://publish.ucc.ie/ijpp/2010/01/considinedukelow/00/en (accessed 10 March 2015).
Cook, D. (2006) *Criminal and Social Justice*. London: Sage.
Corcoran, M. (2014) 'Liveability and the lifeworld of the social housing neighbourhood', in M. Norris (ed.) *Social Housing, Disadvantage and Neighbourhood Liveability: Ten Years of Change in Social Housing Neighbourhoods*. Abingdon: Routledge.

Downes, D. (2013) *The Delinquent Solution: A Study in Subculture Theory.* Abingdon: Routledge.

Dwyer, C. and McAlister, S. (2013) 'Youth justice in Northern Ireland: Post-Good Friday, post-devolution, post-conflict?' Presentation at 'Diverging or merging: Youth justice in five jurisdictions', QUB 12 September 2013.

ESS (2012) 'Welfare Attitudes in Europe: Topline Results from Round 4 of the European Social Survey'. Available at: http://www.europeansocialsurvey.org/docs/findings/ESS4_toplines_issue_2_welfare_attitudes_in_europe.pdf (accessed 11 March 2015).

Fahey, T., Norris, M. and Field, C. (2014) 'Introduction', in M. Norris (ed.) *Social Housing, Disadvantage and Neighbourhood Liveability: Ten Years of Change in Social Housing Neighbourhoods.* Abingdon: Routledge.

Farrall, S., Bottoms, T. and Shapland, J. (2010) 'Social structures and desistance from crime', *European Journal of Criminology*, 7(6): 546–570.

Ferguson, N. and Michaelsen, M. (2013) *The Legacy of Conflict: Regional Deprivation and School Performance in Northern Ireland, Discussion Paper No. 7489.* Bonn: IZA.

Field, S. (1990) *Trends in Crime and Their Interpretation: A Study of Post-War Crime in England and Wales.* London: Home Office.

Fitzduff, M. and O'Hagan, L. (2000) 'The Northern Ireland Troubles: INCORE Background Paper'. Available: http://cain.ulst.ac.uk/othelem/incorepaper09.htm (accessed 3 January 2015).

Fitzgerald, J. (2007) 'Addressing issues of Social Exclusion in Moyross and other disadvantaged areas of Limerick City. Report to the Cabinet Committee on Social Inclusion'. Available at: http://www.limerickregeneration.org/MoyrossReptApr07.pdf (accessed 11 March 2015).

Goldson, B. and Muncie, J. (2006) 'Editors introduction', in B. Goldson and J. Muncie (eds) *Youth Crime and Justice.* London: Sage (pp. ix–xiv).

Goodhand, J. (2003) 'Enduring disorder and persistent poverty: A review of the linkages between war and chronic poverty', *World Development*, 31(3): 629–646.

Griffin, M. and Kelleher, P. (2010) 'Uncertain Futures: Men on the Margins in Limerick City', *Irish Probation Journal*: 24–45.

Grover, C. (2010) 'Social security policy and vindictiveness', *Sociological Research Online*, 15 (2). Available at: http://www.socresonline.org.uk/15/2/8.html (accessed 23 February 2015).

—— (2011) 'Social protest in 2011: Material and cultural aspects of economic inequalities', *Sociological Research Online*, 16 (4). Available at: http://www.socresonline.org.uk/16/4/18.html (accessed 23 February 2015).

Hancock, L. (1998) *Northern Ireland: Troubles Brewing.* Available at: http://cain.ulst.ac.uk/othelem/landon.htm (accessed 12 December 2014).

Harford, K. (2010) 'When poverty flies in the window, love walks out the door': Recessionary times for people experiencing poverty', *Irish Journal of Public Policy*, 2(1). Available at: http://publish.ucc.ie/ijpp/2010/01/harford/05/en (accessed 11 March 2015).

Hargie, O., O'Donnell, A. and McMullan, C. (2011) 'Constructions of social exclusion among young people from interface areas of Northern Ireland', *Youth & Society*, 43(3): 873–899.

Haydon, D. (2014) 'Early intervention for the prevention of offending in Northern Ireland', *Youth Justice*, 14(3): 226–240.

Haydon, D. and McAlister, S. (2015) 'Young People, Crime and Justice', in A.-M. McAlinden and C. Dwyer (eds) *Criminal Justice in Transition: The Northern Ireland Context.* Oxford: Hart Publishing (pp. 301–320).

Haydon, D., McAlister, S. and Scraton, P. (2012) 'Young people, conflict and regulation', *The Howard Journal of Criminal Justice*, 51(5): 503–520.

Healy, D. (2012) 'Advise, assist and befriend: Can probation supervision support desistance?', *Social Policy and Administration*, 46(4): 377–394.

—— (2015) 'The evolution of community sanctions in the Republic of Ireland: Continuity, challenge and change', in G. Robinson and F. McNeill (eds) *Community Punishment: European Perspectives.* Abingdon: Routledge.

Healy, D., Mulcahy, A. and O'Donnell, D. (2013) 'Crime, Punishment and Inequality in Ireland'. AIAS, GINI Discussion Paper 93. Available from www.gini-research.org.

Hillyard, P., Kelly, G., McLaughlin, E., Patsios, D. and Tomlinson, M. (2003) *Bare Necessities: Poverty and Social Exclusion in Northern Ireland, Key Findings.* Belfast: Democratic Dialogue.

Hillyard, P., Rolston, B. and Tomlinson, M. (2005) *Poverty and Conflict in Ireland: An International Perspective.* Dublin: Combat Poverty Agency/ Institute of Public Administration.

Honaker, J. (2008) *Unemployment and Violence in Northern Ireland: A Missing Data Model for Ecological Inference.* Available at: http://tercer.bol.ucla.edu/papers/ni.pdf (accessed 12 January 2015).

Horgan, G. (2005) 'Why the Bill of Rights should protect and promote the rights of children and young people in Northern Ireland. The particular circumstances of children in Northern Ireland', in G. Horgan and U. Kilkelly (eds) *Protecting children and young people's rights in the Bill of Rights for Northern Ireland. Why? How?* Belfast: Save the Children and Children's Law Centre.

Horgan, G. and Monteith, M. (2009) *What can we do to tackle child poverty in Northern Ireland?* York: Joseph Rowntree Foundation.

Horgan, G. and Rodgers, P. (2000) 'Young people's participation in a new Northern Ireland Society', *Youth & Society*, 32(1): 107–137.

Hourigan, N. (2011) (ed.) *Understanding Limerick: Social Exclusion and Change.* Cork: Cork University Press.

Ilan, J. (2007) 'If you don't let us in, we'll get arrested': Class-cultural dynamics in the provision of, and resistance to, youth justice work', *Youth Justice*, 10(1): 25–39.

—— (2011) 'Reclaiming respectability? The class-cultural dynamics of crime, community and governance in inner-city Dublin', *Urban Studies*, 48(6): 1137–1155.

—— (2013) 'Street social capital in the liquid city', *Ethnography*, 14(1): 3–24.

IPRT (2012) *The Vicious Circle of Social Exclusion and Crime: Ireland's Disproportionate Punishment of the Poor.* Dublin: Irish Penal Reform Trust.

JRF (2014) *Monitoring poverty and social exclusion in Northern Ireland 2014.* York: Joseph Rowntree Foundation.

Kingston, B., Huizinga, D. and Elliot, D. (2009) 'A test of social disorganisation theory in high-risk urban neighbourhoods', *Youth and Society*, 41(1): 53–79.

Lea, J. and Young, J. (1993) *What Is To Be Done About Law and Order?* London: Pluto Press.

Leonard, M. (2004) 'Bonding and bridging social capital: Reflections from Belfast', *Sociology*, 38(5): 927–944.

—— (2010) 'What's recreational about 'recreational rioting'? Children on the streets in Belfast', *Children and Society*, 24(1): 38–49.

Lloyd, T. (2009) *Stuck in the Middle: Some Young Men's Attitudes and Experiences of Violence, Conflict and Safety.* Belfast: University of Ulster.

McAlister, S. and Carr, N. (2014) 'Experiences of youth justice: Youth justice discourses and their multiple effects', *Youth Justice*, 12(3): 241–254.

McAlister, S., Scraton, P. and Haydon, D. (2009) *Childhood in Transition: Experiencing Marginalisation and Conflict in Northern Ireland.* Belfast: Queen's University, Prince's Trust and Save the Children.

—— (2014) 'Childhood in transition: Growing up in "post-conflict" Northern Ireland', *Children's Geographies*, 11(4): 297–311.

McAra, L. and McVie, S. (2007) 'Youth justice? The impact of system contact on patterns of desistance from offending', *European Journal of Criminology*, 4(3): 315–345.

McCullagh, C. (1996) *Crime in Ireland: A Sociological Introduction.* Cork: Cork University Press.

McGinnity, F., Russell, H., Watson, D., Kingston, G. and Kelly, E. (2014) *Winners and Losers? The Equality Impact of the Great Recession in Ireland.* Dublin: Equality Authority/ ESRI.

McQuaid, R., Hollywood, E. and Canduela, J. (2010) *Employment Inequalities in an Economic Downturn.* Belfast: Equality Commission for Northern Ireland.

Martin, C. (2010) 'Policy review: National action plans for combating poverty and social exclusion – from 1997 to the present', *Irish Journal of Public Policy*, 2(1). Available at: http://publish.ucc.ie/ijpp/2010/01/martin/06/en (accessed 11 March 2015).

Merton, R. (1938) 'Social structure and anomie', *American Sociological Review*, 3(5): 672–682.

—— (1968) *Social Theory and Social Structure.* New York: Free Press.

Messner, S. and Rosenfeld, R. (1997) *Crime and the American Dream.* Belmont CA: Wadsworth.

Mooney, G. (2011) *Stigmatising Poverty? The 'Broken Society' and Reflections on Anti-Welfarism in the UK Today.* Oxford: Oxfam. Available at: http://oro.open.ac.uk/29714/ (accessed 6 January 2015).

Mulvenna, G. (2012) 'The Protestant working class in Belfast: Education and civic erosion – an alternative analysis', *Irish Studies Review*, 20(4): 427–446.

Muncie, J. (2004) *Youth and Crime.* London: Sage.

NISRA (2014) 'Northern Ireland Poverty Bulletin 2012/13'. Available at: http://www.dsdni.gov.uk/ni_poverty_bulletin_201213.pdf (accessed 25 March 2015).

Nolan, P., Bryan, D., Dwyer, C., Hayward, K. and Shirlow, P. (2015) *The Flag Dispute: An Anatomy of a Protest, Summary Report.* Belfast: Queen's University Belfast.

Norris, M. (2014) (ed.) *Social Housing, Disadvantage and Neighbourhood Liveability: Ten Years of Change in Social Housing Neighbourhoods.* Abingdon: Routledge.

Norris, M. and Fahey, T. (2014) 'Conclusions', in M. Norris (ed.) *Social Housing, Disadvantage and Neighbourhood Liveability: Ten Years of Change in Social Housing Neighbourhoods.* Abingdon: Routledge.

141

O'Connor, N. and Staunton, C. (2015) *Cherishing All Equally: Economic Inequality in Ireland*. Dublin: TASC.

O'Donnell, I. and O'Sullivan, E. (2001) *Crime Control in Ireland: The Politics of Intolerance*. Cork: Cork University Press.

O'Donnell, I., Baumer, E. and Hughes, N. (2008) 'Recidivism in the Republic of Ireland', *Criminology and Criminal Justice*, 8(2): 123–146.

O'Gorman, A. (2014) 'Social (dis)order and community safety', in M. Norris (ed.) *Social Housing, Disadvantage and Neighbourhood Liveability: Ten Years of Change in Social Housing Neighbourhoods*. Abingdon: Routledge.

O'Sullivan, C. (2014) 'How Has Crisis and Austerity Changed the Shape of Public Expenditure?'. Available at: http://www.publicpolicy.ie/how-has-crisis-and-austerity-changed-the-shape-of-public-expenditure/ (accessed 11 March 2015).

Office of Social Inclusion (undated) 'What is Poverty?' Available at http://www.socialinclusion.ie/poverty.html (accessed 27 March 2015).

OFMDFM (2006) *Lifetime Opportunities: Government's Anti-Poverty and Social Exclusion Strategy for Northern Ireland*. Belfast: OFMDFM.

ONS (2013) 'The Effects of Taxes and Benefits on Household Income, 2011/12'. Available at: http://www.ons.gov.uk/ons/dcp171778_317365.pdf (accessed 11 March 2015).

Pfundmair, M., Graupmann, V., Frey, D. and Aydin, N. (2015) 'The different behavioural intentions of collectivists and individualists in response to social exclusion', *Personality and Social Psychology Bulletin*, 41(3): 363–378.

PRT (2014) *Bromley Briefings Prison Factfile*. London: Penal Reform Trust.

Reilly, J. (2004) 'Young men as victims and perpetrators of violence in Northern Ireland: A qualitative analysis', *Journal of Social Issues*, 60(3): 469–484.

Rodger, J. J. (2008) *Criminalising Social Policy: Anti-social Behaviour and Welfare in a Decivilised Society*. Cullompton: Willan.

Shaw, C. and McKay, H. (1942) *Juvenile Delinquency and Urban Areas*. Chicago IL: University of Chicago Press.

Skeggs, B. (1997) *Formations of Class and Gender: Becoming Respectable*. London: Sage.

Smyth, M. (2004) 'The process of demilitarisation and the reversibility of the peace process in Northern Ireland', *Terrorism and Political Violence*, 16(3): 544–566.

Smyth, M., Fay, M. T., Brough, E. and Hamilton, J. (2004) *The Impact of Political Conflict on Children in Northern Ireland*. Belfast: Institute for Conflict Research.

Squires, P. and Stephen, D. E. (2005) *Rougher Justice: Anti-Social Behaviour and Young People*. Cullompton: Willan.

Stamatel, J. (2014) 'Revisiting nations not obsessed with crime', *Crime, Law and Social Change*, 62(2): 113–129.

Taylor, I., Walton, P. and Young, J. (1973) *The New Criminology: For a Social Theory of Deviance*. London: Routledge.

Thornton, S. (1997) *The Subcultures Reader*. London: Routledge.

Tomlinson, M. (2012) 'From counter-terrorism to criminal justice: Transformation or business as usual?', *Howard Journal of Criminal Justice*, 50(5): 442–457.

Treadwell-Shine, K. and Norris, M. (2006) *Regenerating Local Housing Authority Estates: Review of Policy and Practice*. Dublin: Centre for Housing Research.

van Dijk, J., Tseloni, A. and Farrell, G. (2012) *The International Crime Drop: New Directions in Research*. London: Palgrave-Macmillan.

Wacquant, L. (2007) *Urban Outcasts: A Comparative Sociology of Advanced Marginality*. Cambridge: Polity Press.

Wacquant, L., Slater, T. and Pereira, V. (2014) 'Territorial stigmatisation in action', *Environment and Planning A*, 46: 1270–1280.

Watson, D. and Maître, B. (2014) *Social Transfers and Poverty Alleviation in Ireland: An Analysis of the Survey on Income and Living Conditions 2004–2011*. Dublin: Department of Social Protection.

Webber, C. (2007) 'Revaluating relative deprivation theory', *Theoretical Criminology*, 11(1): 97–120.

White, R. and Cunneen, C. (2006) 'Social class, youth crime and justice', in B. Goldson and J. Muncie (eds) *Youth Crime and Justice*. London: Sage (pp. 17–29).

World Bank (2013) Social Inclusion. Available at: http://www.worldbank.org/en/topic/socialdevelopment/brief/social-inclusion (accessed 25 March 2015).

—— (2014/2015) *Global Multidimensional Poverty Index (MPI) Interactive Databank*. Available at http://www.dataforall.org/dashboard/ophi/index.php.

Young, J. (1999) *The Exclusive Society*. London: Sage.

—— (2003) 'Merton with energy, Katz with structure: The sociology of vindictiveness and the criminology of transgression', *Theoretical Criminology*, 7(2): 398–414.

Notes

1 In both jurisdictions, poverty is measured as the percentage of people living in households with an equivalised income at less than 60 per cent of the median.
2 Social transfers refer to state payments such as Jobseekers Allowance, state pensions and child benefit.
3 Flags are symbolic expressions of cultural identity.

7

Gangs and gang-related activity

Niamh Hourigan

Introduction

Much of the blame for the significant increase in crime rates in the Republic of Ireland since the early 1960s has been laid at the door of the country's criminal gangs (Fallon *et al.*, 2012; Reynolds, 2006). High-profile gangs have been involved in robbery, extortion, racketeering and fuel-laundering (Mooney, 2013). Central to this gang activity has been the rise in public demand for illegal drugs (McCaffrey, 2011). In examining the rise of gang-related crime, Ciarán McCullagh (2011) notes:

> An unwavering focus on the individuals and criminal gangs involved is inaccurate and incomplete. Ultimately, the root of this criminal activity is in the continued demand for illegal drugs and the willingness of ordinary citizens to pay high prices for them.
>
> *(McCullagh, 2011: 23)*

In US and UK research, definitions of gangs have tended to highlight the youth of gang participants. For instance, the UK Centre for Social Justice in its report *Dying to Belong* (2009) draws on Hallworth and Young (2004) to define a gang as a:

> Group of young people who
> (1) see themselves ... as a discernible group;
> (2) engage in a range of criminal activity and violence;
> (3) identify with or lay claim over territory;
> (4) have some form of identifying structural feature; and
> (5) are in conflict with other, similar gangs.
>
> *(Centre for Social Justice, 2009: 21)*

In mapping the distinctions between gangs and other groups of youth more randomly engaged in violent behaviour, Ailsa Winton (2014) comments 'what distinguishes gangs from other groups of young people and other delinquent groups is the use of systematic (rather than sporadic) and socially meaningful (rather than instrumental) violence' (Winton, 2014: 4). While gang-related activity in Ireland largely conforms to these models, a review of the organisational development of gangs suggests that a significant proportion of gang members remain involved in gang structures well into adulthood (Duggan, 2009; Williams, 2011; Galvin, 2013). Thus, definitions of gangs which do not link participation to any specific stage in the life-course are more appropriate in this context.

This chapter focuses exclusively on the activities of criminal gangs in the twenty-six counties of the Republic of Ireland, a state which has experienced relative political stability in the last forty years (Ferriter, 2004). During the same period, Northern Irish society has been fractured by much greater levels of violence and political turmoil, with criminal gang-type units operating on both the Republican and Loyalist sides of the Conflict (Maguire, 1993; Silke, 2000). Because gang participation in Northern Ireland is entirely embedded with political/terrorist structures, theoretical frameworks developed to understand criminal gangs are neither adequate nor suitable for understanding gang participation in this context. In mapping more conventional criminal gang activity in the Republic of Ireland however, issues of ethnicity and identity are also visible. Since the 1990s there has been a significant increase in the numbers of Chinese, Eastern European and Asian gangs operating in the Republic of Ireland, whose activities mainly focus on drugs manufacture and distribution as well as people and sex trafficking (Cusack, 2014). As these gangs do not exhibit the distinctive cultural characteristics of Irish criminal gangs, their activities will also not be the primary focus of this chapter. Instead the chapter seeks to establish the key distinguishing features of criminal gangs that are of Irish and Irish Traveller origin. Two key elements of this gang-related activity are highlighted: the role of family and kinship in structuring criminal gangs, as well as the complexities generated by interlinkages with dissident groups which primarily originate within Northern Ireland.

The central role of family in shaping social structures and cultural norms in the Republic of Ireland has been examined in a range of studies (Whelan, 1994; Fine-Davies, 2011; Connolly, 2014). Gang structures reflect this emphasis on kinship relations, with family playing a key role in structuring the hierarchies of a number of prominent criminal gangs (Hourigan, 2011; Williams, 2011). The role of family and kinship in gang activity is therefore quite distinct from its role in the US and UK youth gangs, where policy analysts have repeatedly portrayed gangs as replacement families for marginalised youth alienated from their families of origin (Hirschi, 1969; Loeber and Farrington, 1998; Thornberry, 1998).

A second distinctive feature of Irish gangs is their complex interactions with dissident groups and the role these links play in shaping their engagement with the state. The outbreak of the Conflict in Northern Ireland led to an upsurge in violent activity from the late 1960s onwards. Not surprisingly, a number of violent groups on the Republican, and, to a lesser extent, the Loyalist, side have developed links to gangs south of the border. The Republic of Ireland also has its own tradition of militant Republicanism which has overlapped with gang activity. These interactions have shaped the methods used by gangs and their capacity to access arms. In 1998 the Republic of Ireland's National Crime Forum (1998) acknowledged:

> The emergence of political subversives has meant that more guns have become available to ordinary criminals and there has been a big increase in the number of armed robberies. Disaffected political figures flirting with the regular underworld have made their terrorist skills and their superior weapons available on occasions.
>
> *(National Crime Forum, 1998: 14)*

Interactions with dissident groups have also impacted on attempts by gangs to control pockets of marginalised neighbourhoods in cities (Cusack, 2010). In some instances gangs have paid protection to dissident groups to order to operate in specific areas, while in other cases their attempts to claim territory have been openly challenged by Republican groups (Lowe, 2013). Thus the process of making claims to territory, a practice widespread amongst gangs globally, has become more complex in the Republic of Ireland because of the interlinkages between gangs and dissident groups. The chapter will begin by providing an overview of international gang research and assessing how the key themes developed within this literature are relevant to the analysis of gangs in the Republic of Ireland. This history of gang activity in this jurisdiction and the relatively limited amount of academic and policy research on gangs will be discussed. Finally, two features of criminal gangs – kinship relations and links with dissident groups – will be considered in terms of mapping the distinctive characteristics of gangs and gang-related activity in this jurisdiction.

Gang research

The first major study of gang-related activity was conducted by a member of the Chicago School, Frederic Thrasher who published his seminal analysis *The Gang* in 1927. Thrasher sought to describe the street gangs which were emerging within marginalised urban areas in Chicago. He argued that the activities of these gangs were a response to the severe social disorganisation experienced in these communities. Research on gang participation remained dominated by surveys of American gangs for the next forty years. After World War II a series of studies were conducted by researchers attached to intervention programmes funded by federal and state authorities. This research yielded a number of important publications including Cloward and Ohlin's *Delinquency and Opportunity* (1960) and David Matza's highly regarded *Delinquency and Drift* (1966). These books spearheaded an emerging field of research which sought to examine why young people participate in gangs, how gangs are structured, what type of activities they engage in and how they view the state (Cohen, 1955; Miller, 1958; Miller *et al.*, 1961). By 1971 however, Malcolm Klein in his study *Street Gangs and Street Workers* (1971) expressed concern that this type of research was increasing gang cohesion and effectively glamorising participation, rather than eliminating gang activity.

As gang research evolved from the 1970s onwards, a greater attempt was made to contextualise the emergence and operation of gangs within broader patterns of change in American society. John Hagedorn's landmark study *People and Folks* (1988) drew on interviews with the 'top dogs' of nineteen Milwaukee gangs to investigate the role of de-industrialisation and unemployment in gang emergence. Other analysts have considered the role of poverty and negative school experience (Curry and Spergal, 1992) as well as institutional racism (Hayden, 2004). However, Katz and Jackson-Jacobs (2004) have criticised US gang research for its narrow focus on gang units, which, they argue, ignores the broader social ecology in which these groups emerge. They note:

> Gang research has also remained separate from sociological studies of youth social life and culture outside of gangs. Gang studies refer primarily to other gang studies but not to studies of young male, or female social life, violence or even criminality outside gangs.
>
> *(Katz and Jackson-Jacobs, 2004: 97)*

While there may be some truth in these accusations, there have been a range of studies of disadvantaged neighbourhoods in the United States which have provided this deeper ecological understanding of communities which generate gangs. The work of William Julius Wilson (1997) which stresses the role of joblessness in creating ghettos of urban poverty in US cities and Philippe Bourgois (1999) on the related rise of drugs distribution networks in these neighbourhoods has provided a much deeper understanding of these contexts. Elijah Anderson's (2000) mapping of the 'code of the street' in Philadelphia has demonstrated the enormous challenges which residents face in negotiating the public spaces of these districts. Finally, Loic Wacquant's (2008) comparative research on 'urban outcasts' in Chicago provides specific insights into the role of state and federal policy in creating this marginalisation and points to some important differences with similar contexts in France.

The difficulty in applying frameworks developed by American researchers to the activities of European gangs was highlighted by Klein *et al.* (2001) in their book *The Eurogang Paradox*. Conducted under the auspices of the Euro-gang programme, this project led to a mapping of the distinctive features of European gangs. New comparative studies of the activities of American and European gangs were conducted, most notably, Huizinga and Schumann's (2001) comparison of gangs in Denver, Colorado, and Bremen, Germany. Esbensen and Weerman (2005) also undertook a large-scale comparison of gang participation in the Netherlands and the United States. From this research, it is clear that both the differing welfare regimes and firearm availability policies have generated pronounced differences between European and American gangs (Giora Shoham *et al.*, 2010).

Until the 1980s gangs were rather neglected within British sociology and criminology, despite some significant stand-alone studies (Mays, 1954; Patrick, 1973). However, British sociology historically devoted much attention to the cultural and stylistic elements of youth delinquency which manifested in tension between gangs of mods and rockers, skinheads and football hooligans (Pearson, 1983; Cohen, 2002). The potential for education systems to reproduce the social marginalisation which contributes to gang participation has also been superbly portrayed in Paul Willis's *Learning to Labour* (1977). The recent upsurge in scholarly interest in gangs in the UK is linked to public and political concern about inter-gang violence which increased during the late 1980s and early 1990s (Alleyne and Wood, 2014; Young, Fitzgibbon and Silverstone, 2014). The volume of gang research has surged with projects interrogating the specific features of British gangs as well as important studies examining the specific role of race, religion and gender in contributing to gang participation (Aldridge and Medina, 2008; Bullock and Tilley, 2002; Hallsworth and Silverstone, 2009; Deuchar and Holligan, 2010; Goldson, 2011).

Aside from this international literature, academics and policy analysts attempting to understand gang participation in the Republic of Ireland have four main sources of information. Firstly, media reports and the associated 'true crime' publishing genre have provided a detailed narrative of the activities of the state's most notorious gangs since the 1960s. As most of this material has been written by journalists reporting on gangs for national newspapers, the focus of these descriptions tends to be on 'daring heists', infamous court cases and the lifestyles of gang leaders rather than the underlying structural inequality which produces gang participation (Williams, 2004, 2011, 2014; Duggan, 2009; McCafferty, 2011; Foy, 2012; Mooney, 2013; Galvin, 2013). There have been a smaller number of academic studies of community violence and systems of intimidation in disadvantaged neighbourhoods. Under the auspices of the Health Research Board, Johnny Connolly (2006, 2014) conducted research on the activities of gangs involved in drugs distribution networks. In 2009 Megan O'Leary provided a brief overview of the intimidation of families in Dublin for the Family Support Network (O'Leary, 2009). Marie-Claire Van Hout and Tim Bingham (2012) used crime statistics to map the 'public nuisance' impact of drugs gangs on inner-city Dublin. Given this limited scale of these studies, their primary focus has been to map the nature and extent of intimidation by gangs involved in drugs distribution in marginalised communities in Dublin and recommend potential policy responses. Finally, a more in-depth three-year study of fear, feuding and intimidation by criminal gangs in Limerick city was published as part of my own contribution to the *Understanding Limerick* collection in 2011 (Hourigan, 2011).

Legal scholars examining the development of organised crime legislation provide a third source of information. Liz Campbell (2013) has conducted a systematic review of organised crime law which has been enacted as a result of the activities of high-profile gang crimes. She highlights the distinction between British and Republic of Ireland crime legislation and explores the tension between due process and protecting the public in the recalibration of the criminal law which impacts on gangs in the Republic of Ireland. Finally, studies of policing demonstrate how the operation of An Garda Síochána has changed in response to the activities of criminal gangs (Brady, 2014; Conway, 2013). These studies highlight how the modernisation of criminal gangs from the 1960s onwards forced a related modernisation of approaches to policing criminal gangs.

A much broader range of studies have examined motivations for participation in Loyalist and Republicans groups in Northern Ireland. This research is quite distinct from the organised crime/gang research in the Republic but has drawn on international gang participation literature at certain points (McClung Lee, 1975; Short, 1980; Harland and McCready, 2014). Although no systematic review of gang activity south of the border has ever been published, by combining the four sources of material outlined above, it is possible to provide an overview of gang activity in the Republic of Ireland since the 1960s.

Gangs

Gang participation in the Republic of Ireland predates the foundation of the state in 1922. During the seventeenth, eighteenth and nineteenth centuries secret societies were gangs involved in a range of vigilante activities against landlords and tenants who rented the land-holdings of those evicted (Christianson, 1972; Feeley, 1980). This gang activity was coupled with a strong pattern of feuding and faction-fighting at community level, which thrived in an environment where many Catholics preferred to resolve their problems amongst themselves rather than turn to the official criminal justice system (O'Donnell, 1975). As the Irish Diaspora spread in the late nineteenth century, Irish gangs made their presence felt in the United States, where they were involved in the draft riots of the Civil War period. In New York, Irish youth were involved in 'voting gangs' which sought to intimidate the political rivals of favoured Irish or Irish–American political candidates (Hagedorn, 2006). While the Irish abroad were involved in gangs, indigenous gang-related activity was also evident on the island of Ireland in the late nineteenth and early twentieth centuries. Tenement life created the conditions for the emergence of youth gangs similar to those described by Thrasher in 1927. These gangs ranged from the play-groups of local children and adolescents to the more formal groups such as the Animal Gang which engaged in street fights with other gangs in disadvantaged Dublin neighbourhoods in the 1930s (Quinlan, 2012). While these gangs were deeply embedded in their own communities, the country, post-Independence, lacked the ethnic diversity which provided much of the spark for inter-gang violence in the United States during this period.

Contemporary gang culture in the Republic of Ireland is rooted in the parallel processes of modernisation, urbanisation, secularisation and industrialisation which transformed society from the 1960s onwards (McCullagh, 2011). Fifty years after the 1916 Rising, the economy experienced unprecedented prosperity, and Irish society was being transformed by free education and globalisation (Lee, 1989; Ferriter, 2004). However, 1967 marked the dawn of a new associated era of gang crime, with the Republic of Ireland's first armed robbery conducted on a bank, in Drumcondra in Dublin, by a Republican/Socialist gang describing itself as Saor Éire. The core members of Saor Éire had left the ranks of the IRA in the early 1960s and claimed they were starting a movement which would encourage workers and small farmers to rise up against the state. They conducted a spate of armed robberies south of the border in the late 1960s, a period when it became clear that deepening political unrest in Northern Ireland was inspiring more directly criminal forms of gang participation south of the border. The complexity of these North–South relationships is even more striking when the web of relationships leading to the 1971 Arms Trial were ultimately revealed. Martin Casey and Christy Dunne, two members of Saor Éire, assisted senior politicians in the Republic in purchasing arms for the use of Catholics in Northern Ireland (Williams, 2011). While Casey's presence highlighted the difficulty in distinguishing between gang activity and political insurgency at official level, Dunne's role foreshadowed the increasing prominence of family gangs at the core of gang-related crime in the Republic of Ireland.

Christy Dunne has been described as the godfather of gang crime in the Republic of Ireland (O'Toole, 2012). He grew up in inner-city Dublin, the eldest of a large family of neglected children. He and six of his seven brothers were admitted to industrial schools during the course of their childhood. Their experience of industrial school life not only resulted in the creation of strong bonds with other figures who were to become leaders of Dublin gangs, but also resulted in experiences of abuse which they themselves claimed had a marked hardening effect on their personalities. In an interview given to RTÉ in 1990, Christy Dunne's brother Henry claimed '[t]hey beat us and abused us so much, they made animals of us' (quoted in Williams, 2011: 50). During the early 1970s the Dunnes developed a reputation as one of Dublin's most notorious family gangs. They were involved in a succession of armed robberies; however, after a raid on a Tipperary pharmaceutical plant in 1978, they realised that drugs were a more lucrative source of revenue (Byrne, 2011). In a society experiencing rapid modernisation, the market for illegal drugs was growing. Between 1978 and 1980 the Dunnes built a network of international contacts with cannabis and heroin suppliers, taking advantage of the international glut in supply due to political turmoil in the Middle East and Afghanistan (Haq, 1996). They developed an extensive network of local dealers throughout North inner-city Dublin and solidified their links with other upcoming family gangs. Martin Cahill later known as 'The General' had been an inmate of Daingean industrial school with Larry Dunne in 1965, and he and the Dunnes were at the centre of an emerging network of family gangs in the city at this time.

The depth of Conflict in Northern Ireland during the 1970s resulted in the diversion of Garda resources to the border region, leaving a policing vacuum in marginalised neighbourhoods in the Republic of Ireland which was fully exploited by emerging criminal gangs. Aogán Mulcahy (2002) argues that aside from the depletion of policing resources, there was an official indifference to the plight of communities experiencing the negative consequences of Dublin's burgeoning drugs market. He states 'the fact that such inaction continued into the 1980s, when heroin began to exert such a massive influence, speaks volumes about the lack of police engagement with community concerns' (Mulcahy, 2002: 228). The bulk of criminal gangs during the 1970s emerged from three neighbourhoods in Dublin, Crumlin, Drimnagh and Ballyfermot, and unfortunately much of their activity was focused on disadvantaged Northside neighbourhoods. By 1981 the rapid spread of heroin addiction in Dublin's inner city had led to an upsurge in street crime, child neglect and related health issues. There was increasing disquiet within these communities about the activities of drugs-related criminal gangs which resulted in the election of Tony Gregory as a TD in 1982. He ran on a political mandate to tackle inner-city poverty and drugs. When little changed after his election, local residents began to take matters into their own hands and formed *Concerned Parents Against Drugs* (CPAD) in 1983. The group initially became involved in marching on the homes of known drug-dealers. However, as the movement developed, speculation emerged that Republican elements were using the group to build a power-base in Dublin. A number of prominent members of CPAD left the organisation, claiming that some members of the group were asking drug-dealers to pay protection money (Ferriter, 2004).

Although Dublin was the heartland of gang activity in the Republic of Ireland, similar criminal gangs were emerging in other parts of the country. The social exclusion experienced by residents in local authority housing estates was exacerbated in the mid-1980s by the €5,000 grant scheme which enabled the most affluent residents to move into the private housing sector (O'Connell, 2011). After such residents left, a political vacuum was created in these neighbourhoods. In some cases, it was filled by local gangs with varying levels of sophistication and organisation. Small-scale versions of Dublin's criminal gangs appeared in Cork, Galway and, most notably, Limerick city, where individual families used their involvement in the horse trade to make connections with drugs suppliers at national and international level (Duggan, 2009). In Limerick, the family gang structure was interwoven with a pre-existing tendency towards inter-family feuding, which had been a long-standing feature of tenement life in the city (Hourigan, 2011).

As the country's economy began to boom in the early 1990s, increased disposable income in the general population led to a growing demand for club drugs such as ecstasy and cocaine (Mooney, 2013; McCaffrey, 2011). As a result, family gangs experienced a new level of affluence and a related increase in confidence. The activities of gang leaders became more visible and were described frequently in the national media, most notably by the *Sunday World* and by the *Sunday Independent*'s crime correspondent Veronica Guerin. When she was shot by a member of a criminal gang in 1996 the Republic's government began to realise that the intimidation of individuals by criminal gangs, a problem which had been confined to disadvantaged communities, was spilling over into the wider society. A range of new measures to tackle gang crime were announced, most notably the establishment of the Criminal Assets Bureau – the CAB, as it became known – which achieved some success in stripping members of criminal gangs of assets. The model was reproduced in a range of other European countries where concerns were growing about the activities of criminal gangs (O'Mahony, 2002; see also Campbell, *infra*). While legislative change was occurring in the Republic of Ireland, the peace process was gaining momentum in Northern Ireland. The signing of the Good Friday Agreement in 1998 altered the structure of Republicanism and created divisions between those who accepted the new status quo and dissident groups who rejected the agreement (Horgan, 2013). These internal conflicts within Northern Republicanism, combined with the growing number of non-Irish gangs operating south of the border, greatly increased the complexity of gang activity as the country moved into the twenty-first century.

Even after the murder of Veronica Guerin a certain public tolerance for the activities of criminal gangs continued, perhaps because it was the public who were consuming the drugs and other commodities they were selling (McCullagh, 2011). This public tolerance diminished considerably after two murders in Limerick city. In 2008 Shane Geoghegan, a local rugby player, was murdered when he was mistaken for an associate of a local family gang. The following year Roy Collins, the son of a local Limerick businessman who had given evidence against a Limerick gang, was shot (Galvin, 2013; Williams, 2014). In the wake of both these murders, there was a public outcry about gang activity in Limerick city. The Criminal Justice Act (Amendment) 2009 was introduced, which provided the state with a range of new powers to prosecute gang members (see, further, Campbell, *infra*). In her speech to the Dáil in 2014, outlining the reasons why the Act was introduced, Minister for Justice Frances Fitzgerald stated, '[o]rganised criminal gangs were behaving as though they were untouchable by the Gardaí and the Courts. They even appeared to be taunting those tasked with preventing and investigating criminal acts' (Irish Government News Service, 2014: 11). The Criminal Justice Act 2006 allowed the state to use the non-jury Special Criminal Court for a limited number of gang-related offences including:

(1) directing the activities of a criminal organisation (section 71A);
(2) participating or contributing to certain activities of a criminal organisation (section 72);
(3) committing a serious offence for a criminal organisation (section 73);
(4) liability for the offences committed by the body corporate (section 76).

These legislative changes were accompanied by a number of targeted policing measures including the deployment of armed response units, the use of CCTV surveillance, the placing of witnesses in witness-protection programmes and significant investment of resources in community policing (Hourigan, 2011). These changes resulted in a number of high-profile convictions of senior members of criminal gangs.

As well as criminal justice measures, there was some limited official recognition that the deep social exclusion which characterised the urban areas generating gangs may have contributed to the problem (Fitzgerald, 2007). Although the Republic of Ireland became much wealthier between 1995 and 2007, it also became much more unequal (Allen, 2000; Kirby, 2001; O'Hearn, 2003). The rapid increase in employment, wage levels and property prices during this period made barely any impact on marginalised communities in Dublin, Limerick and other cities. Young people living in these neighbourhoods were just as attracted to the luxury consumer goods such as cars, clothes and gadgets as their more affluent fellow citizens. Becoming involved in drugs distribution or other illegal activities through a gang was a direct route to gaining these objects of desirability for a group largely excluded from Celtic Tiger affluence. Regeneration projects were established in both West Dublin and Limerick which aimed to unpick this marginalisation. However, much of the initial focus of these projects was on building new physical infrastructure, such as houses and community facilities (Bisset, 2008). The Limerick Regeneration project was sharply affected by the 2007–2008 collapse in the property market and was forced to re-orient its activities towards youth intervention projects. Given the subsequent decrease in crime rates in the city, it is probable that this approach was more effective (Prenderville, 2013).

As the Irish economy moved into recession in 2010, the demand for cocaine decreased significantly as disposable income contracted, and some gangs turned their attention to heroin and other commodities, such as fuel (Pike and King, 2013). While the commodities traded by gangs have changed, the structures of more established gangs are also in flux as a result of new legislation and policing approaches. Increasingly, the more senior members of criminal gangs reside outside the state in countries which have less robust legislation governing organised crime. These senior figures are leading gangs which are truly transnational, with links across a number of European states including the Republic of Ireland and Northern Ireland (McCaffrey, 2011; Mooney, 2013). Within the state itself, foot-soldiers of these transnational gangs compete with gangs from other ethnic groups to control their share of lucrative markets. The border region has also become an increasingly important focus for gang activity. Criminal gangs in this area are focusing their attention on the laundering of fuel, foodstuffs and other commodities, as well as drugs (PSNI and An Garda Síochána, 2012). Yet, despite these changes, at least two underlying characteristics of gang activity remain constant: the role of family relationships in structuring gang hierarchies and the complex interactions between gangs and dissident groups.

Family and gang participation

Research conducted in the United States and Britain on the reasons for gang participation has consistently highlighted lack of integration into family structures as a key contributory factor. In his seminal study *Causes of Delinquency*, Hirschi (1969) argued that a child's strong positive attachment to their family acts as a protection against delinquency and gang participation. In contrast, when the attachment to the family is weak, children are more likely to become involved in gangs. These findings have been supported by a range of subsequent studies on gang participation (Loeber and Farrington, 1998; Thornberry, 1998). In their 2011 study of gang participation in England, Alleyne and Wood (2014) found:

> Young people look to their parents for guidance and support, and if left to their own devices, they succumb to the antisocial pressures from their peers … parental management can be considered a protective factor, and pressure from deviant peers, individual delinquency, and neighbourhood gangs can be considered a risk factor.
>
> *(Alleyne and Wood, 2014: 560)*

McCord (1991) emphasised the relational quality of parenting in protecting against gang participation. She argues that children with engaged, attentive mothers are less likely to become involved in gangs, while fathers can also have a positive, preventative influence, particularly during puberty and adolescence. Young, Fitzgibbon and Silverstone (2014) note that the implication of these studies is that:

> Youngsters are attracted to gangs because they seek a surrogate family to fulfil their emotional needs … children from 'dysfunctional families' join gangs to fill a void where 'the gang', for a significant number of young people growing up in our most deprived communities, has become a substitute family.
>
> *(Young et al., 2014 : 172)*

However, a review of the limited literature on gang participation in the Republic of Ireland suggests that this analysis of the link between family and gang participation may be at odds with the Irish experience. A survey of the 'true crime' narratives which describe the activities of the more prominent gangs reveals the centrality of family relationships to gang participation. Family gangs such as the Dunnes, the McCarthy-Dundons and the Keane-Collopys all featured prominently in this literature. Even the reviews of the activities of individual high-profile criminals such as Martin Cahill, John Gilligan and, more recently, Christy Kinahan are notable because of the involvement of family members in their networks of operation. These gang members have not, by and large, been alienated from their families despite, in some cases, poor parental management. Instead, they are deeply integrated into their immediate and extended families, and their gang participation is embedded in these links.

Why have family relationships played so integral a role in the structure of criminal gangs in this country? David Lloyd (2000) has argued family can be a very important unit in societies which have experienced colonialism, because they are secure sites where challenging understandings of power can be developed. Because of the deep trust that exists within families, they are units where information can be tightly controlled and behaviour monitored. Therefore, the family provides, in some ways, an ideal basic unit for a criminal gang.

Aside from the trust and loyalty that characterises family relationships, the extended family is also one of the primary sources of identity in marginalised communities. In neighbourhoods where long-term intergenerational unemployment is not unusual, occupation rarely carries the same significance in terms of defining identity that it does for the middle class (Doherty, 2009). In my three-year study of disadvantaged communities in Limerick, the extended family emerged as the primary means through which individuals were positioned in terms of status and identity within local communities. One gang member described his 'buddy' Keith in the following terms:

'[w]hen I see a guy like Keith, or any guy on the street, I'm thinking of his family, his brother, his mother, what crowd he hangs with, I don't really see him as separate, no-one is separate or on their own here' (Hourigan, 2011: 62). Because the rate of marriage is low and the number of lone parents high, blood relationships play a particularly important role in shaping family ties in marginalised neighbourhoods in Limerick (McCafferty, 2011). However, a proportion of those involved in gang activity in Limerick were drawn from the Irish Traveller community. Within this community, the bonds of marriage are of much greater importance (Hourigan and Campbell, 2010). Therefore, family ties formed through marriage may have a more significant impact on Traveller gang participation. In the gangs considered as part of the Limerick study, no member could achieve a really senior role in the gang hierarchy without a family relationship to the other members.

There are points however, where elements of the US/UK analysis can be applied to the Republic of Ireland. As part of the Limerick study, the capacity of criminal gangs to use the anti-social behaviour of children as means of controlling territorial pockets of estates was highlighted (Hourigan, 2011). The position of children and adolescents as a distinct stratum of gangs has also recently been highlighted by Johnny Connolly (2014). In some cases these children have blood ties to gang members. However, in other cases they are simply neglected children from deeply dysfunctional families who are available for exploitation. Sharon, a woman interviewed for the *Understanding Limerick* study, described her son Tom's friend who was being gradually drawn into a local criminal gang. She said:

> Tom is a nice enough kid but his dad has moved on long ago. His mam has got a new fella who doesn't like him very much and gives him the odd clip round the ear. Sometimes he sleeps rough on the streets, sometimes he stays here or with other friends but I know he's lonely and when he's with the gang, he has a kinda escape from all that. Instead of feelin' sorry for him, we're all afraid of him

(quoted in Hourigan, 2011: 81)

In these cases, the gang does appear to be operating as a surrogate family for the neglected child or adolescent, a function which converges more closely with the Anglo-American analysis.

The importance of family relationships in embedding, rather than challenging, gang participation raises significant questions about the juvenile justice intervention strategies developed by the Department of Justice and the Health Services Executive. A number of these strategies rely heavily on parental intervention in tackling gang participation (Leahy, 2009). However, if children involved in gangs are strongly embedded in families which support their gang participation because other family members are also involved in the gang, it is unlikely that these interventions will be successful. The critical role of family also significantly complicates witness protection. In theory, if the state places a witness in a protection programme, it shields them from reprisals as a result of their testimony. However, if members of the witnesses' extended family are viewed as legitimate targets, the task of protecting witnesses becomes much more complex. This difficulty was clearly evident in the state's attempt to protect members of the Collins family who testified against members of the McCarthy-Dundon gang (Baker, 2012). In this case, the whole family eventually had to opt for witness relocation outside the country, even though only a few members actually gave evidence against the gang. Finally, the significance of family relationships in Irish gangs suggests that research which explores crime rooted in amoral familialism (the prioritisation of one family's interests over the collective interests of the community) may hold specific insights for understanding the operation of gangs in the Republic of Ireland (Basham, 1996; Osgood and Ong, 2001; Pine, 2012).

Gangs and contested sovereignty

A key feature of gangs is their tendency to lay claim to territory particularly in the urban neighbourhoods in which they operate. This tendency was evident in Thrasher's (1927) first study of gangs in the United States and has profoundly shaped inter-gang conflicts in America, most notoriously between the Crips and the Bloods (Sullivan, 2001). However, the primary targets in these violent conflicts are usually other gangs in contexts where control of territory determines capacity to engage in lucrative drug-dealing activities. Gangs may have oppositional relationships with the state at local level which shapes their engagement with the criminal justice system. However, they rarely coherently challenge the state's legitimacy at a macro-level. Indeed, Ailsa Winton (2014) notes that gangs are generally more concerned with their own survival than with political change. She argues that the key characteristic that 'distinguishes gangs from other non-state armed groups in conflict studies is precisely that they do not seek to overthrow the state' (Winton, 2014: 9). Even in South Africa where the state is relatively new, Jensen and Rodgers (2008) found that local gangs are:

> [R]eally not fighting 'for' anything but themselves. Although they can plausibly be said to be fighting 'against' wider structural circumstances of economic exclusion and racism, most of the time the behaviour patterns of gang members are clearly motivated principally by their own interests.
>
> *(Jensen and Rodgers, 2008: 231)*

The desire of gangs to promote their own interests over collective political interests within communities shapes the means by which they seek to control residents in neighbourhoods which are part of their territory. In some cases this need to control can lead to attempts to establish themselves as the effective sovereign power-holders in these areas. Gangs who succeed in convincing local residents that the state is remote and does not care about their welfare can effectively sever the relationship between the citizen and the state at community level. As a consequence, residents are discouraged from co-operating with the police and the criminal justice system in a manner which benefits gang activities (Anderson, 2000; Hourigan, 2011).

The capacity of gang members to establish themselves as power-holders is greatly increased if the police are not effective at responding to the low-level anti-social behaviour. In the *Understanding Limerick* study, one interviewee, Vinnie, illustrated how quickly criminal gangs can occupy a political vacuum when policing is ineffective. He said:

> I was out washing the van one day and this young fella from down the road comes over to me an' asks me for a lift into town. He was out of his fuckin' head so I wasn't goin' to give him a lift. Anyway, that night my tyres got slashed. The next day the community Gardaí came round an' they said they'd look into it and they'd see what they could do. That night my windows got broken. I rang looking for the Guard the next day, but they weren't working … Monday morning I rang looking for the Guard again, but the Guard was sick this time, so I rang my brother to ask him 'what should I do' and he said 'Why don't you get one of the [local gang] on to it?' Now I'm not gonna do that 'coz I know better, but lots of people round here would do exactly that in my shoes.
>
> *(quoted in Hourigan, 2011: 130)*

Blom Hansen and Stepputat (2006) argue that the capacity of gangs to contest sovereignty and assume territorial control in urban marginalised areas may be particularly pronounced in post-colonial societies. In the Republic of Ireland, the model of the nation historically enshrined within Irish nationalism is a thirty-two-county model which is at odds with the twenty-six county structure of the administrative state (Todd *et al.*, 2006). This disjuncture has not only had a significant role in shaping political cleavages but also allowed members of gangs to borrow Republican ideology in order to challenge the state's legitimacy in responding to their activities. This ideological borrowing was particularly evident during the early 1970s, when heightened gang activity coincided with a period of deep violence in Northern Ireland. Brendan Halligan, a Labour TD in the Fine Gael/Labour coalition government between 1973 and 1977, said: 'The IRA at that point did not recognise the legitimacy of the State, it referred to us all as quislings and traitors' (quoted in Williams, 2011: 97).

By 1979, Conor Brady, security editor of the *Irish Times*, had identified three pathways through which violence in Northern Ireland had influenced gang-related activity in the Republic of Ireland. As well as the diversion of Garda resources to the border, he noted that there was a direct spill-over of crime from Northern Ireland, with crimes being committed by Republicans on the run in the Republic of Ireland. He also identified a strong imitative trend, with criminal gangs in the Republic adopting the methods of Northern Republicans (Brady, 1979).

There has been no major scholarly analysis of the relationship between criminal gangs and Republicans/Loyalists in the Republic of Ireland. However, a survey of media analysis and court proceedings since the 1970s demonstrates some long-standing patterns:

(1) GANG STRUCTURE: Irish gangs appear to operate along a spectrum. At one end of the spectrum are dissident and paramilitary groups from Northern Ireland and the Republic of Ireland who may engage in criminal activities but whose focus is primarily political. At the other end of the spectrum are gangs whose focus is solely criminal but who will engage with dissidents around issues of protection payments, arms deals, etc. There would appear to be a considerable number of groups in the middle of the spectrum where there is a significant overlap between criminal gangs and dissident Republicans.

(2) GANG ACTIVITIES: Gangs and dissident groups have traded a range of commodities since the 1970s. However, the most significant part of this trade would appear to be weapons, which were traded to Northern Ireland in the early 1970s and were traded by Republicans to groups south of the border from the late 1980s onwards.

(3) PROTECTION: Criminal gangs pay protection to dissident Republican groups in exchange for being allowed to continue with their activities. Resistance to this practice on the part of gang members has led to considerable conflict between gang leaders and Republicans, a practice which resulted in the murder of dissident Republican leader Alan Ryan in Dublin during 2012 (Lowe, 2013).

(4) VIGILANTISM: In Dublin, Limerick and other towns, Republicans have been involved in vigilantism to halt the activities of gangs. No sustained research has been conducted on this vigilantism, but anecdotal evidence suggests that it is usually targeted at youth gangs rather than more organised family gangs, who pay for 'protection'.

One of the few cases where this vigilantism became public occurred in Cavan town during 2009 (McMahon, 2009). A local youth gang known as The Cavan Rebellion Group (TCRG) had engaged in a series of attacks on individuals and property during the summer of that year. TCRG graffiti appeared in the town, and the group had a presence on the online social media network Bebo. In response to the slow official response to their activities, the Cavan Fermanagh Branch of the 32 County Sovereignty Movement released a statement saying that they were going to respond to the TCRG. They stated, '[w]e will not stand idly by while there are unprovoked and violent attacks on innocent members of the Cavan public by a drugged-up drunken hooligan anti-social element' (McMahon, 2009: 3). Local county councillors and the Gardaí quickly moved to reassure the community that they were in control of the situation. However, this incident was indicative of how quickly a dissident Republican group could move to fill a vacuum created by a slow state response to a gang problem in the border region.

The increase in gang-related activities in the Republic of Ireland since the late 1960s has occurred against the backdrop of the Conflict in Northern Ireland. Given the protracted and violent nature of that Conflict, it is not surprising that each period of change in Northern Ireland has had a corresponding impact on criminal gangs in the Republic of Ireland. John Hagedorn (2007, 2008) has highlighted the distinctive characteristics of gangs which operate in post-colonial contexts in terms of their more subversive stance in relation to the state. This research has brought the relationship between gangs and the state to the fore as a key theme of contemporary global gang studies, although it has been largely ignored in European and North American research (Winton, 2014). As the Republic of Ireland is a post-colonial state, and Northern Ireland is emerging from a protracted period of Conflict about the legitimacy of the state, this literature on gangs in post-colonial societies offers a range of potential insights into the operation of criminal gangs in this context.

Conclusion

The phenomenon of gang activity is almost universal. However, analysis of gangs has tended to be culturally specific, with a strong focus on the experience of US gangs during the earliest period of sociological and criminological research. Scholarly analysis of gangs in the Republic of Ireland has been relatively limited, though gang-related activity has been described in some depth by journalists in the media. At a policy level there has been a tendency to look towards the US and UK in order to understand the operation of gangs in this country (Irish Penal Reform Trust, 2014). This is not surprising, given the geographical location and language orientation of Irish society. However, a brief survey of research on gangs in these contexts suggests that the insights to be gleaned from these frameworks are relatively limited. While the activities of criminal gangs have expanded as part of modernisation and urbanisation, there are a number of distinctive features of gang participation in the Republic of Ireland which have not been widely considered in US and UK contexts. Firstly the role of family relationships in embedding gang participation is a significant feature of gang activity. In US and UK gang analysis, gang members are often portrayed as individuals who are alienated from their families and seeking to establish a surrogate family through the gang. While gang members in the Republic of Ireland may be poorly parented, a number of high-profile gang members have been strongly integrated into their families, and their position in the gang has been closely tied to their kinship relations.

Neither the US nor the UK literatures consider the relationship between gangs and the state in much depth, apart from analysis of relations between gangs and police at local level. The contested sovereignty of Northern Ireland has had a long-standing impact on gang activity in the Republic of Ireland, which shapes the distinctive operating contexts of criminal gangs and their mode of relating to the state. In understanding the operation of gangs, therefore, it is possible that a range of insights might be gained from comparing the experiences of gang members to gang participation in other post-colonial countries. Indeed, a survey of gangs and gang-related activity in the Republic of Ireland indicates how much scope there is for further research on gang participation in this jurisdiction. It is to be hoped that understanding gangs will become a core theme in the field of Irish criminology as it expands and develops in the coming years.

References

Aldridge, J. and Medina, J. (2008) *Youth Gangs in an English City: Social Exclusion, Drugs and Violence*. Full Research Report ESRC End of Award Report, RES-000-23-0615. Swindon: ESRC.

Allen, K. (2000) *The Celtic Tiger: The Myth of Social Partnership*. Manchester: Manchester University Press.

Alleyne, E. and Wood, J. (2014) 'Gang Involvement: Social and Environmental Factors', *Crime and Delinquency* 60 (1): 547–568.

Anderson, E. (2000) *Code of the Street: Decency, Violence and the Moral Life of the Inner City*. New York: Norton.

Baker, N. (2012) 'Witness Protection: History and Reality', *Irish Examiner*, 27 March 2012, p.7.

Basham, R. (1996) 'The Roots of Asian Organized Crime', *IPA Review*, 48 (4): 1–4

Bisset, J. (2008) *Regeneration: Public Good or Private Profit*. Dublin: Tasc /New Island.

Blom Hansen, T. and Stepputat, F. (2006) 'Sovereignty Revisited', *Annual Review of Anthropology*, 35: 295–315.

Bourgois, P. (1999) *In Search of Respect: Selling Crack in El Barrio*. Cambridge: Cambridge University Press.

Brady, C. (1979) 'Crime', *Irish Times*, 28 December 1979, p.10.

—— (2014) *The Guarding of Ireland*. Dublin: Gill and Macmillan.

Bullock, K. and Tilley, N. (2002) *Shooting, Gangs and Violent Incidents in Manchester: Developing a Crime Reduction Strategy*. London: Home Office.

Byrne, C. (2011) 'Bronco Dunne – How I ran guns with the General', *The Herald*, 26 March. Available at http://www.herald.ie (accessed 1 November 2014).

Campbell, L. (2013) *Organized Crime and the Law: A Comparative Analysis*. London: Hart Publishing.

Centre for Social Justice (2009) *Dying to Belong: An In-depth Review of Street Gangs in Britain*. Available at: http://www.centreforsocialjustice.org.uk/publications/dying-to-belong (accessed 25 October 2014).

Christianson, G. (1972) 'Secret Societies and Agrarian Violence in Ireland 1790–1840', *Agricultural History*, 46 (3): 369–384.

Cloward, R. and Ohlin, L. (1960) *Delinquency and Opportunity*. Glencoe IL: Free Press.

Cohen, A. (1955) *Delinquent Boys: The Culture of the Gang*. Glencoe IL: Free Press.

Cohen, S. (2002) *Folk Devils and Moral Panics: The Creation of Mods and Rockers*. 3rd ed. London: Routledge.

Connolly, J. (2006) *Drugs and Crime in Ireland*. Dublin: Health Research Board.

—— (2014) 'Drugs-related intimidation and community violence', *Drug-net Ireland*, 51: 17–18.

Connolly, L. (ed.) (2014) *The Irish Family*. London: Routledge.

Conway, V. (2013) *Policing Twentieth Century Ireland: A History of An Garda Síochána*. London: Routledge.

Curry, D. and Spergal, I. (1992) 'Gang involvement and delinquency in Hispanic and African-American adolescent males', *Journal of Crime and Delinquency*, 29: 273–292.

Cusack, J. (2010) 'Dissidents find new cause in drugs war', *Irish Independent*, 19 September. Available from http://www.independent.ie (accessed 20 October 2014).

—— (2014) 'Ireland? It's a great country for a criminal', *Irish Independent*, 21 November. Available from http://www.independent.ie (accessed 30 November 2014).

Deuchar, R. and Holligan, C. (2010) 'Gangs, Sectarianism and Social Capital: A Qualitative Study of Young People in Scotland', *Sociology*, 44 (1): 13–30.

Doherty, M. (2009) 'When the working day is done: The end of work and identity?', *Work, Employment and Society*, 23 (1): 84–102.

Duggan, B. (2009) *Mean Streets: Limerick's Gangland*. Dublin: O'Brien Press.

Esbensen, F. and Weerman, F. (2005) 'A Cross-National Comparison of Youth Gangs and Troublesome Youth Groups in the United States and the Netherlands', *European Journal of Criminology*, 2: 5–37.

Fallon, D., McGrath, S. and Murray, C. (2012) *Come Here to Me: Dublin's Other History*. Dublin: New Island.

Feeley, P. (1980) 'Early Agrarian Societies: Whiteboys and Ribbonmen', *Old Limerick Journal*, 4: 23–27.

Ferriter, D. (2004) *The Transformation of Ireland 1900–2000*. London: Profile Books.

Fine-Davis, M. (2011) *Attitudes to Family Formation in Ireland*. Dublin: Family Support Agency & TCD.

Fitzgerald, J. (2007) 'Addressing issues of social exclusion in Moyross and other disadvantaged areas of Limerick city: Report to the Cabinet Committee on Social Inclusion'. Available at http://www.limerickregeneration.org/fitzgeraldreport.html (accessed 12 December 2011).

Foy, K. (2012) *CSI: Crime Scene Ireland*. Dublin: Independent Publishing.

Galvin, A. (2013) *Blood on the Streets: A Murderous History of Limerick*. London: Mainstream Publishing.

Giora Shoham, S., Knepper, P. and Kett, M. (2010) *International Handbook of Criminology*. Boca Raton FL: CRC Press.

Goldson, B. (ed.) (2011) *Youth in Crisis: Gangs, Territoriality and Violence*. London: Routledge.

Hagedorn, J. (1988) *People and Folks: Gangs, Crime and the Underclass in a Rustbelt City*. Chicago: Lakeview Press.

—— (2006) 'Gangs and Politics' in L. Sherrod (ed.) (2006) *Youth Activism: An International Encyclopaedia*. Santa Barbara CA: Greenwood Publishing.

—— (2007) *Gangs in the Global City: Alternatives to Traditional Criminology*. Urbana IL: University of Illinois Press.

—— (2008) *A World of Gangs: Armed Young Men and Gangsta Culture*. Minneapolis MN: University of Minneapolis Press.

Hallsworth, S. and Young, T. (2004) 'Getting real about gangs', *Criminal Justice Matters*, 55, 12–13.

Hallsworth, S. and Silverstone, D. (2009) 'That's life innit: A British perspective on guns, crime and social order', *Criminology and Criminal Justice*, 9 (3): 359–377.

Haq, I. (1996) 'Pak-Afghan Drug Trade in Historical Perspective', *Asian Survey*, 36 (10): 945–963.

Harland, K. and McCready, S. (2014) 'Rough Justice: Considerations on the Role of Violence, Masculinity and the Alienation of Young Men in Communities and Peace Building', *Youth Justice*, 143: 269–283.

Hayden, T. (2004) *Street Wars: Gangs and the Future of Violence*. New York: New Press.

Hirschi, T. (1969) *Causes of Delinquency*. Berkeley: University of California Press.

Horgan, J. (2013) *Divided We Stand: The Strategy and Psychology of Ireland's Dissident Terrorists*. Oxford: OUP.

Hourigan, N. (ed.) (2011) *Understanding Limerick: Social Exclusion and Change*. Cork: Cork University Press.

Hourigan, N. and Campbell, M. (2010) 'The TEACH Report: Traveller Education and Adults – Crisis, Challenge and Change'. Available at: http://www.researchgate.net/publication/50431819_The_TEACH_report_traveller_education_and_adults_crisis_challenge_and_change (accessed 21 March 2011).

Huizinga, D. and Schumann, K. (2001) 'Gang membership in Bremen and Denver: Comparative longitudinal data' in M. Klein, H. Kerner and C. Maxson (eds) *The Eurogang Paradox*. Dordrecht: Kluwer Academic.

Irish Government New Service (2014) 'Speech by the Minister for Justice and Equality Ms. Frances Fitzgerald T.D. – Resolution on the continuation in operation of Section 8 of the Criminal Justice (Amendment) Act 2009'. Available at: http://oireachtasdebates.oireachtas.ie/debates%20authoring/debateswebpack.nsf/takes/dail2014061900011?opendocument (accessed 1 November 2014).

Irish Penal Reform Trust (2014) 'Catch 22 Report, Gangs in Prison'. Available at: http://www.iprt.ie/contents/2680 (accessed 21 November 2014).

Jensen, S. and Rodgers, D. (2008) 'Revolutionaries, barbarians or war machines? Gangs in Nicaragua and South Africa', *Socialist Register: Violence Today*, 45: 220–227.

Katz, J. and Jackson-Jacobs, C. (2004) 'The Criminologists Gang' in C. Sumner (ed.) *The Blackwell Companion to Criminology*. London: Blackwell.

Kirby, P. (2001) *The Celtic Tiger in Distress: Growth with Inequality in Ireland*. London: Palgrave.

Klein, M. (1971) *Street Gangs and Street Workers*. Englewood Cliffs NJ: Prentice Hall.

Klein, M., Kerner, H. and Maxson, C. (2001) *The Eurogang Paradox*. London: Springer.

Leahy, W. and Partners (2009) *Anti-Social Behaviour and the Law*. Limerick: Limerick Regeneration.

Lee, J. (1989) *Ireland: Economy and Society 1912–1985*. Cambridge: Cambridge University Press.

Lloyd, D. (2000) 'Colonial Trauma/ Post-colonial Recovery', *Interventions*, 2 (2): 212–228.

Loeber, R. and Farrington, D. (eds) (1998) *Serious and Violent Juvenile Offender Risk Factors and Successful Interventions*. Thousand Oaks CA: Sage.

Lowe, D. (2013) 'Radicalization of Terrorist Causes: The 32 CSM/IRA Threat to UK Security' in D. Lowe, A. Turk and D. Das (eds) *Examining Political Violence: Studies in Terrorism, Counterterrorism and Internal War*. London: Taylor and Francis.

McCafferty, D. (2011) 'Divided City: The Social Geography of Post-Celtic Tiger Limerick' in N. Hourigan (ed.) *Understanding Limerick: Social Exclusion and Change*. Cork: Cork University Press.

McCaffrey, M. (2011) *Cocaine Wars*. Chichester: Summersdale.

McClung Lee, A. (1975) 'Northern Irish Socialization in Conflict Patterns', *International Review of Modern Sociology*, 52: 127–134.

McCord, J. (1991) 'Family Relationships, Juvenile Delinquency and Adult Criminality', *Criminology*, 29 (3): 397–417.

McCullagh, C. (2011) 'Getting a Fix on Crime in Limerick' in N. Hourigan (ed.) *Understanding Limerick: Social Exclusion and Change*. Cork: Cork University Press.

McMahon, S. (2009) '32csm says it will put stop to Cavan attacks', *The Anglo-Celt*, 5 August, p. 3.

Maguire, K. (1993) 'Fraud, Extortion and Racketeering: The Black Economy in Northern Ireland', *Crime, Law and Social Change*, 20: 273–292.

Matza, D. (1966) *Delinquency and Drift*. New York: John Wiley.

Mays, J. (1954) *Growing Up in the City: A Study of Juvenile Delinquency in an Urban Neighbourhood*. Liverpool: Liverpool University Press.

Miller, W. (1958) 'Lower-class culture as a generating milieu of gang delinquency', *Journal of Social Issues*, 4: 5–19.

Miller, W., Geertz, H. and Cutter, H. (1961) 'Aggression in a boy's street corner group', *Psychiatry*, 24 (4): 283–298.

Mooney, J. (2013) *Gangster*. Dunshaughlin: Maverick House.

Mulcahy, A. (2002) 'The Impact of the Northern Troubles on Criminal Justice in the Republic of Ireland' in P. O'Mahony (ed.) *Criminal Justice in Ireland*. Dublin: IPA.

National Crime Forum (1998) *Report of the National Crime Forum*. Dublin: IPA.

O'Connell, C. (2011) 'City, Citizenship and Social Exclusion' in N. Hourigan (ed.) *Understanding Limerick: Social Exclusion and Change*. Cork: Cork University Press.

O'Donnell, P. (1975) *Irish Faction Fighters of the 19th Century*. Dublin: Anvil Books.

O'Hearn, D. (2003) 'Macro-economic policy in the Celtic Tiger: A critical reassessment' in C. Coulter and S. Coleman (eds) *The End of Irish History? Critical Reflections on the Celtic Tiger*. Manchester: Manchester University Press.

O'Leary, M. (2009) 'Intimidation of Families'. Available at http://fsn.ie/uploads/research_files/ IntimidationofFamilies_000.pdf (accessed 13 November 2014).

O'Mahony, P. (ed.) (2002) *Criminal Justice in Ireland*. Dublin: IPA.

Osgood, N. and Ong, B. (2001) 'Social Capital Formation and Development in Marginal Communities with Reference to Post-Soviet Societies', *Progress in Development Studies*, 1(3): 205–219.

O'Toole, J. (2012) 'Was He the Godfather?', *Hot Press*, 25 July 2012, p. 15.

Patrick, J. (1973) *A Glasgow Gang Observed*. London: Methuen.

Pearson, G. (1983) *Hooligan: A History of Respectable Fears*. Basingstoke: Macmillan.

Pike, P. and King, D. (2013) 'Responding to addiction in a time of recession', *Drugnet Ireland*, 47: 2–4.

Pine, J. (2012) *The Art of Making Do in Naples*. Minneapolis MN: University of Minnesota Press.

Police Service of Northern Ireland and An Garda Síochána (2012) 'Cross-Border Organised Crime Assessment'. Available at http://www.justice.ie/en/JELR/doj-cross-border-threat-assessment.pdf/ Files/doj-cross-border-threat-assessment.pdf (accessed 10 November 2014).

Prenderville, N. (2013) 'Positive Developments as Crime Figures Fall in County Limerick', *Limerick Leader*, 18 March, p. 15.

Quinlan, A. (2012) 'The Animals Who Prowled 1930s Dublin', *Irish Independent*, 22 July, p. 20.

Reynolds, P. (2006) 'Crime in Ireland'. Available at http://www.ceifin.com/resources/paper/PaulReynolds_ CrimeCorrespondentRTE.pdf (accessed 26 January 2015).

Short, J. (1980) *Political Implications of Juvenile Delinquency: A Comparative Perspective*. Lanham MA: Lexington Books.

Silke, A. (2000) 'Drink, Drugs and Rock n'Roll: Financing Loyalist Terrorism in Northern Ireland', *Studies in Conflict and Terrorism*, 23 (2): 107–127.

Sullivan, J. (2001) 'Gangs, Hooligans and Anarchists: The Vanguard of the Netwar in the Streets' in J. Arquilla and D. Ronfeldt (eds) *Networks and Netwars: The Future of Terror, Crime and Militancy*. Santa Monica CA: Rand Corporation.

Thornberry, T. (1998) 'Membership in youth gangs and involvement in serious and violent offending' in R. Loeber and D. Farrington (eds) *Serious and Violent Juvenile Offender Risk Factors and Successful Interventions*. Thousand Oaks CA: Sage.

Thrasher, F. (1927) *The Gang: A Study of 1,313 Gangs in Chicago*. Chicago: University of Chicago Press.

Todd, J., Muldoon, O., Trew, K., Canas Bottos, L., Rougier, N. and McLaughlin, K. (2006) 'The Moral Boundaries of the Nation: Nation, State and Boundaries in the Southern Irish Border Counties'. Available at http://researchrepository.ucd.ie/bitstream/handle/10197/4645/moral_boundaries_of_ the_nation._finalrev.pdf?sequence=1 (accessed 14 November 2014).

Van Hout, M. and Bingham, T. (2012) 'A Rapid Assessment Research (RAR) of drug and alcohol related public nuisance in Dublin City Centre'. Available at http://www.drugsandalcohol.ie/19010/ (accessed 19 October 2014).

Wacquant, L. (2008) *Urban Outcasts: A Comparative Sociology of Advanced Marginality*. Cambridge: Polity.

Whelan, C. (1994) *Values and Social Change in Ireland*. Dublin: Gill and Macmillan.

Williams, P. (2004) *The General – Ireland's Mob Boss*. Dublin: O'Brien Press.

—— (2011) *Badfellas*. Dublin: Penguin Ireland.

—— (2014) *Murder Inc: The Rise and Fall of Ireland's Most Dangerous Criminal Gang*. Dublin: Penguin Ireland.

Willis, P. (1977) *Learning to Labour: How Working Class Kids Get Working Class Jobs*. Farnborough: Saxon House.

Wilson, W. (1997) *When Work Disappears: The World of the New Urban Poor*. New York: Vintage Books.

Winton, A. (2014) 'Gangs in a Global Perspective', *Environment and Urbanisation*, 26 (2): 1–16.

Young, T., Fitzgibbon, W. and Silverstone, D. (2014) 'A Question of Family? Youth and Gangs', *Youth Justice*, 14 (2): 171–185.

8

State crime

Elaine A. Byrne, Kristian Lasslett and Bill Rolston

Introduction

Over the course of the twentieth century, states have organised violence on scales which far exceed the accumulative effects of street crime, employing their unparalleled power to perpetrate genocides, ethnic cleansing, war crimes, torture and terror. Equally, the state's intricate, and often opaque, financial organs have frequently been used, with impunity, to redistribute vast portions of the national wealth to senior public officials and their private clients, through a range of illicit transactions. The nascent literature on state crime bears witness to the fact that authoritarian regimes and liberal democracies alike are prolific offenders (see, for example, Green and Ward, 2004; Kramer and Michalowski, 2005; Lasslett, 2014b).

Yet for most of criminology's disciplinary life, illicit state practices have been ignored in favour of street crime and the administrative response to these offences (Green and Ward, 2005). State crime on the island of Ireland is not exempt in this respect. With that in mind, the following chapter will draw attention to the importance of state crime studies for Irish criminology by examining two major instances of state deviance that have confronted the island of Ireland over the course of the twentieth century. The first case focuses on the different, illicit forms of state violence employed in Northern Ireland during the conflict, and the intricate forms of institutional power that have been employed to shield the state from censure. The second case study will historically trace the development of state-organised corruption in the Republic of Ireland, including the regulatory frameworks (or lack thereof) that have allowed it to flourish.

While both cases differ with respect to form and perpetrator, they are united by the serial nature of the offending and the impunity criminal state actors enjoy. Moreover, each case represents one of the most formidable examples of state crime in the jurisdiction concerned. Indeed, while this chapter may not provide an exhaustive analysis of state crime on the island of Ireland, nonetheless, the subject matter dealt with here does capture some of the most potent types of state crime witnessed over the last century. Thus it provides important insights into the challenges associated with detecting, documenting and controlling state crime in Northern Ireland and the Republic of Ireland, including patterns that are common to both jurisdictions.

Conceptualising state crime

While the calamities prompted by illicit state actions have been the subject of scholarly scrutiny extending back into the nineteenth century, as a distinctly criminological pursuit, state crime's origins are more recent (Green and Ward, 2012a). When the catalysing events of the Vietnam War coincided with the emergence of critical criminological scholarship during the 1970s and 1980s (Kramer *et al.*, 2002: 265), the organisational deviancy of state actors became a growing focus (see Michalowski, 1985; Pearce, 1976; Schwendinger and Schwendinger, 1975). These critical interventions culminated in William Chambliss's (1989) Presidential address to the American Society of Criminology, where he called upon criminologists to interrogate one of the greatest challenges facing global peace and security, state criminality. This call prompted a series of innovative attempts to define state criminality as a criminological focus.

Two core methods for defining state crime have emerged. The first employs international law as the preferred framework for distinguishing criminal state practices. A recent example of this method can be found in the work of Mullins and Rothe (2008) who argue:

> [T]he use of international law – customary law, treaties, charters, international humanitarian law, and international human rights law – constitutes the strongest foundation for defining state crime, as this framework includes standards such as human rights, social and economic harms, as well as providing a solid legalistic foundation.
>
> *(Mullins and Rothe, 2008: 8)*

International law's suitability here stems from the fact it contains an authoritative set of codified norms which encompass a wide range of harmful practices that are broadly accepted by states and citizens. As a result, it offers defensible, independent criteria that criminologists can employ to credibly identify criminal state practices.

However, this is not the only approach that has gained currency within state crime studies. One of the most widely cited alternatives, first advanced by Green and Ward (2000, 2004), challenges criteria-driven approaches. In one critical respect, Green and Ward (2000: 108) agree with the above authors – there are, they argue, conduct norms that modern states must adhere to if they are to govern with a 'degree of consent'. For most contemporary states, Green and Ward (2000: 108) suggest, this requires a 'real or nominal commitment to human rights'. However, the contravention of fundamental conduct norms by state actors, in Green and Ward's (2000) view, is not enough to render illegitimate state practices criminal. For this stigmatising social quality to attach to specific state practices there must be an *active moment* of censure and sanction.

In this respect, Green and Ward (2000: 105) challenge criminology's traditional bias towards the official judgments of the state, arguing: '[d]eviancy labels and informal sanctions can ... be applied "from below" to state action that is perceived as illegitimate'. From this vantage point, popular action organised through civil society is an essential part of the framework through which illegitimate state conduct obtains the attribute of being criminal (Lasslett, 2014a). Green and Ward's (2000) approach also implies that the boundaries of state crime studies is an open-ended historical question. For example, there is nothing to prevent harmful practices perpetrated by the state today, which have become normalised, from being stigmatised as criminal in the future through prolonged and effective normative campaigns; nor does Green and Ward's (2000) approach prevent criminologists from asking why certain contemporaneous state practices fail to be censured as wrong by civil society, despite being illegitimate.

This particular conception of state crime advanced by Green and Ward (2000) preludes a recently emerging literature that specifically focuses on how communities resist illicit state practices. Stanley and McCulloch (2013: 4–5) argue resistance is epitomised by 'four essential elements … opposition, intention, communication and transformation'. Accordingly, to be considered resistance, not only must acts be motivated by some form of conscious opposition to illegitimate state practices, they also need to be undertaken in order to communicate disapproval to a wider social audience, and bring about some form of emancipatory change (Stanley and McCulloch, 2013). Critically, the literature on resistance also recognises that the state has specific capacities which allow it to challenge and suppress censure from below. This evolving rhythm of resistance and denial, under the Green and Ward approach, constitutes a vital dimension of the complex social struggle that defines certain state practices as criminal. Clearly, there is no black-and-white moment where state practices become criminal; rather, it is a social quality that progressively attaches to certain practices through the momentum of historical struggle, whose tenor is shaped by the capacity of communities to strengthen conduct norms and prosecute censure, and by the state's ability to deploy obfuscating countermeasures. In drawing this conclusion, state crime studies has developed a compelling response to an important critique levelled by social harm scholars, who contend that crime is an ideological construct lacking an objective existence (see Hillyard and Tombs, 2007). If we follow the Green and Ward approach, state criminality may indeed be conceived of as an objective quality historically activated through a normatively mediated process of struggle from below.

With that process in mind, we will now present two case studies on state crime in the island of Ireland. Both examples reveal not only systemic and systematic instances of illegitimate state practice, but also highly organised, official attempts to manage the process of resistance, in order to limit censure and shield state actors from meaningful sanctions. They reveal how the state is especially well positioned to not only engage in illicit activities, but to manage the subsequent process of exposure and condemnation. This reality, we argue, underlines the importance of building organised forms of resistance within Irish civil society, which can challenge denial.

State crime: violence in Northern Ireland

In Irish history, there is a 'relentless reciprocity'[1] which binds together the violence of the state and that of insurgents, traditionally republican insurgents whose goal is a sovereign, united nation-state. This relationship means that the violence of the insurgent stimulates that of the state; but what is frequently missed in historical and political commentary is that the converse also is true, namely that the violence of the state stimulates that of the insurgent. Given such reciprocity, it is impossible to hold rigidly to the standard hegemonic view that the state, having the monopoly on the use of force, is always legitimate in its use of violence, while insurgents – or in a later era, terrorists – are by definition capable only of illegitimate violence. The recognition of reciprocity allows space for the conclusion that, as elsewhere, Irish insurgents, in their opposition to colonisation, discrimination and political disenfranchisement, have turned historically to violence but cannot automatically be judged as irrational or unjustified in doing so. Conversely, allowance has to be made for the fact that the state's violence can be illegitimate, even criminal.

For the most part in what follows, the focus will not be on the violence of the insurgents, either republican, as traditionally in Irish history, or, more recently, loyalists determined to maintain the link with Britain (Moloney, 2002; Wood, 2003). This is not to excuse all their actions as justifiable and irreproachable. In fact, especially in relation to policies such as the direct targeting of civilians through assassination or disappearance, there is a plausible case to answer by both loyalist and republican insurgents in relation to the issue of war crimes.

Instead, the focus here is on the state in Northern Ireland. At an analytical level, there is something qualitatively different when the state, charged with the care and protection of its citizens, breaks its own rules and engages in criminality. In particular, three practices will be considered: torture, extrajudicial killings and collusion. The aftermath of the conflict will then be examined and the problems involved in calling the state to account for its previous illegitimate behaviour. This will entail the assessment of a 'package of measures' said to be designed to deal with contentious state actions of the earlier period.

Insurgency and state violence

Arguably, from a republican perspective, the very creation of the Northern Ireland state in 1920 was itself the original and overarching act of violence from which much else flowed in subsequent years. In deciding on the borders of their new state, the unionists in the north drew them to ensure 'the largest possible area within which the Protestants could expect to maintain a safe majority' (Beckett, 1971: 125). This decision meant the abandonment of fellow unionists in three Catholic-dominated counties on the other side of the border, in the newly-created Irish Free State, whose inclusion would have threatened the unionist majority in Northern Ireland. It also ensured that northern nationalists were trapped in a state which they did not choose and to which their allegiance was either withheld or sullenly conceded. Maintaining the unionist majority required the relegation of nationalists to a permanent minority status, numerically, socially and culturally. Discrimination in electoral arrangements and the allocation of state jobs and housing were commonplace, especially in the western part of the new state, where nationalists were in a majority (Cameron Report, 1969). In addition, laws that were not in themselves obviously discriminatory were applied in ways which disadvantaged nationalists. For example, a 1954 Act outlawed the display of any flag or symbol which might lead to a breach of the peace.[2] In practice this was taken to apply only to symbols of Irish identity, such as the Irish tricolour, rather than those of British identity, such as the Union flag.

By the 1960s nationalists and liberal unionists instigated a civil rights movement to counter discrimination, and the Northern Ireland state responded in standard repressive mode. Although led by a number of able political activists, the movement represented a genuine popular mass movement of resistance. The British state intervened, supposedly as an arbiter, but soon took the same repressive route. In January 1972 the actions of British paratroopers in Derry led to the death of 14 unarmed civil rights marchers and to any hopes of a non-violent solution to the problem of discrimination and inequality. The guns were out in force on all sides – republican, loyalist and state – from the early 1970s and were not silenced until the end of the millennium.

In this conflict there were atrocities on all sides – such as the Irish Republican Army (IRA) bombing of a Remembrance Day event in Enniskillen in 1987 (McDaniel, 1997), the Ulster Volunteer Force (UVF) bombings in Dublin and Monaghan in 1974 (Mullan, 2000), which led to the biggest daily single death toll in the Conflict, or the state's massacre of civil rights activists on Bloody Sunday 1972 (Mullan, 1997). In its efforts to counter insurgency, the state turned to many tried and tested violent methods, including torture, extrajudicial killings and collusion.

Torture

In August 1971 internment without trial was introduced in Northern Ireland. Three hundred and forty-two nationalists (but no unionists) were rounded up by the British army, and 11 of them were selected for a sustained period of ill-treatment known as 'the five techniques': hooding, 'white noise', long periods of standing, sleep deprivation and deprivation of food and drink (McGuffin, 1974).

Eventually the government of the Republic of Ireland initiated a case against the UK in the European Court of Human Rights (ECHR), alleging that the men had been tortured. The court found that the men had been ill-treated, but stopped short of labelling this torture, referring to it instead as 'inhuman and degrading treatment'.[3] In response, the British government vowed to cease employing the techniques, which had been used since the Second World War, but later evidence indicates that they continue to employ them in places such as Iraq and Afghanistan up to the present day (Cobain, 2012).[4]

In 2014 the government of the Republic of Ireland was compelled to bring the first ever application back to the ECHR for reconsideration as a result of new information, found in the British public archives at Kew, which inferred the British government misrepresented the facts to the court in 1978 (see Amnesty International, 2014).

Extrajudicial killings

Throughout the Conflict in Northern Ireland there have been numerous occasions when British troops and police have been accused of involvement in extrajudicial killings. Particular attention was focused on this issue when it became clear that a specialist police squad, the Special Support Unit, was involved in what was popularly known as a 'shoot to kill' operation where five unarmed members of republican military organisations and one civilian were shot dead in November and December 1982. Not only was no effort made to arrest the men, but official lies were immediately broadcast by the police that the men had been shot while resisting arrest.[5]

A senior police officer from Manchester, John Stalker, sent in to investigate the killings, found that his efforts were stymied from the top of the Royal Ulster Constabulary (RUC) down. He was removed from the investigation as he became increasingly critical, and his report has never been made public. Despite that, he is on record as concluding that the killings were unlawful. Moreover, the fingerprints of the RUC Special Branch were evidenced in every aspect of the killings:

> The Special Branch targeted the suspected terrorists, they briefed the officers, and after the shootings ... removed the men, cars and guns for a private de-briefing ... they decided at what point the CID were to be allowed to commence the official investigation and decided what was, or was not, evidence.
>
> *(Stalker, 1989: 56)*

He concludes: 'I have never experienced, nor had any of my team, such an influence over an entire police force by one small section' (Stalker, 1989: 56).

Collusion

Allegations of collusion between the British army and RUC on the one hand and loyalist paramilitary groups on the other, have been common since the early days of the Conflict. Overwhelming evidence that this was systemic and not simply a matter of periodic unprofessional behaviour on the part of individual security force members now exists – whether in relation to the operations of the so-called Glenanne Gang, which included a number of serving police and army personnel and was responsible for the killing of 120 nationalist civilians in the 1970s (Cadwallader, 2013), or the shocking revelation that in the mid-1980s 85 per cent of the intelligence used by the Ulster Defence Association (UDA) in targeting nationalists for assassination came from state forces (De Silva Report, 2012).

One case of collusion has remained prominent in the public domain over a number of decades, the killing of lawyer Pat Finucane in November 1979. Key members of the UDA who set up the killing and carried it out were agents of RUC Special Branch and British intelligence (Rolston, 2005). A major investigation by a British policeman, Sir John Stevens, concluded that collusion was involved not merely in the killing of Finucane but also in the failure to properly pursue his killers afterwards. However, although the 'Overview and Recommendations' of the Stevens Report were made public in 2003, the main report itself has never been released (Stevens Enquiry, 2003).

The Finucane case has continued to rumble on in the decades since. Canadian judge Peter Cory, called in to examine six cases of suspected collusion, concluded that collusion existed in relation to the killing of Pat Finucane (House of Commons, 2004). And although he recommended legal inquiries in this and four other cases, an inquiry regarding the Finucane murder is the only one which has not yet materialised. The Finucane family continue to push the British government, who consistently resist conceding a full and open inquiry. When pressed by the family to explain why this reluctance continues, Prime Minister David Cameron pointed to the walls in 10 Downing Street and said, '[b]ecause there are people all around this place who won't let it happen' (McCaffery, 2012b).

Aftermath: calling the state to account

Many of these issues continue to haunt Northern Ireland society two decades after the ceasefires of 1994. One such instance is the killing of the six men in 1982, mentioned above. Twenty years later, the case reached the European Court of Human Rights.[6] In a cluster of judgments around this and other cases on the use of lethal force by the state in Northern Ireland and of collusion, the Court ruled that Article 2 of the European Convention had been breached because the state had failed to carry out an effective and robust investigation of their killings.

The Court does not prescribe a blueprint for the state; instead the onus is on the state to respond in its own way. One way would have been for the British state to respond to the McKerr judgment by going down the route of other transitional societies attempting to deal with the past by establishing an overarching truth-recovery mechanism. The British state chose not to go down this route. Whether that was because of the complexity involved in establishing a valid truth-recovery mechanism such as a truth commission, or because of the potential for such a mechanism to unravel the truth of the state's involvement in abuses remains unanswered. Instead, the British state responded to the Council of Ministers in Europe by noting that it had developed a 'package of measures' which could guarantee Article 2 compliance in relation to legacy issues. These included the Historical Enquiries Team of the Police Service of Northern Ireland (PSNI), the additional responsibility given to the Police Ombudsman's Office to investigate historic instances of police involvement in the use of lethal force and the reform of the coroner's court to allow for inquests in historic cases. We will consider the record of each in turn.

Historical Enquiries Team (HET)

The HET was set up as a unit within the PSNI to review all deaths in the conflict – excluding those that involved the police as perpetrators – almost 3,300 deaths. Over time, many questions were raised about the ability of the HET to conduct an independent and accountable investigation of the deaths, as required under Article 2 (Lundy, 2009). But it was in relation to state offences that the most problematic aspects of the HET became apparent. Where the British army were the perpetrators in historic killings, they were treated much more favourably than other perpetrators. Often they were not pursued for statements or were interviewed as witnesses rather than under caution; their legal representatives were also provided with total disclosure of HET documentation on the killing prior to interview (Lundy, 2012). The HET was not reticent in justifying this differential treatment: 'HET maintains it is not appropriate to compare the review processes in military cases with murders committed by terrorists' (Her Majesty's Inspectorate of Constabulary, 2013: 12).

Eventually, Her Majesty's Inspectorate of Constabulary was called in to investigate the HET and its procedures and produced a damning report, finding the HET guilty of failing to comply with Article 2.[7] Specifically, it found the HET's differential treatment of state perpetrators to be 'illegal and untenable' (Her Majesty's Inspectorate of Constabulary, 2013: 85). Subsequently, the PSNI announced that the HET would fold by the end of 2014, with any outstanding investigation of historic cases to revert to a proposed Legacy Investigations Branch within the PSNI (Cromie, 2014). This decision was in turn overtaken by an agreement by all parties in protracted political talks in December 2014 to propose the establishment of a Historical Inquiries Unit in the PSNI with full powers to investigate all conflict-related deaths, including those previously handled by the HET, the Ombudsman and the bespoke PSNI investigation into the Bloody Sunday killings.[8]

Police Ombudsman

The Police Ombudsman was originally established to oversee current matters in the PSNI. However, after the Article 2 judgment of the European Court in 2001, the Office was handed an additional responsibility, to examine historical cases where the police were involved in conflict-related deaths. The original Ombudsman (Nuala O'Loan) was principled and consistent in pursuing the police in a number of cases of collusion. But the second holder of the post (Al Hutchinson) ran afoul of lawyers and human rights NGOs. The Criminal Justice Inspector (2011) found that the Office was fatally flawed in terms of an Article 2 requirement of independence from the police it was investigating. Many of the investigators with the Ombudsman's office were themselves former RUC officers. Moreover, in terms of gathering essential information from the PSNI, they dealt with gatekeepers who were themselves former members of Special Branch (Committee on the Administration of Justice, 2011). Following these reports the operations of the Office were suspended and Hutchinson resigned. The new Ombudsman still faces structural problems in relation to policing the past, not least a chronic lack of resources to investigate the 238 historic cases on his desk. Moreover, the Ombudsman's office initiated a judicial review of the Chief Constable of the PSNI in June 2014 on the grounds that investigations surrounding more than 60 deaths 'have now been stalled by a PSNI refusal to provide certain material' (McCaffery, 2014: paragraph 6).[9] This matter seems to have been resolved with the appointment of a new Chief Constable.[10]

Inquests

As stated above, the case of the six men killed by police in 1982 reached the European Court of Human Rights in 2001. It did so again in 2013. Numerous attempts had been made to conduct an inquest into the deaths, but the coroner had been constantly thwarted by the state. Thirty years on, the inquest had still not occurred, a delay which the Court found to be incompatible with the state's Article 2 obligations.[11] One judge went further in a concurring judgment:

> The period of demonstrated, if not deliberate, systemic refusals and failures to undertake timely and adequate investigation … seem as a matter of principle to make it possible for

at least some agents of the state to benefit from virtual impunity as a result of the passage of time.

(Committee on the Administration of Justice, 2015: 113)

One major blockage for the inquest system is the reliance on the PSNI to provide necessary documentation. This has turned into a frustratingly lengthy process as the police vet and redact every piece of information and classify it as 'top secret', thereby requiring additional ministerial involvement (see McCaffery, 2013). In addition, the PSNI has set up a Legacy Unit to service the coroner's court. This is a six-person team, four of whose members are former Special Branch officers and one a former RUC intelligence officer (McCaffery, 2012a). In addition, between them, these former officers served with 92 of the potential police witnesses whom the coroner may wish to call.[12]

Conclusion

Two conclusions result. First, there is a clear pattern of bias on the part of the state which serves to protect state perpetrators of crime – 'virtual impunity', to quote the judge in the European Court judgment of 2013 cited above. This conclusion was emphasized by Nils Muiznieks, the Council of Europe's Commissioner for Human Rights, on a visit to Belfast in November 2014:

Until now there has been *virtual impunity* for the state actors involved, and I think the government has a responsibility to uphold its obligations under the European Convention to fund investigations and to get the results.

(cited in Kearney, 2014: paragraph 16)

The equally disturbing second conclusion is that this bias remains and continues to distort the legal system, as we have seen in relation to the HET, the Ombudsman and the inquest system. As regards the package of measures, the whole is less than the sum of its parts in terms of a robust approach to transitional justice. In short, the issue of state violence is not just historical, because the business of calling the state to account for past violence is compounded by current state policies and action.

This demonstrates why struggle from below remains such a critical part of the historical process through which state actions become stigmatised as criminal. Left alone, government agencies in the UK have a poor record of judiciously documenting and censuring the criminal conduct of the British state. As a result, the mobilisation of civil society through community groups, victims associations, NGOs and scholarly institutions remains vital for correcting investigative shortcomings and spearheading forms of action that can materially inscribe wrongfulness on the British state for its deviant conduct in Northern Ireland.

On that note, we will now turn our attention southwards where the themes of state criminality and impunity can be witnessed in a different form.

State crime: corruption in the Republic of Ireland

The literature on corruption in the Republic of Ireland has traditionally emphasised the importance of distinguishing clientelism and brokerage (Carty, 1981; Collins and O'Shea, 2000; Komito, 1984; Sacks, 1976). It is said that Ireland's parochial political culture, small size of society and inefficient administrative structures necessitated the legitimate intervention of a broker in order for citizens to access their rightful entitlements. As Chubb (1963: 272) famously advanced, politicians are merely busy 'going about persecuting civil servants' on behalf of constituents.

This useful, though narrow, analytical framework provided for a limited understanding of corruption. The direct exchange of public goods and state resources to reward, support and bestow privilege to individuals for their political support are said to be 'simply not present in (contemporary) Irish electoral politics' because these direct benefits 'are simply not in the gift of TDs' (Gallagher and Komito, 2009: 242).

This premise may account for why the Irish academic literature has neglected to empirically research or theorise on the extent to which design features of the Irish economic policy-making system made it prone to corruption (McCarthy, 2003). Despite the quantity of official inquiries (Davitt, 1944; O'Byrne, 1946; O'Byrne, 1947; Costello, 1980; Hamilton, 1994; McCracken, 1997; Flood, 2002; Morris, 2008; Mahon, 2012; Moriarty, 2006, 2011; Smithwick, 2013) into state malfeasance, the literature preoccupies itself with petty corruption, the presumed outcome of brokerage and the clientelistic intricacies of the Irish political system. The absence of discussion on state crime, state capture and grand corruption is indicative of a refusal to countenance it. However, a growing body of scholarship is beginning to address this deficit from legal (Higgins, 2012), corporate governance (Brennan, 2013; Hardiman, 2012; Horan, 2011), historical (Byrne, 2012) and economic perspectives (Barry, 2008) as well as varying political science approaches (MacCarthaigh, 2005; McMenamin, 2013; Suiter, 2010). For instance, Barry (2008) maintains that parliamentary, judicial, press and civil-society scrutiny of government has not been sufficient to ensure that economic policy decisions were made expeditiously. Brennan (2013) analyses the corporate governance mechanisms which influence auditing and concludes that human weakness is at the centre of corporate failure. Hardiman (2012) argues from a historical institutionalist perspective that Irish institutions are resistant to meaningful reform, while Higgins (2012) presents a legal analysis of Irish corruption law and concludes that corruption is as much a problem of systemic failure as of individual morality.

State crime is defined in the context of the Republic of Ireland by legal corruption. That is, we are looking at the undue, but not necessarily illegal influence exercised over public policies, laws, regulations and decisions, by self-interested actors (Byrne, 2012). Self-interest is defined broadly as a direct benefit such as financial gain or power, prestige, authority and symbolic capital. For political actors the benefit may be support which influences the outcome of an election, or secures promotion within the ranks of a political party or government structure; it could also include the preservation of existing political support. Moreover, self-interest may be indirect and benefit family, friends, political associates, a political party, constituency or other affiliates associated with the public or private actor. Corruption, therefore, is the use of public office for private gain; it need not be directly linked to a precise favour but may be undertaken in anticipation of future benefits.

As noted, this informal misuse of power, or state capture, occurs where personal relationships, patronage, lobbying, political favours and political donations unduly influence the decision-making process of government, even if no laws are broken. To that end, the literature on state crime recognises that state actors in particular have the capacity to influence the legality of their own behaviour. Indeed, criminologists have long recognised that harmful and deviant state behaviour may be nominally legal from a domestic perspective, while nonetheless violating fundamental norms – such as international human rights – to which the state is expected to adhere (Schwendinger and Schwendinger, 1975). In such situations it is the extra-normative character of the conduct, and the historical struggle to have it sanctioned as criminal, which forms the basis of criminological analysis (Green and Ward, 2000).

With that in mind we will now trace the historical evolution of corruption in the Republic of Ireland, looking at the official inquiries it has provoked, and the enduring ability of state actors to eschew stigmatising labels. It is important to remember here that state crime is an emerging social property that gradually attaches itself to certain political practices through a historical process of struggle. Therefore, corruption in the Republic of Ireland must be understood within the *longue durée*, where the status of certain state practices are changing in character – from questionable to clearly deviant – as the conduct in question comes up against increasingly powerful normative criteria, operationalised through a range of judicial, bureaucratic and civil society mechanisms.

Protectionism

First of all it should be emphasised that changes in the Republic of Ireland's political, economic and social structures have been intimately linked to the type of corruption perpetrated by business interests and political associates. Initially, the state's central role in the regulation of economic life provided rent-seeking opportunities for political parties through granting favours to business interests and political associates, using discretionary powers contained within protectionist instruments.

Indeed, the economy in the first half of the twentieth century was heavily protected, largely subsidised and principally controlled by the state. For example, the list of tariffs on indigenous goods covered 68 articles in 1931. By 1938 the number of articles subject to state restriction or control had risen to 1,947 (Whitaker, 1983). As a consequence of the problematic use of discretionary decision-making powers, enabled by protectionism, three tribunals and a parliamentary inquiry were established to examine allegations of conflict of interest, kickbacks, improper disclosure of confidential information, use of position to ascertain favourable access to key decision makers and the circumvention of normal bureaucratic procedures.

This included the Wicklow Gold Inquiry in 1935, which was the first official investigation into allegations of corruption since the foundation of the state in 1922 (see Byrne, 2012). In short, the Mines and Minerals Act 1931 gave the Minister for Industry and Commerce, Sean Lemass, the authority to issue mining leases for state-owned minerals. Lemass granted two prospecting leases with exclusive mining rights to two political representatives of his own party, Fianna Fáil. Senator Michael Comyn and Robert (Bob) Briscoe TD were the only applicants for the 2,982 acres mining lease, the availability of which was not advertised.

Comyn and Briscoe then sub-leased their interest in 1935 to a London syndicate on the expectation of receiving £12,000 in shares and a royalty of 2¼ per cent on all minerals found. This was a significant mark-up on the original terms of the lease that Comyn and Briscoe had secured from the Department, which was set at £5 annual rent and a ½₅ part of the value of the minerals in royalties. The syndicate's intention was to sell shares in the mining leases through the stock market.

The Fine Gael opposition spokesperson on Industry and Commerce, Patrick McGilligan, alleged that Lemass was selling valuable state mining rights at token value for the private gain of his Fianna Fáil colleagues. A cross-party parliamentary select committee established to inquire into McGilligan's claims rejected the allegations. That said, the select committee did note its reservations regarding the receipt of government contracts by parliamentarians and recommended greater transparency in the allocation of leases.

Nonetheless, Comyn and Briscoe were elected public figures whose private business interests benefited from a ministerial decision. At the time, the concept of a conflict of interest where politicians had competing professional and personal interests was uncharted waters. Codes of ethics and procedures for disclosure were not introduced until 1995, sixty years after this incident. The response by Prime Minister Éamon de Valera was indicative of a political culture that narrowly defined self-interest as direct financial gain. De Valera said that corruption in this incident did not arise, as it meant 'using one's political office, one's public office, for personal gain. It was not personal gain the Minister [Lemass] was accused of, but partisanship and giving gain to his friends' (House of the Oireachtas, 1947: paragraph 51).

Aside from the Wicklow Gold Inquiry, three corruption tribunals were established in a four-year period to examine the abuse of discretionary decision-making powers, enabled by protectionism. For example, following the 1943 Great Southern Railways (GSR) Tribunal, a mid-ranking civil servant at the Department of Industry and Commerce was compulsorily retired for insider share-dealing. The chair of the GSR acknowledged that he had personally contacted and given advance information about government plans to heavily invest and nationalise the railways to Dr. John Charles McQuaid, Archbishop of Dublin, the Representative Body of the Church of Ireland and the Bank of Ireland. The Tribunal did not examine if these private entities had benefited from this insider information. Examination of the Archdiocese accounts suggests that McQuaid invested heavily in GSR shares around the time he had received this advance information (Byrne, 2012).

The political regulation of economic activity was exacerbated by a spike in population growth during the 1960s. This led to demands for increased housing in the context of severe shortages of serviced land with sewage, water and drainage amenities. The Planning Act 1963 required citizens to obtain planning permission from their local authority which now had the power to zone unserviced agricultural land for residential and commercial purposes. The Act enabled state actors to seek rents from those wishing to circumvent regulation.

The organisational networks that facilitated the corrupt rezoning of these lands involved a nexus of developers, politicians, local authority officials and lobbyists. The 1997–2012 Flood/Mahon Tribunal made findings of corruption within the local government planning process over a thirty-year period. Criminal proceedings were brought against three former councillors, one serving councillor and a businessman named in the final report of the Mahon Tribunal. The trial collapsed in 2013. However, in May 2009 former lobbyist and government press secretary Frank Dunlop was sentenced to two years, with the final six months suspended, after pleading guilty to five sample charges of bribing Dublin city councillors on behalf of property developers in the early 1990s.

Finally, instruments of economic intervention, such as the allocation of capital expenditure, continued to be utilised by political parties for self-interest in the second half of the twentieth century. The collective benefits of roads, housing, education buildings and sports facilities have been exchanged for electoral backing. Suiter (2010) determined that the constituencies of the Minister for Arts and Sports and the Minister for Finance were statistically predisposed to receive more in capital grants to sports clubs than other constituencies. A similar pattern was observed when examining capital grants to primary schools within the constituencies of the Minister for Education and the Minister for Finance. In the period 2001–07, the constituency of the Minister for Finance received €7.4 million a year in grants to primary schools while the constituency of the Minister for Education received €4.1 million. The figure for other constituencies was €3.7 million. This disproportionate allocation of public money to specific constituencies for political purposes amounts at the very least to an inappropriate political gain.

Privatisation and European integration

Throughout most of the twentieth century, the state has been perceived as a resource to be exploited by economic actors seeking advantages over national and international competitors.

The instruments of impropriety utilised by state and private actors included improper application of contracts, tariffs, quotas, subsidies, tax deductions, foreign exchange allocation, planning permission and passports. Also included were economic control mechanisms, such as monopoly arrangements and the inequitable distribution of state resources: e.g. rights to offshore oil and gas exploration.

However, key parts of the economy were wholly or partially opened to private-sector competition in the late 1980s and early 1990s, a process which coincided with a proliferation of EU funds distributed through complicated and poorly monitored channels (Barrett, 2004). In a comparative analysis with other European states, Chari and McMahon (2003: 38) have described the Republic of Ireland's experience of privatisation as one defined by the closed and 'rather elitist' nature of the negotiation process where 'disproportionate influence by capital actors' is exercised.

The first major inquiry during this period of transition was the Hamilton (Beef) Tribunal (1991–94), which examined allegations of state deviance by the Fianna Fáil government of 1987–89. In particular, it investigated irregularities within the beef processing industry and accusations of regulatory capture and special dispensations given by the Minister for Industry and Commerce, Albert Reynolds, to a private beef company, Goodman International. Reynolds's Department underwrote almost IR£120 million in beef export credit insurance to Iraq for Goodman International in 1987 and 1988. This amounted to a third of all available credit on exports, which was at the disposal of just one company. The Hamilton Tribunal documented a pattern of large campaign contributions by the beef company to Fianna Fáil, the government party. This included IR£50,000 on the day of the 1989 general election and another IR£25,000 two days later (Byrne, 2012).

Reynolds was found not guilty of wrongdoing. Although the Hamilton Tribunal was aware that Fianna Fáil received substantial donations, it was 'satisfied that such contributions were normal contributions made to political parties and did not in any way affect or relate to the matters being inquired into by the tribunal' (Hamilton, 1994: 12). Instead, the Hamilton Tribunal determined that Reynolds's decision was motivated by the national interest rather than personal gain.

The Iraqi government substantially defaulted on its beef debts. Accordingly, the government, as the underwriter of the export credit insurance scheme, subsequently paid €67 million, of which €27 million was never recovered. In 1995 the European Commission anti-fraud agency made findings of sustained abuse of Common Agricultural Policy funds within the Irish beef intervention scheme. It imposed an IR£68 million (€86.3 million) fine in 1996. In an out-of-court settlement in 2003 Goodman agreed to pay €3.81 million in compensation for beef intervention scheme irregularities. Ultimately, the state suffered a loss of some €83 million.

These liberties with public finances were taken at a time when the country was undergoing a severe recession. In 1987 GDP per person was 69 per cent of the EU average, unemployment was at 17 per cent and government debt was 112 per cent of GDP. Funding for school capital projects fell 50 per cent from IR£40 million in 1987 to around IR£20 million a year from 1988 to 1992. The long-term consequence of halving the commitment to educational infrastructure came home to roost in the 1990s and 2000s. The existing stock of schools is in a state of extensive disrepair and unable to meet demographic challenges. The unrecovered €27 million the state was owed from the insurance scheme would have kept the school capital programme intact for one full year. Indeed, Ó Gráda and O'Rourke (1996) see sectorial misallocation of investment and an excessive scope for rent-seeking behaviour as contributing to economic underperformance since 1945.

State organised corruption and impunity

It is evident from the previous section that those senior officials involved in using government powers to benefit clients and their own business concerns have largely enjoyed impunity from meaningful sanction. There are a number of pillars underpinning impunity. First, whistle-blowers have been vilified. For example, in 1974 the journalist Joe McAnthony revealed that Fianna Fáil politician Ray Burke voted on planning decisions within local government while at the same time being in a beneficial financial relationship with those seeking the rezoning. Thirty years later the Mahon Tribunal corroborated McAnthony's evidence. Nevertheless, McAnthony was forced to emigrate after the Burke story: '[m]y life was pretty much over as a journalist ... I was essentially expelled from Ireland' (Byrne, 2012: 234).

Indeed, those who have blown the whistle on impropriety have frequently been labelled informers and traitors. The Protected Disclosures Act 2014 seeks to address these failings by offering legal protections for workers who report concerns about wrongdoing in the public, private and non-profit sectors. The Act, also known as the Whistle-blowers Charter, will safeguard the identity of whistle-blowers. The broader objective of the legislation is to promote public accountability and openness. This is no small task, given the entrenched cultural and institutional hostility to those who expose or allege illegality or misconduct within public life.

Nevertheless, even where state officials are shown to have engaged in inappropriate transactions, often the sanctions applied are minimal. For example, the Moriarty Tribunal 1997–2012 focused on the circumstances surrounding the largest single procurement award in the history of the state. The Tribunal found that the Minister for Transport, Energy and Communications, Michael Lowry, had 'irregular interactions with interested parties at its most sensitive stage ... and thereby not only influenced, but delivered, the result' that allowed Esat Digifone to win the evaluation process (Moriarty, 2011: 1050). Furthermore, it was found that Minister Lowry was the recipient of clandestine payments and loan support from Esat Digifone CEO Denis O'Brien between July 1996 and December 1999. These came in three separate instalments, which the tribunal determined 'were demonstrably referable to the acts and conduct of Mr Lowry in regard to the GMS process, that inured to the benefit of Mr O'Brien's winning consortium, Esat Digifone' (Moriarty, 2011: 1056). Lowry was expelled from his political party, Fine Gael, in 1996 but remains an independent Member of Parliament. He has faced no criminal sanction. Both Lowry and O'Brien strongly contest the findings of the Tribunal.

The government has more recently promised a robust response to tribunal findings, saying it would not remain passive. There is, however, a perception that, following the findings of the Moriarty Tribunal, the government did not properly distance itself from persons involved in the case (European Commission, 2014). For example, seven months after the report's publication, O'Brien was a guest of the Government at the Global Ireland Forum. A year after the report was published he accompanied the Fine Gael Prime Minister when he opened the New York Stock Exchange to mark St Patrick's Day in March 2012.

Legislative responses to state organised corruption

Attempts to prohibit corruption in the Republic of Ireland have been characterised by inertia. Indeed, for a substantial period the country's anti-corruption framework consisted of archaic legislation in the form of the eight British corruption statutes implemented between 1854 and 1916. The Ethics in Public Office Act 1995 was the first substantive anti-corruption law since the foundation of the state. Indeed, the previous self-regulatory approach was transformed between 1995 and 2005, when approximately 25 pieces of legislation focusing directly or circuitously on corruption were initiated. A crisis-led approach introduced new laws on codes of conduct, internal reporting, bribery, freedom of information, misconduct in public office and money-laundering. Nonetheless, only one corruption-related conviction has arisen subsequent to the four corruption tribunals established in the 1990s to investigate impropriety in public life dating back several decades.

The country's corporate enforcement and white-collar crime framework have also been characterised historically by an absence of legislation, political will and resources (see, further, McCullagh, *infra*).

Conclusion

The island of Ireland, like many regions of the world, has been marked in profound ways by state crime. In this chapter we have touched upon several significant examples, but by no means all. For instance, omitted is the significant evidence that has come to light on the criminogenic relationship between the Irish state and the church (Murphy, 2009). Also, we have omitted examples of international crimes, like the use of Shannon airport as both a staging-point for the US-led invasion of Iraq and Afghanistan and a stop-over point for extraordinary rendition flights (see www.shannonwatch.org); in addition, attention might be turned to the Northern Irish government's criminogenic involvement in the arms-trade (Lasslett *et al.*, 2014). Nevertheless, this chapter has demonstrated the systematic and systemic character of state crime.

We have also, crucially, observed in both case studies that *official* attempts to inquire into and remedy these crimes in Northern Ireland and the Republic of Ireland have failed to meaningfully sanction state wrongdoings. This would seem to reinforce the argument made by Green and Ward (2012b) that censure, if it is to have lasting effect, must be organised from below in the form of committed social movements. Indeed, Green and Ward (2012b: 28) note, 'civil society is both the most important counterweight to state crime and one of the most important sources of the norms that define state crime'. Accordingly, it is through the mobilisation of civil society that norms can be best translated into robust instruments against which state conduct can be judged, and it is a strong and vibrant civil society that is well placed to enact condemnation when these norms are violated, including by placing pressure on state accountability organs. On the other hand, it should not be overlooked that popular pressure from below can be managed and marginalised by the state through formal processes of inquiry which eschew mass participation and ensure any form of accountability takes place in a manageable way without threatening state interests, or the interests of organisational clients.

Criminologists are not neutral actors in this respect. Allowing street crime to assume its historic stranglehold over criminology while elite offending goes unchecked only serves to reinforce a profound imbalance in the administration of criminal justice, which sees punitive sanctions applied against largely poor and working-class offenders, while private speculators, corporations, state agencies, banks and religious institutions enjoy impunity. However, criminologists can help to correct this historical imbalance through the production of new data sets on state crime and developing concepts which infuse this data with meaning. In both respects, a special burden now lies with emerging criminologists, who have an opportunity to use the growing body of work in state crime studies to illuminate and resist the different forms of state violence and corruption that have burdened the island of Ireland for much of the twentieth century.

References

Amnesty International (2014) 'Ireland: Decision to reopen "Hooded Men" court case a triumph of justice after four decades of waiting', 2 December. Available at: http://www.amnesty.org/en/news/ireland-re-opens-landmark-hooded-men-torture-case-2014-12-02 (accessed 5 January 2014).

Barrett, S.D. (2004) 'Privatisation in Ireland', *CESifo Working Paper*, 1170: 1–44.

Barry, F. (2008) 'Institutional capacity and the Celtic Tiger economy' in M. Pickhardt and E. Shinnick (eds) *The Shadow Economy, Corruption and Governance*. Cheltenham: Edward Elgar.

Beckett, J.C. (1971) 'Northern Ireland', *Journal of Contemporary History*, 6(1): 121–134.

Brennan, N. M. (ed.) (2013) *Corporate Governance and Financial Reporting, Volumes I–III, Sage Library of Accounting and Finance*. London: Sage.

Byrne, E.A. (2012) *Political Corruption in Ireland: A Crooked Harp?* Manchester: Manchester University Press.

—— (2013) 'Ireland's white-collar crime oversight agencies: Fit for purpose?' Working Paper. Available at: http://elaine.ie/wp-content/up/Fit-for-Purpose-.pdf (accessed 4 April 2014).

Byrne, E., Arnold, A.K. and Nagano, F. (2010) *Building Public Support for Anti-Corruption Efforts Why Anti-Corruption Agencies Need to Communicate and How*. Washington DC: World Bank.

Cadwallader, A. (2013) *Lethal Allies: British Collusion in Ireland*. Cork: Mercier Press.

Cameron Report (1969) *Disturbances in Northern Ireland*. Belfast: Her Majesty's Stationery Office.

Carty, R.K. (1981) *Party and Parish Pump: Electoral Politics in Ireland*. Ontario: Wilfrid Laurier University Press.

Chambliss, W. (1989) 'State-organized crime', *Criminology*, 27: 183–208.

Chari, R.S. and McMahon, H. (2003) 'Reconsidering the patterns of organised interests in Irish policy making', *Irish Political Studies*, 18: 27–50.

Chubb, B. (1963) 'Going about persecuting civil servants: The role of the Irish parliamentary representative', *Political Studies*, 11: 272–286.

Cobain, I. (2012) *Cruel Britannia: A Secret History of Torture*. London: Portobello Books.

Collins, N. and O'Shea, M. (2000) *Understanding Corruption in Irish Politics*. Cork: University Press.

Committee on the Administration of Justice (2011) *Human Rights and Dealing with Historic Cases: A Review of the Office of the Police Ombudsman of Northern Ireland*. Belfast: Committee on the Administration of Justice.

—— (2015) *The Apparatus of Impunity?* Belfast: Committee on the Administration of Justice

Costello, Mr Justice D. (1980) *Report of the Tribunal of Inquiry into the Disaster at Whiddy Island*. Dublin: Stationery Office.

Cox, A. (1958) *Report of the Company Law Reform Committee*. Dublin: Stationery Office.

Criminal Justice Inspector (2011) *An Inspection into the Independence of the Office of the Police Ombudsman for Northern Ireland*. Belfast: Criminal Justice Inspection Northern Ireland.

Cromie, C. (2014) 'PSNI cuts 300 jobs and axes Historical Enquiries Team', *Belfast Telegraph*, 30 September. Available at: http://ww.belfasttelegraph.co.uk/news/local-national/northern-ireland/psni-cuts-300-jobs-and-axes-historical-enquiries-team-30626460.html (accessed 5 January 2015).

Davitt, Mr Justice C. (1944) *Report of the Tribunal of Inquiry into Dealings in Great Southern Railway Stocks between the 1st day of January and the 18th day of November 1943*. Dublin: Stationery Office.

De Silva Report (2012) *Pat Finucane Review*. London: Stationery Office. Available at: https://www.gov.uk/government/publications/the-report-of-the-patrick-finucane-review (accessed 29 June 2014).

European Commission (2014) *EU Anti-Corruption Report: Ireland*. Available at: http://ec.europa.eu/dgs/home-affairs/what-we-do/policies/organized-crime-and-human-trafficking/corruption/anti-corruption-report/index_en.htm (accessed 4 April 2014).

Flood, Mr Justice F.M. (2002) *Tribunal of Inquiry into Certain Planning Matters and Payments: Second Interim Report*. Dublin: Stationery Office.

Gallagher, M. and Komito, L. (2009) 'The constituency role of Dáil deputies' in J. Coakley and M. Gallagher (eds) *Politics in the Republic of Ireland*. London: Routledge.

Green, P. and Ward, T. (2000) 'State crime, human rights, and the limits of criminology', *Social Justice*, 27(1): 101–115.

—— (2004) *State Crime: Governments, Violence and Corruption*. London: Pluto Press.

—— (2005) 'Introduction', *British Journal of Criminology*, 45(4): 431–433.

—— (2012a) 'State crime: A dialectical view' in M. Maguire, R. Morgan and R. Reiner (eds) *The Oxford Handbook of Criminology*, 5th ed. Oxford: Oxford University Press.

—— (2012b) 'Civil society, resistance and state crime', in E. Stanley and J. McCulloch (eds) *State Crime and Resistance*. London: Routledge.

Hamilton, Mr Justice L. (1994) *Report of the Tribunal of Inquiry into the Beef Processing Industry*. Dublin: Stationery Office.

Hardiman, N. (ed.) (2012) *Irish Governance in Crisis*. Manchester: Manchester University Press.

Her Majesty's Inspectorate of Constabulary (2013) *Inspection of the Police Service of Northern Ireland Historical Enquiries Team*. Available at: http://www.hmic.gov.uk/media/inspection-of-the-police-service-of-northern-ireland-historical-enquiries-team-20130703.pdf (accessed 29 June 2014).

Higgins, I. (2012) *Corruption Law*. Dublin: Round Hall.

Hillyard, P. and Tombs, S. (2007) 'From "crime" to social harm?', *Crime, Law and Social Change*, 48(1–2), 9–25.

Horan, S. (2011) *Corporate Crime*. Dublin: Bloomsbury Professional.

House of Commons (2004) *Cory Collusion Inquiry Report: Patrick Finucane*. London: Stationery Office.

House of the Oireachtas (1947) 'Financial Resolutions Report (Resumed) – Proposed Sale of Distillery – Motion for Select Committee Resumed', *Dáil Éireann Debates*, vol. 108 (8). Available at: http://oireachtasdebates. oireachtas.ie/debates%20authoring/debateswebpack.nsf/takes/dail1947103000020?opendocument (accessed 31 March 2015).

Kearney, V. (2014) 'UK must pay for Troubles killings investigations says European official', *BBC News*, 6 November. Available at: http://www.bbc.co.uk/news/uk-northern-ireland-29941766 (accessed 5 January 2015).

Komito, L. (1984) 'Irish clientelism: A reappraisal', *Economic and Social Review*, 15: 173–194.

Kramer, R. C. and Michalowski, R. J. (2005) 'War, aggression and state crime: A criminological analysis of the invasion and occupation of Iraq', *British Journal of Criminology*, 45(4): 446–469.

Kramer, R. C., Michalowski, R. J. and Kauzlarich, D. (2002) 'The origins and development of the concept and theory of state-corporate crime', *Crime & Delinquency*, 48(2): 263–282.

Lasslett, K. (2012) 'State crime by proxy: Australia and the Bougainville conflict', *British Journal of Criminology*, 52(4): 705–723.

—— (2014a) 'Understanding and responding to state crime: A criminological perspective' in I. Bantekas (ed.) *International Criminal Law and Criminology*. Cambridge: Cambridge University Press.

—— (2014b) *State Crime on the Margins of Empire: Rio Tinto, the War on Bougainville and Resistance to Mining*. London: Pluto Press.

Lasslett, K., Green, P. and Stańczak, D. (2014) 'The barbarism of indifference: Sabotage, resistance and state-corporate crime', *Theoretical Criminology*, advance online publication. doi: 10.1177/1362480614558866.

Lundy, P. (2009) 'Can the past be policed? Lessons from the Historical Enquiries Team Northern Ireland', *Journal of Law and Social Challenges*, 11: 109–171.

—— (2012) *Research Brief: Assessment of the Historical Enquiries Team (HET) Review Processes and Procedures in Royal Military Police (RMP) Investigation Cases*. Available at: http://eprints.ulster.ac.uk/21809/ (accessed 29 June 2014).

McCaffery, B. (2012a) 'Coroner told former Special Branch officers in charge of redacting "shoot to kill" files', *The Detail*, 19 October. Available at: http://www.thedetail.tv/issues/137/stalker-update/coroner-told-former-special-branch-officers-in-charge-of-redacting-shoot-to-kill-files (accessed 5 January 2015).

—— (2012b) 'What stopped a public inquiry into Finucane murder?', *The Detail*, 12 December. Available at: http://www.thedetail.tv/issues/156/finucane-preview/what-stopped-a-public-inquiry-into-finucane-murder (accessed 5 January 2015).

—— (2013) 'Coroner warns PSNI delays threatens his ability to hold proper inquiries', *The Detail*, 31 May. Available at: http://www.thedetail.tv/issues/215/shoot-to-kill-leckey/coroner-warns-psni-delays-threatens-his-ability-to-hold-proper-inquiries (accessed 5 January 2015).

—— (2014) 'Police Ombudsman takes legal action against PSNI', *The Detail*, 3 June. Available at: http://www.thedetail.tv/issues/333/ombudsman-legal-action/police-ombudsman-takes-legal-action-against-psni (accessed 5 January 2015).

MacCarthaigh, M. (2005) *Accountability in Irish Parliamentary Politics*. Dublin: Institute of Public Administration.

McCarthy, C. (2003) 'Corruption in public office in Ireland: Policy design as a countermeasure', *Economic and Social Research Institute, Quarterly Economic Commentary*, 3: 1–15.

McCracken, Mr Justice B. (1997) *Report of the Tribunal of Inquiry (Dunnes Payments)*. Dublin: Stationery Office.

McDaniel, D. (1997) *Enniskillen: Remembrance Day Bombing*. Dublin: Merlin Publishing

McDonald, H. (2014) 'Six men's families compensated for delayed Troubles killings inquests', *The Guardian*, 20 May. Online. Available at: http://www.theguardian.com/uk-news/2014/may/20/northern-ireland-six-mens-families-compensated-delayed-troubles-killings-inquests (accessed 5 January 2015).

McDowell, M. (1998) *Report of the Working Group in Company Law Compliance and Enforcement*. Dublin: Stationery Office.

McGuffin, J. (1974) *The Guineapigs*. Harmondsworth: Penguin.

McMenamin, I. (2013) 'Business financing of politics in Ireland: Theory, evidence and reform', *Irish Political Studies*, 28: 20–38.

Mahon, Mr Justice A.P. (2012) *Final Report of the Tribunal of Inquiry into Certain Planning Matters and Payments*. Dublin: Stationery Office.

Mauro, P. (1997) *Why Worry About Corruption?* Washington DC: International Monetary Fund.

Memmi, A. (1990) *The Colonizer and the Colonized*. London: Earthscan.

Michalowski, R. (1985) *Order, Law and Crime*. New York: Random House.

Moloney, E. (2002) *A Secret History of the IRA*. New York: Norton.

Moriarty, Mr Justice M. (2006) *The Moriarty Tribunal Report. Report of the Tribunal of Inquiry into Payments to Politicians and Related Matters. Part I*. Dublin: Stationery Office.

Moriarty, Mr Justice (2011) *Report of the Tribunal of Inquiry into Payments to Politicians and Related Matters. Part II*, 2 vols. Dublin: Stationery Office.

Morris, Mr Justice (2008) *Report of the Tribunal of Inquiry*. Dublin: Stationery Office.

Mullan, D. (1997) *Eyewitness Bloody Sunday*. Dublin: Wolfhound Press.

—— (2000) *The Dublin and Monaghan Bombings*. Dublin: Wolfhound Press.

Mullins, C. W. and Rothe, D. L. (2008) *Blood, Power and Bedlam: Violations of International Criminal Law in Post-Colonial Africa*. New York: Peter Lang.

Murphy, Ms Justice Y. (2009) *Report by Commission of Investigation into Catholic Archdiocese of Dublin*. Dublin: Stationery Office.

O'Byrne, Mr Justice J. (1946) *Report of the Tribunal of Inquiry into Allegations Regarding Dr. Francis Con Ward*. Dublin: Stationery Office.

(1947) *Locke's Distillery Kilbeggan, Purchase by Aliens 1947*. Dublin: Stationery Office.

Office of the Director of Corporate Enforcement (2013) *Annual Report 2012*. Available at: http://www.odce.ie/Portals/0/EasyDNNNewsDocuments/528/ODCE-FullReport-2012-English-v4.pdf (accessed 4 April 2014).

Ó Gráda, C. and O'Rourke, K. (1996) 'Irish economic growth, 1945–88' in N. Crafts and G. Toniolo (eds) *Economic Growth in Europe Since 1945*. Cambridge: Cambridge University Press.

Pearce, F. (1976) *The Crimes of the Powerful*. London: Pluto Press.

Rolston, B. (2005) '"An effective mask for terror": Democracy, death squads and Northern Ireland', *Crime, Law and Social Change*, 44: 181–203.

Sacks, P. (1976) *Donegal Mafia: An Irish Political Machine*. New Haven: Yale University Press.

Saville Inquiry (2010) *Report of the Bloody Sunday Inquiry*. Available at: http://webarchive.nationalarchives.gov.uk/20101103103930/http:/report.bloody-sunday-inquiry.org/ (accessed 29 June 2014).

Schwendinger, H. and Schwendinger, J. (1975) 'Defenders of order or guardians of human rights' in I. Taylor, P. Walton and J. Young (eds) *Critical Criminology*. London: Routledge and Kegan Paul.

Smithwick, Mr Justice P. (2013) *The Smithwick Report. Report of the Tribunal of Inquiry into Suggestions that Members of An Garda Siochana or Other Employees of the State Colluded in the Fatal Shootings of RUC Chief Superintendent Harry Breen and RUC Superintendent Robert Buchanan on the 20th March 1989*. Dublin: Stationery Office.

Stalker, J. (1989) *The Stalker Affair*. London: Penguin Books.

Stanley, E. (2013) 'Resistance to state-corporate crimes in West Papua', in E. Stanley and J. McCulloch (eds) *State Crime and Resistance*. Abingdon: Routledge.

Stanley, E. and McCulloch, J. (2013) 'Resistance to state crime' in E. Stanley and J. McCulloch (eds) *State Crime and Resistance*. Abingdon: Routledge.

Stevens Enquiry (2003) *Overview and Recommendations*. Available at: http://www.cain.ulst.ac.uk/issues/collusion/stevens3/stevens3summary.htm (accessed 29 June 2014).

Suiter, J. (2010) 'Chieftains delivering: Political determinants of capital spending in Ireland 2001–07', unpublished thesis, Trinity College Dublin.

Tanzi, V. and Davoodi, H. (1998) *Roads to Nowhere: How Corruption in Public Investment Hurts Growth*. Washington DC: International Monetary Fund.

Transparency International (2009) *National Integrity Systems: Country Study Report on Ireland*. Dublin: Transparency International.

—— (2012) *National Integrity Systems Study*. Dublin: Transparency International.

Walker Report (1981) *Interchange of Intelligence between Special Branch and CID*. Reference C352/70. Available at: http://www.patfinucanecentre.org/policing/walker1.html (accessed 29 June 2014).

Ward, T. and Green, P. (2000) 'Legitimacy, civil society, and state crime', *Social Justice*, 27(4): 76–93.

Whitaker, T. K. (1983) *Interests*. Dublin: Institute of Public Administration.

Wood, I. (2003) *God, Guns & Ulster: A History of Loyalist Paramilitaries*. London: Caxton.

Notes

1 The phrase is used by Sartre in his introduction to Memmi (1990: 26): 'A relentless reciprocity binds the colonizer to the colonized…'.

2 Flags and Emblems (Display) Act (Northern Ireland) 1954, chapter 10, article 2.1.

3 *Ireland v U.K.* (Application no. 5310/71), Judgment, Strasbourg, 18 January 1978. Available HTTP: http://hudoc.echr.coe.int/sites/eng/pages/search.aspx?i=001-57506 (accessed 5 January 2014).

4 Interestingly, the European court conclusion that the five techniques represented merely inhuman and degrading treatment, rather than torture, was the legal authority proposed by US government lawyers seeking to deploy similar techniques at Guantanamo.

5 These lies were eventually acknowledged by a court as the basis for overturning the conviction against one man, Martin McCauley, who had survived a police ambush; see *Belfast Telegraph*, 14 May 2014. Available online at: http://www.belfasttelegraph.co.uk/news/local-national/northern-ireland/colombia-three-appeal-against-a-weapons-conviction-will-not-be-opposed-by-chief-prosecutor-30274649.html (accessed 5 January 2014).

6 *McKerr v U.K.* (Application Number 28883/95), Judgment, Strasbourg, 4 May 2001. Available HTTP: http://hudoc.echr.coe.int/sites/eng/pages/search.aspx?i=001-59451 (accessed 5 January 2014).

7 Interestingly, the former Chief Constable of the PSNI, Sir Hugh Orde, the architect of the HET, stated that the HET was not designed to be Article 2 compliant, and that he had never claimed that it could be so. See http://sluggerotoole.com/2014/08/07/sir-hugh-orde-in-conversation-with-john-ware-relsforjustice-feilebelfast-timefortruth-feile2014/.

8 See 'Stormont House Agreement', paragraphs 30–40. Available at: https://www.gov.uk/government/uploads/system/uploads/attachment_data/file/390672/Stormont_House_Agreement.pdf (accessed 5 January 2015).

9 The court action became unnecessary when a newly-appointed Chief Constable agreed to make the information available to the Ombudsman.

10 'Ombudsman/PSNI legal action: George Hamilton and Michael Maguire in talks', *BBC News*, 27 June 2014. Available at: http://www.bbc.co.uk/news/uk-northern-ireland-28058542 (accessed 5 January 2015).

11 *McCaughey v U.K.* (application no. 43098/09), Judgment, Strasbourg, 16 July 2013. Available at: http://hudoc.echr.coe.int/sites/eng/pages/search.aspx?i=001-122370 (accessed 5 January 2015). In May 2014 a Northern Ireland court awarded damages to families of the victims because of the 'unlawful delays' involved in concluding an inquest (McDonald 2014).

12 Letter from Crown Solicitor's Office, RE: Former Officers' Involvement in the Disclosure Process, 28 May 2013.

9

Desistance, recidivism and reintegration

Understanding change and continuity in criminal careers

Deirdre Healy

Introduction

It is well-established that the majority of offenders eventually desist from crime, yet researchers have only recently begun to investigate the mechanisms and contexts that facilitate this process. The phenomenon was first documented by Adolphe Quetelet (1842/2003) who found that criminal behaviour peaks in adolescence and then declines rapidly in early adulthood. The so-called 'age-crime curve' has been observed in many countries and historical periods, which suggests that desistance is a universal feature of criminal careers. This chapter critically reviews the Irish literature on this topic and situates its findings in the context of international theory and research.

Before beginning, some caveats and clarifications are required. First, there is no clear and agreed definition of desistance (see Maruna *et al.* (2004) for a detailed discussion of conceptual issues). Early researchers characterised desistance as an *event*, which implied that it involved an abrupt and complete cessation of criminality. However, contemporary research suggests that desistance is better understood as a *process* consisting of a slow and incremental reduction in the frequency and severity of offending. While this definition represents a significant advance on earlier ideas, it poses its own conceptual challenges. For example, the processes of deceleration and de-escalation can signal the beginning of the desistance process but do not always result in permanent transformation, leading some theorists to argue that they should be treated as separate phases in the criminal career.

Second, there is disagreement about the parameters that should be applied to the study of desistance. Pathways to desistance are dynamic and uncertain, and it is quite common for offenders to experience periods of intermittency, or gaps, in their criminal careers before they desist completely. This makes it difficult to establish with certainty whether a person has truly desisted until after his or her death. As Maruna (2001:17) observed, 'desistance from crime is an unusual dependent variable for criminologists because it is not an event that happens, rather it is the sustained *absence* of a certain type of event'; i.e. re-offending. In addition, there is disagreement about the types of offender that should be studied. Laub and Sampson (2003) claimed that desistance among low-rate offenders was of little theoretical interest and proposed that investigators should concentrate their attention on serious and persistent offenders, a convention that has been adopted by the majority of researchers.

Third, the distinction between offenders and desisters is not always clear-cut, because people in conflict with the law do not always self-identify with – or conform to – either label (Maruna, 2001). This raises important questions regarding the criteria that an ex-offender must fulfil in order to be labelled a 'desister'. For example, can a person who has stopped offending but continues to engage in antisocial behaviour, such as alcohol misuse or gambling, be described as an ex-offender? What about a person who continues to offend but self-identifies as a desister? Or someone who has stopped offending but expresses no remorse for their criminal actions? In other words, it is unclear whether a person who has stopped offending without undergoing an identity or lifestyle change can be classified as an ex-offender. While some believe that desistance is achieved with the cessation of criminal activity, others, including most ex-offenders, regard desistance as a stepping-stone on the journey towards other valued goals, such as employment, parenthood or social inclusion (Weaver, 2012).

Maruna *et al.* (2004: 19) attempted to resolve these issues by differentiating between primary desistance, defined as 'any lull or crime-free gap in the course of a criminal career', and secondary desistance, which refers to 'the movement from the behaviour of non-offending to the assumption of the role or identity of a "changed person"'. This framework is useful because it enables researchers to study periods of intermittency as well as more permanent identity transformations.

Theoretical perspectives

In their quest to enhance understanding of desistance, researchers have drawn inspiration from a variety of disciplines, including sociology, psychology and philosophy. In addition, they have used a diverse array of methodologies, ranging from large-scale quantitative studies to single-case qualitative studies. Consequently, the desistance literature has produced a comprehensive and multi-dimensional analysis of pathways through crime. This section critically evaluates three of the most influential theories, namely Laub and Sampson's (2003) age-graded theory of informal social control; Maruna's (2001) theory of the redemptive self; and Giordano *et al.*'s (2002) theory of cognitive transformation.

Laub and Sampson's age-graded theory of informal social control

Laub and Sampson (2003) provided the most detailed account of the age-graded theory of informal social control in their book *Shared Beginnings, Divergent Lives: Delinquent Boys to Age 70*. The book presented the findings of a longitudinal study which followed 500 boys who were sent to a reformatory school in Boston during the 1940s up to the age of 70. The results suggested that desistance was facilitated by important turning points in the men's life histories, such as forming a family, gaining employment, moving to a new area or joining the military. As they aged, the men gradually accumulated pro-social bonds which appeared to reduce offending through the mechanism of informal social control. The bonds had to be meaningful, stable and of high quality in order to encourage desistance.

Social bonds can exert informal social control over putative desisters' behaviour in several ways. First, relationships create emotional attachments which may be jeopardised by further offending. Thus, a person may stop offending because they know that they will lose a valued job if they are arrested and sent to prison. Second, pro-social bonds alter daily routines in ways that reduce exposure to criminal opportunities. For example, an individual who spends the day at work has less time to associate with criminal peers. Third, they provide access to new non-criminal networks, including prospective partners or employers. Fourth, pro-social others monitor and supervise daily activities which reduces the likelihood that a person will engage in antisocial behaviour. Finally, social bonds alter offenders' self-concepts by encouraging them to strive towards non-criminal identities. Although Laub and Sampson (2003: 278) characterised ex-offenders as active participants in the change process, they argued that desistance occurs primarily 'by default'. In their view, desistance does not result from an intentional process of self-change but arises indirectly from a desire to preserve cherished relationships.

This theory has made a number of important contributions to knowledge. By adopting a life-course perspective, the authors focused attention on offenders' entire criminal careers and, in doing so, revealed that offenders and desisters are not different 'types' of people but are simply being studied at different stages of the desistance process. In fact, they found that even the most persistent offenders ultimately desisted from crime. Furthermore, the study demonstrated that children who experience adverse childhood events are not predestined to become adult offenders. In reality, human lives are characterised by change as well as continuity, and positive adult experiences can dramatically alter a person's offending trajectory. In addition, the theory has received widespread empirical support, although it has also been subjected to some important criticisms.

Because Laub and Sampson (2003) focused exclusively on male offenders, they were unable to explore the impact of gender on desistance. This is an important omission, since pathways to desistance appear to be highly gendered. Messerschmidt (1997) claimed that contemporary female identities are fluid enough to accommodate non-traditional feminine behaviours, such as criminality, as well as more stereotypical feminine roles, such as motherhood. This flexibility may facilitate desistance by enabling female offenders to avoid full immersion in criminal subcultures. In contrast, male identities, which are often built around hegemonic masculine ideals, appear to increase the likelihood of criminal behaviour. Carlsson (2013) discovered that age-specific norms surrounding masculinity shaped pathways to and from crime. He found that persistent offenders' identities espoused adolescent versions of masculinity, manifested through a concern with being a 'party animal' or a 'risk-taker'. Conversely, desistance identities emphasised adult masculine roles, such as being a 'good worker' or 'family man'.

Individual life stories are shaped by particular socio-cultural contexts, and it is important to examine whether social bonds exert the same impact across time and space. In other words, are the factors that influenced desistance among a group of boys who grew up in Boston in the early twentieth century universally relevant, or are they specific to that time and place? Giordano et al. (2002) tested the age-graded theory of informal social control using a contemporary American sample and found that marriage and employment did not influence desistance. Further analysis revealed that only a small proportion of the sample had acquired high-quality social bonds, although those that had attained the full 'respectability package' were more likely to have desisted (Giordano et al., 2002: 1013). These findings suggest that social bonds may play a more circumscribed role in contemporary society.

Social bonds may also have been less influential in earlier historical periods. Farrall et al. (2009) examined pathways to desistance among a sample of repeat offenders who lived in Crewe, England, between 1880 and 1940, using a combination of census data, trial records, newspaper reports and employment files. Surprisingly, they found that marriage and employment did not engender desistance but actually increased criminality. The authors offered several explanations for these results. They noted that during the nineteenth century people married primarily for economic, rather than romantic, reasons. A lack of emotional investment meant that marital relationships could not increase the 'costs' associated with continued criminal behaviour. In addition, high levels of gender inequality ensured that women did not have sufficient social power to control their husbands' behaviour. Furthermore, most of the samples' offences related to drunkenness, which can be explained by the local railway industry's tolerance for a heavy drinking culture among its workers. In fact, many non-offenders began to offend after they took up employment in this industry. Overall, this study showed that the impact of informal social control mechanisms is mediated by wider structural arrangements as well as by local cultural values.

It is also unclear whether Laub and Sampson's (2003) findings are relevant outside Anglophone cultures. To investigate this issue, Adorjan and Hong Chui (2012) studied desistance among a sample of ex-prisoners in Hong Kong and discovered that some features of the process were culturally specific. For example, family and marital bonds were more significant than employment, due to the influence of Confucian values. These ties were often strengthened through the mechanism of religion, which has a special status in Hong Kong society. Organised religion also offered ex-offenders a template for a moral life, emotional support and access to rehabilitation programmes. On the other hand, some elements of Hong Kong culture impeded desistance, including the emphasis on material success, a competitive labour market, high inequality and the presence of organised gang networks.

Finally, researchers have criticised the theory's lack of attention to the subjective causes of desistance. Vaughan (2007) argued that the theory's emphasis on situational factors implies that desisters' commitment to change is contingent on their proximal social circumstances. In other words, it suggests that a person's propensity to offend remains stable, and it is only their external circumstances that change. This fails to explain why the majority of ex-offenders remain committed to desistance even when a relationship or period of employment ends and suggests that other, more subjective, factors are involved.

Maruna's theory of the redemptive self

Maruna (2001) employed a narrative approach to explore the subjective dimensions of desistance. Narrative psychologists believe that personal myths, or self-narratives, provide important insights into a person's core motives, values and aspirations. Self-narratives are malleable, which means that people can change their thoughts and behaviour to accommodate new information and experiences. In his landmark book, *Making Good: How Ex-Convicts Reform and Rebuild Their Lives*, Maruna (2001) studied the narrative scripts adopted by desisters as they negotiated the journey to a crime-free life. He concluded that ex-offenders require a plausible story that explains how they made the transition from 'offender' to 'desister' if they are to persuade themselves and others that they have truly changed. To achieve this, they construct a redemption script which links 'past experiences to the present in such a way that the present good seems an almost inevitable outcome' (Maruna, 2001: 87).

The redemption script begins by emphasising ex-offenders' positive personal qualities to demonstrate that they are intrinsically good people who became trapped in criminality by circumstances beyond their control. Narrators then describe how they transcended these circumstances through the assistance of an external advocate, perhaps a counsellor or family member. At the same time, they strongly emphasise their own role, or agency, in the change process. According to Maruna (2001), agency consists of four key elements: a heightened sense of control over life chances; special recognition for personal achievements; the attainment of important goals; and empowerment through association with a higher power. Finally, desisters highlight the benefits that accrued from their criminal experiences in order to imbue an otherwise meaningless life with purpose and direction. Indeed, many ex-offenders engage in generative activities in an effort to redeem themselves; for example, using their knowledge to help other people overcome criminality or addiction. In contrast, persistent offenders adopt a condemnation script which is characterised by an absence of agency and generativity. They claim to have been permanently 'doomed to deviance' by chance events or childhood adversity and distract themselves from feelings of emptiness and alienation through wishful thinking, a hedonistic lifestyle or excessive consumption (Maruna, 2001: 74).

Maruna's (2001) theory has made a number of important contributions to knowledge. As one of the first to explore the subjective dimensions of desistance, his study provided unique and unprecedented insights into the psychological mechanisms that underpin the process, including agency, generativity, shame and redemption. His work has also influenced rehabilitation practice, and strengths-based approaches, inspired by his ideas, are now commonly used in many jurisdictions (see e.g. Laws and Ward, 2011). In addition, Maruna (2001) recognised that ex-offenders play an active role in the desistance process, which represents a significant advance on the passive model offered by Laub and Sampson (2003).

There is significant support for Maruna's (2001) contention that narratives offer important insights into people's thoughts, values and behaviour. For example, Vaughan (2007: 396) studied the cognitive structures that facilitate the construction (or modification) of narrative identities, proposing that 'human agents constitute their identity by plotting their own lives within a narrative that exists between a past that is denounced and a future ideal toward which they strive'. He suggested that, when presented with an opportunity to change their lives, putative desisters engage in an internal conversation which progresses through three distinct phases. During the *discernment* phase, they consider whether the desired conventional self is compatible with current criminal concerns. If the identities are perceived to be in conflict, offenders experience a general openness to change. They then evaluate the costs and benefits associated with both the criminal and conventional lifestyles in the *deliberation* phase before committing themselves to a nascent conventional identity in the final *dedication* stage. Vaughan (2007: 390) concluded that desistance can only be understood through an appreciation of the actor's ultimate concerns, defined as 'the commitments that matter most and dictate the means by which he or she lives'.

Despite its popularity, some aspects of Maruna's (2001) theory require further investigation. For example, Healy and O'Donnell (2008) replicated his study with a sample of Irish probationers to examine whether the redemption script was relevant during the transition to desistance. They found that early-stage desisters were preoccupied with 'ordinary' goals, such as getting a job or finding a home, rather than generative concerns. The authors suggested that basic needs may need to be satisfied before ex-offenders can embrace higher-order goals like generativity. In addition, early-stage desisters lacked a language of agency, which suggests that an agentic outlook may emerge gradually as ex-offenders accumulate real-world experiences of achievement, empowerment and self-mastery. Overall, the findings indicated that the redemption script was not present during the early stages of change and suggested that it may be an outcome, rather than a cause, of desistance. Moreover, Liem and Richardson (2014) found that offender and desistance narratives both contained elements of the redemption script although desisters were significantly more likely to employ agentic language in their narratives.

In addition, the theory does not explain how offenders make the transition from the fatalistic condemnation script to the agentic redemption script. Paternoster and Bushway (2009) added an interesting dimension to Maruna's (2001) work by suggesting that the initial motivation to change is inspired by the desire to avoid an unwanted fate. The authors proposed that offenders become disillusioned with the criminal lifestyle when they realise that it invariably entails frequent spells of imprisonment, risks to health and wellbeing and fractured relationships. This realisation weakens their attachment to the criminal identity and triggers a shift in readiness to change. Once they have embraced a new conventional identity, offenders re-evaluate their attitudes towards crime and begin to move towards pro-social relationships. The authors concluded, however, that motivation to change cannot be sustained in the long term unless the putative ex-offender fashions a valued alternative identity.

Some scholars argue that psychological theories fail to account for the role of structural factors in the development of a new desistance identity. For example, King (2013a; 2013b) discovered that putative desisters began to formulate a desired conventional self during the early stages of change but recognised that structural barriers could impede access to their desired selves and, consequently, experienced a diminished sense of agency and autonomy. This indicates that, both internal and external change processes are required to initiate and sustain a desistance narrative. Recent scholarship has endeavoured to take account of the impact of social opportunities and constraints on identity formation. For example, Rajah et al. (2014) found that narratives tend to adapt to changing social contexts. In their study, some of the prisoners who adopted a redemption script while in custody subsequently rejected the narrative when they discovered after release that valuable goals were unattainable.

Giordano et al.'s theory of cognitive transformation

Recently, theorists have begun to develop integrated models that emphasise the reciprocal relationship between subjective and social processes. The most influential of these is Giordano et al.'s (2002) theory of cognitive transformation, which suggested that offenders must experience a subjective readiness to change which enables them to capitalise on desistance opportunities, or hooks, in their environment. These hooks may emerge from a variety of sources, including rehabilitation programmes, religious communities or family relationships. To facilitate change, they must direct the actor's attention towards the future, provide access to pro-social networks and contain a blueprint for a conventional identity. Once these conditions are met, the hooks can act as catalysts for the creation of a meaningful substitute self that replaces the criminal identity. In a later article, Giordano et al. (2007: 1611) proposed that these cognitive and social transformations are accompanied by an 'emotional mellowing' process which occurs during the transition to adulthood. While criminal behaviour can generate emotional rewards during adolescence, such as excitement or respect, these emotional associations begin to fade once young people enter pro-social adult domains and develop better emotional coping skills.

The theory has gained significant support. Simons and Barr (2012) found that the acquisition of high-quality social bonds elicited dramatic and immediate cognitive shifts among putative ex-offenders, which in turn precipitated desistance. Interestingly, these cognitive shifts occurred relatively quickly after the formation of a relationship, which corroborates Giordano et al.'s (2002) argument that cognitive changes are critical during the early stages of change when emerging identities are not strong enough to exert informal social control over prospective desisters' behaviour.

The perspective is compatible with the two theories reviewed earlier but there are important areas of disagreement. Giordano et al. (2002) situate agency at the forefront of change and suggest that the environment plays a critical, but secondary, role. This contrasts with Laub and Sampson's (2003) argument that desisters respond passively and unconsciously to environmental cues (although it is possible that these theoretical differences are due to social changes, i.e. putative ex-offenders have to exercise greater levels of agency in contemporary society because they possess fewer social resources than earlier generations). Furthermore, Giordano et al.'s (2002) contention that cognitive transformations are paramount in the change process contradicts Laub and Sampson's (2003) view that desistance does not require significant internal shifts. Finally, Giordano et al. (2002) dispute Maruna's (2001) claim that ex-offenders strive to uncover a lost self in their life histories, suggesting instead that they construct a brand new identity.

More recently, Bottoms *et al.* (2004) proposed a multi-dimensional model of desistance consisting of five inter-related processes. They argued that the individual's 'programmed potential', which consists of static background factors such as age, gender and criminal history, exerts an important influence on criminal behaviour in the short-term (Bottoms *et al.*, 2004: 372). Next, structural arrangements, particularly those relating to employment and relationship formation, create a matrix of social opportunities and constraints which either help or hinder desistance. Additionally, cultural contexts generate norms, values and beliefs which shape what is regarded as socially acceptable or normative behaviour; while situational contexts determine the extent to which people encounter opportunities to offend within their immediate environment. Finally, desisters' subjective experiences of the desistance process must be considered. In a test of their model, Bottoms and Shapland (2011) found that future criminal behaviour was predicted by participants' prior criminal history, the number of obstacles they expected to face and their perceived self-efficacy (defined as their belief that they will overcome life's challenges or achieve valued goals).

Desistance and recidivism in the Republic of Ireland and Northern Ireland

Desistance research in Northern Ireland and the Republic of Ireland is still in its infancy, although there has been a marked increase in scholarly interest in recent years. At the time of writing there have been no longitudinal, comparative or quantitative studies of desistance. However, a number of qualitative studies have provided insight into the mechanisms, processes and contexts that underpin the change process. In the following sections, their findings are reviewed and discussed in the context of the international literature in this area. First, the findings of recidivism studies are analysed to explore short-term trends in recidivism (although there are similarities between these phenomena, it is important to stress that desistance is not simply the opposite of recidivism).

Northern Ireland's Department of Justice regularly publishes detailed information on adult reconviction rates. The most recent statistics relate to the 2011/12 cohort, which contained around 28,751 individuals who received either non-custodial or custodial disposals (DOJNI, 2014). The report found clear differences in outcomes across disposals. For example, 33 per cent of offenders under community supervision were reconvicted within one year, compared to 48 per cent of prisoners and 14 per cent of those who received a diversionary disposal. Reconviction rates also varied according to offender and offence characteristics. The groups with the highest reconviction rates were young offenders, male offenders and those with previous convictions. In addition, people who were convicted of robbery, burglary or weapons offences were more likely to be reconvicted. Because offender characteristics were not controlled, it is not clear whether the variations in recidivism rates are explained by the impact of the disposals or other factors.

Reconviction statistics for criminal justice populations are published in the Republic of Ireland on an annual basis; however, the series only began in 2012 with an analysis of the 2007 cohort. The most recent figures relate to the 2008 cohort and show that 32 per cent of the 3,761 offenders serving probation or community service orders that year were reconvicted within two years, with the figure rising to 41 per cent after three years (CSO, 2013a). Breaking this figure down by sentence type, around a third of probationers and 30 per cent of offenders serving community service orders were reconvicted within two years. These figures compare favourably to prisoner reconviction rates in the Republic of Ireland where 51 per cent of the 5,489 prisoners released in 2008 were reconvicted within two years (CSO, 2013b). Reconviction rates among prisoners and probationers also varied according to offence and offender characteristics. Prisoners who had committed public order, burglary or theft offences and probationers who had committed public order, theft or drugs offences had the highest rates of reconviction. In both cohorts, males and younger offenders were more likely to be reconvicted.

Unfortunately, recidivism rates cannot be accurately compared because the two jurisdictions use different follow-up periods. Besides, it is impossible to make meaningful comparisons without controlling for the personal and social factors that are known to affect re-offending, including, *inter alia,* age, gender, criminal history, offence type, employment status and family circumstances. Furthermore, reconviction rates can be affected by differences in legislation, policing practices, crime reporting and sentencing patterns; for example, a police crack-down on public order offences will increase the number of recorded offences in that crime category (see Maguire (2012) for a detailed discussion of the difficulties involved in the interpretation of crime statistics). Finally, reconviction statistics may be influenced by variations in the ways that data are collected, collated and analysed. Indeed, a recent Garda Inspectorate (2014) report revealed that crimes are not always properly recorded or correctly classified by police in the Republic of Ireland. Official figures thus provide useful information about general patterns of re-offending but must be interpreted with caution. Although they reveal little about the differential impacts of socio-cultural contexts north and south of the border, useful insights can be gleaned from single-jurisdiction studies whose findings are explored next.

Social context, transitions and turning points

Braithwaite (1989) theorised that communitarian societies – societies with close communal bonds and a strong sense of mutual obligation – would experience lower re-offending rates because they tend to practise reintegrative shaming. Reintegrative shaming refers to 'shaming which is followed by efforts to reintegrate the offender back into the community of law-abiding or respectable citizens through words or gestures of forgiveness or ceremonies to decertify the offender as deviant' (Braithwaite, 1989: 100–101). It differs from disintegrative shaming, which concerns practices that punish, stigmatise and exclude offenders from full participation in society. O'Donnell *et al.* (2008) examined whether prisoners in the Republic of Ireland, considered by many to fit the profile of a communitarian society, experienced low recidivism rates compared to other jurisdictions. They collected information on almost 20,000 prisoners who were released between 2001 and 2004 and found that around half received a new prison sentence within four years of release; a rate which very closely approximated that found in other, non-communitarian, societies. Furthermore, the factors that predicted re-imprisonment were very similar to those reported in other jurisdictions. Specifically, the prisoners most likely to be re-imprisoned were younger males who had problems with unemployment, literacy and education prior to committal and who had previously been imprisoned. These findings suggest that a communitarian social structure has a limited effect on re-offending and thus, desistance.

The research team also collected information on the home addresses of a sub-set of the sample in order to study the geography of reintegration (O'Donnell *et al.*, 2007). They found that the majority of prisoners were concentrated in a relatively small number of severely deprived urban areas. In fact, 24 per cent of prisoners lived in just 1 per cent of the communities included in the study. The link between poverty and crime was, however, less pronounced in rural areas. The geographical spread of prisoners also varied according to offence type. Prisoners who had been convicted of violent, drug-related or property crimes tended to live in disadvantaged urban areas, whereas prisoners convicted of sexual or driving offences were more evenly spread throughout the country. The authors concluded that pathways to desistance are likely to be more challenging for people who live in disadvantaged communities with high densities of ex-prisoners, because these neighbourhoods lack the social resources required to fully reintegrate ex-offenders.

As discussed earlier, high-quality social bonds can promote desistance by fostering stronger ties to conventional institutions. In both Northern Ireland and the Republic of Ireland, ex-offenders often find their efforts to attain full social inclusion hampered by a range of structural barriers. As a result, many experience problems with educational and vocational attainment (O'Donnell *et al.*, 2008; Davies and Gailey, 2005; Roberson and Radford, 2006), family formation (O'Donnell *et al.*, 2008; McIlwaine, 2011), addiction (Drummond and Codd, 2014; Horgan, 2013; NIPS, 2013; PBNI, 2012), homelessness (Seymour and Costello, 2005; NIHE, 2012) and mental health (Kennedy *et al.*, 2005; CJINI, 2010). Given the substantial barriers they face, ex-offenders must exercise high levels of agency in order to improve their life chances.

Corr (2011: 183) studied offenders' and desisters' responses to the key turning points that occur during the transition to adulthood in the Republic of Ireland, and found that desisters responded more agentically to these 'critical moments'. In particular, negative life events, such as serving a prison sentence, prompted desisters to engage in a period of reflection which engendered a growing awareness of the costs of crime and the recognition that its benefits are ephemeral and short-lived. In addition, desisters became increasingly concerned that continued criminality would interfere with the achievement of valued goals, such as finding a job or home. Conversely, persistent offenders did not engage in any re-evaluation after a negative life experience but expressed a heightened sense of frustration over their failure to attain conventional life success. Their 'fractured' adult transitions motivated them to continue offending in order to obtain the monetary and symbolic rewards that they believed could not be attained through legitimate means (Corr, 2011: 207). In particular, they offended to fund excessive consumption or drug addiction and to obtain status and respect among their peers. The study also highlighted the role of local cultures in initiating and perpetuating criminality, revealing that it is much harder for putative desisters to resist the temptation to offend when they live in communities that embrace criminal values and support informal criminal economies.

These studies show that the structural climate shapes pathways through crime but suggest that its impact is mediated by the opportunities and constraints within the immediate social context as well as offenders' differential responses to environmental conditions. The findings also reveal that criminal justice populations continued to experience substantial barriers to reintegration despite the favourable macro-economic climate that existed north and south of the border during the Celtic Tiger years, when these studies were conducted. It is likely that the recession which began in 2008 has further increased barriers to reintegration.

Gender

Other structural factors can also shape pathways to desistance. Byrne and Trew (2005, 2008) studied the impact of gender on offending patterns in Northern Ireland and discovered that male offenders used crime to achieve masculinity when legitimate avenues were perceived to be unavailable. In contemporary Western society masculinity is thought to be associated with the achievement of personal autonomy, financial independence, risk-taking and aggression (see e.g. Messerschmidt, 1997). Byrne and Trew (2005, 2008) discovered that the commission of theft provided socially excluded men with the financial wherewithal to participate in youth cultural activities, such as consumption; joyriding enabled them to display risk-taking behaviours; while vandalism demonstrated a capacity for violence. For the most part, men held positive attitudes towards crime and highlighted the intrinsic rewards associated with offending behaviour. In contrast, women offended primarily for practical reasons and mainly to provide for their children. They felt ashamed of their actions but believed that being seen as a bad mother was worse than being labelled a criminal. Their experiences show that crime is not an effective way to achieve femininity in a society where women are expected to conform to traditional feminine stereotypes.

At the same time, the researchers observed many similarities between male and female desistance narratives. For both groups, pathways out of crime were influenced by a growing sense of maturity, the development of conventional social bonds and changing attitudes towards criminality. However, social bonds appeared to influence men and women's behaviour in different ways. Men typically emphasised the positive impact of social ties, explaining that family, partners and friends encouraged them to stop offending. Conversely, women's relationships often increased criminality, especially if their partner was already involved in crime. This study adds an important dimension to Laub and Sampson's (2003) research by showing that the impact of social bonds is governed by broader structural factors, such as gender roles and social exclusion, as well as personal factors, such as the criminal history of a prospective romantic partner.

Hourigan's (2012) ethnographic research in the Republic of Ireland also implicated masculine ideals in gangland criminality (see also Hourigan, *infra*). Many of the men in her study adopted a 'hard man' identity to gain a modicum of status and respect despite their marginalised social position. Furthermore, community members often encouraged their children to adopt this identity as a protective measure, but, rather than increase their safety, this strategy merely perpetuated the climate of fear and violence. Interestingly, family bonds also emerged as a crucial factor in the onset and maintenance of criminality because gang membership was open only to those with blood ties to criminal families. This study shows that high-quality social bonds are not always conducive to desistance and, in certain cases, may even increase the likelihood of criminality. Moreover, pro-social masculine identities are not always available to men living in disadvantaged communities. For example, many face barriers to being a good father, such as poor accommodation and insufficient income (Griffin and Kelleher, 2010).

The Conflict

Although the majority of structural factors discussed in this section are pertinent to both jurisdictions, some issues, such as the legacy of the Conflict, pose unique challenges. Dwyer (2013a, 2013b) studied pathways to desistance among politically motivated ex-prisoners in Northern Ireland. This group constitutes a theoretically interesting case study because, unlike most putative desisters, they do not regard themselves as offenders and therefore do not experience a shift in identity, values or beliefs when they decide to change their behaviour. However, they face similar barriers to reintegration, including a permanent criminal record which makes it difficult to obtain employment. Dwyer (2013a, 2013b) found that their refusal to accept the offender label engendered a reluctance to attend state-run rehabilitation programmes. Instead, they established their own self-help organisations which provided rehabilitation services to other politically motivated ex-prisoners. These organisations ultimately developed into a powerful social movement which campaigned for greater social acceptance of former political prisoners.

Whereas Maruna's (2001) desisters sought redemption, the politically motivated ex-prisoners who participated in Dwyer's (2013a, 2013b) research pursued equality and social inclusion. Their involvement in self-help programmes enabled them to create new non-violent identities as peacemakers and leaders and provided them with a sense of purpose and direction. They did not reject their former selves but claimed that they were now using peaceful means to attain their political goals. Although this group followed unique pathways to desistance, their stories resemble those of ordinary desisters in important ways. For example, the benefits that they attributed to their advocacy work echo the generative concerns espoused by ordinary desisters (Dwyer and Maruna, 2011). Generative activities enable former political prisoners to view themselves as assets to the community and provide them with opportunities to develop meaningful non-criminal identities. Furthermore, the enactment of positive social roles allows them to gain positive social recognition from their communities. This study illustrates the important role played by the local socio-cultural context in desistance; in this case, the peace process provided both a context for and a pathway to change. These findings support the argument put forward by several scholars (e.g. Farrall *et al.*, 2009; Adorjan and Hong Chui, 2012) that the shape of individual desistance pathways is influenced by cultural factors. However, the study also raises important questions about the applicability of desistance theories in transitional societies where the label of 'criminal' is contested.

Re-entry and reintegration

State policies, particularly those relating to the criminal justice system, can also influence pathways to desistance. Hughes (2012) drew on Visher and Travis' (2003) theoretical framework to study experiences of desistance, recidivism and re-entry among prisoners in the Republic of Ireland. Visher and Travis (2003) divided the re-entry process into four distinct phases, namely pre-prison, in-prison, immediate post-prison and long-term integration. They proposed that prisoners' experiences during each phase were shaped by individual, family, community and societal factors. Hughes (2012) interviewed 60 male prisoners aged between 16 and 20, five weeks before their release from prison. An examination of their pre-prison experiences revealed that their lives were characterised by low educational attainment, literacy issues, family problems, alcohol and drug misuse and social deprivation. Despite these challenges, the men were optimistic about their future prospects and believed that it would be easy to desist, stop using drugs and find work after release. During their time in custody, they participated in a range of educational, vocational and leisure activities. However, almost half were re-imprisoned within two years, which suggests that their optimistic intentions were not always realised.

The only factors that statistically predicted re-imprisonment were age and perceived likelihood of re-offending. Interestingly, prisoners who expressed uncertainty about their ability to desist believed that their life stories had been scripted by factors beyond their control, a sentiment that is reminiscent of Maruna's (2001) condemnation script. Despite the existence of some therapeutic supports within the prison environment, the shortage of formal post-release programmes may have made it harder to surmount obstacles to desistance. In addition, it is likely that adverse pre-prison experiences diminished prisoners' ability to make a successful transition from prison to community. Hughes (2012) argued that social factors were paramount in the re-entry process but concluded that an integrated model offered the most complete explanation of the findings.

The desistance process may be more challenging for certain offender groups, such as child sex offenders, who, if apprehended, are often subjected to harsh treatment by the state, the public and the criminal justice system. Child sex offenders are regularly portrayed in the media as uniquely dangerous individuals from whom the public must be protected at all costs. Stringent legal and extra-legal measures, including employment vetting schemes, harsh sentences, post-release supervision and sex offender registers, have been introduced in many jurisdictions to manage these risks. McAlinden (2012) observed that such measures do not prevent crime but tend to heighten public fears about child sexual abuse and militate against offender reintegration. She examined the state response to child sex offenders in several jurisdictions, including Northern Ireland and the Republic of Ireland, and found that each jurisdiction faced individual challenges in relation to child protection. Due to its Catholic heritage, the Irish state was unwilling to interfere with the privacy of the family or discuss sexual matters, while public distrust of the state in Northern Ireland meant that paramilitary groups often assumed responsibility for the punishment of sex offenders.

McAlinden (2012) also found that the work of professionals, such as social workers, police officers and treatment providers, was influenced by populist stereotypes that demonised child sex offenders. Some professionals claimed that offenders routinely attempted to subvert police investigations and therapeutic interventions through manipulative behaviours; for example, by presenting themselves as victims to evoke sympathy or by adopting a language of change to create the impression that they were moving away from crime. In reality, many offenders employ these tactics for benign reasons, namely to escape the legal and social consequences incurred by the 'offender' label, to demonstrate their rejection of criminal values or to escape their criminal pasts (Maruna and Mann, 2006).

It is clear from the preceding review that putative ex-offenders face significant obstacles to change. However, the effects of social problems can be ameliorated by effective rehabilitation programmes. Cleere (2013) found that prisoners who participated in prison education in the Republic of Ireland were more likely than non-participants to experience a sense of agency, hold generative ambitions, express confidence in their ability to desist and develop realistic plans for release. These psychological resources not only enabled them to acquire and maintain social capital but also protected them from becoming embedded in prison sub-cultures. Overall, education broadened their horizons by helping them to pursue valued goals through legitimate avenues. In this way, education can act as a 'hook' for change, but only if the actor is willing and able to capitalise on this opportunity (see also Giordano et al., 2002).

While further comparative work is required, the research reviewed in this section suggests that there are similarities (e.g. reintegration barriers) as well as differences (e.g. the impact of the Conflict) in the socio-cultural arrangements that operate north and south of the border. Since international evidence suggests that socio-cultural factors influence pathways to change, it is likely that the desistance process varies at least to some extent within the two jurisdictions. The wider literature also suggests that putative desisters use personal agency to navigate socio-cultural opportunities and constraints. The relevance of psychological and agentic factors in the Irish context is explored in the next section.

The psychology of desistance

During the desistance process, ex-offenders construct new narratives that integrate their past, present and future experiences into a coherent adult identity. Healy (2012) interviewed 72 adult males who were under probation supervision in the Republic of Ireland. She compared the narrative identities of offenders and desisters and discovered important differences between them. Although both groups expressed regret about their criminal history, desisters were more likely to imbue the past with meaning. For example, many claimed that their criminal experiences had provided them with wisdom, compassion and a sense of relatedness. In contrast, persistent offenders failed to find meaning in the past and believed that criminality had caused permanent damage to their personalities, relationships and future prospects. Offenders and desisters also held different visions of the future. While almost all of the participants aspired to conventional adult roles in employment, education and family life, desisters were more confident that they could achieve these desired selves.

Furthermore, desisters tended to employ an agentic approach in their daily interactions with the social world and used a range of coping strategies to capitalise on desistance opportunities in the environment, including reflection, problem-solving, cognitive reframing, expectation management and help-seeking. In contrast, offenders felt trapped by circumstances beyond their control and, believing that there were no alternatives to the criminal lifestyle, adopted a passive approach in their social interactions. These results suggest that prospective ex-offenders must find ways to successfully navigate opportunities and constraints within the present if they are to escape the past and achieve meaningful conventional identities in the future.

Many researchers believe that the early stages of desistance are of limited theoretical interest; however, recent research indicates that desisters inhabit a rich landscape during the preliminary stages of change. Healy (2012) found that the transition to desistance was influenced by negative events, such as the desire to avoid further imprisonment, as well as positive experiences, such as the wish to be a good father. These experiences initiated a period of reflection which led offenders to make an intentional decision to change their lives. Interestingly, desisters appeared to experience sudden and dramatic psychosocial shifts during the early stages of change. These gains were consolidated over time and ultimately enhanced their psychological, social and emotional wellbeing (see also Healy, 2010; Healy and O'Donnell, 2006). This finding contrasts with popular conceptions of desistance as a gradual and tentative process. It is possible that the initial decision to desist generates a long-term momentum towards lasting change, even though prospective desisters may experience doubts, reversals and setbacks in the short-term.

More recently, Healy (2013) investigated the role of agency in the desistance process, noting that little is known about its content (the 'what'), origins (the 'why'), mechanisms of operation (the 'how') and goals (the 'wherefore'). In a later article, Healy (2014: 874) defined agency as 'a dynamic interaction between the person and their social world that is directed towards the achievement of a meaningful and credible new self' and 'supported by a range of cognitive, emotional and social resources which mature during the transition to adulthood'. Her research suggested that the ability to imagine a meaningful and credible new self can activate latent agentic potential and enable desisters to employ coping skills consistently and effectively in pursuit of their goals. Healy (2012) also analysed the dimensions of agency identified by Maruna (2001), namely self-mastery, responsibility, status/victory and empowerment, but found that these themes were largely absent from early-stage desistance narratives (see also Healy and O'Donnell, 2008). This is unsurprising, since Maruna's (2001) definition conceptualises agency as a sense of achievement, which is arguably more relevant to the latter stages of change. Diverging findings such as these highlight the need for greater scholarly consensus concerning the nature of agency.

Overall, the results of Healy's (2012) research are most consistent with Giordano et al.'s (2002) cognitive transformation theory, which emphasises the reciprocal relationship that exists between the actor and the environment and highlights the important role played by agency in the early stages of change. The study also confirms key tenets of Maruna's (2001) theory, especially the importance of meaning-making, optimism, agency and narrative identity formation. However, there was little evidence of 'agency as achievement' or generativity in participants' narratives, which suggests that these features of the redemption script are not characteristic of the early stages of change.

Other studies provide additional insights into the content, origins and functions of desistance narratives in the Republic of Ireland. Marsh (2011) analysed the life stories of five established desisters who were also recovering addicts and found that their personal accounts were influenced by the theory of change espoused by the Alcoholics Anonymous (AA) programme. According to the AA script, addicts must first eschew responsibility for their actions by accepting that they are suffering from an incurable disease. They must then relinquish control to a higher spiritual power before cataloguing the harms caused by their actions and endeavouring to make amends; for example, by acting as a sponsor for other recovering addicts. Similarly, the men's desistance narratives portrayed addiction as a powerful force that could not be contained and described how their surrender to a higher power prompted a shift towards a pro-social identity that was incompatible with continued offending and drug use. Assuming the role of sponsor was regarded as a critical step, because it signalled to society that they had truly changed and also helped to sustain their motivation and capacity to desist. These findings show that rehabilitation programmes can provide putative desisters with a template for a conventional narrative identity. Moreover, many of the narrative themes that emerged from this study resemble key elements of Maruna's (2001) redemption script, particularly the denial of responsibility for harmful behaviour, the reliance on an external force to empower the individual and the desire to engage in generative and restorative activities. However, it is unclear whether individuals can ever become 'ex-addicts' if they view addiction as an incurable disease.

Evidence suggests that agentic behaviour is facilitated by the psychosocial resources that young people accumulate during the transition to adulthood. Seymour (2013) found that the maturation process provided desisters in the Republic of Ireland with an altered perspective on their past and future selves, a greater sense of autonomy and a growing awareness of the costs of crime. These resources helped them to resist the myriad temptations that exist in a high-crime neighbourhood and to capitalise on positive opportunities in their environment. Although the journey to desistance was long and arduous, ex-offenders claimed that their decision to change generated significant psychological, emotional and social rewards. In particular, strong social bonds with parents, siblings, partners and children imbued their lives with meaning and purpose, provided a source of social recognition for their change efforts and exerted informal social control over their behaviour. Seymour's (2013) study also highlighted the impact of the legal context on desistance. For example, motivation to change was often prompted by feelings of fatigue that resulted from frequent contact with the youth justice system, as well as concerns about entering the adult system. Overall, these findings support Giordano et al.'s (2002) cognitive transformation theory, because they emphasise agency but recognise the important secondary role played by the wider social context.

Psychological profiles of offenders also provide useful insights into the cognitive, emotional and social correlates of crime and desistance. Marsa et al. (2004) compared three prisoner groups in the Republic of Ireland, namely child sex offenders, violent offenders and non-violent offenders, to a sample of non-offenders. They found that child sex offenders' failure to form secure parental attachments during childhood generated social anxiety, insecure attachments and loneliness, which led them as adults to satisfy their emotional needs through crime. Overall, participants with secure interpersonal attachments experienced the highest levels of emotional wellbeing and the strongest sense of control over their lives. These findings corroborate Giordano et al.'s (2007) claim that adolescents who experience negative emotions, usually in response to family problems, are more likely to engage in offending behaviour. If these emotions persist beyond adolescence, they create a dysfunctional adult self-image (e.g. the angry self) that reduces an offender's openness and ability to change. Marsa et al. (2004) also suggest that dysfunctional bonding experiences during childhood may adversely affect long-term outcomes by impeding the formation of stable, high-quality bonds during adulthood. This is consistent with Laub and Sampson's (2003) argument that persistent offending is engendered by weak social bonds.

Gudjonsson and Bownes (1991) studied prisoners' attributions, or causal explanations, for their criminal behaviour in Northern Ireland. They found that prisoners who attributed their behaviour to internal causes expressed greater levels of remorse and felt personally responsible for their actions. There were significant differences between prisoners according to offence type. Sex offenders tended to attribute the causes of their behaviour to internal, psychological factors, whereas violent offenders attributed the causes of their actions to external, social factors. The study also found that attributions can be shaped by the wider socio-cultural context. Compared to English prisoners, violent prisoners in Northern Ireland reported lower levels of personal responsibility and remorse and were more likely to make external attributions. The authors suggested that the legacy of the Conflict in Northern Ireland may have normalised a culture of violence among certain offender groups. Despite predating his work, these findings substantiate Maruna's (2001) research which found that persistent offenders attribute their behaviour to internal causes and feel permanently doomed to deviance as a result. Conversely, desisters externalise blame for criminal actions but internalise responsibility for changing their behaviour and consequently experience a sense of control over their lives. These findings have important implications for offender rehabilitation because they suggest that encouraging people to accept responsibility for their criminal actions might in fact be harmful (Maruna and Mann, 2006).

Conclusion

International scholarly interest in desistance from crime has burgeoned in the last twenty years, and the topic is beginning to attract the attention of researchers on the island of Ireland. This chapter has critically reviewed the emerging literature in this field and discussed its implications for international theory and research. Although the indigenous literature largely supports existing theoretical ideas, it has made several unique contributions to knowledge. In particular, research on the role of agency (e.g. Healy, 2013, 2014), communitarian social structures (O'Donnell et al., 2008), gender (Byrne and Trew, 2005, 2008), state policy (McAlinden, 2012; Seymour, 2013) and the Troubles (Dwyer, 2013a, 2013b) have influenced international scholarship in this field.

Future research priorities should include theory-testing to establish whether key constructs, such as 'social bonds', 'redemption' and 'agency', are relevant in Northern Ireland and the Republic of Ireland. In addition, a comparative study would help to identify similarities and differences in the experience of desistance on both sides of the border. Finally, the dearth of quantitative and longitudinal research represents a significant methodological omission, since these methodologies have multiple strengths. For instance, quantitative designs are easily replicated and produce generalisable findings, while longitudinal designs are ideal for studying change and continuity over the life-course. Although qualitative approaches also have numerous advantages, a mix of methods is necessary to produce a comprehensive picture of the desistance process.

Nevertheless, the future of desistance research looks promising, and there are a number of important projects currently under way that have the potential to further advance knowledge in this field. For example, a research team at Queen's University Belfast, led by Anne-Marie McAlinden and Shadd Maruna, is investigating desistance among child sex offenders with a particular focus on the psychosocial factors that enable ex-offenders to overcome the stigma associated with this type of crime. In addition, a study funded by the European Forum for Restorative Justice is studying the mechanisms and contexts that facilitate change among restorative justice participants in three European countries, including Northern Ireland. Finally, the Desistance Knowledge Exchange Project aims to translate desistance theory into a set of policy and practice recommendations (see Maruna et al., 2012). To date, this group has produced a documentary film and held a series of workshops for key stakeholders, including academics, practitioners, policymakers and service users.

In conclusion, the study of desistance has produced a rich and multi-faceted literature, and Irish scholars are beginning to contribute to key debates in this field. It is hoped that this chapter will become a useful resource for academics, policymakers and practitioners working is this field by consolidating existing Irish research and identifying important gaps in knowledge.

References

Adorjan, M. and Hong Chui, W. (2012) 'Making sense of going straight: Personal accounts of male ex-prisoners in Hong Kong', *British Journal of Criminology*, 52(3): 577–590.

Bottoms, A. and Shapland, J. (2011) 'Steps towards desistance among male young adult recidivists' in: S. Farrall, M. Hough, S. Maruna and R. Sparks (eds) *Escape Routes: Contemporary Perspectives on Life After Punishment*. Abingdon: Routledge.

Bottoms, A., Shapland, J., Costello, A. *et al.* (2004) 'Towards desistance: Theoretical underpinnings for an empirical study', *Howard Journal of Criminal Justice*, 43(4): 368–389.

Braithwaite, J. (1989) *Crime, Shame and Reintegration*. Cambridge: Cambridge University Press.

Byrne, C. and Trew, K. (2005) 'Crime orientations, social relations and involvement in crime: Patterns emerging from offenders' accounts', *Howard Journal of Criminal Justice*, 44(2): 185–205.

—— (2008) 'Pathways through crime: The development of crime and desistance in the accounts of men and women offenders', *Howard Journal of Criminal Justice*, 47(3): 238–258.

Carlsson, C. (2013) 'Masculinities, persistence and desistance', *Criminology*, 51(3): 661–693.

CJINI (2010) *Not a Marginal Issue: Mental Health and the Criminal Justice System in Northern Ireland*. Belfast: Criminal Justice Inspection Northern Ireland. Available at: http://www.cjini.org/CJNI/files/24/24d6cd45-20bb-4f81-9e34-81ea59594650.pdf (accessed 12 March 2015)

Cleere, G. (2013) '*Prison education, social capital and desistance: An exploration of prisoners' experiences in Ireland*', unpublished thesis, Waterford Institute of Technology.

Corr, M.-L. (2011) '*Widening the lens: A biographical analysis of young people's offending careers*', unpublished thesis, Trinity College Dublin.

CSO (2013a) *Probation Recidivism 2008 Cohort*. Dublin: Central Statistics Office.

—— (2013b) *Prison Recidivism 2008 Cohort*. Dublin: Central Statistics Office.

Davies, P. and Gailey, Y. (2005) *Risk and Need in Offender Populations in Ireland*. Dublin: Probation and Welfare Service.

DOJNI (2014) *Adult Reoffending in Northern Ireland – 2011/12 Cohort*. Research and Statistical Bulletin 18/2014. Belfast: Department of Justice, Statistics and Research Branch. Available at: http://www.dojni.gov.uk/index/statistics-research/stats-research-publications/reoffending-stats-and-research/18-2014-adult-reoffending-in-northern-ireland-_2011-12-cohort_.pdf (accessed 12 March 2015).

Drummond, A. and Codd, M. (2014) *Study on the Prevalence of Drug Use, Including Intravenous Drug Use and Blood-borne Viruses among the Irish Prisoner Population*. Dublin: NACD.

Dwyer, C. (2013a) 'Sometimes I wish I was an 'ex' ex-prisoner: Identity processes in the collective action participation of former prisoners in Northern Ireland', *Contemporary Justice Review*, 16(4): 425–444.

—— (2013b) 'They might as well be walking around the inside of a biscuit tin: Barriers to employment and reintegration for 'politically motivated' former prisoners in Northern Ireland', *European Journal of Probation*, 5(1): 3–24.

Dwyer, C. and Maruna, S. (2011) 'The role of self-help efforts in the reintegration of "politically motivated" former prisoners: Implications from the Northern Irish experience', *Crime, Law and Social Change*, 55(4): 293–309.

Farrall, S., Godfrey, B. and Cox, D. (2009) 'The role of historically-embedded structures in processes of criminal reform: A structural criminology of desistance', *Theoretical Criminology*, 13(1): 79–104.

Garda Inspectorate (2014) *Report on Crime Investigation*. Dublin: Garda Inspectorate.

Giordano, P., Cernkovich, S. and Rudolph, J. (2002) 'Gender, crime and desistance: Toward a theory of cognitive transformation', *American Journal of Sociology*, 107(4): 990–1064.

Giordano, P., Schroeder, R. and Cernkovich, S. (2007) 'Emotions and crime over the life course: A neo-Meadian perspective on criminal continuity and change', *American Journal of Sociology*, 112(6): 1603–1661.

Griffin, M. and Kelleher, P. (2010) 'Uncertain futures: Men on the margins in Limerick city', *Irish Probation Journal*, 7: 24–45.

Gudjonsson, G. and Bownes, I. (1991) 'The attribution of blame and type of crime committed: Data for Northern Ireland', *Journal of Forensic Psychiatry*, 2(3): 337–341.

Healy, D. (2010) 'Betwixt and between: The role of psychosocial factors in the early stages of desistance', *Journal of Research in Crime and Delinquency*, 47(4): 419–438.

—— (2012) *The Dynamics of Desistance: Charting Pathways through Change*. Abingdon: Routledge.

—— (2013) 'Changing fate? Agency and the desistance process', *Theoretical Criminology*, 17(4): 557–574.

—— (2014) 'Becoming a desister: Exploring the role of agency, coping and imagination in the construction of a new self', *British Journal of Criminology*, 54(5): 873–891.

Healy, D. and O'Donnell, I. (2006) 'Criminal thinking on probation: A perspective from Ireland', *Criminal Justice and Behaviour*, 33(6): 782–802.

—— (2008) 'Calling time on crime: Motivation, generativity and agency in Irish probationers', *The Probation Journal*, 55(1): 25–38.

Horgan, J. (2013) *Drug and Alcohol Misuse among Young Offenders on Probation Supervision in Ireland: Findings from the Drugs and Alcohol Survey 2012.* Dublin: Probation Service.

Hourigan, N. (2012) 'Juvenile justice, crime and early intervention: Key challenges from the Limerick context', *Irish Probation Journal*, 9: 64–74.

Hughes, N. (2012) '*Re-entry and young offenders: Exploring the circumstances, expectations and motivations of young offenders prior to their release*', unpublished thesis, University College Dublin.

Kennedy, H., Monks, S., Curtin, K. *et al.* (2005) *Mental Illness in Irish Prisoners: Psychiatric Morbidity in Remanded and Newly Committed Prisoners.* Dublin: National Forensic Mental Health Service. Available at: http://www.drugsandalcohol.ie/6393/1/4338_Kennedy_Mental_illness_in_Irish_prisoners.pdf (accessed 12 March 2015)

King, S. (2013a) 'Transformative agency and desistance from crime', *Criminology and Criminal Justice*, 13(3): 317–335.

—— (2013b) 'Early desistance narratives: A qualitative analysis of probationers' transitions towards desistance', *Punishment and Society*, 15(2): 147–165.

Laub, J. and Sampson, R. (2003) *Shared Beginnings, Divergent Lives: Delinquent Boys to Age 70.* Harvard: Harvard University Press.

Laws, R. and Ward, R. (2011) *Desistance from Sex Offending: Alternatives to Throwing Away the Keys.* New York: Guilford Press.

Liem, M. and Richardson, N. (2014) 'The role of transformation narratives in desistance among released lifers', *Criminal Justice and Behaviour*, 41(5): 692–712.

Maguire, M. (2012) 'Criminal statistics and the construction of crime' in M. Maguire, R. Morgan and R. Reiner (eds) *Oxford Handbook of Criminology.* Oxford: Oxford University Press (pp. 206–244).

Marsa, F., O'Reilly, G., Carr, A. *et al.* (2004) 'Attachment styles and psychological profiles of child sex offenders in Ireland', *Journal of Interpersonal Violence*, 19(2): 228–251.

Marsh, B. (2011) 'Narrating desistance identity change and the 12-step script', *Irish Probation Journal*, 8: 49–68.

Maruna, S. (2001) *Making Good: How Ex-Convicts Reform and Rebuild Their Lives.* Washington DC: American Psychological Association.

Maruna, S. and Mann, R. (2006) 'A fundamental attribution error? Rethinking cognitive distortions', *Legal and Criminological Psychology*, 11(2): 155–177.

Maruna, S., Immarigeon, R. and LeBel, S. (2004) 'Ex-offender reintegration: Theory and practice' in: S. Maruna and R. Immarigeon (eds) *After Crime and Punishment: Pathways to Offender Reintegration.* Cullompton: Willan.

Maruna, S., McNeill, F., Farrall, S. and Lightowler, C. (2012) 'Desistance research and probation practice: Knowledge exchange and co-producing evidence-based practice models', Irish *Probation Journal*, 9: 42–55.

McAlinden, A-M. (2012) *Grooming and the Sexual Abuse of Children: Institutional, Internet and Familial Dimensions.* Oxford: Oxford University Press.

McIlwaine, P. (2011) 'Diversity profile of offenders under the supervision of the Probation Board for Northern Ireland', *Irish Probation Journal*, 8: 82–92.

Messerschmidt, J. (1997) *Crime as Structured Action: Gender, Race, Class and Crime in the Making.* Thousand Oaks CA: Sage.

NIHE (2012) *Homelessness Strategy for Northern Ireland 2012–2017.* Belfast: Northern Ireland Housing Executive.

NIPS (2013) *Quarterly Drugs Report 1 June 2013– 31 August 2013.* Belfast: Northern Irish Prison Service.

O'Donnell, I., Baumer, E. and Hughes, N. (2008) 'Recidivism in the Republic of Ireland', *Criminology and Criminal Justice*, 8(2): 123–146.

O'Donnell, I., Teljeur, C., Hughes, H., Baumer, E. and Kelly, A. (2007) 'Punishment, social deprivation and the geography of reintegration', *Irish Criminal Law Journal*, 17(4): 3–9.

Paternoster, R. and Bushway, S. (2009) 'Desistance and the "feared self": Toward an identity theory of criminal desistance', *Journal of Criminal Law and Criminology*, 99(4): 1103–1156.

PBNI (2012) *Press Release 27/12/12.* Belfast: Probation Board of Northern Ireland.

Quetelet, A. (1842/2003) *A Treatise on Man.* Edinburgh: Chambers. Extract reprinted in E. McLaughlin, J. Muncie and G. Hughes (eds) *Criminological Perspectives*: Essential Readings. London: Sage.

Rajah, V., Kramer, R. and Sung, H.-E. (2014) 'Changing narrative accounts: How young men tell different stories when arrested, enduring jail time and navigating community re-entry', *Punishment and Society*, 16(3): 285–304.

Roberson, B. and Radford, E. (2006) 'The reintegration needs of women prisoners in Northern Ireland', *Irish Probation Journal*, 3: 110–115.

Seymour, M. (2013) *Youth Justice in Context: Community, Compliance and Young People*. Abingdon: Routledge.

Seymour, M. and Costello, L. (2005) *A Study of the Number, Profile and Progression Routes of Homeless Persons Before the Courts and in Custody*. Dublin: DJELR.

Simons, R. and Barr, A. (2012) 'Shifting perspectives: Cognitive changes mediate the impact of romantic relationships on desistance from crime', *Justice Quarterly*, 31(5): 793–821.

Vaughan, B. (2007) 'The internal narrative of desistance', *British Journal of Criminology*, 47(3): 390–404.

Visher, C. and Travis, J. (2003) 'Transitions from prison to community: Understanding individual pathways', *Annual Review of Sociology*, 29: 89–113.

Weaver, B. (2012) 'The relational context of desistance: Some implications and opportunities for policy', *Social Policy and Administration*, 46(4): 395–412.

Part II
Responding to crime

10

Crime prevention and community safety

Matt Bowden and John Topping

Introduction

It may be argued that any discussion on crime prevention and community safety necessarily involves engagement with wider criminological, and indeed, social and political debates about the nature of the state, the relationship between the state and civil society and the manner through which security as a 'public good' is produced and distributed. At least within the criminological field, crime prevention and community safety have emerged as part of what may be imagined as the 'preventative turn' (Hughes, 1998; 2007) – as a means of capturing the governmental tendency towards the decentralisation of crime control from central institutions and towards the outer edges of the criminal justice system. Critics of such localising agendas argue that it is not only an extension of governing rationalities – 'government at a distance' (Garland, 2000) – but also a part of broader neo-liberal agendas to dismantle welfare apparatuses in favour of 'governing through crime' (Simon, 2007). In this regard the resocialisation of the subject as 'self-governing' is, in effect, a path towards creating the conditions for private security proliferation (Rose, 1999).

Furthermore, critical realist authors on community safety have argued that this neo-liberal model of crime control is subject to regional and national variations, shaped by professional habitus as a function of practice cultures and local political traditions (Edwards and Hughes, 2005; Hughes, 2007). Hence social research in this field needs to identify the 'deep grammar' of 'practice-in-context' in order to capture the nuanced and eclectic nature of crime prevention and community safety in different settings (Stenson, 2008).

Bearing in mind these wider debates, the present chapter attempts to discuss the history and development of crime prevention and community safety in Northern Ireland and the Republic of Ireland – as two distinct, yet closely related jurisdictions – aiming to identify convergences and divergences, continuities and discontinuities. In relation to Northern Ireland, where police reform has been a central component underlying the transition from conflict, the chapter identifies the recent history of crime prevention and community safety together with a critical appraisal of key developments. Critical here is the existence of an active, grass-roots civil society as a key factor underpinning community safety at the level of government policy. In the Republic, where police reform has been a more muted affair, crime prevention and community safety is an emerging area of practice, related to funding, government and governance arrangements including drug prevention, youth justice and urban regeneration. While taking note of recent analyses of crime prevention and community safety in the UK and Ireland, the chapter plots the nature and scope of crime prevention and community safety through case studies of Ireland, North and South. These show that in practical terms, crime prevention and community safety are uniquely shaped by the circumstances in which they are conceived (Edwards et al., 2013; Gilling et al., 2013).

A central contention of the chapter from the outset, underpinned by its layout, is the fact that the two jurisdictions have developed (in a community safety sense) in an entirely distinct fashion. It is therefore contended that a simple thematic or comparative approach defies the complex evolution of the preventative turn within the two jurisdictions. In this regard, the evidence presented highlights that community safety is in fact a function of governmental agendas and policy, rather than rational or criminological approaches to dealing with late modern society (Garland, 2001).

Crime prevention and community safety in the Republic

Rather than any seismic ideological shift in policy, the preventative turn in the Republic of Ireland has resulted from a series of pragmatic yet crucial reforms. Of primary relevance here is juvenile justice and the shift from custodial sanctions to early intervention and social crime prevention in the community. Increasing shifts towards community services, more generally, in a range of areas including mental illness, the expansion of probation services and the development of a proto-youth service, are all critical developments in the shift from incarceration as the primary means of regulating deviance. In addition, it is impossible to establish an understanding of crime prevention and community safety without reference to developments in policing and security more generally. Reforms in policing from about 2005 are leading to new and interesting developments in this field but there is, as yet, an insufficient evidence base from which to get a clear and objective picture of their impact. Developments are also advancing outside the direct sphere of policing – for example in housing and estate management, and in local development and social inclusion strategies where problem-solving and dispute resolution strategies are being used in public housing estates (see Kearns et al., 2013).

Historical development: from incarceration to community prevention

A key development stimulating the emergence of crime prevention and community safety in contemporary historical context is the slow slide towards reform of juvenile incarceration. Socio-historical accounts of this process vary in emphasis as to where the shift from incarceration to the community begins, but one recent comprehensive study (Sargent, 2014) underlined two critical developments. The first was the setting in train of a scheme in An Garda Síochána that cautioned offenders, which subsequently became the Garda Juvenile Liaison Officer scheme. Sargent (2014: 25) points out that the scheme emerged from a number of penal reform measures initiated under an interdepartmental committee set up in 1962, chaired by the Secretary of the Department of Justice.

Developments in the professions of psychology and social work, together with public consciousness raised by journalists during the 1960s, played a significant role in the shift towards prevention and developing the care system (Sargent, 2014). This culminated in a second key development – the *Report on Reformatory and Industrial Schools Systems in 1970* – the Kennedy Report. This report drew greater attention to prevention, in that it highlighted the need for greater emphasis on family services and educational interventions. The Report effectively led to the closure of the industrial and reformatory school system and its replacement with smaller group homes (Sargent, 2014) and ultimately welfarist principles were introduced into the juvenile justice system. Another critical historical development in the preventative turn was the report of the Government Task Force on Child Care Services in 1980, which emphasised the development of a system of personal social services to support children and families (see Burke *et al.*, 1981). The extension of such services, including neighbourhood-based youth projects, was a response to particular groupings of disorderly youth in the inner city of Dublin.

Many of these early developments were critical in framing the shape of an emerging modern youth justice system which was eventually enshrined in the Children Act 2001, which established the Garda Youth Diversion Programme on a statutory basis, and introduced a range of restorative preventative mechanisms including restorative justice (Kilkelly, 2006; see also O'Dwyer and Payne, *infra,* and Convery and Seymour, *infra*). These developments also shaped wider policy and practice, most especially in the emphasis on community-based approaches. This was evident in the emergence of the Garda Special Projects, latterly the Garda Youth Diversion Projects (GYDPs), as well as other preventative initiatives like the Copping On Crime Awareness Initiative (see Bowden, 1998).

Social change and urbanisation

Bowden (2006) has documented the emergence of youth crime prevention and community-based crime prevention in the Republic since the 1990s. Bowden linked this directly to critical incidents surrounding youth disorder in peripheral housing estates, developed between the 1970s and 1980s, that were generally remote from services and where the traditional family and kin networks of inner city communities no longer acted as informal crime control. Drawing from an urban political economy, Bowden (2006) pointed out that youth crime and disorder prevention was effectively a fusion between an underdeveloped youth service and the crime control functions of the formal criminal justice institutions. Thus, according to Bowden (2014), the mode of governing youth in these peripheral settings through crime prevention had the effect of hybridizing youth work into youth-crime prevention work. Using Bourdieu's theory of symbolic power (Bourdieu and Passeron, 1977), Bowden demonstrates how the imposition of this curriculum was arbitrary, manipulative and conniving, and thus constituted a form of 'symbolic violence'. The peripheralisation of the Dublin working class from the late 1970s had profound implications for how conduct rules were established and agreed, given that households were dispersed from traditional forms of labour and its self-regulating capacities (see Byrne, 1984). Similar themes were reported by other researchers who emphasised the invisible nature of the local authority housing estates in particular (Saris *et al.*, 2002; Bartley, 1999).

Bowden (2006) pointed out that the institutional vacuum created by the absence of modern youth justice legislation in the 1990s, the apparent incapacity of An Garda Síochána to effectively police urban peripheral communities and constriction of youth services, gave rise to the Garda Special Projects. The Projects originally sought to divert young people from crime and improve police–community relations. An evaluation report drew attention to the positive potential of the Projects to engage young people, but found that they did little to enhance greater engagement of the community and had little impact on policy development for crime prevention and community safety more generally (Bowden and Higgins, 2000). In their earliest incarnation these youth crime and disorder prevention initiatives were directly concerned with managing the impact of the 1980s recession and its enduring impact into the 1990s. By the late 1990s the Garda Special Projects were incorporated within the labour market supply-side strategies under a series of National Development Plans. In the context of full employment at the time, the emphasis shifted towards those considered unemployable. The Projects were later placed under the aegis of the Youth Justice Service soon after its establishment in 2006 and shifted towards a more evidence-based, behavioural-outcomes and risk focused model (Irish Youth Justice Service, 2010).

Policing, community policing and anti-heroin movements

A further key historical dimension in relation to the formation of crime prevention and community safety in the Republic relates to the emergence of a scheme of community policing within An Garda Síochána from the mid-1980s and leading to the formation of a National Model of Community Policing. By 2013 more than 1,100 gardaí were dedicated to community policing duties. These and other developments might be read as, in effect, an attempt to correct the downsides of greater technicisation in the police force, and consequently less presence on beats, and greater regularisation in the organisation of policing units after the Conroy Commission (Commission on the Garda Síochána, 1970). This Commission's recommendations resulted in changes to the pay and conditions of service of gardaí and hence to the structure and organisation of garda units. This reorganisation coincided with greater suburbanisation and lower densities in planned communities, and, hence, a shift towards greater mechanisation – i.e. greater use of vehicles rather than foot patrols. An early critique of the original proposals argued that the garda community policing model fell short of democratic reforms that were required, given the relative powerlessness of communities within these schemes (McCullagh, 1985). This factor has remained constant in police accountability, despite an impressive roll-out of community policing resources and the significant work that such officers contribute to the public policing process (Connolly, 2002; Bowden, 2014). Reiner's (2010) observation that the working class and the poor are over-policed and under-protected echoes in some of the Irish literature, in that it has been noted that working-class areas and socially marginal groups are policed differently (Mulcahy and O'Mahony, 2005; Institute of Criminology UCD, 2003; Mulcahy, 2008).

In keeping with its community policing strategy and its crime prevention mandate, An Garda Síochána initiated the Neighbourhood Watch Scheme in urban areas in the mid-1980s and the Community Alert Scheme in rural areas. Both schemes were operating in more than 3,500 locations throughout the country. While Neighbourhood Watch achieved an extensive spatial dispersal, working-class participation in the scheme was poor. McKeown and Brosnan (1998) suggested that the scheme was more suited to low-risk settings: part of an extension of the garda community-relations strategy to create a more face-to-face engagement with the public. The authors found that Neighbourhood Watch had no measureable impact on safety or security. The scheme was conceived as a way of softening the excesses of mechanisation and had little impact in working-class areas where police legitimacy and credibility was most challenged. Both schemes were effective at community building through their affective impact, but did little in the reduction or detection of crime (McKeown and Brosnan, 1998: 110). Despite the continuance of the Neighbourhood Watch Scheme, no further evaluation has been carried out since this time.

Both community policing and neighbourhood watch schemes coincided with challenges to An Garda Síochána posed by the protracted heroin epidemics in working-class neighbourhoods in Dublin in the 1980s. The Concerned Parents Against Drugs (CPAD) emerged as a citizen anti-heroin movement in Saint Teresa's Gardens flat complex in Dublin south inner city in 1983 and quickly became a city-wide working-class social movement that was noted for its direct democratic style of ordering working-class communities (Bennett, 1988; Cullen, 1990).[1] Policy developments in this period moved partly in reaction to the emergence of this movement and partly in response to the Bradshaw Report (Dean et al., 1983), which showed a higher prevalence of heroin use in inner-city Dublin wards than those of Harlem in New York. In 1983 the Government Task Force on Drug Abuse denied that there was a socio-spatial class basis to the heroin epidemic, yet it set up the funding of youth workers to undertake prevention in 'community priority areas' (see Butler, 2002). Early innovation with the Community Policing Forum in Dublin's North Inner City in the wake of a seemingly intractable heroin problem revealed that local activists and residents remained fearful of reprisals from drug dealers if they were seen to co-operate with the police (Connolly, 2002).

In later developments in the drug crisis in the 1990s, which affected both the inner city and the urban periphery in the context of greater urban restructuring (Punch, 2005), a similar movement, COCAD (Coalition of Communities Against Drugs), was set in train that reignited concerns within the state that these anti-heroin groups were a front for paramilitary organisations. Amidst this concern and in an attempt to recognise the basis of the heroin economy as an embedded issue of class, the then centre-left 'Rainbow' government set up a committee, chaired by Minister of State Pat Rabbitte, to examine this issue. Their report (Government of Ireland, 1996) led to the establishment of the National Drug Strategy and to the local structures that would implement it. The Local Drug Task Forces (LDTFs) were established to focus efforts in treatment, prevention and rehabilitation in the working-class districts where heroin addiction was most acute. The Task Forces brought together the health services, local authorities, police, local development companies, vocational training and education agencies along with organisations and activists in local communities. One spin-off effect was to incorporate local anti-heroin activists, and, in some areas, local Task Forces actively funded some of their proposals in order to regularise their activities. A critical development also working alongside the National Drug Strategy was the Young People's Facilities and Services Fund, which helped to create a broad preventative infrastructure of public buildings in the most affected communities The LDTFs remain a critical player in the development of community safety and community policing in the Republic today as they have progressed into examining strategies to effect supply reduction.

These historical routes to the preventative turn were critical for what we see as the emergence of crime prevention and community safety as discourses and action in a variety of settings. They shape the patchwork in which the field is currently beginning to take shape.

Key challenges, developments and policies

Despite the existence of a range of measures, activities and programmes, crime prevention and community safety in the Republic of Ireland remains *ad hoc*, resulting in a local and institutional miscellany of initiatives. On the one hand this results from the absence of a solid and coherent legislative basis. On the other hand, that absence of state direction has enabled a diversity of bottom-up practices to emerge, resulting in some interesting innovations. A further complication of the picture is the absence of empirical research to map the field: relatively little is formally written or disseminated in the social scientific literature and, as such, both crime prevention and community safety are largely practice-based traditions. In this regard, the following section is an attempt to provide a brief overview of the field and to identify developments, lessons and knowledge gaps. Thinking about local contexts and the potential for a community governance of crime prevention and safety also needs to take account of the global and local challenges facing the field.

The politics of anti-social behaviour

An ongoing issue for the past fifteen years or so has been the experience of uncivil behaviour, especially (but not exclusively) by young people in public housing estates (Fahey, 1999), where the existence of such behaviour was a determining factor in quality of life and liveability (O'Gorman, 2013). This has coincided with the residualisation of public housing as a share of tenures (down to approximately 7 per cent since 2005, as compared with one-third in the 1980s) (Drudy and Punch, 2005). Hourigan (2011:53) noted that in the case of Limerick, the Surrender Grant Scheme, whereby a substantial incentive grant was given to local authority tenants if they surrendered their tenancy and purchased a dwelling privately, gave rise to the flight of those tenants most likely to support law and order, leaving behind cohorts of residents coping with poverty and marginality. In this sense, anti-social behaviour had structural routes, as government housing policy effectively gave rise to the context in which it flourished.

Two pieces of legislation were introduced in the last fifteen years to deal with anti-social behaviour. The first was the Housing Miscellaneous Provisions (Amendment) Act 1997, which gave the power to local authorities to take proceedings for an exclusion order against those engaged in anti-social behaviour and illegal tenants, which included behaviours such as drug dealing from council premises (see Mulcahy, 2012). While these were initially utilised by councils, the number of orders issued had significantly reduced in numbers five years on (97 in 1998 to 23 in 2003) (Mulcahy, 2012: 186). The second piece of legislation was the provision of 'behaviour warnings' and 'behaviour orders' for anti-social behaviour in the Criminal Justice Act 2006, which also allowed youth justice law to be amended so that civil cases could be brought for such orders with lower evidential standards. These were essentially the same as those introduced in the UK after the Crime and Disorder Act 1998 (Hamilton and Seymour, 2006). Since then it appears that there has been negligible use of the orders – a total of seven in the period from 2006 to 2012 (O'Connell, 2012). From the outset there was considerable resistance to them by police officers, who saw them as 'window dressing' for the lack of resources to implement what they saw as the sufficient provisions in youth justice legislation to deal with such behaviour (O'Keefe, 2005). The Children Act 2001 introduced a framework for youth justice including measures such as cautioning and conferencing based upon restorative principles adopted from policy and practice in New Zealand (Kilkelly, 2006). Behaviour orders are complex to initiate, as the provisions of the Children Act render them a last resort. Indeed, a range of more preventative approaches including estate management by local authorities, complemented by local drugs task forces, may have been a critical factor in offsetting the need to revert to punitive anti-social behaviour orders.

National crime prevention strategy: proposed and abandoned

The government established the National Crime Council (NCC) in 1999 to advise it on aspects of crime policy. One of its primary projects was to consult widely and propose a National Model of Crime Prevention. The Council recommended that the national crime prevention model would integrate with the priorities and policy initiatives of all government departments and that it would be broad and inclusive of early intervention. All agencies were asked to streamline services so that they would complement the work of others. Critically, the council recommended that crime prevention be co-ordinated at local authority level through City and County Development Boards (CDBs) (National Crime Council, 2003). The CDBs were cross-sectoral bodies at local authority level who were also mandated to co-ordinate a range of social inclusion and local development measures and to unite local government institutions with local development programmes. While the crime prevention strategy did not set out new measures, it proposed a more co-ordinated effort amongst local providers and that their actions would be connected with the emerging local development and local government systems. These developments did not gain much traction, and crime prevention co-ordination between the gardaí and the local authorities was subsumed by the Joint Policing Committees after 2005 (see below). The

National Crime Council was effectively abolished in 2010 in the cull of state agencies after the introduction of austerity measures.

The CDB was also the key development structure for the implementation of the RAPID programme (Revitalising Areas through Planning, Investment and Development). A key theme for RAPID, which was to be implemented in the most socially and economically disadvantaged communities, was anti-social behaviour and community safety. The programme commenced in the early 2000s, but government support was discontinued by 2010. The government proposed replacing the CDB structures with Social and Economic Committees (Department of Environment, Community and Local Government, 2013), and provision for this has been recently signed into legislation under the Local Government Reform Act of 2014.

Police and reform after 2005

A Tribunal of Inquiry (the Morris Tribunal) was set up by the government in 2002 to inquire into complaints concerning some gardaí in the Donegal division. Its various reports from 2004 onwards created an atmosphere conducive to policing reform. Two key reforms under the Garda Síochána Act 2005 which have the potential to provide a more sound system for the governance of local crime prevention and safety were the establishing of Joint Policing Committees (JPCs) and Local Policing Fora (LPF). The JPCs were initially piloted between 2006 and 2008 and were then extended to each local authority area. Guidelines were issued by the Minister for Justice in 2008. A review process was initiated in late 2012 (but is unfortunately not available for this iteration of the chapter).

The JPCs are tasked with identifying underlying issues in relation to patterns of crime and anti-social behaviour within the local authority area, and they advise both local authorities and the police authorities on how to address them. As yet there has been no systematic empirical evaluation of the JPCs, and so their range of interventions, practices and impacts remain uncertain. Similarly the Garda Síochána Act 2005 envisaged the establishment of LPF at neighbourhood level in certain areas in which gardaí, local authorities and the community could informally engage on aspects of crime prevention and safety. Again we know little about their overall impact. An exploratory study revealed that they initially began in a didactic fashion, with local councillors seeking to use them as a forum for police accountability, which was not in the spirit of the partnership-forming guidelines issued by the Minister. However at LPF level, the researcher found a greater level of engagement compared to the JPC process that involved more genuine community participation (Harrington, 2011).

The JPCs, while offering the potential for a democratisation of safety and security with a strong community input, fall short of the accountability and participative developments in Northern Ireland. The reforms remain police-centred, emphasising the important symbolic and historic role that An Garda Síochána plays in the national narrative (Bowden, 2014; Conway, 2013).

Crime prevention officers and situational prevention

An Garda Síochána now has a network of crime prevention officers operating at national, divisional and district level. A national office co-ordinates the work of regional officers at Harcourt Square in Dublin. The officers give advice to the public on how to protect their properties and businesses. The emphasis is on preventing victimisation through target hardening.

An Garda Síochána also operates a scheme of CCTV in various communities and in town centres across the country. In addition, a community-driven CCTV scheme operates by providing financial aid from the Department of Justice and Equality to community organisations to install surveillance cameras in their neighbourhoods. One clear issue here is the absence of co-ordination between these schemes. Donnelly's (2012) study pointed out that, despite the poor evidence for crime reduction, there was public support and some value given to greater effective security. Donnelly recommended further evaluation of all CCTV schemes presently operated, to examine effects on crime and displacement.

The recent report by the Garda Inspectorate pointed to many gaps in the organisation, conceptualisation and implementation of crime prevention within the force. The report points, for example, to the lack of research skills for executing local crime surveys; the reliance upon key individuals to respond to text alerts; and the fact that An Garda Síochána did not publish a crime prevention strategy (Garda Inspectorate, 2014). These, and observations on other aspects of policing in the Inspectorate's report, highlight the extent to which crime prevention and community safety within policing has had a rather amateur quality to it to date.

More recent experiments with community safety

Community safety as a specific cross-agency modality of crime prevention is a relatively recent concept in the Republic. There remain clear conceptual, empirical and normative questions about the practice, including the following:

(1) what current practices constitute community safety;
(2) who is doing it; what effect and impact is it having on crime reduction; and
(3) who should be charged with the responsibility for community safety?

Currently, community safety is practised within a wide range of governmental and nongovernmental sectors. These appear to reflect a diverging range of government policies and their concomitant funding lines. In this regard community safety initiatives have sprung up in three identifiable domains: the national drug/substance misuse strategy; large-scale urban regeneration programmes; and childhood and family support developments stressing early intervention.

Local Drugs Task Forces

As noted above, the National Substance Abuse Strategy is implemented by a number of Local Drugs Task Forces (LDTFs) who are involved in community-safety-related actions as part of their supply reduction and drug prevention mandates under the National Substance Abuse Strategies. These appear in areas in Dublin such as the Finglas Safety Forum (2014), which aims to reduce anti-social behaviour and the fear of crime. Its partners include the LDTF, itself a multi-agency body, the Garda Síochána and the local community. Evaluations of such initiatives have yet to be conducted, so the empirical evidence on their penetration and impact has yet to become available.

Urban regeneration

Government policy has supported major regeneration programmes in troubled areas such as public housing estates in Limerick and flat complexes in Dublin's inner city. The latter has been dogged by failures ranging from public private partnerships that did not deliver (Bissett, 2008), to the impact of the recession on available funding to complete promised regeneration (for a more recent account see Norris, 2013). The de-tenanting of flat complexes in the inner city has led to empty units as a site for anti-social behaviour.

The State established large-scale regeneration programmes in Ballymun in Dublin and in Limerick City over the last decade. In the case of the latter, urban regeneration, it might be argued, was in direct response to the perception that organised crime in Limerick had serious negative effects on social housing areas in the city; the destructive impact on the community organisations building local resources and programmes; and the reputation of the city as a productive region. The Limerick Community Safety Partnership was initiated as part of the wider process of regeneration, to 'increase community safety; improve the environment; and promote community spirit' (Limerick Community Safety Partnership, 2014). The multi-agency configuration differs from the model operated in Finglas, in that its partners include agencies such as the Health Service Executive, the local authority, An Garda Síochána and the local community. Its principal funding line, given the focus on regeneration, is from the Department of Environment, Community and Local Government. Similarly, under Ballymun Regeneration, the Ballymun Community Safety Strategy was initiated in 2005 and involved the same group of promoters, underlining its attachment to urban regeneration (McCrann and Scanlon, 2007).

As in LDTFs, evaluations of the process and outcomes of community safety in regeneration programmes have yet to emerge. A study undertaken in the Limerick regeneration areas (Power and Barnes, 2011) revealed that the concerns of residents were based upon fear. The study also pointed out that the physical development of these neighbourhoods was an important signal from the authorities to their residents that they were not being abandoned, perhaps underlining the centrality of the issue of fear-reduction and effective security in relation to community safety.

Early childhood development

The third domain in which community safety has been developed has been in the context of early childhood and family support interventions. An example is the Tallaght West Childhood Development Initiative (CDI) which has put together a comprehensive framework for child, family and community interventions (Canavan et al., 2014). CDI put together a Community Safety Initiative in 2008 after an extensive community consultation process (Cahill et al., 2008). The Initiative proposed the use of community safety contracts as a means of helping communities to agree codes of behaviour to underpin safety. The evaluation outlined the extent of the resources mobilised but also the lack of engagement with the process, reflected in the fact that no community safety contracts were implemented in the period in which the Initiative operated (Kearns et al., 2013).

As can be seen, crime prevention and community safety are recent modalities that remain underdeveloped and under-analysed in the Republic. An empirical base in this field is critical to influence the shape of prevention and local security practice in terms of how security is produced and fairly distributed in the future.

Community safety and crime prevention in Northern Ireland

Reflections on crime prevention and community safety in Northern Ireland can almost not be imagined without reference to the central – if not pivotal – position of policing and security as part of that picture. With the country having emerged from a protracted, internal armed conflict lasting over three decades, 'normal' understandings of efforts to deal with crime and criminality have tended to be marginalised and subsumed under the 'master status' of the Conflict and all it has come to represent (Bew, 2007; Campbell, Ní Aoláin and Harvey, 2003; Topping and Byrne, 2012c).

Yet at the same time, it would be inaccurate to unquestioningly characterise Northern Ireland as some kind of criminological aberration, whose comportment and circumstance render it *entirely* remote from the vagaries of 'everyday' crime prevention and community safety concerns (Ellison and Mulcahy, 2001). With significant progress made in the country following the Good Friday Agreement 1998, it can more accurately be viewed with reference to its dichotomous, post-conflict criminological phase. On the one hand, it cannot be forgotten that Northern Ireland is still stricken with sectarian division, a severe terrorist threat and a polarised political system which, in many regards, sustains pockets of social and political liminality across the country (Frampton, 2010; Mulcahy, 1999; Shirlow and Murtagh, 2006; Topping and Byrne, 2012b).

Yet on the other hand, the country is simultaneously underpinned by one of the most advanced and well-funded policing 'systems' in the Western world. Indeed, reforms to policing under the Independent Commission on Policing for Northern Ireland (ICP) were undoubtedly centred on laying the foundations for a new police organisation, replacing the Royal Ulster Constabulary (RUC) with the Police Service of Northern Ireland (PSNI) on the 4th November 2001 (ICP, 1999; Mulcahy, 2006; O'Rawe, 2003; Topping, 2008a). But the reforms under the ICP also set in train a range of additional changes designed to embed a variety of democratic social, political and community decision-making powers into policing through the vehicles of the District Policing Partnerships (DPPs – now Policing and Community Safety Partnerships) and community safety partnerships, in part mirroring policy in England and Wales through the Criminal Justice Review (CJR) of 2000 (CJR, 2000; Feenan, 2000; Topping and Byrne, 2012c).

In this regard, the remainder of the section will seek to examine the developments associated with crime prevention and community safety in Northern Ireland outside the strict confines of police reform, *per se*; and as part of what may be termed the 'preventative turn', discussed above, associated with contemporary, UK-centric developments around community safety (Hughes, 2007; Newburn, 2002; Squires, 2006). With the post-ICP phase of police reform having come to an end, it is appropriate to consider contemporary shifts away from the dominant policy and academic focus on the PSNI. Additional developments form part of the ever-normalising crime prevention and community safety landscape in Northern Ireland, though it must be stressed that such developments are substantially different from those witnessed in the Republic of Ireland (Topping and Byrne, 2012c).

The context of policing, crime and community

Policing in Northern Ireland has always been central to the social and political development of the jurisdiction (Dickson, 2000; Topping, 2008a). In this regard, O'Rawe and Moore (2001:181) note that progress around peace achieved through the Good Friday Agreement on 10th April 1998 was crucially and critically tied to the consensus that if policing could somehow be 'got right', then the other pieces of the peace process jigsaw would fall into place. The 1998 Agreement created the ICP as an international body broadly tasked not just with reforming the RUC in a police-organisational sense, but also designing an entirely new policing infrastructure for the country. Indeed, a central goal of the ICP and its 175 recommendations was to create a 'new beginning' for policing in Northern Ireland, underpinned by an effective, efficient, accountable and community-oriented police service (ICP, 1999; Mulcahy, 2006; O'Rawe, 2003; Tomlinson, 2000; Topping, 2008b).

Beyond the changes achieved by the ICP in terms of creating this new policing landscape, the political importance of the task may be further observed insofar as 2007 marked a watershed in Northern Irish history, with the policing institutions commanding cross-party support for the first time in their history, as a political endorsement of progress on the police reform process

(*Belfast Telegraph*, 2007 a;b;c). Additionally, policing and justice powers were devolved to the Northern Ireland Executive in April 2010 for the first time since 1972, cementing the contention that policing still remains wedded to wider political progress (McDonald and Watt, 2010).

However, below the level of *general* change to the policing landscape brought about under the ICP, it is the *specific* nature of changes encoded within the ICP recommendations that are of interest in the context of this chapter. In this regard, the ICP's 175 recommendations are viewed as both a 'commitment to a fresh start' and one of the most complex blueprints for police reform ever attempted (Office of the Oversight Commissioner, 2007). At the same time, they are often viewed as a singular 'block' of change brought about to policing arrangements in the country. But when examined in more detail, it is in fact important to consider the reform process as two inter-related, but distinct 'streams' of policing change (Kempa and Shearing, 2005).

The first stream, which has largely reached the end of its life-span, is that related to the physical 'system' of policing, or that attributable to the visible manifestations of police change, including for example: the name of PSNI, badges, uniform, recruitment processes and human rights training, as evidenced in the publication of the nineteenth and final report of the Office of the Oversight Commissioner (OOC) (OOC, 2007; Ellison, 2007). But it is the second 'stream', 'concerned with broader questions around the governance of security, or policing more broadly conceived' (Kempa and Shearing, 2005: 5), which resonates more fully with issues of community safety and laterally, security governance, as part of a more rounded perspective (Johnston and Shearing, 2003).

In this regard, the following sections seek to consider key developments which relate to, and underpin the basis for, community safety and crime prevention in Northern Ireland as related to this second stream. With the focus of academic and policy discourse having centred on PSNI and police reform *per se*, it is appropriate to adopt an approach which encompasses a range of perspectives relating to the direct and indirect evolution of community safety in Northern Ireland as part of a broader appreciation of such developments (Mulcahy, 2006; Ellison, 2007; Topping and Byrne, 2012c).

District Policing Partnerships

The ICP's second stream sought to embed a community policing ethos within the PSNI (Topping, 2008b), but also set out (at least in part) to develop their broader vision of policing (and variant of 'classic' community safety policy) by creating District Policing Partnership Boards (DPPBs) (Crawford, 2008; Newburn, 2002; Topping, 2008a). Intended to have a much wider remit as part of *policing* (in the widest possible sense) rather than merely *police* objectives (as that related solely to the police organisation), ICP Recommendation 32 stated that:

> District Councils should have the power to contribute an amount initially up to the equivalent of 3p in the pound towards the improved policing of the district, which could enable the District Policing Partnership Board to purchase additional services from the policing or other statutory agencies, or from the private sector (ICP, 1999: para 6.33).

But, under a barrage of (mainly) political criticism that these DPPBs could provide a channel for paramilitary actors to manipulate publicly-funded policing arrangements, Recommendation 32 was the only provision of the ICP never to have been enacted in legislative form (Mulcahy, 2006; Bayley, 2007; Topping, 2009). Instead, the Northern Ireland Office (NIO) opted for a 'watered down' version called the District Policing Partnerships (DPPs) with a statutory remit under Part III of the Police (Northern Ireland) Act 2000 to consult, identify, monitor, engage and act within the community in accordance with the policing plan set by the Northern Ireland Policing Board (NIPB), as the police authority in Northern Ireland set up under the same Act.

As a tool for the PSNI to engage with local populations on local matters and insert community oversight into policing delivery, the DPPs (at least in principle) arguably outstripped previous efforts to engage with communities in Northern Ireland, or indeed the UK more generally. However, as the evidence would suggest, there are many underlying tensions with regard to how the DPPs operated, in terms of whether they actually ensured policing was accountable to local communities, with transparency on policing matters central to their operation (NIPB, 2007: 6).

As part of the ICP's vision of the DPPs, it was envisaged that partnership on crime and policing (rather than police) issues would involve:

> [C]reating a real partnership between the police and the community, government agencies, non-governmental organisations, families, citizens; a partnership based upon openness and understanding; a partnership in which policing reflects and responds to community needs (ICP, 1999: 8).

However, for the duration of their lifetime, DPPs were something short of the representative forums envisaged by the ICP.

With Sinn Féin having only taken their seats on the DPPs in 2007, a significant proportion of the Republican/Nationalist community remained absent from *any* local policing debate by their absence from the less than stringent DPP *monitoring* rather than accountability function (Mulcahy, 2006). Even those Nationalists from the more moderate Social and Democratic Labour Party (SDLP), who took their seats in 2003 following the establishment of the DPPs, were subjected to an ongoing campaign of intimidation, harassment, assault and bombings in recent years (*Belfast Telegraph*, 2007a). Indeed, following the appointment of Sinn Féin DPP members in 2007, they too have also been publicly issued with death threats by dissident Republicans (*Belfast Telegraph*, 2007c).

Merely three years after their creation, a barely minimal public attendance at DPP meetings was observed, despite running costs spiralling to approximately £12 million (*Belfast Telegraph*, 2006). With 268 out of 300 meetings between May 2003 and March 2006 with less than 20 members of the public in attendance, the DPPs in fact mirrored their pre-ICP predecessors – community police liaison committees (CPLCs) – as 'talking shops' which were 'staged managed to avoid controversy…' (Mulcahy, 2006: 175).

As Topping (2008b) has contended, the DPPs have had a negligible impact upon local policing operations. And in this respect, they have summarily been described as shallow and sad reflections of the ICP's original vision, with a lack of ability to critically engage and challenge the police (Topping, 2009).

Thus, while in principle the DPPs to some extent laid the foundations for modern iterations of partnership working around crime prevention and policing in Northern Ireland, they were only a small part of the wider political landscape in which policing and community safety were delivered; and were only one element of what may be described as a 'split' community safety agenda, as shall be discussed below.

Community Safety Partnerships

While the delivery of 'policing more broadly conceived' through the DPPs may have been limited, an oddity of the policing arrangements in Northern Ireland relates to the fact that community safety, as a specific policy focus, was run as a parallel and distinct enterprise by the

Northern Ireland Office (NIO) throughout the pre and post-ICP years. And while superficially community safety in Northern Ireland remains broadly comparable to England and Wales as an overarching government policy objective related to the 'preventative turn', the progress and trajectory of community safety in Northern Ireland has also been substantially different, as shall be observed (Hughes, 2007).

Aside from the efforts geared towards police reform during the immediate ICP era, the Criminal Justice Review (CJR) of 2000 (set up in the aftermath of the Good Friday Agreement 1998 to review the policy and practice of the criminal justice system in the country) noted that as early as 1977 a Crime Prevention Panel was formed between the NIO, RUC and representatives of the civic and business sector to look at co-ordinated approaches to dealing with crime (CJR, 2000: 256; Brunger, 2011). In 1993, the NIO also published a paper on community safety entitled 'Crime and the Community' (NIO, 1993; Feenan, 2000). Furthermore, in 1996 a Community Safety Centre (CSC) was set up within the NIO as part of broader community safety efforts. But the modern-day origins of community safety in Northern Ireland can be traced back to the publication of the CJR implementation plan in 2001 (NIO, 2001) with Recommendation 196 of the CJR, proposing that Community Safety and Policing Partnerships (CSPPs) be set up. These eventually became Community Safety Partnerships (CSPs) in their modern form.

Out of the creation of the CSPs it is important to note some distinct features of what was a 'new' model of community safety in Northern Ireland. First, and beyond their parallel approach to the ICP reform process, the legislative provision for the CSPs under the Justice (NI) Act 2002 (as drafted) lacked any of the strength of its Crime and Disorder Act 1998 counterpart for England and Wales. Indeed, there was never any section 17 equivalence which dictated that local authorities and service providers incorporate crime and disorder reduction into their everyday, core activities. Neither did any section 115 powers exist to mandate the sharing of vital information between partner agencies. And of significant note, the legislative provisions relating to CSPs in Northern Ireland under the 2002 Act were *never* brought into force – creating a *de facto* voluntary basis for the current operations of CSPs (CJINI, 2006) – up until their replacement by the PCSPs in April 2012 under the Justice Act (Northern Ireland) 2011 (see below).

Secondly, the Community Safety Unit (CSU) created under the CJR (and now transferred to the Department of Justice for Northern Ireland) has also been subject to criticism from the Criminal Justice Inspection Northern Ireland (CJINI) in terms of the level of central control exerted upon individual CSPs at the council level, reducing the potential for wider public engagement on community safety matters. Furthermore, in terms of these bureaucratic constraints placed upon the CSPs, Brunger (2011) highlights the top-down, Public Service Agreement (PSA) targets to guide CSPs in the Northern Ireland Community Safety Plan. On the one hand, these may be observed as helping to unify the different agencies involved in local partnership, but on the other hand:

> [T]he role of PSAs then, links directly into the debates surrounding central and local control of CSPs. Their pervasive influence ensures that … a large amount of central control is firmly administered over CSP planning … plans are motivated towards addressing these targets and less by dealing with local issues (Brunger, 2011:280).

Thirdly, the democratic nature of, and public input into, community safety issues through the CSU and CSPs has, at best, been a moot point during the period of their existence. With the CSU staffed and run exclusively by civil servants, it is reflective of the CSPs in terms of their composition (Brunger, 2011) – the Criminal Justice Inspection Northern Ireland (CJINI) (2006) noted that statutory bodies accounted for 50 per cent of CSP membership; elected and voluntary members 20 per cent; and the private and community sector merely 3 per cent. Additionally, with the administration and cost of the CSPs running at approximately £1.15 million out of a budget of £3.28 million as part of their operations, when combined with the lack of independent scrutiny to minutes of meetings and funding processes, the space in which local community concerns and priorities on community safety may be considered is undoubtedly limited (Brunger, 2011; Topping, 2009).

Finally, a point which must be reiterated is the fact that CSPs were conceived in parallel to the reforms under the ICP (Ellison and O'Rawe, 2010). In this regard, as part of the wider 'political' constraints limiting membership of the former DPPs prior to Sinn Féin acceptance of the policing institutions in 2007, there was an implicit recognition through the CJR that the NIO had deliberately created a 'two-tier' policing/community safety approach so as to 'manage' the lack of (willingness for) effective engagement and partnership with the (then) estranged Republican (and to a lesser extent Loyalist) communities. The strategy was therefore a deliberate one to perpetuate the 'separateness' between the PSNI and (mainly) Republican communities during this period. It may thus be argued that the dual DPP and community safety partnership system was set up, as a means of encouraging Republican communities to engage on policing issues, but without having to work directly with the police or police structures (Topping 2009).

Policing And Community Safety Partnerships

Outside the immediate issues of DPPs and CSPs as part of community safety evolution in Northern Ireland, the most recent milestone for community safety in the country has been the creation of the new Policing and Community Safety Partnerships (PCSPs), as set out in Part 3 of the Justice Act (Northern Ireland) 2011. Coming into existence in April 2012, under the 2011 Act the roles and functions of the CSPs and DPPs have been merged into a single unit PCSP, with the strategic priorities and objectives of both the NIPB's Policing Plan and the Department of Justice's community safety objectives agreed and aligned under a new Community Safety Strategy (Department of Justice, 2011).

Similar to the structure of DPPs, the new PCSPs comprise eight, nine or ten councillors selected by local councils; and seven, eight or nine independent members selected by the NIPB – providing a political majority. One PCSP exists for each of the 29 council areas in the country. Independent members receive a £60 stipend as part of their roles and responsibilities for each meeting attended. While the majority of the roles and functions of the DPPs and CSPs remain intact under the 2011 Act, a key feature of the Department of Justice policy strategy is the increased emphasis on the role of the voluntary and community sector, noting that PCSPs will build upon efforts to date and 'continue to work with the third sector to explore its role in the delivery of community safety solutions at a strategic and local level' (DoJ, 2011:35). However, none of the legislative shortcomings identified in terms of information sharing or partnership working through a 'national mandatory model' (as with England and Wales) have been amended under the 2011 Act (Hughes et al., 2013; Crawford, 2008).

Contained within the main body of the PCSP there also exists a 'policing committee' comprised of councillors and independent members to perform the more technical PSNI-monitoring functions inherited from the DPPs, including making arrangements for obtaining cooperation of the public with the police. The policing committee must report directly to the NIPB on the exercise of its police-centric functions.

Looking at the overall functions of the new PCSPs, the main statutory obligations include:

- Making arrangements for obtaining the view of the public about matters concerning the policing of the district and enhancing community safety;
- Acting as a general forum for discussion and consultation on matters affecting the policing of the district and enhancing community safety;
- Preparing plans for reducing crime and enhancing community safety;
- Identifying targets or other indicators by reference to which it can assess the extent to which those issues are addressed by action taken in accordance with any such plans; and
- Providing any such financial or other support as it considers appropriate to persons involved in ventures designed to reduce crime or enhance community safety.

Looking specifically at the fourth function in relation to 'measuring' success, there has been a real attempt by the Department of Justice to depart from statistical definitions and 'target culture' of policing and community safety success – so long a source of contention with respect to the function of the DPPs (Byrne and Monaghan, 2008; Topping, 2008b). As noted in the consultation document:

> [W]e do not propose to set arbitrary targets...we will monitor recorded crime levels in order to respond to any emerging issues, and use other robust sources such as recorded crime statistics and the Northern Ireland Crime survey to measure crime levels and confidence in a more holistic way (Department of Justice, 2011: 36).

Significantly for the PCSPs and their function in terms of the post-devolution policing and community safety landscape in Northern Ireland, for the first time since the ICP in 1999, they have the potential to embed *policing* as part of the ICP's original vision of policing more broadly conceived. With the current Justice Minister, David Ford, noting that crime, anti-social behaviour and quality of life issues cannot be separated from housing, the environment, health, social care or employment, the new PCSPs signify a symbolic shift in governmental focus away from narrow debates on police reform and towards the 'preventative turn' – albeit fifteen years behind counterparts in England and Wales.

As may be observed, the focus in the country related to *all* matters policing, community safety and security have been dominated by the necessary physical changes to the PSNI as an organisation, along with the parallel process of 'nurturing' the political landscape to facilitate all-party support for the policing institutions. Thus, the new era of community safety as symbolised through the PCSPs may be viewed as a 'roadmap' to facilitating wider, inclusive action in relation to the delivery of *policing* and laterally community safety, which as Bayley (2007) contends, underpins the ICP's understanding that policing was always too important to be left to just the police alone. Having said that, the most recent CJINI report on the function and effectiveness of the PCSPs suggests it is a case of 'all change, no change'. With the potential innovation of PCSPs for community safety stifled under the weight of bureaucracy, administration and inertia, it appears to be 'window dressing' rather than purposeful change for the new community safety landscape in Northern Ireland (CJINI, 2014).

Community safety from 'below'

Outside the structural and policy evolution of policing and community safety in the country, a crucial (if underdeveloped) issue relates to crime prevention from 'below' through Northern

Ireland's legitimate civil society. With the bulk of academic focus having rested upon 'security' as generated by the formal state policing apparatus or paramilitary 'justice', little attention has been given to the role and capacity of community-level actors in terms of their crime prevention and community safety capacities (Ellison, 2007; Topping, 2008b). Thus, with police reform and change having dominated debate, chances to conceive crime prevention and community safety in language (or by actors) *other* than that set by the policing institutions have remained limited – especially where the centrality of the PSNI's organisational 'expertise' on crime control is contested (Johnston and Shearing, 2003; Topping and Byrne, 2012c).

However, as highlighted by one of the ICP commissioners, Clifford Shearing, in terms of non-state contributions to the broad policing landscape:

> Here in Northern Ireland – and in many other unsettled political contexts – another form of 'non-state' agent is particularly important in challenging the monopoly over the business of policing of the public police: civic bodies of various forms, including, but certainly not limited to, agencies that deploy violence as part of their practices of control (Kempa and Shearing, 2005: 7).

In this regard, it may be observed that such non-state 'policing' in Northern Ireland developed out of the unique circumstances of the Conflict, often as an 'alternative' to the provision of policing by the state – either because of legitimacy issues; or due to the highly polarised security environment within Republican and Loyalist areas (Brogden, 2005; Hamilton *et al.*, 1995; Topping and Byrne, 2012a). More specifically, and developing out of this policing and security 'vacuum', the historical separation of mainly working-class Republican and Nationalist communities from state police interaction and engagement has further generated liminal 'spaces' into which a variety of actors and organisations outside the state have stepped (and continue to exist) (Byrne and Monaghan, 2008; Mulcahy, 2006; Topping, 2008b). As may be observed:

> Where the state could not provide protection, which was the starting point for many Catholics and Nationalists and could easily emerge for less well protected working-class Protestant communities…there was an enormous reservoir of understanding for extra state [policing] (Morrow, 2006: 73).

Thus, when this state of policing affairs is juxtaposed with the *de facto* efforts and attention devoted to formal policing and community safety arrangements

> [D]oes it [non-state policing] constitute a vital assistance to weak states faced with under-resourced police, or does it constitute a threat to the state by allowing a function to be conducted by private elements over which the state should have monopoly? (Baker, 2002: 30).

As reflected in a study by Acheson *et al.* (2004), there are in fact a plethora of voluntary and community sector organisations in the country involved in a variety of roles and responsibilities. In this regard, the nature of civil society organising is an indisputable part of the social fabric of Northern Ireland (NICVA, 2005; CJINI, 2006). Although with approximately 4,500 to 5,000 such organisations in the country, as Acheson *et al.* caution, the 'extent and nature of community action is neither self-evident nor securely defined within clear boundaries' (2006:19) – and especially so with regard to that which constitutes 'policing' or 'community safety' work *per se* (Topping and Byrne, 2012c).

Specifically in regard to this tranche of community-based community safety, little empirical attention has been paid to outlining, mapping these against the broader policing landscape, or correlating those with the country's 'low crime' status (Toner and Freel, 2010). With state reluctance to recognise this 'soft power', it may be viewed as symptomatic of the state-institutional approach, trumping community involvement and ownership in the process of policing and justice throughout the post-ICP era (McEvoy *et al.*, 2002; Vaughan, 2007). Thus, chances to engage in what has been termed a 'fascinating experiment' in utilising community energies as part of community safety and policing initiatives have been largely dismissed in favour of the ICP's much lauded first 'stream' of change, so crucial to the political 'success' of policing in the country (Gormally, 2004; McEvoy *et al.*, 2002; Ellison and O'Rawe, 2010).

In terms of more concrete examples of civil society contributions to the policing and community safety landscape, at present there are only a limited number of empirical studies specifically examining non-state policing provision in Northern Ireland (Topping, 2009; Topping and Byrne, 2012c; Topping and Byrne, 2014). Noting that beyond the strict activities of any one organisation or grouping which may or may not be defined as police or community safety work, it is the collective ability of such civil society organising, mainly within urban, socio-economically deprived Loyalist and Republican areas, to mediate the 'gaps' of policing need which is of significance.

Across eight broad areas of community safety delivery – including community advocacy; education and intervention; emergency response; interface violence; partnership working; crime prevention; mediation; and restorative justice – the research to date indicates that not only is such community safety 'from below' highly focused, but so too the communities where such work exists tend to be highly organised in terms of community infrastructure (Acheson *et al.*, 2004; Morrow, 2006; Topping and Byrne, 2012c). It should be noted, however, that much of this organising is based upon sectarian lines – creating 'parallel' systems of community safety distinguishable only by ethno-national identification between Republican and Loyalist communities respectively (Shirlow and Murtagh, 2006; Topping and Byrne, 2012c).

It must also be considered that outside attempts to situate such non-state community safety efforts within formal state definitions of policing or community safety, 'security' in this respect should be viewed on a more human level, insofar as many of the deep-rooted social, economic and sectarian issues – for so long hidden under the veil of 'bigger' conflict-related issues – are now starting to emerge within post-conflict space. Thus, evidence points to the fact that, while such organising may on one level be seen as community safety or policing *per se*, on another level it may be defined as 'community development', 'good relations' or 'social justice' (Topping and Byrne, 2012c; 2014).

Though outside debates as to the existence of such community 'layers' – as symptomatic of continuing state legitimacy issues (Byrne and Monaghan, 2008) – they in fact exist because of the complex and nuanced nature of local community safety and social problems. In this regard, local, non-state actors are often the only ones with the capacity to deal with the problem in terms of community knowledge, capacity and respect (Topping and Byrne, 2012c). In reference to interface violence in Belfast for example, local efforts at community safety are seldom linked directly to the *politics* of policing delivery, but rather to the need to provide an immediate and effective response as part of making communities safer. As argued by one organisation, society would in fact be worse off without such community sector contributions. And while not wishing to overstate such claims, it may be observed that, 'the cutting edge work on policing and security and parading and interfaces and all that. Frankly, no one else would have been *able* to do it' (Topping, 2009: 249).

Therefore, as part of a reflective look at community safety 'from below', it should be considered that no automatic 'formula' exists in terms of simply 'merging' or co-opting such community-centric bodies into the more formal state-based community safety or policing structures, as outlined above. From a policy perspective, this could in fact destabilise community vitality and infrastructure by limiting or removing local, community 'ownership' of community safety issues – the very basis which sustains their success in the first place (Tonkiss and Passey, 1999). Thus, quite how to utilise this 'soft', non-state power from a state perspective has yet to be resolved as part of the complex and evolving policing and security landscape in Northern Ireland (Topping and Byrne, 2012c; 2014).

Conclusion

In providing an overview of community safety and crime prevention in Ireland, North and South, it is clear that the two jurisdictions have evolved in their own distinct and unique ways as part of dealing with crime and criminality. On the one hand, these divergences are simply a product of the unique social, political and environmental circumstances out of which community safety and policing have evolved. Yet on the other hand, such differences would point to the malleability of the community safety concept and its 'success' when delivered as part of contrasting policy and organising paradigms.

One of the key issues for the delivery of community safety in the Republic of Ireland has been its direct response to increasing socio-economic marginalisation associated with Ireland's evolving late modern condition over the past fifty years. We note the critical influence in this regard is the prominence of drug problems since the 1980s and the prominence of the heroin economy for a significant time during this period. On both community and criminal justice fronts, shifts away from central government control in relation to crime prevention have become a defining feature of the broad community safety landscape; though in view of the organic nature of developments, response and reaction rather than strategic planning would appear to have driven the direction of policy. The recent report of the Garda Inspectorate (2014) underlines the haphazard and rather unfocused nature of crime prevention and community safety within the police in the Republic. Thus, that jurisdiction may be characterised as a collective 'mass' of inter-related movements (both policy and community) which fall under the broad community safety banner.

Looking to Northern Ireland however, it may be observed that a much more centralised, prescriptive and formalised approach to community safety has become the governing mode of crime prevention. Yet in spite of central government drives to embed a uniform approach to the 'preventative turn' within the criminal justice family, the tendency still remains at community and political levels to conflate all crime issues with the PSNI. Thus, while community safety in the South may be viewed as encompassing elements of community relations in addition to more holistic crime prevention efforts, in the North it is defined almost exclusively in terms of crime, policing and anti-social behaviour.

Additionally, the structural and formalised approach to community safety in Northern Ireland has, over the past twenty years, excluded the community-centric and organic stakeholders in civil society, so vital to community safety in the Republic. With politics and sectarianism at the core of this dilemma, it has in fact created and sustained three parallel, but interlinked 'systems' of policing and crime prevention: namely, that run by the Department of Justice as part of formal policy and structures; that of policing, in the form of the PSNI; and that associated with community safety 'from below' through civil society organising in the country. In this regard, while structurally successful through the PCSPs and policy evolution, for example, community safety in the North has become overprescribed and underdeveloped in terms of the necessary collaborative approaches between these three stakeholders. Thus, community safety in the North may be characterised as 'window dressing' for the policing 'normalisation project' more generally.

Ultimately, many of the divergences between community safety in the two jurisdictions can be traced back to the 'normality' (or otherwise) of crime and policing issues – and especially so with regard to the Conflict in Northern Ireland. Arguably, community safety, policing and crime prevention in the Republic were allowed to develop organically because of the fact that there were social – rather than political issues – as in Northern Ireland. For that reason in particular, all such matters in Northern Ireland needed a robust, 'neutral' and controlled framework within which they could be considered.

In this sense, with the 'public good' of security between the two jurisdictions representing very different 'orders', the experience of community safety in Ireland signifies that community safety is more a product of governmental attitudes, agendas and policy 'will' than a rational, social, scientific or evidence-based approach to dealing with the issues thrown up by late modern society (Garland, 2001; Hughes, 2007).

References

Acheson, N., Harvey, B., Kearney, J. and Williamson, A. (2004) *Two Paths, One Purpose: Voluntary Action in Northern Ireland, North and South*. Dublin: Institute of Public Administration.

Baker, B. (2002) 'Living with Non-State Policing in South Africa: The Issues and Dilemmas', *Journal of Modern African Studies*, 40(1): 29–53.

Bartley, B. (1999) 'Spatial Planning and Poverty in North Clondalkin' in D. Pringle, J. Walsh and M. Hennessy (eds) *Poor People, Poor Places: A Geography of Poverty and Deprivation in Ireland*. Dublin: Oak Tree Press.

Bayley, D. H. (2007) *Police Reform on Your Doorstep: Northern Ireland the World*. Seminar held at the Transitional Justice Institute, University of Ulster, Jordanstown, 19 February.

Beck, U. and Ritter, M. (1992) *Risk Society: Towards a New Modernity*. London: Sage.

Belfast Telegraph (2006) 'Threat to DPPs as Public Shuns Meetings', 13 June.

—— (2007a) 'Bomb Bid DPP Man Considers Position', 12 April.

—— (2007b) 'IMC Praises Sinn Fein Policing Commitment', 31 January.

—— (2007c) 'Threat to Sinn Fein Councillors', 22 October.

Bennett, D. (1988) 'Are They Always Right? Investigation and Proof in a Citizen Anti-Heroin Movement' (pp. 21–40) in C. McCullagh, T. Varley and M. Tomlinson (eds) *Whose Law and Order?* Belfast: Sociological Association of Ireland.

Bew, P. (2007) *The Making and Remaking of the Good Friday Agreement*. Dublin: Liffey Press.

Bissett, J. (2008) *Regeneration: Public Good or Private Profit?* Dublin: TASC at New Island.

Bourdieu, P. and Passeron, J. C. (1977) *Reproduction in Education, Society and Culture*. Beverly Hills CA: Sage.

Bowden, M. (1998) *Review of the 'Copping On' Crime Awareness Initiative*. Dublin: Children's Research Centre, Trinity College Dublin.

—— (2006) 'Youth, Governance and the City: Towards a Critical Sociology of Youth Crime and Disorder Prevention', *Youth Studies Ireland*, 1(2): 19–39.

—— (2014) *Crime, Disorder and Symbolic Violence: Governing the Urban Periphery*. London: Palgrave Macmillan.

Bowden, M. and Higgins, L. (2000) *The Impact and Effectiveness of the Garda Special Projects: Final Report to the Department of Justice, Equality and Law Reform*. Dublin: Stationery Office.

Brogden, M. (2005) '"Horses for Courses" and "Thin Blue Lines": Community Policing in Transitional Societies', *Police Quarterly*, 8(1): 64–98.

Brunger, M. (2011) 'From Police to Policing: Policing Reform in Northern Ireland and the Vision of Partnership' (doctoral thesis). Queen's University Belfast.

Burke, H., Carney, C. and Cook, G. (eds) (1981) *Youth and Justice: Young Offenders in Ireland*. Dublin: Turoe Press.

Butler, S. (2002) *Alcohol, Drugs and Health Promotion in Modern Ireland*. Dublin: Institute of Public Administration.

Byrne, D. (1984) 'Dublin – a Case Study of Housing and the Residual Working Class', *International Journal of Urban and Regional Research*, 8(3): 402–420.

Byrne, J. and Monaghan, L. (2008) *Policing Loyalist and Republican Communities*. Belfast: Institute for Conflict Research.

Cahill, J., Murphy, T. and Guerin, S. (2008) *Community Safety Initiative: Consultation Report*. Dublin: Childhood Development Initiative.

Campbell, C., Ní Aoláin, F. and Harvey, C. (2003) 'The Frontiers of Legal Analysis: Reframing the Transition in Northern Ireland', *Modern Law Review*, 66(3): 317–345.

Canavan, J., Coen, L., Ozan, J. and Curtin, C. (2014) *Leading Community Change: Delivering Better Outcomes in an Irish Community – Childhood Development Initiative Final Process Evaluation Report*. Dublin: Childhood Development Initiative.

Connolly, J. (2002) *Community Policing and Drugs in Dublin: The North Inner City Community Policing Forum*. Dublin: North Inner City Drugs Task Force.

Conway, V. (2013) *Policing Twentieth Century Ireland: A History of An Garda Síochána*. London: Routledge.

Crawford, A. (2006) 'Networked Governance and the Post-Regulatory State?: Steering, Rowing and Anchoring the Provision of Policing and Security', *Theoretical Criminology*, 10(4): 449–479.

—— (2008) 'Plural Policing in the UK: Policing Beyond the Police', in T. Newburn (ed) *Handbook of Policing* (2nd ed.) Cullompton: Willan.

Criminal Justice Inspection Northern Ireland (2006) *Added Value? A Review of the Voluntary and Community Sector's Contribution to the Northern Ireland Criminal Justice System*. Belfast: Criminal Justice Inspection Northern Ireland.

—— (2014) *Policing and Community Safety Partnerships: A Review of Governance, Delivery and Outcomes*. Belfast: Criminal Justice Inspection Northern Ireland.

Criminal Justice Review Group (2000) *Review of the Criminal Justice System* in J. Davis and B. Gray (2010) *The Meeting Room: The Rise and Fall of the Concerned Parents*. Dublin: Whitethorn Productions.

Cullen, B. (1990) 'Community Action in the Eighties: A Case Study' in *Community Work in Ireland. Trends in the 80s. Options in the 90s*. Dublin: Combat Poverty Agency.

Dean, G., Bradshaw, J. and Lavelle, P. (1983) *Investigation in a North Central Dublin Area*. Dublin: Medico-Social Research Board.

Department of Environment, Community and Local Government, Ireland. (2013) *Putting People First: Action Plan for Effective Local Government*. Dublin: Department of Environment, Community and Local Government.

Department of Justice (2011) *Building Safer, Shared and Confident Communities: A Consultation on a New Community Safety Strategy for Northern Ireland*. Belfast: Department of Justice.

Dickson, B. (2000) 'The Protection of Human Rights: Lessons from Northern Ireland', *European Human Rights Law Review*, 3: 213–226.

Donnelly, A. (2012) *To CCTV or Not? An Examination of Community-Based CCTV in Ireland*. Dublin: Dublin Institute of Technology.

Drudy, P. J. and Punch, M. (2005) *Out of Reach: Inequalities in the Irish Housing System*. Dublin: Tasc New Island.

Edwards, A. and Hughes, G. (2005) 'Comparing the Governance of Safety in Europe: A Geo-Historical Approach', *Theoretical Criminology*, 9(3): 345–363.

—— (2013) 'Comparative European Criminology and the Question of Urban Security', *European Journal of Criminology*, 10(3): 257–259.

Edwards, A., Hughes, G. and Lord, N. (2013) 'Urban Security in Europe: Translating a Concept in Public Criminology', *European Journal of Criminology*, 10(3): 260–283.

Ellison, G. (2007) 'A Blueprint for Democratic Policing Anywhere in the World: Police Reform, Political Transition, and Conflict Resolution in Northern Ireland', *Police Quarterly*, 10(3): 243–269.

Ellison, G. and Mulcahy, A. (2001) 'Policing and Social Conflict in Northern Ireland', *Policing and Society*, 11: 243–258.

Ellison, G. and O'Rawe, M. (2010) 'Security Governance in Transition: The Compartmentalising, Crowding Out and Corralling of Policing and Security in Northern Ireland', *Theoretical Criminology*, 14(1): 1–27.

Fahey, T. (ed) (1999) *Social Housing in Ireland: A Study of Success, Failure and Lessons Learned*. Dublin: Oak Tree Press.

Feenan, D. (2000) *Community Safety: Partnerships and Local Government* (Report to the Criminal Justice Review Group, Northern Ireland. No.13). London: Stationery Office.

Finglas Safety Forum (2014) http://www.finglassafetyforum.ie (accessed: 9 July 2014)

Frampton, M. (2010) *The Return of the Militants: Violent Dissident Republicanism*. London: ICSR. Available at: http://www.icsr.info/publications/papers/1289498383ICSR_TheReturnoftheMilitantsReport.pdf (accessed 5 December 2010)

Garda Inspectorate (2014) Crime Investigation: Report of the Garda Síochána Inspectorate. Available at: http://www.gsinsp.ie/index.php?option=com_docman&task=doc_download&gid=243&Itemid=152 (accessed 30 November 2014)

Garland, D. (2000) 'The Culture of High Crime Societies: Some Preconditions of Recent Law and Order Policies', British Journal of Criminology, 40: 347–345.

—— (2001) The Culture of Control: Crime and Social Order in Contemporary Society. Oxford: Oxford University Press.

Giddens, A. (1991) The Consequences of Modernity. Cambridge: Polity Press.

Gilling, D., Hughes, G., Bowden, M., Edwards, A., Henry, A. and Topping, J. (2013) 'Powers, Liabilities and Expertise in Community Safety: Comparative Lessons for "Urban Security" from the United Kingdom and the Republic of Ireland', European Journal of Criminology, 10(3): 326–340.

Gormally, B. (2004) 'Tough Questions on Community Policing from Northern Ireland', Community Safety Journal, 3(3): 23–30.

Government of Ireland (1996) Report of the Ministerial Taskforce on Measures to Reduce the Demand for Drugs. Dublin: Government Publications.

Hamilton, A., Moore, L. and Trimble, T. (1995) Policing a Divided Society: Issues and Perceptions in Northern Ireland. Coleraine: Centre for the Study of Conflict.

Hamilton, C. and Seymour, M. (2006) 'ASBOs and Behaviour Orders: Institutionalised Intolerance of Youth?', Youth Studies Ireland, 1(1): 61–76.

Harrington, D. (2011) Partners Against Crime: A Review of Partnerships in Joint Policing Committees. Dublin: Dublin Institute of Technology.

Hourigan, N. (ed) (2011) Understanding Limerick: Social Exclusion and Change. Cork: Cork University Press.

Hughes, G. (1998) Understanding Crime Prevention: Social Control, Risk and Late Modernity. Buckingham: Open University Press.

—— (2007) The Politics of Crime and Community. Basingstoke: Palgrave Macmillan.

Hughes, G., Bowden, M., Henry, A., Gilling, D. and Topping, J. (2013) 'Powers, Liabilities and Expertise in Community Safety: Comparative Lessons for Urban Security from the United Kingdom and Republic of Ireland', European Journal of Criminology, 10(3): 326–340.

Independent Commission on Policing for Northern Ireland (1999) A New Beginning: Policing in Northern Ireland. Belfast: HMSO

Institute of Criminology UCD (2003) Public Order Offences in Ireland. Dublin: Stationery Office.

Irish Youth Justice Service (2010) Designing Effective Local Responses to Youth Crime: A Baseline Study. Dublin: Irish Youth Justice Service.

Johnston, L. and Shearing, C. (2003) Governing Security: Explorations in Policing and Justice. London: Routledge.

Kearns, N., Reddy, J. and Canavan, J. (2013) Evaluation of the Community Safety Initiative of the Childhood Development Initiative. Dublin: Childhood Development Initiative.

Kempa, M. and Shearing, C. (2005) 'Post–Patten Reflections on Patten', Public Lecture, 8 June. Belfast: Queen's University of Belfast.

Kilcommins, S., O'Donnell, I., O'Sullivan, E. and Vaughan, B. (2004) Crime, Punishment and the Search for Order in Ireland. Dublin: Institute of Public Administration Publications.

Kilkelly, U. (2006) Youth Justice in Ireland: Tough Lives, Rough justice. Dublin: Irish Academic Press.

Limerick Community Safety Partnership (2014) Available at: http://communitysafety.limerick.ie (accessed 9 July 2014)

Loader, I. (2007) Civilizing Security. Cambridge: Cambridge University Press.

McCrann, A. and Scanlon, P. (2007) Safer Ballymun: A Community Safety Strategy. Dublin: Ballymun Regeneration Ltd.

McCullagh, C. (1985) 'Community Policing: A Critique of Recent Proposals', Economic and Social Review, 16(3): 169–185.

McDonald, H. and Watt, N. (2010) 'Stormont Votes to Take Over Northern Ireland Policing Powers', The Guardian, 9 March.

McEvoy, K., Gormally, B. and Mika, H. (2002) 'Conflict, Crime Control and the "Re"-Constitution of State–Community Relations in Northern Ireland', in G. Hughes, E. McLaughlin and J. Muncie (eds) Crime Prevention and Community Safety: New Directions. London: Sage.

McKeown, K. and Brosnan, M. (1998) Police and Community: An Evaluation of Neighbourhood Watch and Community Alert in Ireland. Dublin: Department of Justice, Equality and Law Reform.

McLaughlin, E. (2007) The New Policing. London: Sage.

Morrow, D. (2006) 'Sustainability in a Divided Society: Applying Social Capital Theory to Northern Ireland', *Shared Space: A Research Journal on Peace, Conflict and Community Relations in Northern Ireland*, 2: 63–79.

Mulcahy, A. (1999) 'Visions of Normality: Peace and the Reconstruction of Policing in Northern Ireland', *Social and Legal Studies*, 8(2): 277–295.

—— (2006) *Policing in Northern Ireland: Conflict, Legitimacy and Reform*. Cullompton: Willan.

—— (2008) 'Policing "Community" and Social Change in Ireland 1990–2008', (pp. 190–208) in J. Shapland (ed) *Justice, Community and Civil Society*. Cullompton: Willan.

—— (2012) 'Exceptional or Local? The Governance of Crime and Security in Ireland', (pp. 175–195) in N. Hardiman (ed) *Irish Governance in Crisis*. Manchester: Manchester University Press.

Mulcahy, A. and O' Mahony, E. (2005) *Policing Social Marginalisation in Ireland*. Dublin: Combat Poverty Agency.

National Crime Council (2003) *A Crime Prevention Strategy for Ireland: Tackling the Concerns of Local Communities*. Dublin: National Crime Council.

Newburn, T. (2002) 'Community Safety and Policing: Some Implications of the Crime and Disorder Act 1998' in G. Hughes, E. McLaughlin and J. Muncie (eds) (2002) *Crime Prevention and Community Safety: New Directions*. London: Sage.

Norris, M. (ed) (2013) *Social Housing, Disadvantage and Neighbourhood Liveability*. London: Routledge.

Northern Ireland Council for Voluntary Action (2005) *State of the Sector IV*. Belfast: NICVA.

Northern Ireland Office (1993) *Crime and the Community*. Northern Ireland Office Discussion Paper. Belfast: NIO.

—— (2001) *The Criminal Justice Review: Secretary of State's Implementation Plan*. London: HMSO.

Northern Ireland Policing Board (2007) *Reflections on District Policing Partnerships*. Belfast: Northern Ireland Policing Board.

O'Connell, H. (2012) 'Explainer: Why Have Just Seven ASBOs Been Issued in Ireland in Five Years?', *TheJournal.ie*, 17 June 2012. Available at: http://www.thejournal.ie/asbos–ireland–asbo–criminal–justice–alan–shatter–485523–Jun2012/.

O'Gorman, A. (2013) 'Social (Dis)order and Community Safety', in M. Norris (ed) *Social Housing, Disadvantage and Neighbourhood Liveability: Ten Years of Change in Social Housing Neighbourhoods*. Abingdon: Routledge.

O'Keefe, C. (2005) 'Gardaí criticize ASBOs as "just window dressing"', *Irish Examiner*, 23 May 2005. Available at: http://www.irishexaminer.com/archives/2005/0523/ireland/gardai–criticise–asbos–as–aposjust–window–dressingapos–235130608.html (accessed 7 December 2014)

O'Rawe, M. (2003) 'Transitional Policing Arrangements in Northern Ireland: The Can't and Won't of Change Dialect', *Fordham International Law Journal*, 22, 1015–1073.

O'Rawe, M. and Moore, L. (2001) 'A New Beginning for Policing in Northern Ireland?' in C. Harvey (ed) *Human Rights, Equality and Democratic Renewal in Northern Ireland*. Oxford: Hart Publishing.

Office of the Oversight Commissioner (2007) *Overseeing the Proposed Revisions for the Policing Services of Northern Ireland Report 19*. Belfast: Office of the Oversight Commissioner.

Power, M. J. and Barnes, C. (2011) *Feeling Safe in Our Community*. Limerick: Limerick Regeneration Agencies and Faculty of Arts, Humanities and Social Sciences, University of Limerick.

Punch, M. (2005) 'Problem Drug Use and the Political Economy of Urban Restructuring: Heroin, Class and Governance in Dublin', *Antipode*, 37(4): 754–774.

Reiner, R. (2010) *The Politics of the Police*. New York: Oxford University Press.

Rose, N. (1999) *Powers of Freedom : Reframing Political Thought*. Cambridge: Cambridge University Press.

Sargent, P. (2014) *Wild Arabs and Savages: A History of Juvenile Justice in Ireland*. Manchester: Manchester University Press.

Saris, A. J., Bartley, B., Kierans, C., Walsh, C. and McCormack, P. (2002) 'Culture and the State: Institutionalising "the Underclass" in the New Ireland', *City*, 6(2): 173–191.

Shearing, C. and Wood, J. (2003) 'Nodal Governance, Democracy, and the New "Denizens"', *Journal of Law and Society*, 30(3): 400–419.

Shirlow, P. and Murtagh, B. (2006) *Belfast: Segregation, Violence and the City*. London: Pluto Press.

Simon, J. (2007) *Governing through Crime: How the War on Crime Transformed American Democracy and Created a Culture of Fear*. Oxford: Oxford University Press.

Squires, P. (2006) *Community Safety: Critical Perspectives on Policy and Practice*. Bristol: Polity Press.

Stenson, K. (2008) 'Surveillance and Sovereignty' (pp. 279–301) in M. Deflem (ed) *Sociology of Crime, Law and Deviance*. Bingley: Emerald.

Tomlinson, M. (2000) 'Frustrating Patten: Commentary on the Patten Report', *Irish Journal of Sociology*, 10: 103–109.

Toner, S. and Freel, R. (2010) *Experience of Crime: Findings from the 2009/10 Northern Ireland Crime Survey*. Belfast: Department of Justice Northern Ireland.

Tonkiss, F. and Passey, A. (1999) 'Trust, Confidence and Voluntary Organisations: Better Values and Institutions', *Sociology*, 33(2): 257–274.

Topping, J. R. (2008a) 'Community Policing in Northern Ireland: A Resistance Narrative', *Policing and Society*, 18(4): 377–398.

—— (2008b) 'Diversifying from Within: Community Policing and the Governance of Security in Northern Ireland', *British Journal of Criminology*, 48(6): 778–797.

—— (2009) 'Beyond the Patten Report: The Governance of Security in Policing with the Community' (doctoral thesis). University of Ulster, Northern Ireland.

Topping, J.R. and Byrne, J. (2012a) *Community Safety: A Decade of Development, Delivery, Challenge and Change in Northern Ireland*. Belfast: Belfast Conflict Resolution Consortium.

—— (2012b) 'Paramilitary Punishments in Belfast: Policing Beneath the Peace', *Behavioral Sciences of Terrorism and Political Aggression*, 4(1): 41–59.

—— (2012c) 'Policing, Terrorism and the Conundrum of "Community": A Northern Ireland Perspective' in B. Spalek (ed) *Counter–Terrorism: Community-Based Approaches to Preventing Terror Crime*. Basingstoke: Palgrave Macmillan.

—— (2014) 'Shadow Policing: The Boundaries of Community-Based "Policing" in Northern Ireland', *Policing and Society*, DOI:10.1080/10439463.2014.989152.

Vaughan, B. (2007) 'The Provision of Policing and the Problem of Pluralism', *Theoretical Criminology*, 11(3): 347–366.

Wacquant, L. J. D. (2001) 'The Penalisation of Poverty and the Rise of Neo–Liberalism', *European Journal on Criminal Policy and Research*, 9: 401–412.

—— (2008) *Urban Outcasts: A Comparative Sociology of Advanced Marginality*. Cambridge: Polity Press.

Wood, J. and Shearing, C. D. (2007) *Imagining Security*. Cullompton: Willan.

Young, J. (2007) *The Vertigo of Late Modernity*. London: Sage.

Note

1 Jim Davis's and Brian Gray's (2010) film *The Meeting Room* is a superb documentary depiction of the emergence and impact of the CPAD, together with the disillusionment of key members with the potentially violent implications of their *modi operandi*. In addition, the film portrays the political strategies used to thwart the movement, culminating in the trial and imprisonment of some leaders.

11

Restorative justice

Kieran O'Dwyer and Brian Payne

This Chapter comprises four parts. The first introduces the concept of restorative justice as a way of responding to crime and examines the international literature. The second provides an overview of the development of restorative justice practices in Northern Ireland, where the particular conditions created by the Conflict and subsequent period of transition have led to the evolution of parallel restorative justice initiatives from both a community-based and statutory origination. The third part examines the development and use of restorative justice in the Republic of Ireland, where it is located within the criminal justice system. And the fourth is a concluding critical analysis of restorative justice in the two jurisdictions.

Restorative justice: an introduction

In Western criminal justice systems, criminal offences have long been considered to be transgressions against the state (Christie, 1977). Crime, therefore, is construed as behaviour that is deemed to be so wrong that it deserves public censure, with the state enjoying a sense of ownership of criminal justice (Zehr, 1990). Restorative justice, in contrast, conceives of crime primarily as a breakdown of private relationships, with ownership of conflicts devolved to a broader range of stakeholders including the victim, offender and the community (Zehr, 2002; Braithwaite, 1989). It has been described as a 'paradigm shift that is changing the focus of the work of the criminal justice system away from the offender and towards the community and victims of crime' (Barajas *et al.*, 1996:1) and as an approach that 'does not primarily ask what should be done to the offender, but how the harm can be repaired' (Walgrave, 2008: 23). The restorative process is based on a range of practices which have evolved from victim–offender mediation to now also include family group conferencing, 'circle' processes and various types of citizen panels (see, for example, Bazemore and Schiff, 2001).

Some advocates of restorative justice propose it as an alternative to the conventional criminal justice system (Zehr, 1990; Walgrave, 2002) involving a transfer of some level of decision-making authority from government to victims and offenders, their families, friends and other supporters, and community members (Kurki, 2003). In reality, however, many formulations see it as an adjunct rather than an alternative, allowing for greater involvement of parties directly affected by an offence in a process that remains firmly under the auspices of the criminal justice system or subject to its oversight. A transfer of decision-making authority to participants in such manifestations of restorative justice is not envisaged to any significant degree.

Restorative justice is not a new concept, though it has enjoyed a very large surge in popularity over recent decades (Braithwaite, 2002). The modern origins of restorative justice can be traced to North America and mainland Europe and Scandinavia in the 1970s, under the title of victim and offender reconciliation programmes or victim–offender mediation programmes. In several countries restorative justice tended to be used widely for young offenders and less serious offences, at least initially. Restorative justice practices, however, are not restricted to these categories, and their use with adult offenders is now fairly common and is increasing in serious cases of violent crime, including sexual and domestic violence (Hudson, 2002; McAlinden, 2007; Keenan, 2014). Restorative justice can also be applied in many everyday situations and is being used increasingly in classrooms and workplaces under the labels of restorative practice and dispute resolution (McCluskey *et al.*, 2008; Cameron and Thorsborne, 2001; Hopkins, 2004).

Restorative justice: definitions and underlying theories

Restorative justice is a difficult concept to define, as it refers to a wide range of practices (Crawford and Newburn, 2003) and lacks a unitary concept (Dignan and Cavadino, 1996). It has been described as a global social movement with huge internal diversity (Johnstone and Van Ness, 2007). Nevertheless, Marshall (1998: 1) has provided a definition that has been quoted extensively: 'a process whereby parties with a particular stake in an offence, collectively resolve how to deal with the aftermath of the offence and its implications for the future'. In the Republic of Ireland, the National Commission on Restorative Justice (2009: 34) referred to it as 'a victim-sensitive response to criminal offending, which, through engagement with those affected by crime, aims to make amends for the harm that has been caused to victims and communities and which facilitates offender rehabilitation and integration into society'. This broader definition embraces forms of restorative justice that do not necessarily involve victim participation. Other views focus on restorative justice as an outcome rather than a process (Bazemore and Walgrave, 1999) and would consider community service and reparation as restorative even where imposed as a coercive sanction (Walgrave, 2001).

At the heart of the restorative justice process, regardless of format, is a structured, facilitated dialogue between the offender and those most affected by the offence or interested parties. Adherence to stated restorative values such as respect, fairness, proportionality, inclusiveness, voluntariness, confidentiality, personal accountability and facilitator neutrality is seen as key. The main focus is on understanding what happened, identifying who was affected and how, and repairing any harm caused or relationships damaged. Avoidance of future offending is also a primary focus, especially in conferencing and citizen panels; this is achieved largely through offender reintegration and community support (Zehr and Mika, 1997; Marshall, 1998; Johnstone, 2002; McCold, 2004). Crawford (2002: 123) states that 'the deliberative potential of restorative justice should be its primary raison d'être and overarching principle'.

Ashworth (2002: 578) notes that 'the theory of restorative justice has to a large extent developed through practice'. Marshall (1998: 32) comments that restorative justice lacks a 'definitive theoretical statement' but that many academic theories and approaches have been incorporated in or associated with restorative justice at different stages, including control theory (Hirschi, 1969; Gottfredson and Hirschi, 1990) and neutralisation theory (Matza, 1964). Braithwaite (2002: 73) proposes a number of 'theories that might explain why restorative justice works', including reintegrative shaming (Braithwaite, 1989) and procedural justice (Tyler, 1990).

Main goals of restorative justice

Because of the diversity of models and understandings of restorative justice, universal consensus on the stated or assumed goals of restorative justice has not been achieved, although there is much common ground. Many scholars highlight the goals of participation and consensual decision-making, healing what is broken, accountability of offenders, reducing recidivism and avoiding further harms (Van Ness *et al.*, 2001; Maxwell *et al.*, 2006). Johnstone (2002) summarises the desired outcomes of restorative justice as: offenders repairing the harm that results from their criminal acts, offenders experiencing and expressing repentance, offenders being fully reintegrated into communities of law-abiding citizens and victims being healed of the trauma from their experiences. Dignan and Lowey (2000: 4) identify four key attributes of restorative justice as inclusivity of process and outcomes, balancing different sets of interests, non-coercion and a problem-solving orientation.

The personal, participative nature of restorative justice is often contrasted with the impersonal nature of the formal criminal justice system, where the voice of those most affected is largely suppressed. Zehr (2002) argues that the traditional Western model of criminal justice normally marginalises the victim to, at best, a secondary concern of the criminal justice process, as it is concerned primarily with making sure offenders get what they deserve. Offenders are often themselves passive observers, rather than active participants (Dignan and Lowey, 2000). Roche (2003) suggests that this occurs because a traditional criminal justice process is not based on the needs of the stakeholders (victims, offenders, community) but on formal legal procedures and statutes.

Claimed benefits for victims are that restorative justice better meets their needs by offering a less formal process where their views count, providing more information about processing and outcome of their cases, allowing participation, ensuring respectful and fair treatment and offering opportunities for material and emotional restoration, especially apology (Pranis, 1997; Zehr, 1990). For offenders, claimed benefits are that they can regain the respect of the community rather than its perpetual scorn, although they may experience restorative justice as more challenging than other options. For communities, restorative justice is claimed to render offenders less dangerous, be more cost-effective and foster citizenship (Strang, 2002; Johnstone, 2002).

Issues in restorative justice

Restorative justice raises a series of thematic questions surrounding its application. These include the proximity of restorative justice to formal criminal justice systems, the possible erosion of offenders' rights, the extent to which community is involved and the perceived limits to restorative justice practices (Hudson, 2002; Roche, 2003). Regarding proximity to formal criminal justice systems, concerns have been raised about the compatibility of the ethos of restorative justice with retributive forms of justice. For example, it has been argued that restorative justice may widen the net of social control by receiving cases that the formal court system would not have received or by imposing sanctions not utilised by the formal justice system (Galaway and Hudson, 1996) or giving rise to a 'new professionalism, expanding the sphere of social intervention' (Walgrave, 1992: 348). Kurki warns that the popularity of labelling a variety of actions 'restorative justice' could cause programmes that were true to restorative values and principles initially 'to lapse, over time, into mechanical sanctioning processes' (2003: 307). The risk may be higher in programmes where criminal justice professionals play key roles. Particular concerns have been voiced in relation to police officers acting as facilitators (Young, 2001; Ashworth 2002) although others see advantages (McCold, 1998; O'Dwyer, 2006).

As regards erosion of offender rights, critics of restorative justice have argued that the inclusion of victims and the community in criminal justice matters may deprive offenders of the safeguards and rights that would normally be afforded them in conventional criminal justice processes (Ashworth, 2002; Johnstone, 2002). Advocates argue that adherence to restorative justice values, ethos and principles and observance of proper procedures offers adequate protection. Morris (2002: 601) comments that 'there is nothing inherent in restorative justice values that would lead to denial or concern regarding rights'. Marshall (1998: 24), on the other hand, posits that, no matter how well established good practice may be, there is still a need to ensure that it is always observed and '[u]ltimately there is no alternative to some form of judicial oversight'.

As regards community involvement, considerable debate exists as to the role of the 'community' in any restorative justice intervention with some arguing that restorative justice loses much of its effectiveness when community members are not afforded a key role. In restorative justice scholarship, 'community' is often portrayed as an unproblematic solution to issues of justice legitimacy, yet there is comparatively little literature that explores the role of community beyond the superficial (Pavlich, 2005). How 'community' is defined has an important bearing on attempts to establish a restorative justice programme (Crawford, 1999). However, in contemporary Western societies, there are few meaningful interrelationships among people living in the same area and little common interest (Putnam, 2000). Consequently, Dhami and Joy (2007) contend that new state-led restorative justice programmes must first define the relevant 'community' and then somehow create and strengthen a sense of connectedness, common concern and responsibility for crime and victimisation among its members.

As regards limits to restorative justice, many scholars reject its use as a response to serious or violent crime, lest it produce outcomes that fail to reflect the gravity of the offences. An outcome might be acceptable to the parties directly involved, yet fail to address broader community concerns, such as the risk of further serious offences and the need for incapacitation of dangerous offenders (Zedner, 1994; Roche, 2003), and there may be some crimes that are so serious that compensation or reparation is insufficient to put them right (Ashworth, 1986). These arguments may have greater validity when considering restorative justice as an alternative to the criminal justice system, rather than as an adjunct or integral part. Furthermore, there is increasing evidence of the effectiveness of restorative justice in respect of very serious offences, including family and sexual violence (Hudson, 2002; Daly, 2002; Keenan, 2014).

Other concerns relate to the ability of restorative justice to actually 'restore' victims and offenders, risks of secondary victimisation, the extent to which participation can be truly voluntary, the level of accountability, the nature and proportionality of sanctions, the role of punishment, the neutrality of facilitators and effectiveness with respect to deterrence and reduced re-offending. Good practice can address many of the concerns and much attention has been given to ensuring quality of service, for example through promulgation of standards and accreditation of practitioners. There is also now a body of evidence that shows reductions in re-offending where practice is of a high standard. For example, Aertsen et al. (2006) note a growing number of studies that demonstrate a modest but positive effect on re-offending. Latimer et al. (2001) report on a meta-analysis of 32 international studies that showed an average 7 per cent reduction. Sherman et al. (2000) report a 38 per cent decrease in re-offending for youth violence cases. Shapland et al. (2011), reporting on three UK projects, note a modest reduction in reconviction rates but a significant decrease in the frequency of reconviction over a two-year period. A focus on re-offending is understandable but risks overlooking other benefits of restorative justice, such as consistently high satisfaction levels by victims.

Restorative justice in Northern Ireland

The context of transition

One of the most positive developments to have come from Northern Ireland's recent history has been the formation of a vibrant restorative justice movement which has flourished during the jurisdiction's much publicised transition from conflict. Restorative justice in Northern Ireland has evolved both through formal measures that have been put in place to further the peace process by improving conditions in wider society, and also through informal community-led responses to some of the most destructive symptoms of the Conflict, such as the use of punitive paramilitary justice practices.

The principal instrument of the peace process, the Good Friday Agreement, contained a number of measures that supported the growth of restorative justice in Northern Ireland. In particular, section 6 set out proposals which were designed to bridge the gap between the state and communities in Northern Ireland. These included encouraging 'the development of special community-based initiatives based on international best practice' and providing support and encouragement to community and statutory-based programmes (Good Friday Agreement 1998: 6.12). A critical aspect of reform centred on the need to reconstruct the legitimacy of policing by facilitating greater engagement between the police and communities, a recommendation that would have a profound impact on existing community projects.

A major review of the criminal justice system made 294 recommendations for change across the system including in the area of restorative justice (Criminal Justice Review Group, 2000). A programme of research was conducted as part of the review, and one commissioned report (Dignan and Lowey, 2000) recommended the formal integration of restorative principles into the heart of the official juvenile justice system. Subsequently, the application of restorative justice practices for young offenders, including a conferencing model, became a core recommendation of the review, and a new system of youth conferencing based around the principles of restorative justice was duly adopted under the Justice (Northern Ireland) Act, 2002. Finally, the devolution of justice powers from Westminster to the Northern Ireland Assembly in April 2010 has helped create an atmosphere where local stakeholders can exert more influence on criminal justice policy. Overall, the unique context of transition has had a profound impact on the development of restorative justice, encouraging the growth of restorative justice, while providing a series of challenges for those who embraced restorative justice models in their work. Throughout this period, two main systems of restorative justice have been developed – the community system and the state system. Each will be considered in turn.

The community system

The community-based restorative justice projects in Northern Ireland were founded in 1998 in Republican and Loyalist communities, led by political ex-prisoners and former combatants of the Provisional Irish Republican Army (PIRA) and the Ulster Volunteer Force (UVF) respectively. The projects originated as alternatives to paramilitary punishment violence which involved 'policing' activities such as beatings, shootings, threats and exclusions undertaken by Republican and Loyalist groups in the working-class communities that they live and operate in (McEvoy and Mika, 2001; 2002). Such practices have their roots in the Northern Ireland conflict. One of the visible symptoms of this conflict was the extent to which the police were preoccupied with security-orientated policing as a response to the activities of the paramilitaries and consequently paid less attention to 'ordinary' crime (McEvoy and Mika, 2001). To fill the policing vacuum that had been left, paramilitary groups attended to crime and conflict at a community level at the same time as carrying out their 'military activities' (Bell, 1996; Feenan, 2002).

As the peace process progressed, important changes in Northern Ireland's political make-up led to increased international and local scrutiny and criticism of informal practices of punishment violence and a rethink of the use of such punitive sanctions in local communities (Auld *et al.*, 1997; McEvoy and Mika, 2001; 2002). In response to these concerns, key community activists in both Republican and Loyalist areas began looking for a way to disengage from violent forms of community justice and quickly focused on a framework based on general restorative justice principles (McEvoy and Mika, 2001). Innovative restorative justice programmes emerged through direct dialogue between restorative justice advocates, community leaders and Republican and Loyalist groups. A new approach for dealing with offending behaviour was implemented which ensured that cases were now handed over to volunteers and staff trained to employ non-violent restorative justice techniques, such as mediation, shuttle negotiation and family group conferencing, to resolve disputes (McEvoy and Eriksson, 2007). There are two main community-based restorative justice projects operating in Northern Ireland: Northern Ireland Alternatives (NIA), which works in predominantly Unionist/Loyalist areas, and Community Restorative Justice Ireland (CRJI), which operates in largely Catholic/ Republican areas. Both of these organisations proved effective in preventing punishment violence. For example, Mika (2006) reported that CRJI stopped 82 per cent and NIA 71 per cent of potential paramilitary attacks within their respective geographical areas of remit between 2003 and 2005.

Despite this comparatively narrow initial focus on preventing punishment violence, the reality in practice is that both CRJI and NIA projects have significantly extended their remit to include a range of community mediation, offender reintegration, youth intervention and other restorative work. The volume of cases processed is significant. For example, in 2013 CRJI worked on a total of 1,806 cases, with suicide intervention/support and advice (14 per cent) and neighbourhood disputes (12 per cent) making up the two largest categories (CRJI, 2014). NIA have also expanded their traditional focus on intensive youth work to include a range of ambitious new projects which work to provide conflict transformation, community mediation and victim awareness and address anti-social behaviour (CJI, 2010a).

However, despite the evident success of these projects their progression has been beset by a series of difficulties. The 'community' character of the projects and the fact that from their origins they have involved former members of armed groups in their work has placed the groups in a unique position in Northern Ireland's transitional environment. In one sense the projects have been described as having the potential to make an important contribution to the peace process by helping to reconfigure the relationship between state and community (McEvoy and Mika, 2002). However, the extent to which the projects, and CRJI in particular, have traditionally operated independently of the formal criminal justice system ensured that relations between these groups and the police and other state agencies have been highly strained.

Community-based restorative justice schemes in other jurisdictions are normally reliant on state partnerships for financial and in-kind support, and in some cases for referrals (Dhami and Joy, 2007). Northern Ireland's transitional landscape has made accessing such support a complicated undertaking. The community-based schemes have, in the past, been able to operate in parallel to the criminal justice system with funding from a number of external sources including Atlantic Philanthropies (Gormally, 2006). When this funding ceased, the community-based schemes had little option but to apply for public funding, which, in turn, left them open to a series of stipulations, including the need for formal 'accreditation', a process of inspection and adherence to a set of protocols (McEvoy and Eriksson, 2007).

The development of the relevant protocols to regulate relations between CRJI and state justice agencies was a heavily politicised process. In the particular circumstances of transition, the existence of such an informal community-based justice system operating independently of government was viewed (in some quarters at least) as a challenge to the very legitimacy of the state justice system (Feenan, 2002). Perhaps inevitably, the desire by different state agencies to develop a regulatory framework for the projects was viewed by the projects as an effort to impose state control and correspondingly to mitigate community ownership of justice in Northern Ireland (McEvoy and Eriksson, 2006). The production of protocols also became linked to divisive arguments in Nationalist/Republican communities on whether police reforms had gone far enough to justify supporting the new arrangements. The fact that CRJI (like many other community-based projects in Republican areas) were unwilling to formally cooperate with the police until this political situation had been resolved ensured that they attracted extraordinary levels of political scrutiny highly disproportionate to the size of their projects (McEvoy and Eriksson, 2007). At this time CRJI were also unable to secure state funding, as full cooperation with the police was one of the main requirements of the protocol, placing the very future of the organisation at risk.

Once the political uncertainty around policing had been resolved in 2007, CRJI were able to follow the example of NIA and forge new partnerships with the police. For both organisations these partnerships have, in a short space of time, far exceeded the requirements of the protocols, and been praised repeatedly by the Criminal Justice Inspectorate (CJI) for their contribution to combating crime and anti-social behaviour in local communities and in helping to re-engage the police with previously estranged communities (CJI, 2010b; 2011). More recently, the Inspectorate carried out a pre-accreditation inspection of the new CRJI North Belfast and South/East Belfast schemes and found high levels of PSNI involvement in cases and a high clear-up rate, with over 86 per cent of cases achieving a successful resolution in North Belfast alone (CJI, 2014). In particular, the Inspectorate praised the contribution of the projects to community-building and in forging links with the PSNI.

These partnerships have therefore had a significant positive impact on the legitimacy of both the community-based projects and the police in local communities and in wider society. That said, some questions remain with respect to the organisational consequences for the community projects from these partnerships and wider government regulation. In particular, it remains to be seen if working closely with the police and other criminal justice bodies will lead to the community projects moving too far away from their community mandate. Wider questions have also been asked of the commitment of the PSNI to continue to grow and develop their capacity for engaging with local communities. The vast majority of partnership work with CRJI and NIA has been through local neighbourhood policing teams, and there remains uncertainty as to whether the rest of the organisation shares this commitment to community engagement. From such a perspective, the good work carried out by neighbourhood policing teams can be undermined by the less community sensitive approach of other response teams in the PSNI (Byrne et al., 2014; Topping, 2008).

In addition to the much publicised community-based projects, there is also a thriving restorative practice scene operating in local schools and in children's services in Northern Ireland. At the school level, much of the momentum for using restorative practices has been provided by integrated secondary schools which cater for pupils from both main religions in Northern Ireland. Restorative justice can be used in a variety of scenarios within the school setting to improve relationships, avoid repetition of behaviours, increase student accountability and responsibility, as well as teach the students a vital life skill. In particular, great emphasis is also placed on the use of restorative language among students, staff and parents (Payne *et al.*, 2010). The children's charity Barnardos has also deployed a restorative practices project with Looked After Children since 2005. This project originated in response to the high numbers of young people transferring from the residential setting to the criminal justice system. The project works in a variety of children's homes and attempts to create restorative living communities underpinned by an array of restorative practices.

The state system

The statutory system of restorative justice in Northern Ireland was established by the Youth Justice Act 2002 and is administered by the Youth Conference Service. This legislation is unique in the United Kingdom in that it ensures restorative justice is the mainstream response for children or young people who find themselves in conflict with the law, severely constraining judicial discretion in such cases (Maruna *et al.*, 2007). Youth conferencing can be operated both as an alternative to prosecution or as a court-ordered process and is applied to any young person aged 10–17 who has pleaded guilty or been found guilty of an offence (O'Mahoney and Campbell, 2006). The youth conferencing model that is used is drawn from the experiences of other jurisdictions, most pertinently the New Zealand family group conferencing model. The focus is on enabling victims of an offence and their supporters (or representatives) to be brought together with offenders and their supporters in a structured meeting facilitated by professionals, with the principal aim to provide all participants with the opportunity to discuss the offence and its repercussions and to agree on an action plan for the offender.

Underpinning this approach are a number of key principles first proposed by the Criminal Justice Review Group, including meeting the needs of victims, promoting rehabilitation and preventing re-offending, maximising the potential for re-integration and devolving power to conference participants by involving them in the outcome. In practice, a typical conference plan will include an apology, reparation, compensation, community service of some kind, restrictions on conduct or the whereabouts of the offender, or involvement in interventions such as drug and alcohol activities or programmes (CJI, 2010b). In short, the Northern Ireland model of youth conferencing is designed to encourage young people to recognise the effects of their crime, to take responsibility for their actions and to empower participants by engaging victim, offender and community in the restorative processes (Campbell *et al.*, 2005). The workload for practitioners is extensive. In 2012/13 some 1,556 referrals were made to youth conferences, with 83 per cent of referrals resulting in a ratified conferencing plan (Youth Justice Agency, 2014).

The Youth Conference Service has been subject to a number of major reviews. For example, in late 2009 the Prison Reform Trust reported that the Service was working well and making a highly positive contribution to the delivery of youth justice across Northern Ireland (Jacobson and Gibbs, 2009). The report highlighted evidence that victims who attend conferences tend to be satisfied with both the process and outcomes, and levels of victim participation were reasonably high. Of particular note was the finding that the Service had contributed to an overall decline in the use of custody for young offenders and to an increasing rate of diversion of young people out of the formal criminal justice process. The report also quoted findings from research by Tate and O'Loan (2009) which suggested that combined re-offending figures for all restorative justice disposals in 2006 were 42 per cent, in comparison to re-offending rates of 71 per cent for those placed in custody, albeit based on small-scale analysis and a lack of comparable control groups.

The Youth Conference Service was also evaluated in 2011 by the Department of Justice (Youth Justice Review, 2011). The Review praised the impact that youth conferencing has had on the wider system of youth justice. Particular strengths that were identified included the ability to enable offenders to participate in the process and draw links between their behaviour, the conference procedures and the final outcomes; the training and professionalism of staff members; and the incorporation of a strong community service element which enabled offenders to 'do good' in a way that encouraged their reintegration back into society. The review also made a number of recommendations designed to improve future performance. These included the need to maximise the direct participation of victims in the process. A second recommendation involved the need to continue to ensure that conference outcomes are proportionate and relevant to the scale of offending. Such concerns did not go as far as to suggest that net-widening was taking place, but did indicate that some minor adjustments to conferencing procedures were required to enhance proportionality and take account of the needs of the offender.

Previous commentators have focused on problems such as a deficit in levels of engagement by young people, a lack of individual responsibility and oppressive and punitive proceedings (Maruna et al., 2007; O'Mahoney and Campbell, 2006). It has also been noted that the proximity of the Youth Conference Service to the criminal justice system has created some difficulty for practitioners in getting restorative conferencing orders approved by the courts or prosecutors, as such orders were often perceived as being too lenient in more serious cases (Maruna et al., 2007; Campbell et al., 2005). Subsequently it has become a key aim of the Criminal Justice Inspectorate to ensure that proceedings do not result in excessive conference orders. It is worth noting in that regard that since 2009 the Youth Conference Service have given considerable time and resources to responding to the problem of priority youth offenders: that is, young people who exhibit offending behaviour which is either persistent or serious, or both. This initiative involves the Youth Conference Service working with partners to implement a much broader range of measures and has had some success.

Both forms of restorative justice intervention end with a criminal record for the young person involved. Diversionary youth conference disposals do not count as convictions but do attract a criminal record. Similarly, a court-ordered conference results in a Youth Conference Order, which is a sentence of the court and therefore constitutes a criminal conviction. It may be queried whether providing offenders with a criminal record is compatible with the ethos of restorative justice, as it may hinder their reintegration into society once the conditions of their restorative plan have been met. It is interesting to note that the Youth Justice Review (2011) recommended that rehabilitation policy and legislation should be reviewed to ensure that some 18-year-olds are provided with the opportunity for a fresh start by having their criminal records removed. In response the Northern Ireland Justice Minister recently announced publicly that eligible cases would now be automatically referred to have their criminal record reviewed.

A number of other state-led restorative justice initiatives are currently employed in Northern Ireland including police-led restorative cautioning for minor offences, which works in a similar manner to the diversionary scheme administered by the Youth Conference Service. The police scheme is notable in part because it can also be applied to adults, providing they have admitted their guilt and the case is adjudged to be minor in nature by the Public Prosecution Service (PSNI, 2014). The Northern Ireland Prison Service, along with the Probation Board for Northern Ireland, also regularly use restorative justice for the purposes of aiding the rehabilitation and resettlement of prisoners and for providing support to victims of crime. Practitioners go to great lengths to ensure that both the victim and offender are motivated properly and to make sure that any victims are not re-victimised (Payne et al., 2010). Although information on the effectiveness of these schemes is limited, the Criminal Justice Inspectorate described the restorative conferencing scheme in Hydebank Wood Young Offenders Centre as 'very good' and noted that the service had been used on 64 occasions during 2012 (CJI, 2013: 6).

Restorative justice in the Republic

Evolution of restorative justice policy and practice

The genesis of restorative justice in the criminal justice system in the Republic lies in the Children Act 2001. It can be argued that restorative elements were part of earlier practice in the Probation Service (through, for example, community service and victim awareness programmes for offenders) and in the Garda Síochána (through its diversion programme for young offenders), but these practices do not meet all the criteria of generally accepted definitions of restorative justice, including – notably – structured dialogue about repair of harm and engagement with victims. The Act, without making explicit mention of restorative justice, introduced the possibility of restorative interventions at two key stages of processing child offenders: in cases diverted from prosecution under the Garda Diversion Programme and in cases brought before the Children Court. Family group conferencing was the main model, drawing on and adapting the New Zealand model, as in Northern Ireland. A restorative element was also introduced to police cautioning, described in political debate at the time as a form of 'mini-conferencing' (Dáil Eireann, 2000). Around the same time, two pilot community-based restorative justice schemes for adult offenders were established with funding from the Probation Service: one in Nenagh, Tipperary, in 1999 and one in Tallaght, Dublin, in 2000. The Nenagh project was based exclusively on an offender reparation model, while the Tallaght programme operated both a victim–offender mediation model and, since 2004, an offender reparation model.

Political interest in restorative justice re-emerged in the mid-2000s. In 2006 the all-party Joint Committee on Justice, Equality, Defence and Women's Rights examined the potential of restorative justice and held oral hearings. It reported in January 2007 and recommended development of restorative justice as a more regular feature of the criminal justice system. As a result a National Commission on Restorative Justice was established in March 2007. Its final report in July 2009 provided a blueprint for development and remains influential in framing the official discourse and shaping the general understanding of the subject.

The Commission recommended application of restorative justice at all stages of the criminal justice system, beginning with court referrals at the pre-sanction stage and targeting cases involving custodial sentences of up to three years' imprisonment. It concluded that restorative justice was suitable in principle for all but the most serious crimes, such as murder and rape, but also recommended the exclusion of offences such as domestic violence and sexual assault from the initial phases of implementation, pending development of specialist expertise. It sought availability of the options of victim–offender mediation, restorative conferencing and reparation panels in all District and Circuit courts. It recommended that restorative justice be given a statutory base and be available nationwide no later than 2015. It concluded that the Probation Service should be the lead agency in implementing restorative justice for adult offenders in partnership with other criminal justice agencies, non-governmental organisations and local community resources (National Commission on Restorative Justice, 2009).

The economic downturn effectively ruled out any significant roll-out of restorative justice. While the Government welcomed the Commission's report and endorsed its recommendations, the immediate follow-up was limited: expansion of the two adult pilot projects within existing budgets and a focus on offences that would attract sentences of less than 12 months imprisonment. A subsequent internal Probation Service review found that the expanded projects represented significant value for money relative to custody and other traditional community-based sanctions. It recommended further expansion, use in respect of higher tariff offences, continued prioritisation of engagement with victims and increased involvement of volunteers (Probation Service, 2012). In November 2013 the Probation Service published its restorative justice strategy (Probation Service, 2013). Among other things, it commits to building capacity for delivery of restorative justice programmes and exploring opportunities for further development of projects and programmes nationally and for specific categories of offenders. The strategy puts a particular emphasis on offender reparation and states that restorative justice should only be used when it is appropriate to the needs of both offender and victim.

Political interest has continued meanwhile. In March 2013 the Seanad (Senate) approved a motion calling for the development and extension of restorative justice as a nationwide non-custodial sentencing option. The Joint Committee on Justice, Defence and Equality has undertaken a study of restorative justice and invited written submissions. The Joint Committee also invited submissions on the Heads of the Criminal Justice (Community Sanctions) Bill 2014 which includes limited provision for reparation in minor offence cases where the victim so wishes.

The juvenile system

Restorative justice for offenders aged under 18 has statutory underpinning in the Children Act 2001 and has become a significant part of the landscape for such offenders, mostly for those diverted from prosecution under the Garda Diversion Programme and to a lesser extent for those appearing in court.

The Diversion Programme allows for the diversion from prosecution of young offenders who accept responsibility for their actions. Diversion can be by means of formal caution (generally reserved for more serious offences or repeat offenders) or informal caution (generally given for minor offences or first-time offenders). Recipients of formal cautions are placed under the supervision of a Garda juvenile liaison officer for a period of 12 months.

The Act provides for restorative justice under the Diversion Programme in two ways. Both apply where formal cautions are administered. First, Section 26 provides for invitation of the victim to a formal caution and participation in a discussion about the child's criminal behaviour. It also states that the child may be invited to apologise orally or in writing and make financial or other reparation to the victim. Second, Sections 29–43 of the Act provide for a conference after a formal caution to establish the reasons for the offending behaviour, discuss how to prevent further offending, review recent behaviour, 'mediate' between the offender and the victim and formulate an action plan for the child. Victims and their supporters must be invited, unless their attendance would not be in the interests of the conference. It is not mandatory to formulate an action plan, and if a plan is agreed the offender cannot be compelled to comply with it, although the conference can reconvene to examine reasons for non-compliance and to encourage the child to comply with the plan or any amended version.

The scale of the Garda restorative justice programme is of note. It is a nationwide programme and is overseen by a national monitoring committee that includes non-Garda members. The Monitoring Committee's annual report for 2012 shows that 1,036 children referred under the Garda Diversion Programme were dealt with by 'restorative caution', representing 36 per cent of the 2,840 children who received formal cautions that year. The annual reports show a steady increase in restorative events in the period 2003 to 2009 (from 118 to 416) and a more significant acceleration in numbers since then (792 in 2010 and 903 in 2011) (Garda Síochána, 2004–2012). The reports show that many of the cases dealt with by restorative caution involved repeat offenders and more serious offences. The statistics in the annual reports do not distinguish between cautions and conferences.

The Garda programme of restorative justice for young people was evaluated in 2004 (O'Dwyer, 2006). The evaluation examined all restorative events from 1 May 2002 to 31 December 2003. In that period 147 events took place, comprising 134 cautions and 13 conferences. Some cautions were found to be simple affairs focusing primarily, if not exclusively, on apology and reparation, while others resembled conferences in terms of both process and outcomes. On the other hand, some conferences were found to be rather limited, and conferences where no victim was involved were in fact not very different from traditional formal cautions. The blurring of distinctions between cautions and conferences may reduce the significance of an apparent recent shift to exclusive or at least predominant use of cautions – the 2012 annual report, unlike earlier reports, referring only to restorative cautions.

Overall, O'Dwyer (2006) concluded that the Garda restorative justice programme produced benefits along expected lines for offenders, victims and their supporters. Victim participation levels were high by international standards, with victims attending in 73 per cent of cases involving a direct victim. Concerns in the literature about aspects of restorative justice, including possible infringement of offenders' rights and re-victimisation of injured parties, were not substantiated. High rates of satisfaction (e.g. 93 per cent of victims and 94 per cent of offenders giving a score of four or five on a five-point Likert scale) and observed adherence to restorative justice principles and values provided comfort in this respect. Agreements were judged to be fair and proportionate. The most common agreement elements were apologies, compensation and undertakings about future behaviour. Compliance rates were high (89 per cent), especially as regards victim-oriented elements. A third of offenders re-offended within 12 months but most new offending was minor and of short duration. It was not possible, for methodological reasons, to establish a link between the restorative justice interventions and re-offending.

The study found little to suggest a problem with the role of police officers as facilitators and noted a number of features in the Garda programme that distinguish it from other police-led programmes. For example, the fact that interventions take place in the context of the Diversion Programme, where a prior decision has been taken not to prosecute, ensures that the principle of voluntariness as regards participation, formulation of an action plan and compliance with any plan is not diluted by a threat of court looming in the background. Furthermore supervision under the Diversion Programme provides support for the offender over a protracted period, complementing the restorative intervention.

The second provision for restorative justice in the Children Act (2001) relates to child offenders before the courts. Section 78 provides for family conferences similar to those provided for under the Diversion Programme. These are organised on the direction of the Children Court by the Probation Service. They are required to be convened within 28 days, although this can be extended by a further 28 days on application to the Court. If the conference agrees an action plan for the child, the Court may approve or amend it and order compliance under supervision. If the conference does not agree an action plan, the Court may itself formulate a plan or resume prosecution proceedings. Compliance is reviewed within a six-month period. If the child complies with the action plan the Court may dismiss the charge on its merits. If the child fails to comply, the Court may resume proceedings. The National Commission on Restorative Justice recommended greater use of this conference option, and some expansion has begun to occur in recent times. Court referrals have been low in recent years – 19 in 2011 and 15 in 2012 – but were substantially higher in 2013 (50) (Probation Service, 2014). To help put the figures in context, Garda statistics show that in 2012 some 1,822 offenders were deemed unsuitable for inclusion in the Diversion Programme and therefore sent for prosecution. No comprehensive independent evaluation of the programme appears to have been undertaken to date (see, further, Convery and Seymour, *infra*).

The landscape of restorative justice for young people is completed by a growing number of community-based organisations which provide restorative justice services or whose practice is informed by restorative principles. For example, the Le Chéile project in Limerick has, since 2011, been working restoratively with young people who are under Probation Service supervision. It has two facilitators and a capacity to deal with 40 cases per annum. It uses a variety of models, including victim–offender mediation and conferencing. The project can call on a panel of victims where the direct victim does not wish to be involved or cannot be contacted (Le Chéile, 2014). Many other youth-focused organisations and programmes have likewise adopted restorative practices in their dealings with young people, and several schools are adopting restorative practices in ways already described in relation to Northern Ireland.

The adult system

Availability of restorative justice for adults is limited to the two services already mentioned, those that originated in Nenagh and Tallaght. Both services are independent, not-for-profit companies with charitable status, although their independence is perhaps constrained by their reliance on state funding. Both services take referrals from the courts, where a decision on sentencing is deferred under judicial discretion to allow the restorative intervention, and where a positive outcome is taken into account, usually through dismissal, application of the Probation Act or a lesser sentence than might otherwise have been handed down. Repairing harm caused to victims and others has been a key focus of both services, and offenders are encouraged to learn from their behaviour and make positive choices for the future. Detailed information from annual reports or in-depth evaluations is not yet publicly available.

The Nenagh reparation panel, now operating as Restorative Justice in the Community, serves District Courts in Counties Tipperary and Offaly and Cork City. The model involves a meeting between an offender and a panel that comprises two community volunteers, a local Garda member and the project co-ordinator/case worker. Agreed reparation plans are presented to court and, if approved, a further adjournment is granted to allow completion, and a report on the offender's performance is furnished on the return to court. The majority of referrals were until recently in respect of first-time offenders and less serious offences that would not normally attract a custodial sentence. According to the National Commission on Restorative Justice (2009: 46), public disorder and drugs possession accounted for 80 per cent of offences between 1999 and 2007, and contracts were completed in 86 per cent of 105 cases referred. Referrals thus averaged about 15 cases per annum, and victims were seldom involved. Recent years have seen a considerable increase in the number of cases (120 in 2014), a greater mix of offences and increased victim involvement; the programme now also includes options of direct or indirect victim–offender mediation and restorative conferencing (Restorative Justice in the Community, 2014).

Restorative Justice Services (RJS) was established in Tallaght in 2000 and, following expansion in 2011, serves the Criminal Courts of Justice in Dublin and all outlying District Courts in the Greater Dublin area. It operates two programmes – a victim–offender mediation programme and an offender reparation panel. Both programmes are almost exclusively court-referred at pre-sentencing stage. The mediation service dealt with a total of 51 referrals in 2004–2007, with an agreed outcome in 45 per cent of cases (National Commission on Restorative Justice, 2009: 47). Victims declined to participate in many cases, and outcomes typically included verbal or written apologies, financial reparation or donations to charity. The number of referrals to the mediation programme has diminished in recent years, but mediation has re-emerged as an element in action plans under the offender reparation programme. This latter programme operates on the basis of panel hearings, with a case worker assigned to support each offender in preparing for the panel and in completing agreed actions. The panel make-up and process differ from the model of Restorative Justice in the Community. RJS panels have three members (a community volunteer as chair and Garda and Probation representatives) and meet twice, first to discuss the offence with the offender and case worker and agree an action plan and then to review progress before returning to the court for final disposal. Referrals to the offender reparation programme totalled 81 in 2007, and 75 completed their contracts (National Commission on Restorative Justice, 2009: 47). About 300 new cases are now dealt with annually. Originally cases tended to involve first-time offenders and less serious offences, and most cases resulted in a dismissal or application of the Probation Act. Now panels are dealing with a higher proportion of repeat offenders and more serious offences, including referrals from the Circuit Court, and judges occasionally impose a sanction with a criminal conviction rather than dismiss the case, as was the norm in earlier years (Restorative Justice Services, 2014).

An element of restorative justice could be said to be also involved in the Garda Adult Cautioning Scheme, introduced in 2006, although the extent to which the caution is delivered within a restorative framework is not clear. The scheme adopts a diversionary approach and applies generally to first-time offenders involved in relatively minor offences. The restorative element, apart from diversion itself, is that the views of any victim involved must be sought and taken into consideration in deciding on whether or not to caution. The National Commission recommended expansion of the restorative dimension of such cautions (2009: 48).

Conclusion

This concluding section critically examines restorative justice in both jurisdictions in Ireland under two headings:

(i) the extent of use of restorative justice and scope for expansion; and
(ii) the experience of use vis-à-vis issues raised in the literature.

As regards extent of use within the criminal justice system, restorative justice can potentially be applied at any stage: pre-charge, pre-trial, pre-sentence and post-sentence. In a study of 12 European countries, Miers (2001: 79) noted that restorative justice applied at all four stages in Belgium, while the most common combination was at the pre-trial and sentencing stages. The National Commission on Restorative Justice recognised this potential and did not exclude the notion that adult offenders might be referred to a restorative justice process other than by the courts (2009: 98). Restorative justice can potentially be used for adult and young offenders across the full range of offences. It can be used in many formats, including (but not confined to) victim–offender mediation, family conferencing/restorative cautioning and citizen panels. And it can potentially be initiated by victims rather than by criminal justice professionals.

The extent of use to date is quite modest overall when looked at against this full potential. As regards adult offenders, restorative justice is hardly applied at all within the formal criminal justice system in Northern Ireland, save for the PSNI's diversionary scheme and its use within the Prison Service. Importantly, victims do have a possibility to initiate a restorative process with offenders after sentence. Use in the Republic for adult offenders is largely confined to court referrals at the pre-sentence stage, to perhaps the least restorative model (offender reparation panels), to limited geographical areas and, until recently, to relatively minor offences. A restorative process involving victim–offender dialogue is not available (readily or at all) at the pre-charge/pre-trial stage, at the post-sentence stage in prison or on post-release supervision.

The picture is somewhat different as regards young offenders. In Northern Ireland, consideration of restorative justice options is mandatory at prosecution and sentencing stages for all but a small number of exceptional cases and also features in police cautioning for minor offences. In the Republic, conferencing is a core element of formal cautions under the Garda Diversion Programme, although the extent to which victims are currently involved is not known. The option of conferencing at court stage has been little used until recently.

There are signs of welcome development. In the Republic, the report of the National Commission on Restorative Justice provides a blueprint for expansion, there is cross-party political interest and the Probation Service has published its restorative justice strategy. Within existing services, geographical expansion has occurred, higher-tariff offences are being referred, and there is growing awareness and use of restorative practice in domains other than criminal justice. The EU Directive on victim rights (European Union, 2012), due to be implemented by November 2015, may also provide impetus in both parts of Ireland. However, despite this progress, the bottom line is that there are significant gaps in access to restorative justice, and the ultimate policy objectives and vision are not clear.

What can experiences to date tell us about issues raised in the restorative justice literature, and how Irish practice measures up? The available Irish research evidence is somewhat limited. Independent evaluations of existing services need to be carried out in the interests of public awareness, understanding and debate and achievement of excellence. Such evidence as is available (e.g. Jacobson and Gibbs, 2009; Youth Justice Review, 2011; O'Dwyer, 2006) relates to young offenders and, as discussed above, has been broadly positive about practice and impact.

Three main sets of issues and tensions relating to restorative justice were identified in Section 1. As regards the first, proximity to formal criminal justice systems and possible erosion of offenders' rights, widening the net of social control and imposing inappropriate sanctions were seen as risks. It is possible that restorative justice interventions are used unnecessarily in cases of relatively minor offences, or where offenders are considered at low risk of re-offending. The risk is perhaps highest for young offenders in Northern Ireland, since it is mandatory to consider restorative interventions in all but a few types of case. The risk may be mitigated in the Republic to the extent that restorative justice for young offenders is used primarily within a context of police diversion, where practitioners have considerable discretion in case selection and where courts also have discretion as regards referral to restorative justice services for both adult and young offenders. The possibility of net-widening cannot be discounted entirely, of course. There is evidence that some net-widening occurred in the early years of the Garda programme (O'Dwyer, 2006).

As regards sanctions imposed, restorative processes emphasise consensual agreement and voluntary participation. Court-supervised programmes offer safeguards to ensure fairness and proportionality, but even in diversion and community-based programmes, the available empirical evidence is that few agreements could be regarded as excessive. In the Garda programme, for example, O'Dwyer (2006) reported that three-quarters of agreements had three or fewer elements, with a verbal apology the most common element in agreements (74 per cent), followed by making promises (69 per cent), money/gift for the victim (35 per cent) and a written apology (34 per cent). Money for the victim almost invariably related to compensation for loss or damage. In fact, there appeared to be scope to encourage the inclusion of additional elements, such as education about crime and victim awareness, without agreements becoming punitive, disproportionate, counter-productive or unfeasible. The high rate of voluntary compliance in all programmes provides reassurance. In Northern Ireland, the Youth Justice Review Group (2011) recommended fine tuning the youth conferencing system to ensure that conference plans remained proportionate and took account of the needs of the offender, but expressed concern over the length of plans, the number of plans extending over six months having increased from 12 per cent in 2006/2007 to some 41 per cent in 2010/2011 (Youth Justice Review, 2011: 96).

The success of restorative justice is also dependent on adherence to core values and principles, and there needs to be an on-going commitment to quality standards, adequate staff support and supervision and protection against pressure to generate unduly high caseloads. The Garda evaluation (O'Dwyer, 2006) noted the importance of sufficient time within restorative events for respectful dialogue and mutual understanding that is too easily compromised. Ensuring process integrity is vital to protecting against any erosion of offender rights or restorative justice ideals.

As regards the second set of issues and tensions, community involvement, the role of community in restorative justice programmes in the Republic is limited, and many of the concerns around community-based programmes do not arise. The challenge in the Republic may be more to widen the community role, rather than guard against possible dangers. The continued existence of parallel state and community-based schemes in Northern Ireland has led to some discussions on how the state scheme, in particular, can provide greater input from community members, especially those who hail from the kind of working-class neighbourhoods that have traditionally been the preserve of the community-based schemes. One solution implemented by the Youth Conference Service is to allow young people access to one of the community-based projects as part of a wider partnership arrangement with CRJI and NIA.

Finally, as regards the third set of issues and tensions, perceived limits of restorative justice, the reality in the Republic is that all programmes fall within the criminal justice system. Current programmes for adults are subject to court oversight (apart from the limited restorative justice element of police cautioning), and the programmes for children operate predominantly within the Garda Diversion Programme, while the small remainder are subject to court oversight. Both adult and juvenile programmes have been targeted primarily at lower-end offences and offenders, and the more pressing concern and challenge may be to include more serious cases. The National Commission on Restorative Justice (2009) did not think that any class of offence should be excluded in principle from the scope of restorative justice but recommended against its immediate use in cases of sexual assault and domestic violence and did not foresee its use in cases of murder or rape. This view, however, excludes the possibility of restorative justice post-sentence and makes no allowance for victim choice, where victims or their families are cognisant of the risks and willing to take them on. In Northern Ireland, the community-based schemes are a significant feature, but their operations are subject to the protocols agreed with the criminal justice agencies, and the services are inspected by the Criminal Justice Inspectorate. A major brake on their operations has in fact emerged from a perceived reluctance of the Public Prosecution Service to allow diversionary procedures to be initiated under the protocols, except in very few cases of a minor nature. The community-based projects have negated this problem to some extent by developing effective partnerships with a range of statutory agencies including the PSNI.

Other concerns expressed in the literature included doubts over the ability to 'restore' victims and offenders, the risk of secondary victimisation, the voluntary nature of participation and effectiveness in terms of deterrence and reduced re-offending. These are largely matters for empirical research. The available evidence would at least suggest that practice, where measured, adhered to a reassuring degree to important restorative values, and high satisfaction levels would also suggest that victim and offender rights were upheld and expected outcomes were achieved. The voluntary nature of participation is particularly strong under the Garda Diversion Programme, where a prior decision is made to divert the offender from prosecution, and subsequent prosecution is not an option if the offender fails to participate or complete an agreement. The impact of the programmes in terms of reduced re-offending has not been established through rigorous evaluation with control groups, but international evidence would suggest that restorative justice at least avoids negative impacts on re-offending, is a more cost-effective way of processing cases and responds better to participant needs. However there is a need to improve transparency of operations and conduct robust, up-to-date evaluations of programmes to ensure best practice and consistently high standards. The community schemes and youth justice provisions in Northern Ireland and the offender reparation panels and Garda restorative justice programme in the Republic have unique features that are likely to be of interest internationally and are worthy of particular investigative study.

References

Aertsen, I., Daems, T. and Luc, R. (eds) (2006) *Institutionalizing Restorative Justice*. Cullompton: Willan.
Ashworth, A. (1986) 'Punishment and Compensation: Victims, Offenders and the State', *Oxford Journal of Legal Studies*, 6(1): 86–122.
—— (2002) 'Responsibilities, Rights and Restorative Justice', *British Journal of Criminology*, 42 (3): 578–595.
Auld, J., Gormally, B., McEvoy, K. and Ritchie, M. (1997) *Designing a System of Restorative Justice in Northern Ireland*. Belfast: self-published.
Barajas, E. (1996) *Community Justice: Striving for Safe, Secure, and Just Communities*. Washington DC: US Department of Justice.
Bazemore, G. and Schiff, M. (eds) (2001) *Restorative Community Justice: Repairing Harm and Transforming Communities*. Cincinnati OH: Anderson Publishing.
Bazemore, G. and Walgrave, L. (eds) (1999) *Restorative Juvenile Justice: Repairing the Harm of Youth Crime*. Monsey NY: Criminal Justice Press/Willow Tree Press.
Bell, C. (1996) 'Alternative Justice in Ireland' in N. Dawson, D. Greer and P. Ingram (eds) *One Hundred and Fifty Years of Irish Law*. Belfast: SLS Legal Publications (NI).
Braithwaite, J. (1989) *Crime, Shame and Reintegration*. Cambridge: Cambridge University Press.
—— (1999) 'Restorative Justice: Assessing Optimistic and Pessimistic Accounts', *Crime and Justice: A Review of Research*, 25: 1–127.
—— (2002) *Restorative Justice and Responsive Regulation*. Oxford: Oxford University Press.
Byrne, J., Topping, J. and Martin, R. (2014) *Northern Ireland Policing Board: Confidence in Policing Research 'The Key Drivers of Public Confidence in NI'*. Northern Ireland Policing Board.
Cameron, L. and Thorsborne, M. (2001) 'The School System: Developing Its Capacity in the Regulation of Civil Society' in H. Strangand and J. Braithwaite (eds) *Restorative Justice and Civil Society*. Cambridge: Cambridge University Press.
Campbell, C., Devlin, R., O'Mahoney, D., Doak, J., Jackson, J., Corrigan, T. and McEvoy, K. (2005) *Evaluation of the Northern Ireland Youth Conference Service*. Belfast: Northern Ireland Office.
Christie, N. (1977) 'Conflicts as Property', *British Journal of Criminology*, 17(1): 1–15.
CJI (2010a) *Northern Ireland Alternatives: A Follow-Up Review of the Community Restorative Justice Schemes Operated by Northern Ireland Alternatives*. Belfast: Criminal Justice Inspection Northern Ireland.
—— (2010b) *Youth Conference Service, A Follow-Up Review of the Youth Conference Service*. Belfast: Criminal Justice Inspection Northern Ireland.
—— (2011) *Community Restorative Justice Ireland: A Follow-Up Review of the Community Restorative Justice, Ireland Community Restorative Justice Schemes*. Belfast: Criminal Justice Inspection Northern Ireland.
—— (2013) *Report on an Announced Inspection of Maghaberry Prison 19–23 March 2012*. Belfast: Criminal Justice Inspection Northern Ireland.
—— (2014) *A Pre-Accreditation Inspection of North Belfast and South and East Belfast Community Restorative Justice Ireland Schemes*. Belfast: Criminal Justice Inspection Northern Ireland.
Crawford, A. (1999) *The Local Governance of Crime: Appeals to Community and Partnerships*. Oxford: Oxford University Press.
—— (2002) 'The State, Community and Restorative Justice: Heresy, Nostalgia and Butterfly-Collecting' in L. Walgrave (ed.) *Restorative Justice and the Law*. Cullompton: Willan.
Crawford, A. and Newburn, T. (2003) *Youth Offending and Restorative Justice – Implementing Reform in Youth Justice*. Cullompton: Willan.
Criminal Justice Review Group (2000) *The Review of Criminal Justice in Northern Ireland*. Belfast: Northern Ireland Office.

CRJI (2014) *Annual Report and Accounts 2013*. Belfast: Community Restorative Justice Ireland.

Dáil Éireann (2000) (517:36) Available at: http://debates.oireachtas.ie/dail/2000/03/29/00010.asp (accessed 31 March 2015).

Daly, K. (2002) 'Sexual Assault and Restorative Justice' in H. Strang and J. Braithwaite (eds) *Restorative Justice and Family Violence*. Cambridge: Cambridge University Press.

Dhami, M. K. and Joy, P. (2007) 'Challenges to Establishing Volunteer-Run, Community-Based Restorative Justice Programs', *Contemporary Justice Review*, 10 (1): 9–22.

Dignan, J. and Cavadino, M. (1996) 'Towards a Framework for Conceptualising and Evaluating Models of Criminal Justice from a Victim's Perspective', *International Review of Victimology*, 4:153–82.

Dignan, J. and Lowey, K. (2000) *Restorative Justice Options for Northern Ireland: A Comparative Review*. Research Report Number 10. Norwich: HMSO.

European Union (2012) *Directive 2012/29/EU of the European Parliament and of the Council of 25 October 2012*. Official Journal of the European Union L315/57–73.

Feenan, D. (2002) 'Researching Paramilitary Violence in Northern Ireland', *International Journal of Social Research Methodology*, 5 (2): 147–63.

Galaway, B. and Hudson, J. (eds) (1996) *Restorative Justice: International Perspectives*. Monsey NY: Criminal Justice Press.

Garda Síochána (2004–2012) *Annual Reports of the Committee Appointed to Monitor the Effectiveness of the Diversion Programme*. Available at: www.garda.ie or www.iyjs.ie.

Good Friday Agreement (1998) *The Agreement Reached in the Multi-Party Negotiation*. Belfast: HMSO.

Gormally, B. (2006) 'Community Restorative Justice in Northern Ireland – An Overview'. *Restorative Justice Online*, April 2006 edition.

Gottfredson, M. and Hirschi, T. (1990) *A General Theory of Crime*. San Francisco CA: Stanford University Press.

Hirschi, T. (1969) *Causes of Delinquency*. Berkeley CA: University of California Press.

Hopkins, B. (2004) *Just Schools*. London: Jessica Kingsley.

Hudson, B. (2002) 'Restorative Justice and Gendered Violence: Diversion or Effective Justice?', *British Journal of Criminology*, 42(3): 616–34.

Jacobson, J. and Gibbs, P. (2009) *Making Amends: Restorative Youth Justice in Northern Ireland*. London: Prison Reform Trust.

Johnstone, G. (2002) *Restorative Justice: Ideas, Values, Debates*. Cullompton: Willan.

Johnstone, G. and Van Ness, D.W. (2007) *Handbook of Restorative Justice*. Cullompton: Willan.

Keenan, M. (2014) *Sexual Trauma and Abuse: Restorative and Transformative Possibilities?* Dublin: School of Applied Social Science, University College Dublin. Available at: http://facingforward.ie/wp-content/uploads/2014/11/FAFO_Final_Lo_Res.pdf (accessed 18 December 2014).

Kurki, L. (2003) 'Evaluating Restorative Justice Practices', in A. Von Hirsch, J.V. Roberts, A. Bottoms, K. Roach and M. Schiff, *Restorative Justice and Criminal Justice: Competing or Reconcilable Paradigms*. Oxford: Hart Publishing.

Latimer, J., Dowden, C. and Muise, D. (2001) *The Effectiveness of Restorative Justice Practices: A Meta-Analysis*. Ottawa: Department of Justice. Available at: www.justice.ca/en/ps/rs/rep/2001/meta.pdf (accessed 28 November 2005).

Le Chéile (2014), personal communication with the author, May 2014.

McAlinden, A.M. (2007) *The Shaming of Sexual Offenders: Risk, Retribution and Reintegration*. Oxford: Hart Publishing.

McCluskey, G., Lloyd, G., Kane, J., Riddell, S., Stead, J. and Weedon, E. (2008) 'Can Restorative Practices in Schools Make a Difference?', *Educational Review*, 60 (4): 405–417.

McCold, P. (1998) 'Police-Facilitated Restorative Conferencing – What the Data Show', Paper to the Second Annual International Conference on Restorative Justice for Juveniles. Florida: Atlantic University.

—— (2004) 'What Is the Role of Community in Restorative Justice Theory and Practice?' in H. Zehr and B. Toews (eds) *Critical Issues in Restorative Justice*. Cullompton: Willan; Monsey NY: Criminal Justice Press.

McEvoy, K. and Eriksson, A. (2006) 'Restorative Justice in Transition: Ownership, Leadership and "Bottom-Up" Human Rights' in D. Sullivan and L. Tifft (eds) *The Handbook of Restorative Justice: Global Perspectives*. Abingdon: Routledge.

—— (2007) 'Who Owns Justice? Community, State and the Northern Ireland Transition' in J. Shapland (ed.) *Justice, Community and Civil Society: A Contested Terrain*. Cullompton: Willan.

McEvoy, K. and Mika, H. (2001) 'Punishment, Politics and Praxis: Restorative Justice and Non-Violent Alternatives to Paramilitary Punishment', *Policing and Society*, 11 (1): 359–382.

—— (2002) 'Republican Hegemony or Community Ownership? Community Restorative Justice in Northern Ireland', in D. Feenan, *Informal Criminal Justice*. Aldershot: Ashgate.

Marshall, T. (1998) *Restorative Justice: An Overview*. London: Restorative Justice Consortium; St Paul MN: Center for Restorative Justice and Peacemaking. Available at: http://rjp.umm.edu/img/assets/18492/Restorative_Justice_%20Overview_%20Marshall.pdf. (accessed 28 November 2005).

Maruna, S., Wright, S., Brown, J., van Marle, F., Devlin, R. and Liddle, M. (2007) *Youth Conferencing as Shame Management: Results of a Long-Term Follow-Up Study*. UK: Youth Justice Agency.

Matza, D. (1964) *Delinquency and Drift*. New York: Wiley.

Maxwell, G., Morris, A., Hayes, H. (2006) 'Conferencing and Restorative Justice' in D. Sullivan and L. Tifft (eds) *The Handbook of Restorative Justice: Global Perspectives*. Abingdon: Routledge.

Miers, D. (2001) *An International Review of Restorative Justice*, Crime Reduction Research Series Paper 10. London: Home Office.

Mika, H. (2006) *Community-Based Restorative Justice in Northern Ireland*. Belfast: Institute of Criminology and Criminal Justice, Queen's University Belfast.

Morris, A. (2002) 'Critiquing the Critics: A Brief Response to Critics of Restorative Justice', *British Journal of Criminology*, 42: 596–615.

National Commission on Restorative Justice (2009) *Final Report*. Dublin: Department of Justice and Equality. Available at: http.justice.ie/en/JELR/NCRJ%20Final%20Report.pdf/Files/NCRJ%20Final%20Report.pdf (accessed 16 December 2014).

O'Dwyer, K. (2006) 'Restorative Justice in the Garda Síochána – An Evaluation of the Garda Programme of Restorative Justice 2002–2003'. Unpublished thesis. National University of Ireland, University College Dublin.

O'Mahoney, D. and Campbell, C. (2006) 'Mainstreaming Restorative Justice for Young Offenders through Youth Conferencing: The Experience of Northern Ireland' in J. Junger-Tas and S. Decker, *International Handbook of Youth Justice*. New York: Springer.

Pavlich, G. (2005) *Governing Paradoxes of Restorative Justice*. London: Glasshouse Press.

Payne, B., Conway, V., Rice, F., Bell, C., McNeill, C., Flynn, H. and Falk, A. (2010) *Restorative Practices in Northern Ireland: A Mapping Exercise*. Belfast: Queen's University School of Law.

Pranis, K. (1997) 'Rethinking Community Corrections: Restorative Values and an Expanded Role for the Community', *ICCA Journal*, 3(43): 36–9.

Probation Service (2012) *Report on Pilot Expansion of Probation Funded Adult Restorative Justice Projects, July 2012*. Dublin: Probation Service.

—— (2013) *Restorative Justice Strategy 2013*, www.probation.ie.

—— (2014) *The Probation Service Annual Report 2013*, www.probation.ie.

PSNI (2014) *Youth Diversion*. Available at: www.psni.police.uk/youth_diversion.pdf (accessed 27 July 2015).

Putnam, R. (2000) *Bowling Alone: The Collapse and Revival of American Community*. New York: Simon and Schuster.

Restorative Justice in the Community (2014), Personal communication with the author, November 2014.

Restorative Justice Services (2014), Personal communication with the author, November 2014.

Roche, D. (2003) *Accountability in Restorative Justice*. Oxford: Oxford University Press.

Shapland, J., Robinson, G. and Sorsby, A. (2011) *Restorative Justice in Practice – Evaluating What Works for Victims and Offenders*. London: Routledge.

Sherman, L., Strang, H. and Woods, D. (2000) *Recidivism Patterns in the Canberra Reintegrative Shaming Experiments (RISE)*. Australia: Centre for Restorative Justice, Australian National University. Available at: www.aic.gov.au/rjustice/rise/recidivism/report.pdf (accessed 4 April 2006).

Strang, H. (2002) *Repair or Revenge: Victims and Restorative Justice*. Oxford: Clarendon Press.

Tate, S. and O'Loan, C. (2009) *Northern Ireland Youth Reoffending: Results from the 2006 Cohort*. Belfast: Northern Ireland Office.

Topping, J. (2008) 'Community Policing in Northern Ireland: A Resistance Narrative', *Policing and Society*, 18(4): 377–96.

Tyler, T. (1990) *Why People Obey the Law*. New Haven CT: Yale University Press.

Van Ness, D., Morris, A. and Maxwell, G. (2001) 'Introducing Restorative Justice' in A. Morris and G. Maxwell (eds) *Restorative Justice for Juveniles – Conferencing, Mediation and Circles*. Oxford: Hart Publishing.

Walgrave, L. (1992) 'Mediation and Community Service as Models of a Restorative Approach: Why Would It Be Better? Explicating the Objectives as Criteria for Evaluation', *Restorative Justice on Trial*, 64: 343–53.

—— (2001) 'On Restoration and Punishment: Favourable Similarities and Fortunate Differences' in A. Morris and G. Maxwell (eds) *Restorative Justice for Juveniles – Conferencing, Mediation and Circles*. Oxford: Hart Publishing.

—— (2002) 'Restorative Justice and the Law: Socio-Ethical and Juridical Foundations for a Systemic Approach' in L. Walgrave (ed.) (2002) *Restorative Justice and the Law*. Cullompton: Willan.

—— (2008) *Restorative Justice, Self Interest and Responsible Citizenship*. Cullompton: Willan.

Young, R. (2001) 'Just Cops Doing Shameful Business? Police-Led Restorative Justice and the Lessons of Research' in A. Morris and G. Maxwell (eds) *Restorative Justice for Juveniles: Conferencing, Mediation and Circles*. Oxford: Hart Publishing.

Youth Justice Agency (2014) *Annual Workload Statistics 2012/13*. Belfast: Statistics and Research Branch, Youth Justice Agency.

Youth Justice Review (2011) *A Review of the Youth Justice System in Northern Ireland*. Belfast: Department of Justice.

Zedner, L. (1994) 'Reparation and Retribution: Are They Reconcilable?', *The Modern Law Review*, 57 (2): 228–50.

Zehr, H. (1990) *Changing Lenses: A New Focus for Crime and Justice*. Scottdale PA: Herald Press.

—— (2002) *The Little Book of Restorative Justice*. Intercourse PA: Good Books.

Zehr, H. and Mika, H. (1997) 'Fundamental Concepts of Restorative Justice', *Contemporary Justice Review* 1(1): 47–56, reproduced in E. McLaughlin, R. Fergusson, G. Hughes and L. Westmarland (eds) (2003) *Restorative Justice: Critical Issues*. London: Sage.

12

Children, crime and justice

Una Convery and Mairéad Seymour

Introduction

This chapter critically analyses the recent development of the youth justice systems in Northern Ireland and the Republic of Ireland. Developments are set within a brief history of the systems from their shared origins in the nineteenth and early twentieth centuries. It traces the enduring aspects of responses to children in conflict with the law up to the emergence of the contemporary systems in the 1990s. Next, separate sections for each jurisdiction consider the wider context impacting on children and within which the contemporary legislative frameworks were introduced. Legislative provision is charted against competing youth justice paradigms, and the operation of the system in relation to the police, courts, community sentences and detention is critiqued. It is argued that legislation, practice add-ons and rhetorical commitments mask prevailing concerns about the treatment of children in conflict with the law.

Brief history of the development of the youth justice systems: 1850s–1990s

The origins of the youth justice systems in both jurisdictions can be traced to pre-partition British legislative and institutional developments relating to children. Due to increasing concerns about 'the related evils of child destitution and criminality' (Barnes, 1989: 16), British statutes were extended to Ireland by the Reformatory Schools (Ireland) Act 1858 and the Industrial Schools (Ireland) Act 1868. These concerns were influenced less by the processes of industrialisation and urbanisation as in Britain, but more by extreme levels of destitution exacerbated by repeated famines. Notions of 'child-saving' and reform legitimated the incarceration of thousands of impoverished children in state funded and regulated reformatory and industrial schools (O'Sullivan and O'Donnell, 2012). Despite variations in their respective post-partition development, the institutions in both jurisdictions share a history, borrowing from Goldson (2009: 89), 'characterised by a catalogue of failure, misery, scandal, human suffering, abuse and violence'.

In addition to reformatory and industrial schools, the English Borstal system, introduced at the start of the twentieth century for training young offenders, was extended to Ireland in 1906 when a borstal opened in Clonmel gaol. It aimed to reform 16- to 21-year-old males in a secure environment via 'a harsh and repetitive regime' (Reidy, 2009: 112); however, its enduring legacy was the ineffective and destructive imprisonment of children in the adult penal systems (Moore, 2011). Post-partition borstal provision in Northern Ireland was replaced by Hydebank Young Offenders' Centre (YOC) for males and redesignated prison wings for females, provided at Hydebank since 2004 (Convery, 2014). In the Republic, borstal provision was never established for girls, and Clonmel was relocated and renamed as St Patrick's Institution in 1960, with no change to the regime (O'Sullivan and O'Donnell, 2012). The practice of imprisoning children in the adult penal system prevailed in Northern Ireland until 2012 and is due to end in the Republic in 2015.

A British development, the Probation of Offenders Act 1907, provides 'a common heritage' for the contemporary Probation Board for Northern Ireland (PBNI) and Probation Service in the Republic (Donnellan and McCaughey, 2010). It consolidated arrangements for offenders, particularly juveniles, released by the courts to be supervised by a probation officer (Gelsthorpe and Morris, 1994). A probation order was the only community sentence for children, with the exception of an attendance centre order in Northern Ireland, until community service orders for those aged 16 or over were introduced in Northern Ireland in 1979, and in the Republic in 1983. Community sentence provision was later extended under legislation introduced in 2002 and 2001, respectively.

The British Children Act 1908, which was also extended to Ireland, was 'largely concerned with protecting children from "moral danger" and dealing with the very small number of crimes committed by children' (Buckley and O'Sullivan, 2007: 62). *Inter alia*, it confirmed the minimum age of criminal responsibility at seven, created the juvenile court for those aged up to 15, prohibited imprisonment for children under 14 and restricted its use for those aged 14 and 15. 'The prevailing idea was that the juvenile was a wrongdoer' (Morris and Giller, 1987: 11) and, rather than 'an unalloyed reflection of humanitarian ideals', restrictions on imprisonment were motivated by concerns about destroying its deterrent value if used too soon (Gelsthorpe and Morris, 1994: 951).

Post-partition, juvenile justice provisions under the 1908 Act were largely re-enacted in the Children and Young Persons Acts (NI) 1950 and 1968, and not repealed in the Republic until the Children Act 2001. Legislative developments in Northern Ireland resulted in the rebranding of reformatory/industrial schools as 'training schools', an increased age of criminal responsibility of ten years, the definition of 16-year-olds as juveniles and a direction to courts to have regard to juveniles' welfare. Whilst O'Mahony and Deazley (2000: 64) described the last as 'a shift away from a policy of punishment', the only new sentence was an attendance centre order, which required the completion of a programme of work for 12 to 24 hours at the one attendance centre provided until 1995. The adult mode of trial, trial at adult courts and adult penal system imprisonment were retained. Also, Pinkerton (2003) argues that the 1968 Act was hurried through to avoid the welfare-oriented approaches envisaged by the 1969 English Act. The dominance of political conservatism, often attributed to Northern Irish people's conservative religious traditions (Boyle *et al.*, 1975), may partly explain this. Moreover, the outbreak of violence stimulated an official moral panic about juvenile crime in the 1970s (Caul, 1985) and was used to legitimise the 1973 opening of the former borstal, Lisnevin, as a secure training school which remained in use until 2003.

A further significant development was Whitefield House, opened in 1977 to provide non-residential assessment and intermediated treatment for children at risk of custody (McAuley and Cunningham, 1983). Whilst seen as 'a policy shift towards the development of community-based provision, stimulated by concern about the numbers [in training schools]' (Dawson *et al.*, 2004, cited in Seymour, 2013: 71), Lockhart (1995: 82) argues that 'diversionary services were allowed to develop piecemeal with no clear government strategy or funding'. He attributes this to training schools having thwarted the 1979 Black Report on a review of legislation and services relating to children. The report advocated diversion from prosecution and custody and proposed replacing training schools with a single secure unit for serious and persistent offenders. Delays in reform were also attributed to an 'alarming' lack of public debate, symptomatic of other preoccupations with poverty, violence and unemployment or, more cynically, due to apathy or smugness (McAuley and Cunningham, 1983: 95).

In the Republic of Ireland, the 1908 Act, as amended in 1941, defined a child as under 15 and a young person as 15 or 16, and age limits for prohibiting and restricting imprisonment were raised accordingly (Burke *et al.*, 1981). Also, the Criminal Justice Act 1960 provided for young offenders to be remanded to custody in institutions outside the formal criminal justice system rather than prison (Kilcommins *et al.*, 2004). Arguably, both developments reflect 'the changing use of coercive confinement' (O'Sullivan and O'Donnell, 2012: 256), rather than a change in its use, because the use of confinement persisted, albeit in alternative institutions. The state-sanctioned incarceration of thousands of children in institutions managed by religious orders, combined with 'a general inertia in relation to youth justice matters . . . left a vacuum of formal community-based criminal justice responses to young people in conflict with the law' (Seymour, 2013: 65). Although youth, voluntary and community sectors worked with young people in communities, this was 'often on an informal basis with limited resources and formal recognition' (Seymour, 2013: 65). Political neglect of the system persisted for over three decades, despite calls in a series of reports for fundamental juvenile justice reform (CRISS, 1970; Burke *et al.*, 1981; CIPS, 1985). While these reports and the Black Report languished, the UK and the Republic ratified the United Nations Convention on the Rights of the Child 1989 (CRC) in 1991 and 1992 respectively.

It is also noteworthy that reform was progressed in the absence of empirical research and robust statistical data relating to youth justice. As McCord *et al.* (2012: 13) note, despite 'recurrent criticism' and developments in this area, significant gaps remain in the knowledge base relating to youth crime and justice across both jurisdictions.

Northern Ireland

Political and social developments

Following over thirty years of conflict, the peace process was formally initiated by the 1998 Belfast/Good Friday Agreement. Developments included the devolution of political power, general economic improvements and criminal justice reform and oversight (Convery *et al.*, 2008). Reform was advanced by the devolution of criminal justice and policing matters following the 2010 Hillsborough Agreement, which included a commitment to ensure a children's rights compliant system (CLC, 2011). Whilst developments in youth justice are discussed in the next section, the context within which children live, from which they are drawn into the system and within which the system operates are discussed here. This discussion is particularly pertinent given the increasing evidence of substantial victim–offender overlap and concerns that offender, rather than childhood and victimhood, status dominates responses to children (Heber, 2014). Also, it is recognised that children are more likely to be victims than perpetrators of crime, and children with trauma experiences, mental health and special educational needs, learning difficulties and from looked-after care are over-represented in the youth justice system (YJRT, 2011; Kilpatrick, 2013).

Despite general economic improvements and reductions in conflict-related violence, the transition to a normalised society is ongoing. In particular, concerns have been raised about responses to the personal, social, educational and economic difficulties which marginalised children face (Horgan, 2011; Browne and Dwyer, 2014). Research demonstrates the negative impact of the conflict on children, including intergenerational trauma and paramilitary-style threats, assaults and shootings (McAlister, Scraton and Haydon, 2009), poor mental health, suicide and self-harm (Horgan, 2011). The state's response to these issues is regarded as inadequate (McClelland, 2006; RQIA, 2011). More recently, concerns have been raised about the proposed exclusion of under-16-year-olds from mental capacity legislation (DoJ, 2013) and shortfalls in provision for children with disabilities (Byrne *et al.*, 2014).

The political will to respond to concerns about segregated and underresourced communities has been questioned (McAlister, Scraton and Haydon, 2014). Ongoing issues for children include violence, rioting, joyriding, sectarianism, racism and negative views of the police (McAlister *et al.*, 2009; McAlister, Haydon and Scraton, 2013), demonisation and criminalisation (McAlister *et al.*, 2014), manipulation by adults to riot and negative policing experiences (Byrne and Jarman, 2011).

Many children's lives are also characterised by high levels of poverty, debt, limited access to facilities (Kent, 2014), drug and alcohol use (Kilpatrick, 2013), sexual abuse and exploitation (Marshall, 2014) and poor educational attainment and standards of health (Browne and Dwyer, 2014). Further concerns have been raised about the potential negative impact of welfare reforms on thousands of children (Horgan and Monteith, 2012) and high unemployment rates among 16- to 24-year-olds (Kent, 2014).

Evidence strongly indicates that concerns prevail about 'insufficient progress being made to improve the lives of our most marginalised and disadvantaged children and young people' (OFMDFM, 2006: 3). Indeed, most responses to a consultation on delivering social change advocate 'additional, targeted policies and services ... for all children and young people ... , including ... children in the youth justice system' (OFMDFM, 2014: 87).

Development of the youth justice framework

The Criminal Justice (NI) Order 1996 replicated the English sentencing framework for children (and adults). It determined that a sentence should primarily reflect the seriousness of the offence(s), with children who offend receiving their 'just deserts'. Probation and community service orders were placed at the upper end of the seriousness scale and aim to rehabilitate and protect the public from harm. Custodial sentences were to be restricted to 'genuinely serious offenders and not ... petty, yet troublesome, young offenders' (O'Mahony and Deazley, 2000: 60).

The emphasis on principles of proportionality and determinacy in sentencing complies with international benchmarks, but controversial aspects of the system were retained. The commitment to punishment prevailed, and the notion that children who have reached the age of ten have the same capacity for criminal intent as adults was reinforced by the removal of *doli incapax*, under the Criminal Justice (NI) Order 1998. Also, the Criminal Justice (Children) (NI) Order 1998 did not incorporate the CRC primacy of the child's best interests, or raise the age of criminal responsibility. Furthermore, 17-year-olds were treated as adults in the criminal justice system until 2005 (Moore, 2011). For the most part, the 1998 (Children) Order re-enacted 1968 provisions but renamed training schools as juvenile justice centres (JJC) and replaced indeterminate with determinate sentences, with half the sentence spent under probation supervision (Convery, 2014). In 2003 the JJC estate was rationalised to one centre (since 2007, Woodlands JJC), and secure custody was emphasised, despite research findings that higher security levels increase the possibility of re-offending (Curran *et al.*, 1995). The juvenile court was also renamed the youth court, but the requirement that courts have regard to the child's welfare, as opposed to their best interests, was retained (Moore, 2011). A further reform raised the age limit for prison custody from 14 to 15, but the imprisonment of children 'likely to injure themselves or others' was legislated for, despite criticism of such practices (HMCIP, 1995; 1997).

There is room for suspicion that the 1998 Act was hurried through in an attempt to exclude youth justice from the Criminal Justice Review (CJR), which followed from the Belfast/Good Friday Agreement (Convery, 2014). However, the Criminal Justice (Children) Lobby Group successfully campaigned for its inclusion, and CJR recommendations on restorative justice practices were enacted under the Justice (NI) Act 2002 (Moore, 2011). Whilst this represented 'fundamental reform of the system' (Seymour, 2013: 59), the justice-orientated framework of youth justice was reflected in the system's principal aim, namely public protection. The minimum age of criminal responsibility remains ten years, and agencies have to consider the welfare of children, rather than their best interests. The principal aim of the Youth Justice Agency (YJA), established under the Act, is to reduce youth crime and build confidence in the youth justice system. Woodlands JJC and restorative justice provisions come under its authority.

Restorative measures include diversionary youth conferences and youth conference reparation and community responsibility orders. A diversionary conference provides for a child to be diverted from court proceedings by the Public Prosecution Service (PPS) to a youth conference if s/he admits to the offence and consents to participate. Though not a conviction, it attracts a criminal record (YJRT, 2011) and the Children's Law Centre (CLC, 2011) has questioned the extent to which restorative approaches are truly diversionary as envisaged by the CJR.

For children proceeded against, with some exceptions, the court is required to offer a youth conference order on an admission or finding of guilt and pending consent. Where consent is not given, reparation or community responsibility orders or another disposal may be imposed. Statutory responsibility for restorative orders lies with the YJA, while the PBNI is responsible for probation and community service orders and the community element of the JJC Order (JJCO). However, 'most, if not all' children under supervision during the JJCO community element also work with the YJA 'as they look to complete other community sentences such as youth conference orders' (DoJ, 2014a: 16).

Seymour (2013: 59) recognised that, though 'restorative conferencing has been positively endorsed ... some concerns have been raised about its impact and effectiveness for persistent or prolific offenders who may be subject to repeat conferences'. Maruna (2008, cited in Muncie, 2011: 47) also found that conferencing could 'be received as demeaning, punitive and primarily designed to induce disintegrative "shame"'. Further concerns include changing trends in the length and use of conference plans, which waste resources and may increase risk of offending and undermine children's rights (YJRT, 2011).

The 2002 Act brought 17-year-olds within the jurisdiction of the youth court, but restricted the use of JJCOs and maintained prison custody for them (Moore, 2011). In response to criticism by the NI Human Rights Commission and prisons and criminal justice inspectorates, girls were removed from adult custody under the Criminal Justice (NI) Order 2008 (Moore, 2011). Following recommendations in 2011 by the Youth Justice and Prison Review Teams, all children were removed from the adult prison system during 2012. This is an extremely significant development and, whilst an administrative fix, legislative reform has been proposed to ensure all 16- and 17-year-olds serve any custodial sentence in the JJC (DoJ, 2014b). This includes public protection sentences (indeterminate and extended custodial sentences) introduced under the 2008 Order for sexual and violent offences with risk of serious harm.

The 2008 Order also introduced new powers for the use of curfews, supported by electronic monitoring as a condition of bail or supervision under licence, or as a requirement of a probation or combination order, a youth conference order or the community element of a custody probation or JJC order (Seymour, 2013). The CLC (2011) raised concerns that the electronic monitoring of children was introduced in the absence of proper consideration of human rights, its operation in England and Wales and the particular circumstances of Northern Ireland. It also noted the 'substantial use' and 'apparent disproportionate overuse' of electronic tagging of children (CLC, 2011: 105). Arguably, such approaches bring into question the extent to which a philosophy of restorative justice truly underpins youth justice. As Seymour (2013: 76) observes: 'Northern Ireland has not been immune from policy influences from other parts of the UK that emphasize strategies of risk assessment, management and control in the supervision of young offenders in the community'.

Youth justice responses

In 2011/12 offences by children accounted for 9 per cent of all offences, and 43 per cent of offences by children were first offences (Graham and Damkat, 2014a). In 2011/12, one year proven re-offending rates were 26 per cent for diversionary disposals, 48 per cent for non-supervised community disposals and 56 per cent for community supervision. In relation to custody, of 36 children released, 25 re-offended (percentage is not shown where total number is less than 50) (Duncan, 2014).

Policing

The Police Service of Northern Ireland (PSNI) plays a key role in the diversion of children from prosecution. The PPS also has a central role, with prosecutors taking decisions to prosecute or impose formal diversionary approaches on children who admit guilt (CJINI, 2011). In 2011/12 65 per cent of offences committed by children were diverted from prosecution (Graham and Damkat, 2014a). PPS-ordered conferences accounted for 40 per cent of diversionary measures, but a breakdown of cautions and informed warnings is not provided. Re-offending rates for each in 2011/12 were 36 per cent, 28 per cent and 17 per cent respectively (Duncan, 2014).

As Kilpatrick (2013) notes, Youth Engagement Clinics, initiated in 2012, require the PSNI, the PPS and YJA to identify cases suitable for formal diversion before the prosecution stage. Clinics involve a PSNI Youth Diversion Officer (YDO) and YJA practitioner meeting eligible children, with their parent/guardian and potentially their solicitor, to discuss their options. The diversionary options available following an admission of guilt (informed warnings, restorative cautions, youth conferences and referrals to community-based restorative justice schemes) are recorded on children's criminal records. To 'speed up' case processing times in the youth court and to allow children 'to understand the consequences of their offending behaviour and get the support they need to move on with their lives', clinics will be rolled out to all police Districts (DoJ, 2014c).

Police discretion not to take formal action in dealing with low-level offending has also been re-introduced (CJINI, 2011). Furthermore, the 2010 PSNI Speedy Justice policy provides for on-the-spot discretionary disposals for minor offences or penalty notices for disorder. Its implementation has raised a number of concerns, including lack of YDO consultation (McCracken, 2013), potential 'net-widening' effects and disclosure on criminal record checks (Kilpatrick, 2013).

Despite some positive developments, additional concerns remain, including, *inter alia*, the over-use of stop and search practices, inappropriate use and disclosure of discretionary and other diversionary disposals, officers' poor knowledge and skills base and the differential treatment of children by location (Kilpatrick, 2013). Further concerns about diversionary measures include the equitable treatment of children and children's understanding of, and reasons for, admissions of guilt and consent (CLC, 2011).

Additional concerns relate to the use of custodial remands, particularly their over-use for looked-after children and inconsistent practices across policing Districts (McCracken, 2014). The Police and Criminal Evidence (NI) Order 1989 (PACE) provides for the custodial detention of a child pending a court appearance when the child is charged with an offence and bail cannot be granted or any place of safety secured. Whilst the Criminal Justice Inspection (CJINI, 2013: 34) 'found ongoing evidence that numbers [on PACE] were being kept down', as documented below, there has been a significant increase in PACE remands to the JJC.

Courts

The youth court deals with children charged with any criminal offence except murder, and can commit children charged with serious offences to the adult Crown Court. In 2013 the youth court disposed of 2,256 cases, 32 of which were committed to the Crown Court (NICTS, 2014). Statistics for 2012 show that 1,185 children were convicted at the youth court and 14 at the Crown Court (Graham and Damkat, 2014b). Orders imposed on an admission or finding of guilt included 521 youth conference orders, 52 community responsibility orders, 5 attendance centre orders and 124 JJCOs. Monetary and other orders, such as Probation, were not reported in relation to age, but McCaughey (2011) notes that 148 orders were supervised by the PBNI in 2009/10.

The CLC (2011) draws attention to a range of concerns regarding children's experiences of court, including the extent of their understanding and participation; the absence of safeguards for children with mental health difficulties, literacy or language problems, special educational needs or disabilities; lawyers' limited training and skills; security firms escorting children to court from the JJC; the use of handcuffs; poor conditions in court cells; use of live links from the JJC; and avoidable delays. The CLC (2011: 120) noted the particular impact of delay on children remanded to custody and that 'youth summons cases took on average 84 days from first appearance at court to disposal – almost twice as long as adult summons cases'. Figures for 2013 (NICTS, 2014) highlight continued delays, with an average waiting time of 70 days from date of first hearing to date of disposal. The impact of proposed Statutory Time Limits, namely the setting of limits within which cases should be completed, remains to be seen (CJINI, 2013).

An area of 'great concern' for the CLC (2011: 109) relates to bail and remand decisions, which indicate that custody is not being used as a last resort. The CLC (2011: 111) also criticises the courts' imposition of unrealistic bail conditions and advocates 'a renewed emphasis and investment on the development of bail fostering and appropriate accommodation schemes for all children and young people as an alternative to detention while pending trial'. The CJINI (2013) notes substantial progress in the provision of the YJA bail information and support scheme, but limited progress in relation to accommodation schemes. However, it believes that the situation should improve pending the introduction of the Draft Bail Bill which proposes the best interests of the child is a primary consideration and prohibits the use of custody on the grounds of lack of alternative accommodation.

These proposals should not mask the persistent failure to adopt the principle of decriminal-isation and raise the minimum age of criminal responsibility. Similarly the focus on reparative disposals should not detract from concerns about children's access to justice and the extent to which restorative justice ideals are reflected in practice. Arguably, apparent progressive restorative practices fail to address concerns about unjust responses to children and reflect the prevailing idea that the child is a 'wrongdoer' and worthy of punishment.

Community sentences

The most common community-based order imposed on children is a youth conference order. In 2013/14, 44 per cent of referrals from the courts and PPS to the YJA, Youth Justice Services, were court-ordered conferences and 4 per cent were attendance centre, community responsibility and reparation orders (Decodts and O'Neill, 2014). The number of referrals applied to 977 individual children, a rate of 5.2 per 1,000 children aged 10 to 17 (Decodts and O'Neill, 2014). The highest proportion of children were male, aged 17, Roman Catholic and from Belfast.

According to Decodts and O'Neill (2014: 26), the aims of youth conferencing are 'to balance the needs of the victim and the young offender by agreeing plans of action which satisfy the victim and create opportunities for the young person to make amends and stop committing crime'. A child must admit the offence and be willing to participate in a court-ordered conference, which normally leads to an agreed plan for the child. Plans comprise various elements, 'relevant to the child, the impact of the offence and their offending behaviour' (Decodts and O'Neill, 2014: 26). They may require an apology, payment of compensation, reparation or community service, the use of curfews or electronic monitoring, or participation in supervised or specialised programmes or treatments (Seymour, 2013). The CJINI (2013: 27–28) found a 're-balancing and re-direction of conferences' compared with 'the previous trend ... towards creating an onerous list of tasks; an increasing number of plans ... longer than six months; and conferences disproportionate to the offences committed'. For example, 60 per cent of plans in 2012/13 were for six months or more compared with 73 per cent in 2010/11 (Decodts and O'Neill, 2014). Further concerns raised (CLC, 2011) include the need for a child to understand the consequences of a guilt admission.

In relation to children under probation supervision, the court may also impose other conditions. Rather than the routine use of offending behaviour programmes, the focus tends to be on the one-to-one supervisory relationship, supported by community-based programmes, such as family support and mentoring, vocational and educational services, substance abuse treatment and community-based restorative justice projects (Seymour, 2013). PBNI youth cases comprise older children who have exhausted other statutory community-based disposals or refused to consent to them, or where offence seriousness is deemed to justify a higher-tariff response (Seymour, 2013).

Detention

Woodlands JJC, with staff capacity for 36 children, provides for the detention of 48 boys and girls on remand, sentenced or under PACE (Decodts and O'Neill, 2014). The Youth Justice Review Team (2011) commends it as a 'state-of-the-art' facility and notes the dramatic fall in the daily population of children detained in custody since the late 1990s. However, it raises concerns that the JJC is not used as a last resort or for its primary intended purpose, namely the detention of children serving a JJCO for six months to two years, with half the sentence spent in custody and half under supervision.

A total of 196 children were detained in the JJC in 2013/14 (Decodts and O'Neill, 2014). Whilst this equates to 1 in every 1,000 children aged 10 to 17, the rate varies from 0 to 2.9, depending on the area from which children are admitted. The largest proportion of children detained were from Belfast, male, aged 16 and Roman Catholic. The proportion of looked-after children (36 per cent) is clearly disproportionate to the 2 per cent of 10- to 17-year-olds living in care (McCracken, 2014). In 2013 looked-after children were detained more than twice as often as in 2011 and represented 44 per cent of PACE admissions (McCracken, 2014).

The over-representation of looked-after children, and apparent over-use of remand and PACE, brings into question the extent to which recurrent concerns (Convery and Moore, 2006; YJRT, 2011) have been addressed. As Decodts and O'Neill (2014) note, whilst 2013/14 was the first year since 2009/10 that the number of children detained did not exceed 200, JJC workloads increased by over a third (34 per cent) compared with 2012/13, due to an increase in PACE, remand and sentence transactions. Of the total average daily population of 27 children, 52 per cent were on remand, which is twice the reported proportion of the juvenile custodial population on remand in England and Wales (YJRT, 2011). Also of concern is that about half of the children detained on PACE in 2013/14 were released, rather than remanded or sentenced to custody (Decodts and O'Neill, 2014). Questions, therefore, remain about the use of the JJC as a holding centre rather than as a last resort.

Republic of Ireland

Youth justice

Diversion forms the cornerstone of the Children Act 2001 (heretofore described as the 2001 Act), which is the primary legislative mechanism for youth justice and which emphasises the use of detention as a measure of last resort. Youth justice has sidestepped some of the more punitive youth justice trends characteristic of other Anglophone countries in recent decades. One explanation is that political neglect of the youth justice agenda for almost a hundred years and the slow pace at which the 2001 Act was implemented may have buffered the system from the worst excesses of punitiveness. The first structure to co-ordinate youth justice service delivery – the Irish Youth Justice Service (IYJS) – was only established in 2005, and this signalled the commencement of many of the provisions under the 2001 Act. The roll-out of youth justice over the last decade has coincided with a period of profound public anger in the aftermath of the publication of the Ryan Report detailing the harsh regimes and abusive treatment of children in institutions between 1922 and 2000 (Commission to Inquire into Child Abuse, 2009). It is suggested that the painful legacies of unfettered institutionalisation stand as a contemporary reminder of the importance of retaining children within their homes and communities except in extenuating circumstances. With some limited exceptions, the 2001 Act as amended restricts the reporting, publishing or broadcasting of any identifying information about children's involvement in criminal proceedings, and, as a result, their involvement in crime tends not to be sensationalised through media outlets or politicised to any great extent.

This jurisdiction has not been completely immune from punitive elements in the development of the youth justice system. The minimum age of criminal responsibility was increased to 12 years under the 2001 Act. However, retrograde amendments to the Act under the Criminal Justice Act (CJA) 2006 resulted in the abolition of the presumption of *doli incapax* and a lowering of the age of criminal responsibility to ten years for children charged with murder, manslaughter and serious sexual offences. Furthermore, introduction of the Behaviour Order under the CJA 2006 mirrored many of the aspects of the anti-social behaviour orders (ASBOs) in England and Wales, but, in a case that demonstrates the unpredictable relationship between law, policy and practice, only three orders have been made against children since their inception in 2008. While the kernel of the youth justice system may be described as welfare-orientated, it embodies a spectrum of theoretical underpinnings ranging from rehabilitative to actuarial justice. The risk-factor-prevention paradigm was relatively inconspicuous on the youth justice landscape until very recently, when uniform risk assessment was introduced on diversionary projects for children at the entry point to the criminal justice system and for children deemed 'at risk' of offending.

Information on the nature of children's offending is largely restricted to official crime data published on an annual basis (see An Garda Síochána, 2013). In 2012, 24,069 offences by children were recorded, most of which were minor in nature. Public order, theft and damage to property and the environment are the main categories, accounting for almost two-thirds of all crimes by children. Alcohol underpins much of the narrative that emerges on children's involvement in crime and anti-social behaviour (Horgan, 2013; IYJS, 2009). The role of alcohol must be viewed against the backdrop of a cultural acceptance of excessive alcohol consumption and public tolerance of drunkenness (see Seymour and Mayock, 2009). While a considerable proportion of alcohol-related offending relates to minor public order incidents, such incidents have the potential to escalate into more serious and violent events (National Crime Council, 2003). The proliferation of organised crime and associated violence in recent decades has revolved around vicious struggles for the control of the drugs market (Hourigan, 2012). Children in a small number of communities have been drawn into peripheral gang involvement in an attempt to gain status with their peers, to acquire financial resources, as a result of fear and intimidation, or to repay drug debts (Griffin and Kelleher, 2010). The implications of such activities include an elevated risk of violent victimisation for these children, as well as an increased risk of re-offending.

Pre-court diversion

The statutory Garda Juvenile Diversion Programme (GJDP) is the primary mechanism employed to divert children aged ten to 17 years from further offending. All offences are eligible for referral to the GJDP, and the Director, who is a senior police officer, is responsible for deciding the outcome of each case. In 2012 over half of the 12,246 children referred received an informal caution, and a further 15 per cent were formally cautioned. Children subject to formal cautions are placed under the supervision of a Juvenile Liaison Officer (JLO) for a period of up to 12 months and may have conditions attached. A victim or victim representative may attend the formal caution or make a written submission, and, under these circumstances, the caution becomes known as a restorative caution (1,036 restorative cautions were given in 2012). Although legislative provision exists for a restorative conference to be facilitated as part of a formal caution, available evidence suggests that it is rarely utilised (An Garda Síochána, 2010).

The operation of the GJDP has been criticised over its lack of transparency and accountability, due process and compliance with international children's rights standards (Kilkelly, 2011; Walsh, 2008). Discretion is a key facet of decision-making about children in the criminal justice system given variances in their ages, levels of maturity and the circumstances of their personal lives and offending behaviour (Seymour, 2013). At the same time, research suggests that a high level of discretion must be counterbalanced with a corresponding level of accountability to mitigate actual or perceived unfair or discriminatory practices (Eadie and Canton, 2002). It is concerning, therefore, that, despite the GJDP being entirely administered and managed by An Garda Síochána, and the wide-ranging discretion afforded to the Director in deciding the outcomes for children referred to the Programme, it is not subject to any form of independent monitoring. In addition, the GJDP has never been independently evaluated. As a result, little is known about the decision-making processes for children referred to the Programme.[1] A further concern is that there is almost no opportunity for children or their parent(s)/guardian(s) to appeal decisions about their treatment. The only option available is to make a complaint to the Garda Síochána Ombudsman Commission (GSOC). However, the complaint procedures are neither 'age-appropriate [n]or fully accessible to those under 18 years' (Kilkelly, 2011:148). This assertion is supported in Feeney and Freeman's study (2010: 9), which found that a very small proportion of young people aged 15–19 years in the Dublin Metropolitan North police district complained after being subjected to what they considered unacceptable behaviour by police, and none had made a complaint to GSOC.

Net-widening refers to the process whereby the youth justice system expands so that it draws in greater numbers of children who may not otherwise have entered the realm. In the absence of empirical data, it is not possible to comment with authority on the extent to which children who in the past may have been dealt by way of 'a telling-off' from a member of the Gardaí are now brought under the remit of the youth justice system via the GJDP. What can be said is that provisions introduced under the CJA 2006 to extend the remit of the GJDP to include 10- and 11-year-olds and children engaged in anti-social behaviour provide the foundation for net-widening in theory, if not in practice.

Garda Youth Diversion Projects

In addition to the Garda Juvenile Diversion Programme (GJDP), a network of 100 crime prevention initiatives known as Garda Youth Diversion Projects (GYDP) has developed over the last two decades. These projects work with children aged 10–17 and focus on diversion through addressing personal development, promoting civic responsibility and improving long-term employment prospects (IYJS, 2009). In 2011 just over half of the 5,673 referrals consisted of children who had been cautioned for an offence, and the remainder were described as 'at risk' of offending (IYJS, 2012a). The projects are managed locally by a range of youth and community-based organisations and are centrally resourced by the IYJS in cooperation with An Garda Síochána.

The policy rhetoric underpinning these projects is distinct from other strands of youth justice to the extent that it emphasises actuarial principles of risk and behavioural management and control: specifically, potential threats posed by children to social order. A report by the IYJS (2012a: 6) identifies, for example, that the aim of the projects is 'to support An Garda Síochána at local level by impacting upon the attitudes, behaviours and circumstances that give rise to youth offending'. Furthermore, it states that, by working with children 'significantly at risk', the projects contribute 'to improving the quality of life within communities and enhancing Garda/community relations' (IYJS, 2012a: 8). Following changes introduced by the IYJS in 2009, organisations involved in delivering projects are obliged to gather local youth crime data annually from Gardaí when planning their interventions. The practice of formalised risk assessment was introduced in 2010, and, while data are used to target individual interventions, organisations must also include aggregated risk assessment data in their annual plans. A further requirement is that organisations must describe progress in relation to three standard behavioural outcomes: reduced impulsiveness, improved empathy and improved pro-social behaviour in addition to their individual project outcomes (IYJS, 2012b; IYJS, 2012c). These requirements are not insignificant given that each project's annual plan is reviewed by the IYJS and An Garda Síochána, and funding is contingent on satisfactory compliance with the stipulated criteria. These changes represent a new departure in the governance of children deemed 'at risk' of offending or re-offending. The approach resonates with the type of payment-by-results models introduced in England and Wales in 2010 with the stated purpose of 'incentivising' criminal justice partners with responsibility for youth justice service delivery at local level to achieve greater reductions in offending rates (Ministry of Justice, 2010). Success is predicated on the metrics of crime reduction and behavioural change, and consequently the space within which children's interests can be prioritised over risk and behavioural management concerns is considerably narrowed for the organisations tasked with delivering the projects.

The Children Court

The Children Court has jurisdiction over all minor offences and a discretionary power to deal summarily with children charged with indictable offences. The exceptions are murder, rape and related offences, which are tried by the Central Criminal Court. Data on outcomes for defendants dealt with by the Children Court shows that approximately 3 to 4 per cent of children – accounting for an average of 115 children – are sent forward for trial in a higher Court each year (Courts Service, 2009–2013).

There are a number of provisions contained in the 2001 Act that in practice should acknowledge and protect the special status of children, such as: that the time children have to wait for proceedings should be kept to a minimum, that only those directly related to the proceedings are permitted to attend, that the Children Court should sit in a different building or room or at a different time to other court proceedings, and that children should be kept separate from adult defendants. Existing research identifies substantive gaps between the legislation and its application and blames an absence of implementation guidance and standards (Kilkelly, 2008). Not only does this disjuncture deviate from legislative requirements and international children's rights standards (see Kilkelly, 2008), it also reduces potential opportunities for the courtroom to act as a platform for responding to children's offending behaviour. Weijers (2004: 27) argues that engaging children in the courtroom in 'moral communication' or 'dialogue … about the moral consequences of their wrongdoing' creates the foundation upon which the consequences of offending behaviour may be better understood. With the exception of a practice directive relating to cases involving children under 18 in the Dublin Metropolitan Children Court (DC04) in 2014, there have been no advancements made to implement the provisions of the 2001 Act as they pertain to the Children Court.

The length of time to finalise cases in the Children Court is an enduring problem in the youth justice system. In a study of children on remand, Seymour and Butler (2008) concluded that undue delay in case processing placed children at greater risk of re-offending, of breaching their bail conditions and, consequently, of being detained on remand. Furthermore, there is no designated bail support provision for children, making the issue of delays in finalising cases all the more problematic.

Court-ordered conferencing

Two family conference options were introduced under the 2001 Act. The first, a Family Welfare Conference, is convened where serious concerns exist about the welfare of a child involved in criminal proceedings. In such circumstances, the court may dismiss the charge. Under the second option the court instructs the Probation Service to convene a Family Conference where a child accepts responsibility for the offence and consents to the conference. The conference is based on restorative justice principles and involves the child, the family, the victim and relevant others (see Burke, 2006). One of the most notable features is how infrequently it has been used, with an average of 28 referrals annually between 2011 and 2013 (Probation Service, 2014).

Sentencing principles and community sanctions

The courts are obliged to consider a number of principles specific to the rights of child defendants under Section 96 of the 2001 Act. These include that children have the same rights in law as their adult counterparts, that they have the right to be heard and to participate in any court proceedings that affect them, and that criminal proceedings should not be used for the sole purpose of providing for their care or protection needs. Furthermore, the Act stipulates that any sanction imposed on the child should take account of their age and level of maturity, not exceed that which would be given to an adult and cause the least possible amount of interruption to the child's legitimate activities. To this end, explicit reference is made to the use of detention as a measure of last resort. While these principles are a commendable aspect of the legislation, the absence of guidance with regard to their implementation is a notable gap, and one which likely contributes to disparities in court practices.

The 2001 Act makes provision for a number of community-based sentencing options (see Seymour, 2012). However, these orders are used only in a small number of cases, and the standard probation order, as adjudicated for under the Probation of Offenders Act 1907, remains the most common community-based supervised order. The youth division of the Probation Service known as Young Persons' Probation has responsibility for assessing and supervising children on community-based orders. The court has discretion to strengthen probation orders through the use of additional requirements, but there are no specific community-based provisions for children at the higher end of the sentencing scale, with the exception of the Community Service Order. Due to a dearth of guidance and robust data on sentencing outcomes, it is not possible to ascertain if the courts exhaust less restrictive options before imposing detention. More generally, limited provision of services to address specialist care needs or mental health and addiction problems compounds the risk of detention for vulnerable children (Seymour and Butler, 2008).

A common judicial practice in the Children Court is the practice of adjourned supervision, whereby the judge postpones sentencing and places the child under the supervision of the Probation Service (Probation Service, 2014). Cases may be adjourned for varying lengths of time, from weeks to months, and sometimes involve multiple adjournments (Seymour, 2013). Where multiple adjournments occur, children are retained under the radar of the criminal justice system for undefined periods of time. Such practices potentially constitute a breach of international guidance on children's rights to an expedient finalisation of criminal proceedings against them.

Detention

Boys up to the age of 17 and girls under 18 are detained on remand or under sentence in the Children Detention School system, which operates a regime based on care, education and rehabilitation. The numbers of detained children declined dramatically following the implementation of the 2001 Act, and snapshots of the daily population between 2009 and 2013 point to an average daily occupancy of 39 children (HIQA, 2012; 2013; IYJS, 2010). Noteworthy, however, is that the vast majority of admissions (over 80 per cent) involve children on remand (IYJS, 2011). This is concerning given that many children detained on remand are not subsequently given a custodial sentence, nor are the reasons for their detention necessarily related to the seriousness of their offence or risk of re-offending (Freeman, 2008; Seymour and Butler, 2008).

In contrast to their female counterparts, males aged 17 are detained within the prison system at St Patrick's Institution (remand) and Wheatfield Place of Detention (sentenced). Previously all males were detained at St Patrick's Institution, a place of detention that has endured despite persistent calls for its closure (CIPS, 1985; Ombudsman for Children's Office, 2011). However, a report from the Inspector of Prisons in May 2013, highlighting serious concerns about the safety and protection of detainees, acted as the catalyst for transferring most children and young people out of the facility. The detention of children within the prison estate will continue until the completion of a new National Children Detention facility in 2015. It is anticipated that for 17-year-old males the new facility will mark the end of harsh and punitive regimes of detention that violated basic rights and were entirely inadequate to meet their needs (Inspector of Prisons, 2013).

Convergence and divergence across the jurisdictions

Despite a shared legislative history, both the youth justice systems have taken diverse pathways in their contemporary growth. According to Goldson (2011: 15) restorative justice 'has induced a paradigm shift in global criminal justice (in general) and transnational youth justice (in particular)'. As outlined earlier, restorative justice – in the form of youth conferencing – forms the cornerstone of the youth justice system in Northern Ireland, but remains on the periphery of the system in the Republic, where welfare is the dominant philosophy. In practice, both youth justice systems incorporate elements of welfare, justice, restorative justice, children's rights, actuarial justice and punishment. In this regard, they follow a growing international trend towards complex and multi-faceted systems, differentiated only by the extent to which they emphasise a particular philosophy (Dünkel, 2013).

The unique histories and circumstances from which modern youth justice evolved in Northern Ireland and the Republic created the backdrop from which the punitive philosophy underlying youth justice in England and Wales from the mid to late 1990s onwards was circumvented. However, neither jurisdiction emerged unscathed from the influence of their nearest neighbours, and examples of legal and policy transfer include the abolition of the presumption of *doli incapax*, the introduction of ASBOs/Behaviour Orders and provision for electronic monitoring in Northern Ireland. Similarities also exist with regard to the age of criminal responsibility. Northern Ireland, alongside England and Wales, has the lowest age threshold for criminal responsibility in Europe, and while the age of criminal responsibility is 12 years in the Republic, children as young as 10 and 11 years can be held criminally responsible for offences of murder, manslaughter and serious sexual crime. This places both jurisdictions out of line with their European counterparts where the minimum age of criminal responsibility is more commonly 14 years and above (Goldson, 2013).

There appears to be greater convergence with the rest of Europe in the practice of transferring children from the juvenile to the adult criminal courts. In both jurisdictions, the cases of children charged with murder and other serious offences are heard in adult criminal court. Furthermore, cases can be transferred from the jurisdiction of the Children Court in the Republic and the Youth Court in Northern Ireland to the adult courts. In reality, the numbers of children transferred in both jurisdictions is modest which resonates with the broader European experience (Dünkel, 2013). Nevertheless, the practice risks exposing children to the full rigour of the criminal justice system and reduces the protections afforded to them in the youth justice system.

One of the most noteworthy features about both youth justice systems is the substantial decline in the population of children detained under sentence since the mid- to late 1990s. As discussed earlier, reform occurred in very particular contexts: against the background of post-Conflict transition in Northern Ireland and the legacy of an institutionalised past in the Republic. In tandem, the committee established to monitor the implementation of the CRC, and children's rights and penal reform organisations in both jurisdictions, were, and are, important instigators and invigilators of change. The legislation provided the structural basis for reform in embedding the principle of detention as a measure of last resort. However in the absence of specific sentencing guidance, its implementation both in theory and practice has relied on the commitment of the judiciary and criminal justice practitioners to diversion (Seymour, 2013). The high numbers of children detained on remand in both jurisdictions, relative to the sentenced population, cautions against complacency. Furthermore, while the majority of children are diverted out of the formal justice system in both jurisdictions, caution must be exercised in the absence of research that could offset disquiet about due process and net-widening concerns. Notwithstanding these issues, the modest numbers detained under sentence is seen as a very positive outcome from processes of reform instigated in both jurisdictions more than twenty years previously.

Goldson and Hughes (2010: 212) suggest that the CRC and a number of other human rights instruments including the Beijing Rules, the Riyadh Guidelines and the Havana Rules provide 'a unifying framework for youth justice policy on a global scale'. Junger-Tas (2006: 526) further opines that the importance of the CRC is located within the values it espouses and 'its moral appeal to realize these values in practice'. The language of children's rights is evident in the discourse relating to children in conflict with the law in Northern Ireland and the Republic, and without question has been influential in framing the narratives of the systems. Unfortunately, the extent to which the values underpinning children's rights have translated into practice has been slow, resulting in an over-emphasis on responsibility without corresponding recognition of children's rights to protection from poverty, violence and victimisation, as well as access to basic education, health and social services. These concerns are echoed to varying degrees in youth justice systems internationally and have been identified as obstructions to the development and sustainability of progressive youth justice regimes (Goshe, 2015).

References

An Garda Síochána (2010) *Annual Report of the Committee Appointed to Monitor the Effectiveness of the Diversion Programme 2009*. Dublin: Garda Office for Children and Youth Affairs.

—— (2013) *Annual Report of the Committee Appointed to Monitor the Effectiveness of the Diversion Programme 2012*. Dublin: Garda Youth Diversion Office.

Barnes, J. (1989) *Irish Industrial Schools, 1868–1908*. Dublin: Irish Academic Press.

Boyle, K., Hadden, T. and Hillyard, P. (1975) *Law and State: The Case of Northern Ireland*. London: Martin Robertson.

Browne, B. and Dwyer, C. (2014) 'Navigating Risk: Understanding the Impact of the Conflict on Children and Young People in Northern Ireland Studies', *Conflict & Terrorism*, 37(9): 792–805.

Buckley, H. and O'Sullivan, E. (2007) 'The Interface between Youth Justice and Child Protection in Ireland' in M. Hill, A. Lockyer and F. Stone (eds) *Youth Justice and Child Protection*. London: Jessica Kingsley.

Burke, H., Carney, C. and Cook, G. (eds) (1981) *Youth and Justice: Young Offenders in Ireland*. Dublin: Turoe Press.

Burke, M. (2006) 'Implementing Probation and Welfare Family Conferences', unpublished MSc thesis, IPA, Dublin.

Byrne, B., Harper, C., Shea Irvine, R., Russell, H. and Fitzpatrick, B. (2014) *UNCRPD: Shortfalls in Public Policy and Programme Delivery in Northern Ireland Relative to the Articles of the UNCRPD*. Belfast: Equality Commission for Northern Ireland.

Byrne, J. and Jarman, N. (2011) 'Ten Years After Patten: Young People and Policing in Northern Ireland', *Youth Society*, 43(2): 433–452.

Caul, B. (1985) 'A Comparative Study of the Juvenile Justice Systems of Northern Ireland and the Republic of Ireland', unpublished PhD thesis, Trinity College Dublin.

Children and Young Persons Review Group (1979) *Report of the Children and Young Persons Review Group (The Black Report)*. Belfast: The Stationery Office.

CIPS (Committee of Inquiry into the Penal System) (1985) *Report of the Committee of Inquiry into the Penal System (The Whitaker Report)*. Dublin: Stationery Office.

CJINI (Criminal Justice Inspection Northern Ireland) (2010) *Not a Marginal Issue: Mental Health and the Criminal Justice System in Northern Ireland*. Belfast: CJINI.

—— (2011) *Youth Diversion: A Thematic Inspection of Youth Diversion in the Criminal Justice System in Northern Ireland*. Belfast: CJINI.

—— (2013) *Monitoring of Progress on Implementation of the Youth Justice Review Recommendations*. Belfast: CJINI.

CLC (Children's Law Centre) (2011) *Response to the Independent Youth Justice Review Team's Review of Youth Justice in Northern Ireland*. Belfast: DoJ.

Commission to Inquire into Child Abuse (2009) *Report of the Commission to Inquire into Child Abuse*. Available at: http://www.childabusecommission.ie/rpt/pdfs/ (accessed 23 July 2014).

Committee of Inquiry into the Penal System (CIPS) (1985) *Report of the Committee of Inquiry into the Penal System (The Whitaker Report)*. Dublin: Stationery Office.

Convery, U. (2014) 'Locked in the Past: An Historical Analysis of the Legal Framework of Custody for Children in Northern Ireland', *European Journal of Criminology*, 11(2): 251–269.

Convery, U. and Moore, L. (2006) *Still in Our Care: Protecting Children's Rights in Custody in Northern Ireland*. Belfast: NIHRC.

Convery, U., Haydon, D., Moore, L. and Scraton, P. (2008) 'Children, Rights and Justice in Northern Ireland: Community and Custody', *Youth Justice*, 8(3): 245–263.

Courts Service (2009–2013) *Annual Reports of the Courts Service 2009–2013*. Dublin: Courts Service.

CRISS (Committee on Reformatory and Industrial Schools Systems) (1970) *Reformatory and Industrial Schools Systems Report (The Kennedy Report)*. Dublin: Stationery Office.

Curran, D., Kilpatrick, R., Young, V. and Wilson, D. (1995) 'Longitudinal Aspects of Reconviction: Secure and Open Intervention with Juvenile Offenders in Northern Ireland', *The Howard Journal*, 34(2): 97–123.

Dawson, H., Dunn, S., Morgan, V. and Hayes, A. (2004) *Evaluation of Youth Justice Agency Community Services, NIO Research and Statistical Series: Report No. 11*. Belfast: Northern Ireland Office, Statistics and Research Branch.

Decodts, M. and O'Neill, N. (2014) *Youth Justice Agency Annual Workload Statistics 2013/14*. Belfast: YJA.

Department of Justice (DoJ) (2013) *Consultation on Proposals to Extend Mental Capacity Legislation to the Criminal Justice System in Northern Ireland: Report on Responses and Way Forward*. Belfast. DoJ.

—— (2014a) *Consultation: Custodial Arrangements for Children in Northern Ireland*. Belfast: DoJ.

—— (2014b) *Custodial Arrangements for Children: Summary of Responses and Way Forward*. Belfast: DoJ.

—— (2014c) 'Justice Minister David Ford Has Announced Plans to Roll-Out Youth Engagement (YE) Clinics to All Police Districts Across Northern Ireland, Following a Successful Pilot in Belfast'. Available at: http://www.dojni.gov.uk/ford-announces-innovative-new-approach-to-youth-offending (accessed 30 September 2014).

Donnellan, M. and McCaughey, B. (2010) 'The Public Protection Advisory Group: A Model for Structured Co-operation', *Irish Probation Journal*, 7: 6–14.

Duncan, L. (2014) *Youth Reoffending in Northern Ireland (2011/12 Cohort)*. Belfast: Department of Justice.

Dünkel, F. (2013) 'Youth Justice Policy in Europe – Between Minimum Intervention, Welfare and New Punitiveness' in T. Daems, D. van Zyl Smit and S. Snacken (eds) *European Penology?* Oxford: Hart.

Eadie, T. and Canton, R. (2002) 'Practising in a Context of Ambivalence: The Challenge for Youth Justice Workers', *Youth Justice*, 2(1): 14–26.

Feeney, N. and Freeman, S. (2010) 'What Do Young People Think of the Gardaí? An Examination of Young People's Attitudes and Experiences of An Garda Síochána', *Youth Studies Ireland*, 5(1): 3–17.

Freeman, S. (2008) 'Surviving on Remand: A Study of How Young People Cope in Remand Custody in Ireland', unpublished PhD thesis. Dublin Institute of Technology. Available at: http://arrow.dit.ie/appadoc/15/ (accessed 25 July 2014).

Gelsthorpe, L. and Morris, A. (1994) 'Juvenile Justice 1945–1992', in M. Maguire, R. Morgan and R. Reiner (eds) *The Oxford Handbook of Criminology*. Oxford: Clarendon Press.

Goldson, B. (2009) 'Child Incarceration: Institutional Abuse, the Violent State and the Politics of Impunity' in P. Scraton and J. McCulloch (eds) *The Violence of Incarceration*. Abingdon: Routledge.

—— (2011) '"Time for a Fresh Start", but Is This It? A Critical Assessment of the Report of the Independent Commission on Youth Crime and Antisocial Behaviour', *Youth Justice*, 11(1): 3–27.

—— (2013) '"Unsafe, Unjust and Harmful to Wider Society": Grounds for Raising the Minimum Age of Criminal Responsibility in England and Wales', *Youth Justice*, 13(2): 111–130.

Goldson, B. and Hughes, G. (2010) 'Sociological Criminology and Youth Justice: Comparative Policy Analysis and Academic Intervention', *Criminology and Criminal Justice*, 10(2): 211–30.

Goshe, S. (2015) 'Moving Beyond the Punitive Legacy: Taking Stock of Persistent Problems in Juvenile Justice', *Youth Justice*, 15(1): 42–56

Graham, I. and Damkat, I. (2014a) *First Time Entrants to the Criminal Justice System in Northern Ireland 2011/12*. Belfast: Department of Justice.

—— (2014b) *Northern Ireland Conviction and Sentencing Statistics 2010–2012*. Belfast: Department of Justice.

Griffin, M. and Kelleher, P. (2010) 'Uncertain Futures: Men on the Margins in Limerick City', *Irish Probation Journal*, 7: 24–45.

Heber, A. (2014) 'Good Versus Bad? Victims, Offenders and Victim-offenders in Swedish Crime Policy', *European Journal of Criminology*, 11(4): 410–428.

HIQA (Health Information and Quality Authority) (2012) *Inspection Report of a Children Detention School on Oberstown Campus Inspection Report ID Number 584*. Available at: http://www.hiqa.ie/social-care/find-a-centre/childrens-centre/oberstown-campus (accessed 25 July 2014).

—— (2013) *Inspection Report of a Children Detention School on Oberstown Campus Inspection Report ID Number 636*. Available at: http://www.hiqa.ie/social-care/find-a-centre/childrens-centre/oberstown-campus (accessed 25 July 2014).

HMCIP (HM Chief Inspector of Prisons) (1995) *Report on HM Young Offenders' Centre Hydebank Wood (Northern Ireland)*. London: Home Office.

—— (1997) *HM Prison Maghaberry (Northern Ireland): Report of an Unannounced Full Inspection*. London: Home Office.

Horgan, G. (2011) 'The Making of an Outsider: Growing Up in Poverty in Northern Ireland', *Youth & Society*, 43(2): 453–467.

Horgan, G. and Monteith, M. (2012) *A Child Rights Impact Assessment of the Impact of Welfare Reform on Children in Northern Ireland*. Belfast: NICCY.

Horgan, J. (2013) *Drug and Alcohol Misuse among Young Offenders on Probation Supervision in Ireland: Findings from the Drugs and Alcohol Survey 2012*, Probation Service Research Report 3. Available at: www.probation.ie (accessed 19 June 2014).

Hourigan, N. (2012) 'Juvenile Justice, Crime and Early Intervention: Key Challenges from the Limerick Context', *Irish Probation Journal*, 9: 64–74.

Inspector of Prisons (2013) *Office of the Inspector of Prisons Annual Report 2012*. Nenagh: Office of the Inspector of Prisons.

IYJS (Irish Youth Justice Service) (2009) *Designing Effective Local Responses to Youth Crime: A Baseline Analysis of the Garda Youth Diversion Projects*. Dublin: IYJS.

—— (2010) *Irish Youth Justice Service Annual Report 2009*. Dublin: IYJS.

—— (2011) *Irish Youth Justice Service Annual Report 2010*. Dublin: IYJS.

—— (2012a) *Progress Report on Garda Youth Diversion Project Development 2009–2011*. Dublin: IYJS.

—— (2012b) *Garda Youth Diversion Project Annual Plan for 2013*. Available at: http://www.iyjs.ie/en/IYJS/Pages/WP09000002 (accessed 27 July 2014).

—— (2012c) *Garda Youth Diversion Project Annual Plan Explanatory Notes for 2013*. Available at: http://www.iyjs.ie/en/IYJS/Pages/WP09000002 (accessed 27 July 2014).

Junger-Tas, J. (2006) 'Trends in International Juvenile Justice: What Conclusions Can Be Drawn?' in J. Junger-Tas and S. Decker (eds) *International Handbook of Juvenile Justice*. Dordrecht: Springer.

Kent, G. (2014) *Hard Times 3: Youth Perspectives*. Belfast: Community Foundation for Northern Ireland.

Kilcommins, S., O'Donnell, I. and Vaughan, B. (2004) *Crime, Punishment, and the Search for Order in Ireland*. Dublin: Institute of Public Administration.

Kilkelly, U. (2008) 'Youth Courts and Children's Rights: The Irish Experience', *Youth Justice*, 8(1): 39–56.

—— (2011) 'Policing, Young People, Diversion and Accountability', *Crime, Law and Social Change*, 55(2–3): 133–151.

Kilpatrick, A. (2013) *Human Rights Thematic Review: Policing with Children and Young People – Update on PSNI Implementation of Recommendations*. Belfast: Northern Ireland Policing Board.

Lockhart, W. (1995) 'Diversion – Community Schemes: An Overview', in IAJFCM *Growing Through Conflict: The Impact of 25 Years of Violence on Young People Growing Up in Northern Ireland*. Conference Proceedings Regional Seminar, Belfast, 3–7 April.

McAlister, S., Scraton, P. and Haydon, D. (2009) *Childhood in Transition: Children and Young People Experiencing Marginalisation in Northern Ireland*. Belfast: Queen's University/Save the Children/Prince's Trust.

McAlister, S., Haydon, D. and Scraton, P. (2013) 'Violence in the Lives of Children and Youth in "Post-Conflict" Northern Ireland Children', *Youth and Environments*, 23(1): 1–22.

McAlister, S., Scraton, P. and Haydon, D. (2014) 'Childhood in Transition: Growing Up in "Post-Conflict" Northern Ireland', *Children's Geographies*, 12(3): 297–311.

McAuley, M. and Cunningham, G. (1983) 'Intermediate Treatment and Residential Provision for Juvenile Offenders in Northern Ireland – A Whitefield House Perspective', in B. Caul, J. Pinkerton and F. Powell (eds) *The Juvenile Justice System in Northern Ireland*. Jordanstown: Ulster Polytechnic.

McCaughey, B. (2011) *PBNI Submission to the Youth Justice Review Group*. Belfast: PBNI.

McClelland, R. (2006) *The Bamford Review of Mental Health and Learning Disability: A Vision of a Comprehensive Child and Adolescent Mental Health Service*. Belfast: DHSSPS.

McCord, J. and Irwin, T. with Martynowicz, A. (2012) *Reviewing the Provision of Education for Young People in Detention: Rights, Research and Reflections on Policy and Practice*. Coleraine: University of Ulster.

McCracken, N. (2013) 'Prosecutors Criticise PSNI's Use of "Speedy Justice"', *The Detail*, 14 November.

—— (2014) 'Increase in Detention of Vulnerable Young People', *The Detail*, 3 September.

Marshall, K. (2014) *Child Sexual Exploitation in Northern Ireland: Report of the Independent Inquiry*. Belfast: CJINI, ETI, RQIA.

Maruna, S. (2008) *Youth Conferencing as Shame Management: Results of a Long-Term Follow-Up Study*. Belfast: Youth Justice Agency.

Ministry of Justice (2010) *Breaking the Cycle: Effective Punishment, Rehabilitation and Sentencing of Offenders*. London: Stationery Office.

Moore, L. (2011) 'The CRC Comes of Age: Assessing Progress in Meeting the Rights of Children in Custody in Northern Ireland', *Northern Ireland Legal Quarterly*, 62(2): 217–34.

Morris, A. and Giller, H. (1987) *Understanding Juvenile Justice*. London: Croom Helm.

Muncie, J. (2011) 'Illusions of Difference: Comparative Youth Justice in the Devolved United Kingdom', *British Journal of Criminology*, 51: 40–57.

National Crime Council (2003) *Public Order Offences in Ireland: A Report by The Institute of Criminology, Faculty of Law, University College Dublin for The National Crime Council*. Dublin: Stationery Office.

NICTS (Northern Ireland Courts and Tribunals Service) (2014) *Judicial Statistics 2013*. Belfast: Northern Ireland Courts and Tribunals Service.

Northern Ireland Office (NIO) (1996) *Scoping Study for Review of Juvenile Justice Provision*. Belfast: NIO Criminal Justice Policy Division.

Office of the First Minister and Deputy First Minister (OFMDFM) (2006) *Our Children and Young People – Our Pledge: A Ten Year Strategy for Children and Young People in Northern Ireland 2006–2016*. Belfast: OFMDFM.

—— (2014) *Delivering Social Change for Children and Young People: Summary and Analysis of Consultation Responses*. Belfast: OFMDFM.

O'Mahony, D. and Deazley, R. (2000) *Juvenile Crime and Justice: Review of the Criminal Justice System in Northern Ireland*. London: HMSO.

Ombudsman for Children's Office (2011) *Young People in St Patrick's Institution: A Report by the Ombudsman for Children's Office*. Dublin: Ombudsman for Children's Office.

O'Sullivan, E. and O'Donnell, I. (eds) (2012) *Coercive Confinement in Ireland: Patients Prisoners and Penitents*. Manchester: Manchester University Press.

Pinkerton, J. (2003) 'From Parity to Subsidiarity? Children's Policy in Northern Ireland under New Labour: The Case of Child Welfare', *Children & Society*, 17(3): 254–260.

Probation Service (2014) *Annual Report of the Probation Service 2013*. Dublin: Probation Service.

Raftery, M. and O'Sullivan, E. (2001) *Suffer the Little Children: The Inside Story of Ireland's Industrial Schools*, 2nd ed. Dublin: New Island Books.

Reidy, C. (2009) *Ireland's 'Moral Hospital': The Irish Borstal System, 1906–1956*. Dublin: Irish Academic Press.

RQIA (Regulation and Quality Improvement Authority) (2011) *RQIA Independent Review of Child and Adolescent Mental Health Services (CAMHS) in Northern Ireland*. Belfast: RQIA.

Seymour, M. (2012) 'The Youth Justice System', in C. Hamilton *Social Work and Social Care Law*. Dublin: Gill and MacMillan.

—— (2013) *Youth Justice in Context: Community, Compliance and Young People*. Abingdon: Routledge.

Seymour, M. and Butler, M. (2008) *Young People on Remand. The National Children's Strategy Research Series*. Dublin: Stationery Office.

Seymour, M. and Mayock, P. (2009) 'Ireland', in P. Hadfield (ed.) *Nightlife and Crime: Social Order and Governance in International Perspective*. New York: Oxford University Press.

Stewart, G. and Tutt, N. (1987) *Children in Custody*. Aldershot: Avebury.

Walsh, D. (2008) 'Balancing Due Process Values with Welfare Objectives in Juvenile Justice Procedure: Some Strengths and Weaknesses in the Irish Approach'. *Youth Studies Ireland*, 3(2): 3–17.

Weijers, I. (2004) 'Requirements for Communication in the Courtroom: A Comparative Perspective on the Youth Court in England/Wales and the Netherlands', *Youth Justice,* 4(1): 22–31.

Youth Justice Review Team (YJRT) (2011) *A Review of the Youth Justice System in Northern Ireland.* Belfast: Department of Justice.

Note

1 The only available information refers to general criteria used in decision-making, such as the seriousness and persistence of children's offending and/or previous involvement in the GJDP (An Garda Síochána, 2013).

13

Trajectories of policing in Ireland

Similarities, differences, convergences

Aogán Mulcahy

Introduction

At first glance, policing in Northern Ireland and in the Republic of Ireland appear radically different. Certainly, the scale of political division and political violence, and the consequent impact of these issues on the field of policing, has been much greater in Northern Ireland than in the Republic, even if the impact in both jurisdictions has been fundamental (Mulcahy, 2005). However, the two police forces share a number of similarities that easily can be overlooked. Both forces – the Royal Ulster Constabulary (RUC) in Northern Ireland, until its replacement by the Police Service of Northern Ireland (PSNI) in 2001, and An Garda Síochána in the Republic – emerged from the ashes of the Royal Irish Constabulary (RIC) in the aftermath of the partition of Ireland. While the RIC had widely been regarded as an effective and efficient police force, its role in maintaining state security and countering subversion brought it into conflict with much of the population (Malcolm, 2006; O'Sullivan, 1999). With the partition of Ireland, the disbandment of the RIC led to the establishment and development of new police forces in both jurisdictions. If the RIC was the same point of origin in both contexts, the trajectories to be followed differed greatly. The subsequent development of policing in each jurisdiction would greatly affect how each state responded not just to issues of crime, but also to political violence, and the respective police forces would remain prominent symbols of social and political cultures in each state, albeit in notably different ways.

In this chapter I examine the trajectories of policing in both parts of the island. For each juris-diction I consider: the origins and development of policing; how legitimacy was pursued and the impact this had on levels of public support and the dynamics of police–community relations; the crises and challenges they faced and the reform measures put in place to address these. In doing so, I highlight the similarities, differences and convergences in the field of policing in Northern Ireland and the Irish Republic, particularly those arising from political division. I conclude by considering the wider lessons that policing in Ireland has for issues of accountability, legitimacy and police–community relations.

Policing in Northern Ireland

When the state of Northern Ireland was created, it was stamped with an unambiguously unionist identity, yet the fact that approximately one-third of the population were Catholics whose loyalty to the new state was in doubt, ensured that it was fixated on its security (if not its very survival) from the outset (Ruane and Todd, 1996). The establishment of Northern Ireland was marked by considerable and widespread violence that, while concentrated in Belfast, extended across the state. Over 450 people were killed in Belfast between July 1920 and July 1922, while 23,000 of the city's 93,000 Catholics were forced from their homes during this period (Cunningham, 2013; Farrell, 1980; Parkinson, 2004). Once this subsided, however, and with some obvious exceptions,[1] Northern Ireland was characterised thereafter by extremely high levels of stability. This reflected a number of political, social and security factors.

Unionists enjoyed a significant numerical advantage, and in electoral terms this generated enduring political dominance. Northern Ireland was governed by a single political party (the Official/Ulster Unionist Party) from its establishment until 1972. The segregated nature of Northern Ireland also meant that the electoral outcome in many constituencies was entirely predictable; Ruane and Todd (1996: 131) note that in 1933, the successful candidates in 33 of the 52 constituencies were unopposed. Northern Ireland was also a deeply conservative society, with relatively high levels of religious affiliation and practice, and in respect of a range of issues, such as homosexuality and abortion, the moral and legal landscape of Northern Ireland was signifi-cantly more constrained than that which prevailed in Britain (Mitchell, 2006). The differences between unionists/loyalists and nationalists/republicans in political orientation and affiliation were amplified through extremely high levels of segregation in the spheres of education, housing and employment.

In addition, Northern Ireland was characterised by a significant security apparatus, of which the Royal Ulster Constabulary was a key component. As well as dealing with 'ordinary' crime and related matters, the RUC also had responsibility for maintaining the security of the state, and policing levels were relatively high. In 1924 Northern Ireland's ratio of one police officer for every 160 people was a much higher level of policing than that in England and Wales (a ratio of 1:669), Scotland (1:751) (Weitzer, 1995: 34), or the Irish Republic (1:412 in 1926) (McNiffe, 1997: 65). Further security was provided by the Ulster Special Constabulary (the 'B-Specials'). These officers served on a part-time basis and mostly focused on patrolling the border, providing security for key installations and maintaining public order. Farrell (1980: 50) estimates that in the 1920s approximately 20 per cent of all adult male Protestants served in the USC (although many of these were demobilised later in the 1920s as violence levels subsided). The legal powers available to the security forces were nothing if not impressive. This was particularly evident in the iconic Civil Authorities (Special Powers) Act 1923 which, for instance, enabled the Minister for Home Affairs 'to take all such steps and issue all such orders as may be necessary for preserving the peace and maintaining order' (see Farrell, 1980: 93–4).

Political violence, police legitimacy and public confidence

Up until the 1960s, an uneasy peace generally prevailed in Northern Ireland, but growing dis-quiet over discrimination across a range of spheres led to the emergence of an increasingly vocal civil rights movement. Civil rights marches were aggressively policed and often met with loyalist counter-marches. This escalated into major riots, and disturbances and violence spread across Northern Ireland. The police were roundly criticised for their actions – actions that Lord Scarman noted led to 'the fateful split between the Catholic community and the police' (1972:

15) – but they also were overwhelmed by the scale of the disturbances, and, in August 1969, the British Army was deployed to maintain order, with the RUC moved to a largely supporting role. The 1969 Hunt Report outlined a series of measures to modernise the RUC and enhance its reputation. The B-Specials were duly disbanded – prompting a loyalist riot at which an RUC officer was killed – but the proposals that the RUC should be disarmed and no longer play a role in state security fell by the wayside as the scale and intensity of the conflict grew dramatically.

While the army's introduction was considered a means to stabilise the situation, its role in maintaining order on a day-to-day basis proved controversial and often counter-productive, and, as paramilitary organisations increased the intensity of their campaigns, levels of violence rose dramatically. The annual number of homicides in Northern Ireland averaged 2.7 between 1962 and 1968; in 1972 alone, over 450 conflict-related deaths were recorded, and over 200 were recorded annually until 1976 (Brewer *et al.*, 1997). In the face of this crisis the British government developed a new conflict management strategy in the mid-1970s, based around the themes of criminalisation and police primacy. In broad terms, this entailed responding to the conflict through the 'normal' criminal justice system, rather than through the emergency measures (such as internment and various military operations) which had escalated rather than contained the conflict. The police would move to the fore in responding to paramilitary campaigns, with the army playing a largely supporting role, and those convicted of paramilitary-related offences would be held in prisons as 'ordinary' criminals rather than 'special category prisoners', a status that previously had been accorded to members of paramilitary organisations convicted of crimes related to the Conflict (Ellison and Mulcahy, 2001). This required a considerable expansion of the RUC's capacity in dealing with paramilitary violence and public order (involving more officers, and enhanced powers, equipment and training). It also involved sustained efforts to enhance the RUC's legitimacy and levels of public support by demonstrating its commitment to impartiality, accountability and to building positive relations with all sections of the public (see generally, Ellison and Smyth, 2000; Ellison and Mulcahy, 2001; Mulcahy, 2006; Weitzer, 1995).

Levels of violence diminished, and in only five subsequent years did the number of conflict-related fatalities exceed 100 (the last of these in 1988). In some parts of Northern Ireland, policing was relatively 'normalised' (Brewer, 1991), but in many places it became increasingly militarised, and between 1969 and 1998 302 RUC officers were murdered. A range of surveys in the 1980s and 1990s show that police primacy did appear to yield rewards in terms of the public's attitudes towards the police, with consistent findings that an overall majority of both Catholics and Protestants expressed satisfaction with the police. Yet, the RUC's expanded role placed it centre-stage in terms of an array of security policies that were extremely controversial – as well as scandals surrounding police interrogations, allegations of a shoot-to-kill policy and collusion in particular – and largely directed towards the Catholic community (Mulcahy, 2006: 69–75). As a consequence, while the RUC was often highly rated by Catholics and Protestants alike for the manner in which it dealt with ordinary crime, when we consider security policing (see Table 13.1), the gulf between the attitudes of Catholics and Protestants becomes apparent (McGarry and O'Leary, 1999; Weitzer, 1995: chapters 4–5).

As Whyte (1990: 88) noted: '[t]here is an even greater degree of disagreement between Protestants and Catholics on security policy than there is on constitutional questions. Security issues remain an unhealed sore'.

In the peace process that followed the 1994 paramilitary ceasefires, the subject of policing generated extensive and often heated debate. Throughout the conflict, policing had been a uniquely controversial issue for the manner in which it epitomised so many of the fault lines in Northern Ireland – encapsulating issues of state, political affiliation and identity, safety and security – and it remained so during the peace process. Parading had long been a contentious event,

Table 13.1 Public attitudes towards security measures in Northern Ireland

	Catholics agreeing (%)	Protestants agreeing (%)
House searches are used too little	3	26
House searches are used too much	35	3
Random searches of pedestrians are used too little	6	32
Random searches of pedestrians are used too much	41	3
Vehicle checkpoints are used too little	9	34
Vehicle checkpoints are used too much	40	8
Approve of 'shoot-to-kill' actions against terrorist suspects	7	61
Approve of increased use of undercover surveillance operations	25	90
Approve of use of plastic bullets during riot situations	9	86

Source: Adapted from Weitzer (1995: 137).

but in the uncertainty of the peace process it assumed a greater significance, epitomised by events at Drumcree in Portadown. In previous years protests by nationalist residents had been matched by unionist determination that the parade would continue to march along its traditional (though controversial) route. In 1996, for several days the security forces prevented the parade from marching down the Garvaghy Road route. As the protests escalated, the security forces took the decision to push the parade through on the basis that they no longer were able to contain the protesters without resorting to live fire. This in turn sparked a furious reaction among nationalists across Northern Ireland. More plastic baton rounds were fired during those days than at any time since the 1981 hunger strike. The RUC was criticised for yielding to the threat posed by loyalist protesters and the issue of police impartiality once again dominated debates about the future of policing. In a survey in February 1997 conducted for the Police Authority, 11 per cent of Catholic respondents agreed that the RUC should be 'allowed to carry on exactly as it is now', compared to 68 per cent of Protestant respondents; 86 per cent of Catholic respondents indicated they thought the RUC should be reformed, replaced or disbanded (Mulcahy, 2006: 104).

The Patten Report and the transition from RUC to PSNI

As part of the 1998 Good Friday Agreement, an Independent Commission on Policing (ICP) was established to make recommendations for future policing arrangements in Northern Ireland. Chaired by Chris Patten, the ICP's report *A New Beginning* (popularly known as the Patten Report) acknowledged the depth of divisions that existed over policing:

> In one political language they are the custodians of nationhood. In its rhetorical opposite they are the symbols of oppression. Policing therefore goes right to the heart of the sense of security and identity of both communities and, because of the differences between them, this seriously hampers the effectiveness of the police service in Northern Ireland.
>
> *(ICP, 1999: 2)*

While the ICP's focus was on the future of policing in Northern Ireland, its overall approach was to outline a model of policing which could apply in any society. As such, its recommendations were designed to adhere to a series of 'first principles': promoting effective policing; ensuring impartiality and accountability; enhancing representativeness; and protecting the human rights of all. Some of the recommendations addressed different aspects of organisational structures and practices, and coalesced around proposals to modernise the *police institution* in various ways and render it more efficient. Others focused on the issue of *policing* more broadly, particularly in terms of institutions of governance and oversight and the ethos of policing more generally.

The ICP recommended the establishment of a Policing Board (NIPB) to replace the Police Authority, which had been roundly criticised for adopting a minimalist approach to police oversight. At local authority level it recommended that District Policing Partnerships (DPPs) be established to facilitate consultation and provide a measure of local accountability. It endorsed an earlier report's recommendation for a Police Ombudsman to be created to provide an independent police complaints system. It also recommended that an Oversight Commissioner be appointed to provide independent verification that the recommendations were being implemented. With a nod to the political opposition that the ICP's recommendations faced, Patten subsequently described this as 'one of our best ideas' (Patten, 2010: 25). In addition, it called for human rights to be integrated into all aspects of policing, and recommended that 'policing with the community should be the core function of the police service and the core function of every police station' (ICP, 1999: 43).

In 2001 the Police Service for Northern Ireland formally came into being. When the dust settled on what was a bruising and contentious implementation process, the new structures of policing in Northern Ireland were given enormous acclaim. The NIPB Chairperson described the reform programme as a 'blueprint for democratic policing anywhere in the world', and characterised the PSNI as 'the most scrutinized and accountable police service probably anywhere in the world today' (Ellison, 2007; Mulcahy, 2013). Members of the ICP concurred, describing the PSNI as 'the best working example of how to police a divided community' (Patten, 2010: 25) and as 'an exemplary police organisation' (Shearing, 2010: 29).

While the 'Northern Ireland policing model' quickly gained in reputation as a solution to problems of policing worldwide – although the scale of the difficulties in Northern Ireland paled in comparison to the level of conflict, division and social collapse in many other 'divided societies' (Bayley, 2008) – much of this acclaim specifically reflected the establishment of robust new institutions of police governance. Locally, the Patten Report's recommendations initially were highly contested. Unionist opposition coalesced around a sense of betrayal at the loss of 'their' police service (Mulcahy, 2006; see also ICP, 1999: 16), while within the RUC there was considerable resentment and resistance towards the reform agenda and its implementation (Murphy, 2013; see also Mulcahy, 1999). Moreover, the implementation process itself was enormously contentious, and revealed the enduring divisions that remained over the practice, oversight and symbolism of policing. Nationalists viewed the British government's approach as grudging and minimalist, and two separate Police Acts and two further implementation plans were required before the SDLP participated in the Policing Board and the DPPs. It was not until 2007 that Sinn Féin formally endorsed the new policing structures.

Current and future challenges

The ICP's recommendations were based on their congruence with a set of principles that could command universal support. While 'policing with the community' was identified as the core police function, translating this ethos into practice has proven difficult. First, the wider political environment remains volatile. If the political structures were largely designed around the principle of power-sharing, relations between the parties comprising the Northern Ireland Executive, and between the two largest parties – the Democratic Unionist Party and Sinn Féin – in particular, are characterised by hostility and belligerence. Even though the devolution of policing and justice to the Northern Ireland assembly in 2010 was an important symbol of political stability, tellingly, the Minister of Justice is the only position on the executive whose appointment requires cross-community support, and at present that role is held by an Alliance Party representative, David Ford.

Second, concerns remain about wider social conflict. Paramilitary violence is only a small fraction of what it was in previous years, but the threat posed by republican paramilitary groups opposed to the Belfast Agreement remains. While these groups are relatively small, their activities have the capacity potentially to destabilise the political environment, and since 2009 they have been responsible for the deaths of two PSNI officers, two soldiers and a prison officer. Moreover, violence is not confined to dissident republicans. In recent years, large-scale rioting has erupted over contentious parade routes and also other symbolic events (as in 2012 when Belfast City Council reduced the number of days on which the Union flag would be flown above the city hall).

Third, despite the acclaim given to the new framework of policing in Northern Ireland, enacting the vision of 'policing with the community' articulated in the Patten Report has proven to be highly problematic. At times there has been considerable police and political resistance to an enhanced role for communities within the wider field of security provision (Mulcahy, 2008a; Topping, 2008a), while there is also a danger that 'community policing' has been cast in managerial terms rather than as a means of enacting tangible changes in policing practice (Ellison and O'Rawe, 2010; Topping, 2008b).

Moreover, there are considerable challenges in building productive relationships between the police and communities that had been largely hostile to them during the conflict. These difficulties are exacerbated by what the Oversight Commissioner (2007: 3) described as the mismatch between heightened expectations and the realities of 'normal' policing, noting that the goal of meeting 'the expectations of the communities and residents of Northern Ireland ... has not yet been reached':

> The reality of capacity issues such as resource restraints, call and response management, crime and clearance rates, coupled with the time it takes to build trust relationships, all point to an 'expectation gap'. Normalised policing is quite simply a complex, difficult and expensive business that can never fully satisfy client demand.
>
> *(Oversight Commissioner, 2007: 212)*

Clearly the impact of such issues varies from locale to locale, but one study conducted in a republican area in North Belfast, the New Lodge, found that in the years following the ceasefires, many residents were concerned that problems of crime and disorder were not being addressed adequately, whether by the police or paramilitary organisations. This concern was exacerbated by victimisation levels that were far above the average for Northern Ireland and by low levels of reporting crime to the police (Ellison et al., 2013). Moreover, following decades of overt conflict and embedded hostility to the police, the difficulties of engaging productively with the PSNI were tangible. Even though the new institutions of police governance were well-established, residents' assessments of whether policing had improved strongly reflected their assessments of police performance, and, faced with the realities and limitations of 'normal' policing, they were highly critical of police responsiveness and effectiveness (Ellison et al., 2013; Topping and Byrne, 2014).

Fourth, in addition to the above factors, one issue in particular cast a long shadow over the new structures of policing and over Northern Irish society generally: dealing with the legacy of the past. While various initiatives were launched to consider how to address unresolved aspects of the conflict and to deal with the harrowing – and often competing – narratives of victimhood that convulsed Northern Irish society (see, for example, Consultative Group on the Past, 2009), these issues were especially contentious in respect of policing (Lawther, 2014). One strand of this process involved the PSNI establishing a Historical Enquiries Team (HET) to investigate unsolved killings from the conflict (Lundy, 2009; 2011). This largely involved reviewing the original police investigations and any other available evidence, and, while it was possible to bring charges against suspects, generally the outcome of HET investigations was to provide any relevant information to victims' families with a view to giving them some degree of closure. Subsequently, however, the HET was criticised for being less rigorous in investigations where members of the security forces were alleged to be involved (HMIC, 2013: 100). As a result of financial cutbacks, the HET was effectively shut down at the end of 2014, although it was envisaged that a smaller investigative unit would continue to review the outstanding historical cases (*Irish Times*, 30 September 2014). The Police Ombudsman also became involved in investigating historical cases, including high-profile incidents in which collusion between the police and the perpetrators was alleged to have taken place. However, allegations surfaced that the Northern Ireland Office had sought to influence some investigations and to minimise any criticisms of the RUC Special Branch. As a result of this controversy, the Ombudsman, Al Hutchinson, resigned in 2011 (CJINI, 2011; McCusker, 2011), and while the Office of the Police Ombudsman continued to conduct historical investigations, such events demonstrate the potential for controversy that attends this role.

Policing the past is a costly enterprise in terms of resources and capacity. The Criminal Justice Inspectorate of Northern Ireland estimated that, in addition to HET resources, 'some 40% of the PSNI overall serious crime capability was being used in legacy matters' (CJINI, 2013: 6). As the cases of the HET and the Ombudsman demonstrate, the legacy of the past can also implicate institutions in damaging controversies, a point noted by the PSNI Chief Constable in 2014 when he described the challenges of addressing legacy issues as 'debilitating and toxic to confidence' (*Irish Times*, 6 June 2014). In December 2014, amidst concerns that the Northern Ireland Assembly was in danger of collapsing due to disagreement over budgetary and policy matters, talks between all the parties in Northern Ireland and with the British and Irish governments led to the Stormont House Agreement, of which measures to deal with the past were one component, including the establishment of a Historical Enquiries Unit to take forward outstanding cases from the HET and the Police Ombudsman's legacy work. It is clear that the legacy of the past remains deeply contentious, and it is equally clear that this cannot be resolved through policing institutions alone, even though policing is likely to be central to much of this process in the coming years (see also Committee on the Administration of Justice, 2015).

Policing in the Republic of Ireland

As with Northern Ireland, the creation of the Irish Free State led to the establishment of a new police force. In the political upheaval of the time – a War of Independence, followed by a Civil War – competing imperatives shaped this process. Nationalist sentiment demanded that policing institutions should be identifiably 'Irish' in orientation and reflect the ethos of the newly independent state, while pragmatism required prudent choices, given the other pressing needs which the new administration faced. The outcome, therefore, was a compromise of sorts between ideology and expediency.

The RIC had been recognised as a very capable organisation and, in non-political matters at least, it was generally well-regarded. However, its role in supporting the colonial administration brought it into overt conflict with much of the population, and during the War of Independence its officers were consistently targeted by the IRA. Between 1919 and 1922, Conway (2013: 19) notes, 493 were killed during the political conflict, while 18 more were missing and presumed dead; a further 77 died in accidents or other conflict-related incidents. Political independence saw the disbandment of the RIC and the exodus of most of its officers, yet its organisational structures provided a ready-made template for the new police force.

The Civic Guard was established in 1922, and this merged with the Dublin Metropolitan Police in 1925 to form An Garda Síochána, creating a single national police force that survives to the present day. Yet, if the RIC provided the skeleton for this new policing body, the flesh on the bones was decidedly nationalist in political orientation. As McNiffe (1997) demonstrates in his detailed analysis of Garda recruits over the period 1922–52, in clear ways they epitomised the western/rural/nationalist vision of Ireland celebrated by those who fought for independence. No fewer than 38 per cent of recruits joined from the counties of Cork, Kerry, Clare, Galway and Mayo; despite the difference in population, as many recruits joined from Clare as from Dublin (5.6 per cent in each case) over this period. Most recruits came from agricultural (38 per cent) or unskilled/manual labour backgrounds (25 per cent). As few as '2 per cent of the Civic Guards had policing experience' (Conway, 2010: 5), while the vast majority of initial recruits – '96 per cent of the first 1,500 civic guards' (McNiffe, 1997: 33) – had served in the IRA during the War of Independence; it therefore seems reasonable to assume that they brought a similarly nationalistic ideology with them into the police.

During the 1920s and 1930s An Garda Síochána faced considerable violent opposition from those who were opposed to partition. When Fianna Fáil, largely comprised of those opposed to partition and on the 'anti-treaty' side during the Civil War, won the 1932 general election, the police's continued support for the institutions of government was a key point in stabilising the political environment (Brady, 2000; Conway, 2013). Once the conflict over the establishment of the state began to subside, policing generally assumed a less contentious character. The conditions within which officers worked often were appalling, and 'pay and conditions' remained a source of tension between the force and successive governments, but in many other respects the challenges facing the police during the middle of the twentieth century were minimal, due to a number of features of Irish society.

First, levels of recorded crime were low, conspicuously so in comparison to other western societies. In 1950 the Minister of Justice described Ireland as 'very free from crime' and suggested that the population merited a 'pat on the back for being a law-abiding people' (Kilcommins et al., 2004: 62). Later that decade, the Justice Minister described Ireland as 'freer from crime than almost any other country' (quoted in Allen, 1999: 153). Second, Irish society was in the main characterised by stability and conservatism, with extraordinarily high levels of religious observance (Inglis, 1998; see also Ferriter, 2012).[2] Third, beyond the formal structures of policing, a variety of ostensibly 'welfare' institutions administered what O'Sullivan and O'Donnell (2012) term a system of 'coercive confinement' that far surpassed the scale of the formal criminal justice system (see also Brennan, 2015). In 1956, for instance, approximately one per cent of the population was 'confined'. Of this group, however, only 574 people were detained in the formal criminal justice system, while 29,308 people were held in various 'welfare' institutions, including Magdalene laundries, industrial schools, mental hospitals and so on. For every person detained within the criminal justice system, fifty others were detained in this institutional archipelago. All in all, then, the formal policing conducted by An Garda Síochána was complemented, if not extended considerably, by a vast enterprise of moral policing.

Crime and conflict

From the 1970s onwards, policing became an increasingly prominent aspect of public life in the Republic, spurred in part by a six-fold increase in crime levels in the twenty-year period between 1964 and 1983. Within this, illegal drugs played a very significant role. Before the late 1970s, problems related to illegal drugs were minimal by international standards. However, a rapid increase in the availability of heroin in particular in the late 1970s and early 1980s had a devastating impact on many communities, particularly in marginalised areas in Dublin. While drugs contributed significantly to crime levels – Keogh (1997) estimated that between September 1995 and August 1996 two-thirds of all crime in the Dublin area was committed by known drug-users – it also impacted on relations between the police and residents in those areas. Residents were highly critical of what they perceived as an entirely inadequate response on the part of the police and the political establishment. One senior Garda officer acknowledged this criticism, describing the 1970s as 'largely a decade of inaction' (quoted in Mulcahy, 2002: 287). Brewer *et al.* (1997: 46–7) noted that government officials were 'shaken' by the scale of the drugs problem, particularly in relation to heroin use in Dublin, while senior Garda officers described drugs as 'the biggest single influence on the crime profile during their time in service'. Groups such as 'Concerned Parents Against Drugs' conducted a direct action campaign against alleged drug-dealers, which in turn led to ongoing conflict with the police (see, for example, Bennett, 1988; Connolly, 2002; Cullen, 1991; Murphy-Lawless, 2002).

In this changing social climate, the issue of police–community relations emerged as a matter of public concern, particularly in the context of economically marginalised communities (Mulcahy and O'Mahony, 2005). In 1982 the Association of Garda Sergeants and Inspectors expressed its concern that 'things are getting out of control' in light of police officers being 'set upon' in various locations. It noted that in parts of Dublin, 'the Gardaí are, to put it mildly, unwelcome' (AGSI, 1982: 5, 7). Outbreaks of serious disorder in parts of Dublin during the 1980s and 1990s were the subject of a Dáil Committee investigation which linked the high levels of social marginalisation in those areas with the development of antagonistic relations between residents and the police (Interdepartmental Group on Urban Crime and Disorder, 1992; see also Bowden, 2014).

The outbreak of widespread violence in Northern Ireland also had an enormous effect on policing in the Republic (Conway, 2013; Mulcahy, 2005). In addition to the increased risks it posed to Garda officers, it involved significant changes in police practice, including increased checkpoints along the border, responding to the challenges of a huge increase in bank robberies by paramilitaries, and also involving the police in conflict with some sections of the public, including in 1972 when the British Embassy in Dublin was burnt down by protesters following the events of Bloody Sunday in Derry that January. Significantly, the Conflict also cast the police in a 'heroic role', protecting the state and its citizens from the onslaught of paramilitary violence. This bolstered the standing of the force, while also insulating it from much criticism. Many politicians and public figures were reluctant to be seen to undermine the force, given the role it played and the challenges its officers faced (Conway, 2013; Manning, 2012; Walsh, 1999).

However, the police response to serious crime and to paramilitary activity also came under scrutiny in the face of mounting allegations that Garda detectives (termed 'the heavy gang') were using violence to extract confessions from suspects. In a number of high-profile cases – such as the case of Nicky Kelly and others accused of involvement in the Sallins train robbery – compelling evidence was presented that undermined the police officers' accounts (Amnesty International, 1977; Conway, 2013; Dunne and Kerrigan, 1984; see also Ó Briain Committee, 1978). Further controversy emerged from the police investigation into the 'Kerry babies' case, in which Joanne Hayes and her family made detailed confessions admitting to the murder of a newborn baby, even though medical evidence showed that it was all but impossible for her to have been the mother of that baby, and the body of her own baby was found buried in the garden near her home, where she had maintained it was all along (Inglis, 2003). Alleged paramilitaries and serious criminals might be considered 'disreputable' in the eyes of the law, but the Hayes family were from a farming background in rural Ireland and had no history of criminal involvement; in many ways they were precisely the kind of family that An Garda Síochána was, by its ethos and tradition, bound to support and protect. In response to these events, a new police complaints body – the Garda Síochána Complaints Board (GSCB) – was established in 1986 to strengthen the system of police accountability. However, the GSCB repeatedly criticised the powers and resources available to it, highlighting the danger of creating the appearance of a system of police accountability, but not the reality of one (Conway, 2010; Walsh, 1999).

Legitimacy and public support

The legitimacy of policing in the Republic was pursued in parallel ways at national and community level. At the national level, An Garda Síochána embodied the cultural nationalism that underpinned the independence movement. At the community level, it sought to become embedded within local life, through active involvement in other institutions such as the Gaelic Athletic Association (Brady, 2000). This yielded a system of policing in which considerable latitude was given to informal action (Mulcahy, 2008b) and low-level use of violence seems to have been widely accepted and practised within the police (Conway, 2013; Kearns, 2014). Successive governments proved reluctant to establish robust institutions of accountability and oversight. Thus, there developed a system of policing characterised by informalism and discretion, violence, lack of accountability and political interference. Perhaps paradoxically, this system also attracted widespread public support.

While public attitudes to An Garda Síochána have not received sustained attention historically, most commentators conclude that levels of public support for the police were notably high. McNiffe (1997: 175) described An Garda Síochána as 'one of the striking successes of the new state', while Allen (1999: 136) stated that 'their place in the social life of the community could not reasonably have been higher'. For MacGréil (1996: 271), the police were one of Ireland's 'in-groups'. During the 1980s and 1990s a number of surveys found extremely high levels of public satisfaction with the police: 86 per cent in 1986; 89 per cent in 1994; 86 per cent in 1996; and 89 per cent in 1999 (O'Donnell, 2004: 19). Between 2002 and 2008, the Garda Research Unit ran an annual series of public attitude surveys (see Table 13.2), and while these survey findings highlight a relatively high (and *relatively* enduring) level of satisfaction with policing, they also reveal a noticeable decline during the 2000s. Furthermore, it is clear that such figures mask a more nuanced reality in relations between the police and public.

First, a high overall satisfaction rating must be distinguished from confidence in police propriety, and support for the police can co-exist with a range of concerns about police conduct. Bohan and Yorke (1987), for instance, conducted a survey in which 85 per cent of respondents

Table 13.2 Public satisfaction with the police in the Republic of Ireland

	Very Satisfied	Satisfied	**Total Satisfied**	Dissatisfied	Very Dissatisfied	**Total Dissatisfied**
2002	17	69	**86**	11	2	**13**
2003	17	64	**81**	15	4	**19**
2004	15	69	**84**	11	4	**15**
2005	16	67	**83**	14	3	**17**
2006	13	67	**80**	16	4	**20**
2007	14	67	**81**	16	3	**19**
2008	11	70	**81**	14	5	**19**

Source: Adapted from Browne (2008: Table 1).

expressed satisfaction with the police. In the same survey, however, 57 per cent of respondents agreed with the statement that 'the Garda Síochána sometimes exceed their powers by abusing suspects physically or mentally', while 40 per cent agreed that 'in court, some Gardaí would rather cover up the facts than lose face' (Bohan and Yorke, 1987: 79).

Second, people's experiences of policing are mediated by a range of factors, including community profile and socio-economic status, with residents of local authority housing being more critical of the police and more likely to report negative experiences of policing (Browne, 2008; Mulcahy and O'Mahony, 2005). A study by the UCD Institute of Criminology found that the profile and reputation of an area affected the interaction between police and public. It found that the manner of policing in 'Parkway', a Dublin suburb which the police viewed as having an 'established, negative history', was significantly 'more confrontational' than the policing style in the city centre. The authors found that in 'Parkway' the police responded to public order situations with such language as 'f**k off home now'. Officers 'simply asserted their authority and appeared unconcerned about the nature of the reaction that might be elicited as a consequence' (UCD Institute of Criminology, 2003: 67–9).

Relations between the police and Travellers are especially problematic, reflected in satisfaction levels strikingly lower than that found for the settled population. A Garda Research Unit survey exploring the attitudes and experiences of ethnic minorities found that Traveller respondents reported much more negative attitudes than other ethnic minority groups (whom the survey found to have very high levels of satisfaction with the police, perhaps implausibly so). The survey found that 52 per cent of Traveller respondents were satisfied with the police while 48 per cent were dissatisfied, a stark contrast with the findings from the other national surveys. The survey also reported that 43 per cent of Traveller respondents agreed with a statement that a Garda officer had behaved towards them in an unacceptable way. In contrast, only 6 per cent of 'migrants' and 12 per cent of 'refugees', and 7.5 per cent of respondents in the general survey conducted in the same year, made a similar claim (Browne, 2008: Table 49; Walker, 2007: Table 38; see Mulcahy, 2012).

Scandal and reform

By the end of the twentieth century the Republic of Ireland seemed a far different country to that of previous decades. From being an archetypically 'local' society, it now was designated the 'most globalised' society in the world (Inglis, 2008). The 'Celtic Tiger' economy heralded a wide range of social changes in terms of: income, wealth and consumerism; residential patterns and urban development; and culture, identity and ethnic diversity. Disclosures over the sexual and physical abuse of children rocked the Catholic Church and the state itself. Meanwhile the peace process in Northern Ireland led to a relaxation of many of the security measures put in place during the conflict. In terms of policing, a range of organisational and managerial measures were introduced to modernise the force, and an increase in police numbers and powers formed part of a new political crime-control agenda (Brady, 2014; Kilcommins et al., 2004). Migration patterns and the growing ethnic minority population resulted in various initiatives to ensure that policing arrangements were suitable for an increasingly multicultural society, including the appointment of Ethnic Liaison Officers and measures to increase recruitment from ethnic minority groups (McInerney, 2004; Walsh, 2000).

If the challenges of policing were mounting from the 1970s onwards, allegations surrounding a series of events in Donegal led to a full-blown crisis and were the subject of a tribunal established in 2002 and chaired by Justice Morris. The volumes of reports laid bare a range of misconduct as well as a failure of management to address them effectively. These included police officers planting explosives which they then 'discovered' in an effort to advance their careers; planting a firearm on a Traveller encampment to justify a search; conducting an extensive campaign of harassment against one family; and numerous other instances of misconduct, indiscipline and mismanagement (Conway, 2010; Morris, 2004–2008).

A range of other events also highlighted concerns over police actions and accountability. In 2000 John Carty was shot dead in Abbeylara, Co. Longford, by members of the Garda Emergency Response Unit following a stand-off. Carty was known to be mentally disturbed, and over the course of the siege he discharged his shotgun over twenty times. Nevertheless the circumstances in which he was shot provoked controversy and formed the subject of several investigations. In 2002 a 'Reclaim the Streets' protest in Dublin city centre escalated into conflict between police and members of the public. Media coverage appeared to show use of excessive force on the part of Garda officers. In a subsequent investigation, the Chairman of the GCSB criticised a 'general lack of cooperation' from officers present, highlighting the fact that none proved able to identify other Garda officers who were using their batons inappropriately. He stated that this led him to believe that 'many Gardai had put loyalty to their colleagues ahead of that to the force' (*Irish Times*, 19 November 2002).

The Garda Síochána Act 2005 emerged in response to the Donegal scandal and other events. Described as the largest change to policing in the history of the state, the Act provided for the establishment of the Garda Síochána Ombudsman Commission to investigate complaints against the police, and the Garda Inspectorate to address issues of organisational efficiency and effectiveness. It also provided for police–public consultation through the establishment of Joint Policing Committees at local authority level (also making provision for the establishment of Community Policing Fora at neighbourhood level). In other respects though, the Act arguably enhanced central government control over policing policy (Conway, 2009; Walsh and Conway, 2011).

If the 2005 Act was intended to provide a robust response to scandals in Donegal and elsewhere, particularly through a tightening up of internal and external controls, it is unclear what precise impact this has had on the cultural values and practices of Garda officers. Manning (2012: 347) suggested that while An Garda Síochána engaged with the new landscape of accountability at a rhetorical level, the organisation itself is 'very resilient and resistant to change'. Charman and Corcoran (2015: 500), on the other hand, found evidence that the 'cultural change demanded by Justice Morris is evident and that this may have primarily happened because the rationale for the reforms being internally implemented was accepted by most of the Gardaí we interviewed'.

Whatever officers themselves may suggest, it is undeniable that the following years witnessed a succession of further policing controversies and scandals that cumulatively demonstrated that police practices and structures of oversight remained highly problematic. Some of this related to historical incidents. The Smithwick Tribunal (2013), for instance, investigated events surrounding the IRA murder of two senior RUC officers in 1989; it found that there was collusion, and that someone in Dundalk Garda station was 'assisting the IRA'. Other controversies related to the policing of protests against the construction of a gas pipeline in Rossport, Co. Mayo (Garda Research Institute, 2013). More recent events also shook the force to its core, and Charman and Corcoran (2015: 501) surely were correct when they stated that 'more needs to be done to encourage the cultural validation of whistle-blowing in An Garda Síochána'.

Two Garda whistle-blowers, Sergeant Maurice McCabe and Garda John Wilson, alleged that significant numbers of penalty points arising from road traffic offences were cancelled without good reason, and they also alleged that in a number of other instances the police response to what were serious criminal allegations was entirely inadequate. After failing to have these issues addressed satisfactorily within the force, they provided information on these allegations to a number of TDs. From 2012 onwards, these allegations generated much media and political debate, but the whistle-blowers found themselves ostracised within the force. The Garda Commissioner dismissed the substance of their allegations, and in one televised parliamentary committee hearing he described their actions as 'disgusting'. A subsequent investigation (the Guerin Report, 2014) suggested that the scale and gravity of their allegations warranted an Inquiry, and in December 2014 a Commission of Investigation led by Justice O'Higgins was established to investigate a series of events in Bailieboro, Co. Cavan, including allegations that a number of serious crimes were not investigated properly, thereby allowing further serious crimes to be carried out.[3]

A further scandal developed when it emerged that the Garda Síochána Ombudsman Commission, the body tasked with investigating complaints against the police, had hired a UK security company, Verrimus, following concerns that its offices were under surveillance. An inquiry by Judge Cooke did not find proof of bugging (which, given the technology available, is perhaps not surprising), but the report nevertheless included details of a number of occurrences that – to put it mildly – left many questions unanswered (Cooke Report, 2014). For instance, it remains unclear why an unlisted telephone used for conference calls in the office of the GSOC chairman rang several times at 1.45 a.m. immediately after Verrimus personnel conducted an 'alerting test'.

In a separate development, it emerged that in some Garda stations arrangements had been put in place to allow for the recording of phone calls, including calls between individuals in police custody and their legal representatives. A Commission of Inquiry led by Justice Nial Fennelly was established to investigate this practice over the time period 1980–2013.[4] The recording system came to light following the discovery process in a civil action brought by Ian Bailey, who was suing the Garda Commissioner and the state for wrongful arrest and the fabrication of evidence surrounding the police investigation into the murder of Sophie Toscan du Plantier in West Cork in 1996. Among other things, Bailey alleged that Garda officers pressured a witness into making a false statement placing him at the scene of the murder (Bailey lost the case in the High Court in March 2015).

On the heels of this avalanche of scandal and controversy, in March 2014 the Garda Commissioner resigned, and in May the Minister for Justice did likewise. Amidst this turmoil, debate over how best to ensure the integrity of policing institutions (and to repair the damage caused by these scandals) highlighted the need for robust institutions of governance and oversight to enhance accountability and protect against political interference. Yet it was not only issues of governance and oversight that appeared sorely in need of attention. In a major Garda Inspectorate report on crime investigation published in 2014, routine practices of policing were also found to be wholly inadequate. In a wide-ranging analysis, the Inspectorate found alarming deficiencies and widespread inconsistencies across a range of areas, including: officer training, the recording and classification of crimes, the claiming of detections, investigative practices, management support to officers and levels of support and information provided to victims. Overall, the Garda Inspectorate highlighted:

> [A] police service in critical need of modernisation of its crime investigation operational and support infrastructure. The absence of up to date technology and dated inefficient investigative processes and policies, combined with poor internal audit controls, inconsistent case management and poor supervisory practices have led to the systemic operational deficiencies identified in this and other recent government initiated reports. As a result, potentially hundreds of thousands of Garda staff hours and resources, which should be spent on front-line policing, are currently allocated to those inefficient processes.
>
> *(Garda Inspectorate, 2014: i)*

Draft legislation providing for the establishment of a Policing Authority, and to clarify and enhance the powers of GSOC, was published in late 2014,[5] and it seems inevitable that the coming years will see further debate on the governance and accountability of An Garda Síochána.

Conclusion

This chapter has examined the trajectories of policing across Northern Ireland and the Republic of Ireland, exploring the origins and development of policing in each state, the nature of police–public relations and a range of contemporary challenges. While the field of policing in both jurisdictions is characterised by clear differences, there also are striking similarities and a degree of convergence that often has been occluded, due not least to the impact of the Conflict.

The most immediately striking area of comparison is the differences between policing across jurisdictions. Although political violence affected both police forces, the scale of political division and its impact on policing was simply of a different order in Northern Ireland. Responding to these challenges was a defining feature of policing there: officers were routinely armed, were based in heavily fortified stations and often patrolled with military support. Moreover, security concerns and intelligence-gathering influenced all aspects of policing in Northern Ireland. Police–community relations reflected the contested political backdrop, with sharp differences in the attitudes of nationalists and unionists. In the Republic, a more tranquil model of policing prevailed, in which police officers were (and remain) routinely unarmed, and the integration of the police into the fabric of community life – rather than its technical capacity – became a prominent theme in the official narrative of policing.

Notwithstanding these differences, the similarities are also noteworthy, even if they generally pass without remark. The police forces north and south share the same point of origin, even if subsequently they pursued different pathways in the search for legitimacy. Historically, both police forces epitomised the 'imagined community' (Anderson, 1983) whose interests each state explicitly represented, and they largely functioned under the shadow of the dominant political structures. Their ethos, activities and legitimacy were also shaped fundamentally by issues of state security. In both states, political violence was a reflection of the disputed constitutional status of the partition of Ireland, and the police's role in maintaining state security (and symbolising each state) drew it into conflict. This implicated both police forces in recurring controversies, even as simultaneously it cast them in a heroic light, bolstered their standing among some sections of the public at least and shielded them from many of the criticisms they otherwise would have faced. Beyond the specific impact of political violence, both police forces operated in a climate of stability and conservatism; had little by way of independent oversight; were characterised by great latitude in terms of police practice on the ground, particularly when applied to groups of lower social capital; and enjoyed considerable – if fluctuating – levels of public support.

As the Conflict in Northern Ireland has slowly wound down since the 1990s, there is greater scope for moving beyond the constraints and security measures which so deeply affected policing in both jurisdictions. Clearly one possible outcome here is a greater level of cooperation, leading to convergences in structure, activity and ethos. Throughout the Conflict, there was considerable cooperation at local level, but the political context meant that any move towards developing this at a strategic level was highly controversial and operated with little oversight (Dunn *et al.*, 2002; Walsh, 2011). Yet, whether in relation to ethnic diversity or organised crime, in recent years there seems greater scope for cross-border cooperation. Insofar as peace also leads to the gradual dismantling of their role as state-protector, and with it the relative freedom from scrutiny that each police force experienced, it also may mean that the future relationship both forces develop with their respective publics is likely to be based more on the banal issues of police practice and accountability, rather than on police symbolism reflective of the dominant nationalisms of the day. In that context, it seems plausible to expect greater convergence in the treatment of a range of common challenges, and perhaps a greater degree of formal cooperation to sustain this.

On a final point, the example of policing in both jurisdictions highlights a number of issues in relation to accountability and legitimacy. First, both jurisdictions demonstrate the importance of robust accountability structures. The history of police accountability in each state is one of failure and of gradual and grudging moves towards institutions that are independent and have sufficient powers and resources. The central role the police occupied in each society – particularly in respect of state security – made legislators reluctant to be seen to inhibit its activities. As a consequence, both environments are littered with a variety of policing scandals, many of which relate to state security either directly (in terms of particular practices) or indirectly in terms of the latitude that was applied to other areas. In either case, problems that might have been avoided at the time were stored up for the future, and it is striking that 'legacy' and accountability issues continue to dominate policing debate in both contexts. One can but speculate how different things might be if accountability had been given due attention in earlier years.

Second, while recent literature highlights the role that 'fair procedure and just treatment' (Bradford, 2011: 197; see generally Jackson et al., 2013) play in shaping public attitudes towards (and especially confidence in) the police, the analysis outlined here suggests that legitimacy can be pursued by a variety of means (see Herbert, 2006) – whether through a greater emphasis on the formal aspects of professionalism in Northern Ireland (and the distancing from its traditional support base within unionism that this entailed), or an emphasis on informal community links in the Republic (to the detriment of the development of formal and robust structures of public-consultation and oversight). In the case of Northern Ireland, this professionalism was evident in survey findings which continually found that a majority of Catholic and Protestant respondents expressed satisfaction with the 'ordinary crime' role of the RUC, and respondents always rated the performance of the police locally higher than they rated the police across Northern Ireland as a whole (Mulcahy, 2006; Weitzer, 1995). In the contested setting of Northern Ireland, assessments of the performance of the police were subservient to assessments of the police's wider role. In the case of the Republic, even in the absence of any formal structures of police–community consultation, public satisfaction levels remained strikingly and stubbornly high (Mulcahy, 2008b), due partly at least to the social capital An Garda Síochána accrued for the manner in which it was embedded in and affiliated with local communities. In this sense, legitimacy derived from 'proximity' to community structures and national ideals rather than from propriety or professionalism. Whether a resolution to the conflict means that policing north and south will be extricated from all the difficulties that arose from political division, and that legitimacy increasingly will coalesce around issues of service provision and procedural justice, remains to be seen.

References

AGSI (Association of Garda Sergeants and Inspectors) (1982) *A Discussion Paper Concerning Proposals for a Scheme of Community Policing*. Dublin: AGSI.

Allen, G. (1999) *An Garda Síochána: Policing Independent Ireland 1922–1982*. Dublin: Gill and Macmillan.

Amnesty International (1977) *Report of an Amnesty International Mission to the Republic of Ireland in June 1977*. London: Amnesty International.

Anderson, B. (1983) *Imagined Communities*. London: Verso.

Bayley, D. (2008) 'Post-conflict police reform: Is Northern Ireland a model?', *Policing*, 2: 233–40.

Bennett, D. (1988) 'Are they always right?: Investigation and proof in a citizen anti-heroin movement', in M. Tomlinson, T. Varley and C. McCullagh (eds) *Whose Law and Order?* Belfast: Sociological Association of Ireland.

Bohan, P. and Yorke, D. (1987) 'Law enforcement marketing: Perceptions of a police force', *Irish Marketing Review*, 2: 72–86.

Bowden, M. (2014) *Crime, Disorder and Symbolic Violence: Governing the Urban Periphery*. London: Palgrave.

Bradford, B. (2011) 'Convergence, not divergence? Trends and trajectories in public contact and confidence in the police', *British Journal of Criminology*, 51: 179–200.

Brady, C. (2000) *Guardians of the Peace*, 2nd ed. London: Prendeville.

—— (2014) *The Guarding of Ireland: The Garda Síochána and the Irish State 1960–2014*. Dublin: Gill and Macmillan.

Brennan, D. (2015) 'Mental illness and the criminalisation process', in D. Healy, Y. Daly, C. Hamilton and M. Butler (eds), *Routledge Handbook of Irish Criminology*. Abingdon: Routledge.

Brewer, J. with Magee, K. (1991) *Inside the RUC: Routine policing in a divided society*. Oxford: Clarendon.

Brewer, J., Lockhart, B. and Rodgers, P. (1997) *Crime in Ireland 1945–1995: Here be dragons*. Oxford: Clarendon.

Browne, C. (2008) *Garda Public Attitudes Survey 2008 (Research Report 1/08)*. Templemore, Co. Tipperary: Garda Research Unit.

Charman, S. and Corcoran, D. (2015) 'Adjusting the police occupational cultural landscape: The case of An Garda Síochána', *Policing and Society*, 25: 484–503.

Committee on the Administration of Justice (2015) *The Apparatus of Immunity? Human Rights Violations and the Northern Ireland Conflict: A Narrative of Official Limitations on Post-Agreement Investigative Mechanisms*. Belfast: CAJ.

Connolly, J. (2002) 'Policing Ireland: Past, present and future' in P. O'Mahony (ed.) *Criminal Justice in Ireland*. Dublin: Institute of Public Administration.

Consultative Group on the Past (2009) *Report of the Consultative Group on the Past*. Belfast: Stationery Office.

Conway, V. (2009) 'A sheep in wolf's clothing? Evaluating the impact of the Garda Síochána Ombudsman Commission', *Irish Jurist*, 43: 109–30.

—— (2010) *The Blue Wall of Silence: The Morris Tribunal and Police Accountability in Ireland*. Dublin: Irish Academic Press.

—— (2013) *Policing Twentieth Century Ireland: A History of An Garda Síochána*. Abingdon: Routledge.

Cooke Report (2014) *Inquiry into Reports of Unlawful Surveillance of Garda Síochána Ombudsman Commission*. Report by Judge John D. Cooke. Dublin: Department of An Taoiseach.

Criminal Justice Inspection Northern Ireland (CJINI) (2011) *An Inspection into the Independence of the Office of the Police Ombudsman for Northern Ireland*. Belfast: CJINI.

—— (2013) *A Review of the Cost and Impact of Dealing with the Past on Criminal Justice Organisations in Northern Ireland*. Belfast: CJINI.

Cullen, B. (1991) 'Community and drugs: A case study of community conflict in the inner city of Dublin', unpublished M.Litt. thesis, Trinity College Dublin.

Cunningham, Niall (2013) '"The doctrine of vicarious punishment": Space, religion and the Belfast Troubles of 1920–22', *Journal of Historical Geography*, 40(1): 52–66.

Dunn, S., Murray, D. and Walsh, D. (2002) *Cross Border Police Co-Operation in Ireland*. Limerick: University of Limerick.

Dunne, D. and Kerrigan, G. (1984) *Round Up the Usual Suspects: Nicky Kelly and the Cosgrave Coalition*. Dublin: Magill.

Ellison, G. (2007) 'A blueprint for democratic policing anywhere in the world: Police reform, political transition, and conflict resolution in Northern Ireland', *Police Quarterly*, 10: 243–69.

Ellison, G. and Mulcahy, A. (2001) 'The "policing question" in Northern Ireland', *Policing and Society*, 11: 243–58.

Ellison, G. and O'Rawe, M. (2010) 'Security governance in transition: The compartmentalizing, crowding out and corralling of policing and security in Northern Ireland', *Theoretical Criminology*, 14: 31–57.

Ellison, G. and Smyth, J. (2000) *The Crowned Harp: Policing in Northern Ireland*. London: Pluto.

Ellison, G., Pino, N. and Shirlow, P. (2013) 'Assessing the determinants of public confidence in the police: A case study of a post-conflict community in Northern Ireland', *Criminology and Criminal Justice*, 13(5): 552–576.

Farrell, M. (1980) *Northern Ireland: The Orange State*. London: Pluto.

Ferriter, D. (2012) *Occasions of Sin: Sex and Society in Modern Ireland*. London: Profile.

Garda Inspectorate (2014) *Crime Investigation*. Dublin: Garda Inspectorate.

Garda Research Institute (2013) *Making Policing History: Studies of Garda Violence and Resources for Police Reform*. Dublin: Workers Solidarity Movement.

Guerin Report (2014) *Review of the Action Taken by An Garda Síochána Pertaining to Certain Allegations Made by Sergeant Maurice McCabe*. Dublin: Department of the Taoiseach.

Her Majesty's Inspectorate of Constabulary (HMIC) (2013) *Inspection of the Police Service of Northern Ireland Historical Enquiries Team*. London: HMSO.

Herbert, S. (2006) 'Tangled up in blue: Conflicting paths to police legitimacy', *Theoretical Criminology*, 10: 481–504.

Hunt Report (1969) *Report of the Advisory Committee on Police in Northern Ireland* (Cmd. 535). Belfast: HMSO.

Independent Commission on Policing for Northern Ireland (ICP) (1999) *A New Beginning: Policing in Northern Ireland (the Patten Report)*. Belfast: Stationery Office.

Inglis, T. (1998) *Moral Monopoly: The Rise and Fall of the Catholic Church in Modern Ireland*, 2nd ed. Dublin: University College Dublin Press.

—— (2003) *Truth, Power and Lies: Irish Society and the Case of the Kerry Babies*. Dublin: University College Dublin Press.

—— (2008) *Global Ireland: Same Difference*. Abingdon: Routledge.

Interdepartmental Group on Urban Crime and Disorder (1992) *Urban Crime and Disorder: Report of the Interdepartmental Group*. Dublin: Stationery Office.

Irish Times (2002) 'Cases against gardai could be prejudiced – GRA', 19 November.

—— (2014) 'PSNI chief announces departure date with plea for new approach to the past', 6 June.

—— (2014) 'Cutbacks lead to "effective closure" of Historical Enquiries Team', 30 September.

Jackson, J., Bradford, B., Stanko, B. and Hohl, K. (2013) *Just Authority? Trust in the Police in England and Wales*. Abingdon: Routledge.

Kearns, K. (2014) *The Legendary 'Lugs Branigan' – Ireland's Most Famed Garda*. Dublin: Gill and Macmillan.

Keogh, E. (1997) *Illicit Drug Use and Related Criminal Activity in the Dublin Metropolitan Area*. Dublin: An Garda Síochána.

Kilcommins, S., O'Donnell, I., O'Sullivan, E. and Vaughan, B. (2004) *Crime, Punishment and the Search for Order in Ireland*. Dublin: Institute of Public Administration.

Lawther, C. (2014) *Truth, Denial and Transition: Northern Ireland and the Contested Past*. Abingdon: Routledge.

Lee, J. (1989) *Ireland, 1912–1985: Politics and Society*. Cambridge: Cambridge University Press.

Lundy, P. (2009) 'Can the past be policed? Lessons from the Historical Enquiries Team Northern Ireland', *Law and Social Challenges*, 11: 109–71.

—— (2011) 'Paradoxes and challenges of transitional justice at the "local" level: Historical enquiries in Northern Ireland', *Contemporary Social Science*, 6: 89–105.

McCusker, T. (2011) *Police Ombudsman Investigation Report*. Belfast: Office of the Minister for Justice.

McGarry, J. and O'Leary, B. (1999) *Policing Northern Ireland: Proposals for a New Start*. Belfast: Blackstaff Press.

Mac Gréil, M. (1996) *Prejudice in Ireland Revisited: Based on a National Survey of Intergroup Attitudes in the Republic of Ireland*. Maynooth: Survey and Research Unit, St Patrick's College.

McInerney, D. (2004) 'Intercultural Ireland: Developing the role of ethnic liaison officers within An Garda Siochana', unpublished M.Phil. thesis, Trinity College Dublin.

McNiffe, L. (1997) *A History of the Garda Síochána*. Dublin: Wolfhound.

Malcolm, E. (2006) *The Irish Policeman, 1822–1922*. Dublin: Four Courts Press.

Manning, P. (2012) 'Trust and accountability in Ireland: The case of An Garda Síochána', *Policing and Society*, 22: 346–61.

Mitchell, C. (2006) *Religion, Identity and Politics in Northern Ireland: Boundaries of Belonging and Belief*. Aldershot: Ashgate

Morris, Justice Frederick (2004–2008) *Reports of the Tribunal of Inquiry Set Up Pursuant to the Tribunal of Inquiry (Evidence) Acts 1921–2002 into Certain Gardaí in the Donegal Division*. Dublin: Stationery Office.

Mulcahy, A. (1999) 'Visions of normality: Peace and the reconstruction of policing in Northern Ireland', *Social and Legal Studies*, 8: 277–95.

—— (2002) 'The impact of the Northern "Troubles" on criminal justice in the Irish Republic' in P. O'Mahony (ed.) *Criminal Justice in Ireland*. Dublin: Institute for Public Administration.

—— (2005) 'The "other" lessons from Ireland? Policing, political violence and policy transfer', *European Journal of Criminology*, 2: 185–209.

—— (2006) *Policing Northern Ireland: Conflict, Legitimacy and Reform*. Cullompton: Willan.

—— (2008a) 'Community policing in contested settings: The Patten Report and police reform in Northern Ireland' in T. Williamson (ed.) *The Handbook of Knowledge-Based Policing*. Chichester: Wiley.

—— (2008b) 'Policing, "community" and social change in Ireland' in J. Shapland (ed.) *Justice, Community and Civil Society*. Cullompton: Willan.

—— (2012) '"Alright in their own place": Policing and the spatial regulation of Irish Travellers', *Criminology and Criminal Justice*, 12: 307–27.

—— (2013) 'Great expectations and complex realities: Assessing the impact and implications of police reform in Northern Ireland' in J. Brown (ed.) *The Future of Policing*. Abingdon: Routledge.

Mulcahy, A. and O'Mahony, E. (2005) *Policing and Social Marginalisation in Ireland* (Working Paper 05/02). Dublin: Combat Poverty Agency.

Murphy, J. (2013) *Policing for Peace in Northern Ireland: Change, Conflict and Community Confidence*. Basingstoke: Palgrave Macmillan.

Murphy-Lawless, J. (2002) *Fighting Back: Women and the Impact of Drug Abuse on Families and Communities*. Dublin: Liffey Press.

Ó Briain Committee (1978) *Report of the Committee to Recommend Certain Safeguards for Persons in Custody and for Members of An Garda Síochána*. Dublin: Stationery Office.

O'Donnell, T. (2004) 'Building public confidence through the deliberation of police strategy'. *Communique*, December: 17–29.

O'Sullivan, D. (1999) *The Irish Constabularies, 1822–1922*. Dingle: Brandon Books.

O'Sullivan, E. and O'Donnell, I. (eds) (2012) *Coercive Confinement in Ireland*. Manchester: Manchester University Press.

Oversight Commissioner (2007) *Overseeing the Proposed Revisions for the Policing Services of Northern Ireland – Report 19* (Final Report). Belfast: Office of the Oversight Commissioner.

Parkinson, A. (2004) *Belfast's Unholy War: The Troubles of the 1920s*. Dublin: Four Courts Press.

Patten, C. (2010) 'Personal reflections on chairing the commission' in D. Doyle (ed.) *Policing the Narrow Ground: Lessons from the Transformation of Policing in Northern Ireland*. Dublin: Royal Irish Academy.

Ruane, J. and Todd, J. (1996) *The Dynamics of Conflict in Northern Ireland*. Cambridge: Cambridge University Press.

Scarman Report (1972) *Violence and Civil Disturbances in Northern Ireland in 1969* (Cmd 566). Belfast: HMSO.

Shearing, C. (2010) 'The curious case of the Patten Report' in D. Doyle (ed.) *Policing the Narrow Ground: Lessons from the Transformation of Policing in Northern Ireland*. Dublin: Royal Irish Academy.

Smithwick Tribunal (2013) *Report of the Tribunal of Inquiry into Suggestions That Members of An Garda Síochána or Other Employees of the State Colluded in the Fatal Shootings of RUC Chief Superintendent Harry Breen and RUC Superintendent Robert Buchanan on the 20th March 1989*. Dublin: Stationery Office.

Topping, J. (2008a) 'Diversifying from within: Community policing and the governance of security in Northern Ireland', *British Journal of Criminology*, 48: 778–97.

—— (2008b) 'Community policing in Northern Ireland: A resistance narrative', *Policing and Society*, 18: 377–96.

Topping, J. and Byrne, J. (2014) 'Shadow policing: The boundaries of community-based "policing" in Northern Ireland', *Policing and Society*. Advance Access – DOI: 0.1080/10439463.2014.989152 (accessed: 15 February 2015).

UCD Institute of Criminology (2003) *Public Order Offences in Ireland*. Dublin: Stationery Office.

Walker, M. (2007) *Traveller/Ethnic Minority Communities' Attitudes to the Garda Síochána 2007* (Research Report No. 9/07). Dublin: An Garda Síochána.

Walsh, David (2000) 'Policing pluralism' in M. MacLachlan and M. O'Connell (eds) *Cultivating Pluralism*. Dublin: Oak Tree Press.

Walsh, Dermot. (1999) *The Irish Police: A Legal and Constitutional Perspective*. Dublin: Round Hall.

—— (2011) 'Police cooperation across the Irish border: Familiarity breeding contempt for transparency and accountability', *Journal of Law and Society*, 38: 301–30.

Walsh, Dermot. and Conway, V. (2011) 'Current developments in police governance and accountability in Ireland', *Crime, Law and Social Change*, 55: 241–57.

Weitzer, R. (1995) *Policing Under Fire: Ethnic Conflict and Police-Community Relations in Northern Ireland*. Albany NY: New York Press.

Whyte, J. (1990) *Interpreting Northern Ireland*. Oxford: Clarendon.

Notes

1 This included large-scale rioting in the 1930s, the IRA campaign during the Second World War and its 'border campaign' of 1956–62.

2 Kevin O'Higgins, a minister in the years immediately following independence, once claimed that: 'We

were the most conservative minded revolutionaries ever to put through a successful revolution' (quoted in Lee, 1989: 105).

3 The terms of reference for the Commission are available at: http://www.justice.ie/en/JELR/Pages/PR14000376.

4 The terms of reference for the Fennelly Commission are available at: http://www.taoiseach.gov.ie/eng/News/Government_Press_Releases/Government_Announces_Terms_of_Reference_for_Commission_of_Investigation_to_be_Conducted_by_Mr_Justice_Fennelly.html.

5 This is available at: http://www.justice.ie/en/JELR/Pages/PB14000310.

14

The criminal justice process
From questioning to trial

Yvonne Daly and John Jackson

Introduction

The manner in which criminal offences are investigated, prosecuted and tried varies greatly from jurisdiction to jurisdiction. The particular criminal process or criminal justice system which operates is arrived at over time and results from the convergence of many factors as varied as the historic background of the jurisdiction, the international human rights instruments to which the state has acceded, the cases which happen to have come before the courts, current or past crises or perceived crises which have occurred therein and the political leanings of its current government.

A particular distinguishing feature of the development of the criminal processes in Northern Ireland and the Republic of Ireland has been the impact of security threats on the ordinary corpus of criminal procedure. Ever since the partition of Ireland, the island has been blighted by periodic bouts of political and paramilitary violence, met on the part of governments on both sides of the border by emergency legislation which has spilled over into the criminal justice systems of both jurisdictions. In Northern Ireland, the old Stormont government's response to security threats was to resort to detention without any form of trial at all under the infamous Special Powers legislation (Boyle *et al.*, 1975). After direct rule was imposed by the British government in 1972, non-jury trials on indictment were introduced into the criminal justice system in so-called 'Diplock' courts, and such trials can still take place.[1] Powers designed purely for security were invested in the ordinary criminal justice agencies which were given responsibility for countering the security threat in Northern Ireland in a strategy known as 'criminalisation' (Boyle *et al.*, 1980: 31). In the Republic *Bunreacht na Eireann*, the Irish Constitution, specifically provides for special non-jury courts to be established by legislation, and the Offences Against the State Act (OASA) 1939 made provision for a Special Criminal Court to come into operation when the government deemed the ordinary courts inadequate to secure the effective administration of justice. Proclamations to this effect, in response to security threats linked to the Conflict in Northern Ireland, were made for prolonged periods of time: 1939–46; 1961–62; and 1972 to the present day.[2] As we shall see, this non-jury court gradually came to be used in the trial of offences with no link to paramilitary activity.

This is one example of how the normalisation of emergency powers has played a significant role in the development of the criminal process in both jurisdictions. The result of the security legislation spill-over into the criminal justice systems in both jurisdictions was that for many years law was, as Kilcommins and Vaughan (2008: 67–69) have put it, 'in the shadow of the gunman'. While Mulcahy (2005: 186) has cautioned against the overstatement of the 'contagion thesis' he, like others, accepts that emergency measures introduced in the context of addressing paramilitary activity in the Republic and in Northern Ireland displayed a tendency 'gradually to influence the entire legal landscape' (Mulcahy, 2005: 189). Although a peace process has been in place on both parts of the island since the signing of the Good Friday Agreement in 1998, many of these measures continue in force and, by a process described by one of us (in the context of expanding legislative incursions on the right to silence) as 'function creep' (Daly, 2011: 32; 2014: 74), have come to be used to combat other threats to the state such as that of 'gangland' crime.

This chapter considers the manner in which certain aspects of criminal procedure both north and south of the border have developed and changed in the course of the past four decades. While the period from partition up to the 1970s was marked by 'slow deliberate change in the basic principles, structures and processes of the criminal justice system', within the last forty years the pace of change has quickened significantly (Walsh, 2002: x). Structural changes have included the introduction of the Office of the Director of Public Prosecutions (DPP) in 1972, which transformed prosecution arrangements in the Republic (Hancock and Jackson, 2008), and a number of changes following the Good Friday Agreement in Northern Ireland including: a new Public Prosecution Service in 2005; the devolution of policing and criminal justice functions to the Northern Ireland Assembly; and the introduction of Criminal Justice Inspection Northern Ireland – a body responsible for inspecting all aspects of the criminal justice system other than the judiciary. However, the central focus of this chapter is not on structural changes, but on significant shifts observed over the course of four decades in the manner in which suspects are brought to trial. Our discussion is loosely structured around Packer's (1968) famous models of 'crime control' and 'due process', which were used to illustrate the tensions between certain 'value-clusters' (Kraska, 2006: 179) within the American criminal process. His models have been widely applied elsewhere, and, for all the criticisms made of them (e.g. Reed, 1985; Smith, 1997; 1998; Roach, 1999), they provide a useful starting point for any discussion of the criminal process.[3]

The 'crime control' model views the repression of crime as the primary goal of the criminal process and places emphasis on speed and efficiency within the criminal process over the protection of individual rights, in order to achieve that goal. The 'due process' model, by contrast, considers that, even though the repression of crime is a laudable and important goal, other issues such as the protection of individual rights and the prevention of state oppression of the individual must also be considered. Although Packer (1968) was at pains to emphasise that his models were not based upon entirely opposing values, and there was common ground between them, one of the criticisms of his approach is that he 'failed to give a clear explanation of the relationship between his models' (Ashworth and Redmayne, 2010: 40). This has allowed an arguably 'artificial opposition' to be set up between the models in subsequent criminal justice discourse, with the 'crime control' model being assigned the role of the public interest and the 'due process' model asserting the private interest of the individual accused. This has set the parameters for how these interests should be 'balanced' (Dennis, 1989: 30). Another limitation of Packer's models, which were designed in the 1960s, is that they are not cognisant of the rise of victims' rights (Roach, 1999). The perspective of victims now also has to be accommodated alongside other competing values within the criminal process (Ashworth and Redmayne, 2010), although as we shall see, there has been a tendency to assume that the interests of victims are always in opposition to the interests of the accused.

One of the most notable changes in the criminal process of both the Republic and Northern Ireland over the last forty years has been a decided shift of focus from the courtroom to the police station, as arrested suspects can be detained for longer periods and are systematically questioned in police custody, with anything they say or do not say recorded and, in many cases, able to be used against them in court.[4] After questioning, large numbers of defendants who are charged with criminal offences and prosecuted as a result plead guilty, with no forensic examination in court of the evidence against them.[5] The minority who persist in pleading not guilty are faced with a trial where the prosecution faces fewer obstacles in attempting to prove their guilt than used to be the case. These shifts in the direction of crime control are not unique to the Republic or Northern Ireland, which raises the question whether criminal justice policy in each of the jurisdictions over the past forty years has been driven primarily by global developments seen elsewhere or by peculiarly 'local' factors.

The shift towards crime control may be indicative of more general institutional and cultural changes that Garland has argued have taken place in the USA and the UK where 'penal welfarism' has been displaced by a politicisation of crime and a growth in popular punitiveness (Garland, 2001). But it is clear that not every country has experienced such a 'punitive turn' (Zedner, 2002; Downes, 2011), and commentators have highlighted the comparatively low rates of imprisonment and the general resistance to punitiveness in the Republic of Ireland (e.g. Kilcommins *et al.*, 2004; O'Sullivan and O'Donnell, 2007; Hamilton, 2014). We will argue that domestic 'home-grown' crises, such as the emergence of so-called 'gangland' crime in the Republic or paramilitary violence in Northern Ireland, provide a better explanation for the shifts of policy in the direction of crime control, but that these crises have been fomented by a rhetoric that is familiar in other jurisdictions, namely that the traditional focus on due process for the individual accused must be 'rebalanced' in the interests of safeguarding security, protection and the rights of victims. In other words, *both* the domestic and the global contexts have served to reinforce the shift towards crime control. In the context of this apparent shift, questions arise about the influence of the Constitution in the Republic of Ireland and of the European Convention on Human Rights, to which both jurisdictions are signatories, in upholding 'due process' values. These issues are also examined within the chapter.

In the next section we set out the 'due process' underpinnings of the criminal processes in the Republic and Northern Ireland, highlighting the impact of the Constitution in particular in the Republic and the influence of the European Convention on Human Rights in both jurisdictions. Next we look to the rise of crime control measures and compare the position of a criminal suspect in the early 1970s with the modern-day suspect. We examine the 'front-loading' of criminal cases from the trial to the pre-trial process, an experience not unique to the two jurisdictions under consideration here, and we analyse notable shifts which have occurred at the trial stage. We finally consider the strength, or otherwise, of base-line protections, the need for legitimacy in the criminal processes of the two jurisdictions and their future shape.

Due process: the constitutionalisation of the criminal process and human rights

Bunreacht na Eireann, the Irish Constitution, contains several express rights which relate to the prosecution and trial of criminal offences, e.g. Article 38.1, the right to a fair trial; Article 38.5, the right to trial by jury on serious criminal charges; Article 40.4.1, the right to liberty; and Article 40.5, the inviolability of the dwelling (relevant in the context of Garda search and seizure). Constitutional status has also been conferred upon a number of other rights not expressly stated within the document itself, through the interpretation of the superior courts from the mid-1960s onwards. The doctrine of unenumerated rights was first established in *Ryan v AG*,[6] wherein the Supreme Court recognised a constitutional right to bodily integrity. Other unenumerated rights were recognised in criminal cases and, indeed, O'Malley (2009: 1) states that some of the leading decisions 'were motivated by a concern for the rights of suspects and accused persons who found themselves facing the coercive power of the State'. Examples include the presumption of innocence; the right to silence; the right of reasonable access to legal advice; the right to trial within a reasonable time; and the right to proportionality in sentencing.[7] While the courts have been less inclined to expand the list of recognised unenumerated rights since the mid-1990s,[8] O'Malley (2009: 2) suggests that there is an advantage to allowing due process values to be developed through judicial interpretation as 'the rights of suspects, defendants and, nowadays, victims, can evolve in accordance with emerging concepts of justice and progress'. Of course, one of the main drawbacks of this method of rights recognition, besides arguments relating to the legitimacy of such decisions being made by an unelected judiciary, is that it is reliant on the somewhat arbitrary happenstance of which cases make it as far as the superior courts and the specific questions they raise.

Until very recently, one of the strongest protections for suspect rights within the criminal process of the Republic of Ireland was the strict approach adopted by the courts towards the exclusion of unconstitutionally obtained evidence. If only legal rights were breached in obtaining evidence the trial judge held a discretion to admit or exclude such evidence, based on a number of considerations. If the rights breached were of constitutional status, however, the evidence had to be excluded except in extremely limited 'extraordinary excusing circumstances' (*People (AG) v O'Brien*[9]). This rule, 'one of the strictest exclusionary rules (if not *the* strictest one) in the common law world' (Daly, 2011: 63), had considerable impact, since, from the moment an individual comes into contact with the criminal process, it is primarily constitutional rights which come into play: most Garda misconduct in the investigative, pre-trial phase is classified as infringing constitutional, as opposed to purely legal, rights (Daly, 2009). A strong protectionist rationale was expressly adopted for the rule, despite its potential to remove relevant, probative evidence from trial. In *People (DPP) v Kenny*, Finlay CJ stated that 'the detection of crime and the conviction of guilty persons, no matter how important they may be to the ordering of society, cannot … outweigh the unambiguously expressed constitutional obligation "as far as practicable to defend and vindicate the personal rights of the citizen"'.[10] Despite the legislative introduction of many crime control-oriented measures, and the suggestion from Kilcommins and Vaughan (2004: 56) that 'in terms of a devaluation in due process values, [the Republic of] Ireland is now a lodestar for other jurisdictions', this strong due process rule remained in place for 25 years.

However, it was not universally popular: in the *Kenny* case itself there were two particularly strong dissents; the harshness of the rule received judicial criticism in later cases (see, for example, the judgment of Charleton J. in the High Court in *DPP (Walsh) v Cash*[11]); and calls for its replacement with a rule based on balancing and judicial discretion were made by the majority of the Balance in the Criminal Law Review Group (2007). In April 2015, these criticisms found traction in the Supreme Court in *DPP v JC*[12] and, with a 4:3 majority, the Court expressly overruled its own previous decision in *Kenny*, replaced the protectionist rationale with deterrence and set out a new rule relating to unconstitutionally obtained evidence. Essentially this rule provides for a good faith exception such that evidence obtained in inadvertent breach of constitutional rights will not be excluded. It remains to be seen how the new rule will be applied in practice and the definitional parameters of 'inadvertence' are likely to be tested in appropriate cases. Whatever way one looks at it though, the new rule overtly and expressly provides less protection for constitutional rights than its predecessor.

In contrast to the Republic of Ireland, Northern Ireland has no written constitution to which the courts are required to adhere. Traditionally, a number of the rights which have been recognised as unenumerated constitutional rights under the Irish Constitution existed as common law rights developed by the judiciary. Examples relevant to the criminal process include the right to a fair trial, the right to silence and the right to private communication with one's lawyer. Other rights have been underpinned by statute, most notably a suspect's right of access to a lawyer recognised under article 59 of the Police and Criminal Evidence (NI) Order 1989 (PACE). Since the passage of the Human Rights Act 1998, the courts may also make a declaration of incompatibility in respect of any legislative act that is considered to breach the European Convention on Human Rights (ECHR). Although the Northern Irish courts cannot strike down primary legislation in breach of the human rights in the Convention, they must interpret such legislation in a Convention-compliant manner 'in so far as it is practicable to do so'.

The ECHR had an influential effect on the Northern Irish criminal process before it became directly applicable under the Human Rights Act. The landmark judgment of the European Court of Human Rights (ECtHR) in *Ireland v UK*,[13] which ruled that detainees held under the Special Powers legislation in Northern Ireland had been subjected to inhuman and degrading treatment in breach of Article 3 of the ECHR, sent a strong message about the need for ECHR compliance. The ECHR provided a benchmark for assessing the proportionality of the emergency powers that were introduced into the criminal process as part of the criminalisation strategy in response to the "Conflict". When the ECtHR delivered a crushing blow to this policy in *Brogan v UK*,[14] by holding that Article 5 (the right to liberty) was infringed by the detention of terrorist suspects for seven days before bringing them before a court, the UK was forced to derogate from its Convention obligations until the emergency powers were scaled down following the Good Friday Agreement. The ECtHR has continued to intervene on issues since the Agreement and the incorporation of the ECHR into UK law. Thus Article 6(2) of the ECHR which enshrines the presumption of innocence has been applied to require that certain reverse onus clauses putting the burden of proof on the defence be 'read down' as evidential rather than legal burdens (see, for example, *Attorney General's Reference (No 4 of 2002)*[15]), and Article 5 has been applied to circumscribe the circumstances under which the police may stop and search persons under the Terrorism Act 2000 when there is no suspicion that they are in possession of prohibited articles (*Gillan and Quinton v UK*[16]). We shall see, however, that a broad application of the proportionality principle enabling the courts to balance certain rights, such as the right to a fair trial, against other public interests has led to uncertainty about their scope and reach. There is also uncertainty over the degree to which the ECHR requires evidence obtained in breach of Convention rights to be excluded in a criminal trial (Jackson, 2012).

The ECHR has also been influential in the Republic of Ireland since entering into force there in 1953. In the context of the criminal process, a number of state violations of Article 6 ECHR (the right to a fair trial) have been found by the ECtHR, specifically relating to the privilege against self-incrimination/right to silence (e.g. *Heaney and McGuinness v Ireland*[17]) and to delays in criminal proceedings (e.g. *Barry v Ireland*[18]). While it was at one point envisaged that the ECHR might ultimately be adopted directly into law at a constitutional level in the Republic, or that it might be enacted at a legislative level with superiority over ordinary legislation, the legislature in fact chose to import much of the framework for its domestic rights-protection from the Human Rights Act in the UK and enact it as a piece of 'indirect/interpretive legislation' which simply obliges the organs of the state to take account of its provisions and guarantees (Egan, 2003). The European Convention on Human Rights Act 2003 allows for ECHR issues to be directly litigated before the domestic courts, requires that every organ of the state shall perform its functions in a Convention-compliant manner (s 3(1)), provides that judicial notice should be taken of the jurisprudence of the ECtHR (s 4) and allows for the superior courts to make a declaration of incompatibility with the Convention under certain circumstances (s 5). The impact of the Act on domestic rights-protection has, however, been minimal, due to the fact that most rights-based disputes in the Republic can be resolved on the basis of the Constitution, without the need for recourse to the Convention. De Londras (2014: 58–59) suggests that in the Republic rights stemming from the ECHR 'have always played second fiddle to constitutionally enshrined rights' and that the former are really only called into play when recourse to the latter has been unsuccessful. Indeed, since the introduction of the 2003 Act, the courts have insisted that constitutional matters should be considered first, and Convention matters only addressed if the Constitution affords no resolution (*Carmody v Minister for Justice, Equality and Law Reform*[19]). This has raised the concern that the declaration of incompatibility with the ECHR, provided for under the 2003 Act, might become a non-remedy in the Republic, given the somewhat 'awkward fit of a Declaration … designed to instigate political contestation as to rights in a structure of constitutional supremacy in which rights – or at least "rights that matter" from a political perspective – are legally determined and minimally contestable' (de Londras, 2014: 64). While not entirely toothless to date, the incorporation of the ECHR at a domestic level in the Republic has effected no sizeable shift in the criminal process, though members of the Oireachtas have long been aware of their responsibility to uphold both the Constitution and the ECHR in developing legislation.[20]

As a result of the Good Friday Agreement, both jurisdictions have remained committed to human rights protection. It was envisaged that a joint committee of representatives of the two Human Rights Commissions which the governments agreed to establish would consider the possibility of establishing a charter reflecting and endorsing agreed measures for the protection of fundamental rights of everyone living in the island of Ireland (Egan and Murray, 2007). This has yet to see the light of day but there remains a commitment to the Human Rights Commissions remaining in place. With constitutional protection in the Republic and human rights protection in both jurisdictions, the question remains why crime control measures have taken such a hold over the criminal justice agenda over the last four decades.

Crime control: rebalancing the criminal process

In order to see the full measure of change that has taken place in the way suspects are dealt with in both jurisdictions over the last four decades, we need to go back to the criminal process of the early 1970s. At that time a person suspected of a serious criminal offence could not be arrested for the purpose of questioning (except within the context of emergency legislation, such as the OASA 1939 in the Republic and the special powers legislation in Northern Ireland). Within the ordinary criminal justice system, arrest was only for the purposes of bringing the suspect to court to be charged. If charged, a suspect could only be refused bail in the Republic of Ireland on the basis of a risk that he might abscond or interfere with witnesses or evidence; no issue arose as to his propensity to commit crime while on bail. In Northern Ireland, bail could be refused in order to prevent further offences, but here too there was a long tradition in favour of bail (Northern Ireland Law Commission, 2010). The suspect would be tried by a judge and jury (unless charged in the Republic under the 1939 Act) and would not need to provide the prosecution with any advance information as to what defence he might lead at trial. At trial the jury could not be invited to draw any particular conclusions from any failure on the accused's part to answer questions the police might have put to him before trial. If a witness who had spoken to the police about the accused's involvement in the alleged offence told the court that he could no longer remember what he had seen or heard, no evidence as to his prior statement could be introduced. If the accused was acquitted that was the end of the matter, and, under the rule against double jeopardy, he could not be retried in relation to the same offence, even if new evidence came to light.

For the modern-day suspect on both parts of the island much has changed. A suspect can be arrested for interrogation and detained before being brought to court for much longer periods of time (in the Republic for up to 24 hours in relation to most serious offences, and as long as 168 hours (or seven days) in relation to drug-trafficking offences or 'organised crime' offences; in Northern Ireland for up to 96 hours in the case of indictable offences and up to 14 days in terrorist cases). After an initial police-authorised limit is reached (36 hours under PACE in Northern Ireland, 48 hours under various statutes in the Republic), the police must apply to court to further extend detention, but the detained person may not be entitled to attend or have his legal representative attend any such hearing.[21] During detention a suspect can be questioned by the police, and fingerprints and 'non-intimate' samples including swabs from any part of the body (including the mouth, but excluding other body orifices and the genital region) may be taken without consent. Failure to agree to give 'intimate' samples including samples of blood, pubic hair or urine can give rise to adverse inferences at trial. If charged, bail may now be denied in the Republic if there is a risk that the accused might commit offences while on bail. Most indictable offences are still tried by a judge and jury, but, whereas the Special Criminal Court was previously used for subversive crime, it is now also specifically designated to hear certain 'organised crime' offences (see Criminal Justice (Amendment) Act 2009 s 8 and Campbell, 2013). The 'Diplock' courts have been scaled back by the abolition of scheduled offences (offences that were presumptively tried without a jury), but trials on indictment without a jury can still take place for 'certified' trials when the DPP certifies that the offence in question appears to be connected to a proscribed organisation or to religious or political hostility of one person or group towards another person or group (Justice and Security Act 2007, ss 1–9: see Dickson, 2013; Jackson, 2009).

Another change is that there are greater obligations on the defence to co-operate with the police and prosecuting authorities. In both jurisdictions, cautions dating back to the early twentieth century informing suspects that they have a right to remain silent are now outdated, as a failure to answer police questions may in fact harm a suspect's defence (Daly, 2011; Jackson, 2001). Furthermore disclosure obligations in the Republic of Ireland now require the defence to provide the prosecution with advance notice of any alibi on which they will seek to rely at trial (Criminal Justice Act 1984, s 20), if seeking to adduce evidence of a mental condition (Criminal Law (Insanity) Act 2006 s 19(1)), if intending to call an expert witness or adduce expert evidence (Criminal Procedure Act 2012, s 34), or, on a charge of membership of an unlawful organisation under the Offences Against the State Acts, advance notice of any witness to be called (Offences Against the State (Amendment) Act 1998, as amended, s 3(1)). In Northern Ireland, defendants charged with an indictable offence are now required to give to the court and the prosecutor a defence statement setting out what their defence is (Criminal Procedure and Investigations Act 1995, s5(5)). The pressures on the defence to participate prior to trial have gone hand in hand with a general lowering of the evidentiary barriers erected against the prosecutor in having to prove guilt beyond reasonable doubt when cases go to trial. Examples include the growth in the number of 'reverse onus clauses' which interfere with the presumption of innocence by imposing burdens of proof upon the accused in respect of certain issues (Ní Raifeartaigh, 1995; Hamilton, 2007). We shall see that a general relaxation of the evidentiary rules relating to opinion evidence and hearsay have enabled prosecutors to admit evidence that would have been inadmissible forty years ago, including prior contradictory statements of witnesses, and that inroads have been made into the double jeopardy rule. Although we shall see that some of these changes in the direction of crime control can be attributed to the process of 'function-creep' arising from emergency-powers legislation, a large number of them mirror changes that have occurred in the neighbouring jurisdiction of England and Wales and invite a discussion of how exactly they came to be imported on to Irish soil.

'Front loading' the criminal process

Over a number of years there has been a general policy across many common law jurisdictions to 'front load' the forensic enterprise into the pre-trial phase of proof in order to expedite criminal proceedings and keep cases out of court. One of the starting points in this drive towards crime control efficiency has been to give the police powers to make arrests and hold suspects for questioning so that they can be questioned about their suspected criminal activity before any court appearance.

The OASA 1939 can be viewed as the forebear of a number of measures which illustrate the shift from due process ideals towards a crime control orientation in the Republic. That Act was introduced as a response to the declaration of the IRA in late 1938/early 1939 that its Executive Council was the legitimate and legal government of every part of Ireland and to its purported declaration of war on the United Kingdom. Amongst its provisions were the first to allow for detention for the purposes of interrogation (s 30), interference with the right to silence (s 52) and use of the Special Criminal Court (ss 35–53). Following their initial introduction, expanded use of Garda powers under the 1939 Act led to their normalisation and eventual acceptance in a broader context (see de Londras and Davis, 2010; Gross and Ní Aoláin, 2006; Walsh, 1989). This is particularly true of the power to arrest a suspect under the 1939 Act for the purposes of detention for questioning. Within the ordinary corpus of criminal law such a power did not exist until the mid-1980s, whereas it was provided for under s 30 of the 1939 Act. While it was confined to the offences covered by the Act, the Garda Síochána developed certain practices to circumvent this difficulty and broaden its application. First, the Gardaí began to employ the anti-subversive legislation in cases which lacked any element of a subversive nature. Secondly, they began to use 'holding charges', i.e. they would arrest and detain suspects for offences covered by the 1939 Act where their real investigative interest in the suspect related to a wholly different offence which was not covered by the Act. A number of conflicting judgments were initially issued by the courts in relation to the legality of these Garda practices (e.g. *People (DPP) v Towson*;[22] *State (Bowes) v Fitzpatrick*;[23] and *State (Trimbole) v Governor of Mountjoy Prison*[24]), but the Supreme Court ultimately gave them legal *imprimatur* in *People (DPP) v Quilligan*.[25] Walsh (1989: 1110–1111) has suggested that this effected a 'silent, but very significant, shift in the traditional balance built into the criminal process'. Eventually, the exception provided for under the 1939 Act was adopted as the norm, as later legislation introduced a more general power of arrest for detention (Criminal Justice Act 1984 s 4) and allowed for extensive periods of potential detention for suspects in particular types of cases (Criminal Justice (Drug Trafficking) Act 1996 s 2; Offences Against the State Act 1939 s 30 as amended by the Offences Against the State (Amendment) Act 1998; and the Criminal Justice Act, 2007 s 50(1)).

The Conflict in Northern Ireland and the emergency powers that arose from it also provided the backcloth for many increased police powers there. The criminalisation strategy introduced in the 1970s divided the criminal justice system into two tiers – an emergency tier where suspects were arrested and questioned under emergency powers and processed through the 'Diplock' courts; and an 'ordinary' tier reserved for the euphemistically described 'ordinary decent criminals' who were processed under ordinary powers and tried by judge and jury. In the late 1980s, however, this two-tiered system began to fragment when powers that were justified as necessary to deal with the 'emergency' seeped into the ordinary criminal justice process and the gap between the two tiers began to narrow. The catalyst for this fragmentation was the introduction of legislation across the entire criminal process to enable adverse inferences to be drawn when suspects refused to mention facts to the police later relied on in their defence, or refused to account for incriminating facts linking them to crimes (Criminal Evidence (NI) Order 1988; Jackson,

1989). The provisions have their genesis in the recommendations of the report of the Criminal Law Revision Committee in England and Wales (1972). The report was shelved at the time because of widespread opposition to such deep-rooted inroads into the right of silence (although they were introduced in Singapore in 1977). Curtailment of the right to silence was justified in the 1980s by the need to break down the 'wall of silence' erected by terrorist suspects when they were questioned by the police. As in the Republic of Ireland, measures justified for an emergency context became the norm across the entire criminal justice spectrum. The legislation pre-empted a package of measures known as PACE which had been introduced in England and Wales in 1984 and came to be enacted in Northern Ireland under the Police and Criminal Evidence (NI) Order 1989, giving greater powers of arrest and detention to the police in ordinary criminal cases balanced by safeguards such as a right of access to a lawyer in detention (Greer, 1989).

When the curtailment of the right of silence came to be challenged before the ECtHR, the Court held that although the right to remain silent under police questioning and the privilege against self-incrimination were recognised standards which lay at the heart of a fair procedure under Article 6 ECHR, the right to silence was not absolute, and it could not prevent a court taking into account an accused's silence in situations which clearly called for an explanation (*Murray (John) v UK*[26]). However, the Court considered that the scheme contained in the legislation made it of 'paramount importance' for the rights of the defence that an accused had access to a lawyer at the initial stages of police investigation. This helped to narrow the gap still further between the processing of terrorist and ordinary suspects and meant that in time terrorist suspects were given very similar rights of access to a lawyer as those given to ordinary suspects. There continue to be separate codes of practice governing the two kinds of suspect, and non-jury courts still continue for terrorist suspects. Under the Terrorism Act 2000 anti-terror powers were put on a permanent footing along with anti-terror powers in the rest of the UK, and responsibility for terrorism law remains with the UK government, rather than with the Department of Justice in Northern Ireland. However, the interchange between the ways the two types of suspect are processed has resulted in a normalisation and convergence of treatment.

The acceptance by the ECtHR in *Murray* that there might be some legitimate interference with the privilege against self-incrimination or the right to silence, reiterated by that Court in *Heaney and McGuinness v Ireland*,[27] legitimised the use of similar inference-drawing provisions in the Republic of Ireland. Under the Criminal Justice Act 1984, inferences can be drawn at trial from the pre-trial failure of the accused to account for his presence in a particular place or for objects, substances or marks on his person or in his possession or in the place where he was arrested. In 1996, following the high-profile murders of investigative journalist Veronica Guerin and Detective Sergeant Jerry McCabe and a resultant public outcry (see O'Donnell and O'Sullivan, 2001; O'Mahony, 1996), a more extensive inference-drawing provision was introduced as part of a package of legislative measures, though it only operated in the context of drug trafficking offences. This provision allowed for inferences to be drawn from the failure of the accused to mention, during the pre-trial process, a fact which he later relied on in his defence which he ought reasonably to have mentioned at the time of questioning or charging (Criminal Justice (Drug Trafficking) Act 1996 s 7). This was replicated under the Offences Against the State (Amendment) Act 1998. In 2007, a broader provision of the same nature was applied to all arrestable offences (Criminal Justice Act 1984 s 19A, as inserted by the Criminal Justice Act 2007), and in 2009 an even more wide-ranging inference-drawing provision was added to the statute-book in the Republic permitting inferences to be drawn at trial directly from a failure to answer any question material to the investigation of an offence of participating in or contributing to any activity of a criminal organisation (Criminal Justice Act 2006 s 72A, as inserted by the Criminal Justice (Amendment) Act 2009).

These inference-bearing provisions in both Northern Ireland and the Republic of Ireland represent an important shift in the balance of power between the police and the suspect in the police station, breaking with tradition by making the police station and not just the courtroom a legitimate forum for holding suspects to account for their actions and giving the police the moral authority to do so. They gave formal endorsement to a view propounded particularly in England and Wales that as suspects are given increasing access to legal advice in the police station, the balance should shift towards curtailing the right of silence and set an important precedent for other jurisdictions to follow. Although the United States, Canada and most of the territories of Australia continue to hold out against adverse inference provisions, the Northern Ireland provisions were adopted in England and Wales in 1994 (ss 34–37 of the Criminal Justice and Public Order Act 1994), and in 2013 New South Wales embraced the concept of drawing inferences when accused persons charged with indictable offences fail to mention facts relied on in their defence (Evidence Amendment (Evidence of Silence) Act 2013).

Shifting the balance at trial

While one of the most prominent changes in the criminal process has been the shift in focus from the courtroom to the police station, the trial stage remains important in those cases where guilt is contested. Writing over forty years ago, Damaška (1973) argued that across the common law world there were significant barriers mounted against prosecutors at trial in proving the guilt of the accused which contrasted with European continental trial practice. In the intervening forty years these barriers have been lowered across many common law jurisdictions. In the Irish context the use of the Special Criminal Court and the 'Diplock' courts resulting in the withdrawal of the jury to deal with subversion has led in practice to an 'adversarial deficit' for the defence in terms of narrowing the scope for challenging the prosecution evidence (Jackson and Doran, 1995). In Northern Ireland the threshold for admitting confessions in 'Diplock' cases was lowered from the old voluntariness standard at common law to the minimum standard of the absence of torture, inhuman and degrading treatment, although this was raised to conform with the PACE standard based upon reliability and the lack of oppression in 2002 (see article 74 of the PACE (NI) Order 1989). In the Republic the provision permitting Gardaí to give opinion evidence that the accused was a member of an unlawful organisation continues in force (OASA (Amendment) Act 1972 s 3(2)), and a new provision has been introduced permitting Gardaí to give an opinion on the existence of a criminal organisation in organised crime cases (Criminal Justice Act 2006 s 71B, as inserted by the Criminal Justice (Amendment) Act 2009 s 7). The former provision has withstood constitutional and human rights challenge in a number of cases (e.g. *DPP v Donnelly and Others*[28]).

The provisions discussed above permitting judges and jurors to draw inferences from silence are a further example of measures introduced on the basis that they were necessary to deal with the Conflict that have remained on the statute book as permanent, normalised measures. However, it can be argued that these measures have had more impact at the pre-trial stage, because of their psychological impact in persuading suspects to answer questions, than at the trial stage, where the ECtHR has scrutinised very carefully the inferences that judges have drawn and the kinds of directions to be given to juries (e.g. *Condron v UK*[29]). In Northern Ireland the provisions have gone further than in the Republic by permitting inferences to be drawn from an accused's failure to testify at trial (Criminal Evidence (NI) Order 1988, Article 4), and research suggests that this provision has had a considerable impact in encouraging defendants in both jury and non-jury trials to give evidence (Jackson *et al.*, 2000).

Although these measures have their provenance in the need to deal with particular security threats arising from the Conflict, a number of other measures lowering the evidentiary barriers for proving guilt at trial can be attributed to a broader demand, evident across a number of other jurisdictions, that the criminal justice system be 'rebalanced' in favour of victims. Within the last four decades there has been a growing recognition of the importance attached to those who are victims of crime. Forty years ago, the offending individual was the focus of much criminological concern, and the individual victim hardly featured at all (Garland, 2002). Today these positions have been reversed, with the process of individualisation shifting away from the defendant towards the victim and centring upon keeping victims informed, offering them support, consulting with them prior to decision making and involving them in the judicial process (see Kilcommins and Moffett, *infra*). Within the jurisdictions under consideration here, attempts to put the victim more at the centre of the criminal process have included giving the victim a right to make a personal statement informing the court of the impact that a crime has had. A number of reforms have additionally focused on the concerns of vulnerable witnesses. Special measures have been introduced to provide support to witnesses and enhance their ability to achieve their best evidence such as the giving of evidence via video-link, the use of recorded pre-trial statements and the removal of the public from the courtroom (Criminal Evidence Act 1992 in the Republic and Criminal Evidence (NI) Order 1999 in Northern Ireland).

While these changes have not particularly impacted on defendants, others have had the effect of undermining defendants' rights, as they have gone hand in hand with conscious efforts to rebalance the criminal justice system in favour of victims and against defendants. Thus in Northern Ireland in the early 2000s, before the devolution of criminal justice functions to the Northern Ireland Assembly, a package of reforms was introduced as a result of a deliberate policy on the part of the 'New Labour' government in the UK to put victims at the core of criminal justice at the expense of defendants. This included major incursions on the hearsay rule, allowing for the admission of the written statements of witnesses who are unable to be cross-examined in court, and changes aimed at expanding the circumstances in which juries can be informed about a defendant's previous convictions and bad character whilst reducing the circumstances under which witnesses' bad character may be revealed to the jury (Criminal Justice (Evidence) (NI) Order 2003). While the value of these measures for victims has been questioned (Jackson, 2003), they have made major inroads into traditional common law safeguards protecting defendants at trial. A human rights challenge to the hearsay provisions on the basis that they infringed the defendant's right to examine witnesses resulted in an adverse finding by the ECtHR against the UK in 2009[30] – although this was partially reversed in 2012 by a later ruling of the Grand Chamber that convictions could be based 'solely' or 'decisively' on written statements, provided there were sufficient counter-balancing measures in place, including the existence of strong procedural safeguards.[31] A further break with tradition was made in 2003 when the double jeopardy rule was curtailed by permitting a retrial of defendants who have been acquitted of certain serious criminal offences where there is 'new and compelling evidence' (Criminal Justice Act 2003 s 78).

In the Republic, concerns about the need to protect victims have given rise to a similar rhetoric of 'rebalancing' the criminal justice system. In 2006, the Minister for Justice established the *ad hoc* Balance in the Criminal Law Review Group (2007: 3) aimed at:

> [S]triking a fair balance between the rights of the community in general and those of victims of crime in particular on the one hand and the traditional rights of an accused as protected by the Constitution, the ECHR, statute and, indeed, the common law on the other.

The Final Report of this Group called for changes to the right to silence, the exclusionary rule relating to unconstitutionally obtained evidence, character evidence and the rule against double jeopardy amongst other matters. Most, but not all, of these recommendations were implemented.

As in Northern Ireland, changes to the hearsay rule allowing for the admission of previous witness statements have come about in the Republic also, though their introduction in that jurisdiction was prompted by the high-profile collapse of the Liam Keane murder trial in November 2003, through the apparent intimidation of witnesses. Legislation was enacted to admit the previous statement of a witness who is available for cross-examination but refuses to give evidence, denies making the statement or gives evidence which is inconsistent with it (Criminal Justice Act 2006 s 16). Despite coming into existence in the context of so-called 'gangland' crime, the statutory language was sufficiently broad to encompass 'a panoply of scenarios involving uncooperative witnesses who have made pre-trial statements' outside the particular setting of gangland crime (Heffernan, 2014: 5.32). Accordingly, a measure apparently targeted at a specific difficulty has again been normalised and broadly applied. Despite its wide scope and the ramifications of the provision for the tradition of relying on oral witness testimony in criminal trials, this measure would likely withstand any constitutional or human rights challenge because the witness must be tendered for cross-examination (see *DPP v O'Brien*[32]).

The rhetoric of victims' interests has also been cited in the Republic as the reason for introducing other measures in recent years. Announcing proposals for what ultimately became the Criminal Procedure Act 2010 the then Minister for Justice stated that the criminal justice system must be responsive to the needs of society generally 'but it must be especially aware of the trauma and distress of the victims of crime' (Department of Justice, Equality and Law Reform, 2008). In the context of victims' interests, that Act included certain amendments and additions to the law on victim impact statements, and it provided for an accused at trial to lose his shield against the admission of bad character evidence if he or his advocate makes imputations against a deceased or incapacitated victim. Beyond this, the Act also allowed for appeals to the Supreme Court on a point of law following an acquittal at a trial on indictment, and it altered the long-established rule against double jeopardy by allowing for a retrial in relation to specific offences where there is 'new and compelling evidence' and it is in the public interest to allow a retrial. These are most significant changes to the criminal process in the Republic, made more palatable perhaps by their professed provision for the interests of victims.

Recalibrating the balance: base-line protections, legitimacy and the future

This chapter has outlined some of the significant changes which have occurred in the criminal processes of both jurisdictions on the island of Ireland in the course of the past forty years. Whether initially introduced to address subversive activity and later assimilated into the ordinary corpus of the criminal law; enacted in an effort to address victims' interests; or brought about in some other circumstance, many of the changes affecting both the pre-trial and trial stages can be said to have shifted criminal processes in the direction of crime control. The legislature has played a clear role in initiating these changes. Writing in the context of American criminal procedure, Packer (1968) recognised that this organ of government would be the validating authority for the crime control model, an affirmative model that emphasises the existence and exercise of official power. On the other hand, he suggested that the due process model, which asserts the limits on official power, would find its validation in the judiciary and in the law of the Constitution (Packer, 1968: 173). Within the Irish constitutional context, Conway *et al.* (2010) have argued that the courts guard rights which have constitutional status with particular care and are slow to allow any practices to develop which would breach those rights. For example, the courts would not allow pre-trial detention for questioning under the common law or the Constitution until the introduction of the OASA 1939 initially, and then the more mainstream Criminal Justice Act 1984 (see *Dunne v Clinton*;[33] *People (DPP) v O'Loughlin*;[34] *People (DPP) v*

Walsh[35]). However, once legislative measures were put in place, the courts did not interfere with them.

This has been the general experience: where legislation is enacted which interferes with constitutional rights, the courts have usually endorsed it, so long as certain base-line protections are in place to protect the suspect who is subjected to increased risks of lengthy custody and questioning as a result of expanding police powers. In the recent Supreme Court case of *DPP v Gormley; DPP v White*,[36] for example, the Supreme Court unanimously held that an arrested person is entitled to legal advice prior to the commencement of any interrogation. Hitherto the right of access to a lawyer in the Republic had been rather narrowly interpreted as a right to *reasonable* access only. But in a shift of constitutional emphasis away from viewing such a right as embedded in the constitutional lawfulness of custody towards viewing it as a right embedded in the right to a trial in the due course of law, the Court considered that, once the power of the State has been exercised against a suspect in the form of an arrest, deprivation of liberty and subjection to mandatory questioning, it was proper to regard the process thereafter as being intimately connected with a potential criminal trial, rather than being one at a purely investigative stage. This shift in emphasis seems to be a reflection of the shift of the centre of gravity of the criminal process backwards into the police station and a judicial view that due process protections should follow that crime control-oriented realignment. In reaching its decision, the Court noted that both the ECtHR and the US Supreme Court took the position that norms of procedural fairness apply from the point of arrest. It noted the Strasbourg benchmark developed since *Murray* requiring access to a lawyer before and during police questioning in custody (*Salduz v Turkey*[37]) and it also noted the importance stressed by the US and Canadian Supreme Courts of holding off any questioning until a suspect has had an opportunity to consult with counsel (*Miranda v State of Arizona;*[38] *R v Sinclair*[39]). The Supreme Court considered that a 'clear international view' had developed to refrain from interrogating a suspect at a time after the suspect has requested a lawyer which was based upon the vulnerability of the accused in custody and upon the need to protect him or her from self-incrimination. Following the decision in *Gormley and White* and in light of the forthcoming provisions of the EU Directive on the right of access to a lawyer in criminal proceedings (2013/48/EU) along with the decision of the ECtHR in *Salduz v Turkey* and the related UK Supreme Court case of *Cadder v HM's Advocate*,[40] the DPP directed the Garda Síochána that, as of April 2014, suspects were entitled to have a requested solicitor present during Garda interrogation. A Garda Code of Practice on Access to a Solicitor by Persons in Garda Custody was issued in April 2015 (Garda Síochána, 2015). This development represents a significant strengthening of due process, brought about to a large extent by external pressures and international comparisons.

The willingness of the Irish courts to have regard to the legal cosmopolitanism of other foreign judgments in interpreting the Constitution and the legislative requirement on the courts on both sides of the border to take account of Strasbourg jurisprudence are positive indications of the lengths to which the courts will go to ensure that due process baselines are factored into any legislative expansion of police powers. Beyond these baselines, however, the courts have tended to accept the normalisation of increasing police powers and have, in certain contexts, employed the concept of proportionality to allow the state to encroach on citizens' rights in pursuit of legitimate aims such as maintaining public peace and order, provided the rights are affected as little as possible (e.g. *Heaney and McGuinness v Ireland*[41]). The ECtHR has also embraced principles of proportionality and subsidiarity when considering the extent to which Article 6 ECHR rights may be restricted.[42]

Deference to the legislature can account for some of the judicial acceptance of interference with individual rights. There has been a tendency for the courts to accept proportionality arguments based on the need to balance individual rights against the legitimate public interest in crime control. A persistent theme of our review of the criminal justice processes on both parts of the island of Ireland has been the introduction of 'exceptional' measures, justified in terms of the need to respond to 'home-grown' attacks on the security of the state but applied across the criminal justice system as a whole, as they have resonated well with a view expressed across a number of jurisdictions that there needs to be a recalibration away from the traditional focus on defendant's rights (see, for example, Tonry, 2010). One way of giving greater priority to defence interests is to see them not merely in terms of protecting the individual accused but in terms of a public interest legitimating the whole system of criminal justice. In this manner the rights of the suspect or the accused do not merely qualify the legitimate aims of criminal justice as constraints on crime control; they are themselves part of these legitimating aims. Although legitimacy was long neglected by criminologists, it is now recognised that where legal authority is regarded as legitimate by the citizen, compliance is more likely to ensue (Tyler, 1990; Bottoms, 2002; Bottoms and Tankebe, 2012). Part of that legitimacy may be seen in securing verdicts that are not merely accurate in terms of controlling crime but are based upon a process that adheres to the rule of law (cf. Dennis, 2013).

One specific measure which continues to apply both in the Republic and in Northern Ireland, despite constituting a serious challenge to legitimacy in the criminal process, is the use of special, non-jury courts. These may be viewed as a hangover from the darker side of recent Irish history, but we have seen that they remain as an almost permanent feature of the Irish criminal landscape, reinvigorated in the Republic by the assignment of 'organised crime' cases to their jurisdiction and available on an ongoing basis in Northern Ireland for cases relating to paramilitary activity. On both sides of the border the DPP has an unreviewable power to refer classes of offences to non-jury trial. The continued use of non-jury courts for classes of cases rather than on the basis of a case-specific threat of intimidation was found to violate the right to equality pursuant to Article 26 of the International Covenant on Civil and Political Rights on foot of an individual application to the UN Human Rights Committee (UNHRC) (*Kavanagh v Ireland*[43]). The UNHRC found that the Republic of Ireland was obliged to provide the applicant with a remedy for a breach of this right and to ensure that in future persons are not tried before the Special Criminal Court unless reasonable and objective criteria for the decision to use that Court are provided. The same applicant was not successful before the Irish courts, however, (*Kavanagh v Ireland*[44]) and no such change has come about. As recently as August 2014 the UNHRC expressed concern about the expansion of the general remit of the Special Criminal Court in the Republic to include organised crime and recommended the abolition of the Court (UNHRC, 2014). In our view, the use of such wide unreviewable powers to remove offences from the purview of jury trial remains a stain on the legitimacy of the Irish criminal process. It may be hard to argue that those caught up in subversive activity or organised crime are going to be affected in any way by whether they are tried by jury or by a juryless court, but so long as those accused of such crimes are treated differently from other criminal defendants and are able to escape the particular moral censure that is attached to defendants who are convicted by their peers, the criminal justice system has less of a moral claim to command their compliance.

Conclusion

It is clear that there has been immense change in the criminal processes of the Republic and Northern Ireland in the course of the past forty years. We have seen that a decided shift in the direction of crime control has been prompted by pressing domestic needs to combat subversion and gangland crime and bolstered by a global rhetoric which has subjugated defence interests in favour of victims' interests. It may seem somewhat paradoxical that this shift has taken place alongside greater recognition of the need to have regard to 'due process' constitutional and human rights. In its application of these rights, however, the judiciary has sought to ensure that the legitimate aims of crime control can be pursued proportionately. As criminal behaviour, policing and prosecution develop into the future there is likely to be much further change, not least occasioned by advances in technology which allow for different types of offending, investigations, detection and prosecution. Further changes are likely to come about as a result of increasing EU influence on the criminal process, including provisions for victims and defendants, as well as measures aimed at enhancing the movement of criminal intelligence between member states (see further, Ryan and Hamilton, *infra*). The criminal processes on the island of Ireland in forty years' time are likely to be very different from those currently in operation. The challenge for those who work within these processes will be to manage this change in a manner that inspires confidence, both in dealing with crime and in safeguarding the values embedded in the rule of law.

References

Ashworth, A. and Redmayne, M. (2010) *The Criminal Process*. Oxford: Oxford University Press.

Balance in the Criminal Law Review Group (2007) *Final Report*. Dublin: Stationery Office.

Bottoms, A. (2002) 'Morality, Crime, Compliance and Public Policy', in A. Bottoms and M. Tonry (eds) *Ideology, Crime and Criminal Justice*. Cullompton: Willan.

Bottoms, A. and Tankebe. J. (2012) 'Beyond Procedural, Justice: A Dialogic Approach to Legitimacy in Crimmaiinal Justice', *Journal of Criminal Law and Criminology*, 102:119.

Boyle, K., Hadden, T. and Hillyard, P. (1975) *Law and State: The Case of Northern Ireland*. London: Martin Robertson.

—— (1980) *Ten Years On in Northern Ireland: The Legal Control of Political Violence*. Nottingham: Cobden Trust.

Campbell, L. (2013) *Organised Crime and the Law: A Comparative Analysis*. Oxford: Hart.

Conway, V. Daly, Y.M. and Schweppe, J. (2010) *Irish Criminal Justice: Theory, Process and Procedure*. Dublin: Clarus Press.

Courts Service (2013) *Annual Report 2013*. Dublin: Courts Service.

Daly, Y.M. (2009) 'Unconstitutionally Obtained Evidence in Ireland: Protectionism, Deterrence and the Winds of Change', *Irish Criminal Law Journal*, 19(2): 40.

—— (2011) 'Police and Judicial Functions: Recent Developments in Criminal Procedure', *Criminal Law and Procedure Review*, 1: 22–47.

—— (2014) 'The Right to Silence: Inferences and Interference', *Australian and New Zealand Journal of Criminology*, 47(1): 59.

Damaška, M. (1973) 'Evidentiary Barriers to Conviction and Two Models of Criminal Procedure: A Comparative Study', *University of Pennsylvania Law Review*, 121: 506.

Davis, F. (2007) *The History and Development of the Special Criminal Court 1922–2005*. Dublin: Four Courts Press.

de Londras, F. (2014) 'Declarations of Incompatibility under the ECHR Act 2003: A Workable Transplant?', *Statute Law Review*, 35(1): 50.

de Londras, F. and Davis, F. (2010) 'Controlling the Executive in Times of Terrorism: Competing Perspectives on Effective Oversight Mechanisms', *Oxford Journal of Legal Studies*, 30(1): 19.

Dennis, I.H. (1989) 'Reconstructing the Law of Criminal Evidence', *Current Legal Problems*, 21.

—— (2013) *The Law of Evidence*. 5th ed. London: Sweet & Maxwell.

Department of Justice, Equality and Law Reform (2008) Press Release. Available at: http://www.justice.ie/en/JELR/Pages/Government%20Approves%20Major%20Legislative%20Package%20that%20will%20meet%20Concerns%20of%20Victims%20of%20Crime (accessed 21 Jan 2015).

Dickson, B. (2013) *Law in Northern Ireland*, 2nd ed. Oxford: Hart.

Downes, D. (2011) 'Comparative Criminology, Globalisation and the "Punitive Turn"' in D. Nelken (ed.) *Comparative Criminal Justice and Globalisation*. Farnham: Ashgate.

Egan, S. (2003) 'The European Convention on Human Rights Act 2003: A Missed Opportunity for Domestic Human Rights Litigation', *Dublin University Law Journal*, 31(1): 230.

Egan, S. and Murray, R. (2007) 'A Charter of Rights for the Island of Ireland: An Unknown Quantity in the Good Friday/Belfast Agreement', *International & Comparative Law Quarterly*, 65: 297.

Garda Síochána (2015) *Code of Practice on Access to a Solicitor by Persons in Garda Custody*. Available at http://garda.ie/Documents/user/code%20of%20Practice%20on%20Access%20to%20a%20Solicitor%20by%20Persons%20in%20Garda%20Custody.pdf (accessed on Sept 2015).

Garland, D. (2001) *The Culture of Control: Crime and Social Order in Contemporary Society*. Oxford: Oxford University Press.

—— (2002) 'Ideology and Crime: A Further Chapter' in A. Bottoms and M. Tonry (eds) *Ideology, Crime and Criminal Justice*. Cullompton: Willan.

Greer, D.S. (ed.) (1989) 'The Police and Criminal Evidence (NI) Order 1989', *Northern Ireland Legal Quarterly* (special issue) 40: 319–440.

Gross, O. and Ní Aoláin, F. (2006) *Law in Times of Crisis: Emergency Powers in Theory and Practice*. Cambridge: Cambridge University Press.

Gwynn Morgan, D. (2001) *A Judgment Too Far? Judicial Activism and the Constitution*. Cork: Cork University Press.

Hamilton, C. (2007) *The Presumption of Innocence in Irish Criminal Law: Whittling the Golden Thread*. Dublin: Irish Academic Press.

—— (2014) *Reconceptualising Penality: A Comparative Perspective on Punitiveness in Ireland, Scotland and New Zealand*. Farnham: Ashgate.

Hancock, B. and Jackson, J. (2008) *Standards for Prosecutors: An Analysis of the National Prosecuting Agencies in Ireland, New South Wales (Australia), The Netherlands and Denmark*. Nijmegen: Wolf.

Hardiman, A. (2004) 'The Role of the Supreme Court in Our Democracy' in J. Mulholland (ed.) *Political Choice and Democratic Freedom in Ireland: 40 Leading Irish Thinkers*. MacGill Summer School.

Heffernan, L. with Ní Raifeartaigh, Ú. (2014) *Evidence in Criminal Trials*. Haywards Heath and Dublin: Bloomsbury Professional.

Jackson, J. (1989) 'Recent Developments in Criminal Evidence', *Northern Ireland Legal Quarterly*, 40: 105.

—— (2001) 'Silence and Proof: Extending the Boundaries of Criminal Proceedings in the United Kingdom', *International Journal of Evidence and Proof*, 5: 145–173.

—— (2003) 'Justice for All – Putting Victims at the Core of Criminal Justice?', *Journal of Law and Society*, 30: 309–326.

—— (2009) 'Many Years On in Northern Ireland: The Diplock Legacy', *Northern Ireland Legal Quarterly*, 60: 213.

—— (2012) 'Human Rights, Constitutional Law and Exclusionary Safeguards in Ireland' in P. Roberts and J. Hunter (eds) *Criminal Evidence and Human Rights*. Oxford: Hart.

Jackson, J. and Doran, S. (1995) *Judge without Jury: Diplock Trials within the Adversary System*. Oxford: Clarendon.

Jackson, J., Quinn, K. and Wolfe, M. (2000) *Legislating against Silence*. London and Belfast: NIO.

Jackson, J. and Summers, S (2013) 'Confrontation with Strasbourg: UK and Swiss Approaches to Criminal Evidence,' *Criminal Law Review*, 60: 114.

Kilcommins, S. and Vaughan, B. (2004) 'A Perpetual State of Emergency: Subverting the Rule of Law in Ireland', *Cambrian Law Review*, 35: 55.

—— (2008) *Terrorism, Rights and the Rule of Law: Negotiating State Justice in Ireland*. Cullompton: Willan.

Kilcommins, S., O'Donnell, I., O'Sullivan, E. and Vaughan, B. (2004) *Crime, Punishment and the Search for Order in Ireland*. Dublin: Institute of Public Administration.

Kraska, P.B. (2004) *Theorizing Criminal Justice: Eight Essential Orientations*. Waveland Press.

—— (2006) 'Criminal Justice Theory: Toward Legitimacy and an Infrastructure', *Justice Quarterly*, 23(2): 167.

Langer, M. (2014) 'The Long Shadow of the Adversarial and Inquisitorial Categories' in M. Dubber and T. Höernle (eds) *Handbook of Criminal Law*. Oxford: Oxford University Press.

McConville, M. and Wilson, G. (eds) (2002) *The Handbook of the Criminal Process*. Oxford: Oxford University Press.

McDermott, P.A. and Murphy, M. (2008) 'No Revolution: The Impact of the ECHR Act 2003 on Irish Criminal Law,' *Dublin University Law Journal*, 30(1): 1.

Mulcahy, A. (2005) 'The "Other" Lessons from Ireland? Policing, Political Violence and Policy Transfer', *European Journal of Criminology*, 2(2): 185.

Ní Raifeartaigh, Ú. (1995) 'Reversing the Onus of Proof in a Criminal Trial', *Irish Criminal Law Journal*, 5(2): 135–55.

—— (2004) 'The European Convention on Human Rights and the Irish Criminal Justice System', *Judicial Studies Institute Journal*, 4(2): 20.

Northern Ireland Courts and Tribunals Service (2012) *Judicial Statistics 2012*. Belfast: Department of Justice.

Northern Ireland Law Commission (2010) *Consultation Paper: Bail in Criminal Proceedings*, NILC 7. Belfast: Northern Ireland Law Commission.

O'Donnell, I. and O'Sullivan, E. (2001) *Crime Control in Ireland: The Politics of Intolerance*. Cork: Cork University Press.

O'Mahony, P. (1996) 'Taking Liberties: Repression by Stealth' in *Criminal Chaos: Seven Crises in Irish Criminal Justice*. Dublin: Round Hall Sweet & Maxwell.

O'Malley, T. (2009) *The Criminal Process*. Dublin: Thomson Round Hall.

O'Sullivan, E. and O'Donnell, I. (2007) 'Coercive Confinement in Ireland: The Waning of a Culture of Control', *Punishment and Society*, 9(1): 27–48.

Packer, H.L. (1968) *The Limits of the Criminal Sanction*. Stanford: Stanford University Press.

Reed, T.E. (1985) 'In Defense of the Social Learning Model: A Synthesis of the Packer-Griffiths Ideologies', *International Journal of Comparative and Applied Criminal Justice*, 9(1): 141.

Roach, K. (1999) 'Four Models of the Criminal Process', *Journal of Criminal Law and Criminology*, 89(2): 671.

Sanders, A. and Young, R. (2012) 'From Suspect to Trial' in M. Maguire, R. Morgan and R Reiner (eds) *The Oxford Handbook of Criminology*, 5th ed. Oxford: Oxford University Press.

Sanders, A., Young, R. and Burton, M. (2010) *Criminal Justice*. Oxford: Oxford University Press.

Smith, D. (1997) 'Case Construction and the Goals of Criminal Process', *British Journal of Criminology*, 37(3): 319.

—— (1998) 'Reform or Moral Outrage – The Choice Is Yours', *British Journal of Criminology*, 38(4): 616.

Tonry, M. (2010) 'The Costly Consequences of Populist Posturing: ASBOs, Victims, 'Rebalancing' and Diminution in Support for Civil Liberties', *Punishment and Society*, 12(4): 387–413.

Tyler, T.R. (1990) *Why People Obey the Law*. New Haven CT: Yale University Press.

UNHRC (2014) *Concluding Observations on the Fourth Periodic Report of Ireland*. Available at: http://daccess-dds-ny.un.org/doc/UNDOC/GEN/G14/141/79/PDF/G1414179.pdf?OpenElement (accessed 23 Jan 2015).

Walsh, D. (1989) 'The Impact of Anti-Subversive Laws on Police Powers and Practice in Ireland: The Silent Erosion of Individual Freedom', *Temple Law Review*, 62: 1099.

—— (2002) *Criminal Procedure*. Dublin: Thomson Round Hall.

Whyte, G. (2006) 'The Role of the Supreme Court in Our Democracy: A Response to Mr Justice Hardiman', *Dublin University Law Journal*, 28: 1.

Zedner, L. (2002) 'Dangers of Dystopia in Penal Theory', *Oxford Journal of Legal Studies*, 22(2): 341.

Notes

1 See Justice and Security Act 2007, ss 1–7 described in Dickson (2013). For an analysis of the workings of such courts, see Jackson and Doran (1995).

2 For an analysis and history of the Special Criminal Court, see Davis (2007).

3 According to Langer (2014), it is hard to exaggerate the influence of Packer's models on thinking about criminal procedure throughout the world. Kraska (2004) included the models in a comprehensive listing of eight theoretical orientations which are routinely employed in the field of criminal justice research.

4 For an analysis of the impact of the changes to the right to silence on this process in Northern Ireland, see Jackson (2001).

5 Not surprisingly there are significant variations in plea rates according to how serious the offence is. In the Republic of Ireland, for example, a guilty plea rate of only 33% was recorded in the case of offences that were proceeded with in the Central Criminal Court (which tries homicide and sexual offences), while 80% of defendants pleaded guilty to cases in the Circuit Court (which tries less serious offences) (Courts Service, 2013). Plea rates were not recorded for offences in the District Court, which tries the least serious offences. In Northern Ireland, 39% of defendants tried in the Crown Court (where the most serious offences are tried) pleaded guilty to all the charges against them, compared to 60% of defendants tried in the magistrates' court (which tries summary cases) (Northern Ireland Courts and Tribunals Service, 2012).

6 [1965] IR 294.

7 Some of these rights have been read into the general protection of the right to a fair trial under Art. 38.1, which allows for no derogation, while others have been judicially located within the general

protection of individual rights set out in Art. 40.3, which requires that such rights be protected only 'as far as practicable' and therefore does allow for some legitimate limitation of rights.

8 On the decline in judicial recognition of unenumerated constitutional rights see Gwynn Morgan (2001); Hardiman (2004); and Whyte (2006).
9 [1965] IR 142.
10 [1990] 2 IR 110, at 134, quoting Art.40.3.1 of the Constitution.
11 [2007] IEHC 108.
12 [2015] IESC 31.
13 (1979–80) 2 EHRR 25.
14 (1989) 11 EHRR 117.
15 [2004] UKHL 43.
16 (2010) 50 EHRR 45.
17 (2001) 33 EHRR 334.
18 Application no 18273/04 (15 December 2005).
19 [2010] 1 IR 635.
20 For more on the influence of the ECHR on the criminal process in the Republic of Ireland see McDermott and Murphy (2008) and Ní Raifeartaigh (2004).
21 This would only arise, in the Republic, in the context of offences under the Offences Against the State Acts, the Criminal Justice (Drug Trafficking) Act 1996, or s.50 of the Criminal Justice Act 2007. In Northern Ireland, legal representatives may attend the hearing but may be excluded where the court is to be informed about intelligence information: see *Ward v Police Service of Northern Ireland* [2007] UKHL 50.
22 [1978] ILRM 122.
23 [1978] ILRM 195.
24 [1985] IR 550.
25 [1986] IR 495.
26 (1996) 22 EHHR 29.
27 (2001) 33 EHRR 334.
28 [2012] IECCA 78
29 (2000) 31 EHRR 2.
30 *Al-Khawaja and Tahery v UK* (2009) 49 EHRR 1
31 *Al-Khawaja and Tahery v UK* (2012) 54 EHRR 23. For critique see Jackson and Summers (2013).
32 [2011] 1 IR 273.
33 [1930] IR 366.
34 [1979] IR 85.
35 [1980] IR 294.
36 [2014] 1 ILRM 377.
37 (2009) 49 EHRR 19.
38 384 US 436 (1966).
39 [2011] 3 SCR 3.
40 [2010] UKSC 43.
41 [1996] IR 580.
42 Cf. *Janosevic v Sweden* (2004) 38 EHRR 22 at [101] (restrictions on presumption of innocence have to be 'reasonably proportionate to the legitimate aim sought to be achieved'); *Van Mechelen and others v Netherlands* (1998) 25 EHRR 647 at [59] (any measures which restrict the rights of the defence in a criminal case should be strictly necessary; if a less restrictive measure can suffice then that measure should be applied).
43 819/1998, ICCPR, A/56/40 vol. II (4 April 2001) 122.
44 [1996] 1 IR 348.

15

Sentencing

Niamh Maguire

Introduction

Sentencing represents a key symbolic moment in a larger criminal justice process when the outcome of this process, the offender's punishment, is declared in public for all to hear. As the declaration of sentence occurs at the end point of a process that begins with the police decision to arrest and charge, it is undoubtedly influenced by the stages that have gone before. As Garland (1990) has observed, sentencing involves many more people than just the sentencers and those who are sentenced. It also involves the onlookers (the general public) and a range of other actors including prosecutors, defence solicitors and probation officers. To add to its complexity, sentencing systems are embedded within and influenced by specific social, political, cultural, historic and economic contexts (Hogarth, 1971; Hutton, 2006).

As a result of this complexity, it is not possible to comprehensively discuss all matters related to sentencing in both jurisdictions here. Therefore, this chapter takes a thematic approach and highlights some of the key themes and developments in sentencing relevant to both Northern Ireland and the Republic of Ireland. To set the scene, it opens with a brief exploration of the specific contexts of sentencing unique to Northern Ireland and the Republic of Ireland. It then thematically examines the sentencing frameworks currently operative in each jurisdiction and forgoes a general discussion of punishment philosophies on the basis that they are more than adequately dealt with elsewhere (Ashworth, 2010; Easton and Piper, 2008; O'Malley, 2006). Although relevant to sentencing this chapter will also not be concerned with how the courts use community sanctions or issues relating to imprisonment – addressed in Butler (Chapter 17), Behan and Bates-Gaston (Chapter 18), Rogan (Chapter 22), Quinlan (Chapter 26), and others, below. Instead, the final sections of this chapter will highlight two inter-related issues that are particularly topical in both the wider sentencing literature and in current criminological debates. First, developments in the sentencing of dangerous and persistent offenders require attention, as they represent a departure from the traditional system of individualised sentencing that has dominated common law jurisdictions until recently and they pose important questions about the contemporary nature of punishment. Secondly, the important and inter-related issues of judicial sentencing discretion, consistency in sentencing and recent developments north and south of the border relating to sentencing guidelines will be examined.

The context of sentencing

Politics and politicisation of sentencing

According to Tonry (1996: 3), during the last three decades the political salience of sentencing has changed, and it has now become 'a recurrent subject of ideological conflict, partisan politics and legislative action'. However, it is fair to say that in relation to both Northern Ireland and the Republic of Ireland, the debate around the issue of sentencing has been somewhat muted and dependent on stimulation from sporadic outbreaks of public concern and mini-moral panics related to actual sentencing cases reported in the media. It is possible to isolate specific examples of moral panic that led to change in sentencing laws in each jurisdiction. In the Republic the murders of a police officer and journalist in 1996 changed the tone of the debate about crime and punishment and led to a raft of legislative changes, including the introduction of presumptive minimum sentences for drug dealers in 1999 (Kilcommins *et al.*, 2004). In Northern Ireland, the public outcry that followed the rape and murder of Attracta Harron in 2003, by a convicted violent and prolific sex offender who had just been released from custody, led to the introduction of new sentencing laws designed to enhance public protection against dangerous offenders (Ellison and Mulcahy, 2009: 328). Outside of these relatively sporadic events, it could be argued that sentencing has been somewhat neglected in deference to other aspects of criminal justice policy such as policing and even prisons.

In part at least, this neglect can be attributed to the wider neglect and delayed development of criminal justice matters attributable to the ongoing conflict that impacted both jurisdictions for the best part of three decades. In Northern Ireland sentencing policy was shaped by the need to respond to both ordinary criminality and politically motivated crime (Ellison and Mulcahy, 2009). Legitimacy in sentencing was also damaged by the establishment of the Diplock Courts (Ellison and Mulcahy, 2009). While similar courts were established in the Republic of Ireland (the Special Criminal Court) to deal with subversive crime, the context was profoundly different in that the fundamental legitimacy of the state was not in issue (Mulcahy, 2002). While large numbers of convicted terrorists received relatively long sentences, sentencing policy in the Republic of Ireland was not shaped as much by the 'Conflict' as was the case in Northern Ireland. According to Ellison and Mulcahy (2009:328) 'the overall picture of sentencing policy in Northern Ireland is distorted by the relatively high numbers of people given custodial sentences for the commission of a scheduled offence prior to the signing of the Belfast Agreement in 1998'.

Stagnation versus change

Evidence of the historical neglect of sentencing can be found in both jurisdictions. In the Republic, the neglect of sentencing reform is related to the general inertia characteristic of penal policy formulation in the Republic following independence (Kilcommins *et al.*, 2004; Rogan, 2011). One reason for this inertia was the fact that the Republic remained a low-crime country and thus unconcerned about responding to the problem of crime for at least the first 45 years after independence (Rottman, 1984). This, plus a complete lack of information on the criminal justice system, represented a serious hindrance to the analysis, policy-making and reform of sentencing in the Republic of Ireland (Rottman, 1984). While sentencing reform began in other countries in the 1970s and 1980s, it only reached the Republic by the 1990s (Maguire, 2010), and even then the programme of reform outlined by the Law Reform Commission (1993, 1996) was largely ignored and never implemented. As a result, the Irish sentencing system has not been fundamentally altered since independence in 1922 (O'Malley, 2006; Bacik, 2002; Maguire, 2010).

Indeed, the Republic lacks a statutory sentencing framework that sets out how custody and community sentences should be used, and limited legislative steps have been taken to respond to the threat of dangerous offenders, although mandatory sentencing laws were introduced recently for organised crime (see Criminal Justice Act 2007). Further, the Probation of Offenders Act 1907, despite its longevity, is still the main legislative instrument governing the use of probation (Maguire and Carr, 2013), although there are plans to replace this with new statutory provisions. However, in the Republic, while the legislature has generally pursued a policy of non-intervention in the formulation of sentencing policy (O'Malley, 2013), the judiciary, perhaps in order to preserve its traditionally very broad sentencing discretion, has been to the forefront of the development of sentencing policy by championing the principle of proportionality, formulating new sanctions and, most recently, by issuing guideline judgments.

In contrast to the legislative stagnation in the Republic, in recent years developments in sentencing in Northern Ireland could be described as prolific. A relatively structured sentencing framework was first introduced by the Criminal Justice (Northern Ireland) Order 1996 (the 1996 Order), and after the Good Friday Agreement in 1998, the sentencing framework was scrutinised in greater detail, with the operations of the courts being brought into line with standards in England and Wales (Ellison and Mulcahy, 2009). The sentencing framework was recently amended by the Criminal Justice (Northern Ireland) Order 2008 (the 2008 Order), which introduced a range of sentences to deal with dangerous sexual and violent offenders. A key question regarding legislative innovation in Northern Ireland is the extent to which it is driven by the agenda in England and Wales more than by developments at home.

Policy transfer and the culture of control

While both jurisdictions have been affected by elements of criminal justice policy transfer from England and Wales, Northern Ireland has been much more overtly influenced than the Republic. The sentencing framework introduced in Northern Ireland by the 1996 and 2008 Orders is almost entirely based upon the Criminal Justice Acts of 1991 and 2003 in England and Wales. This is undoubtedly due to the late transfer of devolution powers in relation to criminal justice policy. Even so, it is still somewhat surprising that there appears to be little, if any, debate about the fact that sentencing policy has been so directly influenced by developments in England and Wales. Although Northern Ireland is part of the United Kingdom, it is a separate legal jurisdiction to England and Wales, with its own unique social, political and cultural identity. In relation to the Republic of Ireland, the issue of policy transfer is much more subtle and difficult to delineate. Thus, while the Republic has not completely succumbed to the 'new penology' and still retains many aspects of penal-welfarism (Kilcommins et al., 2004; Rogan, 2011; Maguire and Carr, 2013), core features of the 'culture of control' (Garland, 2001) such as harsher sentences for dangerous offenders may be observed in Northern Ireland, largely on account of the close association with England and Wales.

Overview of sentencing frameworks

Understanding the sentencing framework underpinning a particular sentencing system is an important starting point for appreciating how a system works in theory and in practice. This section provides a brief overview of the key features of the sentencing frameworks in each jurisdiction.[1]

The sentencing systems in both jurisdictions can be described as individualised sentencing systems. However, while the Republic of Ireland has one of the most unstructured sentencing systems in the common law world (O'Malley, 2006, 2011), sentencing discretion is more structured in Northern Ireland. This can be explained by the fact that sentencing policy in the Republic has been developed largely by judges on an *ad hoc* basis, whereas in Northern Ireland the current sentencing framework is established by a series of legislative Acts and Orders. These legislative enactments do more than simply outline statutory maxima and minima for a variety of cases. They go much further and set out the general sentencing principles the courts must follow, and, of particular import, they set the sentencing thresholds (largely based upon seriousness) for the imposition of custodial and community penalties. Furthermore, while legislative guidance provides a reasonably coherent sentencing structure, judicially developed guidelines also play an important role in Northern Ireland. The Court of Appeal in Northern Ireland issues guideline judgments and, where appropriate, either adopts or distinguishes guidelines issued by the Court of Appeal in England and Wales and the Sentencing Council (formerly the Sentencing Guidelines Council).

The situation in the Republic of Ireland is different in that there is no coherent legislative sentencing framework to speak of. Such framework as does exist is based on the judicially developed principle of proportionality (O'Malley, 2006, 2011). While the legislature sets out the maximum, and in some cases the minimum, sentences that judges may impose in relation to certain types of offences, it stops short of providing specific guidance regarding how particular (custodial and community) penalties should be used. The lack of sentencing guidance provided by the legislature reflects a policy, pursued by successive Irish governments, of non-intervention in sentencing policy that may in part be motivated by respect for (or a misunderstanding of) the separation of powers. However, as noted by O'Malley (2006, 2011), legislative involvement in the formulation of sentencing policy is compatible with the doctrine of the separation of powers, which merely requires that there be no direct interference in how judges exercise their sentencing discretion in individual cases. With the publication of the *General Scheme of the Criminal Justice (Community Sanctions) Bill 2014*, it appears that the legislature may have missed another opportunity to provide greater sentencing guidance to judges. While the Bill ostensibly introduces a new range of 'supervised community sentences' no guidance is provided on how judges should use these new sentences. This omission shows that the legislature is still reluctant to take a greater role in the formulation of sentencing policy by providing more guidance to judges in terms of how they should exercise their very broad sentencing discretion. As a result, judges must rely heavily on the judicially developed principle of proportionality to guide them when exercising their sentencing discretion, particularly when deciding between custodial and non-custodial sanctions. Understanding the sentencing framework in the Republic of Ireland therefore involves becoming familiar with the main features of the principle of proportionality.

Having outlined some of the general features of the two sentencing systems under discussion the next two sections will examine the sentencing framework of each system in more depth, beginning with Northern Ireland and then turning to the Republic of Ireland.

Northern Ireland

As mentioned earlier, Northern Ireland's sentencing framework is legislatively established and can be found in two main orders: the 1996 Order (which is modelled on the 1991 and 1993 Criminal Justice Acts introduced in England and Wales); and the 2008 Order (which is influenced by the Criminal Justice Act 2003 introduced in England and Wales, particularly its provisions relating to the sentencing of 'dangerous offenders').[2] The 1996 Order prioritises proportionality in sentencing, which in the context of Northern Ireland means that, as a general rule, the seriousness of the offence is the most important factor influencing the type and severity of sentence that judges may impose. Reflecting the emphasis on proportionality, the 1996 Order, like the 1991 Criminal Justice Act that it was modelled on, introduced custody and community sentence thresholds based on crime seriousness. The community sentence threshold provides that a judge must be satisfied that the offence is serious enough to warrant a community sentence. In relation to community sentences, once the seriousness threshold has been met, judges may be guided by other sentencing philosophies, including rehabilitation, public protection and crime prevention. The custody threshold on the other hand provides that a custodial sentence cannot be imposed unless the court believes the offence is 'so serious that only such a sentence can be justified' (1996 Order). The 1996 Order also sets out the main types of disposals available to the courts as well as the conditions and procedures associated with their use.

The provisions aimed at violent and sexual offenders, contained in Article 20 of the 1996 Order, represent an important exception to the prioritisation of proportionality as they allow the courts to impose a prison sentence that exceeds the seriousness of the offence on the grounds of deterrence and public protection. While more advanced provisions were later introduced by the 2008 Order to deal with dangerous offenders, it is interesting to note that some provision for longer-than-proportionate sentences had already existed under the 1996 Order. In this sense the 1996 Order very much mirrors the policy of punitive bifurcation adopted in England and Wales by the 1991 Criminal Justice Act whereby the 'approach to punishment ... distinguishes between 'ordinary' offenders with whom less severe measures can be taken and serious or dangerous offenders who are subjected to much tougher measures' (Cavadino et al., 2013: 327).

However, it would be incorrect to assume that the 1996 Order is a direct copy of the 1991 Act, as, by the time it was introduced in Northern Ireland, some aspects of the 1991 Act had already caused great upset amongst certain sections of the public, the tabloid media and the judiciary, and as a result had been repealed (Ashworth, 2010; Easton and Piper, 2008). Three provisions of the 1991 Act stand out: the new system of unit fines; the emphasis on the current offence (for proportionality reasons); and the prohibition contained in section 29(1) of the Act against taking previous convictions and failure to respond to previous sentences into account when assessing seriousness (Worrall, 1997; Easton and Piper, 2008). In England and Wales, dissatisfaction with these provisions led to intense political pressure for their amendment under the Criminal Justice Act 1993, and as a result these provisions never made their way into the Criminal Justice (NI) Order of 1996. In relation to fines, the 1996 Order simply provides that the amount of any fine fixed by the court must reflect the seriousness of the offence. Similarly, the custody and community sentence thresholds contained in the 1996 Order allow the court to consider other offences in addition to the immediate offence. Lastly, the 1996 Order allows the court to take previous convictions and the failure to respond to previous sentences into account when considering the seriousness of the offence. Therefore, many of the original provisions that supported the prioritisation of proportionality in sentencing and restraint in the use of imprisonment contained in the 1991 Act never made their way into the 1996 Order.

On the other hand, other legislative changes introduced in England and Wales that were designed to further undermine the original basis of the 1991 Act were not adopted by Northern Ireland. For example, the presumptive minimum sentences introduced by the Crime (Sentences) Act 1997 for repeat burglars and drug dealers were never transposed into law in Northern Ireland. Similarly, certain provisions of the Criminal Justice Act 2003 relating to previous convictions (discussed later under Sentencing Persistence) were not adopted by Northern Ireland.

However, the Criminal Justice (Northern Ireland) Order 2008 did adopt the controversial sentencing powers for dealing with dangerous offenders introduced by the Criminal Justice Act 2003 in England and Wales. These new powers, contained in Articles 13 and 14 of the 2008 Order, are almost identical to the three new sentences that had been introduced by sections 224–228 of the

2003 Act aimed at incapacitating 'dangerous' offending and included life sentences, indeterminate custodial sentences (ICS) and extended custodial sentences (ECS). The only difference is that the 'dangerous offender' provisions of the 2003 Act were amended in England and Wales before the 2008 Order introduced these sentences in Northern Ireland. As we will discuss later (under Sentencing Dangerousness), the most controversial of these dangerous offender laws, imprisonment for public protection (IPP) sentences (or ICS in Northern Ireland), were abolished in England and Wales in 2012 but still remain on the statute book in Northern Ireland.

Another significant change introduced by the 2008 Order was the abolition of the automatic right to remission of 50 per cent for all sentenced prisoners and its replacement with a system of automatic release on licence under supervision. Before the 2008 Order, all prisoners were entitled to 50 per cent remission as a matter of right. Momentum for its abolition grew after the murder of Attracta Harron by Trevor Hamilton, a convicted rapist, who had been released early after serving only half of his sentence (Craig, 2008). The abolition of remission and the introduction of tougher sentencing laws for dealing with dangerous offenders that followed this tragic event serve as a good example of 'penal populism', whereby governments pursue 'a set of penal policies to win votes rather than to reduce crime or promote justice' (Pratt, 2007: 16; see also Bottoms, 1995).

Republic of Ireland

In comparison to Northern Ireland, or indeed any other UK jurisdiction, the legislative sentencing framework in the Republic of Ireland is limited. Legislation typically outlines the maximum, and in some cases the minimum, sentence that judges may impose in relation to particular offences, but rarely indicates a type or quantum of penalty for specific offences (O'Malley, 2006; Maguire, 2010). For example, while legislation setting out punishments typically refers to the maximum fine and maximum period of imprisonment that may be imposed for a particular offence, in reality judges have a plethora of other sanctions that they may choose from in relation to most offences, such as compensation orders, probation orders, community service orders and suspended sentences.

In the absence of a coherent sentencing framework from the legislature, the main source of sentencing guidance in the Republic has been provided by the superior courts, particularly the Court of Criminal Appeal (now known as the Court of Appeal) in the form of its jurisprudence on the principle of proportionality (O'Malley, 2006, 2011, 2013).

The principle of proportionality

Unlike Northern Ireland where proportionality in sentencing was adopted through legislation, in the Republic the principle of proportionality developed instead at common law and has only relatively recently been declared by the superior courts to have constitutional status. Denham J. (as she then was) elaborated on the nature of the principle of proportionality in sentencing and stressed its constitutional character in the Supreme Court case of *People (DPP) v M*:[3]

> Sentences should be proportionate. Firstly, they should be proportionate to the crime. Thus, a grave offence is reflected by a severe sentence … However, sentences must also be proportionate to the personal circumstances of the appellant. … Thus, having assessed what is the appropriate sentence for a particular crime it is the duty of the court to consider then the particular circumstances of the convicted person. It is within this ambit that mitigating factors fall to be considered.

The way in which the Irish judiciary has developed the principle of proportionality in sentencing is somewhat unusual. Rather than requiring proportionality simply between the seriousness of the offence and the severity of the sentence, in the Republic it is a constitutional requirement that the sentence must be proportionate to the circumstances of the crime *and* to the circumstances of the criminal (O'Malley, 2006; Maguire, 2010). The constitutional nature of the principle was reaffirmed recently in *Lynch v Minister for Justice, Equality and Law Reform*.[4] In this case, the Supreme Court took the opportunity to state that where judges have a sentencing discretion then they *must* follow the principle of proportionality when exercising their discretion. However, as O'Malley (2013) argues, the court also limited the application of the principle of proportionality by emphasising that it *only* applies where judges *have* a sentencing discretion, and it could not, therefore, be relied upon to challenge the mandatory life sentence for murder.

At one point it was unclear whether judges should adopt a structured or an 'instinctive synthesis' approach when applying the principle of proportionality in sentencing (O'Malley, 2006; Bacik, 2002). Instinctive synthesis is an approach to sentencing whereby judges decide the appropriate sentence by considering all factors of the case together and then come to a decision about the sentence without assigning a precise weight to individual factors. More recently, the Court of Criminal Appeal in the *People (DPP) v Kelly*[5] explained that the proper approach involved a more structured two-step approach: 'one looks first at the range of penalties and locates where on the range the particular case should lie and one then applies the mitigating factors after having performed that exercise'. The first step then is to decide where on the overall scale of gravity the particular offence lies. When making this decision, judges may have regard to factors that aggravate and mitigate the seriousness of the offence.[6] Once the decision regarding seriousness has been made, the next step is to examine the range of penalties applicable to the offence and decide whereabouts on this range the particular offence should lie, having regard to its seriousness.

Once a judge has decided the type and quantum of penalty to impose, consideration and due weight *must* then be given, where appropriate, to any mitigating factors related to the personal circumstances of the offender that might warrant a reduction in the severity of the otherwise proportionate sentence. Again, there is no exhaustive list of factors that mitigate the proportionate sentence; examples include: a guilty plea, co-operation with the police in apprehending others involved in the crime, successful attempts at rehabilitation, genuine remorse and credit for previous good character (Law Reform Commission, 1993, 1996; O'Malley, 2006). While it is well established that a judge must consider and give due weight to factors that mitigate sentence, and that a failure to do so represents an error in law, until recently it was not clear if the presence of mitigating factors *must always* result in a reduction of sentence. While Section 29(2) of the Criminal Justice Act 1999 provides that a court, when passing sentence, is not precluded from passing the maximum sentence even if a plea of guilty has been entered, if it is satisfied that there are exceptional circumstances present that warrant the maximum sentence, it was not clear whether this approach might apply more generally to other mitigating factors. The Supreme Court considered this issue in *People (DPP) v McC and D*[7] and clarified the position by explaining that, although there is an obligation on a court to consider and give due weight to all mitigating factors when present, and while this should usually result in a reduction in the proportionate sentence, a court may exercise its discretion not to give a reduction in sentence in exceptional circumstances.

The fact that mitigation of the proportionate sentence is a requirement of the principle of proportionality is peculiar to Irish law. In most jurisdictions, the principle of proportionality in sentencing merely requires that the severity of the sentence be related to the seriousness of the crime (Ashworth and von Hirsch, 2005). For example, in Northern Ireland, even though judges may consider factors that might mitigate an offender's sentence (indeed, this is specifically provided for by Article 36 of the 1996 Order) they are not obliged to consider mitigation of sentence in the same way as judges in the Republic are.

Another feature of the Republic's proportionality principle is that judges may choose from multiple sentencing philosophies, and, while retribution, deterrence and public protection are important, rehabilitation is also emphasised in the case law.[8] Somewhat confusingly, there is no stated hierarchical relationship between these aims, but the fact that proportionality is the guiding principle suggests that retribution is the primary aim of sentencing and thus presumably trumps other philosophies. However, incapacitation, beyond what is considered proportionate to the offence, is generally not permitted in Irish law on the grounds that preventive detention is contrary to the Irish constitution (O'Malley, 2009; Maguire, 2010; see further the discussion on Sentencing Dangerousness below).

Taking these features together, the Irish principle of proportionality in sentencing is some-what difficult to categorise. It comes close to the theory of limiting retributivism developed by Norval Morris (Morris, 1974; Morris and Tonry, 1990) in that it allows for upward (previous convictions) and downward departures (mitigation of sentence) from the strictly proportionate sentence and allows room for multiple sentencing objectives to be considered. However, the Irish principle differs from limiting retributivism in that it does not allow any room for incapacitation as a sentencing objective and its emphasis on mitigation is a constitutional guarantee rather than a discretionary exercise of mercy.

In the absence of legislative guidance, the development by the judiciary of the principle of proportionality in sentencing as a guide to judges exercising their sentencing discretion is a considerable achievement. However, the ability of the principle to guide judicial sentencing discretion is undermined by a number of factors. First, as discussed above, in Ireland judges are free to choose from a number of different sentencing aims, each requiring a different approach, and this may give rise to inconsistencies in approach. Secondly, the principle of proportionality remains relatively broad in nature and therefore lacks the specificity to truly guide the exercise of sentencing discretion (O'Malley, 2011, 2013; Maguire, 2010).

Proportionality as a constraint on the severity of sentencing?

On closer inspection, it is apparent that both jurisdictions share reasonably similar recipes for proportionality in that the seriousness of the offence guides the choice and quantum of punishment, and each provides for some form of mitigation of sentence. The versions of proportionality applied in the two jurisdictions also share similar weaknesses, the most important of which relates to their (in)ability to act as effective constraints on sentence severity. In both jurisdictions previous convictions are recognised as factors that may aggravate the seriousness of the offence and thereby increase the severity of the sentence (Allen and McAleenan, 1998, 2003; Maguire, 2010, 2014). Apart from the statutory maximums imposed by legislation, the proportionality principles, as they currently stand in Northern Ireland and the Republic of Ireland, provide no ceiling on the extent to which these aggravating factors can increase the severity of the offence on the grounds of retribution.

Aside from these common features there are also important differences between the principles that set them apart. First, in Northern Ireland legislation specifically allows for exceptions to proportionality for dangerous sexual and violent offenders, and this has implications for the range of offences and offenders to which the proportionality principle applies. Secondly, in the Republic of Ireland proportionality acts as a form of constitutional guarantee (O'Malley, 2006, 2011, 2013; Maguire, 2010), which has two specific implications for its application in practice. The first is that judges are constitutionally bound, when exercising their sentencing discretion, to consider the factors that might mitigate the proportionate sentence. The second is that judges may not extend the length of a sentence much beyond what can be justified on punitive grounds – in other words the extent to which longer-than-proportionate sentences can be justified on the grounds of public protection and incapacitation is limited. This latter point will be explored in more detail in the next sections which explore the sentencing of persistence and dangerousness.

Sentencing persistence

Concern about how to respond to persistent offenders has a long history. For example, in England and Wales, whilst early criminal statutes made no reference to repeat offenders or even to an offender's culpability (Roberts, 2008), by the sixteenth century, awareness of an offender's previous record usually resulted in harsher penalties (Ingram, 2004). Interest in recidivist sentencing premiums reached its high point during the Victorian period, when some argued for a ratio between severity of sentence and previous character (Roberts, 2008). Near the end of the nineteenth century Section 6(1) of the Prevention of Crime Act 1871 provided that registers had to be kept of all person convicted of crime in the UK. By the early twentieth century preventive detention laws were introduced in the UK by Part II of the Prevention of Crime Act 1908, which provided that habitual offenders should be imprisoned for an additional five to ten years. This Act remained on the statute books in the Republic of Ireland until it was repealed by the Criminal Law Act 1997. These types of habitual offender laws are the precursors to a range of presumptive minimum and 'three strikes' sentencing laws, introduced in recent decades in many countries to provide enhanced punishment as a way of responding to public concern about persistence (Roberts, 2008; Ashworth, 2010; Law Reform Commission, 2013).

There is much debate in the sentencing literature about how to justify and incorporate previous convictions as an element of a sentence, but the two approaches most relied upon are cumulative sentencing and progressive loss of mitigation (Roberts, 2008; Roberts and von Hirsch, 2010). Cumulative sentencing involves increasing the severity of the sentence with each new conviction; however it often leads to punishment being heaped upon petty persistent offenders, and some argue that this is clearly disproportionate (Ashworth, 2010). Progressive loss of mitigation provides that, on a first offence, a substantial reduction in severity of sentence should be received by an offender based on their previous good character (O'Malley, 2006). However, this reduction should decline on the second and subsequent convictions to a point where no reduction is allowed. Importantly, this approach does not allow for an increase in severity based upon previous convictions and the current offence acts as a 'ceiling' for the severity of the sentence (Thomas, 1979; von Hirsch and Ashworth, 2005).

Regardless of which justification is preferred, research on sentencing has shown that previous convictions play an important role in sentencing practice and that judges are influenced in the direction of a custodial sanction by their presence (Hough et al., 2003; Millie et al., 2007; Tombs and Jagger, 2006; Maguire, 2010, 2014). At the same time, empirical evidence about the nature of the typical persistent offender suggests that most suffer from a range of difficulties and do not rationally assess their chances of being caught and incapacitated (Home Office, 2001). Pursuing a policy of enhanced punishment for persistent offenders therefore might be counter-productive. Additionally, it may also be a waste of resources, as research suggests that up to 40 per cent of persistent offenders desist from crime each year and are replaced by a new cohort of persistent offenders (Carter, 2003). This conclusion is supported by research emerging from desistance studies, which suggests that most offenders desist naturally in their late twenties (Bottoms et al., 2004).

In relation to the sentencing of persistence, neither jurisdiction examined here has taken a particularly punitive stance on punishing persistence, especially when compared to the approach adopted in England and Wales. While the 1991 Act in England and Wales originally provided that previous convictions should not be permitted to increase the seriousness of the current offence, this position was reversed by the Criminal Justice Act 1993, which provided that previous convictions and the failure to respond to previous sentences could be taken into account when sentencing. Article 37(1) of the Criminal Justice (Northern Ireland) Order 1996 adopted this approach. It provides that when 'considering the seriousness of any offence, the court may take into account any previous convictions of the offender or any failure of his to respond to previous convictions'.

Although Northern Ireland has essentially adopted a cumulative sentencing approach to persistence, it is notable that it stopped short of following England and Wales when it introduced tougher sentencing laws for punishing persistence, including presumptive sentences for repeat burglars and drug dealers, in its Crime (Sentences) Act 1997 and a requirement on judges in section 143(2) of the Criminal Justice Act 2003 to treat each relevant previous conviction as a factor aggravating seriousness. Also, apart from the mandatory life sentence for murder and presumptive minimum sentences for firearms offences and for dangerous offenders,[9] Northern Ireland is relatively free of habitual offender laws (Law Reform Commission, 2013: 149). Unlike the Republic of Ireland, it has not yet introduced recidivist premiums in the form of mandatory or even presumptive minimum sentences for those convicted of drug offences (Law Reform Commission, 2013).

In the Republic of Ireland certain statutory provisions provide for enhanced punishment for recidivist offenders. For example, Section 3 of the Criminal Law (Sexual Offences) Act 2006 (as amended by the Criminal Law (Sexual Offences) (Amendment) Act 2007) provides for higher penalties for offenders reconvicted of defiling a child under the age of 17. Under Section 15(a) of the Misuse of Drugs Act 1977 (as inserted by the Criminal Justice Act 1999), persons convicted of possessing drugs with a market value of more than €13,000, for sale or supply, face a presumptive sentence of ten years. Those reconvicted of this offence face a mandatory ten-year sentence under Section 15(b) of the same Act (as amended). Similar laws were introduced amid heightened concerns about organised crime by Section 25 of the Criminal Justice Act 2007 (Campbell, 2013; O'Malley, 2009, 2011).

Apart from these extraordinary provisions, the legislature has provided no guidance on how previous convictions should impact the sentencing of the current offence (O'Malley, 2009, 2011; Maguire, 2008). According to O'Malley (2006, 2009) the courts in the past have shown support for both cumulative sentencing and progressive loss of mitigation, with recent case law suggesting that the courts are undecided between these two approaches.[10] While there is some contradiction in the case law, empirical evidence suggests that in practice judges in the District and Circuit Courts routinely treat previous convictions as factors aggravating the seriousness of the offence (Maguire, 2008, 2010, 2014).

Sentencing 'dangerousness'

Public protection has arguably always been a legitimate aim of the criminal justice system (Dingwall, 1998), and according to Hart (2008), it may well be the general justifying aim of criminal law. The idea of being able to predict dangerousness and selectively incapacitate dangerous offenders came about in the 1980s when Greenwood and Abrahamson's (1982) study suggested that it was possible to distinguish between those who commit large volumes of crime and those who do not. A key element of dangerousness laws is that the court must find the offender in question 'dangerous'. However, the definition of 'dangerous' itself is contested. According to Floud (1982: 214) 'dangerousness is a thoroughly ambiguous concept', whereas Pratt (2000: 35) defines dangerous offenders as 'that group of offenders whose propensity to repeatedly commit crimes of a non-capital but otherwise serious nature puts the well-being of the rest of the community at risk'. Dingwall (2009) writes that, although references are usually made to danger and dangerousness, in practice the focus invariably falls upon 'risk'.

The distinction between risk and dangerousness involves the court making two separate assessments regarding the risk of reoffending and the risk of causing serious harm (Ashworth, 2010). Courts must take all the information available to them into account, including the current offence, previous offences and the circumstances of the offender. Increasingly courts rely upon risk assessments made by probation officers in pre-sentence reports (Tata *et al.*, 2008; Beyens and Scheirs, 2010; Wandall, 2010). Indeed, probation practice has seen a shift in emphasis away from its traditional welfare orientation towards a more public protection stance, which is reflected in the importance placed upon risk assessment (Kemshall, 2003; Maguire and Carr, 2013). This is linked to the emergence of risk as a central organising principle in the criminal justice system as a whole, which raises particular concerns and has been subject to considerable commentary and analysis (Feeley and Simon, 1994; Kemshall, 2003).

Chief amongst these concerns is the fact that predictions of dangerousness are notoriously unreliable. A number of studies carried out in the 1980s found that the existing methods of prediction had at best a 50 per cent and at worst a mere 20 per cent success rate at predicting dangerousness (Floud and Young, 1981; Brody and Tarling, 1981; Blumstein *et al.*, 1986). Furthermore, another problem with selective incapacitation of dangerous offenders is that most offenders, even dangerous ones, tend to reduce their criminal activity over time, thus reducing the incapacitative yield of such policies (Kazemian and Farrington, 2006). Modern risk assessment tools aimed at identifying 'dangerous' offenders or those who represent a high risk of 'serious harm' have not proven any more successful (Brown, 1998; Brown and Pratt, 2000). Apart from important issues of empirical effectiveness, preventive detention raises issues of morality and human rights (O'Malley, 2009; Ashworth, 2010). Given the acknowledged difficulties with accurately predicting dangerousness and the high levels of false positives associated with risk assessments, some contend that it is unfair to incapacitate an offender who has already served the punitive element of their sentence (von Hirsch *et al.*, 2009a). Preventive sentences also breach the Kantian principle that one should not be used as a means to an end (Ashworth, 2010). However, if preventive incapacitation can be justified, some argue that a form of civil, rather than punitive, confinement would be more ethically acceptable, given that the person has already served the punitive element of their sentence (O'Malley, 2009; Ashworth, 2010; Harrison, 2012).

Northern Ireland has taken a relatively proactive approach to the sentencing of dangerous offenders. It followed England and Wales in the 1990s by adopting a policy of punitive bifurcation, in that the 1996 Order allowed for longer sentences than would be proportionate to the seriousness of the offence on grounds of public protection. In the same Order it also introduced the custody probation order, whereby the offender would spend a period of time after release being supervised by a probation officer. Carr (2015) describes the emphasis on public protection contained in the 1996 Order as a 'hardening' of criminal justice, and Fulton and Carr (2013) pinpoint this period as a moment when the move away from welfarism towards public protection was clearly evidenced in Northern Ireland. Although it did not immediately adopt similar provisions to England and Wales following the introduction of the controversial Criminal Justice Act 2003, as discussed earlier, Northern Ireland did eventually follow suit in 2008 and introduced three new prison sentences aimed at incapacitating dangerous offenders including:

a discretionary life sentence; extended custodial sentences (ECS); and indeterminate custodial sentences (ICS).

The most controversial of these new disposals is the indeterminate custodial sentence (ICS) which is a direct replica of the controversial imprisonment for public protection (IPP) sentence introduced in England and Wales by Section 225 of the Criminal Justice Act 2003. The IPP sentences were heavily criticised in England and Wales, and as a result they were amended by the Criminal Justice and Immigration Act 2008 and then eventually repealed by the Legal Aid, Sentencing and Punishment of Offenders Act 2012 (Ashworth, 2010; Harrison, 2012). The original complaint was that the 2003 Act cast the net too wide, leading to the imprisonment of many more offenders and for much less serious crimes than originally envisaged (Jacobson and Hough, 2010; Barnes, 2012; Harrison, 2012).

However, even after the 2008 amendments, which restricted the application of the IPP sentences and gave the court greater discretion over the definition of dangerousness, concern remained that prisoners serving IPP sentences with no release dates needed to satisfy the Parole Board that they had reduced their risk but did not have adequate access to rehabilitation programmes in prison to allow them to do this (Jacobson and Hough, 2010). In 2012, three prisoners serving IPP sentences won their case against the UK government arguing that their right to liberty under Article 5 of the European Convention of Human Rights had been breached by the delay in accessing appropriate rehabilitation programmes in prison.[11]

Despite the criticism that IPP sentences attracted in England and Wales they remain on the statute books in Northern Ireland. Recent case law suggests that, while they are still available as a sentencing option in the North, they must only be used as a last resort, and that the role of pre-sentence and psychological reports will be extremely important in determining the appropriateness of their use.[12] One unintended consequence of these new sentences is that they are likely to increase the incidence of recall to prison for breach of the conditions of supervision. The significance of back-door routes into prison has been highlighted in many European jurisdictions (Padfield and Maruna, 2006; Herzog-Evans and Boone, 2013). In relation to Northern Ireland, Carr (2015) notes that recent prison and parole statistics show that recall to prison for breach of conditions is already on the increase and is contributing to the significant growth in the prison population in Northern Ireland since 2001.

In contrast, while public protection and assessment of risk are important issues in the Republic of Ireland, there is a strong constitutional prohibition against preventive detention. More specifically, detention much beyond the punitive element of a sentence in order to prevent the commission of further offences is thought to be contrary to the Irish Constitution. This prohibition is based on the decision in *People (Attorney General) v O'Callaghan*,[13] and, though the immediate context of this case was bail rather than sentencing, its application to sentencing was confirmed by later cases including the *People (DPP) v M*[14] and more recently in *People (DPP) v GK*.[15] The position seems to be that while judges, when sentencing, may take the need for incapacitation into account, on the grounds of public protection, they may not impose a disproportionate sentence purely on the grounds of preventing the commission of future crimes (O'Malley, 2009). The court can therefore take account of the propensity to reoffend only to a limited extent. Indeed, the High Court recently refused to surrender a person to the UK under the European Arrest Warrant Act 2003 on the basis that he would be subject to preventive detention in the form of an IPP sentence.[16]

Furthermore, it would appear that if the government in the Republic decided to introduce a form of preventive detention, for example extended sentences for dangerous offenders, it might be necessary to address the constitutional prohibition against indeterminate sentences on the grounds of public protection by having a constitutional referendum, similar to the approach applied to the situation of bail in the 1990s (O'Mahony, 2002; O'Malley, 2009). Perhaps for this reason, the Republic, unlike Northern Ireland and many other countries, has not yet introduced specific provisions to deal with 'dangerous' offenders.

Judicial discretion and sentencing guidelines

International developments

The current wave of sentencing reform began in the early 1970s in the United States and was inspired by four factors: concern about unwarranted disparities in sentencing on the basis of racial and class bias; concern that rehabilitation programmes did not work to reduce recidivism and that indeterminate sentencing could not be justified on the grounds of rehabilitation; concern to make legal decision-makers more accountable and more rule-bound; and a concern amongst conservatives to address 'lenient' or 'soft' sentencing practices (Tonry, 1996). As the project of sentencing reform gathered pace a clear, three-pronged agenda emerged which is still influential today and includes:

(1) the need to develop a principled approach to sentencing;
(2) parsimony; and
(3) fairness (von Hirsch, 2001).

In relation to the first item on the agenda, Frankel (1972) made an important, early contribution to the debate. He argued against arbitrariness and the lack of fairness in sentencing and advocated the establishment of a sentencing commission to develop rules on sentencing. In the United States at least, the sentencing commission was enthusiastically adopted by many states: by 1996 twenty-five states had created sentencing commissions, and another twenty had some form of guidelines in place (Tonry, 2001).

Tonry (1996, 2001) has written extensively about the comparative lessons that can be learned from the great American experiment with sentencing reform and two points are worthy of mention here. First, he argues that there is a need to tailor the type of sentencing reform to meet the needs of the specific jurisdiction in question and, in particular, to take account of the punishment context (Tonry, 2001). So, for example, he contends that the need for detailed sentencing standards is less pronounced in jurisdictions with lower incarceration levels. Secondly, he argues that there is a need to 'reconcile both parts of the equality principle': that is, to achieve a balance between treating like cases alike and different cases differently (Tonry, 2001: 6). An over-emphasis on achieving consistency in sentencing may have unintended consequences and reduce, rather than increase, justice in sentencing as well as increasing already high prison populations.

Since its early beginnings in the US, many other jurisdictions have engaged in the modern project of sentencing reform, including Sweden (Jareborg, 1995), Finland (Lappi-Seppala, 2001), Canada (Doob, 1997), Australia (Freiberg, 2001), New Zealand (Thorp, 1997), South Africa (Terblanche, 1997) and England and Wales (Ashworth and Roberts, 2013). Reform in England and Wales has been particularly eventful (Ashworth, 2010; Ashworth and Roberts, 2013) and serves as a useful comparator to developments in Northern Ireland and the Republic. Traditionally sentencers in England and Wales had a very broad sentencing discretion. This was, in part, related to the limited role played by legislation in structuring sentencing discretion: for much of the twentieth century legislation was limited to providing sentencing powers and setting outer limits on their use (Ashworth, 2010). More recently, sentencing legislation in England and Wales has increased in frequency and complexity, making it difficult for the courts to navigate, and the legislature has increasingly made inroads into areas previously left to the judiciary (Ashworth, 2013). As a result of the wide discretion traditionally available to sentencers, the Court of Appeal in England and Wales first began to lay down sentencing guidelines in the early 1980s, although it was not until the 1990s that this became common practice (Ashworth and Roberts, 2013). Since then the arrangements for structuring sentencing discretion in England and Wales have changed three times and have included a Sentencing Advisory Panel (SAP) established by the Crime and Disorder Act 1998, a Sentencing Guidelines Council (SGC) established by the Criminal Justice Act 2003, and most recently an amalgamation of these bodies into a new Sentencing Council (SC) created by the Coroners and Justice Act 2009 (Ashworth and Roberts, 2013).

An important theme underpinning the developments in England and Wales has been the struggle for ownership of sentencing (Ashworth, 2010; Ashworth and Roberts, 2013). Indeed, the experience in England and Wales has led to interesting questions about who owns sentencing – the judiciary, the executive or the legislature. In England and Wales, after a long period during which parliament followed a policy of non-intervention in sentencing policy, the judiciary at first found it difficult to accept the involvement of the SAP (Ashworth, 2010; Ashworth and Roberts, 2013). As Ashworth (2010) argues, the judiciary has to accept that the legislature has the right to make sentencing policy and, provided it does not interfere in the sentencing of individual cases, it also has the right to delegate the formulation of sentencing policy to a body other than the judiciary.

Due to a lack of research on sentencing reform, it is difficult to tell what impact the new system of sentencing guidelines will have on actual sentencing practice (Ashworth and Roberts, 2013). Comparative research on the custody threshold in Scotland and also in England and Wales found that sentencers from England and Wales expressed concern about the inflationary effect of guideline judgments and expressed the view that attempts to produce greater uniformity had resulted in lenient sentences becoming more severe, so that they met the recommended norm (Millie et al., 2007). Another key question is the extent to which sentencing guidelines act as an algorithm, supplanting judicial discretion, or merely as a way of producing external accountability for discretionary decision-making (Franko Aas, 2005; Hutton, 2013).

Guidelines in Northern Ireland and the Republic of Ireland

Northern Ireland and the Republic of Ireland remain two of the only common law jurisdictions that have yet to embrace some form of structured sentencing guidelines system. Arguably Northern Ireland is slightly more advanced in terms of its approach to structuring sentencing, for at least two reasons. First, it has a highly structured legislative sentencing framework which provides much more detailed guidance to judges about the circumstances in which it is appropriate to use the various sanctions available to the courts. Secondly, there seems to be a greater acceptance amongst the judiciary in Northern Ireland of the importance of judicially-developed sentencing guidelines: the Court of Appeal of Northern Ireland has issued a number of guideline judgments and, where appropriate, sometimes draws upon guidelines developed by the Court of Appeal in England and Wales (Allen and McAleenan, 1998, 2003). However, this is not to suggest that the judiciary in Northern Ireland would be any more welcoming than their counterparts in England and Wales towards what might be perceived as outside interference in the formulation of sentencing guidelines.

As discussed earlier, the Republic of Ireland has practically no legislative sentencing framework, and until very recently the superior courts doubted the appropriateness of laying down guideline judgments. In the *People (DPP) v Tiernan*[17] the Supreme Court was reluctant to embrace the idea of sentencing guidelines, citing two principal concerns: the lack of sentencing statistics and the danger of interfering with judicial sentencing discretion. In the intervening years the Court of Criminal Appeal (CCA) and the Supreme Court have endeavoured to produce greater guidance on how to apply the principle of proportionality in practice. Detailed sentencing guidelines now exist in relation to rape and manslaughter (O'Malley, 2006, 2011) and, very significantly, the CCA recently affirmed the appropriateness of issuing detailed sentencing guidelines in the *DPP v Ryan*[18] and *DPP v Fitzgibbon*,[19] opining that the original concerns expressed by the court in *Tiernan* no longer applied. The CCA also decided in these cases that counsel for the Director of Public Prosecutions should have a role in highlighting existing relevant sentencing guidelines to the court. While the announcement that the CCA is now favourably disposed towards issuing guideline type judgments is very welcome, there is a sense in which it may be too little, too late (O'Malley, 2013).

The Law Reform Commission (2013), while noting the progress and contribution made by the courts in developing sentencing guidance, doubted the capacity of the courts to further this project through its appellate jurisdiction for a number of reasons. First, the Commission noted the findings on inconsistency in sentencing (see Hamilton, 2005; Maguire, 2010) and suggested that in the light of these the existing guidance structure was insufficient, due to the unstructured nature of the current system and to the fact that very little of the existing guidance appears to be relevant to the lower courts, particularly the District Court. More significantly it suggested that the reasons underpinning the apparent inconsistencies could not be dealt with on a once-off basis, or by new legislation, or by judicial guidance alone. Instead it recommended the establishment of a Judicial Council to oversee the formulation of sentencing guidelines as the way forward.

It is unlikely that the subsequent pronouncement by the CCA in *Ryan* would have led to a different recommendation, as the Commission expressed the view that a Judicial Council (and more specifically a Judicial Studies Institute that would be a member of the Judicial Council) would be in a better position than the courts to develop and disseminate the appropriate structured guidance. It also opined that the Irish Sentencing Information System (ISIS), a searchable digital database of Circuit and District Court sentencing decisions, while a valuable pilot project, was limited in a number of respects and needed further development (Law Reform Commission, 2013: 36). The ISIS database introduced by the Courts Service in 2006 on a pilot basis was completed in 2010 (Law Reform Commission, 2013). Its main aim was to provide judges with access to information on previous sentencing decisions. While the database is now publicly available at http://www.irishsentencing.ie, it has a number of limitations. First, the range of sentencing decisions available relates only to a limited number of courts and over a limited period of time. Secondly, only a small number of criteria are available in relation to each decision, which limits any understanding of the choice of sentence, and thus reduces comparability. Thirdly, at the moment there is very little analysis of the decisions (with the exception of rape, robbery, drugs and manslaughter) that are available and of how representative they are. Lastly, as O'Malley (2013) argues, strict adherence to previous practice can obscure the need to change course in relation to levels of severity and use of particular sanctions.

However, there is every possibility that the new Court of Appeal will have delivered a range of guideline judgments before the establishment of a Judicial Council. Although the government published the *Scheme of a Judicial Council Bill* in 2010, little progress has been made since then, and this is, unfortunately, typical of sentencing related reform (Department of Justice, 2015). The functions of the Council envisaged in the Bill include the preparation and dissemination of bench books and information on sentencing. The Bill also envisages membership of the Council being made up primarily of senior members of the judiciary. The judiciary would thus lead the Judicial Council and so preserve judicial independence and judicial discretion. O'Malley (2013), writing before the CCA's recent announcement, observed that the judiciary had not capitalised on the opportunity to be at the forefront of developing guidelines. However, if the Judicial Council Bill is anything to go by, it seems clear that the government's intention is to involve the judiciary heavily in any future mechanism adopted to structure sentencing discretion. This represents a continuation of the traditional policy of non-intervention adopted by the Irish legislature in the field of sentencing, which is most likely underpinned by the view that sentencing still belongs primarily to judges.

Despite its early familiarity with judicially developed sentencing guidelines, Northern Ireland has yet to establish a dedicated body to formulate sentencing guidelines. The *Hillsborough Castle Agreement* (Northern Ireland Office, 2010: 6) provided for the devolution of justice matters to the Northern Ireland Executive and Northern Ireland Assembly. It included a provision on the need to establish a sentencing guidelines council. The Lord Chief Justice of Northern Ireland, meanwhile, had already established a Sentencing Working Group (SWG) that produced a report in 2010 recommending the establishment of a Sentencing Group (SWG, 2010). The new group was to be chaired by the Lord Justice of Appeal, and its membership was to be drawn from the judiciary (SWG, 2010). Its functions included the drawing up of a list of priority areas for the development of sentencing guidelines and making arrangements for such guidelines to be produced (SWG, 2010).

At the same time, the Northern Ireland Minister for Justice published a *Consultation Document on a Sentencing Guidelines Mechanism* in 2010 setting out three options for consultation in relation to developing a sentencing guidelines system (Department of Justice Northern Ireland (DoJNI), 2010). They included: a Sentencing Guidelines Council, which would produce guidelines; a Sentencing Advisory Panel, which would draft guidelines for the approval of the Court of Appeal; and an approach to the Lord Chief Justice, which involved measures to enhance procedures for developing sentencing practice. The preferred option following the consultation was the development of a Sentencing Guidelines Council. However, in 2012 the Minister for Justice stated that given the poor economic climate, the establishment of a guidelines council would be too costly.[20] Instead he favoured the Lord Chief Justice's Sentencing Group, which would draw up a list of priority areas for the development of sentencing guidelines and make arrangements for these guidelines to be produced (SWG, 2010).

Both jurisdictions are clearly in the early stages of developing a structured system of sentencing guidelines, but, remarkably, both tend to favour an approach led by the judiciary, despite evidence from England and Wales, and from elsewhere (Tonry, 1996), that judge-led commissions and councils are not necessarily the most effective for structuring judicial sentencing discretion.

Future directions?

Sentencing is a human process (Hogarth, 1971) very much influenced by social practices, contexts and cultures (Hutton, 2006). As we noted in the introduction of this chapter, sentencing involves many more people than just the sentencers and those who are sentenced (Garland, 1990). Nonetheless, in Northern Ireland, and perhaps even more so in the Republic, sentencers still effectively 'own' sentencing. This is illustrated by the breadth of judicial sentencing discretion and by the extent to which the legislatures in both jurisdictions have pursued policies of limited intervention in sentencing matters.

The extent of judicial ownership of sentencing in both jurisdictions may be due to certain contextual factors that have provided a protective influence against legislative encroachment upon judicial discretion. In the Republic of Ireland the existence of a written constitution provides strong support for the doctrine of the separation of powers, and thus judicial independence. The historical legacy of the Diplock Courts may serve to highlight the importance of an independent

313

judiciary in Northern Ireland. However, another more mundane possibility is that the historical neglect of sentencing reform in these jurisdictions, due to the Conflict and to decades of unconcern about crime, may also explain the continued strength of judicial ownership of sentencing.

Having said that, the extent to which other parties play an active role in sentencing is growing. In recent times the influence of probation officers in sentencing, through the provision of pre-sentence reports and risk assessments, has increased significantly in importance. Further changes outside the scope of this chapter are unquestionably afoot. For instance, the role of victims in sentencing, though controversial, has been enhanced by the introduction of victim impact statements in both jurisdictions (Conway *et al.*, 2010; DoJNI, 2011) and will undoubtedly continue to grow after the transposition of the EU Victim's Directive 2012/29/EU. The emergence of a dedicated Drug Treatment Court in the Republic of Ireland (Farrell, 2002; National Crime Council, 2007; Butler, 2013), although not without its critics, highlights another potential for transformation in the nature of sentencing – the advent of problem-solving courts (Donoghue, 2014). However, it will be some time yet before it is possible to discern the extent to which these nascent transformations will reshape the sentencing landscape in Northern Ireland and in the Republic of Ireland.

References

Allen, M. J. and McAleenan, F. (1998) *Sentencing Law and Practice in Northern Ireland*, 3rd ed. Belfast: SLS Legal Publications.

—— (2003) *Supplement to Sentencing Law and Practice in Northern Ireland*, 3rd ed. Belfast: SLS Legal Publications.

Ashworth, A. (2010) *Sentencing and Criminal Justice*, 3rd ed. Cambridge: Cambridge University Press.

—— (2013) 'The Struggle for Supremacy in Sentencing' in A. Ashworth and J. Roberts (eds) *Sentencing Guidelines: Exploring The English Model*. Oxford: Oxford University Press.

Ashworth, A. and Roberts, J. (2013) 'The Origins and Nature of the Sentencing Guidelines in England and Wales' in A. Ashworth and J. Roberts (eds) *Sentencing Guidelines: Exploring The English Model*. Oxford: Oxford University Press.

Ashworth, A. and von Hirsch, A. (2005) *Proportionate Sentencing: Exploring the Principles*. Oxford: Oxford University Press.

Bacik, I. (2002) 'The Practice of Sentencing in the Irish Courts' in P. O'Mahony (ed.) *Criminal Justice in Ireland*. Dublin: Institute of Public Administration.

Barnes, S. (2012) 'Indeterminate Sentences: A "Stain" on the Criminal Justice System'. *The Guardian*, 12 September 2012. Available at: www.theguardian.com/law/2012/sep/18/prisoners-indeterminate-sentences-ipps (accessed 14 January 2015).

Beyens, K. and Scheirs, V. (2010) 'Encounters of a Different Kind: Social Enquiry and Sentencing in Belgium', *Punishment and Society*, 12(3): 309–328.

Blumstein, A., Cohen, J., Roth, J. A. and Visher, C. A. (eds) (1986) *Criminal Careers and Career Criminals*. Washington DC: National Institute of Justice.

Bottoms, A. E. (1977) 'Reflections on the Renaissance of Dangerousness,' *Howard Journal of Penology and Crime Prevention*, 16:70–98.

—— (1995) 'The Philosophy and Politics of Punishment and Sentencing' in C. Clarkson and R. Morgan (eds) *The Politics of Sentencing Reform*. Oxford: Oxford University Press.

Bottoms, A. E., Shapland, J., Costello, A., Holmes, D. and Muire, G. (2004) 'Towards Desistance: Theoretical Underpinnings for an Empirical Study', *Howard Journal of Criminal Justice*, 43: 368.

Braithwaite, J. and Pettit, P. (1990) *Not Just Deserts*. Oxford: Oxford University Press.

Brody, S. R. and Tarling, R. (1981) *Taking Offenders Out of Circulation*. Home Office Research Study 64. London: HMSO.

Brown, M. (1998) 'Serious Violence and Dilemmas of Sentencing', *Criminal Law Review*, 710.

Brown, M. and Pratt, J. (eds) (2000) *Dangerous Offenders: Punishment and Social Order*. London: Routledge.

Butler, S. (2013) 'The Symbolic Politics of the Dublin Drug Court: The Complexities of Policy Transfer', *Drugs: Education, Prevention and Policy*, 20(1): 5–14.

Cahillane, L. (2013) 'Are Sentencing Guidelines Needed in Ireland?', *Irish Criminal Law Journal*, 23(1): 1–7.

Campbell, L. (2013) *Organised Crime and the Law: A Comparative Analysis*. Oxford: Hart.

Carr, N. (2015) 'Probation and Community Sanctions in Northern Ireland: Historical and Contemporary Contexts' in A. McAlinden and C. Dwyer (eds) *Criminal Justice in Transition: The Northern Ireland Context*. Oxford: Hart.

Carter, P. (2003) *Managing Offenders, Reducing Crime: A New Approach*. London: Home Office Strategy Unit.

Cavadino, M., Dignan, J. and Mair, G. (2013) *The Penal System: An Introduction*, 5th ed. London: Sage.

Conway, V., Daly, Y. and Schweppe, J. (2010) *Irish Criminal Justice: Theory, Process and Procedure*. Dublin: Clarus Press.

Craig, R. (2008) 'Remission Revision', *New Law Journal*, 158: 7302. Available at: www.newlawjournal.co.uk/nlj/content/remission-revision (accessed 31 August 2014).

Department of Justice (2015) *Scheme of a Judicial Council Bill*. Available at: www.justice.ie/en/JELR/General%20Scheme%20Judicial%20Bill.pdf/Files/General%20Scheme%20Judicial%20Bill.pdf (accessed 15 January 2015).

Department of Justice Northern Ireland (DoJNI) (2010) *Consultation on a Sentencing Guidelines Mechanism*. Belfast: Northern Ireland Office.

—— (2011) *Provision of Victim Impact Statements and Victim Impact Reports: A Department of Justice Consultation*. Belfast: DoJ.

Dickson, B. (2013) *Law in Northern Ireland*. Oxford: Hart.

Dingwall, G. (1998) 'Selective Incapacitation After the Criminal Justice Act 1991: A Proportional Response to Protecting the Public', *The Howard Journal*, 37(2): 177–87.

—— (2009) 'Sentencing' in A. Hucklesby and A. Wahidin (eds) *Criminal Justice*. Oxford: Oxford University Press.

Donoghue, J. (2014) *Transforming Criminal Justice? Problem-Solving and Court Specialisation*. Abingdon: Routledge.

Doob, A. N. (1997) 'Sentencing Reform in Canada' in M. Tonry and K. Hatlestad (eds) *Sentencing Reform in Overcrowded Times: A Comparative Perspective*. Oxford: Oxford University Press.

Easton, S. and Piper, C. (2008) *Sentencing and Punishment: The Quest for Justice*, 2nd ed. Oxford: Oxford University Press.

Ellison, G. and Mulcahy, A. (2009) 'Crime and Criminal Justice in Northern Ireland' in A. Huckelsby and A. Wahidin (eds) *Criminal Justice*. Abingdon: Routledge.

Farrell, M. (2002) *Final Evaluation of the Pilot Drug Court*. Available at: http://www.drugs.ie/resourcesfiles/research/2002/2601-2765.pdf (accessed 12 January 2015).

Feeley, M. and Simon, J. (1994) 'Actuarial Justice: The Emerging New Criminal Law' in D. Nelkin (ed). *The Futures of Criminology*. London: Sage.

Fletcher, G. P. (1978) *Rethinking Criminal Law*. Boston: Little, Brown.

Floud, J. (1982) 'Dangerousness and Criminal Justice', *The British Journal of Criminology*, 22 (3): 213–228.

Floud, J. and Young, W. (1981) *Dangerousness and Criminal Justice*. London: Heinemann.

Frankel, M. (1972) 'Lawlessness in Sentencing', *University of Cincinnati Law Review*, 41(1), 1–54.

Franko Aas, K. (2005) *Sentencing in the Age of Information: From Faust to Macintosh*. London: Glasshouse Press.

Freiberg, A. (2001) 'Three Strikes and You're Out-It's Not Cricket: Colonization and Resistance in Australian Sentencing' in M. Tonry and R. Frase (eds) *Sentencing and Sanctioning in Western Countries*, Oxford: Oxford University Press.

Fulton, B. and Carr, N. (2013) *Probation in Europe: Northern Ireland*. Available at: http://www.cepprobation.org/uploaded_files/Probation-in-Europe-2013-Chapter-Northern-Ireland.pdf (accessed 26 November 2014).

Garland, D. (1990) *Punishment and Modern Society: A Study in Social Theory*. Oxford: Clarendon Press.

—— (2001) *The Culture of Control*. Oxford: Oxford University Press.

Greenwood, P. W. and Abrahamson, A. (1982) *Selective Incapacitation*. Santa Monica CA: Rand Corporation.

Hamilton, C. (2005) 'Sentencing in the District Court: Here Be Dragons', *Irish Criminal Law Journal*, 15:9.

Harrison, K. (2012) *Dangerousness, Risk and the Governance of Serious Sexual and Violent Offenders*. Abington: Routledge.

Hart, H. L. A. (2008) *Punishment and Responsibility*, 2nd ed. Oxford: Oxford University Press.

Healy, D. and O'Donnell, I. (2010) 'Crime, Consequences and Court Reports', *Irish Criminal Law Journal*, 20(1): 2–7.

Herzog-Evans, M. and Boone, M. (2013) 'Decision-Making and Offender Supervision' in F. McNeill and K. Beyens (eds) *Offender Supervision in Europe*. Basingstoke: Palgrave Macmillan.

Hogarth, J. (1971) *Sentencing as a Human Process*. Toronto: Toronto University Press.

Home Office (2001) *Criminal Justice: The Way Forward*. London: Stationery Office.

Hough, M., Jacobson, J. and Millie, A. (2003) *The Decision to Imprison: Sentencing and the Prison Population*. London: Prison Reform Trust.

Hutton, N. (2006) 'Sentencing as a Social Practice' in S. Armstrong and L. McAra (eds) *Perspectives on Punishment: The Contours of Control*. Oxford: Oxford University Press.

—— (2013) 'The Definitive Guideline on Assault Offences: The Performance of Justice' in A. Ashworth and J. Roberts (eds) *Sentencing Guidelines: Exploring the English Model*. Oxford: Oxford University Press.

Ingram, M. (2004) 'Shame and Pain: Themes and Variations in Tudor Punishments' in S. Devereux and P. Griffiths (eds) *Penal Practice and Culture, 1500–1900: Punishing the English*. London: Palgrave.

Jacobson, J. and Hough, M. (2010) *Unjust Deserts: Imprisonment for Public Protection*. London: Prison Reform Trust.

Jareborg, N. (1995) 'The Swedish Sentencing Reform' in C. M. Clarkson and R. Morgan (eds) *The Politics of Sentencing Reform*. Oxford: Oxford University Press.

Kazemian, L. and Farrington, D. P. (2006) 'Exploring Residual Career Length and Residual Number of Offences for Two Generations of Repeat Offenders', *Journal of Research in Crime and Delinquency*, 43: 898.

Kemshall, H. (2003) *Understanding Risk in Criminal Justice*. Buckingham: McGraw-Hill/Oxford University Press.

Kilcommins, S., O'Donnell, I., O'Sullivan, E. and Vaughan, B. (2004) *Crime, Punishment and the Search for Order in Ireland*. Dublin: Institute of Public Administration.

Lappi-Seppala, T. (2001) 'Sentencing and Punishment in Finland: The Decline of the Repressive Ideal' in M. Tonry and R.S. Frase (eds) *Sentencing and Sanctions in Western Countries*. Oxford: Oxford University Press.

Law Reform Commission (1993) *Consultation Paper on Sentencing*. Dublin: Law Reform Commission.

—— (1996) *Report on Sentencing*. Dublin: Law Reform Commission.

—— (2013) *Report on Mandatory Sentencing*. Dublin: Law Reform Commission.

McGuire, J. (2002) (ed.) *Offender Rehabilitation and Treatment*. Chichester: Wiley.

McNeill, F. and Beyens, K. (eds) (2013) *Offender Supervision in Europe*. Basingstoke: Palgrave Macmillan.

Maguire, N. (2008) *Sentencing in Ireland: An Exploration of the Views, Rationales and Sentencing Practices of District and Circuit Court Judges*, Ph.D. thesis, Trinity College Dublin, Ireland.

—— (2010) 'Consistency in Sentencing', *Judicial Studies Institute Journal*, 10(2): 14–54.

—— (2014) 'When Is Prison a Last Resort? Definitional Problems and Judicial Interpretations', *Irish Criminal Law Journal*, 24(3): 62–72.

Maguire, N. and Carr, N. (2013) 'Changing Shape and Shifting Boundaries: The Media Portrayal of Probation in Ireland', *European Journal of Probation*, 5(3): 3–23.

Millie, A., Tombs, J. and Hough, M. (2007) 'Borderline Sentencing: A Comparison of Sentencers' Decision-Making in England and Wales, and Scotland', *Criminology and Criminal Justice*, 7: 243.

Morris, N. (1974) *The Future of Imprisonment*. Chicago: University of Chicago Press.

Morris, N. and Tonry, M. (1990) *Between Prison and Probation*. New York: Oxford University Press.

Mulcahy, A. (2002) 'The Impact of the Northern Ireland "Troubles" on Criminal Justice in the Irish Republic', in P. O'Mahony (ed.) *Criminal Justice in Ireland*. Dublin: Institute of Public Administration.

National Crime Council (2007) *Problem Solving Justice: The Case for Community Courts in Ireland*. Dublin: Stationery Office.

Northern Ireland Affairs Committee (2007) *The Northern Irish Prison Service: Volume II* (HC 118-II). London: HMSO.

Northern Ireland Office (2000) *Review of Criminal Justice System in Northern Ireland*. Belfast: Northern Ireland Office.

—— (2010) *Hillsborough Castle Agreement*. Belfast: Northern Ireland Office.

O'Mahony, P. (2002) 'The Constitution and Criminal Justice' in P. O'Mahony (ed.) *Criminal Justice in Ireland*. Dublin: Institute of Public Administration.

O'Malley, T. (2006) *Sentencing Law and Practice*, 2nd ed. Dublin: Thomson Round Hall.

—— (2009) 'Sentencing Recidivist Sex Offenders: A Challenge for Proportionality' in I. Bacik and L. Heffernan (eds) *Criminal Law and Procedure: Current Issues and Emerging Trends*. Dublin: Firstlaw.

—— (2011) *Sentencing – Towards A Coherent System*. Dublin: Round Hall.

—— (2013) 'Living without Guidelines' in A. Ashworth and J. Roberts (eds) *Sentencing Guidelines: Exploring The English Model*. Oxford: Oxford University Press.

Padfield, N. and Maruna, S. (2006) 'The Revolving Door at the Prison Gate: Exploring the Dramatic Increase in Recalls to Prison', *Theoretical Criminology*, 6(3): 329.

Pratt, J. (2000) 'Dangerousness and Modern Society' in M. Brown and J. Pratt (eds) *Dangerous Offenders: Punishment and Social Order*. London: Routledge.

—— (2007) *Penal Populism*. Oxon: Routledge.

Roberts, J.V. (2008) *Punishing Persistent Offenders*. Oxford: Oxford University Press.

Roberts, J.V. and von Hirsch, A. (2010) (eds) *Previous Convictions at Sentencing*. Oxford: Hart.

Rogan, M. (2011) *Prison Policy in Ireland*. Abingdon: Routledge.

Rottman, D. B. (1984) *The Criminal Justice System: Policy and Performance*. Report No. 77. Dublin: National Economic and Social Council.

Rottman, E. (1990) *Beyond Punishment: A New View of Rehabilitation of Criminal Offenders*. New York: Greenwood Press.

Sentencing Working Group (SWG) (2010) *Monitoring and Developing Sentencing Guidance in Northern Ireland – A Report to the Lord Chief Justice from the Sentencing Working Group*. Belfast: Sentencing Working Group.

Tata, C., Burns, N., Halliday, S., Hutton, N. and McNeill, F. (2008) 'Assisting and Advising the Sentencing Decision Process – The Pursuit of Quality in Pre-Sentence Reports', *British Journal of Criminology*, 48, 835–855.

Terblanche, S. (1997) 'Sentencing in South Africa' in M. Tonry and K. Hatlestad (eds) *Sentencing Reform in Overcrowded Times: A Comparative Perspective*. Oxford: Oxford University Press.

Thomas, D. A. (1979) *Principles of Sentencing*. London: Heinemann.

Thorp, T. M. (1997) 'Sentencing and Punishment in New Zealand, 1981-1993' in M. Tonry and K. Hatlestad (eds) *Sentencing Reform in Overcrowded Times: A Comparative Perspective*. Oxford: Oxford University Press.

Tombs, J. and Jagger, E. (2006) 'Denying Responsibility: Sentencers' Accounts of Their Decisions to Imprison', *British Journal of Criminology*, 46: 803.

Tonry, M. (1996) *Sentencing Matters*. Oxford: Oxford University Press.

—— (2001) 'Unthought Thoughts: The Influence of Changing Sensibilities on Penal Policies', *Punishment and Society*, 3(1): 167.

Tornudd, P. (1994) 'Sentencing and Punishment in Finland', *Overcrowded Times*, 5(6): 1, 11 13, 16.

von Hirsch, A. (2001) 'The Project of Sentencing Reform' in M. Tonry and R.S. Frase (eds) *Sentencing and Sanctions in Western Countries*. Oxford: Oxford University Press.

von Hirsch, A. and Ashworth, A. (2005) *Proportionate Sentencing*. Oxford: Oxford University Press.

von Hirsch, A., Ashworth, A. and Roberts, J. (2009a) 'Incapacitation' in A. von Hirsch, A. Ashworth, and J. Roberts (eds) *Principled Sentencing: Readings on Theory and Policy*, 3rd ed. Oxford: Hart Publishing.

—— (2009b) 'Deterrence' in A. von Hirsch, A. Ashworth and J. Roberts (eds) *Principled Sentencing: Readings on Theory and Policy*, 3rd ed. Oxford: Hart.

von Hirsch, A., Bottoms, A., Burney, E. and Wikstrom, P. (2009c) 'Deterrence Sentencing as a Crime Prevention Strategy' in A. von Hirsch, A. Ashworth and J. Roberts (eds) *Principled Sentencing: Readings on Theory and Policy*, 3rd ed. Oxford: Hart.

Wahidin, A. and Carr, N. (2013) *Understanding Criminal Justice: A Critical Introduction*. Abingdon: Routledge.

Wandall, R. (2008) *Decisions to Imprison: Court Decision-Making Inside and Outside the Law*. Aldershot: Ashgate.

—— (2010) 'Resisting Risk Assessment? Pre-Sentence Reports and Individualized Sentencing in Denmark', *Punishment and Society*, 12: 329.

Worrall, A. (1997) *Punishment in the Community: The Future of Criminal Justice*. London: Longman.

Notes

1 For more detailed accounts readers are referred to Allen and McAleenan (1998; 2003) and Dickson (2013) for Northern Ireland and to O'Malley (2006; 2011) for the Republic of Ireland.

2 For an in-depth analysis of the sentencing laws in England and Wales see Ashworth (2010) and Easton and Piper (2008).

3 [1994] 3 IR 306, at 317.

4 [2010] IESC 34.

5 [2005] ILRM 19 at 22, Hamilton J.

6 For detailed accounts of all aggravating and mitigating factors recognised in Irish law see Law Reform Commission, 1993, 1996; O'Malley, 2006.

7 [2007] IESC 47.
8 For instance, in 1999 the Court of Criminal Appeal in *Director of Public Prosecutions v McBride* (unreported, Court of Appeal, 5 July 1999) stated that it was one of the 'major purposes of sentencing policy'. See also O'Malley, 2006, 2011; Maguire, 2010; Healy and O'Donnell, 2010; Kilcommins *et al.*, 2004.
9 See Firearms (Northern Ireland) Order 2004 in relation to presumptive minimum firearms offences, and the Criminal Justice (NI) Order 2008 in relation to dangerous offenders.
10 For example, see the contrasting approaches of the court in *People (DPP) v GK* [2008] IECCA 110 and *People (DPP) v PS* [2009] IECCA 1.
11 *James, Wells and Lee v UK* ECHR 340 (2012).
12 *R v Paul Pollins* [2014] NICA 62.
13 [1966] IR 501.
14 [1994] 3 IR 306.
15 [2008] IECCA 110.
16 *Minister for Justice v Nolan* [2012] IEHC 249.
17 [1988] IR 250.
18 [2014] IECCA 11.
19 [2014] IECCA 12.
20 Hansard, Northern Ireland Assembly, 11 June 2012, vol. 75, no. 5 at 311.

16
Community sanctions and measures

Nicola Carr

Introduction

This chapter explores the use of community sanctions in the Republic of Ireland and in Northern Ireland. The Council of Europe's (CoE) definition of Community Sanctions and Measures demarcates the field under study:

> The term 'community sanctions and measures' refers to sanctions and measures which maintain the offender in the community and involve some restriction of his liberty through the imposition of conditions and/or obligations, and which are implemented by bodies designated in law for that purpose. The term designates any sanction imposed by a court or a judge, and any measure taken before or instead of a decision on a sanction as well as ways of enforcing a sentence of imprisonment outside a prison establishment
>
> *(Council of Europe, 1992, Appendix para. 1)*

Included within the ambit of this definition are community sentences imposed by a court and post-custodial restrictions following release from prison (e.g. on licence). These are sometimes referred to as 'front-end' sentences and 'back-end' sentences respectively. Notably the definition above specifies that community sanctions and measures involve 'some restriction of liberty' through the imposition of conditions, which are overseen by a body designated in law.[1] In the Republic of Ireland this body is the Probation Service, in Northern Ireland it is the Probation Board for Northern Ireland (PBNI). Both organisations carry out similar functions but their constitution and governance arrangements differ, as does the extent of their reach (evident in the differing proportions of people under forms of community supervision), and the legal frameworks in which they operate.

The chapter locates the Republic of Ireland and Northern Ireland within a wider international landscape, where the numbers of people subject to supervision in the community has risen markedly. It explores some of the reasons for this growth alongside the rationalities that are deployed to promote the use of community sanctions over time. The differing trajectories of the two jurisdictions in respect of the evolution and use of community sanctions are explored, as are some of the factors that explain areas of divergence and commonality. The chapter concludes by critically considering penal reductionism as a point of policy convergence in the two jurisdictions.

An expanding sphere

Internationally the numbers of people subject to forms of supervision in the community has expanded exponentially (McNeill and Beyens, 2013). Yet, despite the rise in their use, and in some cases the increasing strictures placed on people within the community, this sphere of penality has been subject to relatively limited scholarly attention or public discourse. One reason for this oversight may be the attention directed towards imprisonment in much of the criminological literature, particularly in light of the rise of 'mass incarceration' in the United States and prison expansionism elsewhere (Robinson et al., 2013; Clear and Frost, 2014; DeMichele, 2014). Yet, if one takes the hyperactive incarceration rates of the US as one example, even there the numbers of people subject to community sanctions and measures is more than three times the numbers imprisoned (Herberman and Bonczar, 2014; Carson, 2014).[2] Similarly in many European countries the numbers subject to sanctions in the community far exceeds the numbers imprisoned (see McNeill and Beyens, 2013, for an overview).

Another reason for the neglect of community sanctions may be their lack of visibility particularly when compared with the powerful visual iconography and cultural purchase of the prison (Brown, 2009). In one sense this is understandable, community sanctions are by their nature more spatially diffuse. They are not bounded by a physical structure in the same manner as a prison, and the spaces and places where supervision occurs are not usually made publicly visible. It is therefore harder to picture what they entail, and their penal character appears more oblique (Robinson, 2015). Furthermore, the language or 'branding' (Maruna and King, 2004) of community sanctions often renders their purpose unintelligible to the wider public. All these factors contribute to what Robinson (2015) characterises as their 'Cinderella' status.

Lack of visibility combines with mutability to further obscure this field. Reflecting broader socio-cultural and penal trends the rationale for community sanctions has changed over time. In an analysis of what they describe as the 'improbable persistence of probation', Robinson et al. (2013: 321) identify a number of shifts in the function and legitimation of community sanctions and measures from the beginning of the twentieth century into the present. Initially grounded in penal welfarism with an emphasis on the reform of the individual, the stated purposes of community sanctions have shifted in tandem with wider penal trends. The crisis in penality from the 1970s onwards, most famously described by Garland (2001) in the *Culture of Control*, notes in particular the demise of rehabilitation in favour of more punitive approaches. Following the so-called 'decline of the rehabilitative ideal' (Allen, 1981) and the rise in the use of imprisonment, community sanctions have been repositioned and reframed in response.

Robinson et al. (2013) note four distinct (although not necessarily mutually exclusive) strategies of adaptation: managerial, punitive, rehabilitative and reparative. To take each of these in turn, the managerial adaptation refers to the increased emphasis placed on the categorisation and management of individuals in the most cost-effective manner. The emphasis on *management* is instrumental and mutes any wider ambition for the transformation of the individual. Examples include the advent of 'offender management', perhaps best typified in the integration of prison and probation services in England and Wales under a National Offender Management Service (NOMS). Here as Worrall (2008:120) observes, the concept of 'offender management' serves to create 'a narrative of "joined up" penal thinking and cost-effective delivery': a narrative which she argues is imaginary, invoking an illusion of social control – 'both impossible to achieve but also undesirable' (Worrall, 2008: 113).

Punitive adaptations include the recasting of community sanctions as 'punishment in the community'. In addition to public messaging about the 'toughness' of such sanctions, this has been associated with more intense supervisory requirements and increased penalties for non-compliance. Given the expanded reach of post-custodial supervision, the conditions attached to licences and recall practices can have a significant influence on the prison population through the so-called 'backdoor' sentencing route (Padfield and Maruna, 2006; Padfield, 2012).

The rehabilitative potential of community sanctions was given a renewed focus by an emphasis on 'evidence-based' approaches from the late 1980s onwards. The 'What Works?' initiative, which has advanced particular methodologies and approaches premised on the 'Risk–Need–Responsivity' (RNR) model of offender rehabilitation has been particularly influential (Ward and Maruna, 2007). With its emphasis on risk assessment as a means to target resources and the recasting of 'need' as criminogenic need (i.e. interventions should only be targeted at factors relating to risk of re-offending), we can see that this revived rehabilitation model intersects with the managerialism adaptation.

Reparation, the last adaptation described by Robinson *et al.* (2013), is most closely associated with interventions, which allow some form of repair for the harm caused by offending (McIvor, 2011). Sentences, such as community service, involving unpaid work in the community may be regarded as reparative (although for a discussion about how they can be recast as expressly punitive sanctions see McNeill, 2009). Other forms of reparation include restorative justice approaches, which have gained increasing currency in many countries in recent years (Morris, 2002; Wood, 2015).

Similarly in Northern Ireland and the Republic various legitimations have been deployed over time to support the use of community sanctions (Carr, 2015a; Healy, 2015). In both jurisdictions there has been a rise in the use of community sanctions linked to increased resourcing and an expanded legislative remit. However, the rate of use of community sanctions compared to the numbers imprisoned differs across the two jurisdictions. In Northern Ireland the rate of use of imprisonment compared to community sanctions is broadly equivalent (Graham and Damkat, 2014).[3] In the Republic of Ireland committals to prison exceed community sentences imposed by a rate of more than two to one (Probation Service, 2014; Irish Prison Service, 2014).[4] Importantly a significant proportion of committals to prisons in the Republic of Ireland are as a result of non-payment of a court-ordered fine (DoJE, 2014). Understanding the variance in the use of community sanctions directs attention towards, social and cultural contexts, historical trends, sentencing practices, the purpose and character of these sanctions and their interrelationship with other forms of penality – most notably the use of imprisonment.

Historical context

Both Northern Ireland and the Republic share a common antecedent legislation in the form of the Probation of Offenders Act 1907. Reflecting a welfarist (or perhaps paternalist) orientation, this Act famously refers to the probation role as one of 'advising, assisting and befriending'. Evidence of the inertia in criminal justice policy in the Republic of Ireland, this statute continues to provide the core legislative basis for probation there, despite a recent commitment towards legislative reform in the form of the Criminal Justice (Community Sanctions) Bill 2014.

For much of the twentieth century legislation governing the administration of community sanctions in Northern Ireland followed legislation introduced in England and Wales. However, in relative terms probation in Northern Ireland was poorly resourced and concentrated in the main urban areas (Fulton and Carr, 2013). The establishment of a trainee scheme linked to a social work qualification led to an increased emphasis on professionalization and an expansion of probation services in the 1970s. However, this coincided with the outbreak of the Troubles, which profoundly affected all aspects of Northern Irish society including the administration of criminal justice.

Many agencies within the criminal justice system became embroiled with the Conflict, most notably the prisons and police, but the probation service adopted a stance of 'neutrality' (Carr and Maruna, 2012). Essentially this meant that the probation officers did not work with people whose offences were of a political nature (unless on a voluntary basis regarding welfare concerns). The reasons put forward for this stance, which was endorsed by the National Association of Probation Officers (NAPO), were both principled and pragmatic. It ultimately meant that probation continued work at a community level, and probation officers were not viewed as 'legitimate targets' by paramilitary organisations (Carr and Maruna, 2012).

Legislation enacted in 1982 established the Probation board for Northern Ireland (PBNI) as a non-departmental public body. This meant that direct governance of probation moved from a government department to a separate body overseen by a board. Addressing deficits in legitimacy in state-administered criminal justice during the course of political conflict formed part of the rationale for the establishment of an independent board comprising community representatives (Carr, 2015b). Today, however, this issue is arguably more symbolic than tangible. PBNI receives its entire funding from government and is required by legislation to 'give effect' to the directions of the Department of Justice; therefore the extent of independence or community involvement in its operations is limited in scope.[5] This realignment is evident in its budgetary allocation. When it was first established the PBNI allocated 20 per cent of its budget to community-based organisations; by 2009 this proportion had declined to just 7 per cent (O'Mahony and Chapman, 2007; Carr, 2015a).

Throughout the 1990s and the 2000s a series of legislative measures were passed which further extended provisions for community sanctions and the role of the PBNI. The Criminal Justice Order (Northern Ireland) 1996 updated the law in relation to the main community sentences – Probation Orders, Community Service Orders (CSOs) and Combination Orders – and set out the dual purpose of such orders (protecting the public and securing the rehabilitation of the offender). Following the Good Friday Agreement, the Criminal Justice Review (2000) focused on the administration of justice in Northern Ireland and considered the feasibility of amalgamating prisons and probation into a unitary offender management service, akin to the model that was eventually adopted in England and Wales (Mair and Burke, 2012; Raynor, 2012). Ultimately the Review team did not recommend such an approach in Northern Ireland, largely because of the difficulties facing the prisons (Blair, 2000).

These difficulties followed from the manner in which the prisons had been so closely entwined in the Conflict. The prisons were battlegrounds for many of the key events of the Conflict, including internment without trial and the death of ten men on hunger strike (Gormally et al., 1993). Prison staff were considered 'legitimate targets' by paramilitaries, and 29 prison officers were killed in the course of the Conflict.[6] In the post-Conflict period the prisons were required to significantly downsize, prompted in part by a prisoner-release scheme (McEvoy, 2001). It was also necessary to move from a highly securitized model towards more 'normalised' operations. However, as the Owers' Review of the Prison Service (2011) and subsequent inspection reports make clear (CJINI, 2013; 2014), this process has been painstaking, and the challenges involved are still evident in the present day.

Further legislation throughout the 2000s consolidated probation's public protection role, and throughout this period the systems and processes developed by PBNI placed a strong emphasis on risk assessment. The Criminal Justice Order (NI) 2008 introduced so-called 'public protection' sentences, in certain circumstances extending the periods of post-custodial supervision. The effects of this legislation on the work of PBNI is discussed further below. While probation in Northern Ireland followed some of the similar trends evident in England and Wales, including an increased focus on risk and public protection, it did not do so to the same degree. Some of the reasons for this divergence include the impact and legacy of political conflict on all aspects of the criminal justice system and the fact that historically such a strong emphasis had been placed on probation's community-based role (O'Mahony and Chapman, 2007; Carr, 2015a).

In the Republic of Ireland the pace of legislative change has been much slower. As already noted, the main legislative instrument is more than a century old. Various analyses have put forward reasons for the torpor in criminal justice policy (Kilcommins *et al.*, 2004; O'Sullivan and O'Donnell, 2012; Rogan, 2011). These include low crime rates for much of the twentieth century, the role of wider institutions of social control, and poorly developed governance and administrative infrastructures. These analyses have variously been applied to prisons, youth justice and wider social policy, and in this respect the position of community sanctions, while remarkable, is not especially unique (Healy, 2015).

Evidence of the underdevelopment of the Probation Service in the Republic of Ireland is provided in McNally's (2007) historical account, which notes that until the 1940s there were just four probation officers employed in the entire country, and until 1968 there was no full-time officer working outside Dublin. By 1973, following some investment in the service, the numbers of probation officers employed across the country rose to 47 (Kilcommins *et al.*, 2004; McNally, 2007). In the latter part of the twentieth century, where community sanctions have garnered policy attention, it has largely been in the context of their potential to act as a penal reduction mechanism. Most notably the Whitaker Report (Committee of Inquiry into the Penal System, 1985) recommended that prison should be used as a sentence of last resort and that community sanctions should be used to a greater degree.

The government's five-year plan for the *Management of Offenders* (Department of Justice, 1994) further recommended an expanded role for the Probation Service, again positioned as an alternative to custody in the context of an escalation in the prison population. In parallel, various reports have also decried the lack of investment in the service. For example the *Final Report of the Expert Group on the Probation and Welfare Service* (Expert Group, 1999), the first substantial review of Probation in the history of the State, noted:

> Mechanisms to maximise non-custodial sanctions for offenders are seriously underdeveloped and under-funded in the Irish context relative to custodial options.
>
> *(Expert Group, 1999:5)*

The most significant expansion in the role of the service to date came with the passage of the Criminal Justice (Community Service) Act 1983, which introduced Community Service Orders (CSOs) (McCarthy, 2014). The Irish legislation was largely modelled on English legislation enacted in 1972 (similar legislation had been introduced in Northern Ireland in 1976). In 2011 amending legislation (the Criminal Justice (Community Service) Amendment Act 2011) was enacted which required the court to consider the imposition of a CSO as an alternative to custody for sentences of 12 months or less. The legislation also allowed for the imposition of a CSO as an alternative to prison sentences exceeding this length; however, it is not a requirement that the courts make this consideration when imposing a longer sentence of imprisonment. The evident intention of the 2011 Act was to encourage a greater use of community service by the judiciary and consequently to reduce the resort to short prison sentences.

Legislation enacted in the 2000s (Children Act 2001; Sex Offenders' Act 2000; Criminal Justice Act 2006; Fines Act 2010) has further expanded probation's mandate. By 2007 the number of probation officers in the Republic had risen to 260 (O'Donovan, 2008). In tandem with this widening remit, there has been an increased emphasis placed on risk assessment and public protection, evident in the introduction of standardised risk assessment tools and a greater systemisation of practice (Maguire and Carr, 2013; Fitzgibbon et al., 2010).

With divergent historical pathways, legislative frameworks and resources, community sanctions in the two jurisdictions on the island of Ireland have developed in different ways. The following sections detail current trends in the use of community sanctions highlighting points of variance and commonality.

Trends in community sanctions and measures in Northern Ireland

On 31 March 2014 there were 1,890 people detained in prison in Northern Ireland. On the same date there were approximately 3,443 people under supervision in the community.[7] One of the main roles of the Probation Board is the provision of reports to court, with PBNI preparing almost 6,000 Pre-Sentence Reports (PSRs) per year (PBNI, 2014).[8] PSRs are requested by the court after conviction but before sentencing. These reports provide background information on the defendant's social and personal circumstances, including education, employment and living arrangements. Linked to the advance of risk-oriented approaches, an assessment of the defendant's likelihood of re-offending and risk of causing serious harm is also included, with the assessment of risk being informed by the use of risk assessment tools. In Northern Ireland the ACE (Assessment, Case Management and Evaluation) assessment tool is used by probation officers to assess likelihood of re-offending within a specific time period. Further specialised risk assessment tools are used based on the offence (e.g. sexual or domestic violence) and where there are concerns regarding serious harm.

The community sanctions available to the court are prescribed in legislation. The Criminal Justice (Northern Ireland) Order 1996 outlines that the purpose of a Probation Order is to 'secure the rehabilitation of the offender' to ensure the protection of the public from harm by preventing the commission of further offences (Article 10, 1). A Probation Order involving supervision by a probation officer can be for a minimum duration of six months and a maximum of three years. Within this legislation Community Service Orders (unpaid work in the community) are set out as alternatives to custody, to be considered when the offence is otherwise 'punishable by imprisonment'. Combination Orders (combining probation supervision and community service) are also provided for within this legislation.

As Robinson et al. (2013) note, different rationales to legitimise the use of community sanctions are deployed to varying effects over time. As will be evident from the above, community sentences in Northern Ireland embody differing penal purposes including rehabilitation, public protection and reparation. First introduced in 1976, Community Service Orders are also framed as 'alternatives to custody',[9] thereby ostensibly serving a penal reductionist function. It is notable that in recent years the numbers of Community Service Orders have declined in Northern Ireland, while other forms of sanctions, in particular those that meld elements of custody and community supervision, have come increasingly to the fore. To a certain extent this has been driven by an increased focus on risk management and public protection (Carr, 2015a).

Figure 16.1 shows the rise in the number of people supervised by PBNI in recent years. It illustrates that since 2010 the number of people supervised has risen by over 14 per cent. The

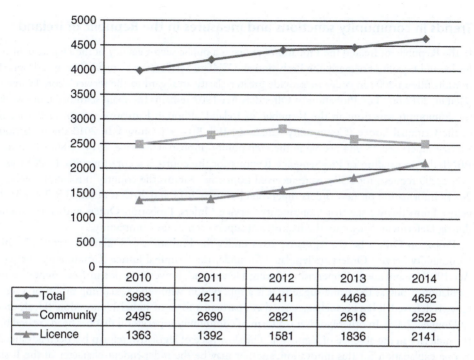

	2010	2011	2012	2013	2014
Total	3983	4211	4411	4468	4652
Community	2495	2690	2821	2616	2525
Licence	1363	1392	1581	1836	2141

Figure 16.1 Northern Ireland: number of people under supervision by sentence type (2010–2014). Source: PBNI caseload statistics (PBNI, 2014)

number of people subject to supervision as a result of a community sentence has risen, as have the number of people supervised on licence. However, the number of people supervised on licence has grown at a faster rate, accounting for an increased proportion of PBNI caseload over time.[10]

This trend illustrates an increased movement towards post-custodial supervision. This is driven in part by an increase in dual sentences such as Determinate Custodial Sentences (DCS), which combine an element of prison with post-custodial supervision. These sentences were introduced under the Criminal Justice (Northern Ireland) Order 2008, and their number rose by 32 per cent between 2013 and 2014 (from 1,130 to 1,497) (PBNI, 2014). The Criminal Justice (Northern Ireland) Order 2008 also introduced so-called 'public protection' sentences – Extended Custodial Sentences (ECS) and Indeterminate Custodial Sentences (ICS).[11] This allows a court to impose prison sentences with longer periods of post-custodial supervision for specified offences of a violent and/or sexual nature. In the case of Indeterminate Custodial Sentences no release date is given, instead a tariff date is set at which point the prisoner *may* become eligible for consideration for release by the Parole Commissioners for Northern Ireland (PCNI, 2014). The numbers of Extended and Indeterminate custodial sentences have also risen in recent years (Graham and Damkat, 2014).

However, the rise in the population under supervision in the community has not been matched by a reduction in the use of imprisonment. In tandem with the increase in numbers of people under some form of community supervision, the prison population in Northern Ireland has also grown. Between 2009 and 2013 the prison population rose by 28 per cent (DoJ, 2014). Some of the reasons for this expansion include increased sentence lengths and a rise in the number of people recalled to prison as a consequence of breach of their licence conditions (DoJ, 2014).[12]

Trends in community sanctions and measures in the Republic of Ireland

In the Republic of Ireland the Probation Service is a public sector agency of the Department of Justice and Equality. Formerly the Probation and Welfare Service, the term 'welfare' was dropped from its title in 2006 in order to 'provide greater clarity' in regard to the service's core business (Geiran, 2012:66). The Probation of Offenders Act 1907 remains the main statutory framework for community sanctions in the Republic of Ireland, although legislative reform in the form of the Criminal Justice (Community Sanctions) Bill 2014 is promised. In 2013 the Probation Service supervised 15,984 people in the community (Probation Service, 2014).[13] Similar to the PBNI, the preparation of Pre-Sentence Reports for the courts is a core function. In 2013 just over 5,000 requests for PSRs were received from courts across the country (Probation Service, 2014). Information on new orders supervised between 2011 and 2013 is outlined in Table 16.1 below. From this we see that Community Service Orders, Probation Orders and 'Supervision during Deferment' constitute the majority of supervision in the community.

Probation Orders have a legislative basis under the Probation of Offenders Act 1907, and Community Service Orders are legislated for under the Criminal Justice (Community Service) Act 1983 (as amended). 'Supervision during Deferment', however, is not in fact a sentence in legislation,[14] but, as the name suggests, it is a supervision while the actual imposition of a sentence is deferred. It has been characterised as a particular form of 'judicial innovation' (Healy and O'Donnell, 2005). In other words it is a form of community supervision that has been created by the judiciary in the absence of legislation. The slow pace of legislative reform has been advanced as one explanation for this innovation; another may be the independent character of the Irish judiciary (Healy and O'Donnell, 2005; Maguire, 2010) and the lack of sentencing guidelines (see Maguire, Chapter 15, *infra*).[15] Whatever its basis, it remains popular and, as Figure 16.2 shows, in the last year for which figures are available (2013), it outstripped the numbers of Probation Orders issued in the same year.[16]

Following the recommendation of the Thornton Hall Project Review Group (DoJ, 2011),[17] Community Service has also been developed as a 'back-door' mechanism for prisoner release. Under the 'Community Return Scheme', a joint initiative of the Irish Prison Service and the Probation Service, prisoners are granted early release under the condition that they engage in unpaid work in the community. Since the establishment of the initiative in 2011 and up until December 2013, 761 released prisoners have participated in the scheme. The majority of people

Table 16.1 Republic of Ireland: new orders supervised by the Probation Service (2011–2013)

	2011	2012	2013
Probation Orders	2,033	1,742	1,640
Supervision during deferment	1,882	1,695	1,732
Community Service Orders	2,738	2,569	2,354
Fully suspended sentence with supervision	570	599	753
Partially suspended sentence with supervision	434	389	440
Post-release supervision orders	25	43	40
Other orders	131	131	126
Life sentence supervision	70	73	76
Sex offender supervision	173	209	211

Note: Figures derived from Probation Service Annual Report (2013).

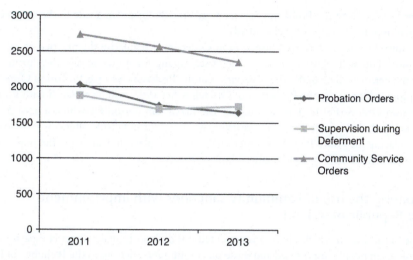

Figure 16.2 Republic of Ireland: comparison of community sentences by type (2011–2013).
Note: This table is based on figures provided in Table 1 (Healy, 2015) with further data added
for 2013.

successfully completed the scheme, and 11 per cent of participants were returned to prison for
breaching the terms of their release (Irish Prison Service and Probation Service, 2014).

Proposed legislative reform

While yet to be enacted, the Criminal Justice (Community Sanctions) Bill 2014 proposes to
update and regularise practice in respect of community sanctions in the Republic of Ireland. Long
awaited, it will overhaul legislation, which is now over a century old. It plans to address some areas
of practice which do not currently have a statutory basis, including the practice of 'adjourned
supervision' and the use of the court 'Poor Box'. It also proposes a system for the inspection of
Probation Services by a designated person appointed by the Minister for Justice and Equality.

The Bill provides for 'Discharge Orders' and 'Binding Over Orders', where a court 'may be
satisfied of the guilt of the person', but views it as inexpedient to impose any punishment. In
these circumstances the court may impose a 'Discharge Order' or 'Binding Over Order' without
proceeding to conviction. The latter entails a degree of conditionality, requiring a person to enter
into a recognisance to comply with the order.[18] The proposed orders replace the provisions set
out under Section 1 of the Probation of Offenders Act 1907 which allow for discharge without
a recorded conviction. The legislation also provides for the adjournment of criminal proceedings
to facilitate restorative justice measures in relation to minor offences dealt with in the District
Court. Here it is envisaged that restoration will take the form of financial reparation to the
victim of the offence.[19]

The legislation also clarifies the circumstances in which Probation Assessment Reports
should be requested by the courts, including: when the court is considering the imposition of
a supervised community sanction; a sentence of imprisonment (in specific circumstances)[20]; a
suspended sentence subject to probation supervision; or making an order imposing post-release
supervision under the Sex Offenders Act 2001. The intention is to ensure that assessment by the
Probation Service is mandatory before the imposition of a sanction by the courts that requires
probation supervision. The need for such a requirement is evidenced by the fact that in 2013, 11

per cent of referrals to the Probation Service were directly for orders made in the absence of an assessment report (Probation Service, 2014).

The introduction of 'Deferred Supervision Orders' will regularise the practice of adjourned supervision. This will allow the court to defer sentencing for up to six months, during which period the person will be under the supervision of the Probation Service. Probation Orders, currently provided for under the Probation of Offenders Act 1907, will be replaced with Probation Supervision Orders (PSOs). This will reduce the maximum period for which a person can be placed under such an order from three years to two years (for indictable offences). A 'Reparation Fund' replacing the court 'Poor Box' system will be put in place and allow for the imposition of Reparation Orders with specific financial limits.[21]

Comparing the use of community sanctions with imprisonment in the Republic of Ireland

Because of the way in which the data is presented it is difficult to make direct comparisons with the numbers of people imprisoned and those on community sanctions in the Republic of Ireland on any one day.[22] However, comparisons can be made with sentences under supervision in a given year. Table 16.2 provides information on the numbers of community sanctions for selected years alongside the total committals to prison. From this we see that the use of imprisonment as a sanction far outstrips the use of community sanctions over time, and, with the increased rates of committals to prison, this differential has become even more marked.

Further information available in the Probation Service's Annual Report 2013 highlights significant regional variation in the use of community sanctions and measures across the Republic.

Table 16.2 Community sanctions and prison committals 1980–2013 (selected years)

Year	Probation Order	Supervision during deferment of penalty	Community Service Order	Other[1]	Total committals to prison[2]
1980	479	642	–	–	2,317
1984	1,326	583	–	–	3,284
1988	1,257	1,341	1,080	–	3,814
1992	1,039	1,062	1,745	–	4,756
1996	1,280	1,815	1,386	–	–
2000	1,345	2,625	998	116	–
2004	1,878	5,623	843	79	10,657 13,557
2008	2,676	2,045	1,413	356	(8,043) 17,026
2012	1,742	1,695	2,569	1,436	(12,991) 15,735
2013	1,640	1,732	2,354	1,646	(12,489)

[1] Following Healy's (2015) typology: 'The "other" category includes suspended sentences (part/full), post-release supervision orders, supervision of life sentence prisoners, young person's probation orders and supervision of sex offenders in the community. Caution is advised when interpreting trends in this category because the figures relate to different combinations of sanctions.'

[2] This figure includes committals on remand and under sentence. Where committals under sentence are available (which is a more accurate comparator) this is included in parentheses.

The rate of referrals to the Probation Service varies significantly across counties.[23] In 2013 in Louth there were more than 250 referrals to probation per 100,000 in the population, compared to Kerry with a referral rate of less than 50 people per 100,000. Similar disparities are evident in the use of Probation Orders and Community Service Orders. Relatively high rates of Probation Orders are imposed in Cavan (90 per 100,000) compared to Leitrim, where the rate is less than 10 per 100,000. The highest rates of Community Service Orders are imposed in Monaghan (almost 120 per 100,000), while in Kerry, Leitrim, Kildare and Kilkenny less than 20 CSOs per 100,000 are imposed (Probation Service, 2014).

The reason for such significant variation is not explained. However, given that caseload in the District Courts accounts for the bulk of sentences in the Republic of Ireland, and in particular a significant proportion of the committals to prison (O'Malley, 2010; O'Nolan, 2013), one can surmise that community sanctions find favour with some judges more than others. Whether this relates to a history of relatively underdeveloped Probation Service provision, judicial confidence in community sanctions or judicial punitiveness are topics that are subject to debate (DoJE, 2014; Maguire, 2014).

Comparing the use of community sanctions in the Republic of Ireland and Northern Ireland

Because of recording differences it is difficult to make direct comparisons of the overall rate of use of community sanctions between Northern Ireland and the Republic of Ireland. However, when one takes into account the differences in population size (4.61 million in the Republic of Ireland compared to 1.84 million in Northern Ireland), the available data show a much higher use of community sanctions in Northern Ireland than in the Republic. Table 16.3 below provides information on new referrals to the respective services over the course of one year. The use of pre-sentence reports by the courts is evidently higher in Northern Ireland than in the Republic, as is the use of Probation Orders and Community Service Orders. Possible reasons for these differences include the stronger legislative basis underpinning probation and community sanctions in Northern Ireland when compared to the Republic of Ireland and the fact that historically Probation within the Republic of Ireland has been under-resourced. Supervision during deferment comprises a significant proportion of the population under supervision in the

Table 16.3 Comparing the use of community sanctions across borders

2013/2014	Pre-sentence reports	Probation Orders	Community Service Orders	Supervision during deferment	Post-custodial supervision
Northern Ireland[1]	5,877	1,260	1,456	N/A	972[2]
Republic of Ireland[3]	5,027	1,640	2,354	1,732	767[4]

The figures provided in this table are the total numbers of reports and orders, rather than a rate per population.

[1] Data for year 1 April 2013–31 March 2014. Source: PBNI Annual Caseload Statistics Report 2013–14.

[2] This figure includes the following sentences: Determinate Custodial Sentences; Juvenile Justice Centre Orders; Life Licences; Sex Offender Licences; GB Licence; Extended Custodial Sentences; and Indeterminate Custodial Sentences.

[3] Data for 2013. Source: Probation Service Annual Report.

[4] This figure includes Post Release Supervision Orders; Part-Suspended Sentence Supervision Order; Life Sentence supervisees; and Sex Offender supervisees. In the latter two categories, Life Sentence and Sex Offender supervisees, the figure presented in the annual report represents the total number of people supervised, rather than all new orders issued that year.

Republic, while there is no equivalent in Northern Ireland. The uptake of post-custodial supervision is markedly higher in Northern Ireland, influenced by legislative changes in recent years.

Probation across borders

Notwithstanding the variance in both jurisdictions, a number of joint initiatives between their respective probation services have been developed over recent years. These include the establishment of a Public Protection Advisory Group (PPAG) under the auspices of the North–South Intergovernmental Agreement on Co-operation on Criminal Justice Matters. This agreement provides for North/South co-operation in the area of criminal justice, including meetings between the Ministers for Justice in both jurisdictions and the establishment of priority areas for joint working.[24] Identified priority areas of specific relevance in the area of community sanctions include: a focus on the production of fast-track probation reports aimed at 'speeding up justice'; best practice in offending behaviour programmes; and putting in place mechanisms for the transfer of prisoners and probation supervision between the two jurisdictions.

The latter priority reflects a requirement to implement the 2008 Framework Decision (FD 2008/947/JHA) of the European Commission 'on the application of mutual recognition to judgments and probation decisions with a view to the supervision of probation measures and probation sanctions'.[25] Essentially this Framework Decision involves the transfer of supervision arrangements between different European states. This means that in practice, for example, a person from the Republic of Ireland who receives a community sanction in Spain could complete this sanction under the supervision of the Probation Service in the Republic of Ireland if he so wished. All EU member states should have transposed this directive into law by the end of 2011. However, to date only a limited number of countries have done so, and neither the Republic of Ireland nor the United Kingdom have done so as yet (see Morgenstern and Larrauri, 2013, for an overview; see also Ryan and Hamilton, *infra*).

Van Zyl Smit *et al.* (2015) note some of the inherent difficulties in the imposition of European norms across a continent with different legal traditions and differing penal philosophies. Similarly, Morgenstern and Larrauri (2013) highlight some of the complexity of practical implementation. Notwithstanding this, and given many of the similarities between the structures of probation in Northern Ireland and the Republic, an informal scheme has been in place since 2007 allowing transfer of orders across the border (McNally and Burke, 2012). Similar information exchange arrangements also exist for the preparation of court reports.

Published on an annual basis, the *Irish Probation Journal* is a joint-initiative of the PBNI and the Probation Service. The stated mission of the journal is to provide: 'a forum for sharing theory and practice, increasing co-operation and learning between the two jurisdictions and developing debate about work with offenders'. The journal includes contributions from practitioners and academics on topics relating to probation and the wider criminal justice system. In a review of research on offender supervision in both jurisdictions, Carr *et al.* (2013) note the journal has provided a forum for the discussion and dissemination of probation work rendering it more visible.

Conclusion: advancing community sanctions as mechanisms for penal reduction

The divergent development of community sanctions between the Republic of Ireland and Northern Ireland provides an interesting comparative case study. Variations in the use of these sanctions in both jurisdictions over time reflect differential resourcing and legislative frameworks, but more fundamentally, different modes of governance. As other chapters in this edition testify, the political context is inextricably linked to the character of penality. This is equally the case for community sanctions, and the legitimations that are deployed to give them effect (Robinson *et al.*, 2013; McNeill and Dawson, 2014).

Healy (2015) observes that for most of its history the story of probation in the Republic of Ireland is one more of continuity than of change. In latter years, however, there has been increased attention paid to this field and a consequent expansion. In Northern Ireland the criminal justice system has faced more fundamental questions regarding its legitimacy. While the Probation Board forged a particularly distinctive path in this respect, in recent years it too has witnessed expansionism driven in part by the emphasis placed on public protection (Carr, 2015a). Despite the different relationships between the use of prison and community sanctions, in both jurisdictions the increased use of community sanctions are advocated as a means of penal reductionism.

The recent *Strategic Review of Penal Policy* (DoJE, 2014) places an emphasis on the need to reduce the use of imprisonment in the Republic of Ireland. Significantly, it identifies increasing the use of community sanctions as a means to achieve this and observes:

> In order, however, to support a recommendation to reduce prisoner numbers, there must be appropriate non-custodial sanctions available to sentencing judges. These sanctions must be cost effective, credible and command public confidence in managing both those who pose a general risk of re-offending and those presenting a real risk of harm and danger to the public.
>
> *(DoJE, 2014: 44)*

Similarly in Northern Ireland a consultation on community sentences conducted by the Department of Justice in 2011 noted the need to reduce the overuse of ineffective short prison sentences by encouraging a greater use of community sentences by the judiciary (DoJNI, 2011). The arguments put forward to support this view were two-fold: community sentences are both less expensive and more effective in reducing re-offending. Cost and effectiveness, therefore, serve as legitimating discourses for community sanctions and measures, particularly when set against a prison service that has demonstrably been failing in both respects.

However, lessons from other countries suggest that caution should be exercised in viewing community sanctions as *merely* a mechanism of penal reductionism. When community sanctions are positioned as 'alternatives to prison', prison is viewed as the 'norm' to which the 'alternative' should be provided. The result is that community sanctions are 'toughened' up to give them an associated punitive bite that may make them potentially more attractive to sentencers and to the public. The net result of this approach may not yield the reduction that is required, but result in precisely the opposite effect (Bottoms *et al.*, 2004; Phelps, 2013).

Increasingly stringent community penalties see people being brought into the ambit of probation services where they may previously have been given a lesser sentence. An emphasis on enforcement of these 'tougher sanctions' results in greater numbers of people being sent to prison for failure to comply with the conditions of their orders. Constituted in these terms, probation functions as a net-widening rather than a penal reduction mechanism. In an analysis of the differential relationship between probation and prison populations across the United States, Phelps (2013) characterises this as the 'paradox of probation'.

Research on what may enhance both public and sentencer support for community sanctions shows that attention needs to be paid to the ways in which the purposes of justice can be served by such sentences (Maruna and King, 2008). This involves both evidence-based arguments (typically premised on rational considerations of what is most effective) and, critically, a wider consideration of what values and functions of justice community sentences should serve. An example of such evidence-based arguments is the recent data on recidivism, published respectively by the Irish Prison Service and Central Statistics Off (2013) and the Probation Service (2013), which shows lower levels of re-offending for those subject to community sanctions when compared with imprisonment. However, appeals to the wider purposes and values of community justice should also involve an increased focus on how community-based sanctions can provide greater opportunities for reparation and change. Some commentators have even argued that such 'affective' approaches should appeal to sentiments regarding redemption and a belief in forgiveness (Maruna and King, 2008).

Central also to leveraging support for community sentences is focussing on the potential for people to change. Given the complex and interrelated nature of issues faced by many who are processed through our criminal justice systems – including drug and alcohol addictions, mental health difficulties and homelessness – such processes of change are often likely to be complex and to take time. However, importantly, as the *Strategic Review of Penal Policy* notes, these challenges cannot be met solely by agencies within the criminal justice system.

References

Allen, F.A. (1981) *The Decline of the Rehabilitative Ideal: Penal Policy and Social Purpose*. New Haven CT: Yale University Press.

Blair, C. (2000) *Prisons and Probation. Research Report 6. Review of the Criminal Justice System in Northern Ireland*. Belfast: Criminal Justice Review Group.

Bottoms, A., Rex, S. and Robinson, G. (2004) *Alternatives to Prison. Options for an Insecure Society*. Abingdon: Routledge.

Brown, M. (2009) *The Culture of Punishment. Prison, Society and Spectacle*. New York: New York University Press.

Carr, N. (2015a) 'Contingent Legitimacy – Community Sanctions in Northern Ireland', in: G. Robinson and F. McNeill (eds) *Community Punishment in Europe*. Abingdon: Routledge.

—— (2015b) 'Probation and Community Sanctions in Northern Ireland: Historical and Contemporary Contexts', in: A. McAlinden & C. Dwyer (eds) *Criminal Justice in Transition: The Northern Ireland Context*. Oxford: Hart Publishing (pp. 229-250).

Carr, N. and Maruna, S. (2012) 'Legitimacy through neutrality: Probation and the conflict in Northern Ireland', *Howard Journal*, 51(5): 474–87.

Carr, N., Healy, D., Kennefick, L. and Maguire, N. (2013) 'A review of the research on offender supervision in the Republic of Ireland and Northern Ireland', *Irish Probation Journal*, 10: 50–74.

Carson, E.A. (2014) *Prisoners in 2013. Bulletin: NCJ 247282*. US Department of Justice, Office of Justice Programmes, Bureau of National Statistics. Available at: www.bjs.gov/content/pub/pdf/p13.pdf (accessed 24 January 2015).

CJINI (Criminal Justice Inspection Northern Ireland) (2013) *Report on an Announced Inspection of Hydebank Wood Young Offenders Centre*. Belfast: CJINI.

—— (2014) *The Safety of Prisoners Held by the Northern Ireland Prison Service. A Joint Inspection by Criminal Justice Inspection Northern Ireland and the Regulation and Quality Improvement Authority*. Belfast: CJINI.

Clear, T. and Frost, N. (2014) *The Punishment Imperative: The Rise and Failure of Mass Incarceration in the United States*. New York: New York University Press.

Committee of Inquiry into the Penal System (1985) Report [*Whitaker Report*]. Dublin: Stationery Office.

Council of Europe (1992) *Recommendation No. R (92) 16 of the Committee of Ministers to Member States on the European Rules on Community Sanctions and Measures*. Available at: jp-eu.coe.int/documents/3983922/6970334/CMRec+(92)+16+on+the+European+rules+on+community+sanctions+and+measures.pdf/01647732-1cf7-4ea8-88ba-2c041bc3f5d6 (accessed 24 January 2015).

DeMichele, M. (2014) 'Studying the community corrections field: Applying neo-institutional theories to a hidden element of mass social control', *Theoretical Criminology*, 18(4): 546–64.

Department of Justice (DoJ) (1994) *The Management of Offenders: A Five-Year Plan*. Dublin: Stationery Office.

Department of Justice and Equality (DoJE) (2014) *Strategic Review of Penal Policy. Final Report.* Dublin: DoJE.

Department of Justice Northern Ireland (DoJNI) (2011) *Consultation on a Review of Community Sentences.* Belfast: DoJNI.

—— (2011) *Report of the Thornton Hall Project Review Group.* Available at: www.justice.ie/en/ JELR/ThorntonReviewReportRedacted.pdf/Files/ThorntonReviewReportRedacted.pdf (accessed 24 January 2015).

—— (2014) *Prison Population Review. A Review of the Factors Leading to the Growth in Prisoner Numbers between 2009 and 2013.* Belfast: DoJ.

Expert Group (1999) *Final Report of the Expert Group on the Probation and Welfare Service.* Dublin: Stationery Office.

Fitzgibbon, W., Hamilton, C. and Richardson, M. (2010) 'A risky business: An examination of Irish probation officers' attitudes towards risk assessment', *Probation Journal,* 57(2): 163–74.

Fulton, B. and Carr, N. (2013) 'Probation in Europe: Northern Ireland.' Available at: http://www. cepprobation.org/uploaded_files/Probation-in-Europe-2013-Chapter-Northern-Ireland.pdf (accessed 24 January 2015).

Garland, D. (2001) *The Culture of Control: Crime and Social Order in Contemporary Society.* Oxford: Oxford University Press.

Geiran, V. (2012) 'Managing change in Irish Probation: Prioritising resources through evidence-based principles, organisational development and collaboration', *Eurovista,* 2(2): 61–9.

Gormally, B., McEvoy, K. and Wall, D. (1993) 'Criminal justice in a divided society: Northern Ireland prisons', *Crime and Justice,* 17: 51–135.

Graham, I. and Damkat, I. (2014) *Court Prosecutions, Convictions and Out of Court Disposals Statistics for Northern Ireland, 2013. Research and Statistical Bulletin 14/2014.* Belfast: DoJ. Available at: www.dojni. gov.uk/de/court-prosecutions-conviction-and-out-of-court-disposals-statistics-for-northern-ireland-2013-published (accessed 16 February 2015).

Healy, D. (2015) 'The evolution of community sanctions in the Republic of Ireland: Continuity, challenge and change', in: G. Robinson and F. McNeill (eds) *Community Punishment in Europe.* Abingdon: Routledge.

Healy, D. and O'Donnell, I. (2005) 'Probation in the Republic of Ireland: Contexts and Challenges', *Probation Journal,* 52(1): 56–68.

Herberman, E.J. and Bonczar, T.P. (2014) *Probation and Parole in the United States, 2013. Bulletin: NCJ 248029.* US Department of Justice, Office of Justice Programmes, Bureau of National Statistics. Available at: http://www.bjs.gov/content/pub/pdf/ppus13.pdf (accessed 25 January 2015).

Irish Prison Service (2014) *Irish Prison Service Annual Report 2013.* Available at: http://www.irishprisons.ie/ images/pdf/ar_2013.pdf (accessed 27 January 2015).

Irish Prison Service and Central Statistics Office (2013) *Irish Prison Service and Central Statistics Office Recidivism Study 2013.* IPS and CSO. Available: http://www.irishprisons.ie/index.php/component/ content/article/81-info/199 (accessed 1 December 2014).

Irish Prison Service and Probation Service (2014) *Community Return: A Unique Opportunity. A Descriptive Evaluation of the First Twenty-Six Months (2011–2013). Irish Prison Service and Probation Service Research Report 5.* Available at: http://www.justice.ie/en/JELR/Community_Return_Study_Report_v3_9. pdf/Files/Community_Return_Study_Report_v3_9.pdf (accessed 27 January 2015).

Kelly, D. (forthcoming) 'Impact of Organizational Reforms in Northern Ireland Prison Service on Staff Attitudes, Occupational Cultures and Working Practices'. Queen's University Belfast: Unpublished PhD.

Kilcommins, S., O'Donnell, I., O'Sullivan, E. and Vaughan, B. (2004) *Crime, Punishment and the Search for Order in Ireland.* Dublin: Institute of Public Administration.

Law Reform Commission (2005) *The Court Poor Box: Probation of Offenders.* Dublin: Law Reform Commission.

McCarthy, J. (2014) 'Community Service at the Crossroads in Ireland', *Irish Probation Journal,* 11: 124–155.

McEvoy, K. (2001) *Paramilitary Imprisonment in Northern Ireland: Resistance, Management and Release.* Oxford: Oxford University Press.

McIvor, G. (2011) 'Reparative and restorative approaches', in: A. Bottoms, S. Rex and G. Robinson (eds) *Alternatives to Prison. Options for an Insecure Society.* Abingdon: Routledge (pp. 162–194).

McNally, G. (2007) 'Probation in Ireland: A brief history of the early years', *Irish Probation Journal,* 4: 5–24.

McNally, G. and Burke, I. (2012) 'Implementation of the Framework Decision on the Transfer of Probation Measures between States in the European Union', *Eurovista,* 2(2): 70–77.

McNeill, F. (2009) 'Probation, Rehabilitation and Reparation', *Irish Probation Journal*, 6: 5–22.

McNeill, F. and Beyens, K. (eds) (2013) *Offender Supervision in Europe*. Basingstoke: Palgrave Macmillan

McNeill, F. and Dawson, M. (2014) 'Social solidarity, penal evolution and probation', *British Journal of Criminology*, 54(5): 892–907.

Maguire, N. (2010) 'Consistency in sentencing', *Judicial Studies Institute Journal*, 2: 14–54.

—— (2014) 'When is prison a last resort? Definitional problems and judicial interpretations', *Irish Criminal Law Journal*, 24(3): 62–72.

Maguire, N. and Carr, N. (2013) 'Changing shape and shifting boundaries – the media portrayal of probation in Ireland', *European Journal of Probation*, 5(3): 3–23.

Mair, G. (2004) 'Diversionary and non-supervisory approaches to dealing with offenders', in: A. Bottoms, S. Rex and G. Robinson (eds) *Alternatives to Prison. Options for an Insecure Society*. Abingdon: Routledge (pp. 135–161).

Mair, G. and Burke, L. (2012) *Redemption, Rehabilitation and Risk Management. A History of Probation*. Abingdon: Routledge.

Maruna, S. and King, A. (2004) 'Public Opinion and Community Penalties', in A. Bottoms, S. Rex and G. Robinson (eds) *Alternatives to Prison: Options for an Insecure Society*. Cullompton: Willan (pp. 83–112).

—— (2008) 'Selling the Public on Probation: Beyond the Bib', *Probation Journal*, 55(4):337–51.

Morgenstern, C. and Larrauri, E. (2013) 'European Norms, Policy and Practice', in: F. McNeill and K. Beyens (eds) *Offender Supervision in Europe*. Basingstoke: Palgrave Macmillan (pp. 125–54).

Morris, A. (2002) 'Critiquing the critics: A brief response to the critics of restorative justice', *British Journal of Criminology*, 42(3): 596–615.

Northern Ireland Prison Service (NIPS) (2014) *Analysis of NIPS Prison Population from 01/10/13 to 31/12/14*. Available at: http://www.dojni.gov.uk/index/ni-prison-service/nips-population-statistics-2/population-snapshot-2014.pdf (accessed 27 January 2015).

O'Donovan, D. (2008) 'Ireland', in: A.M. Van Kalmhout and I. Durnescu (eds) *Probation in Europe*. Nijemgen: Wolf Legal Publishers.

O'Mahony, D. and Chapman, T. (2007) 'Probation, the state and community – delivering probation services in Northern Ireland'. In: L. Gelsthorpe and R. Morgan (eds) *Handbook of Probation*. Cullompton: Willan (pp. 155–78).

O'Malley, T. (2010) 'Time served: The impact of sentencing and parole decisions on the prison population'. Paper delivered to the Irish Penal Reform Trust, Morrison Hotel Dublin, 28 June. Available at: http://www.iprt.ie/files/Tom_OMalley_Presentation_IPRT_Open_Forum_28062010.pdf (accessed 27 January 2015).

O'Nolan, C. (2013) *The Irish District Court. A Social Portrait*. Cork: Cork University Press.

O'Sullivan, E. and O'Donnell, I. (2012) *Coercive Confinement in Ireland: Patients, Prisoners and Penitents*. Manchester: Manchester University Press.

Owers, A., Leighton, P., McCrory, C., McNeill, F. and Wheatley, P. (2011) *Review of the Northern Ireland Prison Service. Conditions, Management and Oversight of all Prisons*. Belfast: Prison Review Team.

Padfield, N. (2012) 'Recalling conditionally released prisoners in England and Wales', *European Journal of Probation*, 4(1): 34–45.

Padfield, N. and Maruna, S. (2006) 'The revolving door at the prison gate: Exploring the dramatic increase in recalls to prison', *Criminology and Criminal Justice*, 6(3): 329–52.

Parole Commissioners for Northern Ireland (PCNI) (2014) *Parole Commissioners for Northern Ireland. Annual Report 2013–2014*. Available at: http://www.parolecomni.org.uk/index/downloads-publications/annual-reports/pcni_annual_report_2013-14.pdf (accessed 27 January 2015).

PBNI (2014) *PBNI Caseload Statistics 2013/14*. Available at: http://www.pbni.org.uk/archive/pdfs/About%20Us/Statistics%20and%20Research/Caseload%20Statistics/Caseload%20Statistics%20Report%202013_14_Internet%20(3)%2007.05.14.pdf (accessed 27 January 2015).

Phelps, M. S. (2013) 'The Paradox of Probation: Community Supervision in the Age of Mass Incarceration', *Law and Policy*, 35(1–2): 51–80.

Probation Service (2013) *Probation Service Recidivism Study 2008–2013*. Dublin: Probation Service.

—— (2014) *Annual Report, 2013*. Dublin: Probation Service.

Raynor, P. (2012) 'Community Penalties, Probation, and Offender Management', in: M. Maguire, R. Morgan and R. Reiner (eds) *The Oxford Handbook of Criminology*. Oxford: Oxford University Press (pp. 928–54).

Robinson, G. (2015 forthcoming) 'The Cinderella Complex: Punishment, Society and Community Sanctions', *Punishment and Society*.

Robinson, G., McNeill, F. and Maruna, S. (2013) 'Punishment *in* Society: The Improbable Persistence of

Probation and Other Community Sanctions and Measures', in: J. Simon and R. Sparks (eds) *The Sage Handbook of Punishment and Society*. London: Sage (pp. 321–40).

Rogan, M. (2011) *Prison Policy in Ireland. Politics, Penal-Welfarism and Political Imprisonment.* Abingdon: Routledge.

Van Zyl Smit, D., Snacken, S. and Hayes, D. (2015) '"One cannot legislate kindness": Ambiguities in European legal instruments on non-custodial sanctions', *Punishment and Society*, 17(1): 3–26.

Ward, T. and Maruna, S. (2007) *Rehabilitation.* Abingdon: Routledge.

Wood, W.R. (2015) 'Why restorative justice will not reduce incarceration', *British Journal of Criminology*, doi: 10.1093/bjc/azu108.

Worrall, A. (2008) 'The "seemingness" of the "seamless management" of offenders'. In: P. Carlen (ed.) *Imaginary Penalties.* Cullompton: Willan (pp. 113–34).

Notes

1 It is worth mentioning that fines, the most common sanction imposed by the courts in both the Republic of Ireland and Northern Ireland, are not included in this definition, *unless* there is a supervisory or 'controlling activity' to secure their implementation. More generally, Mair (2004) among others has critiqued the lack of attention to this form of sentence in penological scholarship.

2 At the end of 2013, there were an estimated 4,751,400 adults under community supervision in the United States. This equates to 1 in 51 of all adults in the US. This compares with an estimated 1,574,700 people imprisoned in the same time period (Carson, 2014).

3 Sentencing statistics from 2013 show that 3,769 prison sentences were issued by the courts, compared to 2,823 community orders (probation orders, community service orders and combination orders). Separate information is not provided in this data set on sentences combining elements of community and custodial supervision (Graham and Damkat, 2014).

4 In 2013 there were 12,849 committals to prison under sentence, compared to 5,726 community sentences (Irish Prison Service 2014 and Probation Service 2014).

5 The relevant legislation specifies: 'The Department of Justice may, after consultation with the Board, give the Board directions of a general character as to the exercise and performance of its functions, and the Board shall give effect to any such directions'. (Probation Board (Northern Ireland) Order, 1982, Part: 6).

6 Since 1994, following the official ceasefires one prison officer has subsequently been killed. In 2012 David Black, a prison officer, was murdered on his way to work: http://www.theguardian.com/uk-news/2014/feb/05/charge-murder-prison-officer-northern-ireland-david-black.

7 This figure is derived from PBNI caseload data, which notes that on 31 March 2014 there were 4,652 people subject to supervision. Of these, some three-quarters (74 per cent) were supervised in the community; the remainder were in prison (PBNI, 2014).

8 A much smaller number of Short Pre-Sentence Reports are also prepared (880 in 2013). These reports are prepared within a shorter time frame and usually in relation to a specific sentence (e.g. assessment for suitability for a community service order) (PBNI, 2014).

9 Community Service Orders were initially introduced under *The Treatment of Offenders (Northern Ireland) Order 1976*. The Northern Ireland legislation was largely modelled on legislation introduced in England and Wales in 1972.

10 The data in this table is derived from PBNI caseload statistics (PBNI, 2014). It is based on the number of people under supervision on 31 March 2014 by sentence type. The PBNI note that a person is counted once for each type of supervision to which they are subject. There may be some double counting, because a person may be subject to more than one type of order at any one time.

11 This legislation was largely modelled on the Criminal Justice Act 2003 in England and Wales. It also led to the establishment of the Parole Commissioners for Northern Ireland, replacing Life Sentence Review Commissioners. An Extended Custodial Sentence (ECS) can be imposed when a person has committed a specified violent or sexual offence and where the court believes that there is a likelihood of re-offending. The sentence involves time spent in custody (minimum one year), followed by a period supervised in the community (extension period). Similar conditions apply for Indeterminate Custodial Sentences (ICS); however, the court must first determine that an ECS is not an appropriate sentence.

12 By December 2013 people who had been recalled to prison accounted for 11 per cent of the prison population (DoJ, 2014).

13 This number includes people released from prisons, including those involved in the Community Return Scheme and 'repatriated offenders' (Probation Service, 2014).

14 Limited provisions allowing a sentence of imprisonment to be deferred in conjunction with the issue of a fine were introduced in the Criminal Justice Act 2006.

15 Healy and O'Donnell (2005) also cite the use of the 'Poor Box' by judges as another form of judicial innovation. Again without a statutory basis, a person can be required to pay money to the 'Poor Box', which is ultimately distributed to charitable causes. Courts use this measure in tandem with the provisions of Section 1 of the Probation of Offenders Act, allowing the person to be convicted but not to acquire a criminal record. Measures set out in the Criminal Justice (Community Sanctions) Bill 2014 propose to place the use of the 'Poor Box' on a statutory basis.

16 Previous analysis of the use of 'supervision under adjournment' reported in Healy and O'Donnell (2005) shows the popularity of this form of liminal sanction over time. It was used more often than Probation Orders in the years 1990–1999. In 1999, 1,568 people were placed on 'adjourned supervision'.

17 The Thornton Hall Project Review Group was established following a decision by a new government that plans to build a large-scale prison on the outskirts of Dublin were not affordable in the context of the economic crisis. Noting the poor conditions within prisons exacerbated by a rising prison population, the group recommended: 'Further steps are required to reduce the prison population. We are of the view that there is scope within the prison system to introduce a form of structured "earned release" for suitable offenders so as to encourage active engagement by prisoners in rehabilitation and progression, prior to release into the community. This would involve prisoners being eligible for consideration for a programme of work in the community and thereby reduce some of the pressure on the system'. (DoJ, 2011:iii).

18 The type of circumstances that a court may consider when making such an order are set out in the Heads of Bill and include:
    a) the character, circumstances, previous convictions, age, health or mental condition of the person;
    b) any previous similar sanctions;
    c) the trivial nature of the offence;
    d) any extenuating circumstances;
    e) the need to have due regard to the interests of the victim;
    f) that the person has accepted responsibility and expressed remorse (cf. Head 9 re. Restorative Justice Criteria).

19 The Explanatory Notes under Head 9 specify: 'It is intended that the provision will deal with cases such as minor assaults or minor criminal damage where the offender accepts responsibility for the wrong-doing, offers to make reparation, e.g. by paying for medical expenses or repairs to a vehicle, and, very importantly, the victim is willing to accept the reparation'.

20 I.e. where a person is aged 18–21 and has not previously been sentenced to imprisonment of 12 months or more.

21 Under the proposals an adult cannot be required to make a payment exceeding €5,000, and a child cannot be required to make a payment exceeding €2,500 in reparation. This is in line with the *Law Reform Commission's* (2005) recommendations to regularise the use of the 'Poor Box' scheme.

22 The Irish Prison Service provides an average daily occupancy rate. In 2013 it was 4,158 (Irish Prison Service, 2014). A similar daily caseload rate for the Probation Service is not available.

23 Information presented in the Probation Service's Annual Report for 2013 is provided at county level rather than by Court District (Probation Service, 2014).

24 North/South Cooperation on Criminal Justice Matters Work Programme (2010–2011; 2011–2012 and 2013–2014. Available at: http://www.justice.ie/en/JELR/Pages/Publications_Northern_Ireland?OpenDocument&start=1

25 Council Framework Decision 2008/947/JHA of 27 November 2008. Available at: http://www.cepprobation.org/uploaded_files/Council_Framework_Decision_2008_947_JHA.pdf (accessed 24 January 2015).

17
Prisoners and prison life

Michelle Butler

Countries with similar economies, cultures, languages and politics tend to have similar penal systems, albeit with some surprises and anomalies (Cavadino and Dignan, 2006). The purpose of this chapter is to explore the penal systems in the Republic of Ireland and Northern Ireland to see if they converge with other Western, developed, industrialised democracies and what lessons can be learnt from the anomalies that emerge. The chapter is divided into five sections. Imprisonment in pre-partition Ireland is reviewed before moving on to examine how the penal systems in the Republic and Northern Ireland developed after partition. Next, everyday prison life is explored to investigate how order and control is maintained as well as the extent to which prisoner needs and quality of life issues are addressed. Lastly, the suitability of the accountability mechanisms employed are reviewed to determine their ability to promote change and encourage ongoing improvements and reform in Irish and Northern Ireland prisons.

Imprisonment in pre-partition Ireland

Up until the mid-nineteenth century the primary methods of punishment in the island of Ireland were public punishments (such as executions) and transportation. In 1775 transportation to America was discontinued, due to the American War of Independence, and the use of public punishments were no longer deemed desirable because of their failure to deter criminality, increased questioning of the legitimacy of public executions and the potential for such displays to agitate national unrest and uprisings against English and Scottish gentry, who had colonised the island of Ireland since the sixteenth and seventeenth centuries (Kilcommins *et al.*, 2004). This led to an increased interest in the prison as a place of punishment, with the introduction of legislation to promote prison reforms and establish a prison inspectorate. Before this, prisons had primarily been viewed as holding cells for people awaiting trial, sentencing, transportation or public punishment and were managed locally, with conditions varying depending on a prisoner's ability to pay (Ignatieff, 1981). Prison reforms provided an official salary for jailers and required local authorities to provide food and medicine to prisoners at public expense (Kilcommins *et al.*, 2004). Failures to adhere to these reforms led to the appointment of local prison inspectors and an Inspector-General who reported to parliament (Kilcommins *et al.*, 2004).

Unfortunately, this interest in prison reform was short-lived, as the colonisation of Australia from 1788 to the 1850s meant that transportation was reintroduced as the primary means of punishment (Kilcommins *et al.*, 2004). In addition, national uprisings and rebellions in the island of Ireland at this time meant that the use of corrective methods and reforms were postponed in favour of suppression (Kilcommins *et al.*, 2004).

Nonetheless, attempts were made to restructure imprisonment so that it could be used as an alternative to transportation. The penitentiary system was introduced to reform individuals through solitary imprisonment, labour and religious instruction, with Millbank in London and Richmond in Dublin chosen as the sites for the first penitentiary prisons in Britain and Ireland (Heaney, 2003). While the penitentiary system operated in Millbank between 1816 and 1843, it was less successful in Richmond due to an inappropriate prison design, lack of planning, insufficient supervision, staff malpractice as well as tensions between the Catholic Chaplain and Protestant Governor (Heaney, 2003). Further, prisoners tended to prefer transportation to the strict discipline, lengthy periods of detention and unfamiliar evangelical atmosphere (Heaney, 2003). For these reasons, Richmond penitentiary was closed after eleven years (1820–1831) and transportation continued to be a popular punishment, with approximately 26,500 prisoners transported to Australia between 1791 and 1853 (Kilcommins *et al.*, 2004).

By the 1840s, concerns about the cost of transportation and a perception that it represented free passage to a more prosperous life for offenders meant that it was replaced with penal servitude as the main method of punishment in 1853, refocusing attention on the prison as a place of punishment and possible behavioural change (Kilcommins *et al.*, 2004). This led to a significant increase in the number of prisoners detained in Britain and Ireland, and the two jurisdictions differed in their management of this increase (Dooley, 2003). The Irish solution to managing this increase became known as the 'Irish system' and played a major role in shaping penal systems internationally, including in America, Europe, Brazil, Ecuador and Australia (Roth, 2006).

The 'Irish system' was developed by Sir Walter Crofton and was influenced by the work of Alexander Maconochie and Sir Joshua Jebb (Dooley, 2003). Sir Walter Crofton was appointed chairman of the newly established Prison Convicts Board in 1854, whose responsibility it was to oversee convict prisons and deal with the increasing convict prison population (Dooley, 2003). At this time, prisons on the island of Ireland consisted of local jails (also known as gaols), debtors' prison, houses of correction and convict prisons (Dooley, 2003; Kilcommins *et al.*, 2004).

The 'Irish system' involved three stages, beginning with approximately nine months of solitary confinement in Mountjoy prison in Dublin, after which time individuals were transferred to a different prison and engaged in work and education. Prisoners could earn marks for their general conduct and demeanour, performance in education and industry at work, but political and agrarian prisoners were excluded from participation (Tomlinson, 1995). Upon earning sufficient points, they moved to the intermediate stage which was unique to the 'Irish system' and involved minimal supervision, paid work, education and religious instruction (Dooley, 2003). These intermediate establishments are similar to open and semi-open prisons used today in the Republic of Ireland, Northern Ireland and internationally (Kilcommins *et al.*, 2004). It was Crofton's intention that individuals would spend the final third of their sentence in these intermediate establishments and would be released under supervision in the community once they had obtained employment (Dooley, 2003). The 'Irish system' was unique in its individualised use of rewards and incentives to prepare prisoners for release and its focus on prisoners earning privileges. Previous attempts at prisoner reform tended to be en masse, and earning of incentives was not imposed in this manner (Dooley, 2003).

Statistics for the first group of individuals released under the system reveal that five years after release approximately 5 per cent had their release revoked, primarily due to a failure to adhere to the conditions of their release rather than committing new crimes (Dooley, 2003). Others claim that up to 10 per cent of people were reconvicted (Kilcommins *et al.*, 2004).

Critics argued that the apparent success of the system was due to specific social and economic conditions at that time. Some believe that many people released under this system were destitute due to the famine (1845–1852) and not delinquent, and it is for this reason that reconviction rates are lower (Kilcommins *et al.*, 2004). Indeed, although the number of people imprisoned in 1867 dropped by 50 per cent compared to during the famine, re-imprisonment rates for those released at this time trebled, leading prison administrations to believe that they were dealing with more delinquent individuals in the late 1860s compared to those who they believed had been driven to commit crime for economic reasons during the famine in the 1850s (Kilcommins *et al.*, 2004). Also, the deaths and emigration associated with the famine meant that there was a smaller pool of potential employees for employers to choose from, increasing the availability of employment opportunities and the willingness of employers to hire prisoners (Dooley, 2003). This has been argued to have been key to the success and reduced reconvictions of those released under the 'Irish system', employers might not have been as willing to employ those who had been imprisoned if as many of the population had not emigrated or died as a result of the famine (Dooley, 2003). However, after the passing of the 1865 Prison Act, the 'Irish system' crumbled (Dooley, 2003).

The 1865 Prison Act represented an attempt to ensure a uniformity of prison conditions across the various prison establishments on the island of Ireland and Britain, and was followed by a desire to centralise the administration of all prisons in 1877. This led to the creation of a General Prisons Board under the Prisons (Ireland) Act 1877, replacing the Prisons Convict Board and Inspector-General of Prisons (Kilcommins *et al.*, 2004). The General Prisons Board was in charge of prison administration until 1928 when, after partition, responsibility for prisons south of the border was transferred to the Irish Department of Justice (Kilcommins *et al.*, 2004). Prisons in Northern Ireland remained under British control until the devolution of justice powers to the Northern Ireland Assembly in 2010 (Tomlinson, 1995; Prison Review Team, 2011a).

Although the 'Irish system' was only in operation between 1854 and 1865, it has played a major role in shaping the penal philosophies and administration of prison systems internationally (Heffernan, 2004; Roth, 2006). In particular, it played a significant role in shaping American penal policies and reform, and remnants of the 'Irish system' remain today in the form of prison incentive schemes, individualised prison discipline and rehabilitation programmes, education and behaviour modification programmes, parole and the use of open and semi-open prisons (Dooley, 2003; Heffernan, 2004).

Irish penal system

After partition, many politicians in the Republic of Ireland expressed a desire for penal reform, having themselves been imprisoned during the fight for independence from British rule and subsequent civil war over partition (Kilcommins *et al.*, 2004; Tomlinson, 1995). However, there was a dearth of academic research and reform of Irish prisons until the 1960s (Kilcommins *et al.*, 2004; Rogan, 2011). A detailed exploration of the main drivers for penal policy is beyond the scope of this chapter, but these are explored in depth in other chapters of this Handbook (see e.g. Hamilton, *infra*; Rogan, *infra*). While the prisoner population was low until the 1960s (excluding the civil war), the Republic of Ireland nonetheless confined large sectors of its population in institutions other than prison (see O'Sullivan and O'Donnell, 2007, 2012, as well as Brennan, *infra*). Political prisoners continued to be a feature of Irish imprisonment during this time, and the Department of Justice began reducing opportunities for independent public scrutiny of prison conditions (Kilcommins *et al.*, 2004; Rogan, 2011; Tomlinson, 1995). Also, in 1958 Mountjoy female prison, which had been the largest female prison in the state since it opened in 1858, was given over to young male offenders and became known as St Patrick's Institution (Quinlan, 2008). The small number of women detained there at the time were moved to a basement of one wing of St Patrick's Institution and held there until 1990 (Quinlan, 2008).

In the 1960s there was a renewed focus on rehabilitation, and improvements were made to prisoner accommodation, staff training, education, treatment programmes, medical care and prisoner welfare, as well as the establishment of a prisoner training unit and hostel in Mountjoy prison, creating more open conditions for prisoners, similar to the last stage of the 'Irish system' (Kilcommins *et al.*, 2004; Rogan, 2011). While rehabilitation remained an official aim of Irish penal policy during the 1970s, the outbreak of the Troubles in Northern Ireland led to an increase in political prisoners as well as a general increased suspiciousness of outsiders, a focus on security and the suppression of subversion in the Department of Justice (Rogan, 2011). The increase in the number of political prisoners led to prisoner protests, hunger strikes, escapes and a greater focus on security (Kilcommins *et al.*, 2004; Rogan, 2011). MacBride (1982) argued that the detention of political prisoners hindered penal reform, as the priority of government was security and deterrence. In addition, serious indictable crime rose considerably between the 1970s and 1980s, and the daily average prison population doubled in size (Rogan, 2011). This led to overcrowding concerns, to which the Department of Justice responded by seeking to expand prison places (Rogan, 2011).

The 1980s brought limited financial resources due to an economic recession, concerns about drug use, AIDS, poor prison conditions, poor prison industrial relations and an increase in deaths in custody (Rogan, 2011). Government recognised these concerns and established the Whitaker Committee to report on prison conditions and prison policy (Whitaker, 1986). This Committee recommended a cap on prison places, more use of alternatives to imprisonment, reduced use of short-term prison sentences, changes to industrial relations practices, collecting more statistical data on crime and imprisonment, better educational and training facilities, improved rehabilitation, treatment, re-integration and after-care as well as highlighting the poor physical conditions of prison buildings (Whitaker, 1986). However, these recommendations were not acted on.

In the 1990s and 2000s growing public concerns about crime rates, high-profile killings due to gangs/organised crime and the politicisation of crime led to changes within policing, sentencing and imprisonment (see Hourigan, *infra*). The Irish Prison Service (IPS) was established in 1996 as an independent agency of the Department of Justice and was given responsibility for the day-to-day management of Irish prisons. During this time, elements of control and order become increasingly apparent as the IPS became more focused on risk management, encouraging individual responsibility, monitoring prisoner progression and developing specific offender-focused strategies (IPS, 2014). This move reflected a shift towards a more administrative, risk-management approach to dealing with offenders observed in many Western, developed countries as they attempted to manage larger prison populations with limited resources (Feeley and Simon, 1992). Yet, these processes have not been as advanced in the Republic of Ireland as elsewhere, due to limited technological and research infrastructure investment amongst other explanations (e.g. Department of Justice and Equality, 2014; O'Donnell, 2008; O'Donnell *et al.*, 2008).

In addition, the prison population increased significantly due to a reduction in the use of temporary release (frequently used in previous decades to reduce prison accommodation pressures), longer prison sentences and an increase in the number of people detained on remand (O'Donnell, 2005a; Rogan, 2011). The number of women detained in the IPS also increased and led to the transfer of female prisoners from the basement of one wing of St Patrick's Institution to their own wing in St Patrick's Institution in 1990 (Quinlan, 2008). They remained there until 1999, when they were moved to a specially designed progressive centre for female prisoners called the Dóchas Centre (Quinlan, 2008). At the time, this centre was seen as an example of best practice in meeting the needs of female prisoners in Europe and incorporated aspects of the 'Irish System' through their ability to earn extra privileges and process to more open prison conditions (Quinlan, 2008; Rogan, 2010).

During the early 2000s the government continued to view prison expansion as the primary means of addressing the accommodation pressures within the prison system and an increase in financial resources available to the government (due to the Celtic Tiger) facilitated this approach, despite numerous objections from academics and community organisations (e.g. O'Donnell, 2005b, 2008; IPRT, 2008, 2009). However, following the economic crisis of 2008 and the subsequent need for financial assistance from the International Monetary Fund and EU in 2010, government plans for prison expansion were reviewed and a government commitment was given to reduce the costs associated with imprisonment (Government of Ireland, 2011; Thornton Hall Review Group, 2011). This contributed to a renewed emphasis on prison as a last resort, reducing the use of short-term prison sentences, increasing alternatives to imprisonment, developing community sanctions and increasing the use of semi-open and open prisons (Department of Justice and Equality, 2014).

Nevertheless, despite the increase in Irish imprisonment in the last few decades, the Republic of Ireland is consistently ranked as a country with a relatively low use of imprisonment (ICPS, 2013).

Northern Ireland penal system

Similar to the Republic of Ireland, there was little reform of the prison system in Northern Ireland after partition up until the 1960s (Tomlinson, 1995). Low crime rates and low prisoner numbers have been put forward as the main explanations for why there was little interest in developing the prison system, improving prison conditions or providing education and welfare (Tomlinson, 1995). In addition, as in the Republic, coercive detention in institutions other than prison was a feature of life in Northern Ireland. But less is known about these activities, and there are growing calls for a public inquiry (Amnesty International, 2013). Internment without trial continued to be used during outbreaks of political unrest, and until the late 1960s the prison population grew at a steady pace (notwithstanding some fluctuations due to the use of internment) (Tomlinson, 1995).

The outbreak of the Troubles in the late 1960s had a significant impact on the Northern Ireland penal system, as official imprisonment rates dramatically increased due to the internment of individuals under emergency legislation, and the prison population grew by 400 per cent over five years (McEvoy, 2001; Tomlinson, 1995). In addition, the number of staff working in the prisons dramatically increased, with 292 prison staff employed in 1969 growing to 2,184 in 1976 (McEvoy, 2001). The outbreak of the Troubles also impacted on prison research in Northern Ireland, with the majority of research focusing on the issue of political imprisonment.

Up until 1972 political prisoners were held in the same conditions as non-political prisoners and were subjected to sporadic forcible attempts by prison staff to make them wear a prison uniform (McEvoy, 2001). Between 1972 and 1976 political prisoners were granted special category status and were detained separately from non-political prisoners and given more autonomy to regulate day-to-day activities (McEvoy, 2001). In 1976 political changes again impacted heavily on Northern Ireland prisons as government officials embarked on a policy of criminalisation (McEvoy, 2001). This resulted in prison staff attempting to regain control from political prisoners and treating incoming political prisoners the same as ordinary prisoners (McEvoy, 2001). This meant that distant staff–prisoner relationships became more hostile as staff began using physical force and prison disciplinary procedures to compel political prisoners to comply with prison rules (McEvoy, 2001). This time is associated with a deterioration in prison conditions, threats and deliberate killing of prison staff, brutality, violence, dehumanisation of staff and prisoners, insufficient accountability mechanisms and human rights abuses, although experiences varied depending on prisoner group and institution (Amnesty International, 1978; Bates–Gaston, 2003; McEvoy, 2001).

Our theoretical understanding of how prisoners resist prison authority has been greatly enhanced by research into the strategies used by political prisoners at this time. McEvoy (2001) identified the use of escape, self-sacrifice (hunger strikes, protests), violence and intimidation as well as the use of litigation to challenge and transform prison administration as key resistance strategies used by political prisoners. These strategies impacted heavily on prison conditions and continue to have repercussions today. For example, the resistance strategies used by political prisoners during the Troubles, especially the use of violence, intimidation and litigation, continue to shape the behaviour of ordinary prisoners in Northern Ireland as well as those claiming political status throughout the island. Furthermore, prison staff continue to receive death threats, and David Black was killed in 2012 because of his profession as a Northern Ireland prison officer.

Rapid expansion of the prison population in the late 1960s and 1970s not only meant that staff training and prison accommodation were particularly inadequate at this time, but it also changed the profile of those detained (Tomlinson, 1995). The distribution of short-term and long-term committals changed rapidly, with long-term committals representing 29 per cent of all committals in 1977 compared to a maximum of 2 per cent during the 1960s (Tomlinson, 1995). Likewise, by 1987 lifers represented 28 per cent of all sentenced committals and 40 per cent of political prisoners (Tomlinson, 1995). As such, Northern Ireland prisons had to deal with two distinct prisoner groups, those serving short sentences for non-politically motivated offences and political prisoners serving long sentences (Tomlinson, 1995).

From 1981 onwards, political moves by the Thatcher government to ensure organisations became more efficient, economical and effective, combined with an increasing acceptance that prison could not serve as a mechanism to defeat/deny the political nature of the Conflict, led to the adoption of a managerialist approach to prisons (McEvoy, 2001). This meant there was an acceptance of the existence of political groupings and an attempt to manage them in a way which limited their influence and focused on risk and security (McEvoy, 2001). Moreover, in 1986 Armagh prison, which had been used to hold female prisoners since it opened in the 1780s, was closed, and female prisoners were moved to a new purpose-built facility called Mourne House within the high security Maghaberry prison estate (Moore and Scraton, 2014).

The 1980s also saw the number of people imprisoned for fine default significantly increase from 14 per cent of all committals at the beginning of the 1980s to 55 per cent of all sentenced committals in 1988 (Tomlinson, 1995). Research at the time suggested that people imprisoned for fine default typically had committed offences of disorderly behaviour or driving without insurance, were unemployed and had insufficient funds to pay substantial fines (Jardine et al., 1986). More recently, high numbers of fine defaulters continued to be an issue, with fine defaults comprising 31 per cent of all receptions into Northern Ireland prisons in 2012 (NISRA, 2013). Since early 2013 the number of fine defaulters admitted to prison has been temporarily suspended following a judicial review challenging the arrangements for imposing and enforcing fines and confiscation orders (NISRA, 2014). This suspension is believed to have contributed to a 33 per cent fall in the number of receptions to prison during 2013 (NISRA, 2014).

In the 1990s the average daily prison population continued to decline from its peak in 1978 to closer to pre-Troubles levels, until 2001. This decrease is attributed to a reduction in the use of internment, ceasefires, the release of political prisoners and decreasing levels of politically motivated violence (McEvoy, 2001; Prison Review Team, 2011a, 2011b). The subsequent rise in the prison population from 2002 onwards corresponds to a global increase in prison populations evident in 78 per cent of countries, including the Republic of Ireland (ICPS, 2013). The average daily prison population in 2013 was over double that of 2001 but was still substantially lower than it was in 1978 (approximately 35 per cent) (McEvoy, 2001; NISRA, 2014). This rise in the prison population in recent decades reflects a global trend towards an increased use of imprisonment but, despite this, both Northern Ireland and the Republic of Ireland remain in the bottom half of the world for their use of imprisonment (ICPS, 2013).

In addition, in 2004 female prisoners were again transferred to a different facility amid concerns about their treatment in Mourne House (Moore and Scraton, 2014). Female prisoners were moved to Ash House in Hydebank Wood young offender centre, and concerns remain about the appropriateness of this facility for female prisoners, as they must share this site with young male offenders (CJINI, 2013a; Moore and Scraton, 2014; Prison Review Team, 2011a, 2011b).

Life in prison

Radical and critical criminologists argue that law and criminal justice institutions, such as prison, are used by capitalist societies to control the subordinated social classes and protect the interests of the powerful (Chambliss, 1975; Taylor *et al.*, 1973). Research on imprisonment in the Republic of Ireland and Northern Ireland reveals that it is those from the most deprived, disadvantaged areas and/or those that challenge the legitimacy of the state that tend to be imprisoned (see Convery and Moore, 2006; O'Mahony, 1997; Scraton and Moore, 2005, 2007; and McCullagh, *infra,* on white-collar and corporate crime). Further, these individuals are usually young men, experiencing more problems than the general population with addiction, mental health, reading, writing, employment, homelessness and learning difficulties (Convery and Moore, 2006; JCFJ, 2012; O'Mahony, 1997; Prison Review Team, 2011b; Scraton and Moore, 2005; Whitaker, 1986). This parallels international research which has found that it is predominantly young socially and economically disadvantaged men who are imprisoned (Morgan and Liebling, 2007).

This poses a number of challenges for the maintenance of order and control, quality of life and rehabilitation needs of prisoners, which will be explored next in order to understand how the Republic of Ireland and Northern Ireland have attempted to respond to these issues, given the historical context and constraints shaping their penal systems.

Order and control

Sparks *et al.* (1996) theorise that the key to maintaining order and control depends on the legitimacy of the prison system, the quality of staff–prisoner relationships and the manner in which security and risk management measures are implemented. However, the security and risk management measures that are adopted are linked to wider economic, political and social concerns (Drake, 2012).

Staff generally use their discretion when enforcing prison rules, but this leaves them open to perceptions of bias and inconsistency, so 'right' relations between prisoners and staff are important to avoid potential conflict (Liebling *et al.*, 2011; Sykes, 1958). 'Right' relationships are respectful, have clear boundaries, are consistent, recognise the power imbalances in prison, address conflict rather than avoid it, and explain deviations from the norm (Liebling *et al.*, 2011). According to theories of procedural justice, authority is viewed as legitimate when individuals feel their 'voices' have been heard, rules are consistently and neutrally applied, that those in authority are sincerely concerned about their well-being and that they have been treated with dignity and respect (Jackson *et al.*, 2010; Tyler and Huo, 2002).

While the quality and nature of interpersonal relations between prisoners and staff can vary depending on the individual, prison and offence, staff in the IPS have historically been viewed as more willing to engage with and develop interactions with prisoners than in the NIPS (NIPS, 2006). Relations between IPS staff and prisoners have been described by some as largely positive (Council of Europe, 2011; NIPS, 2006). Others, however, have expressed concerns about harassment, bullying, intimidation and discrimination (e.g. Inspector of Prisons, 2013; IPRT, 2014). These concerns raise questions about the accountability mechanisms within the IPS which will be explored later in the chapter.

Irish prison staff have been expected to ensure order through the exercise of discretion in their application of prison rules, knowing prisoners' names, being considerate and fair in their dealings with prisoners, keeping abreast of developments between prisoners, while simultaneously ensuring that they do not become too intimate with prisoners (McGowan, 1980; NIPS, 2006). However, this was not always the case in Northern Ireland due to political issues, security threats against staff and their families, concerns about staff being conditioned by prisoners to reveal personal information (which could be used to threaten them or their families) and the possibility of becoming lax in their adherence to security procedures (Hennessy, 1984; McEvoy, 2001; Prison Review Team, 2011a).

In particular, threats and deliberate killings of Northern Ireland prison staff undermined the confidence and ability of staff to fully implement security procedures (especially dynamic security methods) and had a substantially negative impact on their psychological well-being (Bates-Gaston, 2003; Hennessy, 1984; Ramsbotham, 1998). Dynamic security methods involve using staff–prisoner interactions to identify, prevent and defuse risk (see Prison Review Team, 2011a). The deliberate killing of Northern Ireland prison staff peaked between 1976 and 1981, with 20 of the 31 prison staff murdered because of their profession killed during this time (NIPS, 2014). Brian Stack, a prison officer in the IPS, was also deliberately killed in 1983 (McKittrick, 2013). As such, the Troubles contributed to fractious staff–prisoner relations, perceptions of illegitimacy and a lack of procedural justice in Northern Ireland, as well as an over-reliance on physical security procedures to maintain order and control (CAJ, 2010; McEvoy, 2001; Prison Review Team, 2011a; Scraton and Moore, 2005, 2007). Physical security procedures were also used by the IPS but, where possible, a desire was expressed to use interpersonal relations to resolve tensions (McGowan, 1980; NIPS, 2006). It is worth noting though that prisons in the Republic of Ireland have not been exposed to the same level of scrutiny as prisons in Northern Ireland, so less detailed information is available on their operation. This increased level of scrutiny on Northern Ireland prisons can be attributed to the Troubles and its continuing legacy (Butler and Maruna, 2012; CAJ, 2010; McEvoy, 2001; Prison Review Team, 2011a).

Events in Northern Ireland resulted in a very risk-averse, security-focused regime with strict policies on staff–prisoner ratios, excessive use of full-body searching, predominantly security-focused staff training and problematic staff–prisoner and staff–management relationships (Butler and Maruna, 2012; CAJ, 2010; McEvoy, 2001; Prison Review Team, 2011a, 2011b; Scraton and Moore, 2005, 2007). Order and control were largely maintained through extensive security procedures, risk management techniques and coercive displays of power, rather than perceptions of legitimacy and/or staff–prisoner relationships (Butler and Maruna, 2012; CAJ, 2010; McEvoy, 2001; Prison Review Team, 2011a, 2011b).

Further, from 1972 to 1976 a political decision in Northern Ireland was taken to grant special category status to political prisoners, resulting in political prisoners being detained in separate compounds and left to run these compounds themselves (McEvoy, 2001). Staff–prisoner interactions were kept to a minimum, and prison officials recognised the command structure of these groups and sought to negotiate with them for the smooth functioning of the facilities (McEvoy, 2001). This meant that prison staff could not impose their will on these compounds without considerable resources and the potential for serious disorder (McEvoy, 2001). Prisoners maintained order and control by self-policing (McEvoy, 2001). This experience of self-policing can be observed elsewhere (Dias and Salla, 2013; Lindegaard and Gear, 2014). Research in Brazil demonstrates how mass incarceration, deterioration in living conditions and the failings of prison management led to the emergence of an organised prison group which began policing prisoners and, while there are many concerns about its operation, it did lead to a reduction in prison violence (Dias and Salla, 2013). Sparks *et al.* (1996) consider how some prisoners can be in a position of power over others and use that power to achieve their own goals, but the role of prisoner groups in maintaining order was not explored in-depth. More thought needs to be given to the varying conditions under which prisoner groups play a role in order maintenance, what role they should play and the potential consequences of such events. This is especially important given the variation in size, design, management and conditions of prison systems internationally.

Other factors such as prisoner characteristics, drug use, vendettas and tensions between different prisoners, overcrowding, staff surveillance and training, prison design and the frustrations and deprivations associated with life in prison also play a significant role in maintaining order and control in the IPS and NIPS (Butler, 2010; JCFJ, 2012; McMorrow, 2014; Prison Review Team, 2011a, 2011b; Council of Europe, 2011; UNODC, 2013). This corresponds to international research which links drugs, prison architecture, prison frustrations and deprivations, staff supervision, prisoner characteristics, overcrowding and gang involvement to the occurrence of violence (Bottoms, 1999; Edgar *et al.*, 2003; Sykes, 1958; Wortley, 2002). Additionally, these factors shape the quality of life and needs of those detained in prisons and these issues will be explored next.

Quality of life and rehabilitation needs

As previously stated, prisoners are predominantly young men from the most disadvantaged communities with a higher prevalence of substance misuse, mental health issues, learning difficulties, unstable family backgrounds and employment and accommodation problems compared to the general population. Accordingly, prisoners in the Republic of Ireland and Northern Ireland need services and supports which will address their substance misuse, employment, education, mental health, accommodation and, in certain cases, specific offence-related needs (JCFJ, 2012; Inspector of Prisons, 2013; Prison Review Team, 2011a, 2011b).

While such services and supports are available in both the IPS and NIPS, places are limited as there is not the space, resourcing or capacity to accommodate all prisoners in these activities (Committee for Justice, 2014; JCFJ, 2012). In particular, concern has been expressed about the inadequate provision of mental health and drug addiction services for prisoners in the IPS and NIPS (Committee for Justice, 2014; JCFJ 2012; Prison Review Team, 2011a, 2011b; Scraton and Moore, 2005, 2007). This situation has been further exacerbated by overcrowding which has been a particular problem for the IPS and has become a problem in Maghaberry Prison in the NIPS (Committee for Justice, 2014; JCFJ, 2012).

In the IPS, overcrowding has been especially problematic for women, with the governor of the Dóchas Centre resigning in 2010 because of the 'serious undermining' of her efforts to deliver a progressive regime in overcrowded conditions and the consistent failure of the IPS to address the issue (Rogan, 2010). The Dóchas Centre was originally designed as a progressive female prison, and was an example of best practice in Europe, but chronic overcrowding led to it being overloaded, resulting in increased tensions, self-harm, bullying, diminished services and fewer rehabilitative opportunities (Rogan, 2010). Significant overcrowding across the IPS has led to similar problems throughout the prison system and prisoners 'doubling up' and sharing cells that were originally designed for one (JCFJ, 2012; Rogan, 2011). Indeed, chronic overcrowding within the IPS has led to the inclusion of two-person occupancy cells as a formal part of Irish prison accommodation policy, in contravention of European Prison Rules, and despite the sharing of prisoner cells contributing to prisoner violence, bullying, intimidation and homicide (JCFJ, 2012; McMorrow, 2014; Rogan, 2011).

In addition to the usual problems associated with overcrowding, the lack of in-cell sanitation in Irish prisons is particularly concerning (JCFJ, 2012). All prisoners in Cork prison and some prisoners detained in Limerick and Mountjoy prisons do not have access to in-cell sanitation and must therefore 'slop out' (JCFJ, 2012). 'Slopping out' refers to the practice of prisoners using a bucket/chamber pot to collect human waste while locked in their cells overnight and emptying these buckets/chamber pots the following morning (IPRT, 2011). Due to overcrowding in the IPS, some prisoners must 'slop out' in front of other prisoners (IPRT, 2011). 'Slopping out' has been deemed 'inhuman and degrading treatment' for both Irish prisoners and staff by the Irish Inspector of Prisons, UN Human Rights Committee and the European Convention on the Prevention of Torture and Inhuman or Degrading Treatment or Punishment, especially when combined with overcrowding (IPRT, 2011). However, an Irish High Court judgment declared that while the conditions of 'slopping out' in the particular case appearing before it were unacceptable, it did not breach the prisoner's rights under the Irish Constitution or the European Convention on Human Rights (*Mulligan v Governor of Portlaoise Prison*[1]). Nonetheless, the IPS is currently working towards refurbishing its prisons to remove the need to 'slop out' (JCFJ, 2013).

In the NIPS a consistent problem that has negatively affected prison quality of life is the extent to which prisoners are locked in their cells for long periods of time and are not engaged in constructive activity (Amnesty International, 1978; CJINI, 2013a, 2013b; McEvoy, 2001; Prison Review Team, 2011a, 2011b; Scraton and Moore, 2005, 2007). Recent inspections reveal that, while prisoners should be out of their cell on average 9.5 hours, in practice some are only getting between 3 to 4 hours, with young people and women averaging between 5.2 to 7 hours (CJINI, 2013a, 2013b). These inspections revealed that in the previous 3 months for young offenders, 3,000 out-of-cell hours were lost due to staff shortages, while 800 hours had been lost for women on that basis (CJINI, 2013a, 2013b). These figures are likely to have worsened towards the end of 2014, as staff overtime was withdrawn and lock-down increased due to staff shortages and budget restrictions over time.[2] Reasons for these lock-downs have varied but include security concerns, higher staffing levels compared to other high security prisons internationally, high levels of staff absenteeism, the use of confinement as the primary means of dealing with prisoner protest, dissent or prison rule infractions, problematic staff management relationships and resourcing constraints (Butler and Maruna, 2012; CAJ, 2010; Prison Review Team, 2011a, 2011b; Scraton and Moore, 2005, 2007).

Concerns about the use of lock-down and restricted out-of-cell time can also be found in the IPS, especially regarding the treatment of prisoners on protection (JCFJ, 2012; Inspector of Prisons, 2013). Prisoners on protection are those who may be at risk of being harmed by other prisoners due to the nature of their offence, acquired debts, gangland feuding or because they have given evidence in a court case (JCFJ, 2012). Because of concerns about their safety, some prisoners on protection will be subjected to a restricted regime such that they are locked in their cell for 22 or 23 hours (IPS, 2014; JCFJ, 2012). Figures for October 2014 reveal that over one-fifth of protection prisoners on a restricted regime and subjected to 22- or 23-hour lock-down (IPS, 2014). Rather than being used as a temporary respite, this approach has been used as a solution in itself to prisoner safety concerns (Inspector of Prisons, 2013; IPRT, 2013; JCFJ, 2012).

These lengthy periods of lock-up negatively affect quality of life, as they limit participation in educational and vocational training, rehabilitative programmes and physical and social activities, contributing to mental health deterioration, self-harm and/or suicide (CAJ, 2010; CJINI, 2013a, 2013b; IPRT, 2013; JCFJ, 2012; Scraton and Moore, 2005, 2007). Such practices greatly hinder the ability of the IPS and NIPS to meet the needs of prisoners and negatively affect their well-being, human rights, quality of life and perceptions of organisational legitimacy and procedural justice (CAJ, 2010; IPRT, 2013; JCFJ, 2012; Prison Review Team, 2011a, 2011b).

The practice of locking prisoners in their cells for lengthy periods of time is a technique used by many penal systems to deal with high-security, problematic prisoners (King, 2007; Ross, 2013). However, as in the Republic of Ireland and Northern Ireland, international research reveals concerns about the potential for mental health deterioration and human rights abuses to occur (Arrigo and Bullock, 2008). Recently, Drake (2012) has argued that the focus on security in prison is misplaced as prisons have not become safer under a security regime, but instead it has increased the pains and frustrations associated with imprisonment, hindered rehabilitative efforts and distracted us from wider ideological questions regarding the use of imprisonment.

There have also been concerns about the imprisonment of women and young people. In the IPS, the detention of young people in St Patrick's Institution was problematic, due to a violation of human rights, bullying, violence, inadequate buildings, detention of under 18s with over 18s, drugs and insufficient service provision (e.g. IPRT, 2012; Ombudsman for Children, 2011; Seymour and Butler, 2008; UN, 2011). Since 2012 prisoners in St Patrick's Institution have been transferred to Children's Detention Centres and dedicated units in Wheatfield (adult male) prison, although young men aged 17 on remand awaiting trial are still detained there (IPRT, 2012; IPS, 2014). This continues to be an undesirable situation. There are also concerns about the detention of young people in Northern Ireland due to the disproportionate number of young people in care who end up in the prison system, over-use of custodial remand, poor regime, inadequate provision of services, security focused regime and use of lock-downs (CJINI, 2013b; Convery and Moore, 2006; Youth Justice Review, 2011).

The detention of females has been especially problematic in Northern Ireland, due to the use of full-body searching, violation of human rights, co-location of the female prison with the young offender centre, excessive security regime, use of lock-downs, inadequate service provision, intimidation and harassment by young offenders, poor health and mental health services, inappropriate techniques for dealing with self-harm and poor purposeful activity (see CJINI, 2013a; Scraton and Moore, 2005, 2007). In particular, the regime and activities experienced by women in the NIPS are restricted in comparison to male prisoners due to the co-location of Ash House with the young offender centre, and this has led to great concerns about the ability of the prison to adequately meet the needs of female prisoners and ensure their human rights are protected (see Moore and Scraton, 2014, and Quinlan, *infra*, for a more detailed discussion of female imprisonment). It was proposed by the Prison Review Team (2011b) that a new female prison should be built, but this has been delayed due to limited finances. There is also a need for a new prison to be built to detain female prisoners in Limerick, and overcrowding in the Dóchas Centre continues to affect regime delivery and quality of life in the IPS (Inspector of Prisons, 2013). Unfortunately, as in Northern Ireland, women detained in Limerick prison experience a restricted regime due to sharing a prison site with adult male prisoners and a tendency to prioritise the needs of the adult male prisoners over females due to their reduced numbers (see

Inspector of Prisons, 2011; Quinlan, 2008). While the facilities in the Dóchas Centre are specifically designed for female prisoners and were once an example of best practice, concerns about resourcing and overcrowding have reduced the quality of the regime and capacity of the centre to meet the rehabilitative needs of females detained there (see JCFJ, 2012; Rogan, 2010). The issue of female imprisonment is explored in more depth in Quinlan (*infra*) in this Handbook.

Problems with overcrowding and delivery of rehabilitative programmes are not unique to Northern Ireland or the Republic of Ireland. The global increase in prison populations has not been matched by a growth in staffing or financial resources, resulting in less availability of services, supports and rehabilitative programmes, reduced ability to effectively segregate prisoner groups, concerns about safety and security, and increasing use of lock-downs (UNODC, 2013). This has not only reduced the quality of prison life for prisoners but also negatively impacted on working conditions of prison staff (UNODC, 2013).

These issues are recognised by both the IPS and NIPS, and steps have been taken to try to address these concerns. Recent innovations to improve the quality of life and provision of services in the NIPS include: the adoption of 'drug-free' landings; use of step-down facilities and working-out schemes to help prisoners reintegrate into society before release; use of restorative justice to allow prisoners to make amends for their crimes and assist the healing process for victims; a 'Family Matters' landing whereby the focus is on improving prisoners' relationships with families to prevent relationship breakdown, discourage the intergenerational transmission of crime and promote desistance; as well as the transformation of Hydebank Wood young offender centre into a 'secure college' emphasising educational and vocational training as key for the rehabilitation and desistance process. In the IPS, similar innovations are evident such as: 'drug-free' units in most prisons; step-down and open prison facilities; use of working-out schemes to help prisoners reintegrate into society; the community return programme, whereby prisoners can earn early temporary release in return for supervised community service; incorporation of restorative justice practices to handle disagreements between prisoners and/or staff; and the Irish Red Cross volunteer project, which uses peer-to-peer learning to improve community health, hygiene awareness and first aid amongst prisoners. These are just some of the activities undertaken in both jurisdictions, and remnants of the 'Irish System' continue to be evident in this work through the use of incentive programmes, individualised schemes, a focus on rehabilitation, education and behaviour modification as well as the use of early release, open and semi-open prisons. However, these activities remain restricted by resourcing and capacity issues.

Futhermore, managing the needs of prisoners can be difficult for prison staff as they attempt to balance order, control and security with 'right' prisoner–staff relationships in a context of increasing prisoner numbers and reduced resources. These issues are evident amongst Republic of Ireland and Northern Ireland staff, with high levels of absenteeism, mental health issues, stress, alienation, feelings of under-appreciation, fears about safety, dissatisfaction with management and insufficient training (Bates-Gaston, 2003; Butler and Maruna, 2012; CAJ, 2010; Clarke, 2014). These experiences have been magnified in Northern Ireland, with staff experiencing particularly challenging working conditions, increases in suicide and ill-health, intimidation, threats, murder as well as feelings of betrayal, alienation and dissatisfaction with prison management and political actors as a result of events and decisions associated with the Troubles (Bates-Gaston, 2003; McEvoy, 2001). In addition, as threats against staff predominantly originated from Nationalist groups, this negatively affected relationships between Catholic prisoners and staff, contributing to concerns about equality and an over-reliance on physical security techniques (Butler and Maruna, 2012; Prison Review Team, 2011a, 2011b). The review of the NIPS in 2011 sought to address this issue by changing its culture. This cultural change was to be achieved through a redundancy package for older staff and a new recruitment campaign (amongst other changes), although the success of this approach has been questioned as half of the new recruits have either left the NIPS or are on long-term sick leave (McMahon, 2014). Issues of staff alienation, dissatisfaction with management, staff safety, well-being and adequate resources are also problematic for the IPS (Clarke, 2014; POA, 2014). The IPS is attempting to address some of these concerns through its 'Dignity at Work' strategy but to date tensions remain with 93 per cent of Prisoner Officers' Association members voting for industrial action in March 2015 (POA, 2015).

There are many lessons that can be learnt from these experiences. For example, prison and political policies can have long-term effects on order, control and everyday life which cannot be easily overcome, even after these policies have been changed, unless their lingering effects are addressed. Staff also need to be supported in moving from a custodial model of engagement to one that requires more interaction and support of prisoners than before by listening to their concerns and anxieties and dealing with these in a constructive manner to avoid potential negative consequences for staff well-being or performance at work. Research reveals that Northern Ireland staff did not feel supported by management and were expected to quickly move from a position of non-engagement with prisoners, on account of conditioning and fears for their personal safety, to one of engaging with prisoners (Bates-Gaston, 2003; Butler and Maruna, 2012; McAloney, 2011). Many staff reported feeling scapegoated by management for failing to make this transition which left them further disengaged and alienated (Butler and Maruna, 2012; McAloney, 2011; Prison Review Team, 2011a, 2011b). Indeed, the introduction of a redundancy package as part of the reform programme reinforced the view that older staff were perceived as the main barrier to change – something that staff felt was unfair and did not reflect the failings of management or political policies or recognise the 'jailcraft' expertise of older staff (Butler and Maruna, 2012; Kelly, forthcoming). By focusing on staff, the reform agenda forgot that staff–prisoner relationships are a two-way process, also influenced by prisoners' views of staff and willingness to engage with them. In Northern Ireland, even before any staff engagement, prisoners' memories/views about the treatment of prisoners during the Troubles continue to shape their willingness to engage with staff and their perceptions of legitimacy and fairness (Butler and Maruna, 2012). As such, attempts to reform penal culture should focus not only on staff but also on prisoners' views, beliefs and expectations if staff–prisoner interactions and quality of life are to be improved.

Prison accountability

As in other countries, there have been campaigns in the Republic of Ireland and Northern Ireland for government to rethink how and when to use imprisonment (CAJ, 2010; JCFJ, 2012; O'Donnell, 2008; Rogan, 2011; Scraton and Moore, 2005, 2007). However, these arguments have not gripped policymakers, politicians or public attention as hoped, as shown by the continued rise in the prison population, despite relatively stable or falling crime rates.

Efforts are made to hold the IPS and NIPS to account for prison conditions, but these endeavours are hampered by the inability of existing external accountability mechanisms to compel change. In the IPS, a recent review of penal policy reiterated the importance of independent oversight, but there appears to be little change to existing mechanisms other than suggesting that a 'Consultative Council' examine the issue (Department of Justice and Equality, 2014). In Northern Ireland, the need for independent oversight has been recognised due to a failure by the NIPS to action many recommendations put forward by external accountability mechanisms. To address this issue, the 2011 review of the NIPS recommended that an oversight group directly answerable to a Justice Committee be established, and that additional resources should be given to the Criminal Justice Inspectorate Northern Ireland to carry out independent monitoring of outcomes (Prison Review Team, 2011b).

Existing accountability methods include internal and external mechanisms. Internal accountability processes include internal disciplinary procedures, data monitoring, audits, reviews, prisoner complaints processes, performance management reviews, performance targets and codes and procedures. While recommendations arising from these processes may be more likely to be actioned, as they involve internal agencies identifying issues within the organisation, this information is not always publicly available. This can contribute to recommendations being neglected in favour of other organisational outcomes and/or issues, and such neglect may go unchallenged because existing practices are ingrained in the organisational culture. Examples can be found in the IPS's and NIPS's over-reliance on lock-downs, management of self-harm, deaths in custody, full-body searching, bullying and monitoring of equality issues (e.g. Barry, 2011; CAJ, 2010; Inspector of Prisons, 2013; JCFJ, 2012; Prison Review Team, 2011a, 2011b; Scraton and Moore, 2005, 2007).

While the internal mechanisms in both the IPS and NIPS are similar, there are some differences that are worthy of note. In particular, serious concerns about the IPS prisoner complaints process have been raised by the Inspector of Prisons (2013) and Council of Europe (2011), with these organisations arguing that the IPS complaints process was not meeting its international obligations for transparency or accountability. While the process has been reviewed and amended based on the Inspector of Prisons (2013) recommendations, concerns remain about its operation, with prison staff in particular expressing disquiet about its implementation (see POA, 2014). Another key difference between the effectiveness of internal accountability mechanisms in the IPS and NIPS is the use of Freedom of Information requests to obtain such information. Due to restrictions on Freedom of Information requests in the Republic of Ireland, it is more difficult to obtain information about the performance of the IPS as measured by internal accountability mechanisms compared to the NIPS, wherein reasonable requests for such information are facilitated at no cost to the public. This means that information about the NIPS performance as measured on internal accountability mechanisms can be, and frequently is, subject to public scrutiny through Freedom of Information requests more so than the IPS performance in the Republic of Ireland.

Independent external accountability mechanisms are also an important part of holding prisons to account, as they challenge assumed working practices and priorities. Examples of external accountability mechanisms include a Prisoner Ombudsman, inspectors, freedom of information requests, Justice Committees, the courts, politicians, media, academic research, prison-visiting committees, community organisations, domestic and international law, inquiries, committees or investigations, and international inspection agencies, such as the European Committee for the Prevention of Torture and Inhuman and Degrading Treatment amongst others (although there is some doubt about the level of independence of some, due to their connection to Justice Departments).

Differences in the use of external accountability mechanisms are also evident between Northern Ireland and the Republic of Ireland. For example, as of 2015 the Republic of Ireland does not have a Prisoner Ombudsman, while the Prisoner Ombudsman for Northern Ireland (PONI) was established in 2005. The PONI investigates prisoner and visitor complaints (although they must first go through the relevant internal complaints process before they are eligible for PONI consideration) and deaths in custody. Numerous concerns have been raised about the adequacy of investigations into deaths in custody in the Republic of Ireland (see Barry, 2011; Inspector of Prisons, 2013; Rogan, 2011). Attempts have been made to address this by increasing the Inspector of Prisons remit to investigate deaths in custody since 2012, and the Inspector of Prisons (2014) has concluded that this process, combined with investigations by the Irish police and the Coroner's Court, is sufficient for the Republic of Ireland to meet its international obligations in this regard (Inspector of Prisons, 2014). Yet concerns remain about this process, given the resourcing of the Inspector of Prisons office. In contrast, imprisonment in Northern Ireland has been subjected to numerous external accountability checks due to the Troubles and the international attention focused on the handling of events associated with prisoner demands for political status as well as the use of ligation as a resistance strategy by those claiming political status (see CAJ, 2010; McEvoy, 2001; Prison Review Team, 2011a, 2011b). However, despite this increased external scrutiny, Northern Ireland was slow to respond to and/ or act on recommendations put forward by these external mechanisms, highlighting that, while external mechanisms can use public exposure to motivate action, they cannot force change. Only government action or court rulings can force change, and these processes can be slow and weak, and the people involved in implementing these processes can be reluctant to intervene (Independent Review Group, 2014).

This means that the majority of prison accountability mechanisms operate on a 'name and shame' policy, hoping to encourage change by publicly highlighting failings. Unfortunately, international research on naming and shaming as an enforcement strategy highlights its ineffectiveness, due to the potential for being labelled propaganda by those with anti-government vested interests, a tendency to prompt minor reforms which are offset by other abuses and/or a lack of governmental capacity to drive change (Hafner-Burton, 2008). In Northern Ireland and the Republic of Ireland, criticisms surrounding political prisoners were sometimes dismissed as propaganda, subversive, ill-informed or politically biased (MacBride, 1982; McEvoy, 2001). In particular, concerns about religious bias have led to defensive reactions whereby the NIPS deny this is an issue, despite statistics indicating worse outcomes for Catholic compared to Protestant prisoners (Butler and Maruna, 2012; Prison Review Team, 2011b). As such, minimising defensive reactions to criticism is important for ensuring that problems are acknowledged and appropriate action taken. Further, a combination of internal and external accountability mechanisms, with the power to compel change when needed, is required to ensure our prisons are sufficiently held to account.

Conclusion

The emerging picture from this chapter indicates that the modern penal systems of the Republic of Ireland and Northern Ireland are similar to other developed, Western, democratic jurisdictions in terms of the management of prisoners, prison regimes and accountability mechanisms. However, there are certain notable features which hold important lessons internationally. For example, the 'Irish System' played a major role in shaping the penal philosophies and administration of prison systems internationally by emphasising individualised schemes, the use of incentive schemes, parole, open and semi-open prison conditions as well as behaviour modification programmes, amongst others (Dooley, 2003; Heffernan, 2004). In addition, research on political imprisonment in Northern Ireland has provided important insights into resistance strategies that can be adopted in prison and the role of prisoner groups in order maintenance, while the potential for political imprisonment to distract from and impede penal reform can be seen in both jurisdictions. The experiences of the Republic of Ireland and Northern Ireland may help to inform theoretical developments and prison practices internationally in these areas, while both the IPS and NIPS continue to learn from international evidence-based best practice which is applicable to an Irish and Northern Ireland context.

References

Amnesty International (1978) *Report of an Amnesty Mission to Northern Ireland.* London: Amnesty International.

—— (2013) *Briefing: Magdalene Laundry-Type Institutions in Northern Ireland. The Case for a Response from the Northern Ireland Executive.* Available at www.amnesty.org.uk/sites/default/files/doc_23218.pdf (accessed 15 August 2014).

Arrigo, B. and Bullock, J. L. (2008) 'The Psychological Effects of Solitary Confinement on Prisoners in Supermax Units – Reviewing What We Know and Recommending What Should Change', *International Journal of Offender Therapy and Comparative Criminology*, 52(6): 622–40.

Barry, C. (2011) *Death in Irish Prisons: An Examination of the Causes of Deaths and the Compliance of Investigations with the European Convention on Human Rights.* Dublin: Dublin Institute of Technology.

Bates-Gaston, J. (2003) 'Terrorism and Imprisonment in Northern Ireland: A Psychological Perspective', in A. Silke (ed.) *Terrorism, Victims and Society: Psychological Perspectives on Terrorism and Its Consequences.* Chichester: Wiley (pp. 233–55).

Bottoms, A. (1999) 'Interpersonal Violence and Social Order in Prison', in M. Tonry and J. Petersilia (ed.) *Crime and Justice: A Review of Research, Vol. 26.* Chicago: University of Chicago (pp. 205–82).

Butler, M. (2010) 'Breaking Out of the Prison Mindset', *Irish Examiner*, 22 October 2010, p. 15.

Butler, M. and Maruna, S. (2012) *Discipline and Disparity: An Independent Report Prepared for the Northern Irish Prison Service.* Cambridge: ARCS Ltd.

Cavadino, M. and Dignan, J. (2006) 'Penal Policy and Political Economy', *Criminology and Criminal Justice*, 6(4): 435–45.

Chambliss, W. (1975) 'Toward a Political Economy of Crime', in T. Newburn (ed.) *Key Readings in Criminology.* Cullompton: Willan.

CJINI (2013a) *Report of an Announced Inspection of Ash House, Hydebank Wood Female's Prison 18–22 February 2013.* Belfast: CJINI.

—— (2013b) *Report of an Announced Inspection of Hydebank Wood Young Offender Centre 18–22 February 2013.* Belfast: CJINI.

Clarke, J. (2014) *Irish Prison Officers' Perceptions of Job Burnout.* Available at http://trap.ncirl.ie/1780/1/joyceclarke.pdf (accessed 21 January 2015).

Committee for Justice (2014) 'Prison Service Reform Programme: Northern Ireland Prison Service', *Hansard 10 April 2014.* Belfast: Northern Ireland Assembly.

Committee on the Administration of Justice (CAJ) (2010) *Prisons and Prisoners in Northern Ireland: Putting Human Rights at the Heart of Prison Reform.* Belfast: CAJ.

Convery, U. and Moore, L. (2006) *Still in Our Care: Protecting Children's Rights in Custody in Northern Ireland.* Belfast: Northern Ireland Human Rights Commission.

Council of Europe (2011) *Report to the Government of Ireland on the Visit to Ireland Carried Out by the European Committee for the Prevention of Torture and Inhuman or Degrading Treatment or Punishment (CPT) from 25 January to 5 February 2010.* Available at www.cpt.coe.int/documents/irl/2011-03-inf-eng.pdf (accessed 18 June 2014).

Department of Justice (2014) *Department of Justice Staff Attitudes 2013.* Belfast: NISRA.

Department of Justice and Equality (2014) *Strategic Review of Penal Policy – Final Report.* Available at www.justice.ie/en/JELR/Strategic%20Review%20of%20Penal%20Policy.pdf/Files/Strategic%20Review%20of%20Penal%20Policy.pdf (accessed 15 January 2015).

Dias, C. and Salla, F. (2013) 'Organised Crime in Brazilian Prisons: The Example of the PCC', *International Journal of Criminology and Sociology*, 2: 397–408.

Dooley, E. (2003) 'Sir Walter Crofton and the Irish or Intermediate System of Prison Discipline', in I. O'Donnell and F. McAuley (eds) *Criminal Justice History: Themes and Controversies from Pre-Independence Ireland.* Dublin: Four Courts Press (pp. 196–213).

Drake, D. (2012) *Prisons, Punishment and the Pursuit of Security.* Basingstoke: Palgrave.

Edgar, K., O'Donnell, I. and Martin, C. (2003) *Prison Violence: The Dynamics of Conflict, Fear and Power.* Cullompton: Willan.

Feeley, M. and Simon, J. (1992) 'The New Penology: Notes on the Emerging Strategy of Corrections and Its Implications', *Criminology*, 30(4): 449–74.

Government of Ireland (2011) *The National Recovery Plan 2011–2014.* Available at www.budget.gov.ie/The%20National%20Recovery%20Plan%202011-2014.pdf (accessed 15 January 2015).

Hafner-Burton, E.M. (2008) 'Sticks and Stones: Naming and Shaming the Human Rights Enforcement Problem', *International Organisation,* 62(Fall): 689–716.

Heaney, H. (2003) 'Ireland's Penitentiary 1820–31: An Experiment that Failed', in I. O'Donnell and F. McAuley (eds) *Criminal Justice History: Themes and Controversies from Pre-Independence Ireland.* Dublin: Four Courts Press (pp. 175–84).

Heffernan, E. (2004) 'Irish (or Crofton) System', in M. Bosworth (eds) *Encyclopedia of Prisons and Correctional Facilities.* London: Sage (pp. 482–4).

Hennessy, J. (1984) *A Report of Inquiry by HM Chief Inspector of Prisons into the Security Arrangements at HMP Maze.* London: HM Stationery Office.

ICPS (2013) *World Prison Brief.* Available at www.prisonstudies.org/sites/prisonstudies.org/files/resources/downloads/wppl_10.pdf (accessed 12 June 2014).

Ignatieff, M. (1981) 'State, Civil Society and Total Institutions: A Critique of Recent Social Histories of Punishment', *Crime and Justice,* 3: 153–192.

Independent Review Group (2014) *Report of the Independent Review Group on the Department of Justice and Equality.* Dublin: Stationery Office.

Inspector of Prisons (2011) *Report on the Inspection of Limerick Prison by the Inspector of Prisons Judge Michael Reilly 25th November 2011.* Dublin: Department of Justice and Equality.

—— (2013) *An Assessment of the Irish Prison Service.* Dublin: Department of Justice and Equality.

—— (2014) *Report by Judge Michael Reilly Inspector of Prisons into His Investigations into the Deaths of Prisoners in Custody or on Temporary Release for the Period 1st January 2012 to 11th June 2014.* Dublin: Department of Justice and Equality.

Irish Penal Reform Trust (IPRT) (2008) *IPRT Position Paper 1 – Thornton Hall.* Dublin: IPRT.

—— (2009) *IPRT Position Paper 6 – Planning the Future of Irish Prisons.* Dublin: IPRT.

—— (2011) *Policy Briefing Paper on Sanitation and Slopping Out in the Irish Prison System.* Dublin: IPRT.

—— (2012) *Policy Briefing Paper on Detention of Children in St Patrick's Institution.* Dublin: IPRT.

—— (2013) *Policy Briefing Paper on Solitary Confinement, Isolation, Protection and Special Regimes.* Dublin: IPRT.

—— (2014) *Travellers in the Irish Prison System: A Qualitative Study.* Dublin: IPRT.

Irish Prison Service (IPS) (2014) *Census of Restricted Regimes Prisoners October 2014.* Available at www.irishprisons.ie/images/monthlyinfonote/oct_restrict_2014.pdf (accessed 16 January 2015).

Jackson, J., Tyler, T., Bradford, B., Taylor, D. and Shiner, M. (2010) 'Legitimacy and Procedural Justice in Prisons', *Prison Service Journal,* 191: 4–10.

Jardine, E., Craig, J. and Geddis, P.W. (1986) *Fines and Fine Default in Northern Ireland.* Belfast: Social Division Policy Planning and Research Unit, Deptartment of Finance and Personnel.

Jesuit Centre for Faith and Justice (JCFJ) (2012) *The Irish Prison System: Vision, Values, Reality.* Dublin: JCFJ.

—— (2013) *Making Progress: Examining the First Year of the Irish Prison Service Three Year Strategic Plan 2012–2015.* Dublin: JCFJ.

Kelly, D. (forthcoming) 'Impact of Organizational Reforms in Northern Ireland Prison Service on Staff Attitudes, Occupational Cultures and Working Practices'. Queens University Belfast: Unpublished PhD.

Kilcommins, S., O'Donnell, I., O'Sullivan, E. and Vaughan, B. (2004) *Crime Punishment and the Search for Order in Ireland.* Dublin: Institute of Public Administration.

King, R. D. (2007) 'Imprisonment: Some International Comparisons and the Need to Revisit Panopticism', in Y. Jewkes (ed.) *Handbook of Prisons.* Cullompton: Willan.

Liebling, A., Price, D. and Shefer, G. (2011) *The Prison Officer.* Leyhill: Prison Service and Waterside Press.

Lindegaard, M. R. and Gear, S. (2014) 'Violence Makes Safe in South African Prisons: Prison Gangs, Violent Acts and Victimisation among Prison Inmates', *Focaal,* 68: 35–54.

McAloney, K. (2011) 'Life after Prison: The Experiences of Prison Officers Serving during the Troubles in Northern Ireland', *Behavioral Sciences of Terrorism and Political Aggression,* 3(1): 20–34.

MacBride, S. (1982) *Crime and Punishment.* Dublin: Ward River Press.

McEvoy, K. (2001) *Paramilitary Imprisonment in Northern Ireland: Resistance, Management, and Release.* Oxford: Oxford University Press.

McGowan, J. (1980) *The Role of the Prison Officer in the Irish Prison Service.* Available at ftp://78.153.208.68/bkp/ipa/PDF/B3_prisonofficer.pdf (accessed 19 August 2014).

McKittrick, D. (2013) 'IRA Finally Admit Killing Prison Officer Brian Stack during the Troubles', *The Independent,* 9 August 2013. Available at www.independent.co.uk/news/uk/crime/ira-finally-admits-killing-prison-officer-brian-stack-during-the-troubles-8755078.html (accessed 20 August 2014).

McMahon (2014) *Half of All Prison Recruits Have Already Quit or Are on Long-Term Sick Leave.* Available at www.mirror.co.uk/news/uk-news/half-prison-service-recruits-already-4706998 (accessed 21 January 2015).

McMorrow, G. (2014) *Report of the Commission of Investigation into Gary Douch*. Dublin: Department of Justice and Equality.

Moore, L. and Scraton, P. (2014) *The Incarceration of Women: Punishing Bodies, Breaking Spirits*. London: Palgrave Macmillan.

Morgan, R. and Liebling, A. (2007) 'Imprisonment: An Expanding Scene', in M. Maguire, R. Morgan and R. Reiner (eds) *The Oxford Handbook of Criminology*. Oxford: Oxford University Press (pp. 1100–38).

NIPS (2006) *Inside View: A Review of Equality of Opportunity of Prisoners on the Basis of Religion in Relation to Our s75 Statutory Duties*. Belfast: NIPS.

—— (2014) *Roll of Honour*. Available at http://www.dojni.gov.uk/index/ni-prison-service/history/roll-of-honour.htm (accessed 25 June 2014).

NISRA (2013) *The Northern Ireland Average Prison Population: Research and Statistical Bulletin 6/2013*. Belfast: DOJNI.

—— (2014) *The Northern Ireland Prison Population 2013: Research and Statistical Bulletin 15/2014*. Belfast: DOJNI.

O'Donnell, I. (2005a) 'Crime and Justice in the Republic of Ireland', *European Journal of Criminology*, 2(1): 99–131.

—— (2005b) *Putting Prison in Its Place*. Available at http://www.iprt.ie/files/putting_prison_in_its_place__ian_odonnell_nov_2005.pdf (accessed 14 January 2015).

—— (2008) 'Stagnation and Change in Irish Penal Policy', *The Howard Journal of Criminal Justice*, 47(2): 121–33.

O'Donnell, I., Baumer, E. and Hughes, N. (2008) 'Recidivism in the Republic of Ireland', *Criminology and Criminal Justice*, 8(2): 123–46.

O'Mahony, P. (1997) *Mountjoy Prisoners: A Sociological and Criminological Profile*. Dublin: Stationery Office.

Ombudsman for Children (2011) *Report on Young People in St Patrick's Institution*. Dublin: Ombudsman for Children.

O'Sullivan, E. and O'Donnell, I. (2007) 'Coercive Confinement in the Republic of Ireland: The Waning of a Culture of Control', *Punishment and Society*, 9(1): 27–48.

—— (2012) *Coercive Confinement in Ireland: Patients, Prisoners and Penitents*. Manchester: Manchester University Press.

Prison Officers' Association (POA) (2014) *Prison Officers' Association Annual Conference 2014*. Available at http://www.poa.ie/annual-conference/annual-conference-2014 (accessed 17 March 2015).

—— (2015) *Press Statement by the Prison Officers' Association 11 March 2015 – Ballot for Industrial Account Has 93% in Favour*. Available at http://www.poa.ie/latest-news/press-statement-by-the-prison-officers-association-11th-march-2015-ballot-for-industrial-action-has-93-in-favour (accessed 17 March 2015).

Prison Review Team (2011a) *Review of the Northern Ireland Prison Service: Conditions, Management and Oversight of All Prisons – Interim Report*. Belfast: Prison Review Team.

—— (2011b) *Review of the Northern Ireland Prison Service: Conditions, Management and Oversight of All Prisons – Final Report*. Belfast: Prison Review Team.

Quinlan, C. (2008) *Ireland's Women's Prisons*. Available at www.workingnotes.ie/item/irelands-womens-prisons (accessed 16 March 2015).

Ramsbotham, D. (1998) *HM Prison Maze (Northern Ireland) Report of a Full Inspection 23rd March–3rd April*. London: HM Stationery Office.

Rogan, M. (2010) 'Governor of Dóchas Centre Resigns', Human Rights in Ireland Blog, 26 April 2010. Available at http://humanrights.ie/criminal-justice/governor-of-dochas-centre-resigns/ (accessed 18 June 2014).

—— (2011) *Prison Policy in Ireland: Politics, Penal-Welfarism and Political Imprisonment*. Abingdon: Routledge.

Ross, J. I. (2013) *The Globalization of Supermax Prisons*. New Brunswick NJ: Rutgers University Press.

Roth, M. (2006) *Prisons and Prison Systems: A Global Encyclopedia*. Westport CT: Greenwood Press.

Scraton, P. and Moore, L. (2005) *The Hurt Inside: The Imprisonment of Women and Girls in Northern Ireland*. Belfast: Northern Ireland Human Rights Commission.

—— (2007) *The Prison Within: The Imprisonment of Women and Girls in Hydebank Wood 2004–2006*. Belfast: Northern Ireland Human Rights Commission.

Seymour, M. and Butler, M. (2008) *Young People on Remand*. Dublin: Stationery Office.

Sparks, R., Bottoms, A. and Hay, W. (1996) *Prisons and the Problem of Order*. Oxford: Clarendon Press.

Sykes, G. M. (1958) *The Society of Captives: A Study of a Maximum Security Prison.* New York: Princeton University Press.

Taylor, I., Walton, P. and Young, J. (1973) *The New Criminology.* London: Routledge.

Thornton Hall Review Group (2011) *Report of the Thornton Hall Project Review Group.* Dublin: Department of Justice and Equality.

Tomlinson, M. (1995) 'Imprisoned Ireland' in V. Ruggiero, M. Ryan and J. Sim (eds) *Western European Penal Systems: A Critical Anatomy.* London: Sage (pp. 194–227).

Tyler, T. and Huo, Y. (2002) *Trust in the Law: Encouraging Public Cooperation with the Police and Courts.* New York: Russell Sage Foundation.

UN (2011) *Concluding Observations of the Committee against Torture – Ireland: Consideration of Reports Submitted by State Parties under Article 19 of the Convention (9th May–3rd June 2011).* Available at http://tbinternet.ohchr.org/_layouts/treatybodyexternal/Download.aspx?symbolno=CAT%2fC%2fIRL%2fCO%2f1&Lang=en (accessed 20 May 2014).

—— (2013) *Concluding Observations on the Fifth Periodic Report of the United Kingdom of Great Britain and Northern Ireland (6–31 May 2013).* Available at http://tbinternet.ohchr.org/_layouts/treatybodyexternal/Download.aspx?symbolno=CAT%2fC%2fGBR%2fCO%2f5&Lang=en (accessed 20 May 2014).

United Nations Office on Drugs and Crime (UNODC) (2013) *Handbook on Strategies to Reduce Overcrowding in Prisons.* Available at www.unodc.org/documents/justice-and-prison-reform/Overcrowding_in_prisons_Ebook.pdf (accessed 28 August 2014).

Whitaker, T. K. (1986) *Report of the Committee of Inquiry into the Penal System.* Dublin: Stationery Office.

Wortley, R. (2002) *Situational Prison Control: Crime Prevention in Correctional Institutions.* Cambridge: Cambridge University Press.

Youth Justice Review (2011) *A Review of the Youth Justice System in Northern Ireland.* Belfast: Department of Justice.

Notes

1   [2010] IEHC 269.
2   The author is aware of these developments from conducting research in the NIPS during this time.

18

Prison education and rehabilitation

What works?

Cormac Behan and Jackie Bates-Gaston

Introduction

This chapter will examine the programmes, activities and opportunities for transformation available to prisoners in the Republic of Ireland and Northern Ireland. It begins with a brief overview of the development of programmes in both jurisdictions. Drawing on academic analyses and practitioner experience, it examines the debates around the contested concepts of rehabilitation. It outlines what is on offer to prisoners in educational and rehabilitative programmes on both sides of the border. The chapter then explores ideas around 'what works' and concludes by considering the context in which these programmes occur. It argues that, while programmes to assist individuals transform their lives are important, it is also imperative to understand the social, structural and political contexts in which education and rehabilitative programmes take place, both within and without the prison.

History

This section begins by sketching out developments in penal policy in the Republic of Ireland and the emergence of educational and rehabilitative opportunities. It will then examine the development of programmes in Northern Ireland.

Republic of Ireland

When the Irish Free State was established in the 1920s there was relatively little change in penal policy, internal prison regimes and the prison system in general (Rogan, 2013). The core structure of the prisons 'did not change ... one iota' (Aylward, 2002: 574). Despite prisoners and ex-prisoners creating the new state, successive governments showed little interest in 'improving conditions or providing education and welfare resources' (Tomlinson, 1995: 200). One of the reasons for this neglect was the reduction in the size of the prison estate and relatively low levels of imprisonment throughout the twentieth century. By 1926, after political prisoners were released, there was a daily average population of 862, and in 1971 the daily average stood at only 926, of whom 23 were women (O'Sullivan and O'Donnell, 2012: 6). In 2001 there were

3,112 prisoners – still at the lower end of the European imprisonment rate at 80 per 100,000. By December 2014 the imprisonment rate in the Republic of Ireland was still relatively low at 81 per 100,000, with 3,760 prisoners compared to its European neighbours; the rate of imprisonment in England and Wales was 149 per 100,000, in Scotland 139 per 100,000, in Northern Ireland 100 per 100,000, and in France it stood at 102 per 100,000 (International Centre for Prison Studies, 2015).

The low level of imprisonment was undoubtedly one reason for the absence of innovation in penal policy. Discussions about rehabilitative programmes and provision of education to meet the needs of prisoners were virtually non-existent, and during the early decades of the state 'prison policy was largely moribund and inert' (Rogan, 2013: 10). Another reason for the lack of innovation was the network of coercive institutions supplementary to prison. These included industrial and reformatory schools, district mental hospitals, County Homes and Magdalene Homes which 'served as depositories for the difficult, the disturbed, the deviant and the disengaged' (O'Sullivan and O'Donnell, 2012: 5). Despite these institutions being austere and at times brutal, the 'expressed aim was to reform or to treat rather than to punish' (O'Sullivan and O'Donnell, 2012: 257). They were in essence houses of correction. Some education and training was offered in the reformatory and industrial schools, with the latter hoping to inculcate habits of 'industry, regularity, self-denial and self-control' (cited in O'Sullivan and O'Donnell, 2012: 23).

The Republic of Ireland was somewhat immune from the influence of the post-war welfarist approach adopted in other Western nations. For decades after independence, much of the legislation governing prisons predated the foundation of the state. The first advance in internal prison organisation and dynamics, the 1947 Rules for the Government of Prisons, was an almost Victorian set of regulations with little concern for educational or rehabilitative programmes (Behan, 2014a). There was a period of innovation in penal policy in the 1960s reflecting a more open, progressive and aspirational society outside the prison walls. In 1962 the Inter-Departmental Committee on Juvenile Delinquency, the Probation System, the Institutional Treatment of Offenders and their After-Care was established 'to investigate methods for the prevention of crime and the treatment of offenders' (Rogan, 2011: 97). Among the suggestions was a proposal to establish a corrective training unit and a hostel in Mountjoy Prison and the reopening of the prison school (see Rogan, 2011).

However, this period of modernisation was short-lived. Despite official (Whitaker, 1985) and unofficial (MacBride, 1982; Council for Social Welfare, 1983; Irish Commission for Justice and Peace, 1986) reports into the penal system suggesting improvements in out-of-cell activities and a whole raft of international declarations and conventions (e.g. the United Nations Standard Minimum Rules for the Treatment of Prisoners, 1955, and the European Prison Rules, 1986, 2006), Ireland's closed institutions would open only slowly to the influences of social change and international practice. Suggestions for improved regimes and more rehabilitative programmes fell on deaf ears. Nevertheless, modernisation and progress in social policy outside led to greater consideration of the needs of those who were sent to prison. One area in which this change occurred was in the provision of educational and rehabilitative programmes.

Northern Ireland

With the creation of Northern Ireland, control and administration of the existing three prisons – Londonderry (closed in 1953), Armagh (closed in 1986) and Belfast (closed in 1996) – were devolved to the Minister of Home Affairs. Since partition there have been nine prison establishments, apart from prison ships (temporary accommodation) and the internment camp at Larne (Challis, 1999). The Prison Service in Northern Ireland has experienced continuous change, and the developments in the estate have been extensive. A borstal was located at Woburn, Co. Down, and there was a Training School at Malone in Belfast (Challis, 1999). There was even an experimental open prison at a large country house at Castle Dillon in Co. Armagh. Those convicted of politically related offences have been accommodated, at various times, at Long Kesh compounds, Maze cellular, Maghaberry and Magilligan, as well as in HMP Belfast, Crumlin Road gaol, where remand prisoners were held.

The prison population in Northern Ireland had been traditionally low (below 700) until August 1971 when internment was reintroduced to cope with the upsurge in politically related community violence (Bates-Gaston, 2003). The next thirty to forty years of civil disturbance in Northern Ireland led to continuous disruption in prisons generally, where local politics and imprisonment have often been interlinked. This was a time of great unrest and frequent rioting by paramilitary groups, on both sides, within Northern Irish prisons, and the pressures on management, staff and prisoners were at times extreme. Because of community and paramilitary activity, between the late 1960s and around 2000 it is estimated that 20,000 to 32,000 people were incarcerated for politically related offences (McEvoy, 2001). This throughput and turnover within Northern Ireland's prisons could have meant that services and interventions to assist rehabilitation for those who were not convicted of politically related offences were simply considered not feasible, ignored or put on hold. Until the early 1990s that may have been partially the case – except for education and vocational training, which continued – as the system often was in crisis and reactive mode.

The role of Northern Ireland Prison Service (NIPS) staff during this period was one of ensuring the secure containment of many high-risk prisoners and maintaining social distance, because of the threats and concerns about their personal safety and often being called upon to be involved in physical reaction to disturbances, fires and riots. Those convicted of politically motivated crimes refused to engage in work, interventions and risk assessments, although education was encouraged by the political leadership. In the early 1990s, despite these ongoing challenges, offending behaviour programmes and interventions for those not convicted of political offences were being actively considered due to the introduction of psychologists into prisons. This led to professional working arrangements between NIPS and Home Office psychologists in the development of national accredited programmes.

Treatment and rehabilitation: contested concepts

Rehabilitation has gone through many manifestations over time, including penitentiary, therapeutic, social learning and rights orientated models (Rotman, 1990). The concept of 'treatment' and 'rehabilitation' in prison is contested (Rotman, 1986, 1990), especially when it follows a politically inspired agenda (see Behan, 2014b; Costelloe and Warner, 2008; Duguid, 2000). Robert Martinson's 1974 paper *What Works? – Questions and Answers about Prison Reform* reviewed 231 studies of prison rehabilitative programmes, and he concluded that '[w]ith few and isolated exceptions, the rehabilitative efforts that have been reported so far have had no appreciable effect on recidivism' (Martinson, 1974: 25). These programmes, he believed, were largely ineffective and '[w]hat we do know is that, to date, education and skill development have not reduced recidivism by rehabilitating criminals' (Martinson, 1974: 28). Despite later repudiating some of the findings, the publication of the article coincided with the rise of right-wing ideologies of the late 1970s and 1980s in the US and UK and 'provided the scientific foundation for what was to become one of the most significant shifts in modern American corrections' (Pratt, Gau and Franklin, 2011: 83). Its impact was felt far beyond the United States. Since the fallout from the publication of Martinson's *What Works?*, rehabilitation has declined internationally, and Garland

(2001) argues that it is no longer the overarching objective of the prison system. However rehabilitation has evolved and survived, and to gain acceptance in the late-modern era there has been a blurring of punitive and rehabilitative discourses, with its reinvention in political discourse '*as* punishment' (Robinson, 2008: 438; emphasis in original). Political parties that pride themselves on strong law and order policies have proudly embraced a 'rehabilitation revolution', not with the avowed objective of reintegration, but based on ideas around reducing cost, lowering crime and increasing public confidence in the penal system (Grayling, 2012). Contemporary rehabilitation practice has moved from viewing the objective as successful reintegration after incarceration to managing risk and social control in the interests of the general public (Crewe, 2012).

Defining what works

While the meaning, definition and efficacy of criminal justice rehabilitation has been debated amongst academics and practitioners for many years, in their book on *Rehabilitation*, Ward and Maruna (2007) suggest that:

> Over the last two decades empirical evidence has increasingly supported the view that it is possible to reduce reoffending rates by rehabilitating offenders rather than simply punishing them. In fact the pendulum's swing back from a pure punishment model to a rehabilitation model is arguably one of the most significant events in modern correctional policy.

The Risk-Need-Responsivity (RNR) model has been the most influential and important body of evidence-based research into international rehabilitation policy over the last forty years. This model suggests that interventions should include three main rehabilitation principles: targeting dynamic risk factors or criminogenic needs that are causally related to criminal behaviour; the risk principle, which states that higher-intensity programmes are required for individuals assessed as at higher risk of re-offending; and the responsivity principle, which takes into account individuals' personal characteristics, such as learning style, motivation and ethnic background, to ensure that the therapeutic approach is delivered in ways that make sense to the recipient (Ward and Maruna, 2007; Gannon and Ward, 2014).

This model has been challenged as being too concerned with criminogenic needs and too constrained and negative in its approach to rehabilitation. Ward and Maruna (2007) argue strongly that the RNR model is limited in several ways including: neglecting the individual's need for personal agency, ignoring the importance of the therapeutic alliance or relationship in programme delivery and being preoccupied with the individual's risks while ignoring the surrounding social and cultural systems. They believe the RNR approach is too prescriptive and non-motivational for participants.

In response to such criticisms, an alternative model – The Good Lives Model (GLM) – has been developed incorporating a strengths-based or restorative approach which builds on positive psychological theory and focuses on how an individual can contribute to society and feel good about his/her life (Ward and Brown, 2004; Ward and Gannon, 2006).

Both of these models have fuelled much debate and discussion and have evolved to an understanding of the strengths of both approaches. Marshall *et al.* (2005) and Looman and Abracen (2013) have expressed concerns about the effectiveness and outcomes of treatment programmes which use the RNR principles. The latter suggest that the incorporation of Good Lives principles, which provide individuals with optimism and also encourage their capacity to change while providing them with goals, will result in their leading more fulfilling and pro-social lives. Gannon and Ward (2014) in their critical review of evidence-based psychological practice in correctional settings draw attention to their perception of prisoner interventions as lacking in individualised and flexible client focus, disregarding the importance of therapeutic alliance (trust and respect in the client/therapist relationship) and an erosion of evidence-based psychological practice in forensic settings. They suggest that there can be tensions in forensic environments due 'to engaging in psychological practice while also obliging the risk and security policies of correctional systems' (Gannon and Ward, 2014: 435). National programmes delivered in NIPS, like Alcohol Related Violence and the Sex Offender Treatment programme, which have traditionally been based on the RNR model, have incorporated GLM principles into the theory manuals, practice and delivery.

In his review of the research into what works in reducing re-offending, McGuire (2013) argues that there is mounting evidence on the number and variety of cost-effective interventions which bring about reductions in rates of criminal recidivism. He analysed one hundred large-scale international studies published between 1985 and 2013, using meta-analyses or systematic reviews. These, according to McGuire, provide evidence indicating effective interventions for prisoners, and he concluded '[p]unitive sanctions repeatedly emerge as a failed strategy in altering offenders' behaviour' (McGuire, 2013: 1965). On the basis of the findings from the accumulated research, McGuire (ibid.) argued that:

> we can be more confident that there is a range of methods which 'work' to bring about reductions in rates of criminal recidivism. Second, there are systematic and replicable variations in effect sizes. These emerge with sufficient consistency to allow identification of features of more effective interventions, to the extent that they can be used to derive a model of 'best practice' for maximising the impact of criminal justice intervention.

McGuire (2013) argues that the most effective and consistent outcomes include structured programmes which are cognitive behavioural interventions derived from cognitive social learning theory. He emphasised the importance of specifically designed aims and targets which focus on high risk of re-offending and are delivered by specially selected and trained staff to prisoners whose needs, risks and responsivity have been assessed. He stressed the need for programmes to be integrated and supported by the organisation and monitored in various ways to ensure that the facilitators are adhering to the programme's standards and format.

However, some critics of offending behaviour programmes argue that they are used by the state to 'responsibilise', 'redeem' or 'normalise' the socially excluded (Ryan and Sim, 2007: 697). Echoing Ward and Maruna (2007), many offending behaviour programmes within contemporary rehabilitation models tend to concentrate more on 'themes of personal responsibility, choice and recognition of the moral implication of these choices' (Robinson and Crow, 2009: 121) to the detriment of the social context of criminality and punishment. There can be an over-concentration on individual factors to the neglect of structural factors. Based on ideas around 'prison works' and 'get tough on crime' agendas, Costelloe and Warner (2008: 137) contend that some of these programmes follow the 'discredited medical model of imprisonment'. They begin with an ethos that 'views the prisoner primarily as something broken in need of fixing or as an object in need of treatment'. This discourse 'frames attempts to change the inmate while ignoring the wider context from which they came and to which they will return'.

Many prisoners have shown an aversion to courses provided within prison (Crewe, 2012; Maruna, 2011), especially what are termed 'offending-behaviour' programmes. For long-term prisoners, especially lifers, participation in programmes is mandatory, and the process of achieving freedom early has become more complicated, even perplexing, leading Crewe (2012) to argue that in the late-modern prison those with 'psychological power' wield enormous influence. Prisoners become objects rather than subjects in the change process (Duguid, 2000). Harris

(2005: 315) argues that many prisoners and ex-prisoners have a negative attitude towards the concept of rehabilitation and correctional treatment programmes:

> In general, the distaste for such programs is linked to a sense that these interventions involve things 'done to' or 'prescribed for' passive recipients who are characterised as deficient, ineffectual, misguided, untrustworthy, possibly dangerous, and almost certain to get into trouble again.

Despite the 'serious questions of justice to be asked about relating the length of time a person spends in prison to the degree to which he or she co-operates with or is involved in such activities' (Coyle, 2008: 230), some of these programmes can facilitate the expression of agency of those who participate, demonstrating a desire to move away from activities that hurt others as well as desisting from criminal activity. Even though the parole and court systems demand that prisoners undertake various interventions, therapy and treatments to reduce their individual risks, they can also give individuals the opportunity of dealing with personal issues at the same time, or before they can move on to other needs. For some prisoners, attending these courses, some of which address victim empathy and restorative practices, is not only challenging their 'offending' behaviour, as desired by the state, but helps them in facing up to their transgression of the rights of others and the hurt and pain they have caused their victims.

Prison programmes

This section examines programmes and activities for prisoners in the Republic of Ireland and Northern Ireland. The latter has been more influenced by the 'what works' ethos coming from the UK Home Office/Ministry of Justice. However, in the Republic of Ireland, programmes have only latterly been developed for specific prisoner groups. In Northern Ireland, prisons became contested spaces (McEvoy, 2001) throughout the Conflict, as those convicted for politically related activities rejected the label of 'offender' or 'criminal', and therefore the need for programmes or specific interventions and supports, although many were keen to engage in education.

Republic of Ireland

There are a range of services and professional disciplines in the Republic of Ireland which provide programmes, educational opportunities and activities to encourage prisoners to move away from criminal activity. Some of these are organised by prison staff, others by outside bodies. Some programmes are offence-focused, others are educational, and some are informal activities organised by prisoners themselves. The Irish Prison Service (2013a: 4) provides programmes and activities based on the 'principles of normalisation, personal responsibility, individualisation, non-discrimination, progression and reintegration'. The Psychology Service 'addresses those factors that put offenders at risk of reoffending' (Irish Prison Service, 2011: 25) and has developed programmes particularly for those convicted of sex offences and drug-related activities. The Lifers Programme is organised for those on life sentence, and groups such as Alcoholics Anonymous, Alternatives to Violence and Grow (Get Rid Of Worry: a mental health charity) are also active in many prisons.

Sex offender programmes

Programmes for those convicted of sexual offences were introduced in prisons in the Republic of Ireland in the 1990s (IPS, 2009). This was partly due to a dramatic increase in the numbers sentenced for sex offences, rising from 183 prisoners in custody in 1994 to 390 by 2001 (Aylward, 2002: 585). A review of the Sex Offender Intervention Programme in 2008 found that participants showed 'statistically significant improvement on some but not all self-report measures of cognitive distortions, empathy, interpersonal skills, and self-regulation skills'. It concluded that among other motivations to change, including conviction and imprisonment, 'they required the additional assistance provided by the intervention program' (O'Reilly *et al.*, 2010: 109). This evaluation concluded that there were deficiencies when it came to the potential for relapse and suggested modifying the programme to provide more post-programme support in relapse management strategies, especially when prisoners return to their community (O'Reilly *et al.*, 2010).

In 2009 the Sex Offender Intervention Programme was revised with the introduction of a new three-stage initiative: Building Better Lives comprises Exploring Better Lives, Practising Better Lives and Maintaining Better Lives. Designed to be 'more flexible and responsive to individual prisoners' needs, risk and capacity' (IPS, 2009: 5), it is a 'therapeutic programme for men who acknowledge that they have committed a sexual offence and who have a desire to build a better life for themselves' (Inspector of Prisons, 2011: 15). Arbour Hill Prison in Dublin was designated as a National Centre for Sex Offenders to offer a therapeutic whole-prison environment. This new initiative recognised that '[p]rison-imposed participation is not considered an option' (IPS, 2009: 17). Nevertheless, a number of incentives to encourage participation were recommended, including the possibility of early release and/or transfer to an open prison at the later stages of sentence. From its inception in January 2009 to the end of 2011, 105 prisoners participated in the programme, 71 completed it and there were 24 prisoners participating at various stages (IPRT, 2012).

Drug treatment programmes

As in other jurisdictions, there are higher levels of illegal drug use among the prison population than the general population (National Advisory Committee on Drugs and Alcohol, 2014). In 1996, the number of heroin users was put at 66 per cent in Mountjoy, the largest prison in the Republic of Ireland (O'Mahony, 1997: 162). A later study found that lifetime cannabis use among all prisoners was 87 per cent, previous-year use was 69 per cent, and previous-month use was 43 per cent. Lifetime heroin use was 43 per cent, previous-year use was 30 per cent, and previous-month use was 11 per cent (NACDA, 2014: 1). This study also reported that '[w]omen were significantly more likely to have a lifetime history of injecting drugs than men' (NACDA, 2014: 59).

The Irish Prison Service has adopted a two-pronged approach to drug use in prison: reducing the availability of drugs through a number of security measures including installing nets over prison yards and the introduction of sniffer dogs to prevent drugs entering prisons. The second approach is at treatment level, including a programme based on the 'trans-theoretical model of behaviour change and principles of motivational and cognitive behavioural psychology' (IPS, 2011: 25). There are 24 full-time drug counselling posts and nine detoxification beds available across Irish prisons. Methadone treatment is provided in eight out of 14 prisons (Jesuit Centre for Faith and Justice [JCFJ], 2012: 78).

In 2002 the then Director General of the Irish Prison Service argued that eradicating drugs from Irish prisons was more than just a security issue. He rejected the concept of 'less-eligibility' and stressed that services to those with drug addiction 'must replicate in prison, to the maximum extent possible, the level of medical and other supports available in the community for drug dependent people' including methadone maintenance programmes, with sufficient numbers of doctors, nurses, psychologists and psychiatrists (Aylward, 2002: 584). Despite improvements in services over the last decade, the provision has been criticised as inadequate and in need of serious upgrading (JCFJ, 2012). The National Advisory Committee on Drugs and Alcohol (2014: 22) recommended improvements in health screening for prisoners on reception, more comprehensive treatment programmes, gender-specific programmes, drug-free wings and ensuring 'that those availing of treatment services in prison have a smooth transition to appropriate services on release, so that there is continuous care provided to avoid relapse or overdose'.

Education

As in other jurisdictions there is a disproportionate level of educational disadvantage among prisoners in the Republic of Ireland (O'Mahony, 1997; Morgan and Kett, 2003). The latest research on literacy levels indicated that nearly 53 per cent were in the Level One or pre-Level One category (highest is 5), and that the average literacy level of the prison population was much lower than the general population (Morgan and Kett, 2003: 35–36). Therefore there is an acute need to provide educational resources to a large constituency of people who have been failed by the education system in earlier years (Keane, 2011; Wallington, 2014).

Prison education in the Republic of Ireland has been provided since the 1970s primarily by Education and Training Boards (local education authorities), public libraries and the Open University and staffed by non-prison personnel. Along with helping people to 'cope with their sentence', the objectives of the Irish Prison Education Service are to help those in custody 'achieve personal development, prepare for life after release and establish the appetite and capacity for lifelong learning' (Irish Prison Education Service, 2007: 4). Drawing on the Council of Europe's (1990: 4) recommendations, it aims 'to develop the whole person, bearing in mind his or her social, economic and cultural context'. The educational ethos is located in an adult education approach, with 'voluntary student participation, a broad curriculum, student autonomy in subject choice, [and] student identification with their own needs' (Prison Education In-service Committee, 2002: 16–17).

Attending school is voluntary, and courses on offer range from literacy to Open University degree programmes. The wide curriculum includes subjects ranging from history and sociology to home economics, art and music. Qualifications available include, amongst others, Junior Certificate, Leaving Certificate, the European Computer Driving Licence (ECDL) and qualifications under Further Education and Training Awards Council (FETAC) schemes. Education is available in all prisons, and participation rates vary, due to the availability of programmes, levels of overcrowding and the prison population, ranging from a high of 69 per cent in Loughan House open prison to 18 per cent in Cloverhill remand prison (IPS, 2011: 23).

Volunteering

The most common form of volunteering in prison (perhaps partly because opportunities are so few) is participating in charitable activities. Sporadically, prisoners themselves – and from time to time, in collaboration with chaplains, teachers or officers – undertake charitable initiatives. The motivation to participate in these activities indicates personal development and concern for others while building human and social capital, which is essential to move away from a life of crime (see Behan, 2014a: 157–61). The activities include making furniture in workshops for children's charities, fun-runs for local children's hospitals, collections for Saint Vincent de Paul and making podiums and flags for the Special Olympics (held in Ireland in 2003). These informal activities are not prescribed, nevertheless, 'strengths-based practices ... provide opportunities ... to develop pro-social self-concepts and identity' (Burnett and Maruna, 2006: 84).

Incentivised regimes

While programmes in Irish prisons have generally been voluntary, incentives have been introduced to encourage prisoners to participate, be of good behaviour and to adopt a more pro-social lifestyle. Following the example of the Incentives and Earned Privileges scheme introduced in England and Wales in the 1990s (Cavadino, Dignan and Mair, 2013: 216–7), the Irish Prison Service introduced guidelines for Incentivised Regimes in 2012 with three levels of privilege – basic, standard and enhanced (IPS, 2012). Newly committed prisoners enter at the standard level, and they have to meet certain criteria to stay at that level. If prisoners meet certain 'standards' they can progress to the enhanced regime and receive additional privileges at that level. These regimes relate to level of gratuity, access to facilities and activities, daily regime, quality of accommodation and contact with the outside world (IPS, 2012: 4). However, a 'consistent pattern of non-compliance with behavioural standards and refusal to engage in structured activity or engagement in behaviour that constitutes a serious breach of discipline' will result in a prisoner being moved to a basic regime (IPS, 2012: 20).

Post-release support

While programmes in prison can support and assist individuals moving away from criminal activity 'the test comes after release, where options for its reinforcement are greater but, equally, so are the temptations for its abandonment' (Wallington, 2014: 18). Roberts and Hough (2005: 300) observed that, if the general public are unaware of daily life in its penal institutions, 'it seems likely that they know little about the many problems confronting ex-prisoners as they make the transition from custody to community'. O'Mahony (2002: 670) argued that the challenge is to create prison conditions and post-release through-care that will assist programmes inside 'in the enablement and empowerment of offenders, who have often serious health, social and personal problems and are seriously hampered by lack of education and employment experience'. While there have been improvements in both in-prison programmes and post-release supports in recent years, prisoners have argued that there is still much room for improvement (IPRT, 2010: 10).

There are a number of organisations and groups supporting former prisoners in their re-integration into the community. These can be broadly separated into three categories: state agencies, not-for-profit voluntary organisations and ex-prisoner projects. The last add experience to practice and provide peer support in the transition from imprisonment to the community. Evidence from ex-prisoners has identified peer-support as one of the most effective ways of supporting released prisoners (IPRT, 2010: 37). Organisations based on peer support include Soilse which primarily works with recovering drug users. The Care After Prison (2014) website describes the organisation as 'a peer-led charity organisation which provides information, referral and support services to people who have been affected by imprisonment'. Other peer-supported initiatives are for those imprisoned during the Conflict, such as Fáilte Abhaile and Abhaile Arís, which support republican former prisoners.

The non-statutory sector includes Prison AfterCare and Education (PACE) which is the largest voluntary organisation working with prisoners and ex-prisoners. The Pathways Project – an educational centre – was established in 1996 to provide continuity for those who were engaged in education in prison (Wallington, 2014). Since then, based on the experience of participants and staff, it provides both a mixture of peer support and professional interventions. Other educational projects outside Dublin include the HOPE project in Cork and the Ex-Prisoners Assistance Committee (EXPAC) in Monaghan (Irish Prison Education Service, 2014: 35).

The Irish Probation Service works both inside and outside prison to encourage prisoners to use their time in prison to address the behaviour that led to their imprisonment. Recognising the need to begin preparing for release at an early stage of incarceration, improvements have been made in connecting with prisoners who will be subject to supervision by the Probation Service after release. Like the Probation Board for Northern Ireland, it has 'resisted some of the more punitive trends' permeating in the Anglo-American approaches to prisoners and ex-prisoners, has avoided managerial influences and 'probation remains grounded in a social-work orientation' (Carr *et al.*, 2013: 69).

Northern Ireland

This section will present an overview of the development of rehabilitation pathways including education opportunities, vocational skills, as well as group and individual treatment interventions in Northern Ireland. The main focus is on prison-based developments since the early 1990s, which began with the introduction of psychologists into prisons for the first time.

Northern Ireland has two adult male prisons – Maghaberry (high security) and Magilligan (low/medium security) as well as Hydebank Wood, which houses adult women and young offenders aged 17 to 23 years. The prison population is just below 1,900, with approximately 60 adult females and 150 young offenders (Department of Justice Northern Ireland, 2014a). Those sentenced for politically motivated crimes make up around 4 per cent, and between 2006/7 and 2008/9 there has been a 202 percent increase in foreign nationals. There is a new juvenile, purpose-built centre, for under-17-year-olds, and there are further plans for step-up and step-down facilities for women at Hydebank Wood and new residential blocks at Magilligan and Maghaberry sites. There is a pre-release unit in Belfast, where mainly life-sentenced male prisoners are released to work in the community, similar to open prisons in England and Wales. The total numbers of those in custody has risen significantly from 1,318 in 2005 to around 1,900 in 2015. Life-sentenced prisoners numbered 89 in 2000 (Bates-Gaston, 2006a) and are currently (2015) just under 200. New buildings are planned on all three sites to address the increasing population, although economic austerity may delay progress.

National and international criminological and psychological research into addressing re-offending and the concept of rehabilitation underwent significant change in the late 1980s and early 1990s. The prison service in England and Wales began to explore the potential of a new rehabilitative approach, cognitive behavioural programmes, based on the "What Works" research. These developments were led by forensic psychologists being informed by contemporaneous research, mostly from North America. The first group programmes introduced into the UK were the Core Sex Offender Treatment Programme (SOTP) and a version of Reasoning and Rehabilitation (R and R) or Thinking Skills (TS), which encouraged prisoners to actively think about how they think and make decisions generally, and how those decisions had led them into criminal behaviours (Fabiano, Porporino and Robinson, 1990). With the appointment of a Chief Psychologist in 1991, the Northern Ireland Prison Service worked closely with the Offender Behaviour Unit in the UK Ministry of Justice and began implementing these programmes.

The role of the Chief Psychologist was to advise senior civil servants and prison officials on staff support, prisoner needs and services and allowed for the development of creative responses. She was given support to conduct an organisational review and prison staff survey which was the first of its kind in the UK (Bates-Gaston, 1996). Out of this research, plans were put in place to develop policies and services for both staff and prisoners within Northern Ireland prisons. This led to the existing internal occupational health and staff welfare units being supplemented by additional psychologists and also identified the need for these staff to undertake prisoner risk and needs assessments, and to provide professional reports, which in turn prompted the requirements for more prisoner-focused services, programmes and interventions in line with those being developed in the rest of the UK.

In 1992–3, the NIPS obtained training from England for prison and probation officers as well as psychologists, which allowed the multi-disciplinary delivery of the National Core Sex Offender Treatment Programme, first at Magilligan and then Maghaberry Prison (Research and Evaluation Services and Social Information Systems, 1994). The Thinking Skills programme was introduced at Maghaberry, Magilligan and Hydebank in the mid-1990s. Both the Sex Offender Treatment Programme and Thinking Skills training were shared with psychology colleagues in the Irish Prison Service, encouraging programmes and interventions in the Republic.

On reflection, these developments were innovative and bold, because they involved prison officers in the multi-disciplinary delivery of group programmes, just like their contemporaries in the rest of the UK, at a time when the Northern Ireland prison environment was very different because of the large numbers of politically related prisoners. It was a defining moment in the determination of significant changes to the work and role of the prison officer in Northern Ireland and laid the foundations for the expansion of a wide range of interventions and positive staff/prisoner engagement to promote successful resettlement. Training was also delivered by the psychologists to staff who were undertaking the role of the personal officer (a nominated officer who supports and mentors an individual prisoner), and this proactive engagement was found to be acceptable with the non-politically related prisoner. Many prison officers, too, had taken advantage of staff support through psychology counselling (over 1,300 prison officers referred from 1991 to 2001) to assist them with challenging and traumatic events in the workplace (Bates-Gaston, 2002). Staff discovered the benefits of psychological expertise in their work and, over time, accepted that psychology interventions could be useful to all. This acceptance and recognition of the usefulness of psychology within prisons had a positive effect on the organisational culture and future challenges. During the 1990s some 'normality' and positive engagement was being developed in prisons in Northern Ireland.

While the prisons and community environment during the 1990s were not always conducive to rehabilitation philosophy, several developments promoted and supported the existing psychology-led interventions further. From 2000 onwards, developments in legislation became the new and more formal motivation for the promotion of rehabilitative approaches in the criminal justice system.

Life Sentence Review Commissioners (LSRC)

The Life Sentence Review Commissioners (LSRC) replaced the Life Sentence Review Board (LSRB), a non-statutory body, as a result of a review of the Northern Ireland Prisons legislation conducted by the government in anticipation of the provisions of the Human Rights Act 1998 coming into effect in 2000. The review concluded that the existing procedures for discretionary life sentenced prisoners and those sentenced to detention at the Secretary of State's pleasure would not meet the requirements of the European Convention on Human Rights (ECHR). The legislation governing the LSRC was contained within the Life Sentences (Northern Ireland) Order 2001 and the Life Sentence Review Commissioners' Rules 2001. An independent judicial body would now make decisions on all life-sentenced prisoners, and all life-sentenced prisoners would have the punitive element of their sentence judicially determined and their suitability for release independently assessed. It led to a significant demand for increased interventions and services for prisoners as the Parole Commissioners make their decision to release based on the statutory test of whether the prisoner poses a risk of serious harm and whether that risk can safely be managed in the community. Without full risk assessments and demonstrated change through interventions, the Parole Commissioners are unlikely to grant an individual's release.

Other legislative changes

Following earlier legislation in England and Wales, the Criminal Justice Order (Northern Ireland) 2008 was introduced, with the focus being on newly created public protection sentences. This included non-life-sentenced prisoners coming under a parole system. The other sentence types are: Indeterminate Custodial Sentence (ICS), Extended Custodial Sentence (ECS) and Determinate Custodial Sentence (DCS). Each sentence had specific requirements, and all except some DCSs with less than 12 months to serve had to come before the Parole Commissioners Northern Ireland (PCNI) (established 2009) before release on licence was granted. Those subject to a DCS usually had short custody elements to their sentences and were released to the community on licence with the added condition that, if recalled, they would have to be reviewed by the PCNI process before re-release. In the period September 2013 to September 2014 DCSs made up just under 50 percent of the adult male sentenced prison population and around 66 percent of the young offender population (Department of Justice Northern Ireland, 2014a). These short sentences do not allow sufficient time to effectively address prisoners' needs in custody and may impede services for those with longer sentences.

This public protection legislation in England and Wales had proved to be problematic, as, in order to be released on licence, prisoners had to demonstrate that they had reduced their risk to society while in custody. This had placed enormous, urgent pressures on prisons to introduce a wide range of interventions to address general and specific offending behaviours, substance use and personality problems. Over 60 per cent of prisoners in England and Wales were estimated to have one or more personality difficulties (Singleton, Gatward and Meltzer, 1998). A CJINI Inspection Report into Safer Custody in NIPS, (Criminal Justice Inspection Northern Ireland, 2014) found that '90% of prisoners have a diagnosable mental health problem, substance misuse problem or both'. Education and vocational services were also under pressure to prepare the individual for release and resettlement. In England and Wales, judicial reviews were common, as legal representatives sought to ensure that their clients had access to interventions to enable them to be released. This legislation in Northern Ireland has had a similar overall impact by increasing the demands for prison and probation interventions and services.

With devolution of powers, including justice, to the Northern Ireland Assembly in 2010 public interest and accountability became enhanced. The new legislation and the establishment of criminal justice oversight bodies, including the Justice Committee, the Criminal Justice Inspectorate Northern Ireland and the Prisoner Ombudsman's office, have focused the attention of criminal justice agencies in both custody and the community on providing opportunities for higher-risk prisoners, not just life-sentenced prisoners, to demonstrate that they have reduced their risk to the public by undertaking interventions.

The response to the legislation has included the organisation of management processes in each prison with individualised sentence plans, the further development of various interventions (education, vocational skills, health-led drug and alcohol use and dependency treatments, and psychology-led therapeutic interventions and offending behavioural programmes) to provide opportunities for the prisoner to change and prepare for re-integration into society. These interventions have prompted the need for the development of various forensic and clinical assessment techniques, and of the tools to measure the individual's behaviour and attitude towards change and reduction in future risk and the need for one-to-one treatment interventions delivered by psychologists to address personality and learning difficulties. Whilst all NIPS psychology-led interventions require written informed consent and are voluntary, the public protection sentences and the parole process encourage the majority of these prisoners to take active steps to address their past law-breaking, both in custody and in the community.

Life-sentenced and offending programme developments

Between 2006 and 2007, in preparation for the new Criminal Justice Order 2008, NIPS undertook two internal psychology-led research projects, the first being a Review of Life Sentenced Prisoners (Bates-Gaston, 2006a), which examined the journey of long-term prisoners and their needs. The other was a Review of Cognitive Behavioural Programmes in NIPS (Bates-Gaston, 2006b), which explored the potential impact on demand for services emanating from the public protection sentences. From a rehabilitation and parole perspective, it was recommended that further offending-focused programmes and facilitators would be needed to deliver services. The best-practice tripartite, multi-disciplinary team approach of prison and probation officers in conjunction with prison psychologists in programme delivery had been under-resourced for some time, and NIPS recruited 20 psychology assistants to work with existing programme staff, to deliver a wider range and number of cognitive behavioural programmes and individual offence-focused therapy sessions.

Joint NIPS and PBNI programme strategy and programmes operations groups

In order to ensure that rehabilitation services, specifically offending behavioural programmes, in custody and probation were more integrated, NIPS established two working groups in the early 2000s: the Joint Strategic Programmes Group (JSPG) and the Programmes Operations Group (POG). The JSPG was to agree a strategy as to which interventions needed to be provided in both organisations to meet the needs of prisoners in transition from custody to the community, and to share resources such as training and development. The POG was to ensure that the implementation of multi-disciplinary programme delivery with probation staff in prisons ran smoothly. These arrangements were innovative and predated the Prison Review Team's (Owers, 2011) recommendation that both agencies should encourage joint working and sharing of resources. Unfortunately, these positive working arrangements were postponed by Probation due to competing priorities in October 2012 and have just been re-instated. However, these two initiatives demonstrated that NIPS had a firm commitment to joint working and the delivery of offending behaviour programmes long before the Prison Review Team's recommendations and before rehabilitation became the 'new' focus of current programmes within the Northern Ireland Prison Service.

With support from the MOJ and, later, the National Offending Management System (NOMS), NIPS had put in place a range of nationally and internationally accredited cognitive behavioural programmes with practice guidelines. The suite of programmes includes cognitive behavioural programmes which address offence-related thinking skills, sexual and intimate partner violence, drugs and alcohol as well as a wide range of motivational, educational, parenting and vocational courses, which cover most of the current population needs, although the volume of opportunities needs to be expanded to meet the growing numbers being sentenced and recalled.

NIPS also piloted a Challenge to Change Programme in 2012, which targeted those prisoners who needed to address hate-fuelled attitudes and behaviours. Since then further programmes – for example, RESOLVE (addressing anger management and violence) and new Thinking Skills – are being added to the range of possible interventions. P-ASRO (substance use) has been replaced by Building Skills for Recovery (BSR), which was delivered in NIPS by an external agency, AD:EPT, on behalf of the South Eastern Health and Social Care Trust, which provides medical health care.

There are plans to introduce an updated intimate partner violence programme in the near future. NIPS supplements and integrates its group programmes with significant, individually tailored treatment sessions delivered by Clinical and Forensic Psychologists (Bates-Gaston, et al., 2009). Most individual sessions are focused on working with those who have challenging personality disorders, past trauma and intellectual difficulties.

Education and other supportive initiatives

A recent CJINI on the Safety of Prisoners (October 2014) held by the Northern Ireland Prison Service, reported that 34 per cent of young offenders in NIPS have entry level 3 or below in literacy and 51 per cent have a numerical ability at the same low levels. Until recently education has been provided by internal teaching teams in each prison. This has now been contracted out to local education colleges, and the Young Offenders Centre has been recategorised (2015) as a secure college in the hope that a new academic ethos will encourage cultural change and educational opportunities for individuals who have been neglected in their past. In order to improve the employability of those in custody a range of qualifications are offered: essential skills in literacy, numeracy, ICT and ESOL up to Level 2, employability, personal and social skills and service industry skills, including hairdressing, retail, hospitality and catering, sport and leisure and ICT support and PC maintenance. As well as the traditional training and attainment of qualifications in trades and manufacturing, there are also plans to provide business administration and enterprise skills for prisoners across all ability levels.

There are a wide range of external providers, funded by NIPS. These organisations supplement the work of prison staff in supporting prisoners with addictions, personal development as well as financial, housing and employment problems. Restorative practices have additionally been developed and championed, with some success, by prison staff who have undertaken specialised university courses and training in the area.

The Workers Education Association established Man Matters courses in personal development, cooking for men and health promotion. A drug-free landing has been trialled at Maghaberry, and prison staff have been specially trained to work with prisoners with addictions. A Family Matters wing has also been set up at Maghaberry to encourage family relationships while a father is in custody. A vulnerable prisoner unit has also been developed at Maghaberry, while greater independence and preparation for resettlement and release has been encouraged within custody by the development of Martin House Lifer wing in Maghaberry. Chaplains and religious volunteers add significant support to prisoners and their families both in custody and in the community.

What works?

Prisoners are not a homogenous collective. They are a diverse group of individuals, in terms of biography, ability, attitudes and even in terms of their common bond: their conviction. Some have a long history of criminal activity and repeated incarceration; others are in prison for the first time. Many have complex histories, with different needs. Among prisoners in Northern Ireland and the Republic of Ireland there are greater levels of educational disadvantage, drug and alcohol addiction, mental health issues, than in the general population. Many face multiple challenges when they leave prison of finding accommodation, employment and connecting with support services as they transition to life outside. Some prisoners use their time to deal with various problems which may have led them to prison in the first place and others, perhaps, feel that they do not need supports and/or interventions. If we determine what works by an individual's change and transformation (including moving away from a life of crime), perhaps no one set of indices are a suitable method of resolving what works. What works for one individual or group may not work with another. Responses need to be tailored to an individual's assessment of needs and the context of their lives at any one time.

For example, there are characteristics like gender, age and sentence length which impact on reconviction. As individuals mature they are less likely to re-offend. Overall re-offending rates in Northern Ireland are 28 per cent for 18–19-year-olds, and only 10 per cent for 50–59-year-olds. Those over 60 have a low reconviction rate of 6 per cent. Additionally, those with significant numbers of previous convictions are also more likely to reoffend (Duncan, 2014). Therefore, understanding the complexities of re-offending and desistence is vital to the development of policies and targeting of rehabilitation services.

In Northern Ireland over the last generation, the unique characteristics of large numbers of politically related prisoners must be borne in mind when considering what works. Like other parts of the world (Israel, Saudi Arabia, Indonesia), Northern Ireland has extensive experience of large numbers of convicted prisoners who were sentenced for politically related offences (Yehoshua, 2014; Porges, 2014; Osman, 2014; Silke, 2014). These prisoners in Northern Ireland rejected the criminalisation of their activities (Campbell *et al.*, 1996; McEvoy, 2001) and therefore usually refused to participate in prison programmes or engage with the authorities in risk assessments, reports on their progress, supervision by Probation on release or the Life Sentence Review process. Compared to the general rates of offending in their jurisdictions, these high-risk prisoners appear to have low rates of reconviction. 'Overall probably less than five percent of all released terrorist prisoners will be reconvicted for involvement in terrorist-related activity' (Silke, 2014). It is useful to consider the characteristics that might set them apart from other prisoners when considering desistence and rehabilitation.

Internationally and locally, most of those convicted of politically related crimes were serving longer or life sentences, around a quarter to two-thirds had no previous convictions (Bakker, 2006; Sageman, 2004). In Northern Ireland all had a strong allegiance and identity with their particular group or faction (for example, UDA, UVF, PIRA, CIRA, RIRA, RHC and INLA) within the overarching larger republican/loyalist proscribed organisations. This cohesiveness created strong group bonds, individual support and resilience, and on release, the self-perception of the former prisoners and how they were perceived by their communities was very different to that usually experienced by other former prisoners. Some were welcomed back as heroes, and government aid in Northern Ireland – and in other countries too (Saudi Arabia, Indonesia) – greatly assisted resettlement. Therefore, it would be misleading to compare politically related prisoners with 'ordinary' prisoners because their sentence length, their age on release and their experiences in prison and resettlement are significantly different. They share many of these characteristics with life-sentenced prisoners who have low reconviction rates of between two to five per cent (Travis, 2013). However, the international consistency of low rates of re-offending in the politically related prisoners' cohort is still worth considering in the intricacies of 'What Works'.

Evaluating the impact of both rehabilitative programmes and educational courses on the change process and desistance from crime is a near impossible task. Reuss (1999: 114) was asked when conducting her research on educational programmes in prison: '"How can you show it?" or "How do you know they've changed?"' Governments and prison systems tend to determine what works by reference to the recidivism rate. The UK government's Green Paper, *Breaking the Cycle: Effective Punishment, Rehabilitation and Sentencing of Offenders* (Ministry of Justice, 2010a: 5), acknowledged that '[d]espite record spending and the highest ever prison population we are not delivering what really matters: improved public safety through more effective punishments that reduce the prospect of criminals reoffending time and time again'. Nearly 50 per cent of those released from prison in England and Wales reoffend within a year, and 25 per cent of those on community sentences did not complete them (Ministry of Justice, 2010a). These figures mirror the levels of reconviction among those released from prison in the Republic of Ireland. O'Donnell *et al.* (2008: 132) found that 49.2 per cent of former prisoners were re-imprisoned within four years of release, and IPS (2013b: 17) research among all prisoners on completion of a sentence in 2007 – based on re-offending and reconviction data up to the end of 2010 – found an overall recidivism rate of 62.8 per cent within three years, with over 80 per cent of re-offending occurring within 12 months of release. Within Northern Ireland the one year reconviction rate for adults released from custody in the 2011–2012 period was 48 per cent (Department of Justice Northern Ireland, 2014a), and for youths who received a community disposal at court requiring supervision, the one-year proven rate of re-offending was 56 per cent (Department of Justice Northern Ireland, 2014b).

To analyse what works simply by using the recidivism rate may cast a negative shadow over the efficacy of interventions and supports in prison and the work undertaken by prisoners. There are many reasons why an individual decides not to commit a crime, and these supports and educational programmes are undoubtedly helpful and in many cases effective. Data on participation in both Reasoning and Rehabilitation programmes and prison education indicate lower levels of recidivism, and graduates of these courses were found to have higher levels of personal stability, evidence of social change and greater rates of employment in comparison to others who do not participate (Duguid, 2000; Esperian, 2010; Haulard, 2001; Ministry of Justice, 2010b; Wallington, 2014). However, results from both rehabilitation and educational programmes must be interpreted cautiously, as those who have voluntarily signed up to these activities already indicate a desire to change, and the impact of participation on their perspectives and future activities is difficult to measure. Determining what works in terms of recidivism may not be appropriate to judge the success or otherwise with a methodology unsuited to the complex development of human change. Why, how and when people desist from crime occurs at the boundaries 'between developing personal maturity, changing social bonds associated with certain life transitions, and the individual subjective narrative constructions which offenders build around these key events and changes' (McNeill, 2006: 47). Accordingly, McNeill continues, '[i]t is not just the events and changes that matter; it is what these events and changes *mean* to the people involved'. However, McGuire (2013: 30–1) believes that there is also increasing evidence that with more effective supports and interventions 'such approaches can be cost effective and in addition to their impact upon recidivism can result in lower criminal justice costs', and he surmises, 'a 10% reduction in crime rates would represent an enormous benefit to any community'.

Goggin and Gendreau (2006: 209) believe that 'one can now state unequivocally that, not only do correctional treatment programmes "work" but many of the requisite conditions for their optimal effect are known'. However, some evaluations have argued that certain programmes and services are not examples of best practice (Lipsey and Cullen, 2007). Andrews and Bonta (2003) drew up best practice guidance principles they believed would create effective correctional programming which emphasised the importance of the design, implementation and maintenance of these interventions. An evaluation of behaviour programmes within prison and probation services found that over several years there was statistically significant evidence for positive movement in pre- and post-psychometric scores in the Enhanced Thinking Skills programme at Maghaberry Prison (Hatcher *et al.*, 2008). At Magilligan, prisoners undertaking the Sex Offender Treatment Programme reported that 'the programme had brought about radical personal transformation' (RESSIS, 1994: 36).

Nevertheless, there are a number of factors that impede work done by and with prisoners and professional staff in the process of change and transformation. In the Republic of Ireland, overcrowding in the prison estate has been a constant feature since the 1980s (JCFJ, 2012). Overcrowding can have a detrimental impact on, among other aspects of prison life, access to rehabilitative and educational programmes and prisoners' dignity and self-perception. The penal system in the Republic of Ireland is characterised by large numbers of prisoners serving short sentences. In 2012 over 60 per cent of committals received a sentence of less than six months, with over 80 per cent of committals under sentence for less than 12 months (IPS, 2013b: 21). This level of short sentences raises serious questions about the need for incarceration in the first instance, and the high turn-over allows little opportunity to deal with issues that may have led individuals to commit crime. In Northern Ireland the volume of short sentences is less than in the Republic. In 2013–14 just over 9 per cent of all prisoners entering prison received a sentence of six months and under, almost 10 per cent received sentences of between six and 12 months, with just under 14 per cent being imprisoned for 12 to 24 months (Department of Justice Northern Ireland, 2014a).

There are structural and institutional impediments to prisoners moving away from a life of crime, barriers that prevent them participating in society after release. However, examining what works in education and rehabilitative programmes from the perspective of a criminal justice construct is too narrow. These are only part of the reintegration jigsaw, and other aspects, especially the transition and through-care into community services are required to be very robust to enable the individual to succeed in their journey of transformation. Burnett and Maruna (2004: 395) found that, prior to their release, 80 per cent of 'persistent offenders' who had been sentenced a number of times said they wanted to 'go straight', but only 25 per cent believed they would definitely be able to do so. Building human and social capital supports and reinforces efforts to move away from a life of crime, but many prisoners and ex-prisoners have 'low social capital and have to work hard to achieve a successful conventional life' (Healy, 2010: 180). On release, some former prisoners are concerned about their own ability to cope after being in an intensely structured environment for a period of time. NIPS recall statistics indicate that many prisoners who are serving public protection sentences are returned for breaches rather than re-offending (NIPS, 2014). This can mean that an individual spends further time in prison going through the recall process with very little constructive work able to be done due to the limited time.

The lived experience of prisoners both before and during their incarceration must be considered in order to understand the dynamics of personal development and change and to determine what works. Individuals cannot be separated from the context in which they are located, or their social, economic and educational background. Otherwise, we might overemphasise or pathologise individual activity, rather than also seeking to understand actions in wider social, political and economic contexts. It is no coincidence that social class, educational disadvantage and imprisonment are related. Areas that need to be considered include the allocation of significant resources to the early years, parenting projects, resettlement, mental health services, mentoring, employment, positive social activities and services to address drug and alcohol use, expungement of sentences and societal attitudes towards ex-prisoners. Some high-risk prisoners are involved in hundreds of hours of structured time in custody (Bates-Gaston et al., 2009) with interventions at group and individual level, and yet they are often released to face limited support from resettlement authorities, restricted access to forensic mental health facilities, significant financial challenges, social isolation, poor support from family or pro-social peers, unsuitable accommodation and little hope of employment.

Change does not occur in a vacuum. Motivation to change and attempts to create a better life are not always simply down to the individual's desire for transformation. Consideration must be given to both the agency of the individual and structural impediments to change. It is arguable that prison is one of the most inappropriate places to engender change and personal transformation. As the Whitaker (1985: 90) report into the penal system in the Republic of Ireland noted, 'the greatest single obstacle to the personal development of prisoners is the nature of prison itself'. Along with the pains of imprisonment (Sykes, 1958), isolation and disempowerment can undermine the potential for putting individuals in a place where they have the space to engage and the support needed in the process of change and transformation. In the experience of those working in Northern Ireland prisons, delivery of interventions to the recommended standards and principles is challenging both in custody and in the community, due to financial constraints, which makes consistency and maintenance challenging at all levels. There is perhaps an unreasonable expectation that the programmes alone can 'fix' the sometimes lifelong and complex issues of each prisoner.

Conclusion

Change is a complex process. For education and rehabilitative programmes to 'work' requires reframing these concepts as part of a wider mosaic that begins with an individual's desire to move away from criminal activity and necessitates adequate provision of programmes, through-care, legislative change, health care services and community support. This chapter has examined the programmes and educational opportunities available to prisoners and former prisoners in the Republic of Ireland and Northern Ireland. It recognises that, despite the best efforts of prisoners themselves and professional staff, some issues are outside their area of expertise or influence. Both structure and agency must be considered. There is also a pressing need to examine ways of diverting more people who break the law away from imprisonment, especially in the Republic of Ireland, with such a high proportion of short sentences. While many programmes and interventions exist in the prison context, it also requires social and political change for individuals who have transformed themselves, either in or through prison, to fulfil their potential and continue with a process of change and transformation outside.

References

Andrews, D. A. and Bonta, J. (2003) *The Psychology of Criminal Conduct*, 3rd ed. Cincinnati OH: Anderson Publishing.

Aylward, S. (2002) 'The Irish Prison Service, past, present and future – A personal perspective' in P. O'Mahony (ed.) *Criminal Justice in Ireland*. Dublin: Institute of Public Administration.

Bakker, E. (2006) *Jihadi Terrorists in Europe, Their Characteristics and the Circumstances in which They Joined the Jihad: An Exploratory Study*. The Hague: Clingendael Institute.

Bates-Gaston, J.I. (1996) *NIPS Staff Survey*. Belfast: Northern Ireland Statistics and Research Agency (NISRA)/Northern Ireland Office (NIO).

—— (2002) *An Evaluation of Staff Support Delivered by NIPS Psychology Services*. Belfast: Internal NIPS Report.

—— (2003) 'Terrorism and imprisonment in Northern Ireland: A psychological perspective', in A. Silke (ed.) *Terrorists, Victims and Society, Psychological Perspectives on Terrorism and Its Consequences*. London: Wiley.

—— (2006a) *A Review of Life Sentenced Prisoners*. Belfast: NIPS Internal Report.

—— (2006b) *A Review of Cognitive Behavioural Programmes*. Belfast: NIPS Internal Report.

Bates-Gaston, J. I., Keown, A., Markey, K. D. and MacAllister, G. (2009) *A Review of Life Sentenced Prisoners Suspended from the Pre-release Scheme*. Belfast: NIPS Internal Report.

Behan, C. (2014a) *Citizen Convicts: Prisoners, Politics and the Vote*. Manchester: Manchester University Press.

—— (2014b) 'Learning to escape: Prison education, rehabilitation and the potential for transformation', *Journal of Prison Education and Re-entry*, 1(1): 20–31.

Burnett, R. and Maruna, S. (2004) 'So "Prison Works", does it? The criminal careers of 130 men released from prison under Home Secretary, Michael Howard', *Journal of Criminal Justice*, 43(4): 390–404.

—— (2006) 'The kindness of strangers: Strengths-based resettlement in theory and action', *Criminology and Criminal Justice*, 6: 83–106.

Campbell, B., McKeown, L. and O'Hagan, F. (1996) *Nor Meekly Serve My Time: The H-Block Struggle 1976–1981*. Belfast: Beyond the Pale Publications.

Carr, N., Healy, D., Kennefick, L. and Maguire, N. (2013) 'A review of the research on offender supervision in the Republic of Ireland and Northern Ireland', *Irish Probation Journal*, 10: 50–74.

Cavadino, M., Dignan, J. and Mair, G. (2013) *The Penal System: An Introduction*, 5th ed. London: Sage.

Challis, J. (1999) *The Northern Ireland Prison Service 1920–1990: A History*. Belfast: Northern Ireland Prison Service/The Northern Whig.

Costelloe, A. and Warner, K. (2008) 'Beyond "offending behaviour": The wider perspectives of adult education and the European Prison Rules', in R. Wright (ed.) *In the Borderlands: Learning to Teach in Prisons and Alternative Settings*, 2nd ed. San Bernardino: California State University.

Council for Social Welfare (1983) *The Prison System*. Dublin: Council for Social Welfare.

Council of Europe (1990) *Education in Prison*. Strasbourg: Council of Europe.

Coyle, A. (2008) 'The treatment of prisoners: International standards and case law', *Legal and Criminological Psychology*, 13: 219–30.

Crewe, B. (2012) *Prisoner Society: Power, Adaptation and Social Life in an English Prison*. Oxford: Oxford University Press.

Criminal Justice Inspection Northern Ireland (CJINI) (2014) *The Safety of Prisoners Held by the Northern Ireland Prison Service – 22 October 2014: A Joint Inspection by Criminal Justice Inspection and the Regulation and Quality Improvement Authority*. Belfast: Criminal Justice Inspection Northern Ireland. Available at www.cjini.org/TheInspections/Inspection-Reports/Latest-Publications.aspx?did=1409 (accessed 14 October 2014).

Department of Justice Northern Ireland (2014a) *Analysis of NIPS Prison Population from 1/07/2013 to 30/09/2014*. Available at www.dojni.gov.uk/index/ni-prison-service/nips-population-statistics-2/060-population-snapshot-2014-10-01-04-00-10.pdf (accessed 5 October 2014).

—— (2014b) *Youth Reoffending in Northern Ireland (2011/2012 Cohort)*, Research and statistical bulletin 19/2014. Available at www.dojni.gov.uk/index/statistics-research/stats-research-publications/reoffending-stats-and-research/r-s-bulletin-19-2014-youth-reoffending-in-northern-ireland-2011-12-cohort.htm (accessed 20 December 2014).

Duguid, S. (2000) *Can Prisons Work? The Prisoner as Object and Subject in Modern Corrections*. Toronto: University of Toronto Press.

Duncan, L. (2014) *Department of Justice Northern Ireland, 2014a) Adult Reoffending in Northern Ireland (2011/2012 Cohort)*. Research and statistical bulletin 18/2014. Available at www.dojni.gov.uk/index/statistics-research/stats-research-publications/reoffending-stats-and-research/r-s-bulletin-18-2014-adult-reoffending-in-northern-ireland-_2011-12-cohort.htm (accessed 14 December 2014).

Esperian, J. (2010) 'The effect of prison education programs on recidivism', *Journal of Correctional Education*, 61(3): 316–34.

Fabiano, E. A., Porporino, F. J. and Robinson, D. (1990) *Rehabilitation through Clearer Thinking: A Cognitive Model of Correctional Intervention* (Research Brief No.B-04). Ottawa: Correctional Service of Canada.

Gannon, T. A. and Ward, T. (2014) 'Where has all the psychology gone? A critical review of evidence-based psychological practice in correctional settings', *Aggression and Violent Behaviour*, 19(4): 435–46.

Garland, D. (2001) *The Culture of Control: Crime and Social Order in Contemporary Society*. Oxford: Oxford University Press.

Goggin, C. and Gendreau, P. (2006) 'The implementation and maintenance of quality services in Offender Rehabilitation Programmes', in C. Hollin and E. Palmer (eds) *Offending Behaviour Programmes: Development, Application, and Controversies*. Chichester: John Wiley.

Grayling, C. (2012) 'Reducing reoffending and improving rehabilitation'. Available at www.gov.uk/government/news/rehabilitation-revolution-next-steps-announced (accessed 10 December 2014).

Harris, M.K. (2005) 'In search of common ground: The importance of theoretical orientations in criminology and criminal justice', *Criminology and Public Policy*, 4: 311–28.

Hatcher, R., Bilby, C., Gunby, C., Hollin, C., Palmer, E. and McGuire, J. (2008) *An Evaluation of Offending Behaviour Programmes within the Prison and Probation Services of Northern Ireland*. Northern Ireland Office Research and Statistical Series Report No. 17, Belfast: Northern Ireland Office.

Haulard, E. (2001) 'Adult education: A must for our incarcerated population', *Journal of Correctional Education*, 52 (4): 157–59.

Healy, D. (2010) *The Dynamics of Desistance: Charting Pathways through Change*. Cullompton: Willan.

Inspector of Prisons (2011) *Report of an Inspection of Arbour Hill Prison*. Nenagh: Inspector of Prisons.

International Centre for Prison Studies (2015) *World Prison Brief*. Available at www.prisonstudies.org (accessed 3 January 2015).

Irish Commission for Justice and Peace (1986) *Response to the Report of the Committee of Inquiry into the Penal System*. Dublin: Irish Commission for Justice and Peace.

Irish Penal Reform Trust (IPRT) (2010) *Reintegration of Prisoners in Ireland*. Dublin: Irish Penal Reform Trust.

—— (2012) *Reports on Arbour Hill Prison Published*. Available at www.iprt.ie/contents/2312 (accessed 1 February 2014).

Irish Prison Education Service (2007) *Directory of Irish Prison Education*. Longford: Irish Prison Service.

—— (2014) *Directory of Prison Education*. Longford: Irish Prison Education Service.

Irish Prison Service (IPS) (2009) *Sex Offender Management Policy: Reducing Re-offending, Enhancing Public Safety*. Longford: Irish Prison Service.

—— (2011) *Annual Report 2010*. Longford: Irish Prison Service.

—— (2012) *Incentivised Regimes*. Longford: Irish Prison Service.

—— (2013a) *Annual Report 2012*. Longford: Irish Prison Service.

—— (2013b) *Recidivism Study*. Longford: Irish Prison Service.

Jesuit Centre for Faith and Justice (JCFJ) (2012) *The Irish Prison System: Vision, Values, Reality*. Dublin: Jesuit Centre for Faith and Justice.

Keane, M. (2011) *The Role of Education in Developing Recovery Capital in Recovery from Substance Addiction*. Dublin: Soilse Drug Rehabilitation Programme.

Lipsey, M. W. and Cullen, F. T. (2007) 'The effectiveness of correctional rehabilitation: A review of systematic reviews', *Annual Review of Law and Social Science*, 3: 297–320.

Looman, J. and Abracen, J. (2013) 'The Risk Need Responsivity Model of offender rehabilitation: Is there really a need for a paradigm shift?', *International Journal of Behavioural Consultation and Therapy*, 8: 30–6.

MacBride, S. (1982) *Report of the Commission of Enquiry into the Penal System*. Dublin: Ward River Press.

Marshall, W. L., Ward, T., Mann, R. E., Moulden, H., Fernandez, Y. M., Serran, G. and Marshall, L. E. (2005) 'Working positively with sexual offenders maximizing the effectiveness of treatment', *Journal of Interpersonal Violence*, 20(9): 1096–114.

Martinson, R. (1974) 'What works? Questions and answers about prison reform', *The Public Interest*, 35: 22–54.

Maruna, S. (2011) 'Why do they hate us?: Making peace between prisoners and psychology', *International Journal of Offender Therapy and Comparative Criminology*, 55: 671–5.

McEvoy, K. (2001) *Paramilitary Imprisonment in Northern Ireland: Resistance, Management, and Release*. Oxford: Oxford University Press.

McGuire, J. (2013) '"What works" to reduce re-offending: 18 years on', in L. A. Craig, L. Dixon and T. A. Gannon (eds) *What Works in Offender Rehabilitation: An Evidence-based Approach to Assessment and Treatment*. Chichester: Wiley-Blackwell.

McNeill, F. (2006) 'A desistance paradigm for offender management', *Criminology and Criminal Justice*, 6(1): 39–62.

Ministry of Justice (2010a) *Do Cognitive Skills Programmes Work with Offenders*. London: Ministry of Justice. Available at www.swmprobation.gov.uk/wp-content/uploads/2010/06/What-works-Cognitive-skills. pdf (accessed 1 February 2014).

—— (2010b) *Breaking the Cycle: Effective Punishment, Rehabilitation and Sentencing of Offenders: Creating a Safe, Just and Democratic Society*. Available at www.justice.gov.uk%2Fconsultations%2Fdocs%2Fbreaking-the-cycle.pdf&ei=83-hVKSUEceBU5WSgKAD&usg=AFQjCNH_jjXJctHTNahobABINZwGFJ8a4A (accessed 18 August 2014).

Morgan, M. and Kett, M. (2003) *The Prison Adult Literacy Survey: Results and Implications*. Dublin: Irish Prison Service.

National Advisory Committee on Drugs and Alcohol (NACDA) (2014) *Study on the Prevalence of Drug Use, including Intravenous Drug Use and Blood-borne Viruses among the Irish Prisoner Population*. Dublin: NACDA.

Northern Ireland Prison Service (NIPS) (2014) *Prison Population Review. A Review of the Factors Leading to the Growth in Prisoner Numbers between 2009–2013*. Belfast: NIPS internal report.

O'Donnell, I., Baumer, E. and Hughes, N. (2008) 'Recidivism in the Republic of Ireland', *Criminology and Criminal Justice*, 8(2): 123–46.

O'Mahony, P. (1997) *Mountjoy Prisoners: A Sociological and Criminological Profile.* Dublin: Government Publications.

—— (2002) 'Introduction to crime prevention, crime reduction and treatment of offenders', in P. O'Mahony (ed.) *Criminal Justice in Ireland.* Dublin: Institute of Public Administration.

O'Reilly, G., Carr, A., Murphy, P. and Cotter, A. (2010) 'A controlled evaluation of a prison-based sexual offender intervention program', *Sexual Abuse: A Journal of Research and Treatment,* 22: 95–111.

O'Sullivan, E. and O'Donnell, I. (2012) *Coercive Confinement in Ireland: Patients, Prisoners and Penitents.* Manchester: Manchester University Press.

Osman, S. (2014) 'Radicalisation, recidivism and rehabilitation: Convicted terrorists and Indonesian prisons', in A. Silke (ed.) *Prisons, Terrorism and Extremism: Critical Issues in Management, Radicalisation and Reform.* Abingdon and New York: Routledge.

Owers, A. (2011) *Review of the Northern Ireland Prison Service.* Belfast: Prisons Review Team. Available at www.dojni.gov.uk/index/ni-prison-service/nips-publications/reportsreviews-nips/owers-review-of-the-northern-ireland-prison-service.pdf (accessed 1 November 2012).

Porges, M. (2014) 'Saudi Arabia's "soft" approach to terrorist prisoners: A model for others?', in *Prisons, Terrorism and Extremism. Critical Issues in Management, Radicalisation and Reform.* Abingdon and New York: Routledge.

Pratt, T., Gau, J. and Franklin, T. (2011) *Key Ideas in Criminology and Criminal Justice.* London: Sage.

Prison Education In-Service Committee (2002) *Report.* Dublin: Irish Prison Service. (pp. 16–17).

Research and Evaluation Services and Social Information Systems (RESSIS) (1994) *A Review of the Sex Offenders' Programme at Magilligan Prison, Report Prepared on Behalf of the Northern Ireland Office (NIO).* Belfast: REISS.

Reuss, A. (1999) 'Prison(er) education', *The Howard Journal,* 38: 113–27.

Roberts, J. and Hough, M. (2005) *Understanding Public Attitudes to Criminal Justice.* Berkshire: Open University Press.

Robinson, G. (2008) 'Late modern rehabilitation: The evolution of a penal strategy', *Punishment and Society,* 10(4): 431–47.

Robinson, G. and Crow, I. (2009) *Offender Rehabilitation: Research and Practice.* London: Sage.

Rogan, M. (2011) *Prison Policy in Ireland: Politics, Penal-welfarism and Political Imprisonment.* Abingdon: Routledge.

—— (2013) 'The Irish penal system: Pragmatism, neglect and the effects of austerity', in V. Ruggiero and M. Ryan (eds) *Punishment in Europe: A Critical Anatomy of Penal Systems.* Basingstoke: Palgrave Macmillan.

Rotman, E. (1986) 'Do criminal offenders have a constitutional right to rehabilitation?', *Journal of Criminal Law and Criminology,* 77, 1023–68.

—— (1990) *Beyond Punishment: A New View of the Rehabilitation of Criminal Offenders.* New York: Greenwood Press.

Ryan, M. and Sim, J. (2007) 'Campaigning for and campaigning against prisons: Excavating and reaffirming the case for prison abolition', in Y. Jewkes (ed.) *Handbook on Prisons.* Cullompton: Willan.

Sageman, M. (2004) *Understanding Terrorist Networks.* Philadelphia: University of Pennsylvania Press.

Silke, A. (2014) 'Risk assessment of terrorist prisoners', in A. Silke (ed.) *Prisons, Terrorism and Extremism. Critical Issues in Management, Radicalisation and Reform.* Abingdon and New York: Routledge.

Singleton, N., Gatward, R. and Meltzer, H. (1998) *Psychiatric Morbidity among Prisoners in England and Wales.* London: Stationery Office.

Sykes, G. (1958) *The Society of Captives.* Princeton NJ: Princeton University Press.

Tomlinson, M. (1995) 'Imprisoned Ireland', in V. Ruggiero, M. Ryan and J. Sim (eds) *Western European Penal Systems.* London: Sage.

Travis, A. (2013) 'Prisons' risk test for temporary freed lifers is inadequate, say watchdogs'. *The Guardian,* 12 September. Available from: http://gu.com/p/3tkpp/stw (accessed 12 September 2013).

Wallington, J. (2014) *Prison Education, the Pathways Project and Desistance Theory.* Dublin: unpublished paper.

Ward, T. and Brown, M. (2004) 'The Good Lives Model and conceptual issues in offender rehabilitation', *Psychology, Crime and Law,* 10: 243–57.

Ward, T. and Gannon, T. A. (2006) 'Rehabilitation, etiology, and self-regulation: The comprehensive good lives model of treatment for sexual offenders', *Aggression and Violent Behavior,* 11(1): 77–94.

Ward, T. and Maruna, S. (2007) *Rehabilitation.* Abingdon: Routledge.

Whitaker, T. K. (1985) *Report of the Committee of Inquiry into the Penal System.* Dublin: Stationery Office.

Yehoshua, S. (2014) 'The Israeli experience of terrorist leaders in prison: Issues in radicalisation and de-radicalisation', in A. Silke (ed.) *Prisons, Terrorism and Extremism: Critical Issues in Management, Radicalisation and Reform.* Abingdon and New York: Routledge.

Part III
Contexts of crime

19

The inclusion and juridification of victims on the island of Ireland

Shane Kilcommins and Luke Moffett

Introduction

Concern for crime victims has been a growing political issue in improving the legitimacy and success of the criminal justice system through the rhetoric of rights. Since the 1970s there have been numerous reforms and policy documents produced to enhance victims' satisfaction in the criminal justice system. Both the Republic of Ireland and Northern Ireland have seen a sea-change in more recent years from a focus on services for victims to a greater emphasis on procedural rights. The purpose of this chapter is to chart these reforms against the backdrop of wider political and regional changes emanating from the European Union and the European Court of Human Rights and to critically examine whether the position of crime victims has actually ameliorated.

While separated into two legal jurisdictions, the Republic of Ireland and Northern Ireland as common law countries have both grappled with similar challenges in improving crime victim satisfaction in adversarial criminal proceedings. This chapter begins by discussing the historical and theoretical concern for crime victims in the criminal justice system and how this has changed in recent years. The rest of the chapter is split into two parts focusing on the Republic of Ireland and Northern Ireland. Both parts examine the provision of services to victims and the move towards more procedural rights for victims in terms of information, participation, protection and compensation. The chapter concludes by finding that despite being different legal jurisdictions, the Republic of Ireland and Northern Ireland have introduced many similar reforms for crime victims in recent years.

Epistemic shifts in knowing the victim in the criminal process

For much of the nineteenth and twentieth centuries, victims were written out of the State-accused justice system, their absentee status quickly acquiring a relative permanency, 'fixity' and immovability. Their experiences were rooted exclusively through an 'equality of arms' epistemic framework, ensuring that they were interpreted and understood around an axis that focused on the accused and his/her safeguards. Their voices were not heard – and were not capable of being understood – given the commitments, value choices and governing principles of this institutional arrangement. In the last four decades, however, victims are again returning to centre stage in western jurisdictions. Justice systems are partially being reconstructed as they demonstrate an increased sensitivity to the needs and concerns of victims of crime. As Garland (2001: 11) has noted:

> The victim is no longer an unfortunate citizen who has been on the receiving end of a criminal harm and whose concerns are subsumed within the public interest... The victim is now ... a much more representative character, whose experience is taken to be collective, rather than individual and atypical.

This 'vision of the victim as Everyman' is part of a 'new cultural theme', a 'new collective meaning of victimhood' (2001: 12) that is increasingly represented in social, political and media circles. The pattern of the representation of the victim is broadly accurate as it relates to Ireland. Victims of crime are now re-emerging again as important stakeholders.

This has been scaffolded by a number of international legal instruments which have also promoted recognition of the needs of victims within criminal justice systems. The United Nations General Assembly, for example, adopted the *Declaration of Basic Principles of Justice for Victims of Crime and Abuse of Power* in 1985. It has been described as providing 'a benchmark for victim-friendly legislation and policies' (van Dijk, 2005: 202; Doak, 2003: 10). The Declaration set forth a number of non-legally binding rights (Aldana-Pindell, 2004: 618), which include the right to be treated with respect and recognition, to be referred to adequate support services and to receive information about the progress of the case. The European Convention on Human Rights has also been interpreted in ways that began to afford rights to victims of crime. Though the Convention does not explicitly refer to victims of crime, the jurisprudence of the Court has placed obligations on member states to criminalise wrongdoing, 'to take preventive operational measures', to investigate and give reasons and to adequately protect victims and witnesses at various stages in the criminal process. In 1996, for example, the Court in *Doorson v The Netherlands*[1] expanded its interpretation of Article 6, primarily concerned with the rights of defendants in criminal proceedings, to take account of the rights of vulnerable witnesses and victims.

A literal, formalistic approach to the Convention has been rejected in favour of a broader reading that encompasses principles which command that 'rules in the rule book capture and enforce moral rights' (Dworkin, 1985: 11–12). Such an expansionary interpretation acts as a counterpoint to the hegemonic dominance of state–accused relations and the exclusiveness, in particular, of accused rights as 'trump cards'. Facilitated by this human rights jurisprudence, we are thus witnessing a very gradual concretisation of the rights of victims of crime (Emmerson et al., 2007: 741–784; Doak, 2008; De Than, 2003), which governments are required to respect 'case by case, decision by decision' (Dworkin, 1998: 223). This jurisprudence has been referred to in the Irish courts. For example, Charleton J., in examining the exclusionary rule in *People (DPP) v Cash*[2] in the Republic of Ireland, noted that 'the entire focus is on the accused and his rights; the rights of the community to live safely have receded out of view'. He drew attention to the European Convention on Human Rights and particularly the decision of *X and Y v The Netherlands*[3] which suggests that rules which hinder a fair prosecution may be incompatible with the Convention. He then emphasised the following principle:

> Criminal trials are about the rights and obligations of the entire community; of which the accused and the victim are members... The cases of *J.T.* [discussed below] and ... *X. and Y.*

make it clear that the victim, being the subject of a crime, can have interests which should be weighed in the balance as well of those of the accused.

The Council of Europe also recognised from the 1970s onwards the importance of preventing secondary victimisation. It has done this through the adoption of a series of conventions (for example, The Convention on Action against Trafficking in Human Beings, 2005) and recommendations (Muller-Rappard, 1990). The European Union has more recently begun to focus on the area of criminal justice. In March 2001, the Council adopted a *Framework Decision on the Standing of Victims in Criminal Proceedings*, which provides for minimum rights (including the right to be heard and furnish evidence, access to relevant information, the opportunity to participate and the right to compensation) to be ensured in all the territories of the EU. Based on a proposal from the EU Commission, the Council also adopted on 29 April 2004 a Directive on *Compensation to Crime Victims*, which is designed to reduce the disparities in the compensation schemes of various member states.[4] More recently the European Commission has identified as a strategic priority the protection of victims of crimes and the establishment of minimum standards. A draft Directive establishing minimum standards on the rights, support and protection of victims of crime – organised around the tripartite dimensions of information, participation and protection – has been adopted and member states are given until 2015 to transpose it into law.[5] This Directive marks the endpoint of a somewhat haphazard transitory phase, commencing in the 1970s. From November 2015, a more sustained, systematised approach is demanded, one where criminal justice agencies are required to take account of the needs and concerns of victims of crime in their decision-making processes. Through its directly binding and enforceable provisions, it will act as an emboldening juristic reference point, ensuring the better accommodation of victims of crime in all criminal processes and practices.

All of this impetus is largely inclusionary. The 'axis of individualisation' in the criminal justice process – which for so long was directed only at accused/offenders, the causes of their wrongdoing (including 'othering') and their right to protection *from* the State – has now bifurcated to embrace the multi-faceted experiences of victimhood. This of course disturbs older, hegemonic ways of doing things (an accused/offender organising logic that infused a police–public interest-prosecutions-prisons model of justice) and the reified, exclusive voices of certain actors that were central to that process (prosecution and defence lawyers, policing authorities and judges). Writing victims into the criminal justice story necessarily creates disturbances and establishes competing tensions (Kilcommins *et al.*, 2004: 150). Most people would accept that these tensions and disturbances are necessary so as to create a more communicative process, one which permits victims to recover, to some extent, their centrality in 'the Conflict'. Some commentators, however, urge caution, pointing to the power inherent in the image of the 'suffering victim' and its potential to embrace punitiveness (O'Flaherty, 2002: 375; Fennell, 2001: 54). As McCullagh has noted, 'victim discourse in Ireland has achieved the status of being both unchallenged and unchallengeable' (McCullagh, 2014). These concerns about the coercive potential of victim discourse are, of course, real. We should be wary of the possibility of political or media manipulation, or the depiction of the criminal justice system as a 'zero-sum game' where gains for victims must be at the expense of those accused of crime. That said, we should also be mindful that victim ideology is not just the manifestation of a sinister state or the product of media-exaggerated alarm about law and order. Instead its recent emergence must be seen much more as a response to a previous scandalous neglect, as a justified attempt to correct an imbalance in which the victim was constituted as a 'silent abstraction, a background figure whose individuality hardly registered' (Garland, 2001: 179).

The experience of crime victims in the Republic of Ireland

The return of the victim

A number of factors have facilitated an increased awareness of victims in western criminal justice systems in the mid to late twentieth century. To begin with, the introduction of state victim compensation programmes can be viewed as an early attempt to move victims away from the periphery of the criminal process. In England and Wales, for example, Margaret Fry proposed a scheme of State compensation for the victims of violence as early as 1957. In 1964, a Criminal Injuries Compensation Scheme actually came into operation following the publication of a White Paper, *Compensation for Victims of Crimes of Violence*. Specific victimological studies became more prominent and began to direct the criminological gaze away from its focus on offenders, towards the victim's experience and responsibility (von Hentig, 1948; Mendelsohn, 1956; Wolfgang, 1958). These studies, among others, were important in generating academic interest in victims of crime. They were followed up by the introduction of mass victimisation surveys, commencing in the 1970s in the US before also being employed in the early 1980s in the UK (Hoyle, 2012), which among other things drew attention to the under recording of crime, repeat victimisation, fear of crime and victims' experiences with various criminal justice agencies such as the police, prosecutors, trial judges and other court personnel (Henderson, 1985: 937–1021).

In the Republic of Ireland, studies such as that undertaken by Breen and Rottman (1985), O'Connell and Whelan (1994) and Watson (2000) all began to highlight the experiences of victims (McCullagh, 1986: 13–14). However, mass crime victimisation studies had a somewhat sluggish trajectory when compared with other jurisdictions (commencing in the US in 1972 and the UK in 1982), hindered no doubt by the absence of a strong criminal justice research culture and successive governments' dismissive attitude towards policy based on crime data and crime statistics (Kilcommins *et al.*, 2004: 72–4; Cotter, 2005: 295). Notwithstanding such inertia, mass crime victimisation surveys commenced in 1998 with the introduction of a crime segment into the Quarterly National Household survey (follow up studies were conducted in 2003, 2006 and 2010). Since 2002, Garda public attitude surveys have also been conducted (though they are not annual); they focus, among other things, on individuals' experiences and fears of crime.

It is argued that the growth in the women's movement also 'raised the consciousness of women to the oppression of criminal violence' (Young, 2006: 3; Moore Walsh, 2013: 182–9).[6] More specifically, increased self-activism also ensured that victims of crime became more visible again (Maguire, 1991: 370). The first domestic abuse shelter, for example, was established in 1974 (Moore Walsh, 2013: 188). The first Rape Crisis Centre was set up in Dublin in 1977, and Derek Nally established Victim Support in 1985 (Cohen, 2006; Coffey, 2006; McGovern, 2002; Rogan 2006a; and Cotter, 2005). Moreover the revelations brought about as a result of inquiries over the last two decades into Church sexual abuse and institutional abuse – which occurred in the carceral archipelago that emerged post-Independence – is now very much part of the *Zeitgeist* (Rafferty and O'Sullivan, 1999). Among other things, it has helped to raise experiences of victimhood in the collective conscience and awareness of illegitimate and abusive hierarchies of dominance. Finally, as a result of increasing concerns about rising crime rates in western countries from the 1970s onwards and the perceived failure of correctionalist criminal justice projects to rehabilitate offenders, it is not surprising, according to commentators such as David Garland, that the 'aim of serving victims has become part of the redefined mission of all criminal justice agencies' (2001: 121).[7] This has resulted in a partial reorientation of the criminal justice system as it 'reinvents itself as a service organisation for individual victims rather than merely a public law enforcement agency' (ibid.: 122; Goodey, 2005: 35). This new emphasis on victims is evident for example in comments by the then Minister for Justice, Equality and Defence, Alan Shatter, who stated:

> The victims of crime and their families must no longer be silent partners in the criminal process. It flies in the face of justice to shut victims of crime out of the very process that is designed to address the wrongs they have suffered. Giving victims a real voice in the criminal process is vital because it contributes to dignity, self-esteem and the potential for moving on with one's life.[8]

Whilst it is clear – particularly when viewed over a long past – that victims are re-emerging as stakeholders, it would be unwise to over sentimentalise the progress that has been made. Many advancements have been piecemeal in nature, their presence often the product of fortuitous, but isolated, determinants. These included the existence of effective lobbyists and claims-makers, the cooperation and commitment of key individual 'voices' in various criminal justice and voluntary support agencies, outlying examples of expansive judicial interpretation and the enactment of various disparate legislative provisions. Sustained progress has been hampered by the absence of any unified field about the plight of victims of crime in the criminal process. This may in part be attributable to the almost inevitable lack of resources, or the excuse thereof (Grozdanova and de Londras, 2014), the constant dissonance that exists between criminal justice policy and practice (C. Hamilton, 2014: 55) and various embedded practices and institutional ways of doing things. The importance of adversarialism, for example, became deeply ingrained over the last 150 years as the appropriate means of resolving criminal disputes (Damaska, 1986: 88). This deep commitment to the reception and observation of unmediated *viva voce* testimony is grounded in the need to uphold the integrity of the adjudicative process and minimise the risk of misdecision. Its reification as the only way of 'doing justice', however, conceals the extent to which it is rooted in a State-accused logic of action, one which is unwilling to countenance the discriminatory assumptions and biases inherent within such an epistemic paradigm. In addition to the obstacles posed by embedded practices, progress has also been stymied by the unwillingness of the body politic, particularly since the late 1990s, to put the inclusion of victims at the centre of the criminal justice agenda, preferring instead to pursue an expressive agenda of 'governing through crime' with its micro focus on the technologies of protection and the adoption of repressive laws against the outside 'enemy' (Vaughan and Kilcommins, 2008: 123–4; C. Hamilton, 2014: 31–55).

Accommodating victims through service provision

Service provision for victims of crime in the Republic of Ireland has expanded in recent decades. The Victims Charter (Department of Justice, Equality and Law Reform, 2010), for example, marked an important policy development (McGovern, 2002: 393; Rogan, 2006a: 153). This Charter was produced by the Department of Justice, Equality and Law Reform in September 1999 (and was revised in 2010), reflecting the 'commitment to giving victims of crime a central place in the criminal justice system' (Department of Justice, Equality and Law Reform, 1999: 2). It sets out the entitlements a victim has from various services such as the DPP, but it does not confer legal rights.[9] The needs of crime victims are also addressed by a wide variety of victims' organisations, alliances and associations. These operate both at the national and local level and include organisations such as Advic, Amen, Victim Support at Court, National Crime Victims' Helpline, National Sexual Violence Helpline, National Domestic Violence Helpine, Rape Crisis Network Ireland, Support after Homicide, Children At Risk in Ireland (CARI), Irish Tourist

Assistance Service, One in Four, Sexual Violence Centre Cork and Women's Aid. Whilst a significant proportion are specialised in dealing with specific types of victim or services, there are also some key national groups. For example, the National Crime Victims Helpline was launched in 2005. Similarly, Victim Support at Court provides support to witnesses and victims both before and during court proceedings, including pre-trial visits and court accompaniment during proceedings. The Victims' Rights Alliance, which was launched in November 2013, is an amalgam of victims' support and human rights organisations with the purpose of ensuring that the new Victims' Rights Directive is implemented within the proposed time frame (by November 2015). SAFE Ireland is an organisation established to raise awareness about the prevalence of domestic violence and to advocate on behalf of its victims. Other associations and groups include the Irish Road Victims Association (established in 2012) and the PARC road safety group (established in 2006), which offer support to road traffic victims and their families.

Furthermore, as far back as 1974, a Criminal Injuries Compensation Tribunal was established by the then Government to administer a scheme designed to alleviate some of the financial difficulties experienced by victims of violent crime and their families. The purpose of this scheme was to compensate individuals for losses arising from personal injuries as a result of violent crime or acquired while assisting another individual in preventing a crime or saving a human life. Individuals eligible to apply for compensation under this scheme include the injured person(s), the immediate family of the injured person(s) if the victim has died as a result of the crime, or those responsible for looking after the injured party. The Office of the Director of Public Prosecutions has also been active in respect of victims' needs and concerns. A *Reasons for Decisions* pilot project, for example, commenced in Ireland in October 2008. Ordinarily the DPP is under no obligation to give reasons in respect of a decision not to prosecute, as established in cases such as *The State (McCormack) v Curran*[10] and *Eviston v DPP*.[11] The project, however, reverses this rule as it relates to homicide offences such as murder, manslaughter, infanticide, fatalities in the workplace and vehicular manslaughter.

The Courts Service offers referral, liaison and support services to victims and has issued a number of publications including *Going to Court* and *Explaining the Courts*. The Committee for Judicial Studies also recently published a guide for the Irish judiciary entitled *The Equal Treatment of Persons in Court: Guidance for the Judiciary* (2011). A pilot pre-trial procedure, aimed at alleviating the trauma for witnesses by reducing delays and adjournments in trials, was commenced in Dublin Circuit Court and in the Midland and South Eastern Circuit Courts in 2013. The introduction of restorative justice in Ireland can also be seen as a response to the dissatisfaction experienced by victims under the ordinary adversarial justice system. Part of its attractiveness is its potential to refocus the problem of crime to the harms caused to individual victims and local communities. By divesting the state of ownership of the crime problem and through dismantling the 'equality of arms' conflict approach, the restorative justice process is designed to empower victims and local communities to give their accounts in their own terms free from the strictures of formal adversarialism (Kilkelly, 2006: 77–84).

The Gardaí have given a number of commitments to victims of crime including an assurance regarding the provision of information on the progress of a case and on the prosecution process, as set out in its *Charter for Victims of Crime*. The Garda Victim Liaison Office, for example, is responsible for developing Garda Policy on victims of crime and for ensuring the implementation of the Garda aspect of the Victims' Charter. Garda Family Liaison Officers have been introduced to keep crime victims informed of developments and provide support to those affected by traumatic crimes such as homicide or kidnap, where this is deemed appropriate by the local Superintendent. Garda Ethnic Liaison Officers are trained to provide specific support and advice to victims of racist incidents, and a liaison scheme is also provided to the Lesbian, Gay,

Bisexual and Transgender Community. The Gardaí have also recently adopted updated policies on domestic violence and on sexual violence, including the sexual abuse of children.

The juridification of victims' inclusion

In recent years, the courts and legislature in the Republic of Ireland have begun to pay greater attention to the interests of victims of crime, though admittedly the trajectory is a fragmented one rather than constituting anything resembling a concerted practice or strategic vision. In detailing examples, one can refer to the introduction of live television links in the courtroom; the admission of video-recordings, depositions and out of court statements in certain circumstances; greater flexibility on the rules relating to eye witness identification of the perpetrators of crime; a more secularised and (somewhat) inclusionary interpretation of the rules relating to the competency of witnesses to testify at trial; and less rigidity and exclusionary bias in the circumstances in which the spouse of an accused could give evidence for the prosecution in a case (Jackson, 1993: 202). Over the years the common law also devised particular corroboration rules in respect of certain categories of 'suspect' witnesses such as sexual complainants, children and accomplices. The previously fossilised exclusionary assumptions underpinning the perception of some victims/witnesses in the Irish criminal justice system is evident, for example, in the law on the corroboration of sexual complaints. In the past the evidence of a complainant in a sexual offence case required a mandatory warning to the jury on the dangers of acting on such evidence alone. This rule was justified 'by the fear that complaints of sexual offences may sometimes be the product of spite, jealousy, psychological denial of having consented, or a reaction to having been jolted; that women with nothing to lose might seek to subject a man of high social standing to blackmail; and that the accusation of rape is easily made, but difficult to defend' (Healy, 2004: 157). More recently, however, these essentialised notions about the traits and motives of sexual complainants have largely been abandoned, and the trial judge now has discretion whether or not to give such a warning to the jury.

In more recent years the system has also witnessed a greater awareness of the reasons why a complainant may not have made a complaint of a sexual offence at first reasonable opportunity but still avail of the doctrine of recent complaint; a relaxation of the exclusionary rule on opinion evidence in certain circumstances; the introduction of a provision which makes it clear that the absence of resistance by a victim in a rape case does not equate with consent; tighter restrictions that offer victims better protection against unnecessary and distressing information being raised about their sexual histories; separate legal representation for sexual offence complainants where an application is made to admit previous sexual history; the abolition of the marital exemption in relation to rape; court accompaniment in sexual offence cases; greater protection of the identity of victims and witnesses in criminal cases; the introduction of measures to restrict unjustified imputations at trial against the character of a deceased or incapacitated victim or witness; the creation of a statutory offence of intimidation of witnesses or their families; the ability of the DPP to appeal unduly lenient sentences; the right to return of property to be used as evidence; and provisions for the payment of compensation to victims through a statutory scheme introduced under section 6 of the Criminal Justice Act 1993 (Rogan, 2006b: 202–8; Fennell, 2009: 250–60; Vaughan and Kilcommins, 2010).

Along with the above evidential changes, the introduction of victim-impact statements has helped to reduce victim alienation. Section 5 of the Criminal Justice Act 1993, as amended, permits the court to receive evidence or submissions concerning any effect of specified offences on the person in respect of whom an offence was committed. These offences relate to most sexual offences and offences involving violence or the threat of violence to a person. Section 5 initially presupposed that the victims of these offences were capable themselves of giving evidence of the impact the crime had on them (O'Malley, 2009: 885). To combat the narrowness of this presumption, the Irish courts began, as a practice, to admit the evidence of family members of homicide victims.[12] Section 4 of the Criminal Procedure Act 2010 provides that a 'person in respect of whom the offence was committed' now includes a family member of that person when that person has died, is ill or is otherwise incapacitated as a result of the commission of the offence.

Continuing problems and repeat victimisation

Notwithstanding the increased recognition of victims in the criminal process, it remains the case that many of the needs of victims continue to be unmet. To begin with, there are many reported difficulties with the provision of information to victims. The European Commission suggested in 2004 that the provision of information was not secured by 'simply issuing information booklets or setting up websites, without the authorities actively providing individual victims with information' (2004: 5). The Irish Council for Civil Liberties (2008: 21) takes a similar position noting the 'lack of initiation on the part of the State actors in their role as information-providers' to victims of crime.[13] Similarly, the SAVI (Sexual Abuse and Violence in Ireland) Report in 2002 identified barriers for accessing law enforcement, medical and therapeutic services for those abused and the families of those abused. Lack of information from the Gardaí and medical personnel was the main source of dissatisfaction with the services provided. Specifically, the Gardaí were seen to provide inadequate explanations of procedures being undertaken, and medical personnel were seen as needing to provide more information regarding other available services and options. In relation to counselling services, time waiting to get an appointment was the major source of dissatisfaction. A lack of knowledge among criminal justice agencies and actors about the needs of victims of crime also remains a central concern. For example, a study by McGrath (2009) showed that 51 per cent of members of the legal profession were unfamiliar with the provisions of the Victims Charter.

There also remains a problem with the under-reporting of crime. O'Connell and Whelan, for example, in a study in Dublin in the early 1990s, noted that 19 per cent of those surveyed did not report the crime (1994: 85). In a follow-up study a few years later, the figure was reported at 20 per cent (Kirwan and O'Connell, 2001: 10). The Quarterly National Household Survey in 2010, which asked 39,000 households about the experiences of crime among those over 18 years of age in the previous 12 months, found that 25 per cent of burglaries, 36 per cent of violent thefts, 45 per cent of assaults and 45 per cent of acts of vandalism (it fell to 45 per cent in 2010) were not reported (Central Statistics Office, 2010). The SAVI Report into sexual abuse and violence in Ireland noted in 2002, after carrying out a study involving 3,120 participants, that disclosure rates to the Gardaí were very low (McGee et al., 2002: 128–132). Regarding experiences of adult sexual assault, only one per cent of men and eight per cent of women had reported their experiences to the Gardaí (six per cent overall). Only eight per cent of adults reported previous experiences of child sexual abuse to the Gardaí (ibid.: xxxvii).

Other issues that cause concern include the level of violence against women;[14] fear of crime (Butler and Cunningham, 2010: 429–60); intimidation (Hourigan, 2011); victimisation by the process (Kelleher and O'Connor, 1999; Riegel, 2011: 200); attrition rates (Leane et al., 2001; Hanly et al., 2009; O'Mahony, 2009; Leahy, 2014; Bartlett and Mears, 2011; J. Hamilton, 2011); the lack of private areas in courts; difficulties with procedural rules, legal definitions and directions (Bacik et al., 1998; Cooper, 2008; Leahy, 2013); delays in the system (Hanly et al., 2009); the lack of protection and security offered by the justice system (Spain et al., 2014); the lack of opportunity to participate fully in the criminal process; the lack of information on the progress of criminal prosecutions (Watson, 2000); an over-emphasis in some instances on adversarialism and its morphology of combat and contest (Keenan, 2014; Kilcommins and Donnelly, 2014); under- and over-criminalisation (Kilcommins et al., 2013; Schweppe et al., 2014); a lack of empathy and understanding in reporting a crime (Guerin, 2014: 335–336); overcrowded court-rooms and an inability to hear the proceedings; low levels of awareness of the Crime Victims Helpline; a lack of information on claiming witness expenses (Kilcommins et al., 2010); a lack of training of stakeholders, such as legal practitioners, who come in to direct contact with victims (Kilcommins et al., 2013); and inadequate resources (Grozdanova and de Londras, 2014) and support services (Bacik et al., 2007; Mulkerrins, 2003; Deane, 2007; Irish Council for Civil Liberties, 2008; and Cooper, 2008).

The lack of recognition of vulnerable witnesses in Ireland has additionally been identified (Bacik et al., 2007: 10–11; Spain et al., 2014). Victims of crime with disabilities, for example, remain largely invisible – not least because of the difficulties they pose in relation to information gathering and fact finding for an adversarial justice system, which for the most part refuses to engage with the ontological dimensions of disability (Kilcommins et al., 2013). A recent study undertaken on victims of crime with disabilities found that they 'are not being strategically identified as a victim group, either by victim support organisations, or those engaged at a central government policy level in dealing with victims' issues' (Edwards et al., 2012: 100). The Irish court process also remains epistemically rooted in mainstream accounts of victims' needs and concerns. Such victims fit more easily within an adversarial paradigm of justice that emphasises orality, lawyer-led questioning, observation of the demeanour of a witness, the curtailment of free-flowing witness narrative, confrontation and robust cross-examination (Kilcommins and Donnelly, 2014). Many of these issues have been reflected in the experience north of the border.

The experience of crime victims in Northern Ireland

The return of the victim

The Northern Irish criminal justice system is shaped by its unique historical, political and constitutional context. Thus while Northern Ireland is a separate legal jurisdiction, it remains strongly influenced by developments in the rest of the UK. Victims of ordinary crime are easily overlooked in Northern Ireland, with victims of political violence being a more visible and vocal constituency that attracts greater political and academic attention. Although political violence has marred Northern Ireland's recent past, the country has relatively low levels of crime in comparison to its UK neighbours (van Kesteren et al., 2000; Police Service of Northern Ireland (PSNI), 2014), and victims of crime in Northern Ireland have been historically satisfied with the criminal justice system (Mawby and Walklate, 1994: 29).

Yet, the Troubles changed the criminal justice system. Courts and police stations were often targets of paramilitary attacks, becoming heavily guarded fortresses and the police more milita-rised (Ellison and Smyth, 2000). Moreover, the Royal Ulster Constabulary (RUC), a predomi-nantly Protestant police force, was perceived as only serving the Unionist community meaning that satisfaction with the police amongst Protestants (over 80 per cent) was notably higher than that amongst Catholics (less than 50 per cent) (Patten, 1999: 3.4; van Kesteren et al., 2000). Individuals were also reluctant to testify in criminal trials, owing to fear of intimidation or retaliation from paramilitary groups (Amelin et al., 2000). Added to this, high levels of political violence and no-go areas prevented the police from detecting crimes in certain locales. Indeed, far from protecting them, to many people the criminal justice system itself was seen as a source of victimisation. Indiscriminate use of internment, notable miscarriages of justice, allegations of torture and ill-treatment[15] and claims of collusion between the police and paramilitaries (Dickson, 2010; Quirk, 2013; Cadwallader, 2013) all undermined trust in the criminal justice system, prompting reform as part of the peace process to prevent future secondary victimisation.

In the rest of the UK, attention to the needs of victims in the 1990s was marked by improving their engagement with the criminal justice system through Victim Charters and enunciation of rights. The purpose of these developments was to 'rebalance the criminal justice system' and take victims' interests into account, in turn reducing crime and bringing more offenders to justice (Home Office, 1998, 2002). These policies reflected, in part, politicians advancing retributive agendas through the utilisation of victims in reporting crimes and providing evidence (Karmen, 2010: 147). In 1998, the Northern Ireland Office, drawing on the experience in the UK, introduced *Victims of Crime: A Code of Practice*, setting out the services available to victims and commitments by the relevant criminal justice agencies, paving the way for greater attention to be paid to this area. While such policies can be discerned in Northern Ireland as having a retributive and functional aspect, reform of the criminal justice system has been part of a wider dissatisfaction with the system in the aftermath of the Troubles.

As part of the Good Friday Agreement, the Criminal Justice Review Group (CJRG) was established to consider improving the 'responsiveness and accountability of and any lay participation in the criminal justice system', which they interpreted to include the needs of victims and witnesses (2000: 13.1). The Review Group found in its public consultation that a common theme was a need to ensure better respect for victims, as they were 'not high enough on the agenda', 'ignored', 'not given a voice in the adversarial system' and had to 'prove their case' (2000: 3.17). That said, those consulted recognised the sensitive nature of the issue and the need to ensure the presumption of innocence of the accused. The Review Group itself acknowledged that victims are integral to the functioning of the criminal justice system, but its traditional focus on punishment of the offender had done little to alleviate the suffering and distress of victims (2000: 13.9). Many victims felt 'alienated' from the system with the state more interested in securing a conviction than establishing the truth (2000: 13.30). This was in part based on the lack of information and assistance, which left victims feeling re-victimised. The Review Group recommended that greater provision should be made to keep victims informed of proceedings, release of prisoners and available assistance; prosecutors should explain decisions not to prosecute to victims and their families; and individuals should have greater access to make impact statements in sentencing.

A number of the Review Group's recommendations were introduced into law through the Justice (Northern Ireland) Acts 2002 and 2004. Criminal justice agencies themselves have also been reformed, the most noticeable being the change from the Royal Ulster Constabulary (RUC) to the Police Service of Northern Ireland under the Police (Northern Ireland) Acts 2000 and 2003, following the recommendations of the Patten Commission (1999). The reformed institutions, such as the PSNI and Public Prosecution Service, have developed their own codes of practice towards victims. These institutional reforms and the decreasing activity of paramilitaries have encouraged more people to report crime to the police in the past few years, as confidence in the PSNI increases, raising the level of reported crime (PSNI, 2007). Devolution agreements have further embedded victim-orientated reform, with the 2010 Hillsborough Agreement outlining that the interests of victims and witnesses are key in developing domestic governance of the criminal justice system (section 1, para. 6).

Following the initial reforms of the criminal justice system, the Criminal Justice Inspectorate (CJINI) has provided an important independent oversight and monitoring function in the continued development of criminal justice reform. Unlike in England and Wales, a Victims'

Commission was felt unnecessary in Northern Ireland for the time being, given that it would duplicate the work of Victim Support, the Department of Justice (DoJ) and the CJINI. The current reforms in the proposed Justice Bill 2014 are part of the efforts by the DoJ to bring the Northern Irish criminal justice system in line with the EU Victims' Directive. This complements the Department of Justice's Victims and Witnesses Strategy, which intends to streamline service provision to victims by being more responsive to their needs and to improve their experience of the criminal justice system (DoJ, 2012). However, as the next section will discuss, there remains room for improvement in terms of compliance with the EU Directive 2012.

Provisions and services for victims and witnesses of crime

Since 2002 there has been a proliferation of legislation reforming the criminal justice system. Within these reforms a number of new victim and witness legal provisions have been created, which seek to express more shared values, rather than responsive redress and legal entitlements (Ashworth, 1998; Doak, 2008). This section will discuss in particular the provisions for victims of crime on information, participation, protection and compensation, broadly reflecting victimological research on crime victims' needs (Walklate, 1989: 133–6; Maguire, 1991). In closing this section, we examine the nature of victims' rights in Northern Ireland.

Information

There are some legal provisions that entitle crime victims to certain information, such as requesting information about the discharge or release of a prisoner under section 68 of the Justice (Northern Ireland) Act 2002. However, this does not apply to juvenile offenders, and the Justice Minister can decline a victim's request, making such a right not absolute or substantive, but more procedural. The information scheme is run by the Northern Ireland Prison Service under its Prisoner Release Victim Information Scheme (PRVIS) established in 2003 and applies to adult prisoners sentenced to six months or more. To complement this programme, in 2005, the Probation Board Northern Ireland established Victim Information Schemes (VIS) under the Criminal Justice (Northern Ireland) Order 2005 to inform victims about the discharge or release of offenders. Both of these are voluntary opt-in schemes, requiring victims to fill out applications. In addition, a Victims' Code of Practice was published in 2011, which sets out a minimum standard of service that criminal justice agencies should provide.

Participation

Overall, victim participation in Northern Ireland, outside of restorative justice and statements on sentencing, remains very much limited to that of a witness (Brienen and Hoegen, 2000; Moffett, 2014a). In relation to sentencing, since the 1980s, Northern Ireland criminal courts and appeal judges have used victim impact reports from medical professionals and impact statements from victims or their immediate family to determine sentences. These confidential victim impact reports and impact statements (predominantly used in sexual and violent offence cases) assist judges to understand the harm caused by the crime so as to impose a proportionate punishment on the convicted person. As in the RoI, victim impact reports and impact statements do not determine or bind judges in deciding appropriate sentences. Proposals contained in the Justice Bill 2014 will mean that victims statements will be treated as evidence, but can also be cross-examined on the contents. In relation to crimes committed by juveniles, a separate system of Youth Conferencing has been devised on the basis of recommendations by the Criminal Justice

Review.[16] There have been reports of high victim satisfaction in youth conferences, particularly where victims felt their views had been taken seriously (Campbell *et al.*, 2005; see further O'Dwyer and Payne, *infra*).

Protection

Greater protection of vulnerable witnesses and victims has been a growing concern in the past 15 years in Northern Ireland with reform of criminal proceedings mirroring developments in the rest of the UK. In 1998 the Home Office report *Speaking up for Justice* called for greater protection of vulnerable witnesses, including victims, to ensure their 'best evidence'. As a result, the Youth Justice and Criminal Evidence Act 1999 was passed in Westminster for England and Wales, with similar legislation passed in the Criminal Evidence (NI) Order 1999 to apply to Northern Ireland. This legislation intended to offer vulnerable witnesses better protection in criminal proceedings so as to facilitate their testimony and to minimise secondary victimisation.

The 1999 Order appears to have contributed to improving victims' satisfaction with the way in which they are treated (70 per cent), and most (56 per cent) said they would testify again (DoJ, 2014). However, only 33 per cent of victims felt defence cross-examination was courteous towards them (ibid.); enacting the unused Article 16 provision on video live-link cross-examination may help to improve victims' satisfaction in this area (McNamee *et al.*, 2012; Hayes *et al.*, 2011). Indeed, Article 25 of the EU Victims' Directive 2012 may demand further engagement with legal practitioners to minimise secondary victimisation and improve victim satisfaction with cross-examination.

Compensation

There are three compensation schemes available for crime victims in Northern Ireland: compensation orders; the Criminal Injuries Compensation Scheme; and compensation for criminal damage. Another compensation scheme is provided for those who suffer loss or damage to property as a result of activities by the security forces in tackling terrorism under the Justice Act 2007. It is worth discussing in further detail the Criminal Injury Compensation Scheme. Historically, it was a source of controversy for excluding victims who had criminal records or failed to report the crime to the police, reinforcing the 'ideal' victim as a good citizen (Bloomfield, 1998; Miers, 2014: 251). The scheme is now governed by the Criminal Injuries Compensation Scheme, established in 2009. It no longer excludes individuals who have criminal convictions, but instead reduces compensation based on the passage of time and seriousness of their conviction. While this reflects the fact that victims have not only rights, but also responsibilities, this stance perhaps does not reflect the non-discriminatory approach exhibited in international human rights law, at least for serious victimisation and the role of the law in offering protection and remedy to all citizens (Moffett, 2014b).

Support services

At 21 per cent, Northern Ireland has one of the highest coverage rates for specialised support agencies for crime victims, following New Zealand (24 per cent) and Scotland (22 per cent), in comparison to 17 per cent in England and Wales (van Dijk *et al.*, 2007: 119). Following the creation of Victim Support in Bristol in 1974 (Mawby and Walklate, 1994: 112), Victim Support Northern Ireland (VSNI) was established in 1981 and provides emotional support, information and practical assistance to victims of crime. The VSNI also runs more specific support services for witnesses and victims claiming criminal compensation. The VSNI Witness Service operates out of six courthouses, offering information to witnesses on court proceedings, familiarisation with the court layout, counselling and court accompaniment, as well as practical help in filling out forms and liaising with the PPSNI. The National Society for the Prevention of Cruelty to Children (NSPCC) similarly delivers a Young Witness Service for those under the age of 18, their parents and carers who testify in criminal proceedings (Hayes *et al.*, 2011). In relation to the Criminal Injury Compensation Service, the VSNI offers free advice and assistance to victims in claims through the Compensation Agency. In 2012/2013, VSNI helped 1,858 people claim £4.8 million in compensation (Victim Support, 2013). It has a high satisfaction rate of 90 per cent amongst victims (DoJ, 2014).

The juridification of victims' inclusion

Since the signing of the 1998 Good Friday Agreement there has been a swathe of legislation and policy introduced to adapt the Northern Irish criminal justice system to victims' needs. The impetus for initial reform post-Agreement came from the Criminal Justice Review Group, but in subsequent years the influence of the rest of the UK, European Court of Human Rights (ECtHR) jurisprudence and EU legislation has continued the reform momentum. With increasing legal regulation in this area, the Northern Irish government has at times used a rights discourse to legitimise these reforms. However, (with the possible exception of reviews of decisions not to prosecute)[17] these 'rights' have not emerged as justiciable ones where victims have legal standing to hold criminal justice agencies to account for failing to consider their interests or challenge decisions of a court. Instead 'service rights' take centre stage in Northern Ireland where crime victims are seen as consumers with policies shaped to improve their satisfaction. Ashworth (1998) believes that victims' rights should remain service in nature so that they do not impinge upon the rights of the accused or undermine certainty in sentencing decisions. Yet as Doak (2008: 10) points out, treating victims as consumers suggests there is a free market and choice. In reality, the criminal process has not been fundamentally altered, with victims only allowed limited entitlements without risking the adversarial trial and the rights of the accused. Hall (2009) suggests that a more holistic change in practice and culture of practitioners is needed, alongside enabling victims a more narrative input in testifying in criminal proceedings. To a certain extent, the EU Victims Directive 2012 encourages such a change in perspective, making such rights more justiciable than service provision.

The Northern Ireland experience in moving from political violence to a settled, peaceful democracy, has had teething problems in creating a criminal justice system which is responsive to victims' needs. While crime may be lower in Northern Ireland in comparison to other neighbouring countries and general victim satisfaction high at 70 per cent in recent years (DoJ, 2014), in some deprived areas this is not the case (see further Ellison *et al.*, 2012: 496–7). New crimes such as human trafficking and hate crimes are also becoming more prevalent in Northern Ireland, and historical crimes, such as institutional child abuse in state and religious care homes, are also coming to light (McAlinden, 2012). There is ongoing room for further reform in this area to further adapt the criminal justice system to the changing nature of crime and victimisation. A role may perhaps be played here by the proposed Northern Ireland Bill of Rights recommended in the Good Friday Agreement, which would give effect to crime victims' right to treatment with dignity and respect, right to obtain redress, etc. Although this section has concentrated on 'ordinary' crime victims, it is worth discussing outstanding issues of victims of political violence in Northern Ireland, whose unresolved issues in dealing with the past continue to cast a long shadow over the criminal justice system.

Continued problems

The Troubles in Northern Ireland between 1969 and 1998 resulted in the deaths of over 3,500 people, with over 40,000 seriously injured (Breen-Smyth, 2012; Commission for Victims and Survivors Northern Ireland (CVSNI), 2014). Such violence has had a ripple effect on families, communities and society in Northern Ireland whether through loss, caring responsibilities, mental health issues or damaging economic development (Bloomfield, 1998; CVSNI, 2012). Only in 2012 was a needs-based assessment carried out by the Commission for Victims and Survivors (2012) finding that many victims, as well as their carers, continue to have social support, mental health, chronic pain management and financial needs and an ongoing desire to seek truth, justice and acknowledgement.

Contention remains around the definition of who is a victim. Section 3 of the Victims and Survivors (Northern Ireland) Order 2006 defines a victim as 'someone who is or has been physically or psychologically injured, [provides substantial amount of care for such a person], or [bereaved] as a result of or in consequence of a conflict-related incident'. This definition has been criticised as too broad, as it includes those paramilitaries and members of the security forces who victimised others but were also victimised themselves. Recognising such individuals as victims is seen by some to absolve perpetrators of their responsibility in causing harm to others. Some groups have sought to distinguish civilians who were caught up in violence as 'innocent' or 'real', thereby being more deserving of victim status and to benefit from remedies (Morrissey and Smyth, 2002: 4). The controversy over the definition of victimhood has inhibited conversations on more substantive issues of redress for victims, such as reparations.

The Good Friday Agreement stated that it is 'essential to acknowledge and address the suffering of the victims of violence as a necessary element of reconciliation'. Moreover, it provided for victims' 'right to remember as well as to contribute to a changed society', recognising the 'provision of services that are supportive and sensitive to the needs of victims will also be a critical element'. These ambiguous phrases do not provide any sort of justiciable rights for victims, but rather make the acknowledgement and remembrance of the past the private act of individuals, rather than a publicly engaged transitional justice process. Since 1998 this discrete service-based approach has defined assistance to victims and survivors of the Troubles. Services provided to victims are funded now through the Victims and Survivors Service (VSS) and reviewed through the Commission for Victims and Survivors under its role to promote the interests of victims and survivors.[18] In terms of accountability, such measures do not publicly acknowledge individuals as victims, as service provision loses the recognition, entitlement and responsibility aspects associated with reparations through their delivery by groups. In terms of remedy, services provided have been criticised for their access issues, location, standard of provision and ability to respond to victims' needs (CVSNI, 2007).

More substantive redress and accountability has been piecemeal. A number of Northern Irish cases before the European Court of Human Rights have found that the UK government violated its obligations under Article 2 on the right to life, by failing to conduct effective, independent, transparent and prompt investigations into contentious deaths by state forces. In order to comply with these judgments, the Office of the Police Ombudsman assumed responsibility for the independent investigation of complaints against the police; the PSNI established the Historical Enquiries Team (HET) in 2005 to re-investigate all conflict-related deaths (HET, 2005); and the coroner continued to conduct inquests into contentious deaths (McEvoy, 2013).

Although crime victims and political victims in Northern Ireland have differing needs, the failure to deal with the past is having a detrimental impact on both. By treating political violence of the Troubles as ordinary crimes, reliance has been placed on the criminal justice system to deal with the past in Northern Ireland. This is burdening the limited resources of the police and prosecution service and has impacted their ability to address contemporary crimes. Indeed, with funding cuts to the police service, the HET and the Ombudsman's, historical investigations ended in 2014. For ordinary, less politically contentious crime victims, however, there have been a plethora of developments that have to some extent improved their position in the criminal justice system. For victims of the Troubles, their needs remain unsatisfied and their rights unacknowledged. There is an acute need for public consciousness to be awakened to this travesty of justice. A more comprehensive approach to dealing with the past that incorporates victim participation and their rights to truth, justice and reparation is crucial to remedy the past and allow justice for the present. The Stormont House Agreement in late 2014, a reboot of the Haass-O'Sullivan proposal, aspires to provide a comprehensive approach to the past. Yet the agreement continues the language of victim 'services', rather than acknowledging victims' rights to truth, justice and reparation. It remains to be seen if this new agreement can substantively reimagine and deliver redress for the past.

Conclusion

The past few decades have seen a noticeable shift in responsiveness to victims' needs in both criminal justice systems. Much of the impetus for this change has been driven by the need to remedy the neglect generated through a State-accused logic of action which acted as an epistemic lodestar in the criminal process for close to 150 years. The often piecemeal changes that have occurred over the last 40 years or so are rooted in the need to more accurately depict the shared reality of any crime conflict by embracing, in different ways, *all* of the effected parties. Though the changes are designed to alleviate the 'outsider' status of victims, they have not, for the most part, sought to dilute the values and principles of fairness and justice for the accused/offender or to compromise the integrity of decision-making in the criminal process. No doubt, in some instances the momentum generated has been manipulated for punitive purposes and has assisted in ratcheting up the stakes in political and media circles. In the main, however, the constitutive threads of the shift have been inclusionary rather than exclusionary in orientation, designed to remedy previous appalling inattention by embedding victims of crime as stakeholders in the criminal process.

This narrative of increased accommodation for victims is true of both jurisdictions, though the pathways in securing it have not always been the same. Northern Ireland, for example, has had to deal more directly with legacies from the Troubles, including the suffering of victims of violence, reconciliation, resolutions and truth recovery mechanisms. The justice system itself was seen as a source of victimisation throughout the Troubles. This set the antennae quivering more acutely, increasing mindfulness about the importance of lay participation and the accommodation of witnesses and victims. This has resulted in the institutional and cultural reform of criminal justice agencies such as the PSNI and the PPSNI, designed to facilitate confidence-building, participation and legitimacy. Northern Ireland was also aided by the strong influence provided by changes in England and Wales, a much larger jurisdiction encountering more victim-related issues at policy, legal and academic levels. In all, both at the community and national level, victims of the Troubles have been a source of concern in improving their legal position in criminal investigations and trials, which has spilt over in advancing procedural justice for 'ordinary' crime victims.

The causal flow in the Republic of Ireland has been different. It has not overhauled or re-examined the cultural or institutional configuration of criminal justice agencies as a result of the Troubles. It has also operated in the absence of a strong criminal justice research culture and successive governments' apathy towards policy based on crime data and crime statistics. Nevertheless, change has occurred through, for example, various legal reforms, many of which were introduced in the early 1990s; the work of victim support organisations which were established initially in the 1970s and 1980s; and government initiatives, such as the establishment of a Victims of Crime Office in the Department of Justice and Equality in 2008. A cultural shift among stakeholders in relation to engagement with victims has taken more time given the embedded nature of old practices and ways of doing things. The new EU Directive will aid change in this area by demanding that such stakeholders re-examine the nature of their engagements with victims of crime. Though Northern Ireland and the Republic of Ireland continue to encounter difficulties in recognising the needs and concerns of victims, it is clear that over the past 40 years both jurisdictions have moved significantly in the direction of creating a more communicative criminal process which better embraces their experiences and voices. It is a trend that is likely to continue as part of a new 'economy of power' in both jurisdictions.

References

Aldana-Pindell, R. (2004) 'An Emerging Universality of Justiciable Victim's Rights in the Criminal Process to Curtail Impunity for State-Sponsored Crimes', *Human Rights Quarterly*, 26(3): 605–86.

Amelin, K., Willis, M. and Donnelly, D. (2000) *Participation in the Criminal Justice System in Northern Ireland*. Review of the Criminal Justice System in Northern Ireland, Research Report No.3. Belfast: Stationery Office.

Ashworth, A. (1998) *The criminal process: an evaluative study*. Oxford: Oxford University Press.

Bacik, I., Maunsell, C. and Gogan, S. (1998) *The Legal Process and Victims of Rape*. Dublin: Dublin Rape Crisis Centre.

Bacik, I., Heffernan, L., Brazil, P. and Woods, M. (2007) *Report on Services and Legislation Providing Support for Victims of Crime*. Dublin: Commission for the Support of Victims of Crime.

Bartlett, H. and Mears, E. (2011) *Sexual violence against people with disabilities: data collection and barriers to disclosure*. Dublin: Rape Crisis Network Ireland.

Bloomfield, K. (1998) *We Will Remember Them*. Belfast: Report of the Northern Ireland Victim Commissioner.

Breen, R. and Rottman, D. (1985) *Crime Victimisation in the Republic of Ireland*, (ESRI paper no. 121). Dublin: ESRI.

Breen-Smyth, M. (2012) *The needs of individuals and their families injured as a result of the Troubles in Northern Ireland*. Belfast: WAVE.

Brienen, M. E. and Hoegen, E. H. (2000) *Victims of Crime in 22 European Criminal Justice Systems*. Netherlands: Wolf Legal.

Butler, M. and Cunningham, P. (2010) 'Fear of Crime in the Republic of Ireland: Understanding Its Origins and Consequences' in S. Shoham, P. Knepper and M. Kett (eds) *International Handbook of Victimology*. Boca Raton, FL: CRC Press.

Cadwallader, A. (2013) *Lethal Allies: British Collusion in Ireland*. Dublin: Mercier Press.

Campbell, C., Devlin, R., O'Mahony, D., Doak, J., Jackson, J., Corrigan, T. and McEvoy, K. (2005) *Evaluation of the Northern Ireland Youth Conference Service*. Northern Ireland: Department of Justice.

Central Statistics Office (2010) *Quarterly National Household Survey 2010: Crime and Victimisation*. Cork and Dublin: Central Statistics Office.

Coffey, G. (2006) 'The Victim of Crime and the Criminal Justice Process', *Irish Criminal Law Journal*, 16(3): 15.

Cohen, R. (2006) 'The Rise of the Victim: A Path to Punitiveness?', *Irish Criminal Law Journal*, 16(3): 10.

Commission for Victims and Survivors Northern Ireland (CVSNI) (2007) *Support for Victims and Survivors: Addressing the Human Legacy*. Belfast: Interim Victims Commissioner's Report on the Services for Victims and Survivors.

Commission for Victims and Survivors Northern Ireland (CVSNI) (2012) *Comprehensive Needs Assessment*. Belfast: Commission for Victims and Survivors.

Commission for Victims and Survivors Northern Ireland (CVSNI) (March 2014) *Advice on Dealing with the Past: A Victim-Centred Approach*.

Committee for Judicial Studies (2011) *The Equal Treatment of Persons in Court: Guidance for the Judiciary*. Dublin: Committee for Judicial Studies.

Cooper, J. (2008) *The Emotional Effects and Subsequent Needs of Families Bereaved by Homicide: A Study Commissioned by Advic and Support after Homicide*. Dublin: the Commission for the Support of Victims of Crime.

Cotter, A. (2005) 'The Criminal Justice System' in S. Quin, P. Kennedy, A. Matthews and G. Kiely (eds) *Contemporary Irish Social Policy*. Dublin: UCD Press.

Criminal Justice Review Group (2000) *Review of the Criminal Justice System in Northern Ireland*. London: HMSO.

Damaska, M. (1986) *The Faces of Justice and State Authority*. New Haven, CT: Yale University Press.

Deane, J. (2007) 'Balancing the Scales in a Homicide Trial', *Judicial Studies Institute Journal*, 7(1): 18.

Department of Justice (2012) *Making a difference: Improving access to justice for victims and witnesses of crime: a five–year strategy*. Dublin: Stationery Office.

Department of Justice (2014) *Victim and Witness Experience of the Northern Ireland Criminal Justice System: 2008/09 – 2013/14*, Research and Statistical Bulletin 3/2014. Northern Ireland: Statistics and Research Agency.

Department of Justice and Law Reform (2010) *Victims Charter and Guide to the Criminal Justice System*. Dublin: Victims of Crime Office, Department of Justice and Law Reform.

Department of Justice, Equality and Law Reform (1999) *Victims Charter and Guide to the Criminal Justice System*, Dublin: Department of Justice, Equality and Law Reform.

De Than, C. (2003) 'Positive Obligations under the European Convention on Human Rights: Towards the Human Rights of Victims and Vulnerable Witnesses', *Journal of Criminal Law*, 67(2): 165–82.

Dickson, B. (2010) *The European Convention on Human Rights and the Conflict in Northern Ireland*. Oxford: Oxford University Press.

Doak, J. (2003) 'The Victim and the Criminal Process: An Analysis of Recent Trends in Regional and International Tribunals', *Legal Studies*, 23(1): 10.

Doak, J. (2008) *Victims' Rights, Human Rights and Criminal Justice: Reconceiving the Role of Third Parties*. Oxford: Hart.

Dworkin, R. (1985) *A Matter of Principle*. Cambridge, MA: Harvard University Press.

Dworkin, R. (1998) *Law's Empire*. Oxford: Hart Publishing.

Edwards, C., Harold, G. and Kilcommins, S. (2012) *Access to Justice for People with Disabilities as Victims of Crime in Ireland*. Cork, Ireland: UCC.

Ellison, G. and Smyth, J. (2000) *The Crowned Harp: Policing Northern Ireland*. London: Pluto Press.

Ellison, G., Shirlow, P. and Mulcahy, A. (2012) 'Responsible Participation, Community Engagement and Policing in Transitional Societies: Lessons from a Local Crime Survey in Northern Ireland', *The Howard Journal of Criminal Justice*, 51(5): 488–502.

Emmerson, B., Ashworth, A. and MacDonald, A. (2007) *Human Rights and Criminal Justice*, 2nd edn. London: Sweet and Maxwell.

European Commission (2004) *Report from the Commission on the Basis of Article 18 of the Council Framework Decision of 15 March 2001 on the Standing of Victims in Criminal Proceedings*. [SEC 2004, 102].

Fennell, C. (2001) 'The Culture of Decision-Making: A Case for Judicial Defiance through Evidence and Fact Finding', *Judicial Studies Institute Journal*, 2(1): 25–65.

Fennell, C. (2009) *The Law of Evidence in Ireland*, 3rd edn. Dublin: Bloomsbury Professional.

Garland, D. (2001) *The Culture of Control: Crime and Social Order in Contemporary Society*. Oxford: Oxford University Press.

Goodey, J. (2005) *Victims and Victimology: Research, Policy and Practice*. London: Pearson Education Limited.

Grozdanova, R. and de Londras, F. (2014) *Protecting victims' rights in the EU: the theory and practice of diversity of treatment during the criminal trial: national report: Ireland*. Durham: Institute of Advanced Legal Studies: Available at: www.courts.ie/Courts.ie/Library3.nsf/16c93c36d3635d5180256e3f003a4580/41fc36c4b 425f33a80257a9b004e85f5?OpenDocument (accessed 21 April 2015).

Guerin, S. (2014) *Report to An Taoiseach Enda Kenny TD on a review of the action taken by An Garda Síochána pertaining to certain allegations made by Sergeant Maurice McCabe (Guerin Report)* (6 May 2014). Available at: www.merrionstreet.ie/en/wp-content/uploads/2014/05/Final-Redacted-Guerin-Report1.pdf

Hall, M. (2009) *Victims of Crime: Policy and Practice in Criminal Justice*. Cullompton: Willan.

Hamilton, C. (2014) *Reconceptualising Penality*. Farnham: Ashgate.

Hamilton, J. (2011) 'Sexual Offences and Capacity to Consent: A Prosecution Perspective', Annual Conference of the Law Reform Commission, Dublin, 7 November 2011.

Hanly, C., Healy, D. and Scriver, S. (2009) *Rape and justice in Ireland: a national study of survivor, prosecutor and court responses to rape.* Dublin: Liffey Press.

Hayes, D., Bunting, L., Lazenbatt, A., Carr, N. and Duffy, J. (2011) *The Experiences of Young Witnesses in Criminal Proceedings in Northern Ireland: A Report for the Department of Justice.* Northern Ireland: Department of Justice.

Healy, J. (2004) *Irish Laws of Evidence.* Dublin: Thomson, Round Hall.

Henderson, L. (1985) 'The Wrongs of Victim's Rights', *Stanford Law Review,* 37: 937–1021.

Historical Enquiries Team (2005) *Standard Operating Procedure.* Belfast: PSNI.

Home Office (1998) *Speaking up for justice: Report of the interdepartmental working group on the treatment of vulnerable or intimidated witnesses in the criminal justice system.* London: HMSO.

Home Office (2002) *Justice for All – A White Paper on the Criminal Justice System,* CM 5563. London: HMSO.

Hourigan, N. (2011) *Understanding Limerick: Social Exclusion and Change.* Cork, Ireland: Cork University Press.

Hoyle, C. (2012) 'Victims, the Criminal Process, and Restorative Justice' in M. Maguire, R. Morgan and R. Reiner (eds) *The Oxford Handbook of Criminology,* 5th edn. Oxford: Oxford University Press.

Irish Council for Civil Liberties (2008) *A Better Deal: The Human Rights of Victims in the Criminal Justice System.* Dublin: Irish Council for Civil Liberties.

Jackson, J. (1993) 'Competence and Compellability of Spouses to Give Evidence', *Dublin University Law Journal,* 15: 202–11.

Karmen, A. (2010) *Crime Victims: An Introduction to Victimology.* Belmont, CA: Wadsworth.

Keenan, M. (2014) *Sexual Trauma and Abuse: Restorative and Transformative Possibilities?* Dublin: Facing Forward.

Kelleher, P. and O'Connor, M. (1999) *Safety and Sanctions: Domestic Violence and the Enforcement of the Law in Ireland.* Dublin: Women's Aid.

Kilcommins, S. and Donnelly, M. (2014) 'Victims of Crime with Disabilities: Hidden Casualties in the "Vision of Victim as Everyman"', *International Review of Victimology,* 20(3): 305–25.

Kilcommins, S., Edwards, C. and O'Sullivan, T. (2013) *An International Review of Legal Provisions and Supports for People with Disabilities as Victims of Crime.* Dublin: ICCL.

Kilcommins, S., O'Donnell, I., O'Sullivan, E. and Vaughan, B. (2004) *Crime, Punishment and the Search for Order in Ireland.* Dublin: IPA.

Kilcommins, S., Leane, M., Donson, F., Fennell, C. and Kingston, A. (2010) *The Needs and Concerns of Victims of Crime in Ireland.* Dublin: Commission for the Support of Victims of Crime.

Kilkelly, U. (2006) *Youth Justice in Ireland: Tough Lives, Rough Justice.* Dublin: Irish Academic Press.

Kirwan, G. and O'Connell, M. (2001) 'Crime Victimisation in Dublin Revisited', *Irish Criminal Law Journal,* 11(2): 10–13.

Leahy, S. (2013) 'Summing Up in Rape Trials: the challenge of guiding effectively and without prejudice', *Irish Criminal Law Journal,* 23(4): 102–7.

Leahy, S. (2014) 'Bad Laws or Bad Attitudes? Assessing the Impact of Societal Attitudes upon the Conviction Rates for Rape in Ireland', *Irish Journal of Applied Social Studies,* 14(1): 18–29.

Leane, M., Ryan, S., Fennell, C. and Egan, E. (2001) *Attrition in sexual assault offence cases in Ireland: A qualitative analysis.* Dublin: Department of Justice, Equality and Law Reform.

McAlinden, A-M. (2012) *'Grooming' and the Sexual Abuse of Children: Institutional, Internet, and Familial Dimensions.* Clarendon Studies in Criminology. Oxford: Oxford University Press.

McCullagh, C. (1986) 'Crime in Ireland: facts, figures and interpretations', *Studies: An Irish Quarterly Review,* 75(297): 11–20.

McCullagh, C. (2014) 'From Offender to Scumbag: Changing Understandings of Crime and Criminals in Contemporary Ireland', *Irish Journal of Sociology,* 22(1): 8–27.

McEvoy, K. (2013) *Dealing with the Past? An Overview of the Legal and Political Approaches.* Belfast: Healing Through Remembering.

McGee, H., Garavan, R., de Barra, M., Byrne, J. and Conroy, R. (2002) *The SAVI Report: Sexual Abuse and Violence in Ireland.* Dublin: Liffey Press.

McGovern, L. (2002) 'The Victim and the Criminal Justice Process' in P. O'Mahony (ed.) *Criminal Justice in Ireland.* Dublin: IPA.

McGrath, A. (2009) *The Living Victims of Homicide: analysing the needs and concerns of the co-victims of homicide within the Irish criminal justice system.* Unpublished Ph.D. thesis, University College Cork.

McNamee, H., Molyneaux, F. and Geraghty, T. (2012) *Key Stakeholder Evaluation of NSPCC Young Witness Service Remote Live Link (Foyle).* Northern Ireland: NSPCC.

Maguire, M. (1991) 'The Needs and Rights of Victims of Crime', *Crime and Justice*, 14: 363–433.

Mawby, R. I. and Walklate, S. (1994) *Critical Victimology: International Perspectives*. London: Sage.

Mendelsohn, B. (1956) 'Une nouvelle branche de law science bio-psycho-sociale: Victimologie', *Revue international de criminology et de police technique*, 10–31.

Miers, D. (2014) 'Compensating deserving victims of violence crime: the Criminal Injuries Compensation Scheme 2012', *Legal Studies*, 34(2): 242–78.

Moffett, L. (2014a) *Justice for victims before the International Criminal Court*. Oxford: Routledge.

Moffett, L. (2014b) 'Navigating Complex Identities of Victim-Perpetrators in Reparation Mechanisms', *European Consortium of Political Research conference*. Glasgow.

Moore Walsh, K. (2013) *Victims' Rights in Ireland: influences, illusions and impacts*. Unpublished Ph.D. thesis. University College Cork.

Morrissey, M. and Smyth, M. (2002) *Northern Ireland after the Good Friday Agreement: Victims, Grievance and Blame*. London: Pluto Press.

Mulkerrins, K. (2003) 'Trial Venue and Process: the victim and the accused', *Judicial Studies Institute Journal*, 3(1): 120.

Muller-Rappard, E. (1990) 'Perspectives on the Council of Europe's approach to the issue of basic principles of justice for victims of crime', *Human Rights Quarterly*, 12(2): 231–45.

O'Connell, M. and Whelan, A. (1994) 'Crime Victimisation in Dublin', *Irish Criminal Law Journal*, 4(1): 85–112.

O'Flaherty, H. (2002) 'Punishment and the Popular Mind: how much is enough?' in P. O'Mahony (ed.) *Criminal Justice in Ireland*. Dublin: IPA.

O'Mahony, P. (2009) 'Ireland' in J. Lovett and L. Kelly (eds) *Different systems, similar outcomes? Tracking attrition in reported rape cases in eleven European countries*. London: Child and Woman Abuse Unit.

O'Malley, T. (2009) *The Irish Criminal Process*. Dublin: Thomson Round Hall.

Patten, C. (1999) *A New Beginning: Policing in Northern Ireland*. The Report of the Independent Commission on Policing in Northern Ireland, Belfast.

Police Service of Northern Ireland (PSNI) (May 2007) 'Research into Recent Crime Trends in Northern Ireland'. Belfast.

Police Service of Northern Ireland (PSNI) (2014) *Trends in Police Recorded Crime in Northern Ireland 1998/99 to 2013/14*. Belfast: PSNI.

Quirk, H. (2013) 'Don't Mention the War: The Court of Appeal, the Criminal Cases Review Commission and Dealing with the Past in Northern Ireland', *The Modern Law Review*, 76(6): 949–80.

Rafferty, M. and O'Sullivan, E. (1999) *Suffer the Little Children*. Dublin: New Island Books.

Riegel, R. (2011) *Shattered: killers do time, victims' families do life*. Dublin: Collins Press.

Rogan, M. (2006a) 'Victims' Rights: Theory and Practice', *Irish Law Times*, 10: 151–5.

Rogan, M. (2006b) 'The Role of Victims in Sentencing – the case of compensation orders', *Irish Law Times*, 13: 202–8.

Schweppe, J., Haynes, A. and Carr, J. (2014) *A Life Free from Fear: legislating for hate crime in Ireland – an NGO perspective*. Limerick: HHRG/CUES.

Smyth, A. (1993) 'The Women's Movement in Contemporary Ireland: 1970–1992' in A. Smyth (ed.) *Irish Women's Studies Reader*. Dublin: Attic Press.

Spain, E., Gibbons, S. and Kilcommins, S. (2014) *Analysis of Text for the Final Review of the National Strategy on Domestic, Sexual and Gender-based Violence, 2010-2014*. Limerick: Centre for Criminal Justice.

van Dijk, J. (2005) 'Benchmarking Legislation on Crime Victims: The UN Declaration of 1985' in E. Vetere and D. Petro, *Victims of Crime and Abuse of Power: festschrift in honour of Irene Melup*. New York: United Nations.

van Dijk, J., van Kesteren, J. and Smit, P. (2007) *Criminal victimisation in international perspective. Key findings from the 2004-2005 ICVS and EU ICS*. The Hague: WODC.

van Kesteren, J. N., Mayhew, P. and Nieuwbeerta, P. (2000) *Criminal Victimisation in Seventeen Industrialised Countries: Key Findings from the 2000 International Crime Victims Survey*. The Hague, Ministry of Justice: WODC.

Vaughan, B. and Kilcommins, S. (2008) *Terrorism, Rights and the Rule of Law: Negotiating Justice in Ireland*. Devon: Willan.

Vaughan, B. and Kilcommins, S. (2010) 'The Governance of Crime and the Negotiation of Justice', *Criminology and Criminal Justice*, 10: 59–75.

Victim Support (NI) (2013) *2012–13 Annual Report*. Belfast.

von Hentig, H. (1948) *The Criminal and His Victim*. New Haven, CT: Yale University Press.

Walklate, S. (1989) *Victimology: The Victim and the Criminal Justice Process*. London: Unwin Hyman.

Watson, D. (2000) *Victims of Recorded Crime in Ireland: Results of the 1996 Survey*. Dublin: Oak Tree Press in association with ESRI.

Wolfgang, M. (1958) *Patterns in Criminal Homicide*. Philadelphia, PA: University of Pennsylvania Press.

Young, M. (2006) 'History of the Victims Movement in the US'. Available at: www.iovahelp.org/About/MarleneAYoung/USHistory.pdf (accessed 21 April 2015).

Notes

1 [1996] 22 EHRR 330.
2 [2007] IEHC 108.
3 [1986] 8 EHRR 235.
4 2004/80/EC.
5 2012/29/EU.
6 The Irish Women's Liberation Movement was established in 1970, for example, and the Council for the Status of Women was formed in 1973. See Smyth (1993).
7 By 1970 in Ireland, over 30,000 indictable crimes were recorded, representing a doubling up over a ten-year period. As a result, 'the state penal system grew in both importance and scale in managing deviance' (Kilcommins *et al.*, 2004: 87). Recorded indictable crime rates continued to rise, reaching circa 89,000 by 1981.
8 Speech given by Alan Shatter at the fifth meeting of the Victims of Crime Consultative Forum, Ashling Hotel, Parkgate Street, Dublin. Available at www.justice.ie/en/JELR/Pages/SP11000031
9 As part of a *Justice for Victims Initiative* designed to increase the level of support to victims of crime, a new executive office in the Department of Justice was established to support crime victims (September, 2008); a reconstituted Commission for the Support of Victims of Crime was introduced (September, 2008); and a forum for victim support organisations was created to put forward the views of victims with a view to shaping strategy and policy initiatives (2009).
10 [1987] ILRM 225.
11 (Unreported, 31 July 2002). On the right of a victim to have a case prosecuted, see *Fowler v Conroy* [2005] IEHC 269.
12 See *DPP v O'Donoghue* [2007] 2 IR 336.
13 See also part 7 of the Garda Inspectorate Crime Investigation Report on victims of crime (2014: part 7: 1–11); Victims Rights Alliance (2014: 11); and Grozdanova and de Londras (2014). In respect of the Criminal Injuries Compensation Tribunal, for example, it was noted in 1991 that 'it trundled along, almost unheard of, almost inaccessible, almost in secretive silence, behind a door which did not open and where somebody spoke to you through an answering machine' (Seanad Debates Vol 129 No 5, col 452, 29 May 1991, as quoted in Moore Walsh (2013: 135)).
14 Almost one in three Irish women (31 per cent or 470,157 women) have experienced some form of psychological violence by a partner, and 15 per cent of Irish women (227,495 women) have experienced physical or sexual violence by a partner (European Union Agency for Fundamental Rights, 2014).
15 These allegations were brought to light before the European Court of Human Rights in the *Ireland v the United Kingdom* case [1978] 2 EHRR 25. Ireland has requested the case to be reopened after new evidence emerged in 2014.
16 S. 57, Justice (NI) Act 2002.
17 See *Mooney's (Christopher) Application* [2014] NIQB 48; the Northern Irish High Court quashed the prosecutor's decision not to prosecute, as he had failed to take into account the victim's interests.
18 Recent reviews initiated by the Commission have found more systemic problems with the funding and assessments carried out by the VSS. *See The Victims and Survivors Service: An Independent Assessment*, WKM, 2014; and *Independent Assessment of the Victims and Survivors Service*, The Chartered Institute of Public Finance and Accountancy, 2014.

20

Media, public attitudes and crime

Lynsey Black

Existing research and theoretical perspectives

Within criminology, the study of media and crime is a vibrant area of research. Certain criminological perspectives such as labelling theory and cultural criminology posit that the representation of phenomena shapes understanding of them. What these perspectives have in common is a belief in the media's power to construct societal perceptions of persons, groups and events (Becker, 1973; Hall *et al.*, 1978; Ferrell *et al.*, 2008). As many people have little direct experience of crime, the media provides a 'window on the world' and exerts influence through its power to shape public opinion (Barrat, 1986).

The chapter provides an overview of media, public attitudes and crime in the Republic of Ireland and Northern Ireland, opening with a rehearsal of key arguments from existing research regarding the content of crime in the media and the potential consequences of this. Following this introduction, relevant research from the Republic of Ireland and Northern Ireland is presented. The chapter closes with a discussion of the possible links between crime in the media and public attitudes to crime, north and south of the border.

Content of crime in the media

Crime comprises a consistent component of media content (Williams and Dickinson, 1993; Reiner *et al.*, 2000); it is a cornerstone of popular entertainment, and the blurring of news and entertainment in television schedules means that crime has become an everyday phenomenon (Garland, 2001). To understand the reliance on crime as content, one must accept the view that certain biases inhere within the media:

> The media do not simply and transparently report events which are 'naturally' newsworthy in themselves. 'News' is the end-product of a complex process which begins with a systematic sorting and selecting of events and topics according to a socially constructed set of categories.
>
> *(Hall et al., 1978: 53)*

Galtung and Ruge (1973) compiled a list of 'news values', qualities of events which gave them priority for inclusion in news reporting, including factors such as: the frequency, whether it was dramatic, whether it was unambiguous or culturally proximate, the attraction of the negative, elite involvement and 'human interest'. Within this framework, serious and atypical crime provides events which are dramatic and unambiguous. These values are subject to change over time; for example, Jewkes (2011) has provided updated news values which incorporate the tabloidisation of news and include sex and celebrity.

The production processes underlying the prioritisation of crime in the media have been subject to a variety of perspectives. Media pluralism argues that the media present a vista of competing viewpoints. In this conceptualisation, the media act as facilitator for both privileged and marginalised voices (McNair, 2006). Alternatively, a critical perspective views the media as the mouthpiece of the powerful, engaged in reproducing consensus (Hall, 1982/1988). The reproduction of dominant hegemonic ideology is said to be aided by media ownership, the status accorded official sources and the devaluing of certain voices (Barrat, 1986; Herman and Chomsky, 1988/1994). The selection of sources is pertinent in relation to crime reporting due to the role of 'primary definers', such as police and official sources (Hall et al., 1978). This reliance has led many to argue that the media entrench dominant viewpoints while further downgrading dispossessed groups. However, recent work has considered the possibility that new media and the rise of the 'citizen journalist' has transferred some of the authority away from traditional agencies to create a greater democratisation of voices; anyone with a smart phone can now participate in a media dialogue (Greer and McLaughlin, 2010).

The media has also been accused of simplifying complex events through the use of stereotypes (Barrat, 1986). One example of this is evident in the portrayal of women. While women commit a minority of crime, women as perpetrators arouse intense media interest, especially when the crime is one of violence. Jewkes (2011) argues that female offenders are constructed around a narrow range of stereotypes which relate to: sexuality, physical attractiveness, maternity, monsterisation and victimhood. Stereotypes also impact how women as victims of crime are portrayed; for example, female victims and victims of sexual homicide are more newsworthy than other homicide categories (Peelo et al., 2004), a hierarchy corresponding to newsworthiness and informed by stereotypical notions of the ideal victim (Christie, 1986).

Consequences of crime in the media

The appetite for crime in the media has been matched by concern about its effects. Many of these concerns centre on the idea that reading about or watching simulations of violence could lead to imitation; concern about 'copy-cat' violence posited a 'hypodermic' model in which media messages were injected into a passive audience (Lee, 2007).

An alternative hypothesis suggests that crime in the media was more likely to provoke fear than imitation. Fear of crime has now become a policy goal in and of itself (Lee, 2007), and the many methodological and ontological issues related to fear of crime have done nothing to reduce its political appeal (Walklate, 1998). Writing in this vein, David Garland's (2001) 'culture of control' thesis argues that in late modernity, as crime became a quotidian reality, the 'crime complex' created an embedded sense of fear, inflamed by political rhetoric and media saturation, which manifested a sense of perpetual crisis. Certainly, media research has suggested that news reporting may have an impact on fear of crime (Williams and Dickinson, 1993). The difficulty in fear of crime research has, however, been in demonstrating the presence of a relationship between fear and media consumption; later analyses have shown that the relationship is often weak and may be reliant on the *reception*, rather than the volume, of crime in the media (Ditton et al., 2004).

The media has also been accused of fuelling moral panics. Moral panic refers to periods of intense concern about an issue, facilitated by alarmist media reporting, wherein social problems are 'defined and shaped' (Cohen, 1972: 7). The concept was popularised by Stan Cohen, who used the term in reference to clashes between the Mods and Rockers in 1960s England. A moral panic occurs when a threat emerges, branded by Cohen as a 'folk devil', which is then portrayed by the media in a limited way and in a manner which exaggerates the threat. The media is also complicit by providing a mouthpiece for 'experts' who contribute to the escalation (Cohen, 1972; Hall et al., 1978) and in terms of the commercial success which flows from many moral panics (Garland, 2008).

The preceding sections have outlined the existing research and theoretical perspectives on media, public attitudes and crime. The following sections apply these perspectives to the particular cases of the Republic of Ireland and Northern Ireland.

Republic of Ireland

Content of crime in the media

In line with existing research, the Irish media tend to prioritise serious, atypical crimes. Michael O'Connell has conducted the most extensive empirical research into the content of crime in the media in the Republic of Ireland. He demonstrated that newspapers in the jurisdiction, at the time, appeared with 'almost chemical purity, to represent crime frequency perfectly negatively' (O'Connell, 1999: 199).

O'Connell analysed 2,191 articles in a two-month period and found that extreme and atypical crimes were more commonly reported and that these offences received greater coverage in terms of word count than other crimes. O'Connell compared certain crimes as a proportion of the total and compared these to the proportion of the same crime in official crime figures. He found that murder was reported at 3,075 times the level of its actual incidence in the official figures. The proportion of armed robbery in the sample was 176 times the proportion of armed robberies recorded in the official figures. The wordage of all articles relating to Irish crimes was then calculated: 25.7 per cent of all words related to the crime of murder, while rape constituted the second largest category with 13.24 per cent of all words. Thus, the crimes which were the most dramatic and yet which were negligible in official crime figures were the most commonly reported in the newspapers.

The preference for atypical crime has also been noted by O'Donnell (2005) who found that while rising levels of violent crime in the 1990s became a focus for media attention, a late-1990s drop in property offences received little coverage. A reporting hierarchy exists even within the category of property crime, with relatively minor but more common offences receiving little attention (McCullagh, 1996). The media preference for negative stories has had a considerable impact in the context of Limerick city; reporting on the city is predominantly negative in the national newspapers, with 70 per cent of print articles prioritising the issue of crime contributing to the 'further stigmatisation and pathologising of the people and the place' (Devereux et al., 2011: 213).

O'Connell (1999, 2002) also found a general tendency towards pessimistic accounts in articles which were written from a 'meta' or 'macro' perspective, i.e. stories written about the criminal justice system rather than a one-off crime event. However, these stories were not typical fare, and most Irish reporting presented crime news as episodic and absent a wider discussion of structural factors (O'Connell et al., 1998; Devereux et al., 2011; Maguire and Carr, 2013).

Irish research also supports existing findings which show that tabloids report more crime news than broadsheets; O'Connell et al., (1998) found that tabloid titles, such as the *Evening*

Herald and the *Star*, carried proportionately more crime news, with fewer stories in the broadsheet *Irish Press* and *The Irish Times*. The *Star* and the *Evening Herald* also devoted proportionately more space to personal violent crime and tended to have more prominent headlines.

There is differential reporting between national and local media in Ireland. Local media is particularly robust in the Republic of Ireland (P. O'Mahony, 2000), and while national titles focus on the most serious crimes, local newspapers provide something akin to a court reporting service which runs the gamut from the most serious to the most mundane offences. Local crime news also deploys less sensationalist language (Healy and O'Donnell, 2010). The sensitivities of local reporters can often provide context; by contrast, the 'parachuting' of Dublin-based reporters has been cited as a cause of sensationalist reporting in Limerick (Devereux *et al.*, 2011).

One limitation regarding the research in the Republic of Ireland has been its focus on press reporting over other media. This is partly due to the ease of access for researchers (McCullagh, 2008) and may be vindicated somewhat by the jurisdiction's high levels of newspaper readership (Elvestad and Blekesaune, 2008). However, it remains the case that the research thus far presents an incomplete picture of the representation of crime in the Republic of Ireland. The most comprehensive research available (O'Connell, 1999) was conducted in 1993–4 and focussed only on print news; follow-up research which explored an expanded range of media would provide an essential comparison point between various media and across a longer period.

Crime sells

As noted above, the prioritisation of bad news is a well-worn theme within media and crime research. In the Republic of Ireland, the commercialisation of crime led to fundamental changes in news reporting. One media group, Independent Newspapers, which exercises considerable influence in the market (McCullagh, 2008), formed a strategy in the early 1980s to place crime at the centre of news content. Editorial changes at the *Evening Herald* ushered in a new era of reporting which conveyed a steady diet of crime news and a sales strategy directed towards a younger, professional, urban market (Kerrigan and Shaw, 1985). Kerrigan and Shaw argue that while there was no 'sinister' motive behind this strategy, a climate of fear can have commercial and electoral benefits. The tangible effects of a deliberate media campaign were evident in the public opprobrium felt towards joyriding, leading to the hasty opening of a detention centre for young persons on Spike Island in Cork. This was in no small part due to the branding of joyriding as a serious social problem by the *Evening Herald* throughout 1985, despite a 2.6 per cent drop in crime – which went unreported by the newspaper (ibid.). The *Evening Herald* was not alone in its changing approach to crime news; an article in *The Irish Times*, which predicted that one-fifth of all Irish households would be burgled in 1984, was based on information provided by an insurance company (O'Mahony, 1998).

The ideology of journalists has also been investigated as a possible influence of media content. O'Connell *et al.* (1998) conducted interviews with the crime correspondents of national newspapers. The correspondents from the *Star* and *The Irish Times* believed that readers understood that crime reporting was unrepresentative; however, while the *Star* correspondent stressed demand for entertainment, *The Irish Times* correspondent stressed journalistic integrity. In contrast, the *Evening Herald* correspondent believed that Ireland was experiencing an acute law and order crisis. These views are in accordance with the policy of crime saturation implemented at the *Evening Herald* in the 1980s (Kerrigan and Shaw, 1985). Irish journalists have ranked themselves to the political left of both readership and ownership (Corcoran, 2004); however, organisational restraints and the financial benefits of crime news (Devereux *et al.*, 2011) may render much personal ideology moot.

1996: An Irish case of moral panic?

While the Republic of Ireland had traditionally been a country 'not obsessed by crime' (Adler, 1983), it experienced something of a moral panic during the mid-1990s on the issue of gangland crime. In early 1996, three murders in rural Ireland appeared to disabuse the notion that crime was an urban preserve (Kilcommins *et al.*, 2004). However, it was the murders of Garda Jerry McCabe and of the investigative journalist Veronica Guerin[1] in June of that year which 'generated the conditions where a harsh response to perceived lawlessness became acceptable', creating 'a textbook case of moral panic' (O'Donnell, 2011: 78).

During this period, the media and politicians engaged in sensationalist discourse as something akin to a 'state of emergency' was declared (Kilcommins *et al.*, 2004). Periodic concerns about rising crime rates are often linked to fear of the 'imminent collapse of the moral order' (Tomlinson *et al.*, 1988: 13), and the events of 1996 provoked agonised questions on the state of Irish society. The shootings sparked a sense of crisis and were believed to be symptomatic of the 'palpable, inner decay of Irish mores and the atrophy of key institutions, such as the Catholic Church' (O'Mahony, 1996: vii).

Key to understanding this reaction is the fact that opposition parties, Fianna Fáil and the Progressive Democrats, had sought to make political gains by promoting the crime agenda, especially since the Fianna Fáil annual conference of November 1995. Meade (2000) cites the party's increasingly sensationalist rhetoric during this period and contends that the Irish public was already primed for a moral panic through a process of sensitisation. O'Mahony (1996) quotes the speech from Fianna Fáil justice spokesperson John O'Donoghue at the 1995 conference, wherein he claimed that '1995 would be remembered as the year of the criminal'.[2] Newspaper interest in crime had also escalated; the number of news stories in *The Irish Times* referencing 'organised crime' rose from 34 in 1994 to 144 in 1996 (Meade, 2000). Crime reporting had become a significant feature of many newspapers by the 1990s, and coverage was frequently gossipy and included in the lifestyle sections of newspapers (O'Brien, 2007). Newspapers led with allusions to the criminals as 'untouchable' mobsters (Hamilton, 2007; O'Brien, 2007), and this language migrated to the Oireachtas (the Irish parliament), where the concept of untouchability was pushed by the opposition parties. The 'framing' of the events did not allow for informed or reasoned debate on alternatives. For example, Hamilton (2007: 102) writes that 'some of the speeches made by TDs were indistinguishable in both their content and style from articles in the tabloid press'. The apparent 'democratisation' of the media afforded uninformed alarmist views equal weighting, and the agenda-setting role of opinion polls contributed white noise over real debate (O'Mahony, 1996). As O'Mahony (1996: 15) has further noted, this led to a self-sustaining process of escalating concern and coverage:

> The circle is complete: media portrayals of crime instil fear and profound concern in the public; the public express their concern to politicians who in turn vie with each other to articulate, in the most sensational language, a tough philosophy of curtailment and containment of crime.

The impact of aggressive media reporting has been linked to a political willingness to act and legislative activity. Hamilton (2005) argues that while the term 'moral panic' has been 'accepted uncritically' by Irish criminologists in relation to the events of 1996, it remains a useful analytical tool especially in the context of the legislative innovations it sparked. The events of the summer of 1996 left a tangible legacy through the 'Summer Anti-Crime Package' of legislation: The Proceeds of Crime Act 1996, the Criminal Justice (Drug Trafficking) Act 1996 and the Bail Act 1997 made serious encroachments into the presumption of innocence through the constitutional amendment authorising preventative detention and by allowing inferences from silence (Hamilton, 2007). Meade (2000: 12) writes that the public 'passively accepted the diagnosis' of a society overrun with crime, so much so that in 1996 almost half of those surveyed in an IMS/*Independent* poll believed that crime was the most important issue facing the country (O'Donnell and O'Sullivan, 2001).

However, the anxiety experienced during this period was unsustainable. While 41 per cent of respondents named crime as the most serious issue in the 1997 election, only 20 per cent of the registered electorate had voted in the Bail Referendum of 1996 (Kilcommins *et al.*, 2004). The months which had elapsed before the Bail Referendum was held in November of 1996 had seen public concern wane such that when the new laws on bail came into effect in 2000, anxiety had dwindled and many of the law and order promises made were forgotten (O'Donnell and O'Sullivan, 2001; Kilcommins *et al.*, 2004; O'Donnell, 2011). The anxiety had passed, but its legislative legacy remained, alongside a new cultural touchstone for the Irish people.[3]

Tabloids and victims

The media landscape in Ireland is now part of a modern, Western trend, which includes a concentration on celebrity news, a fragmentation of audience due to a proliferation of media and the increased prominence of tabloids (McCullagh, 1996; P. O'Mahony, 2000). The increasingly robust Irish tabloid market has faced criticism for its aggressive reporting of criminal trials and its fetishisation of victims (O'Mahony, 1996; O'Brien, 2010).

The prioritisation of the victim would also appear to have a broader resonance among the Irish media. In line with Garland's (2001) 'crime complex', there is some evidence of a turn towards this manner of reporting, for example, in the greater newsworthiness of crimes with a vulnerable victim and invulnerable offender (O'Connell, 1999). McCullagh (2006) too outlines the hierarchy of victims of homicide, concluding that newsworthiness increased in cases with 'middle-class' perpetrators and victims.

The preference for vulnerable victims (O'Connell, 1999) often finds expression in the preference for female victims. Carr and Holt (2010) have explored the issue of femicide in newspaper reporting and found a binary of 'deserving' and 'undeserving' victims. Women deviating from the conventional role of wife and mother were viewed as less 'worthy'. This good/bad dichotomy (Inglis and MacKeogh, 2012), evident in the news reporting of women as victims, is also present in the reporting of women as offenders. Women who commit crimes are often viewed as unnatural because of the stereotype of women as non-aggressive (O'Sullivan, 2008). This is especially so with women in prison who are typically 'represented in a partial, hostile, indeed, mythical manner' (Quinlan, 2011: 244). Research into the treatment of female offenders in the Irish press has also found that women tend to be portrayed in a limited range of roles linked to gender stereotypes (Black, 2009).

Media representation is a double-edged sword. While it can be problematic and one-dimensional, the media has also been instrumental in raising awareness about hidden issues like violent and sexual offences against women and children, issues which were absent from press reporting in the past (Keating, 2012). Increased media coverage of sexual offences has corresponded with increased reporting to the police (O'Donnell, 2005). Media mobilisation has also provoked legislative reform, such as the Criminal Law (Rape) (Amendment) Act 1990 and the Criminal Justice Act 1993 following media outcry over the perceived leniency of sentences for sexual offences (O'Mahony, 1996). It could be argued that these developments are part of a legitimate realignment of understanding about sexual violence and violence against women rather than a punitive project allied to the rise of the victim.

Conservatism

Despite the tabloidisation of the media in the Republic of Ireland, O'Donnell and Jewkes (2011) contend that broadsheets continue to set the agenda, providing insulation against sensationalism. While some research has found a turn towards more punitive commentary, for example, with regard to fears surrounding sex offenders in probation news stories, these concerns were still found to be in the minority (Maguire and Carr, 2013). Therefore, while tabloids continue to make inroads, tabloidisation has not gripped Ireland to the same extent as Britain, due to 'divergent socio-political cultures' (O'Donnell and Jewkes, 2011: 76). Despite some notable exceptions, it remains rare that tabloid titles set the agenda in Irish politics.

Therefore, although the media may resemble Britain's, it is qualitatively different and possessed of a cultural 'Irishness', identifiable by a 'sense of societal familiarity, belonging and ownership' which engenders an awareness of community (P. O'Mahony, 2000: 18). The smallness of the jurisdiction creates a 'national village', wherein the relationship between media and politics can be characterised as both intimate and ruthless (P. O'Mahony, 2000: 18). However, while O'Mahony claims that the Irish media displays a lack of deference towards those in power, others have characterised the Irish media as conservative. Conway (2010), for example, describes the media reaction to a major corruption scandal among the gardaí in the late-1990s as reactive rather than proactive; O'Brien (2007) too stresses that this story was broken by politicians rather than journalists. Conway's analysis of press discourse suggested that the media was keen to adopt explanations which could maintain the status quo. The homogeneity of the Irish media also discourages alternative voices, and the news content across various outlets and titles is remarkably uniform (P. O'Mahony, 2000).

The legacy of censorship in the Republic of Ireland may also underlie the conservatism of media reporting. Restrictions imposed both formally and informally can foster an atmosphere of caution. Section 31 of the Broadcasting Act 1960 empowered the government to prevent the broadcasting of material likely to incite persons to crime, or material which tended to undermine the authority of the state. Dating from the eruption of 'the Conflict' in Northern Ireland in the late-1960s, this legislation was used to prevent the broadcasting of material deemed sensitive. The effects of this were palpable in the jailing of a journalist in 1972 and in a slew of news stories, not directly related to 'the Conflict', which were adversely impacted as a result of these censorship restrictions (Purcell, 1991). The conservatism of the media has also been linked to the influence of the Catholic Church and the imposition of unyielding moral codes which were enshrined by the state in legislation such as the Censorship of Publications Act 1929. Censorship therefore operated not only in relation to political subversion, but also in the realm of perceived moral subversion (Inglis and MacKeogh, 2012; Keating, 2012).

In summary, beyond the events of 1996, crime has tended not to be used as a tool for electoral gain by Irish political parties (Kilcommins et al., 2004). Related to this political reluctance to politicise crime, the Irish media can be categorised more by reference to conservatism than to sensationalism, despite some inevitable elements of tabloidisation.

Northern Ireland

Until recently, discussions of media and crime in Northern Ireland focussed on 'the Conflict' with little discussion of how 'ordinary' crime was represented. This is unsurprising given that political violence in Northern Ireland received blanket coverage from 1970 (McCann, 1973), becoming, in effect, a form of war reporting (Schlesinger, 1978/1987). While in the Republic of Ireland political crime is usually absent from criminological research (Tomlinson et al., 1988, and see for example O'Connell, 1999), in Northern Ireland the situation is reversed, and ordinary crime tends to be pushed out by a focus on the subversive. This ambivalence about categorisation reflects an ontological crisis which sits uneasily with the case of Northern Ireland and highlights the different realities 'crime' assumes. The literature on media in Northern Ireland is therefore signally different from that produced in the Republic of Ireland. The representation of 'ordinary' crime is not directly comparable, as there is little research of this nature. However, the work which has emerged on the media and 'the Conflict' provides a fundamental critical perspective on state–media relations.

Reporting 'the Conflict'

The print market in Northern Ireland is small and competitive, and the marketplace is dominated by three titles: the *Irish News*, the *Newsletter* and the *Belfast Telegraph* (Greer, 2003). Both the *Irish News* and the *Newsletter* are avowedly ideological, serving the Nationalist and Unionist communities respectively, while the *Belfast Telegraph* positions itself as neutral (or 'bias by omission', Rolston, 1991). Greer (2003) has highlighted how newspapers' established ideology determines readership, which can act as a bar to proprietorial interference.

Unlike print journalism, television news reached both communities at once (Spencer, 2004). However, television news has also been accused of being complicit with state interests during 'the Conflict'. The 'reference upwards' system existing at the BBC and ITV from the early 1970s stifled contentious comment, as senior-level approval was required for stories about Northern Ireland; in practice, this form of internal censorship was targeted at pieces which featured Republican or Nationalist perspectives. Curtis writes that this bias gradually solidified as a BBC ban on televising Republican interviews (Curtis, 1984/1996). Schlesinger argues that while the BBC could not be viewed simplistically as an arm of government, its role in 'upholding the legitimate established order ... means that the BBC is essentially for order as it is defined by the state' (Schlesinger, 1978/1987: 222).

Northern Ireland, in common with the Republic of Ireland, has a legacy of censorship. The 1988 Broadcasting Ban, characterised as 'the most stringent piece of peace-time censorship', prohibited statements from representatives of various proscribed organisations, as well as from representatives of Sinn Féin (Moloney, 1991: 27). The 1988 Ban demonstrated the media's role in the 'propaganda war' waged in Northern Ireland; the media was crucial in 'one of the most concerted and concentrated exercises in labelling ever undertaken in peace time' as the British state sought to rebrand IRA activity as criminality rather than political violence (Hillyard, 1982: 37). The 'oxygen of publicity' argument, namely, that coverage of violence lent support to paramilitary organisations, was used to support these restrictions; tabloid titles especially internalised this rationale and were critical of reporting deemed inflammatory (Moloney, 1991). Rolston (1991) also argues that the timidity of regionally-based journalists was rationalised by the fears of inciting further violence.

The self-censorship exercised by journalists in Northern Ireland also had a 'chilling effect' beyond reporting of 'the Conflict'. When allegations of institutional abuse at the Kincora Boys' Home in Belfast first emerged in the late 1970s, the *Belfast Telegraph* took a cautious approach and decided not to run the story (Rolston, 1991). The story was highly politicised, involving the Protestant churches and allegations of a cover-up against the British state (Greer, 2003). A former editor of the *Irish News*, traditionally a newspaper of the Catholic Hierarchy (Rolston, 1991), has also noted the newspaper's process of 'coming to terms' with news stories alleging clerical sex abuse (Greer, 2003: 108). However, by the mid-1990s, institutional and clerical sex abuse had become the 'dominant theme' of the reporting of sexual offences in Northern Ireland. The prevalence of such stories across nationalist *and* unionist newspapers demonstrated the degree to which the reporting of sexual offences transcended community divisions (Greer, 2003).

Media reliance on official sources also contributed to a state-leaning bias (Kelly, 1986). News outlets such as the *Irish News*, which directly challenged the authority of the police and the government, had fractious relationships with these institutions which adversely impacted informal access to police sources (Greer, 2003). This exposes the difficulty of 'manufacturing consent' in a divided society where a consensus cannot be said to exist (Schlesinger, 1978/1987; Greer, 2003). As Greer (2003: 187) observes: 'Northern Ireland is fractured politically, culturally, socially, economically and geographically, and the changing depth and direction of its many fissures influences profoundly the nature of the news that is produced. It is a fundamentally divided society'.

Rolston (1991) found the widest editorial differences between the *News Letter* and *Irish News*, as these titles focussed on British and Republic of Ireland news respectively. Political alignment was also evident in the reporting of specific incidents, as the newspapers downplayed the sectarian nature of killings committed by 'their' side, while highlighting violence perpetrated by the 'other' side. The less politically-aligned *Belfast Telegraph* also perpetuated unarticulated values in its reporting, with different weighting afforded to Protestant and Catholic deaths: 'the presumption is that a Catholic victim *is* a republican unless it is proven otherwise' (Rolston, 1991: 170).

Elements of cultural criminological exploration are also to be found from Northern Ireland, for example, Rolston's (1989) exploration of fictive portrayals of 'the Conflict' which demonstrated that Republican figures were selected as protagonists over Loyalist figures. Rolston's work has also explored how collective memory and identity are reinforced through wall murals. Rolston has documented the evolving use of Loyalist and Republican symbolism in Northern Ireland's iconic wall murals, looking particularly at how they have adapted in response to the peace process. The allocation of state resources with the purpose of 'rebranding' the murals for a shared future has demonstrated the differential ability of the Republican and Loyalist traditions to adapt a new language of community (Rolston, 2010, 2012).

Reporting 'ordinary' crime

Following the ceasefire of 1994, more attention was devoted to 'ordinary' crime (Hollywood, 1997; Greer, 2003). The unfamiliar violence-shaped hole left by the peace process created the vacuum necessary for a moral panic over drug use; dance culture became the new politically acceptable adversary, and those involved 'were automatically "deviantised" by journalists acting as agents of moral indignation' (Hollywood, 1997: 65). Hollywood's six-month analysis of the main print titles showed that following the ceasefire there was a 40 per cent increase in the coverage of drug crime. The moral panic also served to legitimise recruitment to a police force that was otherwise facing rationalisation, while allowing the Nationalist *Irish News* to normalise reporting of policing. This move was in line with new ownership at the *Irish News* in the 1980s during which IRA death notices were no longer printed, while recruitment notices for the RUC were carried alongside more vocal criticism of the IRA and Sinn Féin (Rolston, 1991; Greer, 2003).

In a similar vein, Chris Greer (2003) has documented the increased reporting of sex crime in the Northern Irish print media from 1985 until 1997. This is the first comprehensive research of its kind into 'ordinary' crime and its representation in Northern Ireland. Greer suggested that in a contested society, sexual offences have the potential to garner universal condemnation and offer a neutral role for law enforcement in post-conflict transition. Greer's research demonstrated the importance of news values in determining news content, indicating that while seriousness and novelty were both significant news values, they were superseded in importance by proximity: Once *The Irish Times* was excluded from the sample, 80 per cent of crimes reported were committed in Northern Ireland. Greer's research also demonstrated the different reporting styles between the mostly broadsheet dailies and the tabloid Sunday titles; broadsheets reported serious crimes, while tabloid coverage also encompassed trivial or comedic stories.

In light of comments above regarding the size of the jurisdiction and its impact on reporting, it is notable that Northern Irish journalists considered the smallness and sense of community as a barrier to sensationalist reporting: 'the production of news in a small jurisdiction carries with it a certain sense of social responsibility that serves to restrain the representation of sex crime' (Greer, 2003: 162). However, this sense of responsibility was interpreted by tabloid journalists as engagement with a punitive message on sex crime, leading to a 'moral consensus' mode of reporting which 'explicitly promotes popular fear and loathing' (Greer, 2003: 162). Greer (2003) also found heavy use of well-worn tropes, such as the narrative of the sex offender as monster and as 'other'. The use of stereotypes has also been found in relation to how women were represented in the context of 'the Conflict', as fictive accounts portrayed women who engaged in violence as unnatural (Rolston, 1989). Research in Northern Ireland has also found that reductive ideas about women underpin news reporting; the gendered gaze was particularly noticeable in relation to the salacious portrayal of women who had committed violent offences (Gordon and Black, 2010).

In line with the general literature, research in Northern Ireland has found that crime is reported as episodic. Research examining the representation of hate crime, for example, has shown that it is reported without discussion of racism, as a series of dramatic one-off incidents (Northern Ireland Council for Voluntary Action (NICVA), 2005). Greer found that despite an exponential increase in the amount of sex crime reported across his sample period, the issue had more accurately been covered in 1985 than in 1997. Over this period he found that analysis became less common, with greater focus going to discrete events: '[w]hat is left behind is a news product which aims primarily to shock and frequently, it seems, to entertain' (Greer, 2003: 89).

The chapter has so far outlined research on the content of crime in the media in the Republic of Ireland and Northern Ireland. The following section examines public attitudes towards crime north and south of the border and explores the possibility that crime in the media can provoke fear of crime.

Public attitudes, fear of crime and the media

Crime in the media was initially assumed to inspire copycat offending; more recently the link has been made between crime in the media and fear of crime (Lee, 2007). In the Republic of Ireland, fear of crime became a policy area for government with the establishment of the now defunct National Crime Council in 1999 (Department of Justice, 2009). While a variety of surveys have measured public perceptions of crime in the Republic of Ireland, these are only sporadically undertaken, which makes reliance on official statistics necessary (Healy and O'Donnell, 2010; O'Donnell, 2011). The available figures suggest that Irish society was largely unconcerned with crime until a rise in fear of crime in the mid-1990s (Whelan and Vaughan, 1982; Breen and Rottman, 1985; Kilcommins et al., 2004) perhaps linked to the 'media-orchestrated "moral panic"' of 1996 (P. O'Mahony, 2000: 19). Thereafter, the Republic of Ireland has been characterised by European and international surveys as having a high fear of crime (van Dijk and Toornvliet, 1996; Eurobarometer, 2004, 2008).

In contrast to this categorisation, Irish figures suggest that feelings of safety have remained relatively stable, with approximately three-quarters of respondents feeling 'safe' or 'very safe' walking in their neighbourhood after dark (CSO, 1998, 2010). There is also a general downward trend in the proportion of respondents expressing worry that they or a family member will become a victim of crime (Browne, 2008). However, a perception gap exists; despite stable or increasing feelings of safety, respondents believe that crime nationally is rising. This gap is also evident in the discord between perceptions of crime nationally compared to perceptions of crime in respondents' local areas; consistently, more respondents felt that crime in Ireland generally is getting worse while being much less committed to this view with regard to their own area (Browne, 2008; CSO, 2010). Research from the Republic of Ireland also shows a pronounced age and sex differential, with females and older persons reporting a higher level of fear. In 2010, 41 per cent of men reported feeling 'very safe' walking alone in their neighbourhood after dark compared to just 22 per cent of women. The age differential is also evident: 19 per cent of those aged 65 or over reported feeling 'very safe', compared to 36 per cent of those aged 18 to 24 (CSO, 2010).

North of the border, the Northern Ireland Crime Survey (NICS) has provided data on public perceptions of crime sporadically from 1994 to 1995 (Boyle and Haire, 1996) and on an annual basis from 2005. Like the Republic of Ireland, figures from Northern Ireland also found that respondents considered crime in their local area to be lower than regional crime levels (Boyle and Haire, 1996). Levels of fear in Northern Ireland have experienced a slight rise and fall; the proportion of those feeling 'very unsafe' rose from 8 to 13 per cent between 1998 and 2003 to 2004. However, since then there has been a general downward trend to a low of 7 per cent in 2012 and 2013 (Campbell and Freel, 2013; Cadogan and Campbell, 2014). These feelings of fear and insecurity are not evenly distributed throughout the community in Northern Ireland, however. The most recent NICS suggests that worry about crime and income is inversely proportionate to an individual's income (Cadogan and Campbell, 2014). Geary et al. (2000) found that Catholic communities tended to perceive higher rates of crime and lower levels of reporting to the police than Protestant communities; however, other research has suggested that there were starker differences in levels of fear between urban and rural communities than between religious communities, with urban communities experiencing generally higher rates of fear (D. O'Mahony et al., 2000). Northern Irish research also shows differences by age and sex with higher rates of fearfulness for females and older persons. The most recent NICS found that 11 per cent of females felt 'very unsafe' walking alone in their area after dark versus 3 per cent of males, while 13 per cent of those aged 75 or over would feel 'very unsafe' walking in their area alone after dark compared to just 4 per cent of 25- to 34-year-olds (Cadogan and Campbell, 2014).

Is fear of crime linked to the media?

The link between the media and fear of crime is intuitive; however, it has proved difficult to show definitive media effects (Ditton et al., 2004). More recent research has suggested that the *interpretation* and *reception* of media content may be the key to understanding this link (Reiner et al., 2000; Ditton et al., 2004).

Research north and south of the border has shown a marked disparity between perceptions of crime at a national and local level. In Northern Ireland, Boyle and Haire (1996: 1) have cited media consumption as a means of explaining this perception gap, suggesting that:

> When people are asked to compare crime in their area with their concept of crime as it exists in the rest of Northern Ireland they are most likely to be comparing real first hand local experience with a view which has been formed more generally.

There is no simple linear relationship between crime, media representation and fear of crime. The outpouring of shock following the killing of Veronica Guerin in the Republic of Ireland in

1996 was not matched in Northern Ireland by the assassination of investigative journalist Martin O'Hagan in 2001 (O'Donnell, 2005). Further, despite rising numbers of 'gangland' murders in the early 2000s, concern about crime did not increase as it had done in 1996; Kilcommins *et al.* (2004) suggest that this may be due to the labelling of victims as 'known to the gardaí', which reduced the impact of the killings on middle-class fears. Middle-class insecurity is an element of the 'crime complex' in which fear of crime becomes an 'organising principle' (Garland, 2001). In the Republic of Ireland, it could be argued that this move was deliberately undertaken in the early 1980s when crime news was prioritised at the *Evening Herald* in an attempt to resonate with young, urban professionals (Kerrigan and Shaw, 1985). However, Kilcommins *et al.* (2004) argue that while crime has become a 'staple' of news reporting, fear of crime has not reached endemic levels in the Republic of Ireland and that, outside the mid-1990s panic, concern about crime is easily displaced by other concerns, such as the economy. Crime in the Republic of Ireland is thus generally not a live political issue (O'Donnell and Jewkes, 2011), accordingly situating Ireland some distance from Garland's (2001) 'crime complex'.

It seems that recorded crime is not directly related to fear of crime, but *interpretation* of media reports may be. Concerns about crime rise and fall independent of the actual levels of crime. It is therefore supposed that perceptions of crime derive from some source other than official statistics, and considerable research has been undertaken into the relationship between media representations of crime and fear of crime. O'Connell (1999) linked high fear of crime and high prevalence estimates of crime with distorted newspaper reporting on crime in the Republic of Ireland. O'Connell found that newspaper readership was the most significant variable in prevalence estimates of crime (O'Connell and Whelan, 1996). O'Connell *et al.* (1998) tested this relationship between newspaper readership and perception of crime and found that while the causal relationship was not solely the result of a top-down model of media influence, there was support for this. When the number of crime articles in the sampled newspapers was presented as a proportion of all articles, it correlated to crime prevalence as perceived by newspaper readers; readers who read newspapers with proportionately more crime articles perceived crime as a more serious problem. The Northern Ireland Crime Survey also breaks down figures according to newspaper readership. Generally, readers of national broadsheets and the *Belfast Telegraph* reported lower fear of crime than readers of national tabloids. *Irish News* readers had initially experienced very high levels of fear, but this figure has dropped considerably, as has the fear of crime reported by *Newsletter* readers (Campbell and Freel, 2013; Cadogan and Campbell, 2014). These figures chime with findings elsewhere (Williams and Dickinson, 1993) that broadsheet readers have lower fear of crime than tabloid readers while also corresponding to differences by community in Northern Ireland which have suggested that predominantly Catholic communities have a higher fear of crime (Geary *et al.*, 2000).

Research both north and south of the border shows that females and older persons have a higher fear of crime. The greater fear of crime felt by these groups has been referred to as a paradox due to their lower risk of victimisation. However, older persons may experience less victimisation because of conscious risk-avoidance tactics (McCullagh, 1996). Crime can also have differential *impact*; Irish research found that the emotional disturbance following victimisation was greater in females and older persons (Watson, 2000). Further, the accuracy of the term 'paradox' in relation to female fear of crime has been challenged by research from both jurisdictions which demonstrated the prevalence of female victimisation (McGee *et al.*, 2002; Freel, 2013; EU Agency for Fundamental Rights, 2014). Finally, the media's preference for vulnerable, often female, victims is an unrelenting tool for teaching women that they have much to fear (O'Connell, 1999; Carr and Holt, 2010).

Conclusion

The introduction to this chapter outlined the key arguments from existing research relating to the content of crime in the media and the possible effects of this. The review of the research from the Republic of Ireland and Northern Ireland suggests some immediate conclusions regarding how the relationship between media and crime in these jurisdictions can be situated within this literature.

Existing trends regarding the content of crime in the media would seem to be borne out by the literature from the Republic of Ireland and Northern Ireland. Research from north and south of the border has demonstrated reliance on crime as a feature of media content, the skewing towards serious and atypical crime and the greater proportion of crime news in tabloid newspapers (O'Connell, 1999; Greer, 2003). A preference for vulnerable victims (O'Connell, 1999) and the emergence of a culture of the victim in tabloids both north and south of the border has also been noted (Rolston, 1991; Greer, 2003; O'Brien, 2007). Research has suggested that crime news is rarely contextualised, reporting instead favouring an episodic approach which frames crime as a series of discrete incidents rather than engaging in analysis (O'Connell *et al.*, 1998; NICVA, 2005; Devereux *et al.*, 2011). In Northern Ireland, Greer (2003) suggested that this tendency has only become more pronounced in the recent past, with the media reporting on sex offending becoming *less* contextualised. In both jurisdictions, the deployment of stereotypes has also inhibited meaningful coverage, for example, in relation to women, as both victims and offenders (Carr and Holt, 2010; Quinlan, 2011), and in relation to sexual offenders who are portrayed as inhuman 'others' (Greer, 2003). Further, the downgrading of victims according to social class (McCullagh, 2006) and the perennial fascination with gangland crime post the mid-1990s moral panic (Hamilton, 2007) – for example, in the context of Limerick, which has borne the brunt of relentlessly negative reporting (Devereux *et al.*, 2011) – has created a hierarchy of crime with differential levels of public empathy. The focus on what is 'newsworthy' has created a homogenous yet unrepresentative picture of crime (P. O'Mahony, 2000; Greer, 2003), and it has been lamented that 'in an era of almost unfettered freedom of expression, media, political and public debate on critical issues like crime is often narrow, clichéd and specious' (P. O'Mahony, 2000: 19).

However, it is also the case that these trends have been mediated by specific local factors north and south of the border, to create historically contingent media landscapes. Therefore, while the broad brushstroke findings from existing research are present in the Republic of Ireland and Northern Ireland, these are experienced differentially. For example, conservatism has persisted as a defining characteristic of the media in both jurisdictions, with broadsheet newspapers retaining political salience over the tabloid press (Greer, 2003; O'Donnell and Jewkes, 2011). Underpinning this conservatism, the spectre of censorship has loomed large in both jurisdictions. The shared history of censorship is borne of the political violence which erupted in Northern Ireland, and its inevitable 'chilling effect' has resulted in a conservative media in both jurisdictions (Moloney, 1991; Purcell, 1991; Rolston, 1991; Conway, 2010). Conservatism may also derive from the small size of the jurisdictions and the obligations and shared sense of community that this can create (P. O'Mahony, 2000; Greer, 2003). An added consideration, particularly in the Republic of Ireland, is the influence of the Catholic Church, which has caused tension between traditional and modern discourses and which has also been articulated as a means of explaining a conservative media (Inglis and MacKeogh, 2012). Therefore, while the trends identified elsewhere are present in the Republic of Ireland and Northern Ireland, these are mediated by the nuances of specific local factors expressed as cultural, social and political differences.

Research from the two jurisdictions is less explicit about the extent to which the *effects* of the content of crime in the media are being felt. A spike in public concern about crime was evident in the Republic of Ireland surrounding the moral panic of 1996. However, despite being newly branded as a nation that is fearful of crime by international and European measures, the veracity of this categorisation is doubtful, and fear of crime remains an issue attracting ambivalent interest which erupts only sporadically (Kilcommins *et al.*, 2004). In Northern Ireland, while newspaper readership appears to correspond to expected fear of crime patterns, feelings of safety there are actually increasing (Cadogan and Campbell, 2014). Ultimately, however, the 'perception gap' experienced between fear of crime at a macro level and the fear of crime at a local level may be partially explained by reference to media reporting (Boyle and Haire, 1996; O'Connell *et al.*, 1998).

Finally, for the reasons outlined above, it is important to note the signally different approach taken by the research which has emerged from the Republic of Ireland and Northern Ireland, rendering straightforward comparative work problematic. However, the recent turn towards investigation of the media representation of 'ordinary' crime in Northern Ireland has provided an opportunity to situate the relationship between media and crime there within a broader context. One question for future research is the extent to which the normalising of the media landscape in Northern Ireland will lead to convergence with the trends evident elsewhere and how far the historical legacy of conflict will continue to create a unique media environment. In the Republic of Ireland, while more research exists, the most comprehensive work is some 20 years old, and much of what does exist relates exclusively to the events of 1996. Further research must engage with how the media in the Republic of Ireland continue to depict issues of crime and justice in an era of proliferating media channels such as online and social media.

Bibliography

Adler, F. (1983) *Nations Not Obsessed with Crime*. Littleton, Colorado: Rothman.

Barrat, D. (1986) *Media Sociology*. London: Routledge.

Becker, H. (1973) *Outsiders: Studies in the Sociology of Deviance*. New York/London: Free Press.

Black, L. (2009) *Paper Women: The Representation of Female Offenders in Irish Newspapers*. Unpublished MA dissertation. Dublin Institute of Technology. Available at: http://arrow.dit.ie/cgi/viewcontent.cgi?article=1000&context=aaschssldis (accessed 14 June 2014).

Boyle, M. and Haire, T. (1996) *Fear of Crime and Likelihood of Victimisation in Northern Ireland*. Research Findings 2/96. Belfast: Statistics and Research Branch, Northern Ireland Office.

Breen, R. and Rottman, D. B. (1985) *Crime Victimisation in the Republic of Ireland*. Dublin: Economic and Social Research Institute.

Browne, C. (2008) *Garda Public Attitudes Survey 2008*. Templemore: An Garda Síochána. Available at: www.garda.ie/Documents/User/24.%20GARDA%20PUBLIC%20ATTITUDES%20-%202008.pdf (accessed 14 June 2014).

Cadogan, G. and Campbell, P. (2014) *Perceptions of Crime: Findings from the 2012/13 Northern Ireland Crime Survey*. Belfast: Department of Justice. Available at: www.dojni.gov.uk/index/statistics-research/stats-research-publications/northern-ireland-crime-survey-s-r/nics-2012-13-perceptions-of-crime-bulletin.pdf (accessed 14 June 2014).

Campbell, P. and Freel, R. (2013) *Perceptions of Crime: Findings from the 2011/12 Northern Ireland Crime Survey*. Belfast: Department of Justice. Available at: www.dojni.gov.uk/index/statistics-research/stats-research-publications/northern-ireland-crime-survey-s-r/nics-2011-12-perceptions-of-crime-bulletin.pdf (accessed 14 June 2014).

Carr, N. and Holt, S. (2010) 'Outrageous Provocation? The Media Reporting of Domestic Violence in Ireland' in P. Share and M. Corcoran (eds) *Ireland of the Illusions: A Sociological Chronicle, 2007–2008*. Dublin: IPA.

Central Statistics Office (1998) *Quarterly National Household Survey: Crime and Victimisation September-November 1998*. Cork: CSO. Available at: www.cso.ie/en/media/csoie/qnhs/documents/qnhs_crimeandvictimisationq31998.pdf (accessed 14 June 2014).

Central Statistics Office (2010) *Quarterly National Household Survey: Crime and Victimisation 2010*. Cork: CSO. Available at: www.cso.ie/en/media/csoie/releasespublications/documents/crimejustice/2010/qnhscrimeandvictimisation2010.pdf (accessed 14 June 2014).

Christie, N. (1986) 'The Ideal Victim' in E. Fattah (ed) *From Crime Policy to Victim Policy: Reorienting the Justice System*. Basingstoke: Macmillan.

Cohen, S. (1972) *Folk Devils and Moral Panics: The Creation of the Mods and Rockers*. London: MacGibbon and Kee.

Conway, V. (2010) *The Blue Wall of Silence: The Morris Tribunal and Police Accountability in Ireland*. Dublin/Portland: Irish Academic Press.

Corcoran, M. P. (2004) 'The Political Preferences and Value Orientations of Irish Journalists', *Irish Journal of Sociology*, 13(2): 22–42.

Curtis, L. (1984/1996) 'The Reference Upwards System' in B. Rolston and D. Miller (eds) *War and Words: the Northern Ireland Media Reader*. Belfast: BTP Publications.

Department of Justice, Equality and Law Reform (2009) *Fear of Crime in Ireland and Its Impact on Quality of Life*. Dublin: Stationery Office. Available at: www.justice.ie/en/JELR/Fear%20of%20Crime%20in%20Ireland.pdf/Files/Fear%20of%20Crime%20in%20Ireland.pdf (accessed 14 June 2014).

Devereux, E., Haynes, A. and Power, M. J. (2011) 'Behind the Headlines: Media Coverage of Social Exclusion in Limerick City – the Case of Moyross' in N. Hourigan (ed) *Understanding Limerick: Social Exclusion and Change*. Cork: Cork University Press.

Ditton, J., Chadee, D., Farrall, S., Gilchrist, E. and Bannister, J. (2004) 'From Imitation to Intimidation: A Note on the Curious and Changing Relationship between the Media, Crime and Fear of Crime', *British Journal of Criminology*, 44: 595–610.

Elvestad, E. and Blekesaune, A. (2008) 'Newspaper Readers in Europe: A Multilevel Study of Individual and National Differences', *European Journal of Communication*, 23(4): 425–47.

Eurobarometer (2004) *Eurobarometer 60 Public Opinion in the European Union*. European Commission. Available at: http://ec.europa.eu/public_opinion/archives/eb/eb60/eb60_rapport_standard_en.pdf (accessed 14 June 2014).

Eurobarometer (2008) *Eurobarometer 68 Public Opinion in the European Union*. European Commission. Available at: http://ec.europa.eu/public_opinion/archives/eb/eb68/eb_68_en.pdf (accessed 14 June 2014).

EU Agency for Fundamental Rights (2014) *Violence Against Women: An EU-Wide Survey*. Luxembourg: Publications Office of the European Union. Available at: http://fra.europa.eu/sites/default/files/fra-2014-vaw-survey-main-results_en.pdf (accessed 14 June 2014).

Ferrell, J., Hayward, K. J. and Young, J. (2008) *Cultural Criminology: An Invitation*. London: Sage.

Freel, R. (2013) *Experience of Domestic Violence: Findings from the 2008/09 to 2010/11 Northern Ireland Crime Surveys*. Belfast: Department of Justice. Available at: www.dojni.gov.uk/index/statistics-research/stats-research-publications/northern-ireland-crime-survey-s-r/nics-2008-09-to-2010-11-domestic-violence-bulletin.pdf (accessed 14 June 2014).

Galtung, J. and Ruge, M. (1973) 'Structuring and Selecting News' in S. Cohen and J. Young (eds) *The Manufacture of News*. London: Constable.

Garland, D. (2001) *The Culture of Control: Crime and Social Order in Contemporary Society*. Oxford: Oxford University Press.

Garland, D. (2008) 'On the Concept of Moral Panic', *Crime, Media, Culture*, 4(1): 9–30.

Geary, R., McEvoy, K. and Morison, J. (2000) 'Lives Less Ordinary? Crime, Communities and Policing in Northern Ireland', *Irish Journal of Sociology*, 10(1): 49–74.

Gordon, F. and Black, L. (2010) *Media Profiling of Women in the Criminal Justice System: North and South*. Dublin: ACJRD. Available at: www.acjrd.ie/files/Women_in_the_Criminal_Justice_System_(2010).pdf (accessed 14 June 2014).

Greer, C. (2003) *Sex Crime in the Media: Sex Offending and the Press in a Divided Society*. Cullompton: Willan.

Greer, C. and McLaughlin, E. (2010) 'We Predict a Riot? Public Order Policing, New Media Environments and the Rise of the Citizen Journalist', *British Journal of Criminology*, 50(3): 1041–59.

Hall, S. (1982/1988) 'The Rediscovery of "Ideology": Return of the Repressed in Media Studies' in M. Gurevitch, T. Bennett, J. Curran and J. Woollacott (eds) *Culture, Society and the Media*. London: Routledge.

Hall, S. *et al.* (1978) *Policing the Crisis: Mugging, the State and Law and Order*. London: Macmillan.

Hamilton, C. (2005) 'Moral Panic Revisited: Part One', *Irish Criminal Law Journal*, 15(1): 8.

Hamilton, C. (2007) *The Presumption of Innocence in Irish Criminal Law*. Dublin: Irish Academic Press.

Healy, D. and O'Donnell, I. (2010) 'Crime, Consequences and Court Reports', *Irish Criminal Law Journal*, 20(1): 2–7.

Herman, E. S. and Chomsky, N. (1988/1994) *Manufacturing Consent: The Political Economy of the Mass Media*. London: Vintage.

Hillyard, P. (1982) 'The Media Coverage of Crime and Justice in Northern Ireland' in C. Sumner (ed) *Crime, Justice and the Mass Media*. Cambridge: Cropwood Conference Series 14.

Hollywood, B. (1997) 'Dancing in the Dark: Ecstasy, the Dance Culture and Moral Panic in Post Ceasefire Northern Ireland', *Critical Criminology*, 8(1): 62–77.

Inglis, T. and MacKeogh, C. (2012) 'The Double Bind: Women, Honour and Sexuality in Contemporary Ireland', *Media, Culture and Society*, 34(1): 68–82.

Jewkes, J. (2011) *Media and Crime*, 2nd edn. Los Angeles/London: Sage.

Keating, A. (2012) 'Sexual Crime in the Irish Free State 1922-33: Its Nature, Extent and Reporting', *Irish Studies Review*, 20(2): 135–55.

Kelly, M. (1986) 'Power, Control and Media Coverage of the Northern Ireland Conflict' in P. Clancy, S. Drudy, K. Lynch and L. O'Dowd (eds) *Ireland: A Sociological Profile*. Dublin: IPA.

Kerrigan, G. and Shaw, H. (1985) 'Crime Hysteria', *Magill*, 18 April.

Kilcommins, S., O'Donnell, I., O'Sullivan, E. and Vaughan, B. (2004) *Crime, Punishment and the Search for Order in Ireland*. Dublin: IPA.

Lee, M. (2007) *Inventing Fear of Crime: Criminology and the Politics of Anxiety*. Uffculme: Willan.

McCann, E. (1973) 'The British Press and Northern Ireland' in S. Cohen and J. Young (eds) *The Manufacture of News: Social Problems, Deviance and the Mass Media*. London: Constable.

McCullagh, C. (1996) *Crime in Ireland: A Sociological Introduction*. Cork: Cork University Press.

McCullagh, C. (2006) 'The Acceptable Victim of Murder' in M. P. Corcoran and M. Peillon (eds) *Uncertain Ireland*. Dublin: IPA.

McCullagh, C. (2008) 'Modern Ireland, Modern Media, Same Old Story?' in S. O'Sullivan (ed) *Contemporary Ireland: A Sociological Map*. Dublin: UCD Press.

McGee, H., Garavan, R., de Barra, M., Byrne, J. and Conroy, R. (2002) *The SAVI Report: Sexual Abuse and Violence in Ireland*. Dublin: Liffey Press. Available at: www.drcc.ie/wp-content/uploads/2011/03/savi.pdf (accessed 14 June 2014).

McNair, B. (2006) *Cultural Chaos: Journalism, News and Power in a Globalised World*. London: Routledge.

Maguire, N. and Carr, N. (2013) 'Changing Shape and Shifting Boundaries – the Media Portrayal of Probation in Ireland', *European Journal of Probation*, 5(3): 3–23.

Meade, J. (2000) 'Organised Crime, Moral Panic and Law Reform: The Irish Adoption of Civil Forfeiture', *Irish Criminal Law Journal*, 10(1): 11–16.

Moloney, E. (1991) 'Closing Down the Airwaves: The Story of the Broadcasting Ban' in B. Rolston (ed) *The Media in Northern Ireland: Covering the Troubles*. London: Macmillan.

NICVA (2005) *Reporting on Civil Society: An Assessment of How the Media Portrays the Activities of Civil Society in Northern Ireland*. Available at: www.nicva.org/sites/default/files/MediaReview_Final.pdf (accessed 14 June 2014).

O'Brien, M. (2007) 'Selling Fear? The Changing Face of Crime Reporting in Ireland' in J. Horgan, B. O'Connor, H. Sheehan (eds) *Mapping Irish Media: Critical Explorations*. Dublin: University College Dublin Press.

—— (2010) 'The Court of Public Opinion' in P. Share and M. P. Corcoran (eds) *Ireland of the Illusions: A Sociological Chronicle 2007-2008*. Dublin: IPA.

O'Connell, M. (1999) 'Is Irish Public Opinion towards Crime Distorted by Media Bias?' *European Journal of Communication*, 14: 191–212.

—— (2002) 'The Portrayal of Crime in the Media: Does It Matter?' in P. O'Mahony (ed) *Criminal Justice in Ireland*. Dublin: IPA.

O'Connell, M. and Whelan, A. T. (1996) 'The Public Perception of Crime Prevalence, Newspaper Readership and "Mean World" Attitudes', *Legal and Criminological Psychology*, 1(2): 179–95.

O'Connell, M., Invernizzi, F. and Fuller, R. (1998) 'Newspaper Readership and the Perception of Crime: Testing an Assumed Relationship through a Triangulation of Methods', *Legal and Criminological Psychology*, 3(1): 29–57.

O'Donnell, I. (2005) 'Crime and Justice in the Republic of Ireland', *European Journal of Criminology*, 2(1): 99–131.

O'Donnell, I. (2011) 'Crime and Punishment in the Republic of Ireland: A Country Profile', *International Journal of Comparative and Applied Criminal Justice*, 35(1): 69–84.

O'Donnell, I. and Jewkes, Y. (2011) 'Going Home for Christmas: Prisoners, a Taste of Freedom and the Press', *Howard Journal of Criminal Justice*, 50(1): 75–91.

O'Donnell, I. and O'Sullivan, E. (2001) *Crime Control in Ireland: The Politics of Intolerance*. Cork: Cork University Press.

O'Mahony, D., McEvoy, K., Geary, R. and Morison, J. (2000) *Crime, Community and Locale: The Northern Ireland Communities Crime Survey*. Aldershot: Ashgate.

O'Mahony, P. (1996) *Criminal Chaos: Seven Crises in Irish Criminal Justice*. Dublin: Round Hall: Sweet and Maxwell.

—— (1998) 'Losing the Plot', *Magill*, 1 January.

—— (2000) 'Crime in the Republic of Ireland: A Suitable Case for Sociological Analysis', *Irish Journal of Sociology*, 10: 3–26.

O'Sullivan, C. (2008) 'The Nun, the Rape Charge and the Miscarriage of Justice: The Case of Nora Wall', *Northern Ireland Legal Quarterly*, 59(3): 305–25.

Peelo, M., Soothill, K., Pearson, J. and Ackerley, E. (2004) 'Newspaper Reporting and the Public Construction of Homicide', *British Journal of Criminology*, 44(2): 256–75.

Purcell, B. (1991) 'The Silence of Irish Broadcasting' in B. Rolston (ed) *The Media in Northern Ireland: Covering the Troubles*. London: Macmillan.

Quinlan, C. (2011) *Inside: Ireland's Women's Prisons, Past and Present*. Dublin: Irish Academic Press.

Reiner, R., Livingstone, S. and Allen, J. (2000) 'No More Happy Endings? The Media and Popular Concern about Crime Since the Second World War' in T. Hope and R. Sparks (eds) *Crime, Risk and Insecurity*. London: Routledge.

Rolston, B. (1989) 'Mothers, Whores and Villains: Images of Women in Novels of the Northern Ireland Conflict' in B. Rolston and D. Miller (eds) *War and Words: The Northern Ireland Media Reader*. Belfast: BTP Publications.

—— (ed) (1991) *The Media and Northern Ireland: Covering the Troubles*. Basingstoke: Macmillan.

—— (2010) 'Trying to Reach the Future through the Past: Murals and Memory in Northern Ireland', *Crime Media Culture*, 6(3): 285–307.

—— (2012) 'Re-Imaging: Mural Painting and the State in Northern Ireland', *International Journal of Cultural Studies*, 15(5): 447–66.

Schlesinger, P. (1978/1987) *Putting 'Reality' Together: BBC News*. London: Methuen.

Spencer, G. (2004) 'The Impact of Television News on the Northern Ireland Peace Negotiations', *Media, Culture and Society*, 26(5): 603–23.

Tomlinson, M., Varley, T. and McCullagh, C. (1988) *Whose Law and Order? Aspects of Crime and Social Control in Irish Society*. Belfast: Sociological Association of Ireland.

van Dijk, J. and Toornvliet, L. (1996) *Towards a Eurobarometer of Public Safety: Key Findings of the First Survey on Public Safety among the Residents of the European Union*. Leiden: European Commission. Available at: http://ec.europa.eu/public_opinion/archives/ebs/ebs_100_en.pdf (accessed 14 June 2014).

Walklate, S. (1998) 'Excavating the Fear of Crime: Fear, Anxiety or Trust?', *Theoretical Criminology*, 2(4): 403–18.

Watson, D. (2000) *Victims of Recorded Crime in Ireland: Results from the 1996 Survey*. Dublin: Oak Tree Press.

Whelan, B. J. and Vaughan, R. N. (1982) *The Economic and Social Circumstances of the Elderly in Ireland*. Dublin: ESRI.

Williams, P. and Dickinson, J. (1993) 'Fear of Crime: Read All About It? The Relationship between Newspaper Crime Reporting and Fear of Crime', *British Journal of Criminology*, 33(1): 33–56.

Notes

1 The murder of Veronica Guerin has been seared into the national consciousness; evidenced in the common usage of her name as a general reference point, imbued with its own meaning, and further illustrated in the feature films which detailed her life and death (O'Donnell and O'Sullivan, 2001).

2 O'Donoghue also announced that 1995 was the first time that the number of indictable crimes had exceeded the 100,000 mark, although this had first happened in 1983 (O'Mahony, 1996).

3 The hugely successful RTÉ drama *Love/Hate*, a depiction of the lives of Dublin's 'criminal underworld', may be evidence of a lasting obsession with the folk devil created in 1996.

21

Illicit drugs, criminal justice and harm reduction

Getting the balance right

Johnny Connolly and Andrew Percy

Introduction

This chapter critically reviews the evolution of drug policy and practice in Ireland and how it has responded to the changing nature of consumption amongst Irish adults and young people. The primary focus of the chapter will be on policy responses to illicit substances, as proscribed under the terms of the Misuse of Drugs Act 1977 for Republic of Ireland (ROI) and the United Kingdom's Misuse of Drugs Act 1971 for Northern Ireland (NI) rather than licit drugs such as alcohol. The chapter begins with a review of the global and local burden of illicit substances and notes their impact on the criminal justice system. We then trace the historical emergence of problematic illicit drug use from the late-1970s up to the mid- to late-1990s. The years 1994 to 1998 can be regarded as a watershed moment in Irish drug policy. In the ROI, the murder of journalist Veronica Guerin in the summer of 1996 by drug dealers resulted in the drug issue assuming one of the highest priorities of the state for the first time. In NI, the evolving peace process saw the loosening of both state and paramilitary security controls over local communities, and one unintended consequence of this was the emergence of a more active illicit drug culture. The chapter then traces the development of drug policy in both jurisdictions, focussing on the uneasy combination of criminal justice and harm reduction approaches that have been a characteristic feature of both. This highlights the prevailing tensions that exist between these two conflicting perspectives, one based within a healthcare paradigm and the other within a criminal justice or legal paradigm. The following issues are then examined: the failure of criminal justice approaches to deter the increase in drug availability or use; the negative human rights implications of the many draconian criminal justice measures introduced in response to drug-related crime; the unintended negative effects of criminal justice approaches including their tendency to make drug markets less predictable and potentially more violent; and the manner in which drug law enforcement can undermine harm reduction approaches. Finally, we examine current international debates for reform in this area and the potential for change in Ireland. In particular, debates around drug legalisation or decriminalisation and reforms that seek to reconcile law enforcement and harm reduction approaches are explored.

The burden of substance use

On a global scale, the consumption of licit and illicit substances is associated with a considerable health and social burden. Substance use contributes to around 2.8 million premature deaths per year (2.7 million attributed to alcohol and 157,000 attributed to drug use) and an estimated loss of 121 million disability adjusted life years (DALYs: healthy years lost through premature death or disability) (Lim *et al.*, 2012). This is equivalent to approximately 5 per cent of the total global burden of all disease (Lim *et al.*, 2012; World Health Organisation, 2014). With an estimated 15.5 million dependant users, opioids contribute to the loss of over nine million DALYs (Degenhardt *et al.*, 2014a). Dependency on other illicit drugs (cannabis, amphetamines, cocaine and other drug use disorders) accounts for a further ten million DALYs (Degenhardt *et al.*, 2014b; Degenhardt *et al.*, 2014c).

Between 2004 and 2012, the National Drug-Related Deaths Index (NDRDI) revealed that there were 5,289 drug-related deaths in the ROI, of which 3,112 were due to direct poisoning and the remainder resulting from health complications associated with chronic drug consumption (Health Research Board, 2014). Nearly two-thirds of all victims of drug poisoning in 2012 were male with over half (54 per cent) of all poisoning deaths in that year involving more than one drug (polydrug use). In Northern Ireland, a further 786 illicit drug-related deaths were registered between 2004 and 2012, with the majority (63 per cent) once again amongst men (Northern Ireland Statistics and Research Agency (NISRA), 2013).

The societal burden of drug consumption extends beyond the public health sphere, however, and the relationship between drug consumption and crime is well documented (see for example, Bean, 2001; T. Bennett and Holloway, 2009; Chaiken and Chaiken, 1990; Connolly, 2006; Seddon, 2000, 2006; Seddon *et al.*, 2008; Stevens *et al.*, 2005; White and Gorman, 2000). A Garda Síochána study published in 1997, for example, found that drug users were responsible for 66 per cent of detected indictable crime in Dublin, including over 80 per cent of detected burglaries and 84 per cent of detected thefts from the person and from unattended vehicles (Keogh, 1997). Drug use in Ireland has also been found to be linked with increasing levels of systemic violence associated with the illicit drug trade over the last decade (Campbell, 2010; Connolly and Donovan, 2014; Loughran and McCann, 2006). This violence is not confined only to those directly involved in the trade, whether users or dealers, but also increasingly directed at their family members and the wider community (Connolly and Donovan, 2014; Hourigan, 2011; Jennings, 2013; O'Leary, 2009). Income generated from drug dealing may also be a major source of revenue for paramilitary organisations and other criminal gangs in NI (Silke, 2000). Research has also begun to highlight the corrosive impact such violence and intimidation is having on the broader communities in which drug markets are typically located and the way in which the fear generated can act as a major disincentive to community engagement with locally based responses, including community policing initiatives (Connolly, 2003, 2002; Connolly and Donovan, 2014; Hourigan, 2011; Loughran and McCann, 2006).

A brief history of drug use in Ireland

It was not until the 1960s, described by Butler (2002: 107) as 'a decade which is universally associated with increased drug use as part of a burgeoning youth culture', that health authorities in the ROI became concerned about the use of illicit drugs. Data presented in the Interim Report of the *Working Party on Drug Abuse*, the first official committee to examine drug problems and make recommendations on future drug policy in Ireland, shows that in September 1969:

[T]here were approximately 350 persons known to the Gardai as drug abusers in Dublin; by December 1970 this figure had grown to 940…The most commonly abused drugs at this time were cannabis and LSD; neither heroin nor any of the synthetic opiates were in common use and there was no evidence of large scale commercial drug dealing.

(Butler, 2002: 11)

While there are some retrospective reports of heroin use in NI during the 1960s and 1970s, the number of individuals engaged in significant drug use was very small indeed (McElrath, 2004). In the UK, the early 1980s saw the publication of a number of influential studies documenting the appearance of localised heroin epidemics across various UK cities including parts of London, Liverpool, Manchester, Glasgow and Edinburgh (Ditton and Speirits, 1982; Lewis *et al.*, 1985; Parker *et al.*, 1987; Pearson, 1987). The extensive migration between the UK and Ireland during this period and the large Irish populations based in these various cities led to speculation regarding Ireland's place as a sub-market of the UK, at least with regards to heroin (O'Gorman, 1998). A link was identified between the criminal underworld in London and the emergence of the family-based criminal network widely credited with introducing heroin to Dublin in late-1979, namely, the Dunne family (Butler, 2002; Flynn and Yeates, 1985; O'Mahony, 1993). Members of this family, some of whom were heroin users themselves and had spent most of their lives living in England, were believed to control around 50 per cent of the Dublin heroin trade at one time in the early 1980s (Flynn and Yeates, 1985).

While Belfast had an established, albeit very small, heroin user population during the 1980s, the changes in heroin consumption noted across the remainder of the UK and Ireland did not occur in Northern Ireland until much later (McElrath, 2001, 2004). Even with the close proximity of Belfast to other urban centres with extensive drug markets and increasing levels of problematic heroin use (e.g. Liverpool, Glasgow, Dublin), Northern Ireland avoided the growth in heroin consumption in the 1980s (McElrath, 2004). By way of explanation, we can look towards the impact of 'the Conflict'. The high levels of police and military security that existed in Northern Ireland during the 1970s, 1980s and early 1990s in response to the political and sectarian conflict and the anti-drug stance of a number of influential paramilitary organisations had a significant suppression effect on heroin consumption, importation and distribution, and the movement of heroin users between NI and Great Britain (Higgins and McElrath, 2000; Higgins *et al.*, 2004; McElrath, 2002).

The 1990s saw new developments in drug consumption in Ireland and the UK, where the growth of the dance and club scene fuelled a dramatic growth in the consumption of ecstasy (MDMA) and related dance drugs (Murphy-Lawless, 2002; Ramsay and Percy, 1996; Sherlock and Conner, 1999), leading to what Davies and Ditton (1990: 811) defined as the 'decade of the stimulants'. In Northern Ireland, the 'loved-up' feelings induced by ecstasy consumption have been credited (albeit mainly by ecstasy users) for a significant reduction in sectarian violence in inner city nightclubs during the 1990s (McElrath and McEvoy, 2001) creating some of the first safe shared space experienced by a generation that had grown up during the Conflict.

Like the UK, this growth in ecstasy use also contributed to a resurgence of heroin use, at least in Dublin (Coveney *et al.*, 1999; Murphy-Lawless, 2002). Some users of ecstasy began to smoke heroin to come down from a night's dancing, and consumption of ecstasy facilitated the growth of heroin use beyond its previous confinement to marginalised youth in inner-city communities. As Murphy-Lawless (2002: 14) suggested, 'in many ways, the explosion of dance music enabled heroin to be woven into a new pattern of consumption and new generations of users, far removed in image terms from the addict injecting or "shooting up" as it is known, in a derelict house or street corner'. However, north of the border, for many ecstasy users, heroin remained a drug to be avoided (McElrath and McEvoy, 2001).

Criminalising the drug problem

In the ROI, drug policy in general has largely been shaped by the Misuse of Drugs Act 1977, first introduced as a Bill in 1973 in order to repeal or update existing laws. Introducing the Bill in 1975,[1] the then Minister for Health, Brendan Corish TD, explained:

> This is a complex Bill, which attempts to deal in a balanced way with a very complex problem. A tough approach on the question of criminality and unethical behaviour has been adopted, while, at the same time, I have attempted to meet the treatment and rehabilitation needs of drug users in a humane and enlightened manner.[2]

Originally, the passage of this Act through the Irish parliament was, politically, a very calm and measured affair (Butler, 2002). This can be explained by the fact that the use of drugs was not regarded as a serious political issue at that time and that the Government of the day did not see criminal justice sanctions as the 'primary or most useful way to tackle drug problems' (Butler, 2002: 111). In an effort to strike a balance between control and treatment approaches, the Misuse of Drugs legislation obliged the courts to consider an offender's medical and social needs prior to sentencing and also permitted the courts to commit such persons to a designated custodial treatment centre.[3] The Act also made special provisions for cannabis possession offences to be treated more leniently at the sentencing stage relative to offences involving other, more harmful, drugs. In its approach to the Misuse of Drugs Act, the legislature had, according to Butler (2002: 129), 'avoided the worst excesses of societal over-reaction to this new and controversial social problem'.

Despite the gentle tenor of the debate surrounding the passage of the Misuse of Drugs Act 1977, its significance should not be underestimated, both in terms of the significant powers it conferred on the Garda Síochána (Charleton, 1986) and in terms of its function as the primary policy instrument through which the Irish state would respond to the drugs crisis into the future (O'Mahony, 2008). For O'Mahony (2008: 68), the Misuse of Drugs Act 1977 is at the 'heart of the prohibitionist system and the manner and effectiveness of its enforcement to a significant extent defines the reality of the Irish "war on drugs"', namely, criminal law enforcement taking precedence over health, social or educational approaches to drug use.

Furthermore, the relatively enlightened approach adopted within the Misuse of Drugs Act 1977 did not last very long. The Misuse of Drugs Act 1984, introduced a few years later with surprising haste,[4] made it an offence to publish, sell or distribute literature which advocated the use of controlled drugs,[5] created the offence of drug importation for the purpose of supply[6] and increased the maximum penalty for drug trafficking from 14 years to life imprisonment.[7] The mandatory requirement that judges should defer sentencing convicted drug offenders pending medical and social reports was dropped while the liberal soundings about cannabis heard during the debates on the 1977 Act were replaced by a climate in which legislators 'concentrated on the evil which was deemed to be inherent in all illicit drugs' (Butler, 2002: 143).[8]

The introduction of the Misuse of Drugs Acts of 1977 and 1984 meant that the ROI could now ratify the United Nations Single Convention on Narcotics 1961 and the Convention on Psychotropic Substances 1971, thereby adhering to its obligations within the 'global drug control system'[9] (Bewley-Taylor, 2012: 8).[10] These treaties have been characterised as reflecting the US-inspired 'highly moralistic…war on drugs' approach to drug policy (Butler, 2007: 128), one that is premised on eliminating drug supply by targeting producers and traffickers.

The corresponding legislation in Northern Ireland was the Misuse of Drugs Act 1971, which amalgamated and simplified existing legislation covering the state control of the importation, sale and consumption of illicit drugs. The Act is notable for introducing: a national classification system for illicit substances based on perceived harm (ranked A to C), which is still the source of considerable debate (Nutt *et al.*, 2007); a graded criminal justice response to the various illicit drugs based on their classification; and the establishment of the Advisory Council on the Misuse of Drugs (ACMD) to provide advice to Government on drug policy and strategy. However, the provision of drug treatment services (Drug Dependency Units) and licensed substitute prescribing established in England at this time, generally referred to as the 'British System', was not extended to Northern Ireland due to a perceived lack of need (Yates, 2002).

Responding to the first heroin epidemic – 'denial'

When the heroin problem first began to impact Dublin in the late-1970s and early-1980s, the response from the Department of Health was one characterised by denial (Butler, 2002; Gilligan, 2011). The drug problem was regarded as a temporary phenomenon rooted in individual pathology, the seriousness of which was being greatly exaggerated (Butler, 2002). This perspective dominated official policy until the publication of the report of the *Ministerial Task Force on Measures to Reduce the Demand for Drugs* (The Rabbitte Report) in 1996, thereby dismissing analyses and research that highlighted the structural factors associated with problem drug use such as poverty, unemployment, educational disadvantage and poor housing (Dean *et al.*, 1983; O'Gorman, 1998; O'Kelly *et al.*, 1988).[11]

In Northern Ireland, the official position was similar. Drug use was not considered a sufficient social problem requiring any substantial state intervention beyond traditional law enforcement (Higgins and McElrath, 2000). While worrying trends in drug consumption were observed in other UK jurisdictions, the official advice from the Northern Ireland Committee on Drug Misuse, as late as 1986, was that drug misuse in NI only warranted a low-level approach to prevention and intervention. However, during this period (the 1970s and 1980s), Northern Ireland could rightly be classified as a low-crime- and low-drug-use society relative to the UK and ROI (Brewer *et al.*, 1997).

The denial by the ROI state in relation to the local impact of the heroin epidemic was also reflected in the failure of the Garda Síochána to respond adequately.[12] According to one account, the fact that established criminals were moving into the drug trade and away from armed robberies, shifting the burden of crime away from more politically influential sections of society (banks, jewellers and wealthy home owners) onto already deprived communities, may also have taken some political pressure off the Garda Síochána (Flynn and Yeates, 1985).

The lack of police engagement with community concerns and especially the low priority accorded to meeting the needs of marginalised groups reflected the historical reality of poor police–community relations in such communities (Connolly, 1998, 2002; Conway, 2010; McCullagh, 1996; Mulcahy and O'Mahony, 2005). The absence of an effective state and policing response to open drug dealing and drug-related crime in many housing estates in Dublin, combined with poor Garda–community relations in such areas, led to the emergence of community self-policing in the form of the Concerned Parents Against Drugs (CPAD) movement in the 1980s (D. Bennett, 1988) and the Coalition of Communities Against Drugs (COCAD) in the 1990s (Connolly, 1997, 1998; Lyder, 2005; McCullagh, 1996; Murphy-Lawless, 2002). Organisations such as the CPAD and COCAD became controversial due to their tactics of street patrols, evictions of alleged drug dealers and links with the Republican movement (Mulcahy, 2002). In Northern Ireland, 1994 saw the emergence of Direct Action Against Drugs (DAAD), a vigilante group with close links to paramilitary organisations and responsible for the murder, beating and intimidation of local drug dealers (Hamill, 2010; Monaghan, 2004)

The watershed in Irish drug policy – Veronica Guerin and the NI peace process

The apparent state indifference and inertia in the ROI was severely shaken by events in mid-1996, a year widely regarded as representing a watershed in the evolution of Irish policy on drugs (O'Mahony, 2008). The killing in July of that year of Veronica Guerin (O'Reilly, 1998), a high-profile journalist who had written a number of exposés about criminals linked to the illicit drug trade, was a catalyst for a range of legislative and policy initiatives introduced in response to a drug problem that increasingly appeared to be beyond the capacity of the state and the Garda Siochána to manage (Butler, 2002). These included measures aimed at addressing both the supply of and the demand for drugs.

In NI, the mid-1990s also proved to be a watershed period in the evolution of drug consumption patterns, drug markets and drug policy, albeit for very different reasons than in the ROI. In 1994, NI witnessed the beginnings of a faltering peace process with most of the major paramilitary organisations declaring a cessation of political violence. This process, culminating in the 1998 Good Friday Agreement and associated referenda, also saw a dismantling of the state security system, a reduction in police officer numbers across NI and the devolution of executive powers, including those relating to alcohol and drug policy, to the new NI Assembly (see Tonge, 2013, for a history of the NI conflict and peace process). As NI adjusted to a sustained period of peace, social problems artificially suppressed by the political conflict and state security began to emerge. In particular, 1994 marks the beginning of a period of increasing drug consumption and the establishment of heroin hotspots similar to those that appeared in UK and Irish urban centres in the 1980s (Higgins *et al.*, 2004; McElrath, 2004). Given the speed at which these drug use problems emerged in Northern Ireland, fuelled by the active involvement of certain paramilitary organisations (mainly loyalist groups) in the importation and distribution of drugs and the 'policing' of drug markets (McDowell, 2001; Silke, 2000), NI had insufficient prevention and treatment facilities in place to meet rising demand (McElrath, 2001, 2004).

Responding to the crisis – 'moral panic'

In the ROI, a plethora of new draconian laws were introduced in the wake of Veronica Guerin's death in 1996. According to a number of commentators, this represented a form of legislation by 'moral panic' (Cohen, 1980), primarily in response to drug-related crime (Hamilton 2005a, 2005b; Meade, 2000; O'Donnell and O'Sullivan, 2001).

The Criminal Justice (Drug Trafficking) Act 1996 allowed for the detention of suspected drug dealers for interrogation for up to seven days and placed restriction on the 'right to silence' (D. Keane, 1997; Ryan, 1997). The Criminal Assets Bureau Act 1996 and the Proceeds of Crime Act 1996 established the Criminal Assets Bureau with the power to seize the illegally acquired assets of criminals involved in serious crime including drug dealing and distribution (McCutcheon and Walsh, 1999). This legislation allows the state to remove the property of citizens that it believes to be the proceeds of crime by means of a civil process and without the requirement of a criminal conviction, thereby bypassing the traditional protections of the criminal law (D. Keane, 1997). Other significant changes came in the form of the Bail Act 1997, facilitated by the passage of a referendum. This Act placed restrictions on the right to bail and allowed for preventive detention, something previously unconstitutional under Irish law (Kilcommins

421

et al., 2004). The Criminal Justice Act 1999 introduced mandatory minimum sentences of ten years for the dealing of drugs with a street value of £10,000 (€12,700) or more. According to the Law Reform Commission (2012: 102), these changes 'marked an important turning point in the Irish sentencing regime which had until 1999 – with the exception of the sentences for murder and capital murder – accorded primacy to judicial discretion in the determination of sentences'.

The Housing (Miscellaneous Provisions) Act 1997 enabled local authorities to evict individuals for drug-related antisocial behaviour, while the Non-fatal Offences against the Person Act 1997 included provisions specifically addressing the use of HIV-infected syringes in robberies and aggravated burglaries. These two pieces of legislation were introduced in response to pressure from local communities to address open drug dealing by some residents in local authority housing estates and, with regard to the latter, to address the large increase in such offences between 1994 and 1996 (Connolly, 2006).[13]

While the reaction to Veronica Guerin's murder has been understood as a 'textbook case of a "moral panic"' (O'Donnell and O'Sullivan, 2001: 3), this legislative (over-)reaction can also be viewed in terms of what David Garland (2001: 134) describes as a form of:

> [A]cting out that downplays the complexities and long-term character of *effective* crime control in favour of the immediate gratifications of a more *expressive* alternative. Law making, of this kind, becomes a matter of retaliatory gestures intended to reassure a worried public and to accord with common sense, however poorly those gestures are adapted to dealing with the underlying problem.

While draconian crime control legislation providing the police with significant powers of arrest and detention was already in existence in Northern Ireland due to the political conflict, similar legislation to that enacted in the ROI was passed in NI during the 1990s. The Proceeds of Crime (Northern Ireland) Order 1996 brought Northern Irish legislation in line with the remainder of the UK regarding the confiscation of the proceeds of drug trafficking and other serious crimes. Indeed, due to the perceived problems of racketeering, the police were granted additional financial investigatory powers not seen elsewhere in the UK.[14] Likewise, the Magistrates' Courts (Drug Trafficking Act 1994) Rules (Northern Ireland) 1996[15] permitted the seizure, detention and forfeiture of cash suspected to be the proceeds of drug trafficking following a Magistrates Court Order.

Towards a sustainable response – building a drugs strategy

Outside of this legislative hothouse, the foundations for an alternative and more pragmatic approach to drug policy were also under development in the ROI. The recommendations of the 1996 Rabbitte Report would form the basis of the ensuing *National Drugs Strategy 2001–2008: Building on Experience*, described as 'by far the most lengthy and detailed drugs policy document ever produced in Ireland' (Butler and Mayock, 2005: 419).[16] What was particularly significant about the Report was the 'explicit' and 'unequivocal' acceptance by Irish policy-makers for the first time of the link between problem drug use and social exclusion and, in particular, the need to address the root causes of problem drug use including unemployment, poor housing and low educational attainment (Butler, 2007: 132).

The National Drugs Strategy 2001–2008 (NDS) set out detailed actions and key performance indicators across the four pillars of supply reduction, prevention, treatment and research (Department of Tourism, Sport and Recreation, 2001).[17] It also established an elaborate policy infrastructure through which these aims were to be delivered by incorporating government ministers at cabinet level and representatives at community level in the areas most affected by the drugs problem. Responsibility for implementing the action plan was specifically assigned to various government departments or state agencies. Although they happened in parallel, the National Drugs Strategy can be interpreted as a reasoned alternative to the reactive criminal justice approach described above.[18] It was also reflective of the more pragmatic response that was necessitated by the emergence of the international public health crisis created by HIV and AIDS in the mid-1980s.

The absolutist or fundamentalist rejection of drugs associated with the international control system developed as part of the 'war on drugs' was seriously challenged internationally and in Ireland as a consequence of this new public health crisis. Until this point, the focus of drug services around the world had mainly been directed towards abstinence and the 'curing' of addictions (Moore *et al.*, 2004). The need to respond to the growing risks posed by blood-borne infections, independent from unrealistic expectations about abstinence outcomes for drug users, led to the emergence of harm reduction interventions such as needle exchange schemes, methadone maintenance programmes and outreach work with high risk groups (O'Hare *et al.*, 1992). A harm reduction approach focusses on reducing the harm that substance users cause to themselves and their families through ongoing interventions that do not require abstinence from drugs (World Health Organisation, 2003).

In the ROI, the high incidence of HIV cases linked to the sharing of needles by injecting drug users saw a renewed focus from the mid-1980s onwards on harm reduction practices and services such as drug clinics providing methadone maintenance, needle exchange and outreach services (Butler, 2002; Butler and Mayock, 2005; Clarke *et al.*, 2001; Moore *et al.*, 2004). The National Drugs Strategy 2001–2008, and its successor, the National Drugs Strategy (*interim*) 2009–2016, would build upon these progressive developments.

The first official policy statement released in response to increasing drug consumption in Northern Ireland was issued in 1995 and attempted to set out clear objectives and an organisational framework for addressing drug use (The House of Commons Northern Ireland Affairs Committee, 2003). This statement triggered a series of additional policy statements from relevant government departments and related statutory bodies and was backed by a public information campaign. However, NI did not see the emergence of a more detailed drug strategy until 1999 (Department of Health, Social Services and Public Safety, 1999). Given the ample evidence of the devastation that heroin and other drugs had wrought on urban areas within the UK and Ireland, it was unfortunate that this strategy deemed that standard drug treatments aimed at reducing the harms associated with illicit drug consumption, and in particular the spread of blood-borne viruses such as HIV and Hepatitis B and C (e.g. methadone maintenance, needle exchange programmes and street-based outreach services), were not necessary within NI. While neighbouring jurisdictions were expanding the provision of drug treatment and harm reduction services, albeit mainly through the criminal justice system rather than through public health services (see Buchanan and Young, 2000), similar action was not undertaken within NI. In effect, the only response to problem drug use in NI at this time was a criminal justice response. This initial failure to develop drug services in line with increasing consumption contributed to a significant gap between the demand for and supply of services for drug users within NI. During this time, drug users reported difficulties accessing services, long waiting lists and limited treatment modalities, thus exacerbating risky behaviour amongst users (McElrath, 2001).

It was not until the mid-2000s that harm reduction was fully embraced as an appropriate response to drug use within NI. The 16th International Conference on the Reduction of Drug Related Harm, held in Belfast in March 2005, provided a major stimulus to the inclusion of harm reduction philosophy and methods within alcohol and drug policy development in the jurisdiction. The conference exposed Northern Irish policy-makers and practitioners to: the cost of ignoring drug-related harms, radical innovations in harm reduction theory, the expanding evidence base for the effectiveness of harm reduction interventions, compelling arguments for a human rights perspective in drug policy and the hazards posed by a traditional 'zero-tolerance' approach (Percy, 2005). While a fledgling pharmacy-based needle exchange scheme first began operating in NI in 2001 (McElrath and Jordan, 2005), the conference confirmed the need for a significant 'up-scaling' of NI services.

The following year saw the publication of the revised five-year drug strategy for NI, entitled the New Strategic Direction for Alcohol and Drugs (Department of Health, Social Services and Public Safety, 2006). At the heart of the new NI strategy were the same four pillars of the ROI drug strategy, namely, prevention, treatment, law enforcement and research, together with a fifth pillar – harm reduction.

Tension between criminal justice and harm reduction

The National Drugs Strategy has resulted in a number of significant improvements in policy responses to the drugs issue in the ROI, including a significant increase in treatment and harm reduction services (Butler, 2007; Connolly et al., 2012; O'Mahony, 2008; Pike, 2008). However, these developments in harm reduction, with its nuanced approach to continued drug misuse, sit uneasily within an overall context of prohibition, where drug-dependent drug users remained heavily stigmatized within Irish society. O'Mahony (2008: 82) characterises Irish drug policy from the mid-1980s as involving a combination of a 'cops' (law enforcement) plus 'docs' (harm reduction) approach within a general prohibitionist framework. He asserts, however, that the Irish response to drugs remains 'first and last a matter of criminal justice policy' (2008: 5) and that those

> who work to ameliorate drugs problems in the areas of public health, harm reduction and social inclusion, tend to forget or minimise the powerful, defining role of the criminal law ... [ensuring] that Ireland remains resolutely prohibitionist despite all its concessions to harm reduction.
>
> *(2008: 5)*

Butler and Mayock (2005: 418) describe Irish healthcare policy with regards to drugs as moving, by stealth, from a position of reinforcing 'criminal justice supply reduction measures by only providing treatment and rehabilitation systems which were abstinence oriented' to the adoption of a harm reduction approach, 'one which prioritised HIV prevention and was prepared to tolerate varying levels of ongoing drug use among its clients'. However, Butler (2007: 138) ultimately concludes that the National Drugs Strategy has failed to address the outstanding tension between the two conflicting perspectives inherent in it:

> [O]ne based within a healthcare paradigm and the other within a criminal justice or legal paradigm. In the former, drug users are viewed as pathological and in need of therapy, while in the latter they are viewed as immoral rule-breakers deserving of exemplary criminal justice sanctions.

It can be argued further that many of the public health measures introduced were primarily concerned with protecting non-drug-using society from becoming infected with HIV, as problematic drug users remain heavily stigmatised as a group in Irish society (Lloyd, 2010; M. Keane et al., 2014).

While the inclusion of harm reduction at the centre of NI Drug Policy was welcomed by many, organisations such as the UK Harm Reduction Alliance were critical of the new policy on the grounds of: its failure to acknowledge the delay in developing adequate harm reduction services; the lack of specific focus on harm reduction interventions and outcomes within the policy document; and the attempt to provide harm reduction within a broader framework of conflicting demand and supply reduction approaches (Hunt, 2006). As with the ROI, the development of the NI drug strategy highlights the ongoing tension between criminal justice responses to illicit drug consumption (supply-and-demand-focussed) and harm reduction approaches to drug use.

This tension is not unique to Irish drug policy, and the tendency to prioritise crime prevention and law enforcement over protecting individual and public health within drug policy development has been documented in other jurisdictions (Hunt and Stevens, 2004; Stevens, 2007). While not without its critics (see H. Keane, 2003), harm reduction can provide an innovative solution to the central paradox within a supply-focussed drug policy – the desire to improve society through the reduction in the supply of drugs and drug consumption whilst unintentionally increasing the social harms associated with the drugs trade (corruption, fraud, violence, acquisitive crime), with little or no impact on overall drug consumption (Greenfield and Paoli, 2012). While it is possible to negotiate the tension between law enforcement and harm reduction, international examples of successful projects are limited (Stevens et al., 2010).

A contributory factor relates to the absence of empirical research or analysis in this area. Although the Research Pillar of the National Drug Strategy (NDS) has led to an improvement in the evidence base about the extent and nature of the drug problem, the same cannot be said in relation to the impact of law enforcement efforts. Indeed, there does not appear to be any clear relationship between the many criminal justice measures introduced in response to the drug problem and 'the strategic objectives or goals of the NDS' (Pike, 2008: 93). This is not just an Irish problem, however. Reuter (1997) argues that the absence of an adequate understanding of the effectiveness of the drug prohibition regime in deterring drug use and drug dealing is a consequence of the way in which drug control has become politicised. A recent international review of evidence-based drug policy by a group of leading scholars stated:

> We conclude with one over-riding analytical observation: supply control interventions absorb the bulk of drug control spending in most nations, even nations that have a reputation for tolerating drug use. The evidence base concerning these interventions is distressingly weak. … Governments are still flying blind (in the war on drugs).
>
> (Babor et al., 2010: 162)

The limitations of criminal justice

Seddon et al. (2008) suggest that underlying policy assumptions about the link between drugs and acquisitive crime led British drug policy under the former New Labour Government to become 'crime focused', with an increasing use of legal coercion as the main driver of treatment engagement. Under New Labour, the distinction was drawn between the young, recreational non-problematic and mainly middle-class drug consumers (who were increasingly ignored by the criminal justice system) and the chaotic, problematic and criminal drug users (who experienced increasing severe legal sanctions) (Buchanan, 2010). Similarly, in the ROI, many commentators have argued that, whatever their intended objective, the enforcement of drug laws tends to target already disadvantaged drug using groups and vulnerable people caught up in the drug trade, rather than drug suppliers, thereby intensifying Ireland's already disproportionate punishment of the poor (Bacik and O'Connell, 1998; Connolly and Donovan, 2014; Irish Penal Reform Trust, 2012; O'Mahony, 2008).

The practical effect of many of the laws introduced is also debateable. O'Donnell and O'Sullivan (2001: 127) suggest that a decrease in robberies and aggravated burglaries involving HIV-infected syringes between 1996 and 2002 can be explained, not as a result of the passage of new laws, but as a consequence of the improvement of treatment provision during this period, including methadone substitution treatment and needle exchange services. It may also have been helped by the increase in employment among dependent drug users during this period, something which would have reduced their dependence on crime as a means of paying for drugs.[19]

Drug law enforcement efforts can also have serious unintended negative consequences for drug markets by making them more violent (MacCoun and Reuter, 2001; Reuter and Trautmann, 2009). This relates to what is perhaps the most important distinction between legal and illegal markets – namely, that participants in the latter have 'no recourse to the system of property rights and dispute resolution offered by the civil courts and legal system' (Babor *et al.*, 2010: 64), meaning that market dominance may often be exercised by the seller who can intimidate others most effectively (Caulkins and Reuter, 2006). Successful law enforcement through large drug seizures or the arrest of significant 'players' can create instability in the market and contribute to turf wars and increased 'systemic' violence as new dealers seek to assert control and fill the gap in the market (Connolly and Donovan, 2014).

O'Mahony (2008: 98) suggests that the Criminal Assets Bureau may have had such unintended negative consequences, leading to a situation where 'successful, large-scale dealers have based themselves abroad and the local trade has become a chaotic arena, riven by rivalry and internecine feuding between less well-organised and controlled and even more ruthlessly violent gangs'. Although the Criminal Assets Bureau is one of the most highly praised developments in Irish policing in decades, Kilcommins *et al.* (2004: 228) suggest that, despite its high profile campaigns against criminals involved in drug dealing, it is unlikely to have made 'much of a dent in the drugs market'.[20]

The mandatory sentencing provisions provided for in the Criminal Justice Act 1999 have been criticised by the Law Reform Commission for being, at best, ineffectual and, at worst, perverse and counter-productive (Law Reform Commission, 2012).[21] The LRC (2012: 132) states that, 'the majority of those being caught for offences under section 15A are drug couriers rather than so-called drug "barons"'. Those at the higher levels of the drugs trade have simply adapted to the sentencing regime by using expendable couriers or 'victims of circumstance', such as 'impoverished individuals from African countries or underprivileged Irish citizens' to hold and transport drugs, thus avoiding detection themselves. Indeed, despite the many criminal justice measures introduced since the Misuse of Drugs Acts (1971, 1977) and particularly since 1996, illicit drug markets appear to have penetrated more deeply into the fabric of many communities, with increasing incidents of so-called gangland murders linked to the illicit drug trade and drug-related intimidation directed against the families of drug users to recoup drug debts (City Wide, 2012; Connolly, 2003, 2005; Connolly and Donovan, 2014; Hourigan, 2011, Jennings, 2013; Loughran and McCann, 2006).

In addition to the harms generated by the unintended consequences of law enforcement efforts, drug users (in particular heroin users) in NI have experienced high levels of informal control from organisations with links to paramilitary organisations such as Direct Action Against Drugs, ranging from threats, punishment beatings, shootings and expulsions (Knox, 2001; Monaghan, 2004). Drug users are considered 'undesirables' within local communities and are driven out in an attempt to 'clean up' an area. However, this publicised motivation can often be a cover for the control of drug markets, local feuds and power struggles within criminal organisations (for an insight into the complexities of paramilitary punishment beatings, see Monaghan, 2004).

Current and future debates

The fact that drug prohibition and its delivery through drug law enforcement may create more harm than good should be a serious matter for policy-makers in Ireland, particularly where the ultimate objective of the national drugs strategies is to reduce drug-related harm to individuals and society. The failure of prohibition to significantly reduce drug use and availability, the resilience and adaptability of illicit drug markets in the face of highly-resourced drug law enforcement (relative to drug treatment services), coupled with the negative consequences that can arise from drug law enforcement has led to calls for a fundamental re-examination of the international system of drug prohibition (Pike, 2012a; Room and Reuter, 2012). These calls have come from countries at all levels of the international drug trade: production, transit and consumption (for example, see Pike, 2011). Advocated policy options range from changes to the legal status of drugs, whether through direct legalisation or some form of decriminalisation (Rosmarin and Eastwood, 2012), to a realignment of the balance between criminal justice and harm reduction approaches (Greenfield and Paoli, 2012) and the promotion of approaches that can facilitate recovery from addiction (M. Keane *et al.*, 2014). The most thorough and lucid recent critique of prohibition in an Irish context is provided by O'Mahony (2008). Arguing that the use of drugs is a human right, O'Mahony (2008: 236) calls for an end to prohibition and for the legalisation of drugs, arguing that ending the 'wasteful and futile "war on drugs"' could allow for the promotion of more sensible and legitimate policy options that would promote greater social justice and support for at-risk individuals and for disadvantaged and stigmatised communities.

In September 2011, members of the Oireachtas Joint Committee on Health and Children asked whether it was time to consider the drug policy options adopted in Portugal[22] and the Netherlands,[23] which have eliminated criminal sanctions for illicit drug users (Pike, 2012b).[24] More recently, the City Wide Drugs Crisis Campaign has called for a debate, at least, on drug decriminalisation (City Wide, 2012).[25] This is an important initiative from a community-based organisation that represents the communities most affected by the drugs crisis. Where drug policy aims to alleviate drug-related harms to individuals and society, it must be informed by an understanding of how those harms are unevenly distributed throughout society. The bulk of drug-related harm occurs among dependent drug users and remains concentrated in areas of socio-economic disadvantage (Reuter and Stevens, 2007).

Conclusion

Both jurisdictions in Ireland came late to the issue of illicit drug use, with governments seemingly initially unwilling to face the reality of the problem. When the peace process in Northern Ireland and the murder of journalist Veronica Guerin in the ROI ultimately forced the issue on to the political agenda, a predominantly law enforcement approach was adopted. The HIV/AIDS crisis and its association with injecting drug use in the ROI saw the introduction of a range of harm reduction measures, and a similar approach was belatedly adopted in 2005 in Northern Ireland once it became apparent that problematic drug use, long suppressed as a consequence of the unique circumstances of the Conflict, was to be an unfortunate dividend of peace. In particular, the informal controls that developed in many marginalised communities throughout the Conflict were instrumental in preventing this social problem from emerging. When compared with international policy approaches, a novel feature of the National Drug Strategy in the ROI was the establishment of localised task forces in the communities most affected by drug-related harm. This reflected an, again belated, political recognition at the time of the development of the strategy of the links between problematic drug use and social exclusion. Observers of UK drug policy have identified a recent shift away from a medical and harm reduction approach towards increasing use of legal interventions in response to problematic drug use. This, it is suggested, appears to be designed to protect those sections of society least affected by drug-related harm. In the ROI, many public representatives and community leaders, in line with the growing international debate about the 'war on drugs' and faced with increasingly violent and diversified local drug markets, are now beginning to question, at least, whether the correct balance has been struck between criminal justice and harm reduction approaches to Irish drug policy.

References

Babor, T., Caulkins, J., Edwards, G., Fischer, B., Foxcroft, D., Humphreys, K., Obot, I., Rehm, J., Reuter, P., Room, R., Rossow, I. and Strang, J. (2010) *Drug policy and the public good*. Oxford: Oxford University Press.

Bacik, I. and O'Connell, M. (1998) *Crime and poverty in Ireland*. Dublin: Round Hall Sweet and Maxwell.

Bean, P. (2001) *Drugs and crime*. Devon: Willan Publishing.

Bennett, D. (1988) 'Are they always right? Investigation and proof in a citizen anti-heroin movement'. In M. Tomlinsom, T. Varley and C. McCullagh, eds. *Whose Law & Order? Aspects of crime and social control in Irish society*. Studies in Irish Society. Belfast: Sociological Association of Ireland.

Bennett, T. and Holloway, K. (2009) 'The causal connection between drug misuse and crime', *British Journal of Criminology*, 49(4): 513–31.

Bewley-Taylor, D. (2012) *International drug control: Consensus fractured*. Cambridge: Cambridge University Press.

Brewer, J. D., Lockhart, B. and Rodgers, P. (1997) *Crime in Ireland, 1945–95: Here be dragons*. Oxford: Clarendon Press.

Buchanan, J. (2010) 'Drug policy under New Labour 1997-2010: Prolonging the war on drugs', *Probation Journal*, 57(3): 250–62.

Buchanan, J. and Young, L. (2000) 'The war on drugs – a war on drug users', *Drugs: Education, Prevention Policy*, 7(4): 409–22.

Butler, S. (2002) *Alcohol, drugs and health promotion in modern Ireland*. Dublin: Institute of Public Administration.

Butler, S. (2007) 'Rabbitte revisited: The first report of the ministerial task force on measures to reduce the demand for drugs – ten years on', *Administration*, 55(3): 124–44.

Butler, S. and Mayock, P. (2005) '"An Irish solution to an Irish problem": Harm reduction and ambiguity in the drug policy of the Republic of Ireland', *International Journal of Drug Policy*, 16(6): 415–22.

Campbell, L. (2010) 'Responding to gun crime in Ireland', *British Journal of Criminology*, 50(3): 414–34.

Caulkins, J. and Reuter, P. (2006) 'Illicit drug markets and economic irregularities', *Socio-Economic Planning Sciences*, 40(1): 1–14.

Chaiken, J. and Chaiken, M. (1990) 'Drugs and predatory crime'. In M. Tonry and J. Wilson (eds) *Drugs and Crime*. Chicago: Chicago University Press.

Charleton, P. (1986) *Controlled drugs and the criminal law*. Dublin: An Cló Liúir.

CityWide Drugs Crisis Campaign (2012) *The drugs crisis in Ireland: A new agenda for action*. Dublin: CityWide.

Clarke, S., Keenan, E., Bergin, C., Lyons, F., Hopkins, S. and Mulcahy, F. (2001) 'The changing epidemiology of HIV infection in injecting drug users in Dublin, Ireland', *HIV Medicine*, 2(4): 236–40.

Cohen, S. (1980) *Folk devils and moral panics: The creation of the mods and rockers*. Oxford: Martin Robinson.

Connolly, J. (1997) *Beyond the politics of law and order: Towards community policing in Ireland*. Belfast: Centre for Research and Documentation.

Connolly, J. (1998) 'From colonial policing to community policing', *Irish Criminal Law Journal*, 8(2): 165–96.

Connolly, J. (2002) *Community policing and drugs in Dublin: The North Inner City Community Policing Forum*. Dublin: North Inner City Drugs Task Force.

Connolly, J. (2003) *Drugs, crime and community in Dublin: Monitoring quality of life in the north inner city*. Dublin: North Inner City Drugs Task Force.

Connolly, J. (2005) *The Illicit drug market in Ireland, HRB Overview Series 2*. Dublin: Health Research Board.

Connolly, J. (2006) *Drugs and crime in Ireland, HRB Overview Series 3*. Dublin: Health Research Board.

Connolly, J. and Donovan, A-M. (2014) *Illicit Drug Markets in Ireland*. Dublin: National Advisory Committee of Drugs and Alcohol.

Connolly, J., Galvin, B., Keane, M., Long, J., Lyons, S. and Pike, B. (2012) 'Drugnet Ireland 10 years on: What have we learned?' *Drugnet Ireland*, 40: 12–16.

Conway, V. (2010) *The Blue Wall of Silence: The Morris tribunal and police accountability in Ireland*. Dublin: Irish Academic Press.

Coveney, E., *et al.* (1999) *Prevalence, profiles and policy: A case study of heroin drug use in inner city Dublin*. Dublin: North Inner City Drugs Task Force.

Davies, J. B. and Ditton, J. (1990) 'The 1990s: Decade of the stimulants?', *British Journal of Addiction*, 85(6): 811–13.

Dean, G., Bradshaw, J. and Lavelle, P. (1983) *Drug misuse in Ireland, 1982–1983: Investigation in a north central Dublin area, and in Galway, Sligo and Cork*. Dublin: Medico-Social Research Board.

Degenhardt, L., Charlson, F., Mathers, B., Hall, W., Flaxman, A., Johns, N. and Vos, T. (2014a) 'The global epidemiology and burden of opioid dependence: Results from the global burden of disease 2010 study', *Addiction*, 109(8): 1320–33.

Degenhardt, L., Baxter, A. J., Lee, Y., Hall, W., Sara, G., Johns, N., Flaxman, A., Whiteford, H. and Vos, T. (2014b) 'The global epidemiology and burden of psychostimulant dependence: Findings from the Global Burden of Disease Study 2010', *Drug and Alcohol Dependence*, 137: 36–47.

Degenhardt, L., Whiteford, H. and Hall, W. (2014c) 'The Global Burden of Disease projects: What have we learned about illicit drug use and dependence and their contribution to the global burden of disease?', *Drug and Alcohol Review*, 33(1): 4–12.

Department of Health, Social Services and Public Safety (DHSPSNI) (1999) *The drug strategy for Northern Ireland*. Belfast, UK: DHSPSNI.

Department of Health, Social Services and Public Safety (DHSPSNI) (2006) *The drug strategy for Northern Ireland*. Belfast, UK: DHSPSNI.

Department of Tourism, Sport and Recreation (2001) *National Drugs Strategy 2001–2008*. Dublin: Stationery Office.

Ditton, J. and Speirits, K. (1982) 'The new wave of heroin addiction in Britain', *Sociology*, 16(4): 595–8.

Flynn, S. and Yeates, P. (1985) *'Smack': The criminal drugs racket in Ireland*. Dublin: Gill & Macmillan.

Furey, M. and Browne, C. (2003) *Opiate use and related criminal activity in Ireland 2000 & 2001*. Research report No. 4/03. Templemore, Co Tipperary: An Garda Síochána Research Unit.

Garland, D. (2001) *The culture of control: Crime and social order in contemporary society*. Oxford: Oxford University Press.

Gilligan, R. (2011) *Tony Gregory*. Dublin: O'Brien Press.

Greenfield, V. and Paoli, L. (2012) 'If supply-oriented drug policy is broken, can harm reduction fix it? Melding disciplines and methods to advance international drug-control policy', *International Journal of Drug Policy*, 23(1): 6–15.

Hamill, H. (2010) *The hoods: Crime and punishment in Belfast*. Princeton, NJ: Princeton University.

Hamilton, C. (2005a) 'Moral panic revisited – Part One', *Irish Criminal Law Journal*, 15(1): 8–12.

Hamilton, C. (2005b) 'Moral panic revisited – Part Two', *Irish Criminal Law Journal*, 15(2): 9–14.

Health Research Board (2014) *Drug-related deaths and deaths among drug users in Ireland: 2012 figures from the National Drug Related Deaths Index*. Available at: www.hrb.ie/publications (accessed 22 April 2015).

Higgins, K. and McElrath, K. (2000) 'The trouble with peace: The ceasefires and their impact on drug use among youth in Northern Ireland', *Youth and Society*, 32(1): 29–59.

Higgins, K., Percy, A. and McCrystal, P. (2004) 'Secular trends in substance use: The conflict and young people in Northern Ireland', *Journal of Social Issues*, 60(3): 485–506.

Hourigan, N. (ed) (2011) *Understanding Limerick: Social exclusion and change*. Cork: Cork University Press.

House of Commons Northern Ireland Affairs Committee (2003) *The illegal drugs trade and drug culture in Northern Ireland Eighth Report of Session 2002–2003*, HC1217-I. London: The Stationery Office.

Hunt, N. (2006) *Response to the consultation on the New Strategic Direction for Alcohol and Drugs (2006-2011)*. London, UK: UK Harm Reduction Alliance. Available at: www.ukhra.org/statements/ni_drug_strategy_consultation.html (accessed 18 September 2014).

Hunt, N. and Stevens, A. (2004) 'Whose harm? Harm reduction and the shift to coercion in UK drug policy', *Social Policy and Society*, 3: 333–42.

Irish Penal Reform Trust (2012) *The vicious circle of social exclusion and crime: Ireland's disproportionate punishment of the poor*. Dublin: IPRT.

Jennings, P. (2013) *Melting the iceberg of fear: A collective response*. Blanchardstown: Safer Blanchardstown.

Keane, D. (1997) 'Detention without charge and the Criminal Justice (Drug Trafficking) Act 1996: Shifting the focus of Irish criminal process away from trial court to Garda station', *Irish Criminal Law Journal*, 7(1): 1–17.

Keane, H. (2003) 'Critiques of harm reduction, morality and the promise of human rights', *International Journal of Drug Policy*, 14(3): 227–32.

Keane, M., McAleenan, G. and Barry, J. (2014) *Addiction recovery: A contagious paradigm*. Dublin: HSE Addiction Services.

Keogh, E. (1997) *Illicit drug use and related criminal activity in the Dublin Metropolitan Area*. Dublin: An Garda Síochána.

Kilcommins, S., O'Donnell, I., O'Sullivan, E. and Vaughan, B. (2004) *Crime, punishment and the search for order in Ireland*. Dublin: Institute of Public Administration.

Knox, C. (2001) 'The deserving victims of political violence: Punishment attacks in Northern Ireland', *Criminology and Criminal Justice*, 1(2): 181–99.

Law Reform Commission (2012) *Consultation paper: Mandatory sentences*. Dublin: Law Reform Commission.

Lewis, R., Hartnoll, R., Bryer, S., Daviaud, E. and Mitcheson, M. (1985) 'Scoring smack: The illicit heroin market in London, 1980–1983', *British Journal of Addiction*, 80(3): 281–90.

Lim, S. S., *et al.* (2012) 'A comparative risk assessment of burden of disease and injury attributable to 67 risk factors and risk factor clusters in 21 regions, 1990–2010: A systematic analysis for the Global Burden of Disease Study 2010', *The Lancet*, 380(9859): 2224–60.

Lloyd, C. (2010) *Sinning and sinned against: The stigmatisation of problem drug users*. London: UK Drug Policy Commission. Available at: www.ukdpc.org.uk/publications (accessed 20 September 2014).

Loughran, H. and McCann, M. E. (2006) *A community drugs study: Developing community indicators for problem drug use*. Dublin: Stationery Office.

Lyder, A. (2005) *Pushers out: The inside story of Dublin's anti-drugs movement*. Victoria BC: Trafford.

MacCoun, R. J. and Reuter, P. (2001) *Drug war heresies: Learning from other vices, times and places*. Cambridge: Cambridge University Press.

McCullagh, C. (1996) *Crime in Ireland: A sociological introduction*. Cork: Cork University Press.

McCutcheon, J. and Walsh, D. (1999) 'Seizure of criminal assets: An overview', *Irish Criminal Law Journal*, 9(2): 127–32.

McDowell, J. (2001) *Godfathers: Inside Northern Ireland's drugs racket*. Dublin: Gill & Macmillan.

McElrath, K. (2001) *Heroin use in Northern Ireland*. Belfast, UK: Department of Health, Social Services and Public Safety.

McElrath, K. (2002) *Prevalence of problem heroin use in Northern Ireland*. Belfast: Department of Health, Social Services and Public Safety.

McElrath, K. (2004) 'Drug use and drug markets in the context of political conflict: The case of Northern Ireland', *Addiction Research and Theory*, 12(6): 577–90.

McElrath, K. & Jordan, M. (2005) *Drug use and risk behaviours among injecting drug users*. Belfast: Department of Health, Social Services and Public Safety.

McElrath, K. and McEvoy, K. (2001) 'Heroin as evil: Ecstasy users' perceptions about heroin', *Drugs: Education, Prevention and Policy*, 8(2): 177–89.

Meade, J. (2000) 'Organised crime, moral panic and law reform: The Irish adoption of civil forfeiture', *Irish Criminal Law Journal*, 10(1): 11–16.

Monaghan, R. (2004) 'An imperfect peace: Paramilitary punishments in Northern Ireland', *Terrorism and Political Violence*, 16(3): 439–61.

Moore, G., McCarthy, P., MacNeela, P., MacGabhann, L., Philbin, M. and Proudfoot, D. (2004) *A review of harm reduction approaches in Ireland and evidence from the international literature*. National Advisory Committee on Drugs. Dublin: Government Publications.

Mulcahy, A. (2002) 'The impact of the Northern "Troubles" on criminal justice in the Irish Republic'. In P. O'Mahony (ed) *Criminal Justice in Ireland*. Dublin: Institute of Public Administration.

Mulcahy, A. and O'Mahony, E. (2005) *Policing and social marginalisation*. Dublin: Combat Poverty Agency.

Murphy-Lawless, J. (2002) *Fighting back: Women and the impact of drug abuse on families and communities*. Dublin: Liffey Press.

Northern Ireland Statistics and Research Agency (NISRA) (2013) *Tables for drug related deaths and deaths due to drug misuse registered in Northern Ireland, 2003–2013*. Belfast: NISRA. Available at: www.nisra.gov.uk/demography/default.asp30.htm (accessed 15 September 2014).

Nutt, D., King, L., Saulsbury, W. and Blakemore, C. (2007) 'Development of a rational scale to assess the harm of drugs of potential misuse', *The Lancet*, 369(9566): 1047–53.

O'Donnell, I. and O'Sullivan, E. (2001) *Crime control in Ireland: The politics of intolerance*. Cork: Cork University Press.

O'Gorman, A. (1998) 'Illicit drug use in Ireland: An overview of the problem and policy responses', *Journal of Drug Issues*, 28(1): 155–66.

O'Hare, P., Newcombe, R., Matthews, A., Buning, E. C. and Drucker, E. (1992) *The reduction of drug-related harm*. London: Routledge.

O'Kelly, F., Bury, G., Cullen, B. and Dean, G. (1988) 'The rise and fall of heroin use in an inner city area of Dublin', *Irish Journal of Medical Science*, 157(2): 35–8.

O'Leary, M. (2009) *Intimidation of families*. Dublin: Family Support Network.

O'Mahony, P. (1993) *Crime and punishment in Ireland*. Dublin: Round Hall Press.

O'Mahony, P. (2008) *The Irish war on drugs: The seductive folly of prohibition*. Manchester: Manchester University Press.

O'Reilly, E. (1998) *Veronica Guerin: The life and death of a crime reporter*. London: Vintage.

Parker, H., Newcombe, R. and Bakx, K. (1987) 'The new heroin users: Prevalence and characteristics in Wirral, Merseyside', *British Journal of Addiction*, 82(2): 147–57.

Pearson, G. (1987) *The new heroin users*. Oxford: Basil Blackwell.

Percy, A. (2005) '16th International Conference on the Reduction of Drug Related Harm, Belfast, Northern Ireland, 20–24th March 2005', *International Journal of Drug Policy*, 16(3): 199–202.

Pike, B. (2008) *Development of Ireland's drug strategy 2000–2007, HRB Overview Series 8*. Dublin: Health Research Board.

Pike, B. (2011) 'In brief', *Drugnet Ireland*, 37: 29.

Pike, B. (2012a) '"To prohibit or not to prohibit?" – that is no longer the question', *Drugnet Ireland*, 41: 7–8.

Pike, B. (2012b) 'Politicians and the drugs debate – six years on', *Drugnet Ireland*, 41: 10.

Ramsay, M., and Percy, A. (1996) *Drug misuse declared: Results of the 1994 British Crime Survey*. London: Home Office.

Reuter, P. (1997) 'Why can't we make prohibition work better? Some consequences of ignoring the unattractive', *Proceedings of the American Philosophical Society*, 141(3): 262–75.

Reuter, P. and Stevens, A. (2007) *An analysis of UK drug policy*. Monograph prepared for the UK Drug Policy Commission. London: Drug Policy Commission.

Reuter, P. and Trautmann, F. (2009) *A report on global illicit drugs markets 1998–2007*. Brussels: European Commission.

Room, R. and Reuter, P. (2012) 'How well do international drug conventions protect public health?', *Lancet*, 379(9810): 84–91.

Rosmarin, A. and Eastwood, N. (2012) *A quiet revolution: Drug decriminalisation policies in practice across the globe*. London: Release.

Ryan, A. (1997) 'The Criminal Justice (Drug Trafficking) Act 1996: Decline and fall of the right to silence', *Irish Criminal Law Journal*, 7: 22–37.

Seddon, T. (2000) 'Explaining the drug-crime link: Theoretical, policy and research issues', *Journal of Social Policy*, 29(1): 95–107.

Seddon, T. (2006) 'Drugs, crime and social exclusion – social context and social theory in British drugs-crime research', *British Journal of Criminology*, 46(4): 680–703.

Seddon, T., Ralphs, R. and Williams, L. (2008) 'Risk, security and the "criminalization" of British drug policy', *British Journal of Criminology*, 48(6): 818–34.

Sherlock, K. and Conner, M. (1999) 'Patterns of ecstasy use amongst club-goers on the UK "dance scene"', *International Journal of Drug Policy*, 10(2): 117–29.

Silke, A. (2000) 'Drink, drugs and rock 'n' roll: Financing loyalist terrorism in Northern Ireland—Part two', *Studies in Conflict and Terrorism*, 23(2): 107–27.

Stevens, A. (2007) 'When two dark figures collide: Evidence and discourse on drug-related crime', *Critical Social Policy*, 27(1): 77–99.

Stevens, A., Stover, H. and Brentari, C. (2010) 'Criminal justice approaches to harm reduction in Europe'. In T. Rhodes and D. Hedrich (eds) *Harm reduction: Evidence, impacts and challenges*. Luxembourg: Publications Office of the European Union.

Stevens, A., Trace, M. and Bewley-Taylor, D. (2005) *Reducing drug related crime: An overview of the global evidence*. Available at: www.beckleyfoundation.org (accessed 25 September 2014).

Strang, J. and Gossop, M. (eds) (2005) *Heroin addiction and the British system: Origins and evolution*. London: Routledge.

Tonge, J. (2013) *Northern Ireland: Conflict and change*. Abingdon, UK: Routledge.

White, H. R. and Gorman, D. M. (2000) 'Dynamics of the drug-crime relationship', *Criminal justice 2000: The nature of crime: Continuity and change.* Washington: US Department of Justice.

World Health Organisation (2003) *Harm reduction approaches to injecting drug use.* World Health Organisation. Available at: www.who.int/en/ (accessed 22 April 2015).

World Health Organisation (2014) *Global status report on alcohol and health 2014.* Geneva: World Health Organization.

Yates, R. (2002) 'A brief history of British drug policy, 1950–2001', *Drugs: Education, Prevention and Policy,* 9(2): 113–24.

Notes

1 The Bill had been introduced first by the previous Government in 1972, then reintroduced in 1973. The Bill introduced by Minister Corish in 1975 had retained many of the provisions of the earlier Bills. Dáil Éireann debate, Supplementary Estimate, 1975 – Misuse of Drugs Bill 1973: Second stage. Thursday, 20 February 1975.

2 Dail Éireann debate *Vol 278 No. 6.* Thursday, 20 February 1975.

3 Section 28. This obligation became discretionary upon the enactment of the Misuse of Drugs Act 1984. See discussion in Charleton (1986: Chapter 14).

4 The legislation was introduced in June 1984 and by August of that year it had passed all stages, been signed by the President and the commencement order for its implementation had been made (Butler 2002: 143).

5 Section 5 Misuse of Drugs Act 1984. See discussion of these provisions in Charleton (1986: Chapter 12).

6 Section 7(1)(a). See Charleton (1986: 85).

7 The offences of possession of controlled drugs for the purpose of supply, contrary to section 15 of the Misuse of Drugs Act 1977, and of importation of controlled drugs for the purpose of supply, contrary to section 7 of the 1984 Act, now carried life imprisonment.

8 Butler (2002:143) refers to a paper prepared by Inspector John McGroarty of the drug squad entitled 'Cannabis: A Cultural Poison' that was used as a source by the Minister of State at the Department of Justice, Nuala Fennell TD.

9 Introducing the Bill, Minister Corish explained that it was not possible for the ROI to adhere to these international conventions up until then, as 'our controls were technically unsuited to the control structure provided for in the conventions'. Dáil Éireann debate Vol.266. No 10. Thursday, 28 June 1973.

10 Bewley-Taylor (2012: 8) suggests that the impact of these conventions is to impose an obligation on Nation Parties to 'adhere to the central prohibitive norm of the global drug control system'.

11 Butler (2002: 140–1) explains that the Report of the Special Government Task Force on Drug Abuse (1983), established to 'review and report on the question of drug abuse, with particular reference to the Dublin inner-city area', also argued that 'the epidemic of drug abuse then being experienced in Dublin could be validly explained in terms of the poverty and powerlessness of the neighbourhoods concerned, rather than in terms of individual risk factors'. Butler explains that the full report of this Task Force was never published however and that the Department of Health press releases of the time explicitly downplayed the ideological thrust of the Task Force's conclusions, re-stating individualistic explanations for the drug problem instead (142).

12 Although an exception within the Garda Síochána was the irrepressible Sergeant Denis Mullins of the Garda Drug Squad, which was set up at his behest in 1967. Butler (2002: 109) writes: 'Denis Mullins … had become convinced from the mid-1960s that illicit drug use in the Dublin area was becoming more common and causing more problems, although at this time there was no official acceptance of this point of view'.

13 The policy of evicting drug pushers from local authority housing estates was advocated by a public representative in the north inner city and prominent anti-drugs activist Tony Gregory. See discussion in Gilligan (2011: 125)

14 HL Deb 09 May 1996 vol 572 cc264–6. Available at: http://hansard.millbanksystems.com/lords/1996/may/09/proceeds-of-crime-northern-ireland-order (accessed 2 February 2015).

15 http://www.legislation.gov.uk/nisr/1996/54/contents/made

16 For a detailed analysis of the National Drugs Strategy 2001–2008, the structures established under it and more recent policy developments, see Pike (2008)

17 Following a mid-term review of the first strategy, a fifth pillar for Rehabilitation was added.

18 Butler (2002: 202–4) identifies a number of factors that contributed to this more enlightened policy response: the development of a 'social partnership' approach to governance which saw government more willing to work in collaboration with community drug activist groups; the adoption of a new approach to public policy administration referred to as the Strategic Management Initiative which promoted inter-sectoral and inter-departmental working on 'cross-cutting' social problems such as drugs; and finally, the healthy state of the public finances in 1996 meant that the government could now invest in large-scale community development projects.

19 Two Garda Síochána studies of drugs and crime conducted in 1997 and 2004 revealed a significant decrease in reported drug-related crime by drug users during this period. The studies also reported unemployment rates among their samples as reducing from 84 per cent (Keogh, 1997) to 55 per cent (Furey and Brown, 2003). See discussion in Connolly (2006: 75).

20 Kilcommins *et al.* (2004: 229) argue that 'the kinds of measures against organised crime of which CAB is a typical example have been criticised for confusing output with outcome measures. Measures of success have been based upon police activity, e.g. value of assets seized, rather than final outcomes, e.g. lower consumption of narcotics'.

21 The Law Reform Commission is an independent body established under the Law Reform Commission Act 1975 to keep the law under review and make recommendations for law reform. See www.lawreform.ie

22 Portugal became the first country in the European Union to decriminalise all drugs, including cocaine and heroin, under a statute passed in 2000.

23 For an analysis of recent developments in the Portuguese and Dutch systems, and elsewhere, see Rosmarin and Eastwood (2012).

24 They also discussed whether it was time to consider allowing physically and chemically dependent drug users to get 'their heroin or morphine in well-supervised, clean, incorruptible circumstances, i.e. to establish safe injecting facilities'. (See Pike, 2012a)

25 In calling for an 'open debate about decriminalisation in Ireland', CityWide (2012: 5) states that 'much of the harm related to drug use and drug dealing occurs because of their illicit nature….the global war on drugs has failed and it is time for us to challenge rather than reinforce common misconceptions about drug markets, drug use and drug dependence'.

22

The policymaking process and penal change

Mary Rogan

Using policy analysis to understand penal change

Policymaking is a subject of increasing attention by criminological scholars, with comparative and national studies becoming more common (Jones and Newburn, 2007, 2013). Loader's study (2006) of the attitudes and dispositions of senior civil servants in the Home Office during the hey-day of penal-welfarism is a rare and insightful glimpse into the world of the senior policy-maker. Loader and Sparks (2004) have also called for more investigation into the reasons why 'evidence' does not find its way into criminal justice policy, arguing that the process must be more closely studied. Stevens (2011) has unearthed an account of policymaking processes which use evidence haphazardly and which can operate to silence questions of social justice. Annison (2014) speaks of the Westminster tradition in criminal justice policy change, while Snacken (2010) notes the influence of the European Court of Human Rights and its possibilities to act as a restraint on increasing punitiveness. I have written elsewhere (Rogan, 2010, 2011a, 2011b) about the influence of individual ministers and civil servants and their particular personalities and agendas, including to be seen as progressive, liberal or 'European'.

The great promise held out by policy analysis is that it provides detailed understandings of the factors motivating those most directly responsible for individual instances of penal change – policymakers. On the surface, these kinds of projects are utterly different from the macro-level structural accounts of penal development, particularly the form of theorising found in *The Culture of Control* (Garland, 2001). One deals with the rough and tumble of politics, while the other employs the ostensibly loftier tools of structural and cultural analyses.

A good contrast between the two is offered by Loader and Sparks (2004) when they compare the exhaustive account of the political activity behind criminal justice provided by Windlesham (1993) with that of Garland in *The Culture of Control*, they argue that the former represents 'a painstaking contemporary history of political debates, policy formations and legislative battles', which, unlike that of Garland, gives 'scant reference to either the economic, social or cultural contexts within which they are played out, or the criminological and political ideas that relevant actors implicitly or expressly mobilise and tussle over' (Loader and Sparks, 2004: 11).

Loader and Sparks note, however, a number of problems with Garland's methodology, suggesting that a 'historical sociology' of crime policy is necessary to explore both the actions of those who affect and effect penal policy and the social context in which those actors operated. Loader and Sparks advocate an approach they call 'historical recovery' to understand penal evolution.

In this spirit, the present chapter conducts an assessment of some of the key features of both penal systems in historical and contemporary perspectives by exploring the influences on policy at key moments of change. The chapter then examines the impact of such influences on prison policy in both jurisdictions of Ireland. Since the emergence of two penal administrations on the island, the paths of both prison systems have diverged. However, there are considerable similarities between them at particular points in their history since 1922. Common factors have also influenced their respective courses. That which overshadows, in so many ways, the history of both systems concerns the influence of the Conflict, and, more generally, the relationship of Ireland with Britain. These influences are explored in some depth in this chapter. However, other crucial influences are also examined, including the reasons behind and impact of an increasing prison population in both systems and attempts to create organisational and policy change.

Penal policy in historical perspective

Until independence for what became the Free State in 1922, Ireland had a network of prisons and local jails spread across the island. At independence, the Free State, through its Provisional Government, took charge of several local prisons including those at Dundalk, Galway, Sligo, Waterford, Kilkenny and Tullamore. These held prisoners serving sentences for minor offences. There were also four convict prisons, in which prisoners sentenced to terms of penal servitude were held. These prisons remain in use: Mountjoy in Dublin; Maryborough (now known as Portlaoise); Limerick; and Cork prison (though Cork prison at independence had a section for women which subsequently closed). In Northern Ireland, Belfast Prison, Derry/Londonderry Prison and, for women, Armagh Gaol Prison were used, which were found to be in very poor condition when the Northern Ireland Government took office.[1] Prisoners in Northern Ireland were also sent to Scottish and English prisons.

The penal system in both jurisdictions was, as Osborough has put it, 'the product very largely of English penological thought and practice. The nineteenth century origins of several of its principal features was equally obtrusive' (1985: 181).

Somewhat surprisingly, when compared to the significant changes which occurred in respect of policing in the Irish Free State (Conway, 2014; Walsh, 2009), the government did not instigate a major change in the prison system. Perhaps part of the reason for this lack of innovation in the realm of prison was the sheer physical solidity of the system, but also the financial costs associated with changing the prison system. Kevin O'Higgins, Minister for Home Affairs and, like many of the members of the cabinet, a former prisoner, stated in the Dáil:

> [Penal reform is a] big question and an interesting question, but scarcely a question for a transitional Government. I think that everyone here would agree that we should aim at improvement and reform in the existing prison system. There is not a member of the present Government who has not been in jail. We have had the benefit of personal experience and personal study of these problems, and, although we have never discussed them, I think we would be unanimous in the view that a change and reform would be desirable. Personally I can conceive nothing more brutalising, and nothing more calculated to make a man rather a dangerous member of society, than the existing system. But one does not attempt sweeping reforms in a country situated as this country is at the moment. One does

not build or try to build in the path of a forest fire. This question and many other interesting questions will have to be postponed until the situation alters.[2]

Both jurisdictions were preoccupied by the cost of the prison system during the 1920s. In the interests of saving money, the General Prisons Board, the agency responsible for running the prison system in the Free State, was disbanded in 1928 (National Archives, Department of An Taoiseach Files, S5578). At Stormont, the cost of the officers' wages and food for the prisoners was also giving rise to disquiet. Incidentally, in response to concerns that the price of food was higher at Belfast Prison than at Armagh, the Minister for Finance replied that this may have been due to the fact that women consumed less food.[3] In the 1920s, the average daily prison population in Northern Ireland was around 400,[4] while, interestingly, in the Free State it was around the same (General Prisons Board, 1928).

Little is known about how the prison staff adjusted to these changing times. Brendan Behan perhaps put it best when he said 'all that changed was the badges on the warders' caps' (1958: 14) when the Irish Free State Government took over. However, some prison officers were concerned about the effect of the transition to an independent government on their work and, indeed, their safety. Being associated with the sharp end of British rule was undesirable, and some took early retirement. Members of the Stormont Assembly suggested that some officers should be transferred across the Border with one member expressing concern about the number of Catholic officers in senior positions in Armagh Gaol, arguing that they should be replaced with Protestants or Catholics 'if they are loyal'.[5]

Stagnation, 'reformation' and efforts to put an 'Irish' stamp on penal policy

The question of imprisonment or theories of how punishment should be administered did not excite much official attention in either jurisdiction following 1922. Indeed, both jurisdictions showed a notable lack of interest in penal affairs in the first 40 years or so after partition. In the case of what was by 1949 the Republic of Ireland, this state of affairs has variously been described as 'calcification' (Kilcommins et al., 2004: 41), or 'stagnation' (O'Donnell, 2008). Such a characterisation could equally apply north of the Border. Part of the reason behind this was the small and declining numbers of prisoners in the system, which was cited by both administrations as militating against the possibilities of experimentation. Both jurisdictions also closed prisons in the interests of economy, with Derry/Londonderry prison being closed in the 1950s, leaving only Belfast prison and Armagh Gaol at the time.[6] In the Republic, Cork prison was closed, reopening in the 1970s, while smaller local prisons such as those at Galway and Dundalk were shut down. However, there were some brief interludes of action.

The late 1940s was a time of interest in penal reform in Northern Ireland. Interestingly, this seems to be associated with the Minister for Home Affairs, John Edmond Warnock, who, though by no means a radical, instigated some change. In 1948, a motion was put before Stormont that 'reform of the penal system in Northern Ireland is overdue and that the primary principle of the system should be to restore a prisoner to liberty as soon as is consistent with the public interest'. The Minister noted that he had introduced longer out-of-cell time, the radio and a 'number of relaxations and privileges' and argued that:

> [O]ne of the primary objects of the prison system should be to try to ensure that a man's present term of imprisonment is his last. Emphasis on the reformative side is always right. Taking it all in all, from such experience as I have, I rather think we are doing more for our

prison population than they are doing in England, and that the general spirit in the prison, taking it all in all, is better here than it is almost in any prison in Great Britain.[7]

When rare examples of discussion about what to do with prisoners did arise within Government, on both sides of the Border, however, the emphasis was on how they could be reformed, and, indeed, 'reform' was the predominant motif in official analyses until the 1960s, when the word gradually gave way to 'rehabilitation'. Perhaps reflecting the agricultural nature of both societies, members of the legislatures in both jurisdictions were keen to promote the potential of agricultural labour and 'the land' as a means of encouraging change. In the 1920s, Minister Fitzgerald-Kenney put forward the idea of an agricultural colony as a mechanism of reform within prisons in the Republic,[8] while a Stormont MP in 1948 argued that 'these people should have an opportunity of farming and dealing with animals, birds, and things of that kind'.[9] As late as 1962, one MP in the Northern Parliament recounted a visit to Crumlin Road prison, where he found men working in cramped conditions and in a stuffy atmosphere. Reflecting the changing mood of the time, Mr O'Reilly noted:

> [T]he whole emphasis now is on the reformation of offenders rather than punishment. People cannot be kept in prison all their lives ... prisons should be out in the country. There should be a good many fields around it, where men could go out and see a bit of Nature instead of being closed up day after day. There is only a garden at the Crumlin Road Prison, and a few of the men can go out with a spade and dig.[10]

Of course, while the sentiments may have been progressive, and intended to be so, conditions in prisons in both jurisdictions during the 1940s and at other times were far from ideal. As the Labour Party in the Republic reported following a Government-sanctioned investigation into Portlaoise prison, much of prison life was monotonous, the food was poor and the conditions involving long periods of lock up and drab prison clothing (The Irish Labour Party, 1946). Concerns were expressed about unsanitary conditions in the then-functioning Derry/Londonderry prison and outbreaks of tuberculosis.[11] Both jurisdictions have relied on Victorian prisons to a major extent.

The main legislative basis for the running of prisons in Northern Ireland is the Prison Act (Northern Ireland) 1953, which has been amended on foot of devolution. Around this period, and within a few years of each other, both prison systems sought to create a legislative framework of their own, distinct from that which had been created by a British government for a pre-partition Ireland. In the case of the Free State, reform was by way of secondary legislation, in the form of the Prison Rules 1947. The introduction of these Rules followed a period of unusual interest in the prison system in the first few decades after independence, which was, in a recurring feature of prison policy in the Republic, associated with a time of concern about the activities of 'subversive' prisoners, particularly members of the Irish Republican Army who were a source of threat to the government. Following a particularly high profile incident where an IRA prisoner died on hunger and thirst strike, there was a sense of public concern that the Government was adopting a similar line on republicanism to that under British rule. This was anathema to the then Fianna Fáil government, who, when taunted by the fact that the prison system was still governed by rules made by a British administration, moved to create prison rules for an independent Irish system (Rogan, 2008, 2011a). The Prison Rules 1947, which governed almost every aspect of prison life, were the result.

A desire to modernise the prison system was present behind the introduction of the Prison (Northern Ireland) Act 1953. Legislators there were distressed by the fact that the governing

Act dated from 1826, and it was a matter of some difficulty to determine accurately what the law was. Stormont did not want to follow what was happening in England, where a Criminal Justice Bill contained a section on prisons. Instead, legislators wanted a bespoke piece of legislation for prisons. In an action predating what happened in the Republic by some 44 years, penal servitude, a form of imprisonment for 'convicts', or those convicted of serious offences, was abolished.[12]

A desire to modernise, and to be viewed as 'progressive', was again evident in the Republic in the 1960s and into the 1970s. In a move which combined two of the characteristic features of prison policy in the Republic during the 1970s, namely an official discourse around rehabilitation as well as a crushing need for additional space, Loughan House was one of two institutions opened initially for young offenders, with a rehabilitative ethos enshrined in legislation via the Prisons Act 1970. The particular circumstances leading to the opening of this unit again reveal much about the nature of penal policymaking in the Republic, and the need to pay close attention to the immediate political context, as well as the interests and circumstances of key policymakers. In this case, the Minister for Justice involved was one responsible for many reforms to Irish penal policy: Charles Haughey (Rogan, 2008, 2010). As a Minister at the beginning of his career, and with considerable ambition and skill, Haughey wished to make his mark on his first Ministerial portfolio. The prison system was, in retrospect, an obvious target for reform. Long the subject of neglect, any efforts at change would have seemed momentous, and the political climate was one supportive of, or at least far from overtly hostile to, penal reform. It is also important to note that Haughey sought to associate himself with 'the European way', which was viewed as modern, forward-looking and, no doubt, suave and somewhat glamorous. Haughey would therefore have been comfortable with the idea that Ireland should adopt some of the key themes of the 'European penal imaginary' (Girling, 2006).

Securitisation

The impact of the Conflict on the prisons in Northern Ireland has been well documented, with some ground-breaking work emerging from McEvoy (2001), Wahidin (forthcoming), Tomlinson (1995) and others.

Much less is known about the impact of this dark period in Irish history on prisons in the Republic, both in the immediate context of the 1970s and in the longer term. Moreover, the effects of other periods involving violent responses to the relationship between Ireland and Britain have also been less distinctly sketched.

For example, it is often overlooked that internment was pioneered by the Free State Government at a number of points in its early history. Both Northern Ireland and the Free State used internment in the early 1920s, with the Free State interning around 8,000 people during the Civil War period. This pattern of using detention as a mechanism for overcoming resistance to the rule of government was repeated during the 'Emergency', the name by which World War II came to be known in the Republic, during which internment was again deployed. During that period, the Fianna Fáil government also passed the Offences Against the State Act 1939, a profoundly important piece of legislation which affected all aspects of the administration of criminal justice, both practically in terms of changes to criminal procedure and garda powers, but also in terms of the official mindset concerning responses to threats to the state (Vaughan and Kilcommins, 2008).

During the Emergency, the number of people interned was around 400 to 500 on any given day, while the numbers sentenced to prison increased rather dramatically as the Special Criminal Courts swung into operation.[13] The daily average prison population rose from 545 in 1939 to 740 in 1942. Hunger strikes were also a feature of resistance to penal policy.

This association between threats to the prison system and threats to democracy itself reappeared in 1972 following a riot in Mountjoy prison. Legislation was rushed through the Oireachtas to provide for the transfer of prisoners to a military prison, and the Taoiseach of the day, Jack Lynch T.D., stated in the Dáil that 'the prison system, is now in serious jeopardy',[14] requiring the speedy implementation of the proposed legislation to preserve public order and democracy.

The impact of the Troubles on penal policy in the Republic from the 1970s onwards was considerable. As well as a direct impact on regimes and the re-establishment of Portlaoise prison as the prison with the highest security in the Republic, the Troubles had major effects on the civil service culture concerning prison. The development of a security-driven mindset was in part driven by fear amongst civil service staff. The Secretary General of the Department of Justice at the outbreak of the Conflict was under garda protection, as was his family. Bomb scares took place at government offices. It is perhaps unsurprising that individuals working in such environments would take no chances with state security in the prison context. It is also important to note that many Justice officials would have begun their careers in this environment, and, as senior managers several years later, would continue to recall the threat the Department perceived itself to be under (Rogan, 2011a).

The Conflict also acted, in some respects conveniently, to distract attention from 'ordinary' prison policy, or elements unrelated to security. It also carried a colossal economic cost (Tomlinson, 2012). There were plans to develop a consolidated Prisons Bill in the late 1960s, which did not come to fruition partly because of the pressure on resources within the Department of Justice. The effect of the Troubles was also to create a very defensive and insular Department, which was suspicious of outside interest in the penal system. This endured for many years, resulting in what seems to have been a policy of non-cooperation with groups seeking to research or reform the penal system for a prolonged period (Rogan, 2011a).

Following the establishment of direct rule and the ending of responsibility for prisons on the part of Stormont, prison policy in Northern Ireland was almost entirely infused by security concerns. The extent of this is that literature on the prison system in Northern Ireland, understandably, focused very much on the experience of prisoners who were members of paramilitary organisations. The effect of this on our understanding of prison regimes and on policymakers' interests is significant.

As regards the approaches taken by the Westminster governments, McEvoy (2001) summarises the phases involved succinctly as: reactive containment from 1969 to 1975; criminalisation from 1976 to 1981; and managerialist strategies, which Wahidin et al. argue 'continue to dominate' (2012: 459).

As with the government in the Republic at various points of conflict, a central strategy was the use of detention without trial and the creation of legal structures to support this, for example, via various Special Powers Acts. The criminalisation strategy was influenced by a toughening of approach by the British Government and, through the hunger strikes of the 1980s, was followed by an explosive combination of penal policy and politics playing itself out in the most visceral of ways. The more pragmatic approach which followed involved a refusal to recognise prisoners as 'political', officially, but allowed for separation of paramilitary groups. Efforts to 'normalise' the prison system were most pointedly felt in the introduction of Maghaberry in 1986. The regime and managerialist ethos prevalent in this prison attracted considerable concern, with Wahidin et al. (2012) noting a blunt approach to security categorisation, and Scraton and Moore (2004, 2013) detailing extremely difficult conditions for women prisoners.

Another effect of the various periods of conflict in Ireland was that public interest in penal affairs for many decades was streamed through the prism of security. In the 1930s, for example, groups advocating for penal reform tended to be aligned to the prisoners detained for IRA-related activity. One such group was the Women's Prisoners' Defence League, founded by, amongst others, Maud Gonne MacBride. This group protested regularly in Dublin. While influencing policy was perhaps not the central aim of the group, their association with threats to the state meant that such interest groups had very limited impact on penal policy. In both jurisdictions, when policymakers had to deal with security issues, 'ordinary' prison matters were forgotten. Wahidin *et al.* (2012) also comment on how mobilisation in favour of penal reform in Northern Ireland has tended to be limited to the area of politically-motivated imprisonment.

McEvoy's description of resistance amongst Republican prisoners in Northern Ireland (2001) is also very relevant to the actions of prisoners in the Republic throughout its penal history, with prisoners employing hunger strikes, but also humour, performance, art and legal strategies. However, while often vociferous, prisoner resistance during the Civil War period in particular cannot be said to have had a major impact on the direction of penal policy in the Free State or Republic.

The impact of former prisoners on the formation of penal policy in both jurisdictions is contrasting. Despite the fact that, for decades, members of Cabinet in the Republic had served time in prison, none of them took up the cause of penal reform in their politics. The first Minister to do so was Charles Haughey, part of the new generation of politicians not directly associated with the Civil War. In Northern Ireland, by contrast, the impact of prisoners and former prisoners on securing a political settlement was immense, though again, the Minister currently in charge of the prison system, unlike the First and Deputy First Minister, does not have a direct experience of prison.

Playing politics with prisons

Two major waves of prison openings in the Republic occurred in the 1970s and 1990s to early 2000s. Both jurisdictions experienced an increase in prison numbers during the 1970s. The entire population of the prisons in Northern Ireland in the 1940s was about 400, while Crumlin Road alone was holding 856 in 1972, not including the increasing number of internees. 1972 was a crucial year for both prison systems, being when the prison population in the Republic breached 1,000 for the first time. Both systems also increased their numbers of prison staff considerably during this time. In the space of a few months, the number of staff in the prison system of Northern Ireland was increased by 25 per cent,[15] while the prison system in the Republic sought more prison officers to cope with the pressure of numbers (Rogan, 2011a). Numbers further increased in the Republic during the very difficult decade of the 1980s (Rogan, 2011a). In the same decade, prison numbers began to stabilise in Northern Ireland, standing at 2,038 prisoners in December 1984 and going below 2,000 in 1985 (House of Commons, 7 March 1986, vol 93, col 300).

While the prison population as a percentage of the total population was higher in Northern Ireland during the 1990s than in the Republic, their trajectories have crossed more recently, and now there are more prisoners per 100,000 of the population in the Republic than in Northern Ireland (see figure 22.1).

The chronology for the development of new prisons is revealing. The prisons which have become operational in the Republic since the foundation of the state are the Midlands prison (2001), the Dóchas Centre (1999), Castlerea prison (1999), Wheatfield (1989), Cloverhill (1999), the Training Unit at Mountjoy prison (1974), Loughan House semi-open prison (1973) and Arbour Hill Prison (1973). Cork prison was reopened in 1972 during a period of overcrowding in the Irish penal estate. In Northern Ireland, Maghaberry was introduced in the mid-1980s,

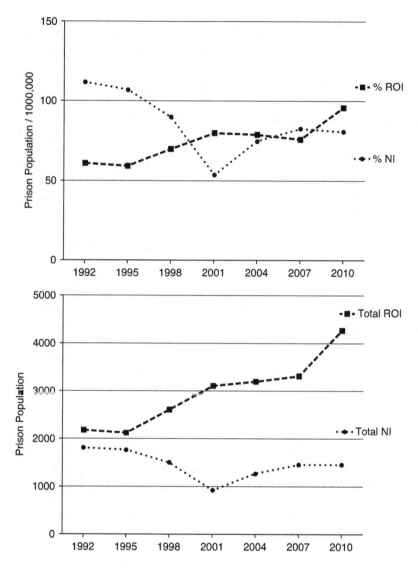

Figure 22.1   Prison populations in Northern Ireland and the Republic of Ireland

following the closure of Armagh prison for women and then Crumlin Road. Magilligan was opened in 1972, initially to accommodate political prisoners.

The financial constraints of the 1970s and 1980s meant that new buildings could not be commissioned in the Republic. No such concerns were present during the following decade, which saw a period of unprecedented penal expansion in the Republic, in comparison to which the prison building programme in Northern Ireland looks rather modest. In a further example of the need to examine the political context for penal change very closely, the period of the mid-90s was a textbook case of political competition leading to increases in the size of the Republic's prison estate, which seemed unstoppable and certainly very difficult to reverse (O'Sullivan and O'Donnell, 2001; Rogan, 2011a). The key figures during this period of penal expansionism were John O'Donoghue T. D., who was an opposition spokesperson on justice for Fianna Fáil (then in a rare period in which it was not in power), and Michael McDowell T. D., who was a member of the Progressive Democrats (an unusual party in Irish terms in the sense of holding an ideological position on economic policy). The mid-1990s was a time of intense political competition in the Republic, with Fianna Fáil opening up crime policy as a front in its battle to be elected. Then Deputy O'Donoghue weaved links between what he argued were rising crime rates, a lack of prison building and tensions between the coalition partners in Government (Fine Gael and Labour) in an effort at portraying the Minister for Justice, Nora Owen T.D., as weak and indecisive.

The effects of this period (the mid-1990s) were profound, and are still being felt. The result was to overturn what was a promising period for Irish penal reform, evidenced by the publication of the *Management of Offenders: A Five Year Plan* (Department of Justice, 1994), which was a frank and considered strategy statement by the Department of Justice acknowledging the considerable problems in the prison system at the time and planning for a modest expansion of prison numbers. That planned increase in numbers (around 230) was quickly replaced in 1997 with a plan to increase spaces by over 800, which figure ballooned to 2,000 by the turn of the century. Many of the penal institutions currently in operation in the Republic therefore have their foundations in the maelstrom of the penal activity of the mid-1990s.

Another planned penal change can also be traced to the mid-1990s. This time the initiative came from Michael McDowell, another highly active and motivated Minister, who had stated his views on the penal system most forthrightly while in opposition. McDowell's position was an interesting mix of an expressed horror at the poor conditions in Irish prisons, especially Mountjoy; disquiet at the use of temporary release to relieve overcrowding; and a zeal for cutting the costs of the budget for staffing and, particularly, overcrowding. The combination of these positions resulted in a plan to build a new prison on a green-field site in North County Dublin. The plan for Thornton Hall prison could also be contemplated because of the then healthy state of the Irish public finances and an appetite for large building projects evident across many aspects of Irish public policy. Thornton Hall was planned to hold up to 2,200 prisoners and, as such, can be read as the symbolic manifestation of a distinctly punitive turn in Irish penal policy. However, as Brangan (2009) has shown, Thornton Hall was driven in part by a desire to save costs through the deployment of modern penal technologies which would require fewer staff.

Thornton Hall was never built and was the subject of a review commissioned by a new Government in 2011 (Thornton Hall Review Group, 2011). As a policy which had become toxic in the fallout from Ireland's economic crisis, a new Government was able to roll back from it without an embarrassing political climb-down.

Strategies of change: contemporary penal policy

Northern Ireland now has three penal establishments: Maghaberry, Magilligan and Hydebank Wood. Maghaberry is a high-security establishment for men; Magilligan is a medium-security prison; and Hydebank Wood YOC is a Category C (low- to medium-security) centre for boys and young men aged 15 to 23. The only institution for women is a unit within the Hydebank Wood, which replaced the old female prison at Maghaberry, despite the warning of Scraton and Moore (2004) regarding moving women from the grounds of one male prison to another. (The conditions in Maghaberry had been the subject of severe criticism by the Prisons Inspectorate (2002) and the Northern Ireland Human Rights Commission (2004)). The Republic has 14 prisons, two of which are for women.

Both prison systems are currently undergoing processes of policy change. The change process which was instigated following the Good Friday Agreement involving the release of prisoners affected prisoners in the Republic too, but on nothing like the same scale seen in Northern

Ireland. The legacy of conflict endures, however, as prisons in Northern Ireland continue to struggle to deal with the demands for segregation between Loyalist and Republican prisoners, and staff cultures formed over decades remain difficult to change (Wahidin *et al.*, 2012).

More recently, penal policy in the Republic has begun to experience some of the most significant changes since the 1960s. Since the General Election of 2011 and under the guidance of yet another influential Minister, Alan Shatter T.D., there has been a raft of policy announcements and concrete developments. As with previous Ministers for Justice who left an important legacy for penal practice, Minister Shatter was energetic and not afraid of swift action. Unlike other Ministers, however, he was also in the latter stages of his political career, which gave him the luxury, perhaps, of being less fearful of what the press or the opposition might make of his proposals for reform. Like Michael McDowell, Alan Shatter came to office with a series of ideas ready to be implemented. In the 1980s, he had been instrumental in the creation of legislation introducing community service orders for the first time (Rogan, 2011a). Spending just over three years in office before resigning in the wake of a policing controversy (Collins, 2014), the pace at which reforms were being announced gives the impression of a Minister with many stored-up policies. Some of the most eye-catching developments have been: the introduction of a requirement on judges to consider community service when a sentence of up to 12 months may be imposed; the introduction of a refurbishment programme to eliminate slopping out in Mountjoy prison (after decades of unfulfilled promises); the introduction of a requirement on the Inspector of Prisons to investigate deaths of prisoners; and the introduction of the 'community return' scheme (whereby certain prisoners are eligible for early release in order to carry out work in the community, brought in to address, in part, severe overcrowding).

There are also signs that the manner in which penal policy is formed in the Republic is changing. Penal policy has long been a subject of criticism for its failure to attend to research, and its *ad hoc*, stop-start nature (O'Donnell, 2008; Kilcommins *et al.*, 2004; Rogan, 2010). As Minister, Alan Shatter T.D. set up three commissions: a review group to examine the plans for Thornton Hall, a Strategic Review Group of penal policy (tasked with a review which should be 'all-encompassing') and a review group examining the question of mental health and the criminal justice system. Crucially, as the experience of the 1960s has shown, each of these groups comprises representatives from the Department of Justice and Equality and the Irish Prison Service. Having such representation is essential for ensuring the credibility of the recommendations made and increasing the likelihood of their acceptance. The report of the Strategic Review Group on Penal Policy was published in September 2014[16] and recommended, *inter alia*, a reduction in the prison population, the development and expansion of alternatives to custody and an increased use of open prisons (Strategic Review Group on Penal Policy, 2014).

Yet again, the history of Irish penal policy demonstrates the importance of the confluence of particular individuals on shaping that policy. As well as a new Minister, the Irish Prison Service received a new Director General, Michael Donnellan, in late 2011. A former head of the Probation Service, he has stated his view that, in prison, 'often we get these adult bodies that are actually empty, and what we have to try and do is fill them back up. And usually the main ingredient is love, care and love, decency and respect' (Donnellan, 2014). Under his leadership, the Irish Prison Service has created a three-year strategic plan (Irish Prison Service, 2012), with goals to develop further strategies around older people in prison and the position of minorities, which are the first strategies of their kind in the history of Irish prison administration. He has also led, with the head of the Probation Service, the development of the first joint strategy with the Irish Probation Service (Irish Prison Service and Probation Service, 2013), as well as the first bespoke strategy for women offenders, again in conjunction with the Probation Service (Irish Prison Service and Probation Service, 2014). It is noteworthy that closer cooperation between the two equivalent bodies was recommended by the Owers report in Northern Ireland (Prison Review Team; 2011).

These developments point to a new focus on developing a long-term and strategic direction for the penal system in the Republic. Importantly, the political context is also quite different from that at any other time in Irish history. The government finds itself in a position where the opposition parties and independents, many of which are broadly left-wing, have proven themselves unlikely to criticise the changes being introduced and often condemn a lack of more progressive measures. In a remarkable move in October 2011, just over six months since the change of Government, the Joint Oireachtas (Parliamentary) Committee on Justice, Equality and Defence established a sub-committee on penal reform. The subcommittee, which comprises representatives of all parties and independents, set itself terms of reference to look in particular at 'back-door' strategies as alternatives to the use of imprisonment and to examine the experience of other jurisdictions in so doing. It received submissions from a wide variety of civil society organisations and academics, and drew on, unusually for an Irish government body, the experience of Finland and Scotland (Rogan, 2013).

The subcommittee's report calls for what it describes as a 'decarceration strategy', designed to reduce the prison population by one-third over ten years (Houses of the Oireachtas, 2013). It argues that all prison sentences of less than six months should be commuted and that standard remission should be increased from the current one-quarter to one-third.

Efforts are also underway to renew the strategic direction of the Northern Ireland Prison Service (NIPS). This change process has its roots in the review of the penal system by Dame Anne Owers, which made 40 recommendations to improve penal culture, policy and practice (Prison Review Team, 2011). A Prison Review Oversight Group was established by the Minister to oversee the implementation of Owers' recommendations, but the process for finalising appointment was slow, and the Committee on the Administration of Justice has criticised the absence of an implementation plan (Committee on the Administration of Justice, 2013).

In 2011, the Northern Ireland Prison Service Strategic Efficiency and Effectiveness (SEE) Programme was published. This is to be a four-year 'change management' programme and was established following recognition by both the Justice Minister, David Ford, and the Director General of NIPS that there is an overwhelming need for the prison service to change. Following a series of highly critical reports regarding NIPS' approach to management, its working practices and organisational culture, the Director General has stated, 'we cannot ignore the fact that NIPS is no longer delivering the necessary values, attitudes, behaviours that this emerging Northern Ireland needs and wants. We need to change' (NIPS, 2011). Dame Owers was subsequently invited to address the Northern Ireland Assembly's Committee for Justice to outline the 40 recommendations contained in the report of the Prison Review Team (Northern Ireland Assembly, Committee for Justice, 2010; Prison Review Team, 2011).

Further to these developments, the Minister has agreed to a new statement of purpose for the Service, with three new strategic priorities, specifically: the provision of safe, decent and secure custody; to reform and modernise to create a more efficient and effective Service; and to reduce the risk of re-offending.

One of the key changes is a 'staff exit scheme', prompted in part by finances, but also in an effort to change cultures, as no new recruits had come into the service in almost 20 years. After launching the strategy in 2011, the Director General described it as a 'critical turning point for NIPS' (NIPS, 2011). In 2014, the final 28 staff of 520 who had applied for voluntary early retirement left the service, while 300 new custody officers were recruited (DOJNI, 2014). At the same launch, the Minister referred to devolution as providing 'an opportunity for a fresh start and a chance to move beyond the constraints of the past to unlock new potential for the future'.

In February 2014, NIPS launched its *Estate Strategy* (NIPS, 2014), which plans to reconfigure Maghaberry, which has been the subject of very damning criticism by the Criminal Justice Inspection and the Chief Inspector of Prisons, including developing a new accommodation block and high-security facility, as well as the redevelopment of Magilligan prison. In further parallels with the Republic, overcrowding is cited as one of the drivers behind this change, along with a desire to move towards the use of dynamic security rather than focus entirely on physical security. The Minister has also expressed his commitment to the development of a separate secure prison for women, though the process for implementing such a change, though sorely needed, does not seem to be advanced.

It seems that in both jurisdictions, policy windows opened up following a change of political responsibility. Devolution in Northern Ireland and a general election in the Republic provided political cover for policymakers to say tough things about the prison system. This is particularly interesting in the northern context when we consider the positions on prison issues adopted by the Democratic Unionist Party and Sinn Féin. The former's stated position is one which emphasises increased sentences and that prisoners should not be 'treated more favourably than law abiding citizens' (Democratic Unionist Party, 2014). Sinn Féin's stated position on safer communities is that prison places should be saved for dangerous offenders and that alternatives to custody for non-offenders should be initiated (Sinn Féin, 2014). Perhaps only a Justice Minister from the Alliance Party can navigate between these two positions. The Alliance Party itself places reform of the prison system first in its list of achievements in the area of justice (Alliance Party, 2013). It is also of note that the Hillsborough Agreement (Northern Ireland, 2010: 7), which paved the way for the devolution of criminal justice powers, stated that, 'a review of the conditions of detention, management and oversight of all prisons' was necessary, while the Committee on the Administration of Justice has argued that, 'with devolution of responsibility for criminal justice, more local pressure for accountability and change can be asserted' (Committee on the Administration of Justice, 2010: 52). In the case of Northern Ireland, we may be seeing an effort, as in Scotland (Morrison, 2012; Scottish Prisons Commission, 2010), to create a new approach to imprisonment, and to differentiate it from the past and, by implication, Westminster rule. In both jurisdictions it was clear that prison policy could not be allowed to continue in the direction in which it had been travelling. The CAJ described the Northern Irish prison system as being in a state of crisis in 2010 (Committee on the Administration of Justice, 2010), while the Irish Penal Reform Trust argued that the prison crisis was 'completely out of control' in the Republic in the same year (Irish Penal Reform Trust, 2010).

It is also important to note that though many organisations, including the Committee on the Administration of Justice and the Northern Ireland Association for the Care and Resettlement of Offenders, do important work on raising awareness of and seeking to influence change on aspects of penal policy, the absence of an organisation with the sole focus on penal reform and prisoners' rights in Northern Ireland is regrettable. Though lobby groups, of course, do not always influence policy in the way that they would like, Stolz (2002) and Rock (2004) have shown that they can obtain the ears of policymakers at pivotal moments. The Irish Penal Reform Trust operates in the Republic only.

Understanding policy landscapes

The history of prison policymaking in Ireland is one in which periods of hyperactivity are interspersed with long periods of neglect (Rogan, 2011a; O'Donnell 2008; Kilcommins *et al.*, 2004). In the Republic, it has been well documented that individual Ministers and civil servants have an influence on specific policy directions which is pronounced and, it seems, much greater than is the case in comparable jurisdictions (Rogan, 2010). This may be a function of being a small jurisdiction, where policy networks are small, though Ryan (2003) suggests that even in a large country, circles of penal policymaking are small and overlapping. It may also be a result of a particular brand of clientist politics practised in Ireland (see further, Rogan, 2011a), which emphasises the practical and here and now, rather than a long-term or more ideological approach to policy. This can lead to very speedy activity within penal policy, but means both jurisdictions are highly vulnerable to the influence of political opportunism on prison issues, the ideological commitments of individual policymakers and moral panics. These factors are difficult to capture without very close reading of the policy processes, and they pose interesting questions of the ability of literature which seeks to explain penal change to do so convincingly without the employment of such laborious methods.

With both systems now emerging from the shadows cast by the Conflict, it seems, tentatively at least, that policymaking processes are improving and policymakers are making efforts to create a more obvious strategic direction for both systems. Perhaps surprisingly, though both processes share many similarities, there does not seem to be significant policy transfer between the two places, nor reference to each other by policymakers[17]. This is a pity in light of the common challenges faced by both administrations.

The histories of both prison systems teach us it is prudent to be cautious about the changes proposed, and Wahidin et al. (2012) are right to express doubt about the possibilities for change in Northern Ireland[18]. However, the combination of new political structures and seismic changes in the political landscape in both jurisdictions; new personnel at the top of each prison service; and penal systems subject to sustained critique in both jurisdictions, means that a rare policy window has opened up for both prison systems. The legacy of this period on the future direction of penal change in Ireland will be of enormous importance. It will also provide an opportunity for scholars to gain an increased understanding of what influences penal change, in Ireland and beyond.

The ability to look closely at the influences on penal change in two small jurisdictions provides a precious opportunity to see policy change at work in sharp relief, but it also poses challenges for theorising about penal politics. Penal policy in Northern Ireland and the Republic of Ireland highlights the crucial role of agency: individual Ministers can have decisive influence, in some cases reversing what seemed to be embedded policy directions, with the actions of Ministers Haughey, Shatter and McDowell in the Republic of Ireland being instructive cases in point. Local factors must always be at the forefront of our understanding of penal change, with the impact of the Conflict being a major and long-lasting factor in the shaping of both penal systems. The 1970s, that decade of crucial importance to many narratives of change in global criminal justice policy, looked quite different in Ireland, where grappling with the difficulties faced by the prison systems and employing the prison system in defence of the state were the animating concerns for policymakers. The role of financial pressures has also been significant throughout this period, restraining penal expansionism in the 1970s and acting to reverse it in contemporary times. Here we see similarities with movements happening in other jurisdictions at present, with unlikely coalitions developing in parts of the United States for example, seeking to reduce mass imprisonment on a combination of principled and economic grounds (see, for example, www.rightoncrime.com). These considerations have important and real effects on penal policy and, of course, on all those affected by the penal system. Penology must pay as close attention to the senior civil servant faced with a slashed budget and a deadline as to changes in the structure of the family.

The importance of such local factors poses a challenge for structural accounts such as those of Garland (2001). While Garland recognises that local factors must also be considered when sketching influences on criminal justice policy, we have yet to see a vigorous school of scholarship analysing local influences in the way that structural accounts seeking to explain change over large geographical areas dominate contemporary criminology. The case of Ireland and its evidence that important shifts in policy direction can take place rapidly and at the behest of a small number of influential individuals suggests that those accounts could be revisited.

It is important to note that debates about analysing influences on penal policy are more than just about method; they are about how we define and understand penal change. This project is hugely significant, as how we carry it out can have enormous consequences for how we think about penal policy, and, as Zedner (2002) points out, it is important to avoid dystopic visions when they are unnecessary. Tonry (2007) also notes the importance of understanding local developments and influences, as well as the role of the makeup of the legal system of a jurisdiction in shaping penal practices.

Policy analysis may seem to be peculiarly useful, and indeed feasible, for small jurisdictions. Policy analysis is painstaking and labour intensive, involving close examination of, amongst other things, White Papers, strategy statements and parliamentary debates. Exploring these sources for more than one policy in a large jurisdiction is a mammoth task. While this is so, the size of the task cannot, surely, mean that penological scholars will accept incomplete understandings of the factors influencing policy change. The Irish case has shown the decisive importance of the political ambitions and personal interests of Ministers and opened up to scrutiny the workings of the civil service in the area of prisons. Perhaps if such methods were employed in larger jurisdictions, we would see similar patterns. Penological scholarship can only be strengthened as a result.

Bibliography

Alliance Party (2013) *What we stand for.* Available at: http://allianceparty.org/page/justice-1 (accessed 23 April 2015).

Annison, H. (2014) 'Weeding the Garden: The Third Way, the Westminster Tradition and Imprisonment for Public Protection', *Theoretical Criminology*, 18(1): 38–55.

Behan, B. (1958) *Borstal boy.* London: Black Swan.

Brangan, L. (2009) *Thornton Hall: A policy analysis: Uncaring or unthinking?* MA thesis. Dublin Institute of Technology.

Collins, S. (2014) 'Alan Shatter's Resignation a Severe Blow to Government', *The Irish Times.* 8 May.

Committee on the Administration of Justice (2010) *Prisons and Prisoners in Northern Ireland: Putting Human Rights at the Heart of Prison Reform.* Belfast: Committee on the Administration of Justice. Available at: www.caj.org.uk/files/2011/01/17/prisons_report_web2.pdf (accessed 27 July 2015).

Committee on the Administration of Justice (2013) 'Prison Reform; 2013 the Year to see Change?', 24 January. Rights NI. Available at: http://rightsni.org/2013/01/prison-reform-2013-the-year-to-see-change/ (accessed 27 July 2015).

Conway, V. (2014) *Policing twentieth century Ireland: A history of An Garda Síochána.* London: Routledge.

Democratic Unionist Party (2014) *Our 7 top priorities.* Available at: www.mydup.com/about-us/priorities (accessed 23 April 2015).

Department of Justice, Equality and Law Reform (1994) *The Management of Offenders: A Five Year Plan.* Dublin: Stationery Office.

Department of Justice Northern Ireland (2014) 'Director General thanks Prison staff for professionalism and dedication', Press Release, 2 May. Available at: www.dojni.gov.uk/index/ni-prison-service/nips-latest-press-releases/director-general-thanks-prison-staff-for-professionalism-and-dedication.htm (accessed 27 July 2015).

Donnellan, M. (2014) *Prevention and Early Intervention Network.* Dublin: Prevention and Early Intervention Network. Available at: www.youtube.com/watch?v=xq1ZNdUWJrc (accessed 27 July 2015).

Garland, D. (2001) *The culture of control: Crime and social order in contemporary society.* Oxford: Oxford University Press.

General Prisons Board (1928) *Annual Report.* Dublin: Stationery Office.

Girling, E. (2006) 'European Identity, Penal Sensibilities, and Communities of Sentiment', in Armstrong, S. and McAra, L. (eds) *Perspectives on Punishment: The Contours of Control.* Oxford: Oxford University Press.

Houses of the Oireachtas (2013) *Joint committee on justice, defence and equality, report on penal reform*. Dublin: Houses of the Oireachtas.

Ireland Department of Justice (1994) *The Management of Offenders: A Five Year Plan*. Dublin: Stationery Office.

The Irish Labour Party (1946) *Prisons and Prisoners in Ireland: Report on Certain Aspects of Prison Conditions in Portlaoise Prison*. Dublin: The Irish Labour Party.

Irish Penal Reform Trust (2010) *Prisons crisis is now completely out of control*. Available at: www.iprt.ie (accessed 23 April 2015).

Irish Prison Service (2012) *Three Year Strategic Plan 2012–2015*. Dublin: Irish Prison Service.

Irish Prison Service and Probation Service (2013) *Joint Irish Prison Service and Probation Service Strategic Plan 2013-2015*. Dublin: Irish Prison Service and Probation Service.

Irish Prison Service and Probation Service (2014) *Joint Probation Service – Irish Prison Service Strategy 2014–2016: An Effective Response to Women Who Offend*. Available at: www.justice.ie/en/JELR/Pages/PB14000059 (accessed 27 July 2015).

Jones, T. and Newburn, T. (2007) *Policy transfer and criminal justice: Exploring US influence over British crime control policy*. Maidenhead: Open University Press.

Jones, T. and Newburn, T. (2013) 'Policy Convergence, Politics and Comparative Penal Reform: Sex Offender Notification Schemes in the USA and UK', *Punishment & Society*, 15(5): 439–67.

Kilcommins, S., O'Donnell, I., O'Sullivan, E. and Vaughan, B. (2004) *Crime, punishment and the search for order in Ireland*. Dublin: Institute of Public Administration.

Loader, I. (2006) 'Fall of the "Platonic Guardians": Liberalism, Criminology and Political Responses to Crime in England and Wales', *British Journal of Criminology*, 46(4): 561–86.

Loader, I. and Sparks, R. (2004) 'For an Historical Sociology of Crime Policy in England and Wales Since 1968', *Critical Review of International Social and Political Philosophy*, 7(2): 5–32.

McEvoy, K. (2001) *Paramilitary imprisonment in Northern Ireland: Resistance, management, and release*. Oxford: Oxford University Press.

Moore, L. and Scraton, P. (2013) *The incarceration of women: Punishing bodies, breaking spirits*. Studies in Prisons and Penology Series. (eds) Crewe, B., Jewkes, Y. and Ugelvic, T. Basingstoke: Palgrave Macmillan.

Morrison, K. (2012) *Penal Transformation in Post-Devolution Scotland: Change and Resistance*. Unpublished PhD thesis. Available at: www.era.lib.ed.ac.uk/bitstream/handle/1842/6435/Morrison2012.pdf?sequence=2 (accessed 27 July 2015).

Northern Ireland Assembly, C. F. J. (2010) *Prison Review Team: Briefing*. Authority of the Northern Ireland Assembly. Belfast: Stationery Office.

Northern Ireland. Government of UK (2010) *Hillsborough Castle Agreement*. Northern Ireland Office. Available at: www.gov.uk/ (accessed 22 April 2015).

Northern Ireland Prison Service (2011) *NIPS SEE Programme Launch – Director General's Speech*. 28 June 2011. Available at: www.dojni.gov.uk/index/ni-prison-service/see-programme-launch-dg-s-speech.pdf (accessed 24 April 2015).

Northern Ireland Prison Service (2014) *Estates Strategy*. Belfast: Northern Ireland Prison Service.

O'Donnell, I. (2008) 'Stagnation and Change in Irish Penal Policy', *Howard Journal of Criminal Justice*, 47(2): 121–33.

O'Sullivan, E. and O'Donnell, I. (2001) *Crime control in Ireland: The politics of intolerance*. Cork: Cork University Press.

Osborough, W. N. (1985) 'An Outline History of the Penal System in Ireland', in Whitaker, T. K. (ed) *Report of the Official Inquiry into the Penal System*. Dublin: Stationery Office.

Prison Review Team (2011) *Review of the Northern Ireland Prison Service: Conditions, management and oversight of all prisons*. Belfast: Prison Review Team.

Rock, P. E. (2004) *Constructing victims' rights: The Home Office, New Labour and victims*. Oxford: Oxford University Press.

Rogan, M. (2008) 'The Prison Rules 1947: Political Imprisonment, Politics and Legislative Change in Ireland', *The Irish Jurist*, 43: 59–80.

Rogan, M. (2010) 'Charles Haughey, the Department of Justice and Irish Prison Policy during the 1960s', *Administration*, 57: 67–99.

Rogan, M. (2011a) *Prison policy in Ireland: Politics, penal-welfarism and political imprisonment*. New York: Routledge.

Rogan, M. (2011b) 'Yes or No Minister: The Importance of the Politician-Senior Civil Servant Dyad in Irish Prison Policy', *The Prison Journal*, 91(1): 32–56.

Rogan, M. (2013) 'Prison Policy in Times of Austerity: Lessons from Ireland', *Prison Service Journal*, 207: 9–16.

Ryan, M. (2003) *Penal policy and political culture in England and Wales: Four essays on policy and process.* Winchester: Waterside.

Scottish Prisons Commission (2010) *Scotland's Choice.* Edinburgh: Scottish Prisons Commission.

Scraton, P. and Moore, L. (2004) *The hurt inside: The imprisonment of women and girls in Northern Ireland.* Belfast: Human Rights Commission.

Sinn Féin (2014) *What Sinn Féin stands for.* Available at: www.sinnfein.ie/what-sinn-fein-stands-for (accessed 23 April 2015).

Snacken, S. (2010) 'Resisting Punitiveness in Europe?', *Theoretical Criminology*, 14(3): 273–92.

Stevens, A. (2011) 'Telling Policy Stories: An Ethnographic Study of the Use of Evidence in Policy-making in the UK', *Journal of Social Policy*, 40(2): 237–55.

Stolz, B. A. (2002) *Criminal justice policy making: Federal roles and processes.* Westport, Conn.; London: Praeger.

Strategic Review Group on Penal Policy (2014) *Report of the Strategic Review Group on Penal Policy.* Dublin: Stationery Office.

Thornton Hall Review Group (2011) *Report of the Thornton Hall Project Review Group.* Dublin: Department of Justice and Equality.

Tomlinson, M. (1995) 'Imprisoned Ireland', in Ruggiero, V., Ryan, M. and Sim, J. (eds) *Western European Prison Systems: A Critical Anatomy.* London: Sage.

Tomlinson, M. (2012) 'From Counter-terrorism to Criminal Justice: Transformation or Business as Usual?' *Howard Journal of Criminal Justice*, 51(5): 442–57.

Tonry, M. (2007) *Crime, punishment, and politics in a comparative perspective.* Chicago; London: University Of Chicago Press.

Vaughan, B. and Kilcommins, S. (2008) *Terrorism, rights and the rule of law: Negotiating justice in Ireland.* Cullompton: Willan.

Wahidin, A. (Forthcoming) *The unofficial story: The experiences of former female politically motivated republican prisoners.* London: Palgrave.

Wahidin, A., Moore, L. and Convery, U. (2012) 'Unlocking a Locked-down Regime: The Role of Penal Policy and Administration in Northern Ireland and the Challenges of Change', *The Howard Journal of Criminal Justice*, 51(5): 458–73.

Walsh, D. (2009) *Human rights and policing in Ireland: Law, policy and practice.* Dublin: Clarus Press.

Windlesham, D. (1993) *Responses to crime: volume 2: Penal policy in the making.* Oxford: Clarendon Press.

Zedner, L. (2002) 'Dangers of Dystopias in Penal Theory', *Oxford Journal of Legal Studies*, 22(2): 341–66.

Notes

1 *Parliamentary Debates of Northern Ireland* (accessed 27 July 2015), Volume 2 (1922), Page 513–14.
2 Dáil Debates, vol 1, cols 2321–2, 28 November 1922.
3 *Parliamentary Debates of Northern Ireland* (accessed 27 July 2015, various dates), Volume 2 (1922), Page 521–2.
4 *Parliamentary Debates of Northern Ireland* (accessed 27 July 2015), Volume 7 (1927), Page 525–6.
5 *Parliamentary Debates of Northern Ireland* (accessed 27 July 2015), Volume 2 (1922), Page 23–5.
6 *Parliamentary Debates of Northern Ireland* (accessed 27 July 2015), Volume 37 (1953), Page 399–400.
7 *Parliamentary Debates of Northern Ireland* (accessed 27 July 2015), Volume 32 (1948-49), Page 1238–9.
8 Dáil Debates, vol 27, col 369, 16 November 1928.
9 *Parliamentary Debates of Northern Ireland* (accessed 27 July 2015), Volume 32 (1948-49), Page 1238–9.
10 *Parliamentary Debates of Northern Ireland* (accessed 27 July 2015), Volume 51 (1962), Page 525–6.
11 *Parliamentary Debates of Northern Ireland* (accessed 27 July 2015), Volume 29 (1945-46), Page 652–3.
12 *Parliamentary Debates of Northern Ireland* (accessed 27 July 2015), Volume 37 (1953), Page 325–6.
13 These courts were established and designed to deal with subversive criminal activity and sit without a jury.
14 Dáil Debates, vol 261, cols 39–40, 23 May 1972.
15 *Parliamentary Debates of Northern Ireland* (accessed 27 July 2015), Volume 83 (1971-72), Page 997–8.
16 The author was a member of this group from February 2014.
17 Individual agencies, however, do share practice and matters of common interest.
18 The policy changes outlined here remain largely in the realm of policy ideas and translation into practice is more patchy. The Minister for Justice has established an Implementation and Oversight Group (chaired by the author) to report on implementation of the recommendations made by the Strategic Review Group. The extent of implementation will be important to monitor.

23

Penal policy in Ireland

Notes from a small country

Claire Hamilton

Introduction

Despite a growing interest in globalisation and an increasingly international academic habitus, criminological writing remains under a strong Anglo-American influence. Writing recently on the problematic universality of criminological writing, Aas (2012) cogently describes the limitations of much theorising from the 'centre', urging the benefits of viewing issues from a more peripheral perspective. While the primary concern of Aas (and Connell, 2006 before her) is to correct the northern hemisphere bias of current scholarship, smaller jurisdictions within the global West have arguably also been marginalised from the debate. Certainly, contemporary work on the sociology of punishment, which forms the focus of this chapter, has been particularly guilty of extrapolating arguments based on the experiences of a few large jurisdictions. Garland (2001), for example, grounds his seminal 'culture of control' thesis in crime policy in the US, UK 'and elsewhere', prompting a response from some European analysts about the specificities of the 'elsewhere' (Albrecht, 2001; O'Donnell, 2004). Wacquant's (2005, 2009) arguments about race, neoliberalism and the 'penal state' are centred around the US and certain large European jurisdictions such as France. While there are advantages to such 'big canvas' accounts, there are costs associated with such a high level of abstraction, not least the danger of presenting an overly monolithic view. Through the more subtle and nuanced learning which can be gained from testing theories across varied political, social and historical contexts, smaller jurisdictions can provide a valid basis for evaluating competing explanations of a given phenomenon. They therefore provide an important area of comparative and international research, not only as a corrective against the 'false universalism' assumed by much penal theory, but also, as Aas observes, in terms of the insights they offer into the 'situatedness' of the global within the local.

Given the value of small country case studies for developing empirical and theoretical approaches, the aim of this chapter is to discuss existing research on Irish penal policy in terms of the broader literature on penal transformation. The question of the 'punitive turn' in the US and whether the dramatic increases in imprisonment in the US will be mirrored in other jurisdictions around the world has been described by Downes (2011: 29) as the 'most important theme in comparative criminology'. The origins of the debate can probably be traced to the early 1990s, when accounts such as those presented by Feeley and Simon (1992, 1994) sought to link contemporary developments such as the new penological focus on risk management to the conditions of late- or post-modernity. While suggestions of a 'new penology' generated much discussion, the real stimulus to debate in a comparative vein came later with the publication of Garland's *magnus opus*, the *Culture of Control* (2001). As is now well known, his thesis situates developments at the level of state sovereignty and explains the state's volatile reaction to crime in recent years in terms of its relative powerlessness to control crime rates. His depiction of the increased punitiveness of the US and UK as a cultural adaptation to late modern economic and social forces (of which higher crime rates were the product) unsurprisingly prompted discussion on the inevitability of change elsewhere.

With the subsequent emergence of more sceptical voices questioning the extent of the transformation and its empirical basis (O'Malley, 1999; Zedner, 2002), it is interesting to note the degree to which the example of the Republic of Ireland has been drawn upon in this scholarly exchange of views. Matthews (2005), for example, cites the case of the Republic in support of his argument that the preoccupation with punitiveness amongst western criminologists is overplayed (see also, Nelken, 2011), and much has been written elsewhere on the idiosyncratic approach taken in many areas of criminal justice in this jurisdiction (Healy and O'Donnell, 2005; Healy, 2012; Vaughan and Kilcommins, 2008; Griffin and O'Donnell, 2012). Drawing on this broad notion of Hibernian exceptionalism or Irish resistance to more punitive trends, this chapter falls into three parts. Part I discusses the literature elaborating the country's divergence in the penal field, particularly the mediating effect of national political and legal cultures, and discusses what it may reveal about contextual factors linked with such divergence. Part II examines work conducted on punishment in the Republic of Ireland which challenges the meaning and scope of the punitiveness concept, particularly narrow views of punishment *qua* sentencing for a criminal offence. Part III then moves to discuss competing trajectories at a global level, namely, universal regulation through human rights instruments, specifically through an examination of the impact of international human rights standards in the youth justice field in Northern Ireland. By using reform of the youth justice system in Northern Ireland as a lens through which to examine the effects of international human rights standards, the tensions between the global and the local are more clearly illuminated. While it is by no means my intention to confine discussion of Northern Ireland to the final part of the chapter, the fact remains that many of the arguments rehearsed below have been applied solely in the context of the Republic of Ireland, and for that reason the preponderance of the discussion in this chapter concerns this jurisdiction. The chapter closes with a conclusion on the evolving dialectic between the global and local, including some brief discussion on criminology's own contribution.

Hibernian resistance

Like many smaller jurisdictions in the West and around the world, the Republic of Ireland has often escaped the criminological gaze. When the spotlight has fallen on the penal landscape, however, it has often (as will be demonstrated below) served to complicate current dystopian analyses of contemporary punishment on the island of Ireland and further afield. It is the consequent aim of this section to examine the existing literature on factors impacting penal variation, with particular regard to the Irish case. Prior to engaging in this analysis, it should be noted that the objective is not to present the jurisdiction as a historical aberration or somehow fixed in aspic. As in several other western jurisdictions, imprisonment rates in the Republic have risen rapidly, legal protections for suspects and defendants have come under attack and evidence of what O'Malley (1992) describes as a 'new prudentialism' is evident in the form of innovations such as the sex offender order (Kilcommins *et al.*, 2004).

Penal change was most clearly evident in the period following the murders of investigative journalist Veronica Guerin and Garda Jerry McCabe in 1996 (ibid.). This period acted as an important watershed in Irish criminal justice history, leading to intense party–political scare-mongering and radical reforms in relation to bail, procedural rights, sentencing, police numbers and prison spaces. The 'zero tolerance' policy upon which the Fianna Fáil party fought the 1997 general election may ultimately have faltered at the implementation stage; however, its adoption as an election ploy spoke quite clearly to the country's vulnerability to changing fashions in criminal justice (O'Donnell and O'Sullivan, 2003). While neither the appetite for such policies nor indeed the desire to use crime as a wedge issue in political campaigns has been sustained (Kilcommins *et al.*, 2004), it is clear that the Republic of Ireland often looks to its larger neigh-bours for inspiration on criminal justice matters. Recent innovations which appear to have originated in either Britain or America include sex offender notification, electronic monitoring and anti-social behaviour orders (Hamilton, 2007).

Despite these sporadic crime crises and the tendency towards 'volatile and contradictory' penal policy (O'Malley, 1999), punitive policies of the kind described by Garland (2001) and others do not appear to have bitten so deep. The Republic of Ireland's rate of imprisonment remains low by international standards (87 per 100,000 population, International Centre of Prison Studies, 2014), rehabilitation and individuated justice remain core aims of the sentencing system, formal risk-assessment tools are less in evidence than in other jurisdictions and the penal system, for all its flaws, retains remnants of humanity (Kilcommins *et al.*, 2004; O'Donnell and Jewkes, 2011). In endeavouring to understand this, it is proposed below to focus in particular on two aspects of Irish penal policy that current research has identified as important in understanding policy trajectories in western jurisdictions, namely, political structures and culture and judicial cultures (Tonry, 2007). Given the evolving understanding in this area, it is suggested that potentially new insights may be afforded by a detailed examination of these two particular contextual factors as they operate in Ireland. In particular, new theoretical perspectives may be acquired through analysing the manner in which local contingencies continue to strongly influence policy choices.

Political culture

The explanatory power which a country's distinctive constitutional and institutional arrange-ments hold for criminal justice policy is slowly gaining recognition in the criminological liter-ature. Savelsberg (1999, 2004), for example, identified the more centralised nature of German democracy as playing an important role in shielding bureaucrats from the force of public opinion, contrasting these arrangements with those in the US. Most recently, work by theorists such as Tonry (2007), Lacey (2008) and Green (2007, 2008) argues for a focus on political culture as the master variable in any analysis of the causes and correlations of punitiveness. While space does not permit a detailed exposition of their arguments, the principal thrust is that multi-party systems with proportional voting may resort less frequently to populist penal politics, resulting in a less punitive criminal justice policy. It is notable that in operationalising political culture, all three choose to adopt Lijphart's (1999) typology based on 'consensus' and 'majoritarian' or 'conflict' democracies. The main distinctions between the two models can largely be derived from the terms themselves (Lappi-Seppälä, 2008). Majoritarian democracies are based on a two-party, 'winner takes all' philosophy where the will of the majority dictates the choices that are made by policymakers. There is little incentive to compromise, as the object is to oust the opposition from power, and coalition government is rare. Consensus-style democracies, on the other hand, seek to protect minorities and share power, with as many views as possible being taken into account. Power is shared and dispersed in various ways such as: through coalitions or minority governments; stronger legislatures; interest group participation; and multiparty systems with proportional representation election systems. Lacey's contention in this regard is that the varying levels of accountability demanded by the need to negotiate with other groups within the political system itself impacts on the 'strength' (in the sense of policy-making autonomy) of the production regime. Her arguments as they subsequently relate to criminal justice policy are neatly encapsulated in the following excerpt:

> In liberal market economies with majoritarian electoral systems, particularly under conditions of relatively low trust in politicians, relatively low deference to the expertise of criminal justice professionals, and a weakening of the ideological divide between political parties ... the unmediated responsiveness of politics to popular opinion in the adversarial context of the two party system makes it harder for governments to resist a ratcheting up of penal severity.
>
> *(Lacey, 2008: 76)*

In her comparative research into the 'new punitiveness' in the Republic of Ireland, Scotland and New Zealand, Hamilton (2013, 2014a, 2014b) collected quantitative data and conducted interviews with key criminal justice stakeholders, including senior civil servants, academics, lawyers, politicians, crime editors and former Ministers for Justice. Adopting a broader conceptualisation of punitiveness than that normally applied, a multidimensional test for punitiveness incorporating seven indices and 34 variables was applied across the three jurisdictions for the period spanning 1976–2006. Her findings are significant for the questions they raise about the utility of political culture, as defined by Lijphart (1999) and subsequently relied on by Tonry (2007), Lacey (2008) and Green (2007, 2008), in explaining differences in a state's level of punitiveness.

In this regard, the first point to note is that the Republic of Ireland's proportional representation election system and strong executive do not fit easily into Lijphart's typology. The unique feature of the system (Proportional Representation by Single Transferable Vote) is that candidates of one party can be elected on the transfers of votes for other parties, a feature which is usually understood to reduce partisanship and enhance the prospect of coalition government. Yet, it was not until 1989 that the largest political party, Fianna Fáil, abandoned its traditional reluctance to form coalition governments. Even with this development, the high level of control wielded by governments over parliamentary business (Döring and Hallerberg, 2004) left little room for consensual politics, as governments saw little need to negotiate with the opposition (MacCarthaigh, 2007). This may be partly explained by the shadow cast on Irish political culture by the Civil War,[1] as the subsequent creation of two large political parties, Fianna Fáil and Fine Gael, has resulted in an adversarial parliamentary politics which the authors of the 1922 Constitution had sought to avoid (see further, MacCarthaigh, 2005). The typology appears similarly challenged when applied to Northern Irish political culture. As discussed in Part III below, the continued polarisation of politics along party lines, despite the introduction of the Single Transferable Vote system in 1998, presents a significant obstacle to continued reform in the area of youth justice. In both jurisdictions, it would seem, therefore, the impact of 'deep historical junctures' (*viz.* the Civil War and the Conflict) has stymied the development of a consensual political culture from consensual institutional arrangements.

While the Republic of Ireland may frequently defy neat categorisation (see, for example, Esping-Anderson (1990) on the Irish welfare system), further analysis of the data presents a more strenuous challenge to Lijphart's binary categories. As Jones and Newburn (2007) have argued, specific national and cultural differences and the views of political actors themselves act as important constraints on policy transfer, and this found strong support in the interviews with policymakers who referenced the need to have regard to domestic sensitivities. Irish and Scottish policymakers both cited criminal justice policies which they rejected on the basis that they would be considered unpalatable to their respective publics. Further, two of the Irish policymakers spoken with cast a sceptical eye on recent US and English criminal justice policies. This is evidenced by the following excerpt from an interview with a former policymaker who, while acknowledging the special influence of English criminal justice policy in the Republic of Ireland, described the difficulties in implementing new managerialist techniques in an Irish context:

> The Blairite stuff of targets and quotas… maybe it's one way of doing it but it's repugnant to the Irish psyche … I mean the Irish media would be horrified if they saw a circular saying you are to catch, you are to increase your detection rate for burglars by 18 per cent…. They'd say what kind of nut decided that.
>
> *(Irish interviewee #8, cited in Hamilton, 2014a: 171)*[2]

It is difficult to capture precisely the cultural values referred to by the interviewee, but it is likely closely allied to the inherent conservativeness of politics in the Republic of Ireland and, more generally, what O'Toole (2009: 217) describes as the 'anarchic attitude [of the Irish] to law and morality'. The less deferential approach taken by Irish people to authority, perhaps an overhang from colonial days, was cited by many interviewees as a critical factor in understanding the way in which criminal justice was done. One referred to the cultural preference Irish people often exhibit for resolving matters informally, without the involvement of the formal criminal justice system; another suggested that it may speak to elements of a Catholic indulgentist tradition. Several respondents mentioned the tradition of Gardaí speaking up for criminal defendants at the sentencing stage or, in the past, withdrawing summary prosecutions in the District Court (this practice has since been discontinued). As one interviewee noted, 'there isn't such a black and white approach to everything' (Irish interviewee #3, p. 4, cited in Hamilton, 2013: 161).

A note of caution must be sounded here, though, lest we should fall prey to a one-dimensional, simplistic view of Irish informalism as something which is 'good', mitigating the effects of more punitive policies, which are 'bad' (see further, Nelken, 2006). It is perhaps the subject of another discussion whether this cultural proclivity towards informal resolutions (even those which are not viewed as sensible or humane) can correctly be described as the country's 'saving grace' (Interviewee #4, p. 7, cited in Hamilton, 2014a: 172). Griffin and O'Donnell's (2012) research into the manner in which the law and policy on parole have operated in the Republic of Ireland, for example, does well to remind us that flexibility and informality in the criminal justice system cut both ways:

> [A]ccru[ing] to the advantage of the prisoner as they did in the 1970s and 1980s, when the average life sentence equated to 7.5 years in custody … [or operating] in the opposite direction, as the lifers now serving an additional decade behind bars might attest.
>
> *(2012: 625)*

Whatever its impact, suffice it to note for present purposes that this informalism or 'colonial habit of playing games with authority' (O'Toole, 2009: 217) was not lost on politicians in making choices over policy.

The data discussed above do little to disturb the argument advanced by Lacey, Green and others in relation to the key role played by political culture in the determination of criminal justice policy. In line with the analysis, however, questions may be raised as to the usefulness of political culture, as defined by Lijphart (1999), in explaining differences in a state's level of punitiveness. In particular, the close relationship between national culture and political culture suggested by the interview data mirrors research in Lijphart's own discipline of political science that seriously questions the applicability of Lijphart's models in different cultural settings (Bormann, 2010). The data are thus less supportive of an understanding of political culture in purely structural terms and more as 'a set of cognitive constraints', (Stokes and Hewitt, 1976, cited in Green, 2007, 2008) determining the range of options open to policymakers. At a conceptual level, this suggests a broader definition of political culture which incorporates 'superficially non-political assumptions' (Green, 2007: 625) as proposed by Elkins and Simeon (1979). Broader cultural values may thus operate to shape policymakers' understanding of criminal justice problems and their solutions in turn militating in favour of more optimistic or pessimistic political strategies (see further, Hamilton, 2013).

Legal culture

A country's legal culture forms another part of the complex tapestry of factors influencing penality in a particular jurisdiction. Both Tonry (2007) and Lappi-Seppälä (2007, 2012) acknowledge this through their identification of elected criminal justice officials (judges, prosecutors) in the American tradition as a risk factor for punitive policies, while a custom of political neutrality in professional legal cultures exerts a protective effect. In a broader sense, however, a country's legal traditions and legal culture are also vital considerations, as exemplified by the influence of the Utrecht School in the Netherlands in the 1950s. In his seminal work on Dutch and English criminal justice policy, Downes (1988) argued that the culture and training of the legal profession (from which the judges were drawn) – and specifically the strong anti-penal influence exerted by the Utrecht School – was critical to the development of Dutch leniency in the 1960s and 1970s. For him, 'the manner of judicial training and socialisation, and the character and timing of the brief ascendancy of rehabilitative policies [are] crucial' (ibid.: 350).

More recently, in an example closer to home, two Irish criminologists (Vaughan and Kilcommins, 2008) have argued that the Irish judicial *habitus* (Hutton, 2006) acts as an important buffer against excessive securitisation on behalf of the state. Its constant affirmation of proportionality and due process values in individual cases sets up a 'legal dialectic' which continues to deliver significant protections to those accused of crime. The authors are surely correct to point to the continued force of liberal constitutionalism in Irish law and its influence in 'legal and judicial craft, if not in the public consciousness more generally' (Vaughan and Kilcommins, 2008: 98). The Republic of Ireland differs from other jurisdictions, such as England, as it is governed by a written constitution placing constitutional rights guaranteeing liberty, due process, proportionate sentencing,[3] etc. on a surer footing. Active judicial interpretation of the due process provisions of the Irish Constitution in the 1960s and 1970s, most notably the development of a stringent exclusionary rule where evidence has been obtained in an unconstitutional manner, *has* provided important advantages to an accused person in the Republic of Ireland, albeit in a context of a distinct legislative shift towards crime control from the 1980s onwards (Walsh, 2005; Hamilton, 2007, see further below). By way of illustration, Vaughan and Kilcommins (2008: 117–8) point to cases concerning alleged or actual sexual misconduct:

> The judgments in *Curtin* (the right to have unconstitutionally obtained evidence excluded), *CC* (the right not to be criminalised for mentally blameless conduct), *O'Donoghue* (the right to have evidence excluded because its positive probative value is outweighed

by its prejudicial effect on the accused) and *WC* (the right to individuated justice) all demonstrate the continued resonance of accused rights, and their capacity to continue to compete for priority and act as a counterpoint to the supremacy of the paradigm of control.

Thus, even in contemporary times, the persistent influence of this judicially embedded rule of law plays out against other more hostile scripts, acting as 'reluctant convert' to the demands of securitisation (Vaughan and Kilcommins, 2008: 11).

In line with Vaughan and Kilcommins's (2008) arguments, Hamilton's (2014a) comparative research on punitiveness in the Republic of Ireland also spoke strongly to the impact of Irish judicial culture or *habitus* on the administration of justice. Indeed, the embedded nature of liberal constitutionalism and the due process model in Irish legal culture is something which emerged in a strong sense from the interviews as a significant protective influence. Respondents noted the jealous manner in which judges guarded their independence, the individualised nature of sentencing and their more 'liberal instincts':

> because again Irish judges I think have a reasonable culture of fair play and even when the Oireachtas [Parliament] has attempted to maybe alter the pitch, judges either by the way they interpreted the legislation or the way they run a trial probably haven't given effect to it in quite the same way as the legislature might have always expected. The judges would have been in many cases practitioners from an early era and would still carry through a lot of the philosophy they were brought up with.
>
> *(Irish interviewee #9, cited in Hamilton, 2014a: 181)*[4]

The argument can be carried further, moreover, in terms of its application to the legal profession as a whole. Several respondents noted that the legal profession constituted a powerful opposition lobby to authoritarian legislation with senior figures speaking out publicly against radical reforms (O'Higgins, 2007; Rogers, 2007).[5] Most interestingly, one senior legal practitioner spoke of the way in which lawyers, like the judiciary, could subvert the intentions of the Oireachtas where legislation conflicted with legal culture:

> If you look at the Criminal Justice Act in 1984, there was this huge resistance to using the inferences [drawing inferences from a suspect's silence] provision in that and I think that a kind of consensus just grew that it was unconstitutional. And then there was the *Rock* case… [Interviewer: which confirmed that it was in fact constitutional] Even after that, there was just no appetite for it.
>
> *(Irish interviewee #5, cited in Hamilton, 2014a: 182)*[6]

What broader lessons does the above discussion hold about the impact of legal culture on punitiveness? In comparing the three jurisdictions, the extent to which judges and the legal profession generally are emboldened to challenge attempts by the executive to introduce harsher legislation marked an important point of distinction between the Republic of Ireland and Scotland on the one hand and New Zealand on the other (Hamilton, 2014a). Again, however, as observed in relation to political culture it would be a mistake to attempt to too readily reify this variable and thus divorce it from its surroundings. The failure on the part of prosecutors in the Republic to apply legislation as enacted by the Oireachtas may well have been informed by an underlying commitment to liberal constitutionalism, but it may relatedly reflect the particular disjuncture which often occurs between policy and practice in this jurisdiction (O'Donnell, 2008; Griffin and O'Donnell, 2012). The interesting marriage of liberal constitutionalism and cultural infor-malism in the Republic of Ireland may therefore do more to explain the particular character of the administration of justice in this jurisdiction than any rigid formulae concerning the *type* of legal system at issue.

Problematising 'punishment'

An often neglected feature of the 'new punitiveness' has been the erosion of the due process rights of suspects and accused persons in an effort to increase the likelihood of conviction. To some extent this is implicit in discussion by Garland (2001) and others of the 'rise of the victim' and of the assumption that anything which is 'against criminals' is by definition 'for victims' (the so-called zero-sum game). Yet, it is arguably an aspect of the new penality which has been con-siderably underdeveloped by many of the contributors to the punitiveness debate (Kilcommins *et al.*, 2004; Campbell, 2008) (with some notable exceptions such as Tonry [2001: 519]). The case of the Republic of Ireland as a jurisdiction which maintains low rates of imprisonment interna-tionally has been discussed above, yet it is also a jurisdiction which in the last 20 years or so has introduced many reforms at the 'front end' of the system enhancing police powers and curtailing defendants' rights (Walsh, 2002, 2005; Hamilton, 2007).

Returning once more to the research conducted by Hamilton (2014a, 2014b) into the new punitiveness in the Republic of Ireland, Scotland and New Zealand, it will be recalled that an important part of her approach to measuring punitiveness is that the test is more holistic than those usually applied, with punitiveness being reconceptualised from the moment of identify-ing a suspect to the point of this person's death. This conceptualisation of punitiveness takes account not only of punitiveness at the point of sentencing, but also system practices impacting on the offender in his or her journey through the criminal justice system. From this broader perspective, it is perhaps easier to consider the different penal choices made by governments in the three jurisdictions. Of particular note are the dramatically different trajectories pursued by New Zealand and the Republic of Ireland over the 30-year period considered; in the former, the 'get tough' movement has concentrated on the 'back end' of the system, (i.e. on the use of imprisonment) with little attention given to 'front-end' reforms, (i.e. increases in police powers and erosions in the rights of defendants). Conversely, the Republic of Ireland has maintained relatively low rates of imprisonment in international terms, while the rights enjoyed by suspects have been increasingly curtailed.

Part of the explanation for this 'front-end' bias may be found in Irish history; a nation accus-tomed to wide ranging powers in an exceptional regime is much more disposed to robust police powers in relation to ordinary crimes. It is therefore unsurprising that the Republic of Ireland – a country which has faced serious threats from subversives within the state since its foundation in 1922 – continues to display a preference for a front-end strategy in its dealings with 'ordinary' criminals. Consider the following excerpts from interviews conducted by Hamilton (2014a: 115), which serve to juxtapose the direction of crime control developments in the Republic of Ireland with those in New Zealand:

> It's a bit of a mixed bag… I don't think we are more punitive in the sort of punishments that we hand down. … The broad feeling I have for it is that we don't go over the top on punishments, but on the other hand I feel we are inclined to adopt, what I would refer to as an authoritarian approach to offending, to criminal justice, unlike some of our other common law countries.
>
> *(Ireland interviewee #7)*

457

I think there's been some increased attention to the right to silence and hostility to that in some quarters to some degree... but I think that in general it's been much more muted than overseas.... One of the issues that we are having to look at with that is the extent to which we should have some of [the] powers that exist in the UK to deal with terrorism situations and I think if we did the public would actually largely go into revolt. I mean I don't think there would be public acceptance of it because we don't have a history of it. A lot of the things in the 2002 UK Act were actually taken over from the old emergency powers and therefore people have got used to them over the last 20 years and dealing with a real threat ... in New Zealand I think there's a lot less public appetite for this because the threat's more removed....

[Interviewer: It's interesting because on the one hand you've got quite a punitive public in relation to punishment practices but that hasn't necessarily translated to the defendants....]
That's a very good point actually. I never thought about that, that's absolutely right.

(New Zealand interviewee #2)[7]

National idiosyncrasies aside, the significance of such data for comparative researchers is to illustrate the limitations of a narrow focus on punitiveness as measured at the point of sentencing. Countries which appear very punitive when viewed through the traditional lens of imprisonment rates may take on quite a different complexion when assessed on a much broader range of criteria, including 'front-end' variables such as the intensity and nature of street-level law enforcement (Neapolitan, 2001). Given the particular salience of such 'front-end' crime-control strategies in certain jurisdictions, researchers should give serious consideration to including front-end variables such as police numbers, powers, procedural protections, etc. in any measure of punitiveness (Hinds, 2005; Tonry, 2007). Not only will this better illuminate systemic punitiveness across the broad range of agencies involved in the criminal process, but it may also provide important clues with regard to the determinants of penal policies such as the struggle against terrorism in the Republic of Ireland (see further, Hamilton, 2014a, 2014b; see also Daly and Jackson, *infra*).

A similar, but perhaps more far-reaching critique of the use of imprisonment rates as a proxy for punitiveness has been launched by O'Sullivan and O'Donnell (2007, 2012) in their work on historical levels of 'coercive confinement' in the Republic of Ireland. Their detailed examination of the rapid decline in the numbers detained in a range of institutions – psychiatric hospitals, mother and baby homes, Magdalene homes, county homes and reformatory and industrial schools as well as prisons and borstals in the latter decades of the twentieth century – provides an important new perspective on the meaning of punishment and exclusion. Indeed, the significant downsizing over this period of the 'captive' population (eight times higher in 1951 than in 2002) turns on its head Garland's arguments about the emergence of a late modern 'culture of control'. As they argue:

[I]f we move away from using imprisonment rates as a proxy for punitiveness and locate the prison in a wider context, as but one of a range of institutions that has been utilised to reform, quarantine or reject... then a different, and indeed less catastrophic, reading of the present becomes possible.

(O'Sullivan and O'Donnell, 2007: 28)

While it could be argued that the express aim of these institutions was to treat or reform rather than punish, there is little doubt that they were experienced punitively, as the following passage cited by the authors testifies (Pallas, 2005 cited in O'Donnell and O'Sullivan, 2007: 37):

I was brought before the Dublin Children's Court at the age of three and (a) charged with being destitute (b) found guilty and (c) sentenced to be detained in industrial schools until my sixteenth birthday... I was 'released' from Artane 'on licence' six weeks prior to my sixteenth birthday. When I queried why 'on licence', I was told that, had I transgressed the law in any way during those six weeks I would have been returned to Artane. Inmates or residents? I think the records speak for themselves.

This punitive and regimented ethos was compounded by a deliberately stigmatising approach, near total social exclusion and in many cases no clear route back to the community. In both a quantitative and qualitative sense, then, it can be said that Irish society in the post-war period represented a much less tolerant place than in contemporary times. While, as noted by the authors, the argument clearly holds relevance for other jurisdictions which operated a similarly coercive infrastructure, the implications are arguably even broader than this. Extending conceptions of punishment beyond the criminal justice system may appear to blur the boundaries between punishment and broader mechanisms of social control, which are sometimes treated as the independent variables in any analysis (Nelken, 2011). Yet, in many cases it is arguable that a satisfactory understanding of the harshness of states or communities at given points in their history cannot be achieved without such an expanded definition. It is difficult to describe pre-Emancipation US, for example, as a more lenient society despite the fact that there were 15 times fewer black people in prison prior to the abolition of slavery than afterwards (Melossi, 2002). The argument also holds much contemporary relevance given criminology's neglect of new forms of confinement such as detention and deportation centres (Aas and Bosworth, 2013), as well as its relative inattention to the qualitative differences in the 'depth' of penal control in different penal facilities (see, for example, Birkbeck's 2011 comparison of penal facilities in North and Latin America). Aas (2012: 13) puts it well in the context of her argument regarding criminology's engagement with the global:

> [C]riminological theory ... faces a challenge of naming and conceptualizing the various forms of confinement around the world which do not 'meet the standards' of imprisonment as seen through the prism of western theory, yet are a formal part of penal systems, are intended as punishments or have distinct punitive elements.

Global meets local

The discussion thus far has focussed on *economic* globalism as generally conceived as a US-inspired 'free market turn' (Downes, 2011) with a concomitant exclusionary and highly punitive logic being adopted in the penal field. The basic assumption of Garland's (2001) thesis, for example, is that the culture of control with its ultimate penal consequence of mass imprisonment takes a certain form which is increasingly globalised (ibid.). However, this form of globalisation also co-exists with *legal* globalism, as inspired by international bodies such as the EU or UN, which simultaneously pushes states towards the protection of individual rights.[8] Small penal systems may prove fruitful arenas for investigation of the global–local nexus in this field also. Aitchison's (2010) examination of the adoption of European human rights norms in Bosnia-Herzegovina, for example, illustrates well the challenges international actors may face in advancing human rights as a governing logic in politically fragmented societies.

The Republic of Ireland provides a particularly interesting case study in this regard as research to date has uncovered instances of both compliance with and resistance to international human rights norms. On the one hand, the influence of European human rights agreements on the Irish criminal justice system has been palpable in certain contexts. The European Convention on Human Rights (ECHR) and accompanying case law has played a key role in the establishment of various accountability mechanisms for the Irish police, both south and north of the border (Vaughan and Kilcommins, 2007, 2008). Following commitments to strengthened protection of human rights in the Good Friday Agreement of 1998 and subsequent recommendations in the Patten Report, the Police Service in Northern Ireland has been established as a model of 'human rights policing' (Mulcahy, 2013). Developments in Northern Ireland also significantly exerted a 'magnetic pull' on the reform of policing oversight mechanisms in the Republic; a combination of domestic events and the process of policing reform in Northern Ireland made radical change in Garda accountability structures difficult for Irish politicians to resist (Vaughan and Kilcommins, 2008). Another interesting example of 'controlled liberalisation' or tactical concession to forestall potential criticisms (Risse and Ropp, 1999 cited in Vaughan and Kilcommins, 2008) followed the judgment of the European Court in *Hirst v UK (No.2)*,[9] where the Irish state took the pre-emptive step of providing all prisoners with the practical means to vote. On the other hand, certain aspects of the penal system such as parole have remained largely impervious to the weight of external pressures from European bodies such as the Council of Europe and European Court of Human Rights, due in no small part to the perhaps unduly conservative approach taken by the Irish judiciary to the incorporating legislation (Farrell, 2013; Griffin and O'Donnell, 2012).

As a microcosm of the broader penal system, a particularly useful insight into the extent to which local modes of governance continue to mediate cosmopolitan trends is provided by Northern Ireland's youth justice system. Following the recommendations of the Criminal Justice Review Group (CJRG) (2000), Northern Ireland fundamentally overhauled its youth justice system in favour of a diversionary, restorative justice model (see further, Convery and Seymour, *infra*; O'Dwyer and Payne, *infra*). The Justice (Northern Ireland) Act 2002 establishes the Youth Justice Agency and provides for youth justice conferences (restorative measures) as the primary response to young people who come into conflict with the law. From the instant perspective, it is notable that the Criminal Justice Review was strongly influenced by international human rights standards in the UNCRC and elsewhere as well as international 'success stories' such as the New Zealand model (Dignan and Lowey, 2000). The human rights focus throughout the report is clear, with a lengthy section devoted to international human rights obligations and a statement by the Review Team that they sought to 'build upon the standards that they set' (CJRG, 2000: 222). The prominence of rights discourse is also evident in more recent policy documents, such as the government initiated *Review of the Youth Justice System* (Youth Justice Review Team, 2011) and in political discourse. Speaking on recommendations made by the Review on the minimum age of criminal responsibility, David Ford, Minister of Justice, opined:

> it is important to live up to our international obligations in relation to children. We do it not out of slavish ideology but because it builds in them a respect for the rights of others and protects them as they develop from the many negative influences to which they may be subjected.[10]
>
> *(Cited in Dwyer and McAlister, 2013)*

Progress in this regard has not been smooth, however, and, while it is important to emphasise the Act's successes in terms of very significant reductions in the number of juveniles in custody (Wahidin and Carr, 2013), it is also true that compliance with international standards in this area is far from secured.

This is most keenly illustrated in relation to key issues of contention such as raising the minimum age of criminal responsibility and the strengthening of the welfare principle in the principal act. The Youth Justice Review (2011) recommended that the age of criminal responsibility in Northern Ireland be raised from 10 years to 12 years with 'immediate effect' and that consideration be given 'after a period of time' to raising the age of criminal responsibility to 14 (Recommendation 29). While this recommendation was 'accepted in principle' by the Minister and the Department of Justice, to date, the minimum age has not been raised. Similarly, the Review recommended that section 53 of the Justice (NI) Act 2002, which contains the aims of the youth justice system, should be amended to state that the 'principal aim of the youth justice system is to promote the best interests of the child, prevent offending by children and protect the public' as espoused in Article 3 of the UN Convention (Recommendation 28). While this recommendation was accepted by the Minister and the Department of Justice, the Implementation Report (Criminal Justice Inspectorate, 2013) notes that the overall elements as set out in section 53 will not change, but that amending legislation will merely extend reference to the welfare of the child in section 53 to include the 'best interests' principle as espoused in Article 3. The section will therefore continue to prioritise public protection, preventing offending and the concerns of victims.

One of the obstacles impeding further progress in this area has been securing the necessary cross-party consensus on the adoption of international norms. Debate in the Northern Ireland Assembly raises important questions about the extent to which universal standards in youth justice have been understood and appropriated by local actors, with many political representatives clearly preferring a more authoritarian approach to youthful misdemeanour. Research recently conducted by Dwyer and McAlister (2013) into parliamentary debates in Northern Ireland revealed references to the 'fear and respect' that young people should have for the law, as well as more punitive sentiments around appropriate punishments. Of particular interest is the following comment from one MLA, Mr. Paul Givan, (incidentally Chair of the Justice Committee), on the extent to which compliance with the UNCRC can be seen as an incursion on local sovereignty:

> We should not pursue the United Nations' agenda on the rights of the child, because it does not have the right way to deal with it. The 'hug a hoody' approach will not solve the problem, and the Minister should remove that from the consultation. If the Minister is going to consult on the age of criminal responsibility, will he look at proposals that will lower the age of criminal responsibility from 10?[11]

The extent to which implementation of human-rights-driven reforms in this area becomes mired in local political issues and generalised resistance to change recalls previous work on reform in transitional societies. Aitchison's (2010) work (referenced above) on post-conflict Bosnia-Herzegovina described how political fragmentation and the lack of hierarchic relationships between entity and state level governments have stymied Council of Europe initiatives relating to the detention of forensic psychiatric patients. Quite aside from the question of compliance with norms at a legislative or policy level, research questioning the extent to which rights discourse has been translated into real change 'on the ground' in the Northern Irish youth justice system also raises the question of a genuine politics of reform (see, for example, Haydon, 2008). As Piacentini (2006) astutely observes in her research on Russian prisons, it is the appearance of making progress which enhances political legitimacy; change itself is a secondary consideration. The most significant point for present purposes, however, is that far from producing uniformity, globalisation may produce segmentation and contestation, even in societies in transition where global human rights norms may retain a particular purchase for historical and political reasons.

Given the dramatic strides taken in the field of policing (albeit not quite the 'transformation' anticipated by Patten; Mulcahy, 2013, *infra*), the story of youth justice in Northern Ireland also illustrates the differential impact of global norms on different sectors of the criminal justice system, even within the same jurisdiction.

Conclusion: the view from the periphery?

The material discussed above does more to deny than to confirm any 'flattening' of national or local differences arising from economic or legal globalism (Muncie, 2005, 2011). As illustrated in the case of youth justice in Northern Ireland, global narratives continue to be mediated by national political cultures, producing diversity rather than convergence. These cultures are of course changing at the same time. A robust judicial and legal culture, for example, currently acts to mitigate the demands of securitisation, etc. in the Republic of Ireland, but often finds itself challenged in a climate that is increasingly hostile to the rights of accused persons (Hamilton, 2007). Thus, while far from immune to global trends, criminal justice in the Republic of Ireland remains firmly embedded within its social context (Melossi, 2001). Indeed, elements of local culture and national psyche appear to act as an important filter in limiting the options available to politicians and other decision makers within the criminal justice system. The role played by this cultural 'wild card' (as well as the manner in which these elements interact) urges caution in the adoption of unduly rigid binary categories between, for example, types of political or legal systems. In striving towards the delicate balancing act between analytic order and relativism, we should be chary of reducing the complex field of penal policymaking to a procrustean checklist of punitiveness risk or protective factors (Tonry, 2007).

Related to this is the recognition that different dependant variables may be relevant in different societies. The case of the Republic of Ireland suggests a distinct 'national signature' in the crime control field which is directed more at the 'front end' than the 'back end' of the criminal justice system. Of course, time and resources are often limited with regard to the range of decision-making points which can be examined throughout the system; however, comparative researchers must ask themselves whether in a given national context the use of imprisonment rates as a singular variable can obscure more than it reveals. An additional issue thrown up by the dramatic decline in 'coercive confinement' in the Republic of Ireland is the place of imprisonment along Foucault's 'carceral archipelago' or institutions of social control. O'Donnell and O'Sullivan's research (2007, 2012), though ostensibly local and historical in focus, holds much value for the global present where increasingly diverse and extra-legal forms of coercion are deployed by states in the name of immigration control or the 'war on terror' (Lazarus *et al.*, 2012; Aas and Bosworth, 2013). In this context, hard questions must be posed as to whether researchers can really afford to ignore a state's approach to immigration or other, more insidious forms of social control. As a concluding thought, it is useful to strike a reflexive note in contemplating the role of the discipline itself in realising the Anglo-American drift towards punitiveness. If global processes ultimately rely on local actors for their activation 'on the ground', the extent to which these actors are equipped with the necessary data and skills to move these processes forward may merit closer attention. Drawing again on the Irish example, O'Donnell (2010) advances the intriguing argument that the underdeveloped nature of criminology may, together with other factors, have played a role in slowing the onset of the 'new penology' or actuarialism. If the absence of a muscular criminology, together with other restraining factors such as sufficient data and an underdeveloped criminal justice bureaucracy, serves to 'dampen the managerialist impulse', questions may properly be raised about the role of (administrative) criminology itself as a 'risk' factor for punitiveness.

References

Aas, K. (2012) 'The Earth Is One but the World Is Not: Criminological Theory and Its Geopolitical Divisions', *Theoretical Criminology*, 16(1): 5–20.

Aas, K. and Bosworth, M. (2013) *The Borders of Punishment: Migration, Citizenship, and Social Exclusion*. Oxford: Oxford University Press.

Aitchison, A. (2010) 'Global Meets Local: International Participation in Prison Reform and Restructuring in Bosnia and Herzegovina', *Criminology and Criminal Justice*, 10(1): 77–94.

Albrecht, H.-J. (2001) 'Post-Adjudication Dispositions in Comparative Perspective', in M. Tonry and R. Frase (eds) *Sentencing and Sanctions in Western Countries*. New York: Oxford University Press.

Birkbeck, C. (2011) 'Imprisonment and Internment: Comparing Penal Institutions North and South', *Punishment and Society*, 13(3): 307–32.

Bormann, N.-C. (2010) 'Patterns of Democracy and Its Critics', *Living Reviews in Democracy*, 2: np. Available at: http://democracy.livingreviews.org/index.php/lrd/article/viewArticle/lrd-2010-3/26 (accessed 24 April 2015).

Campbell, L. (2008) 'The Culture of Control in Ireland: Theorising Recent Developments in Criminal Justice', *Web Journal of Current Legal Issues*, 1. Available at: http://webjcli.org/ (accessed 24 April 2015).

Cavadino, M. and Dignan, J. (2006) *Penal Systems: A Comparative Approach*. London: Sage.

Connell, R. (2006) 'Northern Theory: The Political Geography of General Social Theory', *Theory and Society*, 35(2): 237–64.

Criminal Justice Inspectorate of Northern Ireland (2013) *Monitoring of Progress on Implementation of the Youth Justice Review Recommendations*. Belfast: Criminal Justice Inspection Northern Ireland.

Criminal Justice Review Group (2000) *Review of the Criminal Justice System in Northern Ireland*. Belfast: HMSO.

Dignan, J. and Lowey, K. (2000) *Restorative Justice Options for Northern Ireland: A Comparative Review*. Research Report 10. Belfast: Northern Ireland Office.

Döring, H. and Hallerberg, M. (2004) (eds) *Patterns of Parliamentary Behavior: Passage of Legislation Across Western Europe*. Aldershot: Ashgate.

Downes, D. (1988) *Contrasts in Tolerance: Post War Penal Policy in the Netherlands and England and Wales*. Oxford: Clarendon.

Downes, D. (2011) 'Comparative Criminology, Globalization and the "Punitive Turn"', in D. Nelken (ed) *Comparative Criminal Justice and Globalization*. Farnham, Surrey: Ashgate.

Dwyer, C. and McAlister, S. (2013) 'Youth Justice in Northern Ireland: Post-Good Friday, Post-Devolution, Post-Conflict?' *Youth Justice in the Five Jurisdictions*. Belfast, 12 September.

Elkins, D. J. and Simeon, R. E. B. (1979) 'A Cause in Search of Its Effect, or What Does Political Culture Explain?', *Comparative Politics*, 11(2): 127–45.

Esping-Anderson, G. (1990) *The Three Worlds of Welfare Capitalism*. Cambridge: Polity Press.

Farrell, M. (2013) '10 Years on, Ireland's Human Rights Act Has Failed to Deliver'. *The Journal*, 29 December. Available at: www.thejournal.ie/readme/10-years-on-irelands-human-rights-act-has-failed-to-deliver-1236617-Dec2013/#comments (accessed 23 April 2015).

Feeley, M. and Simon, J. (1992) 'The New Penology: Notes on the Emerging Strategy of Corrections and Its Implications', *Criminology*, 30(4): 449–74.

Feeley, M. and Simon, J. (1994) 'Actuarial Justice: The Emerging New Criminal Law', in D. Nelken (ed) *The Futures of Criminology*. London: Sage.

Garland, D. (2001) *The Culture of Control: Crime and Social Order in Contemporary Society*. Oxford: Oxford University Press.

Green, D. (2007) 'Comparing Penal Cultures: Child-on-Child Homicide in England and Norway', in M. Tonry (ed) *Crime, Punishment and Politics in Comparative Perspective*. Vol. 36 of *Crime and Justice: A Review of Research*. Chicago: University of Chicago Press.

Green, D. (2008) *When Children Kill Children: Penal Populism and Political Culture*. Oxford: Oxford University Press.

Griffin, D. and O'Donnell, I. (2012) 'The Life Sentence and Parole', *British Journal of Criminology*, 52(3): 611–29.

Hamilton, C. (2007) *The Presumption of Innocence and Irish Criminal Law: Whittling the Golden Thread*. Dublin: Irish Academic Press.

Hamilton, C. (2013) 'Punitiveness and Political Culture: Notes from Some Small Countries', *European Journal of Criminology*, 10(2): 154–67.

Hamilton, C. (2014a) *Reconceptualising Penality: A Comparative Perspective on Punitiveness in Ireland, Scotland and New Zealand*. Farnham, UK: Ashgate.

Hamilton, C. (2014b) 'Reconceptualising Penality: Towards a Multidimensional Test for Punitiveness', *British Journal of Criminology*, 52(4): 321–43.

Haydon, D. (2008) '"Do Your Promises and Tell the Truth: Treat Us with Respect": Realising the Rights of Children and Young People in Northern Ireland', *The Journal of the History of Childhood and Youth*, 3(1): 414–42.

Healy, D. (2012) 'Advise, Assist and Befriend: Can Probation Supervision Support Desistance?', *Social Policy and Administration*, 46(4): 377–94.

Healy, D. and O'Donnell, I. (2005) 'Probation in the Republic of Ireland: Context and Challenges', *Probation Journal*, 52(1): 56–68.

Hinds, L. (2005) 'Crime Control in Western Countries, 1970–2000', in J. Pratt, D. Brown, M. Brown, S. Hallsworth and W. Morrison (eds) *The New Punitiveness: Trends, Theories, Perspectives*. Cullompton: Willan.

Hutton, N. (2006) 'Sentencing as a Social Practice', in S. Armstrong and L. McAra (eds) *Perspectives on Punishment: The Culture of Control*. Oxford: Oxford University Press.

International Centre of Prison Studies (ICPS) (2014) World Prison Brief. Available at: www.prisonstudies. org/world-prison-brief (accessed 23 April 2015).

Jones, T. and Newburn, T. (2007) *Policy Transfer and Criminal Justice: Exploring US Influence over British Crime Control Policy*. Maidenhead: Open University Press.

Kilcommins, S., O'Donnell, I., O'Sullivan, E. and Vaughan, B. (2004) *Crime, Punishment and the Search for Order in Ireland*. Dublin: Institute of Public Administration.

Lacey, N. (2008) *The Prisoners' Dilemma: Political Economy and Punishment in Contemporary Democracies*. Cambridge: Cambridge University Press.

Lappi-Seppälä, T. (2007) 'Penal Policy in Scandinavia', in M. Tonry (ed) *Crime, Punishment and Politics in Comparative Perspective*. Vol. 36 of *Crime and Justice: A Review of Research*. Chicago: University of Chicago Press.

Lappi-Seppälä, T. (2008) 'Trust, Welfare, and Political Culture: Explaining Differences in National Penal Policies', in M. Tonry (ed) *Crime, Punishment and Politics in Comparative Perspective*, Vol. 36 of *Crime and Justice: A Review of Research*. Chicago: University of Chicago Press.

Lappi-Seppälä, T. (2012) 'Explaining National Differences in the Use of Imprisonment', in S. Snacken and E. Dumortier (eds) *Resisting Punitiveness in Europe?* Abingdon, Oxon; New York: Routledge.

Lazarus, L., Goold, B. and Goss, C. (2012) 'Control without Punishment: Understanding Coercion', in J. Simon and R. Sparks (eds) *The Sage Handbook of Punishment and Society*. London: Sage.

Lijphart, A. (1999) *Patterns of Democracy: Government Forms and Performance in Thirty-six Countries*. New Haven, Connecticut: Yale University Press.

MacCarthaigh, M. (2005) *Accountability in Irish Parliamentary Politics*. Dublin: Institute of Public Administration.

MacCarthaigh, M. (2007) 'The Recycling of Political Accountability', in M. MacCarthaigh and K. Hayward (eds) *Recycling the State: The Politics of Adaptation in Ireland*. Dublin: Irish Academic Press.

McEvoy, K. (2011) 'What Did the Lawyers Do during the "War"? Neutrality, Conflict and the Culture of Quietism', *Modern Law Review*, 74(3): 350–84.

Matthews, R. (2005) 'The Myth of Punitiveness', *Theoretical Criminology*, 9(2): 175–201.

Melossi, D. (2001) 'The Cultural Embeddedness of Social Control: Reflections on the Comparison of Italian and North American Cultures Concerning Punishment', *Theoretical Criminology*, 5(4): 403–24.

Melossi, D. (2002) *Stato, Controllo Sociale, Devianza*. Milan: Bruno Mondadori.

Mulcahy, A. (2013) 'Great Expectations and Complex Realities: Assessing the Impact and Implications of the Police Reform Process in Northern Ireland', in J. Brown (ed) *The Future of Policing*. London: Routledge.

Muncie, J. (2005) 'The Globalization of Crime Control – The Case of Youth and Juvenile Justice: Neoliberalism, Policy Convergence and International Conventions', *Theoretical Criminology*, 9(1): 35–64.

Muncie, J. (2011) 'On Globalisation and Exceptionalism', in D. Nelken (ed) *Comparative Criminal Justice and Globalization*. Farnham, Surrey: Ashgate.

Neapolitan, J. (2001) 'An Examination of Cross-national Variation in Punitiveness', *International Journal of Offender Therapy and Comparative Criminology*, 45(6): 691–710.

Nelken, D. (2006) 'Patterns of Punitiveness', *Modern Law Review*, 69(2): 262–77.

Nelken, D. (2011) 'Making Sense of Punitiveness', in D. Nelken (ed) *Comparative Criminal Justice and Globalization*. Farnham, Surrey: Ashgate.

O'Donnell, I. (2004) 'Imprisonment and Penal Policy in Ireland', *Howard Journal of Criminal Justice*, 43(3): 253–66.

O'Donnell, I. (2008) 'Stagnation and Change in Irish Penal Policy', *Howard Journal of Criminal Justice*, 47(2): 121–33.

O'Donnell, I. (2010) 'Criminology, Bureaucracy and Unfinished Business', in M. Bosworth and C. Hoyle (eds) *What Is Criminology?* Oxford: Oxford University Press.

O'Donnell, I. and Jewkes, Y. (2011) 'Going Home for Christmas: Prisoners, a Taste of Freedom and the Press', *The Howard Journal of Criminal Justice*, 50 (1): 75–91.

O'Donnell, I. and O'Sullivan, E. (2003) 'The Politics of Intolerance – Irish Style', *British Journal of Criminology*, 43(1): 41–62.

O'Higgins, M. (2007) 'The Practical and Human Rights Implications of New Legislation'. *Human Rights and Criminal Justice Conference*, 13 October. Dublin: Law Society of Ireland.

O'Malley, P. (1992) 'Risk, Power and Crime prevention', *Economy and Society*, 21(3): 252–75.

O'Malley, P. (1999) 'Volatile and Contradictory Punishment', *Theoretical Criminology*, 3(2): 175–96.

O'Sullivan, E. and O'Donnell, I. (2007) 'Coercive Confinement in the Republic of Ireland: The Waning of a Culture of Control', *Punishment & Society*, 9(1): 27–48.

O'Sullivan, E. and O'Donnell, I. (2012) *Coercive Confinement in Ireland: Patients, Prisoners and Penitents.* Manchester: Manchester University Press.

O'Toole, F. (2009) *Ship of Fools: How Stupidity and Corruption Sank the Celtic Tiger.* London: Faber and Faber.

Pallas, P. (2005) 'Industrial Schools'. *The Irish Times*, Letters to the Editor, 23 September.

Piacentini, L. (2006) 'Prisons during Transition: Promoting a Common Identity through International Norms', in L. McAra and S. Armstrong (eds) *Perspectives on Punishment: The Contours of Control*. Oxford: Oxford University Press.

Risse, T. and Ropp, S. (1999) 'International Human Rights Norms and Domestic Change: Conclusions', in T. Risse, S. Ropp and K. Sikkink (eds) *The Power of Human Rights: International Norms and Domestic Change.* Cambridge: Cambridge University Press.

Rogers, J. (2007) 'Elements of the Criminal Justice Bill Do Not Stand Up to Scrutiny'. *The Irish Times*, 4 April.

Savelsberg, J. (1999) 'Cultures of Punishment: USA-Germany'. *American Society of Criminology Annual Meeting*, 17–21 November. Toronto.

Savelsberg, J. (2004) 'Religion, Historical Contingencies, and Cultures of Punishment: The German Case and Beyond', *Law and Social Inquiry*, 29(2): 373–401.

Stokes, R. and Hewitt, J. P. (1976) 'Aligning Actions', *American Sociological Review*, 41(5): 838–49.

Tonry, M. (2001) 'Symbol, Substance and Severity in Western Penal Policies', *Punishment & Society*, 3(4): 517–36.

Tonry, M. (2007) (ed) *Crime, Punishment and Politics in a Comparative Perspective.* Vol. 36 of *Crime and Justice: A Review of Research*. Chicago: University of Chicago Press.

Vaughan, B. and Kilcommins, S. (2007) 'The Europeanisation of Human Rights and the Limits of Authoritarian Policing in Ireland', *European Journal of Criminology*, 4(4): 437–59.

Vaughan, B. and Kilcommins, S. (2008) *Terrorism, Rights and the Rule of Law: Negotiating Justice in Ireland.* Cullompton: Willan.

Wacquant, L. (2005) 'The Great Penal Leap Backward: Incarceration in America from Nixon to Clinton', in J. Pratt., D. Brown, S. Hallsworth, W. Morrison (eds) *The New Punitiveness: Trends, Theories, Perspectives*. Cullompton, Devon: Willan.

Wacquant, L. (2009) *Punishing the Poor: The Neoliberal Government of Social Insecurity*. Durham, North Carolina: Duke University Press.

Wahidin, A. and Carr, N. (2013) *Understanding Criminal Justice: A Critical Introduction*. London/New York: Routledge.

Walsh, D. (2002) *Criminal Procedure*. Dublin: Thomson Round Hall.

Walsh, D. (2005) 'The Criminal Justice Bill: Completing a Crime Control Model of Criminal Justice?'. *Criminal Justice Bill 2004: Implications for Human Rights and Legal Practice*, Trinity College Dublin, 20 April.

Youth Justice Review Team (2011) *Review of the Youth Justice System in Northern Ireland*. Belfast: Department of Justice.

Zedner, L. (2002) 'Dangers of Dystopias in Penal Theory', *Oxford Journal of Legal Studies*, 22(2): 341–66.

Claire Hamilton

Notes

1 The Irish Civil War was a conflict between Irish nationalists which took place between 1922 and 1923 over whether or not to accept the Anglo-Irish Treaty. The Treaty, which followed the Irish War of Independence, established Ireland as a 'Free State', independent from the United Kingdom but within the British Empire.
2 Reprinted by permission of the Publishers from 'Explaining Differences', in *Reconceptualising Penality* by Claire Hamilton (Farnham: Ashgate, 2014), p.171. Copyright © 2014.
3 Though not addressed specifically within the provisions of the Irish Constitution, case law interpreting these provisions has held that there is a constitutional requirement that the sentence must be proportionate to the circumstances of the crime and the circumstances of the offender (See *People (DPP) v M* [1994] 3 IR 306).
4 Reprinted by permission of the Publishers from 'Explaining Differences', in *Reconceptualising Penality* by Claire Hamilton (Farnham: Ashgate, 2014), p.181. Copyright © 2014.
5 The activism of certain senior legal figures in the Republic of Ireland may perhaps be contrasted with what McEvoy (2011) has termed the 'quietism' of Northern Irish lawyers during the Conflict. The obvious distinguishing factor in this regard is the challenge which such activism would pose to the state (and the deeply engrained culture of loyalty to the state) in Northern Ireland; no such considerations operated in the Republic. It is nevertheless interesting to consider McEvoy's discussion on conservatism in smaller jurisdictions and the manner in which the small size of the jurisdiction may facilitate the reproduction of hegemonic understandings (whether 'liberal constitutionalism' or 'quietism/neutrality'). It is also fascinating to contrast the strict Diceyean neutrality (McEvoy, 2011) to which many Northern Irish lawyers adhered during the Conflict with the liberal values, express or implied, held by Hamilton's (2013, 2014) interviewees.
6 Reprinted by permission of the Publishers from 'Explaining Differences', in *Reconceptualising Penality* by Claire Hamilton (Farnham: Ashgate, 2014), p.182. Copyright © 2014.
7 Reprinted by permission of the Publishers from 'The Measurement of Punitiveness', in *Reconceptualising Penality* by Claire Hamilton (Farnham: Ashgate, 2014), p.115. Copyright © 2014.
8 While on the face of it these two processes are oppositional, it may also be that rights agendas implicitly bolster neo-liberal notions of individuality. As suggested by Cavadino and Dignan (2006: 7): 'much of the juristic and political cogence of individual "human rights" can be seen as deriving from the individualization of culture associated with contemporary consumer capitalism'.
9 (2006) 42 EHRR 41.
10 Northern Ireland Assembly, Official Report (Hansard), 26 September 2011.
11 Northern Ireland Assembly, Official Report (Hansard), 26 September 2011.

24

Criminal justice policy and the European Union[1]

Andrea Ryan and Claire Hamilton

Introduction

The role of 'Europe' (broadly conceived) as a penal actor represents a highly current and contested issue in the criminological field. On the one hand, there is an emerging body of work on the significance of European culture and identity and their implications for punishment (Snacken and Dumortier, 2012; Daems, van Zyyl Smit and Snacken, 2013; Body-Gendrot et al., 2013), in turn building on earlier work examining the stark differences in rates of imprisonment between various European jurisdictions and the US (Melossi, 2001; Whitman, 2003; Salas, 2005). In particular, there is a suggestion that the US trend towards increased punitiveness or harshness may be better 'resisted' in Europe (owing *inter alia* to a stronger, more embedded commitment to human rights) (Snacken and Dumortier, 2012; Vaughan and Kilcommins, 2007, 2010). On the other hand, significant concerns have been expressed about the demands of securitisation placed on European Union (EU) Member States, particularly since the events of 9/11 (Loader, 2002; Baker and Roberts, 2005). In this regard it is notable that Baker (2010) characterises the Union's existing role as a penal actor as 'governing through security' rather than 'governing through crime'. The latter term of course refers to Simon's (2007) argument concerning the US state's mobilisation of crime (particularly the ideal subject of the victim) as a framework for normative regulation in response to post war crises in other modes of governance, most notably the welfare state or New Deal political order. Applying this framework to the European Union, Baker (2010) observes some evidence of victim-focussed crime and crime control, thinking in terms of security policies that have been adopted so far, particularly since the creation of the 'area of security, justice and freedom' (ASFJ) in 1999. While she has also acknowledged in later work the strong regard for the rule of law within the Union (Baker, 2013), Baker (2013) raises important questions about the extent to which the Lisbon reforms in the area (since 2009, justice has become subject to supranational EU decision-making procedures) open up the field of possibilities in this regard.

In light of the above, this chapter seeks to assess the manner in which the Republic of Ireland has approached its emerging criminal law and criminal justice obligations deriving from membership of the European Union, an area which of course is regarded as core to the traditional notion of Westphalian sovereignty. As will be seen below, the Irish state has thus far enthusiastically embraced EU-inspired initiatives relating to security, with attendant consequences for due process, but has been slower to implement policies seeking to harmonise procedural protections. In the final section, conclusions will be reached about the factors driving the direction of Irish criminal justice policy in this area, together with some brief comments on issues such as accountability. Prior to embarking upon this analysis, however, discussion follows in the first part on the history of criminal justice policymaking in the European Union to date, including the significance of the recent Lisbon reforms.

Legal framework of the Union and competence in criminal matters

The area of security and justice currently represents one of the fastest growing areas of competence of the European Union (Baker, 2010). This is quite remarkable given that the founding treaties of the 1950s did not confer any competence on the Union in criminal matters, a situation which remained until the entering into force of the Maastricht Treaty in 1993. The situation began to change in the mid-1980s, when moves towards further economic integration compelled the Commission to address the security implications attendant upon removal of cross-border controls (Commission of the European Communities, 1985). The solution whereby Member States would take on reciprocal responsibilities for the internal security of one another was not universally welcomed and ultimately took the form of the 1985 Schengen agreement between just five Member States outside of the formal Treaty structures.[2] This agreement was designed to create a territory without internal borders as well as provide mechanisms to maintain security throughout the region. While Ireland and the UK are not members of Schengen, since 2002 both States cooperate in some aspects of Schengen, namely police and judicial cooperation in criminal matters, the fight against drugs and the Schengen Information System (SIS).[3]

Given this history, and the traditional reluctance of Member States to cede sovereignty in an area which had hitherto been uncontestedly national, the importance of the reforms introduced by the Treaty of Maastricht cannot be understated. The Treaty on the European Union (TEU)[4] created a new principal treaty, which conferred some competence on the Union in the field of 'justice and home affairs'. The provisions relating to justice and home affairs and their related *acquis* (law) became known as the 'third pillar', 'common foreign and security policy' as the 'second pillar' and a consolidated version of the existing treaties as the 'first pillar'. While the creation of a special forum to deal with issues relating to criminal law and sanctions marked a watershed moment in the evolution of Union policy, it should be noted that decision-making in this area remained intergovernmental in nature, i.e. unanimity among all Member States was required before a measure could be adopted. The cumbersome nature of this arrangement was addressed *inter alia* by the Treaty of Amsterdam in 1999, which inched decision-making further towards the methods usual in the Community and introduced the 'framework decision' as a specific instrument of the third pillar. It also represented an important ideological threshold: in committing members to constructing an 'area of freedom, security and justice' (AFSJ), the Treaty marked a break in the Union's approach to justice from a 'reactive means of dealing with those who threatened collective assets' (Baker, 2010: 195) to a common end of the Union in its own right. The significance of these developments for the direction of criminal justice and penal policy should not be lost. As observed by Douglas-Scott (2008–09: 54), it represented an attempt to bring the EU 'closer to its own citizens' through the area of security; as such, the potential for a 'governing through crime' dynamic was heightened.

The 'magic device' (Anagnostopoulos, 2014) for achieving this development was announced at the Tampere summit in October 1999 where the principle of 'mutual recognition' was endorsed as a basis for judicial co-operation in both civil and criminal matters within the Union. This changed the focus in matters of criminal justice co-operation from request to demand, giving States very limited grounds to refuse requests for assistance (including limits on rights arguments) and removing bureaucratic layers by requiring calls for assistance in criminal matters to be made directly between judicial authorities. A body of legislative instruments has since been developed to give effect to the principle of mutual recognition, with a view to replacing the mutual legal assistance regime that had operated heretofore. The first, and most symbolic, manifestation of this policy has been the European Arrest Warrant (EAW), a controversial measure which some argue sailed through a post 9/11 'window of opportunity' (Hassan, 2010), and whose provisions are discussed in further detail below.

Since the adoption of the Lisbon Treaty in 2009, the three-pillar structure has been dissolved, and the areas of competence covered by the third pillar have become vested with a supranational character. Given the supremacy of Community law over national law and the potential for the Commission to bring infringement proceedings against Member States,[5] Members have thus lost a significant degree of control over matters relating to justice and home affairs. Further, the EU can now legislate in the area of criminal law by means of Directives, adopted by a qualified majority vote. The cumulative effect of these measures illustrates why the application of supra-national rather than intergovernmental decision-making procedures to the field of criminal law represents such 'a critical development in the history of the treaties' (Baker, 2013: 80). It should be noted, however, that Ireland along with the UK secured a special position under Protocol 21, allowing them the choice to opt in to proposed legislative instruments. Where they choose not to opt in initially, they may later opt in when the instrument has been adopted or any time thereafter, but will thereby have had no input in the legislative negotiations.[6]

Before moving on to the next part, a point should be made regarding the terminology used to refer to the legal instruments referenced throughout. Prior to the Lisbon Treaty, the most important legislative instruments were known as Regulations, Decisions and Framework Decisions. The first two became law in Member States generally without any domestic legislative action required, but the third category, Framework Decisions, required Member States to transpose the instruments into domestic law by a given deadline, leaving to them the 'choice of form and method' of implementation. Since the Lisbon Treaty, the Framework Decision instrument is now called a Directive; like Framework Decisions, they must be transposed into national law by a given deadline. Other instruments under Lisbon include Regulations and Decisions, both of which are directly applicable.[7]

Ireland's engagement with EU security measures

To date, Ireland has had a good record of transposing legislation with regard to EU instruments on security matters. A notable example is the joint investigation teams' Framework Decision, which was implemented in 2004.[8] Ireland has also implemented the Europol Decision, which replaced the earlier Europol Convention, and exercising its opt in, has chosen to participate in the new Europol Regulation which will become the new framework governing Europol, replacing the prior instruments.[9] Europol, though made up of police officers, is not a police force as would be commonly understood in a domestic setting. It has no operational powers, and its functions are largely 'horizontal' in nature through the gathering, analysing and disseminating of information. The Europol Decision[10] in 2009 expanded its ability to become involved in operational policing, however, giving it power to request national police forces to commence investigations and to participate in joint investigation teams. The proposed Regulation foresees Europol becoming 'the EU hub for information exchange and analysis on serious crime' and 'strengthens and clarifies the obligation for Member States to supply data to Europol'.[11] The

European Data Protection Supervisor will be given responsibility for external data protection supervision of Europol, and the rights of individuals affected by data processing by Europol will be strengthened.

Ireland also wholeheartedly embraced one of the most significant (and controversial) developments in the field of security co-operation in recent years, namely, the Framework Decision on the European Arrest Warrant (EAW). This measure replaced the earlier European Convention on extradition[12] and was transposed into Irish law through the EAW Act 2003. This instrument has been used extensively in all Member States, including Ireland, subjecting thousands of European citizens to fast-track extradition procedures. The number of requests received by Ireland for the execution of warrants has increased with each passing year. In 2013 alone, 223 requests were received, and since the coming into force of the 2003 Act in 2004, a total of 907 orders have been executed.[13] Since 2012, warrants may also be used between EU Member States and third countries.[14] The operation of the EAW is not without difficulty, and a number of stubborn problems have arisen in its first decade. The issue of proportionality, where warrants are issued for relatively minor offences, has been a frequent cause for concern (Hammarberg, 2011). Ireland has been no exception in this regard, with some criticism being voiced by Mr. Justice Peart, who hears many of these cases in the High Court, on the volume of warrants arriving in this State in respect of relatively minor offences such as petty thefts and road traffic offences (Peart, 2011). In part, this is due to the fact that some jurisdictions have a system of compulsory prosecution even for relatively trivial offences, resulting in a disproportionate number of warrants being requested by those jurisdictions. A further problem is the automatic placing of alerts on the SIS whenever a warrant is issued and a failure to revise the SIS as appropriate: if the warrant is refused, it will often remain on the SIS, thus effectively making the person a prisoner in the Member State that has refused the warrant lest he be arrested when entering another Member State. The surrender of persons on foot of a warrant where the trial is not ready to proceed for some time as well as the differing methods of implementation across the various Member States has also attracted criticism from *inter alia* the European Parliament (2014).

The approach of the Irish courts to these problems is somewhat difficult to characterise. On one view, they have followed the approach of other European courts in facilitating execution where possible (Wagner, 2011). This can be evidenced by the manner in which they have 'read down' fundamental rights guarantees in the Irish implementing legislation and through the exacting tests (e.g. 'egregious circumstances') established for denial of surrender where breaches of fundamental rights are alleged (see further, Fahey, 2008, 2012). On the other hand, it is clear that the courts are unwilling to place 'blind faith' in the criminal justice systems of other EU jurisdictions, particularly where fundamental rights such as the right not to be subjected to torture or inhuman or degrading treatment are in issue. In *Minister for Justice, Equality and Law Reform v Rettinger*,[15] for example, the Court held that the principle of mutual trust will not have the effect of nullifying evidence which reveals a 'real risk' that an infringement of fundamental rights will take place in the issuing state following surrender. Indeed, two recent Supreme Court cases in which requests were refused illustrate the potential for injustice, unfairness and unnecessary hardship in this area. While both quite singular in their circumstances, they are discussed in some further detail below given their utility in illustrating the problems inherent in what has been termed a 'checkbox' approach to extradition (MacGuill, 2012).

The first case concerned Ian Bailey,[16] an English national but long-term Irish resident, who was sought by the French authorities in 2009 for the purpose of questioning about the murder of a Frenchwoman in Ireland some 13 years previously. Mr. Bailey had been a suspect in the murder but was never charged with or convicted of any offence, and a decision had been taken by the Irish authorities not to charge Mr. Bailey with any offence. Mr. Bailey's objection to his extradition was based in part on the contention that the purpose of the warrant was investigation rather than prosecution. In rejecting the request for surrender, the Supreme Court agreed with him on this point and also in relation to the issue of extraterritoriality, as Irish murder law would not apply in an equivalent case. An unusual feature of the case is that the state officials were so concerned about the potential for a miscarriage of justice that certain documents were disclosed to Mr. Bailey's legal team (and the French authorities) during the course of the proceedings indicating that the Garda case against Mr. Bailey was highly prejudiced and flawed. Notwithstanding this, and the long period of time which had elapsed between the crime and the request, the State's argument in the Supreme Court was that such matters were irrelevant and that the only consideration for the Court was whether the warrant was for the purposes of prosecution.

The second case[17] also illustrates the potential for unnecessary hardship that can arise from the automatic endorsement of extradition requests, on this occasion compounded by the vague and imprecise drafting of national legislation implementing the Framework Decision. The facts concerned Mr. Tobin, who was convicted of causing the deaths of two small children while driving in Hungary in 2000. While his prosecution was pending, he left Hungary lawfully, fully complying with procedures set down by the Hungarian authorities and was later convicted and sentenced in his absence. In 2007, the High Court held that he had not 'fled' that jurisdiction within the meaning of section 10 of the Irish Act and refused the order for his surrender. That finding was upheld by the Supreme Court in 2008, who noted '"fleeing" necessarily implies escape, haste, evasion, the notion of moving away from a pursuer' and concluded that Mr. Tobin's departure from Hungary came nowhere near such actions. When a second prosecution was brought under amended EAW legislation, which omitted the requirement to have 'fled', the Supreme Court was faced with the question of abuse of process. The Court held by a majority that Mr. Tobin should not be surrendered holding, *inter alia*, that to do so following the previous proceedings in which he was successful would amount to an abuse of process. From the point of view of the coercive effect of the warrant, it is interesting to note that leading counsel for the State did not deny that the result which he sought would be 'terribly harsh' on Mr. Tobin and his family, given the passage of time and also the sense of finality which had attended the previous Supreme Court proceedings. Hardiman J. was additionally very critical of the manner in which the Hungarian proceedings had been conducted, describing the 'mutual trust' vested in other judicial systems as 'an entirely notional respect and confidence which in practice co-exists with an absolute ignorance of the system involved'. It is noteworthy also that in the course of his judgment, the learned judge addressed broader issues relating to the transparency and proportionality of the EAW legislation:

> When the European Arrest Warrant "Framework Document" was first drawn up in 2001 it related exclusively to Terrorist offences. It was subsequently, in the ten day period immediately after the 9/11 outrage in New York, extended to a great number of other offences many of which are not offences of specific intent at all. Again, I do not think that this aspect of the European Arrest Warrant arrangements are widely known, or were widely or clearly explained at the time.

Hardiman J.'s *dicta* reflect concerns within the broader legal community about the 'function creep' evident within European Union security legislation in the post 9/11 period. This involves EU Member States approving a policy to counter terrorism, but subsequently expanding it to a range of other crimes (Hosein, 2005; SECILE, 2013).

A further security measure that has become operational in recent years is ECRIS, a European Criminal Records Information System. The basis for this system is contained in a Framework Decision, which lays down the framework for the development of a computerised system of exchange of information on convictions between Member States, but does not permit Member States to access national criminal records.[18] The Framework Decision calls for the creation of a 'standardised European format', allowing information to be exchanged in a uniform, electronic and easily machine-translatable way. The computerised system referred to in the Framework Decision has been created by a Council Decision on the establishment of ECRIS,[19] which is automatically binding and has been operational in all Member States, including Ireland since 2012. While it does not require transposition, the Decision itself is stated to be 'for the purpose of application of article 11 of the Framework Decision', which does need to be transposed, therefore it cannot be seen as a standalone instrument. Ireland has not yet transposed the Framework Decision even though the ECRIS system has been operational, and used, for two years. In a recent audit of the Garda Síochána by the Office of the Data Protection Commissioner (having been somewhat misleadingly informed that the system has its legal basis in the Framework Decision but making no mention of the Decision), the Office strongly recommended that legislation, currently at draft stage, giving effect to the Framework Decision be passed as soon as possible in order to underpin the legal basis for the operation of ECRIS (Data Protection Commissioner, 2014).

Another instrument, completing the criminal records legislative package, is a Framework Decision that addresses the issue of taking account of criminal convictions in the course of new criminal proceedings.[20] As described in a recital, it:

> [A]ims at enabling consequences to be attached to a previous conviction handed down in one Member State in the course of new criminal proceedings in another Member State to the extent that such consequences are attached to previous national convictions under the law of that other Member State.

Member States are thus free to use the conviction information, just as they would normally do if they were trying a domestic case. Ireland has implemented this Framework Decision, but instead of doing so within the legislation currently being drafted, it has notified the Commission that it has implemented the Framework Decision by way of a 'principle of common law'.[21] It has therefore produced no easily accessible law that could be consulted by the authorities of other Member States. Given the need for Member States to be able to cooperate with each other easily, often in a setting of communicating with each other in different languages, it is regrettable that in their dealings with Ireland they are expected to hunt around the common law in search of a principle, where a clear statement of such a principle could have been included in the criminal records legislation.

Other security measures implemented by Ireland include: a Framework Decision on the execution of orders freezing property or evidence; freezing and confiscation of bank accounts and confiscation of criminal proceeds;[22] a Decision on the exchange of information and co-operation concerning terrorist offences;[23] and a EU Convention and a Protocol that aimed to supplement the mutual assistance regime established under the 1959 Convention.[24] One measure which merits particular mention given its potentially coercive effect is the Directive on the European Investigation Order (EIO) which concerns transferring evidence gathered in one Member State to a Member State seeking to try the accused. Harmonisation in this area has been a longstanding aim that has taken over a decade to materialise in the form of an instrument and will take another four years to implement. It first developed in the form of a proposal for a

Framework Decision on a European Evidence Warrant (EEW), and, after many years of negotiations, the instrument that was finally agreed upon was very limited in its scope as to the types of evidentiary material that could be sought under the warrant. Few Member States transposed the Framework Decision, including Ireland, and in the post-Lisbon period, a new initiative was proposed, namely, a Directive on a European Investigation Order (EIO).[25] This has a much broader scope than the earlier instrument in terms of the types of evidentiary material that can be sought under the Order, covering all types of investigative measures including witness statements, forensic evidence and hearings of suspects through transfer to the requesting State or by video-conference (with the suspects' consent). It repeals the EEW, and aims to entirely replace the existing mutual legal assistance measures: the 1959 Convention on Mutual Legal Assistance and Protocols and more recent EU mutual assistance instruments. When the EIO Directive was originally proposed, the Irish Government decided to opt in; however, with the change in government in 2011, that decision was reversed. The current position is that the UK have decided to opt in to the EIO, but Ireland has not yet reached a decision on whether to opt back in again. Given the implementation deadline of 2017, it is unlikely that a decision will be forthcoming for the immediate future.[26]

Two high profile security measures in respect of which Ireland (together with the UK) has shown much less enthusiasm include new measures relating to Eurojust and the Office of the European Public Prosecutor. Eurojust came into being by way of a Council Decision in 2002,[27] and, in broad terms, it does for public prosecutors what Europol has done for the police. It consists of representatives sent by Member States and is tasked with improving co-operation between criminal justice agencies, facilitating co-ordination of prosecutions with a cross-border element and requesting Member States to initiate investigations and prosecutions in particular cases.[28] Ireland and the UK are both members of Eurojust but have decided not to opt in to the new measures seeking to reform Eurojust, largely on account of its links with proposals for the establishment of a new body, the EPPO or European Public Prosecutor (the Lisbon Treaty provides for the establishment of the EPPO 'from Eurojust'). While the role of the prosecutor's office is limited under the Treaty to 'combatting' crimes affecting the financial interests of the EU, this may be extended where necessary to the area of 'serious crime having cross border dimension'. Once established, the Office shall be responsible for 'investigating, prosecuting and bringing to judgment' perpetrators of offences against the Union's financial interests and 'shall exercise the functions of prosecutor in the competent courts of the Member States in relation to such offences'.[29] A Regulation, currently still at negotiation stage, provides for its establishment as a body of the Union, fully independent and with legal personality. The office and its staff, which will include the European Chief Prosecutor, the Deputy European Chief Prosecutors, the European Prosecutors and the European Delegated Prosecutors (prosecutors nominated by Member States),[30] must act in the interest of the Union as a whole, and Member States and Union bodies must respect its independence. It is accountable solely to the European Parliament, the Council and the European Commission. Currently Ireland and the UK are not opting in to the EPPO Regulation for reasons likely related to the anticipated incursion into national criminal law systems.[31]

Procedural rights protections/measures enhancing the freedom of defendants

While, as noted in the introduction, the Union has been criticised for its excessive focus on security over rights in its approach to justice (see, for example, Douglas-Scott, 2004, 2008–09; Wagner, 2011), recent years have also seen it move towards a series of instruments designed to guarantee various minimum rights for suspects and defendants. These have been officially justified on instrumental grounds – as being necessary to build 'mutual trust' between the criminal justice systems of the Member States – in the absence of which 'mutual recognition' measures, like the European Arrest Warrant, are unlikely to work smoothly. Spencer (2011) also posits the view that they advance a more positive vision of the Union's commitment to an area of justice and freedom as well as security, the idea being an area in all parts of which citizens can enjoy a certain minimal level of humanity, consideration and efficiency. Under the pre-Lisbon legislative arrangements, it proved impossible to obtain unanimity on the numerous proposals that were put forward in this area. Under new post-Lisbon powers to establish 'minimum rules', the Stockholm Programme adopted a 'Roadmap' of measures,[32] a non-exhaustive list of actions addressing procedural rights of suspects including rights to information, to translation and to legal assistance, and called on the Commission to address further procedural rights.[33] In addition, the Union has been active in relation to the development of criminal justice legislation in the field of detention. Both sets of measures will be discussed below.

Procedural rights

Among the first of these measures to be adopted were a Directive on the right to translation and interpretation and a Directive on the right to information. The former provides suspects and accused persons with the right to an interpreter throughout the entire process, from pre-trial through to final disposal of the case, as well as a right to be provided with a written translation of all documents 'which are essential to ensure that they are able to exercise their right of defence and to safeguard the fairness of the proceedings'.[34] The second, the right to information Directive, takes effect as soon a person is made aware that he is suspected or accused of having committed a criminal offence, and it applies to both domestic and cross-border criminal cases.[35] It requires a Member State's authorities to inform suspects of a range of rights as they apply under national law, including: the right of access to a lawyer and any entitlements to free legal advice; the right to be informed of the accusation; the right to interpretation and translation; and the right to remain silent. The arrested person should be given the information 'promptly' by means of a Letter of Rights, which must also contain information about: right of access to the materials of the case; the right to have consular authorities and one person informed; the right of access to urgent medical assistance; and the maximum number of hours or days suspects or accused persons may be deprived of liberty before being brought before a judicial authority. In addition, Member States must make available to the arrested person or his lawyer documents relating to the case in the possession of the authorities that are essential to challenging the lawfulness of the arrest or detention, and ensure that access is granted to suspects and accused persons, or to their lawyers, to all material evidence in the possession of the competent authorities, whether for or against suspects or accused persons, in order to safeguard the fairness of the proceedings and to prepare the defence.[36]

A proposal that encountered much more difficulty in reaching agreement, the Directive on the right of access to a lawyer, has now finally been adopted,[37] although neither Ireland nor the United Kingdom have opted in to the Directive. The Directive clearly defines the precise scope of the right of access, which applies to domestic and cross-border cases. It provides that access must be granted 'without undue delay' and must be granted before the authorities interview a suspect. Member States may determine the investigative acts which a suspect's lawyer may attend, but if the legal system includes procedures of identity parades, confrontations between the suspect and witnesses (a feature that is common in continental jurisdictions), or experimental reconstructions of the scene of crime, and such acts involve the suspect's participation, the suspect 'shall as a minimum have the right for his lawyer to attend'. Member States may make 'practical arrangements' regarding the duration and frequency of meetings by the suspect or accused with a lawyer, but these arrangements must not be so limited as to prejudice the 'effective exercise and essence' of the suspect or accused person's right to meet with a lawyer. Perhaps the most controversial aspect of the Directive is the provision it makes for the right of the suspect or accused to have a lawyer present during any questioning. This was resisted by some Member States but survived the negotiations and provides the clearest statement of the right since it was first addressed, somewhat opaquely, in the European Court of Human Rights (ECtHR) ruling in *Salduz*.[38] That decision was unequivocal in so far as it clearly established a right of access to a lawyer before any questioning begins; however, the wording was ambiguous regarding the issue of a lawyer being present in the interview room during questioning. The Court has more definitively stated this right in subsequent rulings, and, indeed, in a recent decision, the Irish Supreme Court appears to accept that there is a requirement under the European Convention on Human Rights (ECHR) jurisprudence to allow a lawyer to attend questioning.[39]

As to the role played by the lawyer during questioning, Member States must ensure that the suspect or accused has the right for a lawyer to 'participate effectively when he is questioned'; such participation, however, 'shall be in accordance with procedures in national law'.[40] A recital provides that national law may regulate the participation of the lawyer during questioning, provided that such rules do not prejudice the 'effective exercise and essence of the right', and the recital somewhat vaguely suggests that such rules would provide that a lawyer may 'ask questions, request clarification and make statements' during questioning.[41] As noted, the Supreme Court has recently expanded the definition of the constitutional right of reasonable access to a lawyer to include the right not to be questioned by police before consultation with a solicitor.[42] However, since the issue of whether questioning a suspect without a solicitor being present breaches the constitutional right of reasonable access was not raised before the Court, it was unable to rule on the matter. The judgment nonetheless contains veiled indications that it would rule positively on the issue, should it arise in a future case, making special reference to the *Salduz* line. Many jurisdictions in Europe have changed their legislation in response to the ECtHR rulings to require the presence of a lawyer during questioning.[43] Despite much heel-dragging to date, real progress may perhaps soon be made in this area given the recent approval by the Minister of a new Garda station legal aid scheme.[44] It would thus appear that one of the obstacles to the implementation of the Directive – the extra financial burden it would place on legal aid budgets – has been overcome.[45]

The most recent initiative in the area of procedural rights is the proposed Directive on the strengthening of certain aspects of the presumption of innocence and of the right to be present at trial in criminal proceedings.[46] These Directives, along with two other proposals (safeguards for children and vulnerable adult suspects, and legal aid for suspects),[47] complete the current legislative package on procedural rights. Should Ireland decide to opt in to the proposed Directive on the presumption of innocence, it will be faced with a number of difficulties, particularly in relation to its current approach to pre-trial silence. The rationale for a Directive on the presumption arises from the recognition that the presumption of innocence is regularly breached, as evidenced by the number of cases held to be in violation within in a six-year period by the ECtHR.[48] The proposed Directive builds upon Article 6 of the ECHR as interpreted by the ECtHR, which has held that the presumption of innocence established under Article 6(2) encompasses the right not to be publicly presented as convicted by public authorities before the final judgment and that the burden of proof is on the prosecution, with the accused benefitting from any reasonable doubt. In addition, the ECtHR has linked the presumption of innocence with other fair trial rights, the right to silence and the right not to incriminate oneself, on the basis that when such rights are breached the presumption of innocence is inevitably also at stake.

The Directive aims to facilitate the 'practical application' of the right to the presumption of innocence at any stage of the proceedings, even before the person has been made aware that they are suspected of having committed a criminal offence. The right is breached if a person is presented through a public statement by judicial or public authorities as if they were guilty without having yet been proved to be guilty.[49] While the burden of proof is on the prosecution, the shifting of the burden may in limited cases be permitted provided there are safeguards, provided presumptions of fact are confined and provided they are subject to rebuttal. The Directive also provides a right against self-incrimination, and a right not to cooperate in any criminal proceedings, but that does not extend to the use of material obtained through the use of lawful compulsory powers and which has an existence independent of the will of the accused (DNA and fingerprint material, for example). A right to silence is provided to suspects when questioned by police or other authorities, including judicial authorities, and suspects must be informed of their right and any consequences of renouncing or invoking it. An aspect of the Directive that may prove controversial as it proceeds through negotiations is that it provides that the exercise of the right to remain silent (and the same applies to the exercise of the right against self-incrimination or non-cooperation) 'shall not be used against a suspect at a later stage in the proceedings and shall not be considered as corroboration of facts'.[50] What may prove even more controversial, more-so amongst continental jurisdictions than Ireland, is a provision stating that any evidence obtained in breach of the rights 'shall not be admissible, unless the use of such evidence would not prejudice the overall fairness of the trial'.[51] Given the extensive inference provisions that exist under Irish legislation allowing inferences to be used as corroboration where persons fail to mention facts later relied on at trial, or to account for objects, marks, etc. found on their person or premises[52] (see further, Daly and Jackson, *infra*), the prohibition on using the exercise of the right as corroboration will undoubtedly raise difficulties for Ireland.

The second proposed Directive on the right to be present at trial builds upon an earlier Framework Decision that was specifically confined to refining the definition of grounds for non-recognition of orders under instruments implementing the principle of mutual recognition. The Decision did not establish *per se* a right to a re-trial where a decision imposing punishment is taken where the accused is absent and the absence is due to failure by the authorities to effectively notify him about the proceedings, but only allowed a warrant to be executed once certain procedural requirements had been satisfied.[53] The proposed Directive additionally requires Member States to ensure that, where a person is tried in their absence without having been unequivocally informed, the person has the right 'to a new trial at which they have the right to be present and which allows a fresh determination of the merits of the case including examination of new evidence'.[54] Like the provisions on the presumption of innocence, the Directive will likely hold significant implications for the criminal justice systems of Member States. It is not uncommon practice amongst continental jurisdictions to hold trials *in absentia*. Indeed, this is an issue that has arisen in a number of EAW cases that have come before the courts in Ireland, where it is not the practice to hold trials *in absentia* other than in the District Court.

Orders to the benefit of the defendant relating to detention

The arguments of Baker (2010) and others concerning the perceived imbalance between security and justice and freedom in European criminal justice have been noted above. In a striking finding from an audit of mutual recognition measures in the decade between the Tampere European Council 1999 and the entry into force of the Lisbon Treaty 2009, Wagner (2011) notes that only one out of nine of those measures privilege the defendant's interests over those of the executive. The exception he identifies is the Framework Decision on the European Supervision

Order (ESO), which addresses a problem facing persons who find themselves on the wrong side of the law while visiting another Member State. Non-resident accused persons are generally regarded as a flight risk and are therefore less likely to obtain bail than a resident national had they committed the offence in the same jurisdiction. It is also the case that some Member States tend to have long periods of pre-trial detention, in some cases, up to four years. The prospect of an unnecessary or lengthy pre-trial detention also raises difficulties for the operation of the EAW, as it does not foster mutual trust.

The Framework Decision encourages Member States to impose pre-trial supervision measures on a non-resident accused person that could be executed in the person's home State so as to avoid imposing unnecessary custodial detention and differential treatment of residents and non-residents. Its stated dual aim is protecting the general public and their right to live in safety and security by not releasing persons without supervision, while at the same time safeguarding the right to liberty of accused persons by providing alternative measures to custodial detention, especially where the principal reason for detaining them pre-trial is the fact that they are non-residents and therefore a presumed flight risk.[55] It thus enables a non-custodial supervision measure to be transferred from the Member State where the non-resident is suspected of having committed an offence to the Member State where he is normally resident. This allows a suspect to await their trial under supervision in their own resident state, including suspects who have been surrendered following an EAW. It may only be imposed where the suspect consents to return to the State of normal residence, or to a third State.[56] Ireland has not yet transposed this Framework Decision into national law despite the deadline of December 2012 and despite its close nexus with the EAW, an instrument which has resulted in many controversial detentions of persons surrendered.[57] According to the most recent legislative programme of the Irish Government, a Bill was scheduled to be published in 2015.[58]

Another problem that faces convicted persons who have been surrendered on the basis of an EAW, or who have simply been tried and convicted in a Member State where they are not normally resident, is the prospect of serving a sentence far away from home and family, thus compounding the punitive effect of the sanction. Two Framework Decisions address this difficulty. The first applies the principle of mutual recognition to custodial sentences, so that a sentenced prisoner may be transferred to his or her country of residence to serve out the sentence.[59] The second applies to probation decisions and alternative sanctions, again allowing the supervision of these sanctions to be conducted in the person's resident Member State.[60] These instruments were due to have been transposed by December 2011. Two Bills were scheduled for publication in early 2015.[61]

Victims' rights

It would not be appropriate to conclude this chapter without reference to Union measures seeking to strengthen the rights of victims in the criminal process (see further, Kilcommins and Moffett, *infra*). The EU has been active in this area in line with Baker's (2010: 199) arguments concerning the renewed centrality of the (imagined) crime victim in the period since the Amsterdam Treaty. As she goes on to observe, however, it should not be forgotten that the Stockholm Programme simultaneously emphasizes the need to bolster protections for victims *and* defendants, specifically rejecting the 'zero sum game' described by Garland (2001) and others (Kilcommins *et al.*, 2004; Campbell, 2008). Proposed reforms comprise two Directives and a Regulation or a 'legislative package'[62] relating to victims in the criminal process. The Directives constitute a Directive on the European Protection Order[63] (EPO) and a Directive on establishing minimum standards on the rights, support and protection of victims of crime.[64] These were due for implementation by January 2015 and November 2015 respectively.

The EPO Directive applies to protection measures adopted in criminal matters only. The aim of the protection measures is to protect a victim from the criminal acts of another that would endanger them physically or psychologically and applies to all victims, regardless of the nature of the offending conduct. The protection measures established under the Directive are orders preventing the offender approaching or contacting the victim, broadly similar to those that currently exist in Ireland under the Domestic Violence Act. Ireland, however, has not chosen to opt in to this Directive. The Regulation, to which Ireland did opt in, extends the same protections to orders 'adopted in civil matters'. It shall apply from January 2015, and, as a Regulation applies automatically to Member States, it does not require any implementing legislation.[65] The Regulation is designed to 'complement' the Directive on the rights of victims of crime and stipulates that a 'victim' under the Regulation has the same meaning as that under the Directive, despite a protection measure being issued under civil as opposed to criminal proceedings.[66]

The reasons for Ireland's decision not to opt in to the EPO Directive derive specifically from the fact that the matters covered in the Directive are orders obtained in a criminal law context, while in Ireland such orders are generally made in a civil law framework.[67] The move here by Ireland highlights a distinction between continental legal systems where such orders would be routinely made in the context of criminal proceedings – indeed it is the norm that victims would also seek damages in the same proceedings – and adversarial systems. In inquisitorial legal systems there is not the same split between civil and criminal matters as pertains in Ireland where damages and protection orders are dispensed as part of a civil law process. Nonetheless, the nature of the orders under Irish civil proceedings are generally intrinsically connected with criminal matters, aimed at protecting the person from the possible future criminal acts of the person subject to the order. The decision by Ireland not to opt in means that persons coming from other Member States who have had such orders made in their own Member State in the context of criminal proceedings will not be able to avail of any mechanism for mutual recognition of such an order. Such a person would have to commence proceedings in Ireland to obtain an order, precisely the opposite of what the EPO seeks to achieve. Interestingly, the UK, though sharing the same type of adversarial system as Ireland, was content to opt in to the EPO Directive.

The second Directive on minimum standards for victims, to which Ireland has chosen to opt in, gives broad rights to victims of crime: they may be accompanied by a legal advisor during interviews;[68] they are given the right to participation in criminal proceedings in accordance with domestic law;[69] and, again in accordance with national law, they may be entitled to legal aid where they are parties to criminal proceedings (a common feature in continental jurisdictions where a victim will generally be constituted as a *partie civile*).[70] It also provides for the possibility of using video recordings of interviews as evidence in the trial, practical arrangements to prevent secondary victimization during criminal proceedings, such as separate entrances and waiting areas in the court, and for victims to be given information about their case, including any decision not to proceed and on the offender's release from custody. Despite the potentially broad rights afforded under the Directive, it should be noted that it takes account of the different roles that victims are given across Member States, for example, whether they have the role of a party to the proceedings, such as would pertain in many Continental systems, or simply the role of witness as pertains in common law systems. Member states are permitted to take account of the role given to the victim and to determine the scope of rights set out in the Directive when drafting their implementing legislation by reference to that role – if the legal system does not give a victim the right to be represented at trial, the Directive will not confer such a right.

Conclusion

The foregoing discussion shows that there clearly exists an EU criminal justice system, not fully developed, but grown considerably from its fledgling state in the pre-Lisbon era. As revealed in the long list of security measures adopted since the introduction of mutual recognition, justice, or perhaps more correctly *security*, stands apart as an area where the EU has grown most significantly in the first decade of the twenty-first century (Coolaset, 2010). Given that the legislative pace shows little intent of slowing, it is critical that the import of this immense and growing body of law is not lost on criminologists. Most, as Zedner (2011: 279) notes, 'ply their trade without recourse to a criminal law textbook', and these difficulties are further compounded by the fact that even within the legal profession some criminal lawyers have been slow to grasp the increasing relevance of EU law to their area of practice. Such epistemological difficulties, however, should not blind us to the transformative potential of EU law in criminal and penal matters and, particularly its potential for increased punitiveness as discussed in the Introduction. While the 'Europeanisation' of human rights norms may lead to an increasingly 'negotiated' criminal justice sphere 'from above', allowing pressure groups to leverage international norms for domestic change (Vaughan and Kilcommins, 2007, 2010), national executives may also gain from operating in international venues such as the European Union where they face fewer opposition and judicial constraints than in national politics (Lavenex, 2007; Wagner, 2011). Factors such as this may tilt the justice balance further in favour of the sword than the scales, particularly in a post-9/11 era where legislators may not apply strict scrutiny (Hassan, 2010).

In her detailed analysis of European Union criminal justice policy, Baker (2010: 204) writes of the: 'widespread perception of lack of balance in the legislative emphasis that has been given to the constituent elements of the AFSJ'. While not claiming to be exhaustive, the above examination of Ireland's broad approach to this area of Union competence, based on what appears to be a clear intention to participate in the security measures and a more circumspect approach to procedural guarantees, reflects these broader concerns regarding an 'imbalance'[71] between security on the one hand and justice and freedom on the other. The potential for hardship and injustice as these reforms are applied 'on the ground' is also well illustrated by the *Tobin* and *Bailey* cases. In this regard, it is instructive to consider the distinction made by Wagner (2011) between 'negative' and 'positive' integration which has been instrumental in explaining the dynamics of the common market. Applied to the field of criminal law co-operation since the introduction of mutual recognition, Wagner argues that 'negative' (i.e. the abolition of obstacles to enforcement integration) will always be privileged over 'positive' (i.e. the adoption of common standards and rights), as executives themselves are the main subject of regulation in criminal law, and, as such, reforms directly enhance their autonomy. This will be true, he contends, even under conditions of unanimous decision-making as now exist under Lisbon.

On the other hand, it would be false to propose such a neat dichotomy between measures enhancing executive powers and those improving the standing of the defendant. Irish (and British) reticence to commit to 'vertical' as opposed to 'horizontal' harmonization measures in the field of security, such as the European Public Prosecutor, clearly reveal a more complex dynamic at play. Indeed, in many ways, the approach of Ireland reflects what Keohane (2005) refers to as the paradox of the EU's role in security matters: on the one hand, governments agree in principle that co-operation at the EU level is a 'good thing' because of the cross-border nature of the threat from terrorism, transnational crime, etc.; on the other, they are slow to give the Union the powers and resources it would need to be truly effective. Many Member States had a poor record of implementation with regard to third-pillar measures prior to Lisbon, and the resource implications attendant upon doing so, particularly at a time of fiscal crisis, should not be forgotten. It should also be acknowledged that we are relatively early in the days of the post-Lisbon reforms in the ASFJ area. Time will tell whether fundamental rights continue to play second fiddle to security, particularly under the new enforcement mechanisms available to the Union post-Lisbon and the elevated stature of the Union's Charter of Fundamental Rights.[72] Certainly, the provisions in the Lisbon Treaty paving the way for EU accession to the ECHR hold much transformative potential (Douglas-Scott, 2011). Indeed, in the shorter term, measures already in train may have dramatic effect in terms of a reversal of the raft of adverse inference provisions so recently added to the Irish statute book.

Given what it is at stake, one criticism which may be levelled at the Irish government is its failure to clearly articulate a clear policy in this area. There is a distinct lack of political debate in Ireland on EU criminal justice measures, an equal dearth of discussion in the Irish media and general lack of public awareness of EU criminal justice and its implications for Ireland. It has been suggested that the Oireachtas has 'a pretty poor record at European level' of expressing policy views before EU measures are drafted; 'in other words, we are one of the lower performers in terms of contributing to the political dialogue'.[73] These difficulties with accountability and transparency at national level are of course compounded at a European level where many EU or EU-backed initiatives in the AFSJ have been criticised for their deplorable lack of scrutiny and transparency (Douglas-Scott, 2008–09). The opaque manner in which decisions are made at all levels thus renders it all the more incumbent on national governments to ensure that EU-inspired security measures such as the ECRIS and the framework decision on criminal convictions are underpinned by the appropriate national legislation. Given the significance of decisions to be taken over the next five years or so, such as a potential opt in to the EPPO Regulation, it is clear that greater effort needs to be made to bring these matters to a broader audience. The by now familiar 'democratic deficit' may perhaps be tolerated in the area of economic integration, but it is much less acceptable in the context of significant intrusions into privacy and liberty rights through exchanges of data and automatic surrender of suspects.

References

Anagnostopoulos, I. (2014) 'Criminal Justice Cooperation in the European Union After the First Few "Steps": A Defence View', *ERA Forum*, 15(1): 9–24.

Ashworth, A. (1998) *The Criminal Process: An Evaluative Study*. Oxford: Oxford University Press.

Baker, E. (2010) 'Governing through Crime? The Case of the European Union', *European Journal of Criminology*, 7(3): 187–213.

Baker, E. (2013) 'The Emerging Role of the EU as a Penal Actor', in T. Daems, D. van Zyyl Smit and S. Snacken (eds) *European Penology?*. Oxford: Hart Publishing.

Baker, E. and Roberts, J. (2005) 'Globalization and the New Punitiveness', in J. Pratt, D. Brown, M. Brown, S. Hallsworth and W. Morrison (eds) *The New Punitiveness: Trends, Theories, Perspectives*. Cullompton: Willan.

Blackstock, J. *et al.* (2014) *Inside Police Custody: An Empirical Account of Suspects' Rights in Four Jurisdictions*. Cambridge: Intersentia.

Body-Gendrot, S., Hough, M., Kerezsi, K., Levy, R. and Snacken, S. (2013) *The Routledge Handbook of European Criminology*. Oxon: Routledge.

Campbell, L. (2008) 'The Culture of Control in Ireland: Theorising Recent Developments in Criminal Justice', *Web Journal of Current Legal Issues*, Vol. 1.

Commission of the European Communities (1985) *Completing the Internal Market*. COM(85)310. Brussels: Commission of the European Communities.

Coolaset, R. (2010) 'EU Counterterrorism Strategy: Value Added or Chimera?', *International Affairs*, 86(4): 857–73.

Daems, T., van Zyyl Smit, D. and Snacken, S. (eds) (2013) *European Penology?*. Oxford: Hart Publishing.

Data Protection Commissioner (2014) *An Garda Síochána: Final Report of Audit Issued March 2014*. Available at: www.garda.ie (accessed 17 December 2014).

Department of Justice (2013a) *Report on the Operation of the European Arrest Warrant Act 2003 in the Year 2013 Made to the Houses of the Oireachtas.* Available at: www.justice.ie/en/JELR/EAW%20Annual%20Report%20for%202013.pdf/Files/EAW%20Annual%20Report%20for%202013.pdf (accessed 17 December 2014).

Department of Justice (2013b) *Report of Working Group to Advise on a System Providing for the Presence of a Legal Representative during Gardaí Interviews.* p. 26. Available at: www.justice.ie/en/JELR/Pages/Report_Final_15_July_Leg (accessed 17 December 2014).

Douglas-Scott, S. (2004) 'The Rule of Law in the European Union – Putting the Security into the Area of Freedom Security and Justice', *European Law Review*, 29: 219.

Douglas-Scott, S. (2008–09) 'The EU's Area of Freedom, Security and Justice: A Lack of Fundamental Rights, Mutual Trust and Democracy?' *Cambridge Yearbook of European Legal Studies*, 11: 53–85.

Douglas-Scott, S. (2011) 'The European Union and Human Rights After the Treaty of Lisbon', *Human Rights Law Review*, 11(4): 645–82.

European Parliament (2014) *Report with Recommendations to the Commission on the Review of the European Arrest Warrant.* (2013/2109 (INL)). Brussels: European Union.

Fahey, E. (2008) 'How to Be a Third Pillar Guardian of Fundamental Rights?', *European Law Review*, 33: 563–76.

Fahey, E. (2012) *Ireland Report Fide 2012, Questionnaire 3, Area of Freedom Security and Justice and the Information Society. Fida XXV Congress Report 2012.* Available at: http://papers.ssrn.com/sol3/papers.cfm?abstract_id=2096152 (accessed 24 April 2015).

Fair Trials International; Justice; Statewatch; European Parliamentary Research Service (2014) *Revising the European Arrest Warrant*, Micaela del Monte, European Added Value Unit. Available at: www.europarl.europa.eu/committees/en/studies.htm (accessed various dates).

Garland, D. (2001) *The Culture of Control: Crime and Social Order in Contemporary Society.* Oxford: Oxford University Press.

Hammarberg, T. (2011) *Overuse of the European Arrest Warrant – A Threat to Human Rights.* The Council of Europe Commissioner's Human Rights Comment. Available at: www.coe.int/en/web/commissioner/-/overuse-of-the-european-arrest-warrant-a-threat-to-human-rights?inheritRedirect=true (accessed 24 April 2015).

Hassan, O. (2010) 'Constructing Crises, (In)securitising Terror: The Punctuated Evolution of EU Counter-Terror Strategy', *European Security*, 19(3): 445–66.

Hosein, G. (2005) *Threatening the Open Society: Comparing Anti-terror Strategies and Policies in the US and Europe.* London: Privacy International.

Keohane, D. (2005) *The EU and Counter Terrorism.* London: Centre for European Reform.

Kilcommins, S., O'Donnell, I., O'Sullivan, E. and Vaughan, B. (2004) *Crime, Punishment and the Search for Order in Ireland.* Dublin: Institute of Public Administration.

Lavenex, S. (2007) 'Mutual Recognition and the Monopoly of Force: Limits of the Single Market Analogy', *Journal of European Public Policy*, 14(5): 762–79.

Loader, I. (2002) 'Policing, Securitisation and Democratisation in Europe', *Criminology and Criminal Justice*, 2(2): 125–53.

MacGuill, J. (2012) 'European Arrest Warrant in Ireland – An Uneven Playing Field', *European Arrest Warrant and EU-US Extradition Conference*, Irish Centre for European Law, Trinity College Dublin, 19 June.

Melossi, D. (2001) 'The Cultural Embeddedness of Social Control: Reflections on the Comparison of Italian and North American Cultures Concerning Punishment', *Theoretical Criminology*, 5(4): 403–24.

Peart, J. (2011) 'Foreword', in R. Farrell and A. Hanrahan (eds) *The European Arrest Warrant in Ireland.* Dublin: Clarus Press.

Ryan, A. (2014) *Towards a System of European Criminal Justice: The Problem of Admissibility of Evidence.* London: Routledge.

Salas, D. (2005) *La volonté de punir: Essai sur le populisme pénal.* Paris: Hachette.

Securing Europe Through Counter Terrorism: Impact, Legitimacy and Effectiveness (SECILE) (2013) *Catalogue of EU Anti-Terrorism Measures.* SECILE project – GA: 313195. Available at: http://secile.eu/wp-content/uploads/2013/12/Catalogue-of-EU-Counter-Terrorism-Measures1.pdf (accessed 25 April 2015).

Simon, J. (2007) *Governing through Crime: How the War on Crime Has Transformed American Democracy and Created a Culture of Fear.* Oxford: Oxford University Press.

Snacken, S. and Dumortier, E. (2012) *Resisting Punitiveness in Europe?.* Oxon, New York: Routledge.

Spencer, J. R. (2011) 'EU Criminal Law—the Present and the Future?', in A. Arnull, C. Barnard, M. Dougan and E. Spaventa (eds) *A Constitutional Order of States? Essays in EU Law in Honour of Alan Dashwood*. Oxford: Hart.

Vaughan, B. and Kilcommins, S. (2007) 'The Europeanisation of Human Rights and the Limits of Authoritarian Policing in Ireland', *European Journal of Criminology*, 4(4): 437–59.

Vaughan, B. and Kilcommins, S. (2010) 'The Governance of Crime and the Negotiation of Justice', *Criminology and Criminal Justice*, 10(1): 59–75.

Wagner, W. (2011) 'Negative and Positive Integration in EU Criminal Law Co-operation', *European Integration Online Papers*, 15: 1–21.

Whitman, J. Q. (2003) *Harsh Justice: Criminal Punishment and the Widening Divide between America and Europe*. Oxford: Oxford University Press.

Zedner, L. (2011) 'Putting Crime Back on the Criminological Agenda', in M. Bosworth and C. Hoyle (eds) *What Is Criminology?* Oxford: Oxford University Press.

Notes

1 Owing to space constraints, this chapter will address policy in respect of the Republic of Ireland only. Reference will, however, be made throughout to the United Kingdom's approach to many of the EU instruments discussed, which of course includes Northern Ireland. Both Ireland and the United Kingdom obtained the choice to opt in to measures proposed in the area of freedom, security and justice under Protocol 21 to the Lisbon Treaty; both jurisdictions have opted in to a number of measures, but in some cases the UK have gone further than Ireland and opted in where Ireland has not done so.

2 France, Germany, Belgium, Luxembourg and the Netherlands.

3 Approved in Decision 2002/192/EC.

4 Signed at Maastricht 1992, later amended by the Treaty of Amsterdam 1997 and by the Nice Treaty 2001.

5 From December 2014, the Commission will be able to bring infringement proceedings to the European Court of Justice in accordance with Art 258 TEFU.

6 In addition, the UK obtained the choice to opt out entirely from the pre-Lisbon measures under Protocol 36, with the option to opt back in to those they wished to participate in; the UK exercised this general opt out in July 2013, and opted back in to many of the measures, as provided for under the Protocol, in December 2014. For a list of the measures opted in to see [2014] OJ L 354/6.

7 Article 288 TFEU: To exercise the Union's competences, the institutions shall adopt regulations, directives, decisions, recommendations and opinions. A regulation shall have general application. It shall be binding in its entirety and directly applicable in all Member States. A directive shall be binding, as to the result to be achieved, upon each Member State to which it is addressed, but shall leave to the national authorities the choice of form and methods. A decision shall be binding in its entirety. Recommendations and opinions shall have no binding force.

8 OJ No. L 162, 20.06.2002, p. 1; implemented by Ireland under the Criminal Justice (Joint Investigations Teams) Act 2004.

9 The UK chose not to opt in to the draft Regulation having raised concerns that the new body may have powers to direct national police forces to initiate criminal investigations, and might also require the UK to share sensitive intelligence. However, it may opt in once the Regulation has been adopted.

10 Council Decision of 6 April 2009 establishing the European Police Office (Europol), (2009/371/JHA), OJ L 121/37, 15.5.2009.

11 COM (2013) 173, p. 2.

12 The European Convention on Extradition 1957.

13 Department of Justice (2013a) *Report on the operation of the European Arrest Warrant Act 2003 in the year 2013 made to the Houses of the Oireachtas.* Available at: www.justice.ie/en/JELR/EAW%20Annual%20Report%20 for%202013.pdf/Files/EAW%20Annual%20Report%20for%202013.pdf (accessed 17 December 2014). In 2004, two orders were executed; by 2006, this had risen to 45, and since 2010, the number executed is in the region of 150 per year.

14 European Arrest Warrant (Application to Third Countries and Amendment) Act 2012.

15 [2011] 1 ILRM 157.

16 [2012] IESC 16.

17 *MJELR v Tobin (no2)* [2012] IESC 37 Hardiman J.

18 Council Framework Decision 2009/315/JHA OJ L 93/23 7.4.2009.

19 Council Decision 2009/316/JHA OJ L93/33 7.4.2009.
20 Council Framework Decision 2008/675/JHA on taking account of convictions in the Member States of the European Union in the course of new criminal proceedings OJ L220/32 15.8.2008.
21 ANNEX to Report of the Commission to the European Parliament and the Council on the implementation of Council Framework Decision 2008/675/JHA of 24 July 2008 on taking into account of convictions in the Member States of the European Union in the course of new criminal proceedings. Com (2014) 312 2.6.2014.
22 Council Framework Decision 2003/577/JHA; these instruments have been implemented through the Criminal Justice (Mutual Assistance) Act 2008.
23 Council Decision 2005/671/JHA.
24 Articles 4 (formalities and procedures in the execution of requests) and 6 (transmission of requests) of the Convention on Mutual Assistance in Criminal Matters between Member States of the European Union [2000] OJ C 197/1 and Articles 4 (channels of communication) and 8 (procedure) of the Second Additional Protocol to the European Convention on Mutual Assistance in Criminal Matters, 2001.
25 [2014] OJ L 130/1.
26 For detailed consideration of the EEW and the EIO, see Ryan (2014) *Towards a System of European Criminal Justice: The Problem of Admissibility of Evidence*. London: Routledge.
27 Council Act of 29 May 2000 establishing in accordance with Article 34 of the Treaty on European Union the Convention on Mutual Assistance in Criminal Matters between the Member States of the European Union, (2000/C 197/01) OJ 12.7.2000.
28 2002/187/JHA OJ 6.3.2002 amended by Council Decision 2009/426/JHA on the strengthening of Eurojust. OJ L 138/14 16.12.2009.
29 Art 86 TFEU.
30 The European Delegated Prosecutors shall be active members of the public prosecution service or equivalent [judicial] authority of the Member States which nominated them. (Art 15.2 Regulation).
31 See Dail Debates, 23 October 2013; the motion by Dep. Paul Keoghwas carried that the Proposal for a Council Regulation on the establishment of the European Public Prosecutor's Office (COM (2013) 534) does not comply with the principle of subsidiarity (i.e. necessity and proportionality).
32 The measures were put forward in European Council Resolution on a Roadmap for strengthening procedural rights of suspected or accused persons in criminal proceedings, [2009] OJ C 295/1 30.11.2009.
33 In addition to the Roadmap measures, with the coming into force of the Lisbon Treaty, the EU Charter on Fundamental Rights was incorporated into the EU legal order (Art 6 (1) TEU). It should also be noted that since December 2014, the jurisdiction of the Court of Justice of the EU extends to matters relating to justice allowing it to rule *inter alia* on actions brought by a Member State and by individuals, and to give preliminary rulings following a request by national courts on the interpretation of Union Law (Art 19(3) TEU). Potentially, this may lead to an increased reliance on the Charter. Four articles of the Charter relate to justice, (47–50): a right to effective remedy and a fair trial; presumption of innocence and right of defence; principles of legality and proportionality of criminal offences and penalties; and the right not to be tried or punished twice in criminal proceedings for the same criminal offence. While the Charter reflects many of the rights enshrined in the ECHR and provides that 'the meaning and scope of those rights shall be the same' as those laid down by the ECHR, it states that it 'shall not prevent Union law providing more extensive protection' (Art 52(3) Charter).
34 Directive 2010/64/EU of the European Parliament and of the Council on the right to interpretation and translation in criminal proceedings, [2010] OJ L 280/1 26.10.2010; deadline for transposition: 27/10/2013; Ireland and the UK opted to apply the Directive; the costs of interpretation and translation are to be met by the Member States concerned; the Directive applies to domestic and cross-border cases. The Directive was transposed in Ireland by S.I. No. 565/2013 – European Communities Act 1972 (Interpretation and Translation in Criminal Proceedings) Regulations, 2013 and S.I. No. 564 of 2013 – European Communities Act 1972 (Interpretation and Translation for Persons in Custody in Garda Síochána Stations) Regulations, 2013; in Northern Ireland it is awaiting transposition following consultation on a draft Code: www.dojni.gov.uk/index/public-consultations/archive-consultations/pace-code-c-_nov-2014_-consultation-draft.pdf (last accessed 1 March 2015).
35 Directive 2012/13/EU of the European Parliament and of the Council on the right to information in criminal proceedings [2012] OJ L 142/1 1.6.2012; deadline for transposition: 2/6/2014; transposed in Northern Ireland by The Police and Criminal Evidence (1989 Order) (Codes of Practice) (Revision of Codes C and H) Order (Northern Ireland) 2014 no 134. While it is noted on the Irish Department of Justice website that Ireland notified the European Commission of its transposition of the Directive

on 5 June 2014, no statutory instrument has been published (www.justice.ie/en/JELR/Pages/EU_directives). It is apparent from the National Implementing Measures for the Directive listed on the EU legislative database (http://eur-lex.europa.eu) that Ireland's method of transposition has been to simply refer to existing legislation, the Criminal Justice Act 1984, and its accompanying custody regulations. No amendments to reflect transposition of the Directive have been made to these instruments.

36 Art 7. Exceptions noted in Art. 7(4) include where the life or fundamental rights of another person may be at risk, where it might prejudice ongoing investigations or where there are national security implications.

37 Directive 2013/48/EU of the European Parliament and of the Council on the right of access to a lawyer [2013] OJ L 294/1 6.11.2013; Transposition deadline: 27 November 2016.

38 *Salduz v Turkey* [GC] 36391/02 ECHR 2008.

39 *DPP v Gormley & White* [2014] IESC 17.

40 Art 3(3)(b).

41 Ibid. Recital 25.

42 *Gormley & White* above.

43 For France, see Blackstock, J. *et al.* (2014) *Inside Police Custody: An Empirical Account of Suspects' Rights in Four Jurisdictions.* Intersentia; England and Wales and Northern Ireland already provide for presence of a lawyer during police questioning: PACE Code C 6.7; for Ireland, see Department of Justice (2013b) *Report of Working Group to advise on a system providing for the presence of a legal representative during Gardaí interviews.* p. 26. Available at: www.justice.ie/en/JELR/Pages/Report_Final_15_July_Leg (accessed 17 December 2014).

44 The new scheme is available at www.legalaidboard.ie (accessed March 2015).

45 *Report of Working Group* (n45).

46 Brussels, 27.11.2013 COM (2013) 821 final.

47 Proposal for Measures on special safeguards for children and vulnerable adults suspected or accused in criminal proceedings COM/2013/822 final.

48 A total of 26 cases from Jan 2007–Dec 2012, noted in Proposal for Directive on Presumption of Innocence Brussels, 27.11.2013 COM (2013) 821 final.

49 See *Allenet de Ribemont v France* 15175/89 10/2/1995 ECtHR, (statements made at a press conference by minister of interior and police officials).

50 Art 6(3) Proposal for Directive on Presumption of Innocence (n50).

51 A similar inadmissibility rule was opposed during negotiations on the directive on access to a lawyer. See Ryan (n26).

52 Criminal Justice Act 2007 s.30; Criminal Justice Act 1984, ss.15, 16, 18, 19.

53 Council Framework decision 2009/299/ JHA amending FDs 2002/584/JHA, 2005/214/JHA, 2008/909/JHA and 2008/947/JHA, thereby enhancing the procedural rights of persons and fostering the application of the principle of mutual recognition to decisions rendered in the absence of the person concerned at the trial. OJ L 81/2727.3.2009.

54 Art 9 Proposal for Directive on Presumption of Innocence (n50).

55 FD 2009/829/JHA OJ L214/20 11.11.2009.

56 Art 9.

57 See examples in *A Guide to the European Supervision Order* (2012) *Fair Trials International* www.fairtrials.org/publications/training/esoguide/doc (accessed 27 July 2015).

58 Government Legislative Programme Spring–Summer 2015. Available at: http://taoiseach.ie/eng/Taoiseach_and_Government/Government_Legislation_Programme/Government_Legislative_Programme_Spring_Summer_2015.pdf (accessed 27 July 2015).

59 Council Framework Decision 2008/909/JHA on the application of the principle of mutual recognition to judgments in criminal matters imposing custodial sentences or measures involving deprivation of liberty for the purpose of their enforcement in the European Union OJ L 327/27 5.12.2008.

60 Council Framework Decision 2008/947/JHA on the application of mutual recognition to judgments and probation decisions with a view to the supervision of probation measures and alternative sanctions. OJ L 337/102 16.12.2008.

61 Government Legislation Programme Spring–Summer 2015.

62 Europa Press Release 5/03/2013.

63 Directive 2011/99/EU OJ L 338/2 21.12.2011.

64 Directive 2012/29/EU OJ L 315/57 14.11.2012; replacing the earlier Council Framework Decision 2001/220/JHA, OJ L 82/1 22.3.2001, expanding and improving it.

65 Regulation (EU) 606/2013 on mutual recognition of protection measures in civil matters OJ L 181/12 29.6.2013.
66 Ibid. Recital 8; its legal basis, as a civil law measure, falls under the field of judicial co-operation in civil matters and has a different treaty basis (Art 81 TFEU).
67 See statement by Phil Prendergast Labour Party press release, 13.12. 2011; The Non-fatal Offences against the Person Act 1997 makes provision for the criminal court to impose an order prohibiting approach of a victim on a person, even where they have not been convicted of the harassment offence under the Act; the order under s. 10 was described in *DPP v Ramachachadran* [2000] 2 IR 307 as 'an order in the nature of an injunction'– therefore an equitable remedy.
68 Directive 2012/29/EU Art 20.
69 Ibid. Art 10.
70 Ibid. Art 13; see further on role of victim in continental proceedings, Ryan (n26).
71 As observed by both Ashworth (1998) and Douglas-Scott (2008–09), the danger is that the use of this term can marginalise fundamental rights and freedom.
72 Since the Lisbon Treaty changes, the Charter now has the same legal value as the Treaties, rendering it justiciable for the first time. The provisions of the Charter are addressed primarily to the institutions of the Union, and it is important to note it applies to Members States 'only when they are implementing Union law'.
73 Presentation by Dr. Gavin Barrett to the discussion on 'The Oireachtas and the European Union', to Joint Committee on European Union Affairs, Houses of Oireachtas Committee Debates 10.10.2013; available at http://oireachtasdebates.oireachtas.ie/Debates%20Authoring/DebatesWebPack.nsf/committee takes/EUJ2013101000003?opendocument (accessed 17 December 2014).

25

Neo-liberalism, crime and punishment

Barry Vaughan

Introduction

Criminologists may believe that they have harboured some intrinsic truths about neo-liberalism which have only recently been revealed to the public at large. Many people have attributed the onset and severity of the Great Recession to the unregulated freedoms afforded to those manoeuvring complex products in the financial sphere. Even within the Republic of Ireland, there are many who believe that 'light-touch' regulation of the financial sector brought about the downfall of banks and, through the government's guarantee underwriting these institutions, the financial stability of the state. People have experienced considerable austerity thanks to the Irish state's efforts to win back the confidence of the bond markets through prolonged efforts of fiscal consolidation.

Whatever pains and turmoil citizens have suffered due to the scaling back of state spending, criminologists might suggest that it is a weak reflection of the constraints and deprivations brought about by neo-liberalism in the penal sphere. Some influential criminologists have attributed the sustained increase in prison populations and a general coarsening of public sentiment regarding offenders to the ascendancy of neo-liberalism (Wacquant, 2009, 2010).

A common definition of neo-liberalism involves the up-rooting of economic structures from the social relations in which they were embedded and the degradation of collective structures which may impede a market logic based on individualism (Bourdieu, 1998). Often this is associated with a 'rolling-back' of the state. However, for Wacquant (2009, 2010), neo-liberalism is not simply an economic regime whereby the state withdraws from one of its primary roles as collective provider. Instead, there is an explicit re-engineering of the state whereby it embraces two fundamental tasks of: (a) disciplinary welfare or 'workfare' which imposes an obligation to search for and take employment as a condition of receipt of social security payments and (b) punitive prison-fare which both sweeps up those unable or unwilling to adapt to this new economic order of poorly paid precarious employment and erects an insidious alternative of punishment. Emphasising the trope of individual responsibility provides the cultural glue to bind these two tasks together. There is a classic functional argument here in that the latter actions of authoritarianism are there to reinforce the changing features of welfare and to discipline and govern those marginal populations who are unwilling to take up employment, however lowly-paid. Therefore, it is neo-liberalism as a political project that has led to the 'authoritarian state' which maintains the gilded liberty of the few through the intensification of control of the many.

Others have disputed the general applicability of this thesis about the influence of neo-liberalism on the penal sphere. They have queried whether it over-generalises from the American experience of mass incarceration and is not appreciative enough of important institutional and cultural differences that may impede the spread of punitiveness (Lacey, 2008). Other countries have managed to maintain a more inclusive welfare and criminal justice system than that outlined by Wacquant (2009, 2010). Lacey (2008) considers that any adequate explanation of punitiveness, both in the US and elsewhere, must rely on a more finely-grained analysis of the political and institutional factors that condition social relations rather than rely on some monolithic concept such as neo-liberalism which does not have the near-universal relevance often attributed to it. Lacey (2008) relies on what is termed the 'varieties of capitalism' literature with its distinction between 'liberal-market economies' and 'co-ordinated market economies', the argument being that the latter institutional features help to foster penal moderation.

This chapter opened with a brief thumbnail sketch of the most prominent criminological exponent of neo-liberalism and its effects as well as mentioning one of Wacquant's most influential critics. This was done as an orienting device as the author was initially tempted to follow this schema of elaborating and then critiquing Wacquant from the perspective of Irish developments. One could, for example, query whether we have ever had an activist version of workfare in the Republic of Ireland as opposed to a system that is arguably over-reliant on passive transfers (see National Economic and Social Council, 2011).

While such a paper would be valid, mainly in that it would be alive to the importance of jurisdictional differences (this is the principal reason why this chapter concentrates on the Republic of Ireland rather than encompassing developments in Northern Ireland as well), it would suffer from certain limitations. Principally, it would accept the driving role of neo-liberalism within the penal sphere and would essentially be concerned with questioning how deeply its punitive effects had seeped into the criminal justice system. If one was to take Wacquant's account of neo-liberalism as a starting point, the task would then become one of complicating a general portrayal, pointing to overlooked details and features in the particular case of the Republic of Ireland. Thus we start with an explanandum – an alleged rise in punitiveness and increases in the prison population – and seek an explanans, be it neo-liberalism, cultures of control or late modernity (see Garland (2001) for such an approach). Even those who seek to dispute the explanatory force of a category like neo-liberalism, such as Lacey (2008), are essentially on the defensive, pointing out factors that merely moderate punitiveness but do not substantially dispute it.

We would do well to remember Braithwaite's (2003) criticism of Garland's (2001) 'culture of control' thesis, namely that it was a specific narrative about a punishment of the poor project masquerading as a more general depiction of punishment. Not only does this kind of project conflate the particular with the general by ignoring how business is regulated, it also neglects how these practices might moderate the punitiveness being depicted.

Braithwaite's (2003) critique is that whereas Garland (2001) saw the demise of the penal-welfare model as occurring at the hands of neo-liberal models that come from the private sector, many of them actually come from what Braithwaite (2003) labels the regulatory state: institutions established to oversee activities within the private sector. The upshot is that many of the innovations that Garland (2001) sees as occurring for the first time in the criminal justice sphere – restitution, responsibilisation – have been long-standing features in the world of business regulation. There are two important considerations arising from this critique. The first is a general scepticism about the prevalence of neo-liberalism – Braithwaite (2005) goes so far as to label its ascendancy a 'fairy-tale' – since rather than seeing the privatisation of the public, we are witnessing the publicisation of the private whereby state and other powerful actors are increasingly becoming the object of regulation. This hypothesis could be supported with reference to developments in the Republic of Ireland such as the continuing reform of police oversight as well as the monitoring and regulation of crimes like those perpetrated against the environment that had previously been overlooked (Vaughan and Kilcommins, 2010).

A second consideration, which this chapter will develop, is that we can be more cognisant of the complexity of the present if we open our eyes to alternative modes of regulation and see how they intertwine with more traditional models of regulation operative in the criminal justice sphere. Regulatory models influenced by neo-liberalism might be influencing the *modus operandi* of parts of the criminal justice system. In this vein, it can be suggested that indeed we should take neo-liberalism seriously but that the expansion of the prison population might not be the best place to scrutinise its effects. Although penal expansionism is commonly assumed in the criminological literature, when one examines the definition of neo-liberalism, there is no immediate affinity between it and an increasing reliance on imprisonment.

Harcourt (2010) suggests that a defining feature of neo-liberalism is equating the efficiency of the markets with a natural order which sustains and regulates itself and from which governments should keep their distance (a corollary is that governments can legitimately intervene in the penal sphere). O'Malley (2008) agrees that neo-liberalism underlines the role of economic markets as models for social order and that there is an affirmation of individual responsibility and an emphasis on cost-effective, pragmatic government – what works – rather than 'big' government *per se*.

So a plausible starting point for examining the effects of neo-liberalism upon punishment is to analyse the implications of conceiving of the market as the model for social order upon the conception and distribution of criminal sanctions. There is an influential school of thought, known as the law and economics movement, which does precisely this. Becker (1968) was one of the pioneering scholars behind this movement who argued that economics has an application beyond explicit markets and applied economic precepts in relation to punishment. Posner (1985) took up his lead and defined the function of criminal law in a capitalist society as discouraging people from bypassing the market; the threat of punishing pushes up the price of contemplated crimes, making them less likely to be committed and impelling actors to use normal market methods to get what they want. The crucial point is that this is not deterrence as it is normally understood; it is not marked by a commitment to a particular 'substantive' moral order. Instead, the objective of the criminal law is to 'promote economic efficiency' (ibid.: 1195).

This way of thinking finds support from others. For example, the exponents of the theme of 'actuarial justice' note that a moral way of thinking about the individual is being replaced by analysis based on social utility that places an emphasis on the management of incidents and public safety. Such management relies on replacing notions of individual responsibility with those based on strict liability and no-fault doctrines. Feeley and Simon (1992: 455) go on to state that the focus of such doctrines is about

> [I]dentifying and managing unruly groups. It is concerned with the rationality not of individual behaviour or even community organisation, but of managerial processes. Its goal is not to eliminate crime but to make it tolerable through systemic coordination.

In a later paper, Feeley (2006: 221) went on to say that, from the perspective of actuarial justice, 'minor criminal offences were much like fender benders: both are problems to be managed, not moral lapses for which one is to be held accountable. … Events happen and the task is to manage the aftermath effectively and efficiently'. Neo-liberalism then defines criminal incidents as events that need to be managed efficiently rather than actions that require dramatic punishment.

If the goal of neo-liberal doctrines is to manage the flow of offending and minimise disruption, then mechanisms other than imprisonment, such as fines, might be an important means of doing this. Based on an economic analysis, one would expect that imprisonment would be used sparingly and only matched to the most serious offences. Becker (1968: 193) pronounced that 'social welfare is increased if fines are used *whenever feasible*' [italics in original]. Posner (1985) cautions against sanction inflation when he warns that, if the penalty for carelessly injuring someone in an automobile were death, people would drive too slowly or not at all, thereby reducing overall utility. And the converse also holds: 'in cases where tort remedies are an adequate deterrent ... there is no need to invoke criminal penalties' (ibid.: 1204). Posner (1985) does make the distinction between tort damages and criminal fines, noting that the latter are usually more probable and involve more stigma. As one scholar put it, 'criminal law exclusively imposes sanctions, while tort law sometimes prices an activity' (Cooter (1984) quoted in Simons, 2008: 723). But, if the criminal law is partly based on a neo-liberal world view, which is premised on the maximisation of economic efficiency or social utility, then it may be hard to maintain these distinctions, when the end is all important.

On this view, criminal law could become more like tort law and vice versa so that 'everything is contingent ... and all is up for grabs' (Simons, 2008: 731). Becker (1968), the doyen of the law and economics school of thought, thought the same. He considered that the primary aim of all legal proceedings should become the same: not punishment or deterrence, but simply the assessment of the harm done by defendants. The net result would be that much of traditional criminal law would become a branch of the law of torts (Becker, 1968). If this is the case, then many of the distinctions that allegedly hold the two apart might be weakened, such as the existence of intentionality or *mens rea*, the reliance on criminal as opposed to civil procedure, the stigmatising effect of criminal penalties and so on. Returning to the example above, the distinction between the sanctioning and pricing of an activity might break down. It will be argued that this is the case with reference to monetary sanctions or fines which are a neo-liberal 'punishment' *par excellence*.

The fine is an unjustly neglected phenomenon in criminological theorising (but see O'Malley, 2009) with attention devoted more to those penalties that work on the body or psyche of the offender. Thanks to this oversight, it is believed that the work of criminal justice is fundamentally about changing or 'correcting' the offender. If we were to pay more attention to fines or monetary sanctions, we might see that this is not the case. Rather, one might see criminal justice as a process that regulates the flows and distributions of unwanted actions rather than extirpating illegal acts. The net effect is that criminal justice has become, in part, a monetised risk-management system. This result, rather than an alleged rise in imprisonment, may be the most important consequence of neo-liberalism within the criminal justice system.

This point will be underlined by reference to two phenomena: the regulation of traffic offences, which due to their volume may matter more than any other form of intervention by criminal justice agents (O'Malley, 2010a), and the work of the Criminal Assets Bureau (CAB) in confiscating the proceeds of crime. Although the latter has cultivated more commentary, it can be argued that there is a similar dynamic at work in both, namely avoidance of imprisonment, for various reasons, and the reliance on other sanctions and mechanisms that do not involve judicial sanctioning and incarceration.

A road more travelled

To emphasise the prominence of the fine in the panoply of criminal sanctions, it is worth looking at how extensively it is used.[1] In the combined statistics from the Dublin and provincial Circuit Courts for 2012 (Courts Service, 2013), fines were resorted to 97 times out of 8,822 sanctions handed down, which amounts to 1 per cent of all sanctions handed down in these higher courts. In the District Court, fines were handed down in 82,371 cases which amount to 48 per cent of all sanctions dispensed in this court in 2012. In contrast, sanctions of imprisonment and probation or community service combined each represented a little less than 11 per cent respectively of sanctions exercised by District Court judges.[2] And when one examines the nature of offences coming before the District Court, approximately 60 per cent are related to road traffic offences (the next most common offence relates to public order and assault). And in the case of traffic violations, the fine is the most commonly deployed sanction – handed down in 58 per cent of those offences which are prosecuted successfully – although 45 per cent of cases for road traffic offences are struck out. It would seem then that the most commonly used sanction is the fine: it significantly outnumbers the total number of sentences of imprisonment (21,109) and those relating to community service and probation (18,747) handed down in the Irish state in 2012.

However, it is also the case that many road traffic offences are resolved without ever having to resort to courtroom procedures and that the volume of these cases is significantly higher than those appearing before the courts. For example, the Comptroller and Auditor General (2013) reported that during 2011 and 2012, almost 850,000 road traffic offences resulted in the issuing of fixed charge notices. Fixed charge fines were paid within 56 days of issue of the notice in respect of around 71 per cent of the fixed charge penalty notices issued in 2011 and 2012, i.e. there were just over 300,000 fines paid for traffic related offences in 2012, far outweighing the numbers appearing in official court statistics. In about 21 per cent of cases, fines were not paid and court proceedings were initiated (about 7 per cent were terminated before this stage). However, half of the cases that proceeded to summons stage were struck out in court because the related summonses had not been served. In 2011–12, this amounted to 93,500 summons with a potential revenue loss of €7.4m (Garda Inspectorate, 2014: 24).

In reaction to this and other inefficiencies rooted in the discretionary powers of the police, the Garda Inspectorate (2014) has proposed a new system of enforcing road traffic offences to make it more streamlined and less susceptible to manipulation. At the scene of the detection, a garda would request a new driving licence which contains a microchip with all of the driver's personal information. A garda member would scan the licence on a hand-held device and enter the vehicle registration number. This new system would simultaneously and automatically interface with all electronic government databases for verification of the information and any warrants or other information the detecting garda should be made aware of, including driving licence suspensions, car tax arrears, penalty point accumulations and unpaid fines (ibid.: 53).

Not only did the Inspectorate propose streamlining the current system by installing a greater element of automaticity into it, but they also recommended circumventing the criminal process to a much greater extent than before. For example, the Inspectorate recommended that a Criminal Justice Working Group should review the 454 fixed charge offences currently listed and make recommendations on whether certain offences should be designated for adjudication through an administrative process, rather than further congest the local district courts (ibid.: 28). This recommendation had previously been made by the Courts Service (2008: 2) which had opined that one of the objectives of the fixed charge penalty system was to keep cases out of the courts but that this was 'not working'. The Courts Service (2014: 6) has repeated this complaint that the number of people appearing before the courts on road traffic offences is putting a 'great strain' on the system, and 'imaginative ways' should be found to avoid this scenario.

If the proposals of the Garda Inspectorate are implemented, it would represent two significant developments in keeping with the principles of neo-liberalism. The first would be what O'Malley (2009), building on Deleuze (1995), calls the moment of the 'dividual'. Justice in the twentieth century has been considered to operate on the 'individual', seeking to seep into his mental calculations for the purposes of either deterrence or rehabilitation and to effect a change towards a more law-abiding citizen. In Foucault's (1977) terminology, individualised justice would work on the soul of the offender in a 'disciplinary' fashion with intervention modulated to the individual circumstances of the person. This was the ideal at least. But neo-liberal interventions in the field of criminal regulation offer something quite different. Neo-liberal justice deals with a particular aspect of the individual, in this instance a licence holder of a vehicle rather than the whole person. And in the vision of the Garda Inspectorate, this 'dividual' is dissolved and connected, through a licence's microchip, into an electronic flow between all government databases as a search is initiated for any further infractions. Even the apex of sanctioning for traffic-related offences, the automatic disqualification of driving for six months upon accumulation of 12 penalty points, does not involve any explicit work of intervention or correction of the offender. Rather, the offender is simply removed from the flow of traffic.

There is a reason why neo-liberal justice disavows concern with the individual, and that is because the person is not significant in his or her own right but, instead, only matters as part of a potentially risky flow of objects – in this instance, automated vehicles – and the primary concern is with the prudential circulation of this flow. In some ways, prudentialism governs the response since the sheer volume of traffic makes individually intensive intervention impracticable.

The payment of monetary sanctions or fines is crucial in this regard. It has long been recognised that fines are deployed where an action is unwanted, but there is no driving imperative to extinguish it, i.e. the action is to be managed (O'Malley, 2010b). But money not only helps to embed a neo-liberal or marketised conception of justice; it also accentuates it. Since there is no explicit 'disciplining' of the body or soul, exacting monetary penalties excites few qualms in the way that the deprivation of liberty does. Fines point to a form of streamlined justice, away from the courtroom with its attendant procedural safeguards and toward a flow of justice dominated by efficiencies as the Garda Inspectorate (2014) report makes clear.

And this point is the second potentially major ramification of neo-liberalism upon criminal justice in the Republic of Ireland. The operation of the present fixed charge notice system is predicated on keeping cases out of court even though a court summons automatically issues if the fine is not paid after a 56-day period. The prospect of having one's penalty points doubled after conviction in court – from two to four – is meant to diminish this possibility, but various inefficiencies in the system mitigate against this, such as inadequate record-keeping and non-issuing of summonses (Courts Service, 2008). This dissuasive element is intended to encourage people to accept their fate as bearers of a driver's licence rather than argue their fate in court as an individual. Even though, in this instance, the currency of justice is not money but gradations of constraints on one's freedom as a driver, there is still a potentially heavier price to be paid if one wishes to have justice meted out in a courtroom. As O'Malley (2010b: 378) notes, 'it is not the generalised freedom of the liberal subject, but a specific incapacitation of the *licensed dividual* that creates the risk [italics in original]'.

The ideal, as in the Garda Inspectorate's (2014) report, would be for the human element of justice, in the form of the judge, to be diminished and for fines to be calculated and issued via digital technology. If this comes to pass, we would have gone beyond Weber's dystopian vision of the judge operating as a vending machine into which pleadings are inserted and judgments disgorged with reasons derived from a Code (Rheinstein, 1954). Rather, justice would become fully automated with human intervention reserved for those willing to pay the heavier price to argue their individual case before a judge.

The second exemplar of neo-liberalism within the criminal justice sphere, that of the Criminal Assets Bureau, is not characterised by as much automaticity as the penalty points system but is, in its own way, as dispassionate and accepting of crime as the case of traffic policing.

Asset pricing and stripping

The Criminal Assets Bureau was introduced following the killings of the journalist Veronica Guerin and Garda Detective Jerry McCabe in 1996. Guerin had been at the forefront of a campaign to publicise the activity of various criminals, which attached to them monikers such as the 'Monk' and the 'Boxer' amongst others. Whilst this portrayal plundered criminality for its entertainment value, Guerin's murder lent a more menacing appearance to criminals. Compelled by relentless media calls for action against organised crime, the Government passed two significant pieces of legislation: the Proceeds of Crime Act 1996 and the Criminal Assets Bureau 1996.

The Criminal Assets Bureau (CAB) consists of a grouping of members of the Garda Síochána (Irish Police), revenue officials (both from the Customs and Taxation branches), social welfare officers and lawyers. It was established to target the proceeds of any and all types of criminal activity and where possible to forfeit these proceeds to the State. It is most well known for its capacities to confiscate, seize or freeze assets deriving or being suspected as deriving from criminal activity. In doing so, the legislation authorises the confiscation of property in the absence of a criminal conviction; permits the introduction of hearsay evidence; lowers the threshold of proof to the balance of probabilities; and requires a party against whom an order is made to produce evidence in relation to his or her property and income to rebut the suggestion that they are derived from the proceeds of crime. Concerns have been raised about each of these features, based on the fact that a criminal process is being driven forward by civil means, thus depriving suspects of many of the protections that would exist in the criminal sphere proper. In addition to forfeiture powers, CAB also relies extensively on using its revenue powers to ensure that the proceeds of criminal activity are subjected to tax and that revenue acts are fully applied to such proceeds.

This use of revenue powers against the proceeds of criminal activity represents quite a turn-around in attitudes and practices. In 1929 in the case of *Hayes v Duggan*,[3] the Supreme Court held that profits derived from criminal activities were not lawfully taxable – because it would be immoral to benefit from such activity – and this remained case law in the Republic of Ireland until the early 1980s. This prohibition on the taxation of illegal earnings was ended by section 19 of the Finance Act 1983. One of the motives behind the enactment of such legislation was that the arsenal of the Revenue Commissioner could help in 'clearing up some of the big criminal operators' and 'putting them out of business altogether'.[4] However, one politician noted that the putative use of such legislation represented an 'acceptance and blessing of such illegal activities'.[5] Section 19 has now been replaced by the Taxes Consolidation Act 1997 which stipulates that profit or gains shall be taxable even if the source is unknown or unlawful. In addition, the Disclosure of Certain Information for Taxation and Other Purposes Act 1996 enables the Revenue Commissioners to pass on information about gains from suspected criminal activity to the Gardaí. CAB is enabled to utilise both the proceeds of crime route and the taxation route and can also utilise the criminal law through section 1078 of the Taxes Consolidation Act whereby an offender can be dealt with on indictment. A custodial sentence is not considered appropriate if there is full settlement, but it does appear to have the effect of putting additional pressure on people to settle with CAB (Staines, 2004). In other words, the criminal courtroom is a means to an end rather than an end in itself.

The chief concern raised about CAB's work, that it is substantively a criminal process masquerading in civil means, has been largely disregarded by the Irish judiciary. For example, in the case of *Gilligan v Murphy*[6] one of the considerations was the argument that 'the scheme by which property could be "expropriated" by the State as set out in the Act of 1996 would lead to the conclusion that the proceedings were of a criminal nature' (sec. 3.4). However, Feeney J., the judge in the case, rejected this assertion and raised the following points to conclude that the process is civil rather than penal: the legislation is directed against property (i.e. *in rem*) rather than against a defendant or respondent (*in personam*); the proceedings are heard by a civil court, and a defendant's or respondent's guilt is not in issue; and the proceedings can lead to no criminal conviction or any finding of guilt or the imposition of any sentence. Feeney J. went on to cite Scottish jurisprudence to the effect that deprivation of property by an entity like CAB could have no penal character to it because the person in possession had no right to hold that property. In its Annual Report for 2011, CAB construed these findings as meaning that

> A Section 4 Order is not, in any normal sense, an Order of forfeiture as there is no element of a Respondent losing or giving up something as a penalty or of something being taken as a penalty for an offence. The grant of a Disposal Order under Section 4 is not in the true or proper sense a penalty or forfeiture. *The taking of property under the PoC* [Proceeds of Crime] *Act is not and cannot be equated with a punishment* [my italics].[7]

It is here that we can see the affinity with Posner's (1985) marketised or neo-liberal view of justice. People who have profited from illegal activities have, in effect, bypassed the market; therefore, the function of criminal justice is to restore the status quo ante and, because it is depriving people of assets over which they have no legitimate claim, it cannot be construed as punishment. This has two implications: first, there is little concern with the individual offender in terms of meting out a sanction to effect behavioural change; and second, if punishment is not a concern, then there is no obvious reason why the criminal courtroom should be the locus for dispensing justice (with the consequence that embedded due process safeguards do not apply).

If the concern of the penalty points system was with one particular feature of the individual – his or her driving record – the work of CAB is only concerned with the individual as an ancillary to his or her assets. Action is directed *in rem* [against the property] rather than *in personam* [against the person]. As the judgment above makes clear, the respondent's guilt is not an issue or concern. Accordingly, the traditional modality of criminal justice – ascription of responsibility through a judicial process – simply does not figure. Individuals are not there to be deterred or rehabilitated; rather, they are meant to be neutralised. The end result is that neo-liberal justice transforms 'person punishment into threat neutralisation, and criminal law into criminal administration' (Dubber, 2002: 150). From the perspective of this kind of administrative justice, offenders are viewed as the 'subordinates or carriers' (Bottoms, 1983) of criminal activity and its rewards, and it is these assets which are the main object of CAB's attention. It is not surprising then that questions of culpability are never addressed and criminal actions become 'offences of inadvertence' (Walker, 1980) whereby people can be served with tax audits with no concern as to why payments have been minimised or not made at all. The state of mind of the offender does not come into the equation.

The purpose of CAB is 'disruption and discouragement rather than elimination of criminal activity through enforcement of the criminal law' (Barrett, 2007: 229). In other words, it undertakes acts of regulation. A feature of regulatory strategies is their

> [A]cceptance of the normality of crime: hence Felson's well known characterization of crime as a normal social 'fact of everyday life'. This worldview tends towards a larger culture of 'managing crime' rather than responding to it as aberrant or to be suppressed.
> (*Ashworth and Zedner, 2008: 39*)

Prioritising the management rather than suppression of crime has crucial consequences for determining where and how it is handled. A regulatory approach sees little point in persecuting and prosecuting criminals to the bitter end of imprisonment and is conscious of the obstacles to doing so. Accordingly, agents of control may be more sceptical about the value of a criminal trial as the most appropriate venue for managing the problem of 'crime'. Instead, the police respond to the burden of crime by trying to disrupt its occurrence through seizures and audits rather than eliminate it through large-scale imprisonment.

The principal objection to CAB's *modus operandi* is that it represents a 'tooling up' (Lea, 2004: 82) of the state's weaponry in the fight against crime to the extent that criminal and civil distinctions are being fundamentally blurred. Opponents of CAB's methods allege that even though it employs civil means, its function is fundamentally punitive or retributive (Hamilton, 2007), but because CAB pursues its work in the civil sphere, the procedural safeguards are lessened to the detriment of the person concerned. That said, even though the Courts have generally approved how CAB operates, they have queried how it has operated in particular instances. For example, in the case of *Keogh v CAB*,[8] the Supreme Court noted that Keogh was left 'in the dark as to his rights' in relation to a tax settlement. And in the case of *Criminal Assets Bureau v KB*,[9] the Supreme Court agreed with the defendant that there was not sufficient time to mount a defence, as CAB had seized all relevant records which were necessary to make a case (see Campbell, 2006).

However, there are also downsides in stating that the forfeiture of assets does not represent a sanction and that the claiming of tax is simply what the revenue authorities do to ensure compliance. Simply put, it is accepting of crime as a normal social fact with which the authorities must live with as best they can. This attitude was expressed many years ago in the English legal case of *Mann v Nash*[10] which centred on whether the profits from illegal gaming machines should be taxed. The judge considered and explicitly rejected the Irish case law deriving from *Hayes v Duggan*[11] and countered that:

> The Revenue representing the State, is merely looking at an accomplished fact. It is not condoning it; it has not taken part in it; it merely finds profits made from what appears to be a trade, and the Revenue laws happen to say that the profits made from trades have to be taxed, and they say: 'Give us the tax.'

'Give us the tax' could well serve as the motto of CAB in many instances, as it looks at crime as an 'accomplished fact'. But a problem arises when one considers Bentham's (1962) famous adage that a fine is a licence paid in arrears. Considered in this way, a tax audit (or seizure of assets) can be considered as part of the cost of criminal activity which can be weighed against the potential benefits to be derived from the activity in question. They become the price of crime stripped of moral meaning, condemnation or censure. And prices are what economics endorses as the best means of ensuring the optimal flow of goods and activities.

Towards a new architecture of risk?

Contra those who suggest that neo-liberalism is having its most significant effects upon the scale and reach of imprisonment as well as 'coarsening' other non-custodial sanctions, this chapter has tried to suggest otherwise. It has been argued that there is no necessary corollary between neo-liberalism and excessively punitive sanctions, and, in fact, neo-liberalism might well condone a smaller state (see the discussion by the renowned law and economics scholar Gary Becker in Harcourt, 2013). And to substantiate these points, two examples of how neo-liberalism might work in the criminal justice system within the Republic of Ireland were discussed along with their implications.

The three most important ramifications of neo-liberalism upon criminal justice are: (1) a relative acceptance of certain forms of crime; (2) a lack of interest in the 'individual' offender with much more focus dedicated toward the neutralisation of his or her actions; and (3) a certain scepticism about the efficacy and utility of court procedures. The upshot of these three developments, in the two examples analysed above, is that the courtroom is being circumvented, as criminal justice agents see little point in pursuing the traditional methodology of a police investigation that ends up in court for consideration of a custodial or community sanction. It is far more effective to bypass this complex labyrinth of procedure and require the suspect to 'come clean' thanks to more relaxed safeguards.

If this is the case, then it would have some important implications for how we think about change within the criminal justice system. For instance, Walsh (2007: 45) has suggested that with the increased powers granted to gardaí, courts are being presented with a *fait accompli*:

> The centre of gravity of decision-making in the criminal process is moving from the open transparency of the courtroom to the closed … cells of the Garda station. Judicial authorisation and control is being displaced rapidly by police discretion which is expanding and becoming increasingly remote from judicial or independent supervision.

There are perhaps two problems with this kind of analysis. The first is that traditional due process rights are still more vivid in the realm of real crime and its investigation, however strong the political urge to dilute them, than in the world of regulatory crimes. In no small part, this is due to the judicial tendency to uphold the vitality of individual rights against state incursions (Vaughan and Kilcommins, 2008). For example, in the recent case of *People (DPP) v Gormley*,[12] the Supreme Court underlined the necessity of a suspect having access to legal advice prior to legal interrogation in a police station. Previously, the legal position had been that if the Gardaí had made bona fide efforts to contact a solicitor, they were entitled to question the detained suspect. But the Supreme Court cited European Court of Human Rights (ECHR) jurisprudence (*Salduz v Turkey*[13]), which underlined that the defendant's rights would be 'irretrievably prejudiced' if incriminating statements were made without access to a lawyer and would constitute 'a trial otherwise than in due course of law'. This example underlines the potential of the judicial *habitus* (Vaughan and Kilcommins, 2008) to frustrate the executive's wishes to embark on a mission of unadulterated crime control without much reference to due process or, more grandly, the rule of law.

The second problem relates to Walsh's (2007) concern for the general freedom of the individual citizen. This may not be the issue with neo-liberal sanctions which do not necessarily focus on the whole person. Instead, it has been argued, following O'Malley (2009), they focus not on the individual, but on the 'dividual', a particular aspect of the person such as a licence-holder. In both instances of traffic policing and the work of CAB, very rarely is loss of liberty the state's response in managing risks. Rather, there is a specific incapacitation of some function of the person, be it in terms of licensed access to a vehicle or assets, which turns out to be a form of conditional freedom, as they are never constituted as inalienable rights. The person is not incapacitated, but is free to continue life largely unhindered, albeit without access to the vehicle or asset that was previously enjoyed. And as O'Malley (2010b: 378) says, the revocation of these freedoms 'generates little or none of the political angst that is associated with the liberal shibboleth of liberty'.

In part, this is because there is no corporeal punishment involved. And it is also because the flagrant behaviour of the person in question – having multiple penalty points or having ostentatious assets or properties – is seen to almost generate and draw down a response. In the case of traffic policing, those who argue for alternatives do not argue for other forms of punishment but often for better forms of control such as superior forms of road engineering that would render speeding and accidents less likely (O'Malley, 2013). In Deleuze's (1995) terms, this represents a 'society of control' immanently modulating risk by governing circulations and distributions anonymously (O'Malley, 2013) rather than a disciplinary mechanism, such as education, which acts to shape and change individual dispositions from the inside. It is this possibility that leads O'Malley (2013) to opine that digital justice, through electronic detection and payment, is not a necessary future. Rather, some form of engineering could operate as a more effective operator of 'mass preventive justice' and could better manage the flow of traffic and potential offending. Through this construction of a new architecture of risk, one might even move away from adjusting 'dividuals' and concentrate on modulating the aggregate flow of risks in a manner that is less conducive to offences being committed by individual persons.

Contemporary developments might push the society of control in even more radical directions that might minimise the very possibility of offending. Take the case of traffic offences first. Currently, the most significant development in the automobile industry is Google's development of driverless cars, although automobile companies such as Nissan are also developing models. The latter believe that they will be ready to bring an autonomous car to the market by 2020 (O'Brien, 2014). Applications also are being developed that would allow drivers to operate a hybrid model, allowing them to put cars on 'auto-pilot' as they see fit.

One should be wary of making breathless predictions of epochal change and imagining our roads being colonised by thousands of cars that can autonomously navigate traffic. Yet one should also recognise that this is more than a distinct possibility. For example, the British Government has announced that Milton Keynes will, from 2015, host a pilot project that will deliver self-driving 'pods' to carry passengers between destinations. The implications for criminological developments are obvious. If driverless cars become operative on a large scale, then this has the potential to reduce dramatically not only the number of accidents but also road violations such as speeding. To some – as yet unknowable extent – the possibility of offending would be increasingly minimised through design. Obviously there would be resistance to such developments, especially for a product such as the automobile that is sold on the basis of symbolic aspirations such as autonomy and freedom (one writer has predicted that driverless cars would elicit a backlash in the form of a 'National Rifle Association for car owners' (see Buss, 2014)). But for those who live in congested urban environments, being able to divest oneself of owning a car and being able to call on one whenever needed might be a blessing. If this latter scenario occurs, then it would represent the optimal means of managing the circulation and distribution of people whilst negating the attendant ill-effects (and far more effectively than the current system of traffic policing). One would have transitioned from digital justice to digital driving, as the police officer is effectively ever-resident within the automobile.

Contemporary developments in the economy may transform the policing of organised crime. The work of the Criminal Assets Bureau largely revolves around inquiring of suspects the provenance of their property or other assets: in effect, asking them to prove that they have been legitimately obtained. The suspicion is, of course, that they have often been illegitimately procured usually through the medium of 'dirty money' earned outside the arena of the legitimate market economy. CAB's regime of asset pricing and stripping is a form of ex-post control which, it is hoped, will deter others. But what if there was a way to pre-empt the possibility of such crimes, just like driverless cars may make many traffic offences largely a thing of the past?

The obvious way to do so would be to minimise as much as possible the use of physical money and rely on electronic payments, since organised crime has always been an intensive user of cash. In 1969, the US Treasury stopped issuing $500, $1,000, $5,000 and $10,000 bills specifically to impede crime syndicates – the only entities that were still using such large bills after the introduction of electronic money transfers (Lipow, 2010). The Republic of Ireland is the second-highest user of cash in the Euro-area. A National Payments Plan (Central Bank of Ireland, 2013) has been launched to encourage people to make use of electronic payments and move away from cash. This transition has been justified by the fact that it could reduce the size of the shadow economy, whereby people bypass the legitimate market *contra* Posner's (1985) injunction, and diminish the security risk that cash represents. If electronic payments become more prevalent, it would represent a more effective means of ensuring that people do not bypass the market than Posner's (1985) use of criminal law.

Potential developments in both the automobile industry and the monetary economy could transform what is currently a monetised risk-management model. Rather than rely on monetary sanctions to manage the flow of offending, possible changes in the architecture of risk in both fields could effectively forestall a great deal of offending. These are, of course, possibilities, and there is nothing pre-ordained about them. And like all technological developments, new possibilities for offending will open up as some are effectively diminished.

Given the centrality of both driving and payments for modern economies, it is inevitable that a neo-liberal tendency towards control, whereby the emphasis is on the aggregate management of flows and violations, will persist. And the kinds of development sketched above flow from this tendency in that they represent a more efficient means of managing to the extent that they could 'design out' a great deal of potential crime which could dispel some of the fatalism in previous neo-liberal iterations of control. However, there would be a price to be paid, and that would be in the currency of constrained choice. Whether this is a price worth paying for a potentially significant diminution of crime, only the general public can decide.

References

Ashworth, A. and Zedner, L. (2008) 'Defending the Criminal Law: Reflections on the Changing Character of Crime, Procedure, and Sanctions', *Criminal Law and Philosophy*, 2(1): 21–51.

Barrett, R. (2007) 'Proceedings Taken by the Criminal Assets Bureau', *Judicial Studies Institute Journal*, 2: 229–38.

Becker, G. (1968) 'Crime and Punishment: An Economic Approach', *Journal of Political Economy*, 76 (2): 169–217.

Bentham, J. (1962) *The Works of Jeremy Bentham, Vol 1*, J. Bowring (ed) New York: Russell and Russell.

Bottoms, A. E. (1983) 'Neglected Features of Contemporary Penal Systems', in D. Garland and P. Young (eds) *The Power to Punish*. Aldershot: Gower.

Bourdieu, P. (1998) 'The Essence of Neoliberalism', *Le Monde Diplomatique*, December, 1–6.

Braithwaite, J. (2003) 'What's Wrong with the Sociology of Punishment?', *Theoretical Criminology*, 7(1): 5–28.

Braithwaite, J. (2005) *Neoliberalism or Regulatory Capitalism*. RegNet Occasional Paper No 5. Canberra: Regulatory Institutions Network, Australian National University.

Buss, D. (2014) 'Google Jangles Auto Execs; But Will Driverless Cars Really Ever Happen?', *Forbes Magazine*, 30 June.

Campbell, L. (2006) 'Taxing Illegal Assets: The Revenue Work of the Criminal Assets Bureau', *Irish Law Times*, 24(20): 316–21.

Central Bank of Ireland (2013) *National Payments Plan: A Strategic Direction for Payments*. Dublin: Central Bank.

Comptroller and Auditor General (2013) *Report on the Account of the Public Services 2012*, Chapter 7: Management of the Fixed Charge Notice System. Available at: http://audgen.gov.ie/documents/annualreports/2012/report/en/Chapter07.pdf (accessed 3 September 2015).

Cooter, R. (1984) 'Prices and Sanctions', *Columbia Law Review*, 84(6): 1523–60.

Courts Service (2008) Submission by the Courts Service on the *Department of Transport Statement of Strategy 2008–2010*. Dublin: Court Service.

Courts Service (2013) *Annual Report 2012*. Dublin: Courts Service.

Courts Service (2014) *Annual Report 2013*. Dublin: Courts Service.

Deleuze, G. (1995) *Negotiations 1972–1990*. New York: Columbia University Press.

Dubber, M. (2002) 'Policing Possession: The War on Crime and the End of the Criminal Law', *Journal of Criminal Law and Criminology*, 91(4): 1–151.

Feeley, M. (2006) 'Origins of Actuarial Justice', in S. Armstrong and L. McAra (eds) *Perspectives on Punishment: The Contours of Control*. Oxford: Oxford University Press.

Feeley, M. and Simon, J. (1992) 'The New Penology: Notes on the Emerging Strategy of Corrections and Its Implications', *Criminology*, 30(4): 449–74.

Feeley, M. and Simon, J. (1995) 'True Crime: The New Penology and Public Discourse on Crime', in T. Blomberg and S. Cohen (eds) *Punishment and Social Control*. New York: Aldine de Gruyter.

Foucault, M. (1977) *Discipline and Punish: The Birth of the Prison*. London: Penguin.

Garda Inspectorate (2014) *The Fixed Charge Processing System – A 21st Century Strategy*. Dublin: Garda Inspectorate.

Garland, D. (2001) *The Culture of Control: Crime and Social Order in Contemporary Society*. Oxford: Oxford University Press.

Hamilton, C. (2007) *The Presumption of Innocence in Irish Criminal Law: Whittling the Golden Thread*. Dublin: Irish Academic Press.

Harcourt, B. (2010) 'Neoliberal Penality: A Brief Genealogy', *Theoretical Criminology*, 14(1): 1–19.

Harcourt, B. (2013) *Becker and Foucault on Crime and Punishment*. Public Law and Legal Theory Working Paper No. 440. Chicago: University of Chicago.

Lacey, N. (2008) *Prisoners Dilemma: Political Economy and Punishment in Contemporary Democracies*. Cambridge: Cambridge University Press.

Lea, J. (2004) 'Hitting Criminals Where It Hurts: Organised Crime and the Erosion of Due Process', *Cambrian Law Review*, 35: 81–96.

Lipow, J. (2010) 'Turn in Your Bin Ladens', *New York Times*, 17 December.

National Economic and Social Council (2011) *Supports and Services for Unemployed Jobseekers*. Dublin: NESC.

O'Brien, J. (2014) 'The Driverless Car Tipping Point Is Coming Soon'. Available at: http://mashable.com/2014/07/07/driverless-cars-tipping-point/ (accessed 25 July 2014).

O'Malley, P. (2008) 'Neo-Liberalism and Risk in Criminology', in T. Anthony and C. Cunneen (eds) *The Critical Criminology Companion*. Sydney: Federation Press.

O'Malley, P. (2009) 'Theorising Fines', *Punishment and Society*, 11(1): 67–83.

O'Malley, P. (2010a) 'Simulated Justice. Risk, Money and Telemetric Policing', *British Journal of Criminology*, 50(5): 795–807.

O'Malley, P. (2010b) 'Fines, Risks and Damages: Money Sanctions and Justice in Control Societies', *Current Issues in Criminal Justice*, 21(3): 365–81.

O'Malley, P. (2013) 'The Politics of Mass Preventive Justice', in A. Ashworth, L. Zedner and P. Tomlin (eds) *Prevention and the Limits of the Criminal Law*. Oxford: Oxford University Press.

Posner, R. (1985) 'An Economic Theory of the Criminal Law', *Columbia Law Review*, 85(6): 1193–231.

Rheinstein, M. (ed) (1954) *Max Weber on Law in Economy and Society*. Cambridge, MA: Harvard University Press.

Simons, K. W. (2008) 'The Crime/Tort Distinction: Legal Doctrine and Normative Perspectives', *Widener Law Journal*, 719–32.

Staines, M. (2004) 'Criminal Assets Bureau', *Law Society Criminal Law Committee Seminar*. 22 May. Available at: www.michaelstaines.ie/update/data/upimages/L-CRIMINAL_ASSETS_BUREAU-1.pdf (accessed 4 July 2014).

Vaughan, B. and Kilcommins, S. (2008) *Terrorism, Rights and the Rule of Law: Negotiating Justice in Ireland*. Cullompton: Willan.

Vaughan, B. and Kilcommins, S. (2010) 'The Governance of Crime and Negotiation of Justice', *Criminology and Criminal Justice*, 10 (1): 59–75.

Wacquant, L. (2009) *Punishing the Poor: The Neoliberal Government of Social Insecurity*. Durham, NC: Duke University Press.

Wacquant, L. (2010) 'Crafting the Neoliberal State: Workfare, Prisonfare and Social Insecurity', *Sociological Forum*, 25(2): 197–220.

Walker, N. (1980) *Punishment, Danger and Stigma*. London: Basil Blackwell.

Walsh, D. (2007) 'The Criminal Justice Act, 2006: A Crushing Defeat for Due Process Values', *Judicial Studies Institute Journal*, 7: 44–59.

Notes

1 In an ideal world, I would have traced the usage of fines over the decades to see if there have been any evident increases or reduction in how they have been administered. However, information on this issue is not available online before 2000, and even since then, information is not presented in a manner that would facilitate comparison in usage of sanctions. The Courts Service did not provide information on the type of sanctions handed down in the Circuit Court and did not disaggregate the use of probation from a generic category of 'other' which includes cases that were dismissed until 2005. In the District Courts between 2000–2007, the ratio of fines to sentences of imprisonment was typically in the ratio of 5.5:1.

2 About 21 per cent of cases were recorded under the generic category of 'other', which generally means struck out or dismissed, and disqualification amounted to 8 per cent of cases.

3 [1929] I ITR 195.

4 Dáil Debates, May 5, 1983, Vol.342, Cols.463–464 per Mr Molony.

5 Dáil Debates, May 11, 1983, Vol.342, Col.1022 per Mr M. Ahern.

6 [2011] IEHC 465.

7 It might be thought that I am trying to have my cake and eat it in insisting that CAB's work is not a punishment when both the body politic considers it to be such, by depriving people of assets and the recipients of CAB's action which will consider confiscation a disturbing experience. A few points should be made. First, all action can be described from a variety of different perspectives. Intervention, which is designed to be rehabilitative, such as helping a criminal break a drug habit, can be experienced as onerous and an imposition by the individual experiencing it. Second, if CAB is considered a punishment, its modality is such that it extends the meaning of what we usually consider to be a punishment by focusing less on the person and more the consequences of action. Third, what this means is that CAB is not a purely technical exercise of the kinds predicted by the early scholars of actuarial justice. Even Feeley and Simon (1995: 150) admitted that actuarial justice had failed to come up with 'a culturally satisfying story about crime and how to deal with it'. CAB's success lies in the fact that it developed an approach that resonated with people's sensibilities whilst pioneering a model based on efficiency.

8 [2004] IESC 32.

9 [2001] IEHC 93.

10 [1932] 16 TC 523.

11 [1929] I ITR 195.

12 [2014] IESC 17.

13 [2009] 49 EHRR 19.

26

Women, imprisonment and social control

Christina Quinlan[1]

In theory: women, imprisonment and social control

Women have historically lived very different lives to men, and consequently, their pattern of crime and criminality has some unique features (see e.g. Heidensohn and Silvestri, 2012). For instance, the numbers of women engaging in criminal activity differs substantially from the numbers of men. In addition, some argue that male and female experiences of criminal justice and penality are different.

Women constitute a very small minority in Irish prisons. In 2013, there were daily averages of 156 women and 4,158 men in prison in the Republic of Ireland (IPS, 2014) and daily averages of 63 women in prison and 1,780 men, including young offenders, in Northern Ireland in 2013–14 (NIPS, 2014). It is unclear whether it is women's experiences of social control that accounts for the small numbers of women in prison, or whether it is in the nature of women to be more law-abiding than men.

Early theoretical representations of female criminality – among them Lombroso and Ferrero (1958), Pollak (1950) and Thomas (1967) – represented female criminality as deviant femininity. The prevailing discourse suggested that the behaviour of women and men was primarily driven by their biological makeup. Although the study of male criminality quickly moved on to explore the impact of socialisation experiences, women who engaged in crime were portrayed until the 1970s as unnatural and lacking in female instincts.

Many early criminologists claimed that female offenders adopted masculine traits and behaviours and were therefore doubly deviant because they transgressed both social and gender norms. For example, Lombroso and Ferrero (1958) studied the skull, brains and facial and bodily 'anomalies' including tattooing of female criminals in an attempt to identify the traits of the female 'born criminal'. They posited that the female 'born criminal' possessed the deviant characteristics of the criminal male, as well as the worst characteristics of women, among them, cunning, spite and deceitfulness.

Perhaps unsurprisingly then, early theorists explained the underrepresentation of women in crime statistics with reference to what was perceived as women's biological passivity. This is evident in the highlighting by Lombroso and Ferrero (1958: 104) of the conservative tendency of women, the cause of which they located in the immobility of the ovule compared with the activity of the sperm (ibid.: 109). Similarly, Freud characterised women as sexually passive (Klein, 1977: 17), while Thomas (1967) contrasted catabolic male's outward flowing creative energy with anabolic female's storing energy (Smart and Smart, 1978: 38). Finally, Pollak (1950: 128) focused on the psychological imbalance wrought in women by menstruation.

From the 1970s onwards, feminist scholars launched a scathing attack on these perspectives. C. Smart (1976) and Carlen (1985) found misogynous themes throughout, themes evident in the following quote from Lombroso and Ferrero (1958: 151):

> We saw that women have many traits in common with children; that their moral sense is deficient; that they are revengeful, jealous, inclined to vengeances of a refined cruelty. In ordinary cases these defects are neutralised by piety, maternity, want of passion, sexual coldness, by weakness and an underdeveloped intelligence. But when a morbid activity of the psychical centres intensifies the bad qualities of women, and induces them to seek relief in evil deeds, when piety and maternal sentiments are wanting, and in their place are strong passions and intensely erotic tendencies, much muscular strength and a superior intelligence for the conception and execution of evil, it is clear that the innocuous semi-criminal present in the normal woman must be transformed into a born criminal more terrible than any man.

The debate moved on from this low point, and a second wave of criminologists proposed that women are underrepresented in criminal justice statistics, not because they offend less, but because they are treated differently within the criminal justice system. Pollak (1950) posited a chivalry hypothesis, claiming that female crime was underreported and under detected, and when detected and reported, treated more leniently. He suggested that culturally men are protective of women and this cultural norm impacts on the treatment of female criminality and on female-crime statistics. The chivalry hypothesis has been challenged by a number of theorists who highlighted the broad consensus among criminologists that women commit far less crime than men and are therefore underrepresented in official crime statistics because they 'cause less wilful damage to society than men do' (Carlen, 2002; see also Chesney-Lind, 1999; Heidensohn, 1975; Simon, 1975; Klein, 1977).

There is evidence, however, that at least some women are treated more leniently by criminal justice systems. According to Carlen (1988), women who lead lives consistent with hegemonic gender norms, values and behaviours are less likely to be imprisoned, while women who are not controlled by men through marital or other relations, and women who are unemployed or homeless, are more likely to be imprisoned. Worrall (1981) described how women are more likely to be sentenced with a view to their personal circumstances rather than simply in terms of the offence they have committed. Provided a woman is prepared to play the part, the stereotypical female role, she will convince the court that she is out of place there (Worrall, 1981; Hutter and Williams, 1981; Edwards, 1985; Kennedy, 1993).

There is another group of female offenders who, the evidence suggests, tend to be treated leniently by criminal justice systems. Denov (2004) wrote that some female offenders who have committed crimes traditionally perceived as 'masculine,' such as sex offenders, remain invisible in the criminal justice system. She accounted for their invisibility by arguing that there are prevailing 'popular and professional perceptions that sexual abuse carried out by women is relatively harmless as compared to sexual abuse carried out by men' (Denov, 2004: 1138).

Studies in the Republic of Ireland suggest a similar pattern of leniency for female offenders. For example, Bacik and O'Connell (1998) found differential sentencing practices for men and women in the Dublin District Court, where women were less likely to be convicted or to receive prison sentences. Bacik (2002) explained this through socialization theory which posits that women are more controlled by societal norms than men, and it is this that accounts for low levels of female criminality as well as low numbers of women in prison (see also Heidensohn, 1975; Rowett and Vaughan, 1981).

Conversely, others have highlighted the harsh treatment of some women by criminal justice systems. The theory of double deviancy holds that women can be treated harshly because they broke the law by engaging in criminal activity, and also because they contravened societal standards of acceptable female behaviour. Fennell (1993) explained how the legal system in the Republic of Ireland was informed by stereotypical assumptions and myths with regard to male and female roles. These myths operated to disproportionately disadvantage women, since a woman's treatment by the criminal justice system was dependent upon the extent to which she conformed or failed to conform to feminine stereotypical traits, roles and behaviours.

Lyons and Hunt (1983) in their analysis of the effects of gender on sentencing in Dublin concluded that female defendants received lenient sentences for traditional female-type offences such as petty theft, and harsh sentences for non-traditional offences such as assault. This argument was supported by Bacik (2002) who wrote that Irish District Court judges placed more weight on factors such as marital status, family background and parenthood in sentencing women than they did when sentencing men. Overall, however, the evidence about gender differences in sentencing is mixed, with some recent studies even suggesting that sentencing patterns for men and women are beginning to converge (see Bontrager, Barrick and Stupi, 2013).

Gender and power in society

During the 1970s, feminist scholars began to challenge the male-centric, positivistic perspectives espoused by early criminologists (see Chesney-Lind and Morash (2013) for a comprehensive review of feminist criminology). They contended that gender is not a biological or personality trait, but a social construct which is shaped by hegemonic ideals of masculinity and femininity. For this reason, female criminality and criminal justice experiences can only be truly understood when studied within the context of broader structural arrangements, specifically patriarchal structures that place less value on women and exert greater social control over their behaviour. Thus, female crime rates tend to be lower because women are more likely to conform to social norms and are influenced by feminine stereotypes that emphasise passivity, domesticity and maternalism.

In that context, it is worth considering the degree to which there is gender equality in both jurisdictions on the island of Ireland, the Republic of Ireland and Northern Ireland. (Since the partition of Ireland, under the Government of Ireland Act 1920, the north of Ireland has been part of the United Kingdom.) Although the Republic of Ireland and the United Kingdom were ranked at eighth and twenty-sixth respectively out of 142 countries surveyed for the *Global Gender Gap Index 2014* (WEF, undated), overall, rankings may conceal important sites of inequality. For example, studies show that both the Republic of Ireland and the United Kingdom have very low female representation in parliament (Sawer, Tremblay and Trimble, 2006; Galligan, 2006). The remarkable levels of inequality in the upper ranks of academic life in the Republic of Ireland were also recently highlighted by the Higher Education Authority (HEA, 2014).

That being said, the lives of women on the island of Ireland, north and south, have improved dramatically and particularly over the later decades of the twentieth century. Until the twentieth century, women were not allowed to vote; they were not expected or encouraged to participate in education or to earn their own living; and they were required to cede their property to their husband on marriage (Cullen Owens, 2005).[2] They had few employment opportunities (see Quinlan, 2011: 15), and financial security was achieved by many women through marriage (McLoughlin, 2001). In other words, society and culture were patriarchal in nature.

Walby (1990), in her consideration of patriarchy, explored the depth, pervasiveness and interconnectedness of different aspects of women's subordination in contemporary society. She pointed to women's everyday experiences for the causes, citing in particular the family as the site of women's oppression, men's flight from responsibilities and fatherhood, the threat of male violence, patriarchal sexual relations, sexual violence and the sexual double standard. These aspects of women's subordination have long been issues, as will be seen, in women's experiences of prison and social control on the island of Ireland. Inglis (2005) recommended that, in addition to focusing on the State, studies attempting to examine the nature of social control should focus some attention on how ordinary individuals were supervised and controlled in families, schools and communities.

Sexuality and the control of women

Female sexuality has long been fundamental to women's experiences of social control (see Inglis, 1998; O'Sullivan and O'Donnell, 2012). Prior to and in the decades following partition, the control and regulation of female sexuality was very similar north and south of the border. As McCormick (2009) explains, there was considerable unity across the religious and political spectrum in relation to female sexuality, and sexual purity became the fundamental standard of appropriate femininity and female behaviour (Valiulis, 1995). Women who failed to conform to this feminine ideal were often subjected to intense and prolonged forms of social control. The focus, in particular, was on regulating, rescuing and reforming prostitutes, 'fallen women' and unmarried mothers.

As has been well documented, women who were regarded as having engaged in, or been susceptible to, inappropriate sexual behaviour were routinely confined in convents, homes and penitentiaries[3] (Finnegan, 2001; Luddy, 2008; McCormick, 2009; Quinlan, 2011). In their work on coercive confinement in the Republic of Ireland, O'Sullivan and O'Donnell (2012) studied the experiences of prisoners, involuntary psychiatric patients, children in reformatories and industrial schools, as well as unmarried mothers and so-called 'fallen women'. They found that the large daily average numbers of women confined in institutions, such as mother and baby homes and Magdalene laundries, dwarfed the relatively small numbers of women in prison at that time. For example, 2,003 women were confined in these institutions in 1951 compared to a daily average of 43 women in prison (O'Sullivan and O'Donnell, 2007). Moreover, between 1765 and 1993, Luddy (2008; see also Smith, 2007) documented the existence of 32 Magdalen asylums in what is now the Republic of Ireland and eight in what is now Northern Ireland.

Magdalen Homes and Asylums, the carcereal appendage of the convent, were used for over a century to encourage conformity in non-conforming women (Quinlan, 2011). Their widespread use was justified by the State, which, with the Catholic Church, created legislation to develop, propagate and enforce a Catholic construction of sexuality in a gendered project which dedicated almost all actions and energies to the disciplining of women (see Crowley and Kitchin, 2008; see also Beaumont, 1999; Scannell, 1988). This disciplining superstructure was designed to produce 'decent' women, by limiting women's access to work and public spaces, confining them to the marital home, and threatening them with new sites of reformation, emigration or ostracisation if they failed to conform (Crowley and Kitchin, 2008). Female sexuality, it seems, was linked in the public mind with deviance.

Throughout this time, pregnancy outside of marriage was viewed as a scandal because it evidenced proscribed sexual activity which had taken place outside of the bonds of matrimony

(Leane, 1999). Milotte (1997) detailed the stigma attached to unmarried motherhood despite the fact that between the 1920s and the 1970s over 100,000 babies were born in the Republic of Ireland to unmarried parents. While an unmarried mother was a scandal, it was a scandal that could be secreted away. According to Milotte (1997), the nuns who ran the mother and baby homes and the Magdalen Asylums prided themselves on the stealth and concealment they could guarantee in terms of a pregnancy and birth. The secrecy protected the fathers of the babies and prevented the mothers from demanding any maternal rights. The babies of unmarried mothers were routinely forcibly adopted, although this was not an exclusively Irish phenomenon and was also documented in Britain (Roberts, 2013), Australia (Associated Press, 2013) and elsewhere (see The Baby Scoop Era Research Initiative).

Recently, in January 2015, the government of the Republic of Ireland published the Terms of Reference for 'a statutory and independent' commission of investigation into mother and baby homes (Department of Children and Youth Affairs, 2015), an initiative that was influenced by the work of the Justice for Magdalenes Research (JFM) project. Shortly after the establishment of this commission, Amnesty International Northern Ireland (2015) called for the setting up of a similar enquiry in Northern Ireland. Citing their own research into the experiences of women in Magdalen and mother and baby homes (see Amnesty International Northern Ireland), along with the recommendations of the UN Committee Against Torture and the UN Committee for the Elimination of Discrimination Against Women, Amnesty International Northern Ireland called on the Northern Ireland Executive (currently responsible for the governance of Northern Ireland) to establish an enquiry into the abuses suffered by individuals in such institutions.

Consistent with the tenets of early criminological theories, the harshest treatment during this time period was reserved for women that failed to conform to hegemonic feminine stereotypes; among those most severely punished were 'unworthy women', the 'weak willed', incorrigibles, repeat offenders, sexual deviants and prostitutes (see Luddy, 2001; Finnegan, 2001; Crowley and Kitchin, 2008; Quinlan, 2011; O'Sullivan and O'Donnell, 2012). The literature reviewed in this section revealed to some degree the reality of the nature, the experience and the prevalence of female social control. The next sections explore the characteristics and experiences of female prisoners in Northern Ireland and the Republic of Ireland.

A brief historical overview

A key feature in the history of female imprisonment on the island of Ireland is the extraordinary numbers of women imprisoned in the 1800s, in particular through the famine years of the mid-1800s. In fact, the female incarceration rate at this point in time was among the highest in the world. The extreme poverty and lack of opportunity experienced by women, along with the responsibilities of caring for family and children, account for the very large numbers of women in prison (see Quinlan, 2011). This elevated rate of female incarceration may be due in part also to extremely high levels of infanticide during the famine years. O'Donnell (2005) suggested that infanticide was common among women who wanted to avoid the shame attached to unmarried motherhood and women who were too poor to care for the children; he also highlighted the low value placed on infant life by society at that time.

Throughout the nineteenth and twentieth centuries, in the Republic of Ireland (Quinlan, 2011) and in Northern Ireland (Murray, 1998), women were imprisoned for offences which were generally of a petty, personal or sexual nature. Data from the Republic of Ireland (see Annual Prison Reports, relevant years) show that women were imprisoned mainly for drunkenness, simple larceny, soliciting, assault and malicious injury to property. Vagrancy and begging also accounted for substantial numbers of imprisoned women until the 1970s. No more than three or four women were imprisoned in any year from 1930 to the end of the twentieth century for murder or manslaughter (see Kiely, 1999). In the early decades of the twenty-first century, begging again became a feature of women's imprisonment in the Republic of Ireland, particularly in relation to the regular imprisonment for begging of impoverished women immigrants from Eastern Europe.

Throughout the twentieth century, women were imprisoned for politically motivated activity. In the early decades of the twentieth century, politically active women were involved in three substantial struggles: the labour struggle, the struggle for suffrage[4] and the struggle for an independent Irish Republic. Republican women were imprisoned by the British in local jails, in Kilmainham Jail, in Mountjoy Jail and in British prisons following the 1916 rising. During the civil war, Republican women were again imprisoned at these sites but were also incarcerated in the North Dublin Union, a former workhouse used as a concentration camp by the Free State Army during the Civil War (Cooke, 1995; McCoole, 1997, 2003; Carey, 2000; Quinlan, 2011; see also McGowan, 2003[5]).

Given the expectations of women in Irish society in terms of domesticity, piety and purity, as outlined earlier, the radical political roles assumed by these women were extraordinary and they placed them very far beyond the boundaries of normative femininity. Their actions show that it was then possible for women to resist dominant gender norms and the constraints imposed on them by a patriarchal society. Yet, McCoole (1997) records how families were often ashamed of the women's experiences of imprisonment. Consequently, many of the women never again spoke of those experiences after their release. They were women who, within a patriarchal society, had deviated from their feminine roles.

A small number of Republican women were imprisoned in the Republic of Ireland again in the late decades of the twentieth century. Held in Limerick Prison, these women were at the time among some of the more famous female prisoners. A prison officer in Limerick Prison spoke of some of those women (Quinlan, 2011) – Josephine Hayden: 'sentenced to four and a half years, served full time'; Rose Dugdale: 'served more than two years, only dealt with you when she had to'; Marion Coyle: 'served at least three years, background in the IRA, her boyfriend and Uncle were shot by the Brits'; Marie Murray: 'sentenced to death for her part in the murder of off-duty Garda (Police Officer) Reynolds, commuted to life in prison, she left Limerick Prison after 17 years, did loads of degrees here and ran a marathon in the yard at Mountjoy Prison'. The officer said that all these women did hard time in dire circumstances: very restricted visits, no TVs, no phone calls and no kettles. There were no special or separate facilities in the prison for political prisoners. This issue, along with the issue of politically motivated crime and punishment, is most salient in relation to the experiences of women in prison in Northern Ireland, as discussed below.

Northern Ireland

Armagh Gaol, which was built in 1780 (Murray, 1998), was a panopticon-style of prison, which historically contained three prisons, one for women, one for debtors and one for felons. Until it closed in 1986, it was the women's prison in Northern Ireland (Corcoran, 2006). In the decades prior to 1970, it never accommodated more than 12 prisoners (Murray, 1998). Murray (1998: 7) explains that women mainly served sentences for offences such as public drunkenness, assault, theft, fraud and prostitution. There were a few women, 'well known characters', who drifted in and out of the prison. After 1970, the female prisoner population began to rise as the political situation in Northern Ireland deteriorated into civil strife. To cope with rising prisoner numbers, the prison began to accommodate male prisoners in 1971. The numbers of political prisoners held there increased from two in 1971 to more than 100 in the 1972–6 time period (Murray, 1998).

Conditions in Armagh Gaol were described by Corcoran (2006) as overcrowded. There was doubling-up in cells, and the absence of in-cell sanitation meant that the women engaged in the practice of 'slopping-out' every morning. Resources such as education and training were under pressure, and problems with discipline emerged. From 1976, political female prisoners, almost all of them Republican (Corcoran, 1999), demanded the status and treatment of prisoners of war, as did many of their male counterparts. The resistance of these women to penal regimes and penal management led to actions including no-wash protests and hunger strikes. The women's bodies became their instruments of resistance (Corcoran, 2006).

In February 1980, Republican women prisoners in Armagh Gaol began a no-wash protest that would last for nearly one year (Neti, 2003). Throughout that time, the women smeared excrement onto the walls of their cells to draw attention to the conditions of their imprisonment. Male Republican prisoners in Long Kesh Prison had earlier commenced a similar protest. In the women's prison, the smearing of menstrual blood along with excrement, according to Neti (2003), invoked taboo, not only because it was dirty, but also because it was sexualised. She suggests that the British condemnation of the women's dirty protest was politically problematic because it could be read, and it was read, as a condemnation of the sexualised bodies of Northern Irish women. The no-wash protest provided women with a means of resisting the 'normalisation' policies pursued by penal regimes which focused on 'the cultivation of normative aspects of femininity in prisoners who are deemed to have lapsed from that category' (Corcoran, 2006: 175).

Female prisoners also used hunger strike as a weapon. On 1 December 1980, three prisoners – including Mairéad Farrell, who, with two other IRA members, was later shot dead by British Special Forces in Gibraltar – joined the hunger strike of male prisoners in the Maze Prison. The women's hunger strike ended on 19 December, one day after the men's, when the British Government appeared to concede to the prisoners' demands. A second hunger strike in 1981 led to the deaths by starvation of ten Republican men in the Maze Prison. A request by Mairéad Farrell for permission for the women in Armagh Prison to join the hunger strike was refused by Provisional IRA leadership (Corcoran, 2006). Commenting on gender relations in the conflict in Northern Ireland, Dowler (1998) wrote that, in war, men are often positioned as warriors, while women are relegated to the private and domestic sphere and positioned as compassionate supporters of male warriors. The active role of women like Mairéad Farrell challenges this perspective.

The use of random strip-searching by the penal regime in Armagh Prison in the 1980s was viewed by women prisoners as a reassertion of prison authority following no-wash protests and hunger strikes (Corcoran, 2006). In particular, women 'viewed the practice [of strip-searching] as a defining example of State violence against women in prison' (Corcoran, 2006: 184). They connected the exposure of their bodies to sexual domination (see also McCulloch and George, 2009). Consequently, as explained by Corcoran (2006), their resistance to strip-searching placed the female body on the frontline of resistance to coercion, resulting in a collision of the State, sexual violence, penal power and the bodies of imprisoned women.

When Armagh Prison closed in 1986, the women were moved to Mourne House, a women's unit in Maghaberry Prison, which is a high-security adult male prison. Following difficulties in Mourne House, in 2004, the women were moved to Hydebank Wood, a young male offenders' detention centre. A report on the experiences of women in Mourne House (Scraton and Moore, 2004) was commissioned by the Northern Ireland Human Rights Commission because there were serious concerns about possible violations of the human rights of women prisoners. Brice Dickson, Chief Commissioner of the Northern Ireland Human Rights Commission, wrote in the Foreword of the report that 'people held in detention, in prisons and elsewhere, are particularly vulnerable to breaches of their human rights' (2004: 3).

During the fieldwork period for that study, there was one death in Mourne House, two serious suicide attempts and a hunger strike involving a Republican female prisoner. The researchers were concerned too for the well-being of a 17-year-old female prisoner who had been held for four weeks there in strip conditions in isolation in the punishment block. These concerns led to the researchers engaging in legal action against prison authorities, who later suspended and eventually dismissed prison officers who had engaged in 'inappropriate relationships' with imprisoned women (Scraton and Moore, 2004: 10). All of this provides clear evidence of the vulnerabilities of women in prison, as well as the critical need to externally monitor the activities of closed institutions.

At that time, the Northern Ireland Prison Service had no policy for the management and support of women prisoners. According to Scraton and Moore (2004), this resulted in a lack of attention to and sensitivity for their needs as women. The report showed that 80 per cent of the prison officers working in the women's prison were male, and that sometimes all of the prison officers working the night shift were male. Scraton and Moore (2004: 11) concluded that the regime, a restrictive lock-up regime, 'neglected the identified needs of women and girl prisoners. … compromised their physical and mental health…. and caused unnecessary suffering'. Also highlighted were issues of self-harm and suicide, along with 'the pathologisation of girls and women with mental health needs' (see Scraton and Moore, 2006: 67; Scraton and McCulloch, 2009). These same issues were also highlighted by Quinlan (2011: 103–9) in relation to the experiences of women in prison in the Irish Republic.

The history of politically motivated women prisoners provides a critical case study in terms of gender and human rights. More recently, Moore (2010) highlighted the state's failure to reform the women's prison system to establish a rights-based system with gender-specific strategies and policies. Similarly, *Rights Watch* (2013) documented a number of human rights and gender rights abuses in the detention of Marion Price, a member of the Real IRA who was imprisoned in isolation for two years in the all-male Maghaberry Prison before eventually being transferred to Hydebank Wood Women's Prison (CAJ, 2013). Following an inspection of Hydebank Wood Women's Prison in 2011, the Chief Inspector of Criminal Justice in Northern Ireland acknowledged that the environment had improved, but advocated a greater focus on the specific needs of women and highlighted again the need for a specific and separate facility for imprisoned women.

Trends in female imprisonment

Since the beginning of the twenty-first century, there has been a steady increase in the numbers imprisoned. Table 26.1 details the numbers of prisoners, by gender, from 2001 to 2013. The figures include prisoners on remand, those in immediate custody, fine defaulters and other non-criminal detentions. As can be seen, the male prison population increased significantly during this time but appears to be shifting towards a downward trend. Female imprisonment also rose during this period, albeit from a lower base. The number of male prisoners increased approximately 76 per cent between 2001 and 2012, while the number of female prisoners rose by 195 per cent during the same time period. However, it must be noted that small numbers may distort percentage increases, and that women still constitute a tiny proportion of the total prison population.

The small numbers of women imprisoned, relative to men, has implications for the development of gender-specific regimes and policies. When there are relatively few women in prison, it can seem reasonable to accommodate the women in a small unit within a male prison and to provide them with essentially the same regime as the male institution, even when this means more meagre resources for the smaller female institution (Quinlan, 2011). But the need for

Christina Quinlan

Table 26.1 Prison receptions in Northern Ireland by gender

Year	Male	Female	Total
2013	4,992	369	5,361
2012	7,426	578	8,004
2011	7,313	503	7,816
2010	6,591	425	7,016
2009	5,755	332	6,087
2008	5,810	375	6,185
2007	5,691	370	6,061
2006	6,048	424	6,472
2005	5,582	330	5,912
2004	5,124	331	5,455
2003	5,037	272	5,309
2002	4,640	225	4,865
2001	4,220	196	4,416

Source: Compiled from NISRA's Prison Population Research and Statistical Bulletins, various years

gender-specific regimes and policies and women-focused services has been highlighted again and again in the literature on women's experiences of imprisonment (Carlen, 2002; Scraton and Moore, 2004; Hannah-Moffat, 2006; Worrall and Gelsthorpe, 2009; Quinlan, 2011; Irish Penal Reform Trust (IPRT), 2013).

Table 26.2 details the offences for which men and women were committed to prison. Although the numbers of female prisoners were too low for a meaningful analysis, the figures show that violent offences were the most common for both groups. The figures also indicate that men were more likely than women to be imprisoned for sexual offences and robbery. In addition, the figures show that female prisoners are convicted of a range of offences. Diversity in female criminality was also recognised by feminist theorists but was not acknowledged by early theorists, who believed that female offenders engaged solely in 'passive' or 'feminine' crimes such as prostitution and theft.

Table 26.3 highlights the relatively short prison sentences typically imposed on both women and men. These short sentences suggest that the offences are relatively trivial in nature. The high number of women (and men) imprisoned as fine defaulters is, however, particularly noteworthy (see also Scraton and Moore, 2004). This issue is explored later in more detail in relation to the Republic of Ireland.

Having described the characteristics and experiences of female prisoners in Northern Ireland, the discussion now turns to the Republic of Ireland.

Republic of Ireland

The numbers of women and men in prison declined steadily and consistently from the early decades of the 1900s until the 1980s. Carey (2000: 204) writes of the period between 1924 and 1962 as 'the quiet years' in the history of Mountjoy Prison. While in the late 1800s up to 15,000 women were imprisoned annually on the island of Ireland, by 1950 there were on average only 100 women held daily in the Republic of Ireland's prisons. This number fell further to 20 by

Table 26.2 Average daily prison population under sentence of immediate custody by gender and principal offence 2013

Offence	Males	Females
Violence	422	19
Sexual	162	1
Robbery	154	2
Theft	56	6
Burglary	84	1
Criminal damage	56	2
Drugs	76	2
Weapons	20	0
Public order	86	2
Motoring	22	0
Fraud	11	2
Other	137	6
N/A	1	0
TOTAL	1,286	44

Source: Compiled from NISRA Prison Population Research and Statistical Bulletin (2013)

Table 26.3 Average daily prison population under sentence of immediate custody by gender and sentence length 2013

Sentence length	Males	Females
< 3mths	27	3
3 to > 6mths	78	5
6 to > 12mths	131	7
1 to > 5yrs	538	16
5 to > Life	335	4
Life	176	8

Source: Compiled from NISRA Prison Population Research and Statistical Bulletin (2013)

1960 and to 14 by 1970 (Annual Prison Reports, relevant years); as we have already seen, similar numbers of women were imprisoned in Northern Ireland at that time.

One of the effects of the shrinking female prison population was the closure of almost all of the women's prisons and female prison wings: Galway closed in 1930; Waterford and Dundalk in 1935; Cork in 1940; Sligo in 1950; and Port Laoise Prison in 1960. By the latter decades of the twentieth century, there were just two women's prisons in operation, Mountjoy and Limerick Female Prisons. In 1970, Mountjoy Female Prison held a daily average of 15 women, while Limerick Female Prison held three. By 1990, women constituted less than 3 per cent of the prison population.

Interestingly, the phenomenon of low numbers of women in prison through these years was also recorded internationally (see e.g. Chesney-Lind (1991) on the US and Heidensohn (1985) on the UK). In fact, Carlen (1985) noted a Home Office report which estimated in 1970 that fewer women, perhaps no women at all, would receive prison sentences by the end of the twentieth century. While the numbers of women in prison reduced substantially over the twentieth century, there were of course very large numbers of women incarcerated, or 'coercively confined'

(O'Sullivan and O'Donnell, 2012), in the other institutions that went to make up Ireland's peculiarly female carcereal archipelago, as discussed earlier.

Another key feature of women's imprisonment over the twentieth century was the high rate of recidivism. In 1912–13, nearly half of the women committed to Mountjoy had previously been committed to prison under sentence more than 20 times (Carey, 2000). Explaining that recidivism was a particular characteristic of female imprisonment, Carey (2000) draws attention to the fact that in the middle of the twentieth century, female crime and prostitution remained closely linked. A recent study of recidivism showed, conversely, that male prisoners had a slightly higher recidivism rate than female prisoners – 52 per cent of males were reconvicted compared to 46 per cent of females (CSO, 2013). (In Northern Ireland, reoffending rates are 19 per cent for men and 11 per cent for women; see NISRA, 2014b).

Table 26.4 shows trends in committals between 2001 and 2013, the figures include committals under sentence and on remand. As can be seen, there are significantly more male than female prisoners. In 2013, women constituted 17.8 per cent of the prison population. While the numbers of both males and females are rising annually, the numbers of women prisoners are rising at a faster pace.

While the numbers of male prisoners rose from 8,616 in 2001 to 10,729 in 2013, a rise of 24.5 per cent, the numbers of female prisoners grew at a much greater rate over the same time period, rising from 923 in 2001 to 2,326 in 2013, an increase of over 150 per cent. As discussed earlier, similar patterns were observed in Northern Ireland. This could be interpreted as evidencing an extraordinary growth in female imprisonment, at least in relative terms.

Currently women are imprisoned for a range of offences, as seen in Table 26.5 which details the offences for which men and women were imprisoned in 2013. The most common offences among males were drugs, theft, homicide, sexual and other violent offences, with females tending to be imprisoned for theft, assaults and homicide. Again, this shows that the differences between

Table 26.4 Committals to prison in the Republic of Ireland by gender

Year	Male	Female	Total
2013	10,729	2,326	15,735
2012	11,709	2,151	17,026
2011	12,050	1,902	17,318
2010	12,057	1,701	17,179
2009	10,880	1,459	15,425
2008	9,703	1,225	13,557
2007	8,556	1,155	11,934
2006	8,740	960	12,157
2005	7,780	906	10,658
2004	7,914	906	10,657
2003	8,669	1,145	11,775
2002	8,673	1,043	11,860
2001	8,616	923	12,127

Source: Compiled from IPS annual report (2013)

male and female types of offending, at least among the prison population, are much smaller than was believed by early criminologists such as Lombroso.

A full analysis of offence types is beyond the scope of this chapter; however, two categories are considered in more detail next: drug-related offences and the offences of debt and fine default. Drug-related offences – possession, production, cultivation, import or export of drugs for sale and supply – only feature in the recorded offences of women in prison in the Republic of Ireland from 1985 onwards. Currently, substantial numbers of men and women serve relatively long prison sentences because of a presumptive ten-year prison sentence for possession of drugs with an estimated street value of over 13,000 Euro (IPRT, 2009). The Law Reform Commission (2013) recommended that existing mandatory and presumptive sentence regimes be repealed (apart from the mandatory life sentence for murder).[6]

Like Northern Ireland, a significant number of people are imprisoned in the Republic of Ireland for the offences of debt and fine default. For example, in 2013, a total of 12,011 people were committed to prison under sentence, and of these, 8,121 were committed as debtors or fine defaulters (including 1,895 women). In other words, in 2013, 67.6 per cent of all committals to prison under sentence were sentenced for defaulting on fines or for non-payment of debt. A greater proportion of women than men were imprisoned for these offences. In fact, 63.8 per cent (6,226 out of 9,746) of the men imprisoned under sentence in 2013 were imprisoned for these offences, compared to 83.7 per cent (1,895 out of 2,265) of women. The use of imprisonment on such a scale to punish debtors and people defaulting on fines is inappropriate and raises serious issues of justice (IPRT, 2013). Northern Ireland and the Republic are punishing the poor disproportionately (see Wacquant, 2009). The contemporary use of imprisonment as a strategy of social control, coupled with the imprisonment on a large scale of people for debt and fine default, evidences an urgent need for a critical review of the role of the prison and the use of imprisonment in the criminal justice system.

When we add to this picture the data on sentences imposed, an even more accurate picture emerges. As can be seen from Table 26.6, 23 per cent (n=28) of women were serving sentences of 12 months or less, compared to 11 per cent (n=400) of men. Furthermore, 18 per cent (n=604) of male prisoners were serving sentences of ten years or more, compared to just 9 per cent

Table 26.5 Offence groups of prisoners in custody under sentence on 30 November 2013

Offence	Male	Female
Homicide	393	18
Sexual	350	2
Attempts or threats to murder, assaults, harassment, etc.	433	20
Robbery, extortion and hijacking	126	3
Burglary	345	7
Theft	579	34
Fraud and deception	44	3
Drugs	572	17
Weapons and explosives	174	3
Criminal damage	78	5
Public order	54	0
Motoring	35	1
Other	170	8
TOTAL	3353	121

Source: Compiled from Irish Prison Service website (accessed 28 August 2014)

(n=11) of women. Although these figures constitute only a snapshot of the prison population at one point in time, the figures suggest that women tend to serve shorter sentences than men.

Contemporary perspectives

The two women's prisons currently in operation in the Republic of Ireland, the Dóchas Centre (a purpose-built female detention centre located on the Mountjoy prison estate which has been in operation since 1999) and Limerick Prison (predominantly a male prison accommodating 220 men and 28 women, according to the IPS (2014)), between them provide, officially, prison spaces for 134 women. The Dóchas Centre and Limerick Prison have a capacity for 105 and 28 women prisoners respectively (IPS, 2014), and, with a daily average of around 156 women in prison in 2013, the women's prisons are chronically overcrowded.

In Limerick Prison, the women are accommodated on one small wing and held in a basic lock-up regime where they are constantly monitored. They are accommodated in very small double-occupancy cells. The cells have in-cell sanitation, but the fact that each cell is designed for double occupancy renders these sanitation facilities degrading, inappropriate to and completely insensitive to women's needs. The toilets are unhygienic because of their proximity to the work surfaces of the women's cells, along with the fact that in Limerick women eat all meals while locked in their cells. Similar in-cell facilities are provided for both genders; however, broader education and work facilities are provided for male prisoners (see Quinlan, 2011).

The Dóchas Centre, designed specifically for female prisoners, opened in 1999, and the female prisoners moved there from the one wing they occupied of St Patrick's Institution, which has primarily been used as a young offender's facility since 1956. The Dóchas Centre ('dóchas' is the Irish word for 'hope') was deemed to be a model of best practice in Europe when it first opened. Designed to be a 'family' or 'home' style prison, women were accommodated in seven separate houses, surrounding a garden. Each house accommodated ten to 12 women, except Cedar House, which could accommodate 18 women, and Phoenix House, which was the pre-release centre. In the houses, each woman had her own room, and all rooms had en-suite toilet and shower facilities. The women had keys to their rooms so they could lock their rooms, and they had novel degrees of freedom in terms of movement about the prison.

Sadly, with chronic overcrowding and restricted staffing and resource budgets, many of the innovations have been undermined, and some have been entirely eliminated. The Dóchas Centre Visiting Committee (2013) reported that the general state of the prison was shabby. The kitchens

Table 26.6 Sentence length of prisoners in custody on 30 November 2013

Length	Male	Female
< 3 months	33	3
3 to < 6 months	112	5
6 to < 12 months	255	20
1 to < 2 years	362	25
2 to < 3 years	369	24
3 to < 5 years	798	14
5 to < 10 years	820	19
10+ years	293	3
Life sentence	311	8
Total	3,353	121

Source: Table created with data taken from Irish Prison Service website (accessed 28 August 2014)

were in a state of disrepair, with many of the appliances not working. To deal with overcrowding, some communal recreation rooms were being used as bedrooms, and women without medical needs were being accommodated in the Healthcare Unit. In 2013, the Inspector of Prisons again highlighted the problem of overcrowding.

Figure 26.1 depicts a view of the Dóchas Centre, showing the big yard with a playground accessed through the prison's visitors centre. The level of security is evident in the high gates and walls. What cannot be seen is the strip cell (a bare room) and the two padded cells used for control, restraint, surveillance and punishment, located in the Health Care Unit.

An ethnographic study

Ethnographic research carried out by Quinlan (2011) in the women's prisons in the Republic of Ireland provided valuable insights into the characteristics and experiences of, as well as the ways in which women occupy, the prison environment. At the time of the study, the female prison population was comprised of a relatively large number of impoverished chronically addicted women, mostly Irish, and a smaller number convicted of serious offences. The relatively large population of impoverished chronically addicted women tend to constantly come and go, regularly serving short sentences, whereas the relatively small population of women convicted of serious offences serve long years in prison and are typically first-time offenders, found guilty of one serious offence. As a consequence of being cut off from family and home, many imprisoned women can become extremely anxious, and, if they have children, worry and anxiety can overwhelm them. If the woman is from overseas, she will be very far from family and home and will seldom, if ever, receive a visit during her sentence.

Figure 26.1 The Dóchas Centre: the Health Care Unit is on the right, the visiting area on the left. *Source*: Christina Quinlan

Professionals interviewed for Quinlan's (2011) study – among them chaplains, prison governors and probation and welfare staff – spoke of the women's families and their familial obligations. They talked of the women carrying the full burden of the family and the home. They said that they had huge responsibilities in their lives and very little support. They said that it was often the case that at home the women had no security or trust and that within their families, they were subjected to all kinds of suffering and abuse. The women were, they said, the main caregivers in families, and consequently, women in prison tend to need much more intensive work than men.

Along with the large population of women serving frequent and short prison sentences, and Irish and other women serving relatively long sentences, there is another population in the women's prison: those serving life sentences for murder or conspiracy to murder or sentences of ten years or more for manslaughter. A common feature of these crimes is the fact that the women all, without exception, killed or participated in the killing of a family member or someone closely connected to a family member. Almost all of the victims were men, mainly husbands and lovers (Quinlan, 2011). Most tragically, and in a sad echo of earlier times, a very small number of women have been prosecuted for killing their own child. In recent years, for example, there were the cases of the 2014 murder of two-year-old Muhammad Hassan Khan; the 2012 killing of 11-year-old Emily Barut; and the 2012 killing of eight-year-old Anthony Ward. Case by case, at the core of these most serious crimes committed by women, are recurring themes of family and home and romantic and sexual relationships.

Quinlan's (2011) study revealed the ways in which imprisoned women occupied the space allocated to them. They created personal shrines to home, family and relationships in their rooms, which they used to construct and represent their identities, their sense of self. As can be seen in Figure 26.2, the very large and iconic valentine card dominates the shrine created by this

Figure 26.2   A woman's room in the Dóchas Centre. *Source*: Christina Quinlan

woman. The pink and red colours of the card, along with its flowers and expressions of love, signify romance. The size of the card signifies the depth of the romantic attachment that the card represents. The other emblems depicted in the photograph are symbols of family and familial relationships.

Along with romance, of course, comes sex and sexuality. As we have already seen, sex was problematic for women in the early decades of the twentieth century, and over the past two centuries, significant energy was dedicated to controlling women's sexuality. It is worth considering whether and to what degree there has been a cultural shift for women in relation to this. Quinlan (2011) detailed the difficulties experienced by female prisoners who participated in her study with sex and sexuality. All of the women but one were heterosexual in orientation. One woman talked of the deep intimacy that developed between women in prison without, she said, that intimacy becoming sexual. Most of the women expressed a wariness of sex and the possibility of pregnancy.

While unplanned pregnancy is no longer scandalous, the trauma of an unplanned pregnancy and the life changes it engenders prompted caution in relation to sexual activity. Many women, particularly those suffering from addiction, explained that they had endured a range of abuses, including sexual abuse, at the hands of men. There was some discussion in the interviews of sexual relationships between male prison officers and female prisoners, similar experiences were noted earlier in relation to experiences of women in prison in Northern Ireland, and of an experience of sexual abuse suffered by a woman at the hands of a male employee in the Central Mental Hospital in Dublin, the country's only forensic psychiatric facility.

The weak position of the individual incarcerated in relation to the strength of those in control of them opens up the potential for the development of inappropriate relationships, while the closed nature of the institution provides cover enough for such relationships to flourish. The

Figure 26.3 From a wall in a woman's cell in Limerick Prison. *Source*: Christina Quinlan

power differential is all the more pronounced if the prisoner is female and the prison officer male. This power differential can render the women vulnerable to sexual abuse, even if the encounter or relationship appears consensual (Quinlan, 2011).

The final photograph, Figure 26.3, was taken in a woman's cell in Limerick Prison. It provides a montage of the social structures that effectively control the lives of women in contemporary society. The drawings depict the red hearts and flowers symbolic of romance, as well as the sexual embrace between a man and a woman. Family portraits of children are also evident, along with an illustration of the crucifixion of Christ with two figures at the foot of the cross, representing perhaps Mary, the mother of God, and Mary Magdalene, the sinner. The juxtaposition of these two figures could be said to represent the dichotomy between 'good' and 'bad' femininity.

Conclusion

This chapter set out to explore women's experiences of imprisonment and social control on the island of Ireland and also considered the impact of wider issues such as gender, power, politics and women's rights. The analysis found many similarities between women's experiences of prison and social control in Northern Ireland and the Republic of Ireland. As these two jurisdictions were one prior to partition in 1920, this is not surprising.

The low rate of female imprisonment in the Republic of Ireland and Northern Ireland over the twentieth century is broadly similar to patterns of female imprisonment internationally. However, women's experiences of imprisonment and social control are very different and quite unique in some respects. For example, there are the high rates of imprisonment for women in the 1800s, and particularly during the famine years (the mid-years of that century). There is also the fact that the very low numbers of women imprisoned in the mid-twentieth century must be considered alongside the relatively high numbers of women coercively confined in institutions outside of the criminal justice system. In addition, there are the traumatic experiences of politically motivated women imprisoned over the course of political conflict, most recently in Northern Ireland.

As we have seen in the chapter, historically, the linking of female sexuality with female deviance led to the development of very elaborate patriarchal social arrangements designed for the control of women, and particularly for the control of female sexuality. The existence of these practices, along with their power and embeddedness in Church and State structures and in local and community social and cultural practices, undermine the notion that society historically responded with chivalry to female deviance. It was the drive to control female sexuality that led to the mass incarceration of women, albeit outside of the criminal justice system. The women were coercively confined in institutions such as mother and baby homes and Magdalen Homes and Asylums. In these places, the harshest treatment and punishments were reserved for the most intractable women, that is, those who failed to conform to hegemonic feminine ideals.

Throughout the twentieth century, the numbers of women in prison diminished, and the imprisonment of substantial numbers of women in other places accounts in part for this. Then, in the late decades of the twentieth century, the numbers of women in prison, both north and south of the border, began to grow again, but for different reasons. The numbers grew in Northern Ireland in response to the armed conflict and the resultant imprisonment of a relatively large number of its protagonists. The numbers grew in the Republic of Ireland with the development of the trade in illegal drugs. In both jurisdictions, there is also the substantial issue of the imprisonment of large numbers of people for debt and fine default, and, as we have seen, these offences accounted for 83.7 per cent of all of the women imprisoned under sentence in the Republic of Ireland in 2013.

The chapter shows that gender is a key issue in criminal justice on the island of Ireland, as it is elsewhere. The issues of power and control in relation to gender and gendered experiences of crime and punishment are critical in both criminology and in criminal justice. The discussion in this chapter supports the assertion of Heidensohn and Silvestri (2012) that there is a need in criminology and in criminal justice to recognise gender as a social construct rather than treating it as a statistical variable. The significance of gender is clear in the words of Chesney-Lind and Morash (2013: 291), two pioneers in the field, who state that, to gain a full understanding of gender-related issues

> such as the gender gap in crime, as well as the seemingly perplexing responses of the criminal justice system to girls and women as both victims and offenders, we must theorize gender in terms of individual-level identity and interactions embedded in a broader macro-level system of gender arrangements.

Bibliography

Amnesty International Northern Ireland (2015) 'Amnesty calls for inquiry into Mother & Baby Homes in Northern Ireland, as Irish inquiry announced', 09 January 2015. Available at: www.amnesty.org.uk/ (accessed 24 April 2015).

Amnesty International Northern Ireland (undated) *Briefing – Magdalene Laundry-Type Institutions in Northern Ireland: The Case for a Human Rights Response by the Northern Ireland Executive.* Available at: www.amnesty.org.uk/sites/default/files/doc_23218.pdf (accessed 23 April 2015).

Associated Press (2013) 'Julia Gillard apologises to Australian mothers for forced adoptions'. Available at: www.guardian.co.uk (accessed 24 April 2015).

The Baby Scoop Era Research Initiative. Available at: http://babyscoopera.com/ (accessed 23 April 2015).

Bacik, I. (2002) 'Women and the criminal justice system', in P. O'Mahony (ed) *Criminal Justice in Ireland.* Dublin: Institute of Public Administration.

Bacik, I. and O'Connell, M. (1998) *Crime and Poverty in Ireland.* Dublin: Roundhall, Sweet and Maxwell.

Beaumont, C. (1999) 'Gender, citizenship and the state in Ireland 1922–1990', in D. Alderson, F. Becket, S. Brewster and V. Crossman (eds) *Ireland in Proximity: History, Gender, Space.* London: Routledge.

Bontrager, S., Barrick, K. and Stupi, E. (2013) 'Gender and sentencing: A meta-analysis of contemporary research', *Journal of Gender, Race and Justice,* 16(2): 349–72.

CAJ (Committee on the Administration of Justice) (2013) 'Submission no. S411', CAJ's submission to the UN Committee on the Elimination of All Forms of Discrimination against Women (CEDAW) on the UK's 7th Periodic Report. Available at: www2.ohchr.org/English/bodies/cedaw/docs/ngos/CAJ%27sSubmission_UK_ForTheSession_CEDAW55.pdf (accessed 23 April 2015).

Carey, T. (2000) *Mountjoy: The Story of a Prison.* Cork: Collins Press.

Carlen, P. (1985) *Criminal Women.* Cambridge: Polity Press.

Carlen, P. (1988) *Women, Crime and Poverty.* Milton Keynes: Open University Press.

Carlen, P. (2002) *Women and Punishment: The Struggle for Justice.* Cullompton: Willan.

Chesney-Lind, M. (1991) 'Patriarchy, prisons, and jails: A critical look at trends in women's incarceration', *The Prison Journal,* 71(1): 51–67.

Chesney-Lind, M. (1999) 'Media misogyny: Demonizing 'violent' girls and women', in J. Ferrell and N. Websdale (eds) *Making Trouble: Cultural Constructions of Crime, Deviance and Control* (pp. 115–41). Aldine: Transaction.

Chesney-Lind, M. and Morash, M. (2013) 'Transformative feminist criminology: A critical re-thinking of a discipline', *Critical Criminology,* 21(3): 287–304.

Chief Inspector of Criminal Justice in Northern Ireland (2011) *Hydebank Wood Women's Prison.* Belfast: Chief Inspector of Criminal Justice in Northern Ireland.

Cooke, P. (1995) *A History of Kilmainham Gaol 1796–1924.* Dublin: Stationary Office.

Corcoran, M. (1999) 'Mapping carceral space: Territorialisation, resistance and control in Northern Ireland's women's prisons', in S. Brewster, V. Crossman, F. Beckett and D. Alderson (eds) *Ireland in Proximity, History, Gender, Space.* London: Routledge.

Corcoran, M. (2006) *Out of Order: The Political Imprisonment of Women in Northern Ireland 1972–1998.* Cullompton: Willan.

Crowley, U. and Kitchin, R. (2008) 'Producing "decent" girls: Governmentality and the moral geographies of sexual conduct in Ireland (1922–1937)', *Gender, Place and Culture*, 15(4): 355–72.

CSO (2013) *Prison Recidivism: 2008 Cohort.* Dublin: Central Statistics Office. Available at: www.cso.ie/en/media/csoie/releasespublications/documents/crimejustice/2008/prisonrecidivism2008.pdf (accessed 23 April 2015).

Cullen Owens, R. (2005) *A Social History of Women in Ireland 1870–1970.* Dublin: Gill and MacMillan.

Curtin, G. (2001) *The Women of Galway Jail: Female Criminality in Nineteenth-Century Ireland.* Galway: Arlen House.

Denov, M. S. (2004) *Perspectives on Female Sex Offending: A Culture of Denial.* Aldershot: Ashgate.

Department of Children and Youth Affairs (2015) *Commission of Investigation Mother and Baby Homes – Minister O'Reilly Announces the Establishment of the Commission of Investigation into Mother and Baby Homes and Certain Related Matters.* Available at: www.dcya.gov.ie/viewdoc.asp?fn=%2Fdocuments%2FMotherandBabyInfoPage.htm (accessed 23 April 2015).

Dóchas Centre Visiting Committee (2013) *Annual Report 2012 Dóchas Centre Visiting Committee.* Dublin: Department of Justice and Equality.

Dowler, L. (1998) '"And they think I'm just a nice old lady": Women and war in Belfast, Northern Ireland', *Gender, Place and Culture*, 5(2): 159–76.

Edwards, S. (1985) *Gender, Sex and the Law.* Kent: Croom Helm.

Fennell, C. (1993) *Crime and Crisis in Ireland: Justice by Illusion.* Cork: Cork University Press.

Finnegan, F. (2001) *Do Penance or Perish: A Study of Magdalen Asylums in Ireland.* Piltown, Co. Kilkenny: Congrave Press.

Galligan, Y. (2006) 'Women in Northern Ireland's politics: Feminising an "armed patriarchy"', in M. Sawer, M. Tremblay and L. Trimble (eds) *Representing Women in Parliament: A Comparative Study* (pp. 204–20). Abingdon: Routledge.

Hannah-Moffat, K. (2006) 'Pandora's box: Risk/need and gender-responsive corrections', *Criminology and Public Policy*, 5(1):1301–11.

HEA (2014) *Gender and Academic Staff.* Available at: www.hea.ie/news/gender-and-academic-staff (accessed 23 April 2015).

Heidensohn, F. (1975) 'The imprisonment of females', in S. McConville (ed) *The Use of Imprisonment.* London: Routledge and Kegan Paul Ltd.

Heidensohn, F. (1985) *Women and Crime.* London: Macmillan.

Heidensohn, F. and Silvestri, M. (2012) 'Gender and crime', in M. Magure, R. Morgan and R. Reiner (eds) *Oxford Handbook of Criminology.* Oxford: Oxford University Press.

Hutter, B. and Williams, G. (1981) *Controlling Women: The Normal and the Deviant.* Kent: Croom Helm.

Inglis, T. (1998) *Moral Monopoly: The Rise and Fall of the Catholic Church in Modern Ireland.* Dublin: University College Dublin Press.

Inglis, T. (2005) 'Origins and legacies of Irish prudery: Sexuality and social control in modern Ireland', *Eire-Ireland*, 40(3/4, Fall/Winter): 9–37.

Inspector of Prisons (2013) *Interim Report on the Dóchas Centre by the Inspector of Prisons Judge Michael Reilly.* Dublin: Inspector of Prisons.

IPRT (Irish Penal Reform Trust) (2009) *Position Paper No 3: Mandatory Prison Sentences.* Available at: www.iprt.ie/files/IPRT_Position_Paper_3_-_Mandatory_Sentencing.pdf (accessed 28 August 2014).

IPRT (Irish Penal Reform Trust) (2013) *Position Paper 10: Women in the Criminal Justice System: Proposals for Reform.* Available at: www.iprt.ie/contents/2571 (accessed 23 April 2015).

Irish Prison Service (IPS) (2013) *Irish Prison Service Recidivism Study.* Longford: Irish Prison Service. Available at: www.irishprisons.ie/images/pdf/recidivismstudyss2.pdf (accessed 23 April 2015).

Irish Prison Service (IPS) (2014) *Annual Report 2013.* Longford: Irish Prison Service. Available at: www.irishprisons.ie/images/pdf/ar_2013.pdf (accessed 23 April 2015).

Justice for Magdalenes Research (2015) Welcome to Justice for Magdalenes Research. Available at: www.magdalenelaundries.com/ (accessed 19 February 2015).

Kennedy, H. (1993) *Eve Was Framed: Women and British Justice.* London: Vintage.

Kiely, D. (1999) *Bloody Women: Ireland's Female Killers.* Dublin: Gill and Macmillan.

Klein, D. (1977) *The Etiology of Female Crime: The Criminology of Deviant Women.* Boston: Houghton Mifflin.

Law Reform Commission (2013) *Report on Mandatory Sentences (LRC 108-2013).* Available at: www.lawreform.ie/_fileupload/Reports/r108.pdf (accessed 23 April 2015).

Leane, M. (1999) 'Female sexuality in Ireland 1920 to 1940: Construction and regulation', unpublished Ph.D. thesis, University College Cork. Available at: https://cora.ucc.ie/bitstream/handle/10468/545/MI._PhD1999.pdf?sequence=1 (accessed 23 April 2015).

Lombroso, C. and Ferrero, W. (ed) (1958) *The Female Offender.* New York: Wisdom Library.

Luddy, M. (1995) *Women and Philanthropy in Nineteenth-Century Ireland.* Cambridge: Cambridge University Press.

Luddy, M. (2001) 'Abandoned women and bad characters: Prostitution in nineteenth century Ireland', in A. Hayes and D. Urquhart (eds) *The Irish Women's History Reader.* London: Routledge.

Luddy, M. (2008) 'Magdalen asylums in Ireland, 1880–1930: Welfare, reform, incarceration', in I. Brandes and K. Marx-Jaskulski (eds) *Armenfursorge und Wohltatigkeit. Landliche Gesellschaften in Europa, 1850–1930 [Poor Relief and Charity. Rural Societies in Europe, 1850–1930]* (pp. 283–305). Berlin: Peter Lang.

Lyons, A. and Hunt, P. (1983) 'The effects of gender on sentencing: A case study of the Dublin Metropolitan Area District Court', in M. Tomlinson, T. Varley and C. McCullagh (eds) *Whose Law and Order.* Belfast: The Sociological Association of Ireland.

McCoole, S. (1997) *Guns and Chiffon.* Dublin: Dúchas, The Heritage Service, Ireland.

McCoole, S. (2003) *No Ordinary Women.* Dublin: O'Brien Press.

McCormick, L. (2009) *Regulating Sexuality: Women in Twentieth-Century Northern Ireland.* Manchester: Manchester University Press.

McCulloch, J. and George, A. (2009) 'Naked power: Strip searching in women's prisons', in P. Scraton and J. McColloch (eds) *The Violence of Incarceration.* London: Routledge.

McGowan, J. (ed) (2003) *Constance Markievicz: The People's Countess.* Mullaghmore: Constance Markievicz Millennium Committee.

McLoughlin, D. (2001) 'Women and sexuality in nineteenth century Ireland', in A. Hayes and D. Urquhart (eds) *The Irish Women's History Reader.* London: Routledge.

Milotte, M. (1997) *Banished Babies.* Dublin: New Island Books.

Moore, L. (2010) '"Nobody's pretending that it's ideal": Conflict, women, and imprisonment in Northern Ireland', *Prison Journal,* 91(1): 103–25.

Murray, R. (1998) *Hard Time—Armagh Gaol 1971–1986.* Cork: Mercier Press.

Neti, L. (2003) 'Blood and dirt: Politics of women's protest in Armagh Prison, Northern Ireland', in A. J. Aldama (ed) *Violence and the Body: Race, Gender and the State.* Bloomington, Indiana: Indiana University Press.

NISRA (2014a) *The Northern Ireland Prison Population 2013. Research and Statistical Bulletin 15/2014.* Belfast: NISRA.

NISRA (2014b) *Adult Reoffending in Northern Ireland: 2012/12 Cohort.* Belfast: NISRA.

Northern Ireland Prison Service (undated) *Analysis of Prison Population 01/01/2013 to 31/03/2014.* Available at: www.dojni.gov.uk/index/ni-prison-service/nips-population-statistics-2/population-snap-shot-2.pdf (accessed 23 April 2015).

O'Donnell, I. (2005) 'Lethal violence in Ireland 1841–2003', *British Journal of Criminology,* 45(5): 671–95.

O'Sullivan, E. and O'Donnell, I. (2007) 'Coercive confinement in the Republic of Ireland: The waning of a culture of control', *Punishment and Society,* 9(1): 27–48.

O'Sullivan, E. and O'Donnell, I. (2012) *Coercive Confinement in Ireland: Patients, Prisoners and Penitents.* Manchester: Manchester University Press.

Pollak, O. (1950) *The Criminality of Women.* Philadelphia: University of Pennsylvania Press.

Quinlan, C. (2006) *Discourse and Identity: A Study of Women in Prison in Ireland.* Dublin City University: PhD Thesis. Available at http://doras.dcu.ie/19167/1/Christina_Quinlan_20130624093750.pdf (accessed 23 July 2015).

Quinlan, C. (2011) *Inside: Ireland's Women's Prisons Past and Present.* Dublin: Irish Academic Press.

Rights Watch UK (2013) *Marion Price and the Criminal Justice System.* Available at: www2.ohchr.org/english/bodies/cedaw/docs/ngos/RightsWatch_UK55_ForTheSession.pdf (accessed 23 April 2015).

Roberts, Y. (2013) 'Forced adoption: The mothers fighting to find their lost children'. Available at: www.guardian.co.uk (accessed 24 April 2015).

Rowett, C. and Vaughan, P. (1981) 'Women and Broadmoor: Treatment and control in a special hospital', in B. Hutter and G. Williams (eds) *Controlling Women: The Normal and the Deviant.* London: Croom Helm.

Sawer, M., Tremblay, M. and Trimble, L. (eds) (2006) *Representing Women in Parliament: A Comparative Study.* London/ New York: Routledge.

Scannell, Y. (1988) 'The Constitution and the role of women', in B. Farrell (ed) *De Valera's Constitution and Ours* (pp. 123–36). Dublin: Gill and Macmillan.

Scraton, P. and McCulloch, J. (2009) *The Violence of Incarceration*. London: Routledge.

Scraton, P. and Moore, L. (2004) *The Hurt Inside: The Imprisonment of Women and Girls in Northern Ireland*. Belfast: Northern Ireland Human Rights Commission. Available at: www.iprt.ie/files/the_hurt_inside.doc (accessed 23 April 2015).

Scraton, P. and Moore, L. (2006) 'Degradation, harm and survival in a women's prison', *Social Policy and Society*, 5(1): 67–78.

Simon, R. J. (1975) *Women and Crime*. Lexington: Lexington Books.

Smart, C. (1976) *Women, Crime and Criminology: A Feminist Critique*. London: Routledge and Kegan Paul Ltd.

Smart, C. and Smart, B. (1978) *Women, Sexuality and Social Control*. London: Routledge and Kegan Paul Ltd.

Smith, J. M. (2007) *Ireland's Magdalen Laundries and the Nation's Architecture of Containment*. Notre Dame, Indiana: University of Notre Dame Press.

Thomas, W. I. (1967) *The Unadjusted Girl: With Cases and Standpoint for Behaviour Analysis*. New York: Harper and Row.

Valiulis, M. (1995) 'Neither feminist nor flapper: The ecclesiastical construction of the ideal Irish woman', in M. O'Dowd and S. Wichert (eds) *Chattel, Servant or Citizen – Women's Status in Church, State and Society*. Belfast: The Institute of Irish Studies, Queen's University of Belfast.

Wacquant, L. (2009) *Punishing the Poor: The Neoliberal Government of Social Insecurity*. London: Duke University Press.

Walby, S. (1990) *Theorising Patriarchy*. Oxford: Blackwell.

WEF (undated) *Global Gender Gap Index 2014*. Switzerland: World Economic Forum. Available at: http://reports.weforum.org/global-gender-gap-report-2014/rankings/ (accessed 23 April 2015).

Worrall, A. (1981) 'Out of place: Female offenders in court', *Probation Journal*, 28(3): 90–3.

Worrall, A. and Gelsthorpe, L. (2009) '"What works" with women offenders: The past 30 years', *Probation Journal*, 56(4): 329–45.

Notes

1 I am indebted to the editors for their insightful comments on early drafts of the chapter. Without the supportive work of these reviewers, this chapter would not have been possible.

2 In 1932 a marriage bar was introduced which required women who married to resign from all Civil Service positions.

3 Another institution for the control and confinement of sexually deviant women was the Lock Hospital. The word 'Lock' derives from the word 'Loke', which meant a house of lepers. This word was used because of the difficulty in distinguishing venereal disease from leprosy (Luddy, 1995: 105). Lock Hospitals were used in Ireland between 1864 and 1886 for the confinement of women deemed to be prostitutes and found to be infected with venereal disease. The women were confined under the Contagious Diseases Acts (CDAs) (see Finnegan, 2001: 161). These Acts permitted the police to arbitrarily detain women on the streets, prostitutes, and, in the case of the 1866 Act, every woman believed to be a prostitute (see also Curtin, 2001: 83) for medical examination for venereal disease. If the woman was found to be infected, she could be imprisoned in a Lock Hospital for up to nine months. If a woman refused to submit to medical examination, she could be imprisoned for up to one month. The Acts operated only in areas of certain military camps in England and Ireland: in Ireland, Cork, Cobh and the Curragh military camps, and, as Luddy points out, (1995: 109), the acts were designed to eradicate venereal disease but applied only to women; soldiers who infected large numbers of women were not treated for venereal disease in confinement as were women. The Acts remained in force until they were suspended in 1883 and finally repealed in 1886.

4 The Representation of the People Act was passed in 1918, giving the vote to women of 30 years of age and older, and to men over the age of 21. Women in Ireland were granted equal voting rights in 1922.

5 For details of the Countess Markievicz's prison experiences of solitary confinement in Kilmainham Jail following the 1916 rising and proclamation of the Republic, her experience of a life sentence in Aylesbury Jail in England when her death sentence was commuted to life imprisonment, and her experience of the hunger strike in the North Dublin Union in 1923 during the Civil War.

6 The Law Reform Commission noted that consistency of approach in sentencing did not mean uniformity in sentencing outcomes, that each case should be judged on the unique circumstances of the

case; that the principle of proportionality in sentencing requires an individualised approach in sentencing; that mandatory sentencing poses a risk of disproportionate sentencing; that mandatory sentencing regimes have apparently failed to reduce criminality; and that mandatory sentencing regimes are too rigid to keep abreast of evolving penal philosophy (Law Reform Commission, 2013: 212).

Part IV
Emerging ideas

27

Hindsight, foresight and historical judgement

Child sexual abuse and the Catholic Church

Marie Keenan

This chapter draws on the author's 30 years of experience working as a forensic psychotherapist and earlier as a social worker with victims and perpetrators of sexual violence. The discussion is also informed by the author's involvement since the mid-1990s in research on the topic of sexual violence[1] and with treatment programmes that actively respond to it. The author, along with two colleagues, set up a community-based treatment programme for child sexual offenders in the Republic of Ireland in 1996. As well as treating clergy, the programme offered therapy to all men who had sexually abused minors and to their families as well as a smaller number of victims of sexual crime who wished to attend for help. From its inception, the programme attracted a number of Roman Catholic priests and religious brothers for the treatment of sexually abusive behaviour, as the centre was in part a response to a request from the Irish Catholic bishops to establish a treatment facility to help their troubled clergy.

The findings presented in this chapter emerged from a study that explored how priests and religious brothers who were attending the treatment centre made sense of their lives in hindsight. The research generated important insights into how these men understood those aspects of their lives that had given way to their sexual offending (see Keenan (2011) for the full discussion of this topic). Although appearing somewhat irrational to outsiders, deviance is known to have its own internal logic, and it is important to understand that logic. In particular, the study investigated how the men squared their abusive behaviour with their conscience, given that they were 'men of God' and once seen by many, especially Irish Catholics, as 'God's men on earth'. People join the ranks of Catholic clergy for a number of reasons, and, while there is no evidence to suggest that the main reason for joining is the betterment of the human race, the motivation for many is to be of service and to help others. Similar to the finding of the comprehensive John Jay College (2004, 2006, 2011) study on sexual abuse by Catholic clergy in the United States, the findings suggested that gaining access to children to abuse them was not part of the motivation for joining the priesthood or religious life, although some research has suggested otherwise (Sullivan and Beech, 2002). It was clear that whatever else formed the priests' motivation for joining, gaining access to children to abuse them was not part of it. Put simply, the picture of the clergy that emerged from the research did not reveal them to be 'monsters' or individuals who had an 'illness'. Therefore, it was essential to understand what had gone so wrong in their lives, as there was clearly more to their difficulties than individual psychopathology. Indeed, as the research progressed, the situational and institutional dimensions of the abuse problem became increasingly apparent.

Another important dimension to the abuse problem subsequently became evident: the handling of abuse complaints by the Catholic hierarchy. The absence of an adequate response to the abuse complaints by the church leaders has become apparent in almost every country in the world in which sexual abuse by clergy has come to light. Church leaders responded in remarkably similar ways across the globe. This raised questions about these men too. How did they learn to respond almost universally in a similar manner across the Western World? How did the Catholic bishops and church leaders make sense of their own responses to the problem? What forces influenced their decision making? While the research initially focused on understanding the clergy offenders, it subsequently expanded to include the church leaders as well.

While seen by some as two separate and distinct problems, it became clear during the research and clinical engagement that the abuse by Catholic clergy and the responses to it by the church leadership are interlinked. This raises questions as to whether some of the factors that contributed to a climate in which the clerical men could sexually offend also contributed to the climate that made it possible for the church leaders to respond in the manner in which they did. Put simply, they were both part of the same institutional culture. However, within that culture, not all priests were abusive, and it was important to determine the particular dynamic and psychological circumstances that contributed to sexual offending on the part of some clerical men, while at the same time keeping the larger cultural landscape within which this abuse took place in view.

The extent to which the institutional and organisational culture of the Catholic Church played a role in the sexual abuse situation had to be empirically addressed. Whilst the findings from the earlier research with Catholic clergy are presented elsewhere (Keenan, 2011), this paper builds on that earlier work and includes some findings from research with the church hierarchy (Keenan, 2013). Later research (Keenan, 2014) further expanded the focus on these populations and included victims of Catholic clergy by investigating the possible role for restorative justice as an additional justice mechanism for victims.

Brief history

After the Great Irish famine, 1845–52, when the potato crop failed and resulted in a period of mass starvation, disease and emigration, the Catholic Church emerged as a powerful force in Irish society (Whyte, 1980), a force that continued to exert its influence on political and social life until the mid-1990s. In the early years of the Irish Free State, which came into being in 1922, governments made much of their commitment to the Catholic Church with little resistance from the population, the majority of whom were Roman Catholic (Whyte, 1980). In 1937 the first Constitution of the Irish Republic fully embraced Catholic social thinking (Inglis, 1998). The Constitution recognised the 'special position' of the Catholic Church and, some would argue, just stopped short of declaring Catholicism a national religion. Unlike the separation of powers in other jurisdictions, church and state were inextricably linked throughout the twentieth century in the Republic of Ireland.

Nowhere was this bond more in evidence than in matters of social policy and public morality (Inglis, 1998). Huge areas of social policy were ceded to the care of Catholic religious orders with the result that the majority of hospitals, schools, asylums, orphanages and welfare agencies were run by the religious orders. These orders reported directly to the state but also indirectly to members of the church hierarchy. As recently as the mid-1980s, the Catholic hierarchy also wielded enough power to publicly intervene successfully in the constitutional referenda addressing the constitutional ban on abortion and the introduction of divorce legislation. But during the late 1980s and early 1990s, the church's ability to sway public opinion on moral and socio-sexual matters began to decline: contraception was made freely available, homosexuality was decriminalised and divorce was legally provided for in 1995 (Inglis, 1998; Fuller, 2002).

While church influence on society was already beginning to recede in the 1990s, allegations of church collusion in covering up numerous sexual scandals propelled this decline (Keenan, 2011). The scandals centred on a number of revelations, including the sexual abuse of minors by Catholic clergy; the physical, emotional and sexual abuse of children in the care of religious orders at various childcare institutions run by them (Ryan, 2009); and the fact that some Catholic clergy, including a serving bishop, had 'relationships' with women, including fathering children with them (Carroll, 1992: 3).[2] The sudden death of a Dublin priest in a gay sauna added to the moral chaos and served to place the problems of sexuality for the Catholic clergy on the public agenda (O'Toole, 1994). The moral contradictions embodied by these affairs left many questioning for the first time the gap between the preaching and the practice of the ordained and consecrated members of the Catholic Church.

The seeming attempts of the hierarchy to prevent embarrassing controversy for the church, even at the cost of victims' pain, added further to public disillusionment with a religious institution once regarded as all-powerful and untouchable. Further, when it became known that the Attorney General had neglected or ignored an extradition order for a priest convicted of child sexual offences in the Republic to return to Northern Ireland and answer for similar charges, both church and state became inextricably linked in the problem of sexual abuse by Catholic clergy. This led to the collapse of the government in 1995 and to the resignation of its then leader (Moore, 1995). Many began to question the closeness of the relationship between church and state and ask if both had colluded in protecting an abusive priest.

Just as in many other jurisdictions, a series of television programmes in the 1990s helped to focus public attention on clerical abuse beyond national boundaries. The programmes gave voice to adult survivors who provided testimony of their experiences. They documented church and state collusion in the operation of the residential facilities for children, and they underscored the climate of secrecy, denial and deference to the Catholic Church which permeated society (see *Dear Daughter*, RTE, 1996). British, Canadian, American and Australian media outlets also produced programmes for Irish-American and Irish-Australian audiences and helped disseminate word of the scandals throughout the world. In the process, they spoke to victims of abuse amongst the Irish diaspora. As a largely mono-cultural society, rendering the Republic 'the most Catholic country in the world' (Blanshard, 1954), the Catholic Church, once considered the ultimate arbiter of morality in Ireland, now found itself on the margins of influence in public life. That is where it is today.

Sexual abuse and Catholic clergy

Sexual violence is a significant problem internationally, and it is also so in the Republic of Ireland. According to one major study, 42 per cent of women and 28 per cent of men reported experiencing some form of sexual assault over their lifespan; 30 per cent of women and 24 per cent of men experienced sexual abuse in childhood; and 26 per cent of women and 12 per cent of men experienced sexual assault in adulthood (McGee *et al.*, 2002). The study also found that, while the rate of sexual abuse for females is in line with international trends, the high rate of sexual abuse of young males is at the higher end with regard to available international data.

When it comes to sexual abuse by Catholic clergy, there is an absence of official figures internationally; however, from those data that are available, it appears that between 4 and 8 per cent of Catholic clergy have been accused of the sexual abuse of minors (John Jay College, 2004; Loftus and Carmago, 1993). The Republic of Ireland is in line with this international trend (McGee *et al.*, 2002). For the purpose of comparison, studies have indicated that while 1 per cent of the adult male population is convicted of child sexual offences in the United States and the United Kingdom, the real rate of child sexual abuse perpetrated by the general adult male population is about 6 per cent.[3] However, caution must be used in considering this figure. Child sexual abuse is not limited to any one church or to any one profession, and it is difficult to get a clear comparative picture within various professional groupings because of the dearth of international empirical data. Nevertheless, its occurrence at all within the Catholic clergy is worthy of attention because of the distinct features of the Roman Catholic Church and of Roman Catholic clergy.

The Catholic Church is one of the largest religious organisations in the world, comprising approximately 20 per cent of the six billion individuals on the planet (World Religious Statistics, 2006). Because of its size, age and history, it creates an influential force in many societies and in particular in the lives of its many believers. It is a powerful institution, with global reach and a 2,000-year history, and its leadership comprises ordained men who have pledged themselves to work for God and man and to commit themselves to a life of service in a celibate manner. Roman Catholic clergy are all male, similarly educated in philosophy, morality and theology, subject to one authority and vowing obedience to one Supreme Head. As a group of men pledged to celibacy and service to others, the occurrence of sexual activity, especially of an abusive kind, contradicts everything that the institution publicly stands for, such as chastity and protecting the young and vulnerable. The fact that an unusually consistent pattern emerged in the handling of abuse complaints by Catholic leaders across the world added a dimension to a complex problem that has global reach as well as specific national distinctions and variations.

It must, however, be noted that child sexual abuse by Catholic clergy has emerged almost exclusively in First World industrialised nations where legal remedies are more readily available and where the concept of the child has developed into one that includes the idea of vulnerability and the need for protection (Corby, 2000). Yet it is conceivable that both the abuse itself and a similar response of the church leadership have occurred in developing countries too. It is highly likely that this cascading problem is set to continue, as we anticipate the problem showing up in developing countries and in those Catholic-European countries such as Italy, Poland and Spain, where the first appearances of the problem are beginning to be recognised.

Although a full examination of the experiences of the survivors of institutional abuse is beyond the scope of this chapter, the Ryan Report (2009) revealed that emotional, physical and sexual abuse was endemic within institutions. Children were regularly subjected to severe, violent and arbitrary corporal punishments that were designed to maximise pain and humiliation. This created a pervasive climate of fear, as children never knew when or why the next beating would occur. Their emotional trauma was exacerbated by constant ridicule and other practices designed to elicit feelings of shame and degradation. Children were often separated from families, and some were even informed (falsely) that their parents were dead. In addition, malnutrition, inadequate clothing, oppressive regimes, austere accommodation, poor hygiene and limited education and training opportunities contributed to a culture of physical neglect. Sexual abuse was also common in male institutions. Studies have found that survivors of child sexual abuse may experience long-term psychological, economic and social consequences. Carr *et al.* (2010) studied the psychological well-being of 247 survivors of institutional abuse and found that over 80 per cent were suffering from psychological disorders, including anxiety, mood disorders and substance abuse, and had weak social attachments. In addition, Barrett *et al.* (2014) found that male victims of child sexual abuse are three times more likely than the general population to be unemployed as a result of illness or disability in later life. The criminal justice system has not been able to adequately respond to the abuse problem. Approximately 3,000 allegations were made to the Commission to Inquire into Child Abuse; just 11 were sent to the Director of Public Prosecutions, and only three resulted in prosecutions (Holohan, 2011).

A systemic perspective on sexual abuse in the Catholic Church

Over the past three decades, a considerable amount of research has been undertaken into many aspects of the clergy sex abuse problem, producing a library of scholarly articles and books on the topic (see for example, John Jay College, 2004, 2006, 2011; Deetman, 2011; Adriaenssens, 2010; Keenan, 2011). It runs the gamut from the unique kind of particular trauma experienced by clergy victims to the ecclesiological factors that help explain why the Catholic bishops responded in the manner in which they did. However, it is a feature of many areas of academic study that certain perspectives, theories and methods dominate while others are neglected or excluded. Although there are exceptions (such as Adriaenssens, 2010; Deetman, 2011; John Jay College, 2004, 2006, 2011), much scholarly work on abuse in the Catholic Church focuses on the assumed psychopathology of the perpetrator, and much popular writing and Government-commissioned work focuses on failures of named individuals who were in positions of authority in relation to their handling of abuse complaints (Murphy, 2009). There is a need to expand such individualistic perspectives to include cultural, theological and organisational factors in attempting to explain and understand the problem in all its dimensions. As will be shown, it is possible to identify a number of features of sexual abuse within the Catholic Church that have a determining influence, not only on how the priests came to abuse, but on how the church leaders responded as they did. The following is a brief overview of that research.[4]

Sexual abuse by Catholic clergy is best understood as part of the continuum of sexual behaviour of Catholic clergy and not as an unrelated or aberrant sphere of sexual activity. The abuse problem must be considered against the background of the substantial literature on the sexual underworld of 'normal' clergy. The sexual activity of Catholic clergy outside of the abuse situation is of course not of concern for criminologists or the criminal justice system and is more a disciplinary matter for the church itself. However, the sexual underworld of 'normal' clergy and the unhealthy organisational culture which ignores and condones it while at the same time publicly promoting an image of a celibate clerical organisation, forms part of the unhealthy and secretive organisational church culture in which the sexual abuse of children becomes possible. This perspective raises the issue of celibacy as an important area for research in relation to this problem.

An inadequate theology of sexuality and the absence of relational sexual ethics for clergy is also part of the problem of sexual abuse of minors by Catholic clergy. The study found that Catholic clergy were so focused on controlling the 'sex act' that they did not consider the consequences of the act for the child. The men did not engage with the full significance of the young age of the child, beyond the fact that gaining access and compliance was easier with a minor than with an adult, with whom relational negotiation would have been required. Similarly, when disclosures of abuse of minors were made, the responses of the church leaders whose concern with the act that had occurred is evident, as they often sent the perpetrators to confession and therapy, while the child was largely ignored.

The church's theology of scandal also forms part of the context that enabled the abuse by clergy to continue. Church leaders believed that informing the laity of the truth of the sexual activities of clergy was akin to giving scandal and this was to be avoided. The theology of scandal underpins much of the behaviour of senior church clerics who believed that the laity must not be scandalised by the truth of human frailty.

In addition, clericalism appeared to play a significant role in the clergy sexual abuse problem, a finding supported by other research (Doyle, 2014; John Jay College, 2004, 2006, 2011; Bennett,

2004). Clericalism was premised on the idea of clergy as an elite, who are set apart from and above the laity and are closer to God by virtue of their calling and ordination. Both clergy and laity alike were influenced by clericalism. For the Catholic laity, clericalism implied that Catholic clergy could do no wrong, thus children were not believed. For Catholic clergy, it led to the belief that children would never tell and that families would not speak ill of their clergy, giving abusive clergy a false sense of security that the stories of their sexual underworld would never be told. For church leaders, clericalism led to the false belief that the dark secrets of the sexual activities of clergy would remain with the church leaders, as no family or individual would speak badly of their clergy.

The nub of the issue was the interplay of power and powerlessness. This contributed to the genesis of the problem of sexual abuse for Catholic clergy and was also significant in explaining the manner in which the church leaders responded to the abuse disclosures. In the public sphere, clergy appear independent in the exercise of their duties and powerful in the mind of the public. However, despite experiencing the trappings of such a dominant power position in the public realm, many clerical perpetrators revealed personal powerlessness, lack of personal autonomy and frustration in their private lives and in their relationships with superiors. Masked anger and disconnection from the institution to which they had given their lives was the result, with 'comfort' being sought from 'outside'. 'Comfort' often manifested itself in illicit sexual encounters with minors: sexual abuse in everyday parlance. Yet, this response was not inevitable, and other clergy coped by constructing adaptive clerical masculine identities that allowed them to accept their human frailties, form relationships with others and neutralise feelings of guilt and shame.

Bishops also experienced powerlessness vis-à-vis the powerful Roman Curia, and often concealed their problems with clergy abuse from other bishops and from potential sources of support for fear of the poor image it would portray of their diocese. Bishops also feared the wrath of Rome, particularly those who exercised power in the Congregation for the Clergy, the Congregation for Bishops and the Congregation for the Doctrine of the Faith. Power within the Catholic Church was taught and seen to be in one direction only – upwards. Priests feared the bishops, and bishops feared Rome. Neither bishop nor priest feared the laity, certainly not children. This can be related to the power, authority and governance structures of the Catholic Church and to the nature of the relational networks that it fostered.

Finally, and significantly, a moral education that is overly intellectualised and technical and focuses mainly on theoretical or abstract problems does not equip its students to make good moral judgements. As Arendt (2000) observed, the precondition for the kind of judgement that is necessary to prevent wrongdoing is not a highly developed intelligence or sophistication in moral matters, but rather a disposition to live with others and explicitly with oneself and to engage in an ongoing silent dialogue about the consequences of one's actions for another. Good judgement needs the special presence of others in whose place one must think and whose perspectives one must consider. What was absent for too long from the education of Catholic clergy was a relational approach to morality. Instead, the form of morality taught in Irish Catholic seminaries was based on a rulebook that relied on moral absolutes and theoretical understandings. Rule-book morality failed to equip the Catholic clergy and the church leaders for the challenges they would face in their complex ministries, as they encountered real people with real problems of living their human lives and in their relationship with the Divine. Rule-book morality was also easy to get around and re-interpret, as the clergy men could deceive themselves and rationalise their abusive behaviour. Although the use of techniques to rationalise, neutralise or justify criminal acts is common among offenders, these findings suggest that clerical sexual abusers possess particularly well-developed cognitive skills which equipped them to evade responsibility for their actions and quash feelings of guilt. (For a critique of the literature on cognitive distortions, see Ó Ciardha and Ward, 2013.)

The sacrament of Confession could be used on all occasions to clear the conscience, and while many clerics made a firm purpose of amendment never to commit this 'sin' again, their experience would show that this commitment was short-lived. However, fear of being found out and losing their priestly and pastoral ministries prevented them from seeking the help they required. In the end, their biggest fear was to become their reality. It is in the inter-relationship of many of these factors that the genesis of and response to the problem of abuse within the Catholic Church can be found. For the clerical men, the preservation of an image of perfect celibacy had to be maintained, no matter what the personal and psychological cost, or more importantly, the devastating consequences for other individuals, especially minors. Minimising and rationalising and the sacrament of Confession helped to keep such a terrible realisation at bay. For church leaders, the preservation of an image of celibate clergy and a model of institutional perfection and holiness was more important than the reality of anyone's life and ultimately of any individual who could be sacrificed, priest, bishop or child. While children became the sacrificial lambs of an image of celibate living that had to be maintained, the clergy themselves and some bishops became the sacrificial offering that the institutional church was itself willing to make. And nobody who takes an individualist approach to this problem would object to this method of punishment – in fact, they would call for more. Bad priests deserve to be punished severely, with terms of imprisonment, loss of jobs and vocation and a life of poverty and isolation.[5] Erring bishops must be held personally to account, suffer terms of imprisonment and lose their positions in the organisation. Although individuals must be held accountable for criminal wrongdoing within the state and within their own organisation, other approaches to punishment and accountability must also be considered – approaches that fit with a systemic understanding of the problem.

From a systemic perspective, as the integrity of the unsupported, inadequately trained and sometimes psychologically vulnerable priests was sacrificed to an image of priestly perfection that had to be avowed, the offending clergy became both oppressors and oppressed at the same time. As offenders against children, they required therapy and punishment; as victims of the Catholic Church to whom they had given their lives, they required help and support from the institution that failed them. As the individually categorised 'malevolent' bishops became the public and institutional scapegoats of a particular image of institutional church that had to be preserved, the role of the Vatican[6] in the sexual abuse of minors went completely ignored. From a systemic perspective, as long as the 'bad apple' theory of sexual abuse in the Catholic Church is preferred to the more layered 'decaying barrel' theory, with the unwitting 'support' of the public who are outraged by all that has occurred, the organisation will continue as it is, tinkering with procedures and protocols, while individuals are offered on the altar of the sacrifice. In this scenario, the core organisational, cultural and power dynamics within the church, of which the abuse problem is merely a symptom, continues to go unreformed.

At the same time, the church cannot be held solely responsible for the emergence and persistence of clerical sexual abuse. External factors also played a role, for example, the failure of state agencies to monitor the wellbeing of children in institutional care; garda deference towards the church, which engendered a reluctance to pursue allegations against its representatives; and society's ambivalence about the fate of children in care due to their perceived status as second-class citizens (Holohan, 2011).

Sexual abuse, inquiries and commissions of investigation: empirical and justice concerns

In response to the evolving disclosures of the abuse of children by Catholic clergy and the public outcry that followed, institutions of church and state in the Republic and in other jurisdictions have initiated commissions to inquire into the problem, mainly into the handling of abuse complaints by the local church hierarchies. While a good empirical study is badly required by the Vatican, which has both the access and the resources to commission such a work into the genesis and causes of the problem, over the past three decades a strong body of national[7] and church commissioned works has emerged, largely compiled by academics appointed by the church to address the scope of the problem and its causes and context (John Jay College, 2004, 2006, 2011; Bennett, 2004; Deetman, 2011; Goode *et al.*, 2003; Adriaenssens, 2010). In Belgium, one promising church-initiated study, headed by Prof. Peter Adriaenssens (2010), a practicing child psychiatrist and professor of child psychiatry at The Katholieke Universiteit, Leuven, was forcefully and prematurely halted in 2010 when the police raided the offices of the commission and took many of their confidential files on the false belief that the commission was itself involved in cover-up and in hiding clergy 'paedophiles'. In 2013, this raid was deemed to have been unconstitutional in the courts in Belgium, with a lot of trauma caused to victims who had given their testimonies in confidence to the commission (Luxmoore, 2013). Recently the Vatican announced the first Vatican commission into the abuse problem. As the terms of reference of the commission have yet to be defined, it is unclear what aspects of the problem this commission will address. It also remains to be seen whether a Vatican-sponsored commission can be truly objective given its lack of independence, but the appointment of independent-minded advocates for victims to the commission offers some promise here.

National and federal governments internationally have also commissioned inquiries and investigations into the church's handling of abuse complaints, mainly chaired by legal professionals and judges, which have produced large volumes of reports on this aspect of the problem (see for example, Murphy, 2009, 2011; Ryan, 2009; Office of the Grand Jury, Philadelphia, 2005, 2011; Office of the Attorney General, Commonwealth of Massachusetts, 2003). While the results of these statutory inquiries have received universal and largely uncritical attention internationally, the relationship between the statutory investigations and the actual results of these inquiries is not unproblematic. In the Republic, for example, the statutory commissions are not seen as even-handed in their approach to many witnesses, leading to some questionable findings (Sweeney, 2013a, 2013b; McDonagh, 2013; Keenan, 2013). It appears that the global revulsion of the fact that children's lives were used and abused by the clergy who sexually abused them and by the church authorities who failed to respond adequately to their complaints, has served to restrain even academic or legal scholars from essential critical evaluation of these government-commissioned reports. In fact, the response to clerical child sexual abuse resembles a moral panic, which occurs when members of a sub-cultural group come to be perceived as a threat to societal values that must be controlled through harsh measures (Cohen, 1972). The dominant narrative of cover-up by the Catholic Church of the abuse of minors has therefore taken hold internationally without serious critical analysis of the work of the inquiries and commissions of investigation. This issue is now explored in more detail in relation to one commission of investigation in the Republic which highlights key issues concerning the role of hindsight, foresight and the politics of historical judgement.

The Dublin Archdiocese Commission of Investigation was established in 2006 to inquire into the response of church and state authorities to a representative sample of complaints and suspicions of child sexual abuse by priests in the Archdiocese of Dublin between the years 1975 and 2004. It was chaired by a judge with the assistance of two other legal panel members and became known as the 'Murphy Commission'. Its eventual report, in two parts totalling 814 pages, was made public in November 2009 and became known as the 'Murphy Report' (Murphy, 2009). The report investigated the response of the Archdiocese of Dublin and the state authorities to a sub-sample of 46 complaints of child sexual abuse made against priests in the Archdiocese between 1975 and 2004, selected from a total sample of allegations against 172 named and 11 unnamed priests. The authors concluded that the response of the Archdiocese to these complaints was primarily concerned with 'the maintenance of secrecy, the avoidance of scandal, the protection of the reputation of the church and the preservation of its assets. All other considerations, including the welfare of children and justice for victims, were subordinated to these priorities' (Murphy, 2009: 4). They posited that a 'culture of secrecy', legitimated by the provisions of canon law, facilitated the cover-up of child sexual abuse (Murphy, 2009: 8). In particular, authorities in the Archdiocese ignored complaints where possible, failed to report allegations to the gardaí or to deal with them under the provisions of canon law, swore complainants to secrecy and provided incomplete information to psychiatrists and other treatment providers. The report also found that the Archdiocese did not communicate its concerns about particular priests to church authorities or to other dioceses, with the result that these priests were poorly monitored. State authorities who were implicated in the cover-up because their deference to the church meant that allegations were poorly investigated. Furthermore, the report rejected the Archdiocese's claims that it was unaware of the problem, arguing that the relevant authorities had qualifications in canon and civil law and were therefore aware of the gravity of the allegations and the appropriate mechanisms for dealing with them.

The Murphy Report and the reaction to its findings by the Irish media and the Archbishop of Dublin presented an overly-simplistic explanatory narrative. The manner in which the report named and shamed individual bishops raised particular concerns, not least since the terms of reference of the commission was to inquire into the systemic issues and the response of church and state authorities to the abuses that had occurred. The Archbishop's suggestion that the bishops named in the Murphy Report should consider their position was also significant, especially since the Archbishop had been part of the Vatican's diplomatic corps when the abuse crisis began to raise its head in the Republic during the 1980s and 1990s, and since his work was not under investigation by the commission, as his term of office was outside its remit. Pope Benedict's letter to the Catholics of Ireland (Pastoral Letter, 2010) in which the named bishops were effectively blamed for their action and inaction, as though they acted unilaterally against Vatican policy, was also noteworthy. In supporting the simplistic cover-up narrative that dominated public discourse, it seemed that the Archbishop and the Vatican were distancing themselves from the events that had occurred, as though the named bishops had acted in a manner that was deviant and out of sync with the dominant organisational church ethos. However, research findings and professional accounts contradict this narrative (Keenan, 2011). Amongst other things, the commission's approach to the social-scientific process of developing a representative sample on which they entirely based their findings was disquieting, as little of the methodology for developing the sample was evident in the report (McDonagh, 2013). An in-depth analysis of the Murphy Report confirms these concerns (see Sweeney, 2013a, 2013b; Keenan, 2013; McDonagh, 2013).

Sweeney (2013a: 383), from a legal perspective, argued that standards of proof that were legally required as the basis of its claims 'were not always respected by the commission' and that the commission resolved all or any differences of recollection between lay and clerical witnesses by making a finding against the individual cleric without stating the reasons for its judgement. Sweeney (2013a: 382–3) found that, in theory, the clerics (mainly bishops and senior clergy) who appeared before the commission were asked to appear as witnesses to help the commission with its investigation, but from the very tone and content of its report and the experience of the senior clerics who appeared, the commission had embarked on an adversarial approach towards them and they felt themselves to be akin to 'defendants' in a criminal trial, but without the necessary legal protections (see also Keenan, 2013: 437). Sweeney (2013a) argued that in the course of its investigation, the Murphy Commission went well beyond its mandate of being focused only on the institutional response to complaints, suspicions and knowledge of child sexual abuse in the Archdiocese of Dublin by building up and making a case against individual bishops and senior clerics whom it then named and shamed in its report (Murphy Report, 2009: Para. 1.7). Sweeney argues that once the commission had decided to 'name, blame and shame' individual senior clergy, it had a duty to afford these men an opportunity to have their cases presented fully, with the help of their legal advisors, and thus considered carefully, especially if they were at risk of public vilification and censure (Sweeney, 2013a: 384). In going outside its task in this manner, Sweeney's view is that:

> the well accepted minimum rights of natural and constitutional justice were not respected and an individual's constitutional right to his good name was not fully safeguarded.
>
> *(Sweeney, 2013a: 383)*

The report dismissed out of hand any reasons, explanations or mitigating circumstances put forward by those clerics whom it named and shamed, and the commission only referred to such arguments and submissions as were made by the clerics who testified before it 'in order to try to dismantle them' (Sweeney, 2013a: 385; Keenan, 2013: 437). No attempt was made to consider the circumstances facing each senior cleric at the particular time a complaint was made, nor were the matters located in the historical and sociological context of their times. The benefits of hindsight were not borne in mind when assessing behaviour that mostly took place 20 to 30 years prior. Neither was it accepted that the clerics poorly understood the dynamics of sexual abuse and were on a learning curve. According to Sweeney (2013a: 384), the report seems to have looked at the events of 20 to 30 years ago through 'the prism of today's glasses' in its keenness to condemn individual clergy. For him (2013a: 387), it was difficult to avoid the conclusion that the Murphy Commission deviated far from the remit given to it under the terms of the reference, and in carrying out its tasks, fell far short of meeting the requirements of 'natural and constitutional justice'.

In relation to the representative sample, McDonagh (2013: 464) found that there were clear signs in the Murphy Report that the commission was oblivious to the fact that the purpose of representative sampling is to allow statements of fact to be made, not just about the sample, but, within known sampling error, about the whole population. In this failure to understand a fundamental of representative sampling, the commission did not relate at all to the social-science dimension of what was asked of it, and this error inevitably affects the work and judgments of the commission and its findings. It became apparent from an analysis of the report that generalisations were made on the basis of single or selected cases. It is also worrying that reliable aggregate data, normally the outcome of representative sampling in social research, were nowhere to be found in the report, and – not unrelated – the sampling units selected were questionable as to their suitability for the task (McDonagh, 2013: 467). For McDonagh (2013: 466), some of the problem with the representative sampling lay in the fact that the Murphy Commission was totally comprised of legal personnel who failed to adequately open up to the power of social-science approaches to research and to representative sampling in particular on which to base any factual aggregate statements. The demand for the use of representative samples was implicit in its terms of reference. It is therefore shocking how much weight is given to what can only amount to legal opinion, leading to strong judgments in the report while at the same time claiming to be a scientific study, based on a representative sample (McDonagh, 2013: 467).

It is worth considering whether the misuse of a biased sample, that was inappropriately called a representative sample in the Murphy Report, helps to explain the gap between what the senior diocesan officials held to be their truth and what the Murphy Report suggested was the truth in relation to its various findings of fact with regard to the handling of abuse complaints by Catholic bishops. One fact, however, is undeniable: thousands of children were sexually abused by Catholic clergy over decades, both in their parishes and schools and in the industrial and reformatory schools that were supposed to provide for their care (Ryan, 2009). We owe it to them and to their families to get to the full truth of what occurred and to prevent its re-occurrence. The group that carried out the analysis of the Murphy Report (2009) were not convinced that the report had in fact gotten to the core of the problem. (For further information, see the Winter, 2013 edition of *Studies: An Irish Quarterly*).

In her analysis of the workings of a number of commissions and inquiries into organisational disasters, Vaughan (2006) found that the composition and process of each commission is of significance to the final outcome of its work. More importantly, she also found that the manner in which the problem is framed [is to be interpreted] is set early in discussion with one or two people before the full commission is assembled. These internal debates may also never be made known. The timeframe given to commissions to carry out their work was also found to be significant by Vaughan (2006), as this indicated how extensive the inquiry could be and whether shortcuts would have to be taken. Vaughan (2006) also found that many reports of commissions and inquiries are governed by hindsight, with the commission reconstructing what had happened in historical time with contemporary knowledge of the tragic outcome. This body of work also found that many important witnesses and conversations are neither recorded nor available when commissions and inquiries investigate organisational disasters, as historical actions begin to take on a contemporary relevance. A conclusion of this extensive work is the finding that in all commissions of investigation such bias must always be controlled, lest the actions of key actors leading up to the crisis take on an intentionality and direction in retrospect that they did not have at the time.

Interviews with bishops and clergy who had been the subject of the Murphy Commission's work showed that, while they saw some value in the Murphy Report, they were deeply concerned about the many inaccuracies and unfair comments that it contained about them (see Keenan, 2013). From the beginning there was nothing in the terms of reference or in how the problem was to be framed that would locate the response by the church officials in the circumstances of the time and in the context of civil society. There was no meaningful comparison made with other organisations as to how abuse was handled by them in the relevant period. As one respondent said, 'If we mishandled it who handled it better in the 50s, 60s, 70s, 80s and 90s?' The finding of deliberate cover-up of abuse is simply rejected by them and attributed instead to ignorance of the dynamics of sexual violence, lack of knowledge about the effects of abuse, the theology of scandal, fear of Rome and a paternalism towards priests that overruled their response to the children. The role played by the medical and psychiatric profession and their contribution to the plans that were made for clergy who had abused were completely understated in the report. The legal advice that had been given to bishops and diocesan officials for decades was not investigated or even questioned by the Murphy team at all. The legal opinion, which was instrumental to how each case was handled, went completely unscrutinised – an important consideration, given that the commission totally comprised legal professionals.

Murphy failed to grasp the church context in which the senior clerics managed cases, and paid little attention to that context in evaluating their actions. As one bishop said, 'We were pastors not police'. Murphy failed to grasp the church structure and the role of the auxiliary bishop in dealing with a highly centralised church organisation and diocese. Subsequently, former auxiliary bishops were accused of failures to take actions that were not within their role at the time. One senior cleric said that obedience was often mooted as not having been exercised by the Murphy team, who promoted the idea that the bishops and senior clerics did not act decisively in not removing priests from ministry, especially those who refused to stand aside. But according to these men: 'Obedience cannot be used as a means of oppression. This would amount to an abuse of power'. 'One cannot promote the kingdom of justice while acting unjustly' (see also Keenan, 2013: 439).

While the Murphy Report criticized canon law, the commission itself failed to grasp the responsibilities of bishops and senior clergy under canon law and the rights of individuals that it contained. It also failed to completely appreciate the role of the Vatican and the Roman Curia in controlling the actions of the national churches. As one respondent explained: 'It took a long time for Rome to respond to this' (see also Keenan, 2013: 442). The commission also failed to recognise that a vital and primary part of the mission of the church is forgiveness and the emphasis that some senior clerics would have placed on repentance in their dealings with abusive clergy. While Murphy failed to give due weight to these considerations, it opted for attributing the worst of all possible motives to diocesan officials in their handling of allegations of child abuse.

The respondents were clear that the Murphy Report completely failed to understand the complexities involved in dealing with retrospective sexual abuse disclosures, something with which health professionals struggle today and which legal academics question with regard to legal and due process considerations in such cases (see Ring, 2009a, 2009b). Murphy also failed to appreciate the significance of the fact that the majority of allegations of abuse made to diocesan officials were made by adults who had been abused as children. A respondent noted, '[t]he victims came as adults to say would you deal with that priest. They did not want to go to the police' at that time (see also Keenan, 2013: 442). What was also significant for senior clergy was the fact that the report contained many factual inaccuracies that were not corrected in the final draft of the report, even when these inaccuracies were drawn to the attention of the commission and which had significant consequences for some participants.[8] Some of these bishops and senior clergy have left envelopes in safes that can be opened in the event of their death in which they attempt to set the record straight and give account of the decisions they made in responding to abuse complaints. For many of these senior clergy, child sexual abuse has dominated their lives and ministries for the past 30 years. It has also tragically dominated the lives of many of the victims of clerical sexual abuse.

In relation to the Murphy Commission, it can be said that the manner in which the problem was framed produced a rational-choice or regulatory-failure explanatory causal model that became reduced to a dominant narrative of cover-up of the abuse of minors by church leaders. The individualistic narrative may have also served to salve society's conscience by downplaying its complicity in committing children, mostly those on the margins of society, to these institutions. (See O'Sullivan and O'Donnell (2012) on the history of coercive confinement.) An alternative interpretive frame, such as a comparative sociological frame, would have produced a different causal model – for example, an organisational-system failure causal model – with different learnings for the future and different outcome for witnesses.

In coming to this conclusion, it becomes evident that the composition of commissions of investigation is important, and how a problem is framed is not neutral but political in effect. Such knowing therefore casts empirical light on the importance of constructing multi-disciplinary, comprehensively resourced teams of suitably qualified personnel when one is inquiring into matters of public importance, and that their work is audited and subject to supervisory oversight by an independently appointed suitably qualified body.

Conclusions

The findings presented in this chapter suggest that a systemic perspective offers promise for how the problem of sexual abuse in the Catholic Church is best conceptualised, in that a number of inter-related factors coalesced and came together in different individuals and organisational cultures to shape the contours of this particular problem. This premise also has applicability to other organisational cultures and contexts in which sexual abuse of minors has occurred. However, that is for other researchers to pursue. Furthermore, the sociological explanatory frame may offer new insights into the causes of sexual offending more generally by drawing attention to the social factors that precipitate and perpetuate such behaviour. Many theories (and treatment programmes) focus on psychological causes, such as criminogenic attitudes or worldviews (see Mann and Hollin, 2010). However, sex offenders also experience a range of social barriers to reintegration. Many are alienated from friends, families and communities; receive negative media attention; lose access to sources of social capital; experience intense psychological distress; and fear public condemnation (Robbers, 2009). By highlighting the need to address the social as well as psychological causes of sexual offending, these insights offer important lessons for policy and practice. For example, Keenan (2014) found that victims, offenders and criminal justice professionals believed that restorative justice initiatives could complement existing criminal justice responses to sexual offending. In particular, offenders felt that they had a moral obligation to provide their victims with an apology and an explanation for their actions. They also hoped that restorative justice would provide them with an opportunity for redemption, healing and forgiveness.

When one analyses the results of all of the scholarly research on the problem of sexual abuse of minors within the Catholic Church, what begins to emerge is the kind of information that could well be internalised by senior personnel in the church and used as a basis for meaningful change. However, it is also the kind of information that poses the greatest threat to the clerical and hierarchical establishment (Doyle, 2014). For some, this is why the problem of abuse within the Catholic Church has not yet been adequately addressed (Doyle, 2014; Keenan, 2011).

In relation to the investigations into the church's handling of abuse complaints, it is at times when the public is most agitated by the perceived wrongdoings of one sector of society that any statutory investigation and a responsible media have to be seen to carry out its work in a calm, impartial and dispassionate manner. It is at times when a society is experiencing what can be seen as a cultural trauma (Alexander, 2004) that the work of commissions of investigation and statutory inquiries have to be especially careful in how they go about their work. The pull of the dominant narrative must be resisted. The importance of establishing accessible[9] regulatory oversight and accountability mechanisms for all commissions and inquiries therefore cannot be underestimated. The Irish state has already introduced a range of measures in response to the revelations to improve the regulation, management and governance of childcare service delivery. For example, a new statutory body, the Child and Family Support Agency, was established, the Republic of Ireland's constitution was amended by referendum to add a provision that recognises and protects children's rights, new child-protection guidelines were published and additional funding was provided to finance counselling and support services for survivors (Ryan Report Monitoring Group, 2012).

What also emerges when one studies the sexual abuse problem in the Catholic Church is the resilience of children and adults and the power of the human spirit in the face of a fragile, but powerful organisation that seems to have long departed from the messages of its founder. Herein lies the real challenge. In engaging more critically with the messages of its founder, a restorative church could well be one in which victims of sexual abuse would be put at the centre of the church's response; clergy offenders and the church community would be brought together in dialogue; a restructuring of power relations could emerge; and the institutional and organisational factors that contributed to the genesis of this most global of global problems would be addressed.

References

Adriaenssens, P. (2010) *Commissie Voor De Behandeling Van Klachten Wegens Seksueel Misbruik In Een Pastorale Relatie*. Available at: http://deredactie.be/polopoly_fs/1.860520!file/Eindrapport.pdf (accessed 10 March 2015).

Alexander, J. (2004) 'Toward a Theory of Cultural Trauma', in R. Eyerman, J. Alexander, B. Giesen, N. Smelser and P. Sztompka (eds) *Cultural Trauma and Collective Identity*. Berkeley: University of California Press.

Arendt, H. (2000) *The Portable Hannah Arendt* (edited with an introduction by Peter Baehr). New York: Penguin Classics.

Barrett, A., Kamiya, Y. and O'Sullivan, V. (2014) 'Child Sexual Abuse and Later-Life Economic Consequences', *Journal of Behavioural and Experimental Economics*, 53: 10–16.

Bennett, R. and the Staff of the National Review Board for the Protection of Children and Young People (2004) *A Report on the Crisis in the Catholic Church in the United States*. Washington DC: The United States Conference of Catholic Bishops.

Blanshard, P. (1954) *The Irish and Catholic Power*. London: Derek Verschoyle.

Carr, A., Dooley, B., Fitzpatrick, M., Flanagan, E., Flanagan-Howard, R., Tierney, K., White, M., Daly, M. and Egan, J. (2010) 'Adult Adjustment of Survivors of Institutional Child Abuse in Ireland', *Child Abuse and Neglect*, 34(7): 477–89.

Carroll, J. (1992) 'Bishop Must Now Focus on Accountability and Truth', *Irish Times*, 1 July.

Cohen, S. (1972) *Folk Devils and Moral Panics: The Creation of the Mods and Rockers*. London: MacGibbon and Kee.

Corby, B. (2000) *Child Abuse: Towards a Knowledge Base*. Milton Keynes: Open University Press.

Deetman, X. (2011) *Commission of Inquiry into Sexual Abuse in the Roman Catholic Church in the Netherlands*. Available at: www.onderzoekrk.nl/english-summery.html (accessed 10 March 2015).

Doyle, T. (2014) 'Pope's New Abuse Commission Is Another Promise Waiting to Be Broken', *National Catholic Reporter*, 25 March. Available at: http://ncronline.org/blogs/examining-crisis/popes-new-abuse-commission-another-promise-waiting-be-broken (accessed 10 March 2015).

Fuller, L. (2002) *Irish Catholicism since 1950: The Undoing of a Culture*. Dublin: Gill and Macmillan.

Goode, H., McGee, H. and O'Boyle, C. (2003) *Time to Listen: Confronting Child Sexual Abuse by Catholic Clergy in Ireland*. Dublin: Liffey Press.

Hanson, R. K. (2010) Personal communication.

Holohan, C. (2011) *In Plain Sight: Responding to the Ferns, Ryan, Murphy and Cloyne Reports*. Dublin: Amnesty International Ireland.

Inglis, T. (1998) *Moral Monopoly. The Rise and Fall of the Catholic Church in Modern Ireland* (2nd edn). Dublin: University College Dublin Press.

John Jay College (2004) *The Nature and Scope of Sexual Abuse of Minors by Catholic Priests and Deacons in the United States, 1950–2002*. Washington DC: United States Conference of Catholic Bishops.

John Jay College (2006) *Supplementary Report. The Nature and Scope of Sexual Abuse of Minors by Catholic Priests and Deacons in the United States, 1950–2002*. Washington DC: United States Conference of Catholic Bishops.

John Jay College (2011) *The Causes and Context of Sexual Abuse of Minors by Catholic Priests and Deacons in the United States, 1950–2002*. Washington DC: United States Conference of Catholic Bishops.

Keenan, M. (2011) *Child Sexual Abuse and the Catholic Church: Gender, Power and Organisational Culture*. New York: Oxford University Press.

Keenan, M. (2013) 'Senior Diocesan Officials and the Murphy Report', *Studies: An Irish Quarterly Review*, 102(408): 434–46.

Keenan, M. (2014) *Sexual Trauma and Abuse: Restorative and Transformative Possibilities?* Dublin: University College Dublin.

Loftus, J. A. and Carmago, R. J. (1993) 'Treating the Clergy', *Annals of Sex Research*, 6(4): 287–303.

Luxmoore, J. (2013) 'Belgian Bishops Welcome Court Condemnation of 2010 Cathedral Raid', *National Catholic Reporter*, 30 May. Available at: http://ncronline.org/news/global/belgian-bishops-welcome-court-condemnation-2010-cathedral-raid (accessed 10 March 2015).

Mann, R. and Hollin, C. (2010) 'Self-reported Schemas in Sexual Offenders', *The Journal of Forensic Psychiatry & Psychology*, 21(6): 834–51.

Marshall, P. (1997) *The Prevalence of Convictions for Sexual Offending*, Research Findings, no 55. Croydon, UK: Home Office Research and Statistics Directorate.

McDonagh, J. (2013) 'The Representative Sample in the Murphy Report', *Studies: An Irish Quarterly Review*, 102(408): 456–67.

McGee, H., Garavan, R., de Barra, M., Byrne, J. and Conroy, R. (2002) *The SAVI Report: Sexual Abuse and Violence in Ireland. A National Study of Irish Experiences, Beliefs and Attitudes Concerning Sexual Violence.* Dublin: The Liffey Press.

Moore, C. (1995) *Betrayal of Trust: The Father Brendan Smyth Affair and the Catholic Church.* Dublin: Marino Books.

Murphy, Y. (2009) *Commission of Investigation: Report into the Catholic Archdiocese of Dublin* (the 'Murphy Report'). Dublin: Stationery Office.

Murphy, Y. (2011) *Commission of Investigation: Report into the Catholic Diocese of Cloyne.* Dublin: Stationery Office.

Ó Ciardha, C. and Ward, T. (2013) 'Theories of Cognitive Distortions in Sexual Offending: What the Current Research Tells Us', *Trauma Violence Abuse*, 14(1): 5–21.

O'Sullivan, E. and O'Donnell, I. (2012) *Coercive Confinement in Ireland: Patients, Prisoners and Penitents.* Manchester: Manchester University Press.

O'Toole, F. (1994) 'Events That Shook Pillars of Power May Assist Peace', *Irish Times*, 19 November, p. 6.

Office of the Attorney General, Commonwealth of Massachusetts (2003) *The Sexual Abuse of Children in the Roman Catholic Archdiocese of Boston.* Available at: www.bishop-accountability.org/downloads/archdiocese.pdf (accessed 10 March 2015).

Office of the Grand Jury, Philadelphia (2005) *Report of the Grand Jury into Sexual Abuse of Minors by Clergy in the Philadelphia Archdiocese.* Available at: www.bishop-accountability.org/pa_philadelphia/Philly_GJ_report.htm (accessed 10 March 2015).

Office of the Grand Jury, Philadelphia (2011) *Investigation of Sexual Abuse by Clergy II.* Available at: www.phila.gov/districtattorney/PDFs/clergyAbuse2-finalReport.pdf (accessed 10 March 2015).

Pastoral Letter of His Holiness Benedict XVI to the Catholics of Ireland March 19 (2010) Available at: http://w2.vatican.va/content/benedict-xvi/en/letters/2010/documents/hf_ben-xvi_let_20100319_church-ireland.html (accessed 10 March 2015).

Ring, S. (2009a) 'Justice Denied? An Analysis of the Difficulties Facing Applicants for Prohibition in Delayed Prosecutions for Child Sexual Abuse', *First Criminal Law Online*, (6): 83–93.

Ring, S. (2009b) 'Beyond the Reach of Justice? Complainant Delay in Historic Child Sexual Abuse Cases and the Right to a Fair Trial', *Judicial Studies Institute Journal*, 9(2): 162–203. Available at: www.jsijournal.ie/html/Volume_9_No._2/9[2]_Ring_Child_sexual_abuse.pdf (accessed 10 March 2015).

Robbers, M. L. (2009) 'Lifers on the Outside: Sex Offenders and Disintegrative Shaming', *International Journal of Offender Therapy and Comparative Criminology*, 53(1): 5–28.

RTE (1996) *Dear Daughter.* Screened February 1996.

RTE Television (2011) *Would You Believe?* Screened 17 January 2011.

Ryan, S. (2009) *Commission on Child Abuse Report.* Dublin: Government Publications.

Ryan Report Monitoring Group (2012) *Ryan Report Implementation Plan: Third Progress Report.* Dublin: Department of Child and Youth Affairs.

Sullivan, J. and Beech, A. (2002) 'Professional Perpetrators. Sex Offenders Who Use Their Employment to Target and Sexually Abuse the Children with Whom They Work', *Child Abuse Review*, 11(3): 153–67.

Sweeney, F. (2013a) 'Commissions of Investigation and Procedural Fairness', *Studies: An Irish Quarterly Review*, 102(408): 377–87.

Sweeney, F. (2013b) *Commissions of Investigation and Procedural Fairness: A Legal Review of the Commissions of Investigation Act 2004 and the Murphy Report.* Dublin: The Association of Catholic Priests.

Vaughan, D. (2006) 'The Social Shaping of Commission Reports', *Sociological Forum*, 21(2): 291–306.

Whyte, J. H. (1980) *Church and State in Modern Ireland: 1923–1979* (2nd edn). Dublin: Gill and MacMillan.

World Religious Statistics (2006) *Major Religions Ranked by Size.* Available at: www.adherents.com/Religions_By_Adherents.html (accessed 10 March 2015).

Notes

1 In addition to my work on the Catholic clergy, I am the Principal Investigator of a Facing Forward/UCD-collaborative research project, *Sexual Trauma and Abuse: Restorative and Transformative Possibilities*, and am also collaborating with KU Leuven on a Daphne III funded project, *Developing Integrated Responses to Sexual Violence: An Interdisciplinary Research Project on the Potential of Restorative Justice.* My most recent

publications include, *Child Sexual Abuse and the Catholic Church: Gender Power and Organizational Culture* (2012) New York: Oxford University Press, and *Broken Faith: Why Hope Matters* (2013) Oxford: Lang, with Pat Claffey and Joe Egan (eds).

2 I am currently involved in a new organization called Coping, which is a volunteer-led NGO, established to provide support and guidance for children of Catholic clergy, their mothers and the priests themselves.

3 Some researchers have attempted to estimate the extent of sexual offending in the general adult male population, taking into account the many limitations with available data and comparative definitions (Hanson, 2010; Marshall, 1997). Basing his analysis on the actual number of convicted sex offenders in the United States and the United Kingdom as a percentage of adult males, which is 1 per cent in California (Hanson) and 1 per cent to 2 per cent in the United Kingdom (Marshall), Hanson adjusted the figures based on the information already known about conviction rates per victim for child sexual offenders, which is between one in five and one in ten, to suggest that the real rate of child sexual abuse perpetrated by the general adult male population is about 6 per cent. Although this figure is helpful, it must be cautiously interpreted and may be useful as a guide rather than as yet verifiable fact.

4 See Keenan, M. (2011) *Child Sexual Abuse and the Catholic Church: Gender, Power and Organizational Culture* for fuller discussion of this research.

5 I am the Chairperson of the Advisory Board for a Support Group for Catholic clergy out of ministry because of abuse and boundary violations, and we are finding that poverty and isolation are real problems for this cohort of men.

6 The Role of the Vatican has been demonstrated in an RTE documentary, *Would You Believe* (2011), screened 17 January.

7 National Church, such as in the USA, the Netherlands, Belgium, Ireland, as distinct from Vatican-commissioned work.

8 For example, the names of two diocesan officials were mixed up in the draft report with the failure to act attributed to the wrong person, and, while this error was drawn to the attention of the Commission in submissions, the error was not corrected in the Final Report.

9 A procedure that does not require complex and expensive legal proceedings in a High Court.

28

Mental illness and the criminalisation process

Damien Brennan

Introduction

This chapter considers how understandings of, and responses to, mental illness have alternated between the medical and judicial realms on the island of Ireland over the past 200 years. Shaped by law, discourses and practice, it is proposed that there are identifiable shifts in the social construction and management of emotions, behaviours and actions, which are constructed as being deviant or challenging to society. A movement from the moral to the clinical, to the criminal, back to the clinical and once again to criminal is illuminated. During the pre-1840 era, mental illness was constructed as personal tragedy and was managed through 'moral intervention'. Clinical understandings of 'mental illnesses' became dominant during this time in parallel to the medical takeover of asylums. A shift from the clinical to the criminal realm commences with the introduction of the Dangerous Lunatic Acts 1838 and 1867, which moved control over asylum admission from a medical to a judicial process. This established a strong association between mental illness, dangerousness and criminality, which remained intact up to the mid-twentieth century. A reassertion of medical control over the social construction and management of 'mental illness' was driven by the provisions in the Mental Treatment Act (NI) 1932 in Northern Ireland and the Mental Treatment Act 1945 in the Republic of Ireland, the international standardisation of diagnostic criteria and the introduction of new psychopharmacological interventions. This stimulated a continuous decline in the number of mentally ill residents within institutions in the Republic of Ireland from a high point of 21,720 in 1956 to 4,522 at the beginning of the twenty-first century and similarly in Northern Ireland from 5,320 in 1951 to 3,337 in 1991 (Brennan, 2014). The decline of these mental hospitals has been mirrored by a programme of prison building, expanding in the Republic of Ireland from 401 prisoners in 1956 to 2,948 at the close of the twentieth century. (Comparisons in Northern Ireland are more problematic because of the impact of political unrest on prison utilisation during the late twentieth century.) Essentially this heralds a contemporary shift away from the clinical context back to the criminal realm, with mental hospitals being replaced by prisons as the principal sites of confinement.

The comparatively high prevalence of mental health problems amongst the prison population is consistently documented in the international literature (Belcher, 1988; Aderibigbe, 1997;

Singleton *et al.*, 1998; Fazel and Danesh, 2002). This phenomenon is reflected on the island of Ireland, both north and south. For example, the Mental Health Commission (2011) in the Republic reported that:

> Among male prisoners, 15% of those committed to prison in 2003, 25% of remand prisoners and 22% of sentenced prisoners had a mental illness of some kind. ... Among female prisoners, the rates are higher: 37% of sentenced women and 23% of women committed to prison in 2003.

Similarly, the Criminal Justice Inspection of Northern Ireland (2010) reported that around:

> 16% of those individuals who are placed into custody meet one or more of the assessment criteria for mental disorder. In addition, it is estimated that 78% of male prisoners on remand and approximately 50% of female prisoners are personality disordered – a figure seven times that of the general population.

The key sources of data informing this chapter include the Inspector of Lunatic Asylums Reports, the Inspector for Mental Hospitals Reports, Special Parliamentary Papers, early publications of the Medical Press and Circular and The Psychiatric Hospital and Prison Census, focusing on the Island of Ireland up to 1922 and the Republic of Ireland thereafter along with comparative data from Northern Ireland. Methodologically, this data is considered through a fusion of the interpretive and critical traditions within historical sociology.

The Brehon era

An early set of traditions, obligations and provisions for the care and treatment of the 'insane' existed under Brehon Law, an early Irish civil legal system (Robins, 1986). Brehon Law incorporated a complex and wide-ranging body of laws and practices which emerged in the pre-Christian era. Under these laws, individuals who were understood to be insane had reduced rights and responsibilities, which provided a level of safeguard against mistreatment and an acknowledgement that normal social responsibilities may be transgressed in the case of mental illness. However, there is a dearth of research illuminating how these provisions influenced the lived realities of the individuals considered to be mentally unwell during this period. If an incident that challenged social norms did occur, those responsible for the care of a 'fool' or 'lunatic' could be held accountable if they failed to provide appropriate care so as to prevent such wrongdoing. Brehon law also made provisions against the 'insane copulating, marrying or bearing children' (Scheper-Hughes, 1979: 153). During this era, there was an absence of institutional provision for the mentally ill, and as such, Brehon Law worked very much within a community-care context. Human distress, social non-conformity and mental illness were understood to be personal phenomena, experienced and negotiated within the family and community setting. As such, mental illness was not conceptualised at this time as either a judicial, criminal or bio-medical phenomenon. However, a basic diagnostic system did evolve, which:

> [D]istinguished broadly between idiots, fools and lunatics but frequently sub-classified each group in designation of their legal rights and obligations. A major influence of the classification appears to have been the extent to which the individual was adjudged capable of work ... or otherwise useful.
>
> *(Robins, 1986: 14)*

There are some parallels between these early diagnostic categories and contemporary practice; for example, a person could be labelled a 'fool' at the age of seven, which resonates with a category that became known as 'mental handicap' and then 'intellectual disability'. This is a condition characterised by significant limitations in both intellectual functioning and in adaptive behaviour which is usually diagnosed during the early stages of childhood. The category of 'lunatic' or 'mad' was used in cases that would now be described as a 'mental disorder' or a 'psychiatric illness', which refers to disorders generally characterised by dysregulation of mood, thought, or behaviour such as depression, anxiety disorders and schizophrenia.

A key legacy of Brehon Law was the absence of institutional provision for the mentally ill either in asylums or prisons, and hence, there was an absence of selective confinement based on diagnosis. Consequently, the rapid construction of asylums during early nineteenth-century island of Ireland was a 'green field' development, and the systems, structures and bureaucracies that underpinned the new asylum system were not premised on pre-existing practices. This deviates from the system of 'transfer of institutional' function asserted by Foucault (1967), who observed that across Europe the built environment and institutional practice of confinement had their roots in the classification and segregation of individuals suffering from leprosy. Foucault (1967) argues that the management of leprosy entailed a practice of segregation, which encompassed several technologies including classification, labelling and selective confinement. Physical buildings were erected to act as a public place of confinement for lepers, and medical practice established itself as a central agent controlling both diagnoses and intervention. Essentially, Foucault (1967) makes the point that this established a physical setting, diagnostic process and form of intervention that is later adopted in the case of mental illness and asylums.

> Leprosy disappeared, the leper vanished, or almost, from memory; these structures remained. Often, in these same places, the formulas of exclusion would be repeated, strangely similar two or three centuries later. Poor vagabonds, criminals, and 'deranged minds' would take the part played by the leper.
>
> *(Foucault, 1967: 5)*

Foucault (1967) emphasises the professional and institutional drive towards self-preservation. Essentially, professionals had a direct interest in the creation of new markets in deviance so as to continue to legitimate their practice within an expanding set of institutional settings. Foucault (1967) observed this dynamic in the context of various institutional building projects across Europe; however, the island of Ireland did not have a legacy of widespread leprosy, and there was no widespread national construction of leprosaria. In fact, there was an absence of any pre-existing institutional structures, systems or built environments to underpin the development of the Irish asylum system. What was to become the most prolific and enduring programme of institutional confinement on the island of Ireland was initiated from a standing start, proposed by an expert group and purpose built as a new initiative specifically for the care of the insane.

A number of other features of the early development of the island of Ireland's asylum system are atypical when compared to similar institutional trajectories in other European countries (Brennan, 2014). For example, the classic pattern of the development and expansion of asylums during rapid industrialisation is diametrically at odds with the socio-economic reality of Irish life, which remained predominantly rural and un-industrialised through the period of asylum growth in the nineteenth and twentieth centuries. Furthermore, the national asylum system on the island of Ireland was publicly funded and managed centrally, rather than being linked to private enterprise or philanthropic initiative. Lastly, the Irish asylum provision remained outside of church control, which is unusual both internationally and within the context of an expansive pattern of church–state partnerships in other areas of Irish social-service provision.

Moral management

The Act of Union 1800 had the effect of relocating parliamentary decision making from Dublin to Westminster. As a result, social policy and law for the island of Ireland was negotiated and agreed in Westminster and subsequently implemented through the colonial administration at Dublin castle. This had the effect of disconnecting the process of assessing social needs and responding to social problems within a localised community context. Prior to this Act, there was very limited social policy or legislative provision for the care of mentally ill persons on the island of Ireland; however, this was to change radically during the early decades of the nineteenth century.

Internationally, discourse concerning mental illness, human distress and social non-conformity began to promote a more humane approach to mental illness. For example, Samuel Tuke (1813) published *Description of the Retreat, an Institution near York, for Insane Persons of the Society of Friends: Containing an Account of Its Origin and Progress, the Modes of Treatment, and a Statement of Cases*. This text advocated a moral and caring approach to institutional care, which has strong resonance with similar work by Philippe Pinel in Paris around the same period (Saris, 1997). This moral approach emphasised the possibility of cure through institutional care that was characterised by order, calmness and kindness. The availability of such institutional care was seen to be a progressive feature of modernising societies.

Stimulated by such discourse, the Irish Chief Secretary, Robert Peel, in 1814 established an enquiry into the extent of provisions for the insane on the island of Ireland. While the Cork asylum and the Richmond in Dublin provided localised interventions, the enquiry established that provision across the island of Ireland was wholly inadequate and there was an absence of a national system. This intervention led to the establishment of the Select Committee on the Lunatic Poor in Ireland (1817), which was mandated to estimate the level of insanity and to make recommendations regarding the care required at a national level. The report of this Select Committee suggested that levels of insanity were high and that a national network of district asylums was required. The 1817 report drew on the then contemporary discourses concerning insanity, with classification, segregation and moral intervention being the key principles that would underpin the new national asylum system that was to evolve.

Responding to this report, Acts were passed in 1817 and 1821 which provided the legislative structures required to instigate the construction of a national network of asylums for the lunatic poor. These Acts provided for a centralised administrative structure within Dublin Castle with responsibility for overseeing construction, financing and inspection of Irish asylums.

> [I]n 1817, a Committee of the House of Commons gave it as their opinion, that the only mode of effectual relief would be found in the formation of District Asylums, and effect was given to their recommendation by an Act passed in the same year, 57 Geo. III., 106.
>
> *(Inspector of Lunatic Asylums, 1846: 5)*

This Act, along with subsequent enactments, granted the necessary power to the Irish administration to implement the early phase of asylum construction across the country. Asylums were constructed in Armagh, Ballinasloe, Belfast, Carlow, Clonmel, Derry, Limerick, Maryborough and Waterford, all of which were initially relatively conservative in scale with provision for approximately 150 patients in each institution (Finnane, 1981). The Richmond Institution in Dublin and the asylum in Cork complemented these new buildings to form part of the national asylum system. As a system of centrally controlled social intervention, the national asylum system was ground-breaking, predating by 15 years the development of the national primary school system.

There was considerable social deprivation across the island of Ireland during the nineteenth century, which reached appalling levels during the Great Famine of the mid-1840s. As a form of social security, the asylum system provided a major form of institutional intervention that could be employed by families during difficult periods. Asylums also became a larger physical and economic feature within the communities in which they were situated, which further encouraged their expansion. Direct employment within these institutions provided wages that underpinned local economies, which in turn created secondary employment (Brennan, 2014). As these institutions became operational within local communities, they became sites of social assistance for a host of social problems. While individuals were admitted for a multitude of reasons, including mental distress, the rationale for admission was not understood to be a bio-medical or criminal issue. During this early phase, mental distress and social non-conformity were seen as an affliction at the level of the individual with moral, rather than medical, means employed as the primary form of intervention. However, under this moral management there were some bizarre and horrific physician interventions including bleeding, the use of the 'swing chair' and cold water 'baths of surprise' (Robins, 1986; Porter, 2004).

Medicalisation

In the early years of asylum expansion a medical qualification was not required to secure an appointment as asylum manager (Brennan, 2014). Harmonising with the moral management approach, key qualities of asylum managers were their moral character, temperament and caring disposition. These asylum managers were appointed directly by the Lord-Lieutenant (the British monarch's official representative in Ireland) and were answerable to the asylum boards (Finnane, 1981). The physical needs of patients were attended to by visiting medics. However, the asylum system quickly became an institution of major importance, and professional bodies became interested in them as sites in which they could advance professional practice. Up to 1845, the inspection of asylums fell under the responsibility of the Inspector of Prisons, who inspected both sets of institutions. In 1845, there were 177 men and 113 women within the prison system who were identified as having a mental illness, while there were 1,311 men and 1,244 women resident in public asylums (Brennan, 2014). A medical doctor, Francis White, was appointed as Inspector General of Prisons in 1841, and from this position he became one of the most influential individuals in moving the inspection, management and clinical practice of asylums to the medical realm. For example, he was a significant actor in the development of the *Rules for the Regulation of District Asylums* published in 1843, which set out a medical hierarchy for asylum day-to-day management, and he also advanced the case for the separation of the inspection of prisons and asylums, which was realised in 1845. Once these functions were separated, White was appointed as the first inspector of asylums, and from this position he successfully advocated for the reserving of all positions of asylum managers for medically qualified persons. During this period, the conceptualisation of mental illness, human distress and social non-conformity were increasingly moved to the medical–scientific realm. For example, rule 49 for District Asylums Regulations states that every appointed physician

[I]s requested to bear in mind, that the object of the Government is not simply to have the bodily ailments of the patients attended, but to assist their recovery by moral or medical means, and to advance medical sciences in the case of lunacy.

(Inspectors-General, 1844: 46)

545

In parallel with this medical takeover, a new Select committee was appointed in 1843 to examine the general state of Irish asylum provision. This committee reported that the system was inadequate and required substantial expansion, stating that it had formed 'the strongest opinion' of:

> The Necessity of increasing the Accommodation for Pauper Lunatics in Ireland … by an increased Number of the District Asylums or by an Enlargement of those Asylums, or by the Erection of Separate Establishments specially appropriated for these Classes of Patients.
> *(Select Committee of the House of Lords Appointed to Consider the State of the Lunatic Poor in Ireland, 1843: xxv)*

The reports from the newly appointed asylum inspectors echoed this call for expansion as a means of coping with existing overcrowding and to meet what was perceived as a very high demand for asylum admission. These reports instigated a further phase of asylum construction with new asylums erected in Cork, Kilkenny, Killarney, Mullingar, Omagh and Sligo during the 1850s, and Castlebar, Downpatrick, Ennis, Enniscorthy, Letterkenny and Monaghan during the 1860s.

The medical management of asylums was seen as scientifically justifiable while also desirable due to the higher level of 'personal integrity' of medical men. For example, in 1856, the editor of the *Asylum Journal of Mental Science* drew attention to two incidents relating to corruption and the death of a patient, noting that these 'took place in asylums in which there is no resident medical officer, both of the asylums being under the control of non-medical managers' (Bucknill, 1856: 136).

In essence, during the early to mid-nineteenth century, the Irish asylum system was expanding and becoming increasingly medicalised, with medical personnel gaining control over inspection, management and clinical practice. A similar development was occurring in asylum systems across the Western world at this time, driven primarily by professional politics and medical career interests rather than any scientifically justified rationale. Increasingly medical scientific principles were applied, which consolidated the established practice of classification, segregation and selective intervention. Within this milieu, human distress and behaviours that challenged social norms were understood as clinical matters, which could be categorised and managed through a clinical process. However, new legislation was introduced during the mid-nineteenth century which had the effect of moving asylum admission away from the clinical and towards the judicial realms. This recast mental illness, human distress and social non-conformity as criminal events.

'Dangerous lunatics'

A close association between mental illness, dangerousness and criminality was established with the passing of the 1838 Dangerous Lunatics Act. Political calls for better public safety in Dublin acted as a catalyst to the passing of this act. This political concern was simulated by public shock at the murder of a bank director in Dublin who was killed by a wandering 'lunatic' who had been refused admission to the Richmond Asylum (Robins, 1986: 144). While this legislation was enacted in Westminster, its provisions were particular to the island of Ireland, and it was to become a key social force shaping the distinctive trajectory of Irish asylum use.

This Act was intended to be utilised as a preventive measure by providing for the identification and detention of 'dangerous lunatics' who may commit a criminal act at some point in the future. Under this legislation, two magistrates could commit a lunatic directly to a gaol if they were of the view that the lunatic was likely to commit a criminal offence. It should be noted that at this time the criteria for insanity were poorly defined and all-encompassing. In the early years of the application of this legislation, magistrates were not obliged to seek a medical opinion. A person committed to a gaol could be transferred to a district asylum and held until a judicial order effected their release. The operationalisation of this legislation had the effect of relocating the power over asylum admission to a judicial rather than medical context, which, 'in the early years of asylum construction in Ireland, established an intimate link between insanity and criminality' (O. Walsh, 1999a: 225). There were few safeguards against the misuse of this legislation, and it became the predominant route of asylum admission during the mid-nineteenth century (Brennan, 2014).

Furthermore, the Act provided for the committal of all dangerous lunatics regardless of means, which contrasted with work-houses, houses of industry and other institutes which were restricted to the poor. As such, the Dangerous Lunatics Act provided a convenient means of removing family members whose behaviours were viewed as being an affront to social norms, and 'as far as the patient's family was concerned, this was the simplest method of ensuring admission' (Prior, 2003: 531). This Act was applied loosely and extensively in practice, to such an extent that the Lord Chancellor was moved to sending a circular to magistrates complaining about the abuse of this Act and reminding them of its intended narrow use.

> These Abuses ought not to be permitted. The Lord Chancellor has desired that a Return may be regularly made to him of all Lunatics committed to Prison under the Act of Victoria, but he feels assured that the Powers of the Act will in future be exercised with great Caution.
>
> *(Select Committee of the House of Lords Appointed to Consider the State of the Lunatic Poor in Ireland, 1843: xii)*

The 1838 Dangerous Lunatics Act created a situation where both 'lunatic' and 'criminal' were appearing before magistrates, and prison became the location of initial detention. Lunatics were then transferred to asylums when places became available. A further Dangerous Lunatics Act was passed in 1867 which operated in much the same way as the earlier legislation; however, magistrates were required to secure a medical certificate stating that the person in question was a lunatic, and they were also empowered to admit directly to the asylums.

While a medical certificate for admission was required, the cause and nature of insanity remained extremely speculative within medical practice during this time. For example, an article published in the *Medical Press and Circular* in 1866 by the Harveian Society of London includes the following causes:

> Civilisation, overcrowding, speculation in business, effeminacy and luxury, hereditary predisposition, intoxication, sexual excesses, enforced celibacy, self-abuse, injuries to the brain from railway accidents, single women who became violently devout, disappointed affection, Loss of friends, disappointed ambition, damage by blood-clot and tumours, religious zeal.
>
> *(ibid.: 510–11)*

The categories of 'Idiot, Epileptic and Mania' are cited in the first report produced by the Inspector of Lunatics (Inspector of Lunatic Asylums, 1846: 30). The report for 1879 sets out the categories and number of patients for that year as follows: 1,639 cases were classified as 'Moral Causes', 2,006 as 'Physical Causes', 1,898 as 'Hereditary Causes' and 457 as 'Not Known' (Inspector of Lunatic Asylums, 1880: 65). Sub-categories within moral cases included 'Poverty and Reverse of Fortune; Grief, Fear and Anxiety; Domestic Quarrels and Afflictions; Religious Excitement; Study and Mental Excitement, Ill-treatment; Pride; Anger; and Love, Jealousy and

Seduction'. In practice, these categories were so all-encapsulating that any person appearing before a magistrate could be constructed as being a lunatic.

While judicial and medical systems and structures facilitated admission to asylums, it was predominantly family members who initiated the admission process (Malcolm, 2003). For example, with reference to Ballinasloe, O. Walsh (1999b: 140–2) observes that:

> To take just one year as an example: sixty two patients out of seventy two in 1879 were committed on the evidence of family members … The committal process, far from being a disinterested and remote undertaking on the part of official bodies, was mediated through local practice and advice.

The 1838 and 1867 Dangerous Lunatics Acts 'continued to govern Irish committal procedures, at least in the south of the country, until 1945' (Malcolm, 2003: 324). As such, the provisions made in these nineteenth-century Acts provided a legislative framework that underpinned asylum and mental hospital admission in Northern Ireland up to 1932 and in the Republic of Ireland until 1945, when new Mental Treatment Acts were passed. While the Dangerous Lunatics Acts placed mental illness on the island of Ireland within the judicial realm, their effect was to lead to the expansion of asylums as the key location of committal. For example, in 1951 there were 5,320 mentally ill persons resident in various institutions in Northern Ireland, with a further 20,241 in the Republic of Ireland (Brennan, 2014). While these trends are similar, the actual rate per 100,000 of the population is significantly lower in Northern Ireland compared to the Republic of Ireland. This is a continuation of the pre-partition trend, which saw the most intensive asylum usage in the southern part of the island, particularly along the western seaboard (Finnane, 1981). In 1951 there were 684 mentally ill persons resident in mental hospitals per 100,000 of the population in the Republic, compared to 388 per 100,000 in Northern Ireland (see Figure 28.1 below). Interestingly, while the admission of the mentally ill continued to be mediated through a judicial process, mental hospitals rather than prisons were the principal locations of detention.

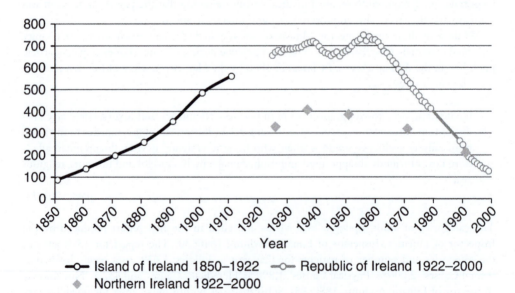

Figure 28.1 Number of 'mentally ill' persons resident in institutions per 100,000 of population 1850–2000

For example, when public mental hospital utilisation reached a peak in 1956 in the Republic of Ireland, with 20,063 residents, only 401 persons were in custody in prisons (Brennan, 2014).

Reassertion of bio-medical control

The passing of the 1945 Mental Treatment Act in the Republic of Ireland had the effect of consolidating medical dominance over matters relating to mental hospitals. Doctors, having previously gained control over key positions of power including directorships, inspection and clinic governance, now also secured direct control over admission and discharge. This served to move the social construction of mental distress and behaviours that challenged social norms into a medicalised context. Under the Mental Treatment Act, three primary modes of admission to psychiatric hospitals were established, referred to as 'voluntary', 'temporary' and 'persons of unsound mind'. These three provisions underpinned most admissions to psychiatric hospitals from 1945 onwards.

Voluntary admission occurred as a result of a direct application being made by the person seeking admission, or by their parents or guardian in the case of the patient being less than 16 years of age. The person seeking admission would be examined and assessed by a psychiatrist and, if deemed appropriate, admitted to the mental hospital to receive treatment until their discharge. However, if the admitted person wished to be discharged, 72 hours' notice was required which gave the hospital administration time to make arrangements for involuntary detention if the psychiatrist believed the person was unfit for discharge.

Temporary admission is involuntary detention. For such an admission to occur, an application was signed by a spouse or close relative of the patient. This form was also to be signed by a medical practitioner, usually the patient's General Practitioner (GP), two practitioners in the case of a private patient. The GP was required to certify that the patient had been examined by them within the previous seven days and that they were satisfied that the patient was suffering from a mental illness or was an addict in need of treatment (Casey and Craven, 1999). Within seven days of such a certificate being obtained, the person would then be moved to the mental hospital, where within 12 hours of arrival they were to be examined by a psychiatrist. This psychiatrist would then decide on whether to make an order for involuntary committal. On admission, the psychiatrist was required to inform the patient of their various rights, including the right to know all details relating to the order and the right to make an objection to an order or any subsequent extension to it. Such an objection could be made to the Inspector of Mental Hospital or the President of the High Court. A person admitted as a temporary patient could be detained for up to six months during which time they may receive treatment for their 'mental illness', administered against their will if deemed necessary. A Temporary Order could be extended up to three times, thus providing for a possible committal of up to two years.

A person could also be admitted as a 'Person of Unsound Mind' under the 1945 Act, which operated in a similar manner to temporary admission with a spouse, relative or a community welfare officer signing a form seeking admission. The Garda Síochána could also use these provisions in order to detain a person if they considered there to be a risk of harm occurring. A medical practitioner would then sign an order stating that they had examined the person within the previous 24 hours and were satisfied that the person was of 'unsound mind' and in need of admission. The person was then taken to the mental hospital within seven days where a psychiatrist would examine them and make a committal order if deemed necessary. Once admitted, the patient could be detained until they were medically discharged, which provided a possibility of long-term committal. The provision of 'Persons of Unsound Mind' was utilised post-1945 for most patients who were resident in mental hospitals prior to the passing of this Act. For example, in 1949 there were 17,332 Persons of Unsound Mind resident in District and Auxiliary Mental Hospitals on 31 December compared with 250 Voluntary patients and 886 Temporary patients (Brennan, 2014).

Reform of mental health legislation in Northern Ireland predated the above developments in the Republic of Ireland. The Mental Treatment Act (NI) 1932 grappled with moving policy and practice in Northern Ireland away from the institutional provisions for insanity of pre-partition Ireland and towards the practices and provisions of prevention and cure that were being pursued in England (Prior, 1993). Similar to the later developments in the Republic of Ireland, this Act introduced new procedures for admission including Voluntary, Temporary and Certified. After the passing of the 1932 Act, the:

> [T]otal number of patients being admitted to mental hospitals did not change very much. But within this the pattern of admission changed radically, with voluntary and temporary admission procedures being used immediately by a significant number of patients and a steady decline in certified admissions.
>
> *(Prior, 1993: 47)*

As can be seen in Figure 28.1, this impacted on rates of residency per 100,000 of population in Northern Ireland, falling from 409 in 1937; 388 in 1951; 322 in 1971; and 211 in 1991.

Such legislation, both in Northern Ireland and in the Republic of Ireland, firmly placed professional and public understandings relating to human distress and non-social conformity within the context of medical practice, particularly psychiatry, with mental hospitals as the key location of intervention. Within an anti-psychiatry thesis, one would expect increased residency to be associated with this consolidation of medical dominance. 'Because psychiatrists were charged with both defining madness and admitting patients to the asylum, they could effectively create the demand for their own services' (Samson, 1995: 59). There was indeed an increase in the level of mentally ill persons resident in institutions in the Republic of Ireland for a full decade following the passing of the 1945 Act, increasing from 19,538 in 1945 to a high point of 21,720 in 1956 (Brennan, 2014). However, similar to Northern Ireland, the number of patients admitted on a voluntary basis steadily increased. This created a pattern of a slow decline in the number of long-stay patients, which subsequently stimulated a gradual decline in overall levels of residency from 1956 onwards. By 2001, the *Irish Psychiatric Hospital and Units Census* found that 'eighty three percent of resident patients on the census night were voluntary … non-voluntary residents decreased from 25% in 1991 to 17% in 2001' (D. Walsh and Daly, 2002: 31). It is interesting to note that mental hospitals were the largest sites of institutional confinement operating within the Republic of Ireland during the second half of the twentieth century and yet admission during this time was predominately voluntary, characterised by self-admission and self-discharge. While family, local communities and professional groups did play a role in the admission process, the reality of voluntary admission in these large locations of confinement deviates from the idea of 'corrective confinement' posited by O'Sullivan and O'Donnell (2012).

Under the 1932 and 1945 Mental Treatment Acts, admissions were required to be based on increasingly standardised medical diagnosis and certification and were now subject to a mandatory second medical opinion. This provided some safeguards against the spurious admissions that were previously possible under the provisions of the 1838 and 1867 Dangerous Lunatics Acts. In practice, several new dynamics emerged as a result of these Mental Treatment Acts. First, self-discharge of voluntary patients was possible, and a system of automatic review for temporary patients was introduced which provided structured points of possible discharge. Secondly, the disjointed judicial and medical system for admissions was replaced with consolidated medical authority, which provided more transparent lines of accountability in the case of involuntary admission. The introduction of these Acts also coincided with the introduction of new 'advances' in clinical interventions during mid-twentieth century such as psychopharmacology and ECT. These forms of treatment were considered to be cutting edge within psychiatric practice, which heightened the focus on cure rather than long-term institutional care. These factors interacted to produce a slow and steady decline of institutional residency for the mentally ill, both in Northern Ireland and in the Republic of Ireland, from the mid-twentieth century to the start of the new millennium (Brennan, 2014). In essence, these Acts would appear to be a significant catalyst to this decline by making involuntary admission more problematic and by making discharge more readily enabled.

In the Republic of Ireland, the declining level of residency that commenced in 1956 was endorsed by a number of social policy documents, originally in the *Report of the Commission of Inquiry on Mental Illness* (Commission of Inquiry on Mental Illness, 1966) and with greater effect in the *Planning for the Future* policy document (Department of Health, 1984), and most recently in the contemporary policy, *A Vision for Change* (Department of Health and Children, 2006). While these documents called for the scaling down of institutional care, they were in fact giving commentary to this reality rather than driving this change. While social policy advocating a reorientating of mental health services towards community care was being articulated from 1966 onwards, the key legislation underpinning this approach was not passed in the Republic of Ireland until 2001, some 35 years later.

Following a protracted legal and political process, which included the drafting of a *Green Paper on Mental Health* (Department of Health, 1992), a *White Paper on Mental Health* (Department of Health, 1995) and a Mental Health Bill 1999, the Mental Treatment Act 1945 was replaced by the Mental Health Act 2001 in the Republic of Ireland. The 1945 Act fell well short of the Republic's obligations under the *Council of Europe Recommendations for the Legal Protection for Persons Suffering from Mental Disorders Placed as Involuntary Patients* (Council of Europe, 1983) and the *UN Principles for the Protection of Persons with Mental Illness and the Improvement of Mental Health Care* (United Nations General Assembly, 1991). These documents required signatories to have laws in place that would ensure the existence of legal provisions for a judicial review for those detained, a right to appeal detention and also a right to be treated with the same ethical and scientific conditions as any other ill person. As such, the passing of the 2001 Act was stimulated as much by external political factors as by concern for the interests of those admitted to mental hospitals. It should also be noted that the passing of this Act occurred during a period of historically low levels of mental hospital residency, with 4,522 persons resident in 2000 compared to 20,863 in 1957.

Under the 2001 Mental Health Act, involuntary admission may be made in cases where, because of the illness, dementia or disability, there is a:

> [S]erious likelihood of the person concerned causing immediate & serious harm to himself or herself or other persons.
> Or
> The judgement of the person concerned is so impaired that failure to admit the person ... would be likely to lead to a serious deterioration of his or her condition.
> *(Mental Health Commission, 2006: Section 2.2: 1)*

In practice, involuntary admission under this legislation is not dissimilar to that of the 1945 Mental Treatment Act. A relative or other suitable person completes a form, along with a medical practitioner and a consultant psychiatrist from the admitting institute. However, the 2001 Act provides much stronger patient safeguards; for example, involuntary admission is made for only 21 days in the first instance, with the possibility for renewal not exceeding three months on first renewal, six months on the second and 12 months thereafter. Furthermore, all admission or renewal orders are subject to review by the Mental Health Commission who refers the matter to a Mental Health Tribunal comprising a practicing barrister or solicitor, a consultant psychiatrist and a person other than a barrister, solicitor, consultant psychiatrist, registered medical practitioner or registered nurse. The patient is also assigned a legal representative and a psychiatrist chosen from a panel of consultants who carries out an examination in order to provide a second opinion regarding the need for admission. The Mental Health Tribunal will consider all matters relating to the case and either affirms or revokes the admission or renewal order. While this legislation did not drive mental hospital de-institutionalisation, it does provide a legal context which acts in a manner to make their future re-expansion less likely, and it copper-fastens the declining trend of mental hospital residence which had commenced in the Republic of Ireland from 1956 onwards.

Criminalisation and prison expansion

The steady decline of mental hospital usage in the Republic of Ireland has been mirrored by a steady increase in the prison population, which grew from 401 in 1956 to a daily average residency of approximately 4,000 in 2014. A direct comparison with the prison population in Northern Ireland is problematic due to the atypical trajectory of prison utilisation in the late twentieth century within the particular context of political and civil unrest during the Conflict.

In the Republic of Ireland the crossing trajectories of decreasing mental hospital populations and increased prison populations suggests that behaviours, emotions and social non-conformity that were previously managed through the mental hospital system are increasingly mediated and experienced through the criminal justice and prison system. However, a closer examination of the data suggests that the sheer gravity of mental hospital closure is not mirrored by increased prison utilisation, and furthermore, there is a very particular gender dynamic in this shift of institutional locations of interventions. An overall decline in the utilisation of institutions of confinement in the Republic of Ireland is observed by O'Sullivan and O'Donnell (2012). The demise of mental hospitals, being the largest sites of institutional confinement in the Republic of Ireland, was the primary driver to this decline, with numbers falling from 21,720 in 1956 to 4,522 in 2000 (Brennan, 2014). The corresponding figures for the expanding prison population are 401 in 1956 rising to 2,948 in 2000 (O'Donnell, O'Sullivan and Healy, 2005). This represents a near fivefold decrease in the institutional confinement of the mentally ill and more than a sevenfold increase in the prison population. However, the actual decrease in numbers is 17,198 for mental patients compared to just a 2,547 increase in the prison population. Hence, while the pattern of declining mental hospital residency set against an increasing population is consistent with that posited by Penrose (1939), it is asymmetric in the Republic of Ireland, with declining rates of mental hospitals usage far outstripping prison expansion.

Furthermore, while gender differences within institutions for the mentally ill have been historically marginal – for example, 11,207 males and 10,531 females resident in the Republic of Ireland in 1956 (Brennan, 2014) – the corresponding gender dynamic in prisons is pronounced, with 371 males and 30 females in prison in 1956 (O'Donnell et al., 2005). While the decline in mental hospital residency for both men and women has been consistent (Brennan, 2014), the increase in the prison population for men is stark, with 2,787 men compared to 84 women in prison in 2000 (O'Donnell *et al.*, 2005). This equates to less than a threefold increase for women compared to more than a sevenfold increase for men. This asymmetric gender dynamic may be driven by historical gender stereotypes, which construct female social non-conformity as sickness or mental illness and male social non-conformity as criminal matters, thus the expanding prison system is primarily driven by male incarceration (see also Quinlan, *infra*).

There are several dynamics at play in this move from the clinical to judicial realms. First, while the scaling down, closure and sale of the old mental hospitals is broadly welcomed, it has had the effect of reducing the availability of accommodation for people whose behaviours and social realities place them at the fringes of society (Brennan, 2014). Furthermore, in cases of acute episodes of mental illness, a person may become very distressed, confused and, in a small number of cases, aggressive. The mental hospital was traditionally the location where the Gardaí or police would bring a person during these times of acute crises, where they would be assessed by a psychiatrist who could decide to admit the individual if deemed necessary. (The author has experience of nursing such cases during the 1980s and 1990s.) The closure of large mental hospitals and the introduction of new routes of admission have resulted in the emergency department of general hospitals now being the path of admission during these times of crises, and these locations are ill-suited to meet the needs of people who are acutely mentally distressed. Gardaí and police who are present at such episodes are placed in a situation where they are required to make a judgment call – whether the person is acting in a criminal fashion, in which case they would be arrested and brought to a cell in the police station, or whether this is a mental health issue that would be resolved by seeking admission through an Emergency department in a local general hospital. The more convenient and possibly less risky option would appear to be direct arrest and detention in the station, which is the doorway into the criminal and judicial realm. There is a dearth of research into this particular moment and axis of institutional trajectory, and further work in this area would appear to be warranted.

Conclusion

Human distress, mental illness and social non-conformity have always been features of human societies, and there is no evidence to suggest that this will change. However, it would appear the social construction, interpretation and response to these phenomena change over time. Historical shifts in the management of social non-conformity and the resulting shifts in institutional locations of confinement have been observed by O'Sullivan and O'Donnell (2012), who argue that a narrow focus on levels of incarceration in prisons can overlook the historical interrelationships between prisons and other places of confinement. O'Sullivan and O'Donnell (2012) posit that shifting levels and locations of corrective confinement in the Republic of Ireland were strongly influenced by a form of 'ruralism', particularly the rural economy, which shaped the nature of social control in Ireland. Such ruralism is characterised by the predominance of small family farms and businesses, low levels of urbanisation and industrialisation and a distinctly localised outlook in terms of social mobility and opportunity. There are tight social controls within such rural societal environments, and non-conformity, it is argued, is managed through institutional incarceration. While this economic milieu was certainly a feature underpinning the spectrum of institutional responses to a host of social situations (Brennan, 2014), other factors, particularly law and professional politics, would appear to have driven the particular dynamic relationship between prisons and mental hospitals.

The moral management of human distress and social non-conformity on the island of Ireland was replaced by clinical practice with the increasing medicalisation of asylums in the mid-nineteenth century. This was in turn reshaped and countered by a judicial process with the introduction of the Dangerous Lunatics Act. A reassertion of medical control over this area of social life was realised in the mid-twentieth century with the introduction of the 1932 Mental Treatment Act in Northern Ireland and the 1945 Mental Treatment Act in the Republic of Ireland, which was a catalyst to the decline of mental hospitals over the past 50 years. However, the rapid pace of prison construction and utilisation, during the same period of mental hospital decline, would appear to signal a recriminalisation of these areas of human experience.

References

Aderibigbe, Y. (1997) 'Deinstitutionalization and Criminalization: Tinkering in the Interstices', *Forensic Science International*, 85(2): 127–34.

Belcher, J. (1988) 'Are Jails Replacing the Mental Health System for the Homeless Mentally Ill?', *Community Mental Health,* 24(3): 185–95.

Brennan, D. (2014) *Irish Insanity 1800–2000.* UK: Routledge.

Bucknill, J. C. (1856) 'Inspector of Lunatics Ireland Seventh Report', *The Asylum Journal. Published by the Authority of the Association of Medical Officers of Asylums and Hospitals of the Insane,* Arial, (17): 129–44.

Casey, P. and Craven, C. (1999) *Psychiatry and the Law.* Dublin: Oak Tree Press.

Commission of Inquiry on Mental Illness (1966) *Report of the Commission of Inquiry on Mental Illness.* Dublin: Stationery Office.

Council of Europe (1983) *Council of Europe Recommendations for the Legal Protection for Persons Suffering from Mental Disorders Placed as Involuntary Patients.* Council of Europe.

Criminal Justice Inspection Northern Ireland (2010) *Not a Marginal Issue: Mental health and the Criminal Justice System in Northern Ireland.* Belfast: Criminal Justice Inspection Northern Ireland.

Department of Health (1984) *The Psychiatric Services – Planning for the Future.* Dublin: The Stationery Office.

Department of Health (1992) *Green Paper on Mental Health.* Dublin: The Stationery Office.

Department of Health (1995) *White Paper: A New Mental Health Act.* Dublin: The Stationery Office.

Department of Health and Children (2006) *A Vision for Change: Report of the Expert Group on Mental Health Policy.* Dublin: The Stationary Office.

Fazel, S. and Danesh, J. (2002) 'Serious Mental Disorder in 23,000 Prisoners: A Systematic Review of 62 Surveys', *Lancet,* 359(9306): 545–50.

Finnane, M. (1981) *Insanity and the Insane in Post-Famine Ireland.* London: Croom Helm.

Foucault, M. (1967) *Madness and Civilization: A History of Insanity in the Age of Reason.* Great Britain: Tavistock.

Harveian Society of London (1866) 'A Paper Read by Dr. Henry Maudsley: On Some Causes of Insanity', *The Medical Press and Circular,* November, 11: 510–14.

Inspector of Lunatic Asylums (1846) *Report on the District, Local and Private Lunatic Asylums in Ireland 1845.* Dublin: HMSO.

Inspector of Lunatic Asylums (1880) *29th Report on the District, Criminal and Private Lunatic Asylums in Ireland.* Dublin: HMSO.

Inspectors-General (1844) *Report of the Inspectors-General on District, Local, and Private Lunatic Asylums in Ireland 1843.* Dublin: HMSO.

Malcolm, E. (2003) 'Ireland's Crowded Madhouses: The Institutional Confinement of the Insane in Nineteenth- and Twentieth-Century Ireland', in R. Porter and D. Wright (eds) *The Confinement of the Insane, International Perspectives, 1800–1965* (pp. 315–33). Cambridge: Cambridge University Press.

Mental Health Commission (2006) *Reference Guide to the Mental Health Act 2001.* Dublin: Mental Health Commission.

Mental Health Commission (2011) *Forensic Mental Health Services for Adults in Ireland: Position Paper.* Dublin: Mental Health Commission.

O'Donnell, I., O'Sullivan, E. and Healy, D. (eds) (2005) *Crime and Punishment in Ireland 1992 to 2003: A Statistical Sourcebook.* Dublin: Institute of Public Administration.

O'Sullivan, E. and O'Donnell, I. (2012) *Coercive Confinement in Post-Independence Ireland: Patients, Prisoners and Penitents.* Manchester: Manchester University Press.

Penrose, L. S. (1939) 'Mental Disease and Crime: Outline of a Comparative Study of European Statistics', *British Journal of Medical Psychology,* 18(1): 1–15.

Porter, R. (2004) *Madmen: A Social History of Madhouses, Mad Doctors and Lunatics.* Gloucestershire: Tempus Publishing Limited.

Prior, P. M. (1993) *Mental Health and Politics in Northern Ireland: A History of Service Development.* Aldershot: Avebury.

Prior, P. M. (2003) 'Dangerous Lunacy: The Misuse of Mental Health Law in Nineteenth-Century Ireland', *The Journal of Forensic Psychiatry and Psychology,* 14(3): 525–41.

Robins, J. (1986) *Fools and Mad: A History of the Insane in Ireland.* Dublin: Institute of Public Administration.

Samson, C. (1995) 'Madness and Psychiatry', in B. S. Turner (ed) *Medical Power and Social Knowledge (2nd edn).* London: Sage.

Saris, A. J. (1997) 'The Asylum in Ireland: A Brief Institutional History and Some Local Effects', in A. Cleary and M. P. Tracy (eds) *The Sociology of Health and Illness in Ireland.* Dublin: University College Dublin Press.

Scheper-Hughes, N. (1979) *Saints, Scholars and Schizophrenics: Mental Illness in Rural Ireland.* Berkeley: University of California Press.

Select Committee to Consider the State of the Lunatic Poor in Ireland (1817) *Report of the Select Committee to Consider the State of the Lunatic Poor in Ireland.* Dublin: Parliamentary Papers.

Select Committee of the House of Lords Appointed to Consider the State of the Lunatic Poor in Ireland (1843) *Report of Select Committee of the House of Lords Appointed to Consider the State of the Lunatic Poor in Ireland.* Dublin: Parliamentary Papers.

Singleton, N., Meltzer, H., Gatward, R., Coid, J. and Deasy, D. (1998) *Psychiatric Morbidity among Prisoners.* London: Stationery Office.

Tuke, S. (1813) *Description of the Retreat, an Institution near York, for Insane Persons of the Society of Friends. Containing an Account of Its Origin and Progress, the Modes of Treatment, and a Statement of Cases.* Philadelphia: Isaac Pierce.

United Nations General Assembly (1991) *UN Principles for the Protection of Persons with Mental Illness and the Improvement of Mental Health Care.* New York: United Nations.

Walsh, D. and Daly, A. (2002) *Irish Psychiatric Hospitals and Units Census 2001.* Dublin: Health Research Board.

Walsh, O. (1999a) '"The Designs of Providence": Race, Religion and Irish Insanity', in J. Melling and B. Forsythe (eds) *Insanity, Institutions, and Society, 1800–1914: A Social History of Madness in Comparative Perspective.* London: Routledge.

Walsh, O. (1999b) 'Lunatic and Criminal Alliances in Nineteenth-Century Ireland', in P. Bartlett and D. Wright (eds) *Outside the Walls of the Asylum: The History of Care in the Community 1750–2000.* London: The Athlone Press.

29

Organised crime in Ireland

Liz Campbell[1]

Defining organised crime

Political discourse across the island of Ireland often emphasises the 'blight' of organised crime (Northern Ireland Office, 2013; Department of Justice and Equality, 2011). As is explored in this chapter, the perceived danger of this form of criminality has prompted significant policy and legislative change and has resulted in the creation of new agencies and processes. However, the certainty and strength of rhetoric on organised crime is not matched by fixed definitional parameters (Van Duyne, 1996).

In this chapter, the theoretical insights of criminologists and penologists such as David Garland, Jonathan Simon and others assist in determining and clarifying the underlying logic of these measures against organised crime. Drawing on Garland (2000), for instance, it will be seen that the criminal justice crisis faced by the state and the associated concern of the electorate drive policy-makers to respond robustly and inventively. Moreover, the characterisation of offenders as incorrigible and rationally motivated steers policy in a particular direction, away from rehabilitation and towards incapacitation as revealed by Feeley and Simon's (1992) work.

As for the central theme of this chapter, the term 'organised crime' may denote specific structures or organisations that are involved in criminality; the provision of illegal goods or services; or a certain type of crime that meets a given level of gravity (Paoli and Fijnaut, 2006; Hamilton-Smith and Mackenzie, 2010). Various constructions of organised crime, its characteristics and definitional prerequisites have been put forward. According to Maltz's (1976) typology, organised crime includes four components: violence, corruption, continuity and variety in the types of criminality engaged in. For Finckenauer (2005: 76), although some crimes may be complex and highly organised, they do not constitute 'organised crime' unless they are committed by criminal organisations. One could argue that such a dichotomous approach fails to recognise that organised crime may be better regarded as involving a spectrum of organisation. Indeed, Levi (2012: 597) recommends a shift in focus and prefers the term 'organising crime' to depict profitable crimes that need a high level of organisation.

Despite these differing scholarly analyses, it is incontrovertible that the central motivating force for organised crime is the generation of wealth and power. Some scholars argue that, conceptually and empirically, organised crime may be difficult to distinguish from other types of serious criminality such as 'white collar' crime and terrorism. In the first instance, the absence of a professional role or status is key. And when compared with terrorism, the classic distinguishing feature is organised crime's lack of ideology (Finckenauer, 2005). Nonetheless, Makarenko (2004) identified some similarities between these two traditionally separate phenomena and posited the existence of a 'Crime-Terror Continuum' on which any particular group may be positioned, depending on its methods, personnel and purposes. Groups may develop into hybrid entities that involve both dimensions of organised crime and terrorism, or may involve the transformation from one to the other (Shelley *et al.*, 2005).

This conceptualisation is of particular relevance in the Northern Irish context, where the distinction between organised crime and terrorist actions is less than clear and a nexus is seen to exist (An Garda Síochána and Police Service of Northern Ireland, 2008; Organised Crime Task Force, 2011). Organised crime groups (OCGs) may supply illegal arms to terrorist groups, while terrorists may seek to generate funds through the sale of illegal goods and services. Persons previously involved in terrorism become 'criminal entrepreneurs' (House of Commons Northern Ireland Affairs Committee, 2003: para. 64), using local and international networks and importation paths to further criminal aims, and their knowledge about weaponry may be disseminated to other criminal groups (House of Commons Northern Ireland Affairs Committee, 2003; House of Commons Northern Ireland Affairs Committee, 2006a; Organised Crime Task Force, 2011). It appears that there is a shift away from a time where certain types of criminality were prohibited by, restricted to or required approval from paramilitary groups. Indeed, despite public denunciations, many dissident republican groups remain dependent on organised crime to fund their terrorist activities (Organised Crime Task Force, 2012).

In the context of legal definitions of organised crime, specific legislation has been enacted in the Republic of Ireland applying to organised criminality, but not in Northern Ireland. Part 7 of the Criminal Justice Act 2006 (ROI) introduced a number of substantive organised-crime offences, and drew implicitly on Finckenauer (2005) in doing so, given that the relevant provisions centre on the concept of a criminal organisation. Section 3 of the Criminal Justice (Amendment) Act 2009 (following the United Nations Convention against Transnational Organised Crime 2000 and amending the 2006 Act) defines a 'criminal organisation' as a structured group, however organised, that has as its main purpose or activity the commission or facilitation of a serious offence, which is that for which a person may be imprisoned for at least four years. A structured group comprises at least three persons and cannot be formed randomly for the immediate commission of a single offence, and the involvement in the group by two or more of those persons must be with a view to their acting in concert. The legislation emphasises that such a group may exist without formal rules or membership, hierarchical or leadership structure, or continuity of involvement by persons in the group. The substantive offences based on this concept include directing the activities of a criminal organisation (Criminal Justice Act 2006 s71A), participating in or contributing to activities of a criminal organisation (s72) and committing a serious offence for a criminal organisation (s73).

No statutory definition of organised crime exists in Northern Ireland. Rather, the Northern Ireland Office (NIO) states that 'generally it involves a group of people involved in serious criminal activities for substantial profit. Violence and threat of violence is used by organised criminals in some cases, the main activity is for financial gain'.[2] The Serious Crime Act (2015) criminalises participation in activities of an organised crime group. The offence, which centres on the notion of such a group rather than on a definition of 'organised crime', applies in England and Wales only. Section 45 provides that an OCG has as its purpose the carrying on of criminal activities, and comprises at least three persons acting together or agreeing to do so to further that purpose. 'Criminal activities' are offences punishable with imprisonment for at least seven years, carried on in England or Wales (or elsewhere as long it is a crime there and is punishable comparably), with a view to obtaining any gain or benefit. It remains to be seen how this is applied in practice.

Obokata, Payne and Jackson (2014) claim that from the point of view of law enforcement, the lack of a legal definition has not caused any difficulty in Northern Ireland, and that all agencies can distinguish organised crime from 'ordinary crime'. This may give rather too much credence to official constructions of the phenomenon and its parameters. Moreover, though Obokata *et al.*'s (2014) observation may well be true, the rationale for separate legislation is to bolster the prosecutorial capabilities of the state, given that the statutory offences echo but do not emulate exactly offences such as conspiracy, and so may capture behaviour that would otherwise not fall within the existing legal framework. A legal definition therefore is of significant value in a substantive and symbolic sense.

Measuring organised crime

The difficulty in ascertaining what the term 'organised crime' means does not preclude statements about the extent of the problem (Levi, 2012: 601). Increasingly, efforts are being made to quantify more precisely the extent, threat and gravity of organised crime, both for operational purposes and for public dissemination. Organised crime 'threat assessments' or 'risk assessments' are carried out annually in the UK and EU (see e.g. National Crime Agency, 2014; Europol, 2013) and aim to assist decision-makers in prioritising threats and devising appropriate strategies. Moreover, OCGs may be mapped to indicate their prevalence, strength and location, as occurs in Scotland (see Scottish Serious Organised Crime Group, 2009).

Due to the definitional problems just discussed, such assessments have been described as 'expressionistic' (van Duyne and van Dijck, 2006: 102). Though Hamilton-Smith and Mackenzie (2010) identify numerous weaknesses in the various forms of risk and threat assessments, they recognise their value in constructing innovative policing practices. So, measuring and mapping OCGs may be of considerable use in an operational sense, but inherent problems remain. For instance, the fluidity of OCGs and the evidence of cooperation and crossover between OCGs (An Garda Síochána and Police Service of Northern Ireland, 2012) may confound efforts to quantify them. And of course, any attempt to ascertain or estimate of the number of OCGs in Northern Ireland is complicated by the involvement of paramilitary groups in crimes such as drug smuggling and extortion (Independent Monitoring Commission, 2006).

Nonetheless, a biennial examination is carried out of organised crime activities on both sides of the border, with the sixth Cross Border Organised Crime Assessment being published in 2014. This report is a multi-agency effort, involving contributions from An Garda Síochána, the Police Service of Northern Ireland (PSNI), the Criminal Assets Bureau (CAB), HM Revenue and Customs (HMRC), the Revenue Commissioners, the National Crime Agency (NCA) and the Border Force. The report found that organised crime north and south of the border is becoming more diverse, complex and global, assisted by developments in technology and telecommunications. The threats posed by cybercrime and human trafficking were found to be comparable across the island of Ireland, but some differences exist in relation to drugs markets. (Northern Ireland, for example, has a smaller market for heroin, but larger for amphetamine, than the Republic of Ireland.)

In addition, Northern Ireland's Organised Crime Task Force (OCTF) (see further below) produces an annual threat assessment, which reports on the impact of organised crime in Northern Ireland. No publicly available threat assessment document or mapping project exists in the Republic of Ireland. Nonetheless, the 2013 annual report of An Garda Síochána (An Garda

Síochána, 2013: 39) noted that '269 Organised Crime Groups were targeted in 2013', indicating a precise quantification of the groups in relation to a particular 'performance indicator'. Moreover, the EU now requires members to include an estimate of illegal economic activities in GDP, including revenue from a range of organised crimes, like prostitution and illegal drug sales. The Republic of Ireland calculates that such activities contributed 0.72 per cent to GDP in 2013 (Central Statistics Office, 2014). While there are comparable figures for the UK as a whole, separate statistics for Northern Ireland are not available publicly.

Categorising organised crime

Despite the difficulties in calculating the number of OCGs, or ascertaining the threat posed, these systematic assessments assist in outlining the types of organised crime that are being perpetrated. In addition, police statistics and court cases also suggest the forms that organised crime takes. Of course, it is important to remain cognisant of the contested nature of the definition of organised crime, and to be mindful of accepting uncritically the state's understanding and narrative. Policing or prosecutorial focus is not linked necessarily to the true extent of the problem and may skew our concerns and perceptions. Bearing all this in mind, it appears that numerous forms of organised crime exist across the island of Ireland, some of which relate directly to the presence of a land border. Importation and sometimes export of licit and illegal goods is commonplace, involving drugs, fuel, guns, tobacco, counterfeit goods, rare animals and people.

A considerable proportion of organised crime across the island of Ireland relates to the illegal drugs market. Overall, the northwest of Europe is regarded as a principal coordination centre for drug distribution (Europol, 2011). Cannabis cultivation in grow houses is becoming more common, and it has been claimed that there is a link between certain communities and this method of cultivation (An Garda Síochána and Police Service of Northern Ireland, 2012).

Alcohol and cigarettes are smuggled into and between the two jurisdictions (An Garda Síochána and Police Service of Northern Ireland, 2008; Europol, 2011). There is a significant difference in the price of alcohol between Northern Ireland and the Republic of Ireland, with that in the former being far cheaper. This is seen to contribute to alcohol smuggling and the counterfeiting of alcohol (OCTF, 2014b). In addition, contraband and counterfeit tobacco is smuggled into the Republic of Ireland and the UK from Europe and Asia (HM Revenue and Customs, 2006). This is seen increasingly as an attractive alternative to the trafficking of illicit drugs because of its lower penalties yet large profits (Europol, 2011).

Fuel-related criminality is a particular issue in both jurisdictions because of the land border and the differential in rates of duty and the currency exchange (An Garda Síochána and Police Service of Northern Ireland, 2014; House of Commons Northern Ireland Affairs Committee, 2006a, 2006b). Fuel is smuggled, as well as 'stretched' (bulked out through its adulteration or mixing) and 'laundered' (whereby marker dye in rebated fuels is removed and it is sold on as road diesel) (An Garda Síochána and Police Service of Northern Ireland, 2010: 14). On this point, the House of Commons Northern Ireland Affairs Committee (2006a: 35) has emphasised the effect on organised crime that a common regime for fuel duty in Northern Ireland and the Republic of Ireland would have, as this would decrease 'racketeering potential' (Goldstock, 2004: para. 3.7). Such criminality involves a significant loss of revenue for the state, as well as grave environmental damage from the effluent and by-products. In a similar vein, the disposal of waste is exploited by cross-border criminality to avail of the difference in the cost of landfill (An Garda Síochána and Police Service of Northern Ireland, 2010). A considerable quantity of household and commercial waste created in the Republic of Ireland but dumped illegally in Northern Ireland is repatriated every year (Organised Crime Task Force, 2011: 9).

OCGs often are involved in extortion, or the demanding of 'protection money' through rack-eteering (Goldstock *et al.*, 1991; Jacobs and Anechiarico, 1992). While this does not appear to be a major issue in the Republic of Ireland (Transcrime, 2008), extortion is a concern in Northern Ireland, affecting small to medium businesses like shops and construction companies (House of Commons Northern Ireland Affairs Committee, 2006b: para. 18; Transcrime, 2008), though this is carried out by both OCGs and paramilitary organisations. Furthermore, the involvement of organised crime groups in the provision of private security is not uncommon, as this may facilitate drug dealing or may be linked to extortion (see Morris, 1998). In fact, it seems to be a specific and enduring problem in Northern Ireland due to the links between certain private security providers and paramilitary groups (Independent Monitoring Commission, 2005).

The land border (like borders all across the EU) is also exploited for VAT (value added tax) fraud, such as where a trader purchases goods VAT-free from another EU state, then sells the goods at a VAT-inclusive price, but fails to pay the tax to the Revenue authorities and absconds (OCTF, 2014b). It has been suggested that this could be mitigated by the harmonisation of tax rates (House of Commons Northern Ireland Affairs Committee, 2006b: para. 18), and this prompts Revenue authorities on both sides of the border to work together (OCTF, 2014b).

Despite Maltz's (1976) inclusion of corruption as a constituent component of organised crime, there is no evidence of any criminal organisation exercising a systematic influence over the political systems or of the judiciary on the island of Ireland. Indeed, no mention is made of corruption in any of the threat assessments. Though corruption is considered in the Irish White Paper on Crime, *Organised and White Collar Crime* (Department of Justice and Equality, 2010: 42), this is in the context of white-collar rather than organised crime. So, it remains unclear whether and to what extent corrupt practices are carried out by OCGs across the island of Ireland to benefit their enterprise.

Policing organised crime

The nature and extent of organised crime has prompted the alteration of policing modes and structures across the island of Ireland. In the Republic of Ireland, there is a fulltime specialist Organised Crime Unit in the Gardaí, which works with the National Drugs Unit and other units, as well as the National Bureau of Criminal Investigation. The PSNI has a Crime Operations Department with a dedicated Organised Crime Branch, in addition to an Extortion Unit. In terms of prosecution, there is a specific assets seizing section in the Office of the Director of Public Prosecutions; this process will often be linked to organised criminality. Unlike the Crown Prosecution Service in England and Wales and the Crown Office in Scotland, there is no dedicated unit on organised crime in either the Republic of Ireland's or Northern Ireland's Public Prosecutions offices (see Obokata *et al.*, 2014).

Northern Ireland's Organised Crime Task Force (OCTF) was established in 2000 and is a forum in which government, law enforcement and various agencies, community and business representatives set priorities and strategy. The three core strands of work agreed by the OCTF are awareness, analysis and action, in an effort to disrupt the activities of OCGs and to reduce the harm that they cause (OCTF, 2014c: para. 8). The OCTF does not have operational capabilities or responsibilities, however. There is no equivalent to the OCTF in the Republic of Ireland, and Obokata *et al.* (2014) suggest that such an entity should be established to strengthen a multi-agency approach to organised crime.

Of course, the most significant structural development in the Republic of Ireland was the establishment in 1996 of the Criminal Assets Bureau (CAB). CAB represents a hybrid of State agencies and authorities, including members of An Garda Síochána, officials of the Revenue

Commissioners and of the Department of Social, Community and Family Affairs (s8, Criminal Assets Bureau Act 1996). CAB was regarded as a significant innovation at the time of its creation and remains a model of best practice. Its structure and *modus operandi* have been used as proto-types for other jurisdictions, with its multi-agency approach in particular attracting considerable international attention. Moreover, CAB was a key initiator of CARIN, the Camden Asset Recovery Inter Agency Network, which is an informal network of practitioners and organisations that cooperate in tackling the proceeds of crime.[3]

CAB acts to confiscate, freeze or seize assets deriving or suspected of deriving from criminal activity, to ensure that the proceeds of (suspected) criminal activity are taxed and to investigate and determine any claim for benefit by any person engaged in criminal activity or where social welfare officers may be subject to intimidation (s5). This capacity to seize assets in the absence of a criminal conviction, and to tax illegal income, has proved remarkably successful, both in real terms and public and political perception.

There has been a series of agencies that impact on the policing of organised crime in Northern Ireland. Drawing on the example of CAB, the Assets Recovery Agency (ARA) was introduced in the UK by Part 1 of the Proceeds of Crime Act 2002. ARA was established to confiscate, recover and tax criminal assets but was unsuccessful in attempting to become self-financing because of the few cases referred to it and its multi-agency structure (House of Commons Committee of Public Accounts, 2007; Harfield, 2008). It appears that the multi-agency structure was problematic and led to a disjointed effort due to limited sharing of information between law enforcement agencies and ARA. So, the Serious Organised Crime and Police Act 2005 established the Serious Organised Crime Agency (SOCA) to replace ARA. SOCA worked to prevent, detect and reduce serious organised crime and to mitigate its consequences, as well as gathering, analysing and disseminating information to law enforcement (ss 2 and 3, Serious Organised Crime and Police Act 2005). Importantly, SOCA could institute criminal proceedings in England, Wales and Northern Ireland and could act, if requested, in support of any activities of a police force or agency (s5, Serious Organised Crime and Police Act 2005).

Now, SOCA has been replaced by the National Crime Agency (NCA), which was established by the Crime and Courts Act 2013 and came into operation in October 2013. Though it may be argued that this is a superficial rebranding exercise, the NCA has an extended remit, albeit with a smaller budget. The NCA differs from SOCA insofar as it can conduct its own operations; it has a national leadership role vis-à-vis UK law enforcement, and it provides operational and specialist support to such forces. However, initially, the NCA operated in Northern Ireland on 'non-devolved' matters only (such as revenue offences). This was due to a lack of political agreement on the appropriate nature of policing in Northern Ireland, which led to two nationalist parties, Sinn Féin and the SDLP (Social Democratic and Labour Party), voting against the NCA's operation. This veto stemmed from nationalists' concerns about oversight of the powerful NCA, given that its director is answerable to the Home Secretary rather than to the Northern Ireland Policing Board as is the case with the PSNI.

This state of affairs had implications in terms of the NCA's ability to support the PSNI in relation to organised crime policing (as occurs elsewhere in the UK). Indeed, there was some inconsistency in the political response given that SOCA could operate fully in Northern Ireland, though it had more limited powers than the NCA. This created a gap in law enforcement, in the support that can be provided to the PSNI, and in respect of civil recovery in devolved cases. The PSNI (2013: 1) stated that 'the NCA should only work in Northern Ireland alongside the PSNI, so that operational control ultimately remains with the Chief Constable and nothing proceeds without agreement'. A settlement was reached in February 2015 when the Northern Ireland

Assembly voted in favour of extending the NCA's powers to Northern Ireland. It remains to be seen how this plays out in practice.

Beyond such specific policing and prosecution units, HMRC, the Serious Fraud Office, the UK Border Force, the Irish Revenue Commissioners, the Social Security Agency and the Environment Agency play an increasingly central and critical role in the context of detecting and policing organised crime, given the diverse and multifaceted nature of the acts perpetrated.

Addressing organised crime

Organised crime is regarded globally as warranting robust legal and policy measures. This reflects both the perception of potential harm and the State's understanding of offenders' criminogenic motivations. Acts by OCGs can be seen as especially problematic and harmful in a number of respects. Such groups cultivate significant power and profit through illegal markets, thereby serving to maintain the group and facilitate further criminality. The joint effort between participants in the group may mean that the offence is more likely to be completed, due to group commitment. In addition, OCGs may evade detection through delegation of tasks and may be capable of withstanding the consequences of detection of particular individuals. Arrest, prosecution or conviction of particular individuals often may be absorbed and withstood by the group, especially if the person is unwilling to provide information to the police or to testify against colleagues. Moreover, preservation of the group is predicated on violence and or corruption, either by coercing or cajoling third parties to assist the enterprise or to remain silent. These are both harms in themselves and are a critical contributor to OCGs' success. Further harm derives from the fact that interactions between different OCGs will displace legitimate means of dispute resolution. This leads to further violence and corruption.

In addition, the dominant narrative on organised crime is grounded in a particular criminological mindset, in which the individuals involved are perceived by policy-makers to behave in a rational and benefit-maximising way. This belief may be an accurate portrayal of the organised crime mindset in some instances, yet is singular and incomplete. While it reflects a body of criminological literature (see e.g. Cornish and Clarke, 2002), it overlooks the significance of criminal opportunities arising from political unrest, enhanced technology (Albanese, 2000), weak states (Makarenko, 2004), the criminalisation of certain markets and the development of subcultures which are sometimes fostered by stigmatisation (Braithwaite, 1989), in the decision-making of organised criminals. Further, it neglects the likely trajectory of careers in organised crime, given that such offenders are likely to be older and to begin their criminality in adulthood (van Koppen et al., 2010).

The characteristics and orthodox understandings of organised crime have led countless jurisdictions and administrations to adopt novel and tough legal measures, which may be categorised as preventative or reactive. As noted, the three core strands of work agreed by the OCTF in Northern Ireland are awareness, analysis and action (OCTF, 2014c). Awareness includes informing the public both about the trends and impact of organised crime as well as the work of the OCTF, while analysis entails research to understand organised crime threats and to facilitate proactive measures. So, it can be seen that not all action against organised crime is reactive, but also seeks to prevent and pre-empt such crime. Action, then, involves 'frustrating, disrupting and dismantling' OCG, through 'prosecuting them [and] removing their assets' (OCTF, 2014c: 8).

A critical action against organised crime is the creation of a suite of legal measures. Beyond the enactment of substantive offences (as discussed above), trial processes, sentencing and civil measures have been altered in an effort to react in an adequate and effective manner. For example, it is possible to hold judge-only trials for some suspected organised crimes, in an effort to protect threatened jurors and to safeguard the administration of justice. In addition, presumptive sentences are imposed, to deter and incapacitate the individuals involved. Concerns about the inability of the conventional criminal justice process to address satisfactorily the central issue of resources and profit motivation in organised crime has led to the use of non-conviction-based asset forfeiture. Analysing these through the lens of criminological theories elucidates the unarticulated logic of the State in enacting these measures. In other words, scholarly reflection may shed light on the unspoken motivations of political actions and may illuminate the issues that are taken as given or uncontested in political discourse.

Protecting the jury

The jury is a critical component of adversarial trials on indictment, but is regarded as a key vulnerability when considering organised crime-related trials in particular. OCGs may seek to ensure impunity through the intimidation of jurors, compromising citizens' safety and leading to difficulties in successful prosecution. Nonetheless, empirical evidence is lacking as to the extent of the problem of juror intimidation across the island of Ireland, and there is no central recording of the number of retrials ordered as a result of jury intimidation.

One response to this unquantifiable problem has been the holding of judge-only trials for serious indictable offences, replicating the approach in counter-terrorism legislation arising from the political violence in Northern Ireland. Despite being predicated on common concerns, and arguably comparable contexts, such trials have been implemented differently in Northern Ireland and the Republic of Ireland. The Irish model is indicative of a categorisation of organised crime as a species of crime *sui generis*, or at least as equivalent to terrorist acts, whereas the Northern Irish scheme (like that in England and Wales) takes a case-by-case approach. The implication of this is that the net is cast rather too widely in the Republic of Ireland, in presupposing the need for an extraordinary mode of trial. This reflects a presumption about the nature and gravity of organised crime and shows less caution in terms of removing the jury.

The jury trial is a fundamental part of the adversarial criminal process: The Magna Carta alluded to trial by one's peers, while in the Republic of Ireland, the jury trial is guaranteed under Bunreacht na hÉireann (the Irish Constitution). Nonetheless, some exceptions are provided in the Irish context, and the right to a fair trial under Article 6 of the European Convention on Human Rights (ECHR) does not guarantee or necessitate trial by jury.

The Republic of Ireland

Judge-only trials for organised crime may be held either at the direction of the Director of Public Prosecutions (DPP) or if the crime falls within certain categories. Article 38.3 of Bunreacht na hÉireann permits restriction of the right to a jury trial where the Executive declares the ordinary courts to be 'inadequate to secure the effective administration of justice and the preservation of public peace and order'. Part V of the Offences Against the State Act 1939 regulates the establishment and operation of special judge-only courts and came into force after Government proclamation about the inadequacy of the ordinary courts (s35). Such a proclamation has been in force since 1972 (Committee to Review the Offences Against the State Acts, 2002: para. 9.8). The 1939 Act allows the DPP to direct the hearing of a trial before the Special Criminal Court on the basis that she believes the ordinary courts to be inadequate to secure the administration of justice and the preservation of public peace and order (ss 47 and 48). Two concerns arise in this context: first, review is possible only if the DPP's decision is *mala fides (Savage and Owen v DPP)*[4], and second, power to limit a constitutional right is vested in a prosecutor.

In addition, organised crime cases may be heard without a jury due to the inclusion of substantive organised crime offences within the scope of counter-terrorism legislation by section 8 of the Criminal Justice (Amendment) Act 2009, so the ordinary courts are deemed automatically to be inadequate. This section has a 'sunset clause' of 12 months, but has been renewed each year since enactment, most recently in June 2014 (see Criminal Justice (Amendment) Act 2009: Motion Seanad Éireann, 19 June 2014). The logic behind such a legislative approach is that organised criminality is distinct from 'ordinary' crime and in fact warrants equivalent measures to those used against suspected terrorists. Despite political support for enactment of these powers and for their ongoing retention, not one case has been brought before the Special Criminal Court under the 2009 Act. This may be a function of the length of time it takes to investigate and construct such cases. Alternatively, it may be argued that this mismatch between governmental rationalities and actual practices is indicative of what has been called a 'governmentality gap' between politicians and policy-makers and prosecutors (McNeill et al., 2009).

Northern Ireland

Jury-less trials have been held in Northern Ireland since the 1970s to deal with juror intimidation by paramilitary organisations and the possibility of perverse acquittals due to religious or sectarian affiliation (Greer and White, 1988). The Emergency Provisions Act 1973 allowed non-jury trials on indictment of scheduled offences (such as terrorism offences, as well as murder and kidnap) in single-judge 'Diplock courts'. Trials on indictment may still be held without a jury where the DPP for Northern Ireland suspects that there is a link to a proscribed organisation or political or religious hostility, and that in view of this, there is a risk to the administration of justice if the trial were conducted with a jury (Justice and Security (Northern Ireland) Act 2007 s1). The legislation was due to expire on 31 July 2013, but was extended for a two-year period by the Justice and Security (Northern Ireland) Act 2007 (Extension of Duration of Non-Jury Trial Provisions) Order 2013.

In addition, the Criminal Justice Act 2003 (ss 43 and 44) established a separate scheme of jury-less trials across England, Wales and Northern Ireland. Such trials may be held where there is evidence of a real and present danger that jury tampering would take place and that despite any reasonable preventative steps there is so substantial a likelihood that tampering would occur as to make it necessary in the interests of justice to hold a jury-less trial. While such trials are not limited to cases of organised crime, it is likely that such applications often will relate to organised crime (HC Deb 19 May 2003 vol 405 c740 per David Blunkett; R v Guthrie[5]).

This mode of trial is little used: just one such trial has been held, in R v Twomey, in the Crown Court sitting in the Royal Courts of Justice. While a real and present danger of tampering was found to exist in R v J, S and M, the Court concluded that necessary protective measures would not impose an unacceptable burden on the jurors.[6] This underlines that a jury-less trial 'remains and must remain the decision of last resort' (para. 8).

Section 46 of the 2003 Act permits a jury to be discharged during a trial and the trial continued without one. This occurred in Northern Ireland in R v Clarke and McStravick, a 'tiger kidnapping' case involving an employee of a security company and his family; the Court of Appeal dismissed the appeal against this decision (R v Clarke and McStravick).[7]

Critiquing jury-less trials

Judge-only trials raise concerns about equality as protected by Article 40.1 of Bunreacht na hÉireann, though not under Article 14 of the ECHR, which is not a freestanding right. Such argument has been raised unsuccessfully before the Irish courts (*Kavanagh v Ireland*).[8] As I have suggested elsewhere (Campbell, 2014), concerns about equality would be remedied by the introduction of a means of review of the DPP's decision and a shift away from such blanket removal of a jury for suspected organised crimes. The case-by-case, risk-based scheme in Northern Ireland (and England and Wales) is preferable in this respect.

In addition, the nature of decision-making may be altered in judge-only courts, especially when this is a single judge acting as arbiter of fact and law as in Northern Ireland (whereas the Special Criminal Court in the Republic of Ireland sits as a bench of three). In their ground-breaking study, Jackson and Doran (1995: 293) found that defendants in the Diplock courts suffered an 'adversarial deficit', on the basis that juries may adopt a broader view of the merits of the prosecution case than an expert tribunal and that a professional approach entails 'case-hardening' through the adoption of an unemotional attitude towards the evidence. In particular, jury-less trials in the adversarial context pose problems regarding inadmissible evidence, when judges may be required to exclude from their minds incriminating material. Of course, District Court judges do this, regularly and uncontroversially. Indeed, this concern may be mitigated if the court provided a written judgment articulating the basis for its factual conclusion, which does not occur in jury trials.

Sentencing organised crime

Concerns about the extent and nature of organised crime have prompted the revision of the traditional scheme of sentencing in the Republic of Ireland, though not in Northern Ireland. There has been a palpable shift from a discretionary, individualised model to a more mechanical and often punitive one involving presumptive sentences. Though this may increase consistency and certainty in sentencing, it also incorporates a legislative drive away from the characteristics and circumstances of the offender, towards a pragmatic emphasis on the type of offence and the protection of the public.

This follows the approach adopted across the US, where mandatory and presumptive sentences are commonplace; other common-law jurisdictions, such as the states of Australia, adopt a more limited and cautious scheme. It is difficult to determine precisely why this development has not occurred in Northern Ireland. Given that Obokata *et al.* (2014) highlight stakeholder concerns about leniency in sentencing for drugs offences, particularly in Northern Ireland, it is curious that this has not translated into political action.

The judiciary across the UK and Republic of Ireland has long enjoyed wide sentencing discretion, but this has been corralled by guidelines and statutory presumptions. Sentencing courts in Northern Ireland are assisted by guideline cases from the English Court of Appeal, but these guidelines are secondary and followed only when they accord with 'local experience' (*Attorney General's Reference (No 1 of 2008) Gibbons et al.* [2008] NICA 41 para. 44). Moreover, a Judicial Sentencing Working Group of judges reported in 2010 as to the improvements that could be made to existing practice (Sentencing Working Group, 2010). The Lord Chief Justice set up a Programme of Action on Sentencing that has sought to introduce new guidelines for a range of offences identified in the consultation (Lord Chief Justice's Sentencing Group, 2012). In addition, there are guidelines for the Magistrates' Court, which includes some drugs and counterfeiting offences (Judicial Studies Board for Northern Ireland, 2014).

Despite calls for sentencing guidelines in the Republic of Ireland (Balance in the Criminal Law Review Group, 2007: 227), none yet exist, though the Irish Sentencing Information System (www.irishsentencing.ie) has been established by the Courts Service to inform judges considering the sentence to be imposed in a given case. There are few formal constraints on judicial discretion, and the system was described as one of the most unstructured in the common-law world (O'Malley, 2000). This began to change with the introduction of presumptive sentences in 1999.

As noted earlier, organised crime is driven by profit, and many OCGs operate in a similar way to legitimate business in terms of management and division of labour. So, the individuals involved are seen as (re)acting in a rational way, and therefore amenable to deterrence through both increasing the likelihood of punishment and decreasing the potential rewards of criminal behaviour. This was one of the animating forces behind the introduction of presumptive sentences for serious drug offences in the Republic of Ireland in 1999. Nonetheless, it does not follow that Northern Ireland takes a different view of organised crime and does not see it as rational choice; rather, it is more likely the case that the extant scheme of sentencing is regarded as sufficient.

Presumptive sentences in the Republic of Ireland

Sections 15A and 15B of the Misuse of Drugs Act 1977 (as inserted by the Criminal Justice Act 1999) provide that any person convicted of the possession of drugs with a value of at least €13,000 with intent to supply or of importation shall receive a minimum term of ten years, unless there are exceptional and specific circumstances which would make such a term unjust. The court may have regard, *inter alia*, to whether that person pleaded guilty, at what stage and in what circumstances, and whether he assisted materially the investigation. The prosecution need not prove that the defendant had knowledge of the value of the drugs or was reckless in this regard (Criminal Justice Act 2006 s82(3)). Amendments by the Criminal Justice Act 2007 ensure that the exceptional circumstances provision is available only to persons convicted of a first offence of drug possession or importation (s15(3E)); and a mandatory minimum sentence of ten years was introduced for a second such offence (s15(3F)). While the prescribed minimum sentence has been imposed in the Republic of Ireland in numerous cases due to the sophistication of drug dealing (*People (DPP) v Byrne*[9]) and the amount of drugs involved (*People (DPP) v Harrison*, unreported, Dublin Circuit Criminal Court, 26 May 2006), for example, the exceptional circumstances caveat has also been used on many occasions (McEvoy, 2005: 8). This demonstrates clearly the tension between politicians attempting to impose punitive measures and judges who are circumventing them. This may derive from the jealously guarded independence of the judiciary due to the separation of powers. Another means of conceptualising this is to view it as a 'governmentality gap' between politicians and the judiciary, with official discourse diverging from the realities of practice (McNeill *et al.*, 2009).

Similarly, for firearms offences (including possession of a firearm in suspicious circumstances, possession of a firearm while hijacking a vehicle and use or production of a firearm to resist arrest), mandatory minimum sentences of between five and ten years are provided for in Part 5 of the Criminal Justice Act 2006. Also, there are robust mandatory minimum sentences for second offences (including certain firearms offences, drug trafficking and organised-crime offences), if the person was sentenced to at least five years for the first offences and then commits another from the range of relevant offences within seven years (excluding any period of imprisonment) from the date of conviction (Criminal Justice Act 2007 s25).

In addition to the enactment of presumptive sentences, a connection to organised crime may lead to an increased sentence. The fact that a serious offence was committed as part of or to further the activities of criminal organisation is an aggravating factor at sentencing (Criminal Justice Act 2006 s74A), and the Court is required to impose a greater sentence than otherwise would be imposed, unless the sentence is one of life imprisonment or there are exceptional circumstances.

Presumptive sentences in Northern Ireland

The situation is rather different in Northern Ireland: Presumptive sentences are in place for some firearms offences but not for drugs offences. The Firearms (Northern Ireland) Order 2004, akin to the Firearms Act 1968 s51A (inserted by the Criminal Justice Act 2003) in the rest of the UK, provides a minimum sentence of five years on offenders aged 21 years or over unless there are 'exceptional circumstances relating to the offence or to the offender which justify its not doing so'. The acts captured by this provision include possessing or acquiring a gun without an appropriate firearm certificate, and possessing, buying, selling or making certain controlled arms or ammunition.

The Misuse of Drugs Act 1971 applies all across the UK, as drugs policy is reserved to Westminster rather than being a devolved matter. However, there are no presumptive sentences in this Act, only maximum terms provided in Schedule 4. Courts in England, Wales and Scotland must impose a minimum sentence of seven years' imprisonment for a third Class A trafficking offence, except where the court is of the opinion that there are particular circumstances relating to the offence or to the offender which would make it unjust to do so (Powers of Criminal Courts (Sentencing) Act 2000 s110; Criminal Procedure (Scotland) Act 1995 s205B, as inserted by the Crime and Punishment (Scotland) Act 1997. There is no equivalent provision in Northern Ireland. In addition, calls have been made for an aggravation in sentencing by virtue of connection to organised crime (Northern Ireland Affairs Committee, 2006: 59–60; Northern Ireland Audit Office, 2010: 30), but no such provision has been enacted. The reason for this is that the courts currently take into account whether a crime was connected with organised crime when passing sentence, and so, such a requirement need not be written into law (House of Commons Northern Ireland Affairs Committee, 2006a: 59).

Unpacking the sentences

Presumptive sentences embody a number of different perspectives in terms of criminology and theories of punishment. The communicative dimension of presumptive sentences is to the fore in Irish political discourse. The unequivocal message that the sentence would send to drug criminals was emphasised in the Dáil, as was its demonstration of society's abhorrence.[10] As Garland (2000: 350) notes, expressive punishments serve as both a cathartic and unifying force for the community.

As for the expression towards the offender, it is hoped that these sentences convey the disapprobation of society and so deter the individual. This is predicated on the rational choice model of human action, whereby the individual weighs up rationally the benefits and disadvantages of acting and the possible consequences. Though this may seem plausible, there is little empirical evidence that presumptive sentences deter drugs and firearms crime. Studies of gun criminals show that the decision to commit the act rarely is driven by rational considerations, *per se* (Matthews, 2002: 37). An individual's decision to commit crime in a broad sense may not be influenced by rational factors, though his choice as to where and when to commit the act may be governed by such reasoning (van Gelder, 2013). And of course, punitive sentences may have an effect only if an individual perceives that they may be imposed on him (Hales, Lewis and Silverstone, 2006: 95). This suggests that police surveillance and intervention are likely to be of more effect than the possible imposition of a robust presumptive sentence. Furthermore, even if one accepts the validity of the rational actor paradigm, a reasonable choice may be to commit the crime despite the possible sentence, as this is less risky or punitive than the alternative, namely retaliation from another OCG (Matthews, 2002; Hales *et al.*, 2006).

In addition to the expressive aspects, it seems that presumptive minimum sentences indicate the (often unarticulated) legislative predilection for a more mechanical application of generalised standards over an individualised approach in which the judiciary have more latitude. These measures embody the concern of legislators about such criminality and about the perceived leniency of the judiciary who are wedded to a different model of sentencing. This maps onto Feeley and Simon's (1992: 449–50) observations about the 'New Penology' in which aggregates and risk are emphasised over personal characteristics, and the offender is categorised according to risk. Bundled up with this is the desire to limit the discretion of the sentencing court and shift the balance back to parliament in prescribing the appropriate sentence. There is a political perception that the judiciary are detached from the reality of the threat posed by organised crime. In addition, the incapacitative component of these sentences is significant, though OCGs may continue to direct activities from prison.

There is no evidence in the Republic of Ireland that the introduction of presumptive sentences has affected crime rates in the past decade, though such a causal link would be difficult to draw. Indeed, the Law Reform Commission (2013: 4.233) has called for their repeal on a number of grounds. The Commission emphasised that such sentences do not advance the sentencing aims of deterrence, retribution and rehabilitation, and so it is unlikely that they further the overarching imperative of crime reduction. The Commission (2013: 4.234–5) also noted their counter-productive results, insofar as these sentences are in tension with the principles of consistency and proportionality in sentencing. In the specific context of drug-trafficking offences, the Commission noted that the sentence seem to impact on low-level drug mules rather than more culpable actors. Nonetheless, change has yet to occur.

Forfeiting criminal assets

In an effort to address the circumvention of the criminal process by organised crime groups and leaders, non-conviction-based asset forfeiture was introduced in the Republic of Ireland in the mid-1990s. This built on the existing powers of criminal confiscation, but differed in that property could be seized and retained in the absence of a conviction. Garland (2001: 105) has spoken of the 'criminological predicament' that states face: This is encapsulated by the seemingly ineluctable problem of organised crime, which requires adaptation and the adoption of a 'radically new and thorough approach' involving evidence on the civil burden of proof.[11] Rather than the traditional approach of investigation, arrest, prosecution and (it is hoped) conviction of a given individual, the focus here is on the money, and the conventional criminal justice chronology is abandoned in favour of a civil process.

As noted earlier, this mechanism and its implementing agency (CAB) were introduced in 1996, after the murders of Garda Jerry McCabe and investigative journalist Veronica Guerin by members of a criminal group. Although the Home Office Working Group on Confiscation (1998) recommended such a civil process for the UK in 1998, the UK Government opted for another review by the Cabinet Office Performance and Innovation Unit (2000) before the enactment of the Proceeds of Crime Act 2002, Part 5 of which provides for 'civil recovery' (the UK equivalent to Irish forfeiture) across the constituent jurisdictions of the UK.

The legislative framework

The schemes are similar in many respects. Civil forfeiture orders may be made against property worth at least €13,000 in the Republic of Ireland and £10,000 in the UK, which are deemed to be the proceeds of crime, that is, obtained as a result of or in connection with the commission of an offence or through unlawful conduct (s1 Proceeds of Crime Act 1996; s240(1) Proceeds of Crime Act 2002). It is not necessary for proceedings to have been brought for an offence in connection with the property (s240(2) POCA 2002); there is no predicate offence. Crucially, the standard of proof is the balance of probabilities (s8(2) POCA 1996; s241(3) POCA 2002).

The NCA, the Public Prosecution Service for Northern Ireland (PPSNI) and CAB, *inter alia*, may apply to the High Court in their respective jurisdictions for a number of orders culminating in asset recovery. Three different civil orders may be granted: In Northern Ireland (as in the rest of the UK), these are freezing (s245A), interim receivership (s246) and recovery orders (s266); and in the Republic of Ireland, interim, interlocutory and disposal orders (ss2–4 POCA 1996). Freezing and interim receivership orders in Northern Ireland and interim orders in the Republic of Ireland prevent a particular person from dealing with the property for a limited period, pending the investigation, and they may be issued *ex parte*. In the Republic of Ireland, an interlocutory order may be applied for instead of an interim order, or within 21 days of the making of the interim order (s3). The High Court must make an interlocutory order if satisfied that the evidence establishes that a person possesses or controls property constituting the proceeds of crime and is of the requisite value, unless this is refuted or if there would be a serious risk of injustice. Furthermore, section 7 allows a receiver to be appointed by the High Court to manage or take possession of the property which is subject to an interim or interlocutory order.

A disposal order deprives the respondent of his rights in the property and transfers the property to the Minister for Finance (s4(4) POCA 1996). In Northern Ireland, if the High Court is satisfied that the property is recoverable, it must make a recovery order (s266(1) POCA 2002), and this must be within 12 years of the date on which the cause of action accrued (s288 POCA 2002). As originally enacted, section 4 of POCA 1996 allowed for the making of a disposal order where an interlocutory order had been in force for not less than seven years; now, disposal may occur after a shorter period with the consent of the parties (s4A).

Given that the civil rules of procedure apply in relation to recovery hearings, hearsay evidence is permitted and previous convictions are admissible automatically in the Republic of Ireland and the UK. In the Republic of Ireland, opinion evidence from a senior police officer or officer of the Revenue Commissioners is admissible in applications for these orders if the High Court is satisfied that there are reasonable grounds for that belief (s8 POCA 1996).

Civil forfeiture has been challenged in numerous respects: The retrospective application of the provisions has been objected to, as has its effect on the right to private property, and the characterisation of the process as civil rather than criminal. None of these arguments has been accepted in the domestic or European contexts. Civil forfeiture has been accepted by the courts as a proportionate and legitimate response to the threat of serious and organised crime and is not regarded as a penalty. Its civil nature has been confirmed judicially due to the absence of criminal process characteristics and its focus on the individual (for critique, see Campbell, 2013a).

As noted above, the NCA is limited in its ability to carry out its civil recovery functions in Northern Ireland. The National Crime Agency (Limitation of Extension to Northern Ireland) Order 2013 permits the NCA to carry out civil recovery functions in Northern Ireland, but only in relation to excepted and reserved offences (namely immigration and customs offences) and transferred offences that are closely connected to such offences. As Obokata *et al.* (2014: 66) identify, the NCA does not address the latter types of closely connected offences in the current political environment, and this may lead to inconsistency in application of the law. Moreover, the PPSNI has limited experience in using its civil recovery powers (Northern Ireland Affairs Committee, 2012), and the PSNI does not have civil recovery powers under the current legislative framework. This undercuts the potential impact of this strategy against organised crime.

Even before such complications in Northern Ireland, the Irish scheme has been far more successful in terms of monies and property recouped, and this galvanises popular and political support. In addition, CAB's funding does not depend on the revenue restrained or forfeit, nor does it represent a proportion of the property seized (s19). In contrast, assets recovered in Northern Ireland were returned to the Home Office, from where 50 per cent was distributed to the agencies involved (Organised Crime Task Force, 2011: 36). Now the full value of assets recovered in Northern Ireland through the criminal recovery process is returned to Northern Ireland, and this distribution is done by the Northern Ireland Department of Justice (Justice Act (Northern Ireland) 2011 s94). Fifty per cent of these assets are directed to community projects that reduce crime or the fear of it; this is called the Assets Recovery Community Scheme. The other half is returned to law enforcement agencies to enhance their asset recovery work under what is known as the Assets Recovery Incentivisation Scheme (see OCTF, 2013: 48). This may compromise equity and fairness by prompting agencies to focus on the revenue-producing capacity of forfeiture (Worrall, 2001), and may undermine the aim of disrupting allegedly criminal behaviour which may not necessarily entail targeting the most lucrative groups.

Assessing civil forfeiture

Civil forfeiture exemplifies proactive, preventative policing, in contrast to traditional reactive means of enforcement, as it seeks to inhibit ongoing criminal enterprises by seizing the capital necessary to develop and maintain illicit markets (Kilcommins et al., 2004). This action against organised crime allows the force of the state and community censure to be visited upon individuals who are believed to transgress the criminal law but who have otherwise evaded prosecution. Though the purported target of the civil action is the property, this seems incomplete at best, disingenuous at worst. It can be suggested that such state action usurps the role of the criminal courts and compromises the presumption of innocence, due to the public expression of censure on the balance of probabilities (see further, Campbell, 2013b). Overall this approach to addressing organised crime favours the objectives of the state in terms of criminal control over the individual's right to due process (Campbell, 2007). Situating these processes in the civil realm limits the available safeguards, notwithstanding the inherent power of the state and the significant impact on the rights of the individual involved. Kilcommins and Vaughan (2007: 136, drawing on Dubber, 2001: 966) aptly describe this approach as 'criminal administration' rather than criminal justice, in which the notion of *mens rea* is circumvented.

Conclusion

In attempting to map and portray the form and extent of organised crime on the island of Ireland, this chapter has underlined the contested nature of this phenomenon. Despite these neighbouring jurisdictions sharing a common legal heritage, historical setting and land border, the diverging sociopolitical contexts have prompted quite different responses to organised crime. In particular, the still-fraught political landscape in Northern Ireland has a direct impact on the capacity of agencies to address organised crime. The measures introduced in the Republic of Ireland fit into a rational actor paradigm in which the organised criminal is regarded as beyond rehabilitation, and are informed by a view of organised crime as an emergency, necessitating the ratcheting up of state powers.

Like numerous jurisdictions, Northern Ireland and the Republic of Ireland seek to confront the problem of organised crime robustly, while retaining and respecting conventional protections for the accused person. Worldwide, radical measures are adopted in an effort to address this form of crime – Scotland, for instance, has an offence of failing to report organised crime (Criminal Justice and Licensing (Scotland) Act 2010 s31), while New South Wales has consorting provisions (Crimes Act 1900, ss93W–Y), which preclude association between certain individuals and are aimed at gangs. Neither approach has been emulated on the island of Ireland. Nonetheless, this does not indicate that the two jurisdictions here have been reticent or conventional in legislating against organised crime. For instance, the removal of the jury is a radical move in common-law jurisdictions, and so it appears that the Republic of Ireland in particular is blazing an unfortunate trail in this respect. In addition, the Republic of Ireland's scheme of civil forfeiture and CAB have been studied and imitated elsewhere.

It is evident from this chapter that the Republic of Ireland and Northern Ireland have not followed criminological insights and penological trends precisely. Elements of the 'New Penology', for instance, are evident, as are aspects of the rational actor model, but policy and practice across the island of Ireland does not map onto theoretical insights directly. So, while these theoretical perspectives help to explicate the rationale for various policies, inconsistencies and gaps remain.

References

Albanese, J. (2000) 'The causes of organized crime: Do criminals organize around opportunities for crime or do criminal opportunities create new offenders?', *Journal of Contemporary Criminal Justice*, 16(4): 409–23.

An Garda Síochána (2013) *An Garda Síochána Annual Report 2013*. Available at: www.garda.ie/Documents/User/Annual%20Report%202013%20-%20English.pdf (accessed 23 April 2015).

An Garda Síochána and Police Service of Northern Ireland (2008) *A Cross Border Organised Crime Assessment 2008*. Belfast and Dublin: Northern Ireland Office and Department of Justice. Available at: www.justice.ie/en/JELR/28350%20final.pdf.PDF/Files/28350%20final.pdf.PDF (accessed 24 April 2015).

An Garda Síochána and Police Service of Northern Ireland (2010) *A Cross Border Organised Crime Assessment 2010*. Belfast and Dublin: Northern Ireland Office and Department of Justice. Available at: www.drugsandalcohol.ie/14537/1/CROSS_BORDER_CRIME_ASSESSMENT_2010%5B1%5D.pdf (accessed 24 April 2015).

An Garda Síochána and Police Service of Northern Ireland (2012) *A Cross Border Organised Crime Assessment 2012*. Belfast and Dublin: Northern Ireland Office and Department of Justice.

An Garda Síochána and Police Service of Northern Ireland (2014) *A Cross Border Organised Crime Assessment 2014*. Belfast and Dublin: Northern Ireland Office and Department of Justice. Available at: www.dojni.gov.uk/index/publications/publication-categories/pubs-criminal-justice/cross-border-crime-assessment-final.pdf (accessed 24 April 2015).

Balance in the Criminal Law Review Group (2007) *Final Report of the Balance in the Criminal Law Review Group*. Dublin: Stationery Office.

Braithwaite, J. (1989) 'Criminological theory and organizational crime', *Justice Quarterly*, 6(3): 333–58.

Cabinet Office Performance and Innovation Unit (2000) *Recovering the Proceeds of Crime*. London: Cabinet Office.

Campbell, L. (2007) 'Theorising asset forfeiture in Ireland', *Journal of Criminal Law*, 71(5): 441–60.

Campbell, L. (2013a) *Organised Crime and the Law: A Comparative Analysis*. Oxford: Hart.

Campbell, L. (2013b) 'Criminal labels, the European Convention on Human Rights and the presumption of innocence', *Modern Law Review*, 76(4): 681–707.

Campbell, L. (2014) 'The prosecution of organised crime: Removing the jury', *International Journal of Evidence and Proof*, 18(2): 83–100.

Central Statistics Office (2014) 'Implementing new international standards for National Accounts and Balance of Payments Statistics', Press Release 3 July 2014. Available at: www.cso.ie/en/newsandevents/pressreleases/2014pressreleases/implementingnewinternationalstandardsfornationalaccountsandbalanceofpaymentsstatistics/ (accessed 23 April 2015).

Committee to Review the Offences Against the State Acts (2002) *Report of the Committee to Review the Offences Against the State Acts 1939–1998 and Related Matters*. Dublin: Stationery Office.

Cornish, D. and Clarke, R. (2002) 'Analyzing organised crimes', in A. Piquero and S. Tibbets (eds) *Rational Choice and Criminal Behavior: Recent Research and Future Challenges* (pp. 41–64). London: Routledge.

Department of Justice and Equality (2010) White Paper on Crime Discussion Document No. 3: *Organised and White Collar Crime.* Available at: www.justice.ie/en/JELR/Pages/WPOC_Doc3_sub_recd_pub (accessed 23 April 2015).

Department of Justice and Equality (2011) *Minister for Justice, Equality and Defence, Mr. Alan Shatter T.D. 9th Annual Cross Border Organised Crime Seminar City North Hotel, Gormanston, Co. Meath.* Available at: www. justice.ie/en/JELR/Pages/PR11000232 (accessed 23 April 2015).

Dubber, M. D. (2001) 'Policing possession: The war on crime and the end of the criminal law', *Journal of Criminal Law and Criminology,* 91(4): 829–996.

Europol (2011) *OCTA 2011: EU Organised Crime Threat Assessment.* Netherlands: European Police Office.

Europol (2013) *The EU Serious and Organised Crime Threat Assessment (SOCTA 2013).* Available at: www. europol.europa.eu/content/eu-serious-and-organised-crime-threat-assessment-socta (accessed 23 April 2015).

Feeley, M. and Simon, J. (1992) 'The new penology: Notes on the emerging strategy of corrections and its implications', *Criminology,* 30: 449–74.

Finckenauer, J. O. (2005) 'Problems of definition: What is organized crime?', *Trends in Organized Crime,* 8(3): 63–81.

Garland, D. (2000) 'The culture of high crime societies: Some preconditions of recent "Law and Order" policies', *British Journal of Criminology,* 40: 347–75.

Garland, D. (2001) *The Culture of Control.* Oxford: Oxford University Press.

Goldstock, R. (2004) *Organised Crime in Northern Ireland: A Report for the Secretary of State.* Belfast: Northern Ireland Office.

Goldstock, R., Marcus, M., Thacher, T. and Jacobs, J. (1991) *Corruption and Racketeering in the New York City Construction Industry: Final Report.* New York: New York University Press.

Greer, S. and White, A. (1988) 'A return to trial by jury', in A. Jennings (ed) *Justice Under Fire: The Abuse of Civil Liberties in Northern Ireland.* London: Pluto Press.

Hales, G., Lewis, C. and Silverstone, D. (2006) *Gun Crime: The Market in and Use of Illegal Firearms.* London: Home Office.

Hamilton-Smith, N. and Mackenzie, S. (2010) 'The geometry of shadows: A critical review of organised crime risk assessments', *Policing and Society,* 20(3): 257–79.

Harfield, C. (2008) 'The organization of "organized crime policing" and its international context', *Criminology and Criminal Justice,* 8(4): 483–507.

HM Revenue and Customs (2006) *New Responses to New Challenges: Reinforcing the Tackling Tobacco Smuggling Strategy.* London: The Stationery Office.

Home Office Working Group on Confiscation (1998) *Third Report: Criminal Assets.* London: Home Office.

House of Commons Committee of Public Accounts (2007) *Assets Recovery Agency Fiftieth Report of Session 2006–07.* London: The Stationery Office.

House of Commons Northern Ireland Affairs Committee (2003) *Eighth Report: The Illegal Drugs Trade and Drug Culture in Northern Ireland.* London: Stationery Office.

House of Commons Northern Ireland Affairs Committee (2006a) *Organised Crime in Northern Ireland Volume I (Third Report of Session 2005–06).* London: The Stationery Office.

House of Commons Northern Ireland Affairs Committee (2006b) *Organised Crime in Northern Ireland: Government Response to the Committee's Third Report of Session 2005–06,* HC 1642. Available from: http:// www.parliament.the-stationery-office.co.uk/pa/cm200506/cmselect/cmniaf/cmniaf.htm.

Independent Monitoring Commission (2005) *Fifth Report of the Independent Monitoring Commission.* London: The Stationery Office.

Independent Monitoring Commission (2006) *Tenth Report of the Independent Monitoring Commission.* London: The Stationery Office.

Jackson, J. and Doran, S. (1995) *Judge without Jury: Diplock Trials in the Adversary System.* Oxford: Clarendon Press.

Jacobs, J. and Anechiarico, F. (1992) 'Blacklisting public contractors as an anti-corruption and racketeering strategy', *Criminal Justice Ethics,* 11(2): 64–76.

Judicial Studies Board for Northern Ireland (2014) *Sentencing Guidelines – Magistrates Court.* Available at: www.jsbni.com/Publications/sentencing-guides-magistrates-court/Pages/default.aspx (accessed 23 April 2015).

Kilcommins, S. and Vaughan, B. (2007) *Terrorism, Rights and the Rule of Law: Negotiating Justice in Ireland.* Cullompton: Willan.

Kilcommins, S., O'Donnell, I., O'Sullivan, E. and Vaughan, B. (2004) *Crime, Punishment and the Search for Order in Ireland*. Dublin: Institute of Public Administration.

Law Reform Commission (2013) *Report on Mandatory Sentences*. Dublin: Law Reform Commission.

Levi, M. (2012) 'The organization of serious crimes for gain', in M. Maguire, R. Morgan and R. Reiner (eds) *The Oxford Handbook of Criminology* (5th edn). Oxford: Oxford University Press.

Lord Chief Justice's Sentencing Group (2012) *Report by Lord Chief Justice's Sentencing Group*. Available at: www.courtsni.gov.uk/en-GB/Judicial%20Decisions/LCJ-sentence-group/Documents/j_lcjsg_Dec12-report/Sentencing-Group-Report-Dec12.pdf (accessed 23 April 2015).

Makarenko, T. (2004) 'The crime–terror continuum: Tracing the interplay between transnational organised crime and terrorism', *Global Crime,* 6(1): 129–145.

Maltz, M. (1976) 'On defining "organized crime": The development of a definition and a typology', *Crime and Delinquency,* 22(3): 338–46.

Matthews, R. (2002) *Armed Robbery*. Cullompton: Willan Publishing.

McEvoy, P. (2005) *Research for the Department of Justice on the Criteria Applied by the Courts in Sentencing under s. 15A of the Misuse of Drugs Act 1977 (as Amended)*. Dublin: Department of Justice, Equality and Law Reform.

McNeill, F., Burns, N., Halliday, S., Hutton, N. and Tata, C. (2009) 'Risk, responsibility and reconfiguration: Penal adaptation and misadaptation', *Punishment & Society,* 11(4): 419–42.

Morris, S. (1998) *Clubs, Drugs and Doormen*. Crime Detection and Prevention Series Paper 86. London: Home Office.

National Crime Agency (2014) *National Strategic Assessment of Serious and Organised Crime 2014*. Available at: www.nationalcrimeagency.gov.uk/publications/207-nca-strategic-assessment-of-serious-and-organised-crime/file (accessed 23 April 2015).

Northern Ireland Affairs Committee (2012) *Fuel Laundering and Smuggling in Northern Ireland. Third Report of Session 2010–12*. London: Stationery Office.

Northern Ireland Audit Office (2010) *Memorandum to the Committee of Public Accounts from the Comptroller and Auditor General for Northern Ireland: Combating Organised Crime*. Belfast: Stationery Office.

Northern Ireland Office (2013) *Ford Praises Recent Organised Crime Taskforce Successes*. Available at: www.northernireland.gov.uk/news-doj-060913-ford-praises-recent (accessed 23 April 2015).

O'Malley, T. (2000) *Sentencing Law and Practice*. Dublin: Round Hall Sweet and Maxwell.

Obokata, T., Payne, B. and Jackson, J. (2014) *AHRC Research Project 2014 North–South Irish Responses to Transnational Organised Crime*. Available at: http://keele.ac.uk/law/research/researchprojects/respondingtotransnationalorganisedcrimeintheislandofireland/AHRC%20OC%20Project%20Final%20Report.pdf (accessed 23 April 2015).

Organised Crime Task Force (2011) *2011 Annual Report & Threat Assessment: Organised Crime in Northern Ireland*. Belfast: Northern Ireland Office.

Organised Crime Task Force (2012) *2012 Annual Report & Threat Assessment: Organised Crime in Northern Ireland*. Belfast: Northern Ireland Office.

Organised Crime Task Force (2013) *2013 Annual Report & Threat Assessment Organised Crime in Northern Ireland*. Belfast: Northern Ireland Office.

Organised Crime Task Force (2014a) *Annual Report & Threat Assessment*, Available at: www.dojni.gov.uk/index/publications/publication-categories/pubs-policing-community-safety/community-safety/organised-crime/octf-annual-report-2014.pdf (accessed 23 April 2015).

Organised Crime Task Force (2014b) *Cross Border Organised Crime Assessment 2014*. Available at: www.octf.gov.uk/Publications/SARS-information-(1)/Cross-Border-Organised-Crime-Assessment-2014 (accessed 23 April 2015).

Organised Crime Task Force (2014c) *Northern Ireland Organised Crime Strategy 2014*. Available at: www.dojni.gov.uk/index/media-centre/northern-ireland-organised-crime-strategy-.pdf (accessed 23 April 2015).

Paoli, L. and Fijnaut, C. (2006) 'Organised crime and its control policies', *European Journal of Crime, Criminal Law and Criminal Justice,* 14(3): 307–27.

Police Service of Northern Ireland (2013) *General: PSNI Statement on National Crime Agency*. Available at: www.psni.police.uk/general__psni_statement_on_national_crime_agency_14_05_13 (accessed 23 April 2015).

Scottish Serious Organised Crime Group (2009) *Preliminary Findings on the Scale and Extent of Serious Organised Crime in Scotland*. Edinburgh: Scottish Government.

Sentencing Working Group (2010) *Monitoring and Developing Sentencing Guidance in Northern Ireland: A Report to the Lord Chief Justice from the Sentencing Working Group*. Belfast: Northern Ireland Office.

Shelley, L., Picarelli, J., Irby, A., Hart, D., Craig-Hart, P.A., Williams, P., Simon, S., Abdullaev, N., Stanislawski, B. and Covil, L. (2005) *Methods and Motives: Exploring Links between Transnational Organized Crime and International Terrorism*. Washington: US Department of Justice.

Transcrime (2008) *Study on Extortion Racketeering – The Need for an Instrument to Combat Activities of Organised Crime: Final Report*. Milan: Transcrime.

van Duyne, P. (1996) 'The phantom and threat of organized crime', *Crime, Law and Social Change*, 24(4): 341–77.

van Duyne, P. and van Dijck, M. (2006) 'Assessing organised crime: The sad state of an impossible art', in F. Bovenkerk and M. Levi (eds) *The Organized Crime Community: Essays in Honor of Alan A. Block*. New York: Springer.

van Gelder, J.-L. (2013) 'Beyond rational choice: The hot/cool perspective of criminal decision making', *Psychology, Crime & Law*, 19(9): 745–63.

van Koppen, M.V., de Poot, C., Kleemans, E. and Nieuwbeerta, P. (2010) 'Criminal trajectories in organized crime', *British Journal of Criminology*, 50(1): 102–23.

Worrall, J. (2001) 'Addicted to the drug war: The role of civil assets forfeiture as a budgetary necessity in contemporary law enforcement', *Journal of Criminal Justice*, 29(3): 171–87.

Notes

1 Senior lecturer in criminal law and evidence, University of Edinburgh, liz.campbell@ed.ac.uk. Thanks to Louise Brangan for research assistance.
2 See www.octf.gov.uk/Areas-Of-Crime.
3 See www.europol.europa.eu/content/camden-asset-recovery-inter-agency-network-carin-leaflet.
4 [1982] ILRM 385.
5 [2011] EWCA Crim 1338 para. 27.
6 [2010] EWCA Crim 1755 para. 7.
7 [2010] NICC 7 47.
8 [1996] 1 IR 348.
9 [2003] 4 IR 423.
10 Dáil Deb, 21 April 1999, vol 503 col 837.
11 Seanad Deb, 27 June 1996, vol 148 col 420.

30

Ethnicity, identity and criminal justice[1]

Denis Bracken[2]

Introduction

Anglo-American criminology has long recognised the role of culture or, more directly, culture-conflict as a source of crime. Nearly 80 years ago, Thorsten Sellin (1938) discussed the idea of crime arising out of a conflict of cultures and, as part of a commentary on research methodologies, wrote about the need to learn about conflict, 'which may be assumed to arise when an immigrant group from another continent settles on our shores...' (Sellin, 1938: 99). In countries with histories of colonization of indigenous minorities and patterns of large-scale immigration, minority ethnic populations were seen as characterised by cultural characteristics that might cause them to come into conflict with a dominant majority's cultural norms (Roberts and Doob, 1997). Assimilation into the dominant 'Settler' society was the preferred solution (Veracini, 2010). When there were racial differences between the dominant culture and various subcultures, the clash might be seen as being much more acute. Racism and racial discrimination becomes a significant part of the narrative. This is not necessarily to make direct causal connections between race or ethnicity and crime, but rather to indicate that in many instances minority ethnic groups are more likely to be processed as offenders than their numbers might suggest as a percentage of a national or regional population. Sellin (1938) seemed to be referring to immigrants from Europe to the United States in the early decades of the twentieth century, but cultural minorities could in a more contemporary American context also mean the African Americans, descendants of Africans brought as slaves to the United States, Latino Americans and recent immigrants. Elsewhere, cultural minorities could include indigenous minorities, the descendants of those present in what is now Australia, New Zealand, the USA or Canada prior to European settlement. In all four countries, indigenous peoples appear in criminal justice statistics in numbers far out of proportion to their representation in national and regional populations. Crime arising out of a conflict of norms could also be identified in the British context related to economic migrants who have come from their countries, formerly a part of the British Empire, to the United Kingdom. The narrative of the 'other', either indigenous or foreign, as different, problematic and in need of control is a pervasive one in Anglo-American criminal justice and beyond. Tonry (1997) provides a good summary of both the thinking and research on the issues of ethnicity and immigration (two related but not identical topics) as they related to crime and criminological thinking 18 years ago. He points out the dangers of over-generalisation (some immigrant and ethnic minority groups in some national contexts have very low crime rates, others much higher), the differences in data collection that make cross-national comparisons difficult and the connections between social and economic disadvantage and crime among minority groups (Tonry, 1997). More recently, Spohn's (2013) research that included race, ethnicity and gender as factors in sentencing suggests that the appropriate research question to ask in this regard is not 'Does race, ethnicity or sex matter?', but 'When do race, ethnicty and sex matter?' in the criminal justice process. Her finding related to sentencing of drug offenders in US federal courts among white, Hispanic and Black offenders was that these factors do matter, but at different stages of the process (especially bail and sentence length) and in different contexts (Spohn, 2013).

This chapter will consider the idea of the criminal 'other' in two forms, indigenous and foreign, in Northern Ireland and the Republic of Ireland. In both instances, the 'other', to use Bauman's (1991: 14) characterisation, is 'the opposite (degraded, suppressed, exiled) side of the first and its creation'. Thus the majority population differentiates themselves from those who are not like them, culturally, perhaps linguistically and possibly racially. The indigenous 'other' in the Republic of Ireland are the Travellers, a specific cultural group with deep historical roots as well as a history of being outsiders and different from the majority Irish population. Characterised as nomadic, they are the opposite of the 'settled' majority. A second 'other' means those who are different because they come from somewhere else and may represent significant cultural traditions that originated in other countries. Each jurisdiction represents a different way in which those who have come from elsewhere, the immigrants and asylum seekers in particular of the past 20 years, have become a part of or remained separate from the dominant cultures of each society. This has particular relevance for the criminal justice systems on the island of Ireland. As will be discussed below, data is very limited on Travellers and ethnic minorities in the criminal justice system. As well, there has been limited scholarly work on these issues in studies of criminology, both in the past (e.g. McCullagh, 1996) or more recently (e.g. Rogan, 2011).

The chapter will begin with an overview of the Travellers and how both the Republic of Ireland and Northern Ireland have defined them as an 'other', a problematic population to be controlled. This will lead to a discussion of the relations between Travellers and aspects of the criminal justice system in each jurisdiction.

The second part of the chapter will examine the ideologies that have appeared to be the dominant narratives by which 'newcomers' to these jurisdictions have been viewed, along with an examination of how both narratives have changed particularly in the past 15 years. Data on immigration to both jurisdictions will be included. This will then lead to a discussion of how parts of the criminal justice systems have responded to the interactions with those who have come to settle on this island. For each topic, data from the criminal justice services in both jurisdictions will be presented, along with data from a study of probation officers' practice experience with Travellers and non-Irish nationals and in particular the Roma, in the Republic of Ireland. The chapter will conclude with some observations on the issue of culture conflict and crime within an Irish context.

Who are the Travellers?

There have been numerous studies and reviews describing the origins of the Travellers on the island of Ireland. One of the more well known of these was by Sharon and George Gmelch, American anthropologists who wrote extensively about Irish Travellers in the 1970s (Gmelch and Gmelch, 1976). Traveller culture has been characterised as based in nomadism, or itinerancy as it was frequently labelled by the Irish government (Commission on Itinerancy, 1963), a strong sense of family including extended family and religious faith, historically Roman Catholicism. Women traditionally had primary responsibility for the home and children. Marriage between Travellers was encouraged and with 'settled people' discouraged (McDonagh, 2000). Provision of accommodation, in particular sites that support the traditional Traveller transient lifestyle, has been an ongoing issue and has had implications for Traveller children and education (Gormally, 2005). Social change from the initial post-independence agrarian society to a more modern urbanized society has also had an impact on the intinerant lifestyle of the Travellers (Gmelch, 1985). The suggestion is that currently for most Travellers, nomadism is at best occasional (Mulcahy, 2012).

Other recent scholarship has moved beyond questions of origin and culture and highlighted the impact of a history of racism and social and economic marginalisation (particularly with respect to housing and accommodation) on members of the Travelling community (Fanning, 2012). Using the notion of the 'other' introduced above, Helleiner (2000: 29) describes how Travellers have been seen by themselves and the wider population and in particular how this notion of the 'other' has placed them outside the majority of Irish society:

> ... Travellers in Ireland have been constructed and have constructed themselves, as an indig-enous minority. Attributions of origin have emphasised the essential 'Irishness' of Travellers and, in contrast to colonized indigenous populations elsewhere, Travellers have not been constructed as racially 'Other'.

Although their identification as an indigenous Irish minority has not been on racial lines, it has not prevented Travellers from being negatively stigmatised, nor shielded them from anti-Traveller discrimination. Travellers are thus seen as 'different' based on lifestyle and culture, although not along racial grounds. Difference was and is interpreted as problematic. At various times after the founding of the State, there have been government commissions and other quasi-official enquiries into what was termed 'the problem of itinerancy'. The remit of the Commission on Itinerancy (1963: 11), for example, was:

(1) to enquire into the problem arising from the presence in the country of itinerants in considerable numbers;
(2) to examine the economic, educational, health and social problems inherent in their way of life;
(3) to consider what steps might be taken—
  (a) to provide opportunities for a better way of life for itinerants;
  (b) to promote their absorption into the general community;
  (c) pending such absorption, to reduce to a minimum the disadvantages to themselves and to the community resulting from their itinerant habits.

Several assumptions underlined the Commission's work as detailed above: that itinerants were a problem, that their way of life created 'social problems', that there was a 'better way of life' for them and that this better way of life was through 'absorption' into the majority community with their way of life extinguished.

Drummond (2007) has pointed out that the focus of the Commission was on how to deal with what was assumed to be a problem: the culture of Travellers based on relatively free move-ment and not being settled in any particular locale. Itinerancy was uncontested and assumed to be a negative phenomenon. The solution, which echoed those of other countries with indige-nous populations defined as problematic (e.g. Australian Law Reform Commission, 1986; Truth and Reconciliation Commission of Canada, 2012), was assimilation, the suppression of distinctive cultures and ways of life.

Although Travellers are to be found throughout the island, Northern Ireland and the Republic of Ireland differ at least in a legal sense on how they are perceived. The difference revolves around whether Travellers are deemed to constitute an 'ethnic minority'. It is a contested area in both jurisdictions, but with different results. In Northern Ireland, 'Irish Travellers are legally recognised as ethnic groups and protected from discrimination by the Race Relations Act (1976, amended 2000) and the Human Rights Act (1998)' (Equality and Human Rights Commission, 2009: 5). This is a relatively recent phenomenon, however. Noonan (1994) suggested that although the legal context might be different, the issue of racism and discrimination against Travellers was very much a fact 20 years ago.

In the Republic of Ireland, Travellers are not a legally recognised ethnic group, although certain protections are afforded to members of the Travelling community, in theory at least, through the Employment Equality Act 1998 and the Equal Status Act 2000.[3] A recent report of the Oireachtas' Joint Committee on Justice, Defence and Equality (2014) recommended that Travellers do constitute an ethnic minority and therefore that the Irish State should recognise Travellers as such.

There are also questions in terms of the size of the Traveller minority. The Central Statistics Office (2012b: 27) estimated the Traveller population in the Republic of Ireland as of 'April 2011 was 29,573 accounting for just over half of one per cent (0.6% of the total population). The figure represents a 32 per cent increase on 2006 (22,435)'. The All Ireland Traveller Health Study (AITHS, 2010) presented a slightly different figure, estimating that the Traveller Population in the Republic of Ireland was 36,224 and 3,905 in Northern Ireland, giving a total of 40,129. However one wishes to view it, these population estimates suggest that the Travellers represent less than 1 per cent of the population. In Northern Ireland, the estimated number of Travellers actually fell between 2001 and 2011 from 1,710 to 1,301. In both years, this represented 0.01 per cent of the Northern Irish population. Ó hAodha (2011), however, offers larger numbers: 36,000 in the Republic of Ireland and 6,000 in Northern Ireland. The variation in population estimates highlights the challenges associated with counting partly mobile populations. Differences in the population numbers, at least in the Republic of Ireland, would appear to be based on whether those doing the counting, so to speak, are aware of the Traveller culture and lifestyle. By working in partnership with the CSO, the primary national Travellers organisation suggested that the CSO in the 2011 census had come closer to an accurate count of the Traveller population, but still has some way to go (Pavee Point, 2013).

Travellers and criminal justice

Data from Northern Ireland on Travellers in the criminal justice system is hard to come by. Drummond (2007), quoting O'Hanlon (2002), suggested that Travellers were 'invisible' in the statistics of the criminal justice system. This is in some ways similar to the findings of the IPRT (2014) study in the Republic of Ireland referred to above, 12 years after O'Hanlon's comment. There are references to Travellers' largely negative experiences with the police (Travellers, undated) and with prison officers in Northern Ireland prisons (Butler and Maruna, 2012). The lack of information may be due to the fact that relatively few Travellers find themselves in prison or on probation. A 2014 inspection report by HMIP suggested that 5 per cent of the prison population in England and Wales were of Gypsy, Romany or Traveller background. However, the report did not separate out the three categories, was based on a survey of England and Wales prison establishments only and suggested that the 5 per cent was possibly an underestimate (HM Inspectorate of Prisons, 2014: 11). Irish Travellers are considered part of the 'white' classification in UK crime statistics, making it difficult to determine their representation in the statistics on offenders. The Ministry of Justice's inspections of prison establishments in Northern Ireland mention Travellers and ethnic minority populations in reports, but the numbers tend to be low. For example, the report on an inspection at Ash House, Hydebank Wood Women's Prison identified two Travellers in the population (Chief Inspector of Criminal Justice in Northern Ireland *et al.*, 2013).

A report by the Irish Penal Reform Trust in 2014 into Irish prisons stated, '[t]he absence of an ethnic identifier makes the actual number of Travellers in prison unknown'(IPRT, 2014: 8). That said, an earlier study suggested that the chances of a Traveller ending up in prison as a result of a court appearance were higher than for a non-Traveller. The All Ireland Traveller Health Study in 2010 (AITHS, 2010: 110) surveyed Travellers in Irish prisons and reached the conclusion that a Traveller was 11 times more likely to be imprisoned than a non-Traveller, and a Traveller woman was 22 times more likely to be imprisoned than a non-Traveller woman. Official data might suggest smaller numbers, but still represented a higher risk of imprisonment for both Traveller men and women:

> When calculated using the Traveller reported prisoner population, the risk of a Traveller being imprisoned was more than 5 times that of a non-Traveller … and for Traveller women, the risk was 18 times that of non-Traveller women
>
> *(AITHS, 2010: 110)*

Drummond's (2007) research referred to earlier details that the various official responses to Traveller culture, beginning with the Commission on Itinerancy in 1963, have generally been recommendations either to eliminate the nomadic aspect of Traveller life all together (for example, through assimilation and 'settlement') or to restrict severely those areas where Travellers could stay (halting sites). This resulted in a tendency to criminalize parts of Traveller culture through, for example, trespass laws, raising the likelihood of criminal justice involvement. Although the responses in Northern Ireland reflect the different jurisdictional context, the 'problem' of the Travellers has generally continued to be identified in terms of transiency and accommodation, and criminality then is attributed to these two problem areas.

Mulcahy (2012) studied relations between the police and Travellers in the Republic of Ireland, both historically and as part of present strategies to recognise diversity in Irish society, while pointing out that the impetus for this recognition of diversity was more related to the influx of immigrants and refugees during the Celtic Tiger. The nomadic lifestyle of the Travellers meant both an ongoing involvement with the police with respect to access to public camping places and concern that the police did not take seriously allegations of victimization of Travellers at the hands of the settled community. He concluded that relations between police and Travellers, despite recognisable progress in some areas, continued to be characterised by mutual distrust (Mulcahy, 2012).

Probation and Travellers

Existing research on probation work with Travellers is from the UK and in general is very limited. Where there has been research, the focus has been on Travellers' experiences of the criminal justice system within the wider context of Irish people living in the UK, or in combination with Roma people (Lewis *et al.*, 2005; Cunneen and Stubbs, 2004). Power's (2003) article from the Probation Journal is one piece of research with a clearer focus on probation, although within the context of England and Wales. More recently, a study for the Thames Valley Probation Trust reported on both probation officers' and Travellers' experiences of probation (Cottrell-Boyce, 2014). It included suggestions for good practice when working with Travellers. The focus was again narrowly within the context of Travellers living in a limited geographic area of England and also of probation practice within a specific probation area. The sample size was relatively small (N=37), and the sample was identified using the category of 'Gypsy or Irish Traveller'. As with the HM Inspectorate of the Prisons (2014) study mentioned above, the category did not appear to permit disaggregation as to who might be gypsy, meaning Roma or Romany, and who might be Irish Traveller. However, the focus of the report was clearly on issues germane to Irish Traveller culture and identity. Both articles, from 2003 and 2014, identified the need for probation officers to be sensitive to the importance of culture to Travellers in the UK, their needs with respect to literacy, employment and transiency. They also indicated that in the view of the authors, risk assessment instruments in use at each time were structured in such a way as to ignore the impact of cultural practices on artificially inflating risk of reoffending scores. As well, both articles, though published 11 years apart, described the concern that the courts could be prejudiced against a Traveller before them for sentencing, because they were Travellers. The report from Thames Valley went so far as to recommend that '[o]fficers should exercise caution when preparing pre-sentence reports, ensuring reports do not contain irrelevant information which could reveal Traveller offenders, cultural identity and leave them open to prejudice in court proceedings' (Cottrell-Boyce, 2014: 27).

In the spring of 2013, the present author conducted research with probation officers of the Probation Service in the Republic of Ireland on the issues related to probation practice with persons from the Travelling community as well as with non-Irish nationals (Bracken, 2014).[4] Focus groups with probation officers were conducted in the cities of Galway, Limerick, Cork, Waterford and Dublin. A total of 37 probation officers participated in the groups. A number of themes emerged from the focus group discussions with probation officers. These themes related to issues of probation practice such as engagement, compliance and risk assessment. Culture and the use of culture in probation work also came through from the focus groups as an important factor. What follows next is a discussion of the findings of this research as it relates to Travellers on probation. Later in this chapter the findings related to non-Irish nationals are discussed.

All focus groups were asked the extent to which they would use a Traveller's ethnic identity as a Traveller in the preparation of reports for court. The intent of the questions was to facilitate a discussion on whether an 'ethnic identifier' at the pre-sentence stage might be helpful to a court's understanding of the Traveller-as-offender's background, or a potential for discriminatory action on the part of the court at sentencing. What emerged were a number of different themes related to the potential for discriminatory sentencing, the need to present a 'full picture' of the offender to the court, an unease about using any form of ethnic identification as well as the need to develop the right discretionary judgement as to when it might be helpful and also when not. These themes are represented in the quotes given below.

> I wouldn't mention it unless the individual [believes] it's important to them that it's mentioned; for instance I worked with a guy who was involved in a community group, a Traveller community group. It was very important for him that it was mentioned. But again I feel that if it isn't going to affect the body of the report and unless the individual brings it up themselves I'd leave it out, because again it could unnecessarily complicate matters....
> *(Bracken, 2014: 50)*

> I would but I always feel uncomfortable about it that's just my feeling as such, cause I kind of just feel that it ... like you're identifying, I don't know I can see the purpose but I am

also a bit uncomfortable with identifying people for everything that they are, you know that kind of way, or where they are coming from. I'm not saying that it can prejudice [others] but on some level it might.

(Bracken, 2014: 50)

You know especially when you're doing a court report and you're saying to the judge well I'm just accepting that because he's a Traveller he's not going to work which is not offering him all the services that are available to the Probation Service, or do you say no we're going to try and get you into work even though we know you're facing discrimination and it's going to be difficult, or are you setting people up to fail. So that's sort of the difficulty that we're kind of working in a lot of the time. And it's a real live issue, that discrimination.

(Bracken, 2014: 51)

The issue of ethnic and cultural identification, combined with the need to educate oneself and others (such as a judge) on the aspects of a minority person's culture that may be important for sentencing and intervention, clearly was something that the probation officers had considered. The IPRT (2014) referenced above recommends that the Irish Prison Service, following the example of some prisons in the UK, create opportunities for ethnic identification so as to encourage suitable services. The probation officers from the present study recognised the importance of ethnic identification as sometimes necessary when presenting the judges with a complete picture of the offender. Yet they also expressed the concern that discrimination exists and that identifying an ethnicity, especially Traveller background, might not always be in the best interest of the offender. There did not seem to be a consensus on the advisability of promoting ethnic identity for Travellers among the probation officers in the focus groups, but the concern expressed in the Thames Valley report resonated with the focus group discussions among Irish probation officers (Cottrell-Boyce, 2014).

Assessing risk and developing strategies, both to reduce where possible and to manage risk, has become the foundation for probation practice in many parts of the world, including the Republic of Ireland and Northern Ireland (Hannah-Moffat, 2005; Fitzgibbon, Hamilton and Richardson, 2010). Methods for assessing risk generally use actuarially based assessment instruments, frequently validated using large-scale samples of male offenders in custody (Bonta and Andrews, 2010). This has raised questions about the applicability of such risk-assessment instruments when they are used with specific ethnic minority offenders. For example, are there aspects of a minority culture that might result in a higher level of assessed risk based on the application of a specific instrument, but are 'normal' aspects of that culture? (see Gutierrez *et al.*, 2013; Webb, 2003). Within that culture, are these aspects in fact 'criminogenic'? (Tauri and Webb, 2012). Focus group participants in the present research were able to identify one specific aspect of the Level of Service Inventory-Revised (LSI-R) instrument that would easily result in a higher risk scored for Travellers – accommodation and changes of address. The LSI-R assumes that the more 'addresses' an offender has had in the past year or more, the higher the risk of committing new offences.

I'm just thinking 'Have you had two or more address changes in the last seven years' like the Travelling communities a lot of them would have moved a lot and that would be the norm for their culture, whereas we're scoring that negatively for the ordinary population, you know we've had five address stages in the last year, so I wonder have you had a job, have you had you know all the things that are scoring people on, you know that the traveller people find harder to achieve a lot of the time.

(Bracken, 2014: 52)

Just by virtue of the fact of the lifestyle, education and not working and into substance abuse, they'll [Travellers] all score fairly high.

I suppose you'd have to use your professional judgment a lot more I think. If you had somebody from the settled community for instance that had three different addresses in the last six months I think your antenna would be hopping, whereas if it's somebody from the Traveller community I think you're beginning to use your professional judgment a little bit and you'll sus it out a little bit more maybe to see why. I suppose you'd have an understanding that that might be part of or attributed to a cultural thing.

(Bracken, 2014: 53)

For the probation officers who participated in the research, moving offenders who were members of the Travelling community from basic compliance to engagement was not dissimilar to working with others on probation, but did require extra attention with respect to establishing trust. There was widespread acknowledgement that relations between Travellers and 'authority' (police, courts, etc.) as well as the media meant Travellers were suspicious of the Probation Service as simply being another part of a highly biased and discriminatory system. It also meant giving greater consideration to what aspects of Traveller culture might inhibit or slow down the process of engagement. To use Bottoms' (2001) characterisation of forms of compliance in community supervision contexts, the discussion centred on moving beyond instrumental or prudential compliance (based on determining what might be the easiest way to complete the bond) or, less frequently, constraint-based compliance, to what Bottoms called 'normative compliance'. This is compliance based on 'a felt moral obligation, commitment or attachment' (Bottoms, 2001: 90). For Travellers to get to this kind of compliance usually took a longer time because of the necessity of getting beyond the distrust of authority as well as accepting that what the probation officer was suggesting would be in some way beneficial to the offender. None of this would be unusual with respect to working with non-Traveller offenders, but the way to achieve this level, if possible, might be different.

In addition, clearly defined gender roles are a part of traditional Traveller culture, although it would appear from the experiences of the research participants' that the traditional Traveller culture may be disappearing. This in turn leads to the need for sensitivity to shifting cultural norms when dealing with Travellers as probationers.

I suppose for me through the years the biggest thing I would have seen is the youngsters growing up and not knowing whether they would align themselves to the Traveller culture or to the settled culture … and sometimes it was a kind of a pull between one and the other. I found it interesting to think about but not interesting for them because they just couldn't pick it out with you, which they were. Now I think we're gone another generation on now so it's probably a little bit more settled.

(Bracken, 2014: 56)

Other examples with respect to gender roles include young male Travellers working at a training centre refusing to wear aprons in a cooking class as that was something that 'only women did' (Bracken, 2014: 58). While one might imagine young males, Traveller or not, rebelling at such a thought, they did eventually come around. It was also difficult for young female Travellers to see themselves as moving forward in education, although there were small examples of this mentioned in various groups where Probation Officers worked with young women.

It was clear that in some instances there were parts of the culture that were still quite strong, and the example given below of a young Traveller man's commitment to a spiritual aspect shows how that may assist in supporting a person's movement away from offending behaviour. It also demonstrates an initial reluctance by the probation officer to engage with the probationer with a part of his culture, but eventually overcoming that reluctance.

> I think one of the things that I have started in my focus is asking them about their spirituality, because the Travellers would have a very strong Catholic ethos ... [commenting on a Traveller young male probationer] all around him there is a lot of criminality so you know what can he do for himself and what's meaningful for him. ... I was kind of going oh I wouldn't ask, but then when I had given it a bit of thought, so now I do. Because it is something that he relies on, because he has said that he's never going to take tablets again because it's a thing that leads him into offending and he's made a solemn promise to Saint someone or other. But for him that works, that's his, you know he had made that commitment to whoever the saint is.
>
> *(Bracken, 2014: 57)*

In other contexts – for example, Aboriginal offenders in Canada – spirituality based in cultural traditions can assist offenders in moving away from crime (Bracken, Deane and Morrissette, 2009). The notions of 'other' also extend to immigrants and refugees, and consideration of their involvement in criminal justice in Ireland follows.

The immigrant 'other' in the Republic of Ireland

The development of the Irish nation both before and after 1922 has been characterised as an exercise in 'the development of exclusionary conceptions of identity and a socio-genesis of homogeneity linked to nationalism' (Fanning, 2012: 30). As part of the struggle to eliminate British colonial rule and subsequently as part of post-1922 nation building, Fanning (2012: 32) suggests that Irish identity was built around religion (Catholicism) with a 'Gaelic cultural base'. This helped to strengthen the view of anyone outside this Irish–Ireland nationalism as an 'other', be they Protestant or Jewish (even if Irish-born) and later virtually anyone else who did not seem to have any family connection to the country. The othering of people who were or are different, that characterised some of the ways of dealing with Travellers mentioned above, was clearly also used for those who did not fit the idealised conception of what it was to be Irish. The policy of the State with respect to refugees from the 1930s onwards at least through the 1980s, according to Fanning (2012: 109), was reflective of this notion that Ireland was at best 'a reluctant host to asylum seekers and refugees'.

There is, however, another narrative that characterises discussion of immigrants. This is the narrative that the Republic of Ireland has for most of the past two centuries been a net exporter of people (Delaney, 2005). Emigration to the USA, the UK and more recently to Australia and Canada has tended to overshadow discussion of immigrants coming to the country, at least until the Celtic Tiger beginning in the mid-1990s. That people did not move *to* the Republic of Ireland, but moved away from it was a dominant theme. Two significant and related factors were at work from about 1995: The first was the previously mentioned Celtic Tiger, when the demand for labour outstripped supply for the first time in living memory. Migration to fill jobs for a time overcame the previous anxiety of being overrun by asylum seekers looking for generous welfare provision. The second and related point was the influx of migrants from EU countries after 2004. Similarly to the UK and Sweden and unlike most of the pre-2004 EU countries, the Republic of Ireland did not place restrictions on the number of EU migrants. The result was significant migration from the newer Eastern European members of the EU. The figures from the 2011 census suggest that the country continues to have an increase in population from immigration, with increases since the 2006 census of people in particular from Poland, India, Brazil and Romania. Non-Irish nationals had increased by 29 per cent from the 2006 census, from 419,733 persons to 544,357 or approximately 12 per cent of the population (Central Statistics Office, 2012a).[5] The need for labour during the years of the Celtic Tiger and immigration from the 2004 and 2007 EU expansion created a division between EU and other economic migrants (Maher, 2010) and asylum seekers. The citizenship referendum of 2004, eliminating the unrestricted constitutional right (*jus soli*) of citizenship to persons born in Ireland of non-Irish parents (Fanning, 2012; Mancini and Finlay, 2008), and the introduction of 'direct provision' for asylum seekers (NASC, 2014), further added to the division. 'Others' came in two broad categories – workers and asylum seekers.

One final point with respect to immigration has to do with migrants from the United Kingdom, as well as Irish returning to the Republic of Ireland after an extended period abroad. It has been suggested that returning Irish made up about 9 per cent of the population in 2006 with British migrants equalling about 2.6 per cent (Ni Laoire *et al.,* 2011). They would likely not be seen in some way as part of the 'others' but rather as somehow more directly connected to the country – in particular the returning Irish – and not considered in discussions about a changing society due to immigration.

Northern Ireland and immigration

The dominant narrative for Northern Ireland with respect to immigration, especially from the 1960s until the Good Friday Agreement, was the division of society into the two communities – Nationalist or Republican and Unionist or Loyalist – which overwhelmed any discussion of anyone who might not fit the popular conception of either category, including immigrants from outside the UK or the Republic of Ireland who might have moved there. The signing of the Good Friday Agreement in 1998 appears to have encouraged discussion on issues of multiculturalism and integration of migrants into the population, issues ignored during the years of sectarian strife. The agreement was part of a decade-or-more-long process to bring an end to sectarian violence through recognition of peaceful democratic means to settle political differences between the Nationalist and Unionist communities (Mansergh, 2006). Section 75 of the agreement required both parties to promote equality of opportunity and monitor if they were discriminating against people on the basis of age, race, ethnicity or religion (Goldie, 2008). Cultural differences among ethno-cultural minorities that were not actively discussed when the divisions into Unionist and Nationalist communities appeared to severely limit such discussion became both acceptable and encouraged (Gilligan, Hainsworth and McGarry, 2011). For example, in 2010 the Office of the First Minister and Deputy First Minister began a consultation process on 'issues impacting on disaffected young people, [to] tackle the conditions that perpetuate urban interfaces and rural segregation, as well as addressing those issues facing both established minority ethnic groups and new arrivals within our community' (Office of the First Minister and Deputy First Minister, 2010: 1). This is not to suggest that the issue of sectarianism has vanished. Indeed, Geoghegan (2008: 190) believes that, despite progress, the divisions continue:

Claims that sectarianism has been eclipsed by racism, and that Belfast is the 'most racist city in the world', seem to represent a displacement from one form of discrimination that is seen as intransigent, namely sectarianism, to another form of discrimination that is …easier to deal with, namely racism.

Since 1998, people have continued to move to Northern Ireland, and more attention perhaps is being paid to ethnic minorities who may well have been there throughout the years of sectarian conflict. Data on movement to Northern Ireland shows a net increase of approximately 25,000 persons between 2000 and 2010 (Russell, 2012). Accounts of ethnic minorities as a percentage of the overall population suggest that 'people from minority ethnic groups number 25,800… and the population born outside the UK is estimated to have increased from 72.2 to 97.9 thousand between 2004 and 2010 accounting for approximately 1.5 per cent of the population' (Owen, undated: 19). Martynowicz (2014), quoting the 2011 census, puts the figure at 4.5 per cent of the Northern Ireland population as having been born outside the UK and Ireland.

Non-nationals, immigrants and criminal justice

Based on media and published reports, it would appear that in Northern Ireland racially motivated crime *against* immigrants and refugees is a greater problem than crimes committed by people who have moved there from elsewhere (Stewart, 2013). The same might be said for the Republic of Ireland. There, data suggests that reported racially motivated crime, including anti-Semitism, peaked in 2007 and has declined to less than half of the peak (217 to 94) in 2013 (Office for the Promotion of Migrant Integration, 2014). Complaints of racial discrimination brought to the attention of the Equality Authority between 2006 and 2009 reflected a much higher number, but what is reported to the Equality Authority are not necessarily crimes as reported to The Gardaí (Taylor, 2010).

Data on the number of non-Irish nationals in prison is easier to come by than data on Travellers. The Irish Prison Service publishes data, for example, that breaks down the committals by year between 2008 and 2013 by 'Nationality group'. The number of EU prisoners (including from the UK) has been between 12 per cent and 13 per cent in that five-year period (Irish Prison Service, 2014). Non-EU prisoners (e.g. African, North American, Asian) showed a steady decline in the same period from a high of 16 per cent in 2008 to a low of 5.6 per cent in 2013, with the largest drop being African nationals.

Martynowicz (2014), in the blog post referenced above, suggests that '[i]n the last ten or so years, the population of foreign national prisoners in Northern Ireland prisons grew from single figures to around 7 per cent of the overall population. The largest group of those are Polish prisoners'. Potter (2011: 1), in a paper for the Northern Ireland Assembly, puts the figures somewhat differently, albeit three years earlier, stating that foreigners in Northern Ireland prisons accounted for 8.9 per cent of the prison population in January of 2011 and that '[t]here are 28 nationalities represented, the most numerous being Lithuanian (37), Chinese (19) and Polish (17) nationals'. In the 12 months ending 31 December 2014, foreign nationals in Northern Ireland prisons (including sentenced and unsentenced) ranged from a high of 140 to a low of 116 (Northern Ireland Prison Service, 2015). Quoting a 2004 study by the Prison Reform Trust, Potter suggests the problems of foreign nationals in N.I. prisons 'include language barriers, isolation, mental health problems, immigration issues and cultural difficulties, leading to the experience of a lack of access to information and legal support, lack of respect and racism and a lack of preparation for release' (Potter, 2011: 4).

Probation data for foreign nationals under supervision is not regularly kept by either the Probation Service (Republic of Ireland) or the Probation Board of Northern Ireland. However, a study of foreigners in the care of each service was jointly undertaken in 2009. It showed that as of 1 May 2009, 3.26 per cent of the Probation Service caseload was made up of what were termed 'foreign nationals' (Probation Service, 2009). Of those, 56 per cent were from Eastern European countries that were part of the EU expansion in 2004 (Poland, Latvia and Lithuania) and 2007 (Romania). UK nationals were excluded from this calculation. For the Probation Board of Northern Ireland, the percentage was 1.6 per cent foreign nationals. Of those, 71 per cent were from the EU (Probation Service, 2009). A follow-up study in 2011 included data only from the Republic of Ireland. It showed an increase to 4.8 per cent of probationers who were foreign nationals over the 3.26 per cent from 2009. As in the earlier study, probationers from the UK are not included in this figure, and four of the top five countries in terms of numbers on probation were Poland, Lithuania, Romania and Latvia (Burke and Gormley, 2012).

Both the Probation Service and the Probation Board of Northern Ireland developed initiatives with respect to understanding the diverse needs of those on probation from other countries. In the case of Northern Ireland, this was part of a larger initiative 'to identify the diversity of the offending population and discover through ongoing longitudinal research whether different groups have differing needs and issues that the PBNI should consider to promote equality of opportunity' (McIlwaine, 2011: 82). Gender, disability, sexual orientation and religious beliefs, along with race and ethnicity, were identified as areas to be considered as part of the promotion of equality. The Probation Service focussed directly on cultural diversity primarily in response to the changing face of the Irish population and also as part of the National Action Plan against Racism 2005–2008 (Department of Justice, Equality and Law Reform, 2001). A review of the process by which cultural diversity was identified as a strategic goal of the Service (Ferneé and Burke, 2010) ended with the interesting question: '[i]s cultural diversity about ensuring people are treated the same or is it about celebrating difference?' (ibid.: 151).

Probation work with non-Irish nationals

As indicated earlier, focus groups were conducted with probation officers of the Probation Service on work with both Travellers and non-Irish nationals under probation supervision. The experiences of the 37 probation officers from the focus groups were mixed with respect to non-Irish nationals as opposed to Travellers. Virtually all probation officers in the groups had experience with Travellers; this was not the case with non-Irish nationals. Similar themes emerged from the focus group discussions with probation officers that related to work with Travellers, such as engagement, compliance and risk assessment. However, cultural differences appeared as a more important factor in working with the non-Irish nationals, possibly because the differences were more obvious than with the Travellers.

Probation officers related a number of experiences wherein the person on probation expressed the view, possibly to minimise their situation, that they had a 'cultural' reason for offending behaviour:

> One of the points that someone made to me a couple of years ago is like 'you think I'm doing bad but I think I'm doing good, compared to where I'm from' … what he was saying to me was that 'the offences that I have committed and I'm been done for were to feed my children because I have nothing to feed my children and I have no social welfare so I see myself as, like you know like what you might see me doing, is actually doing good for

my family, I see a difference' ... I'm not using it as an excuse I'm just saying when you get involved with the family you do see things very different.

The diversity of nationalities and the need to recognise such diversity was also apparent in the conversations:

I mean if you're talking about Africa really we have a representation of about six or seven hundred and they all seem to have a different kind of way of life and living and life experience. Sometimes it can be very difficult to understand all of that. And sometimes I have to get a map and see exactly where they and maybe they begin to talk a little bit more about the kind of cultural stuff from that area so that you kind of get an understanding of where they come from and then you wonder how much of what they're telling you is true or how much of it is fact or have they been through the awful experience that some of them seem to have been through. It's a lot of information coming from a lot of different people.

In both examples, there was expressed an openness to understanding such diversity among probationers from other cultures, as well as a caution being expressed as to how to understand cultural difference and what it might represent. A third example demonstrates the limits to engagement when cultural difference represented in an apparent distrust of authority blocked dealing constructively with the offending behaviour:

I particularly remember one Romanian man who like that had very good English and trying to work with him trying to do some offence focused work looking at the offence ... he would turn up for his appointments he would always be there but that was the limit to his engagement ... there is no way I could come at that whole subject of his offending, he denied that he had done anything wrong, he admitted to a certain extent of it and I felt that that was a level of you know lack of trust there whatever, there was no moving forward and no learning going on for him.

If the probationer could not communicate effectively in English, this presented even more problems. Speaking of a Polish family, one probation officer explained:

But actually the young lad has perfect English and the father had perfect English talking to me. But I think for the nuances of the legal (system) they [interpreters] need to be there. So you have even that piece going on.

Or another, whose experience was that the non-national men might be less likely to learn English, whereas the women do so as to be better able to relate to their children's experiences in school.

[The] wives may speak English perfectly because they look after the children and the children are integrated into the school system, whereas the men have decided 'I'm here six years but I can only speak Polish, I can't speak a word of English'.

One other significant theme that emerged from the group discussions concerned the Roma population. Although the discussion covered a wide range of non-Irish nationals, it was work with the Roma that dominated much of the discussion when it turned to non-Irish nationals.[6] Perhaps because Roma are a clearly identifiable minority culturally and linguistically, most participants in the focus group were able to distinguish between their experiences with them as offenders and other non-Irish nationals. Two examples from the research exemplify this:

> I think the Roma thing I would have noticed from working with the under 18's that would be a very much identifiable piece that we would have put into reports because there was certain I suppose differences with the Roma community versus say other non nationals as in they moved around quite a lot, there would have been a lot of issues around guardianship as well, we would have identified trying to find out who was the actual guardian to them, a guardian in the country, what age they were, what was their date of birth, there was a lot of stuff around child protection as well.
>
> Yeah, there is an awareness of it; it definitely influences decisions particularly with the Roma gipsy culture because the interventions that you would offer to those families are somewhat different.

In 2007, the Probation Service, recognising that Roma were a distinct group for which special attention was necessary, established a program to deal with the specific cultural needs and a pattern of offending behaviour among Roma women in a section of Dublin (Horgan, 2007). The program incorporated the fact that Roma women were 'highly skilled in the craft of hand-sewing … that for the most part they were resilient and resourceful' and that 'the Roma women, in particular, were not used to having their skills and abilities recognised' (Horgan, 2007: 87). A community service program was established, making use of these skills and incorporating language and literacy education.

The culture of the Roma in the Republic of Ireland, reflecting their years of persecution and discrimination in continental Europe, suggested that they were a significant subcategory of 'other'.

Conclusion

Persons who are racially, ethnically or linguistically different from a majority population are often characterised as somehow 'other' than the majority and, possibly, to be feared, resented, excluded or in some way made to feel unwelcome and different. If they appear culturally different, and in most cases this is almost to be expected, the fact that they are somehow 'other' and all that this might entail is brought into something as culturally bound as law. In some circumstances, this 'othering' becomes a part of the criminal justice process, resulting possibly in differential treatment to the detriment of the minorities. In societies that have (or historically have had) a substantial indigenous minority and a history of major migration and settlement, there is recognition in criminology of how society has responded to difference and the impact this has on the criminal justice process. The 'relationship to delinquency of the conflict of norms' that Sellin explored is an accepted part of criminal justice. It would seem that there is just a beginning of recognition with respect to what this might mean for the criminal justice processes in both jurisdictions. Numerically, it is difficult to argue either that Travellers are over- or under-represented in criminal justice statistics such as prison committals or probation cases. Until recently, data was not routinely collected that would point either way. The data from the research with probation officers would suggest that their cultural 'difference' from the rest of the Irish population is clearly recognised and accounted for in terms of probation work. With respect to the Travellers themselves, their increasing confidence in their own position as an ethnic group, formally recognised or not, also suggests that for the criminal justice systems, increasing under-standing and respect for their culture will be crucial to working effectively with Travellers who come into conflict with the law.

In Canada, official recording of indigenous ethnicity enables recognition of cultural difference and the strength inherent in this culture and allows for its use in terms of criminal justice programming both in prison (Correctional Service Canada, 2013) and in the community (Bracken *et al.*, 2009). Australian jurisdictions have had similar experiences (Willis, 2008). Acknowledgement of Travellers within the criminal justice system, as both victims and offenders, may facilitate progress toward addressing their needs.

With respect to foreign or non-Irish national prisoners, in the Republic of Ireland the numbers are close to the percentage of the population born outside of the State. In Northern Ireland, the numbers would suggest that foreigners in prison exceed their representation as a percentage of the population.

Non-nationals are 'others', not as a unified category, but rather as a range of categories both officially in statistics (EU vs. Non-EU) and in terms of probation work. The day-to-day realities of probation practice identified by the research sample require openness to diversity and a flexibility to recognise what these differences might mean in supervision. Roma are an identifiable 'other' that are different, and these differences are evident in probation practice. Africans also are different, but the research identified an awareness that there is a variety of African cultures represented among non-nationals. EU 'others' are also different, but not as different perhaps as Roma or African. Increased movement of people as asylum seekers or as part of the exercise of EU mobility rights suggest that these issues are here to stay. In societies where all but an indigenous minority are immigrants, or descended from people who came from somewhere else, the 'settler societies' (Veracini, 2010), the assumption is that some form of assimilation, perhaps in the context of multiculturalism (Citizenship and Immigration Canada, 2012) or within an assimilationist 'melting pot', (Steinberg, 2014) will occur. On the island of Ireland, the experience of large numbers of immigrants (as economic migrants, asylum seekers or as part of the EU freedom of movement) coming to stay is new. The experience, therefore, of dealing with those who run afoul of the criminal justice system, or, more broadly, who are victims of racially motivated criminal actions, is something to be considered. The review of the development of the Probation Service's strategic initiative on cultural diversity (Ferneé and Burke, 2010) asked: Is this about equal treatment or celebrating difference? For Irish and Northern Irish society in general, understanding that *equitable* treatment is not incompatible with respecting difference may be the first step.

References

AITHS (2010) *All Ireland Traveller Health Study Our Geels. Summary of Findings.* University College Dublin, School of Public Health, Physiotherapy and Population Science. Dublin: University College Dublin.

Australian Law Reform Commission (1986) *3.Aboriginal Societies:The Experience of Contact.* Sydney:Australian Law Reform Commission. Available at: http://www.alrc.gov.au/publications/Recognition%20of%20 Aboriginal%20Customary%20Laws%20(ALRC%20Report%2031/3-aboriginal-societies-experi (accessed 30 October 2014).

Bauman, Z. (1991) *Modernity and Ambivalence.* Ithaca, New York: Cornell University Press.

Bonta, J. and Andrews, D. (2010) 'Viewing offender assessment and rehabilitation through the lens of the risk-need-responsivity model', in F. McNeill, P. Raynor and C. Trotter (eds) *Offender Supervision: New Directions in Theory, Research and Practice.* Abingdon, Oxon, UK:Willan.

Bottoms, A. (2001) 'Compliance and community penalties', in A. Bottoms, L. Gelsthorpe and S. Rex (eds) *CommunityPenalties: Change and Challenges* (pp. 87–116). Cullompton:Willan.

Bracken, D. (2014) 'Probation practice with Travellers in the Republic of Ireland', *Irish Probation Journal,* 11: 44–62.

Bracken, D., Deane, L. and Morrissette, L. (2009) 'Desistance and social marginalization: The case of Canadian Aboriginal offenders', *Theoretical Criminology,* 13(1): 61–78.

Burke, I. and Gormley, A. (2012) *Foreign National Survey – Initial Findings.* Dublin: Probation Service.

Butler, M. and Maruna, S. (2012) *Discipline and Disparity: An Independent Report Prepared for the Northern Ireland Prison Service*. Belfast: ARCS (UK) Limited.

Central Statistics Office (2012a) *Press Release This Is Ireland – Highlights from Census 2011, Part 1*. Available at: http://cso.ie/en/newsandevents/pressreleases/2012pressreleases/pressreleasethisisireland-highlightsfromcensus2011part1/ (accessed 28 September 2014).

Central Statistics Office (2012b) *Profile 7 Religion Ethnicity and Irish Travellers*. Dublin: Stationery Office.

Chief Inspector of Criminal Justice in Northern Ireland, Her Majesty's Chief Inspector of Prisons, the Regulation and Quality Improvement Authority and the Education and Training Inspectorate (2013) *Report on an Announced Inspection of Ash House, Hydebank Wood Women's Prison*. Available at: www.cjini.org/CJNI/files/e9/e919ac2b-4e79-4a80-b1f6-fb753bea3444.pdf (accessed 23 April 2015).

Citizenship and Immigration Canada (2012) *Canadian Multiculturalism: An Inclusive Citizenship*. Available at: www.cic.gc.ca/english/multiculturalism/citizenship.asp (accessed 18 December 2014).

Commission on Itinerancy (1963) *Report of the Commission on Itinerancy*. Dublin: Stationery Office.

Correctional Service Canada (2013) *Strategic Plan for Aboriginal Corrections*. Available at: www.csc-scc.gc.ca/aboriginal/002003-1001-eng.shtml (accessed 18 December 2014).

Cottrell-Boyce, J. (2014) *Working with Gypsy and Traveller Offenders: A Thames Valley Probation Case Study*. Traveller Equality Project. London: ICB Traveller Equality Project.

Cunneen, C. and Stubbs, J. (2004) 'Cultural criminology and the engagement with race, gender and post-colonial identities', in J. Ferrell, K. Hayward, W. Morrison and M. Presdee (eds) *Cultural Criminology Unleashed* (pp. 97–108). London: Glasshouse Press.

Delaney, E. (2005) 'Transnationalism, networks and emigration from post-war Ireland', *Immigrants and Minorities: Historical Studies in Ethnicity, Migration and Diaspora, 23* (2–3): 425–46.

Department of Justice, Equality and Law Reform (2001) *Planning for Diversity: The National Action Plan against Racism, 2005–2008*. Dublin: Stationery Office.

Drummond, A. (2007) 'The construction of Irish Travellers (and Gypsies) as a "problem"', in M. Ó. hAodha (ed) *Migrants and Memory: The Forgotten 'Postcolonials'* (pp. 2–41). Newcastle: Cambridge Scholars Press.

Equality and Human Rights Commission (2009) *Gypsies and Travellers: Simple Solutions for Living Together*. London: Equality and Human Rights Commission.

Fanning, B. (ed) (2012) *Racism and Social Change in the Republic of Ireland (2nd edn)*. Manchester: Manchester University Press.

Ferneé, U. and Burke, I. (2010) 'Cultural diversity and the Probation Service', *Irish Probation Journal*, 7: 140–51.

Fitzgibbon, W., Hamilton, C. and Richardson, M. (2010) 'A risky business: An examination of Irish probation officers' attitudes towards risk assessment', *The Probation Journal*, 57(2): 163–74.

Geoghegan, P. (2008) 'Beyond orange and green? The awkwardness of negotiating difference in Northern Ireland', *Irish Studies Review*, 16(2): 173–94.

Gilligan, C., Hainsworth, P. A. and McGarry, A. (2011) 'Fractures, foreigners and fitting in: Exploring attitudes towards immigration and integration in "post-Conflict" Northern Ireland', *Ethnopolitics*, 10(2): 253–69.

Gmelch, G. (ed) (1985) *The Irish Tinkers: The Urbanization of an Itinerant People (2nd edn)*. Prospect Heights, Illinois, USA: Waveland Press.

Gmelch, S. B. and Gmelch, G. (1976) 'The emergence of an ethnic group: The Irish Tinkers', *Anthropological Quarterly*, 49(4): 225–38.

Goldie, R. (2008) *Law and the Politics of Promoting Equality and Good Relations in the Northern Ireland Peace Process*. Available at: www.qub.ac.uk/sites/QUEST/FileStore/Issue6/Filetoupload,146253,en.pdf (accessed 6 March 2015).

Gormally, E. (2005) *Whiddin to the Gauras: Talking to Our Own – Traveller Researchers Talk to Limerick Traveller Children*. Dublin: Veritas.

Gutierrez, L., Wilson, H. A., Rugge, T. and Bonta, J. (2013) 'The prediction of recidivism with Aboriginal offenders: A theoretically informed meta-analysis', *Canadian Journal of Criminology and Criminal Justice*, 55 (1): 55–99.

Hannah-Moffat, K. (2005) 'Criminogenic needs and the transformative risk subject: Hybridizations of risk/need in penality', *Punishment and Society*, 7 (1): 29–51.

Helleiner, J. (2000) *Irish Travellers: Racism and the Politics of Culture*. Toronto: University of Toronto Press.

HM Inspectorate of Prisons (2014) *People in Prison: Gypsies, Romany and Travellers*. London: HM Inspectorate of Prisons.

Horgan, B. (2007) 'The Roma Project: A case study of community service', *Irish Probation Journal*, 4 (1): 85–92.

IPRT (2014) *Travellers in the Irish Prison System: A Qualitative Study*. Dublin: Irish Penal Reform Trust.

Irish Prison Service (2014) *Nationality of Persons Committed by Year from 2008 to 2013*. Available at: www.irishprisons.ie/images/pdf/nationality_2008_2013.pdf (accessed 28 September 2014).

Joint Committee on Justice, Defence and Equality (2014) *Report on Traveller Ethnicity*. Dublin: Houses of the Oireachtas.

Lewis, S., Lobley, D., Raynor, P. and Smith, D. (2005) 'The Irish on probation in the North-West of England', *Probation Journal*, 52 (3): 293–5.

McCullagh, C. (1996) *Crime in Ireland: A Sociological Introduction*. Cork: Cork University Press.

McDonagh, M. (2000) 'Ethnicity and culture', in E. Sheehan (ed) *Travellers: Citizens of Ireland* (pp. 21–54). Dublin: The Parish of the Travelling People.

McIlwaine, P. (2011) 'Diversity profile of offenders under the supervision of the Probation Board for Northern Ireland', *Irish Probation Journal*, 8: 82–92.

Maher, G. (2010) 'A transnational migrant circuit: Remittances from Ireland to Brazil', *Irish Geography*, 43 (2): 177–99.

Mancini, J. M. and Finlay, G. (2008) '"Citizenship matters": Lessons from the Irish Citizenship Referendum', *American Quarterly*, 60 (3): 575–99.

Mansergh, M. (2006) 'The background to the Irish peace process', in M. Cox, A. Guelke and F. Stephen (eds) *A Farewell to Arms? Beyond the Good Friday Agreement* (2nd edn) (pp. 24–40). Manchester: Manchester University Press.

Martin, M. (2008) 'The Roma population in Europe: A brief look at the situation in Ireland', *Translocations: Migration and Social Change*, 4 (1): 118–27.

Martynowicz, A. (2014) *Foreign-National Prisoners*. Oxford: Border Criminologies – Foreigners in a Carceral Age. Available at: http://bordercriminologies.law.ox.ac.uk/tag/foreign-national-prisoners/ (accessed 28 September 2014).

Ministry of Justice (2013) *Statistics on Race and the Criminal Justice System 2012*. London: Ministry of Justice.

Mulcahy, A. (2012) '"Alright in their own place": Policing and the spatial regulation of Irish Travellers', *Criminology and Criminal Justice*, 12 (3): 307–27.

NASC (2014) *Campaign for Change Direct Provision*. Cork: NASC, The Irish Immigrant Support Centre. Available at: www.nascireland.org/campaigns-for-change/direct-provision/ (accessed 28 September 2014).

Ni Laoire, C., Carpena-Mendez, F., Tyrrell, N. and White, A. (2011) *Childhood and Migration in Europe: Portraits of Mobility, Identity and Belonging in Contemporary Ireland*. Farnham: Ashgate.

Noonan, P. (1994) 'A view from Northern Ireland', in M. McCann, S. Ó. Síocháin and J. Ruane (eds) *Irish Travellers: Culture and Ethnicity*. Belfast: Queen's University Belfast.

Northern Ireland Prison Service (2015) *Analysis of NIPS Prison Population from 01/10/2013 to 31/12/2014*. Belfast: Department of Justice.

Ó hAodha, M. (2011) *'Insubordinate Irish': Travellers in the Text*. Manchester: Manchester University Press.

Office for the Promotion of Migrant Integration (2014) *Reported Racist Crime*. Dublin: Department of Justice and Equality. Available at: www.integration.ie/website/omi/omiwebv6.nsf/page/statistics-RacistIncidentsstatisticscrime-en (accessed 1 November 2014).

Office of the First Minister and Deputy First Minister (2010) *Cohesion, Sharing and Integration – Public Consultation*. Belfast: Office of the First Minister and Deputy First Minister. Available at: www.ofmdfmni.gov.uk/pressrelease.pdf (accessed 29 September 2014).

Owen, D. (undated) *Evidence on the Experience of Poverty among People from Minority Ethnic Groups in Northern Ireland*. Warwick: Joseph Rowntree Foundation.

Pavee Point (2013) *Traveller Numbers 'Up by 32%' in New Census*. Dublin: Pavee Point. Available at: www.paveepoint.ie/traveller-numbers-up-by-32-in-new-census/ (accessed 16 December 2014).

Potter, M. (2011) *Foreign National Prisoners*. Belfast: Northern Ireland Assembly.

Power, C. (2003) 'Irish Travellers: Ethnicity, racism and pre-sentence reports', *Probation Journal*, 50 (3): 252–66.

Probation Service (2009) *Survey of Foreign National Offenders on Probation Service Caseload on 1st May 2009*. Dublin: The Probation Service.

Roberts, J. and Doob, A. (1997) 'Race, ethnicity, and criminal justice in Canada', *Crime and Justice: A Review of Research*, 21 (1): 469–522.

Rogan, M. (2011) *Prison Policy in Ireland: Politics, Penal-Welfarism and Political Imprisonment*. Abington, Oxon, UK: Routledge.

Russell, R. (2012) *Migration in Northern Ireland: An Update*. Northern Ireland Assembly. Belfast: Research and Information Service.

Sellin, T. (1938) 'Culture, conflict and crime', *American Journal of Sociology*, 44 (1): 97–103.

Spohn, C. (2013) 'The effects of the offender's race, ethnicity, and sex on federal sentencing outcomes in the guidelines era', *Law and Contemporary Problems*, 76 (1): 75–104.

Steinberg, S. (2014) 'The long view of the melting pot', *Ethnic and Racial Studies*, 37 (5): 790–4.

Stewart, G. (2013) *An Assessment of Racial Violence in Northern Ireland: 12 December 2013*. London: Institute of Race Relations. Available at: www.irr.org.uk/news/an-assessment-of-racial-violence-in-northern-ireland/ (accessed 1 November 2014).

Tauri, J. M. and Webb, R. (2012) 'A critical appraisal of responses to Māori offending', *The International Indigenous Policy Journal*, 3 (4): 1–16.

Taylor, S. (2010) *Responding to Racist Incidents and Racist Crimes in Ireland*. Maynooth/Dublin: NUI Maynooth/Equality Authority.

Tonry, M. (1997) 'Ethnicity, crime, and immigration', *Crime and Justice: A Review of Research*, 21 (1): 1–29.

Travellers (undated) *Final Report of the PSI Working Group on Travellers 2001*. Office of the First Minister and Deputy First Minister. Belfast: Northern Ireland Assembly.

Truth and Reconciliation Commission of Canada (2012) *Interim Report*. Winnipeg: Truch and Reconciliation Commission of Canada.

Veracini, L. (2010) *Settler Colonialism: A Theoretical Overview*. Basingstoke: Palgrave Macmillan.

Webb, R. (2003) 'Risk factors, criminogenic needs and Māori', *Conference Proceedings of the 2003 Sociological Association of Aotearoa Conference: Knowledge, Capitalism, Critique*. Auckland: Auckland University of Technology.

Willis, M. (2008) *Reintegration of Indigenous Prisoners: Key Findings*. Canberra: Australian Institute of Criminology. Available at: http://aic.gov.au/publications/current%20series/tandi/361-380/tandi364.html (accessed 18 December 2014).

Notes

1 The author is grateful for the kind assistance of the Irish Probation Service, Pavee Point, the Galway Travellers Movement, the Tuam Travellers Education & Development Group and the Tipperary Rural Travellers Project, with the probation research reported here.

2 University of Manitoba.

3 For a more in-depth discussion of these issues, see Drummond (2007).

4 Some of the quotes used in this chapter were also published in Bracken (2014). Reprinted with permission.

5 This figure excludes those born in the UK.

6 Because data is collected in both jurisdictions related to nationality and not ethnicity, it is difficult to estimate the number of Roma in Ireland. Most would have come from Romania; hence, there is frequently confusion over who is non-Roma from Romania and who is Roma, from Romania or somewhere else. See Martin (2008) for further discussion on Roma immigration to Ireland.

Afterword
Why Irish criminology?

Shadd Maruna and Kieran McEvoy[1]

In 1992, when the Northern Ireland Office was considering whether or not it should support the establishment of an Institute of Criminology in Northern Ireland, it commissioned the eminent UK criminologist Professor Ken Pease to review the existing criminological landscape. In the first iteration of his ensuing report, Pease concluded that the 'starting point from criminological research dealing with Northern Ireland was effectively zero' and that, if anything, the situation in the south of Ireland was even more bleak (Pease, 1992: 1). This gloomy assessment was controversial at the time – not least among the criminologists working in academic and policy settings – but a quarter century later, it is now clearly no longer the case.

The depth and breadth of this impressive volume illustrate the utterly changed state of the criminological landscape in Ireland, north and south. In fact, although still small in size and scale, one could argue that criminology has grown from the island's 'absentee discipline' (O'Donnell, 2005: 99) to one of Ireland's most dynamic, creative and increasingly popular areas of research and postgraduate study. The development of a 'handbook' is a clear sign of 'coming of age' in any field of study, and this packed volume is no exception, demonstrating what Irish criminology has to offer. By this, we mean both what criminology has to offer Ireland, as well as what Ireland has to offer criminology. The contents of this volume address both issues, but the latter is probably more interesting.

Of course, all of the chapters draw on North American, British and European criminological foundations (primarily) to help illuminate uniquely Irish subjects and histories. Such analyses are long overdue. The Irish justice system has been badly under-scrutinised for decades, allowing for tragic scandals of abuse and corruption. Whilst the subject of near-endless tabloid fascination, Ireland's marginalised and criminalised communities have been largely invisible to the lens of social science – apart of course from the substantial literature around the political conflict in the north. Considerable lessons can be learned (not least of the cautionary tale variety) from importing theories and frameworks from a century of criminological scholarship from Chicago, Birmingham and beyond into the Irish context. Doing so demonstrates both what is universal and unique about crime and criminal justice issues in contemporary Ireland.

Yet, this book suggests that the international study and understanding of criminology has as much to learn from Ireland as Ireland has to learn from international criminology. Some might interpret the introduction of Western criminology as an indication of the 'normalisation' of Ireland, bringing it in line with 'best practices' developed in the United Kingdom, North America and elsewhere. However, a closer reading of the contributions to this Handbook suggests that the emergent field of Irish criminology is much more intellectually ambitious than that. It is less focused on knowledge importation or mechanistic policy transfer and more on seeking to re-imagine the work of criminology from an Irish perspective. Indeed, readers from outside of Ireland may find in these pages the unformed beginnings of a new and unique approach to understandings of crime and justice.

Different aspects of the criminal justice system play a central role in the competing ways in which community and nation are imagined everywhere, and yet there are particular peculiarities to the Irish context. Most obviously the centuries-long constitutional struggle between self-governance and British rule makes obvious the highly political nature of criminal justice practices from policing to trials to imprisonment.

With regard to policing, scholars like Mulcahy (2005) have argued, for instance, that historically easy assumptions about the Gardaí as an imagined version of *Irishness* built upon a supposed consensual relationship between the police and policed in the Republic were always bound up with simultaneous *othering* of particular communities (such as travellers, Republicans, the urban poor or new immigrant communities) and was subject to the vagaries of local or indeed national corruption. Similarly, the RUC had an equivalent symbolic role in the way in which Unionists imagined the Northern state (and for many nationalists, the exact polar opposite of course), as does the PSNI in the new post-Conflict Ireland.

Of course, all of us, whether we realise it or not, have been touched by the long history of political violence on the island. In the Republic, many families are only three generations away from the widespread experience of political imprisonment; in the North, only one. Our struggles to come to terms with the realities and consequences of that violence still permeate the body politic in both jurisdictions. In a somewhat analogous vein, we are all too aware of the consequences of the extensive reach of the churches in the Republic and to an extent in the North into the penal and disciplinary apparatuses of the state – and the ensuing crimes and abuses that were perpetrated, denied and covered up. The greed, excess and corporate criminality of the economic boom years – and the lack of appropriate regulation or accountability – remain unfortunately vibrant areas of study.

By its nature, criminology requires us to look into these darker corners of our collective psyche, and, judging by the quality of the contributions in this volume, there are Irish criminologists with the intellectual courage to do just that. Yet, the emerging visions of Irish-style criminology are not all doom and gloom; indeed, Ireland can be a beacon for justice studies.

For instance, Ireland has long had a lower rate of incarceration than comparator nations and been seen as a 'nation not obsessed by crime' (Adler, 1983). Although this lack of official state punitiveness is under some threat, surely one reason for this hesitation to over-incarcerate throughout the twentieth century was the remarkable number of Irish political leaders (including most of the Ministers for Justice who served in the mid-twentieth century) who themselves had been incarcerated for war activities by the British. As one of these, Kevin O'Higgins, Minister for Justice from 1922–7, argued:

> There is not a member of this present government who has not been in jail. We have had the benefit of personal experience and personal study of these problems, and although we have never discussed them, I think we would be unanimous in the view that a change and reform would be desirable. Personally I can conceive nothing more brutalizing, and nothing

more calculated to make a man rather a dangerous member of society, than the existing system.

(cited in Kilcommins et al., 2004: 41)

Of course, the island also has a unique relationship with justice practices dating from the Brehon Laws, and there remains a vibrant and growing interest in restorative justice throughout Ireland, with grassroots efforts to control crime without punishment (see McEvoy and Eriksson, 2006). Most importantly, there is a generation of criminal justice researchers and activists emerging who are willing to challenge the accepted status quo internationally and reinvent justice from the ground up.

In short, it is a good time to be an Irish criminologist – even a couple of middle-aged ones – and we hope this Handbook is a signal of more to come.

References

Adler, F. (1983) *Nations Not Obsessed with Crime*. Littleton: Rothman & Co.

Kilcommins, S., O'Donnell, I., O'Sullivan, E. and Vaughan, B. (2004) *Crime, Punishment and the Search for Order in Ireland*. Dublin: Institute of Public Administration.

McEvoy, K. and Eriksson, A. (2006) 'Restorative justice in transition: Ownership, leadership and "bottom-up" human rights', in D. Sullivan and L. Tifft (eds) *Handbook of Restorative Justice: A Global Perspective* (pp. 321–35). London: Routledge.

Mulcahy, A. (2005) 'The "other" lessons from Ireland? Policing, political violence and policy transfer', *European Journal of Criminology*, 2(2): 185–209.

O'Donnell, I. (2005) 'Crime and justice in the Republic of Ireland', *European Journal of Criminology*, 2(1): 99–131.

Pease, K. (1992) 'Establishment of a Criminological Establishment Research Facility in Northern Ireland'. Report Prepared for the Northern Ireland Office. Belfast: Northern Ireland Office.

Notes

1 Shadd Maruna: Rutgers School of Criminology Justice, Rutgers University, New Jersey, USA. Kieran McEvoy: Institute of Criminology and Criminal Justice, School of Law, Queen's University, Belfast, UK.

Index

Page numbers in italics refer to figures. Page numbers in bold refer to tables.